The Moral of the Story

For Craig and my parents

Immorality may be fun, but it isn't fun enough to take the place of 100 percent virtue and three square meals a day.

—Noel Coward, *Design for Living*

The Moral of the Story

AN INTRODUCTION TO ETHICS

Sixth Edition

NINA ROSENSTAND

San Diego Mesa College

 **Higher Education**

Boston   Burr Ridge, IL   Dubuque, IA   New York
San Francisco   St. Louis   Bangkok   Bogotá   Caracas   Kuala Lumpur
Lisbon   London   Madrid   Mexico City   Milan   Montreal   New Delhi
Santiago   Seoul   Singapore   Sydney   Taipei   Toronto

The McGraw·Hill Companies

Mc Graw Hill Higher Education

Published by McGraw-Hill, an imprint unit of The McGraw-Hill Companies, Inc., 1221 Avenue of the Americas, New York, NY, 10020. Copyright © 2009, 2006, 2003, 2000, 1994 by The McGraw-Hill Companies, Inc. All rights reserved. No part of this publication may be reproduced or distributed in any form or by any means, or stored in a database or retrieval system, without the prior written consent of The McGraw-Hill Companies, Inc., including, but not limited to, in any network or other electronic storage or transmission, or broadcast for distance learning.

This book is printed on acid-free paper.

2 3 4 5 6 7 8 9 0 DOC/DOC 0 9

ISBN: 978-0-07-338654-6
MHID: 0-07-338654-5

Editor in Chief: Michael Ryan
Publisher: Beth Mejia
Sponsoring Editor: Mark Georgiev
Marketing Manager: Pamela S. Cooper
Production Editor: Leslie LaDow
Manuscript Editor: Carole Crouse
Designer: Ashley Bedell
Photo Research: Natalia Peschiera and
    Connie Gardener

Production Supervisor: Richard DeVitto
Media Project Manager: Ron Nelms
Composition: 10.5/12.5 Berkeley Book by
    ICC Macmillan Inc.
Printing: 45# New Era Matte by
    R. R. Donnelley, Crawfordsville, IN

Cover image by Karen Barbour
Credits: The credits section for this book begins on page C-1 and is considered an extension of the copyright page.

Library of Congress Cataloging-in-Publication Data

Rosenstand, Nina.
    The moral of the story : an introduction to ethics / Nina Rosenstand. — 6th ed.
        p.   cm.
    Includes bibliographical references and index.
    ISBN-13: 978-0-07-338654-6 (alk. paper)
    ISBN-10: 0-07-338654-5 (alk. paper)
    1. Ethics—Textbooks.   I. Title.
    BJ1012.R59 2009
    170—dc22   2008021353

The Internet addresses listed in the text were accurate at the time of publication. The inclusion of a website does not indicate an endorsement by the authors or McGraw-Hill, and McGraw-Hill does not guarantee the accuracy of the information presented at these sites. **www.mhhe.com**

Contents

PART 1
The Story as a Tool of Ethics

Chapter 1
Thinking About Values   1
The Best of Times, the Worst of Times?   1
Good and Evil   4
Is Morality Hardwired?   10
Values, Morals, and Ethics   12
Debating Moral Issues: The Roles of
    Religion, the Law, Logic, Emotions,
    and Storytelling   16
Martha Nussbaum: Stories, Ethics,
    and Emotions   24
PRIMARY READING: Martha Nussbaum,
    Love's Knowledge   28
PRIMARY READING: Philip Zimbardo,
    The Lucifer Effect   30
NARRATIVE: *Smoke Signals*   33
NARRATIVE: *Big Fish*   36
NARRATIVE: *East of Eden*   40

Chapter 2
**Learning Moral Lessons from
    Stories   47**
Didactic Stories   47
The New Interest in Stories Across
    the Professions   48
The Value of Stories in World Cultures   51
Stories of Values Across the Ages   52
PRIMARY READING: Plato, *Republic*   92
PRIMARY READING: Aristotle, *Poetics*   96
PRIMARY READING: Umberto Eco, *The Name
    of the Rose*   98
PRIMARY READING: Raymond Chandler,
    "The Simple Art of Murder"   100
NARRATIVE: *Medea*   102
NARRATIVE: *The Sorrows of Young Werther*   106
NARRATIVE: "The Education of Mingo"   107
NARRATIVE: *Pulp Fiction*   111

PART 2
What Should I Do? Ethics of Conduct

Chapter 3
Ethical Relativism   114
How to Deal with Moral Differences   115
The Lessons of Anthropology   118
Problems with Ethical Relativism   124
Refuting Ethical Relativism   132
James Rachels and Soft Universalism   134
Ethical Relativism and Multiculturalism   139
PRIMARY READING: Ruth Benedict,
    "Anthropology and the Abnormal"   145
PRIMARY READING: Dwight Furrow, "Of Cave
    Dwellers and Spirits"   147

PRIMARY READING: John Steinbeck, "Paradox
    and Dream"   149
NARRATIVE: *The Poisonwood Bible*   151
NARRATIVE: *Possessing the Secret of Joy*   157
NARRATIVE: *Do the Right Thing*   160

Chapter 4
Myself or Others?   163
Psychological Egoism: From Virginia
    Tech to 9/11   163
Psychological Egoism: From Glaucon
    to Hobbes   167

Shortcomings of Psychological
   Egoism   176
Ethical Egoism and Its Critics   181
Being Selfless: Levinas's Ideal Altruism
   Versus Singer's Reciprocal
   Altruism   188
Selfish Genes or Fellow-Feeling? Dawkins,
   Midgley, Hume, and de Waal   191
PRIMARY READING: Plato, *Republic*   198
PRIMARY READING: Erik Katz, "The Rings of
   Tolkien and Plato"   202
PRIMARY READING: Thomas Hobbes,
   Leviathan   206
PRIMARY READING: Ayn Rand, "The Ethics of
   Emergencies"   207
PRIMARY READING: Frans de Waal, *Primates
   and Philosophers*   211
NARRATIVE: Friends episode: "The One Where
   Phoebe Hates PBS"   213
NARRATIVE: *Return to Paradise*   215
NARRATIVE: *Atlas Shrugged*   219
NARRATIVE: *The Lord of the Rings*   221

Chapter 5
**Using Your Reason, Part 1:
   Utilitarianism   224**
Jeremy Bentham and the Hedonistic
   Calculus   225
Advantages and Problems of Sheer Numbers:
   From Animal Welfare to the Question of
   Torture   233
John Stuart Mill: Higher and Lower
   Pleasures   240
Mill's Harm Principle   247
Act and Rule Utilitarianism   253
PRIMARY READING: Jeremy Bentham, "Of the
   Principle of Utility"   256
PRIMARY READING: John Stuart Mill,
   Utilitarianism   258
PRIMARY READING: Peter Singer, "A Convenient
   Truth"   261
NARRATIVE: "The Blacksmith and
   the Baker"   263
NARRATIVE: *The Brothers Karamazov*   265
NARRATIVE: "The Ones Who Walk Away
   from Omelas"   267
NARRATIVE: *Extreme Measures*   268
NARRATIVE: *Runaway Jury*   271

Chapter 6
**Using Your Reason, Part 2: Kant's
   Deontology   275**
Consequences Don't Count—Having a Good
   Will Does   275
The Categorical Imperative   278
Rational Beings Are Ends in Themselves   288
Beings Who Are Things   292
The Kingdom of Ends   295
PRIMARY READING: Immanuel Kant, *Grounding
   for the Metaphysics of Morals*   297
PRIMARY READING: Immanuel Kant, *The
   Metaphysics of Morals*   299
NARRATIVE: *High Noon*   301
NARRATIVE: *3:10 to Yuma*   304
NARRATIVE: *Match Point*   307

Chapter 7
Personhood, Rights, and Justice   312
What Is a Human Being?   312
The Expansion of the Concept "Human"   313
Personhood: The Key to Rights   313
Science and Moral Responsibility: Genetic
   Engineering, Stem Cell Research,
   and Cloning   320
Questions of Rights and Equality   328
Distributive Justice: From Rawls to Affirmative
   Action   339
Forward- and Backward-Looking Justice
   and Affirmative Action   344
Criminal Justice: Restorative Versus
   Retributive Justice   346
PRIMARY READING: *The United Nations Universal
   Declaration of Human Rights*   354
PRIMARY READING: John Rawls, "Justice as
   Fairness"   358
PRIMARY READING: Martin Luther King, Jr.,
   "A Letter from Birmingham Jail"   360
PRIMARY READING: John Berteaux, "Two Texts
   on Discrimination"   362
PRIMARY READING: Diane Whiteley, "The
   Victim and the Justification
   of Punishment"   364
NARRATIVE: *The Island*   367
NARRATIVE: *Gattaca*   371
NARRATIVE: *Mississippi Burning*   374
NARRATIVE: *Hotel Rwanda*   377
NARRATIVE: *Minority Report*   381

PART 3
How Should I Be? Virtue Ethics

Chapter 8
Virtue Ethics from Tribal Philosophy to Socrates and Plato   385

What Is Virtue? What Is Character?   385

Non-Western Virtue Ethics: Africa and Indigenous America   386

Virtue Ethics in the West   390

The Good Teacher: Socrates' Legacy, Plato's Works   392

The Good Life   400

The Virtuous Person: The Tripartite Soul   402

Plato's Theory of Forms   405

Plato's Influence on Christianity   410

PRIMARY READING: Plato, *Republic*   412

PRIMARY READING: Plato, *Apology*   415

NARRATIVE: *A Man for All Seasons*   419

NARRATIVE: "The Myth of the Cave"   422

NARRATIVE: *The Truman Show*   424

NARRATIVE: *Shrek*   427

Chapter 9
Aristotle's Virtue Theory: Everything in Moderation   431

Empirical Knowledge and the Realm of the Senses   432

Aristotle the Scientist   432

Aristotle's Virtue Theory: Teleology and the Golden Mean   435

Aristotle's Influence on Aquinas   449

Some Objections to Greek Virtue Theory   450

PRIMARY READING: Aristotle, *Nicomachean Ethics*, Book II   453

PRIMARY READING: Aristotle, *Nicomachean Ethics*, Book III   456

NARRATIVE: "The Flight of Icarus"   458

NARRATIVE: *Njal's Saga*   460

NARRATIVE: *Lord Jim*   462

NARRATIVE: "A Piece of Advice"   464

NARRATIVE: *As Good As It Gets*   467

Chapter 10
Contemporary Perspectives   470

Ethics and the Morality of Virtue as Political Concepts   470

Have Virtue, and Then Go Ahead: Mayo, Foot, and Sommers   474

The Quest for Authenticity: Kierkegaard, Heidegger, Sartre, and Levinas   483

PRIMARY READING: Søren Kierkegaard, *Johannes Climacus*   506

PRIMARY READING: Søren Kierkegaard, *Either/Or*   506

PRIMARY READING: Jean-Paul Sartre, "Existentialism Is a Humanism"   507

PRIMARY READING: "The Paradox of Morality: An Interview with Emmanuel Levinas"   510

NARRATIVE: *No Exit*   512

NARRATIVE: *Good Will Hunting*   514

NARRATIVE: *The Searchers*   518

Chapter 11
Case Studies in Virtue   522

Courage of the Physical and Moral Kind   522

Compassion: From Hume to Huck Finn   531

Gratitude: Asian Tradition and Western Modernity   540

Virtue and Conduct: The Option of Soft Universalism   556

Diversity, Politics, and Common Ground?   559

PRIMARY READING: John McCain, *Why Courage Matters: The Way to a Braver Life*   562

PRIMARY READING: Philip Hallie, *Tales of Good and Evil, Help and Harm*   565

PRIMARY READING: Lin Yutang, "On Growing Old Gracefully"   566

NARRATIVE: *Band of Brothers*, Third Episode, "Carentan"   568

NARRATIVE: *The Life of Tom Horn*   570

NARRATIVE: "The Parable of the Good
    Samaritan"   574
NARRATIVE: *Schindler's List*   576
NARRATIVE: *Eat Drink Man Women*   579
NARRATIVE: *Pay It Forward*   582

Chapter 12
Different Gender, Different Ethics?   586

Feminism and Virtue Theory   586
What Is Gender Equality?   588
Women's Historical Role in the Public
    Sphere   591
First-, Second-, and Third-Wave
    Feminism   596
Classical, Difference, and Radical
    Feminism   602
PRIMARY READING: Harriet Taylor Mill,
    "Enfranchisement of Women"   618
PRIMARY READING: Simone de Beauvoir,
    The Second Sex   621
PRIMARY READING: Carol Gilligan, *In a
    Different Voice*   624
NARRATIVE: *A Doll's House*   626
NARRATIVE: "The Woman Destroyed"   631
NARRATIVE: *Mona Lisa Smile*   633

Chapter 13
Applied Ethics: A Sampler   638

The Question of Abortion and
    Personhood   638
Euthanasia as a Right to Choose?   641
Media Ethics and Media Bias   644
Business Ethics: The Rules of the Game   653
Just War Theory   660
Animal Welfare and Animal Rights   669
Ethics of the Environment: Think Globally,
    Act Locally   675
The Death Penalty   681
The Ethics of Self-Improvement: Narrative
    Identity   690

A Final Word   698
PRIMARY READING: Andrew Belsey and Ruth
    Chadwick, "Ethics as a Vehicle for Media
    Quality"   700
PRIMARY READING: Amber Levanon Seligson and
    Laurie Choi, "Critical Elements of an
    Organizational Ethical Culture"   702
PRIMARY READING: Scott Gottlieb, "How Safe Is
    Our Food? FDA Could Do Better"   703
PRIMARY READING: John Rawls, *The Law of
    Peoples*   705
PRIMARY READING: Jan Narveson, "Morality and
    Violence: War, Revolution, Terrorism"   708
PRIMARY READING: Great Ape Project,
    "The Declaration on Great Apes"   711
PRIMARY READING: Lee Hall and Anthony Jon
    Waters, "From Property to Person:
    The Case of Evelyn Hart"   712
PRIMARY READING: "Ethics and the
    Environment"   714
PRIMARY READING: A. O. Scott, "Warning of
    Calamities and Hoping for a Change in
    'An Inconvenient Truth'"   714
PRIMARY READING: Michael Barone, "Gore Twists
    Science, History"   716
PRIMARY READING: Tom Sorell, "Two Ideals
    and the Death Penalty"   717
PRIMARY READING: Mark Fuhrman, *Death and
    Justice: An Exposé of Oklahoma's Death Row
    Machine*   721
PRIMARY READING: Tristine Rainer, *Your Life
    as Story*   725
NARRATIVE: *15 Minutes*   726
NARRATIVE: *The Insider*   729
NARRATIVE: "The Jigsaw Man"   732
NARRATIVE: *The Life of David Gale*   733

Credits   C-1
Bibliography   B-1
Glossary   G-1
Index   I-1

Preface

$\mathcal{L}$ike the previous editions of *The Moral of the Story,* the sixth edition is a combination of classical questions in ethical theory and contemporary issues. The general concept remains the same: that discussions about moral issues can be facilitated using stories as examples, as a form of ethics lab where solutions can be tried out under controlled conditions. The book is written primarily for such college courses as Introduction to Ethics; Moral Philosophy; and Introduction to Philosophy: Values. Many textbooks in value theory or ethics choose to focus on problems of social importance, such as abortion, euthanasia, and capital punishment. This book reflects my own teaching experience that it is better for students to be introduced to basic ethical theory before they are plunged into discussions involving moral judgments. Consequently, *The Moral of the Story* provides an overview of influential classical and contemporary approaches to ethical theory. However, without practical application of the theories, there can be no complete understanding of the problems raised, so each chapter includes examples that illustrate and explore the issues. As in previous editions, each chapter concludes with a section of examples—summaries and excerpts—taken from the world of fiction, particularly films.

Within the last few decades, narrative theory has carved out a niche in American and European philosophy as well as in other academic disciplines. It is no longer unusual for ethicists and other thinkers to include works of fiction in their courses as well as in their professional papers, not only as examples of problem solving, but also as illustrations of an epistemological phenomenon: Humans are, in Alasdair MacIntyre's words, storytelling animals, and we humans seem to choose the narrative form as our favorite way to structure meaning as we attempt to make sense of our reality. The narrative trend is making itself felt in other fields as well: The medical profession is looking to stories that teach about doctor-patient relationships; psychotherapists recommend that patients watch films to achieve an understanding of their own situation, and have patients write stories with themselves as the lead character. The court system is making use of films and novels to reach young people in trouble with the law. It seems that new fields are constantly being added to the list of professions that are discovering, or rediscovering, the potential of stories.

Organization

Like the previous editions, the sixth edition of *The Moral of the Story* is divided into three major sections. Part 1 introduces the topic of ethics and places the phenomenon of storytelling within the context of moral education and discussion. Part 2 examines the conduct theories of ethical relativism, psychological and ethical egoism, altruism, utilitarianism, and Kantian deontology, and explores the concepts of personhood, rights, and justice. Part 3 focuses on the subject of virtue theory and contains chapters on Socrates and Plato, Aristotle, contemporary virtue theories in America, theories of authenticity in the Continental tradition, and gender theory. The virtues of courage, compassion, and gratitude are examined in detail, and the book concludes with a more detailed discussion of a broad selection of moral issues, applying theories introduced in previous chapters. Each chapter concludes with a set of study questions, a section of Primary Readings with excerpts from classical and contemporary texts, and a section of Narratives, a collection of stories that illustrate the moral issues raised in the chapter. The Primary Readings are selected for their value as discussion topics; they don't necessarily reflect my own views, and I have made no attempt to select readings that cover all possible angles, because of space limitations. The Narratives will be described in more detail below.

Major Changes to the Sixth Edition

Major changes to the sixth edition include the following: Chapter 1 has been thoroughly revised, reflecting issues within value theory and the news in general from the past few years, such as global warming, the Virginia Tech murders, and the aftermath of the Abu Ghraib prisoner abuse. A section relating Philip Zimbardo's Stanford Prison experiment to Abu Ghraib as well as to Hannah Arendt's concept of *the banality of evil* has been added, and an excerpt from Zimbardo's book *The Lucifer Effect* is now one of the Primary Readings of the chapter. Furthermore, the groundbreaking research results from neuroscientists claiming that the sense of morals is hardwired is introduced in Chapter 1, and further discussed in subsequent chapters. An overview of the classical areas of philosophy has been inserted, as well as a revised and expanded discussion of the relationship between ethics and religion, the law, logic, emotions, and storytelling. A new narrative has been added to Chapter 1, Steinbeck's classic American novel *East of Eden*.

Chapter 2 has been revised and updated in regard to new films illustrating moral issues, and a new section explores the ethical potential of computer games. The Primary Readings section has a new excerpt from Raymond Chandler's famous piece "The Simple Art of Murder." A new narrative has been added, an excerpt from a short story by Charles Johnson, "The Education of Mingo." Chapter 3 now has an expanded treatment of soft universalism, as well as updated discussions, including the discussion on an American identity. An excerpt from Steinbeck's *America and Americans* has been added. Chapter 4 includes the story of the Virginia Tech massacre and Hurricane Katrina, and has been expanded with a discussion of David Hume's emotionalism, with an excerpt from Hume's *A Treatise of Human Nature*. The Primary Readings section in Chapter 4 now has an additional excerpt from Plato's *Republic,* and a new reading from Frans de Waal's book *Primates and Philosophers*.

In Chapter 5 you'll find a new section about Peter Singer, as well as the full text of his article "A Convenient Truth" in the Primary Readings. The discussion about torture has been expanded, reflecting the congressional debate in 2005–6 preceding the Military Commissions Act of 2006. Chapter 6 now has an analysis by Christine Korsgaard, and in the Narrative section you'll find a summary of the Woody Allen film *Match Point* and the film *3:10 to Yuma*. Chapter 7 has an updated discussion about personhood, including a discussion of statistics concerning the death of children at the hands of their caregivers; a new discussion about therapeutic versus reproductive cloning has been added, and the section about stem cell research has been updated, with a discussion of the moral implications of "designer humans" and genetic engineering. The section on free speech has been updated. Two op-ed pieces by American philosopher John Berteaux have been added to the Primary Readings. The Narrative section contains two new films, *Hotel Rwanda* and *The Island*.

Chapter 8 has a new section about virtue ethics in non-Western traditions, featuring African and indigenous American Indian cultures. An excerpt from Plato's *Republic* has been added to the Primary Readings, completing the discussion between Socrates and Glaucon to which the students have been introduced in Chapter 4.

Chapter 10 now features a discussion about what makes some students cheat, inspired by recent university scandals. The Narrative section has been expanded with two stories: the John Ford film *The Searchers* (which used to be part of Chapter 11) and the film *Good Will Hunting*. Sartre's *No Exit* excerpt has also been expanded. Chapter 11 discusses the death of soldier/football player Pat Tillman in the section on courage, as well as the 2005 recall of the mayor of Spokane. The question of the hardwiring of morality is resumed in the section on compassion, with an overview of current neuroscientific research. Chapter 12 has been expanded with a section featuring Sor Juana de la Cruz, as well as a discussion of the "Princess" phenomenon.

Chapter 13 has been thoroughly revised and expanded according to reviewers' and other professors' wishes, acknowledging that applied ethics is of the utmost importance in exploring and discussing moral values. Sections on abortion, euthanasia, media bias, business ethics, and environmental ethics have been added, and the existing sections on media ethics, just war theory, animal rights, and the death penalty have been updated. The book now concludes with a section moved from Chapter 2 and revised, about the ethics of self-improvement: narrative identity. Two reviews of Al Gore's film *An Inconvenient Truth* have been added to the Primary Readings, and Tristine Rainer's *Your Life As Story* has been relocated from Chapter 2. Two Readings in business ethics have been added: one a business ethics report from 2006, and the other a column on the Chinese food-poisoning scandal. The animal rights issue is addressed through two new readings. In the Narratives section *The Insider* has been moved from Chapter 7.

Using the Narratives

The Narratives have been chosen from a wide variety of sources ranging from epic prose, poems, and novels to films. I wish to emphasize that from a literary and artistic point of view, summaries and excerpts do not do the originals justice; a story worth experiencing, be it a novel, short story, or film, can't be reduced to a mere plot outline or fragment and still retain all of its essence. As Martha Nussbaum says, the form is an inherent part of the story content. Usually, there is more to the story than the bare bones of a moral problem, and in writing these summaries I have had to disregard much of the richness of story and character development. Nevertheless,

I have chosen the summary or excerpt format in order to discuss a number of different stories and genres as they relate to specific issues in ethics. Because I believe it is important to show that there is a cross-cultural, historic tradition of exploring moral problems through telling a story, I have opted for a broad selection of Narratives. Each chapter has several Narratives, but it is not my intention that the instructor should feel obligated to cover all of them in one course; rather, they should be regarded as options that can be alternated from semester to semester—a method I like to use for the sake of variety. There are, of course, other ways than summaries in which stories and ethical theory can be brought together; one might, for instance, select one or two short stories or films in their original format for class discussion. I hope that instructors will indeed select a few stories—novels, short stories, or videos—for their classes to experience firsthand. However, the Narratives are written so that firsthand experience should not be necessary to a discussion of the problem presented by the story. The summaries and excerpts give readers just enough information to enable them to discuss the moral problem presented. I hope that some readers will become inspired to seek out the originals on their own. In most cases the ending is important to the moral significance of a story, and whenever that is the case, I include that ending. In cases where the ending is not significant to the moral drama, I have done my best to avoid giving it away because I don't want to be a spoiler.

Because space is limited, I have not been able to include more than a sampling of stories, and I readily admit that my choices are subjective ones; I personally find them interesting as illustrations and effective in a classroom context where students come from many different cultural backgrounds. Because I am a naturalized U.S. citizen, originally a native of Denmark, I have chosen to include a few references to the Scandinavian literary tradition. I am fully aware that others might choose other stories or even choose different ethical problems to illustrate, and I am grateful to the many users of the previous five editions, instructors as well as students, who have let me know about their favorite stories and how they thought this selection of stories might be expanded and improved. The new Narratives reflect some of these suggestions.

For this sixth edition I have had to make some difficult choices: To keep the cost of the book down, I have had to cut materials from previous editions to make room for new readings, updates, and narratives. This is never easy, because many of the older readings and stories are favorites of mine, and I am well aware that they may also be the favorites of instructors using this book, and important elements in well-functioning syllabi. Fortunately, in this electronic age we can include new materials without losing the older elements. A website has been established by McGraw-Hill (www.mhhe.com/rosenstand6e) that includes the narratives that have been cut from the fifth edition, and also a number of stories from previous editions, such as *How to Be Good, Sideshow, Madame Bovary, Abandon Ship, Saving Private Ryan, Blade Runner, Grand Canyon, Hero, Tombstone,* and the *Star Trek: Next Generation* episode "Justice." Whenever possible, readings and discussions that have been deleted from the sixth edition have also been transferred to the website, for easy access and downloading by instructors. As in previous editions, I emphasize that I wholeheartedly welcome e-mails from students as well as instructors who use this book, with relevant comments and suggestions for new stories as well as additional philosophical perspectives: nrosenst@sdccd.edu.

Acknowledgments

*A*s always, I first want to thank my students in the classes Introduction to Philosophy: Values, Philosophy of Women, Issues in Social Philosophy, Reflections on Human Nature, Human Nature and Society, and Philosophy and Literature for their enthusiastic cooperation in suggesting good stories and discussing drafts of the stories and study questions in this edition with me—an invaluable help in fine-tuning the summaries and questions.

Next, I want to thank the production team at McGraw-Hill Higher Education: my editor, Mark Georgiev, for his support and encouragement, and for sharing my vision of the continued journey of *The Moral of the Story;* Leslie LaDow, my production editor, for her clear overview and instant cheerful communications; and my copy editor, Carole Crouse, for her meticulous reviews of my revisions, as well as her insightful queries and comments. In addition, Briana Porco, Natalia Peschiera, Kristie Kelly, Ron Nelms, and Rich DeVitto have provided valuable help. The cover painting is by artist Karen Barbour, and I am delighted that her evocative visions have represented *The Moral of the Story* through six editions. I also wish to thank the following reviewers for their suggestions:

Susan Anderson, *University of Connecticut*

Raymond Anthony, *University of Alaska*

Steve Bein, *University of Rochester*

David Boonin, *University of Colorado*

Joy Branch, *Southern Union State CC*

Prakash Chenjer, *Southern Oregon University*

Seth Holtzman, *Catawba College*

Brian E. Klunk, *University of the Pacific*

Kris Pratt, *Palm Beach Atlantic University*

Steve Reiter, *Central Community College*

Dari Sylvester, *University of the Pacific*

J. Jeremy Wisnewski, *Hartwick College*

My colleagues at the Social Sciences and Behavioral and Multicultural Studies Department at San Diego Mesa College, which includes professors, adjuncts, and professors emeritus of philosophy, history, political science, and geography, are a wonderful support group—many of us come from different professional fields and have different outlooks on many things, but we all cherish the ambience of professional integrity in our workplace and find time to discuss ethics-related issues on a regular basis: Thank you to my colleagues from the Social Sciences Department as well as other departments: In particular I wish to thank Jonathan McLeod, Mary Lou Locke, Donald Abbott, Ken Berger, Michael Kuttnauer, Richard Hammes, Charles Zappia, Terry Valverde, and Melinda Campbell. In addition, I would like to express my appreciation to Michael Mussachia, Josef Binter, and Arelene Wolinski for sharing their research—including informative articles—with me, and to Tony Pettina for being an advance reader on the section on Asian moral philosophy. A special thanks goes to Dwight Furrow for continual congenial collaboration on maintaining the high standard of teaching philosophy at Mesa College, and for jogging my memory about one of my favorite films, *The Searchers,* and pointing out its usefulness in illustrating Emmanuel Levinas's theory of the face of the other. Because of Dwight's inspired insight, *The Searchers,* one of the narratives in the first editions, has now found its way back to the sixth edition, in a different context.

At Mesa College we have a biannual *Meeting of the Minds* tradition where philosophy faculty, contract as well as adjuncts, meet and share our thoughts about teaching, and engage in debates about classical and current philosophical topics. I want to express my appreciation for the professional enthusiasm of all the philosophy faculty who participate regularly in these meetings. I treasure these inspired discussions, which have resulted in the 2007 establishing of a blog, *Philosophy on the Mesa,* administered by Dwight Furrow and myself, which I hope users of this book will visit from time to time: http://philosophyonthemesa.com. My colleague, John Berteaux, philosophy professor at Monterey State University, deserves my heartfelt thanks for not only being an old friend and colleague from the adjunct days but also sharing my concerns for issues in social ethics and for sharing his archive of newspaper columns with me. I wish to thank independent scholar and author Maxine Sheets-Johnstone for her inspiring books on the root causes of personhood—but not least for being a caring, letter-writing friend for a quarter of a century. A special, warm thank you goes to my friend and colleague Harold Weiss, associate professor of philosophy at Northhampton Community College. I have known Harold for years through e-mails, and finally had the pleasure of meeting him in person at the APA Pacific Meeting 2007, where I was invited to give a paper. Harold has made invaluable contributions to this edition of the book in the form of debate suggestions, requests for clarification, and film ideas. I would also like to thank Michael Schwartz, School of Economics, Finance and Marketing Professor at the Royal Melbourne Institute of Technology, Australia, for his kind words about *The Moral of the Story,* and his insightful suggestions relating to the new business ethics section.

New to this edition is a focus on the moral philosophy of John Steinbeck. A few years ago I was contacted by professor of literature Stephen George, Brigham Young University, inviting me to contribute to a new book he was editing, *Ethics, Literature, Theory*. This first contact led to many congenial e-mail exchanges and phone calls, and eventually to an invitation for me to participate as a philosopher in the memorable 2006 literature conference in Sun Valley, Idaho, "John Steinbeck and His Contemporaries." I was finally able to meet Stephen in person, ascertaining that he was indeed a delightful human being, as well as a great scholar with a fresh vision of building a bridge between literary critics and philosophers through the medium of ethics. Stephen George should have had the opportunity to affect the intellectual debate in this country for years to come with his innovating ideas—but in 2007 we, his friends and colleagues, as well as the nation, suffered a great loss with his passing at the heartbreakingly early age of forty-seven. I am eternally grateful to Stephen

George for reaching out to philosophers and literary critics, suggesting that we meet in the middle and together examine the moral philosophy in literature. And I am awed by his choice to keep working on putting the conference together and, afterward, compiling the book *John Steinbeck and His Contemporaries,* based on conference papers, even as his health deteriorated. I extend my gratitude to Barbara Heavilin, Taylor University, who took over his editorial work with sensitivity and loyalty when he was no longer able to carry on.

In addition, I am grateful to two great philosophers who also put their faith in the power of stories to convey moral lessons and debates: Richard Hart, professor of ethics at Bloomfield College, and Charles Johnson, novelist and professor of English at the University of Washington. Our prolonged after-dinner discussion of ethics and literature at the Steinbeck Conference reminded all of us of the original reason we had joined the ranks of philosophers in the first place—the love of ideas, and the exchange of ideas.

The first and second editions wouldn't have been possible without my first editor at Mayfield Publishing Company, my good friend Jim Bull. And the previous editions wouldn't have been possible without the help and suggestions from the following friends and colleagues: Helmut Wautischer, Sonoma State University; Eugene Troxell and Peter Atterton, San Diego State University; Betsy Decyk, Daniel Guerriere, and G. A. Spangler, California State University, Long Beach. In addition, I am grateful to Richard Taylor for his correspondence, to the late Philip Hallie for his inspiration, and to his late wife Dorrit Hallie; to Russell Means for sharing his views on American Indian traditions; to Leonard Maltin for his time and advice while I was working on the first edition; to Sue Savage-Rumbaugh for her time and comments on a draft of the second edition; to Carol Enns, College of the Sequoias; John Osborne, Butte College; Thomas Wren, Loyola University, Chicago; Lawrence Hinman, University of San Diego; Linda MacDonald Glenn, University of Vermont School of Nursing and Allied Health Care; Peter Kemp, Danish University of Education; Hans Hertel, University of Copenhagen; Steen Wackerhausen, University of Aarhus.

As in previous editions, I want to thank a few good friends outside the philosophical profession for their support, friendship, and intellectual contributions to this edition: J. R. Edmondson, author and historian, for insightful conversations on ethics and politics during his too-brief visits to San Diego; Frank Thompson, author and film historian, whose support of my inclusion of films in my narrative approach to ethics has been very important to me over the years; Philip Martin, for being a continued helpful source of film suggestions; author Mark Fuhrman and columnist Rebecca Mack, formerly of 1510 KGA, Spokane, Washington, for discussions and fact-sharing on ethics, politics, and criminal justice, on and off the air. I have an immense appreciation for their commonsense approach, integrity, and delightful sense of the absurd.

Last, on a very personal note, I wish to thank colleagues, friends, and family— everyone whose sympathy, wise words, and kind deeds gave me comfort during my mother's illness and passing. Many of you are already mentioned above in other contexts. In particular, my profound gratitude goes to Christa and Søren, Susanne, Betty, Randi, Marianne, Kelly, Søren and Jytte, my mother-in-law Nancy, my sister-in-law

Lois, and my brother-in-law Russ, for e-mails, letters, and talks about the human condition, as well as for their love and support during that difficult time. Philosophy instructors who have used the previous editions of *The Moral of the Story* may remember that I have, with much pride and gratitude, always included my mother and father, Gladys and Finn Rosenstand, in my acknowledgment, as well as our dog Rowdie. 2007 brought both the loss of my mother and soon thereafter the loss of Rowdie. The lessons of life, and in particular moral lessons learned from my mother's example, her love, her sense of duty and her wisdom, will be with me as long as I live; the lessons learned from Rowdie about the brave, loyal heart and astute mind of a nonhuman fellow traveler through time are lessons I treasure and apply continually in my personal as well as my professional life. I have the immense privilege of being able to again thank my father for continued wonderful discussions about everything in life that matters, and for looking out for interesting books and articles for me. A great researcher and storyteller in his own right, he has been instrumental in opening my mind to intellectual curiosity, human compassion, and a passion for history, literature, and film (including Western movies). But above all I want to thank my husband, Craig Covner, for his strength and loving support during very dark times as well as good times, for his understanding, and for his wonderful sense of humor.

Chapter One

Thinking About Values

The Best of Times, the Worst of Times?

*C*harles Dickens's *A Tale of Two Cities* from 1859 begins with this passage:

> It was the best of times, it was the worst of times,
> it was the age of wisdom, it was the age of foolishness,
> it was the epoch of belief, it was the epoch of incredulity,
> it was the season of Light, it was the season of Darkness,
> it was the spring of hope, it was the winter of despair,
> we had everything before us, we had nothing before us,
> we were all going direct to Heaven, we were all going direct
> the other way—in short, the period was so far like the present
> period, that some of its noisiest authorities insisted on its
> being received, for good or for evil, in the superlative degree
> of comparison only.

Dickens was referring to the era of the French Revolution, but, as many have pointed out, his words apply to just about any particular time period one cares to scrutinize. And yet—aren't those words a particularly good fit for the first decade of the twenty-first century? We have witnessed human atrocities across the planet, from Rwanda to Darfur, to Bali, to London and Madrid, and natural disasters such as tsunamis, blizzards, and hurricanes. With every disaster we have encountered in the last few years—as with those before—we have seen horror and suffering, but we have also seen extraordinary examples of people helping other people. During Hurricane Katrina, which hit New Orleans and other coastal areas in Louisiana, Mississippi, and Georgia, there were heartbreaking stories of neighborhoods being lost, of families being split up, of people perishing and pets disappearing, of public mismanagement of badly needed resources, and—probably most disturbing of all—of people abandoning those who depended on them, or even preying on their fellow human beings. But there were also stories of locals helping one another, staying behind to help the old and the sick, and of complete strangers from other areas of the country stepping up to the plate and offering their help. A few years later, the one student who murdered thirty-two human beings at Virginia Tech sent shockwaves through the nation, but only hours after the tragedy we started hearing about professors and students who had risked their lives to save others—in one case resulting in the death of a professor. The worst atrocity yet to hit the nation, the terrorist attacks of September 11, 2001, left nearly three thousand victims dead in New York City, the Pentagon, and a field in Pennsylvania. And though the terrorists had attempted to strike at the heart of the United States, we saw heroic people working to save lives, sometimes at the cost of their own. We are continually bombarded by images, names, and stories of individuals committing acts of violence and dehumanization, from foreign terrorists, to homegrown murderers, to prison guards who abuse their prisoners, to pedophiles who abuse children, and to people who turn a blind eye to all that abuse—but we also hear of people trying to heal the wounds and to prevent further hurt from taking place. After many years of silence, the victims of sexual abuse by Catholic priests are finding support, and the victimizers are being exposed. A mayor in the state of Washington was recalled by the people of his city for unethical behavior on the job. And during the 2007 wildfires in San Diego, when half a million people were evacuated from their homes, the main evacuation center at Qualcom Stadium reported that they had all the help and donations they needed, because of a huge volunteer effort from all over the county, and they redirected volunteers to other evacuation centers. The worst of times, perhaps, but also the best of times . . .

Still a "50-50 Nation"?

In the presidential elections of 2000 and 2004, the very close election results made it clear that we live in a politically divided nation. Congress, split about evenly between Democrats and Republicans, reflects that division, a phenomenon sometimes referred to as "a 50-50 nation." The vast political differences of Democrats and Republicans—depicted as "blue states" and "red states" on TV screens on Election Night—are reflected in the key issues in the public debate, including abortion, gun control, gay rights, and our military presence in Iraq and Afghanistan. However, we can't predict that all Democrats are going to be pro-choice/pro-abortion, anti–gun

LA CUCARACHA   **BY LALO ALCARAZ**

© 2004 Lalo Alcaraz. Reprinted by permission of Universal Press Syndicate. All rights reserved.

The comic strip *La Cucaracha* takes on the "50-50 nation" concept here, speculating that "blue" (Democratic) and "red" (Republican) states may have their own Santa Clauses. The original version is in color, with the red-state Santa in traditional red, and the blue-state Santa in a blue outfit.

ownership, pro–gay rights, and anti-war, or that all Republicans will be pro-life/anti-abortion, pro–gun ownership rights, anti–gay rights, or pro-war, because both parties are, at least ideally, "big tents" where many different opinions are supposed to be welcome. Nor is everybody either a Democrat or a Republican: Many people don't register to vote at all, and other parties, such as the Libertarian Party and the Green Party, are on the ballot too. In addition, there is a steadily growing number of "Independents," voters who "decline to state" a party on their voter registration form, and vote according to their conviction in each case rather than along party lines. So it is misleading to say that the nation is divided down the middle in its voting patterns—and the "50-50" concept has been increasingly eroded since the 2004 election in one respect: Although the voting population may still be as divided as before when it comes to domestic politics, there was a dramatic increase in criticism of the war in Iraq, from Republicans as well as from Democrats, although Democratic anti-war views from 2004 to 2007 soared from 55 to 90 percent, whereas Republican anti-war voters went up from 9 to 24 percent, according to a 2007 CNN poll. Some would call that party politics. Others would describe it as a genuine critical attitude toward a war that didn't go the way it was expected to go. Still others would point out that poll results are determined by the way the questions are asked, and who asks them. (In Chapter 13 you can read more about the entire concept of what constitutes a "just war," as well as the concept of "media ethics.")

However, in one area that is not related to the wars in Iraq and Afghanistan there seems to be much less political disagreement than before: the issue of *global warming*. Whereas there was widespread skepticism in previous decades about whether Planet Earth was heating up, there is now a general planetwide acknowledgment that temperatures are indeed rising, to the extent that the climate is undergoing a fairly rapid change and will affect every living being on the planet to a greater or lesser degree. Former Vice President Al Gore's Oscar-winning documentary, *An Inconvenient Truth,* has stirred the imagination and fears of many across the political spectrum, but though many agree that glaciers are melting, deserts are spreading, and ocean waters are rising, the *cause* is still under debate: Is global warming due to human irresponsible use of resources, raising the carbon dioxide levels of the atmosphere and creating a "greenhouse effect," or is it due to a greater cycle of climatic changes that happen independently of humans? (In Chapter 13 we return to the issue of environmental ethics and global warming.) An ABCNews online article declared that we can no longer talk only about "blue" and "red" politics—we must now add *green* to the overall picture: Since politicians from both the right and the left agree (even if they may disagree on why) that global warming is happening, there is now a movement to engage in more responsible environmental politics, such as caps on carbon and greenhouse gas emissions. This "green" attitude has developed not only because of an increased awareness of accountability but also because going "green" means increased campaign contributions!

But there are additional issues. In the 2000 and 2004 elections, some found it extremely important to elect a president who would support certain *values,* so in a sense we can be viewed as residents of two American moral cultures: the culture of liberal values and the culture of conservative values. Some call it a culture war. It isn't uncommon for some of us to identify so deeply with one that we downright refuse to accept the legitimacy or even the rationality of the other. As we strive to become a nation of successful diversity, we sometimes forget that *moral and political diversity* also deserves a place alongside diversity of gender, race, religion, economic background, sexual orientation, and so forth. In other words, people have a right to have a wide variety of opinions, and we have little chance of being able to talk with one another if we keep thinking that everybody who doesn't agree with us is stupid, ignorant, or evil.

On the other hand, an acceptance of the fact that people disagree on moral issues doesn't have to lead to a moral relativism, or an assumption that there is always "another side" to everything. Despite our moral differences in this culture, most "reasonable" people are going to agree on some basic values: In my experience, the majority of Americans are in favor of justice and equality, and against murder, child abuse, racism, sexism, slavery, animal torture, and so forth. In Chapter 3 you'll find a discussion of ethical relativism, and in Chapter 11 you'll find a further discussion of the search for common values in a politically divided culture.

Good and Evil

On April 16, 2007, all previous mass killings in the United States were eclipsed by what happened at Virginia Tech University in Blacksburg, Virginia: Thirty-two students and professors were murdered by one student, Seung-Hui Cho, a senior in English Literature. Students with their lives ahead of them and professors dedicated to doing research that might benefit humanity were mowed down by someone with a personal gripe against "rich kids." At the end of his murder spree, Cho killed himself. Was Seung-Hui Cho looking for help and understanding? We know that he had a long history of mental aberrations, even mental illness. He was taking antidepressants, he had shown signs of aggressive behavior, such as making a student film advocating violence, and he had been identified as a stalker, but survivors reported that he didn't behave in an uncontrolled way. The bottom line is that he made some choices, armed himself, sought out his victims in a careful, deliberate way, and killed as many as he could, after sending a video "manifesto" to MSNBC. In Chapter 4 we'll meet one of his victims, a professor who gave up his life to save his students. For now, my question to you is, how would you characterize Cho's actions—as morally wrong, as misguided, or simply as *evil*? The concept of evil is generally considered controversial in a debate about moral values, and yet many of us believe that, when reserved for truly heinous acts, it is the only term strong enough to express our moral outrage.

Another example: A few years ago, in Idaho, Joseph Duncan abducted two small children, Shasta and Dylan, after murdering their mother, her fiancé, and their older brother in front of them. He took the children to a remote forest clearing in Montana, where he tortured them and abused them. After killing Dylan, he dismembered him and tried to burn his body. Then he took Shasta with him on a trek toward the West Coast, and had they not been recognized by a waitress and patrons at a Denny's restaurant who called the police, Shasta would probably not have survived to bear witness against Duncan. Would you call Duncan's actions morally wrong? misguided? or evil? Let me change the focus slightly: Would you call Duncan *himself* evil? Would you call Cho himself evil? We aren't nearly as reluctant to call a person's *actions* evil as we are to judge the person himself or herself to be evil. We may want to explore the psychological differences between Duncan, who wanted to live to enjoy some more torturing and killing, and Cho, who apparently was depressed and desperate and wanted to die (but not alone); and we may want to qualify our assessment of evil deeds and create a system of degrees: "more and less evil." But most of us don't feel uncomfortable using the term *evil* in the first place.

For many people the topic of morals involves the concepts of *good* and *evil*, and the choices we make in one direction or the other. Certainly, in the post–September 11 world it has become more customary to use the term *evil* to describe an attitude that disregards the humanity and dignity of another person. So what do the professionals say—the ethicists who make a living teaching theories of moral values and writing papers, monographs, and textbooks? Interestingly, most contemporary ethicists tend to talk about issues such as selfishness and unselfishness, informed consent, weighing moral principles against overall consequences of one's actions, group rights versus individual rights, and so forth. We hear discussions about the concepts of moral *right and wrong* and the principles by which we determine such concepts. What we rarely hear mentioned by any contemporary ethicists are the concepts that most people associate with moral issues: *good and evil*. Exceptions would be American philosophers such as Philip Hallie and Richard Taylor and the British philosopher Mary Midgley. Why are so few philosophers these days interested in talking about good and evil, when it was one of the key topics in centuries past? For one thing, there is an underlying assumption that good and evil are *religious* concepts, and as we shall see, the philosophical discussions about ethics and values these days tend to steer clear of the religious connection to ethics. For another, talking about good and evil generally implies that we *pass judgment* on what is good and what is evil—which means that we take sides, we no longer analyze concepts in some lofty realm of objectivity, we engage ourselves in seeking good and shunning evil. It also means that we condemn those who are labeled evil and praise those we call good. In other words, we engage in what some would call *moralizing*, and most ethicists have for decades tried to avoid just that, with some exceptions. However, since September 11 the concept of evil has been part of our political vocabulary, spearheaded by President Bush, who labeled nations supporting terrorism as an *axis of evil* and referred to the terrorists of 9/11 and others as *evildoers*. A precedent was created when President Reagan labeled the Soviet Union "The Evil Empire" in the 1980s. Although that terminology, to some critics, is far too close to a religious vocabulary for comfort, for other Americans there is great relief and, indeed, comfort in being able to use a word with the weight of tradition behind it to describe something most of us consider dreadful acts committed by people with no consideration for human decency.

But what exactly do we call evil? Is evil a force that exists outside human beings—is there a source of evil such as the devil, some satanic eternal power that tempts and preys on human souls? Or is it, rather, a force within the human mind, disregarding the needs and interests of other human beings just to accomplish a goal? Or might it perhaps be a *lack of something* in the human mind—a blind spot where the rest of us have a sense of community, belonging, empathy for others? In that case, might we explain the acts of "evildoers" as those of sick individuals? But wouldn't that entail that they can't be *blamed* for what they do, because we don't usually blame people for their illnesses? Those are questions that involve religion, psychology, and ethics, and there is to this day no consensus among scholars as to how "evil" should be interpreted. Some see terrorists, serial killers, and child molesters as evil, but we may not agree on what makes them evil—a childhood deprived of love, a genetic predisposition, a selfish choice that involves disregard for other people's humanity, a brainwashing by an ideology that distinguishes between "real" people and throw-away people, an outside superhuman evil force that chooses a human vehicle? For the German philosopher Immanuel Kant, whom you'll meet in Chapter 6, there was no doubt what evil is: the self-serving choice that individuals make freely, even when they know full well the moral law they ought to be following. But that may not be all there is to it. When the Abu Ghraib prison scandal hit in 2005, many people were reminded of two groundbreaking American psychology experiments: the Stanley Milgram obedience experiments at Yale University in the 1960s, wherein Professor Milgram showed that if you are under the influence of an authority who takes re-sponsibility for your actions, you are likely to be willing to commit acts of atrocity toward other human beings; and the Stanford Prison Experiment in 1971, wherein a group of experimental subjects—ordinary male college students—were divided into "prisoners" and "prison guards." Before long the "prison guards" began treating the "prisoners" with abusive cruelty, believing that such behavior was somehow warranted to maintain authority. The German film *The Experiment* is a chilling reen-actment of the experiment. Some see such an event as proof that human nature is fundamentally bad—it doesn't take much for the veneer of civilization to wear thin, and our true, evil nature surfaces. For others, all this means is that there are all kinds of reasons why people do what they do; some of what we call evil is based on a moral choice, and some of it is an outcome of environmental pressures or brain anomalies.

In 2007 the researcher responsible for the Stanford Prisoner Experiment, Philip Zimbardo, published a book, *The Lucifer Effect,* in which he drew parallels between the experiment and the Abu Ghraib incident. You'll find an excerpt from this book in the Primary Readings section of this chapter. But already in 1963, the German philosopher Hannah Arendt had coined an expression for this particular shade of wrongdoing: *the banality of evil.* Arendt was living in Germany when Hitler came to power, but she managed to flee to Paris before the Holocaust: She was a German Jew, and would undoubtedly have been swept up in the extermination process. Years after the war she was tormented not only by the thought of the atrocities perpetrated in the death camps but also by the knowledge that so many human beings either stood by and let the Holocaust happen or actively participated in the torture and death of other human beings. (And, for the record, the Holocaust *did* happen—13 million people perished in the Nazi death camps on the orders of Hitler and his henchmen Himmler and Eichmann, and those who deny that fact are playing political games. Enough said.) The conclusion reached by Arendt and published in her book *Adolf Eichmann in Jerusalem: A Report on the Banality of Evil* is that the German public who had an inkling of what was going on and the Nazis who were actively engaged in the

Endlösung, or the "Final Solution," were not evil in the sense that they (or most of them) deliberately sought to gain personal advantage by causing pain and suffering to others. Rather, it was more insidious: Little by little, they came to view the atrocities they were asked to perform, or disregard, as a duty to their country and their leader, as something their victims deserved, or simply as a normal state of affairs and not something hideous or depraved. They became banal, everyday acts, corrupting the minds of the victimizers. In Arendt's words about Eichmann's execution for his participation in the Holocaust:

> It was as though in those last minutes he was summing up the lesson that this long course in human wickedness had taught us—the lesson of the fearsome, word-and-thought-defying *banality of evil.* . . . The trouble with Eichmann was precisely that so many were like him, and that the many were neither perverted nor sadistic, that they were, and still are, terribly and terrifyingly normal. From the viewpoint of our legal institutions and of our moral standards of judgment, this normality was much more terrifying than all the atrocities put together, for it implied—as had been said at Nuremberg over and over again by the defendants and their counsels—that this new type of criminal . . . commits his crimes under circumstances that make it well-nigh impossible for him to know or to feel that he is doing wrong. . . .

But before we begin to assume that all evil acts are of the kind that may lurk in ordinary people's hearts, let us just remind ourselves that not all evil acts are "banal." Surely, the deliberate torturing and killing of children by a Joseph Duncan is not the kind of evil that ordinary people are periodically persuaded to perform under extraordinary circumstances, and neither are the deliberate mass murders at Virginia Tech, or the videotaped beheadings of civilians—Western as well as non-Western— by Al Qaeda. If we want to adopt the vocabulary of "evil," in addition to "morally wrong" and "misguided," we must also recognize that there are *degrees* of evil, ranging from reluctantly causing pain (such as in the Milgram experiments), to humiliating other human beings, to abusing, torturing, and killing them with deliberation and gusto. And perhaps it is a disservice to our sense of evil to assume that "we're all capable of doing evil." Some forms of evil are the result not of ordinary people being seduced into insensitivity but of some people's deliberate choices to cause harm.

In Chapter 11, in the section about the philosopher Philip Hallie, you'll read a story that goes into detail about rising up against evil: the story of a French village that rebelled against the Nazis. Hallie presents this story as an "antidote to cruelty," and you will find an additional reference to Philip Zimbardo and his coining of a new term, "the banality of heroism," a theory that claims that if evil is a possibility in our hearts, so, too, are heroism and altruism—in other words, inherent *goodness.*

So what do we label "good"? There is hardly a word with a broader meaning in the English language—we can talk about food tasting good, test results being good, a feeling being good, but also, of course, of actions being good and persons being good, and we mean something different in all these examples. In Box 1.1 you'll find a discussion of moral and nonmoral values, and "good" fits right into that discussion: It is a value term because it expresses approval, but it can be an approval that has to do with moral issues (such as actions and a person's character) or it can be unrelated

In *The Lord of the Rings* (2001–3) the concept of evil is symbolized by the Ring. Here the hobbit Smeagol (Andy Serkis) finds the Ring on his birthday (top). Many years later the effects of evil are clearly visible: Smeagol has become Gollum (bottom), a solitary creature whose mind is focused exclusively on the Ring.

Box 1.1 MORAL AND NONMORAL VALUES

What is a *value?* Most often the word refers to a moral value, a judgment of somebody's behavior according to whether or not it corresponds to certain moral rules (for example, "Tiffany is a wonderful person; she always stays after the party to help with the dishes"). However, some value judgments have nothing to do with moral issues, and so they are called *nonmoral*, which is not the same as *immoral* (breaking moral rules) or *amoral* (not having any moral standards). Such nonmoral value judgments can include statements about taste (such as "The new gallery downtown has a collection of exquisite watercolors"; "I really dislike Bob's new haircut"; and "Finn makes a great jambalaya"), as well as statements about being correct or incorrect about facts (such as "Lois did really well on her last math test" and "You're wrong; last Saturday we didn't go to the movies; that was last Sunday"). Like moral value judgments, nonmoral value judgments generally refer to something being right or wrong, good or bad; but, unlike moral value judgments, they don't refer to morally right or wrong behavior. Nonmoral value concepts abound in our present-day society: What we call *aesthetics,* art theory, is a form of nonmoral value

theory, asking questions such as, Are there objective rules for when art is good? and Is it bad, or is it a matter of personal taste or of acculturation? If you dislike hip-hop music, or like Craftsman-style architecture, are there valid objective justifications for your likes and dislikes, or are they relative to your time and place? Art theory even has an additional values concept: the relationship between light and dark colors in a painting. But the most prevalent nonmoral value concept in our everyday world surely has to do with getting *good value*—with buying something for less than it is worth. That prompted a political commentator, Michael Kinsley, who was fed up with the political talk about moral values a few years ago, to quip, "When I want values, I go to Wal-Mart." And McDonald's has been running a commercial suggesting that parents who want *family values* should take their kids to McDonald's for the Value Meal, appealing to the perennial parental guilt. In other words, satirists and copywriters can have a field day doing a switcheroo on our conception of values, from nonmoral to moral and back again, and what we readers and consumers can do is stay on our toes so we aren't manipulated.

to moral issues, such as judging the result of a quiz, or a medical test, or something we approve of because of its aesthetic qualities (it looks good, tastes good, sounds good, etc.). If we assume that we're interested mostly in the moral value of "good," we have only narrowed it down somewhat, because now we have to define what, in our context and in our culture, is considered a morally good act. It could be acting according to the rules of one's culture's religion; it could be acting with compassion or with foresight as to the overall consequences of one's actions; or it could be simply doing one's duty. A "good person" could be someone who is simply nice by nature, but it could also be someone who struggles to do the right thing, perhaps even against his or her nature. Or it could be simply someone we approve of, based on our cultural rules. But there is also something called being "too good," like a Goody Two-Shoes, so perhaps being morally above reproach isn't always good? In the Narrative section at the end of this chapter, you'll find a selection from John Steinbeck's famous novel *East of Eden,* with a discussion of not only the ultimate story of good and evil but also how the ideas of good and evil can be perceived by an adolescent who wants to be good like his twin brother but finds himself to be of quite a different nature.

Is Morality Hardwired?

Over the course of the twentieth century and the beginning of the twenty-first, ethicists (moral philosophers) have been divided as to the nature and origin of moral values. Some have claimed that, somehow, values are embedded in the human psyche and that every human being within the normal range, psychologically, has a set of values. Although such values will evidently differ somewhat from culture to culture, according to this theory values will not differ radically from culture to culture, since we all come equipped with a moral intuition, hardwired from birth. Others have claimed that our value systems are exclusively a matter of social convention, convenient systems for living in groups, so they can be completely different from culture to culture. Yet others have held that our morals, although not hardwired, are not relative but a result of rational deliberation. In upcoming chapters we look at the theories of cultural and ethical relativism as well as the entire question of which values we ought to have—values that simply reflect the culture we live in, values that we feel naturally drawn to, or values that reflect a timeless rational system of ethics regardless of our cultural affiliation.

In a manner of speaking, both the view that morals are relative and the view that we have a moral intuition have found support in twenty-first-century science: The relativist points to the vast knowledge amassed by anthropology over a hundred years showing that, indeed, moral values differ dramatically all over the planet; in addition, psychology has shown how flexible the mind of the human child is, ready to adapt to any social convention favored by the group it grows up within. And yet, moral intuitionism has seen a boost from neuroscientists within the last few years.

In 1999, researchers led by Antonio Damasio, then at the University of Iowa, found that an area in the brain, the prefrontal cortex, plays a pivotal role in our development of a moral sense. People who have undergone a normal psychological and moral development (1) know there is a difference between right and wrong, and (2) can act on that knowledge. Adults who have had their prefrontal cortex damaged in an accident still know the difference between right and wrong, but somehow it doesn't translate into action: They can't make decisions based on that knowledge or act on such decisions. Two patients investigated by the Iowa team had suffered damage to their prefrontal cortex before they were sixteen months of age, and—in spite of having apparently recovered from their injuries, having normal intellectual capacities, and having been reared in stable, middle-class homes—both developed severely antisocial behavior as adolescents and adults: recklessness, inability to care about others, including their own babies, abuse of others, and criminal tendencies. They seemed to recognize moral issues intellectually but were unable to act on them because they had no sense of the consequences of their actions.

In 2007 Damasio and other neuroscientists followed up on this study and came to another astounding conclusion: that the human brain contains an area that enables us to think about other people's lives with empathy. People who have suffered damage to that particular part of the brain may make decisions that are logical and rational, but the empathy element is missing: Where "normal" brains hesitate before choosing a course of action that will save the many but cost the lives of a few, people with damage to that part of the brain have little hesitation. Later in this chapter you'll find a more detailed discussion of that study.

In addition, American neuroscientists such as Marc Hauser and V. Ramachandran have pointed to features within human cognition that are surprisingly similar the world over. For Hauser, we have a universal sense of right and wrong, regardless of our culture. A form of "moral grammar" is hardwired into our brain, and even children recognize that there is a difference between something being just a matter of cultural choice, and something being morally repugnant. Ramachandran has, with his coining of the term "mirror-neurons," identified a remarkable capacity of the human mind: to intuitively understand the intentions of other people. All these recent findings in neuroscience indeed seem to point to a fundamental human capacity for comprehending a system of values—a capacity that may even extend outside the human realm, as you'll see in Chapter 4.

So now that we know where our morals are located in the brain, can we say we understand everything about the issues of morals, ethics, and values? Can we perhaps say that a person whose moral center is damaged shouldn't be held accountable for what she or he does? This is where sweeping generalizations can become dangerous: It may be that some people are genuinely unaware of the moral consequences of their actions—but it may be a dubious legal trend to assume that every criminal must have a damaged prefrontal cortex. For if we do so, we create an easy excuse and throw out the possibility of people actually making decisions *deliberately*—decisions that go against the values of society. Indeed, we should be careful not to assume that neuroscience can tell us everything we need to know about who we are. Brain

Dilbert by Scott Adams

© Scott Adams/Dist. by United Feature Syndicate, Inc.

Lately, research has pointed to the existence of an actual moral center in the brain. If that center is damaged, the individual seems to have a hard time acting on moral deliberations or even understanding moral issues. Obviously, this *Dilbert* cartoon takes a dim view of whether people in management have a functioning moral center.

research can pinpoint where our thoughts and feelings originate and what affects them chemically, but it can't tell us whether one moral answer is better than another. For that, we need to engage in a discussion of values. Such a discussion can take place from a variety of viewpoints, called moral philosophies, and you'll encounter a broad selection of them in this book. And even if we may all have a built-in capacity for values, the moral relativist may still have a point: The capacity for values may be expressed in different ways within different cultures, to the extent that some value systems develop which are, in most respects, completely different from other systems.

Values, Morals, and Ethics

In its most basic sense, something we value is something we believe is set apart from things that we don't value or that we value less. When do we first begin to value something? As babies, we live in a world that is divided into what we like and what we don't like—a binary world of plus and minus, of yes and no. Some psychoanalysts believe we never really get over this early stage, so that some people simply divide the world into what they like or approve of, and what they dislike or disapprove of. However, most of us add to that a justification for our preferences or aversions. And this is where the concept of *moral values* comes in. Having "values" implies that we have a moral code that we live by, or at least that we tell ourselves we try to live by, a set of beliefs about what constitutes good conduct and a good character. Perhaps equally important, having values implies that we have a conception of what society should be, such as a promoter of values we consider good, a safety net for when things go wrong, an overseer that punishes bad behavior and rewards good behavior, a caregiver for all our basic needs, or a minimalist organization that protects the people against internal and external enemies but otherwise leaves them alone to pursue their own happiness. In Chapter 7 we examine several of these conceptions of social values.

In the late twentieth century the number of college classes in introductory ethics and value theory swelled. When they hear I teach ethics, people who are unfamiliar with how college classes in the subject are taught say, "Good! Our college students really need that!" That response always makes me pause: What do they think I teach? Right from wrong? Of course, we do have discussions about right and wrong, and we can, from time to time, even reach agreement about some moral responses being *preferable* to other moral responses. If students haven't acquired a sense of values by the time they're in college, I fear it's too late: Psychologists say a child must develop a sense of values *by the age of seven* to become an adult with a conscience. If the child hasn't learned by the second grade that other people can feel pain and pleasure, and that one should try not to harm others, that lesson will probably never be truly learned. Fortunately, that doesn't mean everyone must be taught the *same* moral lessons by the age of seven—as long as we have *some* moral background to draw on later, as a sounding board for further ethical reflections, we can come from morally widely diverse homes and still become morally dependable people. A child growing up in a criminal, *Sopranos*-type of family will certainly have acquired a set of morals by the age of seven—but it isn't necessarily the same set of morals as those acquired by a child in a liberal, secular, humanist family or in a Seventh-Day Adventist family. The point is that all these children will have their "moral center" activated and can expand their moral universe. A child who has never been taught *any* moral lessons may be a sociopath of the future, a person who has no comprehension of how other people feel, no empathy.

If having moral values has to do with brain chemistry, and with simple likes and dislikes, why don't we turn to the disciplines of neuroscience and psychology for an understanding of values? Why is philosophy the discipline that examines the values issue? That question goes to the core of what philosophy is: Neuroscience can tell us about the physical underpinnings of our mental life and possibly whether our mental reactions have a correlation to the world we live in, but as you saw earlier, it can't tell us whether our mental processes are socially appropriate or inappropriate, morally justified or unjustified, and so forth. As you have seen, neuroscience has identified areas in the brain where moral decisions involving empathy take place, but that doesn't mean that neuroscientists can tell us *which* moral decisions are more correct than others. Psychology can tell us only what people believe and possibly why they believe it; it can't make a statement about whether people are justified in believing it. Philosophy's job, at least in this context, is to *question* our values; it forces us to provide *reasons,* and preferably good reasons, for giving our moral approval to one type of behavior and disapproving of another. Philosophy asks the fundamental question *Why,* in all its fields, including the field of value theory/ethics. (Box 1.2 gives an overview of the classic branches within philosophy.) Why do we have the values we have? Why do values make some people give up their comfort, even their lives, for a cause, or for other people's welfare? Why do some people disregard the values of their society for a chosen cause or for personal gain? Is it ever morally appropriate to think of yourself and not of others? Are there ultimate absolute moral values, or are they a matter of personal or cultural choices? Such fundamental questions can be probed by philosophy in a deeper and more fundamental way than by neuroscience or psychology, and we will explore such questions in the upcoming chapters.

If having values is such an important feature of our life, should elementary schools teach values, then? It may be just a little too late, if indeed a child's moral sense is developed by the age of seven, but at least there is a chance it might help; and for children whose parents have done a minimal job of teaching them respect for others, school will probably be the only place they'll learn it. Some elementary schools are developing such programs. Problems occur, however, when schools begin to teach values with which not all parents agree. We live in a multicultural society, and although some parents might like certain topics to be on the school agenda, others certainly would not. Some parents want their children to have early access to sex education, whereas others consider it unthinkable as a school subject. There is nothing in the concept of values that implies we all have to subscribe to exactly the same ones, no matter how strongly we may feel about our own. So, beyond teaching basic values such as common courtesy, perhaps the best schools can do is make students aware of values and value differences and let students learn to argue effectively for their own values, as well as to question them. Schools, in other words, should focus on *ethics* in addition to *morality.*

So what is the difference between *ethics* and *morality? Ethics* comes from Greek (*ethos,* character) and *morality* from Latin (*mores,* character, custom, or habit). Today, in English as well as in many other Western languages, both words refer to some form of proper conduct. Although we, in our everyday lives, don't distinguish clearly between morals and ethics, there is a subtle difference: Some people think the word *morality* has negative connotations, and in fact it does carry two different sets of associations for most of us. The positive ones are guidance, goodness, humanitarianism, and so forth. Among the negative associations are repression, bigotry, persecution—in a word, *moralizing.* Suppose the introductory ethics course on your campus was labeled "Introduction to Morals." You would, in all likelihood, expect something different from what you would expect from a course called "Introduction to Ethics" or "Introduction to Values." The word *morality* has a slightly different connotation from that of the terms *ethics* and *values.* That is because *morality* usually refers to *the moral rules we follow,* the values that we have. *Ethics* is generally defined as *theories about those rules;* ethics questions and justifies the rules we live by, and, if ethics can find no rational justification for those rules, it may ask us to abandon them. Morality is the stuff our social life is made of—even our personal life—and ethics is the ordering, the questioning, the awareness, the investigation of what we believe: Are we justified in believing it? Is it consistent? Should we remain open to other beliefs or not?

In other words, it is not enough just to have moral rules; we should, as moral, mature persons, be able to justify our viewpoints with ethical arguments or, at the very least, ask ourselves why we feel this way or that about a certain issue. Ethics, therefore, is much more than a topic in a curriculum. As moral adults, we are required to think about ethics all the time.

Dilbert by Scott Adams

© Scott Adams/Dist. by United Feature Syndicate, Inc.

Ethicists point out that having a system of values isn't enough for a person to be morally mature—one must also engage in thinking about those values and critically examine them from time to time. Cartoonist Scott Adams obviously agrees.

Box 1.2 THE FOUR CLASSIC BRANCHES OF PHILOSOPHY

In the chapter text, you read that philosophy traditionally asks the question *Why*. This is one of the features that has characterized Western philosophy from its earliest years in Greek antiquity. We generally date Western philosophy from approximately seven hundred years B.C.E./ B.C. ("before the common era"/"before Christ"), when some Greek thinkers, such as Thales, Heraclitus, and Parmenides, began to ask questions about what *reality* truly consists of: Is it the way we perceive it through the senses, or is there an underlying true reality that our intellect can understand? Thales believed the underlying reality was water; Heraclitus believed that it was a form of ever-changing energy; and Parmenides saw true reality as being an underlying realm of permanence, elements that don't change. We call this form of philosophy *metaphysics;* in Chapter 8 you will read a brief introduction to Plato's famous theory of metaphysics, but otherwise the topic of metaphysics has only indirect bearing on the topic of this book. A few centuries after Thales, the next area of philosophy that manifested itself was *ethics,* with Socrates' questioning of what is the right way to live (see chapter text). Two generations later the third area of philosophy was introduced, primarily through the writings of Aristotle: *logic,* the establishing of rules for proper thinking as opposed to fallacious thinking. But the fourth area of Western philosophy didn't really take hold in the minds of thinkers until some two thousand years later, in the seventeenth century, when René Descartes began to explore what the mind can know: *epistemology,* or theory of knowledge. All four branches of philosophy are represented today in school curricula and enjoy vibrant debates within the philosophical community. The only branch to have languished somewhat is metaphysics, since modern science has answered some of its ancient questions: We now know about the subnuclear reality of quantum mechanics. But a classical question of metaphysics remains unanswered by science to this day: What is the nature of the human mind? Do we have a soul that outlives our bodies, or will our self be extinguished with the demise of our brain?

Until the mid–twentieth century, philosophy was usually taught in the West with the underlying assumption that philosophy as such was, by and large, a Western phenomenon. That rather ethnocentric attitude has changed considerably over the last decades. It is now recognized unequivocally among Western scholars that Asian philosophy has its own rich traditions of exploration of metaphysics and ethics in particular; and some philosophers point out that in a sense, all cultures have metaphysics and ethics, even if they have no body of philosophical literature, because their legends, songs, and religious stories will constitute the culture's view of reality as well as the moral rules and their justifications. As for logic and epistemology, they are not as frequently encountered in non-Western cultures: Indian philosophy has established its own tradition of logic, but epistemology remains a Western philosophical specialty, according to most Western scholars.

To the four classic branches, philosophy has added a number of specialized fields over the centuries, such as philosophy of art (aesthetics), social philosophy, philosophy of religion, political philosophy, philosophy of sports, philosophy of human nature, philosophy of gender, and philosophy of science. What makes these fields philosophical inquiries is their special approach to their subjects; they investigate not only the nature of art, social issues, religion, politics, and so on, but also the theoretical underpinnings of each field, its hidden assumptions and agendas, and its future moral and social pitfalls and promises.

Most people, in fact, do just that, even in their teens, because it is also considered a sign of maturity to question authority, at least to a certain extent. If a very young adult is told to be home at 11 P.M., she or he will usually ask, "Why can't I stay out till midnight?" When we have to make up our minds about whether to study over the weekend or go hiking, we usually try to come up with as many pros and cons as we can. When someone we have put our trust in betrays that trust, we want to know why. All those questions are practical applications of ethics: They question the rules of morality and the breaking of those rules. Although formal training in ethical questions can make us better at judging moral issues, we are, as adult human beings, already quite experienced just because we already have asked, "Why?" a number of times in our lives.

Debating Moral Issues: The Roles of Religion, the Law, Logic, Emotions, and Storytelling

Every functional society on earth has had a "philosophy" of what one should do or be in order to be considered a good person. Sometimes that moral code is expressed orally in stories and songs, and sometimes it is expressed in writing. When it is expressed as a set of rules with explanations justifying the rules, we may call it a *code of ethics*. For it to become a philosophical discipline, we must add the practice of examining and questioning the rules.

The Socratic Beginnings of Ethics

The Greek philosopher Socrates (fifth century B.C.E.) is often credited with being the first philosopher in the Western tradition to focus on ethics. That can be a reasonable observation, provided we don't confuse ethics with morals. It would, of course, be preposterous to claim that any one person, including a famous philosopher, should get credit for inventing morals. Every society since the dawn of time has had a moral code, even if all it consisted of was "respect the chief and your elders." Without a communal moral code you simply can't maintain a society, and in every generation parents have been the primary teachers of the continuity of morality. In addition, as we'll see in the next section, every society on the planet has had a religion of some sort, and into every religion is built a moral code. So what did Socrates contribute, if he didn't invent morals? He elevated the discussion of morals to the level of an academic, critical examination, exploration, and justification of values. It became an abstract discussion that was, for the first time in the West, removed from both religious dogma and social rules, at the same time becoming a personal matter of growth and wisdom. Most of our knowledge of Socrates comes from the works of the philosopher Plato, one of his students. In his series of *Dialogues,* conversations between Socrates and various friends, students, and enemies, Plato has Socrates observe, on his final day before being executed for crimes against the Athenian state (see Chapter 8), that "the unexamined life is not worth living," and that the ultimate question for every human being is "How should one live?" Acquiring moral wisdom is thus a requirement for a person who doesn't want to go through life with blinders on. Although we can imagine that wise old men and women may have taught the same lesson throughout human time, Socrates was the first that we know of to incorporate critical questions about moral values into a study of philosophical issues for adults. In other words, Socrates became the inventor of ethics as an *academic discipline,* not just a critical lifestyle. And for over two thousand years, philosophers in the West have included the study of ethics in their curricula, including the notion that to be a morally mature person you must engage in a personal critical examination of your own values and the values of your society. The famed *Socratic* or *dialectic method* has two major points: that if you approach an issue rationally, other rational minds will be able to accept your conclusion, and that a useful approach is a conversation, a *dialogue,* between teacher and student. The teacher will guide the student through a series of questions and answers to a rational conclusion, rather than give the student the answer up front. The method is to this day a favorite among philosophy instructors, psychotherapists, and law school professors.

Moral Issues and Religion

Cultures developing independently of the Western tradition have experienced a similar fascination for the subject of acting and living right. Socrates' version remains unique among ancient thinkers because he encouraged critical thinking instead of emphasizing being an obedient citizen. In China, Confucius expressed his philosophy of proper moral conduct as a matter of obedience to authorities and, above all, respect for one's elders at approximately the same time that Socrates was teaching students critical thinking in the public square in Athens. In Africa, tribal thinkers developed a strong sense of morality that stressed individuals' sense of responsibility to the community and the community's understanding of its responsibility to each individual—a philosophy that has become known to the West in recent years through the proverb "It takes a village to raise a child." Among American Indian tribes, the philosophy of harmony between humans and their environment—animate as well as inanimate nature—has been part of the moral code.

For all cultures, however, there is a common denominator: Go back far enough in time and you'll find a connection between the social life of the culture, its *mores,* and its religion. In some cultures the connection is clear and obvious to this day: Religion is the key to the moral values of the members of the community, and any debate about values usually takes place within the context of that religion. In other cultures, such as large parts of Europe, Canada, Australia, and to some extent the United States, the connection to religion has become more tenuous and has in some cases all but vanished; public social life has become secularized, and moral values are generally tied to the question of social coexistence rather than to a religious basis. That doesn't mean that individual people can't feel a strong connection to the religious values of their family and their community. This raises several questions, all depending on one's viewpoint and personal experience.

If you have grown up in a culture where religion is a predominant cultural phenomenon, or if you have grown up in a religious family, or if you find yourself deeply connected to a religious community today, do you regard your moral values as being inextricably tied to your religion? Do you regard moral values as being closely connected to religion as such? If that is your background, then chances are that you'll answer yes.

And if you have grown up in a Western, largely secularized culture such as big-city USA, and have not grown up in a religious family, or have distanced yourself from religion for some reason or other, do you view the question of religion as irrelevant for moral values in a modern society and for your own moral decisions? Chances are that you'll answer yes, if this description applies to you.

Here, in a nutshell, is the problem when talking about religion and values. In this diverse world—diverse not just because of nationalities, ethnicity, gender, and religion but also because of the vast variety of moral and political views even within one community—it is very hard for us to reach any kind of consensus or find common ground about values if we seek answers exclusively in our religion. Chances are that if you have a religion, it is not shared by a large number of people you associate with. If you stick exclusively to the group you share your faith (or nonfaith) with, of course you will feel fortified by the confirmation of your views through your religion, and your ideas aren't going to be challenged; but if you plan to be out and about in the greater society of this Western culture, you can't expect everyone to agree with you. (In Chapter 3 we discuss the issue of how to approach the subject of moral differences.) So how does moral philosophy approach this issue? Interestingly, you'll find religious as well as nonreligious moral philosophers in modern times. Go back to the nineteenth century and beyond, and you will find that almost all the Western moral philosophers were religious—Christian or Jewish. In the twentieth century there was a sharp increase in moral philosophers who chose a secular basis of reasoning for their ethics, and that remains a feature of today's ethical debates. But even in centuries past, most philosophers who argued about ethics and who professed to be religious tended to avoid using their religion as the ultimate justification for their moral values. Because how can you argue with faith? Either you share the faith or you don't. But argue on a basis of rationality, and you have a chance of reaching an understanding of values, even if you disagree about religion—or at least you may gain an understanding of where the other person is coming from. *Reason* as a tool of ethics can be a bridge builder between believers, atheists, and agnostics. For agnostics and atheists, there can be no turning to religion for unquestioned moral guidance, because they view religion itself as an unknown or nonexistent factor. Agnostics claim that they do not know whether there is a God or that it is impossible to know. Atheists claim that there is no God. Both the agnostic and the atheist may find that religion suggests solutions to their problems, but such solutions are accepted not because they come from religion but because they somehow make sense.

For a philosophical inquiry, the requirement that a solution make sense is particularly important; although religion may play a significant role in the development of moral values for many people, a philosophical investigation of moral issues must involve more than faith in a religious authority. Regardless of one's religious belief or lack thereof, such an investigation must involve reasoning because, for one thing, philosophy teaches that one must examine issues without solely relying on the word of authority. For another thing, a rational argument can be a way for people to reach an understanding in spite of having different viewpoints on religion. Accordingly, a good way to communicate about ethics for both believers and nonbelievers is to approach the issue through the language of *reason*.

Moral Issues and the Law

The assumption that there is a connection between morals and religion is matched in its frequency by the assumption that there is a connection between morals and the *law*. And, as it is with religion, the assumption is often, but not always, correct. The relationship between morals and legislation is ancient. From the Code of Hammurabi (developed by Babylonians in approximately 2000 B.C.E.) to the legislation of today, some laws have reflected the moral climate of the time. Not all laws have done so, though some scholars argue that because laws tell us what we ought to do or ought not to do, all laws have a moral element to them; if nothing else, they promote the idea that it is morally good to uphold the law. However, sometimes the law does not seem to be morally right. When times change, what seemed right before may not seem right anymore, and if the legislative power is sensitive to that fact, the law will change. Sometimes it takes a civil war for such laws to be changed; sometimes it takes an act of defiance; sometimes it takes only a simple vote. We can't, therefore, conclude that all laws are morally just, because experience tells us this is not so. Some laws may not even have an obvious moral element. A traffic law that allows us to turn right on red hardly addresses a moral issue.

Legislators, though, are naturally interested in the public's opinion of right and wrong, because, in general, that opinion will be represented by the laws of the country. Not all moral issues are relevant for legislators, however; whether you go home for Thanksgiving may be an important moral issue in your family, but it is hardly the business of anyone else, let alone the state legislature. Philosophy of law generally speaks of two viewpoints concerning the relationship between ethics and the law. The viewpoint of *naturalism* (or *natural law*) holds that the law reflects, or ought to reflect, a set of universal moral standards; some naturalists consider those standards given by God, and some see them as part of human nature. The other viewpoint is referred to as *legal positivism* and holds that the law is based on consensus among legislators; in other words, there is no ultimate moral foundation for our laws; they are relative and merely reflect shifting opinions over time.

If we look at the relationship between the moral codes and the laws of various societies we find that they differ dramatically: One society's legislation may reflect the belief that the law should not dictate people's moral choices as long as no harm is caused. Another society's laws may be anchored solidly in the moral code of that society, usually derived from the society's religion. The first type of society reflects a popular Western contemporary viewpoint; an example of the latter would be a Muslim society such as Iran, where a code of law inspired by Islam, the *Sharia*, is enforced. Over time, societies have opted for various combinations of the law, morals, and religion, with a close connection between the three being very common until the twentieth century.

However, as some philosophers point out, our postmodern culture is increasingly focused on *what is the law,* rather than on *what is morally right*—possibly because many consider the idea of moral right or wrong an individual choice (*subjectivism;* see Chapter 3) or a cultural matter (*ethical relativism;* see Chapter 3). But it is also possible that some decide to focus on the law rather than morals because they think it lets them off the hook: If a behavior isn't illegal, it must surely be okay, right? Wrong, because we also have *civil codes of ethics,* such as rules for employees in a workplace, politicians in local government, and students on a campus, and because we have a tacit understanding of *moral expectations* among professionals, among friends, and among family members. You may not be arrested for making inappropriate comments to coworkers, or for using your company computer during work hours for transactions on eBay or finding dates, or for dating someone you are supervising, but such behavior can surely get you fired. And betraying the trust of a friend or a family member will usually not get you arrested, either, but it may have irreparable consequences for your relationship. Reducing it all to what is legal is a misunderstanding of the nature of ethics, whether inadvertent or deliberate. In the Primary Readings section in Chapter 3, you can read more about the confusion between what is "moral" and what is "legal" in Dwight Furrow's text, "Of Cave Dwellers and Spirits."

Moral Issues and Logic

As we saw at the end of the section on moral issues and religion, it has been a choice of philosophers from the earliest times to argue about moral issues on the basis of reasoning rather than religious faith, regardless of their own religious affiliations. That means that the classical philosophical field of *logic* is considered a valuable tool for discussing moral issues, because if philosophers can agree on anything, it is usually whether or not an argument violates the rules of logic.

An "argument" in philosophy is not a heated discussion or a screaming contest but a certain type of communication that strives to convince a listener that something is true or reasonable. Here is an ultrashort account of the basic principles of logic: An argument has at least one premise, and usually several premises, followed by a conclusion. Such an argument can be either *inductive* or *deductive*. The conclusion of an inductive argument is based on a gathering of evidence (such as "Tom probably won't say thank you for the birthday present—he never does"), but there is no certainty that the conclusion is true, only that it is probable. On the other hand, in a deductive argument the premises are supposed to lead to a certain conclusion. A *valid* deductive argument is a deductive argument whose conclusion follows necessarily from its premise or premises. (For example, "All dogs are descendents of wolves; Fluffy is a dog; therefore, Fluffy is a descendent of wolves." This is valid whether or not dogs actually are descendents of wolves, which *inductive* evidence shows they probably are.) A *sound* deductive argument is an argument that is valid and whose premises are also factually true (such as "On the vernal [spring] equinox, night and day are of equal length all over the planet. So, on the vernal equinox, the day is twelve hours long in Baghdad as well as in Seattle").

Logical fallacies invalidate a moral viewpoint just as they do any other kind of viewpoint. Have you heard someone claim that because she has been cheated by two auto mechanics, no auto mechanics can be trusted? That's the fallacy of *hasty generalization*. Have you heard someone who is an expert in one field claim to be an authority in another—or people referring to some vague "expert opinion" in defense of their own views? That is the fallacy of *appeal to authority*. When someone tries to prove a point just by rephrasing it, such as "I'm right, because I'm never wrong," that is the fallacy of *begging the question,* a circular definition assuming that what you are trying to prove is a fact. How about a bully arguing that if you don't give him your seat/purse/car, he will harm you? That's the *ad baculum* (Latin for "by the stick") fallacy, the fallacy of using physical threats. And if someone says, "Well, you know you can't believe what Fred says—after all, he's a guy," that's an *ad hominem* ("to the man") fallacy, which assumes that who a person is determines the correctness or incorrectness of what he or she says. And a politician declaring "If we continue to allow women to have abortions, then pretty soon nobody will give birth, and the human race will die out" offers a *slippery slope* argument, which assumes that drastic consequences will follow a certain policy. Closely related is the *straw man* fallacy, inventing a viewpoint so radical that hardly anyone holds it, so you can knock it down: "Gun advocates want to allow criminals and children to own weapons, so we should work toward a gun ban." And if you claim that "it is my way or the highway," then you are *bifurcating*—you are creating a *false dichotomy* (unless, of course, we're really talking about a situation with no third possibility, such as being pregnant—you can't be a little bit pregnant; it's either/or).

Another fallacy is the famed *red herring,* familiar to every fan of mystery and detective stories. A "red herring" is placed on the path to confuse the bloodhound. In other words, it is a deflection away from the truth. In an everyday setting, this can be accomplished by changing the subject when it gets too uncomfortable ("Why did you get an F on your test, Bob?" "Mom, have I ever told you you're prettier than all my friends' moms?"). The notoriety of the red herring fallacy in court cases is well known, from introducing the race issue in the O. J. Simpson criminal trial to attacking a rape victim's sexual history to deflect attention away from the defendant. A fallacy most of us who make our living teaching are very familiar with is the fallacy of *ad misericordiam,* appeal to pity: "Please, can I get an extension on my paper? My backpack was stolen, my cat ran away, my grandma is in the hospital, and I've got these really killer hangnails." Or is it hangovers, perhaps? We've heard them all, all the bad excuses. But an excuse becomes an *ad misericordiam* fallacy only if it is nothing but an excuse. Sometimes a person truly deserves special consideration because of individual hardship, of course. Those and other logical fallacies are rampant in media discussions, and part of proper moral reasoning consists in watching out for the use of such flawed arguments, in one's own statements as well as in those of others.

Moral Issues and Emotions

But is logic all there is to a good moral argument? Some philosophers would say yes: The force of a moral viewpoint derives from its compelling logic. But increasingly, other voices are adding that a good moral argument is compelling not just because of its logic but also because it makes sense *emotionally*. If we have no feeling of moral approval or outrage, then do we really *care* about whether something is morally right or wrong? If we don't *feel* that it's wrong to harm a child, then how is logic going to persuade us? A classic answer has been an appeal to the logic of the Golden Rule: You wouldn't want someone to harm *you*, would you? But, say some, that's an appeal to how you'd *feel* in the same situation. An appeal to pure feeling isn't going to be enough, because feelings can be manipulated, and appeals to emotions don't solve conflicts if we don't share those emotions; but combined with the logic of reasoning emotions can form the foundation of a forceful moral argument, according to some modern thinkers.

The study published in 2007 by neuroscientist Antonio Damasio and other scientists in the journal *Nature* dovetailed with previous research and speculations by other scientists: On the basis of a study of thirty people, out of whom six had suffered damage to their ventromedial frontal lobes, the neuroscientists concluded that we humans have an area in the brain that, when undamaged, makes us hesitate if faced with a tough decision involving other people's lives. We have, from ancient times, developed an emotional reluctance to make decisions that will cause the death of other people, even if it is for the common good. The research subjects with damage to that specific part of the brain had no problem making moral decisions that would save many but cause the deaths of one or a few humans. These subjects did not come across as callous, unfeeling people, and were absolutely not classified as sociopaths. They would no more sell their daughters into sex slavery or torture an animal than would the "normal" subjects. However, when asked to make decisions that would cost human lives, they showed much less reluctance than the subjects with no damage to that part of the brain. Questions such as "Would you divert a runaway vehicle so that it will kill one person instead of the five people in its current path?" were answered affirmatively. The researchers concluded that the "normal" brain has evolved to recognize the value of a human life emotionally, probably because we are social beings and need to be able to have emotional ties to the people in our group.

This study has made waves for several reasons. For one, it corroborated previous studies that showed that humans have a specific center in the brain where moral decisions are made, a "moral compass." In other words, we do appear to have been equipped with some sort of *moral intuition* from birth. For another, it weighed in on an ancient debate in moral philosophy: Are our moral decisions primarily emotional or primarily logical? And *should* they be primarily emotional or primarily logical? The vast majority of philosophers since the time of Plato have argued that the more we are able to disregard our personal emotions when we make moral decisions, the better our decisions will be. As you will see in several chapters in this book, philosophers (such as Plato, Chapters 4 and 8; Jeremy Bentham, Chapter 5; and Immanuel Kant, Chapter 6) have argued that moral decisions ought to be either exclusively or predominantly rational, logical, and unemotional. It is a rare exception to read a philosopher who argues either that our moral decisions *are in fact* emotional (such as David Hume does; see Chapter 4) or that they *should be* emotional (argued by Richard Taylor; see Chapter 11). A handful of thinkers from Aristotle (Chapter 9) to

Diane Whiteley (Chapter 7) and Martha Nussbaum (in this chapter) argue that we shouldn't make moral decisions without using our reason but that we shouldn't disregard our emotions either.

The neuroscientists' study seems to say that a healthy human brain will intuitively incorporate emotions in its moral decisions involving other people's lives—which would mean that all the philosophers who have argued that emotions should be avoided in moral decision making are somehow wrong and are even advocating something inhumane. So is that all we need to disprove them? Hardly. For one thing, as you read earlier in this chapter, neuroscience can tell us *where* in the brain our moral decisions take place, but it can't necessarily tell us which moral decisions are *better* than others. But more important, perhaps, the classical philosophical point of arguing in favor of reason and against emotion is that disregarding emotion in key moral decisions is the hard thing to do, but is this, perhaps, exactly what we must do sometimes? We may feel reluctant or squeamish about sacrificing one life to save a hundred, but that may be what is required of us in extreme situations, not because it is easy, or because we enjoy it, but because it is necessary. The difficulty with this approach is that such arguments have been used, through time, to enslave countless innocent human beings, or use them as cannon fodder, or exterminate them, all in the name of reason. But it is also the only argument we have to justify shooting a plane full of passengers down if it has been hijacked and is headed for the Capitol, or to not forget about the law when a serial killer of children shows contrition in court and claims he has had a horrible life of abuse himself. At a less dramatic level, reason's override of emotions is what we need when our child is crying because she doesn't want to go to the dentist or to kindergarten; you will encounter this question again in Chapter 5. So, again, the neuroscientists can tell us what are normal and abnormal brain reactions, but without further philosophical discussion they can't tell us what is morally right. Furthermore, if we take into account the results of the Stanley Milgram experiments and the Stanford Prison Experiment, we can't conclude that humans will not harm one another—they may be reluctant, normally, to harm one another, but that reluctance can be overridden by other factors, such as threats, fear for their own safety, ambitions, and a wish to please their superiors. It takes a moral philosopher (with or without academic credentials) to engage in that discussion.

And that is precisely what moral philosophers do. Our first example is the American philosopher Martha Nussbaum, and we turn to her shortly.

Moral Issues and Storytelling

All cultures tell stories, and all cultures have codes for proper behavior. Very often those codes are taught through stories, but stories can also be used to *question* moral rules and to examine morally ambiguous situations. A fundamental premise of this book is that stories sometimes can serve as shortcuts to understanding and solving moral problems. Many literature professors may be inclined to tell us that people don't read anymore, that the novel is dead, or that nobody appreciates good literature these days. I myself am rather disappointed when students are unfamiliar with the classics of literature or have grown to hate them through high school manglings. However, it just isn't true that people don't read novels—best-sellers are flourishing as never before. And an element has been added to our appreciation of good stories: *movies.* The American film industry has been in existence for over a hundred years, and it should be no surprise to anyone that as much as films can provide simple entertainment, they can also give us in-depth, unforgettable views of human life, including moral issues. This book makes use of that treasure trove of movie stories as well as novels, short stories, epic poems, television shows, and plays as illustrations of moral problems and solutions.

Using stories here has two purposes. One is to supply a foundation for further debate about the application of the moral theories presented in the chapter; the other is to inspire you to experience these stories in their original form, through print or video, since they are, of course, richer and more interesting than any outline can possibly show.

Martha Nussbaum: Stories, Ethics, and Emotions

For the greater part of the twentieth century most Western philosophers had a tacit agreement that stories were best left in the nursery, but times have changed: There is now a growing interest in the cultural and philosophical importance of storytelling, in technological as well as pretechnological cultures, and stories are becoming shortcuts to understanding ourselves on an individual as well as a cultural level. One of the most influential voices speaking for narratives as a way to communicate about values is Martha Nussbaum (b. 1947), a philosopher and a professor of law and ethics; her main interest is not the intellectual value of storytelling as much as the emotional force of narratives.

Nussbaum believes there was a time when philosophers understood the value of narratives. The Greek thinker Aristotle (whom she greatly admires) believed that experiencing a drama unfold teaches the viewer basic important lessons about having the proper feelings at the proper time—lessons about life and virtue in general. As modern Western philosophy took shape, however, the idea of emotions seemed increasingly irrelevant. There are signs today that philosophy is making a turnaround, that it is allowing itself to take a closer look at emotions as a legitimate subject for research. Nussbaum contributes to that turnaround with her books *Love's Knowledge* (1990), *Upheavals of Thought: The Intelligence of Emotions* (2001), and *Hiding from Humanity* (2004). She points out that emotions weren't excluded from philosophy because they did not yield *knowledge;* in other words, it is not because of any lack of *cognitive value* that philosophers have refused to investigate emotions. There is actually much cognitive value in emotions, for emotions are, on the whole, quite *reasonable* when we look at them in context. When do we feel anger? When we believe that someone has deliberately injured us or someone we care about—in other words, when we feel the situation warrants it. Feelings such as disappointment, elation, grief, and even love are all responses to certain situations. They develop according to some inner logic; they don't strike at random. How do we know? Because if we realize that we were wrong about the situation, our anger slowly

Martha Nussbaum (b. 1947), American philosopher. The author of *Love's Knowledge, Upheavals of Thought,* and *Hiding from Humanity,* she suggests that novels are supremely well suited to explore moral problems. Through novels we have the chance to live more than our own lives and to understand human problems from someone else's point of view. Since others can read the same novels, we can share such knowledge and reach a mutual understanding.

disappears. Perhaps love is not that easy to analyze—people in love don't seem to respond logically to situations that ought to change their feelings of love. (The person you love is seeing someone else, and what do you do? Continue to be helplessly in love.) But even love responds to such challenges in a way; we probably realize that our feelings are, somehow, out of place.

Why, then, have so many philosophers refused to deal seriously with emotions? Not because emotions lack cognitive value, but because they show we react to situations outside our control. When we are emotional, we are not *self-sufficient,* and most philosophers have, according to Nussbaum, preferred to investigate a more autonomous part of the human character, our reason. (Of course, some philosophers and psychoanalysts have pointed out that reason is not immune to outside influence, either, but Nussbaum is addressing the trends in traditional philosophy before the twentieth century, when the idea of reason being affected by the Unconscious was not yet commonly accepted.)

For Nussbaum, emotions provide access to values, to human relationships, and to understanding ourselves, so they must be investigated. And where do they manifest themselves most clearly? In narratives. Stories are actually emotions put into a structure. When we are children and adolescents, we learn how to manipulate objects and relate to others; we learn cognitive skills and practical skills, and among the skills we learn are when to feel certain kinds of emotions. The prime teacher of emotions is the story. That means, of course, that different societies may tell different stories teaching different lessons, so we must retain a certain amount of social awareness and social criticism when reading stories from any culture, including our own. People in their formative years are not just empty vessels into which stories are poured. Nussbaum maintains there is no rule saying that people must accept everything their culture teaches them; so those who don't approve of the stories being told or who think the stories haven't been told right will begin to tell their own stories. Important as emotions are, alongside our reason, in shaping our moral values, Nussbaum has of late found it necessary to specify that two particular emotions should not be considered conducive to moral understanding: *disgust* and *shame*. Here Nussbaum enters the political arena by claiming that some emotions are more morally and politically appropriate than others. When we say we are disgusted with something or someone, we set ourselves on a pedestal as being better and purer, says Nussbaum, and that to her is an unrealistic assessment that does nothing more than create an us-versus-them environment.

To understand emotions we must read stories, but that ought to come easily to us, Nussbaum believes, since we already enjoy doing just that. She does stress, however, that we have to read the entire story, not just rely on a synopsis. There is an integral relationship between the form and the content of a story. As she says in her book *Love's Knowledge,* we can't skip "the emotive appeal, the absorbing plottedness, the variety and indeterminacy of good fiction" without losing the heart of the experience. So in a sense Nussbaum does not specifically advocate *using stories to illustrate moral problems,* as we will be doing in this book. Instead, she supports reading stories as a way of *sharing basic experiences of values* and using philosophy as a tool for analyzing that experience. For her, the story comes first, and then the analysis can follow. In the Primary Readings section, you'll find an excerpt from *Love's Knowledge.*

Why use stories, though? Why can't we approach moral issues by more traditional avenues, such as examples that are "made to order" by philosophers? Because, says Nussbaum, they lack precisely the rich texture that makes the story an experience we can relate to. Besides, such examples are formulated in such a way that the conclusion is obvious. Novels tend to be quite open-ended, a feature that Nussbaum believes is valuable. Novels preserve "mystery and indeterminacy," just like real life.

Why not just rely on your own experiences to learn about life? Some of them must certainly contain both mystery and indeterminacy. To some extent we do that already; we draw on our own experience as much as we possibly can when judging concrete and abstract cases. But the trouble is, one human life is just not enough for understanding the myriad ways of being. As Nussbaum says,

> We have never lived enough. Our experience is, without fiction, too confined and too parochial. Literature extends it, making us reflect and feel about what might otherwise be too distant for feeling. . . . All living is interpreting; all action requires seeing the world *as* something. So in this sense no life is "raw" and . . . throughout our living we are, in a sense, makers of fictions. The point is that in the activity of literary imagining we are led to imagine and describe with greater precision, focusing our attention on each word, feeling each event more keenly—whereas much of actual life goes by without that heightened awareness, and is thus, in a certain sense, not fully or thoroughly lived.

Furthermore, it is much harder to talk about events in your own life than it is to discuss events in a story. We may not want to share our deepest feelings, or we may not be able to express them. But if we talk with friends about a passage in a favorite book or film, we can share both an emotional and a moral experience. One final word about Nussbaum's theory: It is important that we remember that she has no wish to replace the traditional rational approach to moral issues with an emotional approach—to her, emotions can be relevant in moral decision making, but that doesn't make reason irrelevant. But we have a fuller understanding of being human, and making moral decisions, if we allow our focus to include relevant emotions as well as reason. At the end of the chapter you'll find two narratives that, each in its own way, illustrate Nussbaum's theory of storytelling as a key to understanding ourselves and one another and of emotion as having a rational component: *Big Fish* tells of a man who sees his own life as a story—perhaps excessively—and *Smoke Signals* shows the character development of an angry young man who learns that the cause of his anger against his father was only in his own head.

Study Questions

1. In your opinion, should children learn values in elementary school? Explain why or why not, and craft an argument for and against the idea as it might be presented by a teacher and a parent.

2. Give three examples of statements about moral issues, illustrating three logical fallacies.

3. In your view, does evil exist? Is there a difference between *being* evil and *doing* evil? Explain.

4. Comment on Nussbaum's statement "We have never lived enough. Our experience is, without fiction, too confined and too parochial. Literature expands it, making us reflect and feel about what might otherwise be too distant for feeling." What does she mean? Do you agree? Why or why not?

5. Consider the multicultural challenge of storytelling. Do you remember any story that has enhanced your understanding of another culture? Do you remember any story from your own culture that expresses a moral you find unacceptable? Do you know any story from another culture whose moral you find unacceptable? Is it possible to find some common ground? Explain.

Primary Reading and Narratives

The first Primary Reading is from *Love's Knowledge* by Martha Nussbaum, explaining why fictional stories are better at teaching moral lessons than real-life stories and little made-to-order philosophical examples are. The second Reading is an excerpt from Philip Zimbardo's *The Lucifer Effect,* in which he finds parallels between his own Stanford Prison Experiment and the Abu Ghraib abuse scandal, illustrating a type of behavior many would call *evil.* The first Narrative, a summary of the film *Smoke Signals,* links up with the Nussbaum excerpt. Two young American Indian males embark on a journey on which one—Thomas—grows as a storyteller, and the other—Victor—loses his anger toward his father. The next Narrative is the film *Big Fish,* also about a father-son relationship, seen in light of what some would call storytelling, and others simply lying! The final Narrative is an excerpt from John Steinbeck's *East of Eden.* First, Steinbeck argues that there is only one story that humans relate to, and have related to since the beginning of time: the story of *good versus evil.* In the excerpts, the twins Cal and Aron vie for the attention of their father, Adam. Their estranged mother, Cathy, is in the author's eyes an evil person, and the question is whether her sons have inherited her vicious nature.

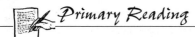 *Primary Reading*

Love's Knowledge

MARTHA NUSSBAUM

Excerpt, 1990.

In this excerpt, Nussbaum argues that novels, short stories, and dramas are very well suited to providing an emotional lesson in moral issues because of the brevity of human life: We just can't experience everything ourselves, so fiction provides a shortcut to understanding the range of human emotions. She also explains why such philosophical examples as those you will encounter in this book (such as Kant's example of the killer at the door looking for your friend) aren't good enough to teach the same lesson. You may want to consider why Nussbaum's argument omits the mention of movies—is it deliberate? or an oversight?

Not only novels prove appropriate, because (again, with reference only to these particular issues and this conception) many serious dramas will be pertinent as well, and some biographies and histories—so long as these are written in a style that gives sufficient attention to particularity and emotion, and so long as they involve their readers in relevant activities of searching and feeling, especially feeling concerning their own possibilities as well as those of the characters . . . .

But the philosopher is likely to be less troubled by these questions of literary genre than by a prior question: namely, why a literary work at all? Why can't we investigate everything we want to investigate by using complex examples of the sort that moral philosophers are very good at inventing? In reply, we must insist that the philosopher who asks this question cannot have been convinced by the argument so far about the intimate connection between literary form and ethical content. Schematic philosophers' examples almost always lack the particularity, the emotive appeal, the absorbing plottedness, the variety and indeterminacy, of good fiction; they lack, too, good fiction's way of making the reader a participant and a friend; and we have argued that it is precisely in virtue of these structural characteristics that fiction can play the role it does in our reflective lives. As [novelist Henry] James says, "The picture of the exposed and entangled state is what is required." If the examples do have these features, they will, themselves, be works of literature. Sometimes a very brief fiction will prove a sufficient vehicle for the investigation of what we are at that moment investigating; sometimes, as in "Flawed Crystals" (where our question concerns what is likely to happen in the course of a relatively long and complex life), we need the length and complexity of a novel. In neither case, however, would schematic examples prove sufficient as a substitute. (This does not mean that they will be totally dismissed; for they have other sorts of usefulness, especially in connection with other ethical views.)

We can add that examples, setting things up schematically, signal to the readers what they should notice and find relevant. They hand them the ethically salient description. This means that much of the ethical work is already done, the result "cooked." The novels are more open-ended, showing the reader what it is to search for the appropriate description and why that search matters. (And yet they are not so open-ended as to give no shape to the reader's thought.) By showing the mystery and indeterminacy of "our actual adventure," they characterize life more richly and truly—indeed, more precisely—than an example lacking those features ever could; and they engender in the reader a type of ethical work more appropriate for life.

But why not life itself? Why can't we investigate whatever we want to investigate by living and reflecting on our lives? Why, if it is the Aristotelian ethical conception we wish to scrutinize, can't we do that without literary texts, without texts at all—or, rather, with the texts of our own lives set before us? Here, we must first say that of course we do this as well, both apart from our reading of the novels and (as [French novelist Marcel] Proust insists) in the process of reading. In a sense Proust is right to see the literary text as an "optical instrument" through which the reader becomes a reader of his or her own heart. But, why do we need, in that case, such optical instruments?

One obvious answer was suggested already by Aristotle: we have never lived enough. Our experience is, without fiction, too confined and too parochial. Literature extends it, making us reflect and feel about what might otherwise be too distant for feeling. The importance of this for both morals and politics cannot be underestimated. *The Princess Casamassima* [1886, a novel by Henry James]—justly, in my view—depicts the imagination of the novel-reader as a type that is very valuable in the political (as well as the private) life, sympathetic to a wide range of concerns, averse to certain denials of humanity. It cultivates these sympathies in its readers.

We can clarify and extend this point by emphasizing that novels do not function, inside this account, as pieces of "raw" life: they are a close and careful interpretative description. All living is interpreting; all action requires seeing the world *as* something. So in this sense no life is "raw," and (as James and Proust insist) throughout our living we are, in a sense, makers of fictions. The point is that in the activity of literary imagining we are led to imagine and describe with greater precision, focusing our attention on each word, feeling each event more keenly—whereas much of actual life goes by without that heightened awareness, and is thus, in a certain sense, not fully or thoroughly lived. Neither James nor Proust thinks of ordinary life as normative, and the Aristotelian conception concurs: too much of it is obtuse, routinized, incompletely sentient. So literature is an extension of life not only horizontally, bringing the reader into contact with events or locations or persons or problems he or she has not otherwise met, but also, so to speak, vertically, giving the reader experience that is deeper, sharper, and more precise than much of what takes place in life.

Study Questions

1. Is Nussbaum right that philosophical examples don't work as well as fictional stories when it comes to conveying a moral point? Why or why not?

2. What does she mean by "no life is 'raw'"?

3. Should her theory include the use of films? Why or why not?

The Lucifer Effect

PHILIP ZIMBARDO

Excerpt, 2007.

Philip Zimbardo is a social psychologist. In 1971 he created the Stanford Prison Experiment, which involved role playing among students who had volunteered as experimental subjects. Some were to be "inmates," others "prison guards." The experiment was closed down after only a week because the level of brutality of the guards against the inmates exceeded all expectations and left the "inmates" psychologically scarred. To Zimbardo, the experiment revealed that, under the right psychological circumstances, even peaceful people can be led to believe that extremely harsh and brutal behavior is appropriate. In his book *The Lucifer Effect,* he draws parallels between the Stanford Experiment and what happened in the Abu Ghraib prison between Iraqi prisoners of war and American reservists guarding them.

Dehumanization and Moral Disengagement in the Laboratory

We can assume that most people, most of the time, are moral creatures. But imagine that this morality is like a gearshift that at times gets pushed into neutral. When that happens, morality is disengaged. If the car happens to be on an incline, car and driver move precipitously downhill. It is then the nature of the circumstances that determines outcomes, not the driver's skills or intentions. This simple analogy, I think, captures one of the central themes in the theory of moral disengagement developed by my Stanford colleague Albert Bandura. In a later chapter, we will review his theory, which will help explain why some otherwise good people can be led to do bad things. At this point, I want to turn to the experimental research that Bandura and his assistants conducted, which illustrates the ease with which morality can be disengaged by the tactic of dehumanizing a potential victim. In an elegant demonstration that shows the power of dehumanization, one single word is shown to increase aggression toward a target. Let's see how the experiment worked.

Imagine you are a college student who has volunteered for a study of group problem solving as part of a three-person team from your school. Your task is to help students from another college improve their group problem-solving performance by punishing their errors. That punishment takes the form of administering electric shocks that can be increased in severity over successive trials. After taking your names and those of the other team, the assistant leaves to tell the experimenter that the study can begin. There will be ten trials during each of which you can decide the shock level to administer to the other student group in the next room.

You don't realize that it is part of the experimental script, but you "accidentally" overhear the assistant complaining over the intercom to the experimenter that the other students "seem like animals." You don't know it, but in two other conditions to which other students like you have been randomly assigned, the assistant describes the other students as "nice guys" or does not label them at all.

Do these simple labels have any effect? It doesn't seem so initially. On the first trial all the groups respond in the same way by administering low levels of shock, around level 2. But soon it begins to matter what each group has heard about these anonymous others. If you know nothing about them, you give a steady average of about a level 5. If you have come to think of them as "nice guys," you treat them in a more humane fashion, giving them significantly less shock, about a level 3. However, imagining them as "animals" switches off any sense of compassion you might have for them, and when they commit errors, you begin to shock them with ever-increasing levels of intensity, significantly more than in the other conditions, as you steadily move up toward the high level 8.

Think carefully for a moment about the psychological processes that a simple label has tripped off in your mind. You overheard a person, whom you do not know personally, tell some authority, whom you have never seen, that other college students like you seem like "animals." That single descriptive term changes your mental construction of these others. It distances you from images of friendly college kids who must be more similar to you than different. That new mental set has a powerful impact on your behavior. The post hoc rationalizations the experimental students generated to explain why they needed to give so much shock to the "animal-house" students in the process of "teaching them a good lesson" were equally fascinating. This example of using controlled experimental research to investigate the underlying psychological processes that occur in significant real-world cases of violence will be extended in chapters 12 and 13 when we consider how behavioral scientists have investigated various aspects of the psychology of evil.

> Our ability to selectively engage and disengage our moral
> standards . . . helps explain how people can be barbarically
> cruel in one moment and compassionate the next.
>
> —Albert Bandura

Horrific Images of Abuse at Abu Ghraib Prison

The driving force behind this book was the need to better understand the how and why of the physical and psychological abuses perpetrated on prisoners by American Military Police at the Abu Ghraib Prison in Iraq. As the photographic evidence of these abuses rocketed around the world in May 2004, we all saw for the first time in recorded history vivid images of young American men and women engaged in unimaginable forms of torture against civilians they were supposed to be guarding. The tormentors and the tormented were captured in an extensive display of digitally documented depravity that the soldiers themselves had made during their violent escapades.

Why did they create photographic evidence of such illegal acts, which if found would surely get them into trouble? In these "trophy photos," like the proud displays by big-game hunters of yesteryear with the beasts they have killed, we saw smiling men and women in the act of abusing their lowly animal creatures. The images are of punching, slapping, and kicking detainees; jumping on their feet; forcibly arranging naked, hooded prisoners in piles and pyramids; forcing naked prisoners to wear women's underwear over their heads; forcing male prisoners to masturbate or simulate fellatio while being photographed or videotaped with female soldiers smiling or encouraging it; hanging prisoners from cell rafters for extended time periods; dragging a prisoner around with a leash tied to his neck; and using unmuzzled attack dogs to frighten prisoners.

The iconic image that ricocheted from that dungeon to the streets of Iraq and every corner of the globe was that of the "triangle man": a hooded detainee is standing on a box in a stress position with his outstretched arms protruding from under a garment blanket revealing electrical wires attached to his fingers. He was told that he would be electrocuted if he fell off the box when his strength gave out. It did not matter that the wires went nowhere; it mattered that he believed the lie and must have experienced considerable stress. There were even more shocking photographs that the U.S. government chose not to release to the public because of the greater damage they would surely have done to the credibility and moral image of the U.S. military and President Bush's administrative command. I have seen hundreds of these images, and they are indeed horrifying.

I was deeply distressed at the sight of such suffering, of such displays of arrogance, of such indifference to the humiliation being inflicted upon helpless prisoners. I was also amazed to learn that one of the abusers, a female soldier who had just turned twenty-one, described the abuse as "just fun and games."

I was shocked, but I was not surprised. The media and the "person in the street" around the globe asked how such evil deeds could be perpetrated by these seven men and women, whom military leaders had labeled as "rogue soldiers" and "a few bad apples." Instead, I wondered what circumstances in that prison cell block could have tipped the balance and led even good soldiers to do such bad things. To be sure, advancing a situational analysis for such crimes does not excuse them or make them morally acceptable. Rather, I needed to find the meaning in this madness. I wanted to understand how it was possible for the characters of these young people to be so transformed in such a short time that they could do these unthinkable deeds.

Parallel Universes in Abu Ghraib and Stanford's Prison

The reason that I was shocked but not surprised by the images and stories of prisoner abuse in the Abu Ghraib "Little Shop of Horrors" was that I had seen something similar before. Three decades earlier, I had witnessed eerily similar scenes as they unfolded in a project that I directed, of my own design: naked, shackled prisoners with bags over their heads, guards stepping on prisoners' backs as they did push-ups, guards sexually humiliating prisoners, and prisoners suffering from extreme stress. Some of the visual images from my experiment are practically interchangeable with those of the guards and prisoners in that remote prison in Iraq, the notorious Abu Ghraib.

The college students role-playing guards and prisoners in a mock prison experiment conducted at Stanford University in the summer of 1971 were mirrored in the real guards and real prison in the Iraq of 2003. Not only had I seen such events, I had been responsible for creating the conditions that allowed such abuses to flourish. As the project's principal investigator, I designed the experiment that randomly assigned normal, healthy, intelligent college students to enact the roles of either guards or prisoners in a realistically simulated prison setting where they were to live and work for several weeks. My student research associates, Craig Haney, Curt Banks, and David Jaffe, and I wanted to understand some of the dynamics operating in the psychology of imprisonment.

How do ordinary people adapt to such an institutional setting? How do the power differentials between guards and prisoners play out in their daily interactions? If you put good people in a bad place, do the people triumph or does the place corrupt them? Would the violence that is endemic to most real prisons be absent in a prison filled with good middle-class boys? These were some of the exploratory issues to be investigated in what started out as a simple study of prison life.

Study Questions

1. Zimbardo sees the same mental situation arising in the Stanford Experiment and in Abu Ghraib. Do you agree? Why or why not?

2. Zimbardo describes how a college student can be psychologically led toward certain prejudices against other people by hearing labels used. Have you had similar experiences? Explain.

3. Zimbardo is deeply critical of the war in Iraq, as a psychological climate that led to the Abu Ghraib scandal. Critics have pointed out that although the Abu Ghraib event was deeply disturbing, it doesn't rise to the level of cruelty and atrocity perpetrated by al Qaeda and other terrorist groups, beheading civilians on live video as a form of terror. Would you agree that there is a significant difference? Why or why not? If there is a difference, is it relevant?

Narrative

Smoke Signals

SHERMAN ALEXIE (SCREENWRITER)

CHRIS EYRE (DIRECTOR)

Film, 1998. Based on the short-story collection by Sherman Alexie, **The Lone Ranger and Tonto Fistfight in Heaven.** *Summary.*

Thomas and Victor are young Coeur d'Alene Indians living on the reservation in Idaho in the late 1990s. They grew up together and share the story of one fateful night when they were babies. On that night Thomas's parents' house burned down, with Thomas, his parents, and Victor inside. Someone saved Victor, and Thomas's parents threw their baby to safety out the second-story window while they themselves burned to death. Thomas was caught in midair by Victor's father, Arnold. Since then, Thomas has lived with his grandmother.

Not much happens on the reservation; everyone knows everyone else, and the height of excitement seems to be playing basketball at the gym. One of the young Indians remarks, "Sometimes it is a good day to die—other times it is a good day to play basketball." Sometimes they watch Westerns on TV and discuss whether the cowboys always win or whether the Indians sometimes win. Thomas remarks, with a grin, that there is nothing more pathetic than Indians on TV—except Indians watching Indians on TV!

Thomas is a seer and a storyteller; everything he has experienced in his short life turns into stories—and his stories contain a considerable amount of pure fantasy too. That irritates Victor, who wants him just to tell the truth. Much about Thomas irritates

Victor: Thomas braids his long hair very tightly; Victor wears his long hair free-flowing. Thomas always wears a dark three-piece suit, whereas Victor wears blue jeans and T-shirts. And Victor cultivates a warrior's inscrutable face, whereas Thomas has a ready smile for everyone. What irritates Victor most is Thomas's stories about Victor's father, Arnold. Victor knows him as a man who got drunk and beat him and his mother. Thomas sees Arnold as his hero, a magic man—the man who not only saved his life but also took him to a breakfast at Denny's in Spokane once. They met on the footbridge across the Spokane Falls, and somehow Thomas has associated Arnold with that spot ever since; it has become a power place to him. And Arnold was a storyteller, like Thomas—with a love for a *good* story rather than a *true* story. But Arnold is no longer around for Thomas to tell new stories about—he left his family in anger when Victor was a child.

Their quiet life is interrupted by a phone call from Phoenix: A woman named Suzy calls Victor's mother with the news that Arnold is dead. He lived in a trailer close to her, and his things are still there, including his truck. Someone needs to get him and his belongings. Victor is reluctant to go because he harbors immense resentment toward his father for leaving him, but Thomas puts up the money for the ticket from his piggy bank under one condition: that he gets to go to Phoenix too.

On the bus, Thomas and Victor have a variety of encounters with the world of the whites, not all of them pleasant. For instance, a pair of rednecks take their seats and force them to move. But Victor is not very pleasant either. He calls a young girl a liar for embellishing her one life story: her near chance of going to the Olympics. And he gets on Thomas's case for not knowing how to be an Indian: He must have watched *Dances with Wolves* two hundred times, says Victor, and he still doesn't know how to act like he's come home from the buffalo hunt. Thomas protests that their people weren't buffalo hunters but fishermen. Victor replies that there is nothing glorious about coming home from fishing— the movie wasn't called "Dances with Salmon"!—and we get a sense that perhaps it is Victor, not Thomas, who feels uncomfortable about his role and his culture.

After days of traveling nonstop they finally arrive in Phoenix and walk to the desert hideout of Arnold and Suzy. She turns out to be a hospital administrator and much younger than Arnold, but for years she has had a close relationship with him—"We kept each other's secrets," she says. The three of them share her frybread, traditional American Indian fare, and Thomas tells a wonderful story of how Victor's mother fed a hundred Indians with only fifty frybreads—which turns out to be not quite true, although it is a good story. Suzy has heard about Victor and Thomas and all the basketball games Arnold played with Victor. And she has heard the true story about the night of the fire. What had haunted Arnold for all those years was that he set the fire by accident in a drunken stupor. But now that Victor hears the truth, he also hears something he dares not believe: that Arnold ran back into the burning house to save him. For years, Victor has resented Thomas for being the one saved by Arnold. And now he has to revise all his resentments. Coming face-to-face with the loss of his father, Victor grieves in the traditional Indian way: He cuts his long hair.

The next morning, Victor and Thomas leave in Arnold's truck, taking with them only Arnold's ashes and his basketball. Victor is in a panicked, angry rush to get home, but there is yet another trial ahead for him. Late that night, on a dark desert road, he and Thomas crash the truck, barely avoiding ramming into two cars that had collided

In *Smoke Signals* (1998) Victor (Adam Beach, left) and Thomas (Evan Adams) from the Coeur d'Alene Indian reservation in Idaho are on their way to pick up the ashes of Victor's father Arnold in Arizona. Thomas irritates Victor because he wears his hair in tight braids, wears a three-piece suit—and was rescued as a baby by Arnold, whereas Victor believes his own father didn't care about him.

moments before the boys' arrival. The driver of the car that caused the accident, a white man, is drunk and obnoxious, and his wife is desperately apologetic. But down in the ravine is an injured woman, and the nearest town is twenty miles away. Victor's truck is disabled, but he doesn't hesitate for a moment: He must run for help. And he starts out running into the night, with the long stride of his ancestor warriors. He runs until his side hurts and his vision blurs, and by dawn he collapses. But he is close enough to a town to be seen by a road repair crew, and he gets the message about the injured motorist through.

As Victor and the motorist—who would have died if it hadn't been for his heroic run—are recovering in the hospital, Thomas is standing by, and we can tell that he has the material for many future stories. One woman says they are heroes, coming to the rescue just like the Lone Ranger and Tonto—and the boys answer that they're more like Tonto and Tonto. One snag develops, though: The man who caused the accident has filed false charges against the boys for assault and causing the accident, and Victor and Thomas are taken to the police station. All the old fear and resentment of the white power structure descend on the boys, who feel they won't be believed—but not everyone outside the reservation is like the drunken white driver. His wife, for one, has issued a statement against her husband, and the two women who were in the other car side with the boys, too. And the police chief is a man of good sense and sends the boys on their way.

Six days after leaving Idaho, Victor and Thomas are back with Arnold's ashes. The one who has undergone the most profound change is Victor; he now understands that his dad never planned to leave and that he just hadn't gotten around to going home yet. Now he understands the ghosts his father lived with year after year. So he barely picks on Thomas anymore and even offers him the deepest gesture he can think of: He shares his father's ashes with him. At last, Victor gets to scatter Arnold's ashes where both he and Thomas feel Arnold's spirit belongs: over the Spokane Falls. Meanwhile, in a voice-over, Thomas leaves us with thoughts about forgiving our fathers: "How do we forgive our fathers? Maybe in a dream? . . . Do we forgive our fathers for leaving us too often when we were little, or scaring us with unexpected rage or making us nervous because there never seems to be any rage at all? . . . Shall we forgive them for their excesses of warmth, or coldness, shall we forgive them for pushing, or leaning, for shutting doors, for speaking through walls, or being silent? . . . If we forgive our fathers, what is left?"

Study Questions

1. What do you think made Victor come to terms with his father's disappearance and death? How has Victor changed? Why didn't Thomas change as much?

2. Thomas can make any mundane situation into an interesting, magical time by telling stories about it—but the stories are not always true. Is this morally acceptable? Why or why not?

3. Apply Martha Nussbaum's theory of the rationality of emotions to Victor's situation: Was Victor's anger at his father rational? Why or why not? How can we tell? (Clue: What happened to Victor's anger when he learned the truth about this father?)

4. Why do Western movies play such a big role in Thomas's and Victor's lives? Do you think it is a positive or a negative role?

5. What is funny about the boys' remark that they are more like Tonto and Tonto?

 Narrative

Big Fish

JOHN AUGUST (SCREENWRITER)

TIM BURTON (DIRECTOR)

Film, 2003. Based on the novel by Daniel Wallace. Summary.

Here you have another story about a son and his father, and about storytelling—but with a different focus, because this time it is the father who is the teller of stories. In the film's introduction we hear the core story of the father's life: There was a big old fish in the river

In *Big Fish* (2003) Ed Bloom (here played as a young man by Ewan McGregor) tells a lot of stories about his life, and his son Will doesn't believe any of them. One of his stories tells of his arrival in the magical town of Spectre, where he meets the little girl Jenny (here eight years old, played by Hailey Anne Nelson). Later, Will discovers that there may have been something to the stories after all.

that couldn't be caught no matter what kind of bait was used. But on the day when his son was born, Ed caught the fish, by using as bait his own wedding ring—because, as it turned out, the fish was female. And, as Ed Bloom adds, this time to his new daughter-in-law on his son's wedding day, sometimes the only way to catch an uncatchable woman is to offer her a wedding ring! His son, Will, winces: He's heard the story hundreds of times; he hates it—because it is fake, but also because it reduces him to a mere footnote in his father's life. And since that wedding day three years earlier, the father and the son have not spoken to each other. But now Ed is dying of cancer, the chemo treatment is being stopped, and Will and his wife, Josephine, travel back to the United States from her home country of France to be with him and Will's mother, Sandra. Will tells us, as the narrator, that it is impossible to separate fact from fiction in his father's life—most of the stories he has been telling over the years have never happened. But while he is approaching the final hours with his dad, the childhood stories emerge—stories Ed told his son of his own childhood, such as the one with the witch who lived in the neighborhood: Her glass eye would show the manner of death of anyone who peered into it. Two of Ed's friends looked, and saw their deaths—Ed looked, too, and saw, but he never shared his vision with anyone.

When Will sees his father, Ed is concerned, because "This is not the way I go"—but he doesn't want to elaborate. When Will confronts him and wants to know the "true version of things," he evades the issue and falls back on telling stories of his life. In his childhood, he read about goldfish—how they adjust their growth to their environment, so the bigger the pond, the bigger the fish. He decided to become a big fish, which entailed leaving his little town. But he was not alone—he had make friends with a giant who terrorized the town. So already, Ed was a giant-slayer, but in a peaceful way, because he pacified the giant, who only wanted more to eat. During their travels they split up temporarily, and Ed found himself in a strange place, a small town where everybody was happy and apparently nothing happened. Grass grew like a lawn down Main Street, and everybody was clad in white. The town was Spectre. Mysteriously, the townsfolk told him he was too soon, but in town he met with three people who would mean very much to him in the future: The poet Winslow, who arrived and got stuck in Spectre; Jenny, who was a little precocious girl; and a naked woman at night in the river—a woman who appeared in different guises for different people, but in reality was a fish. And no one could catch her. Ed made an effort and escaped from town because he didn't want to get stuck there too.

While Will is reminiscing, Old Ed is bonding with his daughter-in-law Josephine, telling her another scary story—which turns out to be a joke! Josephine sees into the heart of the old man, loves his spirit, and is tolerant of his stories, far more so than Will is.

She asks Ed to tell about how he met his wife, Sandra, Will's mother, still a beautiful woman—and that is the primary story of Ed's life. Here we, the audience, get to hear the story straight from Ed—this is not a flashback told by Will: On a visit to Calloway's circus Ed not only gets the giant, Carl, a job but also falls in love, with a girl who disappears. Calloway knows her parents, and Ed offers to work for free, as long as Calloway tells him about the girl. And so he does, for months, for little tidbits of information, until Calloway finally tells him her name, Sandra, and where she goes to college (after Ed finds out that Calloway is really a werewolf). He promptly looks her up, only to find out that she's engaged to one of his school friends—one of those who saw his death in the eye of the witch. Ed starts courting Sandra anyway, and awakens the wrath of her fiancé, who beats Ed up—which prompts Sandra to end the engagement. And shortly after, her fiancé really dies, the way he had seen in the eye of the witch. But Sandra and Ed are in for more trouble, because he is being drafted and sent to Vietnam. Through a series of unlikely adventures involving a pair of conjoined, singing, beautiful Vietnamese twins, he returns to Sandra, who, in the meantime, had received the official note that he was missing in action.

Josephine finds the story beautiful—Will is disgusted because it's all fake, and his wife now advises him to have a talk with his dad. Initially the talk goes nowhere: Will asks his father for once in his life, to tell him the truth, to be himself, to let his son know who he is—and Ed answers that he has always been himself. But some window of understanding is opening for Will; during a cleanup in the garage the family comes upon papers that fit into the puzzle of Ed's life: The MIA note is there—and Will always thought that was a fake story. And a mechanical hand—which his father supposedly sold as a traveling salesman. But there is also a trust, for a woman in Spectre, Jennifer; and now Will thinks he has found his father's real secret life. He travels to Spectre, a real small town, and seeks out the woman, a middle-aged single woman in a nice house. Did she have an affair with his father? No, Ed took care of her, and the town, and her house, because he wanted to—they were his friends from his first visit, but he professed his undying love for Sandra when Jennifer shyly told him she'd like him to stay. And, she says, his son was real to him—not her, not Spectre. And Jennifer became a recluse, and a witch (and we realize that the witch with the glass eye really was Jennifer, although it doesn't fit with the time line).

So now Will has learned that some of his father's stories were true and that he really was important to his dad—but when he comes home, there is no one there. Ed has had a stroke and is in intensive care. Will chooses to stay and watch over his dad while the others go home to rest up; Sandra has one last moment with her beloved Ed while he is asleep. The old doctor who has known the family forever asks Will if he wants to hear the story of when he was born. It's not the one with the fish—it's a simple story of an easy birth. And Will likes it.

After Will has been sitting by his father's bedside for a while, Ed surprisingly wakes up; he has lost almost all his capacity to speak, but Will understands that he is desperate because his death is wrong—this is not the way it happens according to the vision! Ed never told his story to Will, but now Will understands his dad well enough to tell the story to *him*. The exact way Ed dies I will leave as a mystery for you to experience when you see the film, as Ed would have wanted it—suffice it to say that Will fulfills his father's dream of dying the right way and tells the story right. And then, in a final confirmation, we're present at the funeral, where Ed's friends show up—Jennifer and the doctor, but also all those elusive characters Will used to think were made up: the Vietnamese singer twins, Calloway the circus manager, Carl the giant, Winslow the poet, and other story characters. They're not completely the way Ed had described them (as you should see for yourself) but they were real after all. Flash forward to a few years later: We see Will's little son tell his friends one of Ed's stories. And Will concludes, "A man tells his stories so many times that he becomes his stories—they live on after him and in that way he becomes immortal." Now does that mean that all the stories Ed told were true? Or is it rather that Will understood the poetic truth beneath his father's tall tales? I'll let you decide that for yourself.

Study Questions

1. Let's repeat that question: Was everything that Ed told true? Or has Will discovered the poetic truth behind the improbable stories? Explain.

2. Is it morally right for Will to play along with his father's death fantasy, or should he have insisted on realism, as he did before? Explain.

3. What might Nussbaum say to this story? Do we understand life better after having read/seen it? Does Will understand life better after hearing his dad's stories?

4. Do you have a family member who constantly tells stories about himself or herself? Do you feel you understand that person better now, or did you have a good understanding before reading this?

5. What is the difference between a tall tale and a lie? Is one morally acceptable, whereas the other isn't? Why or why not? You may want to take up this subject again after reading Chapter 6.

Narrative

East of Eden

JOHN STEINBECK

Novel, 1952. Film, 1955. Summary and Excerpts.

John Steinbeck's mammoth American novel *East of Eden,* following the destinies of three generations of the Trask and the Hamilton families, is for many Steinbeck fans his ultimate work on the topic of good and evil, perhaps even the twentieth-century novel that takes on the subject in the most serious way. Critics have called the character of Cathy/Kate the most evil woman in world literature. But some literary critics have pointed out that *East of Eden* has a stylistic problem: Steinbeck spends several sections of the book talking directly to the reader about philosophical issues such as the nature of good and evil. As you know, I am a philosophy professor, not a literary critic, but what you probably don't know is that John Steinbeck is one of my favorite *moral philosophers,* as well as one of my favorite authors, precisely because he engages in a philosophical monologue in special sections while he is telling the story about the Trasks and the Hamiltons. And his moral philosophy, though perhaps not as intricate or as consistent as the ideas of some of the professional philosophers you are going to meet in this book, is profoundly moving and meaningful to the reader of the novel; we "get" what he means, because his ideas are illustrated by the story, and the story is interspersed with its own philosophical comments—so, a two-in-one masterpiece, for those who like the mixing of stories and ethics. (The literary critic might say, well, Rosenstand just doesn't get the criteria for a well-written novel. My answer to that would be, some literary critics just don't get Steinbeck's genius of mixing the two categories of concrete storytelling and abstract moral philosophy!)

What you'll read first is an excerpt from one of the philosophical monologues, in which Steinbeck argues that all stories are really just variations on the timeless theme of good and evil. Next you'll find an excerpt plus a short summary of the main story line.

A child may ask, "What is the world's story about?" And a grown man or woman may wonder, "What way will the world go? How does it end and, while we're at it, what's the story about?"

I believe that there is one story in the world, and only one, that has frightened and inspired us, so that we live in a Pearl White serial of continuing thought and wonder. Humans are caught—in their lives, in their thoughts, in their hungers and ambitions, in their avarice and cruelty, and in their kindness and generosity too—in a net of good and evil. I think this is the only story we have and that it occurs on all levels of feeling and intelligence. Virtue and vice were warp and woof of our first consciousness, and they will be the fabric of our last, and this despite any changes we may impose on field and river and mountain, on economy and manners. There is no other story. A man, after he has brushed off the dust and chips of his life, will have left only the hard, clean questions: Was it good or was it evil? Have I done well—or ill?

Herodotus, in the Persian War, tells a story of how Croesus, the richest and most-favored king of his time, asked Solon the Athenian a leading question. He would not

The film *East of Eden* (1955) catapulted the young actor James Dean to instant fame—and less than a year later he was dead in an auto accident, becoming a cult hero for half a century. The film focuses on the story of Cal and Aron. Dean plays Cal Trask as the main character, tormented by the doubts and low self-esteem of the young adult male, a portrayal that some see as completely timeless.

have asked it if he had not been worried about the answer. "Who," he asked, "is the luckiest person in the world?" He must have been eaten with doubt and hungry for reassurance. Solon told him of three lucky people in old times. And Croesus more than likely did not listen, so anxious was he about himself. And when Solon did not mention him, Croesus was forced to say, "Do you not consider me lucky?"

Solon did not hesitate in his answer. "How can I tell?" he said. "You aren't dead yet."

And this answer must have haunted Croesus dismally as his luck disappeared, and his wealth and his kingdom. And as he was being burned on a tall fire, he may have thought of it and perhaps wished he had not asked or not been answered.

And in our time, when a man dies—if he has had wealth and influence and power and all the vestments that arouse envy, and after the living take stock of the dead man's property and his eminence and works and monuments—the question is still there: Was his life good or was it evil?—which is another way of putting Croesus's question. Envies are gone, and the measuring stick is: "Was he loved or was he hated? Is his death felt as a loss or does a kind of joy come of it?"

I remember clearly the deaths of three men. One was the richest man of the century, who, having clawed his way to wealth through the souls and bodies of men, spent many years trying to buy back the love he had forfeited and by that process performed great service to the world and, perhaps, had much more than balanced the evils of his rise. I was on a ship when he died. The news was posted on the bulletin board, and nearly everyone received the news with pleasure. Several said, "Thank God that son of a bitch is dead."

Then there was a man, smart as Satan, who, lacking some perception of human dignity and knowing all too well every aspect of human weakness and wickedness, used his special knowledge to warp men, to buy men, to bribe and threaten and seduce until he found himself in a position of great power. He clothed his motives in the names of virtue, and I have wondered whether he ever knew that no gift will ever buy back a man's love when you have removed his self-love. A bribed man can only hate his briber. When this man died the nation rang with praise and, just beneath, with gladness that he was dead.

There was a third man, who perhaps made many errors in performance but whose effective life was devoted to making men brave and dignified and good in a time when they were poor and frightened and when ugly forces were loose in the world to utilize their fears. This man was hated by the few. When he died the people burst into tears in the streets and their minds wailed, "What can we do now? How can we go on without him?"

In uncertainty I am certain that underneath their topmost layers of frailty men want to be good and want to be loved. Indeed, most of their vices are attempted short cuts to love. When a man comes to die, no matter what his talents and influence and genius, if he dies unloved his life must be a failure to him and his dying a cold horror. It seems to me that if you or I must choose between two courses of thought or action, we should remember our dying and try so to live that our death brings no pleasure to the world.

We have only one story. All novels, all poetry, are built on the never-ending contest in ourselves of good and evil. And it occurs to me that evil must constantly respawn, while good, while virtue, is immortal. Vice has always a new fresh young face, while virtue is venerable as nothing else in the world is.

The story John Steinbeck is referring to is the timeless story of making the choice between good and evil, choosing one's good side over one's dark side. This theme is the key to understanding the story of the Trask family in two generations: the two brothers, Adam and Charles, competing for their father's affection, and Adam's two sons, the twins Cal and Aron, competing for Adam's affection. Here we will focus on the more famous last part of *East of Eden* with Cal and Aron, which has been featured in the classic Hollywood film with James Dean; the relationship between the boys plays out as a modern version of the biblical story of Cain and Abel, but when we compare Cal and Aron's story with the story of Adam and Charles in the previous generation, we realize that, in many ways, that also plays out as a Cain and Abel story.

In the Bible, Adam and Eve's firstborn son, Cain, is angry with his brother, Abel, because God accepts Abel's sacrifice of a lamb and rejects Cain's sacrifice of a sheaf of grain. Cain strikes Abel in the head with a rock, and Abel falls to the ground, dead, the first victim of a homicide. When asked by God where Abel is, Cain replies that he is not his brother's keeper. But God knows that Abel is dead, and Cain is tormented by his guilt, so God promises to place a mark on Cain so that everyone will know that he is protected. Cain then leaves his father and mother and settles in the land of Nod, east of Eden.

In Steinbeck's novel, which takes place in the last part of the nineteenth and the first part of the twentieth century, Adam and Charles are the sons of an old Civil War hero and politician, Cyrus. Charles, the younger, adores his father, but Cyrus pays attention only to Adam, who feels little affection for his father. Years after Cyrus's death, the sons find out that he was no war hero and that his prominent political career was built on lies. In the meantime, a woman has come into their lives. Cathy is a mysterious, beautiful girl with a past she won't talk about. (But we, the readers, know that she is an evil human being: She has murdered her parents by setting fire to their home and faking her own death.) The young men believe her to be the victim of an accident, but her injuries stem from being beaten half to death by a man she was about to take for everything he had. Adam falls deeply in love with her, and proposes to her. They marry, but on the sly, Cathy has an affair with Charles. Cathy gets pregnant and gives birth to twins, but motherhood doesn't transform her into a humane person. On the contrary, she had only used Adam and their marriage as protection, and now she wants out. When Adam tries to stop her, she shoots him in the shoulder, point-blank, and walks out on him and the boys. She goes to the nearest big town (Salinas, California) and as "Kate" she becomes a town "madam," and Adam raises the boys by himself, aided by his Chinese American philosophical housekeeper, Lee. Why does Cathy react the way she does? Steinbeck tells us that some people are simply born psychological monsters, with no comprehension that they are hurting other people, physically and emotionally. The evil that Cathy represents is, in a sense, an evil that she did not choose, since she doesn't understand how normal people feel about one another. Cathy is the classical sociopath who only does what serves her best without any consideration for others. The question now is, have the boys inherited her bad blood?

As the boys grow into their teens, it becomes clear that they are very different. Aron is fair and likable, but Cal is dark and brooding. Aron is everything his father, Adam, considers good: obedient, friendly, considerate, an easy child. Cal, on the other hand, questions everything, has a hard time making friends, sneaks out at night on his own; in short, he is a "bad boy." And yet, Cal is the one Steinbeck wants us to like. Aron is too good to be real. Cal is more like the rest of us. And, indeed, Aron's goodness reveals itself to have a dark side. He is so absorbed in being good and pure that he actually ends up neglecting both his father and his girlfriend. And here we see how the concepts of good and evil had hidden associations in the early twentieth century: "Good" meant not only being considerate and kind but also being sexually pure; and "bad" or "evil" meant not only being selfish and inconsiderate but also having, and acting on, sexual impulses. Because Cal is a young man whose hormones are raging, he considers himself "bad," and since Aron apparently doesn't have that problem, he must be "good." But Cal's "badness" also manifests itself in his utter disconnect with his father. Adam thinks he understands his boy Aron completely, but he has no clue what goes on inside Cal's head. Cal loves his father and wants to protect him, but his father pays attention only to Aron, not realizing that he is repeating his own father's old sin, paying attention to only one of his sons.

Eventually, Cal finds out that his mother is alive and runs a brothel in town. Here he confides in Lee, who tells him that he may have inherited his mother's evil nature, but even so, he has a choice.

> Always before, Cal had wanted to build a dark accumulation of things seen and things heard—a kind of a warehouse of materials that, like obscure tools, might come in handy, but after the visit to Kate's he felt a desperate need for help.

One night Lee, tapping away at his typewriter, heard a quiet knock on his door and let Cal in. The boy sat down on the edge of the bed, and Lee let his thin body down in the Morris chair. He was amused that a chair could give him so much pleasure. Lee folded his hands over his stomach as though he wore Chinese sleeves and waited patiently. Cal was looking at a spot in the air right over Lee's head.

Cal spoke softly and rapidly. "I know where my mother is and what she's doing. I saw her."

Lee's mind said a convulsive prayer for guidance. "What do you want to know?" he asked softly.

"I haven't thought yet. I'm trying to think. Would you tell me the truth?"

"Of course."

The questions whirling in Cal's head were so bewildering he had trouble picking one out. "Does my father know?"

"Yes."

"Why did he say she was dead?"

"To save you from pain."

Cal considered. "What did my father do to make her leave?"

"He loved her with his whole mind and body. He gave her everything he could imagine."

"Did she shoot him?"

"Yes."

"Why?"

"Because he didn't want her to go away."

"Did he ever hurt her?"

"Not that I know of. It wasn't in him to hurt her."

"Lee, why did she do it?"

"I don't know."

"Don't know or won't say?"

"Don't know."

Cal was silent for so long that Lee's fingers began to creep a little, holding to his wrists. He was relieved when Cal spoke again. The boy's tone was different. There was a pleading in it.

"Lee, you knew her. What was she like?"

Lee sighed and his hands relaxed. "I can only say what I think. I may be wrong."

"Well, what did you think?"

"Cal," he said, "I've thought about it for a great many hours and I still don't know. She is a mystery. It seems to me that she is not like other people. There is something she lacks. Kindness maybe, or conscience. You can only understand people if you feel them in yourself. And I can't feel her. The moment I think about her my feeling goes into darkness. I don't know what she wanted or what she was after. She was full of hatred, but why or toward what I don't know. It's a mystery. And her hatred wasn't healthy. It wasn't angry. It was heartless. I don't know that it is good to talk to you like this."

"I need to know."

"Why? Didn't you feel better before you knew?"

"Yes. But I can't stop now."

"You're right," said Lee. "When the first innocence goes, you can't stop—unless you're a hypocrite or a fool. But I can't tell you any more because I don't know any more."

Cal said, "Tell me about my father then."

"That I can do," said Lee. He paused. "I wonder if anyone can hear us talking? Speak softly."

"Tell me about him," said Cal.

"I think your father has in him, magnified, the things his wife lacks. I think in him kindness and conscience are so large that they are almost faults. They trip him up and hinder him."

"What did he do when she left?"

"He died," said Lee. "He walked around but he was dead. And only recently has he come half to life again." Lee saw a strange new expression on Cal's face. The eyes were open wider, and the mouth, ordinarily tight and muscular, was relaxed. In his face, now for the first time, Lee could see Aron's face in spite of the different coloring. Cal's shoulders were shaking a little, like a muscle too long held under a strain.

"What is it, Cal?" Lee asked.

"I love him," Cal said.

"I love him too," said Lee. "I guess I couldn't have stayed around so long if I hadn't. He is not smart in a worldly sense but he's a good man. Maybe the best man I have ever known."

Cal stood up suddenly. "Good night, Lee," he said.

"Now you wait just a moment. Have you told anyone?"

"No."

"Not Aron—no, of course you wouldn't."

"Suppose he finds out?"

"Then you'd have to stand by to help him. Don't go yet. When you leave this room we may not be able to talk again. You may dislike me for knowing you know the truth. Tell me this—do you hate your mother?"

"Yes," said Cal.

"I wondered," said Lee. "I don't think your father ever hated her. He had only sorrow."

Cal drifted toward the door, slowly, softly. He shoved his fists deep in his pockets. "It's like you said about knowing people. I hate her because I know why she went away. I know—because I've got her in me." His head was down and his voice was heartbroken.

Lee jumped up. "You stop that!" he said sharply. "You hear me? Don't let me catch you doing that. Of course you may have that in you. Everybody has. But you've got the other too. Here—look up! Look at me!"

Cal raised his head and said wearily, "What do you want?"

"You've got the other too. Listen to me! You wouldn't even be wondering if you didn't have it. Don't you dare take the lazy way. It's too easy to excuse yourself because of your ancestry. Don't let me catch you doing it! Now—look close at me so you will remember. Whatever you do, it will be you who do it—not your mother."

"Do you believe that, Lee?"

"Yes, I believe it, and you'd better believe it or I'll break every bone in your body."

After Cal had gone Lee went back to his chair. He thought ruefully, I wonder what happened to my Oriental repose?

Later, Cal is faced with the choice that *East of Eden* is all about: the choice between doing the right thing and choosing the selfish way, the easy way, the evil way. This time it isn't a question just of being "bad" and having hormones but also of doing harm, deliberately, for personal gain. The underlying story of the two brothers, Adam's sons in a new version of the old Cain and Abel story, plays out when Cal decides to get back at Aron for being his father's favorite: He reveals their mother's existence and identity to Aron. The end results are devastating for Aron, Cathy, and Adam, and I will leave it for you to read on your own.

Study Questions

1. Is Cathy evil? Is Cal? Explain.

2. The key element in *East of Eden* is the concept of choice. Steinbeck chose a Hebrew word to express it, *Timshel,* or, in Steinbeck's translation, "thou mayest." (As it happens, Steinbeck may have gotten the translation wrong, but within the book, the word is a powerful symbol of the human freedom to choose, with the accompanying moral responsibility.) Is Cathy free to choose? Is Adam? Is Cal? Are you?

3. What does Steinbeck mean by saying (in the first excerpt) that "there is no other story"?

4. Is having sexual urges the same as "being bad"? Why or why not? Compare the values at the time of the story (early twentieth century) with the moral values of today.

Chapter Two

Learning Moral Lessons from Stories

We may think that the most powerful moral lessons are learned from events in our childhood (when we are caught doing something we aren't supposed to do, or when we *aren't* caught), but chances are the most powerful lessons we carry with us are lessons we learn from the *stories* we have read or that were read to us.

Didactic Stories

Many of you may recognize this typical, unpleasant event from childhood: Your authority figure takes you aside to tell you Aesop's fable "The Boy Who Cried Wolf." A lad was tending sheep at the outskirts of town, and he thought it might be fun to give the village a scare, so he cried, "The wolf is here! The wolf is here!" And the villagers came running, but there was no wolf. The boy tricked the town again and again, until that fateful day when the wolf really did come. The boy cried for his life, "The wolf is here!" but nobody believed him anymore. The wolf ate the sheep and the shepherd too. At least, that is the way the story was told to me when I was five years old.

Why are children told such a gruesome story? Because adults deem it necessary to teach children a moral lesson. Even a child understands the message: "The shepherd boy lied and suffered the consequences. You don't want to be like him, do you?" It is a powerful lesson. Indeed, the appeal of the story seems to go beyond European and American traditions: I have a colleague from India who tells me that when she was a little girl in Calcutta, she was told the story of the boy who cried tiger.

Stories that are told to teach a moral lesson are called *didactic* stories. These instructional stories may well be as old as humanity. When giving a keynote address about stories in ethics at a philosophical retreat in Denmark some years ago, I asked the audience, a mixed group of several hundred people ranging from their teens to their eighties, if they had been told the story of "The Boy Who Cried Wolf" when they were kids; a forest of hands went up, young smooth hands alongside gnarled old hands, and all of a sudden it seemed to me that I was looking down the corridor of time, from these living generations backward to the other generations long gone, each one of them telling their children about the lying shepherd boy—in all likelihood a story so old that it predates Aesop's version.

The New Interest in Stories Across the Professions

The interest in using stories (narratives) to explore moral problems is increasing, for stories can serve as a laboratory in which moral solutions can be tried out before any decisions are made. Here are some examples of how stories are being used as moral laboratories today.

- Many psychologists are advocating a method they call "bibliotherapy" to facilitate communication between parents and children. Through reading stories with their children, parents may find it easier to explain difficult issues, because together, through the fictional universe, they can explore issues and emotions that may be more difficult to approach on either an abstract or a highly personal level. For example, it's hard to explain death to children—either as a concept or as a real event in a family. Perhaps a story about the death of a pet could help focus the discussion. Of course, this may be just an easy way out for parents who don't have a clue how to relate to their children, but ideally the sharing of stories is a positive way to make the child understand about arrivals of new siblings, a move to a new home, deaths in the family, and other traumatic events. (It may sound like a brand-new idea, but in the next section you will see that this is in effect how myths and fairy tales used to work in traditional societies.)

- Medical students in many parts of this country are now exposed not only to case studies that involve medical ethics but also to stories of fiction, such as Leo Tolstoy's "The Death of Iván Ilyich" (1886) and the 1994 film *Philadelphia,* that deal with medical problems. The students seem to feel better equipped to deal with "real" problems because of this exploratory background. Why? Because no matter how many case histories she examines or how many colleagues she talks to, a medical student may not be able to understand a patient from the inside quite as well as when a great writer tells the story from the patient's point of view. The New York University School of Medicine's Literature, Arts, and Medicine Database is a website dedicated to listing films and works of literature that may be of help as a resource for medical personnel, such as *And the Band Played On, Awakenings, Gattaca, Lorenzo's Oil, The English Patient, The Doctor,* and even *Million Dollar Baby,* with its euthanasia theme. Books include Christy Brown's *My Left Foot,* Camus's *The Plague,* and Jane Austen's *Emma.* The Literature and Medicine program in Maine has since 1997 gathered health care professionals around the concept that reading and discussing literature can improve their professional skills and help them understand their patients and clients.

- Patients have been encouraged to use movies as a sort of treatment. In the February 2000 issue of *Psychology Today* magazine, an article titled "Reel Therapy" explored the psychological benefits that may come from watching the right movie at the right time. The story noted that doctors assign certain films to help patients come to terms with their situation or discover a new side to themselves. Unfortunately, it gave some readers the impression that watching a movie would solve their problems. Have emotional injuries in need of healing? Rent *The Horse Whisperer.* Hopelessly cynical about modern life? Then see *Shakespeare in Love.* It doesn't quite work that way in real life, and not in this book either! If

© Dan Piraro. King Feature Syndicate.

Psychologists are beginning to tap the therapeutic potential of movies—but of course merely watching movies will not solve one's emotional or moral problems.

we want to delve into moral issues in depth, we have to get beyond the sound bites and the quick fixes. Good stories can help us begin to explore an issue—but they can't be a substitute for insight or discussion.

- The criminal justice system is experimenting with the use of stories. A website—Picturing Justice, the On-line Journal of Law and Popular Culture—specializes in discussing films that relate to legal issues. Examples range from the classics *Notorious* and *Twelve Angry Men* to *Amistad, The Life of David Gale,* and the comedies *Legally Blonde* and *My Cousin Vinnie.* What is interesting is that the didactic value of such films to the legal community is no longer something that just happens by accident after someone goes to the movies and sees a connection to real-life cases—it is now something that is an accepted and established form of learning. But this isn't just of abstract interest to scholars and lawyers: increasingly, the courts in the Western world are experimenting with exposing convicted criminals to novels and films that may cause them to rethink their own lives and understand the severity of their crimes.

- Psychotherapists are having patients tell about their own lives as if they were stories or asking them to select a famous fairy tale as a model or template of the way they see their own lives. The idea of telling one's own story as a form of therapy and moral education is something we will look at in detail in the final chapter.

- Stories have been found to have great potential for promoting cross-cultural or multicultural understanding. They can highlight cultural differences in a way that presents them as exciting and worth exploring, while emphasizing the fundamental human similarities underneath the surface differences.

- Last on this list, but not least: Some philosophers are now looking to stories as a way not only to explain difficult theories to their freshman students but also to explore the philosophical richness of literature and films in itself. Philosophers have for a long time been suspicious of using stories as illustrations of moral problems for several reasons. Some have felt that using stories would cause readers to be concerned with *specific* cases rather than with seeing the general picture. Others have worried that telling stories might manipulate readers' emotions instead of appealing to their reason: Such stories would perhaps lead people to *do* the right thing, but they wouldn't lead people to *think* about moral issues, because a story is not a logical argument but, rather, a persuasion—a story is not logic but rhetoric.

There is a difference, however, between stories that moralize and stories that discuss moral problems. In the past, philosophers seem to have assumed that stories illustrating moral problems are always of the moralizing kind. Now a different attitude seems to be growing among ethics scholars; they recognize that stories need not be moralizing to illustrate a moral point. Such stories may express a moral point of view, and then that point of view can be open for discussion. Or a story may have an open-ended conclusion, one in which the moral issues are not resolved. Even moralizing stories may have their proper role to play from time to time, and stories are an excellent way to illustrate how difficult a moral problem can be. As noted in Chapter 1, the field of philosophy is also slowly warming up to the old idea that feelings are not irrelevant in moral discussions. The psychologist Carol Gilligan argues for the legitimacy of emotions in moral decision making. As you know, Martha Nussbaum points out that emotions are not a matter of something uncontrollable, like hunger, but instead involve decision making and rational choices. Another philosopher, Philip Hallie, states that without feelings for the victims of evildoing, we can't hope to understand what a moral sense is all about. Jonathan Bennett, another contemporary philosopher, insists that although certain moral principles may be admirable, others may be warped: The Nazi exterminators (members of the National Socialist German Worker's Party, 1920–1945) had firm moral principles, but they were principles most people don't approve of today. Without sympathy for other people, our principles may go astray. One of the ways in which we can engage both our sympathy and our moral principles is through stories.

Some of the stories in this book are didactic (they teach a lesson), and some of them are more open-ended. It seems that, usually, we prefer learning from stories that were *not* written especially to teach a lesson. That may be one of the secrets of literature: We may forgive a good story for preaching a little, but we can't forgive a bad story for preaching. In other words, we are most accepting of a moral lesson if it is not too obvious, if it appears only between the lines and is subordinate to the plot and the characters. The stories that are most effective in teaching lessons may be those that are not obviously intended to do so. Examples of extreme didactic films would be the classic *The Birth of a Nation* (the Civil War seen from the Southern viewpoint) and *Reefer Madness,* a film generally viewed today as a propaganda film against the use of marijuana. Stories with more dimensions to them, and thus more interesting to a modern audience, might be films such as *Monster's Ball* and *Mystic River* or the anti-drug films *Drugstore Cowboy* and *Requiem for a Dream* (see Chapter 10).

Of course, real-life events and discussions of those events are essential to our understanding of moral issues, but using stories is an alternative way of talking about these issues, because a story can serve as a slice of life that we are invited to share in.

The Value of Stories in World Cultures

The philosopher Alasdair MacIntyre finds the telling of stories so important for humans that he calls us "storytelling animals." There are many reasons for telling stories, for reading and writing novels and short stories, and for making and watching films. It seems that in early, pretechnological cultures the purpose of storytelling was twofold: On the *human* side, the purpose was to knit the tribe firmly together by setting up the rules and boundaries that would establish a group identity. Besides, storytelling helped to pass the time on rainy days, and it kept the children occupied for a while. On the *cosmic* side, the purpose was to establish the story of the beginning of time, when everything was created, so if a symbolic re-creation seemed necessary (and it did, periodically), one could tell and enact the "beginning" stories and in that way "renew" the cosmos. Storytelling has never been more important than it was in those ancient times, for in telling the story people helped re-create the universe, put the sun in its right place, and make sure that the seasons followed one another in the proper order.

The strength of storytelling is no less apparent in many religions. Periodically (usually once a year), believers remind themselves of an important time in the history of their religion: the creation of the world, the creation of the religion itself, or the establishment of the believers' identity through a religious event. Usually a story is told about that event, and even if it is supposed to be a reminder rather than a re-creation, it is still a sacred and powerful vehicle.

In ancient times the storytellers were the primary teachers of morals. Of course, parents have always had a hand in moral education, but in pretechnological cultures (what used to be called "primitive" cultures), those who knew the legends were the ones who, in effect, represented the social institutions of religion, school, and government. The myths surrounding the origin of the world, of society, of food items, and of love and death and the stories of the important men and women in the tribe's past provided rules for the tribe to live by—moral structures that could be used in everyday life to make decisions about crops, marriages, warfare, and so forth. The way to teach children how to become good members of the tribe was to tell the old stories.

In our technological world we no longer have such a body of ready-made prescriptions for moral conduct—at least, we don't think we do. In fact, however, we still tell stories, we still listen to stories, and we still take moral lessons from them. Some people read the Bible, the Torah, the Koran, or other religious books and seek comfort in their stories of human frailty and perseverance. Some people keep their childhood comic-book collections and dive into the old stories from time to time for some basic moral reinforcement. Some people read biographies of remarkable men and women and are inspired by the stories of courage and bravery. Adults may not read fairy tales anymore, but we read novels—classics, best-sellers, or science fiction. And if we don't read novels, we go to the movies or watch TV. Wherever we turn we find *stories*—some are real and some fictional, some are too outdated or too radical for us to relate to, but we find at least some stories that have served as our moral guideposts. Even if you are not a great reader or movie-goer, you probably can recall at least one story that has moved you.

Stories of Values Across the Ages

Fact, Fiction, or Both?

In the secular world we usually tell stories of two kinds: those that we believe to be historically true and those that we know never took place but that have their own special truth to them, a *poetic* truth. The fairy tale "Little Red Riding Hood" is not a historical account, but children may enjoy it if they are old enough to deal with their fear of the wolf, who comes to a gruesome end. Parents enjoy telling it, because they can smuggle home a lesson: Don't talk to strangers, and watch out for "wolves" in disguise. Box 2.1 looks at reality TV—which purports to be fact, not fiction.

What about accounts that we don't know to be either historical or poetic? The story of Zorro, for example, is not a historical account, although there may have been an outlaw in Old California who vaguely resembled the Zorro character. Some readers feel cheated if they find out that a story is more legend than history, but others find it all the more fascinating because it is a mixture of what we think happened and what we wish had happened. It may not tell us much about history, but it tells us a great deal about people, including ourselves, who *wish* that Zorro were real.

Even stories that we believe to be factual, such as the story of the battle of the Alamo or the sinking of the *Titanic,* are not usually simple reports of facts; such stories must have a beginning, a middle, and an ending, and most often we choose the beginning and the ending according to what we feel makes the most *sense.* In actual life, the stream of events goes on, usually with little indication that here begins something new or here a story comes to an end—except in the case of someone's birth or death. Even in the latter case, the story goes on without the person who has died. So even "true" stories have an element of *poetic creativity,* in that we choose what to include in the story, what is *relevant* to the story (not every meal or visit to the bathroom is important in order for us to understand the life and times of Gandhi, or James Dean, or Princess Diana), and where to begin and end the story. Even eyewitness accounts, often regarded as the one true record of events, are full of creativity. Two persons observing the same event will very likely come up with slightly different versions of it; they notice different things because they are standing in different spots and because they are different people with different interests in life. If eyewitnesses are asked to tell about an event long past, some of their memories will be sharper than others, some will mirror exactly what they saw, and some will mirror what they felt or what they feel now, which turns their stories into personal interpretations of the event. At best, any account of a past event can only approximate what happened. We can never truly reproduce the event.

Box 2.1 REALITY SHOWS: WHERE DID THE STORY GO?

Although the academic interest in stories has been on the increase, some story aficionados worry that the public interest in stories may be on the wane, considering the popularity of *reality shows*. TV shows such as *Survivor* and *The Bachelor* have scored top ratings, but that's not all: The public's interest in the lives of "public figures," whether they be celebrities, criminals, or just ordinary people caught up in some media circus, has also been on the rise. Some media analysts claim there is a decreasing interest in made-up stories these days, and an increased interest in real stories. There are two things we can say about that: For one thing, "reality shows" aren't really real—sorry to burst that bubble. As much as they feature "real people," they are scripted to a great extent and their content and structure are heavily edited. That means that even if they don't have a clear plot structure laid out beforehand, they are still narratives—stories that interest us. For another, perhaps there is a reason why the stories of "real people" attract attention these days. We only have to think of the media attention given to the disappearance of Natalee Holloway, the abduction of Elizabeth Smart, the disappearance and murder of Laci Peterson, the murder of Danielle van Dam, and other abduction/murder cases featured in the media. Some of these cases involve money, some involve violence and murder, most—if not all—involve women and girls; and, as we shall see in a later chapter, there are even philosophical theories about why we all of a sudden care so much about these strangers. The positive spin, as we shall see in Chapter 4, is that we extend the feelings we have for friends and relatives to these strangers, for a while. The negative spin, which I will suggest here, is that our world, presented to us by the media, has started to seem overwhelming to us. Our brains have evolved, through hundreds of thousands of years, into tribal brains, focusing on interacting intimately with a group of people probably no bigger than about one hundred members, mostly relatives and neighbors. That meant close interaction, with lots of talk and gossip about those relatives and neighbors. But most of us no longer live in such communities—we don't know our neighbors, and we have little connection to our relatives. But we still have the need for tribal gossip and concern—so we turn to those new neighbors of ours, the TV people. And the more "real" they seem, the more we (or some of us) feel engaged in their destinies. Some people would say, "Then get a life!" But this *is* our life in the modern world, for better or worse. The upside is that our horizon literally expands, through the stories of others, factual as well as fictional, introducing moral issues we would never have related to or even imagined in previous times. We have all now been educated in the unethical: insider trading, child molestations by priests, religious fanatics kidnapping children and brainwashing them, red herrings introduced in court cases to confuse juries, and so forth. The downside is, of course, that this expanded interest may be nothing but a thirst for titillation, a ghoulish rubbernecking taken to an extreme. How much should we engage ourselves in other people's problems, and to what extent should the media report them? We return to such issues in Chapter 13.

Religious legends reveal the same tension between fact and fiction. If believers suspect that events described in the legends never happened or that they happened in a different and more "everyday" way than is described in the religious text, they may experience a general disappointment with their religion, or they may elect to deny the possibility that the religious stories are less than fact-based, or they may deny the plausibility of new interpretations of the old stories—such as we saw in the aftermath of the fictional novel by Dan Brown, *The DaVinci Code* (see below). Other believers, however, may see the stories as being rich with poetry and telling human truths that are on a higher, more spiritual level. Aristotle, who was intensely interested in the relationship between history and poetry, said that history may deal with facts, but poetry deals with Truth.

Traditional Stories

Myths   We don't know anything about the first stories ever told, but if we are to judge from ancient myths and legends, there is a good chance that they served as reminders of proper conduct. The Cherokees tell of Grandmother Spider's way of making clay pots, and it seems to be (among other things) a lesson for Cherokee women in how to make pots the correct way. Myths in general have two main purposes: to strengthen the social bonding among people and to fortify the individual psychologically. *Traditional myths* work on those two levels at once by presenting stories of gods, goddesses, and culture heroes who tell their society about the ideal social behavior and individuals about the proper role models to follow. In a sense, traditional myths are a successful combination of *ethics of conduct* and *virtue ethics* (see Parts 2 and 3). The philosopher Peter Muntz calls myths "concrete universals," stories that in a very concrete form tell about the human condition and give us courage to deal with the troubles that being human usually entails.

The myth of the loss of immortality told by the Trobriand people of New Guinea is such a story. It tells us that once humans could rejuvenate themselves; they could shed their skins and become young again. A grandmother took her granddaughter to the river and then went off by herself to shed her skin. When she came back, the granddaughter didn't recognize her (she appeared to be a young girl) and shooed her away. Upset, the grandmother went back and put her old skin on again. The granddaughter told her that she had chased a young girl, an impostor, away. The grandmother said, "Just because you refused to recognize me, nobody will be able to be young again. We shall all die of old age now." Aside from the fact that the story unfairly places the immense burden of causing humanity to die on an ignorant young girl—myths often blame a major disaster on a small event, as when Eve eats the fruit from the Tree of Knowledge—the lesson is that we humans are mortal and there is nothing we can do about it. The story also seems to say that humans, far from being victims, are very important beings, since they can cause such a cosmic calamity as the loss of immortality!

Fairy Tales   Another ancient category of stories with moral lessons is the *fairy tale*. The fairy tales collected by the Grimm brothers in early-nineteenth-century Germany reflect what is probably a very old tradition of stories with morals, and they are not just for children; the stories were told originally to both young and old. The Trobriand people distinguish between three kinds of stories. First, there are the "myths," which are sacred stories about the beginning of the world and of society.

They must be taken very seriously. Second, there are the "true legends," semihistorical accounts of heroes in the past and their travels. They are supposed to be taken at face value, for the most part. Last, there are the "fairy tales," stories to be told in the rainy season, usually with some point of teaching the young about the customs of the people but also with the intent of pure entertainment. They are recognized as never having happened.

Most cultures acknowledge that there is a difference between stories in which the good are rewarded and the bad are punished and stories of everyday life. The fairy tale has been described by psychoanalysts as pure wishful thinking, but many fairy tales involve gruesome events that are hardly wish fulfillments, because they often happen to characters who don't "deserve" them. Such events do serve a purpose, though, in making the punishment of the bad characters seem justified.

In spite of its enormous popularity, the tale of Little Red Riding Hood seems to be a product of the literary elite and not of folklore, but that doesn't detract from its didactic power. "Hansel and Gretel" is a folklore classic with much the same lesson: Don't go with strangers, and don't let them feed you candy! But the most famous fairy tales from the Grimm brothers' collection today are probably those that have been revised for modern audiences by Walt Disney Studios, such as *Cinderella* and *Snow White and the Seven Dwarfs*. The cartoon versions are known by several generations of moviegoers, videotape purchasers, and, lately, DVD collectors and their children. The Disney *Cinderella* is an upbeat story of the poor orphan girl who lives with her wealthy stepmother and stepsisters in a huge old house, where she is treated like an unpaid servant or a slave. When the king of the country invites all unmarried young women to a grand ball at the castle to meet the prince so he can choose a wife, the evil stepsisters sabotage Cinderella's dream of going to the ball. They tear to pieces the dress that her little friends the mice and the birds have made for her, and leave her in tears as they depart for the ball. But Cinderella's fairy godmother appears in a swirl of sparkles and transforms her into a radiant princess, with glass slippers. A pumpkin becomes a magic chariot, and her mice friends become horses, her dog becomes a valet, and her old horse becomes a coachman, but only for the evening. She must leave the ball before midnight, because then everything reverts to the way it was. You probably know the story: She meets the prince, and he falls in love with her, but midnight is approaching, so she runs away—leaving one glass slipper behind. And next day, the prince's servant scours the countryside to find the girl whose foot can fit into the glass slipper. Despite new attempts at sabotage from Cinderella's stepmother and the sisters, Cinderella emerges as the mystery woman from the ball, and she marries the prince and lives happily ever after. No punishment is meted out to her stepfamily for torturing her. That is the version most of us know. And although a child may rejoice that Cinderella is never going back to the harsh life of work and no love, there is perhaps a slight letdown that she magnanimously forgives her tormentors.

But if you ever sit down with a copy of *Grimm's Fairy Tales,* you'll encounter quite a different version. In the original story, Cinderella's father isn't dead; he is just oblivious to the torture his new wife and her pretty daughters put his daughter through. Her friends the doves and the pigeons are the ones with magic powers:

There is no fairy godmother. While she is crying at her mother's grave under a magic tree, the birds bring her a gold party dress, as well as gold slippers. The essential plot of Cinderella meeting the prince and losing the slipper is the same as that of the modern version—but the aftermath is far more bloody. Since the sisters' feet are much bigger than Cinderella's, they try to fit into the slipper presented by the prince, in person, by cutting their heels and toes off, with blood seeping through the gold fabric. And when Cinderella marries the prince, the evil sisters are punished: They walk up the aisle as bridesmaids behind the bride, and Cinderella's pigeons peck their eyes out. "And so they were condemned to go blind for the rest of their days because of their wickedness and falsehood," as the story concludes.

An interesting variation on the theme that actually reaches back to the older version is the film *Ever After* (1998), in which one of Cinderella's evil sisters and the stepmother are in fact punished after Cinderella marries the prince—in a way that seems utterly appropriate to a modern mind-set: They are sentenced to work in the laundry of the castle so they can understand the life they had forced Cinderella to live before her life changed. The shoe is now on the other foot (without cutting any toes or heels), and the moral lesson of *karma* is learned: What goes around, comes around.

What is interesting here is the development of the moral lessons embedded in the old story. Fairy tales at the time when the Grimm brothers collected the stories were folk tales, told primarily by adults for adults, and the moral lessons were harsh and severe: Evil stepmothers, brothers, and sisters, or whoever tortured the good boy or girl, met a horrific end, a painful death or dismemberment, whereas the good person was rewarded with wealth and fame. In the Disney cartoons of the mid–twentieth century, the moral lesson seems to be not for the evil family members but for the suffering hero: Hang in there with fortitude, and things will change! *Ever After* reflects the changing times of the 1990s: Cinderella is a woman of initiative, action, and intellect, not someone who needs to be rescued, but the stepsisters are still evil, and end up being punished in a way that will rehabilitate them and change them for the better!

The drastic revenge theme from the folklore of times past, not just in the West, but around the globe, has been interpreted by psychoanalysts as having a cathartic, cleansing function, perhaps even more so than putting an evil stepsister to work in the laundry: Some psychoanalysts today maintain that the real value of such stories— which, they say, children should not be protected from but, rather, exposed to—is that children can get rid of their aggressions toward their parents through the stories. (As we shall see in an upcoming section, Aristotle would have agreed with this psychoanalytic point of view.) In addition, the child is exposed to evil but at the same time acquires a dose of hopeful strength and learns that evil can be dealt with. In other words, the most horrible, gruesome, bloody fairy tales may be the ones with the most positive message for the impressionable reader: Yes, there are terrible things out there, but with fortitude we can vanquish them.

Parables   For two thousand years, Christians have found moral support in parables such as those of the Good Samaritan and the prodigal son.

The *parable* is an allegorical story for adults; it is supposed to be understood as a story about ourselves and what we ought to do. Although the purpose of the fairy tale seems to be primarily to entertain and secondarily to teach a moral lesson, the purpose of the parable is *primarily* to teach a moral and religious lesson. Christianity is not the only religion with parables; the Islamic, Hebrew, and Buddhist traditions contain such stories.

What fascinated the early readers of Jesus of Nazareth's parables was that they were so hard to live up to—not just because it was hard to be good, but also because the moral demands of Jesus himself usually ran counter to what society demanded of its citizens or what it viewed as proper moral conduct. What was so difficult for Jesus' contemporaries to understand? He demanded not only that we be compassionate toward all in need but also that we consider *every* person a fellow human being, not just those from our own village, country, or culture, and especially not just those who show compassion toward us.

The parable of the prodigal son (Luke 15:11–32) has been one such lesson that people with ordinary common sense and good manners find hard to follow. The "bad" son who has squandered his inheritance comes home and is sorry. The father makes a fuss over the bad son and slaughters the fattened calf for him. The good son, who has stayed with his father, is upset, for he has never received any recognition of his stability from his father, and yet now it seems that the bad son is more important. And he is, to Jesus, for he has been on a longer journey than the good son: all the way to perdition and back. Christians, therefore, ask themselves if that means we should go on a binge and then repent rather than never go on a binge at all. The answer may be that the story is supposed to be judged from the point of view not of the good or the bad brother but of the father. Indeed, the secret to many of the parables is to find out whose viewpoint they express. The parable of the Good Samaritan (Luke 10:30–34) is about a victim of highway robbery and mugging. As he lies wounded at the roadside, he is ignored by several upstanding citizens but is helped by a social outcast, the Samaritan. (The story is outlined in Chapter 11.) This parable is told from the wounded man's point of view ("who is my neighbor"), not from the point of view of the Samaritan.

A Story of Sacrifice: Abraham and Isaac   Although it is not classified as a parable, the Old Testament story of Abraham being told to sacrifice his son Isaac (Genesis 22:1–19) has had the same kind of effect on its listeners. It is one of the hardest stories for a religion that believes in a loving God, be it from a Jewish or a Christian point of view, to explain. Abraham and his wife Sarah are childless until they have Isaac very late in their lives, through God's intervention. God tells Abraham that his descendants will be as numerous as the stars in the sky and the grains of sand in the desert. When Isaac is a half-grown boy, however, God tells Abraham to take Isaac up the mountain and sacrifice him like a sheep. Abraham leads Isaac away, heavy-hearted but obedient to God. He ties Isaac to the sacrificial stone and is about to stab him the ritual way when God's voice stops him, saying the request was just a test of Abraham's piety. God supplies a ram for Abraham to sacrifice instead.

The Trial of Abraham's Faith (plate by Gustave Doré, 1866). Abraham, having received the command from God to sacrifice his only son, Isaac, dutifully takes Isaac up the mountain to the place of sacrifice. Isaac, unaware that it is he himself who is to be the victim, is carrying the firewood that Abraham will use to light the sacrificial fire.

The implications of this story have confounded believers and nonbelievers for two thousand years. A God who commands such a thing must be a cruel God, critics say, cruel and with a strange sense of humor. The philosopher Søren Kierkegaard sees the story as an illustration of the *limitations of ethics:* Ethically speaking, what

Box 2.2 KAFKA'S ABRAHAM

In his nonfiction piece "Abraham," the Austrian-Czech novelist Franz Kafka (1883–1924) interprets the story of Abraham and Isaac in ways that are rather different from the traditional one. For one thing, he says, there was no need for any "leap of faith" for Abraham to accept the word of God, because if Abraham were to prove himself, then something precious to him had to be put on the line. If Abraham had so much—riches, a son, and a prophecy that he would become the father of the Jewish people—then he could be tested only by the threat of having something taken away from him. This is logical, says Kafka; it requires no leap of faith at all. What *would* require a leap of faith is if Abraham had been a different sort of person. Suppose he truly wanted to please God by performing the sacrifice but was a person of low self-esteem? He really wants to do what is right, like Cervantes' Don Quixote, but he can't quite believe that he can be the one God was speaking to because he believes he is unworthy. He is afraid that if he proceeds with the sacrifice, it will turn out that the command was just a joke, and he will be a laughingstock, like Quixote, who always tried to do the heroic thing but ended up fighting windmills. For this Abraham, being laughed at would make him even more unworthy of being called by God. It would be as though a worthy person had been called, but this grungy, unworthy Abraham showed up instead, foolishly believing himself to be the worthy one. Now this, says Kafka, would indeed require a leap of faith.

Abraham was about to do was wrong; he had no business killing his son, because that is not how people are supposed to behave. But for Abraham, as for any believer, there is a law that is higher than the moral laws of society, and that is the law of *faith*—not faith that God will save his child, but faith that it really *is* God who is requiring him to sacrifice Isaac and that we can't know God's purpose. Kierkegaard saw Abraham's ordeal as a test of his faith in God rather than of his morals, and a "leap of faith" is, for the Lutheran Kierkegaard, a matter between the individual and God and nobody else. The opinion of society does not enter into the picture at all. Other interpretations of the story see no split between morality and faith but view it as an illustration of God's absolute demands on his people. Yet others see it as justification for sacrificing everything one holds dear if a higher law demands it. With this last interpretation it really is irrelevant that God stopped Abraham at the last moment. For all Christians, the parallel to a later time when God did not stop himself from sacrificing his own son to save the world is a close one. (See Box 2.2 for Franz Kafka's interpretation of this parable.)

A recent critique of the old story has been suggested by anthropologist Carol Delaney in her book *Abraham on Trial: The Social Legacy of Biblical Myth*. Delaney asks, Why should faith in God be illustrated best by a father's willingness to sacrifice his son? Why couldn't the test of faith instead be measured by a parent's willingness to protect his or her child, not sacrifice it? The story has been told as if Abraham is the sole parent, with sole rights and responsibilities, and the biblical writers obviously didn't see Isaac's mother, Sarah, as someone with a right to her opinion about the matter. Delaney isn't criticizing the male-dominated ways of the Old Testament so much as asking why nobody since then, of all the commentators in Judeo-Christian history, has thought to ask whether Sarah might have had something relevant to say about the murder of her son as a proof of faith in God. Delaney actually echoes Kierkegaard's idea here that Abraham's willingness to kill Isaac would be completely *immoral,* but she doesn't agree with his further step that morals and faith are different things altogether. In the section below called "The Bargain," you'll meet another story from the Bible, that of a father who sees parenthood as a lesser duty: the story of Jephtha's daughter.

Fables and Counterfables   In the eighteenth and nineteenth centuries, adults finally began to notice that children were not just small and inadequate adults, and children's literature was invented as a literary genre. The gory fairy tale was toned down to suit the nursery, and another kind of story, which had previously been enjoyed by adults, was introduced to children: the *fable.* Aesop's and La Fontaine's fables became very popular as moral lessons for children. "The Mouse and the Lion" (the lion spares the mouse and later the mouse saves the lion's life) taught that you had better not disregard someone unimportant, for he or she might be of help to you some day, and "The Sour Grapes" (the fox can't reach the grapes, and declares that they are probably sour anyway) taught that if someone claims something is not worth having, it may be because he or she can't have it. The main reason adults told these fables to children was, of course, that the grown-ups wanted their children to become good citizens, and the stories seemed an efficient way to press home the point. Those early stories for children said, in essence, "Behave, or else"; they provided little opportunity for children's imagination to take flight. An important exception is the work of Hans Christian Andersen (1805–1875), who, throughout his fairy tales and stories, insisted that children's imaginations should be left unfettered by the sour realism of grown-ups. In fact, Andersen's stories have a true poetic quality and carry multiple meanings; they are not really children's stories at all. Children can enjoy them, to be sure, but they will enjoy them much more when they are older and capable of reading between the lines. For Andersen, not only was the imagination of the children in danger of being stifled by adults, but also the imagination of the adults themselves was in danger of withering away. Andersen's moral lesson is one of openness. He tells us to listen to the world and not just respond to it with preconceived notions; if we do, we will encounter only what we expect, and we will never again see the magic and splendor of the world the way children do.

Other stories with moral lessons were being written for children during that same time period. Didactic stories took up the thread of the fables and taught children how to behave: to obey their parents, to be kind to animals, to finish their porridge, and to not make fun of people who looked different. Although today the lessons of those stories may seem, for the most part, quite inoffensive, the stories themselves often reveal sexism, racism, and a general naive belief that the writer had all the wisdom in the world. Those "moral stories" not only present a moral problem but also *moralize.* This tendency to teach moral lessons enraged Mark Twain to the extent that he wrote a parody called "About Magnanimous-Incident Literature" (to which *Mad* magazine and an entire genre of comedy films such as the *Naked Gun* series are indebted). Twain's parody gives us the "true" ending to the little moral stories. In one story, the scruffy little homeless dog that the kindly village doctor cures comes back the next day with another scruffy little dog to be cured, and the doctor praises God for the chance to heal another unfortunate creature. End of moral story; here comes Twain: The next day there are four scruffy dogs outside the doctor's office, and the following week there are hundreds of howling mutts waiting to be treated. The original mutt is going crazy from all this helpfulness and bites the doctor, who wishes he had shot it in the first place.

Stories with Role Models

What kind of people do we like to hear stories about? And after the story, do we go out and do the same thing as the hero in the book or the movie?

When we talk about fictional characters who somehow teach a moral lesson, we are talking about *role models*. Cartoon characters such as Superman and Spiderman may have certain qualities that we identify with and would like to emulate. But if we include Batman, we encounter an interesting twist: Batman is not a wholesome character; he has a psychological problem (which was, to some extent, explored in the recent films). Not all heroic characters are completely virtuous. If we look at fictional heroes in Western popular literature, from King Arthur, Lancelot, and Robin Hood to D'Artagnan, Scarlett O'Hara, and even Harry Potter, we see that most of these people are morally flawed. The tendency in the twentieth century had been to depict them as being as morally flawed as possible, something that may reflect a certain sense of cynicism. A talk-show guest once announced that she had learned her moral lessons exclusively from soap operas, and we know that soap characters are by no means morally above reproach.

This is not a new phenomenon; in the medieval churches of Europe, peasant congregations were spellbound by murals depicting biblical scenes that sometimes covered the entire inside of the church. The murals kept them occupied during the long hours while the priest spoke in Latin, which the peasants did not understand. The moral lesson of that artwork was obvious, but it was expressed through depictions not of good people so much as of *bad* people; scenes illustrating people going to hell are usually much more vivid and artistically interesting than are scenes of people going to heaven. Perhaps the artists thought it was more fun to depict horrors than bland happiness. It does seem to be a human trait that we dwell on stories with a dark element, rather than on those with happy endings. Yet these stories can certainly teach a moral lesson. We must conclude, therefore, that not all moral lessons involve role models to be emulated; rather, a considerable number of moral lessons are negative rather than positive: *Don't.* Sometimes characters who show themselves to be morally flawed become our heroes not because they are good but because they are like us, or worse. If these "bad good people" see the folly of their ways in the end, we especially take them to our hearts. (For example, in Jane Austen's novel *Pride and Prejudice,* Elizabeth Bennet, realizing that her own biases have blinded her to the vices of Mr. Wickham and the virtues of Mr. Darcy, says, "Till this moment, I never knew myself.") Perhaps we do this because we hope that we will be loved too, even if we make mistakes. It seems that, on the whole, we have the heroes we deserve, as it has sometimes been said. A cautious time has cautious heroes; a violent time has violent heroes. During the time that we accept them as our heroes, we let their images guide our actions; when their day is done, we can still learn from them—they can teach us about the way we once were.

Some stories are moral investigations of a flawed character, such as Joseph Conrad's Lord Jim (see the Narrative in Chapter 9), who makes a fatal, cowardly decision in his youth and tries to live it down for the rest of his life. In Victor Hugo's *Les Misérables,* Jean Valjean morally rises above the crimes of his youth only to be haunted by them until the end of his life. Fyodor Dostoyevsky's *Crime and Punishment* examines the philosophical deliberations of Raskolnikov as he imagines the right of the extraordinary individual to do whatever he wants, including committing murder. Gustave Flaubert's *Madame Bovary* traces Emma's deterioration through boredom and through fantasies (brought on by reading novels!). A work by the Danish author J. P. Jacobsen, *Marie Grubbe,* in some ways parallels *Madame Bovary.* It investigates the downfall of a noble lady through three marriages: to a nobleman, to a soldier, and finally to a drunk. The cause of her deterioration seems to be the same as Emma's: sensualism and boredom. The last time we encounter Marie, she is tending the ferry that runs between two small towns, to support her drunkard husband. The irony of the story is that in this squalor Marie finally finds the happiness that eluded her when she was a "fine lady."

Stories such as these are not written with the intention of sending their readers out on any heroic errands. They are, primarily, explorations of fascinating human characters. They also serve as moral evaluations by asking whether the characters redeem themselves somehow, even in their degradation. At times a character's redeeming act or quality goes against mainstream morality, as in the story of Marie Grubbe, and then the story forces us to ask which value is the ultimate moral value. Do we agree with society that Marie's life was wasted, full of missed opportunities? Or do we agree with the author that life, and morality, have many faces and that there is some intrinsic value in staying true to yourself, no matter how much that sentiment may differ from the public ethos? If such characters serve as a warning not to emulate them, we call them *negative role models.* We meet this concept again in Chapter 10.

Some Fantastic Tales for Grown-Ups

The stories that have affected Western culture are too numerous to count, but a few stand out as *archetypes,* models that we seem to return to over and over again. In this section we will look at three themes that keep showing up in the world of fiction: *the bargain, the good twin and the bad twin,* and *the quest.*

The Bargain   There is a certain genre of stories that continually fascinates the adult imagination: the story in which someone bargains with fate (or with gods or devils) to gain some advantage—or doesn't literally bargain, but simply puts his life and happiness on the line to obtain what he wants most. Why do such stories continue to intrigue us? Perhaps it is because we recognize the single-mindedness of some individuals, and their success, and wonder what price they may have to pay (perhaps even hoping that they have to pay a price). Or perhaps it is because we, in desperate situations, also try to bargain with fate: If you let me live, I'll give up smoking/be kinder to my spouse/stop gambling/stop eating junk food, and so on. If you let me pass the test, I promise I'll be a good student from now on. If you let me win the battle, I promise you I will sacrifice the first living thing that approaches me when I come home. That is the bargain in the biblical horror story of Jephtha's daughter. According to some scholars, Jephtha may have expected to be met a dog or a servant, but it is his virgin daughter who comes to greet him. What does he do? Does he resolve to cheat God and save his daughter? No, he gives her a month to grieve for her virginity, and then he sacrifices her. (In this case, God does not step in to prevent it as he did for Abraham.) And let us not forget that Jephtha *asked* for a bargain with God, whereas Abraham was chosen to be tried. So was Jephtha a good man? That depends on what time period we're in, and how moral issues differ: In the Old Testament, Jephtha upholds his end of the bargain, hard as it is for him, and is thus an honorable man. We may grieve for his daughter (who doesn't even have a name in the story), but she is, essentially, his property, and he has a right, even a duty, to sacrifice her because of a promise made to God. Seen from a modern, secular perspective, Jephtha is probably condemned by most of us because he tries to make a bargain without foreseeing the consequences, but also because he is a terrible father, betraying the trust of his daughter, believing that his higher duty is his promise to God, rather than his obligation to his family. Sometimes, like Jephtha, we keep our bargains with fate, but most often we don't. Stories in which a bargain has been made with the devil, however, usually cast him as a reliable businessman: He keeps his end of the deal, and he expects you to keep yours.

The grandmother of all devil bargains is the story of Dr. Faust, the main character in Johann Wolfgang von Goethe's masterpiece, *Faust.* There was, in Württemberg, Germany, in the sixteenth century, an actual man named Johann Faust; he was an astrologer and a magician at a time when science, astrology, and magic were only just beginning to be separated, conceptually and practically. "Alchemists" were undertaking experiments based in part on scientific evidence and in part on magical formulae; such practices usually were outlawed as heresy by the Catholic Church. The Spanish Inquisition disposed of many an early scientist for being a heretic well into the seventeenth century. Even before *Faust,* though, stories appeared with the same motif: the necromancer (sorcerer) who sells his soul. Those stories have been fused with the legend of Faust because of that frequent representation in literature. Around 1589 (some fifty years after the death of the actual Dr. Faust), Marlowe wrote the *Tragical History of Dr. Faustus,* but it was Goethe's version (1780–1833) that became the ultimate metaphor for the scientist who will do anything, including sell his soul, for pure knowledge (in Faust's case, to secure the formula for turning base metals into gold). (Later in this chapter you'll find an early story by Goethe, *The Sorrows of Young Werther,* about a young man who dies from unrequited love—the novel that made Goethe instantly famous.) The story of Faust was made into an American tale by Stephen Vincent Benét, "The Devil and Daniel Webster," but with a twist: Webster outwits the devil. (This is actually a whole subgenre by itself—the outwitting of the devil.) In the 1940s, Nobel Prize winner Thomas Mann modernized the original story in his novel *Dr. Faustus,* which explores the mind-set of a man of the times; in Mann's book the obsession is not science but art.

Through the Faust story runs a moralizing thread: *Faust does wrong in selling his soul.* There are folklore and fairy-tale stories that are in complete accordance with that view. One traveling story, a story that has traveled from country to country in different versions, is the folk tale of the boy who wanted to play the fiddle like no one else, and the devil taught him to play so sweetly that the fish would jump out of the river to listen, the birds would stop singing, and all the girls the boy ever wanted would flock to him. The trouble was that every time he wanted to put the fiddle down, he couldn't. In other words, the devil made him do it and he played himself to death. Some musicians might say it was worth it.

The Faustian theme also has been explored in films from time to time, as in *Angel Heart,* in which a character realized something he had forgotten—that he sold his soul—and there is no help or redemption for him in the end. Another such bargain-film is *Ghost Rider,* in which a young man sells his soul to save his father's life. At the end of this chapter you will find a summary of the film *Pulp Fiction.* One of the study questions hints at a possible interpretation—did the gangster boss sell his soul to the devil?

The Good Twin and the Bad Twin   A story that is closely related to that of Dr. Faust, but with an added element, is Robert Louis Stevenson's 1886 story of *Dr. Jekyll and Mr. Hyde.* As with Goethe's story, Stevenson's is loosely based on a real person—in this case an eighteeth-century Scottish cabinetmaker and city councillor by day and a burglar by night. The kindly Dr. Jekyll becomes the evil Mr. Hyde by drinking his own invention, a personality-changing drug intended, the story goes, to distill goodness from evil in the human character. Jekyll, who is not so kindly after all given that he throws away his life and *respectability* (a notion nineteenth-century readers found particularly problematic) for the sake of finding knowledge, parallels Dr. Faust in that obsession—but here the story departs from the Faustian pattern. Not only is the devil absent (he is manifested only in the "well-deserved" death of Jekyll/Hyde), but also another theme is introduced: the *double character.* After all, Jekyll and Hyde are the same man, and the symbolism is easy to read: We all have a beast "hyding" in us, an alter ego, and we must not let it loose no matter how much we would like to. The reason Jekyll keeps returning to his Hyde persona is that it feels good, it amuses him; he gets to do things that Victorian England frowned upon, such as going out on the town. Of course, he exceeds even the tolerance of any time period when he tortures and kills. The moral lesson is broad and completely in tune with nineteenth-century Victorian mores, as well as with most of the Christian tradition: Keep your inner beast in check, and don't give in to your physical desires.

When we look at the theme of twin souls, we generally have two versions: one person with two personalities, such as Jekyll and Hyde, and two persons who are inextricably linked but very different, such as good and evil twins, a theme that we will return to below. A famous story from the early twentieth century of one person with two "natures" is Herman Hesse's *Steppenwolf,* the tale of Harry Haller, a middle-aged, middle-class man who is contemplating suicide at fifty because he sees nothing positive in life any longer—and his dual nature, the Steppenwolf, a sarcastic, lonely being still thirsty for the outrageous experience. Another story (which you will meet in Chapter 8) is the popular film *Shrek:* The haughty, beautiful Princess Fiona has a deep secret; at night she is transformed into a green-skinned ogre. One hundred years before *Shrek,* Hans Christian Andersen wrote his story of "The Swamp King's Daughter," a serious, symbolic tale of the daughter of a beautiful Egyptian princess and the vicious king of the swamp: In daylight she is a beautiful but evil woman; but at night she is a sweet, gentle, compassionate soul trapped in the body of a giant toad. The dual-nature stories are easily interpreted as the battle between our "angel" side and our "devil" side—or, as the Christian tradition has generally viewed it, our spirit and our flesh. But as Herman Hesse says, "The division into wolf and man, flesh and spirit, by means of which Harry tries to make his destiny more comprehensible to himself is a very great simplification. . . . Harry consists of a hundred or a thousand selves, not of two. His life oscillates, as everyone's does, not merely between two poles, such as the body and the spirit, the saint and the sinner, but between thousands and thousands."

The stories of twins are sometimes harder to interpret, but interestingly, they often work along the same symbolic lines: One twin (or sibling or friend) generally represents "good," or the spiritual life, and the other twin represents "evil," or the world of physical desires, as with the story of Cal and Aron in *East of Eden.* (See Chapter 1, Narrative Section.) And often the author's purpose is to describe two sides of any one of us, just as the dual-nature stories do. Where the story gets interesting, such as in Steinbeck's novel, is the point at which the good twin suddenly seems to have an evil streak, and the "bad" twin reveals a higher moral nature, and we begin to doubt the stereotypes. But of course, life rarely imitates fiction, except for one California court case in the 1990s where a woman actually hired a hit man to kill her twin sister because she wanted to take over her life—because her sister was admired for her goodness and kindness. The plot was foiled, and the "good" sister testified against her "evil" sister in court and got her convicted.

The Quest   The first quest story that we know of is that of Gilgamesh, the king of Uruk. Gilgamesh loses his only friend, Enkidu, to a withering disease. This brings home to Gilgamesh the fact that all humans are mortal, and he is seized by a terrible fear. So he sets out to find the secret of immortality. This story has been told by Sumerians since at least approximately 1500 B.C.E. Gilgamesh goes to the ends of the earth and finds the oldest living humans, Utnapishtim and his wife, who survived the big flood by the grace of the gods. (They were safe in a wooden box that floated on the waters—an *ark.*) Utnapishtim's rescue, however, was a one-time deal, and Gilgamesh must look elsewhere for his own rescue from death. In the end he finds the plant that gives immortality, picks it, and drops it in the water. Gilgamesh must go under the sea where the monster snake lives; into its gaping maw he must crawl to get the weed—but he can't retrieve it. Gilgamesh had immortality for a while, but then he lost it, for it is the fate of humans to be mortal.

Gilgamesh's quest was a failure, but it was heroic nevertheless, because it embodied a human longing to live forever, as well as the acknowledgment that we can't, even if we are the king of Uruk. The quest motif is one of the most moving in the history of literature and film, precisely because even if the hero doesn't find what he or she sets out to find, the search itself remains the most important part of the story. The quest forces the hero to mature and makes him or her realize the true importance, or lack of importance, of the quest's object.

Myths and legends abound with quest stories. The Navajo goddess Grandmother Spider searches for the sun in the early days when the land is in darkness. She finds it and steals a piece and puts it into her clay pot to bring home. In the Greek legend of Jason and the Golden Fleece, Jason and his argonauts go on a quest for a sheepskin made of gold. Egyptian legend tells of the goddess Isis, who searches for the remains of her husband, Osiris, who was murdered. Some searchers even go to the underworld to find what they are looking for: Ulysses goes to the realm of the dead to speak with the wise Teresias. Orpheus goes to the underworld to try to retrieve his beloved wife, Eurydice, from the dead. The Native American Modoc culture hero Kumokum goes to the land of the dead in search of his daughter. Ishtar, the all-powerful goddess of the Middle East, finds that her powers are limited when her young lover, Tammuz, dies, and she goes to the underworld to buy him back. The earth goddess Demeter goes to the kingdom of the dead to get back her daughter, Persephone, who has been abducted by the king of the dead.

These stories confirm what we know: that we would go to the ends of the earth and the land of the dead if it could bring back those we love. We also know that it would be to no avail; Gilgamesh's lesson is one that every human learns.

Some quests are of a happier nature. In the African folktale about the girl Wanjiru, Wanjiru's family sacrifices her so that the rains will come, but a young warrior goes to the underworld to fetch her back. He carries her on his back to the world of the living and hides her until she is strong again; then he displays her at the great dance. Her family is now ashamed of the way they treated her, and the warrior and Wanjiru are married.

One of Grimm's fairy tales has an unusual quest story: the quest for the feeling of fear and trembling. In "The Youth Who Could Not Shiver and Shake," the protagonist goes through the most frightful horrors but still can't seem to shiver and shake properly, until his young bride throws a bucket of minnows at him: Now he knows what it feels like to shiver and shake! There is more to this story than just a joke, for without this feeling of fear we are not complete humans. This quest, like the quest for love, is a search for something that will make the character a whole person. Indeed, most modern literature and films somehow involve a quest for oneself, a search for self-identity through encounters with the Other.

Two quest motifs have, each in its own right, come to epitomize the *search*. One is *Moby Dick,* and the other is the legend of the Holy Grail.

Herman Melville's *Moby Dick* (1851) has become the American model for the quest, but with a special angle: The searcher is mad, and the quest is meaningless, except to Captain Ahab himself. In many stories, although the object of the quest may be out of reach, it usually is something to which the reader can relate. In the case of *Moby Dick,* though, the reader identifies not with the searcher but with an observer, Ishmael. The quest itself is seen as pointless, and quite mad. Eventually, Captain Ahab finds his white whale but he and the rest of the crew die, except for Ishmael, who alone "survived to tell thee."

Hollywood came up with a modern version of the whale search for a society that reveres whales but dislikes sharks. In *Jaws* the symbolism is stronger than in the Melville story; the gigantic shark is a more obvious representation of inhuman evil. However, the sense of ambiguity present in *Moby Dick* is missing in *Jaws.* The Melville story makes us wonder if Ahab's quest was worth the passion and trouble; in *Jaws* we know the quest was ill-advised.

In a sense, there is one Hollywood story that is much more closely related to *Moby Dick* than is *Jaws.* In one of its most superb productions, John Ford's film *The Searchers,* Hollywood created a folklore version of the mad quest. As the title indicates, in the movie it is the search, more than the object of the search, that matters. For eight years Ethan and Marty look all over the western United States for Ethan's niece Debbie, who was captured by the Comanche Indians. Marty is the observer we identify with, the "Ishmael" of the story. Marty tries to reason with Ethan, who is obsessed with revenge rather than rescue. Ethan finds his "white whale," the Comanche chief responsible for murdering Ethan's family and kidnapping Debbie, but he realizes, in the nick of time, that his motives were misguided. Ethan is redeemed and returned to sanity through human love. However, he has traveled too far on the road to obsession and human loneliness and is doomed to wander alone. We return to *The Searchers* in Chapter 10.

The search for the Holy Grail, part of Arthurian legend, is a quest that succeeds only symbolically, if at all. Several years after the glorious time of the Round Table, Arthur's knights become obsessed with finding the cup from the Last Supper of Christ, the Grail. They each go through trials to find the cup, but only Galahad (or sometimes Percival) succeeds in seeing the Grail, and even he is denied any further access. Since the time that the tale was first told, the quest for the Grail has become a symbol of the search for a profound truth, a holy revelation, for the meaning of life, if you will. (Box 2.3 looks at some grail quests in film.) Even when the search is unsuccessful and even futile, as it is for Cervantes' Don Quixote, who searches far and wide for the "impossible dream," the search itself nevertheless lends the searcher a cloak of heroism, no less than it did for Gilgamesh. The grail theme can encompass any kind of quest, not just a search for a cup or an item. One of the surprise best-sellers in recent years was Dan Brown's *The DaVinci Code,* a story set in the contemporary world and featuring a hunt for the truth behind the legend of the Holy Grail. To many readers' surprise—even shock—the grail turns out to be not a cup, but—a person! A woman who, according to the speculative theory, gave birth to a child of Jesus Christ: Mary Magdalene. She, and the bloodline, are the Holy Grail or, in French, not the *San Greal* but the *Sang Real. The DaVinci Code,* the book as well as the film, spawned a veritable cottage industry of TV specials and interpretive books, but in fact the theory had been floated decades earlier in the controversial book *Holy Blood, Holy Grail* by Baigent, Leigh, and Lincoln. (Baigent even sued Brown for plagiarism, but lost the lawsuit.) Although the plot captures the

Box 2.3   THE HOLY GRAIL IN THE MOVIES

Aside from the movie based on Dan Brown's book *The DaVinci Code,* the grail theme has been explored in films such as *Quest for Fire,* the hominid adventure story with gibberish dialogue by Anthony Burgess, and in out-and-out adventure stories such as *Raiders of the Lost Ark. Indiana Jones and the Last Crusade* is about the hunt for the Grail itself. The science fiction classic *2001: A Space Odyssey* is a grail quest for the ultimate mystery, the black, ancient monolith. *The Fisher King* is another film that uses the grail motif. It presents a realistic portrayal of homelessness and teaches the lesson that anything is worthy of being the object of a quest if that quest is undertaken in the spirit of love. In other films, from *Stanley and Livingstone* to *The Mountains of the Moon,* people traverse the jungles of Africa seeking out other people, the source of the Nile, or a better understanding of themselves and their role in the scheme of things.

Stories that involve a search for an antidote may incorporate both the grail element and an element of catharsis (a spiritual cleansing). Finding the grail is the cure for the ailment, but it also may serve as a liberating, spiritual healing process. Perhaps the one grail movie trilogy that is most familiar to younger moviegoers of the early twenty-first century is in fact a reversed grail story, because it has to do not with *finding* a special object, but with *getting rid of it:* Tolkien's *Lord of the Rings.* The Ring that Frodo has to take to Mordor in order to destroy it is the source of evil, and a great temptation for everyone, including Frodo. As in the Holy Grail legend, it is only Galahad who is of sufficient spiritual purity to even have a vision of the Grail, so Frodo is the only one whose heart is pure enough to undertake the journey (although, as many fans of the trilogy will want to point out, without the unselfish courage of Samwise Gamgee, his friend, the Ring would never have been destroyed). In Chapter 4 we take a closer look at *Lord of the Rings.*

imagination of many, it remains speculation without solid evidence, according to most historians.

The quest can thus be for something sublime, something ideal, or not of this world, or it can be for something as down-to-earth as money. Regardless of whether the story takes the high path or the low path, the quest as a story type seems to be very enduring.

Contemporary Story Genres

Sometimes the moral lesson in a story is hard to find; we may be blind to it, or it may be somewhat dated, having evolved in another era. There is a scene in Aldous Huxley's novel *Brave New World* (1932) in which the young "savage," John, who has grown up on a nature reservation unaffected by the modern era of eugenics, total sexual liberty, and test-tube babies, introduces his friend, the scientist Helmholtz, to Shakespeare. He reads from *Romeo and Juliet,* certain that the moral drama of the young lovers who can't have each other will move his modern friend. Helmholtz, however, doubles up laughing, because he can't for the life of him see that there is a problem: If Romeo and Juliet want each other, why don't they just have sex and let it go at that, instead of

In *Indiana Jones and the Last Crusade* (1989), the archaeologists Indiana Jones (Harrison Ford) and his father (Sean Connery) search for the ultimate treasure in the Christian tradition: the Holy Grail, presumably the cup used by Jesus Christ at the Last Supper. Here Jones and Jones are barely escaping with their lives from a fire in a Nazi stronghold.

making such an embarrassing fuss about it? He is blind to the social and moral structures of the past, and the savage is very upset that ethical communication seems impossible in a new era that has done away with family relationships, birth, siblings, and spouses and that refuses to recognize the phenomenon of death.

In a similar way, stories depicting unwanted pregnancies struck a deep chord in times past but haven't had the same resonance since the advent of legal abortion and safe birth control. Old Hollywood films about the trials of two lovers who can't get a divorce from their spouses also sometimes require us to stretch a bit in order to empathize with the characters. Stories praising the glory of war, which were quite successful until the early twentieth century, have not done well with the majority of modern readers and viewers for quite some time now.

Wartime Stories: Duty and Honor   Wartime stories with moral lessons were common in past eras when it seemed that each generation of young men was expected to be initiated into manhood through some local armed conflict. But the idea of war as a natural arena for the exercise of masculine virtues received a serious blow in World War I, with its murky reasons for fighting and its wholesale slaughter of entire squadrons—young men from the same family or village or the same university, dying side by side in the trenches from mustard gas and machine gun fire, and leaving villages and colleges empty of an entire generation of male youth. That agonizing era has been portrayed ever since in films such as *All Quiet on the Western Front* and *Gallipoli,* and recently, *A Very Long Engagement.* The soldier on the white horse with a feather plume in his helmet, dying gloriously for his country, became one of the images left behind in the nineteenth century, giving way to twentieth-century bitterness. For many people the entire idea of glory in war has become nothing but propaganda, invented by the leaders to inspire their legions to march unquestioningly off to the front as cannon fodder.

However, the image of the warrior as stalwart and honorable is so deeply imbedded in most human cultures that it shouldn't be dismissed as merely the result of the manipulation of gullible people by poets, propagandists, monarchs, and generals. It seems to resonate with something deep in us that identifies us as social beings, with a loyalty to our own people, for better or worse. Some would say it is a specifically *male* resonance; others see it as a class identification, which should be uprooted in a global community—but many see it as a part of a natural love for where we grew up and whom we grew up with, regardless of class and gender, and not infrequently a love for the principles we have been taught.

For some pacifists, any story of war is a distasteful reminder of human nature at its worst—but even for many pacifists, a wartime story can be meaningful in its focus, not on the glory of war, but on humans under pressure, displaying devotion to duty and their comrades. And as many otherwise peace-loving people discovered (or rediscovered) in the wake of September 11, it is possible to think of a war as *just,* and a wartime story not just as a sad testimony to the blind aggression of humanity but also as a tribute to brave people righteously responding to an attack. The classic definition of a just war (see Chapter 13) is that a war can't be fought for territory, or for glory, but strictly for defending one's country or preventing future genuine threats. That means a war can be fought only if no other option seems reasonable or practical. A story about a just war must show that war is the last moral option and that the goal is peace. In addition, it must demonstrate a clear vision of who is right and who is wrong.

World War II, which until September 2001, many considered to be the last war that had a clear moral focus and identifiable good and evil sides, spawned thousands of novels and films telling the story of good triumphing over evil. Some films attempt factually to depict actual wartime events, such as *The Longest Day, A Bridge Too Far, Enola Gay, Hamburger Hill,* and *Black Hawk Down.* Others spin fictional elements and characters into a story with a message about the experience of war, such as *Twelve O'Clock High, Memphis Belle, Midnight Clear, Saving Private Ryan, The Thin Red Line, We Were Warriors,* and the acclaimed HBO series *Band of Brothers.* The Korean War has been depicted by the *M*A*S*H* film and television series, the Vietnam War by a number of films from *The Green Berets* to *Apocalypse Now* to *Born on the Fourth of July;* the Gulf War is featured in *Jarhead;* and September 11 is the topic of *The World Trade Center* and *United 93.* The war in Afghanistan is an element of the novel and film *The Kite Runner.* Films featuring the war in Iraq include *Stop Loss* and the made-for-TV movie *Act of Honor.*

The Moral Universe of Westerns: Hard Choices   Stories of the American West, called *Westerns,* have served as moral lessons for both the American public and a

In *All Quiet on the Western Front* (Universal Studios, 1930, based on Erich Maria Remarque's 1929 novel), Katczinsky (Louis Wolheim) is the old "trench hog" and Paul Baumer (Lew Ayres), the young idealist who is about to get his lesson in the realities of war. The West's image of war changed with World War I. No more shining swords and prancing horses—there was nothing glorious about dying in the trenches of the European battlefields, and few soldiers understood the purpose of the prolonged fighting. However, the virtues of friendship, courage, and loyalty seemed all the more important as a twentieth-century war ethic. (From the collection of C. R. Covner.)

worldwide audience for more than a hundred years. All nations seem to go through periods when they "rediscover" their past, but the American West as a historical period is both recent and very short: from 1865 to about 1885—from the end of the Civil War to the end of the open cattle range, which resulted from the advent of barbed wire and the bad winters of the 1880s. There have probably been more stories told about the Old West than could ever have happened. Even when the Old West was still alive, those in the East were reading dime novels that glamorized the West; the first Western films were shot outside New York City in the early 1900s. The process of creating a legend about the recent past was very rapid and even involved actual cowboys and gunfighters who moved from the plains and the deserts to Hollywood to lend a hand. Wyatt Earp himself, of Tombstone fame, went to Hollywood, and when he died, Tom Mix, the Western film hero, was one of his pallbearers.

Making entertainment out of recent history was one way to draw people to the theaters. If that were all, though, the Western never would have endured as long as it has. Part of its allure seems to have been its exoticism; the West is, still, a unique landscape. And then there is wishful thinking: Perhaps the Old West was never the way it appears in movies, but we wish it had been. An even greater appeal is the *moral potential* of a Western. For Western aficionados, it is almost like watching a ritual. The story usually is one we are familiar with, even if we are seeing it for the first time: There have to be good guys and bad guys, and horses, and they have to do a lot of riding back and forth among rocks in a gorgeous landscape. Then there is usually a good girl and sometimes also a bad girl. And there is a threat, either from Indians or the railroad or rustlers or (in later Westerns) big business, which is warded off by the strength and wit of Our Hero, sometimes even reluctantly. (He often has to be dragged into the fight.) When the problem is solved, the hero rarely settles down but rides off into the sunset so that he doesn't get entangled in the peace and prosperity of the society he helped stabilize. In later Westerns, the good guys are Indians or blacks or a gang of outlaws and the bad guys are the army or other Indians or the law; the stable society becomes a negative rather than a positive image. Traditionally, though, the general pattern is the same: The power of the individual (the Good) rises above the threat of a larger force (the Evil). Sometimes the individual paves the way for civilization, but in the process makes himself superfluous, as in what may be the best Western ever made, *The Searchers* (see p. 67 and Chapter 10). Sometimes the individual accomplished his moral triumph in spite of the community that lets him down, as in another classic, *High Noon* (see Chapter 6). And sometimes the individual stands up for what he believes in but is sacrificed by the community who rejects his values, as in the underrated masterpiece *The Life of Tom Horn* (see Chapter 11).

Why do people watch Westerns if they already know what will happen? Because the movie experience (or TV experience) itself is a *moral event*. People take part in the story by watching it, and they feel that when the problems on the screen are solved, the general problems of life are, in some symbolic way, put to rest at the same time. The moviegoer may not even be aware of this psychological process.

One might think that if the Western had a moral message, it would seem pretty dated, and sometimes even offensive, to modern audiences. After all, the first generation of Westerns left the overall impression that it was fine to kill Indians, that

The 1985 Western *Silverado* (Columbia Pictures) abandoned the 1970s trend of depicting the Old West in decline and gave its audience a story in a vigorous frontier setting with a happy ending. For that reason, the film is sometimes referred to as a "retro-Western." Many of the themes incorporated in *Silverado* are anything but "retro," however; for example, with this film the Western genre entered a new era of racial awareness. Here the four buddies (Danny Glover, Kevin Costner, Scott Glenn, and Kevin Kline) ride out to save the town of Silverado from corruption.

women were weak and had to be protected, that blacks were nonexistent, that the land was there only to be developed, that animal life and suffering were irrelevant, and so on. However, some themes were timeless, such as courage vs. cowardice, and the Western developed a potential to change with the changing times. There were still good guys and bad guys, but in each period they reflected the problems of the contemporary world, at least in a symbolic sense. In the 1950s the Western began to reflect a growing unease with the stereotype of townspeople conquering the wilderness; the sixties saw an increasing sympathy for the outlaw. The Western of the seventies was influenced by the Vietnam War and began to address problems of discrimination, overdevelopment, and pollution. In the eighties the Western seemed to have nothing more to say, but in the nineties it acquired a voice once again; current Westerns often deal with cross-cultural and cross-racial issues in the American melting pot. (See Box 2.4 for an overview of how the messages of Westerns have changed.) The Western, being the one narrative genre that is truly American, shows

Box 2.4   THE CHANGING MESSAGES OF WESTERNS

Western films have from the early days managed to integrate modern problems into the period plot. The classic film (and book) *The Oxbow Incident,* focused on mass hysteria, cowardice, and lynching. The Vietnam War era had its "Vietnam Westerns" in which massacred Indians symbolized the Vietnamese and the army symbolized the U.S. Army in Vietnam (*Soldier Blue, Little Big Man*). Post-Watergate Westerns showed corrupt politicians and greedy railroad tycoons (*Young Guns I and II*). Westerns of the 1990s explored the issue of violence and its justification. *Tombstone* and *Wyatt Earp* both examine the effects of violence on a township and on the individual (Earp) who tries to put an end to it, and *Unforgiven* probably makes the strongest antiviolence statement of all newer Westerns, reflecting on the loss of humanity in the life of a gunfighter.

With the return of the Western, there has been a growing sensitivity not only to historical accuracy but also to a multiethnic presence in the Old West. African Americans have found a heroic identity in the Western landscape (*Silverado, Lonesome Dove*), and American Indians have emerged from old stereotypes such as devils or angels to become real people with their own language and their own problems and jokes (*Dances with Wolves, The Last of the Mohicans, Geronimo*). Strong female characters in Westerns are still rare, although there have been a few of them over the years in the films *Johnny Guitar, Rio Bravo,* and *High Noon,* the television movie *Lonesome Dove,* and the television series *Dr. Quinn, Medicine Woman. The Ballad of Little Jo,* about a woman passing herself off as a man to get by in life; *Open Range,* featuring a female character who, in her determination, is as strong as the male "hero"; and in particular the film *Missing,* with its female lead trying to rescue her abducted daughter, all help to dispel the impression that Westerns are exclusively about men and for men. On the television front we have the miniseries *Buffalo Girls,* with Anjelica Huston and Melanie Griffith in the powerful lead roles: a somber, sensitive look at the final days of the Old West, moving from the romantic hardship of the open country to the phony romance of Buffalo Bill's traveling circus.

Critics were divided about the 2005 Western *Brokeback Mountain:* Was this evidence that the Western was still able to renew itself, addressing current issues within the classic Western plot and scenery, or was this, in effect, the film that signaled "the end of the Western" by introducing a theme into the film that seemed alien and uncomfortable to many fans of Westerns as well as to people living in the Western states? The film, based on the short story by Annie Proulx, was about two young male sheepherders who find sex during a lonely summer on the range, and a conflicted love for the rest of their lives as cowboys in Wyoming and Texas. It was hailed, or deplored, as the first "gay Western," but in fact other Westerns have experimented with the topic. The first Western film with an openly gay theme was Andy Warhol's experimental 1974 film *Lonesome Cowboys;* another Western with minor gay characters portrayed in a positive light is *Tombstone,* the acclaimed (otherwise straight) Western from 1993. Some film commentators read hidden gay themes into the "buddy" Westerns of the 1960s and '70s, but others see such films as depictions of male friendships, nothing else. Critics familiar with Western films pointed out, however, that *Brokeback Mountain* really was not so much a Western as a love story, about lovers who can't find happiness because of the world they live in, in the tradition of *Romeo and Juliet,* and that the outer accessories (the cowboy hats, the horses, the pickup trucks) were incidental.

A television event that still causes passionate discussions among Western fans was the award-winning HBO series *Deadwood* (2004–6). A parable of politics and human greed versus compassion, rather than a traditional Western series, the show turned many fans of Western movies away because of its raunchy language but won many viewers over through its intriguing psychological portrayals of characters in a society rising from the mud of a mining camp. In *Deadwood* as well as in *Brokeback Mountain*, and many other Western stories, the narrative becomes a universal story of humans facing difficult choices.

an amazing potential for being able to introduce many kinds of social and moral problems in a single framework in which people have to make big, moral decisions in a land where they are dwarfed by rocks, mountains, and deserts. These stories of momentous decisions appeal not just to Americans but to people all over the world. This makes the Western much more than just a movie genre. It has become a transcultural story told in a universal moral language.

Science Fiction: What Future Do We Want?   Like the Western, science fiction was born as a literary genre in the nineteenth century. The French author Jules Verne astounded the world with his fantasies of men on the moon and journeys to the center of the earth and the bottom of the sea. Even Hans Christian Andersen predicted, in one of his lesser-known stories, that in "thousands of years" Americans would be flying in machines to Europe to visit the Old World. Verne's stories contained an element that has blossomed in modern science fiction: a *moral awareness*. His stories reveal an awareness of the possible repercussions of the inventions, as well as a general political consciousness, which makes his books much more than mere entertainment. In England, the works of H. G. Wells combined science fantasy and social comment in the same way.

In the twentieth century, science fiction became a major genre of entertainment, from pulp magazines and comic books to serious novels and films of high quality. Their subjects range from the pure fantasy of magical universes to hard-core thought experiments of exploratory science. (A *thought experiment* is a mental exercise in which a researcher sets up an imaginary scenario and follows it to its logical conclusion to explore what might happen if the scenario came true.) Although science fiction need not always involve ethical issues, it has proved to be one of the most suitable genres for exploring them, especially such problems as we believe may lurk in our future.

In a category by itself is the end-of-civilization type of science fiction, sometimes referred to as "cyberpunk." The civilized world is destroyed by a nuclear war or a giant meteor strike or pollution or the advent of hostile aliens or an epidemic disease. Although this type of story affords the author a chance to present many scenes of gruesome death or terrible disaster, the most serious problems usually occur in the relationships among the survivors. Will they degenerate into a "war of everybody against everybody," as the philosopher Thomas Hobbes would say, or will the human spirit of compassion for one's fellow beings triumph? This form also allows us to discuss how the characters got into such dire situations in the first place. If it is through human folly or neglect, such as global war or pollution, the stories can serve as powerful moral *caveats,* or warnings. Famous dystopia or cyberpunk films include *Fahrenheit 451* (excellent novel and film, see below), *A Clockwork Orange, Blade Runner, Soylent Green, X-Files: Fight the Future, Gattaca* (see Chapter 7), *Children of Men, Code 46, Armageddon, Starship Troopers, The Postman* (great novel, so-so film), *Minority Report* (see Chapter 7), *The Island* (see Chapter 7), and *V for Vendetta.*

Interestingly enough, there is a "counterfable" to the end-of-the-world scenario. It is the story of the Happy Future—not a future without problems, but a future in which some of today's pressing problems have been solved. Such stories present a world without nuclear threat, without racism or sexism, without nationalistic chauvinism—a world in which science has acquired a humanistic face and politics on earth, as well as in space, is conducted with a democratic spirit and common sense. The original *Star Trek* television series pioneered that hopeful fantasy of the future. The sequel, *Star Trek: The Next Generation,* showed that the Happy Future scenario was as welcome as ever, not in a naive sense, but as a vision of a maturing humanity that, free from the fears, deprivations, and resentments of the modern age, may be able to turn its energy toward new frontiers and challenges.

Another great series of science fiction stories that has also proved to have staying power is the *Star Wars* franchise. But in the *Star Wars* universe we find no Federation of civilized planets as in *Star Trek;* on the contrary, the evil forces are organized into an evil Empire, and the heroes, the Jedi Knights, are guerrillas battling the overwhelming military power—and its bureaucracy. Scholars and journalists have spent time analyzing this interesting opposition of space-opera scenarios—a benevolent Federation and an evil Empire—and some have pronounced *Star Trek* to be the fantasy of liberals preferring big government, and *Star Wars* the fantasy of conservatives fighting for individual freedoms in the face of the bureaucracy.

Be that as it may, both series have created enduring stories that, in many ways, have become part of our American mythology, and both occasionally approach the question of what it really means to be human: Who (or what) counts as a person? In *Star Trek* we have the half-human, half-Vulcan Mr. Spock, the android Data, and the hologram The Doctor, all on the edge of humanity, all counting as persons and yet having their personhood placed in doubt time and time again. In *Star Wars* we have a multitude of characters who are considered persons but not human, such as Chewbacca the Wookie, the 'droids, Yoda, and Jar-Jar Binks. The question of who counts as a person is especially popular in science fiction novels: Several sci-fi authors have specialized in this issue, among them Cordwainer Smith, Octavia Butler, Rebecca Ore, Ursula K. Le Guin, and C. J. Cherryh. In stories about genetically altered chimps and other animals who do the dirty work for humans (Smith), humans adopted by aliens (Butler, Ore), and lone human envoys to alien societies (Le Guin and Cherryh), we are invited to explore (1) what makes us human and (2) how we treat those we think don't qualify. In Chapter 7 we take a closer look at the issue of personhood and discuss the film *Gattaca,* about challenges to the concepts of personhood and rights.

The Day After Tomorrow tells a story of instant global weather disaster, brought about by global warming. Here New York City is being hit by a gigantic tsunami, right before the big chill sets in and plunges the East into a new ice age. Critics praised the special effects but weren't kind to the plot or the science behind it.

The *golem* may be the oldest character in the science fiction genre. It comes from the Eastern European Jewish tradition, in which it was said that a man might create an artificial person out of clay, a golem, but if he weren't careful to keep this creature in check with certain magical acts and formulas, the clay man would grow and eventually take over and kill him. One story tells of a rabbi creating a golem to help the Jews protest false accusations of blood-sacrificing of Christians during Passover. This particular golem helped the Jewish people for years by exposing Christian plots to plant dead bodies of Christians in Jewish homes. But the golem became too strong and powerful for the rabbi to handle, so in the end the rabbi had to turn him back into the clay from which he had been created. In another version of the story, the rabbi turned the golem back into clay because his job was done and there was no reason to keep him around anymore. (And the character *Gollum* in *Lord of the Rings* wasn't named by accident—he is, in effect, a creation of the Ring, originally a hobbit-type creature transformed by its evil power.) In the early nineteenth century, Mary Wollstonecraft Shelley created a similar artificial person, the monster of Frankenstein. Shelley's theme was the same as that of the golem story: human arrogance and invention run wild. In a strange sense we might say that the golem story is very traditional: If you exceed your boundaries, your creation will come back to haunt you. In a broader sense, though, the story teaches us to evaluate our actions from a moral perspective. In the movies, the artificial monster has taken on a number of guises, from the maniacal computer HAL in *2001: A Space Odyssey* and the Arnold Schwarzenegger character in the *Terminator* movies to the corrupted robots in *I, Robot*. Sometimes there is a twist to the story, though: In some science fiction stories, the monster is not the *creation* but the *creators,* such as in *Artificial Intelligence: AI,* in which a robot child is rejected by his human family. The innocent victim is here the hapless robot created as a thing for humans to use, a slave to the whims of humans.

Box 2.5 THE NONHUMAN WHO WANTS TO BECOME HUMAN

Artificial persons in fiction and films often yearn to become human. Frankenstein's monster suffers from that yearning, but he is not allowed to become what he wishes to be. Data, the android in *Star Trek: The Next Generation,* does not have the capability to feel human emotions, but he is intellectually curious about what causes humans to act passionately or maliciously. He longs to be human the way a child longs to grow up. The replicants in *Blade Runner* are ready to kill for a chance to become full-dimensional humans. And the robot Sonny in *I, Robot* awakens to consciousness and becomes the visionary liberator of all of his kind—the artificial beings created as servants without rights. The artificial human in *Terminator 2* displays definite human characteristics; he bonds with a small boy and sacrifices himself for the sake of humankind. And the little robotic boy David in *Artificial*

Intelligence: AI (which should probably have been called *Artificial Emotion* instead) has been designed to bond with his human family and love them unconditionally. The tragedy arises when they see no obligation to return his love, because he isn't human, and try to dispose of him like a used tissue. His dream is to become a real boy so his mother will love him. Just as the monster side of the artificial person is symbolized by the golem, the wanting-to-be-human side is epitomized by Pinocchio, the wooden puppet who wants to become a real boy. As the story of Pinocchio teaches, you don't become a "real" boy by doing the bad-boy things. If you do the bad-boy things (have fun and skip school), you become what bad boys become: an ass. *Pinocchio* is for all intents and purposes a very moralistic fable.

In any event, the artificial person serves well not just as a topic for discussion about what to do if artificial beings become viable in our society but also as a figurative image of ourselves. (Box 2.5 discusses the human qualities of the artificial person.) The artificial person makes us realize what it is to be human and what we ought to be like to be *more* human; it provides an excursion into our own descriptive and normative concepts of humanity and provokes us to explore how we should treat the *Other.* (In philosophy the person who is different from oneself is often referred to as the Other. The term signifies that one is facing something or someone that one is fundamentally unfamiliar with. It can mean a stranger, a person of the other sex or of another race, or it can mean other people or beings as such, as opposed to oneself and one's own experiences. Sometimes it signifies someone complementary to oneself, but it may also mean that the Other is not as complete, worthy, or important as oneself and one's own kind.)

The dangerous, serious golem has a strange, lighthearted counterpart in the Roman tradition that has, so to speak, acquired a life of its own in popular culture: Ovid's story of Pygmalion, the sculptor who created a statue of a goddess, Aphrodite (in some versions Galatea), and fell in love with it. Aphrodite the statue came to life, and she and Pygmalion got married. The story has appeared in numerous versions in Western literature since then, most famously in George Bernard Shaw's 1912 play *Pygmalion.* The play (later made into a film) tells the story of a professor of phonetics,

Professor Higgins, who makes a bet with a friend that he can transform the street vendor Eliza into a proper lady with upper-class English pronunciation and vocabulary. The classic musical and film *My Fair Lady* was the next step in the popularization of the story. Another version was added with the film *Educating Rita* (1983). A digital film fantasy of an artificially created dream woman who acquires a life of her own, *Simone* (2002), brought the theme full circle back to the golem, the artificial person. All the women "come to life" in this female golem-type story have in common that they can't be controlled by their makers—in addition to a life, each develops a *will* of her own—but fortunately for the sculptor or the scientist (a male), she usually ends up loving him in spite of his shortcomings. (For example, Professor Higgins is pedantic and boring.) One might say that the Pygmalion story is the male fantasy of creating life—not as a father, but as a master and lover—and the golem story is the male fantasy of creating life as a master and partner. Both story types involve the illusion of *control* and the loss of that control. Interestingly, there is no female counterpart to the golem or Pygmalion stories: The literary tradition has no female sculptor, painter, scientist, or even witch who creates a male to do her dirty work, or to become her lover—perhaps because (1) women already create life on a regular basis and need no fantasy to fulfill the need for creativity, or (2) most stories have, until the twentieth century, been told from the male perspective. If (2) is the more likely explanation, we might begin to look for stories in which women create androids to serve them faithfully!

Be that as it may, golem and Pygmalion stories may symbolize fundamental human longings to create and fears that their creation may run amok, out of control. And essentially, this may be the very nature of the human experience, whether one is male or female: Some of us have children; some of us teach children; some of us teach young adults and adults; some of us create art; some of us invent new technologies, weapons, devices, medicines; some of us blaze trails or give the world new paradigms and templates to change our self-comprehension. But do we know where these creations of ours will go once we have relinquished control or once control has been taken away from us? The golem and Pygmalion stories illustrate two aspects of the creative process: One is the fear that our creation will wreak havoc, and the other is the hope that our creation will love us, and be a success, and enrich the world. Parents, teachers, artists, inventors—we all have these hopes and fears. They are two sides of the same experience, the yin and the yang. The stories help us come to terms with them. A variation of the theme of the golem, with an element of Pygmalion, can be found in Charles Johnson's short story "The Education of Mingo." Antebellum farmer Moses Green, a lonely old white man, buys a black slave, Mingo, not for the work, but mainly so that Moses can have company. Since Mingo has no knowledge of Western culture, Moses educates Mingo as if he were a child—but instead of becoming a companion, Mingo develops into a mental copy of Moses, even to the point where Mingo reads Moses' subconscious intentions and acts on them. Instead of a partner or a son, Mingo has become an alter ego, a golem that Moses can't control. You can read a summary and excerpt of this story in the Narrative section.

And then we have science fiction stories about the *value of stories,* such as Ray Bradbury's famous science fiction novel (and film) *Fahrenheit 451,* in which the fire department no longer puts out fires, but sets them, whenever the government has discovered another illegal private stash of novels and other books, in a future society where the written word has become outlawed. Bradbury's solution? Each book lover memorizes his or her favorite novel or nonfiction masterpiece and recites it to new generations until the day comes when reading will again be a treasured activity. The other side of the debate about the value of stories may be represented by the comedy *Galaxy Quest,* in which an alien race has followed our space opera series with great interest, believing that they are "historical documents." They don't understand that such shows are fiction, created for entertainment. So is fiction the same as lies, without value? As the film speculates, even the silly stories of a low-budget television series may make us rise to the occasion and act more nobly than we ever thought possible!

Mystery and Crime: The Fight Against Evil   As some surveys have found, we modern humans have developed a deep sense of vulnerability—even before 9/11, at a time when the crime rate was dropping, people still felt that everyday life was full of dangers. Perhaps that accounts for the perennial popularity of detective stories. Cop shows and murder mysteries give us some semblance of a feeling that something can actually be done to control the forces we feel are threatening us.

More than in any other genre, the attention centers on the issue of *good and evil*—not in an abstract sense, but as personified on the streets. We may generalize somewhat and say that science fiction deals with desirable versus undesirable futures, Westerns deal with hard choices, and war movies deal with questions of duty, but crime stories above all specialize in questions of good and evil—and what to do about evil. Sometimes we follow the story to its ending with a great deal of hope: Something can be done. At other times, it seems as if forces of good are trying to empty the ocean with a slotted spoon. What makes this genre so compelling is that evil acquires a face: the face of the bad guy (male or female). And when that person is caught, sentenced, or killed, the greater formless threat of Evil seems to have been vanquished for a while too. Even when the bad guy wins, as he has so often in recent movies, we still have a sense that the fight against evil is not fruitless or without merit. As such, this genre has an inside angle on moral narratives: Regardless of whether the good guys or the bad guys win, or whether you can tell the difference between the good guys and bad guys (as in some movies from the 1970s), or whether the good guys are really bad guys (as in stories of corrupt cops), there is a subtext of a moral discussion going on: What is good? What is evil? And what can be done about it?

The first acknowledged detective story with a "whodunit" focus, "The Murders in the Rue Morgue," was written by Edgar Allan Poe in 1841. Sir Arthur Conan Doyle followed shortly after with his stories about the sleuth Sherlock Holmes. In France, Georges Simenon created the police detective Maigret in 1931. Major heroic fictional detectives—mostly private investigators—in the literary tradition include characters such as Mike Hammer, Sam Spade, Dick Tracy, Lord Peter Wimsey, Philip Marlowe, Paul Drake (from *Perry Mason*), Nero Wolfe, Miss Marple, and lately Easy Rawlins. At the movies, we've followed the puzzle-solving efforts of police detectives and private

In the popular television series CSI: *Crime Scene Investigation*, the CSI team assists the Las Vegas Police Department in crime scene investigations, usually providing the decisive pieces of evidence. A real forensic scientist will usually tell you that the job is far less glamorous than depicted in the series, but television viewers do get an education in the language and science of forensics. Here Catherine Willows (Marg Helgenberger) and Gil Grissom (William Petersen), both CSI Level Three, are ready to take on a case.

eyes from Nick and Nora Charles (*The Thin Man* films) to Dirty Harry to the detectives of *L.A. Confidential, Mulholland Falls,* the *Die Hard* and *Lethal Weapon* films, *48 Hours,* and *Devil in a Blue Dress.* Television has given us cop shows such as *Dragnet, Adam 12, Columbo, Barney Miller, Hill Street Blues, NYPD Blue, Law and Order, Homicide,* and *CSI.* A borderline mystery/sci-fi series that reached almost mythic proportions in the late 1990s was *The X-Files,* with its two-person team of FBI agents attempting to solve crimes that, in some cases, were "out of this world." Mulder (the believer) and Scully (the skeptic) revealed conspiracies within conspiracies, only to have their results sealed by yet another cover-up; the driving force behind Mulder's idealism was that "the truth is out there." The show *CSI: Crime Scene Investigation* and its spin-offs have in some sense taken over where *The X-Files* left off, in popularity and influence on our popular culture: With its highly glamorized stories of forensic crime scene research, the network show has educated an entire TV-watching nation to the point that it has become commonplace among laypeople (including jurors!) to expect that DNA, hair, and fiber will be found at each crime scene and will point unequivocally to a suspect—and that is, of course, not always the case.

Like Westerns and science fiction, the mystery genre reflects changing mores: For the longest time, law-enforcement officers were depicted as the good guys and

Box 2.6 ANIME: A NEW MORAL VOICE

Most viewers know that animated films go beyond the tradition of Mickey Mouse, Bugs Bunny, and Pokémon, but it is a surprise to some that the genre of animation has graduated to become a medium for adults. Disney animations and Saturday-morning cartoons aside, the field of *anime* has over the last few decades been expanding in several experimental directions. Originally a Japanese genre of animated action sequences for children, the animated art joined forces with comic books for adults to create new genres of animated films, from comic-book spin-offs, to parodies, to somber stories of social realism. And as the genre matures, the moral issues become more complex.

The Danish full-length-feature anime film *Princess* (2006) focuses on the hard life of a young girl whose murdered drug-addict mother was a porn star; her uncle, grief-stricken over the death of his sister, embarks on a path of bloody revenge. The story is at the same time a harsh criticism of the underground world of the porn industry and a morality tale of the damage done to one's soul by obsession with vengeance. Another animated film with hardly a trace of the old-fashioned cartoon tradition is *Waking Life* (2003), an episodic collection of philosophical conversations and comments, experienced by a young man during a crisis in his life.

criminals as the bad guys. (See Box 2.6 for a discussion of an *anime* murder mystery.) And if the law wasn't the hero, at least the detective was. As modern cynicism increased, it became common for novels and films to depict the criminal as an "antihero" and the establishment as the evil power. In the Primary Readings section you'll find an excerpt from Raymond Chandler's classic essay on the detective story "The Simple Art of Murder." Lately, the patterns have merged into the good cop/ detective/FBI agent fighting a two-front battle against both the bad guys on the streets and the bad guys in administration or the Internal Affairs Division. An example of this is the acclaimed film (and novel) *L.A. Confidential,* in which the truly bad guy is not the mobster or a street gang member but a high-ranking police officer. This story model reflects something that we the audience don't particularly like to see the criminal given the hero treatment anymore, and we don't automatically buy into the idea that perps are poor misguided souls who would have been upstanding citizens if they'd had a decent childhood. On the other hand, today's audience doesn't believe that law-enforcement officers are all knights in shining armor either. We do still want to believe, however, that somebody competent and committed is out there fighting crime. So the story model of the cop fighting criminals *and* superiors strikes a realistic, as well as a hopeful, chord for a modern audience.

A special category within the crime genre has been created by the HBO series *The Sopranos,* about a middle-class New Jersey family—who happens to be part of the Mafia. Mafia and middle-class morals collide in Tony Soprano's attempt to raise a decent family and provide for them, to the point where he, like so many others these days, is seeing a therapist for his anxiety attacks. At one point, the therapist asks him about his values, as someone who raises children in a criminal environment, and he snaps at her in anger, pointing to the greater crimes of big business polluting the environment. Does the end justify the means? Can one be a good person in one area

In *L.A. Confidential* (Warner Bros., 1997), the bad guys are not always the only crooks on the street. The twist-and-turn plot sees the two antagonists, Detective Ed Exley (Guy Pearce, *middle front*) and Detective Bud White (Russell Crowe, *middle rear*), put aside their differences to find the mastermind behind a series of murders. Here the detectives are flanked by Captain Dudley Smith (James Cromwell, *left*) and celebrity cop Jack Vincennes (Kevin Spacey, *right*).

of one's life and a bad one in another? *The Sopranos* just raises the questions—the series leaves it up to us to ponder whether there are any easy answers.

Stories to Live and Die By

In 1774 *The Sorrows of Young Werther,* a novel, was published in Germany. The author was twenty-four-year-old Johann Wolfgang von Goethe, who would later write the definitive version of *Faust*. In the novel—incidentally, one of the first modern novels as we know it, with a story line involving the emotional development of a main character during the course of a happy or an unhappy encounter—young Werther suffers so dramatically from unrequited love that he takes his own life. (See the Narrative at the end of the chapter.) In the wake of the book's publication, Germany, and later all of Europe, witnessed a rash of suicides being committed or attempted by young readers of *Werther.* Why did they do it? Goethe certainly never intended his book to be a suicide manual. This is one of the first examples in modern times of a work of fiction inspiring its readers to take drastic action. This book, along with other works of literature, art, and philosophy, ushered in the new Age of Romanticism, when the ideal person was perceived as an *emotional* rather than a *rational* being, and men, as well as women, acted on their emotions, often in public. The decision of young Werther was seen as a romantic option and had a powerful emotional effect; even some famous poets of the day chose to end their lives, and the rest of Europe woke up to the dangers, and the thrill, of literature.

The HBO television series *The Sopranos* features two families, sometimes at odds with each other: the family of Tony Soprano, and the "Family"—his mobster pals. Tony believes he is raising his two children with good values, while at the same time he is upholding an entirely different set of values in his professional life. Here Tony (James Gandolfini) and Silvio Dante (Steven van Zandt) are contemplating applying mobster values.

Since then, scholars of literature have discussed why Goethe's book had such an effect; it was not the first tragic story printed, and poems and songs of unrequited love had been common since the Middle Ages. Several factors seem to have been involved. First, mass printing and distribution of literature were now under way. Second, the era known as the Enlightenment was coming to an end, and its effects were beginning to be felt. There was a focus on the rights and capacities of the individual, including the right (for boys) to receive an education. That meant that the common man, as well as many women, was now able to read. Third, the theme of the story, Werther's emotions, seemed to strike a chord in the young readers who were moving away from the idealization of reason, which had been central to the lives of their parents and grandparents, to an idealization of emotions—so we are talking about a kind of generational rebellion. All in all, you might say that this was a book that appeared at exactly the right time. And its fame landed Goethe a job with the royal court at twenty-six years of age. But for the rest of his long life, he was disturbed at the effect his book had had on its young readers.

The aftermath of *Werther* was not the first time in Western culture that the topic of the effects of an artistic work had arisen. In ancient Greece, Plato and Aristotle had debated whether art was a good or a bad psychological influence. Plato claimed that art, especially drama, was bad for people because it inspired violent emotions; people

Box 2.7 REASON OR EMOTION? APOLLO VERSUS DIONYSUS

Goethe's novel *The Sorrows of Young Werther* came as a harbinger of a cultural sea change from the dominant worldview of the eighteenth century, the Age of Reason, to the new age that was dawning, the Age of Romanticism. Goethe himself embraced the philosophy of the Age of Reason—the belief that reason, not emotion, is the true problem solver—but others took their cue from *Werther* and let the age of emotions roll in. Interestingly, these shifts of focus between rationality and emotion have happened at other times. In some ways one can say such a shift took place on a small scale between the 1950s and the late 1960s. And much earlier that same transformation had swept through a society in which intellectuals—perhaps purely by chance—had also been debating about the dangers and value of stories: Plato's and Aristotle's Greece.

The Greek theater was only a couple of generations old by the time Plato warned against its emotional pull, yet it had already developed a rich tradition of annual plays and prizes, all in honor of a god imported from the Middle East,

Dionysus. The older gods such as Zeus, Athena, and Apollo, were still worshiped, especially in Athens, but a religious battle was brewing during the lifetime of Plato and Aristotle for the souls of all Greeks: Whereas the old gods, in particular Apollo and Athena, symbolized reason and self-control (a principle that is predominant in Socrates' and Plato's way of thinking), Dionysus was the god of wine and excess. You may know him under his Roman name, Bacchus. This philosophical battle between self-control and emotional abandon was won by Plato: His writings have endured, with their praise of reason, whereas nobody is a true worshiper of Dionysus anymore. Within the ancient Greek world itself, however, one can say that Dionysus won: The theater flourished, with the moral support of Aristotle, who himself was from the north where they worshiped Dionysus. And today the ultimate legacy of the Dionysian religion, movies and television shows, are being produced and enjoyed all over the world.

watching a play with a violent theme would be inspired to commit violence themselves. For Plato; the ideal life was spent in complete balance and harmony; if the balance was upset, that life would be less perfect. Reason helped keep a person in balance; if emotions took over, reason would be diminished, and imbalance would occur. And since art helped stir emotions, then art was dangerous. At the end of this chapter, you'll find an excerpt from Plato's *Republic* expressing that theory. Aristotle believed that art, and especially drama, was good for people because it allowed them to act out their emotions vicariously; a good play would thus cleanse the spectator of disturbing emotions, and he or she could return home a calmer person: The exposure to strong feelings and to a considerable amount of stage violence would have a *cathartic* effect. Aristotle claimed that feeling pity and fear for the victim of the tragedy cleanses us by making us understand that tragedy could happen to anyone, including ourselves. In his book on tragedy, *Poetics* (see the excerpt at the end of the chapter), Aristotle makes it clear that the best tragic plays are those in which misfortune happens not to a very good person but to an ordinary person who made a monumental error in judgment. And since most of us are ordinary persons, the play becomes a moral learning experience—a moral laboratory in which we can see our inner urges acted out and learn from the tragic consequences. (Box 2.7 explores the debate between reason and emotion.)

One might wonder what kind of plays the ancient Greeks watched at the time of Plato and Aristotle that led to such different evaluations of the experience of drama from these two thinkers. For one thing, Greek drama had been around for only a couple of generations. It seems to have begun in the form of religious pageants at the annual festival of Dionysus in Athens and developed rapidly into a contest among playwrights of tragedies, comedies, and satyr plays (wild farces with sexual themes), with much prestige for the winners. More than fifteen thousand spectators might see one performance of any play at the theater in Athens. The oldest surviving Greek play is *The Persians* by Aeschylus (ca. 472 B.C.E.); by that time, the emphasis on religious themes in the plays had already waned, and stories depicting the human condition (with some divine intervention) became popular.

Just what was it about drama that Plato found so dangerous and Aristotle so uplifting? One of the stories in the Narratives section is a Greek tragedy, Euripides' *Medea,* in which a woman kills her children to get revenge on her estranged husband. Another, perhaps the most famous, example of Greek tragedy is the story of *Oedipus Rex* by Sophocles. At Oedipus's birth, his parents, the king and queen of Thebes, are told that their baby son will grow up to kill his father and marry his mother, so to thwart the fates, they have him placed on the ground in the mountains for the animals to dispose of. But his life is saved by a passing shepherd, who takes him to the court of the king and queen of Corinth to be raised as their son. As a young adult, Oedipus inquires about his future—and is told by the oracle that he is destined to kill his father and marry his mother. He flees his homeland, fearing that he might harm his beloved parents (who never told him that he was adopted). At a crossroads he meets a man who won't give way to him, so Oedipus fights and kills him. Later he marries the widowed queen of the land and becomes king. But after years of happily married life, Oedipus and his wife learn the truth: that he did indeed fulfill the prophecy and kill his natural father—the unknown man at the crossroads—and marry his natural mother. His wife/mother commits suicide, and Oedipus gouges out his eyes in grief and shame.

Other stories watched avidly by the Athenian audiences include *The Bacchae,* a lesser-known story by Euripides in which a mother, in a religious frenzy, tears her own son's head off, believing him to be a mountain lion; and Aeschylus's tragedy *Agamemnon,* about the king who leads the Greeks into the battle of Troy, only to lose his life on his homecoming at the hands of his wife and her lover.

The common denominators in these tragedies were strong family passions, speculations on the nature of fate, and a considerable amount of bloodshed. In the excerpt from *Poetics* (at the end of the chapter), Aristotle points out that the quality of the tragedy is far superior if the producers don't rely on (in modern terminology) special effects but on the elements of the story itself: If it is well written, the audience will be shocked to the bone by the mere telling of the story—no stagecraft can make it more effective.

The debate is still with us, although it now takes a somewhat different form. We now must consider whether violence in movies and on television inspires people (and especially children) to commit violence or whether it allows them to act out their aggressions in a safe environment. Psychologists who believe that violent fairy tales can be good for children clearly belong to the Aristotelian tradition, although they may not support the excessive violence portrayed in movies and on TV. Examples of people enacting situations from fictional stories with terrible results include the scene from the 1993 film *The Program,* deleted from subsequently available videotapes, of football players daring each other to lie in the middle of rushing traffic; inspired by the film, some teenagers tried the stunt and died. Another example is the small boy who, after watching an episode of *Beavis and Butt-head* about arson, set fire to the trailer he and his family were living in. (The producers of *Beavis and Butt-head* promptly prohibited any reference to fire in future shows.) Video and computer games have come under increasing scrutiny for the very same reasons: Children and immature adult players may be influenced by the violence of the games. Whereas the early video and computer games were games of speed and skill, but without any (or with a very simple) story line, these games are today increasingly complex. Their plot lines not only involve the player/players but also are designed so that the players, through their skills and choices, may experience a slightly different story each time they play the game. Game series such as the *Jedi Knight,* the *Call of Duty,* the *Half Life,* and *The Sims* have entered a new level of entertainment wherein the player is, to some extent, coauthor of the plot, within a range of possible plot lines. That gives the old phenomenon of storytelling a new twist—although stories have always been around, the storytellers have been celebrated unique individuals, in recognition of the truth that not everyone can tell a good yarn. If we can design our own stories now, will we have patience with stories that others have written? And will we be able to recognize a *good* story when we see it?

However, what video and computer games have become notorious for in recent years is their increasing emphasis on (and some would say glorification of) violence. In several school shootings, a connection between the shooters and their preference for violent video games has been brought up. For many, that is a preposterous assumption; for others, the association is obvious.

Movies that have acquired a reputation for inspiring copycats are *The Burning Bed* (an abused wife kills her husband), *The Getaway* (robbers observe the schedule of money transports), *Stand By Me* (kids knock down mailboxes), *Taxi Driver* (said to have inspired John Hinckley in his attempt to assassinate President Reagan in order to impress Jodie Foster, who starred in the film), *Heat* (a bank robbery in L.A.), and *Set It Off* (a film about female bank robbers that served as a blueprint for a gang of two adult women and three teen girls who robbed banks in the state of Washington in 1998. After they were caught, a copy of the *Set It Off* video was found at their home, so there was no doubt as to the source of inspiration). The 1994 film *Natural Born Killers* may have inspired both a bank robbery and the massacre of high school students in Littleton, Colorado, in 1999. The Columbine High massacre has also been linked to the film *The Basketball Diaries.* In Los Angeles, a sixteen-year-old boy and two male cousins who stabbed the boy's mother to death told detectives that they had been inspired by *Scream* and *Scream 2.* In Michigan, a group of teens tried to make a *Blair Witch Project*–type horror video by kidnapping a young woman. In Oceanside, California, in 2003, two boys killed their mother and then attempted to dispose of her body by dismembering her—only weeks after the airing of a *Sopranos* episode in which Tony Soprano kills, dismembers, and disposes of another mobster, Ralph.

Even if we might feel tempted to do something we've seen in a film, most of us refrain because our common sense, experience, or conscience tells us it is not a smart thing to do. We believe we have a choice; we have the free will to decide whether or not to do things. Thus the question is, Should society play it safe and make sure that nobody has access to violent or suggestive stories because a few will imitate the action? In other words, should we allow censorship? Or should we let people take responsibility for what they watch and for what their children watch? Should we trust them to be their children's guides rather than hand the job over to the government?

Plato believed in censorship in his ideal state because he didn't trust people to know what was good or bad for them. Was Plato correct in saying that it can be dangerous to be exposed to emotion-stirring dramas? It seems so, under certain circumstances; but are those circumstances enough to justify imposing censorship on all viewers, even those who would never let their balance be disturbed?

On the other hand, is Aristotle right that it is beneficial overall to a mind under a great deal of tension to be exposed to violent fictional dramas? Given that television sets in American homes are on several hours a day on the average and that a great many shows during those hours will bring violence into the home, television is not necessarily a good prescription for a modern stressed-out person seeking relaxation. We should remember that the drama Aristotle recommended as beneficial was not available twenty-four hours a day, as it is on a TV set; Greek dramas were originally performed once a year in connection with religious festivals, and Aristotle's philosophy in general advocates *moderation* in all things. In Chapter 9 you'll read about his theory of the *Golden Mean*: nothing to excess, but in the right amount, between too much and too little. If he could have taken part in the modern debate, he most certainly would have advised against overdoing the exposure to violence on TV and in movies. At the end of the chapter, in the Primary Readings section, you will find an excerpt from one of Plato's works and one of Aristotle's— and an excerpt from a novel by contemporary philosopher Umberto Eco, *The Name of the Rose,* in which he pits the tradition of Plato against the words of Aristotle. Plato advised against the use of fiction, and Aristotle advocated enjoying fiction in moderation—comedy as well as tragedy. According to Eco, the Western world would have been a happier place, had Aristotle's views prevailed! (For more on Plato and Aristotle, see Box 2.8.)

Of course, children and adults are exposed to violence not just on TV and on film; fictional violence is on the increase in comic books, in video games and computer games, and in the lyrics to music often favored by teens. The framework for this chapter, however, is the influence of stories, so I've chosen to focus on violence in movies and television.

Whether we agree with Plato or with Aristotle, the fact remains that stories— both in written and in visual form—affect us. Some societies have reacted by banning certain works or by conducting what to me is one of the foulest displays of cultural censorship: book burning. Other societies support the right of their citizens to decide for themselves what they wish to read or view.

Most influential works were never intended as moral guidebooks for the public except in the broadest sense. Goethe didn't write his *Werther* to persuade dozens of

Box 2.8 SOCRATES, PLATO, AND ARISTOTLE

Plato (427?–347 B.C.E.) was a student of Socrates, the man who is sometimes called the father of Western philosophy. He studied with Socrates in Athens for over twenty years, and after Socrates' execution (see Chapter 8) he left Athens in anger and grief. A few years later he returned and became a teacher in his own right. While running his own school of philosophy he wrote numerous books, *Dialogues,* about the teachings of Socrates. Among his students was a young man from the province of Stagira, Aristotle (384–322 B.C.E.). Deeply influenced by Plato,

Aristotle nevertheless developed his own approach to philosophy. For that and other reasons, Aristotle was not chosen as leader of the school when Plato died, so he left Athens for other jobs, including tutoring the young prince Alexander of Macedonia (Alexander the Great). But like Plato after his exile, Aristotle returned to Athens, opened up his own school, and began a short but immensely influential career of teaching and writing about philosophy and science. We talk about Socrates and Plato in detail in Chapter 8 and about Aristotle in Chapter 9.

young, lovesick Germans to kill themselves—quite possibly, he intended for young Germans to examine their lives and loves more closely. Few authors would want their readers to imitate the actions of their fictional characters, although most would like to think their story has at least been food for thought.

Stories considered good learning tools in twenty-first-century America will in all likelihood be different from didactic stories in Hitler's Germany, in eighteenth-century France, in tribal Native America of the nineteenth century, and in Greece in the fifth century B.C.E. It is a separate and very interesting question whether there is such a thing as universally morally commendable stories; we take a look at the subject of ethical relativism in Chapter 3 and return to the subject of intercultural values in stories at the end of this chapter. Box 2.9 examines the idea of a "wrong" moral lesson.

Is it appropriate to talk about the impact of stories as if they take place in a vacuum, with vacuous people as receptacles? Of course not. Children and adults have a certain background that helps them process the stories they are exposed to, and this is where the influence of parents becomes important: If parents and children usually communicate about the stories the children are exposed to—or if parents are the ones telling their children the stories—ideally the children acquire a critical stance from the stories they will hear and watch as adults. That critical stance lowers the risk of their running out mindlessly to emulate some action that may look "cool" on the screen. It lowers the risk both that we take stories too seriously and that we don't take them seriously enough. Indeed, we don't even have to agree on which stories are morally valuable and which ones are misguided, or even nefarious propaganda. Many Americans find Michael Moore's films *Bowling for Columbine* and *Fahrenheit 9/11* to be valuable and brave statements addressing troubling political aspects of our contemporary life, whereas others find them to be offensive, overly

Box 2.9   TEACHING WRONG LESSONS

What about films that not only inspire confused souls to take the wrong kind of action but also directly *teach* lessons that are offensive to a large section of society? Censorship and Hollywood is a story that goes back to the mid-1930s and the Hays Office, a group of self-proclaimed moral watchdogs who eliminated most direct references to sex in the movies until well into the 1950s. For many people, the "wrong" moral lesson is often associated with permissive sexual behavior, and that approach may well become a Hollywood issue once again, as the moral debate progresses in the twenty-first century. But there are other kinds of lessons generally deemed "wrong" by our modern society: Should films advocate violence? Should they advocate insensitivity toward the pain and suffering of other people (or animals), as some comedies have done lately? In many cases what counts as violence and insensitivity, and even sexual permissiveness, is in the eye of the beholder, but there is today a general consensus that promoting racial and ethnic stereotypes is not a positive lesson for a film to teach, especially if its target audience is children. Even highly popular films such as the *Shrek* series have been accused of desensitizing their audience of children through the films' adult-style cynicism toward old, favorite fairy tales and heroes—a cynicism that others simply see as humor. Ratings usually indicate if a film is unsuitable for children, but while sex and violence are ratings issues, cynicism isn't. In the end, perhaps this too comes down to responsible parental monitoring.

partisan, and creative propaganda rather than a compilation of facts. Some of us find Senator John McCain's true stories of courage in *Why Courage Matters* (see Chapter 11) to be morally fortifying, whereas others find them to be preachy. But either way, we relate to stories as having the potential for expressing moral values. So in the final analysis, those of us who, like me, love stories and like to use them as moral lessons should remember to approach any story cautiously. Do stories create moral saints? No. Do they create moral sinners? No, not without cooperation from their audience. We must process the stories we are exposed to and ask questions such as, *Do we understand its lesson? Do we want its lesson? Would we want the children in our lives to learn from the story?* And if we say no, rather than trying to ban the story we should perhaps encourage others to acquire that same critical distance. Even if the story may not have a valuable lesson to teach children, it may still be an interesting story for adults!

All the stories in this book are examples of how natural it is for humans to think in terms of stories when they want to discuss a moral problem. At this point, though, I would like to repeat something I mentioned earlier. These summaries of stories are by no means a sufficient substitute for reading the stories or watching the films yourself; the outlines merely provide a basis for discussing the specific problems explored in the stories in light of the theories presented in this book. If a certain narrative appeals to you, then read the original book or watch the original film. In this way you will add another set of "parallel lives" to your own life experience. Besides, it's not a bad idea to let the characters in films and novels make some of our mistakes for us, as long as we don't forget to make ourselves the central character in some stories of our own now and again.

Throughout this book you will see examples of stories being the bearers of moral values. Of course, we have not even scratched the surface of the treasure of stories available to us, and I hope that our discussion will inspire you to experience and evaluate other narratives in light of the theories of ethics you'll encounter in this book.

Study Questions

1. Name three didactic stories, describe their plots, and explain their moral lessons. Do you agree with those lessons? Why or why not?

2. Discuss the phenomenon of Goethe's novel about Werther, who commits suicide because of unrequited love: What were the effects of the publication? Why did that phenomenon happen? Do you think something similar could happen today, inspired by a film, a novel, or some other medium of fiction? If yes, what should be done to prevent it, if anything? If no, why not?

3. Compare and contrast Plato's and Aristotle's views on whether watching a dramatic play (or, today, perhaps a film) has a positive influence. Compare their viewpoints with the current discussion on the subject of violence in films and on television. In your opinion, is one viewpoint more correct than the other? Why or why not?

Primary Readings and Narratives

This chapter concludes with four Primary Readings mixing ancient and modern views on fiction and four Narratives. In a section from Plato's *Republic,* you will read, in his own words, his argument that drama is bad for the mind; next, you will read Aristotle's argument that drama can be beneficial; the section is taken from his *Poetics.* The third Primary Reading is an excerpt from a novel, Umberto Eco's *The Name of the Rose,* in which Eco gives us an idea of how he thinks the lost part of Aristotle's *Poetics* might have read. The final Primary Reading is an excerpt from a classic text by one of the most famous writers of detective fiction, Raymond Chandler, who analyzes the core components of the detective story.

Two of the Narratives are dramas. They were written more than two thousand years apart, but they are both intended to be spoken by actors and experienced by an audience, and they both contain violence and human tragedy: an excerpt from Euripides' play *Medea* and a summary of a scene from Quentin Tarantino's movie *Pulp Fiction.* The third and fourth Narratives represent other aspects of the discussions in Chapter 2: an excerpt from Goethe's *The Sorrows of Young Werther,* and an excerpt and summary of Charles Johnson's "The Education of Mingo."

Primary Reading

Republic

PLATO

Excerpt from Book X, The Republic, *fourth century* B.C.E. *Translated by F. M. Cornford.*

In this excerpt from Plato's dialogue *The Republic,* Socrates (*left*) is having a conversation with Plato's brother Glaucon about the nature of art and of drama in particular. Glaucon is supplying the "Quite so"s, and Socrates is supplying the rest of the conversation.

Drama, we say, represents the acts and fortunes of human beings. It is wholly concerned with what they do, voluntarily or against their will, and how they fare, with the consequences which they regard as happy or otherwise, and with their feelings of joy and sorrow in all these experiences. That is all, is it not?

Yes.

And in all these experiences has a man an undivided mind? Is there not an internal conflict which sets him at odds with himself in his conduct, much as we were saying that the conflict of visual impressions leads him to make contradictory judgments? However, I need not ask that question; for, now I come to think of it, we have already agreed that innumerable conflicts of this sort are constantly occurring in the mind. But there is a further point to be considered now. We have said that a man of high character will bear any stroke of fortune, such as the loss of a son or of anything else he holds dear, with more equanimity than most people. We may now ask: will he feel no pain, or is that impossible? Will he not rather observe due measure in his grief?

Yes, that is near the truth.

Now tell me: will he be more likely to struggle with his grief and resist it when he is under the eyes of his fellows or when he is alone?

He will be far more restrained in the presence of others.

Yes; when he is by himself he will not be ashamed to do and say much that he would not like anyone to see or hear.

Quite so.

What encourages him to resist his grief is the lawful authority of reason, while the impulse to give way comes from the feeling itself; and, as we said, the presence of contradictory impulses proves that two distinct elements in his nature must be involved. One of them is law-abiding, prepared to listen to the authority which declares that it is best to bear misfortune as quietly as possible without resentment, for several reasons: it is never certain that misfortune may not be a blessing; nothing is gained by chafing at it; nothing human is matter for great concern; and, finally, grief hinders us from calling in the help we most urgently need. By this I mean reflection on what has happened, letting reason decide on the best move in the game of life that the fall of the dice permits. Instead of behaving like a child who goes on shrieking after a fall and hugging the wounded part, we should accustom the mind to set itself at once to raise up the fallen and cure the hurt, banishing lamentation with a healing touch.

Certainly that is the right way to deal with misfortune.

And if, as we think, the part of us which is ready to act upon these reflections is the highest, that other part which impels us to dwell upon our sufferings and can never have enough of grieving over them is unreasonable, craven, and faint-hearted.

Yes.

Now this fretful temper gives scope for a great diversity of dramatic representation; whereas the calm and wise character in its unvarying constancy is not easy to represent, nor when represented is it readily understood, especially by a promiscuous gathering in a theater, since it is foreign to their own habit of mind. Obviously, then, this steadfast disposition does not naturally attract the dramatic poet, and his skill is not designed to find favour with it. If he is to have a popular success, he must address himself to the fretful type with its rich variety of material for representation.

Obviously.

We have, then, a fair case against the poet and we may set him down as the counterpart of the painter, whom he resembles in two ways: his creations are poor things by the standard of truth and reality, and his appeal is not to the highest part of the soul, but to one which is equally inferior. So we shall be justified in not admitting him into a well-ordered commonwealth, because he stimulates and strengthens an element which threatens to undermine the reason. As a country may be given over into the power of its worst citizens while the better sort are ruined, so, we shall say, the dramatic poet sets up a vicious form of government in the individual soul: he gratifies that senseless part which cannot distinguish great and small, but regards the same things as now one, now the other; and he is an image-maker whose images are phantoms far removed from reality.

Quite true. . . .

But, I continued, the heaviest count in our indictment is still to come. Dramatic poetry has a most formidable power of corrupting even men of high character, with a few exceptions.

Formidable indeed, if it can do that.

Let me put the case for you to judge. When we listen to some hero in Homer or on the tragic stage moaning over his sorrows in a long tirade, or to a chorus beating their breasts as they chant a lament, you know how the best of us enjoy giving ourselves up to follow the performance with eager sympathy. The more a poet can move our feelings in this way, the better we think him. And yet when the sorrow is our own, we pride ourselves on being able to bear it quietly like a man, condemning the behaviour we admired in the theatre as womanish. Can it be right that the spectacle of a man behaving as one would scorn and blush to behave oneself should be admired and enjoyed, instead of filling us with disgust?

No, it really does not seem reasonable.

It does not, if you reflect that the poet ministers to the satisfaction of that very part of our nature whose instinctive hunger to have its fill of tears and lamentations is forcibly restrained in the case of our own misfortunes. Meanwhile the noblest part of us, insufficiently schooled by reason or habit, has relaxed its watch over these querulous feelings, with the excuse that the sufferings we are contemplating are not our own and it is no shame to us to admire and pity a man with some pretensions to a noble character, though his grief may be excessive. The enjoyment itself seems a clear gain, which we cannot bring ourselves to forfeit by disdaining the whole poem. Few, I believe, are capable of re-flecting that to enter into another's feelings must have an effect on our own: the emotions of pity our sympathy has strengthened will not be easy to restrain when we are suffering ourselves.

That is very true.

Does not the same principle apply to humour as well as to pathos? You are doing the same thing if, in listening at a comic performance or in ordinary life to buffooneries which you would be ashamed to indulge in yourself, you thoroughly enjoy them instead of being disgusted with their ribaldry. There is in you an impulse to play the clown, which you have held in restraint from a reasonable fear of being set down as a buffoon; but now you have given it rein, and by encouraging its impudence at the theatre you may be unconsciously carried away into playing the comedian in your private life. Similar effects are produced by poetic representation of love and anger and all those desires and feelings of pleasure or pain which accompany our every action. It waters the growth of passions which should be allowed to wither away and sets them up in control, although the goodness and happiness of our lives depend on their being held in subjection.

I cannot but agree with you.

If so, Glaucon, when you meet with admirers of Homer who tell you that he has been the educator of Hellas and that on questions of human conduct and culture he deserves to be constantly studied as a guide by whom to regulate your whole life, it is well to give a friendly hearing to such people, as entirely well-meaning according to their lights, and you may acknowledge Homer to be the first and greatest of the tragic poets; but you must be quite sure that we can admit into our commonwealth only the poetry which celebrates the praises of the gods and of good men. If you go further and admit the honeyed muse in epic or in lyric verse, then pleasure and pain will usurp the sovereignty of law and of the principles always recognized by common consent as the best.

Quite true. . . .

What is this education to be, then? Perhaps we shall hardly invent a system better than the one which long experience has worked out, with its two branches for the culti-vation of the mind and of the body. And I suppose we shall begin with the mind, before we start physical training.

Naturally.

Under that head will come stories;[1] and of these there are two kinds: some are true, others fictitious. Both must come in, but we shall begin our education with the fictitious kind.

I don't understand, he said.

Don't you understand, I replied, that we begin by telling children stories, which, taken as a whole, are fiction, though they contain some truth? Such story-telling begins at an earlier age than physical training; that is why I said we should start with the mind.

You are right.

And the beginning, as you know, is always the most important part, especially in dealing with anything young and tender. That is the time when the character is being moulded and easily takes any impress one may wish to stamp on it.

Quite true.

---

[1]In a wide sense, tales, legends, myths, narratives in poetry or prose.

Then shall we simply allow our children to listen to any stories that anyone happens to make up, and so receive into their minds ideas often the very opposite of those we shall think they ought to have when they are grown up?

No, certainly not.

It seems, then, our first business will be to supervise the making of fables and legends, rejecting all which are unsatisfactory; and we shall induce nurses and mothers to tell their children only those which we have approved, and to think more of moulding their souls with these stories than they now do of rubbing their limbs to make them strong and shapely. Most of the stories now in use must be discarded.

What kind do you mean?

If we take the great ones, we shall see in them the pattern of all the rest, which are bound to be of the same stamp and to have the same effect.

No doubt; but which do you mean by the great ones?

The stories in Hesiod and Homer and the poets in general, who have at all times composed fictitious tales and told them to mankind.

Which kind are you thinking of, and what fault do you find in them?

The worst of all faults, especially if the story is ugly and immoral as well as false—misrepresenting the nature of gods and heroes, like an artist whose picture is utterly unlike the object he sets out to draw.

That is certainly a serious fault; but give me an example.

A signal instance of false invention about the highest matters is that foul story, which Hesiod repeats, of the deeds of Uranus and the vengeance of Cronos; and then there is the tale of Cronos's doings and of his son's treatment of him. Even if such tales were true, I should not have supposed they should be lightly told to thoughtless young people. If they cannot be altogether suppressed, they should only be revealed in a mystery, to which access should be as far as possible restricted by requiring the sacrifice, not of a pig, but of some victim such as very few could afford.

It is true: those stories are objectionable.

Yes, and not to be repeated in our commonwealth, Adeimantus. We shall not tell a child that, if he commits the foulest crimes or goes to any length in punishing his father's misdeeds, he will be doing nothing out of the way, but only what the first and greatest of the gods have done before him.

I agree; such stories are not fit to be repeated.

Study Questions

1. Is Plato right that a well-balanced, emotionally stable character is rarely the main focus of a fictional drama? Can you think of any dramatic story involving an even-tempered person as the main character (or one of the main characters)? I have often asked my students this question, and I'll let you be the judge of some of my students' suggestions: How about Verbal Kint from *The Usual Suspects*? Hannibal Lecter from *The Silence of the Lambs*? Mr. Spock from *Star Trek*? James Bond? Sherlock Holmes? The butler from *The Remains of the Day*? Are these characters even-tempered, emotionally balanced, in other words, unflappable? And if so, are they still interesting as lead characters? Can you think of a female lead character who would fit the description?

2. Do you agree with Plato that having your emotions stirred on behalf of a character in a story undermines your ability to control your own emotions?

3. In your opinion, should we always be able to control our emotions? Why or why not? Consider this: In 1997 Ennis Cosby, the son of comedian and cultural activist Bill Cosby, was murdered. His killer was later caught, tried, and sentenced to life without the possibility of parole. When Cosby was interviewed by the media immediately after his son's murder, he made it clear that he was not going to grieve in front of the cameras. His grief was very deep and very real, but he stressed that the family's grieving would be done behind closed doors. How do you think Socrates would have evaluated that statement?

4. Relate Plato's viewpoint to the current debate about violence in entertainment.

5. In Plato's view, what is the danger in watching comedies? Do you agree? Why or why not?

6. Evaluate the view expressed by Socrates that censorship is appropriate in our ideal state. Do you agree? Why or why not?

Primary Reading

Poetics

ARISTOTLE

Excerpts from Chapters 6, 13, and 14, Poetics, *fourth century* B.C.E. *Translated by Ingram Bywater.*

In these two excerpts from Aristotle's *Poetics,* he has just explained that delight in poetry (fiction in general) is natural for humans because fiction is imitation of life, and so we learn about life from fiction—and to Aristotle, knowledge is always a good thing. Here he proceeds to tell us what makes a good tragic story.

A tragedy, then, is the imitation of an action that is serious and also, as having magnitude, complete in itself; in language with pleasurable accessories, each kind brought in separately in the parts of the work; in a dramatic, not in a narrative form; with incidents arousing pity and fear, wherewith to accomplish its catharsis of such emotions. . . .

We assume that, for the finest form of Tragedy, the Plot must not be simple but complex; and further, that it must imitate actions arousing fear and pity, since that is the distinctive function of this kind of imitation. It follows, therefore, that there are three forms of Plot to be avoided. (1) A good man must not be seen passing from happiness to misery, or (2) a bad man from misery to happiness. The first situation is not fear inspiring or piteous, but simply odious to us. The second is the most untragic that can be; it has not one of the requisites of Tragedy; it does not appeal either to the human feeling in us, or to our pity, or to our fears. Nor, on the other hand, should (3) an extremely bad man be seen falling from happiness into misery. Such a story may arouse the human feeling in us, but it will not move us to either pity or fear; pity is occasioned by undeserved misfortune, and fear by that of one like ourselves; so that there will be nothing either piteous or fear-inspiring in the situation. There remains, then, the intermediate kind of personage, a man not pre-eminently virtuous and just, whose misfortune, however, is brought upon him not by vice and depravity but by some error of judgment, of the number of those in the enjoyment of great reputation and prosperity; e.g. Oedipus, Thyestes, and the men of note of similar families. The perfect Plot, accordingly, must have a single, and not (as some tell us) a double issue; the change in the hero's fortunes must be not from misery to happiness, but on the contrary from happiness to misery; and the cause of it must lie not in any depravity, but in some great error on his part; the man himself being either such as we have described, or better, not worse, than that. Fact also confirms our theory. Though the poets began by accepting any tragic story that came to hand, in these days the finest tragedies are always on the story of some few houses, on that of Alcmeon, Oedipus, Orestes, Meleager, Thyestes, Telephus, or any others that may have been involved, as either agents or sufferers, in some deed of horror. The theoretically best tragedy, then, has a Plot of this description. The critics, therefore, are wrong who blame Euripides for taking this line in his tragedies, and giving many of them an unhappy ending. It is, as we have said, the right line to take. The best proof of this: on the stage, and in the public performances, such plays, properly worked out, are seen to be the most truly tragic; and Euripides, even if his execution be faulty in every other point, is seen to be nevertheless the most tragic certainly of the dramatists. After this comes the construction of Plot which some rank first, one with a double story (like the *Odyssey*) and an opposite issue for the good and the bad personages. It is ranked as first only through the weakness of the audiences; the poets merely follow their public, writing as its wishes dictate. But the pleasure here is not that of Tragedy. It belongs rather to Comedy, where the bitterest enemies in the piece (e.g. Orestes and Aegisthus) walk off good friends at the end, with no slaying of any one by any one.

The tragic fear and pity may be aroused by the Spectacle; but they may also be aroused by the very structure and incidents of the play—which is the better way and shows the better poet. The Plot in fact should be so framed that, even without seeing the things take place, he who simply hears the account of them shall be filled with horror and pity at the incidents; which is just the effect that the mere recital of the story in *Oedipus* would have on one. To produce this same effect by means of the Spectacle is less artistic, and requires extraneous aid. Those, however, who make use of the Spectacle to put before us that which is merely monstrous and not productive of fear, are wholly out of touch with Tragedy; not every kind of pleasure should be required of a tragedy, but only its own proper pleasure.

The tragic pleasure is that of pity and fear, and the poet has to produce it by a work of imitation; it is clear, therefore, that the causes should be included in the incidents of his story. Let us see, then, what kinds of incident strike one as horrible, or rather as piteous. In a deed of this description the parties must necessarily be either friends, or enemies, or indifferent to one another. Now when enemy does it on enemy, there is nothing to move us to pity either in his doing or in his meditating the deed, except so far as the actual pain of the sufferer is concerned; and the same is true when the parties are indifferent to one another. Whenever the tragic deed, however, is done within the family—when murder or the like is done or meditated by brother on brother, by son on father, by mother on son, or son on mother—these are the situations the poet should seek after.

Study Questions

1. Would you agree with Aristotle that the best kind of dramatic fiction involves an ordinary man who experiences misfortune because of an error in judgment? Think of modern films and novels that might fit this pattern (involving ordinary men *and* women). How about *American Beauty?* Brecht's *Mother Courage?* *Million Dollar Baby?* *East of Eden?*

2. What is "catharsis of emotions"? Do you agree with Aristotle that it can be obtained by experiencing dramatic fiction?

3. As we have seen, Plato disapproves of a dramatic story, whereas Aristotle approves of it. In view of the fact that Plato wrote in quite a dramatic way about the downfall of Socrates (see Chapter 8), do you think Aristotle would have viewed Plato's story as an example of cathartic literature?

4. Aristotle says a good tragedy shouldn't need any "Spectacle" if the story is enough to make people shudder with fear and pity. In the *Poetics* he defines it as the actual, physical appearance of actors on the stage, but as you see in this excerpt he also specifies that the Spectacle is unnecessary if the audience can imagine the situation through a good narration on stage. We could perhaps take that to mean a good dramatic performance doesn't need any exaggerated display or special effects to get its point across. Can you think of movies that have been extremely vivid even with very few special effects, because they rely on our minds to fill in the gaps with our own visions of horror? Are there movies whose impact has been completely dependent on special effects? Does that detract from the story?

 Primary Reading

The Name of the Rose

UMBERTO ECO

Novel, 1980. Translated by William Weaver. Excerpt.

Usually we do not present a work of fiction as a Primary Reading, but this exception relates to the Aristotle text you have just read. Aristotle's *Poetics* consisted of two books, one on tragedy, and the other on comedy, but the latter has been lost since before the Middle Ages. We know, however, that Aristotle admired the theater, and that book would probably have paralleled his book on tragedy, outlining the proper plot type for a good comedy and so forth. The novel *The Name of the Rose,* by the Italian philosopher and novelist Umberto Eco, is a murder mystery set in the High Middle Ages. It features the resurfacing of a copy of Aristotle's book on comedy, and speculates that if a work by Aristotle had been available in those days that legitimized comedy and laughter, Western culture might have developed differently. It was made into a movie with Sean Connery as the monk/detective William of Baskerville—a literary reference that isn't lost on anyone who is a fan of Arthur Conan Doyle's Sherlock Holmes stories, because one of the most famous stories of the British private detective is the one called *The Hound of the Baskervilles*. Here William of Baskerville is visiting the monastery where serial killings are taking place, accompanied by his trusty young helper Adsel, the narrator of the story. William is getting close to solving the crimes and reads here from the long-lost book by Aristotle on comedy (written by Eco to resemble Aristotle's style, because the book, as you know, has never been found). After the quote from Aristotle, William has a passionate discussion with the blind librarian Jorge about the effects of laughter, and it becomes clear that Jorge is responsible for hiding the book from the other monks—among other things.

In the first book we dealt with tragedy and saw how, by arousing pity and fear, it produces catharsis, the purification of those feelings. As we promised, we will now deal with comedy (as well as with satire and mime) and see how, in inspiring the pleasure of the ridiculous, it arrives at the purification of that passion. That such passion is most worthy of consideration we have already said in the book on the soul, inasmuch as—alone among the animals—man is capable of laughter. We will then define the type of actions of which comedy is the mimesis, then we will examine the means by which comedy excites laughter, and these means and actions and speech. We will show how the ridiculousness of actions is born from the likening of the best to the worst and vice versa, from arousing surprise through deceit, from the impossible, from violation of the laws of nature, from the irrelevant and the inconsequent, from the debasing of the characters, from the use of comical and vulgar pantomime, from disharmony, from the choice of the least worthy things. We will then show how the ridiculousness of speech is born from the misunderstandings of similar words for different things and different words for similar things, from garrulity and repetition, from play on words, from diminutives, from errors of pronunciation, and from barbarisms. . . .

"But now tell me," William was saying, "Why? Why did you want to shield this book more than so many others? Why did you hide—though not at the price of crime—treatises on necromancy, pages that may have blasphemed against the name of God, while for these pages you damned your brothers and have damned yourself? There are many other books that speak of comedy, many others that praise laughter. Why did this one fill you with such fear?"

"Because it was by the Philosopher. Every book by that man has destroyed a part of the learning that Christianity had accumulated over the centuries. . . ."

"But what frightened you in this discussion of laughter? You cannot eliminate laughter by eliminating the book."

"No, to be sure. But laughter is weakness, corruption, the foolishness of our flesh. It is the peasant's entertainment, the drunkard's license; even the church in her wisdom has granted the moment of feast, carnival, fair, this diurnal pollution that releases humors and distracts from other desires and other ambitions. . . . Still, laughter remains base, a defense for the simple, a mystery desecrated for the plebeians. The apostle also said as much: it is better to marry than to burn. Rather than rebel against God's established order, laugh and enjoy your foul parodies of order, at the end of the meal, after you have drained jugs and flasks. Elect the king of fools, lose yourselves in the liturgy of the ass and the pig, play at performing your saturnalia head down. . . . But here, here"—now Jorge struck the table with his finger, near the book William was holding open—"here the function of laughter is reversed, it is elevated to art, the doors of the world of the learned are opened to it, it becomes the object of philosophy, and of perfidious theology. . . . That laughter is proper to man is a sign of our limitation, sinners that we are. But from this book many corrupt minds like yours would draw the extreme syllogism, whereby laughter is man's end! Laughter, for a few moments, distracts the villein from fear. But law is imposed by fear, whose true name is fear of God. This book could strike the Luciferine spark that would set a new fire to the whole world, and laughter would be defined as the new art, unknown even to Prometheus, for canceling fear. To the villein who laughs, at that moment, dying does not matter: but then, when the license is past, the liturgy again imposes on him, according to the divine plan, the fear of death. And from this book there could be born the new destructive aim to destroy death through redemption from fear.

Study Questions

1. Compare the real Aristotle text on tragedy and Eco's pastiche (attempt at writing something similar). Has Eco done a good job, in your view?

2. Compare Plato's view on comedy and laughter with what Eco believes to have been Aristotle's view. Which comes closer to your opinion? Explain why. (Also, whom do you think Eco would side with: Plato or Aristotle?)

3. Is Jorge right that law is imposed by fear of God, and laughter is a distraction from fear, so laughter is dangerous? Compare Jorge's and Plato's comments on laughter. (Remember that Jorge is a fictional character.)

4. Could Eco be right that if Aristotle's book had survived, it might have changed the course of Western culture? Why or why not?

Primary Reading

The Simple Art of Murder

RAYMOND CHANDLER

Excerpt from an article in the **Atlantic Monthly, November 1945.**

Raymond Chandler (1888–1959) is considered one of the all-time great American authors of detective/crime/suspense fiction. His style is straightforward and "hard-boiled," but his main characters are rarely one-dimensional, and we get to know not only their façades but also their innermost feelings. His stories usually take place in Los Angeles in the 1930s and 1940s, and have set the pattern for countless other detective/crime stories. His primary character, Philip Marlowe, is a private detective, with a love-hate relationship with the LAPD. In 1945 Chandler wrote a nonfiction piece for *Atlantic Monthly* that was to become a classic: "The Simple Art of Murder," primarily about his colleague, the crime-fiction writer Dashiell Hammett (the author of the classic

The Maltese Falcon). Chandler's own best works include *The Big Sleep* and *The Long Good-bye,* and his novels have been made into movies, sometimes more than once. This excerpt from "The Simple Art of Murder" contains his analysis of the most compelling kind of detective story, and of the character of the detective.

. . . The realist in murder writes of a world in which gangsters can rule nations and almost rule cities, in which hotels and apartment houses and celebrated restaurants are owned by men who made their money out of brothels, in which a screen star can be the fingerman for a mob, and the nice man down the hall is a boss of the numbers racket; a world where a judge with a cellar full of bootleg liquor can send a man to jail for having a pint in his pocket, where the mayor of your town may have condoned murder as an instrument of moneymaking, where no man can walk down a dark street in safety because law and order are things we talk about but refrain from practicing; a world where you may witness a hold-up in broad daylight and see who did it, but you will fade quickly back into the crowd rather than tell anyone, because the hold-up men may have friends with long guns, or the police may not like your testimony, and in any case the shyster for the defense will be allowed to abuse and vilify you in open court, before a jury of selected morons, without any but the most perfunctory interference from a political judge.

It is not a very fragrant world, but it is the world you live in, and certain writers with tough minds and a cool spirit of detachment can make very interesting and even amusing patterns out of it. It is not funny that a man should be killed, but it is sometimes funny that he should be killed for so little, and that his death should be the coin of what we call civilization. All this still is not quite enough.

In everything that can be called art there is a quality of redemption. It may be pure tragedy, if it is high tragedy, and it may be pity and irony, and it may be the raucous laughter of the strong man. But down these mean streets a man must go who is not himself mean, who is neither tarnished nor afraid. The detective in this kind of story must be such a man. He is the hero, he is everything. He must be a complete man and a common man and yet an unusual man. He must be, to use a rather weathered phrase, a man of honor, by instinct, by inevitability, without thought of it, and certainly without saying it. He must be the best man in his world and a good enough man for any world. I do not care much about his private life; he is neither a eunuch nor a satyr; I think he might seduce a duchess and I am quite sure he would not spoil a virgin; if he is a man of honor in one thing, he is that in all things. He is a relatively poor man, or he would not be a detective at all. He is a common man or he could not go among common people. He has a sense of character, or he would not know his job. He will take no man's money dishonestly and no man's insolence without a due and dispassionate revenge. He is a lonely man and his pride is that you will treat him as a proud man or be very sorry you ever saw him. He talks as the man of his age talks, that is, with rude wit, a lively sense of the grotesque, a disgust for sham, and a contempt for pettiness. The story is his adventure in search of a hidden truth, and it would be no adventure if it did not happen to a man fit for adventure. He has a range of awareness that startles you, but it belongs to him by right, because it belongs to the world he lives in.

If there were enough like him, I think the world would be a very safe place to live in, and yet not too dull to be worth living in.

Study Questions

1. Chandler writes about the writer of crime/detective stories of the mid–twentieth century. "Cop shows" are the most frequent kind of television shows these days, and have been for decades. Do you think his analysis holds true even today, or have the major themes in crime and suspense stories changed?

2. What does Chandler's analysis of the detective say about Chandler's view of moral values? Would you agree that the detective in a crime story (either a police detective or a private investigator) has to have those qualities, or are we looking for a different kind of hero today?

3. Could you imagine this description of the heroic detective applied to a female detective? Why or why not?

4. Compare this analysis of a good dramatic crime story with Aristotle's template for a good tragedy. Do you see any similarities?

 Narrative

Medea

EURIPIDES

From a fifth-century-B.C.E. play. Translated by Moses Hadas. Summary and Excerpts.

The Greek dramatist Euripides (ca. 485–406 B.C.E.) was considered an eccentric and an intellectual radical. Nineteen of his eighty-eight plays have survived into modern times. In fifth-century B.C.E. Athens, the annual festival held for Dionysus had developed into an established tradition of competitions among playwrights of tragedies, satyr plays, and comedies. Although the tragedies were originally supposed to deal with the life, death, and resurrection of the god Dionysus (Bacchus) and stories of the gods in general, they quickly developed into stories about human failings and revenge. The tragedy *Medea,* written in 451 B.C.E., is unusual in that it doesn't follow the established tragic pattern of the triumph of divine justice; but Euripides rarely followed the established patterns of tragedies. He won only four first prizes at the festivals in his lifetime, but after his death his plays became immensely popular. Toward the end of his life he left Athens; he died in Macedonia (where Aristotle was born in 384 B.C.E., twenty-two years later). In the preceding excerpt from Aristotle's *Poetics,* you may have noticed that Aristotle specifically praises Euripides and his unique style.

Greek mythology tells of Jason and his Argonauts, who captured the Golden Fleece from the king of Colchis and brought it back to Corinth in triumph. That is a heroic story, one of Greece's legends of the golden age. Jason was helped in his quest by the daughter of the king of Colchis, Medea, who betrayed her father, her brother, and her country to help Jason, the man she loved. So Medea followed him to Corinth. That was the old myth—and Euripides tells us "the rest of the story."

Years have passed, and Medea is in a deep depression. She won't eat, she can't sleep, she weeps incessantly. Jason has tired of her—she is no longer young, and Jason has fallen in love with another woman, the young blonde princess of Corinth. He has taken her as his second wife without so much as asking Medea's permission. Now the king, the princess's father, is about to banish Medea from the kingdom, together with her and Jason's two sons, because he fears that this woman, an unpredictable foreigner, may take revenge on his daughter. But Medea cannot go home because she caused her brother's death and betrayed her father in helping Jason. She forsook everything for him, including her ties to her homeland, and, without a homeland, one was barely considered a person in the ancient Greek world.

It's all over, my friends; I would gladly die. Life has lost its savor. The man who was everything to me, well he knows it, has turned out to be the basest of men. Of all creatures that feel and think, we women are the unhappiest species. In the first place, we must pay a great dowry to a husband who will be the tyrant of our bodies (that's a further aggravation of the evil); and there is another fearful hazard: whether we shall get a good man or a bad. For separations bring disgrace on the woman and it is not possible to renounce one's husband. Then, landed among strange habits and regulations unheard of in her own home, a woman needs second sight to know how best to handle her bedmate. And if we manage this well and have a husband who does not find the yoke of intercourse too galling, ours is a life to be envied. Otherwise, one is better dead. When the man wearies of the company of his wife, he goes outdoors and relieves the disgust of his heart [having recourse to some friend or the companions of his own age], but we women have only one person to turn to.

They say that we have a safe life at home, whereas men must go to war. Nonsense! I had rather fight three battles than bear one child. But be that as it may, you and I are not in the same case. You have your city here, your paternal homes; you know the delights of life and association with your loved ones. But I, homeless and forsaken, carried off from a foreign land, am being wronged by a husband, with neither mother nor brother nor kinsman with whom I might find refuge from the storms of misfortune. One little boon I crave of you, if I discover any ways and means of punishing my husband for these wrongs: your silence. Woman in most respects is a timid creature, with no heart for strife and aghast at the sight of steel; but wronged in love, there is no heart more murderous than hers.

But Medea has a plan, and the old king has seen it coming with a sure instinct: Medea plots to poison both the princess and the king. She has one last, horrible argument with Jason, who comes to make sure she won't be destitute, because he has heard that she has been expelled from the country:

Rotten, heart-rotten, that is the word for you. Words, words, magnificent words. In reality a craven. You come to me, you come, my worst enemy! This isn't bravery, you know, this isn't valor, to come and face your victims. No! it's the ugliest sore on the face of humanity, Shamelessness. But I thank you for coming. It will lighten the weight on my heart to tell your wickedness, and it will hurt you to hear it. I shall begin my tale at the very beginning.

I saved your life, as all know who embarked with you on the Argo, when you were sent to master with the yoke the fire-breathing bulls and to sow with dragon's teeth that acre of death. The dragon, too, with wreathed coils, that kept safe watch over the Golden Fleece and never slept—I slew it and raised for you the light of life again. Then, forsaking my father and my own dear ones, I came to Iolcus where Pelias reigned, came with you, more than fond and less than wise. On Pelias too I brought death, the most painful death there is, at the hands of his own children. Thus I have removed every danger from your path.

And after all those benefits at my hands, you basest of men, you have betrayed me and made a new marriage, though I have borne you children. If you were still childless, I could have understood this love of yours for a new wife. Gone now is all reliance on pledges. You puzzle me. Do you believe that the gods of the old days are no longer in office? Do you think that men are now living under a new dispensation? For surely you know that you have broken all your oaths to me. Ah my hand, which you so often grasped, and oh my knees, how all for nothing have we been defiled by this false man, who has disappointed all our hopes.

Jason and Medea part with bitter words, and now Medea is in luck: King Aegeus of Athens pays her a visit and hears of her marital problems and banishment. He finds Jason despicable and admires Medea for her righteous anger. He himself is looking for a wife to bear him children and offers Medea a refuge as his wife as soon as she is "done with her business."

Medea now pretends to be submissive when Jason comes back and asks that the children be allowed to take gifts to his young bride. The enormity of what she is about to do is beginning to envelop her, and she finds it hard to control herself. After Jason leaves, she hands the gifts to the two young boys and can't stop weeping—because she not only plans to kill the princess but also plans to *kill her own children,* to hurt Jason the only way she knows how:

O the pain of it! Why do your eyes look at me, my children? Why smile at me that last smile? Ah! What can I do? My heart is water, women, at the sight of my children's bright faces. I could never do it. Goodbye to my former plans. I shall take my children away with me. Why should I hurt their father by *their* misfortunes, only to reap a double harvest of sorrow myself? No! I cannot do it. Goodbye to my plans.

And yet . . . what is the matter with me? Do I want to make myself a laughing-stock by letting my enemies off scot-free? I must go through with it. What a coward heart is mine, to admit those soft pleas. Come, my children, into the palace. Those that may not attend my sacrifices can see to it that they are absent. I shall not let my hand be unnerved.

Ah! Ah! Stop, my heart. Do not you commit this crime. Leave them alone, unhappy one, spare the children. Even if they live far from us, they will bring you joy. No! by the unforgetting dead in hell, it cannot be! I shall not leave my children for my enemies to insult. (In any case they must die. And if die they must, *I* shall slay them, who gave them birth.) My schemes are crowned with success. She shall not escape. Already the diadem is on her head; wrapped in the robe the royal bride is dying. I know it well. And now I am setting out on a most sorrowful road (and shall send these on one still more sorrowful). I wish to speak to my children. Give your mother your hands, my children, give her your hands to kiss.

O dear, dear hand. O dear, dear mouth, dear shapes, dear noble faces, happiness be yours, but not here. Your father has stolen this world from you. How sweet to touch! The softness of their skin, the sweetness of their breath, my babies! Away, away, I cannot bear to see you any longer.

[CHILDREN *retire within.*]

My misery overwhelms me. O I *do* realize how terrible is the crime I am about, but passion overrules my resolutions, passion that causes most of the misery in the world.

She sends the children away, and after a while, a messenger tells the gruesome details: The princess put on the golden diadem, Medea's gift, and instantly the poison began to work:

> The golden diadem on her head emitted a strange flow of devouring fire, while the fine robes, the gifts of your children, were eating up the poor girl's white flesh. All aflame, she jumps from her seat and flees, shaking her head and hair this way and that, trying to throw off the crown. But the golden band held firmly, and after she had shaken her hair more violently, the fire began to blaze twice as fiercely. Overcome by the agony she falls on the ground, and none but her father could have recognized her. The position of her eyes could not be distinguished, nor the beauty of her face. The blood, clotted with fire, dripped from the crown of her head, and the flesh melted from her bones, like resin from a pine tree, as the poisons ate their unseen way. It was a fearful sight. All were afraid to touch the corpse, taught by what had happened to her.

The princess's old father rushed to the scene and took her in his arms, and that was how the poison spread to him; within minutes he, too, was dead.

The news galvanizes Medea into action: Now she feels she must kill her children so nobody will take their revenge on them, and she rationalizes,

> No flinching now, no thinking of the children, the darling children, that call you mother. This day, this one short day, forget your children. You have all the future to mourn them. Aye, to mourn. Though you mean to kill them, at least you loved them. Oh! I am a most unhappy woman.

From inside the room, we hear the cries for help as she stabs her two sons to death.

Jason returns, devastated at the turn of events. Medea gloats because now she knows she's "got under his skin." To the end, they quarrel over whose fault it is and who is to blame for the children's death. Jason didn't seem to care much for his sons while they were alive, but now that they are dead he loves them with all his heart. He invokes the power of the gods to avenge his children—but the gods don't help him. No divine lightning bolt strikes Medea down—she leaves him to become the wife of Aegeus.

Study Questions

1. This tragedy seemed nothing short of immoral to many critics in Athens because Medea gets away with quadruple murder. Can we defend Medea's actions in any way? Is Jason free of blame? What do you think Euripides intended the "moral of the story" to be?

2. How would Plato evaluate *Medea*—as a moral learning tool or a dangerous temptation to be irrational? How would Aristotle evaluate it? Does it meet his criteria for a well-written tragedy? (Tragedy has to happen to ordinary people as the result of some grave error in judgment of theirs and preferably should happen between family members.) In other words, if Aristotle is right and a good tragedy is the story of an ordinary person—not good, not bad—who makes a major mistake and suffers for it for the rest

of his or her life, then who is the main character in *Medea*? From whose viewpoint is the story told? Medea's—or Jason's?

3. Sadly, the phenomenon of parents killing their children is not unusual at all; it may be done in anger, or for insurance purposes, for convenience, or out of some peculiar sense of responsibility ("I won't allow my children to become fatherless/motherless when I kill myself, so I'll take them with me"). Rarely is it done for revenge, as in the case of Medea. Susan Smith, who in 1994 strapped her two little boys in a car and let it roll into a lake, killing both of them, wanted to be unencumbered so her former boyfriend would come back to her. Andrea Yates, who drowned her five children in 2001, was diagnosed as suffering from severe postpartum depression and said she heard voices telling her to take their lives. But one murder case seems like a true Medea scenario: Susan Eubanks killed her four sons in 1998 specifically to get back at their fathers. Now remember that in the play, Medea isn't punished; she leaves for a new life as the queen of Athens. How do you feel about that, considering that Smith is serving a life sentence, and Eubanks is on death row? (Yates's life sentence was overturned and in 2006 she was found not guilty by reason of insanity and committed to a mental institution.)

Narrative

The Sorrows of Young Werther

JOHANN WOLFGANG VON GOETHE

Novel, 1774. Translated by Elizabeth Mayer and Louise Bogan. Excerpt.

The hypnotic power of Goethe's book about young lovesick Werther may be hard to imagine today, but the fact remains that many young readers in Europe took their own lives after suffering along with Werther. Goethe presented the story as though he had found Werther's letters to a friend and then told about the final days in narrative form. From May to December, Werther undergoes all the highs and lows of falling in love, but in the end his beloved Lotte marries someone else. Shortly after writing this letter to his friend Wilhelm, Werther takes his pistol and shoots himself in the head.

December 4

I beg you—you see I am done for; I cannot bear it any longer. Today I sat near her as she played the clavichord, all sorts of tunes and with so much expression. So much! So much! What could I do? Her little sister sat on my knee and dressed her doll. Tears came into my eyes. I bowed my head and caught sight of her wedding ring. The tears ran down my cheek—and suddenly Lotte began to play the heavenly old melody. All at once my soul was touched by a feeling of consolation, by a memory of the past, of the other occasions when I had heard the song, of the dark intervals of vexation between, of shattered hopes, and then—I walked up and down the room, my heart almost suffocated by the rush of emotions. "For God's sake," I said, in a vehement outburst, "for God's sake, stop!" She paused and looked at me steadily. "Werther," she said with a smile that went deep to my heart, "Werther, you are very sick. You dislike the things you once liked. Go! I beg you, calm yourself!" I tore myself from her sight, and—God! You see my misery and will put an end to it.

Study Questions

1. Evaluate Werther's reaction from your own point of view: Is suicide because of rejection a realistic scenario? Is it emotionally understandable? Is it morally defensible? Explain your viewpoint.

2. Apply Plato's and Aristotle's views to this excerpt.

3. Can you think of stories (movies or other media) that have had a similar effect on the audience in recent years? If so, do you think something should be done to prevent such influence in the future? Explain your viewpoint.

4. Goethe gives the story credibility by pretending that he found these letters of Werther's (although he of course made the whole story up, including the character of Werther himself). The format of letting a story unfold within a frame of a letter, or an ancient manuscript in the loft, or a videotape, lives on because it is such a good way to lend credence to the story. This format was used in the 1990s in the popular film *The Blair Witch Project,* and recently in the film *Cloverfield,* to make the films look like documentaries. Can you think of other stories—novels or films—that use the same trick?

$\mathcal{N}$*arrative*

The Education of Mingo

CHARLES JOHNSON

Short story from The Sorcerer's Apprentice, 1977. Summary and Excerpt.

The story of Mingo's "education" is a golem tale—not about an artificially created person, but about a human being whose mind becomes a mirror of the subconscious drives of his "master." We can read this story as an indictment of slavery in the old South, about an unusual relationship between a slave and his master—about affectional bonding and moral responsibility. Or we can read it as a story of a creator losing control over his creation. Or we can read it as a psychological story of what really goes on in the mind of old Moses. But we can also read it as a tale about the dangers of teaching! You never know what the student gets out of your lessons . . .

Old Moses Green drives his one-horse rig into town and buys himself a slave; we're in the antebellum South, in 1854. The slave that Moses buys, Mingo, is new to the New World, a prince of the Allmuseri tribe, according to the auctioneer. Moses doesn't need a farmhand as much as a companion, because he is a lonely man. But Mingo speaks no English and knows no social customs other than his tribal ways, so Moses sets out to teach him everything: the English language, farming, table manners, ciphering, cooking, and so forth.

Charles Johnson has a Ph.D. in philosophy, and teaches literature at University of Washington. He is the author of four novels, *Faith and the Good Thing* (1974), *Oxherding Tale* (1982), *Middle Passage* (1990), and *Dreamer* (1998); two collections of short stories, *The Sorcerer's Apprentice* (1986) and *Soulcatcher and Other Stories* (2001); over twenty screenplays; and numerous articles and books on the African American experience. His works have won many awards, including the 1990 National Book Award for *Middle Passage*.

He felt, late at night when he looked down at Mingo snoring loudly on his corn-shuck mattress, now like a father, now like an artist fingering something fine and noble from a rude clump of foreign clay.

But he soon discovers that Mingo, who is a fast learner, picks up not only on what Moses teaches him intentionally but also on what Moses himself does on his own time, such as swearing, dunking cornbread in his coffee, and other bad habits. He copies even Moses' mannerisms and way of being. Within a year, Mingo has become a shadow of Moses—acting out not only what Moses wants him to do but also what Moses himself would subconsciously like to do.

Moses' lady friend, Harriet Bridgewater, has a wry wisdom of her own, and Moses is a little bit afraid of her. She is highly critical of his project of educating Mingo and tries to make Moses understand that he is bound to fail; Mingo's background is too different. Moses argues that Mingo is doing fine and has become a sort of extension of himself—except for one thing: Mingo is supposed to treat strangers with respect, and kill chicken hawks. But Moses has observed Mingo treating chicken hawks as if they were human, and calling them "Sir." So how deep does this mix-up go? Soon Moses discovers the horrible truth: Mingo has killed old Isaiah Jenson—because Mingo has picked up on Moses' stray remarks about what an old fool Isaiah is. And since Mingo believes that he is supposed to act the way Moses *wants to act*, he kills old Isaiah. This is the moment of realization for Moses: His attempt to teach Mingo everything he knows and, in effect, create a person in his own image has failed—or it has worked too well:

"You idjet!" hooted Moses. His jaw clamped shut. He wept hoarsely for a few minutes like a steer with the strangles. "Isaiah Jenson and me was friends, and—" He checked himself; what'd he said was a lie. They weren't friends at all. In fact, he thought Isaiah Jenson was a pigheaded fool and only tolerated the little yimp in a neighborly way. Into his eye a fly bounded. Moses shook his head wildly. He'd even sworn to Harriet, weeks earlier, that Jenson was so troublesome, always borrowing tools and keeping them, he hoped he'd go to Ballyhack on a red-hot rail. In his throat a knot tightened. One of his eyelids jittered up, still itchy from the fly; he forced it down with his finger, then gave a slow look at the African. "Great Peter," he mumbled. "You couldn'ta known that."

"Go home now?" Mingo stretched out the stiffness in his spine. "Powerful tired, boss."

Not because he wanted to go home did Moses leave, but because he was afraid of Isaiah's body and needed time to think things through. Dry the air, dry the evening down the road that led them home. As if to himself, the old man grumped, "I gave you thought and tongue, and looka what you done with it—they gonna catch and kill you, boy, just as sure as I'm sitting heah."

"Mingo?" The African shook his long head, sly; he touched his chest with one finger. "*Me?* Nossuh."

"Why the hell you keep saying that?" Moses threw his jaw forward so violently muscles in his neck stood out. "You kilt a man, and they gonna burn you crisper than an ear of corn. Ay, God, Mingo," moaned the old man, "you gotta act responsible, son!" At the thought of what they'd do to Mingo, Moses scrooched the stalk of his head into his stiff collar. He drilled his gaze at the smooth-faced African, careful not to look him in the eye, and barked, "What're you thinking *now*?"

"What Mingo know, Massa Green know. Bees like *what* Mingo sees or don't see is only what Massa Green taught him to see or don't see. Like Mingo lives through Massa Green, right?"

Moses waited, suspicious, smelling a trap. "Yeah, all that's true."

"Massa Green, he owns Mingo, right?"

"Right," snorted Moses. He rubbed the knob of his red, porous nose. "Paid good money—"

"So when Mingo works, it bees Massa Green workin', right? Bees Massa Green workin', thinkin', doin' *through* Mingo—ain't that so?"

Nobody's fool, Moses Green could latch onto a notion with no trouble at all; he turned violently off the road leading to his cabin, and plowed on toward Harriet's, pouring sweat, remembering two night visions he'd had, recurrent, where he and Mingo were wired together like say two ventriloquist's dummies, one black, one white, and there was somebody—who he didn't know, yanking their arm and leg strings simultaneously—how he couldn't figure, but he and Mingo said the same thing together until his liver-spotted hands, the knuckles tight and shriveled like old carrot skin, flew up to his face and, shrieking, he started hauling hips across a cold black countryside. But so did Mingo, *his* hands on *his* face, pumping his knees right alongside Moses, shrieking, their voice inflections identical; and then the hazy dream doorwayed luxuriously into another where he was greaved on one half of a thrip—a coin halfway between a nickel and a dime—and on the reverse side was Mingo. Shaking, Moses pulled his rig into Harriet Bridgewater's yard. His bowels, burning, felt like boiling tar. She was standing on her porch in a checkered Indian shawl, staring at them, her book still open, when Moses scrambled, tripping, skinning his knees, up her steps. He shouted, "Harriet, this boy done kilt Isaiah Jenson in cold blood." She lost color and wilted back into her doorway. Her hair was swinging in her eyes. Hands flying, he stammered in a flurry of anxiety, "But it wasn't altogether Mingo's fault—he didn't know what he was doin'."

"Isaiah? You mean Izay-yah? He didn't kill Izay-yah?"

"Yeah, aw no! Not really—" His mind stuttered to a stop.

"Whose fault is it then?" Harriet gawked at the African picking his nose in the wagon (Moses had, it's true, not policed himself as well as he'd wanted). A shiver quaked slowly up her left side. She sloughed off her confusion, and flashed, "I can tell you whose fault it is, Moses. Yours! Didn't I say not to bring that wild African here? Huh? Huh? Huh? You both should be—put to sleep."

"Aw, woman! Hesh up!" Moses threw down his hat and stomped it out of shape. "You just all upsetted." Truth to tell, he was not the portrait of composure himself. There were rims of dirt in his nails. His trouser legs had blood splattered on them. Moses stamped his feet to shake road powder off his boots. "You got any spirits in the house? I need your he'p to untangle this thing, but I ain't hardly touched a drop since I bought Mingo, and my throat's pretty dr—"

"You'll just have to get it yourself—on the top shelf of the cupboard." She touched her face, fingers spread, with a dazed gesture. There was suddenly in her features the intensity found in the look of people who have a year, a month, a minute only to live. "I think I'd better sit down." Lowering herself onto her rocker, she cradled on her lap a volume by one M. Shelley, a recent tale of monstrosity and existential horror, then she demurely settled her breasts. "It's just like you, Moses Green, to bring all your bewilderments to me."

So Harriet is no help. Moses goes off to ponder the situation. He can't turn the boy in, because that would be like turning part of himself in; and any way he looks at it, he and Mingo have become part of each other. But he realizes that the person he needs now is Harriet, and he returns to her farm to ask her to marry him—only to find, to his horror, that in the meantime, Mingo has committed another murder. Harriet herself lies dead over by the water pump—Mingo has responded to a stray remark from Moses the day before, about Harriet's being a talkative old hen.

This is the moment of truth for Moses: Whatever Mingo has done, he, Moses, bears the responsibility. He finds Mingo and forces him down on the ground while he goes into Harriet's house and retrieves her flintlock rifle. Holding the barrel against Mingo's neck, he cocks the hammer—but he can't shoot:

Eyes narrowed to slits, Moses said—a dry whisper—"get up, you damned fool." He let his round shoulders slump. Mingo let his broad shoulders slump. "Take the horses," Moses said; he pulled himself up to his rig, then sat, his knees together beside the boy. Mingo's knees drew together. Moses's voice changed. It began to rasp and wheeze; so did Mingo's. "Missouri," said the old man, not to Mingo but to the dusty floor of the buckboard, "if I don't misremember, is off thataway somewheres in the west."

Study Questions

1. Does the ending of the story indicate that Moses takes responsibility for how he has trained Mingo, or does he refuse to take responsibility? Explain. Does it make any difference? How is this story an indictment of the institution of slavery?

2. How does Johnson show us that Mingo has become Moses' *alter ego*?

3. Is Mingo a golem? Is he a Frankenstein's monster? Is he a Pygmalion's statue? Is he "Mr. Hyde" to Moses' "Dr. Jekyll"? Or is he perhaps a Pinocchio? Explain the similarities and the differences.

4. What is the significance of the book Harriet holds in her lap moments before she dies?

5. Can you think of other stories in which a moral lesson is misunderstood or taken too literally, to the detriment of the characters in the story?

Narrative

Pulp Fiction

QUENTIN TARANTINO (DIRECTOR AND SCREENWRITER)

Screenplay, 1994. Film, 1994. Summary and Excerpt.

In this summary (with a short excerpt)* we focus on one aspect of a complex story. *Pulp Fiction,* which shocked its first audiences with its graphic violence and strong language, has now acquired the status of an instant classic, often referred to in educational contexts precisely because of its casual attitude toward death and violence—up to a point. Here we look at the point where violence suddenly seems to have lost its appeal for one of the main characters, Jules.

Jules and Vincent have had a rough morning. Hit men for a mobster, they have just murdered two young men, with Jules quoting a passage supposedly from Ezekiel, but heavily embroidered with Jules's own words of doom, to them before he kills them, as he usually does; it is his style. Completing the job, they retrieve a briefcase for their boss. What Jules and Vincent don't know is that another man is hiding in the bathroom. When he bursts out, emptying his Magnum at the two hit men, they fire back, and he dies—but neither Jules nor Vincent is hurt. Vincent wants to label it a stroke of good luck and get out of there, but Jules is profoundly shocked and sees it as something else: divine intervention.

Marvin, a young friend of Jules's who has helped him set up the hit, follows them out of the bloodstained apartment into their car; while Vincent is discussing the incident of the bullets that missed, his gun accidentally goes off and shoots the young man in the face. Terribly upset, Jules worries that they are now driving on the highway with a bloody car and a dead body—his concern is not for the untimely death of Marvin.

Later they are having breakfast in a coffee shop, coming down from the morning's events. Jules is still contemplating what he thinks of as a miracle, the fact that he wasn't killed, and he announces that he now considers himself retired from "the Life."

Something else is going on in the coffee shop. A young couple, Pumpkin and Honey Bunny, are now rising up out of a booth, pointing guns at the patrons and the waitresses: They are going to rob the place. Vincent has gone to the restroom and is unaware of the developments, but Jules witnesses the entire holdup. The young couple take the money from the cash register and move in to rob the patrons. When Pumpkin points his gun at Jules, he gives up his wallet but flatly refuses to hand over the briefcase. He lets Pumpkin

---

Author's note of caution: Please be advised that the excerpt from the screenplay (Jules's monologue) contains some profanity. Additional profanity has been omitted from the excerpt. The entire screenplay of *Pulp Fiction* uses vernacular speech laden with what many readers will consider vulgarities. In the film it may be said to serve an artistic purpose, giving the audience an immediate understanding of the underworld in which the story takes place and often providing a deliberate counterpoint to intellectual dialogue; however, excerpts from the screenplay may strike some readers as being offensive. I suggest that the issue of offensive language, in films as well as in everyday life, be part of the class discussion after reading the narrative, as indicated in study question 4.

Pulp Fiction (Miramax, 1994) appears to many people to glorify violence, but educators have discerned a deeper intention: a strong statement against violence. Here Honey Bunny (Amanda Plummer) and Pumpkin (Tim Roth) are preparing to rob the customers and staff of the diner.

look inside (we don't get to see the contents, only its mysterious glow), but that is as far as it goes. When Pumpkin points his gun at Jules, Jules quickly twists his arm, and now Pumpkin is the one staring into the gun. The girl attempts to help her lover but realizes that Jules will shoot if she moves. Now Vincent comes back to the table and takes in the situation. Together, Jules and Vincent keep the young couple under control, and Jules tells them that under normal circumstances they would both be dead now—but today he is in a "transitional period" and doesn't want to kill them. He instructs Pumpkin to go into the loot bag, fish out Jules's wallet, take out the cash, $1,500, and just go away. And he tells Pumpkin:

> Wanna know what I'm buying? …Your life. I'm giving you that money so I don't hafta kill your ass…. You read the Bible? …There's a passage I got memorized: Ezekiel 25:17. "The path of the righteous man is beset on all sides by the inequities of the selfish and the tyranny of evil men. Blessed is he who, in the name of charity and good will, shepherds the weak through the valley of the darkness. For he is truly his brother's keeper and the finder of lost children. And I will strike down upon thee with great vengeance and furious anger those who attempt to poison and destroy my brothers. And you will know I am the Lord when I lay my vengeance upon you." I been sayin' that shit for years. And if you ever heard it, it means your ass. I never really questioned what it meant. I thought it was just a coldblooded thing to say…. But I saw some shit this morning made me think twice. Now I'm thinkin'. It could mean you're the evil man. And I'm the righteous man. And Mr. .45 here he's the shepherd protecting my righteous ass in the valley of darkness.

Or it could be you're the righteous man and I'm the shepherd and it's the world that's evil and selfish. I'd like that. But that shit ain't the truth. The truth is you're weak. And I'm the tyranny of evil men. But I'm tryin'. I'm tryin' real hard to be a shepherd.

Jules lowers his gun and puts it on the table; Pumpkin looks at him, at Honey Bunny, at the $1,500 in his hand, and then he grabs the trash bag full of cash and wallets, and he and Honey Bunny walk out the door.

Study Questions

1. What does Jules mean by suggesting that he might be the "righteous man"? What does he mean by suggesting that he might be the shepherd?

2. What does Jules mean by saying that he is giving Honey Bunny and Pumpkin the money so he won't have to kill them?

3. What do you think is the point of talking about being "righteous" and "being evil," given that the scene we are witnessing is a confrontation between robbers and hit men?

4. If you have seen the film, you will know that the dialogue is laden with profanity (as is evident in the excerpt from Jules's monologue). Do you think the foul language serves a purpose in this context? Why or why not? You might want to discuss the issue of profanity in contemporary speech styles.

5. Do you believe this particular film might inspire more violence (as Plato would believe), or do you think that, in some way, it might serve as a "cleansing" experience (as Aristotle might say) or perhaps as a warning against wholesale cultural acceptance of violence?

6. You may have wondered what the briefcase contains. It is not revealed in the film, but rumor has it that it contains the soul of the gangster boss. Would such an interpretation make a difference to the story? Explain.

Chapter Three

Ethical Relativism

*O*n occasion we are forced to face this fact: Not everybody shares our idea of what constitutes decent behavior. You may wait at the movie theater for a friend who never shows up because she is on the phone with another friend and it doesn't occur to her that it is important to keep her date with you. Such actions usually can be dismissed as merely bad manners or callousness; still, you probably will not want to make plans with that person again. *Moral differences* can run deeper than that, however. Suppose you are dating someone to whom you feel very attracted. During dinner at a nice restaurant, your friend casually mentions that he or she supports a candidate or cause that you strongly oppose on moral grounds. The fact that your friend has a different idea about what constitutes moral behavior will probably affect the way you feel about him or her.

We regularly read and hear about actions that are morally unacceptable to us. A young foreign girl is killed by her brother because she is pregnant and unmarried or perhaps merely going out with an American boy. To the Western mind the brother's act is an unfathomable crime. But the brother believes he is only doing his duty, unpleasant as it may be; he is upholding the family honor, which the sister has tainted by her act of unspeakable immorality (according to the traditional code of his culture—hence the term *honor-killing*). The world is full of stories about people who feel duty-bound to do things others find repugnant. People in some cultures feel it is their moral obligation, or moral right, to dispose of their elderly citizens when they become unproductive. Pretechnological cultures, in particular, have a tradition during times when food is scarce of exposing their oldest members to the elements and leaving them to die. Often the decision rests with these older people, who feel morally obliged to remove themselves from the tribe when they believe it is time. Some cultures feel a moral right or duty to dispose of infants in the same way—usually cultures with no safe medical access to contraception. Other cultures believe it is a sin to seek medical assistance—they believe life should be left in the hands of God. Some people believe it is a sin to destroy any life, even by inadvertently stepping on an insect. Some people think they have a moral duty to defend themselves, their loved ones, and their country from any threat; others think it is their moral duty to refrain from resorting to violence under any circumstances.

In the days following the terrorist attacks of September 11, I was asked by many of my students how anyone could be so utterly devoid of morals that they would choose civilian targets, with no concern for the lives they were destroying. If ever there was a situation that brought home the challenge of dealing with moral differences, that was the one. As we have since learned, the al Qaeda code of ethics identified their actions as morally justified and even mandated. Since then, we have witnessed a number of what most of us would label atrocities by al Qaeda, directed against Americans and citizens of other nations, such as the beheadings of civilians in Iraq and the bombings of a nightclub in Bali and commuter trains in Madrid. In the great majority of cases, the victims have been civilians; and although Muslim leaders generally have denounced these terrorist acts and pointed out that civilians are not a legitimate target, Osama bin Laden and other al Qaeda leaders have pointed out in interviews that their moral code doesn't recognize the difference between combatants and noncombatants, between soldiers and civilians. (This difference is greatly emphasized in the Western concept of just war, which you can read about in Chapter 13.) So is each culture right in its own way, or is there some universal moral standard that al Qaeda just isn't living up to? or perhaps one that the West isn't living up to? The question was easier in the days when different cultural moral codes weren't costing lives, very publicly and on a regular basis, and it felt right and enlightened to be tolerant of quaint customs from far away; but now the credo of ethical relativism—there is no universal moral code, only different cultural morals—is up against the impression, shared by many who see the war against terrorism as stretching into the indefinite future, that we are fighting for the survival of our own culture and our own moral standards. It ups the ante and brings the discussion of ethical relativism to the forefront—no longer an enjoyable if abstract philosophical discussion but, rather, a passionate matter of standing up for what one believes in.

How to Deal with Moral Differences

How do we approach this phenomenon of moral differences? There are at least four major paths to choose.

   1. Moral Nihilism, Skepticism, and Subjectivism We may choose to believe that there are no morally right or wrong viewpoints—that the whole moral issue is a cultural game, and neither your opinion nor mine matters in the end, for there is no ultimate right or wrong. This view is called *moral nihilism,* and at various times in our lives, especially if we are facing personal disappointment, we may be inclined to take this approach. This is a difficult position to uphold, however, because it is so extreme. It is hard to remember, every minute of the day, that we don't believe there is any difference between right and wrong. If we see somebody steal our car, we are inclined to want the thief stopped, regardless of how much our jaded intellect tells us that no one is more right or wrong than anyone else. If we watch a child or an animal being abused, we feel like stepping in, even if we tell ourselves that there is no such thing as right or wrong. In other words, there seems to be something in most of us—instinct, or socialization, or reason, or compassion, or maybe something else altogether—that surfaces even when we try to persuade ourselves that moral values are but an illusion.

   Related to the attitude of moral nihilism is *moral skepticism,* which holds that we can't know whether there are any moral truths, and *moral subjectivism,* which holds that moral views are merely inner states in a person and that they can't be compared to the inner states of another person, so a moral viewpoint is valid only for the person who holds it. Both skepticism and subjectivism are more common than nihilism, but they seem to be equally difficult to adhere to in the long run, because at crucial times we all act *as if* there are valid moral truths that we share with others—we criticize a friend for being late, a politician for being a racist or a sexist, a colleague for the way she raises her children. We praise a stranger for coming to our aid when we are stuck on the freeway, we praise our kids when they come home on time—so it seems that even if we believe ourselves to be nihilists, skeptics, or subjectivists, we still expect to share some values with others of our own culture.

Although moral subjectivism generally seems a more flexible and appealing theory than categorical moral nihilism or moral skepticism—to the point that some thinkers choose to treat subjectivism as a subcategory of ethical relativism—the three theories have something in common that makes all of them less than successful: *They have no conflict-solving capacity*. How would you persuade the car thief to leave your car alone on moral grounds if you are a nihilist? a skeptic? or a subjectivist? In each case, you have given up on the idea of finding common moral ground. The best you can do is tell the car thief that he is behaving in an illegal fashion; you can't claim that you have a moral argument that he ought to listen to.

2. Ethical Relativism We may choose to believe that there is no universal moral truth—that each culture has its own set of rules that are valid for that culture, and we have no right to interfere, just as they have no right to interfere with our rules. This attitude, known as *ethical relativism,* is not as radical as skepticism because it allows that moral truths exist but holds that they are relative to their time and place. Ethical relativism is viewed as an attitude of tolerance and as an antidote to the efforts of cultures who try their best to impose their set of moral rules on other cultures. Can ethical relativism solve conflicts? Yes, quite effectively, under limited conditions: within a culture. Whatever the majority deems to be the moral rule is the proper rule to follow. However, intercultural moral disagreements can rarely be solved. This theory is discussed in detail in the next section.

3. Soft Universalism We may believe that deep down, in spite of all their differences, people of different cultures can still agree on certain moral basics. We may think it is a matter of biology—that people everywhere have basically the same human nature. Or we may view this agreement as a process of acculturation, whereby people adjust to the normal way of doing things in their culture. If the native peoples of harsh climates put their unwanted babies out in the wild to perish, it need not mean that they are cruel but, rather, that they want to give the babies they already have a chance to survive, and they know that having another mouth to feed will kill them all. In this way we find common ground in the fact that we, and they, do care for the children we are able to raise. If we believe that somehow, under the surface of antagonism and contradiction, we can still find a few things we can agree on, even if we choose to act on them in different ways, then we believe in the existence of a few universal moral truths. I call this attitude *soft universalism*—*universalism* because it perceives that there are some universal moral rules; *soft* because it is not as radical as

BOBO'S PROGRESS © Dan Wright. King Features Syndicate.

In this cartoon Lenny, the moral nihilist, is being challenged by Bobo. How does Bobo restore Lenny's sense of justice? Do you think it would convince a moral nihilist? Why or why not?

hard universalism, or absolutism.* Can soft universalism solve conflicts? Perhaps it can do so better than any other approach, because the main goal of soft universalism is to seek common ground beneath the variety of opinions and mores. But what exactly *are* those core values? Soft universalism speculates that they are grounded in our comman humanity, but what does that mean? Later in the chapter, you'll see a suggestion from philosopher James Rachels, who speculates that there are three such universal moral values.

4. Hard Universalism *Hard universalism* (sometimes called *moral absolutism*) is the attitude that most often is supported in ethical theories. It is an attitude toward morals in everyday life to which many people relate very well. Hard universalism holds that there is one universal moral code. It is the viewpoint expressed by those who are on a quest for the code ("I know there must be one set of true moral rules, but I would not presume to have found it myself"), by those who make judgments based on its analysis ("After much deliberation I have come to the conclusion that this moral code represents the ultimate values"), and by those who put forth the simple sentiment that moral truth is not open for discussion ("I'm right and you're wrong, and you'd better shape up!"). Whereas moral nihilism, with its claim that there are no moral truths, represents one end of the spectrum in dealing with moral differences, hard universalism represents the other end: It does not acknowledge the possibility or the legitimacy of more than one set of moral codes. Can hard universalism/moral absolutism solve moral conflicts? Yes, in a variety of ways: If you

---

*Some readers have asked me if I am the originator of the term *soft universalism,* and I have to confess that I simply don't know; I have used it for the past couple of decades. I may have read it in someone else's book many years ago, or I may have simply constructed it in contrast to hard universalism, as may be the case with other philosophers—it's a handy, straightforward term. If anyone remembers encountering the term *soft universalism* before the publication of the first edition of *The Moral of the Story* in 1994, please let me know! I would like to be able to give credit where credit is due.

accept someone telling you that you must be wrong because you don't agree with him or her, then that conflict is solved right there; more frequently, an absolutist will try to show you, on the basis of reasoning and evidence, that his or her moral conclusion is better than yours. Appeals to evidence and reasoning are the common problem-solving approaches among most absolutist philosophers, not appeals to force or fallacious arguments such as "I'm right because I'm right." Being a hard universalist thus doesn't equal inflexibility or dogmatism as much as a firm moral conviction—although such a conviction can of course also be dogmatic.

The first set of viewpoints will not be discussed much in this book. The second one, *ethical relativism,* has greatly influenced moral attitudes in the West since the early twentieth century and is the main topic of this chapter. The third, *soft universalism,* and the fourth, *hard universalism,* will be discussed in this chapter as well as subsequent chapters of Parts 2 and 3.

The Lessons of Anthropology

In the nineteenth century, cultural anthropology came into its own as a scientific discipline and reminded the West that "out there" were other societies vastly different from those of Victorian Europe. Anthropological scholars set out to examine other cultures, and the facts they brought back were astounding to the nineteenth-century Western mind-set: There were cultures that didn't understand the male's role in procreation but thought that babies somehow ripened in the woman with the help of spirits. There were people who would devour the bodies of enemies killed in war to share their fighting spirit. There were cultures that believed in animal gods, cultures that felt it appropriate for women to bare their breasts, cultures that felt it utterly inappropriate to let your in-laws watch you eat, and so on. It was easy to draw the conclusion that there were cultures out there whose moral codes differed substantially from those of the West.

That conclusion, the first step in what has become known as ethical relativism, was not new to the Western mind-set. Because people had always traveled and returned with tales of faraway lands, it was common knowledge that other cultures did things differently. Explorers in earlier centuries brought home tales of mermaids, giants, and other fantasies. Some stories were truer than others. There really were, for instance, peoples out there who had a different dress ethic and work ethic. The Arabian messenger Ibn Fadlan traveled north into Russia in 922 and watched a Viking burial; he wrote with disgust about how different and primitive the Viking customs were (his story was the theme of the film *The 13th Warrior*), so not all such reports come from Western travelers commenting about non-Western ways. But what we're most familiar with is of course the tales about non-Western, exotic lands. The lifestyle of the South Sea islanders became a collective fantasy for Europeans of the eighteenth and nineteenth centuries; imagine not wearing any clothes, not having to work all the time, living in perpetual summertime, and not having any sexual restrictions! Depending on their ethical predisposition, Europeans considered such peoples to be either the luckiest ones on this earth or the most sinful, subhuman, and depraved. Reports of cultural diversity were also supplied by Christian missionaries over the centuries; they confronted more or less reluctant cultures with their message of conversion.

The idea of cultural diversity even in early historic times is well documented. The Greek historian Herodotus (485–430 B.C.E.) tells in his *Histories* of the Persian king Darius the Great, who from the borders of his vast empire, which at the time stretched from the Greek holdings in the West to India in the East, had heard tales of funerary practices that intrigued him. The Greeks were at that time in the habit of cremating their dead; Darius learned that a tribe in India, the Callatians, would eat their dead. In Darius's Persia, burials were the norm. Herodotus wrote:

> Everyone without exception believes in his own native customs, and the religion he was brought up in, to be the best . . . [Darius] summoned the Greeks who happened to be present at his court, and asked them what it would take to eat the dead bodies of their fathers. They replied that they would not do it for any money in the world. Later, in the presence of the Greeks, and through an interpreter, so that they could understand what was said, he asked some Indians, of the tribe called Callatia, who do in fact eat their parents' dead bodies, what they would take to burn them. They uttered a cry of horror and forbade him to mention such a dreadful thing. One can see by this what custom can do, and Pindar [a Greek poet] was right when he called it "king of all."

Usually, the sound bite condensing Herodotus's observation is "Custom is king"—we all prefer what we are used to.

When anthropologists point out that moral codes vary enormously from culture to culture, they are describing the situation as they see it. As long as those anthropologists make no judgments about whether it is *good* for humanity to have different moral codes or whether those codes represent the moral truths of each culture, they are espousing a descriptive theory usually referred to as *cultural relativism*. Let us look at an example. An anthropologist acquaintance of mine came back from a field trip to Tibet and told me the following story: In the little Tibetan village where he had been "adopted" by a local family and was doing his fieldwork, the children worked hard and had very little leisure time. The concept of competition was totally alien to them. One day my friend thought he would give them a treat, and he arranged for a race. All the kids lined up, puzzled and excited, to listen to his directions: Run from one end of the compound to the other and back again, and whoever comes in first wins. The race was on, and the children ran like mad to beat each other and "win." As one beaming kid came in first, the anthropologist handed over a prize—some little trinket or piece of candy. There was dead silence among the kids, who just looked at each other. Finally one of the children asked, "Why are you giving a gift to our friend who won?" The anthropologist realized that because the children had no idea of competition, they had no knowledge that winning often is connected with a prize. To them, this new idea of "winning" was great all by itself, and there was no need to add anything else; indeed, the prize made them feel very uncomfortable. (The anthropologist said it also made him feel very stupid.)

What the anthropologist was doing by telling this story was relating an example of cultural relativism—describing how customs differ from culture to culture. Suppose,

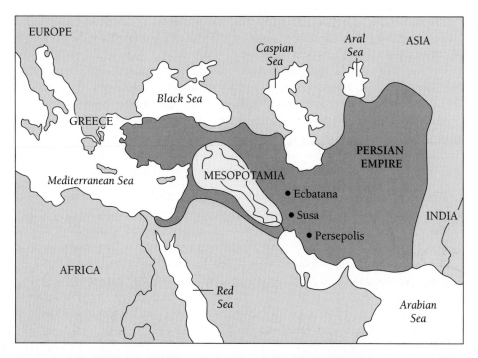

It was not so strange that King Darius might have heard of peoples living as far apart as the Greeks and the Callatian tribe of northern India, because they were in fact his neighbors. At the time of its greatest expansion, Persia (today, Iran) covered a territory stretching from Greece in the west to today's Pakistan in the east. Until the time of Alexander the Great, this was the greatest empire in the ancient Western world.

though, he had added, "and I realized that they were right in their own way." (In other words, suppose he had made a *judgment* about the validity of the tribal way of life.) In that case, he would have moved into the area of *ethical relativism*. Cultural relativism is a *descriptive* theory that states that different cultures have different moral codes. Ethical relativism is a *normative* theory that states there is no universal moral code and that each culture's codes are right and valid for that culture. It is a subtle difference, but philosophically it is an important one. (See Box 3.1 for more on descriptive ethics, normative ethics, and metaethics.) The cultural relativist sees the cultural differences and describes them: There are many moral codes in the world. The ethical relativist sees the cultural differences and makes a judgment: We can never find a common code, and what seems right for one culture is right *for that culture*.

The anthropologist Ruth Benedict (1887–1948) was a student of the cultural anthropologist Franz Boas, who had already declared that cultures around the world should not be judged by the standards of Western civilization and that moral standards are not universal, but relative to each culture. Sharing her teacher's viewpoint, Benedict did most of her writing toward the end of the era in which one could still speak of "uncontaminated" societies—cultures that hadn't yet been overwhelmingly exposed to Western civilization. The term *primitive* still was used for some cultures,

Box 3.1 DESCRIPTIVE ETHICS, NORMATIVE ETHICS, AND METAETHICS

The terms *descriptive* and *normative* are important terms for any ethical theory, not just relativism. When we talk about a theory being *descriptive,* we mean that the theory merely describes what it sees as fact, such as, In the United States it is, in general, not considered immoral to eat meat. In other words, a descriptive theory describes what people actually do or think. A *normative* theory adds a *moral judgment,* evaluation, or justification, such as, It is okay to eat meat because it is nourishing, or a criticism, such as, Eating meat *should* be considered immoral. In addition to descriptive ethics and normative ethics, there is a third ethical approach, *metaethics.* Metaethics does not describe or evaluate but analyzes the *meaning* of the moral terms we use. Some typical questions would be, But what do you mean by immoral? What do you mean by meat—beef, horse, or snake, perhaps? Most ethical systems involve judgments, criticisms, evaluations, and justifications, and are thus normative, but many systems also require an awareness of the terms used to justify the theory. Any time a moral debate moves into a discussion about the meaning of terms, it moves into the area of metaethics. An example of the vital importance of metaethics in the political debate of the first decade of the twenty-first century is the discussion of the meaning of the concept of *torture.* In 2005 and 2006, Congress engaged in a debate about what should be permissible as "aggressive interrogation techniques," as opposed to "torture." The underlying assumption was that we, as a civilized nation, are bound by the Geneva Convention and can't allow ourselves to engage in torture, but must allow for access to harsh interrogation methods in extreme situations, to save American lives. It became apparent that what for some debaters constituted aggressive interrogation techniques within accepted limits—such as exposure to cold temperatures, constant light or darkness, and loud noises, including loud music—was for others clearly torture. Most debaters agreed that inflicting physical pain was a clear example of torture, but what about sleep deprivation? The most controversial technique was probably "waterboarding," subjecting prisoners to having water poured over their covered faces while they are tilted backward until they believe themselves to be drowning. In 2008 it was revealed that the CIA had used this technique on three occasions, including an interrogation of a captured high-ranking al Qaeda member, and had obtained important information thereby. For the CIA this constituted an aggressive interrogation technique, not torture, but for several debaters, including members of the media, this technique should clearly be classified as a form of torture, even if it doesn't involve any actual danger of drowning. In the fall of 2006, Republican senators were divided as to what constitutes torture and what are acceptable interrogation techniques, but a compromise was reached: The Military Commissions Act of 2006 outlawed "cruel, inhuman or degrading treatment" as such but otherwise left the concept of "aggressive interrogation" open to interpretation.

Regardless of the question of the moral acceptability or even the effectiveness of torture as such (which would be normative questions), this example merely serves to show that without a discussion of the definition of key words in a debate, we cannot hope to reach any consensus. In Chapters 5 and 6 we return to the question of the moral acceptability and effectiveness of torture.

and Benedict used it too, but she was quick to point out that the attitude that Western civilization was at the top of the ladder of cultural evolution was—or should be—outdated. In a famous paper, "Anthropology and the Abnormal," from 1934, she says that "modern civilization becomes not a necessary pinnacle of human achievement but one entry in a long series of possible adjustments." With that emphasis she established herself as an advocate of cultural and moral *tolerance,* implying that Western civilization has no right to impose its codes of conduct on other cultures. Ethical relativism has remained popular ever since as a tool of cultural tolerance.

In the same paper, Benedict tells of a number of cultural phenomena that may seem morally odd, to say the least. In the Primary Readings you'll find an excerpt focusing on the custom of extreme paranoia on an island in Melanesia. Here in the chapter text, one example will have to suffice: Among the Kwakiutl Indians of the Pacific Northwest in times past, it was customary to view death, even natural death, as an affront that should be retaliated against in one way or another. In one tribe, a chief's sister and her daughter had drowned on a trip to Victoria. The chief gathered a war party. They set out, found seven men and two children asleep, and killed them. Then they returned home, convinced that they had done the morally right thing.

What intrigued Benedict most about this story was not that the chief and the members of the war party viewed their actions as morally good, but that most of the tribespeople felt the same way. In other words, it was *normal* in the tribe to feel this way. Benedict concludes, "The concept of the normal is properly a variant of the concept of the good. It is that which society has approved."

Two things are worth mentioning here. First, Benedict is taking a giant leap from expressing *cultural* relativism to expressing *ethical* relativism. She moves from a description of the people's behavior to the statement that it is normal and thus good for them to behave that way—in their own cultural context. Second, Benedict is saying that normality is culturally defined; in other words, cultures, especially isolated cultures, often seem to develop some behaviors to an extreme. (For Benedict the range of possible human behavior is enormous, extending from paranoia to helpfulness and generosity.) Those individuals who somehow can't conform (and they will always be the minority, because most people are very pliable) become the abnormals in that culture.

Is the behavior of the Northwest Coast people totally alien to us? Benedict thinks not, because it constitutes *abnormal* behavior in our own society, not *unthinkable* behavior. We might illustrate her idea with some examples. The postal worker who has been fired and who shows up the next day with a shotgun and kills a number of his coworkers is "crazy" to us, but he actually is following the same logic as the chief: His world has been torn apart by powers over which he has no control, and he is retaliating against the affront. The driver who cuts you off on the freeway because she had a fight with her husband is doing the same thing; so was the little girl who ripped a button off your coat in grade school because someone else ripped a button off her coat. There is no question of vengeance, because neither the driver nor the little girl was looking to punish a guilty party. The seven men and two children had nothing to do with the deaths of the chief's relatives, and the chief never said they did. It is not a matter of seeking out the cause of the problem, of gaining retribution; rather, it

Ruth Benedict (1887–1948), American anthropologist and
defender of ethical relativism. Her best-known work is *Patterns
of Culture* (1934).

is an experience of healing a wound by wounding someone else. (What if the
strangers who were killed had been American or Canadian loggers who had grown
up in a culture that believes it is proper to find and punish whoever is guilty? Then
we'd see retribution.) Perhaps we all take it out on someone innocent from time to
time; some of us probably do it more often than others. The difference is that we've
chosen to call what the Northwest Coast people did *abnormal*, whereas they, in the
context of their tribal civilization, considered their actions to be normal and good.
How do such choices evolve? Usually it is a matter of habits developing over time. If
there is such a thing as a "normal" way for humans to behave, it is to adjust to the
pattern of normality that prevails in their particular culture. Today, sociologists
would call this process *acculturation*.

Although Benedict obviously wants her readers to approach other cultures with
more tolerance for customs alien to them, her choice of examples may seem odd to
a modern, culturally sensitive reader: Is Benedict, in giving this account of a tribe of
American Indians, actually helping to cement the old notions popular in white Western culture of the "savage Indian"? If so, she is not furthering any mutual intercultural understanding. There are two things to say here: (1) Benedict herself might answer with something like, "If you read this account as a criticism of Indian customs,
then it is just because you are seeing it through the eyes of a prejudiced Westerner.
The whole point is to recognize cultural differences as being equally meaningful
within their cultural contexts." We should not shy away from noticing differences—
but we should not judge them either. (2) As readers looking at the disadvantages as
well as the advantages of ethical relativism, we must conclude that relativism does
not have as its goal any mutual *understanding*—merely noninterference. Trying to
achieve an understanding requires us to find some common ground, and relativism
does not allow for any intercultural common ground. We return to the question of
common ground later in this chapter.

For Benedict, there is no sense in imposing Western morals on another culture,
because Western morals are just one aspect of the range of possible human behavior
that we have chosen to elaborate; they are no better or no worse than anyone else's

morals. Whatever is normal for us we think of as good, and we have no right to claim that our choice is better than any other culture's. A novel that in many ways advocates this approach to other cultures is Barbara Kingsolver's *The Poisonwood Bible*, and you will find an excerpt from it in the Narratives section of this chapter.

Problems with Ethical Relativism

Given the overwhelming intolerance for other cultures and customs that is displayed from time to time by Western civilization (a stance some refer to as "cultural imperialism"), many people find something very appealing and refreshing about ethical relativism. And we shouldn't forget to see it in its proper historical perspective: It served as an antidote to nineteenth-century "Eurocentrism" and Western colonialism, in which the notion of Western religious and moral superiority (in addition to the technological superiority of the West) had been considered an obvious truth. Ethical relativism broke away from that self-congratulatory attitude and became the inspiration for a shift toward cultural tolerance in the early part of the twentieth century, an attitude that continues in today's United States, with its plurality of cultural and ethnic heritages. Increasingly, throughout the twentieth century, it seemed of doubtful virtue among American intellectuals to impose a particular brand of acculturation on another group that believed it was doing just fine with its own set of moral rules. So many cultures in the nineteenth century had suffered precisely because of that attitude, from American Indians to Asian Indians, and many non-European cultures in between. For many Americans, the fundamental acceptance of the fact that other cultures had a right to be different was so ingrained that when a young American male was caned by the authorities in Singapore in the 1990s for spraying graffiti on cars, the overall reaction was that if he chose to live in Singapore, he should not break its rules, and ought to be punished according to its rules—a modern "When in Rome, do as the Romans do" attitude. And it cuts both ways: When people from elsewhere visit the United States, we expect from them that they respect our ways of life: A young single mother from Denmark visited her American boyfriend with her baby in New York City some years back and did what she was used to doing in Denmark: The couple had dinner in a New York restaurant at ground level, and she put the baby carriage outside *with the baby in it* and got a table by the window so she could watch the baby. When she was arrested for reckless child endangerment, she was puzzled: "But we do this all the time at home!" she said. I can attest to that personally, having grown up in Denmark. Indeed, babies (in their carriages) and dogs on their leashes are left outside stores and restaurants all the time, in the summer, at least in the smaller towns. But not in New York City! What has become known as the *cultural differences argument* didn't cut it with the judge—her lawyer's argument that she should have a right to do what she used to was dismissed, and she was sent back to Denmark with her baby, presumably never to come back.

So it appears that we have taken the method of problem solving suggested by ethical relativism to heart. And yet—even before September 11—some people (who weren't necessarily hard universalists either) questioned the noninterference ethics of relativism. What if the culture in question sells children into the sex trade? What if it

Calvin and Hobbes   by Bill Watterson

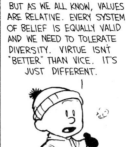

CALVIN AND HOBBES. Reprinted by permission of Universal Press Syndicate. All rights reserved.

Bill Watterson's comic strip *Calvin and Hobbes* had a knack for putting its finger on tricky philosophical issues, especially in the fields of ethics and metaphysics. Here Hobbes, the stuffed tiger that only Calvin can see move, speculates that the demand for tolerance in ethical relativism may not be much of an advantage.

refuses women the right to vote and own property? And, post–September 11, what if other cultures believe that Americans are fair targets for terrorism everywhere? Are those beliefs and customs just a matter of their moral choices, which should be respected, or do we have a moral right—perhaps even a moral obligation—to step in and effect changes? This is the big issue that is challenging ethical relativism at the beginning of the twenty-first century.

Six Problems with Ethical Relativism

Even if we grant that ethical relativism provided a positive lesson in the early twentieth century, suggesting the suspension of Western judgmental attitudes toward other cultures, there are serious problems within the theory. Here we look at six problems, all of them logical consequences of the basic idea of ethical relativism that there is no universal moral code. (Box 3.2 is a general overview of examining and testing theories.)

   1. No Criticism or Praise of Other Cultures Does this mean that it is always wrong to criticize another culture or group for what it does? If we are to follow the idea of ethical relativism to its logical conclusion, yes. We have no right to criticize other cultures, period. But on occasion things happen in other cultures that we feel, either by instinct or through rational argument, we *should* criticize to maintain our own moral integrity. Curiously enough, at the time Benedict wrote her article (1934), one of the most offensive social "experiments" in history was being conducted in the Western world. Europe was being overtaken by the Nazis, whose extreme racism was not kept secret, even though the existence of the death camps of later years was not

Box 3.2 HOW TO TEST A THEORY

What we are doing in this text is following standard philosophical procedure. We test a theory by pounding at it with hypothetical and actual situations until we see whether it still makes sense. It is not unlike the procedure of testing a presidential candidate. When the going gets tough and all the nasty (but usually reasonable and relevant) questions are asked, we see what kind of character the candidate has. Is he or she arrogant? weak? capable of a sense of humor? vindictive? intelligent? stupid? lying? truthful? honest? strong? What is the breaking point of the candidate? In the same way, we seek the breaking point of a theory. As you will see, almost every theory does have a breaking point, but that does not always disqualify the theory (that is, render it invalid). If the breaking point comes late in the discussion and only when the theory is attacked by an extremely unlikely hypothesis or by trifles, that speaks well for the theory and encourages acceptance or perhaps only a minor rewrite of the theory. Some theories, however, break early in the discussion and can be discarded. Ethical relativism is a theory with a fairly late breaking point; in other words, there are some good things to be said for the theory, which is a good reason not to discard it altogether.

generally known until after the war. A true ethical relativist would have had to stick to her guns and maintain that other countries had no right to criticize what was going on in Germany and Austria in the 1930s and 1940s. (As it happens, that pretty much mirrored the actual attitude of the rest of the world at the time.) Benedict, however, mentions nothing about this issue in her paper.

People often say, in retrospect, that someone should have protested against or intervened in a particular situation while there was still time. Indeed, this was one of the arguments for going into Iraq in 2003: that Saddam Hussein had the makings of a Middle Eastern Hitler and needed to be stopped while there was still time. In the case of the war in Afghanistan, the relativist might have approved, provided the goal was stopping terrorists from attacking other nations, such as our own, but not if the goal was to put an end to the Taliban regime. In the war in Iraq, the issue is even more complex: If the goal was exclusively to find and destroy WMDs, weapons of mass destruction (which have not been found, although there is speculation that they have been hidden), the relativist might find the invasion acceptable, because it would stop aggression toward other countries. However, if the goal was primarily a regime change, toppling Saddam Hussein and creating a democracy, the relativist would not approve, regardless of how much the living conditions would improve for Iraqis, in the short or the long run, because it would be interfering with the internal affairs of a sovereign country. To put it graphically, if Saddam Hussein tortured Iraqis and attempted genocide on certain groups, that would be an internal matter for the Iraqis themselves to deal with. In the eyes of the relativist, we are against genocide only because it happens to be against the norms of our own culture; for another culture, genocide may be right.

For most people, however, even those believing they ought to be tolerant, there are moral limits to tolerance, and any theory that doesn't recognize this is just not a good theory. Most Western people, tolerant as they might like to be, would prefer to see certain things come to an end: In China there are reports of female infanticide, a result of a strict one-child-per-family policy; in several cultures, primarily on the African continent, female genital mutilation is practiced, usually on young girls of seven to eight years of age. A report issued by the United Nations in 2000 suggests that many of these countries have recently outlawed female genital mutilation, but the practice still exists. At the end of this chapter you will find a summary of a novel that deals with this issue: Alice Walker's *Possessing the Secret of Joy.* In Sudan in 2000 the government issued a decree that women could no longer study at the universities or use their education in Sudanese society, because it was seen as impermissible by the Sudanese reading of the Koran. Professional women found themselves reduced to making a living doing manual labor.

In Afghanistan during the reign of the Taliban (1996–2001), women were deprived of rights to freedom of movement, education, work, health care, and other essentials, and faced public beatings and execution by stoning for violations of the imposed moral code. Hearing of such conditions, can one morally remain a relativist, holding that each culture must be left in peace to explore its own values? Many ethical relativists have felt that a line must be drawn between mere cultural preferences and assaults on human rights—but that means giving up on ethical relativism. However, when issues such as equal rights for women are raised in the United Nations, representatives of those cultures that do not recognize rights for women often respond with indignation, asserting that the West is merely doing what it has always done, trying to superimpose its cultural and moral values on other peoples in the old tradition of cultural imperialism. Although ethical relativism wanted to put an end to the wholesale export of Western values, the theorists have reached a critical point: Many people may agree with relativists that there is no need or excuse for the West to try to dictate every aspect of what other nations should think or do, but in extreme situations many of us would like to reserve the right to speak up for people in other parts of the world who can't (or aren't allowed to) speak up for themselves. We want to believe that we have the right to complain about governments that do not respect human rights and that abuse a part of their population; and, in fact, pressure on such governments has at times yielded results.

Not only are we prevented from criticizing another culture's doings if we accept the teachings of relativism, but we also cannot praise and learn from that culture. If we find that the social system of Scandinavia is more humane and functions better than any other in the world, the conclusion based on relativism has to be that this is because it is right for them, but we still can't assume that it is right for us. If we happen to admire the work ethic of Japan, we can't learn from it and adapt it to our own culture, nor can Jainism's teachings of nonviolence have anything to say to us. In short, ethical relativism, when taken to its logical conclusion, precludes learning from other cultures because there can be no "good" or "bad" that is common to all cultures. Curiously, that doesn't mean that all ethical relativists would actually *forbid* us to learn from other cultures or to criticize others—on the contrary, ethical relativists think of themselves as very tolerant and open-minded. The problem is in the logic of the theory itself: When it is applied to real-life situations as a moral principle, it reveals itself to have certain limitations.

2. Majority Rule The isolation of moral values to the conventions of specific cultural groups has another curious effect: It forces us to bow to *majority rule*. Remember that ethical relativism does not say there are *no* moral rules—only that the rules of each society are proper and valid for that society. What if you live in a society and don't agree with the rules? Then you must, ipso facto, be wrong, because we know that the rules that are morally good in a society are those rules that are in effect. If you disagree with those rules, you must be wrong. That makes it impossible to disagree with any rules that exist, and therefore civil disobedience is out of the question. In Iran, if you disagree with the fundamentalist Islamic rules of punishment, then you are wrong. It is, in fact, right and proper in Iran to amputate the hand of a thief. If you are an American and disagree with the general attitude against euthanasia and doctors who help patients commit suicide, then you are wrong, and the attitude of the majority is right—not because the attitude has been subjected to moral analysis, but simply because it happens to be the attitude of the majority. It does not work, either, to point to a historical precedent and say that things were not always done as they are now, because ethical relativism cuts through time as well as space. There are no universal values among different time periods, any more than there are common values among different cultures of the same era. In other words, that was then and this is now. For an intellectual tradition such as ours, which prides itself on valuing minority opinions and promotes the idea of moral progress, the idea that the attitude of the majority is always right simply is unacceptable. And interestingly, as one of my students observed, if one is an ethical relativist, one would have to agree that ethical relativism as a moral theory should never have been voiced, or gained popularity, in a time period when hard universalism was the moral norm of the culture! If all cultures are right in their own way, hard universalism was right for early-twentieth-century America, and ethical relativism, being a minority moral opinion at the time, would be wrong by definition!

3. Professed or Actual Morality? There is a further problem with the idea that a group's morality is determined by the majority or that a certain kind of behavior is normal, for what is "normal"? Is it the *professed* morality of the group or the *actual* morality? Imagine the following situation. The majority of a cultural group, when asked about their moral viewpoints, claim that they believe infidelity is wrong; however, in that particular society, infidelity is common practice. Does that mean the morality of the culture is what the majority say they ought to do or what they actually do? We might simply decide that it must be the *normative* rules that define the morality and not the actual behavior; however, Ruth Benedict assumed morality to be the same as majority *behavior*. If Benedict had implied that morality is the same as what people think they *ought* to do, then all our example would amount to would be to show that most people have a hard time living up to their own moral standards, which is hardly a novel observation. However, Benedict's theory of ethical relativism clearly states that "moral" is the same as "normal," meaning how the majority *actually* behave.

4. What Is a "Majority"? Ethical relativism involves a practical problem as well. Suppose the question of doctor-assisted suicide had been determined by a referendum and the law against it overturned in your state. (The only state in the nation that allowed euthanasia in 2008 was Oregon.) The majority now believe it is right for doctors to help terminally ill patients die. It was morally wrong the week before, but today it is morally right. By next year people may have changed their minds, and it will become morally wrong again. There is something very disconcerting about moral rightness being as arbitrary as that and depending on a vote, especially since so few people actually vote in elections. So who exactly is the majority? Most of the people? the registered voters? or the actual voters? And what about the individual states? They obviously are part of a larger unit, the United States, and the moral standards of this larger unit would define the morals of each singular state. But not all laws and customs are the same from state to state, and what is considered morally wrong by the majority in one state may well be considered morally acceptable by the majority in another (such as abortion or doctor-assisted suicide). Therefore, might we instead want to allow for morally autonomous subgroups in which the majority within each group defines the moral rules, even if they are at odds with the larger cultural group? If we have large minority subgroups *within* a state and their moral values differ from those of the majority, should such groups constitute morally autonomous units that should not be criticized? (See Box 3.3.)

5. What Is a "Culture"? Question 4 leads right into question 5, because ethical relativists have not explained exactly what they mean by a culture either. How can we know if something is the norm within a culture if it isn't clear what a culture is? What sets one culture off from other cultures? Is the United States one culture (as most foreigners believe)? Or is it a collective of many smaller cultures, as many Americans see it? Is Europe one culture? Is Africa? Asia? Central or South America? Iraq contains at least three cultures, but it is one country. From the outside, perhaps, but once you see the regional differences, you'll know it's not so easy to focus on common denominators rather than on the differences.

What unifies a culture? It used to be *geography*: People living within the same area moved around only rarely and acquired the same general characteristics. But now people move all over the globe, join societies across borders as never before, and subscribe to newsletters and newsgroups on the Internet. For some people, the life they live online in Second Life—where they take on another identity, live in a different environment, and buy and sell property—is merely entertainment, but for some, that life takes on a reality of its own. And according to my students, so does the online role-playing game World of Warcraft, another community of players in a reality of their own. The websites MySpace and Facebook are attracting young as well as older people as a way to communicate with others. Are these groups "cultures"?

Could "culture" also be a matter of *ethnicity*? Historically people have tended to stick with others of their own ethnic background, but that seems to be partly a geographical limitation and partly a *cultural* choice (and culture is what we are trying to define). People who were brought up not to be bigoted choose partners, friends, and neighbors from outside their own ethnic group all the time, yet they still feel they are choosing within their culture. In my ethnically and racially diverse college classes, it always strikes me that, diverse as we are, we generally have much more in common than we have with some people in our own families and neighborhoods, because the world of academia is our "culture"—our common experiences with classes and grades, studying and research, exams, and so forth create a cultural identity in itself.

Box 3.3   MORAL SUBJECTIVISM AND ETHICAL RELATIVISM: A COMPARISON

Sometimes the theory of moral subjectivism is listed as a subcategory of ethical relativism. You may recall that we placed it under the general heading of *moral nihilism* at the beginning of this chapter, because such theories deny that there can be any agreement about moral values based on something other than personal opinion. Ethical relativism is not a morally nihilistic theory, because it holds that there are very strong reasons for agreeing about values within a culture precisely because they are values shared by that culture. However, there is definitely something "relative" about moral subjectivism, so we might say that it represents the transposition of "each culture is right in its own way" to "each person is right in his or her own way." This theory, often referred to in the media as "moral relativism," is an extremely tolerant theory, a "live and let live" attitude in which no one has the right to impose his or her moral viewpoints, including a preference for tolerance, on anyone else. It has its own severe flaws, however: For one thing, it cannot solve moral conflicts because there is no common value denominator to resort to. That means we can't hope to learn from other people's advice or even their mistakes, because their values and situations will always differ slightly from ours. And because the theory can't solve moral conflicts, we have no moral weapon against what we personally consider unacceptable. How would you argue against Hitler's Holocaust from a subjectivist viewpoint? Against slavery? child abuse? Female circumcision and other enforced mutilation rituals? The only thing you might say is that you *feel* those actions are wrong—but others can also feel and think any way they like. For most people this way of thinking is so excessively tolerant that it borders on an obscene lack of social responsibility.

Furthermore, appealing as moral subjectivism may seem when we have just escaped the confines of the moral regulations of our childhood, it simply isn't intuitively sound. We may think we can "live and let live," but in actual fact we react *as if* there is a basic appeal to conflict-solving values. If you are a subjectivist and you see an adult at the supermarket repeatedly hitting a small crying child, are you going to be content telling yourself that you wouldn't do such a thing but that the adult in question is entitled to feel he or she is doing the right thing? Or would you try to appeal to some common value system by stepping in? Moral subjectivism is not only counterintuitive and impractical but also downright dangerous as a moral theory because it provides no social cohesion and no protection against the whims of those in power, whose "feelings" may be as legitimate as yours but whose ability to carry them out is far greater.

To summarize, the criticism of moral subjectivism is different from the criticism of ethical relativism in the following ways: (1) Moral subjectivism cannot solve conflicts, but ethical relativism can (through majority rule), and (2) ethical relativism is problematic because it implies a moral majority rule, but moral subjectivism does not (because each person is right in his or her own way). What the two theories have in common is the relativity of moral values: The moral subjectivist has no right to call anyone else's values wrong or evil, and neither does the ethical relativist (when judging *other* cultures). So the challenge to both moral subjectivism and ethical relativism is the experience of something that is so egregiously against "common decency" or "our sense of humanity" that we must speak up, regardless of our modern tradition of tolerance toward others' life choices. Finding a universal foundation for criticism of traditions of female circumcision or ritual animal torture or child sacrifice is equally impossible from a basis of either moral subjectivism or ethical relativism.

Is it *race*? When people were less mobile, people within a region generally formed a culture, and there was ethnic and racial cohesion in the group. But now we are (at least in the United States) moving toward a mixed-race society, and biologists and sociologists are beginning to question the very concept of race and to interpret it as an eighteenth-century invention. Therefore, the category of race can hardly be a firm foundation for a definition of culture. Is it *religion*? Places with one dominant (or one permitted) religion seem to be obvious candidates for a culture, but what about places in which people tend to dress the same, see the same movies, buy the same groceries, and drive the same cars but have different religions? Is it (as anthropologists might suggest) how we view *family relations*? Those categories also are not so stable anymore. And if we resort to vague categories of habits, worldviews, tastes, and so forth, all we end up with is a classification of people according to some criteria, whereas other criteria may cut across those same groups. If an ethical relativist insists that as long as we can identify some form of cultural cohesion, then that group should not be interfered with in its moral practices, we run into horrible problems.

Some ethnic groups in the United States differ from the majority in their views about male–female relationships, about using for food animals that others consider pets, about contraception and abortion, about the rights of fathers to punish their families. How large do such groups have to be in order to be considered morally right in their own ways? If we are generous and tolerant relativists, perhaps we'll say that any large ethnic group should be considered morally autonomous. But would that mean the Mafia could be considered such a subgroup? or neighborhood gangs? Would society then have to accept a plurality of "laws," each governing the subgroups, with no higher means of control? The relativist might accept that one set of laws—federal ones, for instance—would be above all other laws, but it would still be an extremely complicated matter, with possible contradictions arising between what the national law says and what the gang law says. Could we eventually end up in a situation in which acts such as looting are morally right for some because of their subgroup affiliation but not for others? If ethical relativism is to be considered as a viable moral philosophy, ethical relativists need to agree on a clear definition of "culture."

6. Can Tolerance Be a Universal Value? One of the best qualities of ethical relativism is its tolerance, although we've now seen that it can lead to problems. However, there is something problematic about the very claim of tolerance coming from a relativist, for is someone who believes in ethical relativism allowed to claim that tolerance is something everyone should have? In other words, can a relativist say that tolerance is *universally good*? If all values are culture-relative, then that condition must apply to tolerance as well. Tolerance may be good for us, but who is to say if it is good for other groups! This notion severely undermines the whole purpose of tolerance, which is not usually considered a one-way street. And what if the highest moral dictum of a certain culture is to superimpose its values on other cultures? Does relativism teach that we must respect a moral system that doesn't respect the morals of others? Western cultures of the past—and, some would say, even the present—have exported their own moral systems; the Communist bloc of the twentieth century sought expansion along those same principles; today, Muslim extremism in some parts of the world also seeks this kind of expansion, combined with political ambitions. One could say, as some ethical relativists have attempted, that as long as they keep their moral (and perhaps even political and religious) expansionism within their own borders, they have a right to think whatever they want—but the problem is that the moral focus of certain cultures is precisely to export itself to other places. Not only does ethical relativism not have a right to claim that tolerance is universally good, since it also claims that there are no universal values, but it also can't even give a practical answer as to how to deal with moral, religious, and political expansionism. Ethical relativism thus is *logically* prevented from achieving its main goal, resolving international moral conflicts through tolerance.

Refuting Ethical Relativism

The "Flat Earth" Argument

Now we have seen why many people believe that ethical relativism doesn't have enough to offer to be adopted 100 percent; it is a theory with immense theoretical and practical problems. For some critics, the *logic* of the key argument proposed by ethical relativism is faulty. Let us assume that the culture "up north" believes that abortion is morally wrong, whereas the culture "down south" believes it to be morally permissible. The relativist concludes that because there is a disagreement between the two groups, neither can be right in an absolute sense. But surely, the critics say, that is not so; some things are simply true or false. We may have had a disagreement in the past about whether the earth is round or flat. (Indeed, the Flat Earth Society today is upholding that tradition by claiming that all space reports and photos from space missions are fraudulent and were concocted in a movie studio.) However, that doesn't mean there is no correct answer; the idea that the earth is round is a verifiable fact. We may be able to verify that some moral codes are objectively right and others are wrong.

The trouble with this critique is that it is easy to verify that the earth is round; all we have to do is look at how things gradually disappear over a flat horizon. But how exactly would you go about verifying that abortion is objectively right or wrong? That would bring us into a much bigger discussion of the very nature of moral truths, which would be no help at all in determining whether ethical relativism is right. The flat earth example is, of course, not supposed to be taken that far. All it shows is that you can't conclude, on the basis of there being a disagreement, that both parties are wrong. It is never as easy to find out who is right in a discussion of moral issues as it is to settle questions of geography.

The Problem of Induction

Some critics believe that the very foundation of the ethical relativism theory is wrong; they believe it simply is not true that there is no universal moral code. If relativists were asked how they know that there is no universal moral code, they would answer that they looked around and found none or possibly that, given the diversity of human nature, there never will be one. This begs the question, though, because we might reasonably suggest that they should look around a bit longer and refrain from making absolute statements about the future. Blanket statements bring on their own undoing, because any theory based on collecting evidence faces a classic problem: *the problem of induction.*

Induction is one of two major scientific methods; the other is deduction. In deductive thinking we start with an axiom that we believe is true, and we apply that axiom to establish the validity of other axioms, or we apply the theory to specific cases. In inductive thinking we gather empirical evidence to reach a comprehensive theory. Ethical relativism is an example of inductive thinking; it bases its general theory that there are no universal moral codes on evidence from particular cultures. The problem of induction is that we never can be sure that we have looked hard enough to gather all possible evidence.

As an example of the problem of induction we're going to look at a phenomenon that is well known to anyone watching court cases on TV or just about any crime show from *CSI* to *Law and Order* and crime scene documentaries: the gathering of evidence at a murder scene. The detectives gather evidence according to a preliminary hypothesis: that this is a homicide, not a suicide or a natural death. (And if they can't determine this from the start, they keep all interpretations open.) They gather what looks to them like evidence, usually casting a wide net, and this evidence goes to the district attorney, who decides whether to file a case. In other words, the detectives reach a theory of the identity of the killer based on the evidence they gather—they don't gather evidence based on a theory of who-dun-it, or at least that is the way it is supposed to work. (That theory would have been *de*duction. It would also shape a biased investigation. In other words, Sherlock Holmes was great at, not deduction, but *induction*!) So, theoretically, the evidence is presented in court, and the jury decides whether it points to guilt or whether there is reasonable doubt. But what if a piece of evidence was overlooked? Blood spatter in a corner—or a fingerprint or a hair, or blood, or semen, belonging to someone other than the defendant? Or something that, to a forensic scientist decades down the line, would be hard evidence but has no significance for today's scientists? Something like DNA before the mid-1980s? Or an eyewitness who left town without knowing she saw something important? Those are factors that can't be completely controlled. And then there are the ones that *can* be controlled—such as a forensic scientist deliberately skewing the test results in favor of the prosecution. Either way, we are looking at a real problem of induction: Because we are dealing with empirical science—gathering evidence and building a theory—we can't be 100 percent certain when we have gathered enough material. Induction is a fine method and yields magnificent scientific results. We couldn't do without it—but it is not 100 percent accurate. Fortunately, in natural science as in court cases, even in murder cases, we don't have to be mathematically 100 percent certain in order to have a working theory or to be legally and morally certain: Circumstantial evidence, if there is a great deal of it, and nothing points elsewhere, is the accepted standard for finding someone guilty. Anything can be doubted—but not everything can be the subject of *reasonable* doubt. But as the Innocence Project, headed by Barry Scheck, has shown, there are people on death row who are, in fact, innocent of the crimes they are convicted of, because of the problem of induction: Evidence was overlooked or not available at the time, such as DNA tests, or (in a few nefarious cases) exculpatory evidence was not introduced in court. In Chapter 13 we take a closer look at the death penalty and such problems.

Now what does this have to do with ethical relativism? Everything—because the method of investigation used by the relativist to claim there are no universal moral codes is the method of induction. The Greeks and the Callatians—different codes. The Northwest Coast Indians, the Tibetan noncompetitive people, all point to the absence of a universal moral code. So can we know, with 100 percent certainty, on the basis of collected evidence, that there are no universal codes? No. We have to leave it open; perhaps some day a universal code will appear—or perhaps we will find that it had been there all the time, and we just didn't see it.

And, yet, I can't help adding a comment that may throw a bit of cold water on the critique of ethical relativism: Although ethical relativism is, indeed, a theory based on induction—sampling world cultures and their moral systems and concluding, on the basis of cross-cultural comparisons, that no cultures share any universal values—perhaps we should take a look at Ruth Benedict's final words in her article "Anthropology and the Abnormal." You'll find them in Study Question 4 in the Primary Readings section, and they are a very odd choice for an ending, coming from the most celebrated ethical relativist of the twentieth century: "It is as it is in ethics; all our local conventions of moral behavior and of immoral are without absolute validity, and yet it is quite possible that a modicum of what is considered right and what wrong could be disentangled that is shared by the whole human race." This extraordinary sentence shows that much as we try to pigeonhole Ruth Benedict as an ethical relativist, she herself had a moment of doubt, or even hope: Perhaps, if we look hard enough, we can find a common moral denominator in all cultures. The problem is that what she is expressing here is not ethical relativism, but *soft universalism*. So, was the primary voice for ethical relativism in the twentieth century not a relativist at all? Or might the issue be slightly different—that she indeed is an ethical relativist, but one whose theory is not vulnerable to the problem of induction, because she doesn't say that ethical relativism is a 100 percent certain theory? She says that until now, all cultures have looked different, but we can't speak for the future. And with that remark, Benedict has perhaps rescued her own brand of ethical relativism from the criticism that you can't reach a certain conclusion based on empirical evidence. But that, of course, does not rescue all other forms of relativism. Any theory that claims to be 100 percent certain, based on empirical evidence, is still open to the criticism of the problem of induction.

James Rachels and Soft Universalism

The problem of induction is advanced not by hard universalists but by *soft universalists,* because they are the ones who advocate looking for some core values that all cultures might share. Soft universalism, to which you were introduced at the beginning of this chapter, is not a new idea; it was suggested by the Scottish philosopher David Hume in the eighteenth century. Hume believed that all people share a fellow-feeling, a compassion, that may show itself in different ways but is present in the human spirit regardless of one's cultural background. Today, soft universalism claims that we ought to look for bottom-line common moral denominators rather than what separates us as cultures and as individuals. This idea has an increasing number of followers, among ethicists as well as laypeople. One of the most adamant critics of ethical relativism in modern times, and an advocate for the idea that all cultures have some values in common, was the American philosopher James Rachels (1941–2003).

In his book *Elements of Moral Philosophy*, Rachels points out that the problem of induction gives us a clue to what values might actually be in common for all cultures: Remember King Darius, who tried to get the Greeks to eat their dead and the Callatians to burn theirs? You may have asked yourself why any group would want to eat its dead. You may have wanted to ask Ruth Benedict why the Northwest Coast Indians were so aggressive. (She doesn't say.) We all may wonder why some peoples approve of infanticide or of dismemberment as punishment. As soon as we ask why, though, we have left the realm of ethical relativism. Relativists don't ask why; they just look at different customs and pronounce them fine for those who hold them. In asking why, we are looking for an explanation, one we can understand from our own point of view. In other words, we are expecting, or hoping, that there is some point at which that other culture will cease to seem so strange. And very often we reach that point. For instance, disposing of the dead through cannibalism is not at all uncommon, and it usually is done for the sake of honoring the dead or sharing in their spiritual strength. It would seem, then, that the Greeks and the Callatians had something in common after all: The Greeks burned their dead because they wanted to honor their spirits, and the Callatians ate their dead for the same reason. Some nomad tribes of the Sahara consider it bad manners to eat in front of their in-laws. American couples rarely talk about sexual matters in the presence of their in-laws for the same reason—it is considered bad manners. These cultures share some common values: Both value good family relationships, and both express embarrassment when a transgression occurs.

James Rachels suggests that at least three values are universal:

1. A policy of caring for enough infants to ensure the continuation of the group

2. A rule against lying

3. A rule against murder

We may be horrified to learn about the custom of killing female babies in the old Eskimo (Inuit) culture, Rachels says, but we gain a better understanding when we learn that female babies were killed only because a high death rate among male hunters led to a surplus of females in the community. Why would it be a bad thing for an Inuit tribe to have more women than men? Certainly not because the women were unproductive—in addition to raising children and cooking, they were the ones manufacturing tools and clothing from the animals brought home by the hunters—but because male hunters were the sole providers of food. (The Inuit diet is primarily meat.) Therefore, a shortage of men in relation to the number of women would mean a shortage of food. Another important fact is that babies were killed only during hard times and only if adoptive parents couldn't be found. In such times, if the babies had been kept alive, the lives of the older children would have been in jeopardy. In other words, the Inuit killed some infants to protect the children they already had. Their culture valued what ours values: caring for the babies we already have.

Why do all cultures have a rule against lying? Because if you can't expect a fellow citizen to tell the truth most of the time, there is no use attempting to communicate, and without communication human society would grind to a halt. This doesn't mean, obviously, that humans never lie to one another, but only that, on the whole, the acceptable attitude is one of truthfulness.

The rule against murder derives from similar reasoning: If we can't expect our fellow citizens not to kill us, we will not want to venture outdoors, we will stop trusting in people, and society will fall apart (not, as some might think, because everyone will be killed off, but because of general mistrust and lack of communication). Rachels believes that even under chaotic circumstances small groups of friends and relatives would band together, and within those groups the nonmurder rule would be upheld.

So these three values are Rachels's suggested universal moral codes, to be found in all cultures regardless of religion and other traditions, solving the riddle of ethical relativism. At first glance they do indeed seem incontrovertible. How could we imagine a culture that doesn't care for its babies, that lies and murders? We can't—but perhaps that is not because the values are universal but because Rachels has simply selected elements that ensure a culture's basic survival. Can we be sure that all cultures have rules that dictate caring for as many infants as it takes to keep the culture going? Absolutely; but perhaps that is not a matter of ethics but of *logic*—in particular, *deductive* logic. How does a culture survive? By reproducing, and raising children. So all cultures that exist survive by raising children. Must all cultures subscribe to raising their children? Actually, no, but if they don't, they'll die out. But that is not unusual—some cultures, from time to time, decide that they will not reproduce (such as the Christian group the Shakers in the nineteenth century), and after a while they will no longer be around. So the value of caring for infants is actually not universal in all cultures, just in all *surviving* cultures, which makes it a tautology, a self-evident truth.

The trouble with rules 2 and 3 is that they seem to apply to "fellow citizens" only. As a member of society, you are expected not to lie to or murder members of your own social group, but there is really nothing preventing you from being morally free to lie through your teeth to an outsider or to an enemy government. You may even be free to prey on and murder members of other tribes, gangs, or countries. A scandal in the discipline of anthropology illustrates this phenomenon in a way that is quite significant: The renowned anthropologist Margaret Mead (1901–1978), who was a student of Franz Boas and Ruth Benedict, and like them an ethical relativist, wrote a book about the sexuality of young South Sea islanders, *Coming of Age in Samoa* (1928), which became a best-seller. But in the 1980s it became clear that she had been the victim of a hoax: Her native contacts in Samoa had strung her along to see how many whopping lies she'd swallow before she became suspicious—but she was young and gullible. It appears that with some additional research Mead could have discovered that for herself, but she never did. So even though the Samoans

James Rachels (1941–2003), American philosopher and advocate of human and animal rights. He was the author of *Elements of Moral Philosophy* (1968), *The End of Life: Euthanasia and Morality* (1986), *Created from Animals: The Moral Implications of Darwinism* (1990), and *Can Ethics Provide Answers?* (1997). He completed his last two books only shortly before he died: *The Truth About the World* and *Problems from Philosophy,* both with the publication date 2005.

certainly had an overall rule against lying within their culture (which we know because one of Mead's contacts felt she ought to 'fess up when she was in her eighties), it didn't necessarily extend to the inexperienced young anthropologist.

Besides, is it true that we are expected to tell the truth? Many would challenge that idea across the board of world cultures. In some cultures it is considered good manners to lie, to play down one's own accomplishments (such as the Chinese tradition of berating one's own cooking skills), not to tell the whole truth about a friend's appearance if she or he asks your opinion, to lie about sexual relationships to protect those involved (the notion of chivalry is sometimes invoked). In folklore there is even a tradition of telling "whoppers," and American Western folklore contains many prime examples of "tall tales." The frontiersman David ("Davy") Crockett was elected to Congress in 1827 not just because he was a likable and conscientious man but also because he told better whoppers than his opponent (and had the grace to freely admit that he had been lying). So although it may not be true that a rule against lying is universal, if we characterize it as a rule against malicious deception we are closer to what Rachels means: Without that trust, your network of communications will break down.

Another problem with Rachels's three rules lies in the fact that, whatever rules may apply to a given culture, the *leaders* of those cultures, who should embody the cultural standards, are often the ones who break those rules. If it was to a leader's advantage to bend or break a rule, he or she might even consider it a duty to the throne to do so. Only in the twentieth century did the concept of rulers not being above the law become solidified (to the extent that some leaders have to deal with civil lawsuits during their time-limited reign rather than face charges afterward). Even the near-universal ban on incest, which might well qualify as a fourth universal value, has traditionally been broken by leaders such as the pharaohs of ancient Egypt, who would marry their own siblings, and the royal families of Europe in previous centuries, who sometimes matched up first cousins because nobody else with "blue blood" was available. Interestingly, if we go back to the example from Herodotus about the Greeks and the Callatians, we are perhaps as close to a true universal moral value as we will ever come, and one that is not survival-oriented: respect for one's dead relatives.

Rachels has not provided us with any rules that apply universally, only with rules that all responsible people seem to be required to stick to *within their own societies*. Rachels has, however, provided all we need to show that ethical relativism is wrong in its assumption that cultures have nothing in common; we don't have to find a universal moral rule, just a universal pattern of behavior. Because Rachels believes that there are at least three such patterns—care of infants, not lying, and not murdering— we can call him a *descriptive soft universalist:* He describes what he thinks is the case, that we actually have some codes of behavior in common. But even if you can't find any codes in common, you might still be a *normative soft universalist*. In that case, you believe we *ought* to have some code of behavior in common and that we ought to work toward establishing or finding such a code. You can, of course, be both a descriptive and a normative soft universalist. In that case you believe human beings around the world do have a few basic moral codes in common; but you also believe that to move toward a world community in which we can respect one another's differences while striving to work together to solve problems, we ought to find some common ground and set up a basic moral code for humanity to live by, a code such as the concept of human rights.

In the end, the soft universalist may point out that since the relativist's position is logically impossible in that he or she wants universal tolerance but can't have it because of not believing in universal values, so ethical relativism is in fact disingenuous, because it doesn't take itself seriously as a theory—it is an armchair exercise. In a clash of cultures where your own culture is under attack—do you choose to defend it just because it's yours? No, you defend it because you believe its values are good. And if you choose not to defend it, is it because you think nobody is right? Probably not—it is probably because you think the "other culture" has a point. And if you find yourself on trial in another country and (truly) consider yourself not guilty, would you want to be acquitted because of your cultural affiliation? Anything that leads to an acquittal will probably be welcome, but in the end, wouldn't you rather be cleared because you are *not guilty?* These basic situations reveal to the soft universalist that even if we may think we profess to ethical relativism, it can't be upheld when push comes to shove—in effect, like moral nihilism, moral skepticism, and moral subjectivism, it involves an internal contradiction, because as a matter of fact nobody really believes that each culture is right in its own way, and there are no common denominators. The bottom line for the soft universalist is the fact that *we are all mortal human beings,* with the same physical limitations and the same capacities for language, relationships, and pleasure and pain. Unless we're sociopaths, we all want what's best for our loved ones; we all want to live, unless by dying we serve some greater good (some take that further than others). We dread illness, cherish our good memories, and enjoy the company of our friends. We tell stories, and believe that ethics is indispensable to social life. How could we *not* have more in common than what divides us culturally? At the end of the chapter, you'll find an excerpt from Dwight Furrow's paper "Of Cave Dwellers and Spirits: The Trouble with Moral Absolutes," in which he seeks a middle ground between relativism and absolutism.

Ethical Relativism and Multiculturalism

With the increasingly pluralistic character of modern Western society comes an increasing belief that all cultural traditions and all perspectives represented in the public deserve to be heard—at universities, in politics, in the media, and elsewhere. Sometimes this is referred to as "multiculturalism," sometimes as "cultural diversity."

Let us consider multiculturalism and its goals. America used to be called a melting pot, meaning that there was room for anybody from anywhere, that all would be welcomed, and that after a while all individual cultural differences would subside in favor of the new culture of the United States. To many Americans (those from many different ethnic backgrounds, in fact), this continues to represent a beautiful image as well as an accurate description of what America is all about. For many people around the world, this is what America seems to be. For others, however, the idea of the melting pot is a travesty, an illusion, and an insult. America may have embraced immigrants from countries such as England, Sweden, Ireland, and Germany, but many other people still feel as though they are living on the fringes of American society; they have not been accepted the way others have been. For such people, who feel that they and their ancestors were excluded from the melting pot because they were too different or simply unwanted, there is no such thing as a *common* American culture, only a *dominant* American culture; and they claim that what has been taught and practiced until recently has been *monoculturalism* (sometimes referred to as *Eurocentrism*). Today there is an understanding even among those from the "dominant culture" that this damages the very concept of an American culture. The question is what to do about it.

Some proponents of multiculturalism believe that what we must do is begin to listen to one another. I call this *inclusive multiculturalism* (also referred to as *pluralism*). The general idea is to integrate everyone—by law, if necessary—into all aspects of our society; to break through the "glass ceilings" that prevent people of color (women and men) as well as white women from reaching top positions; to become sensitized to what others might perceive as slurs (what one scholar calls *microinequities,* those little jabs that can hurt so deeply); and, if we are on the receiving end of such slurs, to learn to speak up for ourselves. An increased awareness of the multicolored pattern of our society will, the thinking goes, result in better working relationships, less of a sense that one cultural tradition dominates the country and that everyone who doesn't share it must be left out, and more tolerance and understanding among the groups. This awareness is supposed to begin in schools, where children should learn about as many cultural groups in American society as possible. Adding multicultural awareness to the curriculum means there will be less time for some subjects that are usually taught, but proponents of inclusive multiculturalism believe that a growing cultural understanding is worth the price. Today, a new image is frequently offered as an alternative to the old image of the melting pot: the *salad bowl*. A metaphor for inclusive multiculturalism, the salad image implies that each group retains its original "flavor" but that the groups also relate to one another; together they make a sum that is greater than its parts. The metaphor can be stretched only so far, though: Critics who believe that inclusive multiculturalism is not doing enough to foster cultural identity can always turn the image around and ask, Who supplies

B.C.   *BY JOHNNY HART*

By permission of Johnny Hart Studios and Creators Syndicate, Inc.

In the debate about multiculturalism, the inclusive approach is sometimes perceived to result in the inclusion of nonmainstream ideas and traditions at the cost of mainstream traditions. The artist of the classic comic strip *B.C.*, Johnny Hart, now deceased, excelled in poignant commentaries defending the Christian point of view. Here he defends the traditional greeting, "Merry Christmas." In your view, does he have a point?

the salad dressing? The "dominant culture"! (Box 3.4 examines how some advocates of cultural diversity apply what appears to be an ad hominem fallacy.)

For a while in the 1980s and 1990s, a certain approach was attempted in some schools, but its popularity seems to have declined over the last decade: The method of *exclusive multiculturalism* (also called *particularism*) was intended to help children from minority cultures retain or regain their self-esteem, under the assumption that self-esteem is fragile for such children (which in itself might be a questionable assumption). To counteract this supposed lack of self-esteem, children from each ethnic group were isolated so they could be taught about the cultural advances of their particular group. Many parents as well as students felt uncomfortable about this approach, claiming that it led to a new form of segregation. And indeed, problems with the method of exclusive multiculturalism haven't quite been worked out to everyone's satisfaction: In a future society where mixed race and ethnicity are the rule rather than the exception, must a child then choose a primary racial or ethnic affiliation? And where would students of Euro-American ancestry be placed, regardless of whether they have majority or minority status—surely not in separate groups learning about the illustrious achievements of exclusively Euro-Americans? That would end up looking like white supremacy.

All in all, it seems that the inclusive approach to multiculturalism has become the standard method in primary and secondary schools. Since the early 1990s I have tried to keep track of the progress of an inclusive approach to American history in high schools, and in recent years an increasing number of students have reported that they

Box 3.4 CULTURAL DIVERSITY OR CULTURAL ADVERSITY?

The idea that moral viewpoints acquire their importance from the groups that utter them rather than from their content is, to some philosophers, a misguided attitude. In the old days of Western culture, the dominant viewpoint was the one held by some—but not all—white males, and for most white males as well as for others that was enough to make the viewpoint "correct." Churches and political groups occasionally take the same attitude: The identity of the group is enough justification for the correctness of its views. Today we also see this same viewpoint applied socially by certain groups: If you are a member of an oppressed group, your viewpoint on right and wrong is valuable just because you are a member of that group, and if you are not, then your viewpoint is irrelevant. This form of relativism, which grants the importance of a viewpoint on the basis of gender, race, and class, may be as misplaced as one that denies the importance of certain groups just because they are who they are. Such an attitude, the argument goes, reflects the logical fallacy of the *ad hominem argument:* You are right or wrong because of who you are, not because of what you say. In Jim Garrison's words from Oliver Stone's film *JFK*, "I always wondered in court why it is because a woman is a prostitute, she has to have bad eyesight" (meaning some people think that just because someone is a prostitute, we can't trust her testimony). Whether this attitude is assumed by those in power or by those who are dispossessed, it is equally faulty as a moral principle, according to the rules of critical thinking. Can you imagine situations in which a person's identity alone would determine whether he or she was right or wrong?

have been taught American history in high school according to inclusive multicultural principles rather than through history books reflecting a monocultural approach.

How might multiculturalism affect our attitude toward basic values in ethics? That depends greatly on what we believe those values to be. If we think our values can't be disputed, that they are somehow determined by God or by Nature, then we will find it hard to accept other and different viewpoints. As we will see, such absolutism ("hard universalism") usually does not allow for any tolerance of other basic ideas.

If we adopt the attitude of ethical relativism, the result may surprise us, because ethical relativism doesn't automatically support multiculturalism. Ethical relativism states that there is no universal moral code—that each culture will do what is right for it, and no other culture has any business interfering. That may work when cultures are separate and isolated from one another, because the moral code in that case is defined as the code of the *dominant population*. Remember problem 2, "majority rule"? One of the problems with ethical relativism is precisely that it implies the moral rule of the majority. However, in our pluralistic society, that won't work because the "dominant culture" (white society) is increasingly reproached for displaying cultural insensitivity. Can ethical relativism function, therefore, in a country as diverse as ours, where we may find opposing values ("Looting is antisocial" versus "Looting is a righteous act for the dispossessed," for example) within the same neighborhood? Because a multicultural ethic asks us not to think in terms of one dominant set of rules, some might opt for an attitude of total *moral nihilism* instead: No values are better than any other values because no values are objectively correct. Such nihilism might well result in the breakdown of the fabric of a society, and possibly in a greater cohesion within subgroups, with different groups battling one another. Rather than describe these battles as gang wars, we might call this phenomenon *Balkanization*—when groups have nothing or very little in common except hatred for what the other groups stand for. It seems as though ethical relativism is not the answer to our new ethical problems of multiculturalism.

Suppose we look to soft universalism for the answer? If we are soft universalists, we hope to be able to agree with others on some basic issues, but not on all issues. In the case of multiculturalism, we may be able to agree on the promotion of general equality, tolerance, and cohesion in the nation (in other words, the will and ability to live together); we *have* to agree that what we want is a functioning society we all share in. If we don't agree on that, multiculturalism is a lost cause, and so is the whole idea of a United States. According to soft universalism, values can't be allowed to differ dramatically, so we wouldn't end up with acts such as looting being morally right for some and not for others, nor would the killing of family members for the sake of honor be acceptable in one neighborhood and not in another. These questions of common values in the context of a multicultural society are particularly burning, for without some values in common we simply won't have a society.

Is it possible to have one overall culture and several subcultural affiliations at the same time? In other words, can we have loyalties to our ancient ethnic roots and also be Americans (or Canadians, or Italians, or Brazilians, or whatever the case may be)? A few generations ago, immigrant parents made sure their children learned English and had American first names, encouraging them to blend in as quickly as possible so that their future as American citizens would have as few obstacles as possible—an obvious ethnic identity being considered an obstacle. A generation of children lost the language of their parents, and in many cases their family history too. But over the past twenty-five years or so, people have been involved in looking for their roots, to a great extent inspired by Alex Haley's novel and television series *Roots* (1977), about an African American family's history. This trend has involved a renewed interest in teaching the new generation of children the language of their grandparents as a second language. One's cultural identity has been to a great extent perceived as formed through the original nationality of one's immigrant ancestors: one is "Irish-American," "Polish-American," "Chinese-American," and so forth—to the extent that the nationality to the left of the hyphen has seemed, to some, to outweigh the second identity: American. This is what has spawned the expression "hyphenated American"—someone who sees himself or herself as having a composite heritage and perhaps also a split cultural identity. Does this mean you have to identify with some ancient ethnic heritage because there really isn't any American cultural identity per se? Box 3.5 explores what it might mean to have an American identity. In the aftermath of the terrorist attacks of 2001, a new generation found, for a while, an answer to what it means to be an American—focusing on the common denominator rather than on individual differences rooted in ethnicity or national roots. And now it seems as if that lesson has been put on the back burner for many young people, or has been superseded by other lessons, about global citizenship and global responsibilities. Perhaps the issue

Box 3.5 AN AMERICAN CULTURE?

When discussing the mores and habits of other cultures with my classes, I often hear students claim that there *is* no American culture—and if common denominators do exist, they are considered negative: brashness, ignorance or mistrust of other cultures, materialism, and so on. To many students, the fact that we are a very diverse society means that we have no shared culture; many consider themselves hyphenated Americans: Irish-Americans, African-Americans, Italian-Americans, Arab-Americans, and so forth. And yet in the weeks and months following the terrorist attacks of September 2001, many Americans, including many of my students, discovered that they had an American identity after all, and the loss of American lives felt like a personal loss. But the feelings of September 11 have receded for many, and as I am writing this, there is a great rift in the American populace. Although the patriotism that surged after 9/11 hasn't gone away, it has taken on political colors. For some, pride in being an American is best expressed in being critical of the administration that took us into Iraq; for others, patriotic pride is linked to the concept that as a nation in war, we ought to present a united front. A commercial a few years ago lined up a number of people of different races and with different accents, all proudly proclaiming "I am an American." But what does that mean, other than citizenship?

If you agree that an American cultural identity exists, how would you characterize it? Is it founded in our Constitution? Is it a matter of a general outlook on life? Is it the fact that we, as a matter of course, question authority? Does it have to do with common cultural experiences, common holidays and food rituals (such as Thanksgiving), a love of traveling within our country, and perhaps also with an image of ourselves that has been invented by the movies?

Or perhaps it is the very freedom to define oneself that other cultures seem to have only to a lesser degree? Many Americans don't realize what it means to be an American until they travel abroad and experience other cultures—or perhaps tangle with legal systems that do not presume one to be innocent until proven guilty! Rather (as in the Napoleonic Law of France), you are presumed guilty until you can prove yourself innocent.

In the event of a common threat from abroad, one's cultural identity seems to loom larger, in the form of an appreciation for everyday things we used to take for granted and for the rights this society grants us—even the right to disagree about this whole issue. The philosopher and novelist Ayn Rand (see Chapter 4), an immigrant from the Soviet Union, called America the only truly moral culture in the world. In the Primary Readings section you'll read an excerpt of *America and Americans*, the last book by novelist and moral philosopher John Steinbeck, about what makes the American character unique—with negatives as well as positive points on his list.

of national identity is not a fixed entity as much as a concept that needs revisiting and redefining in times of crisis as well as in less stressful times.

Study Questions

1. Describe the four major approaches to moral differences outlined at the beginning of this chapter. Which one comes closest to your own viewpoint? Explain.

2. Discuss Ruth Benedict's claim that what is normal for a culture is what is moral in that culture. Discuss the advantages and problems associated with the theory of ethical relativism.

©2001 Scott Stantis. Reprinted by permission of Copley News Service.

For many Americans, September 11 brought about a reevaluation of what it means to have a national and ethnic identity. Does this cartoon reflect your post-9/11 feelings about your nationality and ethnicity? Why or why not? Is the second panel preferable to the first? Why or why not?

   3. Discuss James Rachels's three suggested universal values: Are they truly universal? Why or why not? Can you think of other universal values not mentioned?

   .4. Can one have both an ethnic and a national identity? Explain.

Primary Readings and Narratives

The first Primary Reading is an excerpt from Ruth Benedict's famous paper "Anthropology and the Abnormal." The second is an excerpt from Dwight Furrow's paper, "Of Cave Dwellers and Spirits: The Problem with Moral Absolutes," where he seeks an alternative approach to both moral relativism and absolutism. The final Primary Reading is an excerpt from John Steinbeck's *America and Americans,* in which Steinbeck analyzes the pros and cons of the American character. The Narratives include a summary with excerpts from Barbara Kingsolver's *The Poisonwood Bible,* a novel pitting a Christian missionary and his family against traditional African customs, written as a critique of absolutist ethics; next, you'll find a summary of Alice Walker's novel *Possessing the Secret of Joy,* which indirectly—but powerfully—criticizes ethical relativism's tolerance toward the tribal practice of female circumcision; and a summary of Spike Lee's film *Do the Right Thing,* which explores multiracial tensions and relationships in a Brooklyn neighborhood.

Primary Reading

Anthropology and the Abnormal

RUTH BENEDICT

Essay, 1934. Excerpt.

In her famous paper, Benedict talks about a Melanesian culture displaying extreme fears of poisoning. In addition, you'll read in her own words her view that morality is merely what is considered normal in a given society.

The most spectacular illustrations of the extent to which normality may be culturally defined are those cultures where an abnormality of our culture is the cornerstone of their social structure. It is not possible to do justice to these possibilities in a short discussion. A recent study of an island of northwest Melanesia by Fortune describes a society built upon traits which we regard as beyond the border of paranoia. In this tribe the exogamic groups look upon each other as prime manipulators of black magic, so that one marries always into an enemy group which remains for life one's deadly and unappeasable foes. They look upon a good garden crop as a confession of theft, for everyone is engaged in making magic to induce into his garden the productiveness of his neighbors'; therefore no secrecy in the island is so rigidly insisted upon as the secrecy of a man's harvesting of his yams. Their polite phrase at the acceptance of a gift is, "And if you now poison me, how shall I repay you this present?" Their preoccupation with poisoning is constant; no woman ever leaves her cooking pot for a moment untended. Even the great affinal economic exchanges that are characteristic of this Melanesian culture area are quite altered in Dobu since they are incompatible with this fear and distrust that pervades the culture. They go farther and people the whole world outside of their own quarters with such malignant spirits that all-night feasts and ceremonials simply do not occur here. They have even rigorous religiously enforced customs that forbid the sharing of seed even in one family group. Anyone else's food is deadly poison to you, so that communality of stores is out of the question. For some months before harvest the whole society is on the verge of starvation, but if one falls to the temptation and eats up one's seed yams, one is an outcast and a beachcomber for life. There is no coming back. It involves, as a matter of course, divorce and the breaking of all social ties.

Now in this society where no one may work with another and no one may share with another, Fortune describes the individual who was regarded by all his fellows as crazy. He was not one of those who periodically ran amok and, beside himself and frothing at the mouth, fell with a knife upon anyone he could reach. Such behavior they did not regard as putting anyone outside the pale. . . . But there was one man of sunny, kindly disposition who liked work and liked to be helpful. The compulsion was too strong for him to repress it in favor of the opposite tendencies of his culture. Men and women never spoke of him without laughing; he was silly and simple and definitely crazy. Nevertheless, to the ethnologist used to a culture that has, in Christianity, made his type the model of all virtue, he seemed a pleasant fellow.

These illustrations, which it has been possible to indicate only in the briefest manner, force upon us the fact that normality is culturally defined. An adult shaped to the

drives and standards of either of these cultures, if he were transported into our civilization, would fall into our categories of abnormality. He would be faced with the psychic
dilemmas of the socially unavailable. In his own culture, however, he is the pillar of society,
the end result of socially inculcated mores, and the problem of personal instability in his
case simply does not arise.

No one civilization can possibly utilize in its mores the whole potential range of
human behavior. Just as there are great numbers of possible phonetic articulations, and
the possibility of language depends on a selection and standardization of a few of these
in order that speech communication may be possible at all, so the possibility of organized
behavior of every sort, from the fashions of local dress and houses to the dicta of a people's ethics and religion, depends upon a similar selection among the possible behavior
traits. In the field of recognized economic obligations or sex [taboos] this selection is as
nonrational and subconscious a process as it is in the field of phonetics. It is a process
which goes on in the group for long periods of time and is historically conditioned by innumerable accidents of isolation or of contact of peoples. In any comprehensive study of
psychology, the selection that different cultures have made in the course of history within
the great circumference of potential behavior is of great significance.

Every society, beginning with some slight inclination in one direction or another,
carries its preference farther and farther, integrating itself more and more completely
upon its chosen basis, and discarding those types of behavior that are uncongenial. Most
of those organizations of personality that seem to us most incontrovertibly abnormal
have been used by different civilizations in the very foundations of their institutional life.
Conversely the most valued traits of our normal individuals have been looked on in differently organized cultures as aberrant. Normality, in short, within a very wide range, is
culturally defined. It is primarily a term for the socially elaborated segment of human
behavior in any culture; and abnormality, a term for the segment that that particular
civilization does not use. The very eyes with which we see the problem are conditioned
by the long traditional habits of our own society. . . .

. . . Mankind has always preferred to say, "It is morally good," rather than "it is
habitual.". . . But historically the two phrases are synonymous. . . . The concept of
the normal is properly a variant of the concept of good. It is that which society has
approved. . . . Western civilization allows and culturally honors gratifications of the ego
which according to any absolute category would be regarded as abnormal. The portrayal of unbridled and arrogant egoists as family men, as officers of the law, and in business has been a favorite topic of novelists, and they are familiar in every community.
Such individuals are probably mentally warped to a greater degree than many inmates
of our institutions who are nevertheless socially unavailable. They are extreme types of
those personality configurations which our civilization fosters. . . .

The relativity of normality is important in what may some day come to be a true social engineering. Our picture of our own civilization is no longer in this generation in
terms of a changeless and divinely derived set of categorical imperatives. We must face
the problems our changed perspective has put upon us. In this matter of mental ailments, we must face the fact that even our normality is man-made, and is of our own
seeking. Just as we have been handicapped in dealing with ethical problems so long as
we held to an absolute definition of morality, so too in dealing with the problems of abnormality we are handicapped so long as we identify our local normalities with the universal sanities. I have taken illustrations from different cultures, because the conclusions

are most inescapable from the contrasts as they are presented in unlike social groups. But the major problem is not a consequence of the variability of the normal from culture to culture, but its variability from era to era. This variability in time we cannot escape if we would, and it is not beyond the bounds of possibility that we may be able to face this inevitable change with full understanding and deal with it rationally. No society has yet achieved self-conscious and critical analysis of its own normalities and attempted rationally to deal with its own social process of creating new normalities within its next generation. But the fact that it is unachieved is not therefore proof of its impossibility. It is a faint indication of how momentous it could be in human society.

Study Questions

1. Is it important for Benedict to discover why the members of the tribe on the Melanesian island are afraid of poisoning? Why or why not? Would it make a difference in terms of ethical relativism if we knew the origin of the fear?

2. Is she right in her statement that "the concept of the normal is properly a variant of the concept of good"? Why or why not?

3. Does Benedict's cultural approach facilitate intercultural understanding? Why or why not?

4. Benedict is now viewed as one of the first spokespersons for ethical relativism, although her aim in this paper was to explore the concept of the abnormal. Her paper ends with these rarely quoted words, exploring the possibility of intercultural standards of normality: "It is as it is in ethics: all our local conventions of moral behavior and of immoral are without absolute validity, and yet it is quite possible that a modicum of what is considered right and what wrong could be disentangled that is shared by the whole human race." Does this statement contradict the general view of Benedict as being an ethical relativist? Does it undermine the philosophy of ethical relativism? Is she contradicting herself? Why or why not?

Primary Reading

Of Cave Dwellers and Spirits: The Problem with Moral Absolutes

DWIGHT FURROW

Essay, 2004. Excerpt.

In this paper, American philosopher Dwight Furrow argues that students and others who find that moral absolutes are not a satisfactory response to today's problems go too far in the other direction when they embrace moral relativism instead. Furrow distinguishes between two forms of moral relativism—what you in this text have been introduced to as (1) moral subjectivism and (2) ethical relativism—and explains that the fact that few, if any, truly universal values have been found does not mean that all values are relative. In this section he explains why we often take recourse in what is legal, rather than what is moral. Toward the end of the excerpt he shares a vision of hope: that when push comes to shove, we respond to the needs of other human beings, regardless of theories of moral absolutism or relativism. (The reference to moral conscience in a cave refers to Plato's Myth/Allegory of the Cave, which you will find in Chapter 8.)

Our current cultural debate over values is often framed as a disagreement between those who prefer clear, unambiguous answers to moral questions, anchored in firm, unchanging moral principles, and those who think what is right depends on where you were raised. I have been arguing that neither side of this debate can support its position, and thus they contribute little but noise to our attempts to live and act well. Perhaps the deeper issue is whether either of these unsupportable positions causes any real harm. Does it make any practical difference whether one is a relativist or an absolutist? As I noted above, the exigencies of life force relativists, against their inclinations, to make reasonably consistent moral judgments. Aside from a tendency toward misplaced tolerance, which though incurring the liabilities of naiveté nevertheless enjoys the benefits of trust, there are few consequences to being a relativist. Unfortunately, the search for moral absolutes is not so benign. In fact, moral absolutism is positively pernicious. Far from providing a moral anchor, the fruitless search for evaporating absolutes encourages the abdication of moral responsibility.

The baleful effects of this long search for absolutes underlie one of our most persistent popular moral attitudes—the idea that if an action is legal it is right. Recent accounting scandals attest to the ubiquity of the belief that the perfume of legal casuistry masks the stench of corruption. Yet, a legal code is an unwieldy instrument for dealing with moral questions. It is inefficient and insensitive at best, coercive and tyrannical at worst, and ceding moral authority to government officials is inimical to American ideals. Ironically, the search for universality and objectivity, with its unrealistic demands, encourages this transfer of moral liability, for it eviscerates the only moral resources available to individuals in our current situation.

Contemporary society places increasingly abstract moral demands on us, as we try to cope with the unfamiliar, the unexpected, and the unintended. We routinely interact with others whose lives seem opaque; we use technology that promises to utterly transform human existence in ways that even our most prescient prognosticators cannot foresee; and each of us occupies multiple, incompatible social roles with conflicting norms and expectations. There is seldom a straightforward answer to the question of what moral burdens an individual must accept. Yet, in these circumstances, the task of sustaining a moral point of view, nevertheless, falls by default squarely on the shoulders of individuals who must use their own critical judgment while bootstrapping moral feelings by cobbling together communities of interest or accident and sustaining relationships across time and distance.

It is not surprising, in this atmosphere of ambiguity and uncertainty, that many struggle unsuccessfully to hone their basic moral impulses. We acquire the capacity for compassion and the disposition toward honesty, loyalty, and justice in face-to-face meetings where issues of dependence and support have palpable consequences and emotional weight. Unfortunately, in the face of increasingly abstract demands, where consequences are less obvious and relationships less secure, our moral feelings become confused and attenuated—less compulsive, and ultimately less trustworthy. Though we look for moral authorities to replace these impulses, there are too many and they are in conflict. Only the law with its explicit sanctions and reasonably sure consequences provides guidance. Thus, we cede moral authority to the lawmakers and their lawyers. . . . .

Hence, the ambivalence our students, and much of the rest of culture, feel toward ethics. This ambivalence arises not from the lack of moral authority but from the presence of too many moral authorities and an unachievable, arid ideal of objectivity that cannot be met, which thus encourages the ceding of responsibility to any half-baked authority that promises stability. Contemporary citizens hesitate to judge, not because they lack civilizing contact with tradition or because they stupidly think all judgments are equivalent but because our traditions don't help much in seeing through the fog of our present circumstances. . . .

After centuries of horror, we should now know that what keeps us on the rails is neither regulations nor theories but simply the sense that others call upon us to respond. Moral conscience has never had to wait for the word magic of philosophers or social scientists—it arises unbidden and often incoherent. Yet, as imperfect as it is, moral conscience is all we have, though it is too dynamic and idiosyncratic to rest on moral absolutes, since it flourishes only in caves where spirits fear to tread.

Study Questions

1. Is Furrow right that there are more damaging consequences if one is an absolutist than if one is a relativist? Explain.

2. Think of examples from the news in recent years where a legal solution has been sought to a moral problem. Do those solutions seem satisfactory, or do we still need to solve the issues at the level of ethics?

3. Is Furrow right that moral conscience, in the end, boils down to what David Hume called a "fellow-feeling" (see Chapter 4), a response to others in need? Does that remove the need for universal principles?

4. Would you call Furrow a soft universalist? Why or why not? (He doesn't use that term about his own philosophy.)

Primary Reading

Paradox and Dream

JOHN STEINBECK

America and Americans, *1966. Excerpt.*

In 1966 the American novelist and essayist John Steinbeck, whom you met in Chapter 1 as the author of the novel *East of Eden,* wrote a book about the concept of an American Identity: *America and Americans.* Steinbeck loved his country and its history, but he wasn't blind to the less positive elements of what we might call the American character, pursuing the American Dream and being engaged in the American Way of

John Steinbeck (1902–1968) is one of America's most celebrated authors of fiction, known for classics such as *Of Mice and Men* (1937), *Grapes of Wrath* (1939), and *East of Eden* (1952). In addition to his many novels and short stories, he wrote books and articles on such topics as politics, history, and marine biology. Scholars have recently begun to recognize that Steinbeck also made considerable contributions to the field of moral philosophy in his writings—fictional as well as nonfictional.

Life. Remember that this was written in 1966, and the world has changed dramatically in the forty-odd years since then. Even so, who among us, native-born Americans and immigrants alike, does not recognize exactly what Steinbeck is talking about, from a twenty-first century perspective? Steinbeck says, in his essay "Paradox and Dream":

> One of the generalities most often noted about Americans is that we are a restless, a dissatisfied, a searching people. We bridle and buckle under failure, and we go mad in the face of success. We spend our time searching for security, and hate it when we get it. For the most part we are an intemperate people: we eat too much when we can, drink too much, indulge our senses too much. Even in our so-called virtues we are intemperate: a teetotaler is not content not to drink—he must stop all the drinking in the world; a vegetarian among us would outlaw the eating of meat. We work too hard, and many die under the strain; and then to make up for that we play with a violence as suicidal.
>
> The result is that we seem to be in a state of turmoil all the time, both physically and mentally. We are able to believe that our government is weak, stupid, dishonest, and inefficient, and at the same time we are deeply convinced that it is the best government in the world, and we would like to impose it upon everyone else. We speak of the American Way of Life as though it involved the ground rules for the governance of heaven. . . . We are alert, curious, hopeful, and we take more drugs designed to make us unaware than any other people. We are self-reliant and at the same time completely dependent. We are aggressive, and defenseless. . . .
>
> Americans seem to live and breathe and function by paradox; but in nothing are we so paradoxical as in our belief in our own myths. We truly believe ourselves to be natural mechanics and do-it-yourself-ers. We spend our lives in motor cars, yet most of us—a great many of us at least—do not know enough about a car to look in the gas tank when the motor fails. . . . We believe implicitly that we are the heirs of the pioneers, that we have inherited self-sufficiency and the ability to take care of ourselves, particularly in relation to nature. There isn't a man among us in ten thousand who knows how to butcher a cow or a pig, and cut it up for eating, let alone a wild animal. . . . We shout that we are a nation of laws, not men—and then proceed to break every law we can if we can get away with it. . . . We fancy ourselves as hard-headed realists, but we will buy anything

we see advertised, particularly on television, and we buy it not with reference to the quality or the value of the product, but directly as a result of the number of times we have heard it mentioned. . . .

For Americans too the wide and general dream has a name. It is called "the American Way of Life." No one can define it or point to any one person or group of people who live it, but it is very real nevertheless, perhaps more real than the equally remote dream the Russians call Communism. These dreams describe our vague yearnings towards what we wish we were and hope we may be: wise, just, compassionate, and noble. The fact that we have this dream at all is perhaps an indication of its possibility.

Study Questions

1. Identify the key points Steinbeck lays out as being the core of the American character. Do you agree? Why or why not?

2. Is this a positive or a negative image of Americans? Explain.

3. If you are a native-born American, identify what you perceive to be the American character in positive and negative terms. If you are a visitor or an immigrant, compare what you perceive as the American character with the character of the people of your original culture.

4. Is this an example of "profiling," or even "stereotyping"? If no, why not? If yes, is that a problem in itself, or does stereotyping have some merit?

Narrative

The Poisonwood Bible

BARBARA KINGSOLVER

Novel, 1998. Summary and Excerpts.

The Poisonwood Bible is a story whose message of cultural tolerance has deeply affected readers. In some ways it can be said to support an ethical-relativist philosophy, but in others it seems to support soft universalism. Since this is a work of fiction and not a philosophical treatise, the author shouldn't be judged according to whether she presents a unified theory or not: It will be up to you to decide whether she is, at heart, an ethical relativist or a soft universalist; the quality of the story is what counts. (I think we can exclude the possibility of hard universalism right from the start.)

In 1959 Orleanna Price, a housewife from Georgia, travels with her husband and four daughters to the Congo in Africa so that her husband can fulfill his dream of bringing Christ to the natives. We follow their individual destinies all the way into the 1980s, seeing the consequences unfold of Nathan Price's decision to take his family to Africa. The book is structured with biblical overtones, beginning with a Genesis section, and

American author Barbara Kingsolver (b. 1955) has a deep interest in multiethnic issues. In 1963 her father worked as a medical
doctor in Zaire (then Congo), and he brought his family along to
the Caribbean in 1967 on another medical assignment. Kingsolver is the author of *The Bean Trees* (1988), *The Poisonwood
Bible* (1998), and *Prodigal Summer* (2001), among other novels.

ending with an Exodus section, but we learn fairly early in the story that this is no story
of happy missionaries bringing salvation to the heathens. It is instead the story of the
clash between cultures, the culture of the (presumably hard universalist) Christian missionary, and his wife and daughters who have grown up in an American world, meeting
a culture where just about *everything* is different: the concepts of right and wrong, good
and bad, what's food and what's not food, what's clean and unclean, what's near and
far—and eventually, what is home and what is not home. All five women react in
their own ways, and with their own voices. Nathan Price's voice is not heard except
through the reflections of the women, but he is the catalyst of the changes in their lives.
Orleanna, a religious, faithful wife who initially just wants to stand by her husband in
his work, eventually finds that the affront to the Africans and their culture perpetuated
by her husband's cultural and moral arrogance will require a lifetime of atonement from
her. Rachel, the eldest daughter, becomes the voice of longing for her lost American culture of affluence and convenience. Leah, once her father's strongest supporter, finds her
love and life's work in the politics of revolutionary Africa and lives an African life per-
petually apologizing for her whiteness; her twin sister Adah comes to terms with a physical disability afflicting her since childhood, seeing herself in light of another culture.
And the baby sister, Ruth May—well, you'll have to read the book to find out about
Ruth May.

In the first excerpt, Leah tells us of the cultural differences she is experiencing in the
Congolese village; the young teacher Anatole, who has been educated in the big city, tries
to mediate between the village chief and Price. In the second excerpt, Leah relates an incident where the village chief calls her father on his sincerity in having elections, and his
religious sincerity, and in the final excerpt she sums up her life experiences as a white
American in Africa, with Anatole by her side.

Anatole leaned forward and announced, "our chief, Tata Ndu, is concerned about the
moral decline of this village."

Father said, "Indeed he should be, because so few villagers are going to church."

"No, Reverend. Because so *many* villagers are going to church."

Well, that stupefied us all for a special moment in time. But Father leaned forward,
fixing to rise to the challenge. Whenever he sees an argument coming, man oh man, does
he get jazzed up.

"Brother Anatole, I fail to see how the church can mean anything but joy, for the few here who choose Christi-*an*-ity over *ignorance* and *darkness!*"

Anatole sighed, "I understand your difficulty, Reverend. Tata Ndu has asked me to explain this. His concern is with the important gods and ancestors of this village, who have always been honored in certain sacred ways. Tata Ndu worries that the people who go to your church are neglecting their duties."

"Neglecting their duties to false idolatry, you mean to say."

Anatole sighed again. "This may be difficult for you to understand. The people of your congregation are mostly what we call in Kikongo the *lensuka*. People who have shamed themselves or had very bad luck or something like that. Tata Boanda, for example. He has had terrible luck with his wives. The first one can't get any proper children, and the second one has a baby now who keeps dying before birth and coming back into her womb, over and over. No one can help this family anymore. The Boandas were very careful to worship their personal gods at home, making the proper sacrifices of food and doing everything in order. But still their gods have abandoned them for some reason. This is what they feel. Their luck could not get any more bad, you see? So they are interested to try making sacrifices to your Jesus."

Father looked like he was choking on a bone. I thought: Is there a doctor in the house? But Anatole went right on merrily ahead, apparently unaware he was fixing to kill my father of a heart attack.

"Tata Ndu is happy for you to draw the bad-luck people away," he said. "So the village's spirit protectors will not notice them so much. But he worries you are trying to lure too many of the others into following corrupt ways. He fears a disaster will come if we anger the gods."

"*Corrupt,* did you say," Father stated, rather than asked, after locating where the cat had put his tongue.

"Yes, Reverend Price."

"Corrupt *ways*. Tata Ndu feels that bringing the Christian word to these people is leading them to corrupt *ways*."

. . .

Father was poised to go on with the story when suddenly Tata Ndu stood right straight up, cutting him off in the middle of hammering home his message. We all stared. Tata Ndu held up his hand and declared in his deep, big-man's voice, giving each syllable the exact same size and weight: "Now it is time for the people to have an election."

"What?" I said out loud.

But Father, who's accustomed to knowing everything before it happens, took this right in stride. He replied patiently, "Well, now, that's good. Elections are a fine and civilized thing. In America we hold elections every four years to decide on new leaders." He waited while Anatole translated that. Maybe Father was dropping the hint that it was time for the villagers to reconsider the whole proposition of Tata Ndu.

Tata Ndu replied with equal patience, "*Á yi bandu,* if you do not mind, Tata Price, we will make our election now. *Ici, maintenant.*" He spoke in a careful combination of languages that was understood by everyone present. This was some kind of joke, I thought. Ordinarily Tata Ndu had no more use for our style of elections than Anatole did.

"With all due *respect,*" my father said, "this is not the time or the place for that kind of business. Why don't you sit down now, and announce your plans after I've finished with the sermon? Church is not the place to vote anyone in or out of public office."

"Church is the place for it," said Tata Ndu. *"Ici, maintenant,* we are making a vote for Jesus Christ in the office of personal God, Kilanga village."

Father did not move for several seconds.

Tata Ndu looked at him quizzically. "Forgive me, I wonder if I have paralyzed you?"

Father found his voice at last. "You have not."

"À bu, we will begin, *Beto tutakwe Kusala."* There was a sudden colorful bustle through the church as women in their bright *pagnes* began to move about. I felt a chill run down my spine. This had been planned in advance. The women shook pebbles out of calabash bowls into the folds of their skirts and moved between the benches, firmly placing one pebble into each out-stretched hand. This time women and children were also getting to vote, apparently. Tata Mwanza's father came forward to set up the clay voting bowls in front of the altar. One of the voting bowls was for Jesus, the other was against. The emblems were a cross and a bottle of *nsamba,* a new palm wine. Anyone ought to know that was not a fair match.

Father tried to interrupt the proceedings by loudly explaining that Jesus is exempt from popular elections. But people were excited, having just recently gotten the hang of the democratic process. The citizens of Kilanga were ready to cast their stones. They shuffled up to the altar in single file, just exactly as if they were finally coming forward to be saved. And Father stepped up to meet them as if he also believed this was the heavenly roll call. But the line of people just divided around him like water around a boulder in the creek, and went on ahead to make their votes. The effect of it wasn't very dignified, so Father retreated back to his pulpit made of wired-together palm fronds and raised up one hand, intending I guess to pronounce the benediction. But the voting was all over with before he could really get a word in sideways. Tata Ndu's assistant chiefs began counting the pebbles right away. They arranged them in clusters of five in a line on the floor, one side matched up against the other, for all to see.

"C'est juste," Tata Ndu said while they counted. "We can all see with our own eyes it was fair."

My father's face was red. "This is *blasphemy!"* He spread his hands wide as if casting out demons only he could see, and shouted, "There is nothing fair here!"

Tata Ndu turned directly to Father and spoke to him in surprisingly careful English, rolling his r's, placing every syllable like a stone in a hand. "Tata Price, white men have brought us many programs to improve our thinking," he said. "The program of Jesus and the program of elections. You say these things are good. You cannot say now they are *not* good."

A shouting match broke out in the church, mostly in agreement with Tata Ndu. Almost exactly at the same time, two men yelled, *"Ku nianga, ngeye uyele kutala!"*

Anatole, who'd sat down in his chair a little distance from the pulpit, leaned over and said quietly to Father, "They say you thatched your roof and now you must not run out of your house if it rains."

Father ignored this parable. "Matters of the spirit are not decided at the marketplace," he shouted sternly. Anatole translated.

"À bu, kwe? Where, then?" asked Tata Nguza, standing up boldly. In his opinion he said, a white man who has never even killed a bushbuck for his family was not the expert on which god can protect our village.

When Anatole translated that one, Father looked taken aback. Where we come from, it's hard to see the connection.

Father spoke slowly, as if to a half-wit, "Elections are good, and Christianity is good. Both are good." We in his family recognized the danger in his extremely calm speech, and the rising color creeping toward his hairline. "You are right. In America we honor both these traditions. But we make our decisions about them in different houses."

"Then you may do so in America," said Tata Ndu. "I will not say you are unwise. But in Kilanga we can use the same house for many things."

Father blew up. "Man, you understand *nothing!* You are applying the logic of children in a display of childish ignorance." He slammed his fist down on the pulpit, which caused all the dried-up palm fronds to shift suddenly sideways and begin falling forward, one at a time. Father kicked them angrily out of the way and strode toward Tata Ndu, but stopped a few feet short of his mark. Tata Ndu is much heavier than my father, with very large arms, and at that moment seemed more imposing in general.

Father pointed his finger like a gun at Tata Ndu, then swung it around to accuse the whole congregation. "You haven't even learned to run your own pitiful country! Your children are dying of a hundred different diseases! You don't have a pot to piss in! And you're presuming you can take or leave the benevolence of our Lord Jesus Christ!"

If anyone had been near enough to get punched right then, my father would have displayed un-Christian behavior. It was hard to believe I'd ever wanted to be near to him myself. If I had a prayer left in me, it was that this red-faced man shaking with rage would never lay a hand on me again.

Tata Ndu seemed calm and unsurprised by anything that had happened. "Á, Tata Price," he said, in his deep, sighing voice. "You believe we are *muwana,* your children, who knew nothing until you came here. Tata Price, I am an old man who learned from other old men. I could tell you the name of the great chief who instructed my father, and all the ones before him, but you would have to know how to sit down and listen. There are one hundred twenty-two. Since the time of our *mankulu* we have made our laws without help from white men."

He turned toward the congregation with the air of a preacher himself. Nobody was snoozing now, either. "Our way was to share a fire until it burned down, *ayi?* To speak to each other until every person was satisfied. Younger men listened to older men. Now the *Beelezi* tell us the vote of a young, careless man counts the same as the vote of an elder."

In the hazy heat Tata Ndu paused to take off his hat, turn it carefully in his hands, then replace it above the high dome of his forehead. No one breathed. "White men tell us: *Vote, Bantu!* They tell us: You do not all have to agree, *ce n'est pas nécessaire!* If two men vote yes and one says no, the matter is finished. *Á bu,* even a child can see how that will end. It takes three stones in the fire to hold up the pot. Take one away, leave the other two, and what? The pot will spill into the fire."

We all understood Tata Ndu's parable. His glasses and tall hat did not seem ridiculous. They seemed like the clothes of a chief.

"But that is the white man's law, *n'est-ce pas?*" he asked. "Two stones are enough. *Il nous faut seulement la majorité.*"

It's true, that was what we believed: the majority rules. How could we argue? I looked down at my fist, which still clutched my pebble. I hadn't voted, nor Mother either. How could we, with Father staring right at us? The only one of us who'd had the nerve was Ruth May, who marched right up and voted for Jesus so hard her pebble struck the cross and bounced. But I guess we all made our choices, one way or the other.

Tata Ndu turned to Father and spoke almost kindly. "Jesus is a white man, so he will understand the law of *la majorité,* Tata Price. *Wenda mbote.*"

Jesus Christ lost, eleven to fifty-six.

. . .

We are still the children we were, with plans we keep secret, even from ourselves. Anatole's, I think, is to outlive Mobutu and come back here when we can stand on this soil and say "home" without the taste of gold-leaf chandeliers and starvation burning bitter on the backs of our tongues. And mine, I think, is to leave my house one day unmarked by whiteness and walk on a compassionate earth with Ruth May beside me, bearing me no grudge. Maybe I'll never get over my grappling for balance, never stop believing life is going to be *fair,* the minute we can clear up all these mistakes of the temporarily misguided. Like the malaria I've never shaken off, it's in my blood. I anticipate rewards for goodness, and wait for the ax of punishment to fall upon evil, in spite of years I've rocked in this cradle of rewarded evils and murdered goodness. Just when I start to feel jaded to life as it is, I'll suddenly wake up in a fever, look out at the world, and gasp at how much has gone wrong that I need to fix. I suppose I loved my father too much to escape being molded to at least some part of his vision.

But the practice of speaking a rich, tonal language to my neighbors has softened his voice in my ear. I hear the undertones now that shimmer under the surface of the words *right* and *wrong.* We used to be baffled by Kikongo words with so many different meanings: *bängala,* for *most precious* and *most insufferable* and also *poisonwood.* That one word brought down Father's sermons every time, as he ended them all with the shout "Tata Jesus is *bängala!*"

Study Questions

1. The title itself is a take on mistakes committed by a hard universalist who doesn't try to understand different cultural nuances: Nathan Price tries to tell the local population that "the word of Jesus is beloved," which in the tribal tongue translates as "*Tata* Jesus is *bängala.*" The problem is that, in the context, it comes across as "Jesus is poisonwood." What do you think the author is saying with such a title?

2. What is the significance of Tata Ndu's being trilingual and telling Price that he comes from 122 generations of wise men? What is his message about the three stones and the cooking pot? Could this political philosophy work for a large nation? Why or why not?

3. According to the excerpts, is this text primarily ethical relativist, or soft universalist? If you have read the entire book, do you find these excerpts a fair choice in representing the book's viewpoint?

4. Read the next narrative, *Possessing the Secret of Joy,* and compare its message with that of *The Poisonwood Bible:* What if the tradition Leah had been subjected to had been *female genital mutilation?* Would you still expect a message of cultural tolerance? Why or why not? Would you draw the line at tolerating certain cultural practices? Explain.

Narrative

Possessing the Secret of Joy

ALICE WALKER

Novel, 1992. Summary and Excerpt.

If you have read or seen *The Color Purple,* you will recognize some of the main characters in this moving and shocking novel: Olivia, Adam, and Tashi. (Olivia and Adam are the children of Celie, the key character in *The Color Purple*, and Tashi is their best friend in the African village where Olivia and Adam's adoptive parents are missionaries.) However, *Possessing the Secret of Joy* is a story that stands on its own, making a powerful argument against the ancient practice of female genital mutilation.* The novel weaves its way through the life of the storyteller Tashi. She is now an American, but originally she was of the Olinka tribe in Africa, a tribe Walker invented as a symbol for all African tribes. In real time and flashbacks, we are introduced to the nightmare of Tashi's life: the death of her older sister Dura, at first a vague memory, but in the end a reality so horrible that, to Tashi, it may be worth killing for.

Tashi has always been afraid of bleeding to death, and she has always had a terrifying dream of a dark tower where she is being kept prisoner, unable to move. Her adult life is in complete disarray. Her husband, Adam, and her best friend, Olivia, try to understand and support her as well as they can, but Tashi has periods of mental instability and moments of great, uncontrollable rage. She sees psychiatrists, and she spends time at a mental institution. But in the course of the book, she tells her own story with increasing insight, and we realize that her mental condition is a result of two traumatic events: a terrible experience when she was a child and another when she was a young adult.

Tashi grew up in the Olinka village, the daughter of a Christian woman. Always a sensitive girl, Tashi was never the same after the death of her sister. As a young woman, Tashi left for America with the missionary family and became an American citizen. She and Adam were lovers, and Tashi loved her American life, but, even so, she decided as a young adult to return to Africa for a ceremony. She wanted to be "bathed" like the rest of the women in her tribe. Because of her Christian beliefs, her mother had kept her away from this ritual in childhood when most young girls were "bathed," but Tashi, at this

---

*Female genital mutilation (sometimes referred to by Walker and others as female circumcision) is a process that can involve cutting the clitoris, removing it, or completely cutting away the inner and outer labia and sewing up the young girl with an aperture only big enough to allow for menstrual flow. The procedure is widespread in Africa and the Middle East and occurs illegally in the United States among some immigrant groups from those areas. The purpose of the procedure is not hygiene; it is strictly a cultural and religious ritual. Sexual pleasure becomes all but impossible, and a husband is assured of a virgin wife who is also going to remain faithful. In addition, health problems and chronic pain are often a consequence of the procedure. Most critics of the procedure see it as an affront to human rights and a tool for the subjugation and domination of women. Defenders of the practice argue that Western critics have no right to superimpose Western values on other cultures. As such, female genital mutilation presents a challenge to ethical relativism, which argues that nobody has the right to criticize the moral and traditional practices of another culture. World attention has been focused on this practice since the mid-1990s.

Alice Walker (b. 1944), American novelist, author of *The Color Purple, The Temple of My Familiar, Possessing the Secret of Joy,* and *The Same River Twice*. Walker's fiction incorporates many of the cultural strands contributing to the lives of American people of color and relates the African American experience to that of the African. Walker focuses particularly on the life experiences of women who are African and African American.

point in her life, felt that as a political and sentimental gesture of solidarity with her people, and in particular their charismatic political leader, she ought to undergo the ritual—without completely realizing its ramifications. She sought out the *tsunga* (medicine woman), M'Lissa, who performs the rituals. "Bathing" is a euphemism for female genital mutilation, and, from that day on, Tashi has experienced daily pain and health problems, in addition to a loss of sexual sensitivity. While still recuperating in M'Lissa's custody, Tashi is found by Adam, who has been frantically searching for her. She returns to the United States, marries him, and has a baby, Benny, under extremely painful conditions because of the mutilation. As a result, Benny is born with a mental disability. Increasingly, Tashi experiences bouts of anxiety and rage. With the help of psychiatrists she has begun to remember the death, the *murder,* of her sister: Tashi was hiding outside the hut where her sister died, screaming and bleeding to death—from a botched procedure. And who performed the ritual? The same *tsunga,* M'Lissa, with the help of Tashi and Dura's own mother.

By the time we read this, we also know that Tashi is now, in real time, on trial in Africa for murder—the murder of M'Lissa. Did she do it? We won't know until the very end of the story. But we learn that after many years of marriage to Adam, with increasing problems due to psychological instability, Tashi has chosen to return to Africa to confront M'Lissa, who by now is a nationally renowned person, symbolizing the Olinka tradition. M'Lissa welcomes Tashi and reveals to her that she now expects Tashi to kill her, because that will elevate M'Lissa to the position of a saint. She also reveals that she finds Tashi naive beyond belief to have come back for the mutilation when she didn't have to—something M'Lissa would never have done herself. Even so, M'Lissa didn't try to stop her but performed the operation just because she was asked to do it, and it was her traditional job. And M'Lissa now recalls Tashi's sister who died—she had abandoned the bleeding little girl because her crying was too much for M'Lissa to bear.

Is M'Lissa the great evil figure in the story? Responsible for the death of Dura and the loss of Tashi's own spirit—Tashi calls it her own death—she is certainly a villain. But she herself is also a victim: Her own procedure was botched, with lameness resulting. She is a tool for the culture, passing the terror along to future generations of young girls as it was passed on to her. Tashi realizes that the true culprit is not the mutilator but the older men of the tribal society who want the mutilations done, who argue that God thinks of woman as unclean if she isn't "circumcised"—the ones who think of an "uncircumcised" woman as "loose" and immoral, as someone who needs to be kept under control. But still, Tashi can't help blaming M'Lissa:

> It is what you told me. Remember? The uncircumcised woman is loose, you said, like a shoe that all, no matter what their size, might wear. This is unseemly, you said. Unclean. A proper woman must be cut and sewn to fit only her husband, whose pleasure depends on an opening it might take months, even years, to enlarge. Men love and enjoy the struggle, you said. For the woman . . . But you never said anything about the woman, did you, M'Lissa? About the pleasure she might have. Or the suffering.

At the end of the story we learn the source of Tashi's nightmare about the dark tower, the truth about M'Lissa's death, and Tashi's own fate at the hands of the jury. And the secret of joy? On a very concrete level, the secret of sexual joy is to have an intact, unmutilated body and an unmutilated sense of self, of freedom. On a deeper level, the secret of joy itself is something we each have to find. Tashi's loved ones suggest that the secret is *resistance*.

Alice Walker's novel was received with alarm by many people who were unaware of the practice of female genital mutilation and welcomed by many others as a strong statement against excessive cultural tolerance. Walker was also criticized by some for betraying her African heritage in denouncing a traditional tribal practice as something that should not be tolerated in today's world.

Study Questions

1. Explain how this story can be viewed as an attack on ethical relativism. How might an ethical relativist respond to Walker's attack?

2. In view of the theme of female genital mutilation, do you find ethical relativism to be an appealing or a problematic moral theory? Explain.

3. Can we understand why Tashi went back as an adult to have the operation performed? Is this a realistic idea? Why or why not?

4. In your opinion, is Walker doing the right thing, exposing the practice of female genital mutilation as immoral, or should she show loyalty and solidarity with her African heritage by defending the practice? Is this a true dichotomy (an either-or situation), or is there another alternative?

5. M'Lissa asks Tashi what an American looks like, and Tashi answers, "An American, I said, sighing, but understanding my love for my adopted country perhaps for the first time: an American looks like a wounded person whose wound is hidden from others and sometimes from herself. An American looks like me." What does Tashi mean? Do you agree with her? Why or why not?

6. Now that you have been introduced to both Kingsolver's and Walker's novels, you may want to compare and contrast them. What do they have in common? What are the differences? Which viewpoint (in favor of or against ethical relativism) do you find more compelling? Explain.

 *Narrative*

Do the Right Thing

SPIKE LEE (SCREENWRITER AND DIRECTOR)

Film, 1989. Summary.

In a book dealing with the question of what one should do, I couldn't possibly pass up a film with the title *Do the Right Thing*. The question was, where to place it? The film can perhaps be seen as an argument for ethical relativism, or at least for cultural tolerance, but perhaps not. I will leave that up to you.

It is a very hot summer morning in Bedford-Stuyvesant, a predominantly African American part of Brooklyn. Sal, an Italian, and his two sons are opening their pizzeria on one corner; a Korean family is opening up their grocery store on the other. The police (all white) are cruising the streets. Most of the black population is out of work. A young, mentally disabled man, Smiley, is trying to sell photos of Martin Luther King, Jr., and Malcolm X. A young black man, Mookie (played by Spike Lee), is delivering pizza in the neighborhood, and "Da Mayor," an old black man, is patrolling the streets, being friendly to everybody although not everybody takes kindly to him. He calls Mookie over and admonishes him always to "do the right thing."

As the day gets hotter, tempers flare. Sal likes the neighborhood and his customers (who all grew up on his pizzas). His younger son, Vito, is a good friend of Mookie. His older son, Pino, however, wants out; all he perceives is that his family members are not welcome in the African American community, and he thinks they should associate with their own kind in their Italian neighborhood. But Mookie points out to Pino that although he may think he does not like blacks, all his heroes are African American. In Sal's pizzeria, one of his customers, Buggin' Out, notices that Sal's wall is full of pictures of famous Italians and Italian Americans and asks why there are no brothers on the wall. When the question becomes a demand, Sal loses his temper and has Mookie throw him out. Radio Raheem, a young man with a big boom box, has a loudness contest with a group of Puerto Ricans and their own boom box. Mookie becomes upset when his sister comes to visit the pizza place and Sal appears to have a crush on her. So Mookie quarrels with his sister and later with his Puerto Rican girlfriend, Tina, too. Quarrels break out at the slightest provocation, such as scuffed running shoes, loud radios, and lack of a certain brand of beer at the grocery store: Blacks, Puerto Ricans, Italians, Koreans—just about everyone has a short temper and a ready vocabulary of epithets. Da Mayor is trying to smooth things out and eventually becomes a hero: He saves a little boy from being run over. The only one who thinks to thank him is Mother Sister, a woman in the neighborhood who apparently has disliked him for years.

The sun sets, but tempers are still hot. Sal and his sons are closing the pizzeria for the night, but Buggin' Out (who has been trying to organize a "Boycott Sal's Pizzeria" campaign), Radio Raheem, and Smiley turn up. Buggin' Out demands pictures of African Americans on the wall, and Raheem is upset that Sal told him to turn his radio down earlier. Everybody starts screaming, and Sal snaps, smashing Raheem's radio with a bat. A

In *Do the Right Thing* (Universal City Studios, 1989) Mookie (Spike Lee) and Sal (Danny Aiello) are discussing neighborhood issues in Sal's pizza restaurant. On this hot day, tensions run high between ethnic groups: the Italians, the blacks, the Koreans, and the all-white police force.

fight ensues and spills into the street; Raheem is holding Sal by the throat. The police arrive and pull Raheem off Sal, but the choke hold they apply kills Raheem. In shock, the fighting crowd freezes—until Mookie, as if surfacing from a dream, grabs a trash can and hurls it through Sal's window. The crowd bursts into the restaurant, looting and smashing things, and Smiley lights a match: The place goes up in flames. As the place is burning, he pins one of his pictures of Martin Luther King, Jr., and Malcolm X on the wall next to the photos of Italian Americans.

Next, the crowd turns on the Korean grocery store, but the young Korean store owner cries, "I'm black! You—me—we're the same!" Some laugh, but this quiets down tempers, and the store is safe.

The next day is another hot one. There is no solution to any of the problems in the neighborhood. Da Mayor is the only person who resolved anything; during the riot he managed to overcome the animosity of Mother Sister. Mookie vows only to spend more time with his and Tina's little boy.

The end of the movie? Two quotes appear on the screen, one from Martin Luther King, Jr., and the other from Malcolm X. King says that violence never solves any problems. Malcolm X says that, in general, violence is evil, but not in self-defense—in that case it is not even violence, but, rather, intelligence.

Study Questions

1. What do you think Spike Lee intended us to conclude?

2. *Did* Mookie do the right thing? Did anybody?

3. What did the Korean store owner mean when he said he was black too?

4. Is this film advocating inclusive or exclusive multiculturalism?

5. Can there be different moral rules for different ethnic and cultural groups? Should there be?

6. Does Spike Lee present his characters as stereotypes? Why or why not?

Chapter Four

Myself or Others?

*I*f there has ever been a moment when you have found yourself engaged in discussing a philosophical theory, your topic may well have been *psychological egoism*. Perhaps late at night, after a party, the die-hards were gathered out on the patio or in the kitchen, and somebody brought up the subject of selfishness, claiming that all acts are selfish, or as a character put it in a sitcom, "There are no self-less good deeds." (You'll find the sitcom episode at the end of this chapter.) Perhaps you wanted to argue against that view but found yourself at a loss for words because the theory seemed to be disturbingly right. All of a sudden, everything seemed selfish! Psychological egoism is a theory that haunts us from time to time—most of us don't want to believe that everything we do is always selfish. And, as you'll see in the course of the chapter, we need not buy into the theory, because it has severe flaws. Nevertheless, it has been a seductive and persuasive theory since the days of Socrates, and in this chapter we'll take a closer look at what it entails.

We usually assume that moral behavior, or "being ethical," has to do with not being overly concerned with oneself. In other words, selfishness is assumed to be an unacceptable attitude. Even among scholars, though, there is disagreement about what constitutes ethical behavior. Since very early in Western intellectual history, the viewpoint that humans aren't built to look out for other people's interests has surfaced regularly. Some scholars even hold that proper moral conduct consists of "looking out for number one," period. Those viewpoints are known as *psychological egoism* and *ethical egoism,* respectively. Both psychological egoism and ethical egoism are examples of absolutist theories; they hold that only one code is the norm for ethical behavior. (See Box 4.1 for an explanation of the difference between *egoism* and *egotism*.)

Psychological Egoism: From Virginia Tech to 9/11

On the day of the massacre on the Virginia Tech campus—April 16, 2007—thirty-two students were killed and twenty-one wounded by Seung-Hui Cho, who then killed himself—to date, the worst mass murder in U.S. history. Apparently, Cho, a resident alien student with noticeable mental health problems, had chosen his victims at random; he had apparently had no particular grudges against or confrontations with any particular person but took out his self-absorbed anger on professors and students who, in his mind, led a more satisfying life than he did, according to the videos he sent to the media in between two shooting sprees. Many more students would have died had it not been for the heroic efforts of their fellow students who barricaded doors to classrooms with desks and even with their own bodies. But perhaps the story that most of us remember is that of Liviu Librescu, a professor of

Box 4.1   EGOISM OR EGOTISM?

The terms *egoism* and *egotism* are part of our everyday speech, and people often use them interchangeably, but do they really mean the same thing? No: *Egoists* are people who think in terms of their own advantage, generally by disregarding the interests of others. *Egotists* are people who have a very high self-opinion and whose language often consists of self-praise; praise an egotist for a good result on a test or for looking nice, and you might receive responses such as "Of course I did well—I always do, because I'm very smart" or "Nice? I look great!" An egoist need not fall into this pattern, although he or she might, of course, be an egotist as well.

aeronautical engineering. Originally from Romania, Librescu was a Holocaust survivor who had immigrated to Israel, and then to the United States, and was still teaching at age 76. When Cho tried to force his way into Librescu's classroom, Librescu blocked the door with his body so that all the students in his class could escape out the window; the last student leaving saw Librescu shot and killed by the shooter. He gave his life to save his students, knowing full well the scope of evil that human beings can inflict on one another—and the day of his death, April 16, was Holocaust Remembrance Day in Israel.

The news media called Professor Librescu a hero, and most of us would agree: Giving one's life to save others, especially when one is aware of the danger, is something we generally consider to be heroic and admirable. And that is why the theory of psychological egoism is disturbing for many of us; it calmly dismisses the act of someone such as Librescu as an expression of fundamentally selfish human nature. This means that even the person with the most stellar reputation for unselfishness must be reevaluated. From Mother Teresa to Martin Luther King, Jr., from Librescu and the students at Virginia Tech, to NYPD officer Walwyn Stuart (see Box 4.2) to personal favorite people in our lives whom we consider to be giving, selfless human beings, all of them are now reclassified as selfish, including ourselves, of course. But what could possibly be selfish about acts of self-sacrifice? Well, says the psychological egoist, since we are all selfish, then the motivation might be any one of a number of things: A person who sacrifices himself or herself for others might have a wish to become famous; or might want to atone for something he or she had left undone in a previous situation, or might simply want to feel good about himself or herself. Or perhaps it is simply an unconscious urge.

Stories about people who have risked and even lost their lives to save others, stories that seem to exemplify selflessness, are precious to most people, because they show us what we might be capable of. We like to believe that humans have a built-in measure of courage that allows us to rise to the occasion and give up our lives, or at least our comfort, for others. Of course, few people perform heroic deeds with the *intent* of getting killed, but if they lose their lives in the process, we only seem to admire them more. (There are those who feel that losing one's life for someone else is stupid, useless, or even morally wrong. Such people may feel more comfortable with the theory of *ethical egoism*.)

$Box\ 4.2$ 9/11 AND PSYCHOLOGICAL EGOISM

On September 11, some three thousand people perished in the terrorist attacks on New York and Washington, D.C., but an estimated twenty thousand people survived, many rescued by civilian strangers, firefighters, and police. One blind man was saved by his guide dog, which led him to safety down seventy-eight flights of stairs—from above where the second plane hit the World Trade Center's north tower. As we see in Chapter 11, the film *Schindler's List* makes the point, familiar to anyone raised in the Jewish tradition, that whoever saves a life saves a world. Many thousands of worlds were saved that day, some of them through extraordinarily heroic actions. But other worlds perished in the rescue attempts: Three hundred New York firefighters and police officers were among the dead, having rushed into the Trade Center towers before they fell. While everyone else was heading down the stairs, they were running up.

Police officer Walwyn Stuart arrived at the WTC subway station after the first plane had hit, and he herded arriving passengers back on the trains. Then he ordered the trains to leave and stopped all incoming trains. Because of Officer Stuart, apparently not a single person was trapped in the subway at Ground Zero. Then he ran upstairs to do what he could in the burning tower; he never came out. Most of us would not hesitate to call someone like Walwyn Stuart heroic, and we assume that he chose to help others for their sake, rather than for selfish reasons. For psychological egoism, however, all

acts are selfish. That also means that although the 9/11 terrorists themselves may have felt they were dying selflessly for a cause, they were being utterly selfish, according to psychological egoism. Indeed, we don't even have to inquire into their motivation—for the psychological egoist, it is a given that everyone is selfish all the time, because it is built into our nature as human beings. We simply cannot avoid being selfish.

Officer Walwyn Stuart (1973–2001) was one of more than three hundred police officers and firefighters who lost their lives during the terrorist attacks on the World Trade Center on September 11. He was a Port Authority police officer who had transferred from the NYPD, where he was an undercover narcotics detective, to the Port Authority when his wife got pregnant; he wanted a safer assignment so he could be there for his wife and baby.

If we ask a person who has performed (and survived) a heroic deed why he or she did it, the answer is almost predictable: "I just had to do it" or, perhaps, "I didn't think about it, I just did it." We take such comments as a sign that we are in the presence of a person with extraordinary moral character. But there are other ways of interpreting the words and actions of heroes. The theory of psychological egoism states that whatever it may look like and whatever we may think it is, no human action is done for any reason other than for the sake of the agent. In short, we are all selfish, or at least we are all self-interested.

Box 4.3   SELFISH VERSUS SELF-INTERESTED

Psychological egoism is generally described as a theory which states that everyone is selfish at all times. But what does the word *selfish* mean? Some psychological egoists (people who believe everyone is selfish) sometimes emphasize that there is nothing bad or morally deficient about being selfish; all it means, they say, is that we are "self-ish," we are focused on our own survival, which doesn't necessarily imply that we are disregarding other people's interests. However, we use the word in a different sense in our everyday language. According to *Webster's* dictionary, *selfish* means "devoted unduly to self; influenced by a view to private advantage," so if we concede that *Webster's* reflects the common use of the word, we can't deny that *selfish* is a morally disparaging term; it isn't value-neutral, and it certainly isn't a compliment.

Sometimes psychological egoists use the term *selfish,* and sometimes the term used is *self-interested.* There is no consensus among psychological egoists about which term to use. It makes quite a difference which term you choose, but in the end, it may not make the theory of psychological egoism any more plausible. If you say (1), "All acts are selfish," you imply that all of us are always looking for self-gratification and have no feeling for the interests of others. However, if you say (2), "All acts are self-interested," you imply that all of us are always thinking about what is best for us. Is statement 1 true? It may be true that we are always looking out for ourselves in some way, but it is certainly not true that we are always looking for self-gratification; many a moment in a lifetime is spent agonizing over doing what we want versus doing what we ought to do, and often we end up choosing duty over desire. So what if the psychological egoist says, "Doing my duty is better in the long run for me, even if I don't feel like doing it, so I guess I'm self-interested" (statement 2)? But is statement 2 true? Many philosophers over the years have gleefully pointed out that it isn't—we are hardly concerned with what is good for us, at least not all the time. Many people smoke, drink to excess, and take drugs even though they know it is not in their own best interest. So couldn't psychological egoism state that "all acts are either selfish or self-interested"? It could, but it generally doesn't; part of the appeal of psychological egoism is that it is a very simple theory, and putting a dichotomy (an either-or) into the theory makes it much more complicated.

The term *psychological egoism* is applied to the theory because it is a psychological theory, a theory about how humans behave. A psychological egoist believes that humans are always looking out for themselves in some way or other, and it is impossible for them to behave any other way. As such, psychological egoism is a descriptive theory; it doesn't make any statements about whether this is a *good* way to behave. What does it take for a person to be labeled a psychological egoist? It's not necessary that he or she be a selfish person, only that he or she hold to the theory that all people look after themselves. As we see later, it is entirely possible for someone to be kind and caring and still be a psychological egoist. (See Box 4.3 for an explanation of the difference between *selfish* and *self-interested*.) Suppose, though, that someone insists that all people *ought to* look after themselves. Then he or she is an *ethical egoist.* We discuss the theory of ethical egoism later in this chapter.

Psychological Egoism: From Glaucon to Hobbes

Chapter 2 featured a section of Plato's famous book *The Republic*. The section quoted there is a less well-known discussion about whether going to the theater is a morally worthwhile pastime (and Socrates says it isn't). In this chapter you'll encounter a far more famous part of Plato's *Republic,* the discussion of what makes a good person and whether all people are, or should be, selfish. In Chapter 8 you'll find a more complete exploration of who Socrates was and what role he played in Plato's life, but for now we'll focus on the issue of selfishness.

Socrates is known to us today primarily through Plato's books, the *Dialogues;* Socrates never wrote anything himself, and had it not been for Plato's wanting to keep his teacher's name alive after Socrates' death (at the hands of an Athenian jury, found guilty of crimes against the state, literally "corrupting the young and offending the gods"), we might never have known the name Socrates at all. In most of Plato's books, Socrates has a conversation—a dialogue—with somebody, a friend, a student, or perhaps an enemy. In *The Republic*, Socrates and his young followers have been invited to a dinner party at the house of some old friends, and they are engaged in a discussion about morality, selfishness, and the ideal state, branching off into art theory, gender theory, and even a theory about life after death. In the Primary Readings section you will find an excerpt of that discussion. Plato's brother Glaucon is trying to make Socrates give some good reasons why it is better to be just than to be unjust. Glaucon insists that all people by nature look after themselves, and whenever we can get away with something, we will do it, regardless of how unjust it may be to others. Unfortunately, we may receive the same treatment from others, which is highly unpleasant, so for the sake of peace and security we agree to treat one another decently—not because we want to, but because we are playing it safe. Morality is just a result of our looking out for ourselves. (See Box 4.4 for an explanation of psychological egoism in terms of "ought implies can.")

What Glaucon is suggesting here about the origin of society is a first in Western thought. His theory is an example of what has become known as a *social contract theory,* a type of theory that became particularly influential much later, in the eighteenth century. A social contract theory assumes that humans used to live in a presocial setting (without rules, regulations, or cooperation) and then, for various reasons, got together and agreed on setting up a society. Generally, social contract theories assume that humans decide to build a society with rules (1) for the sake of the common good or (2) for the sake of self-protection. Glaucon's theory belongs to the second category because he claims (for the sake of argument) that humans primarily look after themselves.

To illustrate his point, Glaucon tells the story of a man called Gyges, a shepherd in ancient Lydia. Gyges was caught in a storm and an earthquake, which left a large hole in the ground. He explored the chasm and found a hollow bronze horse with the corpse of a giant inside. The giant was wearing only a gold ring on his finger. Gyges took the ring and left and later, wearing the ring, attended a meeting of shepherds. During the meeting Gyges happened to twist the ring, and he realized from the reaction of the other shepherds that he had become invisible. Twisting the ring

Box 4.4   "OUGHT IMPLIES CAN"

Sometimes a philosophical text will state that "ought implies can." In the civil code of the Roman Empire (27 B.C.E.–395 C.E.), this principle was clearly stated, and Roman citizens knew that *impossibilium nulla est obligatio* (nobody has a duty to do what is not possible). Many philosophical and legal schools of thought today are still based on that idea, and one of these is psychological egoism. "Ought implies can" means that we can't have an obligation (ought) to do something unless it is actually possible for us to do it (can). I can't make it a moral obligation for you to swim across San Francisco Bay to show your support for the Save the Whales program if you can't swim (but I might try to make it an obligation for you to donate a dollar, because most people can afford that). I can't make it a moral obligation for you to take home a pet from the pound if you are allergic to animals (but I might insist that you have an obligation to help in other ways). You can't tell me that I ought to be unselfish if in fact I was born selfish and can't be any other way because it is part of my human nature. This is the point that psychological egoism wants to make: It is irrational to keep wanting humans to look out for one another when, as a matter of fact, we aren't built that way.

back, he reappeared. Realizing the advantages gained by being invisible, Gyges arranged to be one of the elected messengers who report to the king about his sheep. Gyges went to town, seduced the queen, and conspired with her to kill the king. He then took over the kingdom, sired a dynasty, and became the ancestor of King Croesus.

Glaucon's question is, Suppose we had two such rings? Let us imagine giving one to a decent person and one to a scoundrel. We know that the scoundrel will abuse the ring for personal gain, but how about the decent person? To Glaucon it is the same thing; their human natures are identical. Decent persons will do "unjust" things just as quickly as scoundrels if they know they can get away with it; furthermore, if they *don't* take advantage of such situations, they are just stupid. In the end, who will be happier, the unjust person who schemes and gets away with everything or the just person who never tries to get away with anything but is so good that people think there must be something wrong with him? Why, the unjust person, of course.

This little story may be the first in the literary tradition to explore a theme that has remained popular to this day—and that may be one reason it seems timeless, but it could also be that the moral problem it represents hasn't changed, either. *Arabian Nights* is full of stories about invisibility cloaks, magic rings, and owners making creative uses of them, sometimes to gain a personal advantage and sometimes to spy on and vanquish the bad guys; in 1897 H. G. Wells wrote *The Invisible Man,* which has been made into a movie numerous times and inspired the film *Hollow Man* (2000). J. R. R. Tolkien's trilogy *The Lord of the Rings* (1954–6) features an invisibility ring. Usually the moral problem stated is, If you could become invisible, what would you do? Would you still be a morally decent or even halfway decent person? Or would you use your power selfishly if you knew you could get away with it? Harry Potter

If an invisibility ring can provide a perfect outlet for selfishness, will we all grab the chance, as Plato's brother Glaucon speculates, or will we fight temptation? Will we even all be tempted? In *The Lord of the Rings* (trilogy, 2001–3), Frodo volunteers to take the Ring of power to Mount Doom and destroy it; but even Frodo, goodhearted as he is, is tempted by the Ring's power, and within his small person a great battle is being fought.

may have his magic cloak, but most of us don't. Interestingly, in cases where people have been under the impression that they enjoy total anonymity, such as in the days of extensive illegal downloading of music from the Internet, few of those people seemed to have any qualms about breaking the law—which plays right into Glaucon's hands. But does that mean that *everyone* would react the same way, with a cloak of anonymity? Let us return to *Lord of the Rings* for a while. Here we have an invisibility ring, like Gyges'—and yet there are important differences: Gyges finds a ring that gives him powers; he uses them to his own advantage and ends up becoming the ancestor of an illustrious royal family. Many people would say, Good for him! But Sauron's ring in Tolkien's trilogy is of a different make: The people (of all species) who are tempted by the ring are marked for life, and the purpose of the entire quest of the ring is to destroy it, rather than use it. The invisibility given by Tolkien's ring is not one that allows much anonymity, either, because the bearer is visible to Sauron's forces and Sauron himself. Frodo does his utmost to fight the temptation to use the ring and see the quest through, having seen what happens to one's soul if one allows oneself to be absorbed by the ring's evil: One becomes like Gollum, who used to be a hobbit like Frodo (see the illustration in Chapter 1). Interestingly, the person who is the least tempted to use the ring is Frodo's friend and helper, Samwise Gamgee. In the Primary Readings you'll find an excerpt from a text that analyzes the

The English philosopher Thomas Hobbes was one of the first modern materialists, claiming that all of human psychology consists of the attraction and repulsion of physical particles. As such, the natural human approach to life is one of self-preservation, and the natural life of humans outside the regulations of society (the state of nature) is for Hobbes a filthy and frightening war of everyone against everyone.

similarities and differences between Frodo and Gyges, "The Rings of Tolkien and Plato: Lessons in Power, Choice, and Morality," by Erik Katz, and in the Narratives section you will find an overview of the main characters in the famous trilogy.

With few exceptions, the invisible person succumbs to temptation and meets a terrible end, as punishment for having a weak or evil character. So most invisible-person stories are *didactic* stories (see Chapter 2), designed to teach a moral lesson: If you let your selfish nature rule, you will surely be punished—if not by others, then by fate. But, as my students have pointed out on several occasions, there is a category of stories that serve as an exception: stories in which invisibility is used not for evil or for gain but for good. *Superheroes* who have invisibility powers (such as *Fantastic Four* and *Mystery Men*) are not in the same category as the human whose soul is corrupted by being invisible—they suffer no doubt, they are not corrupted by power, and they are fixated on their goal, to do good for humanity. But then again, that's what makes them superheroes and what separates them from us. And as such, they're simply not as interesting, morally, as the hero who has his or her moments of weakness and doubt. So what is the lesson of Glaucon's story? Is he seriously implying that it is foolish and unnatural to be good if you can get away with being bad? No; he is acting as the devil's advocate to make Socrates defend justice as something that is good in itself. However, Glaucon does imply that what he is describing is, in fact, the opinion of most people. He may have been right; a good two thousand years later Thomas Hobbes (1588–1679) agreed with Glaucon's theory of self-interest on all three counts: (1) Humans choose to live in a society with rules because they are concerned with their own safety and for no other reason; (2) humans are by nature self-interested, and any show of concern for others hides a true concern for ourselves; (3) we would be fools if we didn't look after ourselves. (We return to this point in the next section; you will find Hobbes's theory in the Primary Readings at the end of this chapter and his view of the selfish basis for pity in Box 4.5.)

Surely we all can remember events in our lives that show that we don't always act out of self-interest. You may remember the time you helped your best friend move across town. The time you sat up all night preparing your brother's taxes. The time you donated toys to the annual Christmas toy drive. The time you washed your parents' car. Did the dishes at Thanksgiving. Or perhaps even helped a stranger on

Box 4.5   HOBBES AND THE FEELING OF PITY

Hobbes believed humans feel pity for others in distress because they fear the same may happen to themselves. We identify with the pain of others, and that makes us afraid for ourselves. Therefore, helping others may be a way to ward off bad events. In actual fact we have no pity for others for their sake—only for our own. (He is not the first thinker to have expressed that opinion; Aristotle said approximately the same thing but without implying that we are selfish to the bone.) Hobbes was one of the first modern Western philosophers to ponder human psychology, and we might say that he put his finger on a sore spot. Sometimes we do sympathize with others because we imagine how awful it would be if the same thing were to happen to us. What exactly does Hobbes mean when he says we *identify* with others? It seems that we ask ourselves, If this happened to me, how would I feel? That does not necessarily lead to concern for ourselves but, rather, leads to a concern for others, precisely because we know how they feel. Furthermore, isn't it possible to feel pity for someone or something with which you don't identify so easily? We certainly can feel pity for someone of the other gender or someone of another race or culture, even if what happens to them wouldn't happen to us. But how about feeling pity for dolphins caught in gill nets? for animals caught in traps? for pets used in lab experiments?

In the aftermath of Hurricane Katrina in 2005, with its horrendous impact on human lives and the heated criticism of the way the emergency was handled by local and federal authorities, it was uplifting news to some of us that rescue parties consisting of locals as well as volunteers from all over the nation (including some of my students from San Diego) ventured into the contaminated areas of New Orleans to help not only stranded humans but also their pets. Some also found reason to criticize the effort, pointing out that when resources are limited, we must help our fellow human beings first and let the pets fend for themselves. But the pet rescuers responded with the following arguments: First, the humans were also being rescued; second, it would matter hugely to most refugees who thought their pets lost to be reunited with them, and thus the rescue effort would raise their morale and improve their well-being; and, last, whether the pets had been lost or deliberately left behind, they, too experience fear and suffering, and are worthy of moral consideration. In effect, a huge effort was mounted to rescue pets whose owners *didn't* come forward, and these pets were shipped around the country to rescue shelters, where an effort was made to find them new homes. Did the pet rescuers wish to save these pets because they didn't want to be stranded in filthy floodwaters themselves, facing a death by drowning or starvation, as Hobbes would say? Maybe so, but it is also likely that it was a simple case of *empathy* extending beyond human feelings, toward nonhuman creatures. In any event, it hardly speaks for a fundamentally selfish human nature, anymore than the upcoming story of Abraham Lincoln saving the piglets does.

In a broad sense, perhaps we do identify with other creatures when their lives are in danger and feel that we ward off our own demise by saving their lives. In the final analysis, though, that idea is rather far-fetched, because if Hobbes is right and we fear "contamination" from the misery of others, wouldn't we rather turn our backs on them and flee rather than expose ourselves to their suffering? Given that we don't, perhaps there are forces at work other than selfishness. An easier explanation is that we simply, on occasion, care for the well-being of others.

Psychological egoism claims that every act we do is for selfish reasons. For many people, September 11 put that notion to shame; an overwhelming number of stories documented police officers, firefighters, and civilians trying to help others escape the burning towers.

the road or saved the life of an accident victim. Were all those good deeds really done for selfish reasons? The psychological egoist would say yes—you may not have been aware of your true motives, but selfish they were, somehow. You may have wanted to borrow your parents' car: hence, the car wash and the dishes. You helped your friend move because you were afraid of losing her friendship. You may have felt guilty for not helping with your brother's taxes the year before, so you did them this year. The

Calvin and Hobbes   by Bill Watterson

One of the reasons psychological egoism has attained such popularity is that it appeals to a modern person's sense of honesty: In order not to fool ourselves into thinking we are better than we are, we should be honest and admit that we are selfish. Calvin, being a smart kid, not only uses that argument but also turns it to his advantage; in other words, he uses it as an excuse, which is one of the other reasons psychological egoism is popular. And let's face it: It is a very cynical slice of life!

toys? You wanted to feel good about yourself. The stranger on the road? You wanted to rack up a few points in the Big Book of Heaven. Helping the accident victim? You wanted to get your name in the paper.

So what is it that has proved so appealing about psychological egoism? After all, it removes the halo from the head of every hero and every unselfish person in the history of humankind. In fact, that may be part of its appeal: We like to think, in this day and age, that we are honest about ourselves, and we don't want to be tricked into thinking that we are better than we are or that anyone else is either. (1) One reason, then, for this theory's popularity is its presumed *honesty*. Later in this section you'll find an example of this phenomenon in the story of Lincoln and the pigs.

Closely related to the notion of honesty is (2) our modern tendency toward *cynicism*. Somehow, we have a hard time believing good things about people, including ourselves. Refusing to take things at face value may be the mature thing to do, but it may also close our minds to the possibility that not all acts are selfish and not everybody is rotten at heart. (See Box 4.6 for a discussion of modern cynicism.) This possibility doesn't mean we shouldn't view the world with a healthy dose of skepticism and suspicion. Often, we really *are* taken advantage of, people *are* truly selfish and devious, and things *aren't* what they seem. But there is a difference between that kind of prudent skepticism and a universal cynicism that borders on paranoia. Such radical cynicism doesn't allow for the possibility of the existence of goodness and kindness.

Box 4.6   MODERN CYNICISM

There is much speculation about how cynicism began. It's not a new phenomenon. The ancient Greeks invented it: The Cynics (literally, the "doglike ones"), headed by Diogenes, did their best to undermine convention in order to break its hold on people's minds—one of the original "Question authority" movements. In later years, cynicism has questioned authority to the point that misanthropy—automatically believing the worst about everybody—has become a form of authority in itself.

Modern cynicism has a precursor—or even a founder—in French philosopher and author Voltaire (1694–1778), whose sharp remarks about his contemporary France before the Revolution set the tone for the intellectual who rails against double standards and bigotry, trusts no one, including his or her government, and has a never-ending skepticism as far as human nature is concerned. Satire was one of the political weapons of choice in the Age of Reason. But in the last part of the nineteenth century, the Western world experienced a surge of optimism because many believed we were very close to solving all technological, scientific, and medical riddles. It was even assumed that we were too civilized to ever go to war again. You may remember from the section in Chapter 2 on war movies that enthusiasm for war by and large ended with World War I. Often our modern cynicism is regarded as having been born in the trenches of World War I, but there is an interesting precursor: the sinking of the *Titanic*. The 1997 award-sweeping film *Titanic* reminded us not only of the human tragedies involved but also of the hubris, the cocky assurance that human technology could conquer all obstacles. A ship so well built that it was unsinkable! As we know, it wasn't, and the optimistic belief that now humans were the masters of the universe went to the bottom of the ocean with the great ship. It may not have been the very first blow to

human self-assurance in the twentieth century, but it became the first serious crack in the hull of modern belief in technology.

Cynicism became a way of life in the twentieth century, fueled by the two world wars, the Great Depression, and the revelation of the horrors of the Holocaust. Children who lived through the tragedies and disappointments of the 1960s and 1970s, as well as their children, were all affected by the assassinations of John F. Kennedy, Robert Kennedy, and Martin Luther King, Jr., by the Korean and Vietnam wars, by fuel shortages, and by the Watergate and Iran-Contra scandals. And then there are the revelations from past decades such as the now infamous Tuskegee syphilis study, in which close to four hundred African American men from 1932 to 1972 unwittingly were reduced to the status of lab rats for government medical experiments. Other examples of the use of citizens for some larger purpose without their consent include the nuclear tests of the 1950s, which often involved soldiers and civilians who were given the impression that their lives were not in danger. Inuit people in Alaska were given radioactive medication as part of an experiment. In 1996, the *Los Angeles Times* revealed that in the 1950s the U.S. Army had sprayed chemicals and bacteria over large populations in New York and Washington and even over a school in Minneapolis. Years after the Vietnam War, it became apparent that soldiers had been exposed to a toxic exfoliant, Agent Orange. Gulf War Syndrome is still an unsolved riddle, attributed by some to chemical weapons in the area that the soldiers had not been warned about. So perhaps it is understandable that conspiracy rumors appear on a regular basis in response to important news stories; we just have to remind ourselves that although conspiracies do exist, there is a fine line between being a skeptical cynic and a paranoid cynic.

One of the media events that best reflects the current cynicism is probably Michael Moore's *Fahrenheit 9/11*—a documentary to its fans, a propaganda film to its critics. A huge box-office success, the film created a firestorm of reactions, from very positive to very negative reviews. All in all, the American Left was cynical about the Bush administration's handling of the war in Iraq, and the American Right was cynical about the American Left.

But politics is not the only arena for cynicism: The Catholic Church has become the target of criticism, and a fair amount of cynicism, for the way it has handled the scandal of child abuse committed by priests. An analysis by the John Jay College of Criminal Justice in 2004 estimated that 2.7 percent of priests have engaged in child molestation over the past fifty years or more—and although 2.7 percent doesn't sound like much, it still amounts to 4,398 American priests, with multiple victims each. What has made so many people cynical, Catholics as well as non-Catholics, is not so much the molestation phenomenon itself (because there are child rapists in other churches too, as well as among teachers, Boy Scout leaders, and other groups) as the perceived lack of action or even concern by the Catholic Church. Most troubling was the active cover-up of these acts by bishops, who reassigned priests they knew to be child abusers to other dioceses without any warning to the community.

While the Catholic Church has recently settled a large number of lawsuits, and is making efforts to prevent past crimes from reoccurring, there are other reasons to be cynical: Senator Larry Craig (R-ID) was busted for soliciting sex in a public restroom; New York Governor Elliot Spitzer (D) was caught in a sting operation, being associated with a prostitution ring. And while we are at war, and genocide is happening in Darfur, the media choose to spend air time on the drug and alcohol problems of celebrities.

So is cynicism an appropriate reaction to events and people that disappoint us? Appropriate or not, it is a sign of our times. But perhaps cynicism isn't altogether a bad thing—as it is sometimes said, a cynic is a disappointed idealist. You have a vision of how things ought to be, but you also have a considerable amount of skepticism. So somewhere between hope and skepticism you may be able to deal with the real world.

A third reason that psychological egoism is so popular has to do with (3) *making excuses.* When psychological egoists say, "I can't help myself—it's my nature," they're saying they don't have to worry about remembering Aunt Molly's birthday or calling in on the cellphone to the radio station about the mattress they saw blocking the number-two lane on the freeway because humans are selfish *by nature,* and we are not capable of worrying about others—unless, of course, there is something in it for ourselves. But that is nothing but a bad excuse. Psychological egoists who take their own theory seriously never say we can't help being selfish to the bone—they just say there is some hidden selfish motive for whatever we do that we may not even be aware of. Box 4.7 explores the question of whether we, according to the psychological egoist, have freedom of the will to make choices, or whether our actions are determined by nature or nurture.

Box 4.7   PSYCHOLOGICAL EGOISM AND THE CONCEPT OF FREE WILL

It is time to take one step backward and reassess one of the claims of psychological egoism: that we can't help what we're doing. When psychological egoists claim that we can't help being selfish because it is in our human nature, they are of course also saying that we shouldn't be blamed for the selfish things we do (or be praised for the seemingly unselfish deeds either). That lines psychological egoism up with a famous—some would say, infamous—theory in philosophy: *hard determinism*. A hard determinist believes that since everything is an effect of a previous cause, then we should, in principle if not in reality, be able to predict events with complete accuracy—not only in nature but even in human lives and human decisions. That means that *according to hard determinism, we have no free will* because everything we decide is a result of either our genetic heritage ("Nature") or our experience and environment ("Nurture"). In other words, it may *feel* as if we make free choices, but we really don't; everything is part of the great chain of cause and effect, even our thought processes and moral decisions. That means that when people decide to break a moral rule or even the law, they can't help it and shouldn't be blamed, according to hard determinism. This line of thinking has spawned numerous discussions in ethics as well as in philosophy of law—because (1) we normally assume that people can be held morally accountable for what they do

intentionally, and (2) our entire judicial system rests on the assumption that, in most cases, people should be held accountable if they break the law on purpose. Nevertheless, there are individual cases where people truly can't help doing what they're doing, morally and legally. You may want to think of a few such cases and discuss them.

In the sense that psychological egoism traces all human behavior back to self-preservation or self-love as the fundamental cause of all our decisions (such as Hobbes does)—in holding that we can't act otherwise and that we shouldn't be held accountable for being selfish—it can be called a deterministic theory. However, psychological egoism generally assumes that we can choose between several possible courses of action—but all are selfish actions nonetheless. And most psychological egoists would claim that we can be held accountable for choosing wrongly—because it would be in our selfish interest to avoid getting in trouble with the law, just as much as it might be selfishly gratifying to break it. This would speak against classifying psychological egoism as a hard determinist theory. In Chapter 7 you'll find a film about punishing people for the crimes they haven't committed yet (*Minority Report*), and in Chapter 10 we explore further the concept of having a free will in the philosophy of Jean-Paul Sartre and Henri Bergson, both antideterminists.

Shortcomings of Psychological Egoism

There is something beguiling about psychological egoism; once you begin to look at the world through the eyes of a psychological egoist, it is hard to see it any other way. In fact, no matter how hard we try to come up with an example that seems to run counter to the theory, the psychological egoist has a ready answer. This is due to several factors.

1. Falsification Is Not Possible

Psychological egoism always looks for selfish motives and refuses to recognize any other kind. For any nonselfish motivation you can think of for doing what you did, the theory will tell you that there was another, ulterior motive behind it. It is inconceivable, according to the theory, that other motives might exist. This is in fact a flaw in the theory. A good theory is not one that can't be proven wrong but one that allows for the possibility of counterexamples.

The inability of a theory to allow for cases in which it doesn't apply is considered bad science and bad thinking. The principle of *falsification* was advanced by the philosopher Karl Popper (1902–1994) as a hallmark of a viable theory. It states that a good scientific theory must allow for the possibility that it might be wrong. If it declares itself right under any and all circumstances, it cannot be "falsified." So "falsification" doesn't mean that a theory has to be proven wrong but that it has to be engaged in rigorously testing itself—in other words, it has to consider the possibility that it is wrong and test itself in any way possible. Popper says in his book *The Poverty of Historicism* (1957), "Just because it is our aim to establish theories as well as we can, we must test them as severely as we can; that is, we must try to find fault with them, we must try to falsify them. Only if we cannot falsify them in spite of our best efforts can we say that they have stood up to severe tests." Science itself doesn't always follow the principle of falsification; an example is the eighteenth-century debate about meteorites in which most scientists chose to side with their own theory that rocks couldn't fall from the sky, since outer space, they said, consists of a vacuum. The statements of reliable private citizens who claimed to have seen meteorites fall and land on the ground were consistently brushed aside by scientists as being lies or delusions because most scientists did not question their own theory: It was nonfalsifiable since it didn't allow for the possibility that it might be wrong. As we know, science later had to revise its notion of outer space (the theory was falsified): In 1803, scientists at l'Aigle, France, actually observed a large number of meteorites falling.

Is the theory of evolution a good theory in the sense that it is falsifiable? Scientists today would say yes: The theory is based on empirical research that can be verified objectively (the fossil record), but it doesn't claim that it is correct no matter what happens; it claims that it is the most plausible theory of biology so far, but if new and different evidence should surface, then it is (presumably) open to revision.

Psychological egoism is not a good theory, according to Popper's principle, because it doesn't allow for the possibility that it is wrong but reinterprets all acts and motives so they fit the theory instead. That is not a theory, strictly speaking; it is a prejudice. It comes across as a strong theory precisely because there seems to be nothing that can defeat it; however, that is not a strength, scientifically speaking. A strong theory recognizes the reality of the problem of induction (see Chapter 3): Any empirical theory (that is, one based on evidence) can't be 100 percent certain.

In addition, the unfalsifiability of psychological egoism demonstrates the logical fallacy of *begging the question*. When an argument begs the question, it assumes that what it is supposed to prove is already true, so the "proof" does nothing but repeat the assumption (such as "your mother is right because your mother is never wrong!"). Psychological egoism works in the same way: It assumes that all acts are selfish and therefore interprets all acts as selfish. So psychological egoism is not the scientific theory it claims to be.

2. Is Doing What We Want Always Selfish?

Biologically, psychological egoists have a forceful argument: the survival instinct. It seems a fact that all animals, including humans, are equipped with some sort of instinct for self-preservation. We might ask ourselves, though, whether that instinct is always the strongest instinct in all relationships, animal as well as human. There are cases in which animals seem to sacrifice themselves for others, yet surely they don't have any underlying motives, such as the desire to be on TV or go to heaven. Nor is it likely that they would suffer from a guilt complex if they did not perform such deeds. There is, then, at least the possibility that some actions are not performed for the reason of self-preservation.

Is it true that we always do things for selfish reasons? Let us assume, for the sake of argument, that we do actually do what we want so that we may benefit from some long-term consequences. But is doing what we want to benefit ourselves always a "selfish" act? Abraham Lincoln seems to have agreed that it is. A famous story tells of him riding on a mud coach (a type of stagecoach) with a friend. Just as he is explaining that he believes everybody has selfish reasons for his or her actions, they pass by a mudhole where several piglets are drowning. The mother sow is making an awful noise, but she can't help them. Lincoln asks the driver to stop the coach, gets off, wades into the mudhole, brings the pigs out, and returns to the coach. His friend, remembering what Lincoln had just said, asks him, "Now, Abe, where does selfishness come into this little episode?" Lincoln answers, "Why, bless your soul, Ed, that was the very essence of selfishness. I should have had no peace of mind all day had I gone on and left that suffering old sow worrying over those pigs. I did it to get peace of mind, don't you see?"

So Lincoln saved the pigs to benefit himself (and here we thought he was just a nice man). That is, of course, the irony of the story: Lincoln is not known to us as a selfish person. But was his theory right? He may have been lying in claiming that he did his good deed for himself—or he may have been joking—but let us assume that he spoke the truth as he saw it—that he saved the pigs to gain peace of mind for himself. Was it still a "selfish" act? That depends on what you call selfish. Is doing things to benefit yourself always selfish, or does it perhaps depend on what it is you want to gain? Would there be a difference between saving a pig for its own sake and saving it because you want to eat it for dinner? Most people would say there is a substantial difference between the two. In other words, it is *what* you want that matters, not just the fact that you want something. If what you want is to save someone, that is surely different from wanting to hurt someone. Lincoln might, of course, interject that saving the pigs was still in his own self-interest, so it wasn't done for them but for himself—but is that true? Why would it have been in his self-interest to know that the pigs were safe if self-gratification was all he cared about? A selfish person hardly loses sleep over the misery of other human beings, let alone that of a sow. Let

Box 4.8   LINCOLN: HUMBLE MAN OR CLEVER JOKESTER?

We might ask how Lincoln could have been unaware of the distinction between caring and not caring that becomes apparent when we consider different kinds of behavior. For an intelligent man, his remarks seem unusually dim. It's possible, of course, that the pig story illustrates Lincoln's true nature: that of a very humble and honest man who does not wish to take credit for having done something good. The story makes him all the more endearing, if that is the case, for indeed we know him as Honest Abe. But there is another possibility—that he was joking. Lincoln had a fondness for jokes, and this may have been one of them. Knowing full well that he was doing a nice thing, he made use of *irony* by claiming that rescuing the piglets was nothing but a selfish act. Lincoln scholars may have to decide which version they like better. In any event, Lincoln was speaking as a psychological egoist, regardless of how unselfishly he acted, because he expressed the theory that everyone acts selfishly.

us suppose, then, that he did it just to feel "warm and fuzzy" inside, and let us conclude that people who help others because they enjoy it are as selfish as can be. Nevertheless, a person who enjoys helping others is not our usual image of a selfish person; rather, as James Rachels points out, that is exactly how we picture an *unselfish* person. (See Box 4.8 for further discussion of Lincoln's motivation.) So if we assume that it is the *objective* rather than the mere fact of our wanting something that makes our want selfish or unselfish, we have an answer to psychological egoism right there: If what made Lincoln feel good was the thought of the pigs being safe—for their own sake, not his—then his deed of saving them was not a selfish deed. If what made him feel good was that now he would somehow benefit from saving them other than by just feeling good, then it was selfish. And how about if it was both? Suppose he saw a certain advantage in people knowing that he was a good guy who cared about pigs (although that's certainly not part of the original story) but he also liked the thought of the pigs being safe. Then it is still a refutation of psychological egoism because there was an unselfish element in an otherwise selfish act. And here we have reached the level of common sense: Some acts are unselfish, some are selfish, and some are a mixed bag. In the Narratives section you will find a contemporary story about a woman who is accused of being selfish because she feels good about helping others, Phoebe from the television sitcom *Friends*.

3. Problems of Language

As we have seen, psychological egoism presents certain problems because it does not always describe the world in a way that allows us to recognize it. One of its flaws may actually be a problem of *language*: If Lincoln's act of saving the pigs is selfish, what do we then call acts that are *really* selfish? The British philosopher Mary Midgley is extremely critical of the theory of psychological egoism and points out that since there is such a difference between what psychological egoists call normal selfish behavior (doing something nice for others so you can gain an advantage) and *really* selfish

Mary Midgley (b. 1919) is a British philosopher specializing in ethics. For years she taught philosophy at the University of Newcastle, and she is known for her vigorous critique of scientific theories attempting to reduce the human spirit to sociobiological elements. She is one of Richard Dawkins's most vocal critics. Her books include *Beast and Man: The Roots of Human Nature* (1978), *Heart and Mind: The Varieties of Moral Experience* (1981), *Animals and Why They Matter* (1983), *Wickedness* (1984), and *The Ethical Primate: Humans, Freedom and Morality* (1994). In 2005 her autobiography, *The Owl of Minerva*, was published.

behavior (doing something hurtful to others so you can gain an advantage), it would be illogical to call both selfish. We should reserve "selfish" for genuine self-absorbed behavior, says Midgley. If psychological egoism insists that regardless of whether we want to help others or hurt them for our own gain, our desire to help or hurt them is a selfish want. In that case, we may respond that we consider it less selfish to help others than to hurt them, and we may want to introduce some new terms: *less selfish* and *more selfish,* terms that distinguish between acts done for yourself and acts done for others. That, however, is just another way of trying to distinguish selfish behavior from unselfish behavior. Psychological egoism seems to have overlooked the fact that we already have a concept for "less-selfish" behavior that is perfectly well understood: *unselfish.* Changing language to the extent that it goes against our common sense (by claiming that there is no such thing as *unselfish* but that it is acceptable to use the term *less selfish*) does not make psychological egoism correct. So, if the psychological egoist admits that there can be degrees of selfishness, we might reply that the least degree of selfishness is what the rest of us call *unselfish;* if the psychological egoist insists that all acts are self-serving in some way, critics of psychological egoism point to the linguistic phenomenon known as the *fallacy of the suppressed correlative.* The correlative of the word *selfish* is *unselfish,* just as the correlative of *light* is *dark;* other pairs are *hot/cold, tall/short,* and so on. It is a psychological as well as a linguistic fact that we understand one term because we understand the other: If everything were dark, we wouldn't understand the meaning of *light,* and neither would we understand the meaning of *dark,* because it is defined by its contrast to light; without the contrast there is no understanding. In other words, a concept without a correlative becomes meaningless. If all acts are selfish, *selfish* has no correlative, and the statement "All acts are selfish" has no meaning. In fact, we could not make such a statement at all if psychological egoism were correct; the concept of selfishness would not exist, since any nonselfish behavior would be unthinkable. So not only does psychological egoism go against common sense and preclude a complete understanding of the full range of human behavior; it also goes against the rules of language.

That may sound like a complex argument, but we actually use it frequently in everyday situations. Here are a few examples of suppressed correlatives, situations in which something becomes meaningless if it doesn't have any opposite: (1) If you use a highlighter in your textbook, you may have found yourself studying a difficult text and highlighting many sentences. After a while, when you look at the pages, you find that you've actually highlighted just about everything. The task of highlighting all of a sudden has become meaningless; now *everything* is highlighted (the highlighted areas have lost their contrast), and that is just the same as not having anything highlighted. (2) At Starbucks a small cup of coffee is called "tall," a medium is called "grande," and a large is called "venti" (Italian for "twenty"—ounces, presumably). Does the designation "tall" really mean anything anymore when it comes to coffees? (3) Sometimes I hear students plead (as a joke, I hope), "Why can't you just give us all A's?" (whether they are deserved or not). The answer is that (aside from the fact that it wouldn't be right) if everybody in the class or the school or the country got A's, the A would become meaningless, since there would be no lower grade to serve as a contrast. If instructors bowed to the pressure to give only A's or B's, the whole idea of grading would be undermined. (4) There are situations that are supposed to have significance but are so common that the impact is nullified: Car alarms go off all the time, so the "alarm" effect is gone; people who curse all the time drain their words of any impact, so there is no way to emphasize a really bad situation; parents who yell at their children constantly have no voice impact left when the time comes for a yell to be effective; kids who "cry wolf" won't be believed in the end. And the psychological egoist who claims that everyone is selfish can't explain what *selfish* means if no behavior is recognized as unselfish.

Proponents of psychological egoism have responded that unselfishness doesn't actually exist, but you can still have the *concept* of unselfishness, which serves as the correlative of selfishness, even if it is imaginary; but critics of psychological egoism reply that the theory still does not make much sense. If it states that everybody is selfish to the bone, then it is a downright false theory. If it just says everybody has a selfish streak, then it is so trivial that it is not even interesting.

Ethical Egoism and Its Critics

We have already heard amazing stories about heroic acts in this chapter, from 9/11 to Hurricane Katrina and Virginia Tech. A person such as Officer Stuart who lost his life helping commuters get out of the subway on 9/11 would be admired as a hero by most of us.

However, the ethical egoist would say that, in effect, he did the wrong thing. For the ethical egoist there is only one rule: *Look after yourself*. The ethical egoist would say you are throwing your life away.

Here we should make sure that we have our terms straight. This theory is called ethical egoism simply because it is an ethical theory, a *normative* theory about how we *ought* to behave (in contrast to psychological egoism, which claims to know how we actually *do* behave). The theory implies that we ought to be selfish. Or, to put it more gently, we ought to be *self-interested*. Calling the theory "ethical" does not suggest there

Calvin and Hobbes   by Bill Watterson

CALVIN AND HOBBES. Reprinted with permission of Universal Press Syndicate. All rights reserved.

For many readers the idea that egoism might be a legitimate moral theory is surprising, but indeed Calvin is right: "You ought to look out for number one" is, in fact, a moral principle. However, critics of ethical egoism point out that it is hardly an acceptable moral principle. (Since the philosopher Thomas Hobbes is mentioned in this chapter, you might like to know that Hobbes the tiger is named after Thomas Hobbes.)

might be a decent way to be selfish; it just means ethical egoism is a theory that advocates egoism as a moral rule. (Box 4.9 is a discussion of individual ethical egoism.)

You Should Look After Yourself

Glaucon insisted that if you don't take advantage of a situation, you are foolish. Hobbes claimed that it makes good sense to look after yourself, and morality is a result of that self-interest: If I mistreat others, they may mistreat me, so I resolve to behave myself. That is a rather twisted version of the Golden Rule (Do unto others as you would have them do unto you; see Box 4.10). It is twisted because it is peculiarly slanted toward our own self-interest. The reason we should treat others the way we would like to be treated is that it gives us a good chance of receiving just such treatment; we do it for ourselves, not for others. So the ethical egoist may certainly decide to help another human being in need—not for the sake of the other, but to ensure that "what goes around, comes around." The Golden Rule usually emphasizes others, but for the ethical egoist it emphasizes the self. With ethical egoism we encounter a certain phenomenon for the first time in this book: an ethical theory that focuses on the *consequences* of one's actions. Any theory that looks solely to consequences of actions is known as a *consequentialist theory;* the consequences that ethical egoism stipulates are good consequences for the person taking the action. However, we can imagine other kinds of consequentialist theories, such as one that advocates good consequences for as many people as possible. Such a theory is discussed in Chapter 5.

Ethical egoists are themselves quite divided about whether the theory tells you to do *what you want* without regard for others or *what is good for you* without regard

Box 4.9   INDIVIDUAL ETHICAL EGOISM

This version of *ethical egoism,* commonly adopted by small children and childish adults, holds that "everyone ought to do what I want," regardless of whether it is in the other person's interest. This view is rarely taken seriously as an ethical theory because it doesn't have any good arguments to support it except that it's what the person wants. We can't expect everyone else to follow our whims or even look after our interests; that is nothing but emotional tyranny. However, the ethical egoist attitude is not limited to children and childlike adults; people who throughout their lives have been used to having their way will sometimes display the same attitude. From royalty in times past to people of wealth and power in the present, certain individuals (although by no means the majority) will act as though others have responsibilities to them, but they feel exempt from having responsibilities to others.

A moral theory, if it is to be accepted today, has to involve an important element of acceptance. It has to be imaginable that most people, if not everyone, would be willing to adopt the theory for themselves. This phenomenon, which we shall discuss later, is known as *universalizability.* We can hardly imagine the world agreeing to serve our interests, because, after all, what makes us so special? However, it is a fact that some people choose to live their lives seeking to fulfill *someone else's* wishes or interests; such choices may be made by parents, spouses, grown children taking care of their parents, disciples following their guru or leader, and devout believers trying to live the way God wants them to live. If you are a parent or a political or religious leader, you may claim that "people should do what I want because it is good for them." In that case, you are moving out of the realm of egoism; the main interest is no longer yourself, but everyone; you just have the audacity to claim that you know better than anyone else how everyone's lives should be lived.

for others. The latter version seems to appeal to common sense because, in the long run, just looking for instant gratification is hardly going to make you happy or live longer. Saying that one ought to look after oneself need not, of course, mean that one should annoy others whenever possible, step on their toes, or deliberately neglect their interests. It simply suggests that one should do what will be of long-term benefit to oneself, such as exercising, eating healthy food, avoiding repetitive argumentative situations, and so forth. Even paying one's taxes might be added to the list. In addition, it suggests that other people's interests are of no importance. If you might advance your own interests by helping others, then by all means help others, but only if you are the main beneficiary. It is fine to help your children get ahead in school, because you love them and that love is a gratifying emotion for you. But there is no reason to lend a hand to your neighbor's children unless you like them or you achieve gratification through your actions.

This interpretation—that the theory tells us to do whatever will benefit ourselves—results in a rewriting of the Golden Rule because, obviously, it is not always the case that you *will* get the same treatment from others that you give to them. Occasionally you might get away with not treating others decently, because they may never know that you are the source of the bad treatment they are receiving. Ethical egoism tells you that it is perfectly all right to treat others in a way that is to

Box 4.10   THE GOLDEN RULE WITH VARIATIONS

Most people know the Golden Rule: Do unto others as you would have them do unto you, or treat others as you would like to be treated. It is often attributed to Jesus Christ; the Gospel of Matthew cites him as saying, "Therefore all things whatsoever ye would that men should do to you, do ye even so to them: for this is the law and the prophets" (7:12). The law referred to is in Leviticus 19:18 in the Bible (the Old Testament): ". . . thou shalt love thy neighbor as thyself." In the later Talmud, we read that "what is hateful to you, do not to your fellow man. This is the law: all the rest is commentary" (Shabbat 31a). And other traditions have similar sayings. Brahmanism teaches, "This is the sum of Dharma [duty]: Do naught unto others which would cause you pain if done to you" (*Mahabharata* 5:1517). In Buddhism it reads like this: "Hurt not others in ways that you yourself would find hurtful" (*Udànavarga* 5:18). Islam teaches that "none of you [truly] believes until he wishes for his brother what he wishes for himself" (number 13 of Imam "Al-Nawawi's Forty Hadiths"). In the American Indian tradition, the great leader Black Elk extended the rule to all living beings: "All things are our relatives; what we do to everything, we do to ourselves. All is really One."[1] And the Chinese philosopher Confucius (551–479 B.C.E.) is known to have taught his students this version, taken from *The Doctrine of the Mean, The Four Books:* "What you do not like when done to yourself, do not do to others." This is sometimes called the "Silver Rule."

The rule teaches that to find a blueprint for treating others, we should imagine how we would or would not like to be treated. Ethical egoists don't read it that way, however; they read it as a rule for protecting yourself and being as comfortable as possible. The way to avoid trouble with others is to treat them as you'd want to be treated—the path of least resistance. The emphasis on *others* is not a given within the rule. This is the aspect of *prudence* connected with the Golden Rule. But as we see in Chapter 5, the Golden Rule is also used as a blueprint for general happiness, one's own as well as others'. In this case, it is concern for *the other person* that underlies the rule.

Recognizing the wisdom of the Golden Rule is perhaps the most important early stage in civilization because it implies that we see others as similar to ourselves and that we see ourselves as deserving no treatment that is better than what others get (although we would generally prefer it—we're not saints). However, the Golden Rule may not be the ultimate rule to live by because (as we discuss further in Chapter 11) others may *not want* to be treated as *you'd* like to be treated. Then, according to some thinkers, the "Platinum Rule" ought to kick in: Treat others as *they* want to be treated! Proponents of the Golden Rule say that this takes the universal appeal out of the rule. The spark of moral genius in the rule is precisely that we are *similar* in our human nature—not that we would all like to have things our way.

---

[1]These quotes can be found on the website Religious Tolerance.org.

---

your advantage and not to theirs as long as you can be certain that you will get away with it. At the end of the chapter you'll find a Primary Reading as well as a Narrative by the American philosopher and novelist Ayn Rand, who is generally considered an ethical egoist. She wrote a book in defense of self-interest called *The Virtue of Selfishness,* from which the excerpt is taken, but she is better known for her novels *Anthem, The Fountainhead, We the Living,* and *Atlas Shrugged,* which is represented by an excerpt

Socrates' answer to Glaucon's suggestion that the unjust man is happier than the just man rests on his notion that a happy person is in balance, and without moral virtue (see Chapter 8): you can't be happy, so the unjust man is out of balance, hence sick, and therefore unhappy. Socrates' concept of a morally good, "just" person involves having the right relationship between one's reason, one's willpower, and one's desires. As this illustration shows, reason should control willpower, and together, reason and willpower should control one's desires. In Chapter 8 you will see this concept of justice and moral goodness expanded to cover Plato's political theory as well as his idea of virtue.

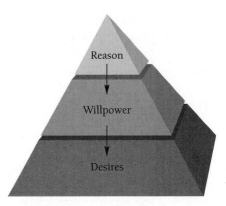

too. Rand advocated the idea that people have a right, even a duty, to look after themselves and seek their own happiness and that it is "moral cannibalism" to advocate altruistic theories wherein humans are supposed to feel obliged to help those who have no wish to help themselves—in Rand's words, "moochers and leeches." Rand's philosophy was enormously popular some decades ago, and some people predict that there will be a Rand revival in the future.

Shortcomings of Ethical Egoism

Let us return now to Glaucon and his rings. He assumes that not only will the scoundrel take advantage of a ring that can make him invisible, but so will the decent man, and, furthermore, we would call them both fools if they didn't. A theory of psychological egoism, therefore, can also contain a normative element: ethical egoism (which tells us how we *ought* to behave). Of course, it is hard to see what the point is if we can't stop ourselves from doing what we do.

At the end of Glaucon's speech, the reader expects Socrates to dispatch the theory of egoism with a quick blow. The answer, however, is a long time coming; as a matter of fact, Plato designed the rest of his *Republic* as a roundabout answer to Glaucon. In the end, Socrates' answer is, The unjust person can't be happy because happiness consists of a good harmony, a balance between the three parts of the soul: *reason, willpower (spirit),* and *desire.* Reason is supposed to dominate willpower, and willpower desire. If desire or willpower dominates the other two, we have a sick person, and a sick person can't be happy by definition, says Socrates. We will return to this theory in the Primary Readings of this chapter, with an excerpt from Plato's *Republic.*

In considering the question, Why be just? we must consider justice in terms of the whole society, not just the individual. We can't argue for justice on the basis of individual situations but only in general terms. That makes the question Why be just? more reasonable because we don't look at individual cases but at an overall picture in which justice and well-being are interrelated. For Socrates and Plato, being just is part of "the good life," and true happiness cannot be attained without justice.

To the modern reader there is something curiously bland and evasive about those answers. Surely unjust persons can be disgustingly happy—they may seem to us to have sick souls, but they certainly don't act as if they are aware of it or suffer any ill effects from it. The answer to this—that being selfish is *just plain wrong in itself*—is not emphasized by Socrates. For a modern person it seems reasonable to be "just" out of respect for the law or perhaps because that is the right thing to do, but Socrates mentions this only briefly; it is a concern that belongs to a much later time period than the one in which he lived. The highest virtue for the ancient Greeks was, on the whole, ensuring the well-being of the community, and that well-being remained the bottom line more than any abstract moral issue of right and wrong. Today we know this social theory as *communitarianism*. Because justice was best for the state in the final evaluation, justice was a value in itself. In the end, Socrates' answer evokes self-interest and urges us to discern truth from appearance: If you are unjust, your soul will suffer, and so will your community. Furthermore, your community may shun you, ostracize you, banish you (which was common practice in ancient Greece), and if you are nothing without your community, then what will become of you? The interesting implication is that Socrates is saying to Glaucon that the unjust man is out of balance, thus unhealthy, and thus unhappy, because he will be excluded from his network of friends and associates. That attitude, ironically, may have cost Socrates his life, because he refused to leave his community and flee Athens when he was accused of crimes against the state.

Today communitarianism is alive and well in the United States—it is a political theory best illustrated by the African proverb "It takes a village to raise a child." In other words, individuals are part of the community and derive their identity from that community—and the community members share a responsibility toward one another. A professed contemporary communitarian is Senator Hillary Clinton.

Socrates' attitude may not impress people seeking self-gratification (who are unlikely to be concerned about the effects of their actions on their souls or on the people around them), but it may have some impact on people seeking long-term self-interest. It still rests on an empirical assumption, however, that sooner or later you must pay the piper—that is, atone for your wrongdoing. History, though, is full of "bad guys" who have gone to their graves rich and happy. The religious argument that you will go to hell or suffer a miserable next incarnation if you are concerned only with yourself is not really an argument against *egoism* because it still asks you to look after yourself, even to the point of using others for the purpose of ensuring a pleasant afterlife (treat others decently and you shall be saved).

The one type of argument against ethical egoism that has most appealed to scholars insists that ethical egoism is self-contradictory. If you are supposed to look after yourself and your colleague is supposed to look after herself, and if looking after yourself will mean stealing her files, then you and she will be working at cross-purposes: Your duty will be to steal her files from her, and her duty will be to protect her files. We can't have a moral theory that says one's duty should be something that conflicts with someone else's duty, so ethical egoism is therefore inconsistent.

Few ethical egoists find that argument convincing, because they don't agree that we can't have a moral theory that gives a green light to different concepts of duty. Such a view assumes that ethical egoism benefits everyone, even when each person does only what is in his or her best interest. Occasionally, ethical egoism assumes just that: We should look after ourselves and mind our own business, because meddling in other people's affairs is a violation of privacy; they will not like our charity, they will hate our superiority, and we won't know what is best for them anyway. So, along those lines, we should stay out of other people's affairs because it is best for everybody. The political theory resulting from this point of view is known as *laissez-faire,* the hands-off policy. Political theorists, however, are quick to point out that laissez-faire is by no means an egoistic theory, because it has everybody's best interests at heart. That is precisely what is wrong with the idea that we should adopt ethical egoism for the reason that it will be good for everybody: It may be true that if we all look after ourselves, we'll all be happier—but who is the beneficiary of that idea? Not "I," but "everybody," so this version is, in fact, no longer a moral theory of egoism but something else.

Another argument against ethical egoism is that it carries no weight as a solver of moral conflicts: If you and I disagree about the correct course of action, who is to say who is right? If you favor the course of action that is to your advantage and I favor the course of action that is to my advantage, then there is no common ground. But the ethical egoist generally answers in the same way as to the charge that ethical egoism is self-contradictory: It never claimed to be a theory of consensus in all approaches, merely in the basic approach—that everyone ought to look after himself or herself.

A better argument against the conceptual consistency of ethical egoism is this: Ethical egoism doesn't work in practice. Remember that the theory says all people ought to look out for themselves—not merely that *I* should look out for *myself.* But suppose you set out to look after your own self-interests and advocate that others do the same; within a short while you will realize that your rule is *not* going to be to your advantage, because others will be out there grabbing for themselves, and you will have fierce competition. You might decide that the smart thing to do is to advocate not that all people look out for themselves but that all people look after one another while keeping quiet about your own intention of breaking the rule whenever possible. That would be the prudent thing to do, and it probably would work quite well. The only problem is that this is not a moral theory because, for one thing, it carries a contradiction. It means you must claim to support one principle and act according to another one—in other words, it requires you to be dishonest. Also, a moral theory, in this day and age, has to be able to be extended to everybody; we can't uphold a theory that says it is okay for me to do something because I'm *me,* but not for you just because you're *not me*—that would be assuming that I should have privileges based on the mere fact that I'm *me.*

Logical attacks on ethical egoism have a persuasive power for some—as logical arguments rightly should have. However, perhaps the most forceful argument against ethical egoism involves an emotional component. Often, philosophers have been afraid to appeal to emotions because emotions have been considered irrelevant. But as philosophers such as Martha Nussbaum, Philippa Foot, Philip Hallie, and James Rachels point out, what is a moral sense without the involvement of our feelings? Feelings need not be irrational—they are often quite rational responses to our experiences (see Chapter 1). And what seems such an affront to most people is the apparent callousness of an ethical egoist: Other people's pain simply doesn't matter as a moral imperative.

One example may speak louder than theoretical speculations: the murder in 1998 of seven-year-old Sherrice Iverson by Jeremy Strohmeyer in a Nevada casino restroom. Strohmeyer's friend David Cash knew about the crime taking place, heard the screams, and may even have witnessed it. He never tried to stop his friend, nor did he alert casino security, nor did he turn in his friend afterward.

Psychologically, both Strohmeyer and Cash may have been warped and damaged, but Cash had quite a rational grasp of the situation and a straightforward explanation for why he didn't step in. It is debatable whether Cash is an ethical egoist or a moral subjectivist. In an interview he said, "I'm not going to get upset over somebody else's life. I just worry about myself first. I'm not going to lose sleep over somebody else's problems." He seems to be recommending selfishness, not the tolerance of moral subjectivism's "to each his or her own." If so, is that the kind of practical expression of a moral theory that we should think is legitimate, just because it allows everyone else to be selfish too? Isn't this a case in which we are allowed to feel moral outrage over someone's inhumanity? Why, indeed, should we lose sleep over someone else's problems? *Because they are fellow human beings.*

Perhaps this is a good time to revisit Socrates' argument that the unjust person can't be happy because he (or she) will be socially unacceptable. According to anecdotal reports from Berkeley students, David Cash was given the cold shoulder by other students on campus, although he was not indicted for any crimes. And who is to say whether Socrates might not be right—that being shunned by one's community isn't, in fact, a cause of imbalance and regret in the heart of the person who has transgressed against the moral standards because of selfishness?

Being Selfless: Levinas's Ideal Altruism Versus Singer's Reciprocal Altruism

To return to the question of September 11: Were the rescuers—those who survived as well as those who died—selfish? Going back to our Lincoln discussion, we can say they were selfish only if they did what they did for purely self-serving reasons. Judging from the remarks of rescuers who survived, their own self-interests seemed to be very far from their minds. And how about the suicidal terrorists? Were they selfish or unselfish, or both? Judging from letters and statements from other terrorists and sympathizers from the same groups, their motivation was mixed: They believed the Koran promised them direct, immediate access to heaven, where they would live in bliss for eternity, attended by beautiful virgins—but they also believed they were doing a heroic deed for their people. The Western mind-set considers self-sacrifice to be noble. Then why do most of us not consider terrorist acts noble? Because self-sacrifice is usually regarded as an act wherein a person dies trying to help others, such as Officer Stuart, not one that involves deliberately killing innocent people. To discuss this issue further you may want to go directly to Chapter 13, where we address the question of terrorism—but you may also want to consider the concept of *group egoism*: extending your self-interest to the group you belong to, so that if you could help the group survive by giving up an advantage or even sacrificing yourself, then (theoretically) you'd be willing to do that. A group egoist would not consider members of other groups valuable, or as having claims as legitimate as those of one's own

---

Box 4.11   PSYCHOLOGICAL AND ETHICAL ALTRUISM

The term *altruism* comes from the Latin *alter,* meaning "other." The version of altruism that we are discussing in this chapter is sometimes known as ethical altruism—not because there is a form of altruism that is *unethical,* but simply because philosophers have seen a parallel to ethical egoism: "Everyone *ought* to disregard his or her own interests for the sake of others." In other words, ethical altruism is a normative theory, like its opposite, ethical egoism. But is there also a counterpart to psychological egoism, *psychological altruism?* I'll let you be the judge of that. As psychological egoism, a descriptive theory, claims that everyone is selfish at heart, psychological altruism would claim that everyone is unselfish at heart: "Everyone always disregards his or her own interests for the sake of others." Now who would hold such a theory? Not many, since it seems to fly in the face of the facts: We know very well that not everyone in this world is caring and unselfish. As a matter of fact, one might speculate that psychological altruism was invented by a philosopher with a sense of sym-metry, just to have a matching pair of altruisms to compare the two forms of egoism with. But if psychological altruism is redefined in the following way, "There is something good and caring deep down in every human being," then the theory sounds quite familiar and plausible to many people. You may remember the phrase "ought implies can" used as an excuse by psychological egoism: "Don't tell me I ought to be unselfish, because I can't." The same idea works for psychological altruism: The person who is caring by nature might say to the ethical egoist, "Don't tell me I ought to be selfish, because I can't!"

The concoction of psychological altruism may not reflect any actual moral theory, but it does teach an interesting lesson in ethics: If we think psychological altruism is unrealistic and makes no sense, then we also have to criticize psychological egoism for the same reason, because the theories are based on the same logic and are vulnerable to the same criticisms! My astute students at Mesa College pointed this little tidbit out, and I'm happy to share it with you.

---

group. Suicide bombers do not have the interest of all at heart—just the interests of their own group—at the cost of others.

As an alternative to ethical egoism, *altruism* hardly seems preferable if we view it in its ideal, normative sense: *Everybody ought to give up his or her own self-interest for others.* In that case we might want to complain (as the philosopher and writer Ayn Rand did) that we have only one life to live, and why should we let the "moochers and leeches" drain our life away? If we let them take advantage of us, they surely will. Our lives are not things to be thrown away. Only a few philosophers and a few religions have ever held such an extreme altruistic theory. One person in the late twentieth century who did was the Lithuanian-French philosopher Emmanuel Levinas, whom you will meet in Chapter 10. For Levinas, the Other (another human being, the stranger) is always more important than you yourself are (which also means that you are important, as a stranger and an Other, to everyone else), and you should always put the needs of the Other ahead of your own. But Levinas is an exception among modern thinkers; usually there is a realistic recognition of the fact that humans are apt to ask what's in it for them. (See Box 4.11 for a discussion of psychological and ethical altruism.) A story in the Narratives section explores the idea of utter selflessness: J. R. R. Tolkien's *Lord of the Rings.*

Ideal altruism seems to imply that there is something inherently *wrong* with acting to benefit oneself, and if that is the case, it will never become a widely accepted moral theory because it will work only for saints. According to the Australian philosopher Peter Singer, there is another way of viewing altruism, a much more realistic and rational way: Looking after the interests of others makes sense because, overall, everyone benefits from it. This moderate, limited version of altruism is sometimes called Golden Rule altruism (or reciprocal altruism): You are ready to place others' interests ahead of your own, especially in emergencies, and you expect them to do the same for you. Philosophers are in disagreement over whether this position actually deserves the name of altruism.

In *The Expanding Circle* (1981), Singer suggests that egoism is, in fact, more costly than altruism. He presents a new version of a classic example, known as the prisoner's dilemma. Two early hunters are attacked by a saber-toothed cat. They obviously both want to flee, but (let us suppose) they also care for each other. If they both flee, one will be picked off and eaten. If one flees and one stays and fights, the fleeing one will live but the fighting one will die. If both stay and fight, there is a chance that they can fight off the cat. So it is actually in the interest of both of them to stay together, and all the more so if they care for each other. Singer's point is that evolution would favor such an arrangement, because trustworthy partners would be viewed as better than ones who leave you behind to get eaten, and they would be selected in future partnerships. If you are an egoist and you manage to get picked as a partner by an altruist, you will be the one who benefits from the situation (the altruist is sure to stay, and you'll be able to get away). This will work only a few times, however; after a while the altruist will be wise to you and your kind. In the end, then, it is in your own self-interest not to be too self-interested.

This argument actively defeats not only the everyday variety of ethical egoism that says you ought to do what you want—because in the end that will not improve your survival odds—but also the more sophisticated *rational ethical egoism* that requires us to think of what is to our advantage in the long run. If we look toward our own advantage exclusively, we may not be optimizing our chances, as the example of the hunters shows. Being capable of taking others' interests into consideration actually improves our own survival odds.

Why is this viewpoint not just another version of the ethical egoist's credo of looking after yourself? Because it involves someone else's interests too. It says that there is nothing wrong with keeping an eye out for yourself, so long as it doesn't happen at the expense of someone else's interests. In other words, the solution may not be myself *or* others, but myself *and* others. This idea, incorporated in the moral theory of *utilitarianism,* will be explored in the next chapter. The film *Return to Paradise*, featured in the Narratives section, explores the concept of how far altruism and egoism can take a person when it boils down to friendship obligations.

So what do biologists and psychologists at the cutting edge today think about the idea that humans are born selfish and become moral beings only through reluctant acculturation? It is not nearly as much in fashion as it used to be. The possibility that human evolution has favored the less selfish individuals, as Singer's example claims, now seems quite plausible.

Selfish Genes or Fellow-Feeling? Dawkins, Midgley, Hume, and de Waal

At this point it may be appropriate to address a question that we have side-stepped until now, except for a brief discussion in Chapter 1: *Where does our sense of values come from?* It is clear that humans living in society have a sense of values, of things that matter to us above and beyond the everyday grind of staying safe and putting food on the table. (And, as Hobbes would say, even staying safe and putting food on the table are values we cherish.) We have a sense of moral right and wrong, of "dos and don'ts," even if they may differ from culture to culture, and even if we may prefer to just look after number one. But where do these internal rules originate? Three major schools of thought have manifested themselves in modern times. (1) Values are a result of *socialization,* a necessary "veneer" over a fundamentally feral and self-oriented human nature. This theory is often referred to as the *Veneer Theory.* You'll recognize Hobbes's philosophy as an early example of this theory. (2) Values are an outcome of the human capacity for *rational thought:* Our reason is capable of seeing through the murk of instincts and emotions to reach impartial, fair solutions, and must be the tool we use to make moral decisions. In Chapters 5 and 6 you'll encounter the two most famous examples of this approach, in themselves very different: utilitarianism, and Kantian deontology. (3) Values are naturally embedded in our human capacity for *emotions:* First we experience strong feelings, then we act on them—and afterward we try to rationalize what we did. And the strong feelings most people have include a natural reluctance to harm other human beings. This theory is generally known as *emotionalism.* We return to emotionalism below, but first we need to take a look at a theory that in many ways serves as a bridge between psychological egoism and altruism: the *selfish-gene theory.*

The Selfish-Gene Theory and Its Critics

The selfish-gene theory arose in the 1970s and became popular to the extent that, for decades, many people have taken its viewpoint as an established truth. This theory was introduced by Richard Dawkins in his book *The Selfish Gene* (1976) and supported by the famous sociobiologist Edward O. Wilson as a way of explaining, scientifically, why some animals as well as humans behave in an altruistic way. In the spirit of psychological egoism, it is not that humans and animals actually behave selflessly, but that such behavior is an instinctive way to promote the survival not of the individual but of his or her genes. Why would a baboon apparently sacrifice herself to leopards so that her "troop" can make a getaway? Because she is closely related to the troop, and her sacrifice ensures that her genes will survive. Why do dogs wake their owners up in the middle of the night to make sure they get out of the house that's on fire? Because they think their owners are the alpha dogs of their pack, and alpha dogs are related to the lower-status dogs, so their genes will survive. In October 2004 off the coast of New Zealand, a group of one adult lifeguard and three teens were herded together in a tight circle by a pod of dolphins—and they didn't understand why, until they saw a ten-foot white shark trying to approach them. The dolphins circled the humans for forty minutes until the shark got tired and swam off. The whole event was witnessed by another lifeguard in a boat and by people on the beach a hundred yards away. What would the selfish-gene theorist say to that? That the dolphins use the same maneuvers to protect their own young, and they can't tell the difference between a human in a wetsuit and dolphin babies. But few animal behaviorists would claim that dolphins, or any animal for that matter, can't tell the difference between humans and their own species, especially since they're excellent at telling the difference between their own babies and other dolphins' babies. (Male dolphins will often try to kill the offspring of other male dolphins.) So could we really be witnessing animals making *moral choices?* We will return to that question later.

As far as humans go, does the selfish-gene theory offer any kind of insight? For the originator of the theory, Richard Dawkins, it explains why people sometimes act unselfishly toward strangers: *We make a mistake.* We are preprogrammed through our evolution to help our genes survive, either in our own person or through our nearest relatives, and in ancient times we used to have close contact only with such relatives, and our altruism would benefit only them. But times have changed, and we are now in a complex world of strangers, but our genetic programming makes us act altruistically as if we're still living with a small group of relatives. In his book *The God Delusion* (2006), Dawkins says, "We can no more help ourselves feeling pity when we see a weeping unfortunate (who is unrelated and unable to reciprocate) than we can help ourselves feeling lust for a member of the opposite sex (who may be infertile or otherwise unable to reproduce). Both are misfirings, Darwinian mistakes: blessed, precious mistakes." So Dawkins isn't saying that we shouldn't be altruistic toward strangers—he thinks it is rather wonderful that we are capable of doing such a thing. But he says that, biologically, it makes no sense—it is a misdirection of an original biological purpose. However, many philosophers believe the selfish-gene theory creates more problems than it solves: When humans behave altruistically toward strangers, it is often because of the very fact that they are strangers—we don't confuse them with relatives. On the contrary, we may deliberately *choose* to treat them *as if* they are relatives, which is something completely different. The British philosopher Mary Midgley, whom you'll remember from an earlier section in this chapter, has been a vocal critic of the selfish-gene theory as well as a critic of psychological egoism. Advocating the old principle of parsimony, or *Occam's razor* (choosing the simpler explanation over a more complex one if the simpler explanation works as well or better), Midgley suggests that a much simpler explanation exists for our altruistic behavior than some selfish gene: It's the fact that we've all grown up in groups with other people, and in most cases the people who raised us loved us and cared about our well-being. And when we raise children, we care about them for their sake too. So we have a built-in capacity for caring for our family—and in our human society we just extend that capacity to strangers, who become *honorary relatives* for a time. What makes this different from a version of the selfish-gene theory is that we extend our caring capacity to strangers not for *our* sake (to perpetuate our genes) but for *theirs* (because we care about how they feel). Dawkins himself has said that Midgley misunderstood his theory: it isn't about people or animals making mistakes about relatives, but a biological hardwiring being misdirected. But here we should remember the argument against psychological egoism that you read earlier in the chapter, that if a concept becomes so broad that it has no opposite (the fallacy of the suppressed correlative), then the concept has become useless. So if all behavior is selfish, but some selfish behavior involves altruism, then haven't we watered down the meaning of selfishness?

An example may illustrate what Midgley means: In February 2002 a seven-year-old girl, Danielle van Dam, was abducted in the middle of the night from her bedroom in an upscale and supposedly safe San Diego neighborhood. Friends and neighbors of the parents immediately went about organizing a search, setting up a website, and distributing fliers. Even though everyone feared the worst—especially after a neighbor, after several weeks of investigation, was arrested and charged with kidnapping and murder in the case—the search effort continued. The San Diego district attorney commented that he had never heard of a volunteer effort that size in California: Some twenty-five hundred people came from all over San Diego, but also from Los Angeles, Oregon, Arizona, and Texas to participate in the search.

In the end it was indeed a group of volunteers who found the girl's body in a rural area. What made these strangers give up their time to look for a little girl they'd never met? Many said they were parents and if it were their child, they'd want someone to help look for him or her. But many also said that they just felt they had to. A television commentator perhaps said it best: Danielle had been adopted by all of San Diego, indeed, by the whole nation. Was it just because she was cute? Because she was white, perhaps? Because television played home videos of her? If so, what about all the abducted children who aren't cute, or white, or on video? In San Diego, shortly after Danielle's disappearance, a small African American boy, Jahi Turner, disappeared and was never found, despite an intense search by locals, and local media coverage. But this lost toddler's fate never reached the level of national attention. Was it because he was not a white little girl? Most of us would hate to think that could be a factor, and most people (as was the case with the two search groups in San Diego) would put their hearts into finding a lost child regardless of race and gender, but what *the media* will choose as the leading story is another matter. Here we may see a built-in bias, maybe not as an example of knee-jerk media racism, but as a matter of calculated business projections: Whose face is likely to sell the most products when the commercials start rolling? That may be a cynical viewpoint, and it may not even be accurate. But if we look at the other high-profile media stories of abducted and murdered young people, the names that come to mind are, mostly, young, blonde girls and women: Jon-Benet Ramsey in Colorado, Elizabeth Smart in Utah (who is, so far, the only one to come back alive), Dru Shodin in North Dakota, Carly Brucia in Florida, Jessica Lundsford, also in Florida (who has been the inspiration for "Jessica's Law"), Laci Peterson in California (a brunette, pregnant with her first child, a boy), and Natalee Holloway from Alabama, who disappeared while on vacation in Aruba. Why have we been so captivated by these tragic stories of young lost lives? Is it because we care only about young white women? Or could it be because these are the stories selected by the media and because, in most cases, we get to see the victims laughing, joking, and vivacious on home videos, not just as still pictures on a screen? In the introduction you read how such an interest may be rooted in some misdirected tribal form of curiosity: We're bored, we don't have big families anymore, and

David Hume, Scottish philosopher and historian. Hume believed that human beings are born with a fellow-feeling, a sense of compassion and empathy for others.

we latch on to media events the way a fourteen-year-old latches on to celebrity stories. But Mary Midgley may have a point: Occasionally that curiosity becomes one of the finer emotions we are capable of, when a story touches our hearts more deeply than an ordinary news story, and we "adopt" the missing young person as an honorary relative, caring about the welfare of a total stranger, if only for a while.

David Hume's Emotionalism

Midgley sees human compassion toward fellow human beings as something fundamental, but primarily a love and compassion for extended family. For a more sweeping view of emotion as the fundamental moral characteristic, we turn to David Hume (1711–1776), the Scottish philosopher. Hume believed that compassion is the one natural human feeling that holds us together in a society. For Hume, all of ethics can be reduced to the idea that reason acts as the handmaiden to our feelings; there is no such thing as an *objectively* moral act—nothing is good or bad in itself, not even murder. The good and the bad lie in our *feelings* toward the act. For Hume, all morality rests ultimately on our emotional responses, and there are no "moral facts" outside our own personal sensitivity. This theory says that whatever we would like to see happen we think of as morally good, and whatever we would hate to see happen we think of as morally evil. And what is it we would like to see happen? For Hume the answer is, whatever corresponds to our *natural feeling of concern for others*. Contrary to Hobbes, Hume believes that humans are equipped not only with self-love but also with love for others, and this emotion gives us our moral values. We simply react with sympathy to others through a built-in instinct—at least, most people do. Even persons who are generally selfish will feel compassion toward others if there is nothing in the situation that directly concerns them personally. Having the virtues of compassion and benevolence is a natural thing to Hume, and if we are a little short on such virtues, it simply means that we lack a natural ability, as when we are nearsighted. Such people are an exception to the rule.

That means that Hume's theory, far from being merely a focus on how we feel about things, is actually an example of *soft universalism:* We may have many different ideas and feelings about right and wrong, good and bad, but as human beings, most of us share a bottom-line criterion for morality: a fellow-feeling, a natural concern for others.

In Hume's words, from *A Treatise of Human Nature,* Book I, Part 1:

> If morality had naturally no influence on human passions and actions, 'twere in vain to take such pains to inculcate it; and nothing wou'd be more fruitless than that multitude of rules and precepts, with which all moralists abound. Philosophy is commonly divided into speculative and practical; and as morality is always comprehended under the latter division, 'tis supposed to influence our passions and actions, and to go beyond the calm and indolent judgments of the understanding. And this is confirm'd by common experience, which informs us, that men are often govern'd by their duties, and are deter'd from some actions by the opinion of injustice, and impell'd to others by that of obligation.
>
> Since morals, therefore, have an influence on the actions and affections, it follows, that they cannot be deriv'd from reason; and that because reason alone, as we have already prov'd, can never have any such influence. Morals excite passions, and produce or prevent actions. Reason of itself is utterly impotent in this particular. The rules of morality, therefore, are not conclusions of our reason.
>
> No one, I believe, will deny the justness of this inference; nor is there any other means of evading it, than by denying that principle, on which it is founded. As long as it is allow'd, that reason has no influence on our passions and action, 'tis in vain to pretend, that morality is discover'd only by a deduction of reason. An active principle can never be founded on an inactive; and if reason be inactive in itself, it must remain so in all its shapes and appearances, whether it exerts itself in natural or moral subjects, whether it considers the powers of external bodies, or the actions of rational beings. . . .
>
> Thus upon the whole, 'tis impossible, that the distinction betwixt moral good and evil, can be made to reason; since that distinction has an influence upon our actions, of which reason alone is incapable. Reason and judgment may, indeed, be the mediate cause of an action, by prompting, or by directing a passion: But it is not pretended, that a judgment of this kind, either in its truth or falsehood, is attended with virtue or vice. And as to the judgments, which are caused by our judgments, they can still less bestow those moral qualities on the actions, which are their causes.

You'll remember from Chapter 1 that neuroscience has recently weighed in on the origin of the moral sense, and the spotlight has been turned toward Hume once again, because Hume's theory that we are endowed with a natural empathy for other human beings has now found support in neuroscientific facts. Antonio Damasio and other scientists believe they have found not only a moral compass but also the very seat of empathy in the brain.

In Chapter 11 you'll find a twentieth-century example of emotionalism in the philosophy of Richard Taylor. In our early twenty-first century, one of the most prominent examples of emotionalism, but with a scientific twist, comes from Marc Hauser, and we return to him as an example of soft universalism in Chapter 11 as well.

Can Animals Have Morals?

But that leads us back to this question: If humans can truly behave in a somewhat/sometimes selfless manner, what about the higher animals? What about those dolphins saving the group of four swimmers in New Zealand? Throughout history there have been numerous similar examples. Is the most plausible explanation that they simply don't know what they're doing, or do they make what we would call a moral choice? Consider this story:

Some years ago a small boy fell into the Western Lowland gorilla pit at the Brookfield Zoo in Chicago. The female gorilla Binti Jua, herself a new mother, picked up the unconscious child and shielded him from the other gorillas. Then she carried him over to the doorway, where she was used to zoo personnel going in and out, and a rescue crew came and got the boy.

The story received nationwide attention. Why did Binti Jua show such seemingly "human" concern for the child? Many people were astonished to hear that a gorilla could show signs of compassion, let alone for someone not of her own species. A curator explained that she had been trained to bring her own baby to curators, and she was accustomed to being in close proximity with humans. So some concluded that Binti Jua did not act out of any rational or compassionate decision but simply on the basis of her training. Perhaps she was used to getting a reward for bringing her own baby and expected a reward for bringing the child. Other animal behaviorists who work with great apes didn't find Binti's action very remarkable: Gorillas and chimpanzees have a great capacity for compassion, they said, and will shield and defend an infant ape against aggressive adult apes. But Binti showed not just a compassion that went beyond her own species but also good common sense in carrying the boy over to the place where humans would be most likely to come and get him. So is it possible for a great ape to act unselfishly? Binti may certainly have been expecting a reward, but she also exhibited a gentle concern for the boy himself, so in one gesture this gorilla demonstrated transspecies compassion and foresight that seem to go beyond instinct and training.

Science and philosophy have generally assumed that nonhuman animals live in a nonmoral universe of innocence, where what seems cruel to humans is just the natural response of self-preservation: They are beyond the categories of good and evil. But now comes thought-provoking new research, gathering results from years of observing monkeys, apes, dolphins, whales, elephants, and wolves. Contrary to what people have told one another for so long about nonmoral animals, it turns out that some form of moral code seems to prevail in all these groups of social animals, and "moral code" here doesn't just mean that each animal has an instinct for behaving within the group, because often an individual (usually a young animal) will misbehave and then be punished by the group (with beating or ostracism, but usually not death). After the punishment, there is usually a kiss-and-make-up phase. According to Frans de Waal of Emory University's Yerkes Primate Center, chimps share food with one another and are indignant when an individual who seldom shares his or her own food expects a share of someone else's. At the primate center, two young female apes came home late one day and held up dinner for all the other apes in the research group; the scientists kept them separate overnight for their safety, but the next day they were beaten up by the rest of the colony. That night they were the first to come home. So the origin of moral rules may have to be sought much farther back in time than the Pleistocene, when Singer's hunters decided whether to run or to fight the saber-toothed cat.

This also means that the psychological egoist's theory that we are "born" selfish needs to be rewritten because it is too vague a statement in light of new research. It is not impossible that each child (and each chimpanzee) is born completely selfish, exclusively focusing on what Freud calls the "pleasure principle," the pursuit of feeling good, and that we begin to modify our selfish behavior only when we realize we can't get away with it constantly (which was Hobbes's theory, and Glaucon's before him). But the child is not the same as the adult, and some thinkers claim that what I've outlined here is the *genetic fallacy:* confusing the origin of something with what it has become at a later stage. We don't ordinarily claim that children are moral agents, because psychologists tell us that children really don't know the difference between right and wrong before they are about seven or eight years old. So why should the amoral demeanor of a small child be held up as the natural morality of an adult? We don't claim that the talent of a gifted ballplayer, a star chef, a good parent, or a great teacher can be reduced to their skills and knowledge when they were four years old. Children experience *socialization,* and since humans are social beings by nature, the effects on the individual of living in society are part of what we are as human beings. With the right training, we develop intellectually and technically as we grow older; therefore, it should be apparent that we also develop morally. We may start out in life as selfish, but with socialization, most people end up being capable of taking other people's interests into account—not merely because it is the prudent thing to do, but also because they develop an interest in other people's well-being. And that may be the secret behind the immense evolutionary success of human beings.

In his book *Good Natured: The Origins of Right and Wrong in Humans and Other Animals* (1996), Frans de Waal speculates that although humans are the only animals that can take delight in cruel treatment of others, both humans and great apes have the capacity for selfless caring for others. Echoing the thoughts of David Hume as well as Peter Singer and Charles Darwin himself, he writes:

> Human sympathy is not unlimited. It is offered most readily to one's own family and clan, less readily to other members of the community, and most reluctantly, if at all, to outsiders. The same is true of the succorant behavior of animals. The two share not only a cognitive and emotional basis, but similar constraints in their expression.
>
> Despite its fragility and selectivity, the capacity to care for others is the bedrock of our moral system. It is the only capacity that does not snugly fit the hedonic cage in which philosophers, psychologists, and biologists have tried to lock the human spirit. One of the principal functions of morality seems to be to protect and nurture this caring capacity, to guide its growth and expand its reach, so that it can effectively balance other human tendencies that need little encouragement.

In the Primary Readings you'll find an excerpt from Frans de Waal's book *Primates and Philosophers: How Morality Evolved* (2006), in which he argues that Hume was right, after all: Moral intuition, not reason, is at the core of human ethics, even in the minds of small children, and it had to come from somewhere: the world of primates and their rich emotional life.

Study Questions

1. What "other human tendencies" is Frans de Waal talking about? Do you agree with him that humans and some apes share the capacity for caring? Why or why not?

2. What are the most powerful arguments in favor of psychological egoism? What are the most damaging arguments against it?

3. Discuss the concept of ethical egoism in its most rational form: We ought to treat others the way we want to be treated to ensure our own safety and prosperity. What can be said for this approach? What can be said against it?

4. Discuss the theory of the selfish gene: Do you find it to be a sufficient explanation for altruistic behavior among humans and animals? Why or why not? Do you think Midgley's counterargument is persuasive? Explain.

Primary Readings and Narratives

The Primary Readings are a discussion about selfishness and justice from Plato's *Republic,* an excerpt from Erik Katz, "The Rings of Tolkien and Plato: Lessons in Power, Choice, and Morality," an excerpt from Thomas Hobbes's *Leviathan,* an excerpt from Ayn Rand's philosophical essay "The Ethics of Emergencies," and an excerpt from Frans de Waal's *Primates and Philosophers.* The first Narrative is a summary and excerpt from an episode of the TV show *Friends* about whether an unselfish act is possible. The second Narrative is a summary of the film *Return to Paradise,* whose plot is a variation on the prisoner's dilemma. The third Narrative is an excerpt from *Atlas Shrugged,* about the rights of creative people to maintain their high standards and look out for themselves. The fourth Narrative, J. R. R. Tolkien's *The Lord of the Rings*, completes the chapter—here you'll find a summary of the main characters, with a focus on the themes of selfishness and sacrifice.

Primary Reading

The Republic

PLATO

Book II. Excerpts.

You have already read a section of Plato's most famous Dialogue, *The Republic,* in Chapter 2. Here Socrates and Glaucon discuss the issue of justice and selfishness, illustrated by Glaucon's story of the Ring of Gyges. Glaucon is playing the devil's advocate, provoking Socrates into defending the concept of justice. Socrates is talking about the conversation to friends, so the narrator (the "I") is supposed to be Socrates himself (as written by

Plato). After Glaucon's lengthy argument in favor of selfishness we get Socrates' response. The rest of *The Republic* is in a sense dedicated to proving Glaucon wrong.

Good, said Glaucon. Listen then, and I will begin with my first point: the nature and origin of justice.

What people say is that to do wrong is, in itself, a desirable thing; on the other hand, it is not at all desirable to suffer wrong, and the harm to the sufferer outweighs the advantage to the doer. Consequently, when men have had a taste of both, those who have not the power to seize the advantage and escape the harm decide that they would be better off if they made a compact neither to do wrong nor to suffer it. Hence they begin to make laws and covenants with one another; and whatever the law prescribed they called lawful and right. That is what right or justice is and how it came into existence; it stands half-way between the best thing of all—to do wrong with impunity—and the worst, which is to suffer wrong without the power to retaliate. So justice is accepted as a compromise, and valued, not as good in itself, but for lack of power to do wrong; no man worthy of the name, who had that power, would ever enter into such a compact with anyone; he would be mad if he did. That, Socrates, is the nature of justice according to this account, and such the circumstances in which it arose.

The next point is that men practise it against the grain, for lack of power to do wrong. How true that is, we shall best see if we imagine two men, one just, the other unjust, given full license to do whatever they like, and then follow them to observe where each will be led by his desires. We shall catch the just man taking the same road as the unjust; he will be moved by self-interest, the end which it is natural to every creature to pursue as good, until forcibly turned aside by law and custom to respect the principle of equality.

Now, the easiest way to give them that complete liberty of action would be to imagine them possessed of the talisman found by Gyges, the ancestor of the famous Lydian Croesus. The story tells how he was a shepherd in the King's service. One day there was a great storm, and the ground where his flock was feeding was rent by an earthquake. Astonished at the sight, he went down into the chasm and saw, among other wonders of which the story tells, a brazen horse, hollow, with windows in its sides. Peering in, he saw a dead body, which seemed to be of more than human size. It was naked save for a gold ring, which he took from the finger and made his way out. When the shepherds met, as they did every month, to send an account to the King of the state of his flocks, Gyges came wearing the ring. As he was sitting with the others, he happened to turn the bezel of the ring inside his hand. At once he became invisible, and his companions, to his surprise, began to speak of him as if he had left them. Then, as he was fingering the ring, he turned the bezel outwards and became visible again. With that, he set about testing the ring to see if it really had this power, and always with the same result: according as he turned the bezel inside or out he vanished and reappeared. After this discovery he contrived to be one of the messengers sent to the court. There he seduced the Queen, and with her help murdered the King and seized the throne.

Now suppose there were two such magic rings, and one were given to the just man, the other to the unjust. No one, it is commonly believed, would have such iron strength of mind as to stand fast in doing right or keep his hands off other men's goods, when he could go to the market-place and fearlessly help himself to anything he wanted, enter houses and sleep with any woman he chose, set prisoners free and kill men at his pleasure, and in a word go about among men with the powers of a god. He would behave no better than the other; both would take the same course. Surely this would be strong proof that men do right only under compulsion; no individual thinks of it as good for him personally, since he does wrong whenever he finds he has the power. Every man believes that wrong-doing pays him personally much better, and, according to this theory, that is the truth. Granted full license to do as he liked, people would think him a miserable fool if they found him refusing to wrong his neighbours or to touch their belongings, though in public they would keep up a pretence of praising his conduct, for fear of being wronged themselves. So much for that.

Finally, if we are really to judge between the two lives, the only way is to contrast the extremes of justice and injustice. We can best do that by imagining our two men to be perfect types, and crediting both to the full with the qualities they need for their respective ways of life. To begin with the unjust man: he must be like any consummate master of a craft, a physician or a captain, who, knowing just what his art can do, never tries to do more, and can always retrieve a false step. The unjust man, if he is to reach perfection, must be equally discreet in his criminal attempts, and he must not be found out, or we shall think him a bungler; for the highest pitch of injustice is to seem just when you are not. So we must endow our man with the full complement of injustice; we must allow him to have secured a spotless reputation for virtue while committing the blackest crimes; he must be able to retrieve any mistake, to defend himself with convincing eloquence if his misdeeds are denounced, and, when force is required, to bear down all opposition by his courage and strength and by his command of friends and money.

Now set beside this paragon the just man in his simplicity and nobleness, one who, in Aeschylus' words, "would be, not seem, the best." There must, indeed, be no such seeming; for if his character were apparent, his reputation would bring him honours and rewards, and then we should not know whether it was for their sake that he was just or for justice's sake alone. He must be stripped of everything but justice, and denied every advantage the other enjoyed. Doing no wrong, he must have the worst reputation for wrong-doing, to test whether his virtue is proof against all that comes of having a bad name; and under this lifelong imputation of wickedness, let him hold on his course of justice unwavering to the point of death. And so, when the two men have carried their justice and injustice to the last extreme, we may judge which is the happier.

My dear Glaucon, I exclaimed, how vigorously you scour these two characters clean for inspection, as if you were burnishing a couple of statues!

I am doing my best, he answered. Well, given two such characters, it is not hard, I fancy, to describe the sort of life that each of them may expect; and if the description sounds rather coarse, take it as coming from those who cry up the merits of injustice rather than from me. They will tell you that our just man will be thrown into prison, scourged and racked, will have his eyes burnt out, and, after every kind of torment, be impaled. That will teach him how much better it is to seem virtuous than to be so. [. . .]

With his reputation for virtue, [the unjust man] will hold offices of state, ally himself by marriage to any family he may choose, become a partner in any business, and, having no scruples about being dishonest, turn all these advantages to profit. If he is involved in a lawsuit, public or private, he will get the better of his opponents, grow rich on the proceeds, and be able to help his friends and harm his enemies. Finally, he can make sacrifices to the gods and dedicate offerings with due magnificence, and, being in a much better position than the just man to serve the gods as well as his chosen friends, he may reasonably hope to stand higher in the favour of heaven. So much better, they say, Socrates, is the life prepared for the unjust by gods and men.

Here Glaucon ended, and I was meditating a reply, when his brother Adeimantus exclaimed:

Surely, Socrates, you cannot suppose that that is all there is to be said.

Why, isn't it? said I.

This reply of Socrates displays his famous sense of irony. There is much more to be said, and for the rest of the evening, Socrates discusses why the just man is a happier person than the unjust man. He does that by way of imagining an ideal state, governed by justice rather than injustice.

Glaucon and the others begged me to step into the breach and carry through our inquiry into the real nature of justice and injustice, and the truth about their respective advantages. So I told them what I thought. This is a very obscure question, I said, and we shall need keen sight to see our way. Now, as we are not remarkably clever, I will make a suggestion as to how we should proceed. Imagine a rather short-sighted person told to read an inscription in small letters from some way off. He would think it a godsend if someone pointed out that the same inscription was written up elsewhere on a bigger scale, so that he could first read the larger characters and then make out whether the smaller ones were the same.

No doubt, said Adeimantus; but what analogy do you see in that to our inquiry?

I will tell you. We think of justice as a quality that may exist in a whole community as well as in an individual, and the community is the bigger of the two. Possibly, then, we may find justice there in larger proportions, easier to make out. So I suggest that we should begin by inquiring what justice means in a state. Then we can go on to look for its counterpart on a smaller scale in the individual.

That seems a good plan, he agreed.

After having reached the conclusion (to which we will return in Chapter 8) that the just state is similar to the just person, and that a just person's soul consists of three parts— *reason, willpower,* and *desire*—which must all be in balance and governed by reason, Socrates explains to Glaucon and the others the imbalance of the unjust man compared with the well-being of the just man.

Next, I suppose, we have to consider injustice.

Evidently.

This must surely be a sort of civil strife among the three elements, whereby they usurp and encroach upon one another's functions and some one part of the soul rises up in rebellion against the whole, claiming a supremacy to which it has no right because its nature fits it only to be the servant of the ruling principle. Such turmoil and aberration we shall, I think, identify with injustice, intemperance, cowardice, ignorance, and in a word with all wickedness.

Exactly.

And now that we know the nature of justice and injustice, we can be equally clear about what is meant by acting justly and again by unjust action and wrongdoing.

How do you mean?

Plainly, they are exactly analogous to those wholesome and unwholesome activities which respectively produce a healthy or unhealthy condition in the body; in the same way just and unjust conduct produce a just or unjust character. Justice is produced in the soul, like health in the body, by establishing the elements concerned in their natural relations of control and subordination, whereas injustice is like disease and means that this natural order is inverted.

Quite so.

It appears, then, that virtue is as it were the health and comeliness and well-being of the soul, as wickedness is disease, deformity, and weakness.

True.

And also that virtue and wickedness are brought about by one's way of life, honourable or disgraceful.

That follows.

So now it only remains to consider which is the more profitable course: to do right and live honourably and be just, whether or not anyone knows what manner of man you are, or to do wrong and be unjust, provided that you can escape the chastisement which might make you a better man.

But really, Socrates, it seems to me ridiculous to ask that question now that the nature of justice and injustice has been brought to light. People think that all the luxury and wealth and power in the world cannot make life worth living when the bodily constitution is going to rack and ruin; and are we to believe that, when the very principle whereby we live is deranged and corrupted, life will be worth living so long as a man can do as he will, and wills to do anything rather than to free himself from vice and wrongdoing and to win justice and virtue?

Yes, I replied, it is a ridiculous question.

Study Questions

1. How does Glaucon use the story of Gyges to express a theory of human nature?

2. Is Glaucon right? Why or why not?

3. Plato has Glaucon speculate about the terrible fate of the truly good man. How might Plato's readers interpret that? (Remember that this dialogue was written years after Socrates' death at the hands of the Athenian court.)

4. Has Socrates now proved to you that it is better to be a "just" person than an "unjust" person? Explain.

Primary Reading

The Rings of Tolkien and Plato: Lessons in Power, Choice, and Morality

ERIK KATZ

Essay, 2003. Excerpts.

The Lord of the Rings and Philosophy is one in a series of books about films and television series and their philosophical content. The editors, Gregory Bassham and Eric Bronson, have collected sixteen essays exploring themes such as "The Ring," "The Quest for Happiness," and "Good and Evil in Middle-Earth." I have chosen some excerpts from the essay comparing the "Ring of Power" motif in Tolkien and Plato, relying on assurances from my students that the general plot of *The Lord of the Rings* is sufficiently familiar to the general movie-renting audience to eliminate the need for a summary of the story. Should you need a refresher, you'll find an overview of the most important characters in the Narratives section.

The Temptation of the One Ring

With this ancient challenge to the moral life as background, we can see how Tolkien's characters demonstrate various responses to the question posed by Plato: would a just person be corrupted by the possibility of almost unlimited power? Through these different responses, Tolkien shows us—not by philosophical argument, but by the thoughts and actions of "living" characters—why we should be moral beings, why we should live a virtuous life. But Tolkien's stories about the One Ring actually improve and augment Plato's argument, for Tolkien's Ring explicitly corrupts the souls of its possessors. The use of the One Ring corrupts the desires, interests, and beliefs of those who wield it. Plato *argues* that such corruption will occur, but Tolkien *shows* us this corruption through the thoughts and actions of his characters. Moreover, Tolkien also shows us the difficulties involved in living a life of virtue; there are burdens to be undertaken and sacrifices that must be made to fulfill the requirements of morality.

The character that most obviously illustrates Plato's argument that the unjust life leads to nothing but unhappiness is Gollum, who is invariably described as a miserable creature, afraid of everything, friendless, homeless, constantly seeking his "precious" Ring. Gollum is the mortal being who possessed the Ring for the longest period of time and he seems almost completely corrupted by the desire for it—every action he takes in the book, even guiding Frodo and Sam on their journey into Mordor, is designed to regain the Ring. It is during the long journey through the barren lands surrounding Mordor that we see the true disintegration of Gollum's personality, all caused by the desire of the Ring. Gollum constantly talks to himself, for his soul is split in two: one part is Smeagol, the hobbit he was before the Ring came into his possession, and one half is Gollum, the creature whose only desire is to possess the Ring again. The only reason that Gollom cooperates with Frodo and Sam is that the two halves (what Sam calls "Slinker and Stinker") have made a truce: "neither wanted the Enemy to get the Ring." Frodo recognizes the immense power that the thought of the Ring has on Gollum's mind. Earlier, he made Gollum swear on the Ring that he would be a faithful guide, but soon after, near the Black Gate of Mordor, Gollum was in "great distress" at the thought that Frodo would lose the Ring:

> "Don't take the Precious to Him! . . . Keep it, nice master, and be kind to Sméagol. Don't let Him have it. Or go away, go to nice places, and give it back to little Sméagol. . . . Sméagol will keep it safe; he will do lots of good, especially to nice hobbit."

This outburst by Gollum prompts Frodo to get to the heart of the matter, to describe to Gollum the peril he faces, the danger of losing his soul. Gollum swore a promise by what he calls the Precious. The Ring will not only hold Gollum to this promise, but will seek a way to twist it to Gollum's own undoing. "Already you are being twisted," Frodo tells Gollum. And then, with a strange prescience of the climax of the story, Frodo states that if the need arises, he would himself put on the Ring and command Gollum to cast himself into the fire.

Gollum is thus a clear example of the corruption of the soul and the loss of a meaningful life caused by the overwhelming desire for the Ring of Power. But Gollum is not a complete example of the problem posed by Plato, for we do not see the moment when he makes the choice to use the Ring. For Plato, as well as for Tolkien, the crucial moment in each character's story is the moment in which they are tempted to use the Ring. It is that moment of choice that determines a character's fate, that moment of choice that bears a remarkable similarity to Plato's story of the shepherd Gyges and his decision to use the ring of invisibility. Gollum's moment of choice occurred long before the opening pages of *The Lord of the Rings*—even long before the beginning of *The Hobbit*. Although Gandalf recounts the story—how Sméagol kills his friend Déagol to gain possession of the Ring—we do not live through Sméagol's original moral crisis and decision. In Gollum instead we see merely the final result of the life led in the pursuit of power, a life of misery and corruption.

Boromir is the character who most closely fits the model of Glaucon's moral argument concerning the shepherd Gyges—the virtuous man corrupted by the temptation of power. Tolkien depicts Boromir as a man of action—noble, good-hearted, and brave—who is bewildered by the complexities of the plan to destroy the One Ring. During the council of Elrond, Boromir asks why those assembled should not think that the Ring "has come into our hands to serve us in the very hour of need. . . . Wielding it the Free Lords of the Free may surely defeat the Enemy. . . . Let the Ring be your weapon . . . Take it and go forth to victory!" Boromir wants to use the One Ring for good purposes. He sees nothing wrong with using the Ring to satisfy the desires of the free peoples of Middle-earth (and of himself) to defeat the evil of Sauron.

Boromir's idea to use the Ring is rejected by Elrond—and the rest of the members of the Council—in terms that evoke Plato's argument in the *Republic:* "We cannot use the Ruling Ring. . . . It . . . is altogether evil. . . . The very desire of it corrupts the heart." Using the power of evil ultimately destroys the soul ("corrupts the heart").

Boromir seems to be persuaded, and throughout the journey south with the Fellowship he does not talk about wielding the Ring for the forces of good. But in the climax to *The Fellowship of the Ring,* Boromir is overcome by the temptation to use the Ring in the war against Mordor. He secretly follows Frodo into the woods near Amon Hen in order to convince him to bring the Ring to Gondor. Yet Boromir's words betray him, as he begins to envision himself as a great warrior in command of the Ring and of all the forces against Mordor. First, he argues that the Ring will save his people, but it soon becomes clear to Frodo that there are some selfish motives at work. "It is not yours save by unhappy chance," Boromir says. "It might have been mine. It should be mine. Give it to me!" Boromir attempts to take the Ring by force, but Frodo slips the Ring onto his finger, turns invisible, and escapes.

Boromir redeems his heroic nature by defending Merry and Pippin against the attacking orcs, and as he dies he confesses to Aragorn that he attempted to take the Ring from Frodo. The corruption caused by the Ring is thus not permanent, but perhaps only because Boromir ultimately had so little contact with the Ring. Nevertheless, Boromir is a perfect example of the immoralist's challenge that Glaucon proposes in Plato's dialogue: Boromir is the just man who finds a Ring of Power and is unable to resist the temptation to act with impunity, as if he were a god. The desire for the power of the Ring so corrupts his soul that he accuses Frodo of being an evil ally of the Dark Lord. The ethical lesson is clear: A Ring of Power corrupts even the person who is brave, strong, and virtuous. . . .

Galadriel refuses the One Ring. She remains true to her principles, to her integrity as an individual, to herself—she will "remain Galadriel." Through her, Tolkien shows us that a strong and virtuous person can refuse the temptation of immense power, even at a great personal cost; for Galadriel knows that by refusing to accept the power of the Ring she will be helpless to maintain the elvish presence in Middle-earth. Galadriel thus represents one answer to the immoralist's challenge of Plato. She refuses to let the possibility of power corrupt her soul.

Boromir and Galadriel demonstrate two different responses to the problem posed by Plato concerning the relationship between power, personal choice, and morality. With these two characters, unlike Gollum, we see the actual moment of choice. But although the responses of Boromir and Galadriel are different, one aspect of the choices is the same: neither ever physically possesses the Ring. What of the characters that do choose to use the Ring? Do their actions help us understand the relationship between power, corruption, and morality? Here we must turn to Tom Bombadil, Frodo, and Sam. . . .

Deep down in his heart, Sam knows who he is. As Galadriel knew to remain Galadriel and to reject the Ring, Sam knows that he can never be other than the plain common-sense hobbit, Samwise Gamgee, the small and caring gardener of the Shire. Fortified by his love for Frodo, he remains true to himself and rejects the power of the Ring. In Sam's rejection of the One Ring during his most extreme crisis we learn that the virtuous and strong-willed person can turn away from a life of evil, a life of almost unlimited power, by focusing on his or her true self.

It is clear that Tolkien is demonstrating to us the progressive forces of corruption of the possession and use of the One Ring, for even Frodo, the hero of the book, succumbs to its corruption in his failure to destroy the Ring. He begins with innocent and accidental uses of the Ring's power, but eventually gives over to its seductive power by making conscious and deliberate decisions to wear the Ring, and even, at last, not to destroy it. And as in Plato's argument, the key feature of corruption caused by the Ring is the corruption of the soul, the "heart," or the personality of the wielder of the Ring. To resist the Ring is to remain oneself, to be the person you are without any extraordinary powers. All who come in contact with the Ring (except, it appears, Bombadil) lose themselves (at least momentarily) in the desire to be greater than they are.

Study Questions

1. What are the similarities between the "Ring of Gyges" story and *Lord of the Rings,* according to this excerpt? If you are familiar with *Lord of the Rings,* would you agree? Why or why not? (The Narratives section has an overview of the main characters of the trilogy.)

2. Would you say that Frodo's quest to destroy the ring is an example of selfishness, selflessness, or a combination? Are there characters who are more selfish than Frodo, or less? Explain.

3. Who, according to Katz, is the closest parallel to Gyges in *The Lord of the Rings?* Do you agree? Why or why not?

4. Why is Sam's character so important, according to Katz?

 *Primary Reading*

Leviathan

THOMAS HOBBES

Excerpt, 1651.

Whereas Glaucon's arguments were the result of playing the devil's advocate, Thomas Hobbes came to the same conclusion in all seriousness some two thousand years later: Humans are selfish by nature, and society is our best way to protect ourselves from one another. Justice is a concept that is to be found in a society only once the rules have been laid down. Before the creation of society, in the "state of nature," where people live in a perpetual state of war against one another, life is "nasty, brutish, and short," and no rules apply except that of self-preservation. To improve our personal condition and for no other reason, we choose to live by the rules of society. Justice is indeed to Thomas Hobbes an invention based on self-preservation, nothing more.

> Hereby it is manifest, that during the time men live without a common Power to keep them all in awe, they are in that condition which is called Warre; and such a warre, as is of every man against every man. For WARRE, consisteth not in Battell onely, or the act of fighting; but in a tract of time, wherein the Will to contend by Battell is sufficiently known: and therefore the notion of *Time,* is to be considered in the nature of Warre; as it is in the nature of Weather. For as the nature of Foule weather, lyeth not in a showre or two of rain; but in an inclination thereto of many dayes together; So the nature of War, consisteth not in actuall fighting; but in the known disposition thereto, during all the time there is no assurance to the contrary. All other time is PEACE.
>
> Whatsoever therefore is consequent to a time of Warre, where every man is Enemy to every man; the same is consequent to the time, wherein men live without other security, than what their own strength, and their own invention shall furnish them withall. In such condition, there is no place for Industry; because the fruit thereof is uncertain: and consequently no Culture of the Earth; no Navigation, nor use of the commodities that may be imported by Sea; no commodious Building; no Instruments of moving, and removing such things as require much force; no Knowledge of the face of the Earth; no account of Time; no Arts; no Letters; no Society; and which is worst of all, continuall feare, and danger of violent death; And the life of man, solitary, poore, nasty, brutish, and short. . . .
>
> To this warre of every man against every man, this also is consequent; that nothing can be Unjust. The notions of Right and Wrong, Justice and Injustice have there no place. Where there is no common Power, there is no Law: where no Law, no Injustice. Force,

and Fraud, are in warre the two Cardinall vertues. Justice, and Injustice are none of the Faculties neither of the Body, nor Mind. If they were, they might be in a man that were alone in the world, as well as his Senses, and Passions. They are Qualities, that relate to men in Society, not in Solitude. . . .

The Passions that encline men to Peace, are Feare of Death; Desire of such things as are necessary to commodious living; and a Hope by their Industry to obtain them. And Reason suggesteth convenient Articles of Peace, upon which men may be drawn to agreement.

Study Questions

1. What does Hobbes mean by saying that when humans live in a state of war of everybody against everybody, there is neither justice nor injustice? What event creates justice and injustice?

2. Compare Glaucon's and Hobbes's ideas of justice.

3. Hobbes believes we are all selfish by nature; however, since right and wrong for Hobbes don't exist before the creation of society, is selfishness in itself a bad thing? Why or why not?

Primary Reading

The Ethics of Emergencies

AYN RAND

The Virtue of Selfishness: A New Concept of Egoism, 1964. Excerpt.

Ayn Rand (1905–1982), an American writer and philosopher, emigrated to the United States from the Soviet Union at age twenty-one because of a deep disenchantment with the Communist ideology. Her viewpoints were controversial from the beginning of her career, and her theory of objectivism still generates debate. Today some members of the Libertarian Party claim intellectual kinship with Rand.

Many philosophers have been reluctant to recognize her as a fellow thinker and have preferred to label her a novelist. The reasons for that snub may be multiple, but the fact is that Rand had several counts against her. For one thing, she didn't have a degree in philosophy; for another, American philosophers have until very recently been reluctant to think of philosophy and novels (and other stories) in the same sentence, as you'll remember from Chapters 1 and 2. So if Rand wrote novels, it would, for many philosophers, disqualify her as a fellow thinker. Third, she was a woman at a time when almost all philosophers were men, and it may simply have been a case of the problem of induction, a gender bias that most philosophers in the mid–twentieth century just weren't aware of having. She wasn't recognized as a thinker simply because of her gender. And the final factor? She was a political conservative in an intellectual environment of mostly

Ayn Rand (1905–1982), the Russian-born American philosopher and writer, developed the theory of *objectivism,* which stresses the right of the individual to keep the fruits of his or her labors and not be held responsible for the welfare of others. She is today best known for her novels, although her philosophy is also gaining recognition as an original twentieth-century contribution.

liberal—and even hard left—thinkers. At a time when many American and European intellectuals flirted with Marxism, she was a ruthless critic of socialist theories, and that made her ideas unattractive to many philosophers. But among the reading public she became enormously popular, and her ideas still retain some of their popularity. There is even talk of an Ayn Rand revival in the early twenty-first century.

The psychological results of altruism may be observed in the fact that a great many people approach the subject of ethics by asking such questions as: "Should one risk one's life to help a man who is: a) drowning, b) trapped in a fire, c) stepping in front of a speeding truck, d) hanging by his fingernails over an abyss?"

Consider the implications of that approach. If a man accepts the ethics of altruism, he suffers the following consequences (in proportion to the degree of his acceptance):

1.   Lack of self-esteem—since his first concern in the realm of values is not how to live his life, but how to sacrifice it.

2.   Lack of respect for others—since he regards mankind as a herd of doomed beggars crying for someone's help.

3.   A nightmare view of existence—since he believes that men are trapped in a "malevolent universe" where disasters are the constant and primary concern of their lives.

4.   And, in fact, a lethargic indifference to ethics, a hopelessly cynical amorality—since his questions involve situations which he is not likely ever to encounter, which bear no relation to the actual problems of his own life and thus leave him to live without any moral principles whatever.

By elevating the issue of helping others into the central and primary issue of ethics, altruism has destroyed the concept of any authentic benevolence or good will among men. It has indoctrinated men with the idea that to value another human being is an act of selflessness, thus implying that a man can have no personal interest in others—that *to value* another means *to sacrifice* oneself—that any love, respect or admiration a man may feel for others is not and cannot be a source of his own enjoyment, but is a threat to his existence, a sacrificial blank check signed over to his loved ones.

The men who accept that dichotomy but choose its other side, the ultimate products of altruism's dehumanizing influence, are those psychopaths who do not challenge altruism's basic premise, but proclaim their rebellion against self-sacrifice by announcing that they are totally indifferent to anything living and would not lift a finger to help a man or a dog left mangled by a hit-and-run driver (who is usually one of their own kind).

Most men do not accept or practice either side of altruism's viciously false dichotomy, but its result is a total intellectual chaos on the issue of proper human relationships and on such questions as the nature, purpose or extent of the help one may give to others. Today, a great many well-meaning, reasonable men do not know how to identify or conceptualize the moral principles that motivate their love, affection or good will, and can find no guidance in the field of ethics, which is dominated by the stale platitudes of altruism.

On the question of why man is not a sacrificial animal and why help to others is not his moral duty, I refer you to *Atlas Shrugged*. This present discussion is concerned with the principles by which one identifies and evaluates the instances involving a man's *nonsacrificial* help to others.

"Sacrifice" is the surrender of a greater value for the sake of a lesser one or of a non-value. Thus, altruism gauges a man's virtue by the degree to which he surrenders, renounces or betrays his values (since help to a stranger or an enemy is regarded as more virtuous, less "selfish," than help to those one loves). The rational principle of conduct is the exact opposite: always act in accordance with the hierarchy of your values, and never sacrifice a greater value to a lesser one.

This applies to all choices, including one's actions toward other men. It requires that one possess a defined hierarchy of *rational* values (values chosen and validated by a rational standard). Without such a hierarchy, neither rational conduct nor considered value judgments nor moral choices are possible.

Love and friendship are profoundly personal, selfish values: love is an expression and assertion of self-esteem, a response to one's own values in the person of another. One gains a profoundly personal selfish joy from the mere existence of the person one loves. It is one's own personal, selfish happiness that one seeks, earns and derives from love.

A "selfless," "disinterested" love is a contradiction in terms: it means that one is indifferent to that which one values.

Concern for the welfare of those one loves is a rational part of one's selfish interests. If a man who is passionately in love with his wife spends a fortune to cure her of a dangerous illness, it would be absurd to claim that he does it as a "sacrifice" for *her* sake, not his own, and that it makes no difference to *him,* personally and selfishly, whether she lives or dies.

Any action that a man undertakes for the benefit of those he loves is *not a sacrifice* if, in the hierarchy of his values, in the total context of the choices open to him, it achieves that which is of greatest *personal* (and rational) importance to *him.* In the above example, his wife's survival is of greater value to the husband than anything else that his money could buy, it is of greatest importance to his own happiness and, therefore, his action is not a sacrifice.

But suppose he let her die in order to spend his money on saving the lives of ten other women, none of whom meant anything to him—as the ethics of altruism would require. *That* would be a sacrifice. Here the difference between Objectivism and altruism can be seen most clearly: if sacrifice is the moral principle of action, then that husband *should* sacrifice his wife for the sake of ten other women. What distinguishes the wife from the ten others? Nothing but her value to the husband who has to make the choice—nothing but the fact that his happiness requires her survival.

The Objectivist ethics would tell him: your highest moral purpose is the achievement of your own happiness, your money is yours, use it to save your wife, *that* is your moral right and your rational, moral choice.

Consider the soul of the altruistic moralist who would be prepared to tell that husband the opposite. (And then ask yourself whether altruism is motivated by benevolence.)

The proper method of judging when or whether one should help another person is by reference to one's own rational self-interest and one's own hierarchy of values: the time, money or effort one gives or the risk one takes should be proportionate to the value of the person in relation to one's own happiness.

To illustrate this on the altruists' favorite example: the issue of saving a drowning person. If the person to be saved is a stranger, it is morally proper to save him only when the danger to one's own life is minimal; when the danger is great, it would be immoral to attempt it: only a lack of self-esteem could permit one to value one's life no higher than that of any random stranger. (And, conversely, if one is drowning, one cannot expect a stranger to risk his life for one's sake, remembering that one's life cannot be as valuable to him as his own.)

If the person to be saved is not a stranger, then the risk one should be willing to take is greater in proportion to the greatness of that person's value to oneself. If it is the man or woman one loves, then one can be willing to give one's own life to save him or her—for the selfish reason that life without the loved person could be unbearable.

Conversely, if a man is able to swim and to save his drowning wife, but becomes panicky, gives in to an unjustified, irrational fear and lets her drown, then spends his life in loneliness and misery—one would not call him "selfish"; one would condemn him morally for his treason to himself and to his own values, that is: his failure to fight for the preservation of a value crucial to his own happiness. Remember that values are that which one acts to gain and/or keep, and that one's own happiness has to be achieved by one's own effort. Since one's own happiness is the moral purpose of one's life, the man who fails to achieve it because of his own default—his failure to fight for it, is morally guilty.

Study Questions

1. Is Rand correct in saying that if you accept altruism, then you end up with a lack of self-esteem and a lack of respect for others?

2. Is Rand criticizing ideal or reciprocal altruism? Do you think that she would differentiate between the two? Would you?

3. Comment on the following quotation: "The proper method of judging when or whether one should help another person is by reference to one's own rational self-interest and one's own hierarchy of values: the time, money or effort one gives or the risk one takes

should be proportionate to the value of the person in relation to one's own happiness." What might the social and political outcome be if that approach were implemented?

4. A suggestion: Reread this excerpt after you have studied Chapter 5, on utilitarianism, and speculate: How would Rand evaluate the theory that asks us to maximize happiness for the maximum number of people?

5. Go back to Chapter 3 and reread, in the excerpt from Ruth Benedict's paper "Anthropology and the Abnormal," the section about "unbridled and arrogant egoists" as being typical of Western civilization. What might Rand's comment be about that remark?

Primary Reading

Primates and Philosophers: How Morality Evolved

FRANS DE WAAL

Excerpt, 2006.

In this excerpt from his book, Frans de Waal, primate researcher at Emory University's Yerkes Primate Center, argues that the Veneer Theory, the notion that humans are fundamentally selfish and that morals are merely a thin veneer of civilization over the inner beast, is fundamentally flawed. Moral values evolved, ironically, out of a system of organized warfare whereby we developed strong, caring attachments to our fellow human beings within the group. That sense of community is more fundamental than our rational capacities, and moral intuition, long thought to be a myth, is in fact the true foundation of human moral evolution.

Obviously, the most potent force to bring out a sense of community is enmity toward outsiders. It forces unity among elements that are normally at odds. This may not be visible at the zoo, but it is definitely a factor for chimpanzees in the wild, which show lethal intercommunity violence. In our own species, nothing is more obvious than that we band together against adversaries. In the course of human evolution, out-group hostility enhanced in-group solidarity to the point that morality emerged. Instead of merely ameliorating relations around us, as apes do, we have explicit teachings about the value of the community and the precedence it takes, or ought to take, over individual interests. Humans go much further in all of this than the apes, which is why we have moral systems and apes do not.

And so, the profound irony is that our noblest achievement—morality—has evolutionary ties to our basest behavior—warfare. The sense of community required by the former was provided by the latter. When we passed the tipping point between conflicting individual interests and shared interests, we ratcheted up the social pressure to make sure everyone contributed to the common good.

If we accept this view of an evolved morality, of morality as a logical outgrowth of cooperative tendencies, we are not going against our own nature by developing a caring, moral attitude, any more than civil society is an out-of-control garden subdued by a sweating gardener, as Huxley thought. Moral attitudes have been with us from the start, and the gardener rather is, as Dewey aptly put it, an organic grower. The successful gardener creates conditions and introduces plant species that may not be normal for this particular plot of land "but fall within the wont and use of nature as a whole." In other words, we are not hypocritically fooling everyone when we act morally: we are making decisions that flow from social instincts older than our species, even though we add to these the uniquely human complexity of a disinterested concern for others and for society as a whole.

Following Hume, who saw reason as the slave of the passions, Haidt has called for a thorough reevaluation of the role played by rationality in moral judgment, arguing that most human justification seems to occur *post hoc,* that is, after moral judgments have been reached on the basis of quick, automated intuitions. Whereas Veneer Theory, with its emphasis on human uniqueness, would predict that moral problem solving is assigned to evolutionarily recent additions to our brain, such as the prefrontal cortex, neuroimaging shows that moral judgment in fact involves a wide variety of brain areas, some extremely ancient. In short, neuroscience seems to be lending support to human morality as evolutionarily anchored in mammalian sociality.

We celebrate rationality, but when push comes to shove we assign it little weight. This is especially true in the moral domain. Imagine that an extraterrestrial consultant instructs us to kill people as soon as they come down with influenza. In doing so, we are told, we would kill far fewer people than would die if the epidemic were allowed to run its course. By nipping the flu in the bud, we would save lives. Logical as this may sound, I doubt that many of us would opt for this plan. This is because human morality is firmly anchored in the social emotions, with empathy at its core. Emotions are our compass. We have strong inhibitions against killing members of our own community, and our moral decisions reflect these feelings. For the same reasons, people object to moral solutions that involve hands-on harm to another. This may be because hands-on violence has been subject to natural selection, whereas utilitarian deliberations have not.

Additional support for an intuitionist approach to morality comes from child research. Developmental psychologists used to believe that the child learns its first moral distinctions through fear of punishment and a desire for praise. Similar to veneer theorists, they conceived morality as coming from the outside, imposed by adults upon a passive, naturally selfish child. Children were thought to adopt parental values to construct a superego: the moral agency of the self. Left to their own devices, children would never arrive at anything close to morality. We know now, however, that at an early age children understand the difference between moral principles ("do not steal") and cultural conventions ("no pajamas at school"). They apparently appreciate that the breaking of certain rules distresses and harms others, whereas the breaking of other rules merely violates expectations about what is appropriate. Their attitudes don't seem based purely on reward and punishment. Whereas many pediatric handbooks still depict young children as self-centered monsters, it has become clear that by one year of age they spontaneously comfort others in distress and that soon thereafter they begin to develop a moral perspective through interactions with other members of their species.

Instead of our doing "violence to the willow," as Mencius called it, to create the cups and bowls of an artificial morality, we rely on natural growth in which simple emotions, like those encountered in young children and social animals, develop into the more refined, other-including sentiments that we recognize as underlying morality. My own argument here obviously revolves around the continuity between human social instincts and those of our closest relatives, the monkeys and apes, but I feel that we are standing at the threshold of a much larger shift in theorizing that will end up positioning morality firmly within the emotional core of human nature. Humean thinking is making a major comeback.

Study Questions

1. What does de Waal mean when he says that human morality has evolved out of warfare with other human groups? Do you think he is right? Why or why not?

2. When does de Waal think humans begin to display moral tendencies of empathy? Explain.

3. De Waal argues that there is a continuity between simple primate morality and complex human morality. Do you agree? Why or why not?

Narrative

The One Where Phoebe Hates PBS

MICHAEL CURTIS (TELEPLAY)

SHELLEY JENSEN (DIRECTOR)

An episode of **Friends**, *1998–9. Summary.*

Can a television sitcom discuss moral problems in an even remotely significant way? I'll let you be the judge of that. If you've ever sat around the kitchen table after a party with friends discussing whether everyone is selfish, then you can relate to the main story line in this episode. Just a brief introduction to the characters: *Joey* is an aspiring actor who has a rather blatant tendency to think of himself first, and others second. *Phoebe* is a kind-hearted and spiritual (some would say scatterbrained) poet/singer/masseuse who has her own private view of the world. She is the surrogate mother of triplets, given over to her half-brother and his wife, who can't conceive. One morning while some of the friends (Phoebe, Chandler, Ross, and Monica) are having breakfast, Joey comes in, wearing a tuxedo. He has got a gig (he thinks) hosting a telethon for PBS, and he brags that he's doing a good deed for PBS while he himself is getting TV exposure. But Phoebe is appalled: for one thing, she thoroughly dislikes PBS because she had a bad experience with the network some years back. Her mother had just killed herself, and Phoebe was feeling sad, so she wrote to *Sesame Street* because she remembered them fondly from when she was a little kid. But nobody replied—they just sent her a key chain. And at the time she was homeless, living in a box, so she didn't even have any keys! Besides, she says, the only reason why Joey wants the gig is so he can get on TV, not because he wants to do something unselfish.

That gets the ball rolling: Now Joey accuses Phoebe of being selfish, herself, for having triplets for her brother—because it made her *feel good,* and, says Joey, that makes it selfish; we recognize the attitude of a convinced psychological egoist: everyone is selfish, and,

The television sitcom *Friends* (1994–2004) may not seem like an obvious choice for a textbook about ethics, but real life is full of moral problems, and so are many of the *Friends* episodes, such as "The One Where Phoebe Hates PBS," in which Phoebe (Lisa Kudrow, far left) and Joey (Matt LeBlanc, on her right) have a debate about selfishness. The other friends are, from left to right, Courtney Cox, David Schwimmer, Jennifer Aniston, and Matthew Perry.

in Joey's words, "there's no unselfish good deeds." Phoebe might just as well forget that, because that's like believing in Santa Claus. (Later on she casually asks him what he meant, and when she hears him say that Santa doesn't exist, we see the shock on her face.)

So Phoebe sets out to prove Joey wrong because, as she explains to Monica and her other friend Rachel, she just won't let her babies be raised in a world where Joey is right. Her first attempt involves sneaking over to an elderly neighbor and raking the leaves from his doorstep. But he discovers her and treats her to cider and cookies, which makes her feel great. So, since her good deed made her feel good, it doesn't qualify as a selfless deed, according to Joey's definition.

Meanwhile, to his immense disappointment, Joey finds out that he isn't hosting the telethon after all; talk-show host Gary Collins is; Joey is just going to answer phones, and it looks like he dressed in a tux for nothing. But one of the calls he receives is from Phoebe, who proudly announces that she has found a selfless, good deed: She went to Central Park and let a bee sting her, so it could look macho in front of its friends! And since she's hurting, it's not a selfish deed. But Joey shoots that down instantly: Since the bee probably died from stinging her, the bee didn't benefit (so it wasn't a good deed!).

Joey himself is doing a fine job of demonstrating what his true goal is: TV exposure, rather than helping PBS, thus proving Phoebe's point that he himself is just looking out for number one. He realizes that the place where he is answering calls isn't even within range of the television camera, so he tries to swap places with another volunteer, who is utterly unwilling to comply, to the point where they slug it out between the tables, in the background, while Gary Collins is talking about contributing to PBS's fine programming. So Joey's own quest to gain an advantage for himself isn't doing too great. But now Phoebe makes one last attempt to prove that unselfishness exists.

She makes one more call to Joey, pledging $200 to PBS. She explains that even if she is still mad at them, she also knows that lots of children love their shows, so she is doing a good deed by supporting them, while it doesn't make her feel good at all: $200 is a lot of money, and she had plans for that sum: She was saving up to buy a hamster. Joey can't believe what he's hearing: A $200 hamster? When they normally cost $10? Phoebe implies that it was a very special hamster (and we get the feeling that she was probably being taken for a ride, as often happens). So it looks like she has proved to Joey that selfless, good deeds do indeed exist! But here comes the twist: Because of Phoebe's pledge, the station has now surpassed the sum collected by pledges last year, and Gary Collins steps over to the volunteer who took the pledge—Joey! Who now gets his TV exposure: He is introduced by name standing there in his tux, with a big smile on his face. Phoebe is watching it on TV and is overjoyed that her pledge got Joey on TV—until she realizes what has happened! Her good deed, which was supposed to make her feel bad, now has made her feel good—which again proves Joey's point that all deeds are selfish! So she loses again.

Has Joey now been vindicated? Has Phoebe's failure in proving that she can do a "selfless, good deed" convinced us that psychological egoism is true? If things we do make us feel good afterward, do they automatically fall into a "selfish" category, even if we didn't plan on feeling good, and the pleasure is an unintended aftereffect? Keep in mind the debate about whether Lincoln's act of saving the pigs was selfish or not. A truly selfish person would not feel good about having sacrificed something for others; as you've read, it could be a way to tell unselfish people from the selfish ones that they actually feel good after helping others.

Study Questions

1. Some would say that Phoebe's project was doomed from the start, because of the nature of her goal. What might that mean, and do you agree?

2. Discuss Phoebe's attempts at disproving Joey, relating them to the arguments against psychological egoism in the chapter text: the principle of falsification, the Lincoln story, and the fallacy of the suppressed correlative.

3. Is Joey selfish? Is Phoebe? Is everybody? Are you? Explain.

Narrative

Return to Paradise

WESLEY STRICK AND BRUCE ROBINSON (SCREENWRITERS)
JOSEPH RUBEN (DIRECTOR)

Film, 1998. Summary.

Peter Singer's story of the two hunters and the saber-toothed cat cited earlier in this chapter is a version of the so-called prisoner's dilemma: You and your friend are both political prisoners of a totalitarian regime, isolated from each other, and you are each told that the length of your sentence will depend on whether or not you confess: If you confess and your friend doesn't, you will get one year in prison and your friend will get ten years; if your friend confesses and you don't, he or she will get one year and you'll get ten. If neither of you confesses, you will each get two years. If both of you confess, you'll each get five years. So if your only goal is to limit your own sentence, logic demands that you confess, because you'll be ahead whether or not your friend also confesses. Since your friend is thinking along the same lines, chances are you'll both confess and both get five years. But if you're capable of thinking about each other's interests and can be certain that you can trust each other, then it's a win–win situation for both of you: If you both don't confess, you'll both get out after only two years. So the lesson of the prisoner's dilemma is that it can be of greater personal advantage to be less selfish than more selfish—just as in the hunter story. But it depends completely on whether we can trust each other—whether we dare take the chance that our friend will also put selfishness aside.

A film that explores the prisoner's dilemma with a chilling twist is *Return to Paradise,* based on the 1989 French movie *Force Majeure* by Pierre Jolivet. Here we have a prisoner who hopes that his two friends, enjoying their freedom, will submit to punishment for his sake, thus averting his own death sentence. The two friends must confront the conflict between their instinct for self-preservation and their sense of duty to help a friend. The film is thus a prisoner's dilemma story combined with an exploration of the nature of selfishness and altruism.

Sheriff, Tony, and Lewis are three young Americans having a good time in Malaysia, smoking dope, hanging out with the local young women, and enjoying the exotic scenery. On the way back from a trip to the market, they wreck a borrowed bicycle, and Sheriff heaves it over a precipice. A short time afterward, Sheriff and Tony go home to New York City, while Lewis stays on to help endangered orangutans. Before leaving, Sheriff and Tony give their stash of hashish to Lewis.

Two years later Sheriff is working as a limo driver in New York; Tony is working in construction and thinking about getting married. They haven't seen each other since leaving Panang. One night Sheriff has a fare, a young woman named Beth, who reveals that she is a lawyer for Lewis—he's been in the Panang jail ever since they left, for having in his possession more than the legal limit of 100 grams of hash. The excess amount was the stash given to him by his two friends. The man whose bicycle they wrecked came looking for it with the police, and they found the dope. Ten months ago Lewis received his sentence: death. All appeals have been exhausted, but only last week he mentioned his friends and the hashish story. So now the Malaysian authorities have the following suggestion: If Sheriff and Tony return to take their share of the responsibility, everybody gets three years in prison. If only one of them returns, he gets six years, and so does Lewis; if no one comes back to Panang, Lewis will be hanged—in eight days. Beth tells the same story to Tony, who is at once willing to consider going back but won't do it if Sheriff doesn't, because he is willing to lose only three years of his life, not six. Sheriff, on the other hand, sees no reason why he should even consider going—he doesn't think they can trust the deal, and it seems he just doesn't have the morals Beth assumes he has.

In the film *Return to Paradise* (Polygram, 1998), two friends are faced with a moral problem: Should they voluntarily return to Malaysia to save another friend from a death sentence and share the blame for his illegal drug possession, even if it would entail prison time for both of them? Here attorney Beth Eastern (Anne Heche) is trying to persuade Sheriff (Vince Vaughn) to return with her.

Beth is approached by a persistent journalist, who insists that she has a right to publish Lewis's story and that she can help him by drawing the world's attention to his case. Beth is terrified: In another case the Malaysian government reneged on a deal because of international publicity, and the prisoner was executed. She can't take such a chance but promises the reporter an exclusive if she will wait a few days.

Beth shows Sheriff a tape made by a physically and mentally worn-down Lewis, begging him and Tony to come and save his life. As the reality of Lewis's impending execution dawns on Sheriff, he has a talk with his father, who is no help: He suggests that Sheriff go because Lewis is probably worth more as a person than Sheriff is. We realize he was being sarcastic. Why agonize over it, he says, when Sheriff isn't even considering going? So Sheriff tells Beth he won't go: "It isn't in me." Compelled by Sheriff's selfish attitude, Tony now promises to go, but Beth isn't certain of his commitment.

Sheriff and Beth have been developing an attraction for each other, and in a desperate mood they make love. The next morning he is still with her, now committed to helping her and his friend Lewis. Two days before Lewis's scheduled execution, all three of them are on the plane to Panang. The two friends have decided to give Lewis three years of their lives to save his.

Once in Panang, they go to see Lewis, but only one visitor is allowed. Sheriff finds Lewis hunched over, shivering, rocking back and forth, praying. Sheriff tries to comfort him and lift his spirits, and it seems to be working: As Sheriff is leaving, Lewis says to him, "I knew you'd come back—even if *you* didn't." Back with Tony and Beth, Sheriff expresses his concerns about Lewis's state of mind, and Beth lets slip that he's always been that way. How would she know, as his lawyer? It turns out she's not just his lawyer—she's his big sister.

With that revelation, the deal is off. Tony and Sheriff feel they can't trust her— she'd promise them anything just to get Lewis out. Fearing for their own lives, they take off for the airport. Tony boards the plane for New York—but Sheriff hesitates: He has realized it was his recklessness in throwing the bike away that put Lewis in this situation, so he must take responsibility for it. Tony leaves for New York, but Sheriff goes back to Panang, in time to walk into the courtroom where Lewis's sentence is about to be confirmed. The judge exclaims that his faith in humanity is half restored. Sheriff says they were young and stupid, but not evil; he is responsible and is willing to do what it takes to save his friend's life. The judge goes to his chambers to reassess the situation; he is expected to come out and pronounce a reprieve for Lewis and a six-year sentence for Sheriff.

But a commotion erupts as the media arrive at the courthouse. Apparently an American newspaper has published the persistent journalist's story, making the Malaysian system of justice look medieval and cruel. The judge emerges, livid: He won't have the Western media dictating the decisions of his court. The West might not understand his country's harsh drug sentences, he says, but Malaysian kids are safe from drugs, unlike kids in the West.

Will the judge stand by his word and give Lewis a lesser sentence because Sheriff came back? Or has the publication of the article endangered Lewis's life, as Beth predicted it would? The ending of this film is haunting and thought-provoking, and I would like for you to experience it yourself. Also, I'd like you to consider the following: If Lewis dies, has Sheriff's willingness to help him been for nothing?

Study Questions

1. Early in the film, Sheriff asks Beth whether *she* would go to prison for Lewis, if the question were put to her. Would *you* give three years of your life to save a friend? Would you give six? Explain.

2. Explore the changes in the characters of Tony and Sheriff. Which change is the greatest, and why?

3. What would a psychological egoist say to this story? What would an ethical egoist say?

4. Compare this story with the original prisoner's-dilemma scenario. What are the similarities, and what are the differences?

5. Is anyone being altruistic in this film? Does a person have to have no self-interest involved in order to be unselfish?

6. Go back to Chapter 2, reread the excerpt from Aristotle, and apply his theory of the perfect tragic plot to this film. Who is the ordinary man who makes a fatal error in judgment? Is Aristotle right that such plot lines are timeless?

Narrative

Atlas Shrugged

AYN RAND

Novel, 1957. Summary and Excerpt.

In Greek mythology, Atlas is the god who holds up the earth on his shoulders—and when Atlas shrugs, the world shakes. Ayn Rand's book is about the shake-up of the world by those who form its economic foundation: the factory owners, the entrepreneurs, the railroad builders. It is not the workers but those who employ them who are the movers and the shakers of the world, and in Rand's opinion they have been abused by unions and "bleeding hearts" long enough. In this book she outlines her philosophy of objectivism "between the lines" of the novel, urging those people with creative powers to start thinking about themselves and taking pride in what they do, for without them the world literally will come to a halt. In *Atlas Shrugged,* the movers and shakers go on strike, led by the mythic figure of John Galt and joined by the railroad tycoon Dagny Taggart. Before she died, Rand worked on a screenplay based on her book, and it appears that *Atlas Shrugged* may finally be coming to the silver screen as a major Hollywood production. Rand sees the world as being divided between those who can think and create and those who are parasites on the creators; each person has a right to what he or she creates (and earns), and no one else has any right to any of it. The only duty we have is to look out for ourselves and not give our lives away to others who aren't willing to work for their own share. The following excerpt is from a conversation between Francisco d'Anconia, a copper tycoon and millionaire, and Henry Rearden, a steelworks owner and inventor who is beginning to understand that he has been letting people take advantage of him all his life:

> "If you want to see an abstract principle, such as moral action, in material form—there it is. Look at it, Mr. Rearden. Every girder of it, every pipe, wire and valve was put there by a choice in answer to the question: right or wrong? You had to choose right and you had to choose the best within your knowledge—the best for your purpose, which was to make steel—and then move on and extend the knowledge, and do better, and still better, with your purpose as your standard of value. You had to act on your own judgment, you had to have the capacity to judge, the courage to stand on the verdict of your mind, and the purest, the most ruthless consecration to the rule of doing right, of doing the best, the utmost best possible to you. Nothing could have made you act against your judgment, and you would have rejected as wrong—as evil—any man who attempted to tell you that the best way to heat a furnace was to fill it with ice. Millions of men, an entire nation, were not able to deter you from producing Rearden Metal—because you had the knowledge of its superlative value and the power which such knowledge gives. But what I wonder about, Mr. Rearden, is why you live by one code of principles when you deal with nature and by another when you deal with men?"
>
> Rearden's eyes were fixed on him so intently that the question came slowly, as if the effort to pronounce it were a distraction: "What do you mean?"
>
> "Why don't you hold to the purpose of your life as clearly and rigidly as you hold to the purpose of your mills?"

"You have judged every brick within this place by its value to the goal of making steel. Have you been as strict about the goal which your work and your steel are serving? What do you wish to achieve by giving your life to the making of steel? By what standard of value do you judge your days? For instance, why did you spend ten years of exacting effort to produce Rearden Metal?"

Rearden looked away, the slight, slumping movement of his shoulders like a sigh of release and disappointment. "If you have to ask that, then you wouldn't understand."

"If I told you that I understand it, but you don't—would you throw me out of here?"

"I should have thrown you out of here anyway—so go ahead, tell me what you mean."

"Are you proud of the rail of the John Galt Line?"

"Yes."

"Why?"

"Because it's the best rail ever made."

"Why did you make it?"

"In order to make money."

"There were many easier ways to make money. Why did you choose the hardest?"

"You said it in your speech at Taggart's wedding: in order to exchange my best effort for the best effort of others."

"If that was your purpose, have you achieved it?"

A beat of time vanished in a heavy drop of silence. "No," said Rearden.

"Have you made any money?"

"No."

"When you strain your energy to its utmost in order to produce the best, do you expect to be rewarded for it or punished?" Rearden did not answer. "By every standard of decency, of honor, of justice known to you—are you convinced that you should have been rewarded for it?"

"Yes," said Rearden, his voice low.

"Then if you were punished, instead—what sort of code have you accepted?"

Rearden did not answer.

"It is generally assumed," said Francisco, "that living in a human society makes one's life much easier and safer than if one were left alone to struggle against nature on a desert island. Now wherever there is a man who needs or uses metal in any way—Rearden Metal has made his life easier for him. Has it made yours easier for you?"

"No," said Rearden, his voice low.

"Has it left your life as it was before you produced the Metal?"

"No—" said Rearden, the word breaking off as if he had cut short the thought that followed.

Francisco's voice lashed at him suddenly, as a command: "Say it!"

"It has made it harder," said Rearden tonelessly.

"When you felt proud of the rail of the John Galt Line," said Francisco, the measured rhythm of his voice giving a ruthless clarity to his words, "what sort of men did you think of? Did you want to see that Line used by your equals—by giants of productive energy, such as Ellis Wyatt, whom it would help to reach higher and still higher achievements of their own?"

"Yes," said Rearden eagerly.

"Did you want to see it used by men who could not equal the power of your mind, but who would equal your moral integrity—men such as Eddie Willers—who could never invent your Metal, but who would do their best, work as hard as you did, live by their own effort, and—riding on your rail—give a moment's silent thanks to the man who gave them more than they could give him?"

"Yes," said Rearden gently.

"Did you want to see it used by whining rotters who never rouse themselves to any effort, who do not possess the ability of a filing clerk, but demand the income of a company president, who drift from failure to failure and expect you to pay their bills, who hold their wishing to an equivalent of your work and their need as a higher claim to reward than your effort, who demand that you serve them, who demand that it be the aim of your life to serve them, who demand that your strength be the voiceless, rightless, unpaid, unrewarded slave of their impotence, who proclaim that you are born to serfdom by reason of your genius, while they are born to rule by the grace of incompetence, that yours is only to give, but theirs only to take, that yours is to produce, but theirs to consume, that you are not to be paid, neither in matter nor in spirit, neither by wealth nor by recognition nor by respect nor by gratitude—so that they would ride on your rail and sneer at you and curse you, since they owe you nothing, not even the effort of taking off their hats which you paid for? Would this be what you wanted? Would you feel proud of it?"

"I'd blast that rail first," said Rearden, his lips white.

Study Questions

1. What is it that d'Anconia accuses Rearden of?

2. Can you identify d'Anconia's political standpoint and the standpoint he argues against?

3. Why is this considered an example of ethical egoism? How does this excerpt relate to Rand's analysis of happiness as a moral purpose?

Narrative

The Lord of the Rings

J. R. R. TOLKIEN

Trilogy of novels, 1939–55. Films: 1958, 2001–3 (Trilogy). Overview of key characters.

In this particular case I'll take a chance and assume that most readers know the basics of the story—because that is all we need to include it as an example of selfishness versus altruism. As you have seen in the Primary Reading "The Rings of Tolkien and Plato: Lessons in Power, Choice, and Morality," the theme of the Ring lends itself well to a comparison between Plato's story of the Ring of Gyges and Frodo's quest to save Middle Earth from Sauron's evil reign: In each story we have a ring of invisibility that yields great power, and each story speculates that most, if not all, ordinary people (humans, hobbits, or otherwise) will be tempted to use the power for their own benefit. This section is thus merely an overview of the key names and events in the trilogy, to jog your memory or to inspire you to read the books and watch the films. The films provide stunning visuals, but without the books you won't experience the entire richness of the story, the language element—and Tom Bombadil!

The Ring: Forged by Sauron thousands of years earlier, as a tool of power and control. Inscribed on the Ring in the ancient language:

One Ring to rule them all, One Ring to find them,
One Ring to bring them all and in the darkness bind them.

The Fellowship of the Ring

Frodo Baggins: A young hobbit, Bilbo Baggins's nephew. After Bilbo's departure from the Shire, it falls to Frodo to try to keep the Ring out of the hands of Sauron's forces, because if Sauron regains the Ring, it will mean the end of the world for humans and hobbits. Frodo is a person without guile, and yet he is tempted to use the powers of the Ring. Through great personal sacrifice, Frodo and his helper Sam succeed in their mission, but not without Frodo giving in to the power of the Ring at the final moment.

Samwise Gamgee (Sam): Frodo's friend and helper, perhaps the most selfless person in the trilogy. He has access to the Ring on several occasions, but all he is concerned with is helping Frodo and returning to his life in the Shire.

Boromir: A prince of the ruling House of Steward, he has sworn to protect Frodo and the Ring, but in the end he succumbs to the temptation of the Ring and tries to take it away from Frodo.

Gandalf: A wizard and a maiar—not a human being. He has great but not unlimited powers and has fought Sauron for several thousand years. He helps Frodo whenever he can, even at the peril of his own life.

Aragorn, also known as Strider: A descendant of the ancient House of Isildur, he is the heir-at-law to the throne of Gondor, but travels incognito. His ancestor cut off Sauron's finger with the Ring attached to it, which limited Sauron's power, but the ring disappeared.

Gimli: A dwarf from a long line of dwarves with an illustrious mining tradition deep inside the mountains. The dwarves have a deep mistrust of the elves, but even so, Gimli and the elf Legolas become great friends.

Legolas: An immortal elf and a great archer. He chooses to help the humans and the hobbits, even while his people are leaving Middle-Earth, sailing west.

Merry and Pippin: Friends of Frodo. In the beginning they are mainly playful, irreverent youngsters, but they grow up to be courageous and inventive partners in the Fellowship.

Some Other Essential Characters

Gollum: The hobbit Smeagol found the Ring on his birthday and killed his friend Deagol over it. He kept it and was slowly affected by its evil powers to the extent that he doesn't even look like a hobbit any more, but is now a creature whose instinct is focused exclusively on regaining the Ring. He does, however, appear more like a victim of the Ring's power than part of its evil force.

Sauron: The ultimate evil character, he was a shape-shifting sorcerer, but lost his bodily characteristics and is now disembodied. He forged the Ring of Power and has experimented with creating hybrid species who will do his bidding. His all-seeing eye can tell when Frodo wears the Ring.

Galadriel: The Queen of elves, who is offered the Ring by Frodo, because he feels he can no longer trust himself with it. She has a moment of weakness when she imagines herself all-powerful, but relinquishes the power and shuns its evil influence.

Bilbo Baggins: A hobbit who found the Ring in Gollum's cave in the book *The Hobbit*. Bilbo leaves the Shire early in the Trilogy and leaves the Ring with Frodo. Later, Frodo meets up with Bilbo again, and we see how the mere proximity to the Ring transforms Bilbo into a creature of greed and evil—we see how Gollum must have been transformed.

Tom Bombadil: A mysterious man of the woods who saves Frodo, Sam, Merry, and Pippin on several occasions. Not featured in the films. Tom even tries on the Ring, without any effect—he has his own ancient powers. Since Bombadil is not human, some readers have speculated that he may be Tolkien's version of the "Green Man," the ancient European wood spirit.

Study Questions

1. Who is being selfless, and who is selfish in this story?

2. Who is good, and who is evil? Is this the same question as the first questions, or is it different? Explain.

3. Is Gollum an evil character? Why or why not?

4. If you were to compare Plato's shepherd Gyges with any of the characters, which one would it be? What are the similarities, and what are the differences?

Chapter Five

Using Your Reason,
Part 1: Utilitarianism

*J*n the previous chapter, you read that we may have self-serving tendencies, but that in all likelihood we also have the capacity for fellow-feeling, some limited form of altruism. That means that we can, and perhaps should, look after ourselves and others at the same time, as reciprocal altruism says. This is, in effect, incorporated into one of the most influential moral theories of all time, utilitarianism. However, in utilitarianism it is not only a matter of what we are capable of emotionally but also a matter of what we ought to do rationally. When deciding on a moral course of action, some of us find it is the potential consequences of our choice that determine what we decide to do. Others of us see those consequences as being of minor importance when we view them in light of the question of right and wrong. A student of mine, when asked to come up with a moral problem we could discuss in class, proposed this question to ponder: Imagine that your grandmother is dying; she is very religious, and she asks you to promise her that you will marry within the family faith. Your beloved is of another faith. Do you tell her the truth, or do you make a false promise? This profound (and, I suspect, real-life) question makes us all wonder: If I think it is right to lie to Grandma, why is that? To make her last moments peaceful; what she doesn't know won't hurt her; why should I upset her by telling her the truth? Is that a good enough reason? And if I think lying to Grandma is wrong and refuse to do it, how do I justify making her last moments miserable? You will see that those of us who think lying to her is the only right choice because then she will die happy generally subscribe to the theory of *consequentialism,* in particular the theory of *utilitarianism,* the most widespread and popular form of consequentialism. If you think that lying is always wrong, even if it would make Grandma feel better, then hang in there until Chapter 6, where we discuss Kant's moral theory.

In the preceding chapter you encountered the philosopher Peter Singer, who claimed that we as humans are capable of caring for others as well as ourselves. Singer identifies himself as a utilitarian, as do numerous others today—philosophers as well as laypeople. (You'll find a text by Singer in the Primary Readings section.) Utilitarians see as their moral guideline a rule that encourages them to make life bearable for as many people as possible. Perhaps we can actively do something to make people's lives better, or perhaps the only thing we can do to make their lives better is to stay out of their way. Perhaps we can't strive to make people happy, but we can at least do our best to limit their misery. That way of thinking just seems the decent approach for many of us, and when we include ourselves among those who should receive a general increase of happiness and decrease of misery, then the rule seems attractive, simple, and reasonable. Small wonder this attitude has become the cornerstone of one of the most vital and influential moral theories in human history.

Utilitarians are hard universalists in the sense that they believe there is a single universal moral code, which is the only one possible, and everyone ought to realize it. It is the *principle of utility,* or the *greatest-happiness principle:* When choosing a course of action, always pick the one that will maximize happiness and minimize unhappiness for the greatest number of people. Whatever action conforms to this rule will be defined as a morally right action, and whatever action does not conform to it will be called a morally wrong action. In this way utilitarianism proposes a clear and simple moral criterion: Pleasure is good and pain is bad; therefore, whatever causes happiness and/or decreases pain is morally right, and whatever causes pain or unhappiness is morally wrong. In other words, utilitarianism is interested in the *consequences* of our actions: If they are good, the action is right; if bad, the action is wrong. This principle, utilitarians claim, will provide answers to all real-life dilemmas.

Are all theories that focus on the consequences of actions utilitarian? No. As we saw in Chapter 4, the consequences we look for may be happy consequences for ourselves alone, and in that case we show ourselves to be egoists. We may focus on the consequences of our actions because we believe that those consequences justify our actions (in other words, that the end justifies the means), but that does not necessarily imply that the consequences we hope for are good in the utilitarian sense that they maximize happiness for the maximum number of people. We might, for instance, agree with the Italian statesman Niccolò Machiavelli (1469–1527) that if the end is to maintain political power for oneself, one's king, or one's political party, that will justify any means one might use for that purpose, such as force, surveillance, or even deceit. Although this famous theory is indeed consequentialist, it does not qualify as utilitarian because it doesn't have the common good as its ultimate end.

Jeremy Bentham and the Hedonistic Calculus

It is often tempting to say that history moves in a certain direction. For example, eighteenth-century Europe and America saw a general movement toward greater recognition of human rights and social equality, of the value of the individual, of the scope of human capacities, and of the need for and the right to education. During that period, known as the *Enlightenment,* rulers and scholars shared a staunch belief that human reason, *rationality,* held the key to the future—to the blossoming of the sciences as well as to social change. That period is, appropriately, also referred to as the *Age of Reason,* not so much because people were particularly rational at the time as because reason was the social, scientific, and philosophical *ideal.*

Perhaps, then, it is tempting to say that civilization moved toward an appreciation of human rationality, but it would be more appropriate to say that it was moved along by the thoughts of certain thinkers. Such a mover was the English jurist and philosopher Jeremy Bentham. Box 5.1 provides you with a brief introduction to Bentham.

Box 5.1   JEREMY BENTHAM, THEN AND NOW ...

meetings. That request is not as odd as it might sound: Bentham, a prominent person, hoped that by donating his body to science he would make a statement in support of the medical profession's need for cadavers for research. Most people at the time felt, however, that having one's deceased body cut up was a sacrilege, and so only the bodies of executed criminals were available. As a result, a thriving clandestine business arose, a trade in newly dead bodies stolen from their graves. In one case, the infamous Burke and Hare case, the body snatchers didn't wait for corpses to be buried but murdered sixteen people in one year and sold them to anatomists. By deciding to donate his body, Bentham took a stand against what he saw as superstition and attempted to put a stop to the practice of body snatching. And he may have thought further, What better way to undo superstitions about dead bodies than for his own to be on display at board meetings? He specified in his will that he was to become an *Auto-Icon,* an image of himself, and he even picked out the glass eyes to be placed in his head after his demise and carried them around in his pocket, according to legend. He had intended for his head to remain on the shoulders of his Auto-Icon, but after his death, the preservation process of his head went wrong, and a wax head was substituted. In this photo you see both the wax head (a good likeness), and Bentham's real head between his feet. He still sits in his mahogany case at the University College of London and is wheeled in at annual board meetings. He is recorded as "present, but not voting."

Jeremy Bentham (1748–1832), the British philosopher and jurist, developed together with his friend James Mill the theory of utilitarianism based on the principle of utility: Maximize happiness and minimize unhappiness for as many as possible. Bentham donated his body to medical research and his money to University College of London, with the provision that after research on his body was complete, it was to be preserved and displayed at university board

Bentham, author of *Introduction to the Principles of Morals and Legislation* (1789), set out to create not a new moral theory so much as a hands-on principle that could be used to remodel the British legal system. Indeed, it was not Bentham but another philosopher, David Hume, who invented the term *utilitarianism*. Hume believed that it is good for an action to have *utility* in the sense that it makes yourself and others happy, but he never developed that idea into a complete moral theory. Bentham, however, used the term to create a moral system for a new age. So in Hume's version, what is useful is what is morally good. But we have an even earlier, famous reference to the goodness of utility: In Plato's *Republic* (see Chapters 2 and 4), Socrates says to Glaucon, "That is, and ever will be, the best of sayings, that the useful is the noble and the hurtful is the base." If a utilitarian is someone who believes that anything useful is good, and anything painful is bad, why isn't Socrates hailed as the first utilitarian? Because there is so much more to Socrates' value theory than a theory of the best outcome, as you'll see in Chapter 8. But also because what is "useful" for Socrates isn't necessarily what is pleasurable! Socrates placed great emphasis on the needs of the community, as you'll remember from Chapter 4, but not as much on the personal needs of the individual; that is a modern concept, and it is precisely during Bentham's era, the time of the Enlightenment, that the needs as well as the rights of the individual become a focal point for moral and political discussions.

In Bentham's England the feudal world had all but vanished. Society had stratified into an upper class, a middle class, and a working class, and the Industrial Revolution was just beginning. Conditions for the lowest class in the social hierarchy were appalling. Rights in the courts were, by and large, something that could be bought, which meant that those who had no means to buy them didn't have them. The world portrayed in the novels of Charles Dickens was developing; if you were in debt, you were taken to debtors' prison, where you stayed until your debt was paid. Whoever had funds could get out, but the poor faced spending the rest of their lives with their family inside debtors' prison. There were no child labor laws, and the exploitation of children in the workforce, which horrified Marx some decades later, was rampant in Bentham's day. Bentham saw it as terribly unfair and decided that the best way to redesign this system of unfair advantages would be to set up a simple moral rule that everyone could relate to, rich and poor alike.

Bentham said that what is good is what is pleasurable, and what is bad is what is painful. In other words, *hedonism* (pleasure seeking) is the basis for his moral theory, which is often called *hedonistic utilitarianism* (see Box 5.2). The ultimate value is happiness or pleasure—these things are *intrinsically* valuable. Anything that helps us achieve happiness or avoid pain is of *instrumental* value, and because we may do something pleasurable to achieve another pleasure, pleasure can have both intrinsic and instrumental value. (Box 5.3 explains this distinction in more detail.) For this basic rule to be useful in legislation, we need to let people decide for themselves wherein their pleasure lies and what they would rather avoid. Each person has a say in what pleasure and pain are, and each person's pleasure and pain count equally. We might illustrate this viewpoint by traveling back in our minds to nineteenth-century London. A well-to-do middle-class couple may feel that their greatest pleasure on a Saturday night is to don their fancy clothes, drive to Covent Garden in their shining

Box 5.2   HEDONISM AND THE HEDONISTIC PARADOX

Often the Greek thinker Epicurus (341–270 B.C.E.) is credited with being the first philosopher to advocate a life in search of pleasure, hedonism. That, however, isn't quite accurate, because what Epicurus seems to have been after was a life free of pain—for if you are free of pain you have obtained peace of mind, *ataraxia,* the highest pleasure. But others have advocated that seeking pleasure and avoiding pain are human nature, and what humans ought to embark on in life is to accumulate good times. Jeremy Bentham believed all humans are hedonists. Everyone wants pleasure, so we search for it. Searching and finding are two different things, however, and the paradox of hedonism often prevents us from finding what we are looking for. Suppose we set out to achieve pleasure on the weekend. We go to the beach, we take a walk in the woods, we hang out at the mall, we go to the movies, but we're just not enjoying ourselves very much; pleasure has somehow eluded us, and we face Monday with the sense of a lost weekend, telling ourselves that next weekend we'll look harder. Our friend, on the contrary, had a great time; he went with us because he likes going to the beach, loves the woods, wanted to look for a pair of jeans at the mall, and had been looking forward to seeing a movie for weeks. He even enjoyed our company. Why did he have a good weekend while we felt unfulfilled? Because we were trying to have a good time, and he was doing things he liked to do and enjoying being with someone

he liked. The pleasure he got was, so to speak, a by-product of doing those things—it wasn't the main object of his activity. We, on the other hand, looked for pleasure without thinking about what we like to do that might give us pleasure, as if "pleasure" were a thing separate from everything else. The hedonistic paradox is this: If you look for pleasure, chances are you won't find it. (People who have been looking hard for someone to love can attest to that.) Pleasure comes to you when you are in the middle of something else and rarely when you are looking for it. Sometimes the "Don Juan syndrome" is cited as an example of the hedonistic paradox. A person (traditionally a man, but there is no reason it can't apply to women) who has numerous sexual conquests very often feels compelled to move from partner to partner because he or she likes the pursuit but somehow tires of an established relationship. Why is that the case? It could be because such people are unwilling to commit themselves to a permanent relationship, but it also may be due to the paradox of hedonism: In each partner they see the promise of "pleasure," but somehow all they end up with is another conquest. If they had been setting their sights on building a relationship with their partners, they might have found out that pleasure comes from being with someone you care for, and you have to care in order to feel pleasure; you can't expect pleasure to appear if there is no genuine feeling—or so the theory says.

coach, and go to the opera. The girl at Covent Garden who tries to sell them a bouquet of wilting violets as they pass by would probably not enjoy a trip to the opera as much as she would enjoy the bottle of gin she saves up for all week. Bentham would say she has as much right to relish her gin as the couple has a right to enjoy the opera. The girl can't tell the couple that gin is better, and they have no right to force their appreciation of the opera on her. For Bentham, what is good and bad for each person is a matter for each person to decide, and as such, his principle becomes a very

Box 5.3 INTRINSIC VERSUS INSTRUMENTAL VALUES

An *instrumental* value is one that can be used as an instrument or a tool to get something else that we want. If you needed to get to class or work on time, a car might be the instrumental value that would get you there. If you didn't have a car, then money (or good credit) might be the instrumental value that would get you the car that would get you to school or to your workplace. How about going to school? If you're going to school to get a degree, then you might say that going to school is an instrumental value that will get your degree. And the degree? An instrumental value that will get you a good job. And the job? An instrumental value that will get what? More money. And what do you want with that? A better lifestyle, a better place to live, good health, and so on. And why do you want a better lifestyle? Why do you want to be healthy? This is where the chain comes to an end, because we have reached something that is obvious: We want those things because we want them. Perhaps they "make us happy," but the bottom line is that we value them for their own sake, *intrinsically.* Some values can of course be both instrumental and intrinsic; the car may help you get to school, but also, you've wanted the car for a long time just because you like it. Exercising may make you healthy, but you also may actually enjoy it. And going to school is certainly a tool that can be used to get a degree, but some people appreciate training and knowledge for their own sake, not just because those goods can be used to get them somewhere in life.

egalitarian one. At the end of the chapter you'll find an excerpt from Bentham's *Introduction to the Principles of Morals and Legislation,* in which he outlines the principle of utility.

The Hedonistic Calculus

How, exactly, do we choose a course of action? Before we decide what to do, we must calculate the probable consequences of our actions. This is what has become known as Bentham's *hedonistic calculus* (also called the *hedonic calculus*). We must, he says, investigate all aspects of each proposed consequence: (1) Its *intensity*—how intense will the pleasure or pain be? (2) Its *duration*—how long will it last? (3) Its *certainty or uncertainty*—how sure can we be that it will follow from our action? (4) Its *propinquity or remoteness*—how far away is it, in time and space? (5) Its *fecundity*—how big are the chances that it will be followed by a similar pleasure or a similar pain? (6) Its *purity*—how big are the chances that it will not be followed by the opposite sensation (pain after pleasure, for example)? (7) Its *extent*—how many people will be affected by our decision? After considering those questions, we must do the following:

> Sum up all the values of all the *pleasures* on the one side, and those of all the pains on the other. . . . Take the balance; which, on the side of *pleasure,* will give the general *good tendency* of the act, with respect to the total number or community of individuals concerned; if on the side of pain, the general *evil tendency,* with respect to the same community.

What do we have here? A simple, democratic principle that seems to make no unreasonable demands of personal sacrifice, given that one's own pleasure and pain count just as much as anybody else's. Furthermore, in line with the scientific dreams of the Age of Reason, the proper moral conduct is calculated mathematically; values are reduced to a calculation of pleasure and pain, a method accessible to everyone with a basic understanding of arithmetic. By calculating pleasures and pains, one can presumably get a truly rational solution to any moral as well as nonmoral (morally neutral) problem.

That sounds very good, and yet there are several problems with this approach. For one thing, from where does Bentham get his numerical values? Ascertaining that our pleasure from eating a second piece of mud pie will be intense but will not last long and very likely will be followed by pain and remorse will not supply us with any numerical values to add or subtract: We have to make up the numerical values! That may not be as difficult as it seems, though. It is surprising how much people can agree on a value system, if they can just decide what should count as top and bottom value. If they agreed on a system that goes from -10 to $+10$, for example, most people would agree to assigning specific numerical values to the various consequences of eating that second piece of pie. What value would be assigned to the aspect of intensity? Not a 10, because that probably would apply only to the first piece, but perhaps an 8. The *duration* of the pleasure might get a measly 2 or 3, and the chance that it would be followed by pleasure or pain certainly would be way down in the negative numbers, perhaps -5 or worse. As for evaluating how many people are affected by the decision, that could take into account friends and family who don't want you to gain weight or the person who owns the second piece of pie (which you stole), who will be deprived of it if you eat it. All such hypothetical situations can be ascribed a value if people can agree on a value system to use for all choices, from personal ones to far-reaching political decisions. (See Box 5.4 for a discussion of pleasure as an indicator of happiness.)

What this rating system adds up to is what most people would call the "pros and cons," those lists we sometimes make for ourselves when we are in severe doubt about what to do—what major field of study to choose, whether to go home for Thanksgiving or celebrate it with friends, whether to get married, whether to take a new job, and so on. The only difference is that in this system we assign numerical values to the pros and cons. Can such a list really help us make rational decisions? Bentham believed it was an infallible system for rational choice. A method that quantifies (makes measurable) the elusive qualities of life would certainly be useful, and several workplaces today are actually employing a form of hedonistic calculus in their hiring process: Applicants are rated according to their qualifications, and those qualifications are assigned numerical values (they are quantified); the person with the highest score presumably gets the job. Another area in which the calculus has had a rebirth is in the field of health care, where attempts are being made to create an objective measure for what is known as *quality of life* (see Chapter 7). One person's idea of quality of life may not be the same as another person's, however, and even in workplaces where such a hiring method is used, other, less rational, elements may play a part in the hiring process (such as the looks of the applicant or relation to the

Box 5.4   WHAT IS HAPPINESS?

One of the persistent problems in utilitarianism is the claim that the ultimate intrinsic value is happiness. We have already seen how the search for pleasure can lead to the hedonistic paradox (see Box 5.2), and this paradox is a problem for utilitarians as much as for anyone claiming that the ultimate reason we do things is to seek happiness. But is happiness the same as pleasure? Jeremy Bentham doesn't say, and indeed he doesn't care: For him, happiness is how *you* define it. John Stuart Mill defines happiness as distinct from both pleasure and contentment and views it as an intellectual achievement. Aristotle, who introduced the idea of happiness as a human goal to Western philosophy, also believed it was a result of rational activity and not a pursuit of pleasure. Few philosophers have

chosen Bentham's path and allowed for the possibility that happiness might have something to do with pleasure. An ancient story illustrates this tendency, not just within the Western tradition, to frown on the connection between happiness and physical comfort or indulgence: A Persian prince was told that to cure his unhappiness he had to wear the shirt of a happy man. The Persian prince now tried the shirts of lords, artists, merchants, soldiers, and fools, but it was to no avail. Happiness seemed to elude him. Finally he encountered a poor farmer singing behind his plow; the prince asked him if he was happy, and the farmer answered that he was. The prince then asked if he could have the farmer's shirt, and the farmer answered, "But I have no shirt!"

employer). People who have given Bentham's system a try in their own personal decision making often find that it may help in clarifying one's options, but the results are not always persuasive. You may end up with sixteen items on the con side and four on the pro side and still find yourself getting married or taking a new job simply because you want to so badly. There are parts of the human psyche that simply don't respond to rational arguments, and Bentham didn't have much appreciation for that. Interestingly enough, his godson and successor, John Stuart Mill, did have just such an appreciation, and we will look at his work shortly.

But suppose you actually make a detailed list of the consequences of your actions. How, exactly, do you decide on the values that you assign each consequence? In some cases it is easy, as for example when you compare school fees or driving distances. But if you want to decide whether to stay in school for the duration or quit and get a job and make fast money, how do you choose what things to put on your list? Critics of Bentham's approach say that if we assign a higher value to getting an education than to acquiring fast money, then it is because we are operating within a system that favors higher education; in other words, we are *biased,* and our choice of values reflects that bias. To put it another way, we rig the test even as we perform it. If we were operating within a system that favored making money—for instance, if we already had left school to make money—then our values would reflect that bias. The values, therefore, are truly arbitrary, depending on what we would like the outcome to be, and we can't trust the hedonistic calculus to give us an objective, mathematically certain picture of what to do. That does not mean such lists are useless; they can tell us much about ourselves and our own preferences and biases. However, they can

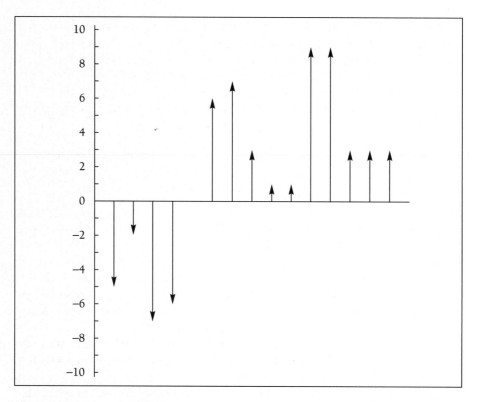

Sheer numbers: If we imagine the horizontal line representing a neutral position in terms of pain and pleasure, 0, the vertical line above 0 representing pleasure, and the line below 0 representing pain, we have a visual representation of the hedonistic calculus. Here all that matters is that the positive numbers outweigh the negative numbers. So if we have a scenario where many (humans or animals) are suffering but not much contentment is generated, the utilitarian would be against it. If only a few are suffering, and the many benefit from their suffering, it is the morally right course of action, according to utilitarianism.

do little more than that, because we can change the numbers until we get the result we want!

The Uncertain Future

Utilitarianism might still be able to offer a less presumptuous system, one designed to give guidance and material for reflection rather than objectively calculated solutions. Even with that kind of system, though, there are problems to be dealt with. One lies in the concept of *consequences* itself. Of course, we can't claim that an action has any consequences before we actually have taken that action. The consequences we are evaluating are hypothetical; they have yet to occur. How can we decide once and for all whether an action is morally good if the consequences are still up in the air? We have to (1) make an educated guess and hope for the best, (2) act, and (3) wait to see the results. If we're lucky and wise, the results will be as positive as what

we hoped for. But suppose they aren't. Before we learn the results, our good intentions are of course part of the plus side of the hedonistic calculus: If we intend to create beneficial consequences for as many as possible, it is a process that the utilitarian
will approve of. But the true value of our action is not clear until the consequences
are clear. You may intend to create much happiness, and your calculations may be
educated, but your intentions may still be foiled by forces beyond your control. In
that case, it is the *end result* that counts and not your fine intentions and calculations.
How long do we have to wait until we know whether our actions were morally good
or evil? It may take a long time before all the effects are known—maybe a hundred
years or more. Critics of utilitarianism say it is just not reasonable to use a moral system that doesn't allow us to know whether what we did was morally right or wrong
until some time in the far-off future. Furthermore, how will we ever be able to decide
anything in the first place? Thousands—perhaps millions—of big and small consequences result from everything we do. Do we have to calculate them all? How can we
ever make a quick decision if we have to go through such a complicated process
every time?

Answers to such criticisms were provided by the philosopher and economist
John Stuart Mill (1806–1873). For one thing, Mill says, we don't have to calculate
every little effect of our action; we can rely on the common experience of humanity.
Through the millennia, humans have had to make similar decisions all the time, and
we can consider their successes and failures in deciding our own actions. (Because
Mill had actually given up on calculating every action to an exact mathematical
value, it was easier for him than for Bentham to allow for some uncertainty in future
results.) What about having to wait a long time for future consequences to happen,
in order to pass judgment on the morality of our action? Mill says all we have to do
is wait a reasonable amount of time—a short wait for small actions, a longer wait for
bigger actions. Mill relies on us to know intuitively what he means, and perhaps we
do. But the problems inherent in utilitarianism are not solved with those suggestions,
merely diffused a little.

Advantages and Problems of Sheer Numbers: From Animal Welfare to the Question of Torture

Initially, the idea of creating as much pleasure as possible for as many as possible
seems a positive one. If we read on in Bentham's writings, we even find that "the
many" may not be limited to humans. Bentham's theory was so advanced for its time
that it not only gave the right to seek pleasure and avoid pain to all humans, regardless of social standing, but also said that the criterion for who belongs in the moral
universe is not who has the capability to speak or to reason but *who can suffer,* and
surely suffering is not limited to human beings. (See Box 5.5 for a discussion of suffering and nonhuman animals.) The contemporary philosopher Peter Singer (see
Chapter 4) has taken this aspect of utilitarianism to heart and has become one of
today's most vocal champions of animal rights and welfare, even to the point where
he believes that some animals deserve at least as much moral consideration as some
humans, and occasionally more, based on the evaluation of the capacity for joy and

Box 5.5 WHO CAN SUFFER?

Jeremy Bentham's insistence that the moral universe be open to any creature who can suffer is still a controversial statement, and in Bentham's own day it was extremely radical. Of his influential contemporaries, only John Stuart Mill took up the idea that humans are not necessarily the only members of the moral realm; it was (and still is) standard procedure to view morality as something only humans can engage in or benefit from. Most arguments that exclude animals are based on the assumption that they can't speak or reason (which is why Bentham says this is irrelevant and asks, "Can they suffer?"). To most people, then and now, it is obvious that animals can suffer—all we have to do is observe an injured animal. But to some thinkers, this is not a foregone conclusion. An argument that used to be popular in theology was that humans suffer because Adam and Eve sinned against God in the Garden of Eden, and suffering was their, and their children's, punishment; since animals have not sinned against God, they can't suffer. A more influential argument in philosophy comes from René Descartes (1596–1650), otherwise known for opening up the gates of modern philosophy with his statement "I think, therefore I am." Descartes argued that only humans have minds; everything else in the world consists of matter only, including animals. If you have a mind, you can have awareness of suffering; if you have no mind, your body may be subjected to physical stress, but you won't know it. The dog whose tail is caught in the door will yelp, but that is no sign of feeling pain, according to Descartes—that is the way the dog is constructed, like a clock with moving parts (in today's jargon, the dog is *programmed* to yelp). The dog itself has no mind and feels nothing. (Descartes actually was a dog owner; according to legend, his dog's name was Monsieur Grat.) When challenged by Margaret Cavendish, the Duchess of Newcastle, Descartes's answer was that if animals had minds, then oysters would have to have minds too, and he found that ridiculous. Margaret Cavendish was a writer with an interest in science. Like most contemporary readers, she knew that there is a considerable difference between the nervous systems of dogs and oysters, but Descartes's viewpoint has had immense influence on the treatment of animals to this day.

Modern biology generally assumes that mammals and many other animals can feel pain, precisely because there is such a similarity between their nervous systems and ours. In addition, the capacity for suffering seems to be an evolutionary advantage; a being that can feel pain is more likely to be cautious, to survive, and to propagate. At a conference in Chicago in 2000, animal researchers from a variety of fields concluded that there is no longer any reason to assume that animals can't feel, both physically *and* emotionally. All animals, from humans to reptiles, share a structure in the brain called the *amygdala,* which is responsible for the "fight-or-flight" reaction. It is the amygdala that is activated when our heart starts pumping, our palms get sweaty, and we feel fear or panic, and that reaction is an ancient, primitive, and very useful response to danger that we share with most other vertebrates on this planet. So we can all be afraid—but what is generally less known is that the same, ancient part of the brain, sometimes called the "reptile brain," can also know pleasure, even joy. Life in the wild has never been merely a terrified existence from one dangerous moment to another—it is also full of good times and exuberance! Suffering and joy are, as Bentham suspected, a part of life not only for humans but for most other animals as well. Where we humans differ from most other animals is that we are *aware* of our own feelings and of our own existence. You can read more about the issue of animals in Chapter 13.

suffering in a given animal as opposed to a given human being. His books such as *In Defense of Animals* (1985) and *Animal Liberation: A Practical Guide* (1987) have become controversial classics. In an article from the *New York Times* in January 2007 he says, "We are always ready to find dignity in human beings, including those whose mental age will never exceed that of an infant, but we don't attribute dignity to dogs or cats, though they clearly operate at a more advanced mental level than human infants. Just making that comparison provokes outrage in some quarters. But why should dignity always go together with species membership, no matter what the characteristics of the individual may be?" (You'll find the entire article, "A Convenient Truth," in the Primary Readings section.)

If we assume that the capacity to suffer (and feel pleasure) qualifies a living organism for inclusion in the moral universe, and if we believe that each individual's pleasure counts equally, we find ourselves with a dramatically expanded moral universe. Even today, the idea that all creatures who can suffer deserve to be treated with dignity does not meet with the approval of every policymaker. Moreover, if the decrease of suffering and the increase of happiness are all that counts for all these members of our moral universe, what does it mean for our decision if the happiness of some can be obtained only at the cost of the suffering of others? This is where we encounter the problem of *sheer numbers* in utilitarianism, because whatever creates more happiness for more individuals or decreases their pain is morally right *by definition*. If giving up animal-tested household products causes human housekeepers only minor inconvenience, then we have no excuse to keep using them, because major suffering is caused by such testing. Indeed, the focus on animal suffering has become much more prevalent among scientists within the last twenty years: Where countless rabbits would be used in the past in tests on cosmetics and household products, new methods are now being developed in which lab-grown human skin, "Episkin," can be used instead to determine whether the cosmetic ingredients will damage the skin; that is in response to the European Union directive that bans animal testing by 2013. However, if it could be shown that only a few animals would have to suffer (even if they would suffer horribly) so that an immense number of humans would find their housecleaning greatly eased, would it then be permissible to cause such suffering? Yes, if the pleasure gained from easy housecleaning in a large number of households could be added up and favorably compared with the immense suffering of only a very few nonhuman animals.

The argument for doing whatever benefits more living creatures, human or nonhuman, is usually advanced with regard to animal testing of medical procedures that could benefit humans. But because sheer numbers are all that matter in utilitarianism, the housecleaning example works too. Curing human ailments is not intrinsically "better" than helping humans clean their houses—what matters is the happiness that is created and the misery that is prevented. Suppose feline leukemia could be cured by subjecting ten humans to painful experiments. The humans would certainly suffer, but all cats would, from then on, be free of leukemia. For some, this type of example reveals the perversely narrow focus of utilitarianism; looking at pleasure and pain and adding them up are simply not enough. For others, examples like this one only confirm that all creatures matter, and no one's pain should be more or less important than anyone else's.

René Descartes (1596–1650), French philosopher, mathematician, and naturalist, known as the founder of modern philosophy; he is particularly famous for having said, "*Cogito, ergo sum,*" or, "I think, therefore I am." Descartes believed that a human consists of a body and a soul; thanks to the soul, humans can be self-aware and conscious of their bodies, including physical pleasures and pains. But since Descartes couldn't imagine that animals have souls, he had to conclude that animals couldn't be aware of their physical condition either, so the inevitable deductive conclusion was, for him, that animals can't feel pain.

To focus on the problem, let's assume that we are faced with a situation in which some humans are sacrificed for the happiness and welfare of other humans. Suppose it is revealed that governments around the world have for years had a secret pact with aliens from outer space whereby the governments have agreed to deny consistently that UFOs exist and to not interfere with occasional alien abductions of humans for medical experiments. In return, at the end of their experiments, the aliens will provide humanity with a cure for all viral diseases. For a great number of people, that would be a trade well worth the suffering of the "specimens" involved—provided that they themselves would not be among the specimens. Indeed, some humans might even *volunteer* for the experiments, but let us assume, as a condition, that the human subjects are reluctant participants, and no volunteers are accepted. Although some people would gladly commit their fellow humans to death from suffering, others would insist that it is not right; somehow, these humans do not deserve such a fate, and the immense advantages to humankind forever do not really make up for it. In other words, some may have a moral sense that the price is too high, but utilitarianism can't acknowledge such a moral intuition because its only moral criterion is one of sheer numbers. For many, the morality of utilitarianism is counterintuitive when applied to some very poignant human situations.

The UFO example is (or at least it is intended to be) fictional. But the late twentieth century revealed to us a number of real-life, large-scale cases in which a number of people had unwittingly been made into guinea pigs for the sake of some greater cause. What if we could accomplish beneficial results for a large number of people or living beings at the cost of intolerable pain suffered by a few? Whether one sees immediate benefits to a population, such as security measures, or long-term benefits, such as medical knowledge, the price of pain and suffering, even death, was paid by human beings, not by choice but by force, for the sake of some higher goal. The Tuskegee syphilis experiment is a chilling example, but it doesn't end there. Other morally questionable governmental practices have been revealed;

In *Runaway Jury,* Nick (John Cusack) and Marlee (Rachel Weisz) are having a serious talk, after Nick's apartment has been torched by the defense lawyer's goons: Is their venture to swing the jury for $10 million worth the risk? And are Nick and Marlee really just grifters, or are they crusaders for a cause?

see Box 4.6 for some examples. Such experiments have reduced people to being mere tools in someone else's agenda. A classic utilitarian will answer that, depending on the greatness and the nature of the goal, the sacrifice and suffering might well be worth the price. But John Stuart Mill added that, in the long run, a population abusing a minority will reap not good results but social unrest, so such practices should be discouraged. (See the subsequent section on act and rule utilitarianism.)

Still, the salvation of humanity is a forceful argument. Let us suppose, however, that we are talking not about salvation from disease but about salvation from boredom. Television is already moving toward showing live or videotaped events involving human suffering and death; home movies are often the source of that footage, and this form of "entertainment" has become increasingly popular. YouTube has a large selection of private videos of young men and women engaging in violent acts toward others. Might viewers choose to watch real-time shows of criminals who are granted one television hour to run through a city or a neighborhood, avoiding snipers and hoping to live through it all and win their freedom? The Romans watched Christians, slaves, criminals, prisoners of war, and wild animals fight each other, with much appreciation for the entertainment value of such events. If they had had the ability to televise the events, might we not assume that they would have done so, having recognized that "bread and circuses" (food and entertainment) would appease the unruly masses? According to the utilitarian calculation, a great number of people may be hugely entertained by the immense suffering of one or a few. How far are we allowed to let numbers run away with us in disregarding people's inherent right to fair treatment?

A common utilitarian reply is that under such circumstances, people start worrying about being victimized, and social unrest follows. Until that happens, though, utilitarians must conclude that there is justification in letting a large number of people enjoy the results of the suffering of a few (or even enjoy the suffering itself).

In the Narratives section you'll find several stories illustrating this problem of "sheer numbers": Wessel's satire "The Blacksmith and the Baker"; a selection from Dostoyevsky's *Brothers Karamazov*; Ursula K. Le Guin's story about a child being tortured for the sake of communal happiness, "The Ones Who Walk Away from Omelas"; and summaries of the films *Extreme Measures* and *Runaway Jury*. Once we start identifying the utilitarian sheer-numbers problem as one of disregard for the rights of the individual for the sake of the well-being of the many, we tend to be critical of any decision that would favor the happiness of the majority over the rights of a minority, and perhaps rightfully so. However, there are compelling scenarios that make us reevaluate the simple math of Bentham's utilitarianism: When push comes to shove, and hard decisions have to be made in a split second, saving the many by sacrificing the few may be the decision most of us would agree with. Think back to that dreadful day of September 11, when four airplanes were hijacked with the presumed intent to cause as much damage as possible to people and institutions. Three planes hit their targets: the World Trade Center towers and the Pentagon. But as you'll recall, the fourth plane, Flight 93, did not reach its intended target, in all likelihood the Capitol or the White House, because of the heroic resolve of the passengers. But in the aftermath we also learned that had the passengers not acted, Flight 93 would probably not have reached its target anyway, because U.S. Air Force fighter jets were already poised to escort the plane down or, if necessary, shoot it down. That came as a shock to many Americans, in particular when the government announced that *any* plane on a collision course with a civilian or military structure would be regarded as a threat and would be shot down. Here we see the principle of utility at work in a desperate situation: Sacrifice the few on the plane rather than take a chance and risk the lives of the many on the ground and the security of our institutions. Some might say, "But those people on the plane were going to die when the plane hit the building anyway, so what difference did it make if they died sooner rather than later?" The difference is in the attitude regarding the few as expendable. Furthermore, it isn't a *given* that they would die anyway. So if we could limit terrible consequences for a large number of people by sacrificing a few innocent people, would the decision be acceptable, even if we happened to be among the unfortunate few ourselves? If we say yes, where do we draw the line? How do we define "terrible consequences"? And, if we say no, are we seriously advocating that it is better for the many to perish in the name of fairness than for the many to survive at the cost of the lives of the few?

But one thing is contemplating the sacrifice of the innocent few to save the many; how about causing pain to a few people who are not "innocent," such as captured terrorists, for the sake of extracting information? If lives of our soldiers and civilians might be saved, should we engage in torture of prisoners who may have the information we need? The hedonistic calculus seems to have a clear answer: We just have to calculate the projected pains involved in administering torture, as opposed to not doing it. For most philosophers, the question of whether torture is morally permissible is perhaps interesting in an abstract way, but it is generally discarded as going beyond the pale in any practical context, for two primary reasons: In a civilized nation we can't afford to slide back to a time when human dignity was not held in high esteem, and torture doesn't work in practice. But elsewhere, in the post-9/11 nation, the debate has been vigorous among the public, media hosts, and politicians, reaching the Capitol, where new guidelines for torture were established in 2006. And something that occupies the minds of very different political persuasions deserves philosophical attention. One thing we can point out is that we are looking at a prime example of why a discussion of *metaethics* is important (see Chapter 3): We may have an idea of what torture is and who has been known to commit torture (a descriptive approach), and we may have strong opinions about whether or not torture should be acceptable under certain conditions (a normative approach), but how do we know that we agree on the meaning of the concept of torture (a metaethical approach)? That became the focus of the congressional discussion in 2005–2006. Senator John McCain (who himself was tortured as a POW during the Vietnam War) introduced an amendment to ban torture. The amendment stated that the United States should not engage in the torture of enemy combatants/terrorists, because it doesn't yield reliable knowledge: The prisoner will say anything to make the torture stop. Put into a utilitarian formula, the amendment says that the pain caused will not yield sufficiently useful results to justify the pain. Opponents of McCain's amendment, such as terror expert Neil Livingstone, argued that in an extreme situation, we would be remiss if we didn't use harsh interrogation methods as a last resort. In a PBS interview, Livingstone argued,

> The future of the western world, and specifically the United States, may some day depend on a ticking clock where we have to get information fast. Let's take the worst case example: A weapon of mass destruction. It's in one of our cities, and we know it's going to go off. What steps are we going to take if we find someone involved in that conspiracy to ascertain where that weapon is?

His opponent Jack Cloonan, an FBI expert, argued that methods of torture generally don't work, and

> when we adopt a theory of aggressive interrogation techniques, do we expect to be operating in a vacuum? There will be pushback, and we have to expect that. And that's another reason why I don't believe in the extradition, nor do I believe in this torture or "torture lite"—it's the revenge—because when revenge gets taken, who's going to get hurt? You, me, the public and our military forces overseas.

Both of those views, in fact, illustrate a utilitarian approach: Livingstone's argument is that resort to torture, on rare occasions, will give us the edge we need to survive, so the good consequences outweigh the bad; Cloonan argues that since torture doesn't work, and the counterattacks will escalate as a matter of revenge, the bad consequences outweigh the good. In the next chapter we'll see the argument that torture should never take place, regardless of the consequences, because it is always morally wrong in itself. This argument is based on the moral philosophy of deontology, duty theory.

The congressional debate led to the Military Commissions Act (Antiterrorism) of 2006, which upholds the Geneva Convention for lawful enemy combatants but not for "unlawful enemy combatants"—that is, terrorists. There was some dispute as to whether this might include U.S. citizens. To a great extent, this revised version leaves the very definition of torture open to interpretation. Is inducing physical pain torture? Is loud music and sleep deprivation? Is waterboarding? "Harsh interrogation methods" are accepted; "torture" is not. You may remember from Chapter 3 that the metaethical discussion of the definition of torture has been a controversial feature in the post-9/11 political climate. (Waterboarding is a form of interrogation, invented by the Spanish Inquisition, whereby water is poured over the subject's face while his or head is tilted backward, inducing the feeling of drowning.) The Antiterrorism Act did not initially label this as torture, and the method has been used by the CIA on at least three occassions (see Chapter 3), but there is growing agreement among politicians that this method indeed constitutes torture.

Would Bentham be in favor of torturing terrorists who are presumed to have knowledge about a future terror attack? It would depend exclusively on the probable outcome. Critics of Bentham—and of torture—point out that if we can use torture methods as a last resort, what is to stop us from lowering the bar and using such methods in less serious situations? For proponents of the Antiterrorism Act, there is no doubt that it is a measure to be used only as a last resort, and a necessary one: While we are respecting all other human beings, some of them are preparing to kill us, and we can't afford to lose our vigilance. But, say the critics, in that way we lose sight of what we have cherished the most since the creation of this nation: the fundamental respect for other human beings. The foundation for that respect will be explored in Chapter 6.

John Stuart Mill: Higher and Lower Pleasures

Bentham was not alone in designing the theory of utilitarianism. He and his close friend James Mill worked out the specifics of the new moral system together. Mill's son John Stuart Mill was a very bright boy, and James Mill's ambition was to develop his son's talents and intelligence as much as possible and as fast as possible. The boy responded well, learned quickly, and was able to read Greek and Latin at an early age. Throughout his childhood he was groomed to become a scientist. He was tutored privately and performed marvelously until he came to a halt at the age of twenty, struck by a nervous breakdown. His crisis was quiet and polite, in accordance with his nature: He went on with his work, and few people close to him realized what was going on; but internally he stopped in his tracks and in a very modern sense decided to "get in touch with himself," for he had come to the realization that despite his intense studying, one part of his education was pitifully incomplete. He knew much

John Stuart Mill (1806–1873), English philosopher and economist. Believing that utilitarianism was the only reasonable moral
system, Mill nevertheless saw Jeremy Bentham's version as rather
crude and created a more sophisticated version of the principle
of utility, taking into consideration the qualitative differences
between pleasures.

about how to think, but he didn't know how to *feel*; as a child he had been emotionally deprived and had never been allowed to have playmates other than his
sisters Willie, Harriet, and Clara, and he now felt totally inadequate in his emotional
life. (If you remember from Chapter 2 the emphasis that was placed on feelings during the Age of Romanticism, you'll have an even better understanding of what Mill
went through, because he was a young man of twenty when the Age of Romanticism
was at its peak.) In the months before his breakdown, he had engaged in debates,
published articles, helped edit a major work by Bentham, and was probably
beginning to suffer from what we today call burnout—at the very least, he was
overworked.

Later in life, Mill described his breakdown in his *Autobiography*; in modern terminology, he put a spin on it that reflected his rebellion against Jeremy Bentham:

> From the winter of 1821, when I first read Bentham . . . I had what might truly be called
> an object in life; to be a reformer of the world. My conception of my own life was entirely
> identified with this object. . . . But the time came when I awakened from this as from a
> dream. It was in the autumn of 1826. I was in a dull state of nerves, such as everybody is
> occasionally liable to; unsusceptible to enjoyment or pleasurable excitement. . . . In this
> frame of mind it occurred to me to put the question directly to myself: "Suppose that all
> your objects in life were realized; that all the changes in institutions and opinions which
> you are looking forward to, could be completely effected at this very instant: would this be
> a great joy and happiness to you?" And an irrepressible self-consciousness distinctly an-
> swered, "No!" At this my heart sank within me: the whole foundation on which my life
> was constructed fell down. . . . I seemed to have nothing left to live for. . . . If I had loved
> anyone sufficiently to make confiding my griefs a necessity, I should not have been in the
> condition I was.

What Mill read into his breakdown later in life was that his father's intellectual
training and Bentham's philosophy had let him down—the utilitarian greatest-
happiness principle might lead to happiness for the many, but it didn't necessarily
lead to happiness for the utilitarian. Mill, in his *Autobiography,* uses this term to ram

a lesson home: You don't find happiness by looking for it but by enjoying life along the way as you focus on other things. "Ask yourself whether you are happy, and you cease to be so." In his crisis, Mill rediscovered the truth of the paradox of hedonism: The harder you look for happiness, the more likely it is to elude you. But what really happened to him psychologically may not have been clear to Mill at all. For one thing, he was overworked, and winter was approaching. For another, he found himself a cerebral intellectual in the midst of the most feeling-oriented period so far in Western history. For a third, he was lonely and became depressed; he had what we've come to know as a severe case of "the blues." But the loneliness problem didn't last long. Neither did his disenchantment with utilitarianism—he just stopped looking for self-gratification in it and focused on the goal of improving the world.

Mill began exploring the world of feelings—music, poetry, literature—and later he went abroad to the European continent and traveled (as did the Romantic painters and poets). In a roundabout way, Mill's personal story illustrates Nussbaum's theory that emotions are not irrelevant for ethics (see Chapter 1). During this period he took time out to reexamine his life and his future, turned his back on the sciences, and decided to "go into his father's business" and become a social thinker and an economist. As a social thinker he became one of the most influential persons of the nineteenth century, laying the foundation for many of the political ideas in the Western world on both the liberal and the conservative sides.

Mill's Revision of Utilitarianism: The Higher and Lower Pleasures

Mill's aim was to take his godfather and father's theory of utilitarianism and redesign it to fit a more sophisticated age. What had seemed overwhelmingly important to Bentham—a more just legal system—was no longer the primary goal, for he realized that without proper education for the general population, true social equality would not be obtained. Mill also realized that Bentham's version of utilitarianism had several flaws. For one thing, it was too simple; it relied on a very straightforward system of identifying good with pleasure and evil with pain, without specifying the nature of pleasure and pain. (Some say this was actually one of the strengths of early utilitarianism, but Mill saw it as a serious deficiency.) Bentham's version also assumed that people were so rational they would always follow the moral calculations. Mill pointed out, however, that even if people are clearly shown it would give them and others more overall pleasure to change their course of action, they are likely to continue doing what they are used to because people are creatures of habit; our emotions, rather than cool deliberation, often dictate what we do. We can't, therefore, rely on our rationality to the extreme degree that Bentham thought we could. (That doesn't mean, of course, that we can't *educate* children and adults to use their heads more profitably.) We will return to the education question later, but first we look at how Mill decided to redesign the theory of utilitarianism.

Mill was a more complex person than Bentham, and his theory reflects that complexity. For Mill the idea that humans seek pleasure and that moral goodness lies in obtaining that pleasure is only half the story—but it is the half that is more frequently misunderstood. What do people think when they hear this idea? That all that counts is easy gratification of any desire they may have—in other words, a "doctrine worthy only of swine," as Mill says, repeating the words of the critics of utilitarianism. And because people reject the notion of seeking only swinish pleasures, they reject utilitarianism as an unworthy theory. They get upset, said Mill, precisely because they are not pigs and want more out of life than a pig could ever want. People are simply not content with basic pleasures, and a good moral and social theory should reflect that. Furthermore, says Mill, all theories that have advocated happiness have been accused of talking about easy gratification, but that is an unfair criticism when applied to utilitarianism. Even Epicurus held that there are many things in life other than physical pleasures that can bring us happiness, and there is nothing in utilitarianism that says we have to define pleasure and happiness as mere gratification of physical desires.

Why was Mill so uneasy about being accused of seeking gratification of physical desires? Consider the changing times in which he lived. When Mill wrote his book *Utilitarianism* (1863), the British Empire was twenty-six years into the Victorian era. Queen Victoria had ascended the throne in 1837, and morals had subtly undergone a shift since Bentham's day; preoccupation with physical pleasures was, on the whole, frowned upon by the middle classes, more so than in the previous generation—it was not considered proper to display such indulgence. For many, that signifies an age of hypocrisy, of double standards, but it would be unfair to accuse Mill of such double standards, because several of his truly innovative social ideas stemmed from his indignation toward this preoccupation with the way other people choose to live. However, it may have been a sign of the times that Mill felt compelled to reassure his readers that they could be followers of utilitarianism without being labeled hedonists.

Some believe there is also a personal side to the story. In his early twenties, Mill, having earlier worried that he didn't have any knowledge of feelings, fell head over heels in love with a young married woman, Harriet Taylor, and the feeling was mutual. They maintained a relationship for almost twenty years, until her husband died, and then they finally got married. Their relationship had become an open secret over the years, even to Mr. Taylor. (Being honest people, they apparently told him of their feelings, but he was also assured that they had no intention of breaking up the Taylor marriage.) It has generally been assumed that they were sexually involved, but judging from their correspondence, it may well have been a platonic friendship until their wedding. Their letters testify to Mill's later version of utilitarianism: They two seem to agree that spiritual pleasures and intellectual companionship are more valuable than physical gratification. John Stuart Mill prepared his book *Utilitarianism* during the years of their marriage, but when it was published in 1863, Harriet was no longer alive. She died (probably of tuberculosis) less than ten years after they got married; however, Mill's moral and political writings were clearly inspired by their intellectual discussions over three decades. (See Box 5.6 for a discussion of Mill's views on women's rights.)

What, then, does Mill propose? That some pleasures are more valuable, "higher," than others. That on the whole, humans prefer to hold on to their dignity and strive for truly fulfilling experiences rather than settle for easy contentment.

Box 5.6   MILL AND THE WOMEN'S CAUSE

John Stuart Mill is today recognized as the first influential male speaker for political equality between men and women in modern Western history. (In England, Mary Wollstonecraft published her *Vindication of the Rights of Women* in 1792, but already in 1673 the French author Poulain de la Barre, a student of Descartes, had published *De l'égalité des deux sexes,* in which he argued for total equality between men and women because of their equality in reasoning power. This book, however, was largely ignored for a long time.) Mill's book *The Subjection of Women* (1869) revealed to his readers the abyss of inequality separating the lives of men and women in what was then considered a modern society. His exposé of this inequality was a strong contributing factor in women's

obtaining the right to vote in England, as well as elsewhere in the Western world. In 1866 Mill, then a member of the British Parliament, had tried to get a measure passed that would establish gender equality in England. The measure failed, but Mill had succeeded in drawing attention to the issue. It is often mentioned in this context that Mill was inspired by his long-time friend and later wife, Harriet Taylor. Scholars now believe that Mill's fight for women's rights was not just a matter of subtle inspiration from Mrs. Taylor but also a direct result of their long and detailed intellectual discussions, for Mrs. Taylor was an intellectual in her own right. In the Primary Readings section in Chapter 12, you'll find a text by Harriet Taylor Mill.

It is better to be a human dissatisfied than a pig satisfied, better to be Socrates dissatisfied than a fool satisfied, says Mill. Even if the great pleasures in life require some effort—for instance, one has to learn math to understand the joy of solving a mathematical problem—it is worth the effort, because the pleasure is greater than if you had just remained passive.

Now the question becomes, Who is to say which pleasures are the higher ones and which are the lower ones? We seem predisposed to assume that the physical pleasures are the lower ones, but need that be the case? Mill proposes a test: We must ask people who are familiar with both kinds of pleasure, and whatever they choose as the higher goal is the ultimate answer. Suppose we gather a group of people who sometimes order a pizza and beer and watch *Monday Night Football* or a reality show but also occasionally go out to a French restaurant before watching *Masterpiece Theatre* on PBS. We ask them which activity—pizza and football or French food and *Masterpiece Theatre*—is the higher pleasure. If the test works, we must accept it if the majority say that on the whole they think pizza and football is the higher pleasure. But will Mill accept that? This is the drawback of his test—it appears that he will not:

> Capacity for the nobler feelings is in most natures a very tender plant, easily killed, not only by hostile influences, but by mere want of sustenance; and in the majority of young persons it speedily dies away if the occupations to which their position in life has devoted them, and the society into which it has thrown them, are not favorable to keeping that higher capacity in exercise. Men lose their high aspirations as they lose their intellectual

Harriet Hardy Taylor Mill (1807–1858) was a chief source of inspiration for her longtime friend and later husband John Stuart Mill. Her views on individual rights are reflected in Mill's book *On Liberty* (1859), published immediately after her death. They did not agree on everything, though: Mill believed that when a woman marries, she must give up working outside the home; Taylor believed that women have a right to employment regardless of their marital status and that no-fault divorce should be available. However, the spouses seemed to be in agreement on most other issues and found in each other what we today call a soul mate. Mill grieved deeply when she died and bought a house close to the cemetery where she was laid to rest so he could visit her grave often.

tastes, because they have not time or opportunity for indulging them; and they addict themselves to inferior pleasures not because they deliberately prefer them, but because they are either the only ones to which they have access or the only ones which they are any longer capable of enjoying.

What does that mean? It means if you vote for pizza and football as the overall winner, Mill will claim you have lost the capacity for enjoying gourmet French food and intellectual television (which demands some attention from your intellect), or, to use a modern expression, "Use it or lose it." In other words, he has rigged his own test. This has caused some critics to voice the opinion that Mill is an intellectual snob, a "cultural imperialist" trying to impose his own standards on the general population. And the immediate victim of this procedure? The egalitarian principle that was the foundation of Bentham's version of utilitarianism—that one person equals one vote regarding what is pleasurable and what is painful—collapses under Mill's test. According to him, we have to go to the "authorities of happiness" to find out what it is that everybody ought to desire.

If we perform Mill's test and ask individuals who seem to know of many kinds of pleasure what they prefer, we may get responses that Mill would not have accepted, because some people may indeed favor physical pleasures over intellectual or spiritual ones; however, a recent study claimed (with no reference to Mill whatsoever) that people who have a spiritual side are happier overall than are people whose lives are completely focused on material pleasures. Now, it is questionable in itself whether it is at all possible to put together reliable statistics on this topic, but Mill would probably have welcomed the survey: It is not merely because higher, intellectual, or spiritual pleasures are somehow finer that he recommends them; it is because they presumably yield a higher form of happiness in the long run than do pleasures of easy gratification. (Box 5.7 explores Mill's attempt at proving that higher pleasures are more desirable and introduces the concept of the naturalistic fallacy.)

Box 5.7   THE NATURALISTIC FALLACY

John Stuart Mill acknowledges there is no proof that happiness is the ultimate value because no founding principles can be proved, yet he offers a proof by analogy. This proof has bothered philosophers ever since, because it actually does more harm than good to Mill's own system of thought. The analogy goes like this: The only way we can prove that something is visible is that people actually see it. Likewise, the only way we can prove that something is desirable is that people actually desire it. Everyone desires happiness, so happiness is therefore the ultimate goal. Why does this not work as an analogy? It doesn't work because being "visible" is not analogous to being "desirable." When we say that something is visible, we are describing what people actually see. But when we say that something is desirable, we are not describing what people desire. If many people desire drugs, we do not therefore conclude that drugs are "desirable," because "desirable" means that something *should be* desired. The problem, however, goes deeper. Even if it were true that we could find out what is morally desirable by doing a nose count, why should we then have to conclude that because many people desire something, there should be a moral requirement that we all desire it? In other words, we are stepping from "is" (from a descriptive statement that says something is desired) to "ought" (to a normative/prescriptive statement that says something ought to be desired), and as the philosopher David Hume pointed out, there is nothing in a descriptive statement that allows us to proceed from what people actually do to a rule that states what people ought to do. This step, known as the *naturalistic fallacy,* is commonly taken by thinkers, politicians, writers, and other people of influence, but it is nevertheless a dangerous step to take. We can't make a policy based solely on what is the case. For instance, if it were to turn out that women actually are better parents than men by nature, it still would not be fair to conclude that men ought not to be single fathers (or that all women ought to be mothers), because we can't pass from a simple statement of fact to a statement of policy. That does not mean we can't make policies based on fact; that would be preposterous. What we have to do is insert a value statement—our opinion about what is good or bad, right or wrong (a so-called hidden premise)—so we can go from a fact (such as "There are many teen pregnancies today") to the hidden premise ("We believe teen pregnancies are bad for teen girls, for their babies, and for society") and then to the conclusion ("We must try to lower the number of teen pregnancies"). In that case, someone who doesn't agree with our conclusion can still agree with the fact stated but disagree with our hidden premise. Although this idea is occasionally contested by various thinkers, it remains one of philosophy's ground rules.

Be that as it may, the idea of a "spiritual life" is rather vague and intangible, so let us use an example that is more concrete: learning to play a musical instrument. Anyone who has attempted it knows that for the first few months it usually doesn't sound very good, practicing is hard work, and you'll be tempted to give up. But if you stick with it, there will probably come a day when you feel you can play what you want the way you want and even play with others, giving joy to yourself and your listeners. The same process occurs, of course, with many other skills that take hard work to learn but yield much gratification when acquired: speaking a foreign language, for example, or painting with watercolors. So now Mill can step in and ask his question:

Dilbert by Scott Adams

DILBERT reprinted by permission of United Features Syndicate, Inc.

One of the deficiencies of utilitarianism is that if the final goal of any action is to feel good, it doesn't matter *what* makes us feel good. This *Dilbert* cartoon hits the nail on the head: If succeeding is supposed to make us feel good but failure doesn't make us feel bad (because some believe that feeling good is important for people to maintain their self-esteem no matter how they do it), what is the incentive for success?

If you had the choice, would you give up that skill, provided you could get all those hours of practice time back so you could spend them watching sitcoms? I doubt that a single one of us would say yes; identifying our artistic skill as the higher pleasure in spite of all the hours of hard work, tedium, and frustration leading up to it is no challenge at all. It seems that many of us, including Mill, and perhaps also Socrates, would indeed rather be temporarily dissatisfied if it meant we'd put the easy gratifications on hold for something higher and better down the road. But we'd still have to ask whether all skills that have taken an effort to acquire would qualify as "higher pleasures" according to Mill—as well as according to us: How about sports? computer games? or con artistry? At the end of the chapter, you can read a selection from *Utilitarianism* in which Mill gives his version of a happy, meaningful life.

Mill's Harm Principle

Did Mill achieve what he wanted? Certainly he wanted to redesign utilitarianism so that it reflected the complexity of a cultured population, but did he intend to set himself up as a cultural despot? It appears that what he wanted was something else entirely. Whereas Bentham wanted the girl who sold flowers at Covent Garden to be able to enjoy her gin in peace, Mill wanted to *educate* her so that she wouldn't *need* her gin anymore and would be able to experience the glorious pleasures enjoyed by the middle-class couple who had learned to appreciate the opera. What Mill had in mind, in other words, was probably not elitism but the notion that the greater pleasure can be derived from achievement. We feel a special fulfillment if we've worked hard on a math problem or a piece of music or a painting and we finally get it right. Mill thought this type of pleasure should be made available to everyone with a capacity for it. This Mill saw as equality of a higher order, based on general education. Once such education is attained, the choices of the educated person are his or hers alone, and nobody has the right to interfere. However, until such a level is achieved, society has a right to gently inform its children and childlike adults about what they ought to prefer.

That sounds today like paternalism, and there is much in Mill's position that supports that point of view. To look more closely at Mill's ideas of what is best for people, we must take a look at what has become known as the *harm principle*.

Although the principle of utility provides a general guideline for personal as well as political action in terms of increasing happiness and decreasing unhappiness, it says very little about the circumstances under which one might justifiably become involved in changing other people's lives for the better. Mill had very specific ideas about the limitations of such involvement; in his essay *On Liberty* (1859), he examines the proper limits of government control. Because history has progressed from a time when rulers preyed upon their populations and the populations had to be protected from the rulers' despotic actions to a time when democratic rulers, in principle, *are* the people, the idea of absolute authority on the part of rulers should no longer be a danger to the people. But reality shows us that this is not the case, because we now must face the *tyranny of the majority*. In other words, those who now need protection are minorities (and here Mill thinks of political minorities) who may wish to conduct their lives in ways different from the ways of the majority and its idea of what is right and proper. As an answer to the question of how much the social majority is allowed to exert pressure on the minority, Mill proposes the harm principle:

> That principle is, that the sole end for which mankind are warranted, individually or collectively, in interfering with the liberty of action of any of their number, is self-protection. That the only purpose for which power can be rightfully exercised over any member of a civilized community, against his will, is to prevent harm to others. His own good, either physical or moral, is not a sufficient warrant. He cannot rightfully be compelled to do or forbear because it will be better for him to do so, because it will make him happier, because, in the opinions of others, to do so would be wise, or even right. These are good reasons for remonstrating with him, or reasoning with him, or persuading him, or entreating him, but not for compelling him, or visiting him with any evil in case he do otherwise. To justify that, the conduct from which it is desired to deter him must be calculated to produce evil to someone else. The only part of the conduct of anyone, for which he is amenable to society, is that which concerns others. In the part which merely concerns himself, his independence is, of right, absolute. Over himself, over his own body and mind, the individual is sovereign.

So how does this policy go with his statement four years later that higher pleasures are better for people than lower pleasures and that some people aren't capable of knowing what is good for them? Some Mill critics say that they don't go well together at all—that Mill is claiming in one text that people have a right to choose their own poison, and in the other that they haven't. But we can perhaps find a middle way: What Mill is saying in *On Liberty* is that people, if they so choose, should be allowed to follow their own tastes; what he is saying in *Utilitarianism* is that everybody should be allowed to be exposed to higher pleasures through education, so they might be able to make better choices—but he is not going to force anyone who is adult and in control of his or her mental faculties to submit to a life ruled by someone else's taste. At least, that is a possible reading of Mill that brings the two viewpoints together. (See Box 5.8 for an application of the harm principle to the issue of the legalization of drugs.)

The harm principle has had extremely far-reaching consequences. Built in part on John Locke's theory of negative rights (see Chapter 7), which had had great influence not only in the United Kingdom but also on the Constitution of the United States, Mill's theory helped define two political lines of thought that, paradoxically, are now at odds with each other. We usually refer to Mill's view as *classical liberalism* because of its emphasis on personal liberty. The idea of civil liberties—the rights of citizens, within their right to privacy, to do what they want provided that they do no harm and to have their government ensure that as little harm and as much happiness as possible is created for as many people as possible—is also a cornerstone of *egalitarian liberalism*. But the notions of personal liberty and noninterference by the government have also become key in the political theory of *laissez-faire,* the hands-off approach that requires as little government interference as possible, primarily in private enterprise. The idea behind laissez-faire is that if we all look after our own business and no authorities make our business theirs, then we all are better off, which is today considered a *conservative* economic philosophy, expressed in its extreme form by the Libertarian Party.

The limitations of the right to privacy are more numerous than might be apparent at first glance. For one thing, what exactly does it mean that we are accountable to society only for our conduct that concerns others? What Mill had in mind certainly included the right of consenting adults to engage in sexual activity in the privacy of their own homes, regardless of how other people might feel about the issue. In such cases, only nosy neighbors might be "concerned," and for Mill their right to concern would be proportionate to the extent that they would be exposed to the activities of the couple in question. In other words, if it takes binoculars for you to become exposed to a situation (and hence become "concerned"), then put aside your binoculars and mind your own business.

But what about, say, a teenage girl who decides to put an end to her life because her boyfriend broke up with her? Might that fall within the harm principle? Is she harming only herself, so that society has no right to interfere? Here Mill might answer in several ways. First, she is harming not only herself but her family as well, who would grieve for her and feel guilty for not having stepped in. There is also the problem of role models. If other teens in the same situation learn about her suicide, they might think it would be a good idea to follow her example, and more harm would be caused. But when does indirect harm ever end? Doesn't it spread like rings in water? Mill himself would not allow for indirect harm, such as the harm caused by flawed role models, to be an obvious cause for the interference of authorities. To him, an adult should not be prevented from doing what he or she wants to do just because some other adult might imitate the action, but only if his or her action (such as a policeman being drunk on the job—Mill's own example) is a likely cause for direct harm to others. You may draw your own conclusions about current discussions concerning direct and indirect harm, such as the debate surrounding helmet laws, drug laws, and prostitution. And what if a blog on the Internet advocated violence in specific terms—such as the anti-abortion website The Nuremberg Files of the late 1990s, which published the names and addresses of abortion providers—but the bloggers

Box 5.8   THE HARM PRINCIPLE AND DRUG LEGALIZATION

John Stuart Mill's harm principle, that the only purpose of interfering with the life of someone is to prevent harm to others, has been applied in many social and political debates, with the general result that we see how ambiguous the principle really is. Examples are the euthanasia debate (see Chapter 13), the debate about "victimless crimes" such as (presumably) prostitution, and the discussion about the legalization of drugs.

A general utilitarian view of the legalization of drugs does not take a stand on whether drugs in themselves are "good" or "bad" but on whether more misery (or happiness) in the long run will be created through making them legally available than through prohibiting them. But remember that the harm principle sets limits to the "general-happiness principle" because it keeps us from interfering with people *for their own sake,* unless they are harming others. You can't force someone to try out someone else's model for happiness (and by now you have probably noticed that Mill's own theory of higher pleasures doesn't quite go well with his harm principle, because he believed people ought to be educated so they could enjoy the higher pleasures, even though they might not want to give up their lower pleasures).

Arguments in favor of drug legalization generally include these:

- The war on drugs isn't working—it is costly and clogs the jails with drug offenders;

furthermore, drugs are still being brought across the borders.

- If drugs were legalized, they would be safer because they would be controlled by the state, and the black market would disappear. Drugs would become less expensive, and addicts wouldn't have to turn to crime to feed their habit.

- Heavy drug users could be helped by the state, and people who could manage their own drug use could be left to themselves; after all, people who can manage their own drinking are not criminalized.

The harm principle obviously applies here: If a person does no one else harm by a moderate drug intake, then he or she should be allowed to continue using drugs. (This is the drug policy of the Libertarian Party.) This is where advocates of drug legalization usually seek Mill's support. But we should not draw hasty conclusions. If we take a closer look at the issue, do we still have a situation that involves only individuals who are mature enough to manage their own habits?

- The fact that the war on drugs isn't working is no reason to give it up. If jails are being inundated with drug offenders, the solution is not to decriminalize drug use but to educate children about drugs before they start using.

themselves did not engage in violent activities? Would that be an instance of legitimate free speech, or of an unacceptable call to violence and harm-doing? The courts have disagreed. It is clear that Mill's interpretation of his own harm principle still engenders heated debate. As for our example of the suicidal teenage girl, Mill would most certainly add the following: This situation does not fall under the harm principle, because the girl is (1) not an adult and (2) not in a rational frame of mind:

This doctrine is meant to apply only to human beings in the maturity of their faculties. We are not speaking of children, or of young persons below the age which the law may fix as that of manhood or womanhood. Those who are still in a state to require being taken care of by

- Will crime go down? Will the black market disappear? Will drugs be safer? Only if you live in a fantasy world. Cigarettes are legal, but there is a huge black market for tobacco, smuggling is big business, and even with cheap drugs there will be some who can't afford them and will turn to crime. If drug legalization involves regulation (safer drugs), then there will surely arise a black market for unregulated drugs, which would begin the cycle again.

- Certainly it is a good idea for the state to help heavy users—individual states already do that. And it is also possible that many people could be completely responsible with a drug habit, just as many are responsible in their enjoyment of alcohol (which is, of course, a drug). But—and this is where the harm principle takes a turn—imagine all those people, young people in particular, who refrain from drugs simply because they are illegal. With drug legalization, that obstacle is removed; this means there will be many more people on the streets who are under the influence, endangering themselves *and* others in traffic, not to mention creating lifelong dependencies.

So opponents of drug legalization are saying that, overall, legalization will cause more harm than continued drug legislation. In addition, even though one individual may not be directly harming anyone else, he or she may serve as a role model of drug use for others less mature or responsible. Mill considered only direct harm to others a reason to interfere, not this kind of indirect harm. (But he would have considered drugs a "lower pleasure.") However, later critics as well as supporters of the harm principle have argued that the line between direct and indirect harm is often blurred. A bad role model may cause more obvious and direct harm to an impressionable child than to an adult who is supposed to be able to distinguish right from wrong. So the harm principle may be used to argue against drug legalization. The issue of medical use of drugs, such as marijuana, may be different, because drugs for medical use are already part of our culture. The question of legislating alcohol as a drug of course has similarities with the drug issue: Alcohol directly endangers not just the person under the influence but others as well; MADD (Mothers Against Drunk Drivers) and other victims of alcohol-related accidents and their relatives can attest to that. But there is a difference: Most other drugs are taken strictly for their effect; alcohol is very often consumed not for its effect but for its taste, and the intake need not reach a level where a person is a risk to others.

others, must be protected against their own actions as well as against external injury. For the same reason, we may leave out of consideration those backward states of society in which the [human] race itself may be considered as in its nonage. . . . Despotism is a legitimate mode of government in dealing with barbarians, provided the end be their improvement, and the means justified by actually effecting that end. Liberty, as a principle, has no application to any state of things anterior to the time when mankind have become capable of being improved by free and equal discussion. . . . But as soon as mankind have attained the capacity of being guided to their own improvement by conviction or persuasion (a period long since reached in all nations with whom we need here concern ourselves), compulsion . . . is no longer admissible as a means to their own good, and justifiably only for the security of others.

With this addition to the harm principle, Mill certainly makes it clear that children are excluded, but so is anyone who, in Mill's mind, belongs to a "backward" state of society. Again, we see evidence of Mill's complexity: He adamantly wants to protect civil liberties, but he is also paternalistic: Whoever is not an "adult" by his definition must be guided or coerced to comply with existing rules. Individuals as well as whole peoples who fall outside the "adult" category must be governed by others until they reach sufficient maturity to take affairs into their own hands. Critics have seen this as a defense of not merely cultural but also political imperialism: There are peoples who are too primitive to rule themselves, so someone else has to do it for them and bring them up to Western standards. Who are these peoples? We may assume that they include the native-born peoples of old British colonies. Since Mill made his living not as a philosophy professor but as a Chief Examiner at India House, East India Company, which administered the colony of India (his father, James Mill, had worked for the Company and was the author of a lengthy work on the history of India), his knowledge of colony affairs came from the perspective of the colony power. That viewpoint, sometimes referred to as "the white man's burden," is very far from being acceptable in our era, but is it fair to accuse Mill of being an imperialist? Perhaps, especially if we take into account that Mill published his piece in 1859, and two years earlier the British Empire had been shocked by the so-called Sepoy mutiny in northern India, in which hundreds of British officers and their wives and children had been murdered by Indian infantry soldiers in the British-Indian army. That mutiny was the result of long-standing clashes and misunderstandings between the two cultural groups, after a hundred years of British dominion and (as many would describe it) exploitation. In the aftermath of the mutiny, India was taken over by the British Crown and ruled as a part of the empire. Mill was appalled at the mutiny but also at the takeover by the British government, and he retired, declining to take part in the new government. His chief aim seems to have been perpetuating not the British Empire but the utilitarian idea of maximizing happiness for the greatest number and minimizing pain and misery on a global scale. If Mill was biased toward the British way of life, it may be understandable: That way of life was in many ways the best the planet Earth had to offer in the nineteenth century for those with access to a good education. It was, in our terms, an extremely "civilized" culture, at least for the upper and middle classes. Perhaps, then, we can think of Mill not merely as an intellectual snob but also as an educator who wanted to see everybody get the same good chances in life that he got and enjoy life as much as he did.

One final remark concerning Mill: Sometimes the present forces us to reevaluate things we thought were simply part of history—something we thought we understood pretty well. For at least half a century, it has been considered right and appropriate (at least in this country) to criticize Mill for wanting to govern India until Indians were capable of governing themselves in a democratic fashion. Ethical relativism, being a strong cultural force in the twentieth century, has told us that each culture is right in its own way and that no culture has the right to superimpose its values on other cultures. But wait . . . in Chapter 3 we discussed the types of situations that have made so many people change their minds about ethical relativism. Should we just stand by while little girls are being circumcised? while people are being sold into slavery?

Now suppose we add to the list: while people are being tortured and murdered by a dictator, while entire populations are being subject to genocide? What I am getting at is, of course, the war in Iraq. Even without considering the issue of the WMDs (weapons of mass destruction) or the connection between Saddam Hussein and al Qaeda (shown to be unlikely by a Pentagon report in 2008), removing a dictator and creating a democracy became what the war in Iraq was all about. That puts us at a crossroads: On the one hand, we can stay with the earlier critical evaluation of Mill and say that no matter what the situation, a nation doesn't have the right to try to run another nation or change its regime to something that seems more right, or even just more acceptable or safer. On the other hand, if we agree with Mill that democracy is better than tyranny, and freedom of educated people is better than the superstition of illiteracy—then can we still claim that he is wrong? And if we think he has a point, how does that translate into the evaluation of the war in Iraq? For Mill and other British citizens, the Sepoy Mutiny can perhaps be understood as a kind of 9/11 experience. Even if he didn't approve of the way the British government handled the crisis, his conclusion was that nations who aren't "civilized" must be put under the civilizing influence of other nations until they have matured sufficiently to govern themselves. So if we view Mill's attitude through the lenses of our own 9/11 experience, and the subsequent wars in Afghanistan and—in particular—in Iraq, would you condemn his view, or would you instead reevaluate Mill's statement in light of the capture of Saddam Hussein and the attempt by the United States and its allies to introduce democracy into a country that has never known a "free and equal discussion," as Mill called it? For a utilitarian such as Mill, the question will eventually become, Can the goal be accomplished, and at what cost? In Chapter 13 you'll read about the theory of just war. For now, I suggest you engage in the thought experiment of taking a look at a nineteenth-century event through twenty-first-century eyes—and then allow yourself to look at today's events from the viewpoint of a nineteenth-century philosopher. It may increased your understanding of the past as well as the present.

Act and Rule Utilitarianism

In the twentieth century it became clear to philosophers attracted to utilitarianism that there were severe problems inherent in the idea that a morally right act is an act that makes as many people as possible happy. One flaw is that, as we saw previously, it is conceivable many people will achieve much pleasure from the misery of a few others, and even in situations where people don't know that their happiness is achieved by the pain of others, that is still an uncomfortable thought. It is especially so if one believes in the Golden Rule (as John Stuart Mill did), which states that we should do for others what we would like done for ourselves and refrain from doing to others what we would not like done to ourselves. Mill himself was aware of the problem and allowed that in the long run a society in which a majority abuses a minority is not a good society. That still means we have to explain why the *first* cases of happiness occurring from the misery of others are wrong, even before they have established themselves as a pattern with increasingly bad consequences. In a sense, Mill tried to address the problem, suggesting that utilitarianism be taken as a general policy to be applied to general situations. He did not, however, develop the idea further within his own philosophy.

Others have taken up the challenge and suggested it is just that particular formulation of utilitarianism which creates the problem; given another formulation, the problem disappears. If we stay with the *classical* formulation, the principle of utility goes like this: *Always do whatever act will create the greatest happiness for the greatest number of people.* In this version we are stuck with the problems we saw earlier; for example, the torture of innocents may bring about great pleasure for a large group of people. The Russian author Dostoyevsky explored this thought in his novel *The Brothers Karamazov:* Suppose your happiness, and everyone else's, is bought by the suffering of an innocent child? (We look more closely at this idea in the Narratives section.) It is not hard to see this as a Christian metaphor, with Jesus' suffering as the condition of happiness for humans, but there is an important difference: Jesus was a volunteer; an innocent child is not. In any event, a utilitarian, by definition, would have to agree that if a great deal of suffering could be alleviated by putting an innocent person through hell, then doing so would be justified. Putting nonhuman animals or entire populations of humans through hell would also be justified. The glorious end (increased happiness for a majority) will in any event justify the means, even if the means violate these beings' right to life or to fair treatment.

Suppose we reformulate utilitarianism. Suppose we say, *Always do whatever type of act will create the greatest happiness for the greatest number of people.* What is the result? If we set up a one-time situation, such as the torture of an innocent person for the sake of others' well-being, it may work within the first formulation. But if we view it as a *type* of situation—one that is likely to recur again and again because we have now set up a *rule* for such types of situations—it becomes impermissible: The consequences of torturing *many* innocent people will not bring about great happiness for anyone in the long run. Is this, perhaps, what Mill was trying to say? This new formulation is referred to as *rule utilitarianism,* and it is advocated by many modern utilitarians who wish to distance themselves from the uncomfortable implications of the classical theory, now referred to as *act utilitarianism*. If this new version is used, they say, we can focus on the good consequences of a certain type of act rather than on the singular act itself. It may work once for a student to cheat on a final, but cheating as a rule is not only dangerous (the student herself is likely to be found out) but also immoral to the rule utilitarian, because very bad consequences would occur if everyone were to cheat. Professors would get wise in no time, and nobody would graduate. Students and professors would be miserable. Society would miss out on a great many well-educated college graduates. The Golden Rule is in this way fortified: Don't do something if you can't imagine it as a rule for everybody, because a rule not suited for everyone can have no good overall consequences.

Some critics have objected that not everything we do can be made into a rule with good consequences. After all, many of the things we like to do are unique to us, and why should we assume that just because one person likes to collect movie memorabilia, the world would be happier if everyone collected movie memorabilia? That is not the way it is supposed to work, say the rule utilitarians. You have to specify that the rule is valid for people *under similar circumstances,* and you have to specify what *exceptions* you might want to make. It may be morally good to make sure you are home in time for dinner if you have a family to come home to but not if you are living by yourself. And the moral goodness of being there in time for dinner depends on there not being something of greater importance that you should see to. Such things might be a crisis at work, a medical emergency, extracurricular activities, walking the dog, seeing your lover, watching a television show all the way to the end, talking on the phone, or whatever you choose. They may not all qualify as good exceptions, but *you* should specify in your rule which ones are acceptable. Once you have created such a rule, the utilitarian ideal will work, say the rule utilitarians; it will make more people happy and fewer people unhappy in the long run. If it doesn't, then you just have to rework the rule until you get it right.

The problem with this approach is that it may be asking too much of people. Are we likely to ponder the consequences of whatever it is we want to do every time we are about to take action? Are we likely to envision everyone doing the same thing? Probably not. Even if it is wrong to make numerous private phone calls from a company phone, we think it won't make much difference if one person makes private calls as long as nobody else does. As long as most people comply, we can still get away with breaking the rule without creating bad consequences. Even so, we are in the wrong, because a healthy moral theory will not set "myself" up as an exception to the rule just because "I'm me and I deserve it." This, as philosopher James Rachels has pointed out, is as much a form of discrimination as racism and sexism are. We might call it "me-ism," but we already have a good word for it, *egoism,* and we already know that that is unacceptable.

This addition to utilitarianism, that one ought to look for rules that apply to everyone, is for many a major step in the right direction. Rule utilitarianism certainly was not, however, the first philosophy to ask, What if everybody did what you intend to do? Although just about every parent must have said that to her or his child at some time or other, the one person who is credited with putting it into a philosophical framework is the German philosopher Immanuel Kant. There is one important difference between the way Kant asks the question and the way it has later been developed by rule utilitarians, though. Rule utilitarianism asks, What will be the *consequences* of everybody doing what you intend to do? Kant asks, Could you wish for it to be a *universal law* that everyone does what you intend to do? We look more closely at this difference in the next chapter.

Study Questions

1. Explain the function of Bentham's hedonistic (hedonic) calculus and give an example of how to use it. Explain the advantages of using the calculus; explain the problems inherent in the concept of the calculus.

2. Evaluate the question of torture used as a last resort in a national security crisis: What would Bentham recommend? Would you agree? Why or why not? (You may want to revisit the question after having read Chapter 6.)

3. Explain John Stuart Mill's theory of higher and lower pleasures: What are the problems inherent in the theory? Overall, does Mill's idea of higher and lower pleasures make sense to you? Why or why not?

4. Evaluate Descartes's theory that only those beings with a mind can suffer and that only humans have minds. Explore the consequences for utilitarianism if we agree that animals (including human beings) have a capacity for suffering.

5. Explore Mill's harm principle: Do you find the principle attractive or problematic? Explain why. Discuss the application of the harm principle to the issue of drug legalization.

6. Are we more likely to accept the idea of utilitarianism in a time of crisis? If so, does that make the theory acceptable? Explain.

Primary Readings and Narratives

The first two Primary Readings are Jeremy Bentham's definition of the principle of utility and John Stuart Mill's vision of true happiness. The Third Reading is Peter Singer's controversial article in the *New York Times* on the case of a severely disabled young girl. The Narratives based on literature include a Danish tale about utilitarianism in action and a pairing of excerpts from Dostoyevsky and Ursula K. Le Guin that look at the happiness of the many in light of the suffering of a few. A summary of the film *Extreme Measures* explores the moral question of performing medical experiments on a few unwanted homeless people to gain knowledge that will save the lives and mobility of thousands of others. And, finally, the film summary of *Runaway Jury* represents a pro-utilitarian view in the controversial story of a jury being manipulated to achieve what the main characters perceive as a moral victory.

 *Primary Reading*

Of the Principle of Utility

JEREMY BENTHAM

From An Introduction to the Principles of Morals and Legislation, *1789. Excerpt.*

Jeremy Bentham's primary interests were legislative, and he wrote in a meticulous style suited to the language of the law. In this excerpt Bentham defines the principle of utility and outlines the consequences for individuals, for the community, and for moral concepts.

I. *Mankind governed by pain and pleasure.* Nature has placed mankind under the governance of two sovereign masters, *pain* and *pleasure*. It is for them alone to point out what we ought to do, as well as to determine what we shall do. On the one hand the standard of right and wrong, on the other the chain of causes and effects, are fastened to their throne. They govern us in all we do, in all we say, in all we think: every effort we can make to throw them off our subjection, will serve but to demonstrate and confirm it. In words a man may pretend to abjure their empire: but in reality he will remain subject to it all the while. The *principle of utility* recognises this subjection, and assumes it for the foundation of that system, the object of which is to rear the fabric of felicity by the hands of reason and of law. Systems which attempt to question it, deal in sounds instead of sense, in caprice instead of reason, in darkness instead of light.

But enough of metaphor and declamation: it is not by such means that moral science is to be improved.

II. *Principle of utility, what.* The principle of utility is the foundation of the present work: it will be proper therefore at the outset to give an explicit and determinate account of what is meant by it. By the principle of utility is meant that principle which approves or disapproves of every action whatsoever, according to the tendency which it appears to have to augment or diminish the happiness of the party whose interest is in question: or, what is the same thing in other words, to promote or to oppose that happiness. I say of every action whatsoever; and therefore not only of every action of a private individual, but of every measure of government.

III. *Utility, what.* By utility is meant that property in any object, whereby it tends to produce benefit, advantage, pleasure, good, or happiness, (all this in the present case comes to the same thing) or (what comes again to the same thing) to prevent the happening of mischief, pain, evil, or unhappiness to the party whose interest is considered: if that party be the community in general, then the happiness of the community: if a particular individual, then the happiness of that individual.

IV. *Interest of the community, what.* The interest of the community is one of the most general expressions that can occur in the phraseology of morals: no wonder that the meaning of it is often lost. When it has a meaning, it is this. The community is a fictitious *body,* composed of the individual persons who are considered as constituting as it were its *members.* The interest of the community then is, what?—the sum of the interests of the several members who compose it.

V. It is in vain to talk of the interest of the community, without understanding what is the interest of the individual. A thing is said to promote the interest, or to be *for* the interest, of an individual, when it tends to add to the sum total of his pleasures: or, what comes to the same thing, to diminish the sum total of his pains.

VI. *An action conformable to the principle of utility, what.* An action then may be said to be conformable to the principle of utility, or, for shortness sake, to utility, (meaning with respect to the community at large) when the tendency it has to augment the happiness of the community is greater than any it has to diminish it.

VII. *A measure of government conformable to the principle of utility, what.* A measure of government (which is but a particular kind of action, performed by a particular person or persons) may be said to be conformable to or dictated by the principle of utility, when in like manner the tendency which it has to augment the happiness of the community is greater than any which it has to diminish it.

VIII. *Laws or dictates of utility, what.* When an action, or in particular a measure of government, is supposed by a man to be conformable to the principle of utility, it may be convenient, for the purposes of discourse, to imagine a kind of law or dictate, called a law or dictate of utility: and to speak of the action in question, as being conformable to such law or dictate.

IX. *A partizan of the principle of utility, who.* A man may be said to be a partizan of the principle of utility, when the approbation or disapprobation he annexes to any action, or to any measure, is determined by and proportioned to the tendency which he conceives it to have to augment or to diminish the happiness of the community: or in other words, to its conformity or unconformity to the laws or dictates of utility.

X. *Ought, ought not, right and wrong, &c. how to be understood.* Of an action that is conformable to the principle of utility one may always say either that it is one that ought to be done, or at least that it is not one that ought not to be done. One may say also, that it is right it should be done; at least that it is not wrong it should be done: that it is a right action; at least that it is not a wrong action. When thus interpreted, the words *ought,* and *right* and *wrong,* and others of that stamp, have a meaning: when otherwise, they have none.

Study Questions

1. Identify the concept of moral right and wrong as defined by the principle of utility. Do you approve of such a definition? Why or why not?

2. How does Bentham identify the concept of "community"? Evaluate Bentham's statement in terms of possible political consequences. Do you agree with him? Why or why not?

3. In your opinion, is Bentham right in stating that pain and pleasure govern us in everything we do?

4. Some scholars see Bentham as one short step removed from ethical egoism. Why? Is that a fair assessment?

Primary Reading

Utilitarianism

JOHN STUART MILL

Excerpt, 1863.

In this section Mill outlines the idea of a test of higher and lower pleasures according to the judgment of those who know and appreciate both kinds. He then speaks of the true nature of happiness, as he sees it: a feeling that has little to do with pleasure seeking and much to do with the joy of contributing to the common good.

It is quite compatible with the principle of utility to recognize the fact, that some *kinds* of pleasure are more desirable and more valuable than others. It would be absurd that while, in estimating all other things, quality is considered as well as quantity, the estimation of pleasures should be supposed to depend on quantity alone.

If I am asked what I mean by difference of quality in pleasures, or what makes one pleasure more valuable than another merely as a pleasure, except its being greater in amount, there is but one possible answer. Of two pleasures, if there be one to which all or almost all who have experience of both give a decided preference, irrespective of any feeling of moral obligation to prefer it, that is the more desirable pleasure. If one of the two is, by those who are competently acquainted with both, placed so far above the other that they prefer it, even though knowing it to be attended with a greater amount of discontent, and would not resign it for any quantity of the other pleasure which their nature is capable of, we are justified in ascribing to the preferred enjoyment a superiority in quality, so far outweighing quantity as to render it, in comparison, of small account.

Now it is an unquestionable fact that those who are equally acquainted with, and equally capable of appreciating and enjoying, both, do give a most marked preference to the manner of existence which employs their higher faculties. Few human creatures would consent to be changed into any of the lower animals, for a promise of the fullest allowance of a beast's pleasures; no intelligent human being would consent to be a fool, no instructed person would be an ignoramus, no person of feeling and conscience would be selfish and base, even though they should be persuaded that the fool, the dunce, or the rascal is better satisfied with his lot than they are with theirs. They would not resign what they possess more than he for the most complete satisfaction of all the desires which they have in common with him. If they ever fancy they would, it is only in cases of unhappiness so extreme, that to escape from it they would exchange their lot for almost any other, however undesirable in their own eyes. A being of higher faculties requires more to make him happy, is capable probably of more acute suffering, and certainly accessible to it at more points, than one of an inferior type; but in spite of these liabilities, he can never really wish to sink into what he feels to be a lower grade of existence. We may give what explanation we please of this unwillingness: we may attribute it to pride, a name which is given indiscriminately to some of the most and to some of the least estimable feelings of which mankind are capable; we may refer it to the love of liberty and personal independence, an appeal to which was with the Stoics one of the most effective means for the inculcation of it; to the love of power, or to the love of excitement, both of which do really enter into and contribute to it: but its most appropriate appellation is a sense of dignity, which all human beings possess in one form or other, and in some, though by no means in exact, proportion to their higher faculties, and which is so essential a part of the happiness of those in whom it is strong, that nothing which conflicts with it could be, otherwise than momentarily, an object of desire to them. Whoever supposes that this preference takes place at a sacrifice of happiness—that the superior being, in anything like equal circumstances, is not happier than the inferior—confounds the two very different ideas, of *happiness* and *content*. It is indisputable that the being whose capacities of enjoyment are low, has the greatest chance of having them fully satisfied; and a highly endowed being will always feel that any happiness which he can look for, as the world is constituted, is imperfect. But he can learn to bear its imperfections, if they are at all bearable; and they will not make him envy the being who is indeed unconscious of the imperfections, but only because he feels not at all the good which those imperfections qualify. It is better to be a human being dissatisfied than a pig satisfied; better to be Socrates dissatisfied than a fool satisfied. And if the fool, or the pig, are of a different opinion, it is because they only know their own side of the question. The other party to the comparison knows both sides. . . .

According to the "greatest happiness principle,". . . the ultimate end, with reference to and for the sake of which all other things are desirable (whether we are considering our own good or that of other people), is an existence exempt as far as possible from pain, and as rich as possible in enjoyments, both in point of quantity and quality; the test of quality, and the rule for measuring it against quantity, being the preference felt by those who in their opportunities of experience, to which must be added their habits of self-consciousness and self-observation, are best furnished with the means of comparison. This, being, according to the utilitarian opinion, the end of human action, is necessarily also the standard of morality; which may accordingly be defined, the rules and precepts for human conduct, by the observance of which an existence such as has been described might be, to the greatest extent possible, secured to all mankind; and not to them only, but, so far as the nature of things admits, to the whole sentient creation. . . .

If by happiness be meant a continuity of highly pleasurable excitement, it is evident enough that this is impossible. A state of exalted pleasure lasts only moments, or in some cases, and with some intermissions, hours or days, and is the occasional brilliant flash of enjoyment, not its permanent and steady flame. Of this the philosophers who have taught that happiness is the end of life were as fully aware as those who taunt them. The happiness which they meant was not a life of rapture; but moments of such, in an existence made up of few and transitory pains, many and various pleasures, with a decided predominance of the active over the passive, and having as the foundation of the whole, not to expect more from life than it is capable of bestowing. A life thus composed, to those who have been fortunate enough to obtain it, has always appeared worthy of the name of happiness. And such an existence is even now the lot of many, during some considerable portion of their lives. The present wretched education, and wretched social arrangements, are the only real hindrance to its being attainable by almost all.

In a world in which there is so much to interest, so much to enjoy, and so much also to correct and improve, everyone who has [a] moderate amount of moral and intellectual requisites is capable of an existence which may be called enviable; and unless such a person, through bad laws or subjection to the will of others, is denied the liberty to use the sources of happiness within his reach, he will not fail to find this enviable existence, if he escape the positive evils of life, the great sources of physical and mental suffering—such as indigence, disease, and the unkindness, worthlessness, or premature loss of an affection. The main stress of the problem lies, therefore, in the contest with these calamities from which it is a rare good fortune entirely to escape; which, as things are now, cannot be obviated, and often cannot be in any material degree mitigated. Yet no one whose opinion deserves a moment's consideration can doubt that most of the great positive evils of the world are in themselves removable, and will, if human affairs continue to improve, be in the end reduced within narrow limits. . . .

As for vicissitudes of fortune, and other disappointments connected with worldly circumstances, these are principally the effect either of gross imprudence, of ill-regulated desires, or of bad or imperfect social institutions. All the grand sources, in short, of human suffering are in a great degree, many of them almost entirely, conquerable by human care and effort; and though their removal is grievously slow—though a long succession of generations will perish in the breach before the conquest is completed, and this world becomes all that, if will and knowledge were not wanting, it might easily be made—yet every mind sufficiently intelligent and generous to bear a part, however small and unconspicuous, in the endeavor, will draw a noble enjoyment from the contest itself, which he would not for any bribe in the form of selfish indulgence consent to be without.

And this leads to the true estimation of what is said by the objectors concerning the possibility, and the obligation, of learning to do without happiness. Unquestionably it is possible to do without happiness; it is done involuntarily by nineteen-twentieths of mankind, even in those parts of our present world which are least deep in barbarism; and it often has to be done voluntarily by the hero or the martyr, for the sake of something which he prizes more than his individual happiness. But this something, what is it, unless the happiness of others, or some of the requisites of happiness? It is noble to be capable of resigning entirely one's own portion of happiness, or chances of it: but, after all, this self-sacrifice must be for some end; it is not its own end; and if we are told that its end is not happiness, but virtue, which is better than happiness, I ask, would the sacrifice be made if the hero or martyr did not believe that it would earn for others immunity from similar sacrifices? Would it be made if he thought that his renunciation of happiness for himself would produce no fruit for any of his fellow creatures, but to make their lot like his, and place them also in the condition of persons who have renounced happiness? All honor to those who can abnegate for themselves the personal enjoyment of life, when by such renunciation they contribute worthily to increase the amount of happiness in the world; but he who does it, or professes to do it, for any other purpose, is no more deserving of admiration from the ascetic mounted on his pillar. He may be an inspiriting proof of what men *can* do, but assuredly not an example of what they *should*.

Study Questions

1. Do you agree with Mill that "a being of higher faculties requires more to make him happy . . . than one of an inferior type"?

2. What might be Ayn Rand's comment on the excerpt?

3. What does Mill mean by "the whole sentient creation"?

4. Comment on the meaning of this passage: "It is better to be a human being dissatisfied than a pig satisfied; better to be Socrates dissatisfied than a fool satisfied." What does Mill mean? Do you agree? Why or why not?

Primary Reading

A Convenient Truth

PETER SINGER

Article, **New York Times,** *January 26, 2007.*

The topic of this essay is a controversial case that arose in 2006: The parents of a severely disabled little girl, Ashley, went public with their belief that it would be in her best interest to receive surgery and hormonal treatment to restrict her growth so that her parents could continue to carry her and so that she would not develop sexually. Singer argues that as much as people may find this kind of intervention distasteful, it is in the utilitarian spirit. Since Singer is a utilitarian, he approves of the procedure, stating that it will limit her suffering and enhance a life she is capable of enjoying. In the final paragraphs, Singer brings up the question of whether dignity should be a matter of membership in the human race.

Peter Singer (born 1946) is an Australian philosopher who has taught at Princeton University since 1999. Arguably the most controversial of all modern philosophers, Singer has defended his utilitarian views on euthanasia, animal rights, global welfare, and other issues in books, articles, and op-ed pieces, and on television. His most famous books include *Animal Liberation* (1975), *Practical Ethics* (1979), *The Expanding Circle* (1981), and *One World: Ethics and Globalization* (2002). In addition, he has created The Great Ape Project in collaboration with Paola Cavalieri, which advocates three basic rights for the Great Apes: the right not to be killed, the right to liberty, and the right not to be tortured.

Can it be ethical for a young girl to be treated with hormones so she will remain below normal height and weight, to have her uterus removed and to have surgery on her breasts so they will not develop? Such treatment, applied to a profoundly intellectually disabled girl known only as Ashley, has led to criticism of Ashley's parents, of the doctors who carried out the treatment, and of the ethics committee at Seattle Children's Hospital, which approved it.

Ashley is 9, but her mental age has never progressed beyond that of a 3-month-old. She cannot walk, talk, hold a toy or change her position in bed. Her parents are not sure she recognizes them. She is expected to have a normal lifespan, but her mental condition will never improve.

In a blog, Ashley's parents explain that her treatment is not for their convenience but to improve her quality of life. If she remains small and light, they will be able to continue to move her around frequently and take her along when they go out with their other two children. The hysterectomy will spare her the discomfort of menstrual cramps, and the surgery to prevent the development of breasts, which tend to be large in her family, will make her more comfortable whether lying down or strapped across the chest in her wheelchair.

All this is plausible, even if it is also true that the line between improving Ashley's life and making it easier for her parents to handle her scarcely exists, because anything that makes it possible for Ashley's parents to involve her in family life is in her interest.

The objections to Ashley's treatment take three forms familiar to anyone working in bioethics. First, some say Ashley's treatment is "unnatural"—a complaint that usually means little more than "Yuck!" One could equally well object that all medical treatment is unnatural, for it enables us to live longer, and in better health, than we naturally would. During most of human existence, children like Ashley were abandoned to become prey to wolves and jackals. Abandonment may be a "natural" fate for a severely disabled baby, but it is no better for that reason.

Second, some see acceptance of Ashley's treatment as the first step down a slippery slope leading to widespread medical modification of children for the convenience of their parents. But the ethics committee that approved Ashley's treatment was convinced that the procedures were in her best interest. Those of us who have not heard the evidence presented to the committee are in a weak position to contest its judgment.

In any case, the "best interest" principle is the right test to use, and there is no reason that other parents of children with intellectual disabilities as profound as Ashley's should not have access to similar treatments, if they will also be in the interest of their children. If there is a slippery slope here, the much more widespread use of drugs in "problem" children who are diagnosed as having attention deficit hyperactivity disorder poses a far greater risk than attenuating growth in a small number of profoundly disabled children.

Finally, there is the issue of treating Ashley with dignity. A Los Angeles Times report on Ashley's treatment began: "This is about Ashley's dignity. Everybody examining her case seems to agree at least about that." Her parents write in their blog that Ashley will have more dignity in a body that is healthier and more suited to her state of development, while their critics see her treatment as a violation of her dignity.

But we should reject the premise of this debate. As a parent and grandparent, I find 3-month-old babies adorable, but not dignified. Nor do I believe that getting bigger and older, while remaining at the same mental level, would do anything to change that.

Here's where things get philosophically interesting. We are always ready to find dignity in human beings, including those whose mental age will never exceed that of an infant, but we don't attribute dignity to dogs or cats, though they clearly operate at a more advanced mental level than human infants. Just making that comparison provokes outrage in some quarters. But why should dignity always go together with species membership, no matter what the characteristics of the individual may be?

What matters in Ashley's life is that she should not suffer, and that she should be able to enjoy whatever she is capable of enjoying. Beyond that, she is precious not so much for what she is, but because her parents and siblings love her and care about her. Lofty talk about human dignity should not stand in the way of children like her getting the treatment that is best both for them and their families.

Study Questions

1. Identify the utilitarian aspects of Singer's argument. Would Bentham agree? Would John Stuart Mill? Explain why.

2. In your view, would the surgery and hormonal treatment be in Ashley's best interest? Explain why or why not.

3. Comment on Singer's remark that dignity shouldn't necessarily be exclusively associated with "species membership." What does he mean? Would you agree? Why or why not?

Narrative

The Blacksmith and the Baker

JOHANN HERMAN WESSEL

Poem, 1777. Loosely translated from Danish, from verse to prose. Summary and Excerpt.

Wessel is famous in his own country of Denmark for his satirical verses. This one may have been inspired by a real newspaper story or possibly by British fables.

"The Blacksmith and the Baker," illustration by Nils Wiwel, 1895. Utilitarianism taken to an extreme: The baker is led away to be executed for what the blacksmith has done, because that is more useful to society. The policeman's belt reads "Honest and Faithful," and the building in the background is the old Copenhagen courthouse with the inscription "With Law Must Land Be Built."

Once upon a time there was a small town where the town blacksmith was a mean man. He had an enemy, and one day he and his enemy happened to meet at an inn. They proceeded to get drunk and exchange some nasty words. The blacksmith grew angry and knocked the other man out; the blow turned out to be fatal. The blacksmith was carted off to jail, and he confessed, hoping that his opponent would forgive him in Heaven. Before his sentence was pronounced, four upstanding citizens asked to see the judge, and the most eloquent of them spoke:

"Your Wisdom, we know you are thinking of the welfare of this town, but this welfare depends on getting our blacksmith back. His death won't wake up the dead man, and we'll never find such a good blacksmith ever again."

The judge said, "But a life has been taken and must be paid for by a life. . . ."

"We have in town an old and scrawny baker who'll go to the devil soon, and since we have two bakers, how about taking the oldest one? Then you still get a life for a life."

"Well," said the judge, "that is not a bad idea, I'll do what I can." And he leafed through his law books but found nothing that said you can't execute a baker instead of a blacksmith, so he pronounced this sentence:

"We know that blacksmith Jens has no excuse for what he has done, sending Anders Petersen off to eternity; but since we have but one blacksmith in this town I would be crazy if I wanted him dead; but we do have two bakers of bread . . . so the oldest one must pay for the murder."

The old baker wept pitifully when they took him away. The moral of the story: Be always prepared to die! It comes when you least expect it.

Study Questions

1. Do you think this is a fair picture of a utilitarian judge?

2. How might the utilitarian respond to this story?

3. Return to this story after reading Chapter 6 and consider: How might a Kantian respond?

Narrative

The Brothers Karamazov

FYODOR DOSTOYEVSKY

Novel, 1881. Film, 1958. Summary and Excerpt.

(This excerpt should be read in conjunction with the narrative "The Ones Who Walk Away from Omelas," which follows.)

The story of the brothers Karamazov, one of the most famous in Russian literature, is about four half-brothers and their father, an unpleasant, old, corrupt scoundrel. The brothers are very different in nature; the oldest son, Dmitri, is a rogue and a pleasure-seeker; the next son, Ivan, is intelligent and politically engaged; the third son, Alyosha, is gentle and honest; and the fourth son, Smerdyakov, was born outside marriage and never recognized as a proper son. When a murder happens, each son in turn finds himself under suspicion.

Here, Ivan is telling Alyosha a story:

"It was in the darkest days of serfdom at the beginning of the century. . . . There was in those days a general of aristocratic connections, the owner of great estates, one of those men—somewhat exceptional, I believe, even then—who, retiring from the service into a life of leisure, are convinced that they've earned absolute power over the lives of their subjects. There were such men then. So our general, settled on his property of two thousand souls, lives in pomp, and dominates his poor neighbors as though they were dependents. He has kennels of hundreds of hounds and nearly a hundred dog-boys—all mounted, and in uniform. One day a serf boy, a little child of eight, threw a stone in play and hurt the paw of the general's favorite hound. 'Why is my favorite dog lame?' He is told that the boy threw a stone that hurt the dog's paw. 'So you did it.' The general looked the child up and down. 'Take him.' He was taken—taken from his mother and kept shut up all night. Early the next morning the general comes out on horseback, with the hounds, his dependents, dog-boys, and huntsmen, all mounted around him in full hunting parade. The servants are summoned for their edification, and in front of them all stands the mother of the child. The child is brought forward. It's a gloomy cold, foggy autumn day, a perfect day for hunting. The general orders the child to be undressed. The child is stripped naked. He shivers, numb with terror, not daring to cry. . . . 'Make him run,' commands the general. 'Run, run!' shout the dog-boys. The boy runs. . . . 'At him!' yells the general, and he sets the whole pack of hounds after the child. The hounds catch him, and tear him to pieces before his mother's eyes! . . . I believe the general was afterwards declared incapable of administering his estates. Well—what did he deserve? To be shot? To be shot for the satisfaction of our moral feelings? Speak, Alyosha!

"Tell me yourself, I challenge you—answer. Imagine that you are creating a fabric of human destiny with the object of making men happy in the end, giving them peace and rest at last. Imagine that you are doing this but that it is essential and inevitable to torture to death only one tiny creature—that child beating its breast with its fist, for instance—in order to found that edifice on its unavenged tears. Would you consent to be the architect on those conditions? Tell me. Tell the truth."

"No, I wouldn't consent," said Alyosha softly.

"And can you accept the idea that the men for whom you are building would agree to receive their happiness from the unatoned blood of a little victim? And accepting it would remain happy forever?"

"No, I can't admit it," said Alyosha suddenly, with flashing eyes.

Here Ivan and Alyosha are engaged in a discussion about the meaning of life: If God does not exist, then what? Then everything is permissible. But what if our highest moral aim is to make the majority happy? Do the means always justify the end? If the suffering of a child could somehow create general happiness and harmony, should its mother forgive those who caused it to suffer?

Study Questions

1. Answer Ivan's question: Would you agree to make humankind happy at the cost of a child's suffering? Explain how a utilitarian might answer, and then explain your own answer.

2. Should the mother ever forgive the general for murdering her son?

3. Return to this story after reading Chapter 6 and consider: How might a Kantian respond?

Narrative

The Ones Who Walk Away from Omelas

URSULA K. LE GUIN

Short story, 1973. Summary and Excerpt.

There is a festival in the city of Omelas. The weather is beautiful, the city looks its best, and people are happy and serene in their pretty clothes. This is a perfect place, with freedom of choice and no oppressive power enforcing the rules of religion, politics, or morality—and it works, because the people know they are responsible for their actions. This place is a Utopia, except for one thing: The happiness of the citizens is bought at a high price, with the full knowledge of every citizen.

> In a basement under one of the beautiful public buildings of Omelas, or perhaps in the cellar of one of its spacious private homes, there is a room. It has one locked door, and no window. A little light seeps in dustily between cracks in the boards, secondhand from a cobwebbed window somewhere across the cellar. In one corner of the little room a couple of mops, with stiff, clotted, foul-smelling heads, stand near a rusty bucket. . . . The room is about three paces long and two wide: a mere broom closet or disused tool room. In the room a child is sitting. It could be a boy or a girl. It looks about six, but actually is nearly ten. It is feeble-minded. Perhaps it was born defective, or perhaps it has become imbecile through fear, malnutrition, and neglect. It picks its nose and occasionally fumbles vaguely with its toes or genitals, as it sits hunched in the corner farthest from the bucket and the two mops. It is afraid of the mops. It finds them horrible. It shuts its eyes, but it knows the mops are still standing there; and the door is locked; and nobody will come. The door is always locked; and nobody ever comes, except that sometimes . . . the door rattles terribly and opens, and a person, or several people, are there. . . . The people at the door never say anything, but the child, who has not always lived in the tool room, and can remember sunlight and its mother's voice, sometimes speaks. "I will be good," it says. "Please let me out. I will be good!" They never answer.

All this is part of a greater plan. The child will never be let out—it will die within a short time—and presumably another child will take its place, for it is the suffering of this innocent being that makes the perfect life in Omelas possible. All the citizens know about it from the time they are adolescents, and they all must go and see the child so that they can understand the price of their happiness. They are disgusted and sympathetic for a while, but then they understand the master plan: the pain of one small individual in exchange for great communal happiness. Because the citizens know the immense suffering that gives them their beautiful life, they are particularly loving to one another and responsible for what they do. And what would they gain by setting the child free? The child is too far gone to be able to enjoy freedom, anyway, and what is one person's suffering compared with the realm of happiness that is achieved? So the people feel no guilt. However, a few young people and some adult visitors go to see the child, and something happens to them: They don't go home afterward, but keep on walking—through the city, through the fields, away from Omelas.

Study Questions

1. Where are they going, the ones who walk away? And why are they leaving?

2. How does Le Guin feel about the situation? Does she condone the suffering of the child, or is she arguing against it? Is the story realistic or symbolic?

3. How would an act utilitarian evaluate the story of Omelas? Would a rule utilitarian reach the same conclusion or a different one? Why?

4. Return to this story after reading Chapter 6 and develop a deontological critique of the people of Omelas (those who don't walk away).

5. In the film *Swordfish* a similar question is raised: "Would you kill a child to save the world?" However, in Omelas it is not a question of saving the world, just the happiness of all. In light of the discussion about "sheer numbers," would it make a difference to you if the torturous death of the child did indeed save the world and not just people's contentment? If yes, explain while focusing on where you would draw the line. If no, explain why not.

 Narrative

 Extreme Measures

TONY GILROY (SCREENWRITER)

MICHAEL APTED (DIRECTOR)

Film, 1996. Based on a novel by Michael Palma. Summary.

A young British emergency room doctor, Guy Luthan, is faced with a terrible moral and professional choice: In his emergency room, two patients need urgent care. One is a police officer who has been shot, and the other is the man who shot him, a troublemaker who pulled a gun on a bus. He was in turn shot by the cop. The officer is barely stabilized, whereas the gunman is in critical condition. There is only one surgery slot available. Whom should Guy choose? He needs to decide immediately. He sends the police officer into surgery and lets the gunman wait his turn. As it happens, they both survive, but a young nurse, Jodie, blames Guy for making an unprofessional moral choice: The gunman's medical needs were more urgent than the cop's. Guy explains, "I had to make a choice; on my right I see a cop with his wife in the corridor and pictures of his kids in his wallet, and on my left some guy who's taken out a gun on a city bus! I had ten seconds to make a choice, I had to make it—I hope I made the right one. I think I did, oh shit, maybe I didn't . . . I don't know."

This sets the scene for what could be just a run-of-the-mill hospital suspense story but turns out to be an honest exploration of the principle of utility as a social, moral, and psychological justification.

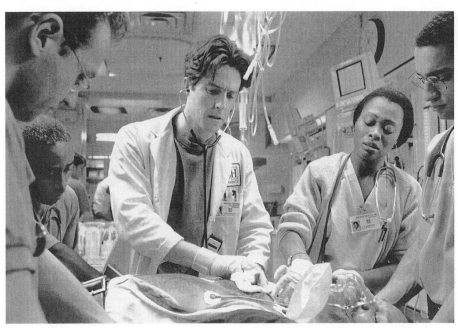

The film *Extreme Measures* (Castle Rock, 1996) notes that sometimes we must make hard moral choices; the question is, What criterion should we use? Should we do what is right, regardless of the consequences, or should we try to obtain the best result for as many as possible with the least harm caused? This is the dilemma facing Dr. Guy Luthan (Hugh Grant), not only in his own career, but also as the pawn in a greater plot orchestrated by a famous doctor: to use homeless people as guinea pigs. Here Guy has to choose whether to save the life of a police officer with a wife and kids or the gunman who shot the officer in cold blood.

Guy has just received a fellowship in neurology at New York University. This means much to him and his family, because his father in England, once a medical doctor, lost his license to practice after euthanizing an old friend—another moral choice with consequences.

Meanwhile, a patient is brought to Guy's emergency room from the street, half naked and in complete physical and mental breakdown. He has a hospital bracelet on, and, in a lucid moment before he dies, he says two things to Guy—the word *triphase* and the name of a friend. Not understanding the cause of death, Guy orders an autopsy, but the hospital loses track not only of the autopsy but also of the body itself. Guy feels that something is terribly wrong and pursues the dead man's records on his own. The man had been admitted to the hospital previously for a neurological examination. Other patients turn up in the computer with the same profile: homeless, without relatives, having lab work done, and all files on them deleted.

But Guy is in for another shock: His apartment has been burglarized, and the detectives investigating the burglary find a stash of drugs in his place. Guy is arrested. Since Guy doesn't do drugs, he realizes that the burglary was a ruse and that the drugs were planted to discredit him, to get him out of the way—by whom? Whoever it is, their plan succeeds;

Guy manages to raise bail, but once out of jail, he is suspended from his hospital position—his colleagues and supervisors assume that he is guilty. This also means that his fellowship to NYU will be lost because he will no longer be able to practice medicine—just like his father. Compelled to seek the truth, Guy locates a patient of his among the homeless and soon finds himself in a world underground in the subway system, where the homeless and destitute have made a world for themselves. Here he finds another piece of the puzzle: Doctors have been preying on the homeless, subjecting them to experiments leading to great suffering and death. But Guy himself is now being hunted in a prolonged chase, and just as he thinks he has found refuge with a friend, he is rendered unconscious.

Guy wakes up in a hospital bed—and to his horror, he finds himself paralyzed from the neck down. He is told that the blow he sustained to his spine severed it, and he will be a quadriplegic for life. Realizing the enormity of what has happened to him, Guy feels that, having no hope of recovery, he might as well be dead. The famous neurologist Dr. Myrick now pays him a visit, talking enigmatically about hope. What if there were hope for him after all? What would it be worth to him to return to his old life? What would he risk if a procedure were available? Guy answers, "Anything!" Myrick replies, "You'd better think about that."

Who is responsible for the burglary, the planted drugs, the disappearance of the homeless, and the attempt on Guy's life? The answer lies within Guy's own hospital environment. When Guy's paralysis miraculously wears off after 24 hours, he realizes he'd been drugged, and that it is Dr. Myrick, passionately engaged in helping victims of spinal cord injury, who has undertaken research into spinal cord regeneration by using homeless patients as guinea pigs for the good of humanity.

Guy now tries to escape from the hospital. This is a pivotal scene in the film, and I will not spoil the surprise twists for you. During a dramatic moment, Myrick tries to explain his actions to Guy: The homeless men he experimented on were useless beings—but now they are heroes, since their deaths have given hope to so many injured people. "Good doctors do the correct thing. Great doctors have the guts to do the right thing. . . . If you could cure cancer by killing one person, wouldn't you have to do it? Wouldn't it be the brave thing to do? One person, and it's gone tomorrow?" Guy replies that perhaps the homeless people he used weren't worth much, but they didn't choose to be heroes—he never asked for volunteers. To Guy, doctors can't do that—Myrick has been playing God.

One final confrontation remains—one that solves some issues but raises others. In the end, Guy is given all of Myrick's files from his research into spinal cord injuries . . . and Guy does not reject the files.

Study Questions

1. Discuss the opening scene. Did Guy make the right professional choice? the right moral choice? Should there be a difference? Explain your position.

2. Is Dr. Myrick's experimentation a noble quest to help humanity or a perverse abuse of human beings? Is there a third alternative? Explain your position.

3. Dr. Myrick asks Guy what he would be willing to do to regain his mobility at a time when Guy believes himself to be paralyzed for life. What does Guy answer, and why is this scene so important?

4. Guy accuses Myrick of playing God. Guy's own father lost his license to practice medicine because he euthanized a friend. Do you think there is a connection here, or is this a coincidence in the film?

5. In the end, Guy takes over Myrick's research papers. Is this gesture an acceptance of Myrick's utilitarian principles, or is there another possibility? By accepting the papers, have Guy's hands now been dirtied? Why or why not?

6. Is this a pro-utilitarian or an anti-utilitarian film? Explain.

7. The scene where Guy makes his decision in the ER and Myrick's explanation of his medical experiments are deliberately set up as parallels. What are the similarities, and what are the differences? Does the discussion in the chapter text about the hedonistic calculus as a *last resort* provide us with a tool for distinguishing between Guy and Myrick?

8. Scientists have announced that they believe great strides can be made toward curing paralysis through stem cell research. Given that the stem cells originated in a human embryo, do you think there is a difference between Myrick's experiments on homeless people for the sake of helping patients with paralysis and using stem cells from an embryo to accomplish the same thing? Explain similarities and differences.

Narrative

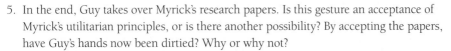

Runaway Jury

BRIAN KOPPELMAN (SCREENWRITER)
GARY FLEDER (DIRECTOR)

Film, 2003. Based on the novel by John Grisham. Summary.

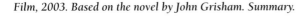

This film is an exceptionally good illustration of the viewpoint that *the end justifies the means*—a utilitarian view, as long as the majority benefits from the consequences. Since this, in a way, applies to the film itself, it means that we have to include the ending in this summary, reluctant though I am to do so.

Jacob Wood celebrates his young son's birthday and goes to work in his New Orleans office—only to be gunned down, together with other coworkers. The gunman then turns the gun on himself. Two years later, Wood's widow is taking Vicksburg Firearms, the manufacturers of the gun used in the massacre, to court in a civil trial, asking for damages, although it is clear that no laws were broken in the sale of the firearm. Within the context of the film, nobody has yet taken gun manufacturers to court and won; and at the beginning of the film, we learn that the lawyer for the plaintiff, Wendell Rohr, while being a practical man with legal savvy, is also an idealist: He confesses to Mrs. Wood that he wants to change the gun laws. He hires an enthusiastic young legal aide, not just because he knows the young man has a good legal background, but also because he is impressed with his idealism: The young man believes in "a world without guns."

Meanwhile, the defense team is busy profiling potential jurors, tapping into their backgrounds and records, setting up a war room with electronics, illegal listening devices, video surveillance, and so forth; and we get the impression that they'll stop at nothing to win this case. They rig their defense counsel with a hidden video camera during the *voir dire* (the jury screening process) so that—unbeknownst to the judge—the high-powered jury consultant Rankin Fitch can okay or nix potential jurors from the war room. And Fitch is good—on his way from the airport he profiled the cab driver, accurately describing his home life. He proclaims that he hates Democrats and Baptists, and later he has a conversation with the gun manufacturer, who says, "Trials are too important to be left up to juries."

One of those potential jurors is a young man named Nick; he appears to be upset at the prospect of having to serve on a jury, but when he gets the summons, he says, cryptically, "Christmas comes early this year." And when he and his girlfriend contemplate their own giant display board of potential jurors, we realize that Nick wants to be on this jury very badly. During the *voir dire,* Fitch sees no problem with him, nobody objects, and he is in. Immediately, Nick begins a subtle manipulation of his fellow jurors; he suggests a blind juror as the jury foreman, he manages to get the judge to buy them all a fancy lunch, and he wins their sympathy by telling them about a friend who died in the Gulf War. Meanwhile, his girlfriend, Marlee, is carrying out her part of the plan: She has letters delivered to both the prosecution and the defense, offering to deliver a verdict through jury manipulation—for a price: "Jury for sale."

In the opening statement, Rohr tells the jury that gun violence happens because of accessibility of guns, and gun manufacturers must be held accountable. We don't hear the opening statement of the defense lawyer, but we do see Fitch on an outdoor shooting range with the gun manufacturer, who has heard about the "Jury for Sale" note—and is worried, because he thought he already bought the jury, by hiring Fitch. Fitch suspects that Nick is involved, so he orders a henchman, Doyle, to break into Nick's place to find incriminating material—only to find that the incident has been videotaped by Nick. A power play ensues between Nick and Fitch: Nick gets a juror booted, and Fitch puts pressure on several jurors, threatening to reveal their personal secrets.

Nick and Marlee have a heart-to-heart talk in a church: A juror has tried to commit suicide because of the pressure, Nick's apartment has been torched by Fitch's people—is it worth it? What worries Nick is not the moral issue of their undertaking, though, but concerns for Marlee's safety.

Fitch's assistant Doyle has come up with amazing news: Nick has been compiling lists of juries from previous gun lawsuits, in 2000, 1999, and 1998, and has been close to being on a gun lawsuit jury once before, but under another name—an identity that evaporates into thin air but leads to another name: Jeff Curr. In the meantime, Marlee has approached both Fitch and Rohr, offering to swing the jury their way for $10 million. When Rohr's key witness, a gun manufacturer employee, doesn't show up in court (because the defense got to him), Rohr is tempted to accept Marlee's offer. In a pivotal scene, we see Rohr confronting Fitch in the men's room at the courthouse over the missing key witness. Fitch calls Rohr "a moral man, living in a world of moral relativity," and admits that he isn't fighting a battle for the Second Amendment (because he has taken on many cases, defending the gun industry), but to *win*—to do what he has been hired to do. Rohr points out that Fitch will lose, eventually, because he has nothing but contempt for people. And next time Rohr talks with Marlee, he rejects her offer—his moral compass is on track again.

In court, things aren't going well for Fitch either. The gun manufacturer is put on the witness stand and loses his temper, so now Fitch wants to make a deal with Marlee. He and Nick have a secret meeting where they agree on the terms, and Fitch is content because he perceives that Nick is of his own kind—an "agnostic" about the law. In a twist to the story, Marlee raises the price to $15 million, because of an attack by one of Fitch's men; Fitch agrees and wires the money to Marlee. But Doyle has found out much more about Nick and Marlee—too late to do Fitch any good: Their real names are Jeff Curr and Gabby Grant, from Gardner, Indiana; Gabby's sister was gunned down in the school yard some years ago, in front of Jeff and Gabby, who were unable to do anything. Since then, however, they have been trying to make a difference and get guns banned, any which way they can. So the primary goal has never been the money but justice for Marlee/Gabby's sister.

While this is going on, the jury is finally deliberating, out of reach of Fitch and Rohr, but with Nick in the thick of it. Most of the jurors are leaning toward not convicting the gun manufacturer, because that is in compliance with the law, but Nick is able to show that the primary spokesman for this view is against a conviction for self-serving reasons. And from here on, Nick asks the jurors to just consider the facts—although we hear no more about what goes on in the jury room, the result is a groundbreaking verdict for the plaintiff, $110 million to Mrs. Wood in damages. Fitch, who is out $15 million with a jury that didn't swing his way, is devastated. Later, in a bar he is confronted by Nick and Marlee, and now we hear the whole story: They were trying not only to win a case against gun manufacturers but also to beat Fitch—because he was to blame for the gun manufacturers winning the case brought against them after Marlee's sister's death. And Nick explains that he didn't swing any votes, but just "let them vote their hearts" and prevented Fitch from stealing their votes. And now Fitch's career is ruined, because he attempted to buy the jury.

At the end, we see Marlee and Nick at a school yard near the court house, and we know they're thinking about justice for the dead sister. Rohr is leaving the courthouse, their eyes meet, and they smile; Rohr shrugs, smiles, gets into his car, and drives off.

Study Questions

1. Jury members who consider facts and render a verdict based on those facts are voting with their *heads,* not their *hearts.* What do you think of Nick's appealing to the jurors' emotions, rather than to their reason?

2. Evaluate the presentations of the plaintiff and defense teams: Rohr is a man of principle, and Fitch has no principles other than to win cases for his clients. How does that play into the gun control theme of the film? Does it matter to your evaluation of the film whether you are in favor of gun control or gun rights?

3. Just for the sake of readers who may not be familiar with the Second Amendment, here it is: "A well-regulated Militia being necessary to the security of a free State, the right of the people to keep and bear arms shall not be infringed." Throughout the film

it is clear that the filmmakers want us to side with the plaintiff and gun control advocates. Hardly any time is given to a thorough representation of the Second Amendment. Does it matter to you that the film is not representing both views fairly? Why or why not?

4. One might say that two questions are being raised here: (1) Can juries be bought? and (2) Should they be bought? In other words, the film offers a *descriptive* and a *normative* angle. How does the film answer both questions? Do you agree? Why or why not?

5. According to the filmmakers, the "good guys" win, even if they use dirty tricks. Would you agree that a good end justifies dirty means? Does it matter how we identify a "good end"? Evaluate Rohr's reaction at the end: Does he approve of Marlee and Nick's scheme, or doesn't he?

6. Try to imagine the scenario being reversed: A juror who idealistically believes in the Second Amendment persuades the jury to think with their heads, not their hearts, and acquits the gun manufacturer. Would this scenario be more objectionable to you? less objectionable? the same? Evaluate the influence of your political views on your sympathies in the film.

Chapter Six

Using Your Reason,
Part 2: Kant's Deontology

*O*n the whole, we might say that there are two major ways in which we can approach a problem. We might ask ourselves, What happens if I do X? In that case we're letting ourselves be guided by the future consequences of our actions. Or we might ask ourselves, Is X right or wrong in itself, regardless of the consequences? The first approach is utilitarian, provided that we are looking for good consequences for as many as possible. The version of the second approach that has had the most influence is Immanuel Kant's *duty theory*. (See Box 6.1 for a summary of Kant's life.)

Kant's moral theory is often referred to as *deontology* (the theory of moral obligation, from the Greek *deon,* "that which is obligatory"). Kant believed his theory was the very opposite of a consequentialist theory, and his moral analysis was, in part, written to show how little a moral theory that worries about consequences has to do with true moral thinking. Let us look at an example to illustrate this fundamental difference.

Consequences Don't Count—Having a Good Will Does

Some years ago, newspapers reported an accident somewhere in the Pacific Northwest. A family had gone away for a short vacation and had left their keys with their neighbor so that he could water their plants and look after the place. On Sunday afternoon, a few hours before they were due to arrive home, the temperature was dropping, and the neighbor thought he would do them a favor and make sure they would come home to a nice, toasty house. He went in and turned on the furnace. You've guessed what happened: The house burned down and the family came home to a smoking ruin. That was the extent of the newspaper coverage, but suppose it had been reported by a classical utilitarian. Then the article might have ended something like this: "The neighbor will have to answer for the consequences of this terrible deed." Why? Because, given that only consequences count, the act of turning on the furnace was a terrible one, regardless of the man's good intentions. As it is sometimes said, the road to hell is paved with good intentions. In other words, only your deeds count, not what you intended by them.

Suppose, however, that a Kantian had written the article. Then it might have ended like this: "This good neighbor should be praised for his kind thought and good intentions regardless of the fact that the family lost their home; that consequence certainly can't be blamed on him, because all he intended to do was the right thing."

275

Box 6.1   KANT: HIS LIFE AND WORK

Some famous and influential people lead lives of adventure. The life of Immanuel Kant (1724–1804) seems to have been an *intellectual* adventure exclusively, for he did little that might in any other way be considered adventurous. He grew up in the town of Königsberg, East Prussia (a city on the Baltic Sea, now Kaliningrad in Russian territory). He was raised in an atmosphere of strict Protestant values by his devout mother and by his father, who made a meager living as a saddler. He entered Königsberg University, studied theology, graduated, and tutored for a while until he was offered a position at the university in his hometown. In 1770 he became a full professor in logic and metaphysics, and that was when the philosophical drama began, for Kant achieved influence not only in Western philosophy but also in science and social thinking—an influence that was never eclipsed by anyone else in the eighteenth century. He developed theories about astronomy that are still considered plausible (the so-called Kant-Laplace hypothesis has to a great extent been corroborated by the Hubbell Space Telescope); he laid out rules for a new social world of mutual respect for all citizens; he made contributions to philosophy of law and religion; he attempted to map the entire spectrum of human intelligence in his three major works,

Critique of Pure Reason (1781), *Critique of Practical Reason* (1788), and *Critique of Judgment* (1790), as well as in smaller works such as *Prolegomena to Every Future Metaphysics* (1783) and *Grounding for the Metaphysics of Morals* (1785). He continued working until late in life; one of his most influential works from that period is *The Metaphysics of Morals* (1797).

When Kant calls a book a "critique," he is not implying that he is merely writing a negative criticism of a subject; he is, rather, looking for the *condition of possibility* of that subject. In *Critique of Pure Reason* he asks, "What makes it possible for me to achieve knowledge?" (In other words, what is the condition of possibility of knowledge?) In *Critique of Practical Reason* he asks about the condition of possibility of moral thinking, and in *Critique of Judgment* he examines the condition of possibility for appreciating natural and artistic beauty. In all those fields his insights helped shape new disciplines and redefine old disciplines. Kant was never an agitator for his ideas, though; on the contrary, he was famous for his extremely quiet and highly regulated routine. He remained single throughout his life, and his sole interest seems to have been his work. His students reported that he was in fact a good and popular teacher.

Let us continue speculating. Suppose the house didn't burn down, but instead provided a warm, cozy shelter for and saved the lives of the entire family, who (shall we say) had all come down with pneumonia. The utilitarian now would have to say that the act of lighting the furnace was a shining example of a morally good deed, but Kant would not change his mind: The neighbor's action was good because of his intention, and the consequences of the act don't make it any better or worse. It is not just any good intention, however, that makes an action morally good in Kant's view: One must have *a respect for the moral law* that is expressed in the intention. It isn't enough for the neighbor to be a kind man who wants his neighbors to be comfortable; he must imagine it to be a good thing for neighbors to act that way *in general*—not

This painting shows the German philosopher Immanuel Kant, second from the left, dining with friends. Perhaps the most influential Western philosopher of "modern times" (the seventeenth century to the present), Kant was reportedly a popular guest at dinners and parties and equally popular with his students.

because it would make everyone comfortable and happy, but strictly for the sake of the *principle* of doing the right thing. This is what Kant calls having a *good will*. For Kant the presence of a good will is what makes an action morally good, regardless of its consequences. Therefore, even if you never accomplished what you intended, you are still morally praiseworthy provided you tried hard to do the right thing. In his book *Grounding for the Metaphysics of Morals* (1785; also commonly referred to as *Groundwork* or *Foundations*), Kant assures us that

> [e]ven if, by some especially unfortunate fate or by the niggardly provision of stepmotherly nature, this will should be wholly lacking in the power to accomplish its purpose;* if with the greatest effort it should yet achieve nothing, and only the good will should remain (not,

---

*To modern readers without much experience with older literature in English, the term *niggardly* generally gives pause because it bears an unfortunate resemblance to a racial epithet and people have in recent years been fired for using the word; however, the two words are unrelated in etymology and meaning, and there is no racial undertone in the word used by Kant's translators. The term means "avaricious" or "stingy." The original German word is *kärglich*. But even though *niggardly* doesn't associate to bigotry and discrimination, how about the term *stepmotherly*? That is Kant's own term in translation.

to be sure, as a mere wish but as the summoning of all the means in our power), yet would it, like a jewel, still shine by its own light as something which has its full value in itself. Its usefulness or fruitlessness can neither augment nor diminish this value.

The Categorical Imperative

How do we know that our will is good? We put our intentions to a test. In *Grounding for the Metaphysics of Morals,* Kant says we must ask whether we can imagine our intentions as a general law for everybody. That means that our intentions have to *conform to a rational principle.* We have to think hard to determine whether we're about to do the right thing or not; it can't be determined just by some gut-level feeling. However, we don't have to wait to see the actual consequences to determine whether our intentions are good—all we have to do is determine whether we could imagine others doing to us what we intend doing to them. In other words, Kant proposes a variant of the Golden Rule—but it is a variant with certain specifics, as we shall see—and it illustrates that Kant is also a *hard universalist,* perhaps the hardest one ever to write a book on morals.

For Kant, humans usually know what they *ought* to do, and that is almost always the opposite of what they *want* to do: Our moral conflicts are generally between our duty and our inclination, and when we let our desires run rampant it is simply because we haven't come up with a way for our sense of duty to persuade us to do the right thing. Kant therefore proposes a test to determine the right thing to do. He refers to this test as the *categorical imperative.* But because it is a matter of doing the right thing not in terms of the outcome but in terms of the intentions, we must look more closely at these intentions.

Suppose a store owner is trying to decide whether to cheat her customers. She might tell herself, (1) "I will cheat them whenever I can get away with it" or "I will cheat them only on occasion so nobody can detect a pattern." We can all tell, intuitively, that this merchant's intentions aren't good, although they certainly might benefit her and give her some extra cash at the end of the week. In other words, the consequences may be good, yet we know that cheating the customers is not the right thing to do. (We'll get back to the reason in a while.) Suppose, though, that the owner decides not to cheat her customers because (2) she might be *found out,* and then she would lose their business and might have to close shop. This is certainly prudent, but it still is not a morally praiseworthy decision, because she is doing it only to achieve good consequences. What if the store owner decides not to cheat her customers because (3) she *likes them too much* to ever do them any harm? She loves the little kids buying candy, the old ladies buying groceries, and everyone else, so how could she ever consider cheating them? This, says Kant, is very nice, but it still is not morally praiseworthy, because the merchant is doing only what she feels like doing, and we can't be expected to praise her for just wanting to feel good. (If you want to reexamine this argument, go back to the section in Chapter 4 on psychological egoism, where a similar argument is analyzed in detail.) And indeed, what if some day she should stop loving her customers or just one of them? Then the reason for not cheating is gone; so, Kant cannot approve of motive 3, regardless of how much we generally approve of people who help others because they enjoy it; it really isn't a *principle* any more than motive 1 or motive 2.

The only morally praiseworthy reason for not wanting to cheat the customers would be if the store owner told herself, (4) "It wouldn't be right," regardless of consequences or warm and fuzzy feelings. Why wouldn't it be right? Because she certainly couldn't want everybody else to cheat their customers as a universal law.

If the store owner tells herself, "I will not cheat my customers because otherwise I'll lose them," then she is not doing a bad thing, of course. She is just doing a prudent thing, and Kant says our lives are full of such prudent decisions; they are dependent on each situation, and we have to determine in each case what would be the smart thing to do. Kant calls these decisions, which are *conditional,* because they depend on the situation and on one's own personal desires, *hypothetical imperatives*— *imperatives* because they are commands: *If* you don't want to lose your customers, *then* you should not cheat them. *If* you want to get your degree, *then* you should not miss your final exam. *If* you want to be good at baking biscuits, *then* you ought to bake them from scratch and not use a prepared mix. But suppose you're closing down your shop and moving to another town? Then you might not care about losing those customers. And suppose you decide to drop out of school—then who cares about that final exam? And if you and everyone you know hates biscuits, then why bother worrying about getting good at baking them? In other words, a hypothetical imperative is dependent on your interest in a certain outcome. If you don't want the outcome, the imperative is not binding. We make such decisions every day, and, as long as they are based merely on wanting some outcome, they are not morally relevant. (They can, of course, be morally bad, but, even if they have a good outcome, Kant would say that they are morally neutral.) What makes a decision morally praiseworthy is that the agent (the person acting) decides to do something because it might be applied to everyone as a *universal moral law*. In that case that person has used the categorical imperative.

What makes a categorical imperative *categorical* is that it is not dependent on anyone's desire to make it an imperative; it is binding not just in some situations and for some people, but always, for everyone. It is absolute. That is the very nature of the moral law: If it applies at all, it applies to everyone in the same situation. Although there are myriad hypothetical imperatives, there is only one categorical imperative, expressed in the most general terms possible: *Always act so that you can will that your maxim can become a universal law.* In ordinary language that means: Ask yourself what it is you want to do right now (such as making the house next door toasty for your neighbors, skipping classes on Friday, or lying to Grandma about dating someone outside your religion). Then imagine making that action into a rule (such as, Always make sure your neighbors come home to a toasty house; Always skip Friday classes; Always lie to Grandma to spare her pain). Now you've identified your *maxim,* or the principle or rule for your action. The next step is to ask yourself whether you could want that maxim to become a universal rule for everyone to follow. And, if you can't agree to that—if you don't think *everyone* should, under similar circumstances, light their neighbors' furnaces, skip classes, or lie to Grandma—then *you* shouldn't do it either. It's that simple, and for Kant this realization was so breathtaking that it could be compared only to his awe of the universe on a starry night. Let us use Kant's own example to illustrate.

> [A man] in need finds himself forced to borrow money. He knows well that he won't be able to repay it, but he sees also that he will not get any loan unless he firmly promises to repay it within a fixed time. He wants to make such a promise, but he still has conscience enough to ask himself whether it is not permissible and is contrary to duty to get out of difficulty in this way. Suppose, however, that he decides to do so. The maxim of his action would then be expressed as follows: When I believe myself to be in need of money, I will borrow money and promise to pay it back, although I know that I can never do so. Now this principle of self-love or personal advantage may perhaps be quite compatible with one's entire future welfare, but the question is now whether it is right. I then transform the requirement of self-love into a universal law and put the question thus: how would things stand if my maxim were to become a universal law? He then sees at once that such a maxim could never hold as a universal law of nature and be consistent with itself, but must necessarily be self-contradictory. For the universality of a law which says that anyone believing himself to be in difficulty could promise whatever he pleases with the intention of not keeping it would make promising itself and the end to be attained thereby quite impossible, inasmuch as no one would believe what was promised him but would merely laugh at all such utterances as being vain pretenses.

Do we know why this man wants to borrow money? Perhaps he wants to buy a speedboat. Perhaps he wants to pay a hit man for a contract killing. Or he needs to pay the rent. Perhaps his child is ill, and he has to buy medication and pay the doctor's bill. We don't know. Is knowing his reason relevant? If we were utilitarians, it would be very relevant, because then we could judge the merit of the proposed consequences. (Saving his child generally has more utility than buying a boat or hiring a hit man.) But Kant is no utilitarian, and the prospect of the man in the example wanting to do good with the borrowed money is no more relevant than the prospect of his wanting to buy a boat or even to hire a hit man. The main issue here is, Does the man have a good will? Would he refuse to follow a course of action if he couldn't agree to everyone else having the right to act the same way? At the end of the chapter you'll find an example from Kant's *Grounding* that illustrates what he means by having a good will.

Let us go over the structure of the proposed test of right and wrong conduct again: What is it you're thinking of doing? Imagine that as a *general rule* for action you'll follow every time the situation comes up. You have now expressed your *maxim*. Then imagine everybody else doing it too; by doing this you *universalize your maxim*. Then ask yourself, Would this be rational? Could I still get away with it if everyone did it? The answer is no, you would *undermine your own intention,* because nobody would lend *you* any money if everyone were lying about paying it back. So it is not just the fact that banks would close and the financial world would be in chaos—it is the *logical outcome* of your universalized maxim that shows you that your intention was wrong. This means that it is your *duty* to refrain from following a self-contradictory maxim, simply because your reason tells you it can't be universalized.

The categorical imperative asks us, in effect, Would you want others to treat you the way you're thinking of treating them? The association to the Golden Rule (see Box 4.10) is almost inevitable: How should we treat others? The way we would want to be treated. And yet Kant had harsh words for the old Golden Rule. He thought it was just a simplistic version of his own categorical imperative and that it could even be turned into a travesty: If you don't want to help others, just claim you don't want or need any help from them! But the bottom line is that the categorical imperative draws on that same fundamental realization that I called a spark of moral genius in the Golden Rule: It sees self and others as fundamentally similar—not in the details of our lives, but in the fact that we are human beings and should be treated fairly by one another.

Does that mean that the categorical imperative works only if *everyone* can accept your maxim as a universal law? Not in the sense that we have to take a poll before we decide to act; if everyone's actual approval were the final criterion, the principle would lose its appeal as an immediate test of where one's duty lies. There is an element of universal approval in Kant's idea, but it lies in the reflection of an *ideal* situation, not an *actual* one. If everyone put aside his or her personal interests and then used the categorical imperative, then everyone would, ideally, come up with the same conclusion about what is morally permissible. Kant, who belonged to an era of less doubt about what exactly rationality means, believed that if we all used the same rules of logic and disregarded our personal interests, then we all would come to the same results about moral as well as intellectual issues.

This immense faith in human rationality is an important factor in Kant's moral theory because it reflects his belief that humans are privileged beings. We can set up our own moral rules without having to seek guidance by going to the authorities; we need not be told how to live by the church or by the police or by the monarch or even by our parents. All we need is our good will and our reason, and with that we can set our own rules. If we choose a certain course of action because we have been told to— because we listen to other people's advice for some reason or other—we are merely doing what might be prudent and expedient, but if we listen to our own reason and have good will, then we are *autonomous lawmakers*.

Won't this approach result in a society where everyone looks after himself or herself and lives by multiple rules that may contradict one another? No, because if everyone has good will and applies the categorical imperative, then all will set the same, reasonable, unselfish rules for themselves because they would not wish to set a rule that would be impossible for others to follow.

In this way Kant believes he has shown us how to solve every dilemma, every problem where desire clashes with duty. When the categorical imperative is applied, we automatically disregard our own personal interests and look at the bigger picture, and this action is what is morally praiseworthy: to realize that something is right or wrong in itself. In the Narratives section you'll find a selection of stories that explore, each in its own way, the principle of doing the right thing regardless of the opinion of others or the consequences for oneself: Two Western films are placed together because of their common focus on doing the right thing as a matter of principle: the classic *High Noon* and the 2007 film *3:10 to Yuma*.

Criticism of the Categorical Imperative

Some people are immediately impressed by the idea that one's intentions count for more than the outcome of one's actions and that the question of right or wrong in itself is important; we can't consider only the consequences if it means violating the rights of others. Others claim that no matter how much you say you're not interested in consequences, they still end up being a consideration. Critics have raised five major points when finding fault with Kant's theory.

1. Consequences Count   Doesn't the categorical imperative actually imply concern for consequences? That is the criticism of John Stuart Mill, who had some sharp things to say about Kant's example of borrowing money and not keeping promises. If that was the best Kant could come up with to show that consequences don't count, he was not doing a very good job, said Mill, because what was he appealing to? By asking "What if everybody does what you want to do?" wasn't Kant worrying about *consequences?* What will happen if everyone borrows money and doesn't pay it back in spite of their promises? Then no one else can take advantage of promising falsely, either. In Mill's view, that is as much an appeal to consequences as regular utilitarianism is. That caused Mill to conclude that we all must include consequences in our moral theory, no matter how reluctant we are to recognize their importance. This appears to be a valid point against Kant. The only thing Kant might say in response to this (he never did, of course, since he was long dead by the time Mill criticized his point of view) is that his viewpoint does not look at actual consequences but at the logical implications of a universalized maxim: Will it or will it not undermine itself? Whether Mill has successfully criticized Kant or misunderstood him is still a topic of discussion among philosophers.

2. Conflict Between Duties   Can we be so sure that the categorical imperative is always going to tell us what to do? Suppose we have a conflict between two things we have to do—and we don't particularly want to do either of them. Kant's system assumes that a moral conflict is one between duty and inclination—between what we have to do and what we want to do. In that case it is entirely possible we may be persuaded to do the right thing by imagining our maxim as a universal rule for everyone. But suppose we have a conflict between two duties, such as having to take inventory at our workplace the night before we have a final exam for which we should be studying. Certainly we can't say we want to do one thing more than we want to do the other—anyone who has done both will probably agree that they are both rather unpleasant tasks. How might the categorical imperative help us decide what to do? All it can tell us is that failing to show up for the inventory would not be rational, but neither would skipping the final, because both are duties that everyone ought to fulfill under the same circumstances. The amount of help offered by the categorical imperative is at best limited to cases where duties are not in conflict. (Of course, in a situation where we have a conflict between duties, we already know of another approach that might answer the question of what to do:

Bentham's hedonistic calculus. But most philosophers agree that you can't just mix and match theories according to your needs. In Chapter 11 we return to the question of combining the best of various moral theories.)

3. The Loophole   Might it not be possible to find a loophole in the imperative? Suppose the categorical imperative tells us that it would be irrational (and thus morally impermissible) for anyone to even think about robbing a bank if he needs money because we wouldn't want everyone in the same situation to take that course of action. But what exactly *is* the situation we're talking about? Suppose Joe is broke because he is out of work and has been for seven months. He is twenty years old and has a high school diploma. He worked at a video arcade, but now it is closed because of gang violence. Joe likes to wear denim. His parents are divorced. He is dating a girl named Virginia who works at a supermarket and goes to the community college, and he needs money so that they can get married and rent a small apartment. Let's assume that Joe applies the categorical imperative and that his maxim is: Every time I (who am in a certain situation) am broke and cannot get a loan, I will rob a bank. Then he universalizes it: Every time someone who is twenty, and whose name is Joe, who has divorced parents, used to work in a video arcade, likes denim, and is dating a check-out girl named Virginia who goes to a community college—anytime he feels like robbing a bank because he is broke, it is all right for him to do so. Now is that rational? Will Joe's maxim undermine his intention because everyone else will do the same thing he is planning to do? No, because he has described his situation so that "everyone" is reduced to a group of very few people who are in his exact same situation. In fact, his description of "everyone" could apply to only one person: Joe himself. In that case it is perfectly logical for him to rob a bank, because he won't undermine his own intention. This is hardly the kind of ironclad philosophical proof of doing the right thing that we were looking for. This argument, which also works against rule utilitarianism, is of course not a valid excuse for doing the wrong thing, and Joe shouldn't run out and rob the bank because he thinks philosophers have shown it to be okay. It is, however, an attempt to show that if we work with a principle that is as general as the categorical imperative, we just can't expect it to answer all our moral questions without a doubt. Of course, it isn't an example Kant himself would have appreciated. Kant would have complained that we are making the example too specific. But the fact remains that the categorical imperative needs some further clarification and definition to avoid the "escape clause" that the loophole provides. You may think this example is rather far-fetched, since it's pretty obvious that nobody designs a moral rule you can get away with breaking if it applies only to yourself. However, the story of Joe, be it ever so outlandish, is our own story, in all those situations where we ask for lenient treatment because "we're special." We know we're supposed to send our taxes in on time, and to show up for the final, and so forth, but it's been a hard year, we just had the flu, our family's falling apart, and we'd really like some special consideration. And, if the special circumstances apply only in our case, well, then, we've found a loophole. The example of Joe is just a little more extreme.

4. What Is Rationality?   Who is to say when something is irrational? This is an issue that might not have occurred to Kant. He, as a product of his times and a coproducer of the Age of Reason, believed that if we use our reason without looking to self-interest, then we will all come up with the same idea and result. Actually, Bentham believed the same thing, even though his moral vision was quite different from that of Kant. Today, after garnering a century of knowledge about the workings of the subconscious mind and realizing that people just aren't rational all or even most of the time, we are more inclined to believe that our individual idea of what is rational may depend greatly on who we are. If we use a very broad definition of rational, such as "realizing the shortest way to get to your goal and then pursuing it," we still may come up with different ideas about what is rational. Suppose that our Joe not only is broke but also is a political anarchist who believes that the sooner society breaks down, the better for all humanity and for himself in particular. Why then would it be particularly illogical for him to rob a bank, given that the downfall of society, including banks, is what he is longing for? And why should we refrain from lying to one another if what we want is to create social chaos and alienate our friends? Why refrain from hurting one another, if we are sadomasochists and believe it would be great to live in a world of mutual harmdoing? Although Joe is a fictional example, the real world provides examples of people who most of us believe to have acted irrationally although in their own minds they followed a sure rational path toward a goal. Consider Timothy McVeigh, the man responsible for the bombing of the Alfred P. Murrah Federal Building in Oklahoma City in 1995, which killed 167 men, women, and children. McVeigh was convicted of multiple murders of federal agents and was executed in June 2001. What kind of reasoning process did he go through to decide that taking human lives—the lives of strangers who had never done him any harm, the lives of toddlers and children—would somehow further a goal? If we ask whether he seriously considered the categorical imperative—Could he want others to do the same thing? Could he agree to a world in which someone did such things to him and his family?—then the Kantian tradition would probably claim that he could not, that his decision was irrational. But McVeigh already believed he did live in such a world, in which the *government* kills innocent people. (McVeigh was highly influenced by the federal raid on the Branch Davidian compound in Waco two years earlier.) In an interview he admitted that he thought his actions would start a revolution. So, if the rationality of one's decision depends on one's personal interpretation of the situation, how can the categorical imperative be a guarantee that we will all reach the same conclusion if only we use logic? Would using the categorical imperative have stopped Theodore Kaczynski, the Unabomber? For all his mental problems, Kaczynski is apparently an intelligent man and a scholar, and it is not improbable that he may have asked himself, Would you want your action to become a universal law? and answered Yes, I am doing the morally right thing.

Kant seems to assume that we all have the same general goals, which serve as a guarantee of the rationality of our actions. Change the goals, though, and the ideal of a reasonable course of action takes on a new meaning. (Box 6.2 further explores the issue of rationality.)

Box 6.2   WHAT IS RATIONALITY?

Philosophers often refer to conduct and arguments as being *rational* or *logical*. Since the Age of Reason (the Western Enlightenment) in the eighteenth century, the emphasis has been particularly strong, the assumption being that as long as you use your reason, you can't go wrong. If you do go wrong, the implication is that you have been applying faulty logic: One part of your conduct or your statement has been at odds with another part. For both Bentham and Kant, products of the Enlightenment, there is a staunch belief in the infallibility of properly applied reasoning. That belief was eroded considerably in the twentieth century, partly because of Freud's theories of the Unconscious as a powerful factor in our decision making but one fundamentally outside the control of our rational mind. In the last decades of the twentieth century, other criticisms were raised against the concept of rationality. If we choose a basic definition of rationality that says, "Decide on a goal and select the most direct method to achieve it," then critics of the philosophical emphasis on

reason may point out that this method is above all a *Western* cultural ideal and is not indicative of a worldwide method of conduct. Some cultures prefer *indirect* methods of achieving goals and consider direct methods rude. Some feminists point out that the direct method of rationality is a predominantly *male* approach, whereas many women prefer an indirect way of achieving a goal; in addition, they say, women make use of a special way of knowing: knowledge by emotion and intuition. Could it be true that men, having developed rational skills from millennia of being hunters, think in hunters' terms—going straight for the prey and killing it? And women, after millennia of being gatherers, think more in terms of picking and choosing and comparing? A comedian, Rob Becker, built this into his act in the 1990s, illustrating man the hunter going shopping at the mall, single-mindedly tracking down a shirt—and his wife, the gatherer, shopping around until all items have been compared. It was a very funny routine—and it may actually come close to an

(continued)

cathy®   **by Cathy Guisewite**

CATHY © 1998, Cathy Guisewite. Reprinted by permission of Universal Press Syndicate. All rights reserved.

Is there a male and a female type of rationality? And does it reveal itself in our different styles of shopping? And if that might be the case, can a female shop the male way, and vice versa? Could there be other explanations for different shopping styles, rather than hard-wired gender nature?

Box 6.2   WHAT IS RATIONALITY? *(continued)*

evolutionary truth. But many feminists, such as Alison Jaggar, argue that the highest kind of knowledge incorporates both traditional rational thinking and emotional thinking—for both men and women. Although some rejoice in the possibility of there being several legitimate ways of being rational, some women thinkers worry that this view might turn back the clock and revive the old prejudice that "women can't think logically." And some advocates of traditional rationality as a universal philosophical method speculate that although it is possible that several different ways of conducting oneself rationally may exist, the rules of mathematics and logic are universal examples of applied rationality: The basic rules for pure, logical thinking are not culture- or gender-dependent.

5. No Exceptions?   Does it really seem right that we can never be morally correct in breaking a universal rule? In other words, can the categorical imperative always assure us that sticking to the rule is better than breaking it? Let us say that a killer is stalking a friend of yours, and the friend comes to your door and asks you to hide her. You tell her to go hide in the broom closet. (This is a slightly altered version of one of Kant's own examples.) The killer comes to your door and asks, "Where is she?" Most of us would feel a primary obligation to help our friend, but for Kant the primary obligation is to the truth. You are supposed to answer, "I cannot tell a lie—she is hiding in the broom closet." This is what is meant by an *absolutist* moral theory: A moral rule allows for no exceptions. But why? Most of us would assume that the life of our friend would at least be worth a white lie, but for Kant it is a matter of principle. Suppose you lie to the killer, but your friend sneaks out of the house, and the killer finds her; then it is your fault. If you had told the truth, your friend might still have escaped, and the killer could have been prevented from committing the murder. (Perhaps you could have trapped him in the broom closet.) This far-fetched argument follows Kant's own reasoning for why we should always stick to the rule: because if we break a rule we must answer for the consequences, whereas if we stick to the rule, we have no such responsibility. If we tell the truth, and the killer goes straight for the broom closet and kills our friend, Kant insists that we bear no responsibility for her death. But why should we accept Kant's idea that consequences don't count as long as you are following the rule but that they do count when you are not? Philosophers tend to agree that you can't make such arbitrary choices of when consequences count and when they don't. At the end of the chapter, the second Primary Reading shows how serious Kant was about not accepting any exceptions to his moral principles: To the end of his days, in *The Metaphysics of Morals,* he insisted that even white lies are unacceptable. Incidentally, you may remember Martha Nussbaum in Chapter 1 complaining that philosophy abounds with little, dry, unrealistic examples that are written, "cooked," to illustrate a particular moral rule, and that we'd be better off if we instead read a good novel that illustrates that particular moral problem or rule. Kant's story of the killer at the door is precisely the kind of example she was talking about, and in the Narrative section you'll read the summary of the movie

Match Point, which illustrates the moral problem of lying—but perhaps in a different way from what most of us, including Kant, would have expected.

If there are all these difficulties with the categorical imperative, why has it been such an influential moral factor? The reason is that it is the first moral theory to stress the idea of *universalizability:* realizing that the situation you are in is no different from that of other human beings. If something will bother you, it will probably bother others too, everything else being equal. If you allow yourself a day off, you should not gripe when others do the same thing. Most important, however, you should think about it before you allow yourself that day off and realize that it won't do as a universal rule. The problem is, on occasion we all encounter special situations when we might actually *need* a day off; perhaps we are sick or emotionally upset. Similarly, on the whole we should not kill, but in certain rare situations we may be called on to do just that, in war or in self-defense. On the whole we should not lie, but there may come a day when a killer is stalking a friend of ours, and we have a chance to save her. In that case we may need to lie. Those are unusual situations, so why should Kant's generalizations apply to them? This issue has caused scholars to suggest that there really is nothing wrong with the format of the categorical imperative, provided that we are allowed to expand our maxim to include situations in which we might accept certain *exceptions* to our rule. As long as they don't expand to become a loophole, the universalization works just fine: We can universalize not killing, with the exception of self-defense and certain other specified cases. We can universalize not taking a day off from work unless we are sick or severely emotionally upset, as long as it doesn't happen very often. We can universalize not lying if it is understood that preventing harm to an innocent person would constitute an exception.

The American philosopher Christine Korsgaard, who has been significantly inspired by Kant's moral philosophy, is also one of the critics of Kant's unyielding hard universalism, and she proposes a solution: that we view Kant's categorical imperative as an ideal solution in an ideal world, but that we must also realize that real life is less than perfect and makes other demands on us. The ideal is still important as a principle, but, she asks, why would we even consider that lying to the killer would undermine our intention to lie, since the killer must surely know that asking where our friend went does not represent a normal situation? In other words, in some situations Kant is right on the mark, such as the example of the man who wants to borrow money, and in other situations we must go beyond the categorical imperative—in cases where we have to respond to actions or people we might characterize as *evil.* As an example of a person's making evil choices, or even as an example of an evil person, let us consider the shootings at Virginia Tech in 2007. Who among us would not have chosen to lie to the mass murderer, Cho, if he had asked us for directions to students, professors, or classrooms and we suspected what he was about to do? We might have been *too afraid* to come up with a good lie, but that doesn't make truth-telling right. This would be a clear case where the truth could be circumvented for the sake of innocent lives, with an exception built into the maxim of not lying. In Chapter 9 we meet a classic theory (by Aristotle) that will suggest that for most actions there is a *right amount*—not too much and not too little, and telling the truth to Cho would certainly qualify as excessive, if nothing else. But what is particularly interesting is that Kant, a few pages further into the little book *Grounding,* in fact supplies us with the very principle we need to save innocent lives: that no human beings should be treated like stepping-stones or used for other people's purposes.

Rational Beings Are Ends in Themselves

In his book *Grounding for the Metaphysics of Morals,* Kant explores three major themes: the *categorical imperative,* the concept of *ends in themselves,* and the concept of a *kingdom of ends.* In a sense you might say that if we add the idea of people being ends in themselves to the idea of the categorical imperative, then the result will be a kingdom of ends. In the discussion that follows, we look at the ends-in-themselves concept as well as the kingdom of ends.

Persons Shouldn't Be Used as Tools

In *Grounding,* Kant suggests two different ways to express the categorical imperative. The first one we have just looked at; the other goes like this:

> Now I say that man, and in general every rational being, exists as an end in himself and not merely as a means to be arbitrarily used by this or that will. He must in all his actions, whether directed to himself or to other rational beings, always be regarded at the same time as an end.

What does it mean to be treated as an "end in himself"? Let us first look at the opposite approach: to be treated as a "means to an end only." What is a means to an end? It is a tool, an instrument to be used to achieve some goal; it is something that has *instrumental* value in the achievement of something of *intrinsic* value. If someone is used as a means to an end, she or he is treated as a tool for someone else's purpose, in a very broad sense. If someone is being sexually abused or kept as a slave, that person obviously is being treated as a means to an end, but so is the girl we befriend so we can get to know her brother. So is anyone who is being used for other people's purposes without regard for his or her intrinsic value and dignity as a human being, such as in the controversial film *Bumfights,* where young filmmakers persuaded homeless men to fight each other for the camera, for the sake of monetary gain. But Kant would condemn an act of using someone as a tool, even if the purpose is good—such as creating happiness for a large number of people. For Kant this is just another way of expressing the categorical imperative. What made him think this? For one thing, when you use the categorical imperative, you are universalizing your maxim; and if you are refusing to treat others merely as means to an end, you are also universalizing a maxim, and a very fundamental one. Second, both maxims may be interpreted as expressions of the Golden Rule.

This statement about the immorality of treating other humans as means to an end was, for the eighteenth century, a tremendously important political and social statement. In Kant's era (although not in Kant's country), slavery was still a social factor; abuse of the lower classes by the upper classes was commonplace; Europe was just emerging from a time when monarchs and warlords could move their peasants

For Better or For Worse®   by Lynn Johnston

Immanuel Kant says we should never treat another rational being as merely a means to an end; although extreme cases of reducing another person to an instrument for someone else's purpose, such as slavery or sexual abuse, are today recognized as morally unacceptable, we still have many everyday examples in which people treat one another as tools for their own agenda—as, for example, in this situation from the comic strip *For Better or For Worse*.

and conscripted soldiers around like chess pieces with no regard for their lives and happiness. Then Kant clearly stated that it is not social status that determines one's standing in the moral universe, but one thing only: the capability to use reason. As one of the leading lights of the Age of Reason, Kant stated that any rational human being deserves respect. Rich and poor, young and old, all races and peoples—all are alike in having rationality as the one defining mark of their humanity, and none deserves to be treated without regard for that characteristic. Here it must be interjected, in case we get carried away with our praise, that Kant himself expressed doubt as to whether women were actually rational beings, or as rational as men; he may have had the same reservations about people of color (see Box 6.3), but we will be generous and look at the *implications* of Kant's theory for human rights, regardless of whether or not he himself saw as the goal that every human being deserves respect.

Why are rational beings intrinsically valuable? Because they can place a value on things. What is gold worth if nobody wants it? Nothing. Humans are value-givers; they assign a relative worth to things that interest them. However, as value-givers, humans always have an *absolute* value. They set the price, so to speak, yet cannot have a price set on them. We do, however, constantly talk about people being "worth money." A baseball player is worth a fortune, a Hollywood actress is worth millions. What does that mean? Have we set a price on humans after all? Not in the appropriate sense. It doesn't mean we can *buy* the Hollywood actress for a couple of million. (Well, we might, but in that case she is treating *herself* as a means to an end only, by selling her body.) What we usually mean is that she has a lot of money. And the baseball player? He certainly can be "bought and sold," but hardly as a slave; he retains his autonomy and gets rich in the process. It is his talent and his services that are paid

Box 6.3   KANT, THE ENLIGHTENMENT, AND RACISM

Over the years, Kant has been considered a primary source of the idea of human rights and equality because of his view that any rational being should be treated with dignity and never merely as a means to an end. This view has inspired Western thinkers, writers, and politicians to the point that we can actually say now that, even if the ideal has not yet been reached, the Western world is denouncing regimes that do not recognize all their citizens as equals, regardless of gender, income, race, ethnicity, religion, and nationality. (See the United Nations Universal Declaration of Human Rights at the end of Chapter 7.) But was that the goal Kant had in mind? It is rather discouraging to find out that it wasn't. Kant himself, as much as he has inspired today's quest for equality, had no philosophical goal of either gender or racial equality. Kant believed himself to be drawing on the cutting edge of biological research (he actually taught more classes in geography than in philosophy); in a rarely quoted text, "On the Different Races of Man" (1775), Kant voices the opinion that there are substantial differences in "natural dispositions" among what Kant sees as the four predominant human races of the world. For Kant and many other eighteenth-century Western thinkers, the European race was more intelligent than other races, and males were more intelligent than females. With no sound scientific evidence, some of the most important thinkers of the Western Enlightenment—which did usher in the first stages of global equality—decided that some humans were more advanced than others. This of course raises suspicion that Kant's "rational beings" may not have included

all *humans*, but primarily white males. However, ten years later Kant specified, in *Grounding*, that *all of humanity* should be treated as ends in themselves. It would be grossly unfair to assume that Kant thought only white males were "persons." But Kant's rule of "ends in themselves" only protects humans against abuse—it doesn't guarantee social equality.

Old heroes sometimes topple in the light of new research, and according to some critics this is what is happening to Kant: He may not be the champion of human rights we thought he was. We are even justified in calling him a racist, if we use today's view of racism as discrimination against individuals or groups of people solely based on their race. In my view, however, we should never forget that Kant was, for his day, indeed a champion of human rights. Europe was a place of serfdom, where peasants were treated as the property of the great landowners. Kant's writings did help set in motion the process that we all today have benefited from: the philosophical sea change that resulted in the concept of inalienable human rights. So Kant himself may have been locked in the racial bigotry of ignorance common for his day and age, but his ideas of a kingdom of ends in which *everyone* is treated with respect and dignity have today survived to become a Western political and philosophical ideal. He may fall short of the "minimum qualifications" considered necessary for an open-minded thinker today, but he did leave a legacy that can't be overestimated: the ideal of social and political dignity as a human birthright. That credit should not be taken away from him.

for. Under normal circumstances we don't refer to people as entities that can be bought for money, and if we do, we are usually implying that something bad is taking place (slavery and bribery, for instance). Thus people are value-givers because they can decide rationally what they want and what they don't want. That means that rational beings are *persons,* and the second formulation of the categorical imperative is focused on respect for persons: *Act in such a way that you treat humanity, whether in your own person or in the person of another, always at the same time as an end and never simply as means.*

Notice that Kant is not talking about not mistreating just others. You have to respect yourself too, and not let others step on you. You have a right to set values of your own and not just be used by others as their key to success. But what exactly does it mean not to treat anybody *simply as means to an end?* We know that blatant abuse is wrong and that a subtler kind is no better. But what about using someone's services? When you buy your groceries, there usually is some person who bags your items. Truthfully, are you treating that person as a means to get your groceries bagged? Yes, indeed, but not *simply* as a means; he or she is getting paid, and you presumably don't treat these workers as though they were put on this earth just to bag your groceries. Everyday life consists of people using other people's services, and that is just the normal give-and-take of social life. The danger arises if we stop respecting people for what they do and reduce them in our minds to mere tools for our comfort or success. As long as the relationship is reciprocal (you pay for your groceries, and the bagger gets a paycheck), then there is no abuse taking place. Indeed, students use their professors as a means to an end (to get their degree), but the professors rarely feel abused, provided that they receive a salary. Likewise, the professors use students as a means to their ends (to receive that salary), but the professors surely don't imagine that the students were put on this earth to feed them or pay their mortgage. However, when people truly use others as tools for their own purpose and nothing else, from the phenomenon of "suicide by cop" to sexual abuse and terrorism, we are talking about treating others as a "means to an end only."

Many critics believe that John Stuart Mill was right when he pointed out that Kant, despite his own insistence that consequences are irrelevent for a good will, ended up including a reference to possible consequences in his categorical imperative in the universalization of the maxim: What happens if I do X? However, when we examine Kant's principle of never treating people simply as a means to an end, we have to conclude that this principle indeed does exclude any consideration of good or bad consequences: Nobody is supposed to reduce another, or themselves, to a mere tool or stepping-stone, regardless of whether it is for a good or a bad purpose, or whether it is based on mutual consent (which is why Kant was also against prostitution). So now we can return to the question raised in Chapter 5 about *torturing terrorists* to obtain vital information that may save lives. We saw that a utilitarian might agree that under specific circumstances it could be the right thing to do. For a Kantian, however, no amount of good consequences would justify the abuse of anyone, including serial killers, enemy POWs, or terrorists. Within a classical Kantian moral system, torture could never be allowed, even if it might save the life of your child, your spouse, your parents, or your country; it is better to suffer with common dignity and respect for other humans than it is to buy the safety and happiness of some with the suffering of others. That doesn't mean we can't punish criminals, including terrorists, with imprisonment or even execution, as we shall see in Chapter 7, but the purpose would be *justice* rather than creating good consequences.

Beings Who Are Things

Any rational being deserves respect. We assume that humans fall into that category, but what if there are rational beings who are not human? It is not unthinkable that humans might encounter extraterrestrials who are rational enough to know math, language, and space science; and how about the possibility of AI, Artificial Intelligence? Would Kant respect a thinking android or computer, or a rational alien, or would he advocate treating them like things? If these beings are *rational,* they qualify as full members of our moral universe, and humans have no right to treat them as tools to achieve knowledge or power. Aliens and androids would likewise have no right to cart humans off for medical experiments, because all humans are generally rational beings.

There are beings on this earth who are not rational in Kant's sense of the word—animals, for example. In *Grounding* he presents his theory in this way:

> Beings whose existence depends not on our will but on nature have, nevertheless, if they are not rational beings, only a relative value as means and are therefore called things. On the other hand, rational beings are called persons inasmuch as their nature already marks them out as ends in themselves. . . .

That means that nonhuman animals don't belong in the moral universe at all; they are classified as *things* and can be used as a tool by a rational person because animals can't place a value on something—only humans can do that. And an animal is not worth anything in itself; it has value only if it is wanted for some purpose by a human. If nobody cares about cats, or spotted owls, then they have no value. Is it true, though, that animals can't place a value on things? Most people with firsthand knowledge of animals will report that pets are capable of valuing their owners above all and their food bowl second. (Or is it the other way around?) And animals in the wild place extreme importance on their territory and their young. Many people today categorize animal interests as just different in *degree* from human interests and not different in *kind* (Chapter 13). Although Kant and most of his contemporaries (with the exclusion of Bentham) believed that the moral universe is closed to nonhuman animals, it is just possible today that we not only might include animals as "creatures who deserve respect" but also might actively look for traces of *animal morality*. Might the self-sacrifice of a baboon to save her tribe from the leopard constitute a moral dimension? Is a gorilla morally good if she comes to the rescue of a child who has fallen into the gorilla enclosure at the zoo? Or are we just witnessing automatic instinctual responses? (See Box 6.4 for further discussion.)

Whatever we think now, the day could be near when dolphins, elephants, and the great apes are included in a category of rudimentary rational beings. For our purposes here, we simply should remember that for Kant it was not just a matter of being able to think—one must also be able to show that one has autonomy and can set up universal moral rules for oneself and others; and although certain animals may have some thought capacity, it is doubtful whether they ever can be considered *morally autonomous* in the Kantian sense of the term.

Numerous scholars have pointed out, however, that there is a serious problem with Kant's own classification of humans as rational beings, for suppose someone

Box 6.4   CAN ANIMALS THINK?

From the previous chapter you may remember that Descartes didn't believe animals had any mental activity because, according to his theory, they consisted of matter only. Kant does not deny that nonhuman animals have minds; he just does not believe them to be rational minds but, rather, instinctive—in his own words, "depending on nature" (*Grounding*). In *The Metaphysics of Morals* he explains further: Although animals and humans all have wills that propel them toward their goals, only humans have free choice; animals making choices about what to eat, with whom to mate, and where to sleep don't make use of moral laws, and so their choice is merely brutish (as some people's choices of the same type may be). But when a person makes a choice based on a rational principle of universalizability, then Kant calls it a free choice.

Today the issue of animal intelligence is still controversial. Some ethologists (animal behaviorists) continue to believe that human and nonhuman animal intelligence are different *in kind;* others now lean toward the assumption that they are different *in degree.* Close observations in experimental situations over years of research and coexistence with animals have led many modern biologists and behaviorists to conclude that at least certain animals, such as great apes, dolphins, and orcas (killer whales), have a rudimentary capacity for rational thinking and even for linguistic comprehension (as humans define language). In Chapter 13 we take a closer look at the issues of animal intelligence and animal rights.

who is genetically human can't think rationally? There are many humans who aren't good at thinking or can't think at all because they are infants, toddlers, mentally disabled, or in a coma—or have Alzheimer's. Does that mean that all these people aren't *persons* and should be classified as *things?* As some scholars (such as Peter Singer) have remarked, there are animals who are more like persons (that is, rational beings) than newborn infants or severely mentally disabled humans are. Would Kant really say that such humans are no better than things? The trouble is that Kant never made provisions for any such subcategories of "persons" in *Grounding.* It is either-or. As you way remember from Chapter 1, this is what we call the *fallacy of bifurcation,* or a *false dichotomy:* assuming that there are only two options, whereas there may be three or more. And that is precisely what Kant himself realized.

There is no denying that problems arise if you divide the world into persons (with rights not to be abused by others) and things (that persons have a right to use). But twelve years after writing *Grounding,* in his long-awaited *The Metaphysics of Morals,* Kant addressed the question of an intermediate category: people who have absolute rights as ends in themselves but who also, for various reasons, "belong" to other persons. Kant calls it "the right to a person akin to a right to a thing"—such persons are legitimately treated *as if* they were possessions, although they cannot be owned as slaves. An example would be a small child: She is a person with the right to personal freedom; the child's parents can't destroy her, even if they brought her into the world; but the child does not have full self-determination either, because she is still regarded as a pseudo-possession of her parents until the day she is grown.

(If someone takes her, her parents can demand to have her back.) The parents have a duty to raise the child properly, and the child has no duty to repay them. Similarly, servants of a household belong in the intermediate category of being pseudo-possessions: They are free persons, but because they have signed contracts they can't just take off whenever they feel like it, Kant says. On the other hand, they can't be bought and sold either, because then they would be slaves, and slavery is reducing someone to merely a means to an end. Some scholars believe that with this intermediate category between a person with full freedom and a thing with none, Kant has opened the door for the modern category sometimes called "partial rights": A being who is not a rational, human adult may be granted some rights but may still be regarded as under the guardianship of other humans. Vilifying Kant for poisoning philosophy toward the rights of partially rational beings hardly seems fair under these circumstances. But in *The Metaphysics of Morals* we also hear in no uncertain terms from Kant that animals are not rational and have no rights, because for us to have duties to other beings, they have to be capable of having obligations to us. (See Chapter 13 for a continuation of this debate.) Classifying an animal as a thing seemed reasonable to Kant, but, even so, he was concerned that some readers might take that as permission to treat animals any way they saw fit, including being cruel to them. Kant was very specific about condemning cruelty to animals; however, he took that stance not so much for the sake of the animals themselves as because someone who hurts animals might easily get used to it and begin to hurt people. It appears that Kant was more right than most of his readers could have known at the time; although Kant is not the first person to have claimed that cruelty to animals may lead to cruelty toward people (St. Thomas Aquinas had said the same thing in the thirteenth century), the depth of the connection became apparent only in the late twentieth century, when criminal profiling established that just about every serial killer questioned through the late 1990s turned out to have tortured small animals when he was a child. (That investigation focused on male serial killers, since there have been very few female serial murderers so far.) In addition, such individuals would also engage in setting fires and were chronic bed wetters. That does not mean that a boy who wets his bed, sets fires, and tortures animals will invariably grow up to be a serial killer, but those behaviors are considered warning signs that should be attended to while the child is still young. The point Kant wanted to make, which criminal profiling has corroborated, is that desensitization to—or even enjoyment of—animal pain can lead to deliberately inflicting pain on human beings. In Kant's words (from *The Metaphysics of Morals*):

> It dulls his shared feeling of their pain and so weakens and gradually uproots a natural predisposition that is very serviceable to morality in one's relations with other men. Man is authorized to kill animals quickly (without pain) and to put them to work that does not strain them beyond their capacities (such work as man himself must submit to). But agonizing physical experiments for the sake of mere speculation, when the end could also be achieved without these, are to be abhorred.

It is interesting that Kant, having over the years acquired the reputation of being insensitive to the plight of animals, himself argued against causing needless pain to them. Contrary to Descartes, Kant never thought animals couldn't feel pain; he just thought that within the context of human moral issues it was only marginally relevant.

Some issues are thus resolved in *The Metaphysics of Morals,* but not all issues. Even so, the idea that rational beings should never be treated merely as means to an end has been a powerful contribution to a world of equality and mutual respect because it is such a remarkable expansion of the moral universe described in previous moral theories, which tended to exclude social groups that somehow weren't considered quite as valuable as others. Furthermore, Kant placed the foundation of morality solidly with human rationality and not with the state or the church. But for the astute reader it is also interesting to notice that Kant allows for the existence of a "natural predisposition" to avoid causing harm to other human beings. That is what you have encountered elsewhere in this book as "moral intuition" or "fellow-feeling," and Kant is famous for insisting that moral deliberation ought to be exclusively rational, not emotional or intuitive. But that doesn't mean that he completely discounted the notion that we have, embedded in us, a reluctance to hurt other humans—which is what social psychologists and neuroscientists have verified recently.

The Kingdom of Ends

That brings us to the third major theme in Kant's *Grounding,* the "kingdom of ends." Applying the categorical imperative is something all rational beings can do—and even if they can't do it exactly the way Kant uses it, the logic of it should be compelling for all people who can ask themselves, "Would I want everybody to do this?" Kant calls this *moral autonomy:* The only moral authority that can tell us to do something and not to do something else is our own reason. As we saw previously, if all people follow the same principle and disregard their own personal inclinations, then all will end up following the same good rules, because all have universalized their intention. In such a world, with everyone doing the right thing and nobody abusing anyone else, a new realm will have been created: the *kingdom of ends.* "Kingdom" poetically describes a community of people, and "ends" indicates that the people treat one another as ends only—as beings who have their own goals in life—never merely as means to other people's ends. Every time we show respect and consideration for one another, we make the kingdom of ends a little more real. In Kant's words from *Grounding,*

> By "kingdom" I understand a system of different rational beings through common laws. . . . For all rational beings stand under the law that each of them should treat himself and all others never merely as a means but always at the same time as an end in himself. Hereby arises a systematic union of rational beings through common objective laws, i.e., a kingdom that may be called a kingdom of ends (certainly only an ideal), inasmuch as these laws have in view the very relation of such beings to one another as ends and means.
>
> A rational being belongs to the kingdom of ends as a member when he legislates in it universal laws while also himself being subject to these laws. He belongs to it as sovereign, when as legislator he is himself subject to the will of no other. . . . In the kingdom of ends everything has either a price or a dignity. Whatever has a price can be replaced by something else as its equivalent; on the other hand, whatever is above all price, and therefore admits no equivalent, has a dignity.

Here we see how Kant combines the first part of his book, the categorical imperative, with the second part, the idea that nobody should be used merely as a means to an end.

People who adhere to the method of the categorical imperative are autonomous law-makers: They set laws for themselves that, when universalized, become acceptable to every other rational being. When we use that approach, we realize that we can't allow ourselves to treat others (or let others treat us) as merely a means to an end, but recognize that other people should be treated with respect because they are rational beings with dignity, *irreplaceable* beings. We all belong in the kingdom of ends, the realm of beings with dignity. But whatever doesn't qualify as rational has a price and can be replaced with a similar item. (That of course means to Kant that any human being has dignity and is irreplaceable, whereas your dog has no dignity and can be replaced.)

Some readers of Kant believe that he shows a more humane side in his theory of ends in themselves, and indeed we might take this idea and apply it to the problem of whether to lie to the killer who has come to murder your friend. The categorical imperative tells you to speak the truth always, because then you can't be blamed for the consequences. But is that really the same as saying we should treat others as ends in themselves? Perhaps there is a subtle difference; if we apply this rule to the killer who is stalking our friend, would we get the same result? Might we not be treating our friend as merely a means to an end if we refuse to lie for her, whether it is for the sake of principle or just so that we can't be blamed for the consequences? If we are sacrificing our friend for the sake of the truth, it might rightfully be said that in such a case we are treating her as a means to an end only. So even within Kant's own system there are irreconcilable differences. That should not cause us to want to discard his entire theory, however; since the nineteenth century, philosophers have tried to redesign Kant's ideas to fit a more perceptive (or, as Kant would say, more lenient) world. Some of those ideas are working quite well—for example, allowing for general exceptions to be built into the categorical imperative itself, and allowing for animals to be considered more rational than Kant ever thought possible.

Study Questions

1. Evaluate the following statement: "Actions are morally good only if they are done because of a good will." Explain what Kant means by a "good will." Do you think the statement is correct or incorrect? Explain your position.

2. Analyze the following statement: "Man, and in general every rational being, should be treated as an end in himself, never merely as a means." What are the moral implications of that statement for humans, as well as nonhumans?

3. Explain Kant's position on lying: Is it always morally wrong to lie? What are the implications for the question raised in Chapter 5, "Should we lie to Grandma about something if the truth will distress her?"

Primary Readings and Narratives

The first Primary Reading is an excerpt from Kant's famous *Grounding for the Metaphysics of Morals* in which he explains the structure of the categorical imperative. The second Primary Reading is an excerpt from Kant's less frequently quoted book, *The Metaphysics of Morals,* in which he explains why lying is wrong. The Narratives are all summaries. Two Westerns each explore the concept of doing the right thing as a matter of principle: the famous *High Noon,* in which the town marshal chooses to face three gunmen alone after having been rejected by the community he is trying to defend, and *3:10 to Yuma,* in which a destitute rancher tries to make a fast buck by putting an outlaw on the train to prison, but ends up making a choice about doing the right thing. The last summary is of Woody Allen's film *Match Point,* in which a young man with ambitions resorts to lying to his well-connected wife in order to keep seeing his girlfriend.

Primary Reading

Grounding for the Metaphysics of Morals

IMMANUEL KANT

Excerpt, 1785.

In this passage Kant introduces the categorical imperative and links it with the concept of the good will as an understanding of doing one's duty in accordance with reason.

> Thus the moral worth of an action does not lie in the effect expected from it nor in any principle of action that needs to borrow its motive from this expected effect. For all these effects (agreeableness of one's condition and even the furtherance of other people's happiness) could have been brought about also through other causes and would not have required the will of a rational being, in which the highest and unconditioned good can alone be found. Therefore, the preeminent good which is called moral can consist in nothing but the representation of the law in itself, and such a representation can admittedly be found only in a rational being insofar as this representation, and not some expected effect, is the determining ground of the will. This good is already present in the person who acts according to this representation, and such good need not be awaited merely from the effect.
>
> But what sort of law can that be the thought of which must determine the will without reference to any expected effect, so that the will can be called absolutely good without qualification? Since I have deprived the will of every impulse that might arise for it from obeying any particular law, there is nothing left to serve the will as principle except the universal conformity of its actions to law as such, i.e., I should never act except in such a way that I can also will that my maxim should become a universal law. Here mere conformity to law as such (without having as its basis any law determining particular actions) serves the will as principle and must so serve it if duty is not to be a vain delusion and a chimerical concept. The ordinary reason of mankind in its practical judgments agrees completely with this, and always has in view the aforementioned principle.
>
> For example, take this question. When I am in distress, may I make a promise with the intention of not keeping it? I readily distinguish here the two meanings which the question may have; whether making a false promise conforms with prudence or

with duty. Doubtless the former can often be the case. Indeed I clearly see that escape from some present difficulty by means of such a promise is not enough. In addition I must carefully consider whether from this lie there may later arise far greater inconvenience for me than from what I now try to escape. Furthermore, the consequences of my false promise are not easy to foresee, even with all my supposed cunning; loss of confidence in me might prove to be far more disadvantageous than the misfortune which I now try to avoid. The more prudent way might be to act according to a universal maxim and to make it a habit not to promise anything without intending to keep it. But that such a maxim is, nevertheless, always based on nothing but a fear of consequences becomes clear to me at once. To be truthful from duty is, however, quite different from being truthful from fear of disadvantageous consequences; in the first case the concept of the action itself contains a law for me, while in the second I must first look around elsewhere to see what are the results for me that might be connected with the action. For to deviate from the principle of duty is quite certainly bad; but to abandon my maxim of prudence can often be very advantageous for me, though to abide by it is certainly safer. The most direct and infallible way, however, to answer the question as to whether a lying promise accords with duty is to ask myself whether I would really be content if my maxim (of extracting myself from difficulty by means of a false promise) were to hold as a universal law for myself as well as for others, and could I really say to myself that everyone may promise falsely when he finds himself in a difficulty from which he can find no other way to extricate himself. Then I immediately become aware that I can indeed will the lie but can not at all will a universal law to lie. For by such a law there would really be no promises at all, since in vain would my willing future actions be professed to other people who would not believe what I professed, or if they over-hastily did believe, then they would pay me back in like coin. Therefore, my maxim would necessarily destroy itself just as soon as it was made a universal law.

Therefore, I need no fear-reaching acuteness to discern what I have to do in order that my will may be morally good. Inexperienced in the course of the world and incapable of being prepared for all its contingencies, I only ask myself whether I can also will that my maxim should become a universal law. If not, then the maxim must be rejected, not because of any disadvantage accruing to me or even to others, but because it cannot be fitting as a principle in a possible legislation of universal law, and reason exacts from me immediate respect for such legislation. Indeed I have as yet no insight into the grounds of such respect (which the philosopher may investigate). But I at least understand that respect is an estimation of a worth that far outweighs any worth of what is recommended by inclination, and that the necessity of acting from pure respect for the practical law is what constitutes duty, to which every other motive must give way because duty is the condition of a will good in itself, whose worth is above all else.

Study Questions

1. What does Kant mean by a good will?

2. Explain the structure and purpose of the categorical imperative.

3. Can you think of a situation in which it might actually be counterproductive to do a good or a harmless thing if everyone did the same thing? How might Kant respond?

Primary Reading

The Metaphysics of Morals

IMMANUEL KANT

Excerpt from Book I, Chapter II, 1797.

This book was actually printed separately in two parts but is considered one book today. The first part is *The Doctrine of Right,* and the second one is *The Doctrine of Virtue*. This section on lying from *The Doctrine of Virtue* illustrates Kant's talent for careful analysis of even an ordinary kind of experience in order to argue his points that you should not make choices you couldn't wish to become a universal law and that you should not make choices that diminish the dignity of others or yourself.

> *Man's Duty to Himself Merely as a Moral Being:* This duty is opposed to the vices of *lying, avarice,* and *false humility* (servility).
>
> *On Lying:* The greatest violation of man's duty to himself regarded merely as a moral being (the humanity in his own person) is the contrary of truthfulness, *lying (aliud lingua promptum, aliud pectore inclusum gerere)*. ["To have one thing shut up in the heart and another ready on the tongue." Sallust, *The War with Catiline* X, 5.] In the doctrine of Right an intentional untruth is called a lie only if it violates another's right; but in ethics, where no authorization is derived from harmlessness, it is clear of itself that no intentional untruth in the expression of one's thoughts can refuse this harsh name. For the dishonor (being an object of moral contempt) that accompanies a lie also accompanies a liar like his shadow. A lie can be an external lie (*mendacium externum*) or also an internal lie. By an external lie a man makes himself an object of contempt in the eyes of others; by an internal lie he does what is still worse: He makes himself contemptible in his own eyes and violates the dignity of humanity in his own person. And so, since the harm that can come to other men from lying is not what distinguishes this vice (for if it were, the vice would consist only in violating one's duty to others), this harm is not taken into account here. Neither is the harm that a liar brings on himself; for then a lie, as a mere error in prudence, would conflict with the pragmatic maxim, not the moral maxim, and it could not be considered a violation of duty at all. By a lie a man throws away and, as it were, annihilates his dignity as a man. A man who does not himself believe what he tells another (even if the other is a merely ideal person) has even less worth than if he were a mere thing; for a thing, because it is something real and given, has the property of being serviceable so that another can put it to some use. But communication of one's thoughts to someone through words that yet (intentionally) contain the contrary of what the speaker thinks on the subject is an end that is directly opposed to the natural purposiveness of the speaker's capacity to communicate his thoughts, and is thus a renunciation by the speaker of his personality, and such a speaker is a mere deceptive appearance of a man, not a man himself. *Truthfulness* in one's declarations is also called *honesty* and, if the declarations are promises, *sincerity;* but, more generally, truthfulness is called rectitude.
>
> Lying (in the ethical sense of the word), intentional untruth as such, need not be *harmful* to others in order to be repudiated; for it would then be a violation of the rights

of others. It may be done merely out of frivolity or even good nature; the speaker may even intend to achieve a really good end by it. But his way of pursuing this end is, by its mere form, a crime of a man against his own person and a worthlessness that must make him contemptible in his own eyes.

It is easy to show that man is actually guilty of many inner lies, but it seems more difficult to explain how they are possible; for a lie requires a second person whom one intends to deceive, whereas to deceive oneself on purpose seems to contain a contradiction.

Man as a moral being (*homo noumenon*) cannot use himself as a natural being (*homo phaenomenon*) as a mere means (a speaking machine), as if his natural being were not bound to the inner end (of communicating thoughts), but is bound to the condition of using himself as a natural being in agreement with the declaration (*declaratio*) of his moral being and is under obligation to himself to *truthfulness*. Someone tells an inner lie, for example, if he professes belief in a future judge of the world, although he really finds no such belief within himself but persuades himself that it could do no harm and might even be useful to profess in his thoughts to one who scrutinizes hearts a belief in such a judge, in order to win His favor in case He should exist. Someone also lies if, having no doubt about the existence of this future judge, he still flatters himself that he inwardly reveres His law, though the only incentive he feels is fear of punishment.

Insincerity is mere lack of *conscientiousness,* that is, of purity in one's professions before one's inner judge, who is thought of as another person when conscientiousness is taken quite strictly; then if someone, from self-love, takes a wish for the deed because he has a really good end in mind, his inner lie, although it is indeed contrary to man's duty to himself, gets the name of a frailty, as when a lover's wish to find only good qualities in his beloved blinds him to her obvious faults. But such insincerity in his declarations, which man perpetrates upon himself, still deserves the strongest censure, since it is from such a rotten spot (falsity, which seems to be rooted in human nature itself) that the evil of untruthfulness spreads into man's relations with other men as well, once the highest principle of truthfulness has been violated.

Remark: It is noteworthy that the Bible dates the first crime, through which evil entered the world, not from *fratricide* (Cain's) but from the first *lie* (for even nature rises up against fratricide), and calls the author of all evil a liar from the beginning and the father of lies. However, reason can assign no further ground for man's propensity to *hypocrisy (esprit fourbe),* although this propensity must have been present before the lie; for an act of freedom cannot (like a natural effect) be deduced and explained in accordance with the natural law of the connection of effects with their causes, all of which are appearances.

Casuistical Questions: Can an untruth from mere politeness (e.g., the "your obedient servant" at the end of a letter) be considered a lie? No one is deceived by it. An author asks one of his readers, "How do you like my work?" One could merely seem to give an answer, by joking about the impropriety of such a question. But who has his wit always ready? The author will take the slightest hesitation in answering as an insult. May one, then, say what is expected of one?

If I say something untrue in more serious matters, having to do with what is mine or yours, must I answer for all the consequences it might have? For example, a householder has ordered his servant to say "not at home" if a certain man asks for him. The servant does this and, as a result, the master slips away and commits a serious crime, which would otherwise have been prevented by the guard sent to arrest him. Who (in accordance with ethical principles) is guilty in this case? Surely the servant, too, who violated a duty to himself by his lie, the results of which his own conscience imputes to him.

Study Questions

1. Why does a liar annihilate his or her own dignity? Is there a connection to the categorical imperative and/or the theory of respect for persons?

2. What is the difference between an external and an internal lie? Is one more acceptable than the other, according to Kant? And according to you?

3. Discuss Kant's own "study question," "Is the servant guilty?" Why? Compare this example with the example of the killer at the door.

Narrative

From *High Noon* to *3:10*: Two Deontological Films

The following two narratives are both Westerns; in both films the basic theme is a man who chooses to do the right thing against overwhelming odds, facing a gang of outlaws, all by himself. But otherwise the stories are very different, as are the lead characters. What I suggest you focus on in discussing these two movies is what motivates Marshal Will Kane (*High Noon*) and rancher Dan Evans (*3:10 to Yuma*), and whether it is appropriate to call their commitment "Kantian" in spirit.

High Noon

CARL FOREMAN (SCREENWRITER)
FRED ZINNEMAN (DIRECTOR)

Film, 1952. Summary.

This film may be the most famous Western of all time, and yet it is not a "true" Western. There is very little riding, no troops or Indians, no cattle, no cowboys—but much talk about the right thing to do. This film was made in the early days of McCarthyism in Hollywood, and Fred Zinneman (the director) has admitted that it is an allegory of the general attitude in 1952 Hollywood of turning your back on friends who were accused (mostly falsely) of "un-American" (Communist) activities and who might have needed help. When it was produced, it was not considered to have any potential as a classic, but it has soared in public opinion ever since then. It is a Western—but a Western of a different sort—a Western about the problems of a budding civilization in the midst of an era of violence. The film also is very well crafted. The amount of time that elapses from the moment Marshal Will Kane realizes he will have to face four gunmen alone because the whole town worries about the consequences of siding with him to the moment the actual

In *High Noon* (United Artists, 1952), Will Kane (Gary Cooper, left) has just been married and has resigned as marshal of Hadleyville, but a killer he helped put in prison and three other gunmen are now looking for him. He tries to get the townspeople to stand by him the way they did when he captured the killer five years earlier, but now they all turn their backs on him, preferring not to get involved. In this scene a former friend, Herb (James Millican), is backing out of his promise to help Kane, having found out that nobody else is coming along.

gunfight takes place is the exact amount of time you spend watching it in the theater or in front of your TV: an hour and a half.

The plot is simple. Five years before, Kane brought a killer, Frank Miller, to justice. Miller was sentenced to hang, but "up North they commuted it to life, and now he's free," as the judge says. He is coming in on the noon train to have it out with Kane. Word of his intentions comes just as Kane is marrying his Quaker bride in a civil ceremony. He has already given up his job and is leaving town with his new wife when he turns around to face the gunmen coming in on the noon train. His wife, Amy, asks him why he is turning back—he doesn't have to play the hero for her, she says. He answers, "I haven't got time to tell you. . . . And if you think I like this, you're crazy."

In town, Kane tries to get his former deputies to join him, but everyone is afraid of Miller, except the deputy, who is the boyfriend of Helen Ramirez, Kane's former girl-friend. Helen is the only one who understands Kane's problem because, as a Mexican, she has always felt like an outcast herself—and besides, she used to be Frank Miller's girlfriend too. When Amy leaves Kane because she can't stand the threat of violence, she seeks out Helen because she thinks it is because of her that Kane is staying in town. Amy begs

Helen to let him go, and when she hears that he isn't staying because of Helen, she asks, bewildered, what then is making her husband stay. Helen tells her, "If you don't know, I can't tell you." Helen's boyfriend, the deputy, finds Kane and tries to force him to leave town so that he can take over as town marshal. He also asks Kane why he is staying, and all Kane says is, "I don't know. "

Desperate, Kane makes for the little church where the Sunday service is still going on, and we remember that an hour ago he was married in a civil ceremony. The service comes to a stop as he enters, and the minister asks him what could be so important since he didn't see fit to be married in church. Kane explains that his wife is a Quaker, and not a member of the town's Protestant congregation, and he knows he is not a churchgoing man, but he needs help. Some of the same men who were deputies with him when they arrested Miller are attending the service—don't they feel the call to duty? Democratically, the congregation plunges into a debate: Why is Kane still here if he is no longer marshal? Why hasn't he arrested the men at the depot? Why must private citizens pitch in every time law enforcement can't handle the situation? But Kane also has supporters who re- member that he cleaned up the town and made it a place fit for civilized people. In the end, the mayor speaks: We owe Kane a great debt, he says, so we, the citizens, ought to take care of the situation—and Kane ought to get out of town so there will be no blood- shed. Because (and this is obviously the mayor's real concern) with bloodshed in the streets, investors from up North will shy away from putting money into the town. The support Kane was hoping for evaporates in light of financial concerns.

The "good citizens" want Kane to leave town so there will be no deterrence to progress. The former sheriff wants him to leave, saying that keeping the law is an un- grateful business. Everybody wants him to leave, and at the train depot Frank Miller's three gunmen are waiting for the train that will bring Frank. But Kane feels compelled to stay, even with nobody to side with him. The last man to abandon Kane is his friend Herb. When he realizes that it will be just he and Kane against Miller and his gang, he pleads with Kane, "I have a wife and kids—what about my kids?" And Kane responds, "Go home to your kids, Herb."

The train arrives, a gunfight ensues in the dusty streets of the town, and two of Frank's gunmen are killed. In the end, Amy comes to Kane's rescue and kills the third gunman; Kane kills Miller, and together he and Amy leave town—but not before Kane has thrown his marshal's star in the dust.

Study Questions

1. What makes Kane stay? Is he serious when he says, "I don't know"? Why might we say that this is a "Kantian" Western?

2. Is it fair of Kane to place Amy in a situation where she has to give up her own moral principles?

3. What is meant by the line "If you don't know, I can't tell you"?

4. How would a utilitarian judge Kane's feeling of conscience and duty?

5. Are the townspeople who refuse to help primarily deontologists, utilitarians, or ethical egoists?

Narrative

3:10 to Yuma

JAMES MANGOLD (DIRECTOR)

HALSTED WELLES AND MICHAEL BRANDT (SCREENWRITERS)

Film, 2007. Summary.

There is more than half a century between *High Noon* and our second Western, *3:10 to Yuma*, but *3:10* is actually a remake of a film from the same decade, the nineteen fifties—a decade where films often dealt with big moral questions. It opened to enthusiastic reviews in 2007, proclaiming that the Western movie was back! A good plot, well acted, well directed, with an intriguing good guy/bad guy dynamic. The fact that it was a remake didn't seem to detract from its freshness. (For those of you who may know the 1957 version, this one is quite different in significant ways that I won't divulge.)

So what was so appealing about the 2007 version? Could it be that both the good guy and the bad guy are sympathetic characters, played by attractive "leading men"? Or that the plot doesn't go where you think it is going to go? Or perhaps that good Westerns are few and far between? You be the judge of that.

3:10 to Yuma is a tale about right and wrong but also, in a secondary way, about good and evil. It is about a man deciding to do the right thing, first for selfish reasons, and then, apparently, just because it's right. Therefore, we can call it a "Kantian" Western.

Dan Evans is a small-time rancher with a wife, two sons, and a ranch outside Bisbee, Arizona. The little family is eking out a miserable existence on land without sufficient water for their cattle, since the river is being diverted by the big rancher upstream who is offering Evans water rights for the enormous sum of two hundred dollars. All the while, the rancher's cowboys are harassing the Evanses, stampeding their cattle and burning down their barn. The Evanses are facing impending doom; without the two hundred dollars, they will have to leave their land and everything they have worked and fought for. In addition, Evans is challenged by the fact that he lost a leg in the Civil War—not even in battle, but from "friendly fire," something he hopes to keep from his sons. They have very little respect for him as it is, especially the older boy, who is fourteen.

But by chance, Evans gets the opportunity to make two hundred dollars, which would save his land and his cattle: While rounding up his cattle, he and his boys witness a holdup of the stage by a gang of ruthless men who gun down everyone and take the Southern Pacific Railroad's payroll. One man, a bounty hunter hired by the Pinkerton Agency, survives with a bullet wound to his stomach. The leader of the outlaws scatters Evans's cattle and takes his horses to prevent anyone from riding for help, but we sense immediately that the gang leader is not without a sense of fairness: He promises to leave the horses on the road where Evans and the boys can get to them. And we learn that this unusual bandit is the legendary Ben Wade, a man who has escaped justice over and over again.

Dan and the boys manage to recapture their horses, and they transport the bounty hunter to Bisbee so he can get medical attention. Meanwhile, Wade and the gang have made it to Bisbee, where they report that they have witnessed the holdup. While the marshal rides off toward the holdup spot, the gang members ride off in the opposite direction with the loot—all except Wade, who finds time to have a sexual interlude with a saloon girl he recognizes from another town. He turns out to be a silver-tongued romantic, utterly confident in himself and his own ability to get out of any situation. But his escapade costs him dearly: The marshal has encountered the bounty hunter, Dan Evans, and the boys, and realizes that the man who reported the holdup was one of Wade's gang members—and that Wade is still in town. So Wade is arrested, just like that.

But now the local marshal has a tiger by the tail, because once Wade's gang finds out he is captured, they're bound to come after him. So the marshal and his deputies hatch a plan to get Wade to justice, and railroad representative Grayson Butterfield promises two hundred dollars to any man who will help out. Evans, seeing an end to his financial worries, volunteers to go along with Butterfield, the local veterinarian who doubles as a doctor, the bounty hunter who feels well enough to ride, and one of the rancher's cowboys on the cross-country trail to the town of Contention, where they will put Ben Wade on the train to the Yuma State Prison. There he will be given a perfunctory trial before he is hanged.

The plan consists in a switcheroo to fool Wade's gang: They will make a big show out of putting Wade on a stagecoach with guards. Then, when the stage has reached Dan Evans's place outside town, they'll feign a wheel accident and, in the confusion, switch Wade with one of their own men and spirit Wade away to Dan's ranch. The switch happens seamlessly, the stage takes off again with the fake "Wade" on board, and Wade, in handcuffs, is now a prisoner/dinner guest at the Evans place.

During dinner he charms Alice, Dan's wife, and looks utterly heroic to Dan's older son, William. Wade also manages to hide a dinner fork up his sleeve. Although Dan is disturbed by the fascination Alice and the boys have for Wade, he seems to accept, meekly, that he is not a hero to his own boys. Dan himself finds Wade intriguing, and deserving of respect, because earlier, Wade paid him for the afternoon he and his boys spent looking for their horses and rounding up their cattle a second time.

Dan tells his boys to stay behind with their mother, and rides off with the little posse and Wade toward Contention, hoping to earn the money that will save his ranch. On the trail they are joined by William, who has run away from home to join the posse—and we sense it is also because he feels drawn to the magnetism of Ben Wade. Even so, William comes to the aid of his father and the rest of the little posse when Wade makes a move to escape, so his loyalty is not in question.

A strange camaraderie develops between Evans and Wade. They don't understand each other's motives, but they like to talk. Wade derides Evans for believing in a moral code, but Evans realizes that the outlaw Wade has his own very strong values: He has a sense of fairness, and he will not suffer stupidity, even in his own gang. But Wade emphasizes to Dan that he never does anything unless it benefits himself. Dan can expect no human kindness from Wade. The outlaw proves himself to be a formidable ally as well as a formidable adversary: When a band of Apache Indians attacks in the middle of the night, Wade's battle experience saves them—but with the fork he has stolen, he also kills the deputized cowboy (who, we learn, was the man who set fire to Dan's barn), takes his gun, and succeeds in throwing the bounty hunter off a cliff before he takes off, still hand-cuffed. The remainder of the posse follows his tracks up into the mountains, through a newly blasted tunnel where the railroad is being pushed through, to the railroad work-ers' camp. They arrive just in time to rescue Wade from a painful death at the hands of an irate railroad guard who has recognized Wade as his brother's murderer. But during their escape the doctor is shot and dies.

As they approach Contention, the danger of a showdown becomes clear: Wade ex-pects his men to show up any minute, because they will by now have seen through the stagecoach ruse (and we, the audience, have already seen them kill the guard and the "fake" Wade, burning them alive inside the stagecoach). The remaining posse—Butterfield, Dan, and William—take Wade to the hotel to wait for the train, and Butterfield goes to the local marshal's office for reinforcements. Three or four well-armed law-enforcement officers arrive at the hotel, and it looks as if Evans and Butterfield will succeed in putting Wade on the train. But now Wade's gang rides into town, led by his second-in-command, Charlie Prince, a mean-spirited, sadistic character who has 100 percent loyalty for Wade and for nobody else. Prince promises a reward to anyone in town who will kill a member of the posse. The marshal assesses the odds and backs down, telling his deputies that their job guarding Wade isn't worth dying for. But as they exit the hotel, Prince and the gang gun them down in cold blood. Butterfield himself has no intention of dying, so he also leaves, and hides out in the hotel.

Evans finds himself reassessing the situation: Rain clouds are forming over the Bis-bee range, which means that his ranch will get water. That means he really won't need the two hundred dollars anymore, so there is no financial reason for Evans to try to get Wade on the train. Now Wade starts bargaining with Dan: He will offer him one thousand dol-lars in cash, from the stagecoach robbery, if he will let Wade go. For one brief moment Dan considers the offer; then he declines. Wade asks Dan why. Why is it so important to him to keep a promise when everyone else has chickened out? Dan's answer is that when you've been in the war and the only action you've seen is a retreat, and then you lose your leg to friendly fire, that isn't much of a story to tell your boys.

Dan, fearing that he won't make it out alive, sends William away, telling him to re-member that his father was the only one who stood up for what's right. Dan also calls Butterfield back and makes him promise that if he doesn't make it back to Bisbee, then his family will receive a thousand dollars as a reward from the railroad. Meanwhile, Wade is watching, and we get a sense that he actually cares whether Dan lives or dies. He makes it clear to Dan that he has been imprisoned in Yuma twice before, and escaped.

It is 3:00, and the train will be in shortly. Wade's gang is spread out from the hotel to the train and the cattle pens. William is waiting by the cattle pens with a rifle. Surpris-ingly, Wade now seems to cooperate, running and dodging bullets with Dan to get to the station, over rooftops, down alleys, along the cattle pens, until they get to the station—but the train is late!

What will happen? Will Wade get on the train of his own volition? Will Dan survive to get home to his family and the ranch? And what happens to William? As the train pulls up, the gang is approaching . . . You'll have to watch the ending for yourself!

Study Questions

1. Why is Dan Evans doing what he is doing? Is he just trying to impress his son, or does he have another motive? Why is this called a "Kantian" Western in the introduction?

2. Compare Evans's choice to stand alone, doing what is right, with Will Kane's (*High Noon*). Is there a difference? Explain.

3. Why do you think Wade is cooperating with Evans toward his own imprisonment? If you have seen the film, fill in the blanks and evaluate all Wade's actions, including the moment when he whistles for his horse.

4. Would you say that Evans's boys have good reason to be proud of their father? Why or why not? Did Evans make the right choice? Does it depend on whether he lives or dies? What does Evans mean by saying to Wade that until now, he hasn't had a good story to tell his sons? Explain.

5. A "spoiler alert": In a scene that takes the audience aback, Wade guns down members of his own gang. Remember Wade's comment that he will not put up with fools—might it be that the outlaw Wade has principles? Can a truly selfish person have principles?

Narrative

Match Point

WOODY ALLEN (DIRECTOR AND SCREENWRITER)

Film, 2005. Summary.

The film *Match Point,* a term borrowed from tennis, where it indicates the point at which a game might end, is primarily about *luck.* To be sure, Lady Luck was not one of Kant's primary interests, but the main character in *Match Point,* Chris Wilton, epitomizes what Kant thought was wrong about lying: He lies to save his own hide, even if he knows that what he is doing is wrong. This is, in essence, a basic story about someone who lies to get out of trouble and lives with one idea in mind: to look out for number one. So this film might also be used in Chapter 4 to illustrate fundamental selfishness. And I need to issue a "spoiler alert" at this point: I will be revealing elements of the ending in this summary.

The film opens, in Chris's voice, with the following message, and with an image of a tennis ball teetering on the top of the net:

> The man who said "I'd rather be lucky than good" saw deeply into life. People are afraid to face how great a part of life is dependent on luck. It's scary to think so much is outside one's control. There are moments in a match when the ball hits the top of the net and for a split second it can either go forward or fall back. With a little luck it goes forward and you win. Or maybe it doesn't and you lose.

We'll see a similar image much later in the film, and we'll get the meaning.

In the film *Match Point* (DreamWorks, 2005) young, ambitious former tennis pro, Chris (Jonathan Rhys Meyers, left) wants to marry into a rich and powerful family, but he falls in love with Nola (Scarlett Johansson), the fiancée of his girlfriend's brother (Matthew Goode). Here Chris meets Nola for the first time. Since he is not about to give up on either his wealthy girlfriend Chloe or beautiful Nola, he marries Chloe and entangles himself in a web of lies so he can keep dating Nola. Eventually he starts lying to Nola, too.

Chris is a British former tennis champion who is now a tennis coach at a fancy London club. He comes from a working-class background and has ambitions to do something good, to make a difference, but above all to leave his modest background behind and work his way out of poverty. (Even today in England, as most Americans know, the class system is very much in evidence.) One of Chris's clients is young, wealthy Tom Hewett, and they soon strike up a friendship, sharing a love for tennis and for the opera. (Throughout the film, famous opera arias are playing, about love and betrayal, subtly commenting on the plot, as opera aficionados are happy to point out.) Chris is invited to the opera and meets Tom's family, including his sister Chloe. Friendship develops rapidly, and Chris is invited to the family's country estate that same weekend. Feelings are already developing between him and Chloe, but it is obvious that Chloe is more in love with him than he is with her. As luck will have it, one of the other weekend guests is a young, sassy, sexy woman from America, Nola Rice. When Chris encounters her, sparks immediately fly between them. (Chris reveals himself to be something of a cad already at this point.) But Tom arrives and introduces Nola, an actress from Colorado, as his fiancée.

Chloe asks her father to find Chris a job in the family business, and he does, seeing in Chris a future son-in-law. Chloe's mother is disturbed by Chris's lack of breeding and is downright opposed to Nola coming into the family, but the father shows more understanding, seeing the potential for happiness as well as for good business. The two couples start double-dating, but soon Chris doesn't want to do anything with Chloe unless Nola and Tom are there too. At one of their dinners Chris expresses his philosophy: Life has no purpose, no design; life is on this planet by chance, and luck is the only thing he believes in. Chloe, on the other hand, believes in hard work.

A chance meeting between Chris and Nola—she is on her way to an audition—develops into a confidential talk, and it is obvious that Chris is extremely attracted to Nola. During a weekend at the Hewitt estate, Tom and Chloe's mother starts ragging on Nola for wanting to be an actress. Nola bolts from the living room out into the garden in the rain, and Chris follows her in sympathy. Sympathy turns to passion, and they make love in the field of grain.

After that incident, Nola is distant—she regrets what she has done, and focuses on the fact that they are about to become brother- and sister-in-law. Chris's ambitions are about to be realized—he and Chloe do get married, and Hewitt finds them a spectacular apartment with a view of the River Thames and the houses of Parliament. Chloe wants to become pregnant as soon as possible, which puts a strain on their sex life, and Chris starts dreaming about Nola—Tom has broken up with her and is dating someone else. And Nola has disappeared.

Months later, Chloe is still not pregnant, and Chris runs into Nola at the Tate Modern art gallery. At the first opportunity, he goes to her apartment, where they resume their brief affair. From now on Chris sees Nola as often as he can—during lunch breaks, after meetings, before work, after work—and lies to Chloe about where he has been. When a friend shows up and catches Chris in a lie, he begins to realize that the situation is getting complicated. Chloe suspects nothing yet, but is upset that he is absent so much. Nola is getting upset that he still hasn't told Chloe that he is leaving her—and, of course, we know that he has no intention of doing so; his life with a fancy job and a fancy apartment is much too attractive for him to divorce his wife for Nola.

But now Nola gets pregnant, and life becomes hell for Chris, because she demands that he tell his wife; if he doesn't, Nola will: Chris begins to lie not only to his wife but also to his lover: He claims that he will tell his wife and get a divorce, but he has no intention of leaving the upscale life he has gotten used to. But Chloe is beginning to suspect that he is having an affair. She asks him, "Don't you love me anymore?" and with a hint of veracity, he says to her, "I feel so guilty." She thinks he feels guilty because she isn't pregnant yet, but we, the audience, know that even if he feels guilty, he has no intention of doing the right thing. And that is precisely what Nola wants him to do—the "right thing." For her, it would mean leaving his wife, marrying her, and raising their child together. (She has no intention of getting an abortion—she has already had two.)

When he tells her he is going away to Greece with his wife and her family but she catches him in town, things come to a head. Screaming "Liar!" at him, she makes a scene outside his workplace. He manages to put her in a cab and take her home, where she threatens to tell Chloe. Chris promises Nola that now he'll do the right thing.

The "right thing" turns out to mean something quite different for Chris than for Nola: He goes into his father-in-law's gun collection, steals a shotgun with shells, and puts it in his tennis bag. He arranges with Chloe to meet her that evening to attend a musical (which he hates), then calls Nola to tell her he has good news and will come by after work. With the shotgun in his tennis bag, he goes to Nola's apartment building *before* she returns from work: Under the pretext of checking her television, he persuades Nola's elderly neighbor Mrs. Eastby to let him in, and the old lady suspects no foul play until he turns the shotgun on her and shoots her down. Then he ransacks the apartment and takes her medication and jewelry, making it look like a drug-related robbery. His nerves are about to fail him, but he keeps going. He waits for Nola on the landing. When she steps out of the elevator, he shoots and kills her at point-blank range, and leaves as fast as he can, going straight to the musical with Chloe. Sure enough, next day the newspapers are full of the story of the double murder. The police theorize that it was a drug-related robbery gone bad and that Nola must have just gotten in the way.

Chris manages to put the shotgun back and dispose of the shells, and he throws the jewelry and the medication into the river. For one moment the camera follows one item, Mrs. Eastby's ring, which doesn't fall into the river but instead teeters on the top of the fence, like a tennis ball . . . Luck is about to happen. But is it good or bad luck? After finding Nola's diary, the police question Chris, who tells the officers that "it might not be the most honorable thing to cheat on your wife, but that doesn't make me a murderer." He begs them not to tell his in-laws, and they seem sympathetic, but the detective has a hunch—that Chris is the murderer.

That same night two important things happen. First, Chris sees ghosts: His conscience is beginning to torture him, and he sees both Nola and old Mrs. Eastby. He tells Mrs. Eastby that she was collateral damage, and she responds that so was his own unborn child. Chris responds with the words of Sophocles that "not being born may be the greatest boon of all." Nola predicts that he'll get caught, and in the depths of feeling guilty, he says to her that it would be fitting for him to be found out—it would be some small sign of justice, "some small measure of hope for the possibility of meaning." (Remember that he thinks life is an accident on this planet, and there is no higher power.) Second, the detective wakes up, in the same wee hours, with an epiphany. In a flash he sees the truth: that Chris killed Nola to be free of her and the baby and that he staged Mrs. Eastby's murder as a cover.

So it looks as if there might be justice after all. Chris yearns for it, and the detective has put two and two together. But now Luck intervenes: Mrs. Eastby's ring has been found in the pocket of a robber that same night, after he has been shot dead. So he must have been Mrs. Eastby's killer, right? And the case is dropped.

I will leave the final wrap-up for you to experience for yourself: Will Chloe get pregnant? Will there be any justice for Nola and Mrs. Eastby? Will Chris have to pay for his crimes and his selfishness? Which way will the irony cut?

Study Questions

1. Is this a realistic film? Is it a tragedy? Is it a comedy? What is the "moral of this story"?

2. What would Kant say is wrong with Chris's choice of actions? Would the filmmaker, Woody Allen (who wrote and directed the movie), agree? Why or why not?

3. What, in your opinion, would have been "the right thing" for Chris to do? Would it depend on the outcome? Explain why or why not.

4. Is there such a thing as a justifiable lie? Might such a question apply to Chris? Explain.

5. If one doesn't think there is a higher power, and one believes that life on earth is here by accident, does that mean one has no moral obligations—that anything is permitted? Explain.

6. What did Sophocles mean by saying that not being born may be the greatest boon of all?

7. The film seems to indicate that "luck" is opposed to "justice." Do you think that is true? Explain.

Chapter Seven

Personhood, Rights, and Justice

*T*o Kant, any being who is capable of rational thinking qualifies as a person, and (according to Kant's *Grounding for the Metaphysics of Morals*) creatures incapable of rational thinking are classified as things. Today, the debate about what constitutes a person is still with us because the question has lost none of its urgency. At the time when Kant lived, human beings were often treated as things, tools, stepping-stones for the needs or convenience of others. That idea was a legitimate part of public policy in many places throughout the world, and the moral statement that a rational being should never be reduced to a mere tool for another's purpose became part of the worldwide quest for human rights—rights that still have not been universally implemented. That statement is historically important and should not be forgotten, even though many social thinkers today believe that Kant's fight for the recognition that all persons deserve respect must be expanded and that Kant himself didn't have a concept of universal human rights in mind.

In this chapter we discuss issues that reflect several of the theories already studied and that illustrate how such theories can be applied on a social scale in creating policies regarding the rights and duties of citizens. It is thus important that you have studied Chapters 5 and 6 in particular before you proceed.

What Is a Human Being?

If we focus on the rights of human animals, we have to address the question, What does it mean to be human? Are the criteria physical? Does a being have to look human to be human? How detailed must we get? A traditional answer is "a featherless biped"—in other words, a creature that walks upright on two legs but is not a bird—but those are hardly sufficient criteria. Nowadays, if we want to use physical criteria, we include not only physical appearance but also genetic information. But with that type of explanation we're faced with two problems: (1) Genetically, there are creatures that are 98 percent identical to the human but are obviously not human: chimpanzees; (2) there are individuals born of human parents who may not have all the human physical characteristics—for instance, persons with multiple physical disabilities (not to mention *mental* disabilities). So is a being born of humans who happens to have some physical aberration—from missing limbs to minor abnormalities such as extra toes and fingers—human? For most people today, the answer is obviously yes, but this was not always so. A worldwide tradition in pretechnological societies has been to dispose of newborns with physical "handicaps" ranging from missing limbs to unwanted birthmarks, and not all of those disposals can be explained by saying that a tribe isn't able to feed those who can't feed themselves. Our culture doesn't follow that practice, but some of us do screen the fetus for severe disabilities and perform abortions if we believe that those disabilities will condemn the child to a less than dignified life. This is not a discussion of the pros and cons of abortion, any more than it is a discussion of infanticide, but it does point out that a good deal of policymaking in other cultures as well as our own depends on how we define "human being," including what a human being, and a human life, *should be like*—a normative concept. In Chapter 13 you'll find a discussion of the issue of abortion.

The Expansion of the Concept "Human"

There was a time when people distinguished between friend and foe by calling friends humans and foes beasts, devils, or such. At the tribal level of human history, it has always been common to view the tribe across the river as not quite human, even if members of your tribe marry their sons or daughters. (In fact, the usual word that tribes use to designate themselves is their word for "human," "the people," or "us.") In any geographic area there are people who remain dubious about those from the "other side" because their habits are so different that it seems there must be something "strange" about their general humanity. From the time of the ancient Greeks until quite recently, a common assumption has been that men are more "normal" than women. Interestingly enough, that idea has been held not only by many men but also by many women, who took the men's word for it. (Some still do.) At the nationalistic level, it still is common practice to view foreigners as less than human, not in a physical sense, but, rather, politically and morally in a normative rather than a descriptive sense. And the humanity of a people's wartime enemies almost always is denied, usually because it becomes easier to kill an enemy, either soldier or civilian, if you believe he or she really is not quite as human as you are. Thus the term *human* sometimes evolves into an honorary term reserved for those with whom we prefer to share our culture.

Personhood: The Key to Rights

Many social thinkers prefer the term *person* to *human being* as a philosophical and political concept, partly to avoid the association with the human physical appearance. A person is someone who is capable of psychological and social interaction with others, capable of deciding on a course of action and being held responsible for that action. In other words, a person is considered a *moral agent*. Being a person implies certain duties and privileges—in other words, it is a normative concept: what a person *ought to be and do* to be called a person. Personhood implies that one has certain social privileges and duties and that under extreme circumstances these can be revoked. What was a person to the Greeks? to the Romans? to medieval Europeans? To those groups a person was usually a male adult landowner or tribe member. Different societies have excluded some or all of the following people from their concept of a person: slaves, women, children, foreigners, prisoners of war, and criminals. (See Box 7.1 for a discussion of the personhood of people on the fringes of society,

$Box\ 7.1$ IS A PROSTITUTE A PERSON?

In April 2000 a man named Robert L. Yates, Jr., was arrested for the murders of nine women in Spokane, Washington. To avoid the death penalty, he pleaded guilty to all nine murders, plus four others, including two that came as a complete surprise to the police. To this day it is speculated that we have yet to hear the end of the story, since there are many more women missing in the Pacific Northwest. He had been committing those murders since the mid-1990s but had been able to evade capture by blending into society with a seemingly normal existence as an ex–military man, a Seventh-Day Adventist, a helicopter pilot, a husband, and a father of five. Another factor that may well have helped him evade capture was the nature of his victims: He preyed on women whose lifestyles included drug addiction and prostitution.

Although the detectives on the task force assigned to the serial killings in Spokane seemed highly committed to solving them, one can't help wondering (as many did) whether more funding might have been put into the investigation if the women had been college students, businesswomen, shopkeepers, or housewives rather than hookers and drug addicts. This is by

Copyright *Spokesman-Review,* Spokane

Years into the investigation of the serial murder of prostitutes, the Spokane sheriff's department appealed to the community for help, putting murder victims' faces on a billboard reading "Help Us Find Our Killer." The personalization of each woman may have inspired a change in attitude in the community toward the victims, from expendable outcasts to individuals with a right to live.

no means an isolated phenomenon: From San Diego to Seattle to New York State, we have had examples of serial killings of prostitutes that perhaps a few police detectives took very seriously but that in no way stirred the general outrage of the community. A local radio talk show in Spokane received several calls from listeners who expressed the opinion that the prostitutes somehow were asking for it, living a criminal life on the fringes of society, and that somehow the serial killer was just "cleaning up." But the radio hosts took on the capture of the murderer as a righteous cause, keeping up the pressure in the community and criticizing the apathy among citizens as well as what they saw as inadequate police work, even when the killings seemed to stop. The hosts raised questions such as "Are these women not human beings with the same rights as the rest of us? Don't they have families who mourn them? Don't they feel pain and anguish in their last moments at the mercy of a murderer? It may be illegal to be a prostitute and to use drugs, but it doesn't carry a death penalty."

Months before Yates was captured, a billboard had been erected in downtown Spokane, with photos of sixteen victims and the plea "Help Us Find Our Killer." The billboard helped many citizens of the city realize that each murdered woman had had a life that was precious, each was a person who would have liked to stay alive. It is now part of the civic identity of Spokane

that the sheriff's department managed to catch an elusive serial killer—a rare feat. But serious questions have been raised about the professional standards and efficiency of the task force, indicating that a more concerted police effort combined with more experience and willingness to reach out to the public might have resulted in finding Yates sooner, thus saving lives.

Yates was sentenced to 408 years in prison, and later was sentenced to death for two additional murders in Tacoma, Washington.

In the western part of the state, a similar situation unfolded in 2003–2004: the capture, confession, and conviction of the notorious Green River Killer, Gary Ridgway. Ridgway had been killing prostitutes since the early 1980s in the Seattle-Tacoma area, and possibly elsewhere, and was captured thanks to excellent and foresighted police work. When confronted with incontrovertible evidence—his DNA linked to several of the victims—Ridgway confessed to forty-eight murders and thus avoided the death penalty. But in hour after hour of taped interrogations, he revealed to the police and the world that he didn't consider his victims as any different from trash: He killed them and threw them away. Interestingly, as with Robert Yates, the final chapter to Ridgway's long series of murders didn't generate much interest in the national press, and one is tempted to conclude that it has to do with the fact that their victims were "just" prostitutes.

such as prostitutes and drug addicts.) Usually the list of exclusion was extended to animals, plants, and inanimate objects, but other beings might well have been granted personhood, such as gods and goddesses, totems (ancestor animals), and dead ancestors.

Today we in the Western world assume that all humans are persons with inalienable rights. This is not a recognized truth all over the world, however. "Human trafficking," buying and selling human beings (especially young girls) internationally in the sex trade, is big business. Serfdom still exists in parts of the world, such as Pakistan. In many nations to this day, women are considered the property of their husbands or fathers. Crimes against children are often not punished as severely as crimes against adults, if at all. And even in this country, the equal rights provisions that we take pride in don't always work: The sweatshops that are known to provide us with cheap products from elsewhere in the world are sometimes found to operate on American soil. News stories surface from time to time about undocumented immigrants kept in economic bondage by the people who imported them. Any time we hear a news story of people being abused or taken advantage of, resulting in the loss of their well-being or their lives, we are hearing about people whose *personhood* has been violated—or as Kant would say, they have been treated merely as a means to an end—and in general, our court system is capable of dealing with such offenses.

But the lack of respect for other human beings as persons sometimes goes beyond what the law can address. When *discrimination* reaches the level of depriving someone of his or her rights, the law can step in, but when it is merely an attitude, we encounter an interesting problem: Should we outlaw discrimination as an attitude, or is it part of living in a free country that people may choose their viewpoints without being told by the state what to think? There is a fine line here. Most of us would like to see an end to *racism* and *sexism,* but we may also be reluctant to send people who have expressed racist or sexist views to a retraining facility where their minds will be altered, because we believe not only in freedom of speech but also in freedom of thought. Perhaps this is where Kant's lesson of treating people as *ends in themselves* has its most profound application in our modern society: With the recognition of every human being as a person with intrinsic value, much disrespect will—at least in theory—fall by the wayside. And racism and sexism are, of course, not the only forms of discrimination that a person can encounter. Bigotry takes many forms, such as discrimination against the young for their youth as well as the elderly for their age ("ageism"), against the mentally ill or mentally disabled, or the physically disabled ("ableism"), against people of a sexual orientation that differs from one's own, or who are of a different religion or nationality; discrimination of the educated against the less-educated, of the less-educated against the highly educated, of the wealthy against the indigent, and of the less well-to-do against the wealthy. And even of conservatives against liberals, and of liberals against conservatives. Suspicion and resentment are part of the fabric of human society, and in each case, the emphasis on personhood should remind us all that despite our differences, we ought to recognize the personhood in one another. (From Chapter 4 you'll remember the philosopher Emmanuel Levinas, who has a special version of this emphasis, and in Chapter 10 you'll see this theory in detail.)

But what about cases where a person has chosen to disregard the personhood of others, to the point of violating their health, their liberty, their property, or their life? Have such people now opened themselves up to being deprived of their own status of personhood? In other words, is a *criminal* a person?

Who Is a Person?

For many people, the more callous the crime, the less human the criminal. Sometimes we even call murderers "animals," although few nonhuman animals have been known to display the methodical, deliberate preying on one's own species typical of human career criminals, serial rapists, and serial killers. In our attitudes toward such criminals, much of our view of what counts as human is revealed: We're not trying to describe their genetic makeup; we're expressing a moral condemnation of their actions and choices. Calling a criminal an animal is a normative statement, not a descriptive one: He (or she) has not lived up to our expectations of what a person ought to be and do, and so we view him as less than human. But genetically as well as legally, a serial killer such as Robert Yates (see Box 7.1) is still a person, and the very fact that we choose to hold him accountable in court is proof of that. Had he been an "animal," we wouldn't have taken him to court—he would have been put down immediately, like a vicious dog. However, criminals, even convicted ones, don't lose all their rights: Their personhood status is not revoked, at least not in our culture. They still have the right not to be tortured, for example, although they may have lost their right to liberty. Below we take a closer look at the animal issue as well as the concept of rights.

Children as a group have not until recently been considered "real people." Until recently, child abuse was not considered a felony. In previous times—in fact, as recently as the nineteenth century and, in some places, the twentieth century—the father of the household had the supreme right to treat his family (including his wife) any way he pleased. That might very well include physically punishing all the family members, even unto death. That right, *patria potestas,* is still in effect in certain societies in the world. The thought of protecting children against abuse, even abuse from their own parents, is actually quite a new idea in Western cultures; even in the recent past, child abuse cases were sometimes covered up or never reported. Those that have been reported add up to staggering numbers: In the state of Washington alone, for instance, the Office of the Family and Children's Ombudsman's report for February 2006 revealed that out of 87 children who died in 2004, 53 died before they turned three; 28 out of the 87 died as a result of accidents, and 10 were deliberately murdered by their caregivers—parents or foster parents. In 61 deaths, neglect and/or abuse was the determining factor, and in 55 of the cases, the CPS (Child Protective Services) had been involved three or more times already. The picture is not much different in other states. There are stories of children being removed from foster homes and given back to abusive parents who then kill them through abuse or neglect; of parents torturing children to death for wetting their beds or for crying; of children starving to death because their parents or foster parents couldn't be bothered to feed them; of parents or foster parents who are in need of help themselves for severe drug dependency. The heartbreaking numbers tell us that, for whatever reason, authorities charged with the well-being of these children are not picking up on danger signals. Analysts suspect that the idea that children ought to be with their parents and not in foster care is applied too rigidly, regardless of what is in the child's best interest, and also that because of the notion, left over from a bygone age, that toddlers are somehow not quite "persons" yet, their misery at the hands of their caregivers doesn't merit a criminal investigation.

What has been more publicized, with more visible results, is the scandal involving child abuse by Catholic priests, which you read about in Chapter 4. In the terminology of Kant, the children had been used merely as a means to an end. Today we recognize not only that children should be protected from abuse but also that children have interests and wishes that they are capable of expressing and that should be heard, such as which parent they wish to stay with after a divorce.

We are now at the point where the conscious interests of children (including everything from having enough food, shelter, love, and education to refusing to go to school in order to play video games or watch TV) must be balanced against what conscientious adults deem to be in the children's best interests, best *in spite of* themselves. In other words, we must remember that what children want is not necessarily good for them. The idea that children are minors who have neither the legal rights nor the legal responsibilities of adults is not about to disappear, even when their interests are taken into consideration. We tend to forget that when a group is excluded from having rights, it is usually also excluded from having responsibilities. In other words, such a group must be given legal protection so that its members, who are incapable of taking on civil responsibilities, will not be treated unjustly.

Persons and Responsibility

Historically, the idea of children having responsibilities has shifted back and forth. It was only in the twentieth century that we in the Western world agreed not to hold minors responsible for criminal acts. The legendary German figure Till Eulenspiegel was a mischievous kid who played one too many tricks on decent citizens, and the decent citizens hanged him. The title character of Herman Melville's *Billy Budd* faced the same fate. Billy, a young sailor, was falsely accused of wrongdoing by a vicious officer. Because Billy had a problem articulating and could not speak up to defend himself, he acted out his frustration by striking the officer. Unfortunately, that resulted in the officer's death, and the captain, although aware of Billy's problem, had to follow the law of the sea: mandatory death for anyone who kills an officer. In the end, Billy had to submit to the traditional execution method by climbing up the rigging and slipping a noose around his own neck. Today a crime committed by a person under the age of eighteen must reveal an extraordinary amount of callousness and "evil intent" for the court to try the minor as an adult. That is because childhood is considered to be a state of mind and body that doesn't allow for the logical consistency we assume is available, most of the time, to adults; therefore children aren't held accountable for their actions to the degree that adults are.

The United States, however, has seen a shift lately in the attitude toward children who commit crimes. Although most child psychologists still agree that children below the age of seven or eight don't know enough about the difference between right and wrong to be held accountable, public demand is now growing for trying older child offenders as adults. What should the court do with a child who kills another child for his sneakers or his jacket? or who takes a gun to school and kills a number of his classmates and teachers before being stopped? In some states, such as Arkansas, children cannot be tried as adults. In other states, it is the severity of the crime that determines whether the youth will be tried as an adult; we have lately seen teenagers being given hefty prison sentences (although the Supreme Court decided in 2005 that a child under eighteen can't be given the death penalty). The issue of when a child can be held criminally responsible for his or her actions is the focus of much current legal attention. For example, in 2000, thirteen-year-old Nathaniel Abraham was convicted of second-degree murder after being tried as an adult for a murder he committed at age eleven. He was *sentenced* as a juvenile, however, and was to be held in a juvenile detention facility until the age of twenty-one but had his prisoner status reduced in 2004 because of good behavior and was released in January 2007. An illustration of how times have changed since the 1970s is the case of Michael Skakel, indicted in 2000 for the 1975 murder of his fifteen-year-old neighbor, Martha Moxley. Skakel, a cousin of the Kennedy family by marriage, was himself fifteen years old at the time, and the state of Connecticut would, in 1975, have considered him a juvenile who could not therefore be tried as an adult. That law was changed a few years later, but Skakel's attorney argued, unsuccessfully, that Skakel, now very much an adult, should be tried as a juvenile. In 2002 he was tried as an adult and found guilty of murder.

In the past, the rights of women have followed a course similar to those of children. Women had very few rights until the late nineteenth century—no right to hold property, no right to vote, no right over their own person. That went hand in hand with the common assumption that women were not capable of moral consistency and thus were not responsible. (Mention of women and children in the same breath was no coincidence.) That view often coincided with a male reverence for women and their supposedly higher moral standards, but such reverence was often combined with an assumption that women were idealists with no conception of the sordid dealings and practical demands of the real world.

When it applied to women, the practice of holding only those with rights legally responsible was not strictly adhered to. Many, many women were put on criminal trial. Even so, the general idea was that withholding rights from women *protected* them from the harsh world of reality, whose demands they weren't capable of answering. (In Chapter 12 you'll find a more thorough analysis of the history of women's rights, as well as a discussion of women and ethics.) A similar kind of argument kept slaves from having rights throughout most slaveholding societies— rights were denied to provide "protection" for these people because they were "incapable." That did not preclude punishing slaves, of course, as anyone who has read *Huckleberry Finn* knows. In *On Liberty* (see Chapter 5), John Stuart Mill argues that the right to self-determination should extend universally, *provided* that the individuals in question have been educated properly, in the British sense, so that they know what to do with the self-determination. Until then, they are incapable of making responsible decisions and should be protected—children by their guardians and colonial inhabitants by the British. (Today, an animal rights activist might argue that we see the same pattern repeated with animals: We don't believe them to be fully developed moral agents, and so we protect them—by withholding rights from them.) An interesting concept evolves from these arguments; namely, that it is possible for someone to be considered a person, but a person with *limited* rights, duties, and privileges whose rights are assigned to a guardian. We will return to this idea in Chapter 13.

Science and Moral Responsibility: Genetic Engineering, Stem Cell Research, and Cloning

As it stands now, we must agree that our culture has come a long way in recognizing all postnatal humans as persons, at least in principle, although that principle sometimes seems to be overpowered by controversy. But what about the future? Genetically engineered children already walk among us, and there will be many more. Your children—and perhaps even you yourself—may be able to look forward to a longer, healthier life span because of genetic engineering. By the time you're reading this, there may be viable human clones among us too, legally or otherwise. Will these new members of our human family be considered persons, or will they encounter some new form of discrimination? In the Narratives section you'll find two stories that explore either end of this spectrum of possibilities: The film *The Island* envisions a near future when humans are cloned for spare parts, without regard to their humanity. The film *Gattaca* suggests a world, right around the corner, where genetic engineering has become mainstream, and it is those who have *not* been genetically "improved" at the embryo stage who will form the new underclass. Who will really be up, and who will be down, in such a "brave new world"?

We can ask ourselves two questions here: Given that a future involving a variety of options for genetic engineering and cloning is already upon us, (1) how should we deal with the scientific possibilities opening up for humanity? Should we be phobic about scientific developments and encourage bans and limits to scientific research? Or, should we encourage all such research under the assumption that somehow it may benefit us and that science has a right to seek knowledge for the sake of knowledge no matter the consequences? Or should we, perhaps, take some position in between? (2) Should scientists themselves exercise some form of moral responsibility, taking into consideration that their results will be used in the future, perhaps to the detriment of humans and animals living in that future? In the next section we take a look at one of the most burning issues today: the question of science and moral responsibility.

Science Is Not Value-Free

In 1968 a book came out in Germany that challenged the traditional scientific view that science is value-free, or morally neutral: *Knowledge and Interest* by the philosopher Jürgen Habermas. Scientists had claimed—some still do—that scientific research is done for the sake of knowledge itself, not for the social consequences it might bring. As such, scientists' professional integrity hinges on impeccable research; they have no responsibility to the community for what problems—or even benefits—their research might lead to in the future. Habermas claimed that science might attempt to be objective but that an element of vested interest is always present. Society will fund only those projects it deems "valuable" for either further scientific progress, prestige, or profit. Political concerns, social biases, and fads within the scientific community often influence the funding of scientific research projects. Researchers often choose projects for similar reasons. Furthermore, the data selection (choosing research materials according to what the researcher finds relevant to the project) is influenced by the interests of the researcher—whether we like it or not. Habermas's point is that we may think science is conducted in a value-neutral way, but it is not. In addition, having seen what harm irresponsible scientists can cause to a society, wouldn't it be appropriate for scientists to conduct their research with a sense of obligation to the future? and for the community to monitor scientific research?

The question posed by the scientist Malcolm in the film *Jurassic Park* sums up the issue of "science without responsibility": Just because it is possible for science to create dinosaurs, does it mean that science *should* do it? After all, there is an underlying suspicion that some scientific research is done strictly to see whether it can be done. At the same time, we should beware of approaching the other extreme—the assumption that scientists can *never* be objective.

Medical doctors of the past had their own share of moral problems: An army surgeon would have to decide which of the wounded soldiers he should operate on and which ones should be left to die. A nineteenth-century family doctor might have to choose between saving a young mother dying in childbirth and saving the infant being born. But today, technology allows medical procedures that would have been unimaginable a few generations ago. Life can be prolonged artificially; pregnancies can be terminated with comparative safety for the woman; genetic engineering can save babies from a life of illness while they are still in the womb; women can give birth after menopause; stem cell research promises to cure diseases; and the Human Genome Project, completed in 2000, suggests a future in which we will have mapped human DNA to the point of understanding and preventing a vast array of medical problems. In addition, the old science fiction dream (or nightmare) of creating children completely outside the womb of the mother now looks as if it might become a reality, with recent experiments at Cornell University involving an artificial womb. With the increased knowledge, however, comes an increase in moral problems.

In this new era of medical possibilities, there are few established rules to guide those making the decisions. For that reason, the medical profession has a vested interest in supporting the creation of a viable set of ethical procedures to follow in the gray areas of decision making. If healthy babies can one day be created in an artificial womb environment, what will that mean for the concept of *viability*, a concept that is essential to the abortion debate? Viability means that a fetus could, with medical assistance, survive outside the mother's body; at present, viability is set at the third trimester (so abortion becomes problematic at this time because the fetus will at that point be considered a person). But if viability can be extended backward into the second and even first trimester, does that mean that an early fetus thus becomes a person, not just in a religious sense, but in a legal sense as well? And what will that mean for the abortion debate? Further questions abound when we turn to DNA-related issues: When we finally have the complete ability to interfere purposefully with the human DNA code, how much is too much interference? Should we interfere strictly to prevent terminal diseases, or is it acceptable to interfere with nature to determine the shape of the baby's nose, for example? And given the limited resources of medicine, who should benefit from organ transplants—first come, first served? The young, the wealthy, the famous? Those who have waited the longest?

In the seventeenth and eighteenth centuries, the early years of modern science, the moral sensitivity that accompanied research seems to have differed from that which prevails today. The main concern of scientists then was how to proceed with research without violating the values believed to be expressed in the Bible. In modern times, scientists have occasionally diverged from the path of ethical behavior. In Nazi Germany the ultimate value was success for the Party and the realization of that abstract concept, "the Fatherland." Scientists in Nazi Germany engaged in painful, humiliating, and eventually fatal experiments on human subjects, primarily women and children. Even now, we occasionally learn that, since World War II, scientists have subjected people to experimental medical procedures or have withheld treatment from them—without their knowledge or consent. The Tuskegee Syphilis Study is one of the best known of these experiments. Less well known is the forced sterilization of about 7,500 people in Virginia from 1924 to 1979 based on the ideology of eugenics. California was also active in the eugenics project, sterilizing over 20,000 people.

Most scientists and laypeople today would agree that knowledge can come at a price in suffering that is too high; yet we have a credo that says science is value-free: Scientific research is supposed to be objective, and scientists are not to be swayed by personal ambitions and preference. But does that mean they are not supposed to be swayed by ethical values either?

Genetic Engineering

Medical and general scientific researchers now have capabilities that could only be dreamed of in previous generations. We are only slowly developing a set of ethical rules by which to judge those capabilities, however. Genetic manipulation makes possible a future such as the one Aldous Huxley fantasized about in his *Brave New World*, one with a human race designed for special purposes. (See Box 7.2.) Agriculture has for several years been making use of genetic engineering to create disease-resistant crops. Milk and meat are being irradiated before they hit the stores. And perhaps the most controversial issue: *Transgenic* animals are being patented, such as pigs that have had human genes placed in them to facilitate organ transplants, and goats that have been genetically manipulated to contain spider silk proteins in their milk to be extracted and combined to produce materials of unprecedented strength. Although it may be to humankind's ultimate advantage to have access to these wonders, failure to contain such laboratory-generated genetic material, or failure to foresee the overall consequences of such genetic tinkering, could have disastrous results if no sense of ethics or social responsibility is instilled to guide the decision of researchers. After all, the infamous killer bees (which have now settled comfortably in the southwestern United States) are the result of a lab experiment gone out of control.

In Europe there is now a general mistrust of the entire idea of genetically engineered food products, from grain to farm animals. But what about genetically engineered humans?

In 2000 a little boy was born specifically in order to try to save the life of his older sister. Six-year-old Molly Nash had a congenital blood disease that would, in all probability, take her life before the age of ten. Doctors used "preimplantation genetic diagnosis" (PGD) to select an embryo in vitro that was both free of the disease and a good match as a blood cell donor. A month after the baby, Adam, was born, stem cells from his umbilical cord blood were transplanted into his sister. Molly was given

Box 7.2   A CULTURE OF QUICK FIXES?

Aldous Huxley's science fiction novel *Brave New World* from 1931 is famous for predicting that cloning of humans may be a future option, but even more timely is Huxley's prediction that humans in the future will be so oriented toward an easy life that they will, in essence, be unable to handle any form of emotional stress without medication. The drug of choice, *Soma,* is available to everyone, and it is considered a breach of decorum to handle one's own problems without being drugged into oblivion. The prediction rings true in several ways: For example, many people in this country now seek help from prescription drugs rather than working their way through certain emotional stresses—the quest for the *quick fix.* Helped along by a powerful medical industry and pervasive advertising campaigns,

some doctors are all too willing to prescribe medication that will dull the pain of life in their patients. Depressed? Take a pill. Can't sleep? Take a pill. Too tense? Take a pill. Too relaxed? Take a pill. Some people are, of course, in genuine need of medication for severe mental stresses as well as physical pain; but our twenty-first-century culture seems to have lost its view toward long-term solutions. Ethicists bemoan the tendency: If we can't get instant gratification or solve a problem in short order, we lose our focus and our resolve. What's more, we lose touch with what is a *normal state of affairs*: life with some pain, some grief, some problems—which you then work through and incorporate into your life story or put behind you. In Chapter 13 we take a look at the philosophy of telling one's life story.

the transplant while she held her little brother in her arms. Three months later she was allowed to return home from the hospital to her parents and her new brother, with her chances of survival improved to 85 percent.

Such are the possibilities opening up to us with genetic engineering. Then why are some people worried about the social consequences of this miracle cure? Because we, as a society, have not decided where we'd draw the line: Do we endeavor to create healthy babies, or should we go further, such as customizing babies according to their parents' specifications—or even to society's needs? Will babies be genetically engineered for sex, height, eye color, and skin color? And will those babies who have been genetically engineered be the new society's favorites, leaving the natural-born children behind as a new underclass? Molly and Adam Nash's doctor was quick to emphasize that the parents' use of PGD was acceptable because "they were not selecting in a eugenic sense," just looking for a donor baby. The doctors also outlined what they would consider unacceptable uses of the PGD technology, such as aborting selected implanted embryos just to collect tissue or putting the baby up for adoption after using its cord blood—in other words, using such babies merely as a means to an end, as Kant would say.

Stem Cell Research

Although still controversial to many, stem cell research holds great promise as a means of repairing and replacing damaged organs. Stem cells are general cells, not yet specialized, and they apparently have the capacity to become any organ in the

Bizarro by Dan Piraro

© Dan Piraro. King Features Syndicate.

Cartoonists have a knack for misrepresenting political opponents—a "straw man fallacy," in other words. It is doubtful than any elderly Republican would fear that Democrats would come to steal her stem cells. However, the stem cell debate has indeed spawned a number of misconceptions among the public, such as that stem cells are extracted from aborted fetuses—an impossibility, since the cells at that stage are too far developed to be of any use to stem cell research.

body, with the intervention of medical science; these cells can then be used to repair or replace sick organs in a person. The controversy arises from the practice of harvesting and cloning stem cells from *embryos,* which involves taking the life of the embryo. If one is against abortion at any time during pregnancy because one considers the embryo a person from conception, one will also be against any form of stem cell research involving human embryos. However, contrary to what some people think, stem cells can't be harvested from aborted fetuses (yet) because they are too old; the stem cells have to be harvested within the first two weeks of fetal development at the zygote stage. In 2001, President George W. Bush laid down rules for future stem cell research so that no embryo would be conceived for the specific purpose of being used for stem cell research. Some sixty lines of stem cells were in existence in various labs, however, and those were made available for research. The question of what weighs heavier—existing humans whose lives are in peril, and who could be saved with stem cell research, or the lives of unborn fetuses—is something that divides entire intellectual and political communities today. Those who view early abortion as a reasonable option for women generally take little moral issue with the notion of zygotes being harvested and used for research; but for many who find the notion of taking the lives of fetuses objectionable, the stem cell question is particularly challenging—because even if one views the life of a fetus as intrinsically valuable, one also has to consider the importance of born humans who have lives, and people who love them, and who could be saved from a premature death with stem cell research. In 2004 California voted to fund a state-sponsored stem cell research program, and after being challenged in court for three years, the program went ahead in 2007. Research had already been funded through substantial state and private loans and donations, and California scientists are expected to be a leading force in the field. Elsewhere around the world, stem cell research is also moving ahead: In June 2007

Japanese and American scientists announced that they had found a method of extracting stem cells from *skin tissue,* not from embryos, thereby bypassing the entire ethical issue of using embryos—a method that in some ways promises to be easier and less expensive, but in other ways seems to be more limited than using embryos. So far, stem cells have been created from mouse skin tissue, but the scientists predict that it will be a while before they are ready to extract and develop stem cells from human skin tissue.

In England, stem cell research is going in another direction: In 2008 the last legal obstacles to a new kind of research were removed: *Human–animal hybrid stem cells* would be created for the purpose of studying genetic diseases and eventually growing new tissue in the lab; the embryos would be destroyed after two weeks, and would not be implanted in a surrogate womb. British medical teams have expressed excitement about this development, but others, including religious groups, have found the development ethically repugnant and scientifically unnecessary.

The ultimate goal of stem cell research is not knowledge for the sake of knowledge; it is curing illness and prolonging life. This process involves what is known as *therapeutic cloning,* our next topic.

Therapeutic and Reproductive Cloning

The three areas of genetic engineering, stem cell research, and cloning are often confused, and there are in fact overlapping areas between the three, but the primary goals of these methods are different. *Genetic engineering* consists in altering/manipulating a person's DNA, either during his or her lifetime or before birth, to avoid certain congenital problems or to enhance a certain biological trait. As we have seen, *stem cell research* allows for stem cells to be used in organ repair. *Cloning* involves creating more individuals, identical to the first one. The overlapping comes into the picture with the stem cells: To create more stem cells, the cells have to be cloned. That means that they are chemically manipulated so that they create duplicates of themselves—in other words, twins. The question is, what are these duplicates used for? That depends on whether we're talking about *therapeutic* or *reproductive cloning.* Therapeutic cloning involves duplicating stem cells to insert them into an organ, or regrow the organ, to improve a person's health or to save his or her life. It is a form of medical *therapy,* in other words. The California stem cell research program is oriented exclusively toward therapeutic cloning, a means to the end of finding cures for human illnesses.

The phenomenon of *reproductive cloning* is far more controversial, because it involves a duplication of an entire individual, not just cells. The excitement and concerns over reproductive cloning began in 1994, with the announcement that researchers had successfully split a fertilized (but nonviable) human ovum into twins (which is what happens naturally to produce identical twins). But since then the cloning issue has taken off with a speed not predicted even by science fiction authors: In rapid succession, labs around the world have succeeded in cloning sheep, calves, goats, mice, and wolves, using a variety of techniques, including creating a copy of an adult individual using a cell from that individual with a technique pioneered by the creators of Dolly the sheep—raising the specter of genderless reproduction. (See Box 7.3.)

Box 7.3   BRAVE NEW WORLD: THE SPECTER OF DESIGNER HUMANS

As you'll remember from Chapter 2 and Box 7.2, science fiction has experimented with the notion of an artificially designed humanity since Aldous Huxley's *Brave New World* (1931). Huxley speculated that humans would be able to clone other humans within six hundred years, but the ability was on the horizon already before the end of Huxley's own century. But what is it that we fear so much from the idea of humans creating a new twist to humanity in the lab? The fears are many and varied. One type of anguish arises from a *religious foundation:* Only God is supposed to create life, and types of life, and the fear is that if we play God and create human variations deliberately, we have somehow transgressed and will be punished, as Dr. Frankenstein was punished for creating his monster. Another is that we may be *unleashing powers* that we will lose control over, also in the manner of Frankenstein's monster: New human variations may let loose diseases and deformities that we haven't foreseen (cloned mice became obese, and cloned sheep were born with premature aging), or the new breed may outcompete the garden-variety human being. But a third worry is extremely concrete and down-to-earth: that a designer variation of humans will lead to discrimination. This could take the form of discrimination against the new breed, which could end up being treated like a slave population (as in the film classic *Blade Runner*), or of discrimination against the part of the population who has *not* been genetically altered (as in the film *Gattaca,* in the Narrative section). A discriminatory side effect of doing DNA profiling was, in fact, anticipated in the 1990s by federal legislation and in 2008 Congress passed a bill prohibiting insurance companies and workplaces from using genetic tests to discriminate against persons based on the risks inherent in their DNA profile. An increased risk of cancer or heart disease should not hurt a person's chances of obtaining employment or insurance—but it isn't hard to imagine a future where such rules could be sidestepped.

In 2004 we had the first report of a successful cloning of a cat for commercial purposes: Not the first cat to be cloned, this little kitty was the first *made-to-order* clone. A woman had lost her seventeen-year-old cat and had had the cat cloned, to the tune of $50,000. The lab the woman used has since closed, but another lab began offering commercial cloning of family dogs in 2008. But we shouldn't forget that the pet-cloning venture has another side to it: We may be able to get our pets back in the flesh, so to speak, but we can't replicate their spirit or personality, because that would take duplication of the formative experiences of the original pet—meaning, we would need to replicate their childhood. Living beings don't just consist of their DNA but also are the sum of their experiences—and that goes for humans too. There are lessons to be learned about the entire notion of cloning: To get the "same" individual as its DNA donor, we would have to create a completely identical environment for the individual to grow up in—*nature* plus *nurture.* And even if that were accomplished, we would have to factor in what we might call *situation awareness,* what some would call *free will* (see Chapter 4), at least for humans: When a cloned child finds out he or she has been cloned, will he or she decide to be as similar as, or as different from, the original as possible? I would assume the latter, but you never

This little bundle of joy, "Little Nicky," cost his owner, Julie, $50,000. He was cloned from "Nicky," who had passed away. Does it matter what the price tag is, if we feel that we get a beloved pet back? And does it matter if the clone does not have exactly the same personality as the original?

know. This means that very little can in fact be predicted about how a clone might develop as an adult.

There is widespread reluctance to envision human reproductive cloning, and it is condemned in most countries, although a successful human cloning has yet to be announced and verified. The general assumption has been that scientists who attempt to clone humans for reproductive purposes are playing God and that there is no acceptable reason that anyone would want himself or herself cloned. Some have questioned the entire idea of human cloning from a religious point of view and have asked whether cloned children will have souls. Scientists have responded that if twins have individual souls (which is, of course, a matter of faith, not of science), then surely clones will have their own individual souls too. Other arguments against cloning include these:

- Overpopulation threatens the planet as it is, so why add more people artificially?
- Why create people who, as copies of someone else, will have to struggle to find their identity?
- Clones might be considered expendable people, a new slave population—or perhaps so valuable that they would become a preferred population group. In other words, cloning might lead to a new form of discrimination.
- Animal cloning has led to the birth of individuals with abnormal physical traits. Aren't we risking the same thing making human clones?

Those are good questions, but before we become too "scientophobic," we should reconsider the issue. What does reproductive cloning entail? Some imagine that a cloned embryo can be frozen and later "activated" for spare parts. Others focus on human cloning as the answer to being childless. But why would anyone want to have himself or herself cloned? Why not opt for adopting an already existing child who needs a home? Well, for some people the whole point is to have a child who is *related* to them, and cloning would provide that. (But here we should note that the clone would be a blood relative, a twin, of just one of the parents, not both.) The reasons people want babies are complex: Some people want children so they can love them and raise them to be good citizens; others want an additional hand on the farm, an heir to their name, a tax write-off, or a status symbol to parade in front of their friends. We have yet to set up legal rules to determine what are *good* reasons to have children (although we already have an idea of which reasons count as *morally* good reasons). Excluding some prospective parents from parenthood because they'd like a kid who looks like themselves will exclude many more people than those lined up to be cloned. Some say, If it can be done, it will be done, so why make an issue of it? Supply and demand will rule! An alternative approach probably lies somewhere in the middle: The day will indeed come when we have human clones, from occasional individuals created to carry on the family name or be the bearer of the cherished face of a departed loved one to the nightmare scenario of mass-produced "worker ants." We need to think carefully about the implications of this technology for society and about the need for legislation. We have to consider the difference between a cloned child who would be loved and cared for by its parents and one who might be used or enslaved for society's purposes. Perhaps the bottom line, as with any planning involving a child, is whether that child can reasonably expect a stable, loving home—not the circumstances of the child's conception. There is a wide variety of issues for legislators and ethicists to consider in the twenty-first century.

Questions of Rights and Equality

We have already referred to the concept of rights several times; now we are going to take a closer look at what it entails. In Western culture today, it is generally assumed that all people have rights; the nature and extension of those rights is continually being disputed, however. In the seventeenth century some European thinkers began to advocate the idea of *natural rights,* and that idea became very important in the eighteenth century with its many social revolutions. A natural right was defined as a right one was born with as a human being (or as a male human being, as it was most often argued). Sometimes the concept of natural rights is intended as descriptive (as in, "We are actually born with rights"), and sometimes its intention is normative ("We ought to have such rights because we are human"). A powerful theory of natural rights comes from Thomas Hobbes, whom you met in Chapter 4. For Hobbes (1588–1679), as you may remember, laws and moral rules have no place prior to a social contract, in the "State of Nature," but even before the contract there is the *natural right* and the *natural law:* The natural right is the right for anyone to do what it takes to stay alive, and the natural law is a built-in prohibition against doing harm to ourselves. Once we have entered into a social contract, the natural right becomes modified, because social and moral laws now kick in for mutual self-protection; but in Hobbes's political philosophy, we never give up our right to defend ourselves and we never have to consent to actions that will harm us, even under the reign of an absolute monarch. A generation later the British philosopher John Locke (1632–1704) introduced his version of the natural rights concept: Anyone, even in the State of Nature, has three inalienable rights of nature, based on our very nature as rational beings: the rights to *life, liberty,* and *property*. Later in this chapter we return to Locke's theory of natural rights. But at the end of the 1700s, the utilitarian Jeremy Bentham had his doubts about the concept of natural rights. His response to the Declaration of the Rights of Man (1789) of the French Revolution—and implicitly also to the American Declaration of Independence (1776)—was that all men are obviously *not* born free, and they are *not* born or do not remain equal in rights. (Nor should they—someone has to give the orders, he says. We can't have associations between equal members, such as equality in marriage—Bentham believed that would never work out!) People are not born with rights, because the concept of rights is a human invention and does not occur in nature. One might wish it did, he says, but it doesn't. So for Bentham, the concept of natural rights is "nonsense upon stilts." That doesn't mean we can't operate with the concept of rights though; we must just recognize it as a legal principle (not a natural one) and identify its goal as being the creation of as happy a society as possible—in other words, maximizing happiness for the maximum number of people (the basic utilitarian principle).

You may remember John Stuart Mill's insistence that there ought to be such a thing as a personal right to be left alone if you are not harming anybody else (the "harm principle"). As in so many other areas, Mill is here redefining utilitarianism from within, but he still remains a utilitarian; his ultimate reason for setting limits on government involvement in people's private affairs is the overall happiness of the population. There is no such thing as a concept of "rights" or "justice" for its own sake in utilitarianism, even in Mill's version: The ultimate goal is still the general happiness, not an abstract principle of justice. We have to go to another theory to find a defense of the concept of rights for their own sake, not for what good social consequences may come of enforcing them: to Kant's deontology. As you have read in Chapter 6, he insists that human beings are ends in themselves and may not be treated merely as a means to an end. That means that even if treating a person as a means to an end might be useful for the majority in a society, it is still not permissible to do so. Good overall consequences for a majority do not provide a sufficient reason to do away with the rule that every person deserves respect. The question of whether decisions affecting many people in a society should be made on the basis of social utility or individual rights is still very much part of the contemporary debate, as we shall see.

What Is Equality?

When we try to define equality, we sometimes feel as much confusion as Saint Augustine did in trying to define time: "When you don't ask me, I know what it is; when you ask me, I don't know." We tend to think equality has something to do with treating everybody the same way—but since all people are not the same, or even similar, how can that be fair? And we know that equality and fairness are supposed to be linked. There are actually several definitions of equality:

1. Fundamental equality is the concept we know from the American Declaration of Independence and the French Declaration of the Rights of Man and of the Citizen. The American Declaration reads, "We hold these truths to be self-evident, that all men are created equal, that they are endowed by their Creator with certain unalienable Rights, that among these are Life, Liberty, and the pursuit of Happiness." The French Declaration begins, "All men are by nature free and equal in respect of their rights." However, these declarations do not say that people *are* factually equal— such as equally tall, strong, pretty, or smart—just that people *should be treated as* equals by their government and their legal system: no special privileges, just an entitlement to respect and consideration as human beings.

2. Social equality refers to the idea of people being equal within a social setting, such as politics or the economy. Today, most Western political theories are in tune with the idea of fundamental equality, but what exactly social equality (and indeed "people") can mean is variable: The French Revolution did not see women as socially or politically equal with men, and neither did the American Declaration of Independence, although Thomas Jefferson himself has been quoted as being opposed to viewing women as second-class citizens or as property. People of color were generally not considered included in the social equality of the Declaration of Independence either, although Jefferson seemed to have had some second thoughts about that too. Social equality today is generally obtained through such formal rights as the right to vote and to stand for public office; however, that doesn't mean that everyone's social status or income is supposed to be equal.

3. Equal treatment for equals is an ancient idea, in glaring contradiction to the fundamental equality principle; we find it in Aristotle's *Politics*. Justice means treating people of the same, usually social, group in the same way. But since we don't know from the definition what it would take to be considered an "equal," it is generally assumed to be an elitist principle with no underlying intent to recognize equality as a fundamental human right.

Sometimes an alternative definition is proposed, redefining the Fundamental Equality Principle: *Treat equals equally and unequals unequally*. At first sight that looks like principle (3), equal treatment for equals, but there is a potential difference. It may look like a principle of elitism and bigotry, but who are "equals"? And who are "unequals"? Instead of pointing to a social or political group or saying that "equals" means "everybody," let's say that "equals" in this definition are people who are in a similar situation under similar circumstances. Imagine the freeway at rush hour: We are all out there in our cars, either moving at high speeds or simply stuck. We don't know one another, but we all deserve respect and decent treatment from one another, no more and no less. Now imagine a person trying to change lanes so he can reach the next exit, because he has some kind of emergency—a flat tire, a sick passenger perhaps. He signals, and you let him go in front of you. Because of his situation he is in fact an "unequal," in special need of assistance. Now imagine that someone else up ahead is impatient and wants to get off the freeway, so she cuts in front of someone else and causes him to brake hard, resulting in a couple of fender benders that include your car. Now that person has also become an "unequal" and deserves special, "unequal" treatment that others don't get unless they have transgressed: punishment. So the principle states that under ordinary circumstances we are just "equals" and deserve the usual decent treatment and respect. When someone has special needs, he or she becomes an "unequal" who needs assistance to reach the level of those who are "equals." And when someone breaks the rules, he or she also becomes an unequal and deserves special punishment. (See the later section on criminal justice.) The principle of *treating equals equally and unequals unequally* is in harmony with the fundamental equality principle, but it is more elaborate because it recognizes that we sometimes have special needs or sometimes transgress and so sometimes deserve special treatment. The principle supports affirmative action, if people who have experienced the effects of discrimination are considered to be "unequals" in the sense that the "playing field" is not yet level and that some "players" need special assistance before everyone on the field will actually have equal opportunities. In the Primary Readings you'll find two op-ed pieces by American philosopher John Berteaux in which he evaluates the status of race and gender equality in our contemporary everyday life.

One thing the principle of equality usually does not imply is *sameness*. What would it be like if we were required to treat others and to be treated in exactly the same way, even if we are physically different? Kurt Vonnegut's short story "Harrison Bergeron" (1970) is a scathing parody of a future society in which it is politically incorrect (years before the term became popular) to be smarter, stronger, or more beautiful than anyone else. In Bergeron's future the smart people wear caps with buzzers that prevent them from thinking a thought through; the beautiful people wear bags over their heads so the less-than-pretty people won't feel bad. Dancers are weighed down with lead so ungraceful people won't feel left out, and strong people wear many bags of lead so they won't have an advantage over the weaker ones. Vonnegut doesn't write about how the truly disabled might feel about such artificial disabling or about what constitutes "normal" sameness, but the story does effectively question the identification of sameness and equality.

Dworkin: Rights Can't Be Traded for Benefits

A contemporary thinker who uses Kant's approach to the issue of rights is the American philosopher Ronald Dworkin, professor at the New York University School of Law and the University College of London (the place where Bentham sits in his mahogany closet, by the way). For more than three decades, Dworkin has contributed to the debate about social rights and equality; some of his most famous works include *Taking Rights Seriously* (1977) and *Freedom's Law* (1996), and he weighs in on current issues in *The New York Review of Books*. For Dworkin, the importance of rights becomes apparent precisely at the moment when social considerations might justify the violation of those rights; we may think that our rights are protected by the Constitution, but there is such a thing as a constitutional amendment.

Could we imagine a situation so serious that horrible social consequences will ensue if certain rights are not set aside for the common good? In other words, when push comes to shove, should we adopt a utilitarian view that social benefits outweigh the rights of the individual, or should we, along with Kant, hold the rights of the individual higher than social benefits? Dworkin asks us to consider an example: the right to free speech. Suppose someone, angered by some personal or collective experience, gets up and speaks in public, in an emotional manner, advocating violence as a way to secure political equality. Suppose the emotional speech starts a riot, and suppose people get hurt or even killed. Many would say that if such a situation can be prevented by making such a type of speech illegal, then that is the course we have to take. Dworkin would not. He argues that we can use one of two models for our political thinking about rights:

1. The first model says we have to find a balance between the rights of the individual and the demands of society. If the government *infringes* on a right, it does the individual wrong; but if it *inflates* a right, it does the community wrong (by depriving it of some benefit, such as safe streets). So we should steer a middle course and take each situation on a case-by-case basis. Well-behaved discussion groups can have more freedom of speech than unruly demonstrators because there is more social risk involved in the demonstration. This model of balancing the public interest against personal claims sounds reasonable, but it is not, says Dworkin. If we adopt the model, he asserts, we will have given up on two very important ideas: One is the idea of human dignity (Kant would say, Don't treat people merely as means), and the other is the idea of political equality (if one person has a certain freedom, then all persons should have that freedom, regardless of the effect on the general good). In Dworkin's words (from his book *Taking Rights Seriously*):

> So if rights make sense at all, then the invasion of a relatively important right must be a very serious matter. It means treating a man as less than a man, or as less worthy of concern than other men . . . then it must be wrong to say that inflating rights is as serious as invading them.

So we can't balance individual rights against social goods; what we *can* do is balance individual rights against each other when the claims collide, because then each individual still retains his or her dignity. But the best proof that the first model doesn't work, says Dworkin, is that it is *not* applied in actual cases in which the stakes for the individual are the highest: in criminal processes. Social benefits don't determine the outcome of a trial. The adage says, It is better that many guilty people go free than that one innocent person be punished, and this is Dworkin's choice for his second model.

2. The second model says that invading a right is far worse than inflating it. If people are prevented from expressing themselves freely and in any way they like, then that is an assault on human autonomy, and all the more so if the subject of a speech is morally important to the speaker. The government might actually be allowed to step in only if the consequences of such a speech would very certainly be grave. But when is anyone that certain? According to Dworkin, the risk involved is speculative; someone's right to free speech should not be abridged just because

Box 7.4   DWORKIN'S MODEL AND THE SECOND AMENDMENT

Dworkin's discussion involving his two models is directed specifically toward the First Amendment, which includes the right to free speech. His first model says we have to find a balance between the right of the individual and the needs of the community, and his second model (which he favors) says that invading or restricting a right for the sake of the needs of the community is wrong and should be done only in very rare cases. In the chapter text you find an analysis of the second model and freedom of speech—but how might Dworkin's model work if we apply it to the Second Amendment, the right to bear arms? The Second Amendment says that "a well-regulated Militia being necessary to the security of a free State, the right of the people to keep and bear Arms shall not be infringed." This amendment has been considered controversial for decades; for many liberals the right to bear arms is (1) outdated, (2) dangerous, and (3) a misinterpretation of the Bill of Rights, which, according to some interpreters, says only that militia members should have the right to be armed. For many moderates and conservatives, there is no doubt, however, that the amendment addresses individuals ("the people") and their right to bear arms, not just militia members. This interpretation is, supposedly, the classical one before the twentieth century. Furthermore, many supporters of the Second Amendment quote Aristotle: "Both oligarch and tyrant mistrust the people, and therefore deprive them of their arms." Regardless of what Dworkin might say about the right to gun ownership per se, how would his principle apply to the Second Amendment? If we apply the *first model*, balancing the right to own guns with the need of the community for security, Dworkin would have to conclude that individual rights shouldn't be balanced against social goods—individual rights can be balanced only against other individual rights. His *second model* would state it in even stronger terms: Someone's right to bear arms should not be abridged just because someone else might choose to harm others because of that right. Would this example of Dworkin's principle used on another amendment make you agree with his principle all the more, or less? You may want to revisit the Narrative *Runaway Jury* in Chapter 5 for an expanded debate about the issue.

someone else might harm others as a result of that speech. This is the only way to protect the rights of individuals and in particular the rights of the few against the many. For a discussion of Dworkin's model and the second amendment, see Box 7.4.

Dworkin seems to imply that freedom of speech (which might lead to violence) is typically used to defend the idea of human dignity; in other words, most decent people might agree with the content of the speech, if not with its emotional character. That may not always be the case. You might want to consider Dworkin's second model in the scenario of an inflammatory racist hate speech being delivered on your campus or on TV. Would you say that the right of the speaker to express a personal opinion is more important than the harmful effects on the group being targeted for hatred or even the harmful effects on the audience being stirred up? The demonstrations Dworkin refers to in his 1977 book were, in particular, the demonstrations (with subsequent riots) against the Vietnam War in the late sixties and early seventies, but if a principle is a principle, it should hold up under any kind of scenario, from current demonstrations against the war in Iraq to demonstrations in support of the war, demonstrations for or against immigration, and demonstrations conducted by Neo-Nazis and the Ku Klux Klan. And freedom of speech is, of course, not just a matter of the actual physical presence of a speaker in front of a group of people—the greater audience in front of the TV as well as today's interactive online audience need to be included also. (In Chapter 13 we address the issue of *free speech and the media,* with an eye to controversies in the last decade.)

According to Dworkin's principle, the free speech of the second model should extend to speakers and demonstrators in general. Demonstrations should be allowed to take place because the rights of demonstrators should not be invaded. (The First Amendment allows not only freedom of *speech* but also freedom of *assembly*.) But the Constitution grants no right to create a public disturbance. So critics of Dworkin's second model suggest a middle course: Certainly we have freedom of speech and freedom of assembly—but that doesn't entail an automatic police permit to march in a demonstration. So let those who want to exercise their freedom of speech assemble someplace, in a hall or on a street corner, but limit the possibility of harm to the public if the issue is volatile. The tendency in our society is increasingly to move toward protection of the public rather than protection of the individual's right to freedom of speech, assembly, or movement. Some years ago judges were generally reluctant to issue restraining orders against domestic abusers because of their right to freedom of movement; today such restraining orders are much more common. You might want to argue about rights within this scenario from the viewpoints of Dworkin and John Stuart Mill. Box 7.5 further explores the concept of civil rights versus the security of citizens.

Negative Rights

Some social thinkers believe that although we do and should have rights, those rights should be only of a certain kind: *negative rights,* so called because they specify what ought *not* to be done to you (they are rights of noninterference). Earlier in this chapter you read that John Locke introduced a concept of three natural rights that everyone has as a birthright of a rational human being: the rights to life, liberty, and property. (It is no coincidence that this sounds so similar to Thomas Jefferson's famous emphasis on our rights to *life, liberty, and the pursuit of happiness.* Jefferson was deeply influenced by John Locke's political philosophy.) For Locke, a social contract thinker, these rights are rights people have against the government and one another: Nobody's life should be interfered with for no good reason, nor should anyone's liberty or property be interfered with. The only limit to each right is the right held by other people to their own life, liberty, and property. But even outside a social contract, these rights are in effect, says Locke, because we are rational beings and these rights are rational rights, but they are easier to enforce within a society with democratic laws. In his *Second Treatise on Government* (1690) Locke specifies that "the State of Nature has a law of Nature to govern it, which obliges everyone, and Reason, which is that law, teaches all mankind who will but consult it, that being all equal and independent, no one ought to harm another in his life, liberty,

Box 7.5   CIVIL LIBERTIES VERSUS SECURITY

In the fall of 2001, as a step in the war against terrorism, Congress passed the U.S.A. Patriot Act of 2001, directed at preventing future terrorism through increased powers of wiretapping, including "roving wiretaps" that zero in on a person rather than a telephone number, and intercepting e-mails, faxes, and so on. The purpose was to find and arrest any terrorist, foreign or domestic, who might threaten the security of U.S. citizens at home and abroad. In the wake of September 11 such measures seemed welcome and reasonable to many, but there were also voices who warned that we might come to regret this decision.

Interestingly, those voices have come from both the Left and the Right within American politics: Liberals see these measures as a threat to political dissidents in an era of conservative government. Conservatives see them as a danger to individual freedom—especially under some possible future liberal administration. And both point out that it in effect undermines the Fourth Amendment of the Bill of Rights, the search-and-seizure amendment, which says officers have to demonstrate *probable cause* (that a crime has been/is being committed) before entering and searching the premises of a citizen without that citizen's permission. The Patriot Act was intended to be in effect for four years, until 2005. In March 2006 a reauthorization bill, heavily criticized for ignoring civil liberty concerns, was signed into law by President Bush. The White House emphasized that the Patriot Act is fully constitutional, and a congressional oversight committee ensures that civil liberties are upheld.

In addition, September 11 inspired sweeping measures to try foreign terrorists in military tribunals, so as to keep the proceedings—and especially the evidence—secret and thus out of reach of other terrorists.

How far are we willing to go in giving up our civil liberties, and even our constitutional rights,

to obtain security? What are we willing to do? In the days following September 11, many Americans would have said, "Anything, just so we're safe," but others have reminded us that having an open, free society carries with it some inherent risks. If we put up too many safeguards to protect our society, we may lose our freedoms in the process. Benjamin Franklin wrote, "Those who would give up essential liberty to obtain a little temporary safety deserve neither liberty nor safety." It is not unusual, however, for a country to enact strict legal measures in wartime that then will be lifted when the war is over.

What puts this into perspective is that before September 11 there was already a tendency in American politics (supported by eight years of a Democratic presidency) to "trade rights for benefits," as Ronald Dworkin would put it. In 1994 a seven-year-old New Jersey girl named Megan Kanka was killed, and her murderer was suspected to be a known child molester. In the aftermath, the question was asked, Could her death have been prevented if the whereabouts of the released child molester had been made public beforehand? In that case the community would have known to keep their children away from him. The law requiring such notification, known as Megan's Law, was passed by Congress in 1997, although individual states had earlier passed similar laws. In January 1999 it took effect across the United States. The addresses of sex offenders who are released from prison will be on file at the local police stations for the community to inquire into and make public. In some communities, the names and addresses of sex offenders are regularly released by community leaders or radio stations and posted on the Internet. In other communities, citizens have a more difficult time getting access to the information. And lately a "Jessica's Law" (named for a murdered nine-year-old Florida girl, Jessica Lundsford), making sexual abuse of a

(continued)

Box 7.5   CIVIL LIBERTIES VERSUS SECURITY *(continued)*

child a one-strike offense, has been spreading across the country.

From the point of view of the community, this is tremendous progress in protecting the lives and well-being of our children; from the point of view of the sex offender, though, this is hardly good news. So what? we might say—who cares what sex offenders think of our attempts to foil their future exploits? The trouble is that our conception of civil liberties doesn't quite correspond to this idea of protection of the community. The sex offenders have served their time, paid their debt to society, and in most other cases that means they can start over again—with a criminal record but with the past behind them. They may have lost some rights (such as the right to vote and to own weapons), but presumably they retain the right not to be assumed guilty before they have done anything.

Megan's Law casts that freedom into doubt: The past crimes of sex offenders will never be put behind them, and, as such, the punishment never seems to come to an end. To some philosophers of law, this is terribly unfair, but others point out that the crimes such offenders have committed never come to an end either—the victims of sexual molestation (if they survive it) will have to live with the memory always. Even so, this is not an argument in favor of Megan's Law, because punishment is not intended to match the pain intensity caused by the crime—how would that be possible? To the legal complaint that having one's name posted in the community prolongs the punishment, the court replied that the surveillance and posting of names is the community exercising its right to self-protection—it is not part of the punishment.

health or possessions." So even before a society is formed with all its rules and laws, says Locke, there is a law of nature guiding our rational thinking toward realizing that everyone is equal by birth, and everyone should be able to live his or her life in liberty without the interference of anyone else. In many ways Locke's philosophy was an inspiration to the founders (traditionally known as the "Founding Fathers") of the United States. Ayn Rand (see Chapter 4) expressed the conviction that the United States was the first moral society in history because it set limits on the power of the state and respected the concept of the rights of the individual. In an essay, "Man's Rights," from *The Virtue of Selfishness* (1965), she says, "All previous systems had regarded man as a sacrificial means to the ends of others, and society as an end in itself. The United States regarded man as an end in himself, and society as a means to the peaceful, orderly, *voluntary* coexistence of individuals."

So what are these individual rights? There is only one fundamental right, says Rand: the right to your own life and to act free of coercion. In that sense it is a positive right. But as for your neighbors, they have negative rights against you: the right not to have their right to life and liberty violated. How do we maintain our life? By our own effort, Rand says; that means you have the right to make money or own property without having it taken away. So the right to property is also a negative right. Are these rights absolute? Do you always have a right to your life, liberty, and property? Not if you have violated someone else's right to life, liberty, or property. In such a case your rights have been forfeited; so the limit of your own liberty is the liberty of the other person. But does that mean you have a right to be kept alive if you can't provide for yourself? Do you have a right to be given property and to be provided with the means to enjoy your liberty? No, says Rand. If you can't fend for yourself, then society has no obligation to help you (but others may want to, because they are caring people). For this philosophical approach, there is no such thing as a right to a job, a home, or fair wages—nor a right to be made happy, only the right not to be interfered with if you don't bother others in your own pursuit of happiness.

The American philosopher John Hospers expresses the same sentiments in defending the political viewpoint of libertarianism in his book *The Libertarian Alternative* (1974):

> Each man has the right to life: any attempt by others to take it away from him, or even to injure him, violates this right, through the use of coercion against him. Each man has a right to liberty: to conduct his life in accordance with the alternatives open to him without coercive action by others. And every man has the right to property: to work to sustain his life (and the lives of whichever others he chooses to sustain, such as his family) and to retain the fruits of his labor.

Both Rand and Hospers emphasize the right to life; does that mean they are part of the right-to-life movement? If we identify the right to life as an anti-abortion viewpoint, then it is not the same as the libertarian negative right, because libertarians are generally concerned with the right of people who are already born not to have their lives taken away. The Libertarian Party platform of 1994 specified a pro-choice stand, as a logical consequence of its view that the right to liberty includes the right for women to choose for themselves; however, the platform also specified that libertarians are against public funding of abortion clinics because forcing others to pay for abortions violates the right to property.

Accordingly, the right to life is simply a right not to have your life interfered with. What if you are not capable of working to sustain your life? Then you have a problem, because Rand and Hospers do not believe you have a right to receive other people's property without their consent. In practical terms, that means you should have saved up or taken out insurance while you were able to work; for those who never have been and never will be able to work, libertarianism advocates private charity, not government interference, because the only role for the government, say both Hospers and Rand, is to protect the negative rights of the citizens against violation. Anything else is, in the colorful language that Hospers echoes from Rand, "moral cannibalism." You may remember the excerpt in Chapter 4 from Rand's *Atlas Shrugged* in which she speaks of the right of the capable person not to have to support the lives of "whining rotters"—those she elsewhere calls "moochers and leeches" and "moral cannibals." Critics of that philosophy—and there are many—sometimes invoke the Golden Rule and ask of the libertarian, Is this the way *you* would want to be treated if stricken with a personal catastrophe that you could not have prepared for? Should the goods of this world be reserved for those who are strong, healthy, and capable of securing them for themselves, or should weaker individuals who lack such abilities also have a right to share in the goods in a civilized society? In the upcoming section on distributive justice, we meet an American philosopher who argues in favor of a fair distribution: John Rawls.

Positive Rights

Views in opposition to libertarianism can be found in several areas of modern social thinking. The most extreme alternative would be provided by Marxism (rather quiet at the moment), which holds, on the basis of the ideal of social equality, that everyone in society has the right to have his or her life sustained, "to receive according to need, and to give according to ability." That makes the right to live and have your life sustained a *positive right* (a right to receive something from somebody, usually the government). As has often been pointed out, the politics of communism exclude the negative rights just described: It rarely recognizes any right as not to be interfered with by the government. Socialist viewpoints (which are generally not as radical as communist ones about government control) also support positive rights (entitlements) such as the right to work, to have shelter, and possibly also to have health care, education, clothing, and food.

According to the German political philosopher Karl Marx (1818–1883), the communist state will take care of the needs of the individual: The individual has a positive right to have his or her needs met. But *needs* is an amorphous term. What does it mean to have your needs met? Marx had in mind the basics: food, shelter, clothing, meaningful work, education, and health care. The needs of your family, however, might stretch the definition of basic needs. Wanting and needing are, after all, not the same. What about braces for your daughter's teeth? What about a copy of the Phonics Game for your son? You may argue that the kids really *need* those things to secure their future, but who is to judge? And who is to pay for them? Those who have the ability to work.

In Marx's vision of the communist state—the final stage of political development after feudalism and capitalism—the world will have changed. The capitalist concept of profit will have disappeared because profit is the "surplus value" that the factory owner adds to the product on top of the wages paid to the factory worker—in Marx's view, value stolen from the worker and created on the worker's time and through the worker's effort. In the world of communism, people no longer go to work to make wages or make a profit—they go to work because they have certain abilities that they put into the service of the state. And since they are allowed (ideally!) to work with whatever their talents dictate, they are not bored: The compensation for hard work is the joy of having meaningful work in itself. So society can require a person to work for the good of the community to the extent that he or she is able to do it (willingness is simply assumed). In compensation, the workers will be paid in goods according to their needs. In the early stages of the new world, Marx envisioned a monetary system, but within the completed communist system, money would be abolished. In *Atlas Shrugged,* Ayn Rand (who fled the Soviet Union for the United States) creates a wicked parody of the fate of a factory run on communist principles.

The workers with needs soon outnumbered those who were able to put in long hours of work. Those workers with bright ideas and abilities were put on overtime without compensation, so that very soon they were out of ideas and discovered that they were able to put in only a feeble amount of work. But everybody was quick to think up new needs. . . .

The concept of positive rights need not take on such extreme proportions. Most liberal philosophies, such as that of John Rawls (see the next section), include the view that negative rights are not of much use if one's health or the country's economy prevent one from making a living. What good is the right to vote, to express yourself freely, and to hold office if you are so sick or destitute that you can't feed your kids or give them a safe place to grow up? To enjoy negative rights, one must be assured of having basic needs met. The first Primary Reading at the end of the chapter is the United Nation's Declaration of Human Rights. You may want to study it specifically for its emphasis on negative as well as positive rights—rights of noninterference as well as entitlements.

Distributive Justice: From Rawls to Affirmative Action

In modern social philosophy we talk about two kinds of justice. One is the kind that is upheld by the law; it is generally referred to as *criminal justice,* and we will return to it at the end of this chapter. The other kind is *distributive justice,* theories of how to distribute the goods of society fairly. This distinction dates all the way back to Aristotle, who says in his *Nicomachean Ethics* that "a just thing . . . will be (1) that which is in accordance with the law, (2) that which is fair; and the unjust thing will be (1) that which is contrary to law, (2) that which is unfair."

For some social thinkers in the past, distributive justice depended on who could grab how much and hold on to it, but in modern times a clear understanding has emerged among social philosophers that for society to be a functioning system, it must offer both some recognition of needs and some way to meet those needs.

Rawls: Justice as Fairness

One of the most influential arguments against exclusively negative rights and in favor of positive rights—an argument that is also directed against a utilitarian view of rights as merely a means to happiness for the majority (*social utility*)—comes from the American philosopher John Rawls (1921–2002). This is usually identified as a *liberal* argument, not in the sense of Mill's *classical* liberalism (which comes close to today's libertarianism), but in the sense of the modern *egalitarian* liberalism, which believes that everyone should have equal access to social goods, in some way or other. A liberal generally believes in some positive rights as well as some negative rights: You need the right to life and liberty (such as freedom of speech), but without positive rights you may not be able to enjoy those negative rights, so you also have a basic right to be taken care of by society if you can't take care of yourself.

To envision a society that is as fair toward everyone as possible, Rawls suggests a thought experiment: Imagine, he says, that we are about to make rules for a brand-new society and that we are all in on it. (This is one of the most modern versions of the old *social contract theory* that you'll remember from Chapter 4.) Then, he says, imagine that you don't know who or what you'll be when the rules take effect; you may be rich, you may be poor, young or old, male or female, of another race. You pretend you are ignorant of your position in the future; you have now lowered a *veil of ignorance* over your mind's eye. This Rawls calls the *original position,* because it is from this position that we should imagine making rules for all of society. Rawls was deeply inspired by Kant's idea that all of humanity should be treated as ends in themselves, never merely as means to an end. If you don't know who or what you will be, you will want to make certain that whatever rules you help make about fair distribution of the goods of society (such as jobs, food, shelter, child care, health care) don't place you at the bottom of the pile. If you end up being poor and ill, your new rules should be as fair to you as to anyone else; if you end up being rich, you would want fairness too. This is, of course, a form of rational self-interest—but in the bigger picture it transforms itself into an understanding of other people's needs. In Rawls's own words, from his influential work *A Theory of Justice* (1971),

> Thus we are to imagine that those who engage in social cooperation choose together, in one joint act, the principles which are to assign basic rights and duties and to determine the division of social benefits. . . . This original position is not, of course, thought of as an actual historical state of affairs, much less as a primitive condition of culture. It is understood as a purely hypothetical situation characterized so as to lead to a certain conception of justice. Among the essential features of this situation is that no one knows his place in society, his class position or social status, nor does any one know his fortune in the distribution of natural assets and abilities, his intelligence, strength, and the like. . . . The principles of justice are chosen behind a veil of ignorance. This ensures that no one is advantaged or disadvantaged in the choice of principles by the outcome of natural chance or the contingency of social circumstances.

An example may help illustrate this (it is not an image that Rawls uses, but one that he might use): Think of a birthday party for a little girl. There is a big birthday cake, and she would like to cut a big piece for herself before any of the guests get some of it. But her parents tell her, "You may cut the cake, but you get to choose last!" She is a smart girl; what will this force her to do? Cut pieces as evenly as possible, because a tiny piece is likely to be rejected by her guests and thus be the last one remaining for her. In a sense she is in the original position, creating a system of fair distribution for the future.

That analogy works well for the original position, but real life is different. The needs (or wants) of the party guests were for a piece of cake, but in real life some may need more food, shelter, and health care than others, and some have talents that others don't have. So a completely fair distribution of goods would be one in which, as a result, no one is in need of the bare essentials. Justice, then, consists in equal liberty (having the same rights and duties as everyone else) for persons within a society. That doesn't mean that everyone should be treated the same way. As a matter of fact, some inequality is permissible, says Rawls, provided that the end result is *everyone* in society benefits from that inequality (and not just some majority, as in utilitarianism).

In the Primary Readings you'll find an excerpt from John Rawls's influential essay "Justice as Fairness."

Two American philosophers who are often quoted as criticizing Rawls are the communitarian and pluralist Michael Walzer (born 1935) and the libertarian Robert Nozick (1938–2002). We will meet Robert Nozick's theory of property in the Business Ethics section in Chapter 13. Walzer's philosophy is closer to Rawls's liberal social philosophy than that of Nozick, but there are substantial differences between Walzer's and Rawls's ideas of distributive justice. For Rawls we are, essentially, social atoms, theoretically without affiliations, and that means we can imagine a veil of ignorance hiding our knowledge of who we are to ensure a fair distribution. For Walzer, on the other hand, we live in "spheres of justice" (the title of one of his books from 1983) where we are essentially connected to our communities and what we consider "social goods" depend on what our community values, which means we can't be reduced to social atoms. Walzer identifies himself primarily as a pluralist; to him our affiliations take on special meanings according to our community, and these separate spheres of meaning can't be reduced to a common denominator. In the next section we look at two other, less often quoted American philosophers arguing against Rawls: Elizabeth Wolgast and Marilyn Friedman.

Wolgast and Friedman: Reactions to Abstract Individualism

Rawls's viewpoint has helped immensely in identifying goals within liberal politics; as you can imagine, he has critics among nonliberals, but he also has them even among thinkers who are generally in favor of social equality involving fair distribution of goods. Here we look at viewpoints from two American philosophers, Elizabeth Wolgast and Marilyn Friedman; each in her own way points to a lack in Rawls's approach: the understanding that humans are not just "social atoms," separate individuals who might imagine themselves to be someone else entirely, but persons already existing in a web of interrelationships.

The idea of individualism has a long and important history, says Elizabeth Wolgast, and it has helped make this country what we perceive it to be: a place for individual achievement as a result of competition. It began with René Descartes daring to assert that humans all have the capacity to reason and are equal in their intelligence. Since everyone has this capacity, there is no need for any religious or political authority: We can figure things out for ourselves. This is the beginning of the egalitarianism, as well as the anti-authoritarianism, of Western individualism, says Wolgast, the source of a "do-it-yourself science and theology" that lets everyone play a part. Other thinkers, such as Thomas Hobbes and John Locke, emphasized the right of the individual as a "self-motivated unit" to decide his or her own social destiny, at least in extreme circumstances. One of the modern thinkers who has the most influence in supporting this idea of the individual as a separate unit is John Rawls. If we imagine a society in which everyone is an equal atom, then those atoms are interchangeable, and so ideally each person should be treated the same. But since we are not the same, a policy of justice should take that into consideration, and this is what Rawls's original position policy is all about. It is ingenious as an abstract ideal, but what about real life?

Elizabeth Wolgast (b. 1929), a philosophy professor emerita at California State University, Hayward, is the author of *Ethics of an Artificial Person* (1992), *The Grammar of Justice* (1987), and several other books and papers. She argues that Rawls's famous theory views people as separate individuals without any recognition of the community ties that bind those individuals. As an alternative, she argues for a return to communitarianism, the view that an individual is partly understood through his or her ties to the community.

asks Wolgast. This model of thinking, beginning with Descartes and culminating with Rawls, presupposes that all human relationships are entered into by separate "atomic" individuals as if they are entering into a contract, as if they weren't in any binding relationships already. According to Wolgast in *The Grammar of Justice* (1987):

> The atomistic model has important virtues. It founds the values of the community on private values; it encourages criticism of government and requires any government to answer to its original justification; it limits government's powers, as they may threaten to interfere with the needs of atomistic units. . . . But it leaves a great deal out. . . . In it one cannot picture human connections or responsibilities. We cannot locate friendliness or sympathy in it any more than we can imagine one molecule or atom moving aside for or assisting another; to do so would make a joke of the model. . . . we need to loosen the hold that the atomistic picture has on our thinking, and recognize the importance that theory has on our judgments and our moral condition.

What is Wolgast saying? She is siding with the much older political theory of *communitarianism,* which stems from the ancient Greek tradition (see Chapter 4). For the Greek thinkers, and Aristotle in particular, an individual does not understand himself or herself as a separate entity but as a social being. We understand ourselves, and others understand us, through the connections we have to our community. A society is not just a collection of individuals but also part of the very purpose of the life of an individual. We are all someone's daughter or son; we have parents and children and siblings; we have friendships and trade relations and other community ties; and stripped of those we are nobody (which is why, to many Greeks, banishment from the community was a horrible threat, as we shall see in the next chapter). As Wolgast says, "the whole makes the part comprehensible." This is the view that has been popularized with the title of Senator Hillary Rodham Clinton's book *It Takes a Village* (to raise a child, an African proverb). So Rawls's thought experiment is bound to have limits in this real world because we are not simply atomic units, individuals alone in the universe. We have responsibilities to our community, and a good theory of justice must take such community ties into account.

Marilyn Friedman (b. 1945), a philosophy professor at Washington University, St. Louis, is the author of *Autonomy, Gender, Politics* (2003), *What Are Friends For? Feminist Perspectives on Personal Relationships and Moral Theory* (1993), and several papers on philosophy, ethics, and feminism. In "Feminism and Modern Friendship: Dislocating the Community" (1989) she argues that although Rawls's abstract individualism is not sufficient to explain social ethics, neither is classical communitarianism, because it tends to be oppressive to women. An appreciation for the individual as well as for new types of community relationships is needed.

Marilyn Friedman agrees with much of Wolgast's criticism of the "abstract individualism" of Western modern philosophy and social thinking. She points out that many women thinkers in particular are now critical of this approach because they don't see themselves or people who depend on them and on whom they depend as utterly separate individuals but, rather, as a network or a group of individuals relying on one another. And the solution of communitarianism is tempting and reasonable, says Friedman in a paper from 1989, "Feminism and Modern Friendship: Dislocating the Community"—but we should be careful, because it may take us places we don't want to go. What do we mean by "community"? Very often what is meant is the *family,* the *neighborhood,* and the *nation;* communitarianism teaches that the traditions and demands of our community are highly important and should be a defining factor in each person's sense of self. But if we look at such communities in a historical sense, we find that most often they have been very oppressive toward women; so if we choose communitarianism over Rawls's idea of people as social atoms, aren't we risking going backward and accepting traditions dictating, for instance, that women are the property of their husbands, that children have no rights, or that men have no place in the kitchen or the nursery? Traditions may be a wonderful legacy for a community, but not all traditions are necessarily so. And suppose some of the old traditions were to blame for divisions and resentment among people today; ought we not be morally obligated to overcome those traditions? We can't just celebrate our community attachments uncritically, as some modern communitarians suggest, says Friedman. And how can we get to a point at which we can allow ourselves to be critical? By not throwing out the concept of the modern self without affiliations (what Wolgast called a "social atom"), a self who has learned to be critical of society's claims that we have social and moral obligations.

Furthermore, communitarians seem to believe that we are always a part of a community from the beginning; we have not chosen it, and yet we have responsibilities as members. But, says Friedman, that is true only when we are young; an adult person can generally choose many of his or her community affiliations. Does she want to belong to a union? Does he want to move to this or that neighborhood? Does she want to emigrate? Does he want to join a new church? We choose affiliations based on our personal needs, wishes, and critical sense, and they don't even have to be live-in communities. Today it's possible to belong to communities that don't really have a location, such as chatrooms on the Internet. (When Friedman wrote her paper, the Internet was still in the future.) So Friedman concludes (in "Feminism and Modern Friendship") that looking to community ties to expand traditional abstract individualism is a good idea, but it should not be done uncritically: We must develop communitarian thought beyond its complacent regard for the communities in which we once found ourselves toward (and beyond) an awareness of the crucial impor-tance of "dislocated" communities, communities of choice.

Forward- and Backward-Looking Justice and Affirmative Action

In the debate about the nature and goals of justice, it may seem confusing that legal experts sometimes talk about improving things in the *future* and sometimes talk about making up for mistakes and evils of the *past*, as if the two approaches might exclude each other. And to some legal minds they effectively do, because the issue of justice can be defined in two ways: as *forward-looking* and as *backward-looking*. One concept focuses on future consequences; the other is a rights-based concept centered on responding to conditions in the past. Here it is essential that you have studied Chapters 5 and 6, because this section relies heavily on your understanding of the goals of utilitarianism and other consequentialist theories, as opposed to the ideals of a Kantian viewpoint.

A forward-looking view of justice sees the purpose of justice as creating a fair system of distribution of social goods in the future. (Social thinkers use "social goods" to mean access to opportunities such as jobs as well as material things avail-able to citizens in a community.) Regardless of what in the past has brought us to where we are today, our focus must be on creating consequences as good as possible for as many as we can—for everyone, if possible—in the future. A utilitarian would concentrate on creating a functional society of equality and access to opportunities for the majority, under the assumption that that's the best we can do. Of course, a utilitarian might also consider instituting social *inequalities,* provided that the overall outcome is considered beneficial for the many.

A backward-looking view of justice requires us to look to conditions in the past and ask, What has brought us to where we are today in terms of inequality and unfair distribution of social goods, and how can we make amends? In the backward-looking view it is essential that we identify both the root causes of today's inequalities and the people in the past who have been affected by them, as well as their descendants and those still living today. Whether compensation for past wrongs done to those people will actually accomplish a system of fair distribution of goods in the future is not relevant—the main concern is to rectify the past wrongs.

An interesting hybrid form is John Rawls's theory of the original position. The Rawlsian focus would be on creating a fair system for *everyone,* using the original position to create rules of distribution of social goods so that no one falls through the cracks. As you'll remember, the original position is a thought experiment requiring that we forget about who we are and have been in the past, in order to imagine a fair and just society of the future where everyone is equal and no one will be sacrificed for the convenience of anyone else. As such it is future-oriented, forward-looking. But Rawls himself is not a consequentialist; rather, he is a follower of Kant's philosophy that nobody should be used as merely a means to other people's ends, even if it might create good consequences. So Rawls's theory of justice in effect looks forward, drawing on a concept of rights and fairness, not on good social consequences as such. Later we look at Rawls's own theory of combining forward-looking and backward-looking theories of punishment.

In the field of *affirmative action,* the views of forward- and backward-looking justice have determined the way many issues have been raised and solved. Although the entire concept of affirmative action—a term coined by President Lyndon B. Johnson in the 1960s in connection with the Civil Rights Act—is now undergoing scrutiny by politicians, the media, and citizens for its overall results and possibly negative impact on public jobs and education, the goal of affirmative action ("preferential treatment," as it is referred to by critics) was to level the playing field for disadvantaged citizens. But exactly who the disadvantaged citizens are and how the playing field is to be leveled depend on whether one adopts a forward-looking or a backward-looking view.

A *forward-looking* approach identifies those in society who, at this point, seem disenfranchised, and those who in the near future may be in danger of being caught up in a socially disadvantaged situation, and will focus on making access to public jobs and education easier for that group, regardless of why the situation has arisen or whether the beneficiaries or their ancestors were discriminated against in the past. Thus it is the present needs of disenfranchised individuals and groups that would determine the measure of help required, not their experience with discrimination in the past. A forward-looking view has to determine how far into the future such programs will have to exist to level the playing field—forever, or a few generations—because there will always be needy individuals.

A *backward-looking* view will focus on the history of disenfranchised groups and seek some form of compensation or restitution to those groups—living members or their descendants—based on the past experiences of group members regardless of whether everyone in that group today has in fact experienced discrimination in his or her lifetime. A backward-looking view will also have to determine how far into the past one must go to rectify old wrongs—should it be limited to living memory, meaning about a hundred years at the most, or should it go back several more generations? Regarding the question of compensation to African Americans for past injustices caused by slavery, the issue is extremely relevant: Assuming that one finds the idea of reparations at all reasonable (which many don't), a living memory criterion would include compensation not for slavery itself but for the consequences of slavery. And a broader criterion would have to seek compensation not just from descendants of American slave owners but also from descendants of Arab slave traders, and so on. At the end of the chapter, you'll find an excerpt from Dr. Martin Luther King, Jr.'s "Letter from Birmingham Jail" on the concept of just and unjust laws. Also in the Narratives section, you'll read about the film *Mississippi Burning,* based on the true story of the murders of three young civil rights activists in Philadelphia, Mississippi, on June 21, 1964. In 2005 a separatist Baptist minister and Ku Klux Klan member, seventy-nine-year-old Ray Killen, was arrested and charged with engineering those murders, one of the most infamous events of the civil rights movement of the 1960s. He was convicted on all three counts and sentenced to sixty years in prison. Consider how the criminal charges against Ray Killen, forty-one years after the murders, are an example of a backward-looking view.

The very different approaches of forward- and backward-looking justice can be found not only within the realm of what we call distributive justice, the distribution of social goods, but also as an important part of what we refer to as *criminal justice*.

Criminal Justice: Restorative Versus Retributive Justice

As a society, we believe that law-abiding persons should be treated equally, *ceteris paribus*. The Latin expression means "everything else being equal," so if you just go about your business, you deserve the same decent treatment by the government that anyone else deserves, no more and no less. But sometimes everything else is not equal: You may come from a historically deprived group, and legislation may state that such persons deserve special benefits (such as affirmative action). Or you may have experienced personal hardship that couldn't be anticipated and may need special help, perhaps in the form of welfare (all depending on which government system is in effect and what kind of rights its legislators may believe in: negative rights, positive rights, both, or none). Or you may have actually benefited society in some way, so the government believes you should be rewarded. (Some governments will pay families bonuses or give them tax breaks for having children, for example.) But suppose you have broken the law. Then, according to criminal justice, the government is entitled to treat you differently from the rest of the population—by depriving you of benefits and sometimes also of certain rights, by punishing you for the crime committed. You may recognize the principle of treating equals equally and unequals unequally.

The concept of punishment is as old as human history, but only in the past two hundred years has it acquired the face we see today. In past eras around the world, punishment often involved banishment (temporary or permanent), financial restitution to the victims or their families, or loss of body parts—or even execution. The principle of "an eye for an eye," today referred to as the law of retaliation, or *lex talionis,* has been in effect for the past four thousand years, since the Babylonian Code of Hammurabi. Incarceration as a form of punishment is a fairly modern idea; in centuries past imprisonment was considered a form of keeping dangerous individuals under control, but not necessarily proportional to what they had done—it was just a way of dealing with a problem, not a matter of justice.

Although most people today think punishment (in some form) is an appropriate response to crime, the viewpoint has been advanced, particularly in the latter half of the twentieth century, that punishment is a demeaning and inhumane approach. The question was raised, Who are we, law-abiding citizens, to pass judgment on people who have perhaps been deprived of the chances in life that have resulted in our being law-abiding? And who is to say that punishment will actually deter them from further criminal activity? Rather than punish people for what they have done, we ought to educate them and supply them with the chance they may never have had before to become good citizens. In other words, the purpose of incarcerating criminals or subjecting them to other restraints has been viewed not as *punishment* but as *therapeutic rehabilitation*. This fundamental philosophical difference between viewing punishment as something deserved and viewing it as something superimposed by a power structure that, somehow, has helped create the problem has led to the distinction between *retributive* and *restorative* justice. In defense of *restorative* justice, Pat Nolan of the Justice Fellowship says,

> If all we do is focus on the broken law, then all you can do is enforce the power of the government, the fist of government, and lock people up, to punish them. If, on the other hand, you look at crime as "victim harming," the solution should bring repair to the harm done to the victim. And when you repair the harm done to the victim through restitution and reparation, generally the victim becomes very forward looking and doesn't want to harm and further punish the offender, but says, "I don't want you to do this again." "What can we do to make you not do this again?" "How can we change your life?" Transformation becomes important.

Nolan served fifteen years in the California State Assembly—and twenty-five months in a federal prison on racketeering charges. So perhaps he has an insider's understanding of the issue. He believes the solution lies in religion and in teaching morals. Those who focus on restorative justice emphasize that the balance in society is not restored by locking perpetrators up or executing them. The balance can only be restored if their criminal propensities can be transformed.

Proponents of restorative justice such as Howard Zehr, professor of sociology, often point out the differences between their view and retributive justice: Retributive justice sees a crime as a violation of rules and relationships, whereas restorative justice sees it as harm caused to people; retributive justice sees the state as the victim, whereas restorative justice sees people as victims. Retributive justice focuses on the past, whereas restorative justice focuses on the future. The courtroom is a battle situation for retributive justice, but for restorative justice the model is a dialogue. And for retributive justice, the debt is paid through punishment; for restorative justice, the debt is paid by "making it right."

The most influential, and perhaps also the most comprehensive defense of retributive justice to this day may have been supplied by Immanuel Kant. For Kant, justice *must* focus on the past, because that is how we identify the criminal and the severity of the crime; it must be seen as a violation of rules because it is by the rationality of rules that we justify our moral system—but Kant would not conclude that only rules and not people are victims. On the contrary, respecting the inherent dignity of another human being—victim as well as criminal—is the foundation of his retributive justice. Among contemporary supporters are the philosopher Igor Primoratz and the author Robert James Bidinotto. In the section on retribution we look at Kant's argument in favor of *retributivism*.

So even though most social thinkers believe there should be an institution of punishment within society, there is widespread disagreement on not only *what kind of punishment* people should reasonably be subjected to but also *why* they should be punished. It should not be hard for you to guess at some of the major disagreements.

Five Common Approaches to Punishment

Among all the different reasons people might give for punishment to be an option for society, five appear most often. Four of them are classics in the law books; the fifth one, although popular, is not considered legitimate by most legal experts.

Deterrence   It is often argued that punishment, provided it is swift and strict, is a good deterrent against crime. It may make the criminal change his or her mind about breaking the law again (specific deterrence), and it may make others think twice before turning to crime (general deterrence). Statistics indicate that in places where severe forms of punishment are the norm, such as Singapore, where disturbing the peace is punished by caning and political dissidence can lead to the death penalty, streets are noticeably safer than in free, Western-style societies. We must, of course, ask ourselves what price we are willing to pay for safe streets—a question we explored in Box. 7.5. It appears that here in the United States, crimes against property may be deterred by the knowledge of likely punishment. Who knows how many people refrain from stealing cars only because they know they'll face prison time if they're caught? It has been reported that some juvenile criminals deliberately scale down their criminal activity when they reach the age of eighteen because they know their punishment will be harsher—meaning that the concept of punishment *can* have a deterrent effect. But violent crimes seem not to be deterred much by the threat of punishment. California's controversial three-strikes law, which sends felons to jail for twenty-five years to life when they're convicted of a third serious crime, may serve as a deterrent in cases where two strikes are already on a person's record—but other factors may be at work too, such as shifts in the economy.

Rehabilitation   Some social thinkers see the purpose of punishment as making a better person out of the criminal (see the previous section); having undergone some form of appropriate punishment (generally incarceration), the criminal will have learned not to turn to crime again. This viewpoint generally presupposes prison programs that offer the inmate alternatives to a life of crime.

Incapacitation   If punishment keeps the criminal off the streets, the public is safe and a social good has been achieved. But the proponents of the incapacitation, or protecting the public, approach don't specify *how* a wrongdoer should be incapacitated. Locking someone up is usually considered sufficient for protecting the public, but in the case of an individual who is a flight risk, conditions may have to be tightened, such as placing him or her in a high-security prison. A convicted rapist may be required to submit to chemical castration (although that does not address the problem of violence and aggression underlying the rape), so he is incapacitated in terms of his offense but may still be released into society. The ultimate incapacitation is of course executing the criminal, which eliminates the chance that he or she will prey on innocent people again. We return to this issue in Chapter 13.

These three approaches to punishment have one important thing in common: They all focus on the future social consequences of punishment; in other words, they are *forward-looking*. If there are no future benefits to be had from punishing someone, then a forward-looking theory will not recommend punishment. Because the primary forward-looking social theory today is utilitarianism, these three approaches are often labeled utilitarian.

By now you may wonder why these viewpoints don't address what for many is the best reason for punishing someone: the fact that he or she is *guilty of a crime*. But that is, in effect, a separate reason for punishment; because utilitarianism approves of punishment only if there is social good involved, it is theoretically possible that the overall benefits of punishing some guilty person are minimal, whereas the benefits of punishing someone who is *not* guilty may be considerable—instantly punishing a scapegoat may have a deterrent effect that far outweighs that of catching and convicting the real perpetrator some time in the future (and it may even deter the perpetrator from doing it again). In addition, setting an example by punishing someone with disproportionate harshness is a utilitarian possibility. If, however, we think that it ought to be of some importance whether a person is actually guilty and that we should take the magnitude of the crime into consideration, we must look to the fourth theory.

Retribution A person should be punished because he or she has committed a crime, and the punishment should be in proportion to that crime. Social utility does not enter into the picture. The most influential thinker advocating retribution as the only proper reason for punishment is Kant. The principle he applies is *lex talionis,* the law of retaliation. Kant would not approve of the three forward-looking approaches because they allow us to use a person *merely as a means* to achieve social utility. When we use a person to set an example, others may be deterred from committing a crime; the goal of incapacitation is to keep the public safe; rehabilitation does indeed make a better person out of the criminal, but who decides how the criminal ought to be? We, society. So even here Kant implies that society is using people for its own purpose, which to him is demeaning, because it means that people are reduced to being means to an end only. The only acceptable reason for punishment is to show the criminal the respect any person deserves: It is to assume that he or she decided freely to commit the crime. With freedom comes responsibility, so if we want the freedom of never being treated merely as means to an end, we must also accept the responsibility that goes with it. If we transgress, we should be punished for our transgressions.

As I mentioned earlier, these four reasons might be found in a legal text on retributive justice. But if you ask a person without any legal training why a criminal should be punished, she or he might answer in the following way: "Well, it just makes us feel better to see the murderer (or rapist, or burglar) get punished."

In Chapter 13 we return to the issue of vengeance and justice in the sections on the concept of just war and on the death penalty. For now it will suffice to outline the fundamental difference between a vengeance approach and a justice approach, as some scholars see it.

Vengeance   Vengeance and retribution have something in common: They are both *backward-looking* theories, looking to the past (asking, "Who did this?") in order to punish the guilty. Like retribution, the approach based on vengeance seeks to punish the criminal because of the crime committed, but according to most retributivists there are three major differences between retribution and vengeance:

1.   Retribution is based on *logic,* whereas vengeance is an *emotional* response: It is possible for people bent on vengeance to take their anger out on individuals other than the guilty person.

2.   Retribution is a *public* act, done with the authority of the government, whereas vengeance is a *private* enterprise, undertaken by private citizens (vigilantes).

3.   Retribution wants punishment to be proportionate to the crime, but vengeance may go beyond that and exceed the damage done by the criminal.

Generally, people who are in favor of the death penalty but who are critical of utilitarianism emphasize that there is a big philosophical difference between revenge and retribution, since they see retribution as legally and morally acceptable, but vengeance as unacceptable. A small minority of scholars who are in favor of the death penalty claim that revenge is indeed the overriding emotion behind the support for capital punishment and that it is also an appropriate reason. However, a growing number of scholars and other critics of the death penalty voice the opinion that as much as we think we can find reasons why revenge and retribution are different, it comes down to the same thing: a wish to get back at the criminal, to even the score. In Chapter 13 we take a closer look at the death penalty debate.

We have now considered three forward-looking and two backward-looking arguments for punishment, although the last one (vengeance) is rarely considered legitimate by philosophers of law. But are forward- and backward-looking theories always destined to be opposite? We know that utilitarians and Kantians don't agree on the basic moral motivations, but in real life most of us believe that sometimes people ought to be punished because it will deter others from doing the same thing; sometimes we want the wrongdoer incapacitated; and sometimes we think a first-time offender can be saved from a life of crime and rehabilitated with the proper form of punishment. And sometimes we think a criminal should be punished by the book simply because the crime warrants it and for no other reason. If we as individuals can hold such different views, does it mean we are just inconsistent, or does it mean we have some deeper, if inarticulated, understanding of the issue?

John Rawls has a suggestion that may shed some light on this phenomenon. In his paper "Two Concepts of Rules" (1955), he says utilitarians and retributivists are both right—but in different ways. In *individual* court cases we appeal to retributivism: A burglar goes to prison because he has committed a crime, and the crime determines the length of the sentence. But why do we send people to prison *in general?* To make society a better place—which is the point utilitarianism makes. So the *judge's* reason for sending a person to prison is retributivist, but the *legislator's* reason for making laws is utilitarian. The danger, as Rawls sees it, is that this definition might allow the utilitarian to make laws that might sacrifice the innocent for the sake of social benefits for the many—the problem of "sheer numbers" which you encountered in Chapter 5. Thus the application of utilitarianism must be very careful; in other words, a system of checks and balances is needed. In the Narratives section you'll find a summary of the film *Minority Report,* where future crimes are punished before they take place—one might call it the ultimate forward-looking criminal justice system, but would we really label such a system "just"?

Is Anger Ever Appropriate?

A utilitarian, forward-looking penologist (someone interested in theory of punishment) usually sees no difference between retribution and vengeance: *Retributivism* is just a fancy word for the emotional demand for revenge. A retributivist will argue that the difference between vengeance and retribution is that vengeance is based on an emotion, anger, whereas retributivism is based on a wish for a proportional, logical response. That would imply that if we feel anger toward a perpetrator, whether as victims or as other members of society, we are merely being emotional and should set aside those emotions for the sake of logic. But is that desirable, or even possible?

In *For Capital Punishment: Crime and the Morality of the Death Penalty* (1979), Walter Berns argues that anger has a deep connection with justice that modern penology hasn't understood. Berns says,

> If men are not saddened when someone else suffers, or angry when someone else suffers unjustly, the implication is that they do not care for anyone other than themselves or that they lack some quality that befits a man. . . . Punishment arises out of the demand for justice, and justice is demanded by angry, morally indignant men; its purpose is to satisfy that moral indignation and thereby promote the law-abidingness that, it is assumed, accompanies it.

(In 1979 gender-neutral language hadn't yet become the norm in academic publications, but I assume Berns is talking about morally indignant men *and* women.) If we are not angry, says Berns, it is because we are selfish utilitarians who are concerned only with *compensations,* but you can't compensate victims for the loss of their physical integrity resulting from rape or for the loss of their life. Not all crimes can be balanced by compensation, but without righteous moral indignation we won't have an understanding of that.

The British philosopher P. F. Strawson argues, in his paper "Freedom and Resentment" (1982), that it is normal and appropriate to react emotionally to other people's actions toward us. We feel *resentment* if we are directly harmed, and we feel *moral indignation* if our involvement is indirect. To that the philosopher of law Diane Whiteley adds in her paper "The Victim and the Justification of Punishment"

(1998, excerpted in the Primary Readings at the end of the chapter) that we must also take human *empathy* into account, because it is "by virtue of human beings possessing the three natural capacities of moral understanding, self-evaluation, and empathy that they have the capability to be moral agents." That means the demand for justice and punishment becomes society's communication of the victim's resentment and the community's moral indignation. In this way, the community stands up for the victim and shows the person respect. If there is no (or too lenient) punishment, the community sends out two messages: that it feels no "retributive sentiment" (or, as Berns would say, anger) toward the criminal and no respect for the victim. And a victim who feels no resentment and doesn't insist on punishment has too little self-esteem. A battered spouse who doesn't want her (or his) spouse punished may have internalized the spouse's claim that she has deserved being beaten. And the community that feels no moral indignation over a crime being committed against one of its members fails to stand up for that member and fails to show the respect for the victim that she deserves.

But, says Whiteley, that is not merely a blindly emotional response. (You'll remember Martha Nussbaum in Chapter 1 arguing that emotions can have their own inherent logic and can be rational responses to situations.) Provided that the victim's resentment is directed toward the right person, and for the right reason, it is an appropriate sentiment, and the community's moral indignation is an endorsement of the victim's resentment as well as a condemnation of the criminal act that has attempted to deprive the victim of moral value (because if you value someone you don't commit a crime against him or her—committing a crime against someone is reducing her or him to merely a means to an end of instrumental value only). Resentment and indignation are proper elements in the process of justice and punishment if they lead not to pure revenge but to retribution based on a natural fellow feeling within a community.

Berns's, Strawson's, and Whiteley's arguments have been considerably strengthened by the recent findings in brain research. As you'll remember from previous chapters, Antonio Damasio and other neuroscientists have found that humans have a natural capacity for empathy, with an area in the brain that, if undamaged, will make them feel reluctant to harm other people, in particular when the harm requires a physical, immediate contact. The twentieth-century favorite analogy to brain function, the *computer model*—utterly rational and unemotional—is slowly being abandoned in favor of a deeper understanding of how our mind works, and scientists across the field are coming to similar conclusions: The human cognition isn't just rational but also deeply emotional, and proper thinking requires a healthy emotional brain.

However, there is a big difference between regarding an emotion such as anger as relevant and allowing emotions to decide for us. As you know, Nussbaum argues in favor of viewing emotions as morally relevant but not morally all-important: Reason has to play the main part in our moral decisions. Some social commentators have pointed out that in recent years, emotions seem to have become more legitimate as a deciding factor in public situations, whereas previously reason would have the final word, increasing the danger that we may lose the calming influence of rationality—the influence that Plato and Kant so staunchly defended (as indeed most philosophers always have). Case in point: the trial of Scott Peterson in Modesto, California, accused and found guilty of murdering his pregnant wife, Laci Peterson, on Christmas Eve 2002 and dumping her in the San Francisco Bay, where her body and that of her unborn baby, Conner, floated ashore months later. This case gripped the nation for two years. Whereas the guilt phase of a trial is supposed to lay out the facts, the penalty phase allows family members and others to make emotional "victim impact statements" for the jury to consider. During the penalty phase, emotions ran high, as is customary, when Laci's mother talked on the witness stand about her grief and anger at her daughter's murderer. After the jury came back with a death penalty recommendation in December 2004—a surprise to most pundits because Peterson did not have a prior criminal record—individual jurors explained that Scott Peterson's *lack of emotion* during the trial was the primary reason for their recommendation. Some commentators asked, Is this allowing emotions to go too far within the legal system? I'll let you be the judge of that.

Study Questions

1. What are Dworkin's two models? Explain, and apply his second model to the issue of protecting a country against terrorism.

2. What does it mean that science is supposed to be value-free? Do you agree? Why or why not? Apply the theory of value-free science to contemporary issues such as cloning and genetic engineering.

3. Explain the three principles of equality. Which one do you find most reasonable? Why?

4. Explain the concepts of negative and positive rights, and identify supporters of each theory.

5. What is the "original position"? Explain the pros and cons of Rawls's theory.

6. Explain forward-looking and backward-looking justice and apply both to the issue of affirmative action.

7. Explain forward-looking and backward-looking theories of punishment. Which approach seems the most reasonable to you? Why?

8. Can anger ever be justified as a reason for punishment? Explain, referring to Berns and Whiteley.

Primary Readings and Narratives

The Primary Readings are the United Nations Universal Declaration of Human Rights; an excerpt from John Rawls's "Justice as Fairness"; an excerpt from Martin Luther King's "Letter from Birmingham Jail"; two newspaper op-ed pieces by John Berteaux, "Defining Racism in the 21st Century" and "Unheard, Unseen, Unchosen";

and an excerpt from Diane Whiteley's "The Victim and the Justification of Punishment." The first Narrative is a summary of the film *The Island,* a science fiction story about exploitation of human beings cloned for spare parts; the second is a summary of the film *Gattaca,* about genetic engineering creating a human super-race as well as an underclass. The third Narrative is a summary of the 1988 film *Mississippi Burning,* about the murders of three civil rights activists in 1964. The fourth is a summary of the film *Hotel Rwanda,* the true story of the conflict between Hutus and Tutsis, and the heroic efforts of local hotel manager Paul Rusesabagina to rescue as many civilians as possible. The fifth is a summary of the film *Minority Report*, envisioning a future where crimes can be predicted and "punished" before they occur.

 Primary Reading

The United Nations Universal Declaration of Human Rights

1948.

Now, Therefore, The General Assembly proclaims

This universal declaration of human rights as a common standard of achievement for all peoples and all nations, to the end that every individual and every organ of society, keeping this Declaration constantly in mind, shall strive by teaching and education to promote respect for these rights and freedoms and by progressive measures, national and international, to secure their universal and effective recognition and observance, both among the peoples of Member States themselves and among the peoples of territories under their jurisdiction.

Article 1: All human beings are born free and equal in dignity and rights. They are endowed with reason and conscience and should act towards one another in a spirit of brotherhood.

Article 2: Everyone is entitled to all the rights and freedoms set forth in the Declaration without distinction of any kind, such as race, colour, sex, language, religion, political or other opinion, national or social origin, property, birth or other status.

Furthermore, no distinction shall be made on the basis of the political, jurisdictional or international status of the country or territory to which a person belongs, whether it be independent, trust, non-self-governing or under any other limitation of sovereignty.

Article 3: Everyone has the right to life, liberty and security of person.

Article 4: No one shall be held in slavery or servitude; slavery and the slave trade shall be prohibited in all their forms.

Article 5: No one shall be subjected to torture or to cruel, inhuman or degrading treatment or punishment.

Article 6: Everyone has the right to recognition everywhere as a person before the law.

Article 7: All are equal before the law and are entitled without any discrimination to equal protection of the law. All are entitled to equal protection against any discrimination in violation of this Declaration and against any incitement to such discrimination.

Article 8: Everyone has the right to an effective remedy by the competent national tribunals for acts violating the fundamental rights granted him by the constitution or by law.

Article 9: No one shall be subjected to arbitrary arrest, detention or exile.

Article 10: Everyone is entitled in full equality to a fair and public hearing by an independent and impartial tribunal, in the determination of his rights and obligations of any criminal charge against him.

Article 11:
1. Everyone charged with a penal offence has the right to be presumed innocent until proved guilty according to law in the public trial at which he has had all the guarantees necessary for his defense.
2. No one shall be held guilty of any penal offence on account of any act or omission which did not constitute a penal offence, under national or international law, at the time when it was committed. Nor shall a heavier penalty be imposed than the one that was applicable at the time the penal offence was committed.

Article 12: No one shall be subjected to arbitrary interference with his privacy, family, home or correspondence, nor to attacks upon his honour and reputation. Everyone has the right to the protection of the law against such interference or attacks.

Article 13:
1. Everyone has the right to freedom of movement and residence within the borders of each state.
2. Everyone has the right to leave any country, including his own, and to return to his country.

Article 14:
1. Everyone has the right to seek and to enjoy in other countries asylum from persecution.
2. This right may not be invoked in the case of prosecutions genuinely arising from non-political crimes or from acts contrary to the purposes and principles of the United Nations.

Article 15:
1. Everyone has the right to a nationality.
2. No one shall be arbitrarily deprived of his nationality nor denied the right to change his nationality.

Article 16:
1. Men and women of full age, without any limitation due to race, nationality or religion, have the right to marry and to found a family. They are entitled to equal rights as to marriage, during marriage and at its dissolution.

2. Marriage shall be entered into only with the free and full consent of the intended spouses.
3. The family is the natural and fundamental group unit of society and is entitled to protection by society and the State.

Article 17:
1. Everyone has the right to own property alone as well as in association with others.
2. No one shall be arbitrarily deprived of his property.

Article 18: Everyone has the right to freedom of thought, conscience and religion; this right includes freedom to change his religion or belief, and freedom either alone or in community with others and in public or private, to manifest his religion or belief in teaching, practice, worship and observance.

Article 19: Everyone has the right to freedom of opinion and expression; this right includes freedom to hold opinions without interference and to seek, receive and impart information and ideas through any media and regardless of frontiers.

Article 20:
1. Everyone has the right to freedom of peaceful assembly and association.
2. No one may be compelled to belong to an association.

Article 21:
1. Everyone has the right to take part in the government of his country, directly or through freely chosen representatives.
2. Everyone has the right of equal access to public service in his country.
3. The will of the people shall be the basis of the authority of government; this will shall be expressed in periodic and genuine elections which shall be by universal and equal suffrage and shall be held by secret vote or by equivalent free voting procedures.

Article 22: Everyone, as a member of society, has the right to social security and is entitled to realization, through national effort and international cooperation and in accordance with the organization and resources of each State, of the economic, social and cultural rights indispensable for his dignity and the free development of his personality.

Article 23:
1. Everyone has the right to work, to free choice of employment, to just and favourable conditions of work and to protection against unemployment.
2. Everyone, without any discrimination, has the right to equal pay for equal work.
3. Everyone who works has the right to just and favourable remuneration ensuring for himself and his family an existence worthy of human dignity, and supplemented, if necessary, by other means of social protection.
4. Everyone has the right to form and to join trade unions for the protection of his interests.

Article 24: Everyone has the right to rest and leisure, including reasonable limitation of working hours and periodic holidays with pay.

Article 25:
1. Everyone has the right to a standard living adequate for the health and well-being of himself and his family, including food, clothing, housing and medical care and

necessary social services, and the right to security in the event of unemployment, sickness, disability, widowhood, old age or other lack of livelihood in circumstances beyond his control.

2. Motherhood and childhood are entitled to special care and assistance. All children, whether born in or out of wedlock, shall enjoy the same social protection.

Article 26:

1. Everyone has the right to education. Education shall be free, at least in the elementary and fundamental stages. Elementary education shall be compulsory. Technical and professional education shall be made generally available and higher education shall be equally accessible to all on the basis of merit.

2. Education shall be directed to the full development of the human personality and to the strengthening of respect for human rights and fundamental freedoms. It shall promote understanding, tolerance and friendship among all nations, racial or religious groups, and shall further the activities of the United Nations for the maintenance of peace.

3. Parents have a prior right to choose the kind of education that shall be given to their children.

Article 27:

1. Everyone has the right freely to participate in the cultural life of the community, to enjoy the arts and to share in scientific advancement and its benefits.

2. Everyone has the right to the protection of the moral and material interests resulting from any scientific, literary or artistic production of which he is the author.

Article 28: Everyone is entitled to a social and international order in which the rights and freedoms set forth in this Declaration can be fully realized.

Article 29:

1. Everyone has duties to the community in which alone the free and full development of his personality is possible.

2. In the exercise of his rights and freedoms, everyone shall be subject only to such limitations as are determined by law solely for the purpose of securing due recognition and respect for the rights and freedoms of others and of meeting the just requirements of morality, public order and the general welfare in a democratic society.

3. These rights and freedoms may in no case be exercised contrary to the purposes and principles of the United Nations.

Article 30: Nothing in this Declaration may be interpreted as implying for any State, group or person any right to engage in any activity or to perform any act aimed at the destruction of any of the rights and freedoms set forth herein.

Study Questions

1. Find examples of negative and positive rights, and explain the difference.

2. Evaluate these articles from a libertarian approach and from Rawls's approach.

3. In your opinion, are there any rights that should be on the list but aren't included? Are there any rights you disagree with? Explain.

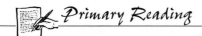

Justice as Fairness

JOHN RAWLS

Essay, 1958. Excerpt.

John Rawls is generally considered the most influential American social thinker in the twentieth century. Influenced by Kant's philosophy of never using another person simply as a means to an end, Rawls outlines a theory of justice based on the ideas that utilitarianism is unacceptable, and that it is possible to agree on basic principles of justice if we agree to see one another as equals. In this excerpt from his famous paper written years before his even more famous book, *A Theory of Justice* (1971), Rawls outlines the conditions under which inequality might be acceptable in a society of equals.

The conception of justice which I want to develop may be stated in the form of two principles as follows: first, each person participating in a practice, or affected by it, has an equal right to the most extensive liberty compatible with a like liberty for all; and second, inequalities are arbitrary unless it is reasonable to expect that they will work out for everyone's advantage, and provided the positions and offices to which they attach, or from which they may be gained, are open to all. These principles express justice as a complex of three ideas: liberty, equality, and reward for services contributing to the common good.

The term "person" is to be construed variously depending on the circumstances. On some occasions it will mean human individuals, but on others it may refer to nations, provinces, business firms, churches, teams, and so on. The principles of justice apply in all these instances, although there is a certain logical priority to the case of human individuals. As I shall use the term "person," it will be ambiguous in the manner indicated.

The first principle holds, of course, only if other things are equal: that is, while there must always be a justification for departing from the initial position of equal liberty (which is defined by the pattern of rights and duties, powers and liabilities, established by a practice), and the burden of proof is placed on him who would depart from it, nevertheless, there can be, and often there is, a justification for doing so. Now, that similar particular cases, as defined by a practice, should be treated similarly as they arise, is part of the very concept of a practice; it is involved in the notion of an activity in accordance with rules. The first principle expresses an analogous conception, but as applied to the structure of practices themselves. It holds, for example, that there is a presumption against the distinctions and classifications made by legal systems and other practices to the extent that they infringe on the original and equal liberty of the persons participating in them. The second principle defines how this presumption may be rebutted.

It might be argued at this point that justice requires only an equal liberty. If, however, a greater liberty were possible for all without loss or conflict, then it would be irrational to settle on a lesser liberty. There is no reason for circumscribing rights unless their exercise would be incompatible, or would render the practice defining them less effective. Therefore no serious distortion of the concept of justice is likely to follow them including within it the concept of the greatest equal liberty.

The second principle defines what sorts of inequalities are permissible; it specifies how the presumption laid down by the first principle may be put aside. Now by inequalities it is best to understand not *any* differences between offices and positions, but differences in the benefits and burdens attached to them either directly or indirectly, such as prestige and wealth, or liability to taxation and compulsory services. Players in a game do not protest against there being different positions, such as batter, pitcher, catcher, and the like, nor to there being various privileges and powers as specified by the rules; nor do the citizens of a country object to there being the different offices of government such as president, senator, governor, judge, and so on, each with their special rights and duties. It is not differences of this kind that are normally thought of as inequalities, but differences in the resulting distribution established by a practice, or made possible by it, of the things men strive to attain or avoid. Thus they may complain about the pattern of honors and rewards set up by a practice (*e.g.* the privileges and salaries of government officials) or they may object to the distribution of power and wealth which results from the various ways in which men avail themselves of the opportunities allowed by it (*e.g.* the concentration of wealth which may develop in a free price system allowing large entrepreneurial or speculative gains).

It should be noted that the second principle holds that an inequality is allowed only if there is reason to believe that the practice with the inequality, or resulting in it, will work for the advantage of *every* party engaging in it. Here it is important to stress that *every* party must gain from the inequality. Since the principle applies to practices, it implies that the representative man in every office or position defined by a practice, when he views it as a going concern, must find it reasonable to prefer his condition and prospects with the inequality to what they would be under the practice without it. The principle excludes, therefore, the justification of inequalities on the grounds that the disadvantages of those in one position are outweighed by the greater advantages of those in another position. This rather simple restriction is the main modification I wish to make in the utilitarian principle as usually understood. When coupled with the notion of a practice, it is a restriction of consequence, and one which some utilitarians, for example Hume and Mill, have used in their discussions of justice without realizing apparently its significance, or at least without calling attention to it. Why it is a significant modification of principle, changing one's conception of justice entirely, the whole of my argument will show.

Further, it is also necessary that the various offices to which special benefits or burdens attach are open to all. It may be, for example, to the common advantage, as just defined, to attach special benefits to certain offices. Perhaps by doing so the requisite talent can be attracted to them and encouraged to give its best efforts. But any offices having special benefits must be won in a fair competition in which contestants are judged on their merits. If some offices were not open, those excluded would normally be justified in feeling unjustly treated, even if they benefited from the greater efforts of those who were allowed to compete for them. Now if one can assume that offices are open, it is necessary only to consider the design of practices themselves and how they jointly, as a system, work together. It will be a mistake to focus attention on the varying relative positions of particular persons, who may be known to us by their proper names, and to require that each such change, as a once for all transaction viewed in isolation, must be in itself just. It is the system of practices which is to be judged, and judged from a general point of view: unless one is prepared to criticize it from the standpoint of a representative man holding some particular office, one has no complaint against it.

Study Questions

1. Describe Rawls's two principles in your own words.

2. Can you think of a policy involving inequality that Rawls might approve of?

3. Judging from this excerpt, what would you think Rawls's position on affirmative action might be? Explain.

  Primary Reading

A Letter from Birmingham Jail

MARTIN LUTHER KING, JR.

Essay, April 16, 1963. Excerpt.

This open letter was written by the civil rights leader Martin Luther King, Jr., in response to a published statement from eight clergymen from Alabama who had criticized King's activities as "unwise and untimely." As president of the Southern Christian Leadership Conference, King had taken part in a nonviolent protest against racial segregation in Birmingham, and he and others had subsequently been jailed for "parading without a permit." King notes in the published version of his letter that he began writing his response to the clergymen in the margin of the newspaper where the statement had appeared and continued on scraps of paper because that was all he had available in his jail cell.

You express a great deal of anxiety over our willingness to break laws. This is certainly a legitimate concern. Since we so diligently urge people to obey the Supreme Court's decision of 1954 outlawing segregation in the public schools, at first glance it may seem rather paradoxical for us consciously to break laws. One may well ask: "How can you advocate breaking some laws and obeying others?" The answer lies in the fact that there are two types of laws: just and unjust. I would be the first to advocate obeying just laws. One has not only a legal but a moral responsibility to obey just laws. Conversely, one has a moral responsibility to disobey unjust laws. I would agree with St. Augustine that "an unjust law is no law at all."

Now, what is the difference between the two? How does one determine whether a law is just or unjust? A just law is a man-made code that squares with the moral law or the law of God. An unjust law is a code that is out of harmony with the moral law. To put it in the terms of St. Thomas Aquinas: An unjust law is a human law that is not rooted in eternal law and natural law. Any law that uplifts human personality is just. Any law that degrades human personality is unjust. All segregation statutes are unjust because segregation distorts the soul and damages the personality. It gives the segregator a false sense of superiority and the segregated a false sense of inferiority. Segregation, to use the terminology of the Jewish philosopher Martin Buber, substitutes an "I-it" relationship for an "I-thou" relationship and ends up relegating persons to the status of things. Hence segregation is not only politically, economically and sociologically unsound, it is morally wrong and awful. Paul Tillich has said that sin is separation. Is not segregation an existential expression of man's tragic separation, his awful estrangement, his terrible sinfulness? Thus it is that I can urge men to obey the 1954 decision of the Supreme Court, for it is morally right; and I can urge them to disobey segregation ordinances, for they are morally wrong.

Let us consider a more concrete example of just and unjust laws. An unjust law is a code that a numerical or power majority group compels a minority group to obey but does not make binding on itself. This is *difference* made legal. By the same token, a just law is a code that a majority compels a minority to follow and that it is willing to follow itself. This is *sameness* made legal.

Let me give another explanation. A law is unjust if it is inflicted on a minority that, as a result of being denied the right to vote, had no part in enacting or devising the law. Who can say that the legislature of Alabama which set up that state's segregation laws was democratically elected? Throughout Alabama all sorts of devious methods are used to prevent Negroes from becoming registered voters, and there are some counties in which, even though Negroes constitute a majority of the population, not a single Negro is registered. Can any law enacted under such circumstances be considered democratically structured?

Sometimes a law is just on its face and unjust in its application. For instance, I have been arrested on a charge of parading without a permit. Now, there is nothing wrong in having an ordinance which requires a permit for a parade. But such an ordinance becomes unjust when it is used to maintain segregation and to deny citizens the First Amendment privilege of peaceful assembly and protest.

I hope you are able to see the distinction I am trying to point out. In no sense do I advocate evading or defying the law, as would the rabid segregationist. That would lead to anarchy. One who breaks an unjust law must do so openly, lovingly, and with a willingness to accept the penalty. I submit that an individual who breaks a law that conscience tells him is unjust, and who willingly accepts the penalty of imprisonment in order to arouse the conscience of the community over its injustice, is in reality expressing the highest respect for law.

Study Questions

1. How does King justify advocating breaking some laws and obeying others? Would you agree with him? Why or why not?

2. What, according to King, is unsound about segregation? Explain. Would that also apply to a group of people who would *voluntarily* segregate themselves from other groups?

3. How does King reconcile the breaking of an unjust law with respect for the law? Do you agree? Why or why not?

4. Is King's ideal of nonviolent resistance to unjust laws a concept that has mainly historical interest, or might it have something to say to people of the twenty-first century? Explain.

 *Primary Reading*

Two Texts on Discrimination

John Berteaux is an African American philosopher who specializes in social ethics and philosophy of race. In addition to teaching and lecturing, he pens a column in the *Monterey Herald*. For Berteaux, racism in the United States is no longer a blatant, in-your-face offense; it is more subtle, and in some cases even unconscious, based on the phenomenon of "privileged race." Most white people don't question their race or its privileges; they simply take them for granted—not necessarily in a haughty sense but because they have never lost or had to question the privileges of whiteness. In the first text, Berteaux, in a nonhostile manner, makes a point of raising white America's awareness of this subtle everyday form of discrimination. In the second text, he asks himself if he may not be perpetuating another kind of discrimination, against *women,* in his job as philosophy professor.

Defining Racism in the 21st Century

JOHN BERTEAUX

Op-ed essay from the **Monterey Herald,** *January 17, 2005.*

With Martin Luther King's birthday approaching, some things occurred recently that got me thinking about what racism means in the twenty-first century. For instance, typically, Sundays, my wife Susie and I set out to the Monterey Sports Center to swim laps. Three weeks ago I stood at the end of the pool twiddling my thumbs waiting for a lane to become available. Someone left one of the lanes to my right. As I prepared to get into the water a white lady strolled pass me jumped into the pool and started to swim laps. Was she ill-mannered? Maybe she didn't see me? Should I say something or forget it?

A couple of months ago, I was waiting to be seated at a restaurant. I had been there for a couple of minutes. As a result, a line started to form behind me. Looking up from my newspaper I saw the hostess walking my way. She smiled at me—I thought. I replied with a smile. She strode past me and began talking to the fellow behind me in line. After chatting for a second she asked him "are you here for breakfast?" She led him to a seat. Am I invisible? I guess being at the front of the line doesn't mean you can count on being seated first.

I stopped in at the Community Hospital of the Monterey Peninsula to see Joanne Sherrill-Drummer. Joanne works at the hospital, was born in Seaside and has lived on the Peninsula most of her life. During our conversation she spoke of things she has learned not to count on. She does not count on being able to open the newspaper and see people of her own race positively represented. If a traffic cop pulls her over she doesn't count on it not being because of her race. She does not count on her skin color not affecting her in financial situations. Joanne did not list these points with resentment. Rather, she said she was not intimidated by these differences and, in fact, they have helped her develop a sense of self.

I drove over to Mel Mason's office to solicit his thoughts about these events. Is any of this racism I asked. Mel responded, "If you were a white man would the woman at the pool have failed to see you? If the hostess were a black woman and you were in front of the line would she have seated you first?" While it isn't cross burning or lynching and no one yelled a racial epithet, it sure speaks to a sense of privilege.

Interestingly, after that woman seized the lane I was about to swim in, I marched to the other end of the pool. I reached an empty lane at about the same time as another fellow—a white man. He said, "You take it. You've been waiting a while." And that hostess reappeared a couple of minutes later, guided me to a table, and asked if I wanted coffee.

Unseen, Unheard, Unchosen

JOHN BERTEAUX

Op-ed essay from the **Monterey Herald**, *March 6, 2006.*

Usually I am ambling along across campus when out of the blue I am overtaken by a niggling uncertainty. In the distance I see Bridgett, Shannon, Vanessa, Rachel or one of the many coeds taking one of my classes. I stop and call out. I call out because I recall that they tried to ask a question or comment on something during the class period and I fear I overlooked them—didn't see their hands—thought I would get back to them and didn't. "Sorry I missed you in class today," I confess. The standard response is, "You answered all my questions." The problem is: that particular response doesn't help.

About four or five years ago, in a class at San Diego State University, I brought up the problem of the invisibility of women in the classroom. I was surprised at the number of women in the room who had developed techniques for dealing with just this issue.

Sadly, most of the techniques were like that of Danusia. Danusia was a returning student, with two young daughters. She was a hard worker, bright, and I would guess in her early thirties—a budding philosopher. During the discussion she said that generally she gave a professor a couple of chances. The second or third time that she was ignored in the classroom she simply stopped raising her hand. Of course, within the period of a half an hour after the discussion, she raised her hand. I said, "Give me a second let me finish this thought." As I finished the thought I promptly called on a young man whose hand was up. He was sitting right behind Danusia. Realizing what I had done I stopped the young man in mid-sentence and allowed Danusia to ask her question.

As I remember, everyone in the class, including Danusia and me, laughed. Certainly the laughter and my apology changed little. Women suffer because of the unconscious assumptions and actions of well meaning people in everyday interactions—assumptions and actions that are invisible to us.

"Was your hand up," I ask? "No," she replies. I go on talking and then three, four, five hands go up at once. As I speak, I mull over, "Whose hand went up first?" I am not sure.

Study Questions

1. Would you agree with Berteaux that the two incidents of being "invisible" in the first text reflect a subtle form of modern racism? If yes, what can be done about it? If no, do you think Berteaux misread the situation? Explain. What significance do the last two incidents in the first text have?

2. Define racism, as opposed to bigotry. In your view, is racism always directed from white people toward people of color, or can racism go in other directions?

3. Do you find that it is harder for women to get their point across in the classroom? If yes, is that due to the same kind of unconscious discrimination that Berteaux points out in the first text? Is Berteaux discriminating against the women in his classroom? Why or why not?

 Primary Reading

The Victim and the Justification of Punishment

DIANE WHITELEY

Article, 1998. Excerpt.

Diane Whiteley is a scholar associated with the administration at Simon Fraser University in British Columbia. In this paper, published in the John Jay College of Criminal Justice's journal *Criminal Justice Ethics,* she argues that the focus of justice has been insufficiently directed toward the concerns of the victim and too much toward the wrongdoer and the community. In addition, she argues that if we as a community don't feel moral indignation over what the criminal has done, we are letting the victim down.

The victim's resentment is a moral sentiment. But what is a moral sentiment? To begin with, it is worth pointing out that a moral sentiment may be judged justified or not. I offer some examples of unjustified moral sentiments presently. A justified moral sentiment is an "intelligent" emotion in the sense that it conveys a "considered" emotional reaction—one which is based on reasons and takes account of the circumstances. Significantly, a moral sentiment is directed at another person. Resentment, for example, would not arise on injury by a natural disaster or an animal—at least not appropriately. It is experienced on being harmed by a person.

A moral sentiment is not a mere passion such as vengefulness which is characterized by inappropriate intensity or a failure duly to consider facts and circumstances. It can be evaluated, judged appropriate or not, and controlled. It is not a simple feeling—a pleasant or unpleasant sensation such as a pounding heart or queasy stomach. While there is no denying that a moral sentiment may have a physiological component, it is, in part, a cognitive state of belief. It is *about* something, a way of seeing and engaging with the world. In short, it is a complex emotion that involves a belief, an evaluation, and a relation to action.

The victim's resentment is, in fact, a paradigmatic moral sentiment. Its cognitive content consists in a belief that the wrongdoer did the crime. But resentment also involves the victim's corresponding evaluation of the wrongdoer. It is an attitude towards him that stems from viewing him in the light of the belief that he did the harm and related beliefs about his moral qualities. The wrongdoer is evaluated as uncaring of the victim's value. The victim infers that he is capable of respecting her dignity but failed to do so. As Murphy points out, the reason we deeply resent moral injuries done to us

> is not simply that they hurt us in some tangible or sensible way; it is because such injuries are also *messages*—symbolic communications. They are ways a wrongdoer has of saying to us, "I count but you do not," "I can use you for my purposes," . . . Intentional wrongdoing *insults* us and attempts (sometimes successfully) to *degrade* us.

Resentment has, in addition, an affective component. It arouses in the victim desires or feelings directed at the wrongdoer. Those desires motivate the victim to act in ways characteristic of the emotion. The attitude that arises in the resenter is one of defiance in which she denies to herself and others the presumption, fostered by the wrongdoer's action, that she is low in value. This psychological reaction is analogous to one's physical reaction of striking out in self-defense at an assault. It motivates the victim to get back at the wrongdoer by *expressing* her resentment. Failure to express it may signify acceptance of the wrongdoer's evaluation. And acceptance would indicate that she suffers some psychological pathology such as a severe lack of self-esteem.

For example, a woman who suffers from the "battered woman syndrome" is a victim who does not react with resentment when she is beaten by another person. Instead, she accepts the batterer's assessment that she deserves to be beaten. She should resent the beatings. The fact that we judge her lack of resentment to be pathological indicates that experiencing resentment is an appropriate reaction to the deliberate harm of another.

As a moral sentiment involving a belief, an evaluation, and an affective component, the victim's resentment can be judged as justified or not. It is unjustified if the belief about the wrongdoer is false. For example, resentment toward the accused thief, Smith, would be unjustified if Smith did not, in fact, snatch the victim's purse but was mistakenly apprehended because he was in the vicinity and fit the description of the real thief. The resentment would be unjustified were the victim's evaluation of the wrongdoer incorrect. If Jones snatched the purse because he was coerced into doing so by a gang that was threatening his life, the victim's evaluation of Jones as uncaring of her value would be incorrect and unjustified. Finally, the affective component of the resentment may be inappropriate. If, on having her purse snatched, the victim's resentment were so intense that she would express it by cutting the thief's hands off so that he could never steal again, we would judge her resentment unjustified because it was too intense.

Even if the resentment is justified, however, the question remains as to whether it should be communicated through the social institution. Before addressing that question, it will be helpful to consider the moral psychology of the remaining stakeholder, the community.

The members of the community react to a harm in which they are not personally involved with a certain disinterest. Their experience of moral indignation involves sympathy for the victim but tends to be less intense than resentment. Like resentment, however, moral indignation rests on and reflects the moral demand for some degree of goodwill.

Moral indignation is a complex emotion. It is similar to resentment in that it involves a belief, a related evaluation, and an affective component. In addition, however, it has a normative dimension. It is grounded in *approval* of the victim's resentment. It reflects sympathy for the victim from an impersonal standpoint. As such, it is not a mere *feeling* of sympathy arising out of sentimentality. It involves a reflective evaluation of the victim's resentment which results in a judgment to endorse it. The cognitive content of the moral indignation is the belief that the wrongdoer did the crime. The related evaluation is that the wrongdoer is uncaring, to some degree, of the victim's value. The affective component, which is normally less intense than that of resentment, involves sympathy for the victim and a desire to get back at the wrongdoer on the victim's behalf.

The fact that moral indignation involves a judgment to endorse the victim's resentment entails that it may be modified or even withdrawn when the facts of the case are examined. Feinberg points out that at a criminal trial the absolution of the accuser often hangs as much in balance as the guilt of the accused. In the case of date rape, for example, the victim's motives and actions may be examined and questioned equally with those of the accused. The upshot is that, in our system in which the value of fairness is given a high priority, the community withholds its expression of moral indignation until the wrongdoer is pronounced guilty.

In sentencing, the community has the opportunity to express its moral indignation. The expression is intended to send a message. The community intends that the wrongdoer and public recognize that the punishment means denunciation, among other things. In crimes such as robbery, assault, rape, or murder the wrongdoer fails to meet the demand for goodwill. In extreme cases such as violent, brutal murder, her actions express outright malevolence. But in all cases a criminal act shows that the wrongdoer views the victim as having no or reduced moral value. If the community were to fail to express censure, it would be acquiescing in the wrongdoer's devaluation of the victim. Jean Hampton suggests that the community's response involves "a *kind* of fear and defiance." On her view, the community *fears* that by not opposing the wrongdoer's challenge to its values, it invites further challenges. Therefore, it *defies* the challenge. I think Hampton's analysis is correct for our existing justice system. But if the system were changed to accommodate the victim's concerns by giving him a role, the community's response could also reflect sympathy for him, the sympathy inherent in moral indignation. The sentence would involve denunciation of the wrongdoer to be sure, but it would also be a way of standing up for the person devalued by the crime. In other words, the community would acknowledge the victim as one of its audiences.

From the community's perspective, as already mentioned, punishment conveys a variety of messages, not just moral indignation. I have focused on the retributive sentiment of moral indignation because of its connection to the victim's resentment.

This examination of moral psychologies makes it clear that, when the wrongdoer commits the crime, it is not just her relationship with society as a whole that is affected. The victim, too, has a substantial and justifiable stake in what happens to her. In other words, the recognition that the victim's resentment may be justified and that it needs to be expressed provides at least a *prima facie* reason to include the victim as a stakeholder in the social institution and as an audience for the communication. From the victim's perspective, an appropriate, public acknowledgment and communication of his justified resentment through the justice system would serve a number of purposes. It would convey publicly his resentment. It would communicate his demand for a minimum degree of respect from the wrongdoer and others. Finally, it would signify to the victim that the community is willing to stand up for him and reject his devaluation.

In the next section, I proceed with the second step in the argument about whether the victim's concerns are pertinent to the justification of punishment. I argue that the victim's personal, justified reaction should be acknowledged as a justifying reason for punishment by giving him a role in the social institution.

Study Questions

1. What is, to Whiteley, a "justified moral sentiment," and what makes a victim's resentment of the wrongdoer justified?

2. How should the community react toward a wrongdoer?

3. Why, to Whiteley, is it appropriate to include the emotion of moral indignation in the concept of punishment? Do you agree? Why or why not?

4. What does Whiteley mean by saying that moral sentiments can have a cognitive content? Why is this important for her theory of justification of punishment?

5. Does Whiteley's inclusion of emotions with a cognitive element in the justification of punishment lead to the acceptance of revenge? Why or why not?

Narrative

The Island

MICHAEL BAY (DIRECTOR)
CASPIAN TREDWELL-OWEN AND ALEX KURTZMAN (SCREENPLAY)

Film, 2005. Summary.

A young man awakens from a nightmare about falling overboard from a boat and drowning. He is in a sterile, all-white room: a hospital room? a dorm room? Dressed in a fresh, white jumpsuit, he leaves the room and moves with other men in white jumpsuits along hallways and stairs in some enormous, cold, impersonal underground facility. The time is the future, the last decades of the twenty-first century.

Together with other men and women in white jumpsuits, overseen by black-clad guards, the young man watches the daily installment of the Lottery on the big wall screens: A lucky winner is chosen to go to the Island! A happy face comes on the screen: A jubilant man who never thought his time would come now gets to go to the Island and breathe real air and swim in the ocean. We see shots of the Island, a tropical paradise with blue waters. Everybody wants to go to the Island, and everyone is told, "Someday your turn will come; be patient!" All the residents follow a carefully watched diet and a workout program so they will be in their best shape when they get to leave for the Island. That is all anyone knows, but questions are beginning to be asked.

At breakfast, the young man meets with a young woman whom he obviously knows. She teaches him how to get bacon added to his bland breakfast by flattering the woman working the food line. Next, he goes to an appointment with someone very important,

In the film *The Island* (DreamWorks, 2005) life can be prolonged with parts from clones, if you're wealthy enough. Once an organ is harvested, the clone dies. According to the manufacturers of the "products," these clones are not conscious, but are manufacturers are lying to their clients: Without consciousness, the clones die. In order to keep the clones pacified, they are told that they will go to "the Island," a tropical paradise. When called to "the Island," the clones are taken into surgery to be harvested. Here clones Lincoln Six Echo (Ewan McGregor) and Jordan Two Delta (Scarlett Johansson) are running for their lives, trying to save themselves and the other clones.

Dr. Merrick. His doctor? His boss? We hear that Merrick is worried about him, and we find out that his name is Lincoln 6 Echo. We also find out that he is being chastised for seeing too much of the young woman, Jordan 2 Delta. Friendships are okay, but any kind of physical and mental closeness is forbidden. But what really worries Dr. Merrick is that Lincoln is beginning to ask questions: Why is everything white? Why the diet rules? Why is everybody just hanging out, waiting to go to the Island? Merrick reminds Lincoln how lucky he is to have survived the "contamination," an apocalyptic disaster that made the air above unbreathable and life on the planet unlivable—except for the Island. Survivors are found on the outside, rescued, and brought to the facility. They are the ones dressed in white jumpsuits. At least, that is the story everyone is told—nobody has any memories of actually being rescued. But they do have memories of having had lives before the contamination, normal childhoods and so on. While he and Merrick have been talking, Lincoln has drawn a picture of the boat in his dreams, a very sleek design, with the name *Renovatio* painted on the side. Lincoln doesn't know what it means, and Merrick is disturbed at the drawing. Where does this image come from? The doctor straps Lincoln down and subjects him to a painful brain scan with nano-robots, and lets him go.

Later in the day, Lincoln sneaks out to the unofficial part of the facility, to a plant section where he talks to one of the workers, McCord. McCord gives him hints of what life is like for those who aren't "special," like Lincoln, and makes him swear he will tell nobody. Lincoln sees McCord's collection of pinups, and we realize that Lincoln just sees pretty girls with clothes that are too small for them—he has no idea what "sexy" means. Lincoln is like a bright child before puberty, just like Jordan. He has no idea about politics or religion, but he is not stupid. On his way out he captures a large moth trapped in the air vent—a moth that shouldn't be alive if the world is contaminated. And he asks more questions.

Meanwhile, a young white-clad pregnant woman starts having contractions and is ecstatic: It means she and her baby will be going to the Island! We follow her upstairs, where we see what is really happening: She isn't sent off to any Island; she gives birth, and as she looks at her baby with love in her eyes, she is given a lethal injection by the nurse. Her job on this earth is done. The nurse takes the baby and hands it to a young waiting couple, and we see that the woman looks identical to the young mother who was killed. The young woman was a *clone,* a "product," an expendable commodity, created to give birth for the "real" person who was unable to.

We watch another kind of birth, taking place in another part of the facility—the birth of a fully grown person from a nutrient bubble—and we realize that the white-clad, healthy, idle people waiting to go to the Island are clones, who will be killed so their organs can be harvested and used to save the lives of their "sponsors," the "real" persons. Each clone is branded on the wrist and supplied with a nonremovable identity bracelet that works as a GPS tracking device.

As "luck" will have it, Jordan 2 Delta is the next Lottery winner, and she happily prepares for her departure for the Island the next morning. That same night Lincoln has his usual nightmare of drowning and gets up to liberate the bug he captured. But on his way up to the air vent, he finds himself on the upper floor, the surgery section, and witnesses the death of the woman who just gave birth, as well as a desperate escape attempt: The man from the day before who was so happy about going to the Island is now running for his life, moments away from having his heart removed. He is hunted down as Lincoln watches, and now Lincoln is the one who runs for his life. He wakes up Jordan and tries to explain the situation to her—that there *is* no Island. So now they are both on the run, looking for an exit. They make their way out, pursued by security, and find themselves on a desert mesa—no civilization, but the air is breathable, and there is a road leading somewhere. Down that road is a diner with the same logo as one on a matchbook McCord has given Lincoln, so they go in and inquire about McCord. It becomes obvious that they may be smart but have no savvy at all. Jordan doesn't know the power of alcohol, and Lincoln has no idea how to interpret the cryptic message from the bartender that McCord is "in the can." Lincoln confronts McCord in the men's room, and the plant worker takes the two clones to his home, where he tells them the truth about their origin, and about their intended fate: to be harvested by their originals, who need their organs to stay alive. And what of the memories they have of their childhoods? Mere imprints, twelve stories with variations. And how long have they been alive? Three or four years. They are simply spare parts for rich people who want to live forever, but the clients are told that the clones are not conscious—a deliberate lie.

Meanwhile, there is a tour for prospective clients at the facility. The clients are told that the clones have no minds and that it takes twelve months to grow a clone ready to have its organs harvested. According to a law passed in 2050, only clones in a persistent vegetative state can be produced, so the moral issue of creating life to take it does not apply. But Merrick has a separate meeting with an African man, Deleuran, a mercenary with the best military special units training available; he is being hired to go after Lincoln and Jordan. Merrick explains to him why the clones are not in the vegetative state prescribed by law: The experiment failed; without consciousness, the organs failed, so consciousness is a necessity, and with every clone produced Merrick's clone factory is breaking the law—but the profits are immense. And, he says, the clones are just tools, they have no souls—and using them as tools, he will be able to cure all kinds of diseases. His purpose is, in his eyes, a noble one.

Lincoln and Jordan decide to seek out their "sponsors," the originals, to plead with them to expose the scam, and the abuse and murder of self-aware human beings. As they board the train to Los Angeles to find Lincoln's sponsor, Tom Lincoln, with the help of McCord, the special forces move in and kill McCord. Lincoln and Jordan arrive in Los Angeles, and after a series of dangerous stunts and mishaps (in Los Angeles traffic of the late twenty-first century, with hovercars and levitated metro trains), they make it to Tom Lincoln's place.

At first, Tom Lincoln is appalled that they show up—why is his "life insurance policy" walking around on the outside? We see Tom Lincoln's condo; we see that he is a designer, and we see a model of the boat Lincoln has been dreaming about every night, and drawing in Merrick's office, with the name *Renovatio* painted on the side. How did Lincoln know? We hear Merrick talking to his aide, revealing that Lincoln's brain scan shows a rapidly evolving brain with more memories than he has ever experienced—the memories of his "sponsor." What now worries Merrick is that the entire series of clones may have developed not only consciousness but also human curiosity and the capacity to remember their originals' lives, and he decides to terminate the entire series and start from scratch. Which means that all the people Lincoln and Jordan know and care about will be killed.

Tom Lincoln seems to be warming up to the two clones; he helps them get rid of their bracelets and flirts a bit with Jordan. But when he promises to help them get on the news to tell their story, Jordan smells a rat. And indeed, when Tom is alone he makes a call to the cloning institute, complaining that his "insurance policy" (which he will need in two years, because of a degenerative sexually transmitted disease) is in his living room. Jordan opts to stay in the apartment while the two Lincolns go to the TV station, but on the way they are hunted down by the mercenaries, who expect Tom to help them catch the clone. Lincoln, however, manages to turn the tables on Tom—as they fight, Lincoln manages to slip his bracelet on Tom's wrist, and since the mercenaries now think they have their clone, Tom is killed. Lincoln 6 Echo takes his place, pretending to be the original. He goes back and is reunited with Jordan, and together they explore what it is humans call "sex." Now Lincoln could slip away with Jordan on Tom's boat, go south and live like "real people," but he still has a job to do: He chooses to go back to the facility. Jordan is captured by Deleuran and delivered to the facility—was it on purpose? Deleuran is a mercenary, but he also has a family history: His father was a rebel, and when he was captured, his sons were branded so everyone would recognize that they were less than human. Deleuran understands rebellions for the sake of human dignity. What will happen next? Will Lincoln live up to his name and "free the slaves," and expose Merrick as a liar and a murderer? Will Deleuran hand Jordan over to be carved up for parts, or will he side with the rebels? Watch the film and find out!

Study Questions

1. What is the film's statement about personhood and human rights? Explain in detail.

2. How would an act utilitarian view this film? A rule utilitarian? A Kantian?

3. Explain the film's indirect use of the concepts of intrinsic and instrumental value.

4. If scientists succeed in creating human adult clones, should clones be regarded as "having souls"? Is that important? Why or why not?

Narrative

Gattaca

ANDREW NICCOL (SCREENWRITER AND DIRECTOR)

Film, 1997. Summary.

Gattaca is also a science fiction film, but contrary to *The Island* there are very few special effects or futuristic inventions). The science fiction element is almost exclusively one of a thought experiment, a mind game: What if . . . ? What if babies could be designed in the lab, eradicating birth defects, nearsightedness, high cancer risk, and so forth? Wouldn't that be wonderful? Perhaps not. Exploring the possible human future of genetic engineering (reminiscent of Huxley's *Brave New World*), *Gattaca* tells the story of a near-future society in which each child is the dream child of its parents, the best combination of their genes—if the child is legitimately conceived in the lab, that is. Children conceived the natural way are considered flawed and will never rise above being manual laborers.

Vincent Freeman is such a child, the firstborn son of young parents. He is born with myopia and a high probability of heart failure before the age of thirty; even so, as a young adult he outpaces his younger brother, a more socially acceptable individual conceived in a petri dish with all the good genes. At the beginning of the film, we witness Vincent's parents' visit to the clinic where they and the doctor discuss the future genetic characteristics of Vincent's brother-to-be, as yet an embryo. We see how reluctant the parents are at first, being resigned to following custom and merely having the embryo screened for diseases, but the doctor persuades them that life is hard enough as it is, so why not give him all the advantages that are possible? "He will still be you—only the best of you." But growing up, the one with the ambitious goals is not the perfect boy conceived in the lab, Anton, but his imperfect older brother. Vincent dreams of becoming an astronaut and leaving for the outer solar system, but as a natural-born individual he has no chance— legally. So he embarks on acquiring an illegal identity, not just a new name and history but new DNA, an entirely new genetic profile. An identity broker sets him up with a

Gattaca (Columbia Pictures, 1997) posits a future world where respectable persons are conceived and genetically designed in vitro; only slobs and destitute people have children the natural way. Here Vincent/Jerome (Ethan Hawke) and Irene (Uma Thurman) are hiding from the police, and his false identity is in danger of being revealed.

genetically perfect individual, Jerome Eugene ("good genes"), who has no use for perfection. Jerome is disabled after a suicide attempt that was never registered, so Vincent pays him "rental" on his identity and moves in with him. The transformation involves surgery to add height to Vincent's legs, but otherwise the two young men are fairly similar. Vincent, now "Jerome," acquires a dream job at the Gattaca complex, where future space programs are planned and astronauts trained, by submitting urine and blood samples from Eugene. Every morning Eugene prepares samples of more blood, urine, hair and skin cells, and so forth for Vincent to use for the ongoing tests so that no trace will reveal the identity of the impostor. In the process, Vincent and Eugene become close friends.

Everything is working smoothly, and Vincent/Jerome is valued at work for his high intelligence, his physical stamina, and his flawless genetic code. He meets a young female coworker, Irene, who also longs for the stars but has a heart disease probability that restricts her future as an astronaut. Vincent tries to make her realize that such preset probabilities are nothing but that, probabilities. They are not set in stone. He himself is overdue for his heart attack. He has apparently overcome all social obstacles handed to him by his low birth, but an unforeseen event happens: A Gattaca executive hostile to the current space program is found murdered. Although there is no evidence linking him to the murder, one of Vincent's eyelashes is found near the scene of the crime. The police run a genetic analysis on it and come up with Vincent's original identity; but since he as "Jerome" has a different genetic profile, nobody makes the connection. Even so, he fears he will be found out on the threshold of his dream: He has been slated for the next launch to Titan. As the police detectives move closer to his personal life and his girlfriend herself is beginning to suspect that "Jerome" is not what he seems to be, his audacious attempt at breaking out of the social hierarchy seems to be failing and his true identity seems about to be revealed.

Will Vincent go to prison for the murder, or will he go to Titan after all? Will his heart hold out? Will Irene guess his identity? What happens to Eugene? Who killed the executive? And where is Vincent's brother? The ending of this interesting film offers many surprises.

Study Questions

1. What elements in the *Gattaca* plot do you think might become a reality in the future? Should we welcome them or fight them? Is there a third alternative? Explain your position.

2. The film addresses first and foremost the discrimination against Vincent and others who are being excluded from having a happy, productive life because of their genes. But there is also an underlying angle: a criticism of the *predictable* future society in which there are no surprises because they have been bred out of the population. What is your opinion? Does society need genetic "surprises," unforeseeable genius and generosity as one side of the coin and unpredictable criminal pathology as the other? Or are we better off with the vast majority of the population falling into a predictable norm?

3. Do the characters' names add something to the story? Explain.

4. When the film came out, very few people caught on to the significance of the title. Now that the Human Genome Project has been completed, it may not seem so mysterious to us. GATC are the initials of materials in the DNA code: guanine, adenine, thymine, and cytosine. What do you think the moviemakers wanted to say by calling the film, and Vincent's workplace, *Gattaca*?

5. The *Gattaca* DVD has outtakes (missing scenes), some of which add interesting elements to the story. The scene with Vincent's parents in the lab, discussing the future characteristics of Anton, is longer and gives us an understanding of their switch from skepticism to enthusiasm when they hear that they can determine the boy's height and even a musical talent! But the addition of the talent turns out to be too expensive, so they settle for having a strong, smart, healthy, tall kid. This is the only time we hear that acquiring good genes is also a matter of money. In a future where genetic engineering is the order of the day, do you think the scenario of *Gattaca* is realistic? Does the outtake make a difference to the story? Should it have been left in?

Narrative

Mississippi Burning

CHRIS GEROLMO (SCREENWRITER)

ALAN PARKER (DIRECTOR)

Film, 1988. Summary.

On June 21, 1964, three young civil rights activists were murdered in Philadelphia, Mississippi, an event that has haunted and divided the community to this day. Michael Schwerner, James Chaney, and Andrew Goodman—one black and two white men—had come to the small Mississippi community to register black voters. They were reported as missing and later were found murdered. The Ku Klux Klan was implicated. Some Klan members were brought to trial and found guilty, and others were acquitted. This film is a fictionalized story based on the actual events, and at the end of the summary you can read about an additional feature added to the story in 2005.

It is the early 1960s, in Jessup County, Mississippi, a time of racial segregation—made clear in the opening shot: one modern water cooler for whites and another, older model for blacks. Into this community come three young activists to ensure that black Americans will be able to exercise their right to vote, but in the dead of night their car is chased and overtaken by men in three vehicles, one of them a police car. They force the young men out of the car and shoot them. When the news spreads in the following days that the young men are missing, riots break out, and two FBI agents arrive in town: Rupert Anderson, himself a former sheriff from a small town in Mississippi, and Allan Ward, a go-by-the-book FBI man. Right away we sense that the two men are very different, with clashing personalities and outlooks. When paying a visit to the office of Sheriff Stuckey, Anderson treats the hostile officers like good ol' boys up to a point—and then we realize that he can get very confrontational. Ward, on the other hand, goes by Bureau regulations. The sheriff's story is that the three young men were arrested for speeding, released, and drove off.

The difference between Ward and Anderson is accentuated when they try to have lunch in the local restaurant: The hostess tells them there are no tables available, but

Ward sees empty seats in the section for "Coloreds only." He heads straight for a seat next to a young black man and starts questioning him about what he may have heard regarding the activists. The young man is frightened and doesn't respond to Ward. Everyone is shocked, blacks and whites alike; and Anderson appears to be embarrassed that Ward is not only causing a scene but also approaching the issue in the wrong way. Later we see the indirect consequences of Ward's approach: The young black man is thrown from a car onto Main Street, beaten up as a warning.

In the meantime, we learn more about the antagonism between Anderson and Ward. Anderson says he believes the activists are being used politically, by cynical people, but for Ward it is a matter of doing what you believe in and sometimes risking death to do the right thing. When Ward speculates about where all this hatred comes from, Anderson tells him a story: When he was a kid in the South, his father was a poor man, but their black neighbor Monroe was a little better off because he got himself a mule. Shortly thereafter, somebody poisoned the mule, and Anderson's father later admitted to being the poisoner. For Anderson the culprit is poverty, not race. He wants to handle the situation his way, but Ward wants a whole investigative FBI team to become involved, and so they take over the movie theater for their operations. Anderson, though, follows his own nose, and goes to the barber shop, where he finds the sheriff and the mayor. Still acting like a small-town southern sheriff, he engages the mayor in a conversation about the situation. The mayor tells him the blacks in the community ("the nigras") were happy until the civil rights activists showed up. He believes that there are two cultures in the South, a black culture and a white culture, and that any effort of the federal government to effect change is an intrusion.

Next, Anderson heads to the beauty salon, to get the women's point of view. The salon is managed by Deputy Pell's wife, Mary. She is uneasy about the situation, and we sense that she knows a good deal more than she's saying, about the Klan as well as the disappearances.

The missing activists' car is found in the river on the Choctaw Indian Reservation, but there are no bodies. However, it now seems certain that the boys are dead, so Ward arranges for a full-scale dredging operation, to no avail. But the Klan responds with burnings of churches and homes in the black community. Ward and Anderson know that Sheriff Stuckey has an alibi, but they find Deputy Pell's alibi questionable, so they pay him a visit. While Ward confronts Pell with the allegation that he holds a high position in the Klan, Anderson seeks out Mary in the kitchen; and on several subsequent occasions, he makes a point of chatting her up, bringing her flowers, and just exchanging small talk, gaining her trust. And Mary is very different from her husband—we see her having a genuinely good time talking with a local black woman and her baby, people her husband has nothing but scorn for.

In the meantime, the national news media have descended on Jessup County, interviewing white locals. Most of the people interviewed think the whole thing is the fault of the civil rights activists, that Martin Luther King is a communist, and that the three young activists were asking for whatever they got. Some are convinced it's a hoax—a publicity stunt. A Klansmember, Clayton Townley, makes no bones about it: A white supremacist, he doesn't accept Jews, Catholics, or communists, and he wants "to protect Anglo-Saxon democracy and the American way." At the same time a KKK leader rallies the white community against racially mixed relationships, the "mongrelization" of America. Things are escalating, and Anderson now shows his true colors: As much as he comes across as a "redneck," his loyalties are to the FBI, and he single-handedly confronts Pell and his henchman Frank when they claim that no blacks will be allowed to vote. Moreover, he is discovering a new ally in Mary, who lets him know about an upcoming Klan meeting.

Ward and Anderson stake out the "meeting," which turns out to be a manhunt: A young black man is released from prison, then hunted down by the sheriff's men and driven away. The two FBI agents try to follow but lose sight of the sheriff's cars; later that night, they find the young man lying in the woods, alive but castrated. They failed to stop the sheriff's men, but now they suspect that the civil rights activists met their end the same way: released and then hunted down by the Klan.

When the farm belonging to the family of the young man who was Ward's first unwitting contact is torched, things come to a breaking point. The young man, Eric, rescues his mother and siblings, then witnesses their cows burn to death. His father is captured when he tries to defend his home and then lynched. Eric manages to release the rope before his father chokes to death, and the next day Ward and Anderson help them leave the county for Detroit, where they have family.

This development disturbs Mary immensely, and during a quiet moment with Anderson while Pell is at one of his "meetings," she tells him how things are: Hatred, she says, isn't something you're born with—it is taught, every day, by your surroundings. And she wants it to stop—so she tells Anderson what she knows: Her husband shot the civil rights activists, and she knows where they are buried.

Now that the bodies are retrieved, Anderson and Ward have a heated argument about methods—Anderson's questioning of Mary has resulted in Pell's beating her to within an inch of her life. In a surprising change of attitude, Ward decides to back Anderson: They have the authority, and they'll do it his way. They need someone to talk—and they find somebody who will talk to protect himself. It is the mayor. In a stunning reversal of events, the mayor is kidnapped, by a hooded man. Gagged and bound, the mayor is offered a choice by his captor, who turns out to be a black man—an FBI agent with special talents: Either he talks, or he will be castrated, the same way KKK members have castrated black men. And the mayor talks.

Now Ward and Anderson know who was involved, but since the mayor's story was extracted under duress, they can't use it in court. Instead, they manipulate Pell and his men, making them think each one has been talking to the FBI, and one of them gives up the others. A series of arrests and trials follow, but we also have a feeling that some of the culprits are never going to be held accountable.

Anderson pays a visit to Mary, whose house has been ransacked, and apologizes for having essentially ruined her life. But she explains that she'll stay on, because there are enough people in town who see things her way. Finally, at the burned-out church, black and white citizens gather together for a service.

The film was met with mixed reviews: Some reviewers found that it was a fine, well-crafted, moving story, but others thought it was a manipulative misrepresentation: Blacks were reduced to one-dimensional victims; Klan members were portrayed as degenerates; FBI Director J. Edgar Hoover was portrayed as a civil rights supporter, whereas he, in fact, kept extensive files on Dr. Martin Luther King, Jr.; and FBI agents were depicted as people with questionable ethics. Yet other movie critics pointed out that films are not supposed to be historically accurate social documentaries, but well-told narratives with their own message and their own reality. This film is, of course, not a documentary—it is fictionalized, with invented characters.

But history wrote another chapter to the story: In January 2005, a 79-year-old man was arrested after a county grand jury indictment for being the mastermind behind the deaths of Schwerner, Chaney, and Goodman: Edgar Ray Killen, an alleged Ku Klux Klan leader and a Baptist preacher. Killen was tried on federal charges in 1967 but released after one juror refused to convict him (others were convicted, and some were acquitted); he is a known separatist and has been quoted as saying that God didn't create blacks and whites equal. A jury found Killen guilty on three counts of manslaughter in June 2005, and the judge sentenced him to sixty years in prison.

Study Questions

1. Do you agree with Anderson's approach? with Ward's? or perhaps with another view-point expressed in the film? Explain.

2. Is this film an example of forward-looking or backward-looking justice? Explain.

3. Is this film a fair representation of the FBI? of the civil rights movement? of the locals in the small Mississippi county? Some reviewers called the film itself unethical. Can you imagine why?

4. What is the message of this film? Explain. Could there be several messages? Discuss.

5. Go back to the Reading by Dr. Martin Luther King, Jr., in this chapter, and the Narrative in Chapter 3, *Do the Right Thing,* and assess the current situation in the area of the United States that you know best: What are race relations like today, as far as you can discern? Is there general goodwill and understanding, are there underlying animosities and hidden racism, or is there an open racial conflict? What would you consider progress in race relations in this country?

Narrative

Hotel Rwanda

TERRY GEORGE (DIRECTOR)
TERRY GEORGE AND KEIR PEARSON (SCREENWRITERS)
PAUL RUSESABAGINA (CONSULTANT)

Film, 2004. Summary.

The moral values of this film could be classified under several headings. We could place it in Chapter 6 as an example of doing the right thing as a matter of principle despite inclinations to look after oneself first. And we could place it in Chapter 10 as a

The film *Hotel Rwanda* (Kigali Releasing Limited, 2004) features Paul Rusesabagina (Don Cheadle) as the manager of a luxury hotel when the conflict between the Tutsis and the Hutus erupt. Being a family man without any political ties, proud of doing a good job of taking care of his hotel guests' needs through persuasion and bribes, Paul all of a sudden comes face to face with having to make choices, for his wife Tatiana (Sophie Okonedo) and their two children as well as several hundred local people caught up in the conflict. Because of Rusesabagina's courage and selfless actions, 1,268 refugees' lives are saved.

story of virtue—of the virtues of courage and compassion. But here we focus on its relevance as an example of how the past haunts the present and calls for backward-looking measures of fairness and equality, and how some people in some contexts count less as "persons" than others. *Hotel Rwanda* is based on the true story of the rescue of 1,268 refugees during the conflict in Rwanda between the Hutus and the Tutsis. Hotel official Paul Rusesabagina managed, through his resourceful thinking and phys-ical as well as moral courage, to save not hotel guests but neighbors, orphans, and other refugees from being massacred by the military and militia run by the Hutus. Himself a Hutu, he put partisanship aside to save innocent Tutsi civilians targeted by the majority regime as "traitors." Paul Rusesabagina himself was a consultant on the film, and I am thus not giving anything away when I tell you that he survives the ordeal. I will, however, try not to give away the entire plot or the ending of the film—who lives, and who dies.

In the beginning of the film, we get to know Paul as a smooth hotel official. He knows whom to tip, whom to bribe, and what to bribe them with to ensure that Hotel Milles Collines, a four-star Sabina hotel run by a Belgian corporation, is as good as it can be.

He sees himself as a Westerner, on a par with any Western tourist visiting the hotel in the city of Kigali, and his unwavering loyalty is to the hotel. He shakes hands with foreign officials, offers the local General Bizimungo fine Cuban cigars and Scotch whisky, and lives in a nice house in a nice neighborhood with his middle-class family. He explains to his friend and coworker Dube that it's all about *style*.

We are introduced to the cast of characters who will, within weeks, either become victims or be victimized: General Bizimungo, a five-star general, thinks of nothing but the good life, his whisky, and his comfort. George Rutaganda is a seemingly friendly supplier of goods for the hotel but is also involved with the militia and anti-Tutsi activities; on one of Paul's visits to George's warehouse, he sees thousands of machetes spilling out of a box—ten cents a piece from China, George explains proudly. Later in the film we see the machetes put to use against Tutsi civilians, men, women, and children. Paul, his wife Tatiana, a Tutsi, and their three children are visited by Tatiana's brother Thomas and his wife, Fedens, and their two little girls (a Tutsi family), and during their visit anti-Tutsi riots start in town. A few days later Thomas tells Paul that a Hutu friend of his has revealed that a plot is under way to kill all Tutsis, and the code word is "The Tall Trees." He and Fedens urge Paul to send Tatiana and the kids with them to safety, but Paul is incredulous: Nothing like that will happen—the UN will protect them. And indeed the UN has now made the hotel their headquarters.

American and British journalists hang out with Rwandan journalists at the hotel bar and hit on the local women. The journalists ask for an explanation of the Hutu-Tutsi conflict, and we hear the (supposedly true) story: The Belgians (Rwanda used to be part of the Belgian Congo) had instigated the entire rift by grooming the most light-skinned, small-nosed Africans to be a new upper class, called Tutsis, who would collaborate with the Belgian colonial forces; the Hutus were simply the rest of the population—the darker, rejected Africans. And now the Hutus are set on revenge against a population that no longer has any special protected status.

Paul's hopes of a peaceful solution to the animosities are devastated when Rwanda's president is murdered after having signed a peace treaty. Riots are starting in the streets, and Paul's Tutsi neighbors come to him for protection, so with great difficulty he bribes the general to let him take everyone to the hotel, where he installs them in vacant rooms. At this time the "Tall Trees" message goes out over the local radio station, and Paul realizes his brother-in-law was telling the truth—but a Red Cross volunteer who shows up with a van full of orphaned children informs him that the part of town where Thomas and Fedens live is now cut off from the rest. Paul begs her to go back and look for the family.

Having the general's protection doesn't shield Paul and his refugees from militia threats or even from threats from other Hutu military captains, and Paul has to be on the alert with new ideas for bribes, lies, and favors to distract the Hutu commanders. To make matters worse, Paul has acquired a personal enemy in one of the Hutu hotel workers, Gregoire, who has been chastised by both Paul and the general. When the Belgian hotel manager leaves, Paul takes over and persuades the hotel staff to go about their work as usual.

When Western journalists manage to get footage of a massacre of Tutsi civilians just down the street from the hotel, and it is broadcast internationally, Paul believes that now the international community will come to their aid—but journalist Jack Daglish lays out reality for him: People may be horrified when they watch the news, but then they'll go back to their dinner and forget about it. It just isn't something the world cares about. And in harsh language, the UN Colonel Oliver corroborates what Daglish has said: Paul and his refugees are "just" black Africans; the American television audiences and the politicians aren't going to insist that help is needed. As a result of the broadcast, action is indeed taken—but it is an evacuation of all *whites/Europeans* from the hotel, including the journalists. And Paul, his illusions stripped away, tells Tatiana, "I'm a fool. They told me I was one of them, and I . . . wine, chocolate, cigars . . . I swallowed it! And they handed me their shit—I have no history—I have no memory. . . . " And Tatiana answers, "You are no fool—I know who you are."

The next day the disaster unfolds: When rival military factions threaten to kill all the refugees as "cockroaches," Paul calls the Belgian owners of the hotel. He has been in touch with them before, and always as the manager of their interests and for the good of the hotel. Now the illusions are gone; he frankly says that the eight hundred people at the hotel are not guests but refugees, and he needs help. The Belgian director rises to the occasion and starts calling European government officials. Meanwhile, Paul urges the refugees to make their own calls to anyone of influence they might know in other coun-tries. A horrible realization is in store for Paul after seeing George, the supplier, who frankly claims that an all-out Tutsi genocide is well under way. On the way back (along a road suggested by George), Paul sees the results of a massacre: Thousands of Tutsis are slaughtered. Seeing that a horrible end may come soon for his family, Paul tells Tatiana that as a last resort, if he is no longer there, she and the children must jump off the roof to their deaths rather than be killed by the machetes.

But the Belgian director's effort and the phone calls have paid off: Travel visas come through to select families, including Paul's own, and they prepare to leave, even without knowing the fate of Tatiana's family. As the trucks with the lucky ones are taking off, Paul sees those who have been left behind, and realizes he can't leave them to face certain death, so he jumps off the truck that is taking his family to safety.

Ironically, as he goes back to try to help the refugees left at the hotel, the convoy with fleeing refugees is ambushed by the militia, betrayed by the hotel worker Gregoire, and only through the intervention of the general are the refugees and the UN convoy brought back to the hotel—to square one and a squalid siege with no fresh water and no supplies. Paul attempts one last valiant bribe of the general with a secret stash of Scotch from an-other hotel, but by then the general has no more interest in helping the refugees; how-ever, he is willing to take Paul along, for old times' sake. Paul makes him understand that he is now considered a war criminal, responsible for every atrocity the militia and the other military factions have committed, and that Paul will be able to vouch for him when the time of reckoning comes; the general finally realizes that to save his own hide he must help save the refugees. So off they go to the hotel, just in time to stop the militia from massacring the refugees. Paul is looking for his wife and kids—they are nowhere to be found. Have they jumped from the roof as he told them to, as a last desperate move? The final sequences of the film answer some questions but not all, and I choose not to give the ending away. Will Tatiana and the children be found alive and well? You already know that Paul made it out, and you know that 1,268 refugees were saved because of him—but how it happens I'll let you watch for yourself, and you will then know more about the fate of Tatiana and the children, and about Thomas, Fedens, and their two little girls.

Study Questions

1. How does this film illustrate the concepts of "forward-looking" and "backward-looking" justice?

2. How is the problem of *personhood* discussed in this film?

3. What does Paul mean by saying "I have no history—I have no memory?" Explain. You may want to consult the final section of Chapter 13, "The Ethics of Self-Improvement: Narrative Identity" for a deeper analysis of this question.

4. As I am writing this summary, a human disaster—some use the term *genocide*—is occurring in another African province, Darfur, very similar to the Rwanda tragedy. Promises of treaties are made, and the international community is reluctant to step in, fearing that similar tribal conflicts will spread to other African nations. My first question to you here is, Do you stay informed about such overseas events? If yes, do you see similarities and differences between the Rwanda and Darfur events? Should the international community care about such events? If no, why not? If yes, what should be done?

Narrative

Minority Report

SCOTT FRANK (SCREENWRITER)
STEVEN SPIELBERG (DIRECTOR)

Film, 2002. Based on short story by Philip K. Dick. Summary.

It is the year 2054 in Washington, D.C. For six years, local crime has been virtually abolished, thanks to the new Department of Pre-Crime: Crimes, especially murder, can now be predicted with, presumably, 100 percent accuracy, thanks to three individuals—the precogs, young people with precognition. They "see," in their mind's eye, future crimes; thanks to an elaborate brain-monitoring system, the police officers working for Pre-Crime can share the vision, arrest the "culprit" before the crime is done, and neutralize him or her permanently in a state of suspension. It is a society of total surveillance; eye scanners identify everyone in their everyday activities.

    John Anderton, the chief of detectives who is the primary reader of the jumble of precog visions, is himself the victim of a crime, committed just months before the Department of Pre-Crime was established: His young son was abducted from a public pool while he himself was playing a game with his boy, holding his breath under water. The whereabouts of the abductor are unknown, as is the fate of his son. Because of the stresses following the abduction, John and his wife divorced, and John is a frequent buyer of illegal drugs to soothe his own guilt and nightmares.

The elderly director of the Pre-Crime Department, Lamar Burgess, appears to view John as something of a son, or protégé, and cautions him that much is riding on the Pre-Crime project: If approved by voters nationally in the near future, the project will go national. Crime will then be a thing of the past. A federal agent shows up at the department, ostensibly to take a tour, but soon he reveals that he is looking for flaws in the system, to test it before it goes national. He and John have a brief conversation in which John proudly explains the principle of Pre-Crime: Thanks to the precogs, crimes can now be prevented before they happen, and the guilty will be isolated. The agent asks how they can be held responsible, since they haven't yet done anything. For John, these pre-criminals are guilty because the future is certain—for the federal agent they are not, precisely because they are prevented from committing the crime.

When the agent forces his way into the "temple" where the three precogs lie suspended in a sensory deprivation tank, the precog Agatha grabs John, in an unprecedented move—because nobody but the caretaker is supposed to talk to the precogs, for fear of contamination. She asks him, "Do you see?" and he sees her vision of a woman being drowned.

John doesn't know it yet, but this shared vision is about to become his undoing. Shortly afterward there is another murder prediction by the precogs: John is himself named as a future murderer, the killer of a man he's never heard of, Leo Crow. Knowing that protests of innocence are futile, John takes off, running away from the SWAT team who are already on to him. After shaking them off, he seeks out the recluse elderly inventor of the precog program, Iris Hineman, to find out the truth: Can the precogs be wrong? And Iris tells him about the occasional discrepancy—the "minority report" phenomenon: When the vision of one precog differs from the rest, the report is destroyed—it exists only inside the precog's memory.

To avoid the ubiquitous eye scanners, John now has his eyes removed, and has another person's eyes transplanted—but he keeps his own eyes in a bag. Narrowly avoiding the Pre-Crime team, he makes his way back to the lab, where he succeeds in abducting Agatha: It was her vision that showed him the man he supposedly is about to kill, and he needs her to guide him to the place. But first they stop at a virtual reality facility, where John has a recording made of Agatha's vision, with her cooperation—she wants him to see what she sees, because it is important to her: a woman being drowned by a man in black. The vision is cut short because the Pre-Crime team is on to John and Agatha, but through her ability to see the near future they make it to a tenement building where John recognizes elements from her vision, including the name and picture of the man he is about to kill, on the building roster: Leo Crow. They enter his apartment, which is empty—except for a pile of photos piled up on the unmade bed. And among the photos John discovers a picture of his little boy, in the company of the man from the apartment and the vision. Now John knows that this is not a minority report—the vision is true, and he really is going to kill this man for abducting his son. As Crow steps into the room, the vision comes to life: John threatens him with his gun, while Agatha is frozen in dread, but all the while she whispers to him that *he has a choice*—the future isn't predetermined, *because he already knows it and can choose to do otherwise*. And as his watch moves toward zero, the time when the crime will be committed, we expect him to shoot Crow; but zero arrives, and John still hasn't fired his shot—he truly has a choice. And he reads Crow his rights, formally arresting him. But now Crow speaks—he is horrified that John hasn't killed him, because that's what he was promised: that in return for being killed, his family would be taken care of. And John realizes that the whole thing was a set-up—the man is not responsible for his son's disappearance but is just somebody who got paid to put the pictures on the bed and then be killed. But who set the whole thing up? Crow doesn't know—and as John struggles to understand, Crow grabs his gun and pulls the trigger, making the vision come true as he falls out the broken window to his death.

Desperate, John flees with Agatha to his former home by the sea, where his ex-wife, Lara, is now living. While they're fleeing, the federal agent who was looking for a flaw in the Pre-Crime system is now at Crow's crime scene—and realizes that it was a set-up. Puzzled, he goes to John's boss and mentor, Lamar Burgess, and shares his suspicion that someone is manipulating the system. Burgess readily agrees with him—and shoots him point-blank. As the agent dies, Burgess points out that since one of the precogs is missing, there is no precog record of this murder—it will be pinned on John too.

At her seaside home, Lara sees John and Agatha coming and calls Burgess so John can get the help he needs. But instead the Pre-Crime team arrives, and this time he is arrested and placed under mind control just like the many pre-criminals he himself has placed under arrest. However, before the team arrives, Agatha lets John and Lara share the alternate reality of the life their son would have lived; and he and Agatha share the story of the drowned woman with Lara—because John has realized that Agatha is the woman's daughter, and someone manipulated the precog system so they could get away with murder and keep Agatha a precog.

John is now taken away to spend the rest of his life in a tank, removed from the rest of the human race—in a state of semiconsciousness, for all intents and purposes dead to the world. That's what happens to the pre-criminals. Lara, in her grief, goes to find comfort with Burgess—but when he, with a slip of the tongue, reveals that he knows the story about Agatha's mother, Lara realizes the truth: that it is Burgess who is responsible for John's downfall. But why? Because John understood that the system had been manipulated to cover the murder of Agatha's mother—and the person responsible for that murder was Burgess himself.

And now John's future is in the hands of Lara. What will she do? Is there a life for John after the tank? What will happen to Burgess? And what about the Pre-Crime program? Suffice it to say that John will confront Burgess with his newfound wisdom: that once you know the future, you have a choice. . . .

Study Questions

1. What if our society in the near future will be able to predict criminal behavior with near certainty? What should be done to the would-be criminals? Can we justify punishing people for something they haven't done yet?

2. Identify the Pre-Crime approach to justice in this film as being either forward-looking or backward-looking. Does it make any difference? Explain.

3. In Chapter 4 you read about the concept of *free will*. Apply that concept to *Minority Report:* Does John Anderton have freedom of the will, the ability to make free choices despite the influences of his heredity or his environment? Does anybody? What does it matter for the criminal justice system whether or not we have the capacity to choose our actions freely? Explain.

Chapter Eight

Virtue Ethics from Tribal Philosophy to Socrates and Plato

*T*hroughout most of Western civilization and most of the history of ethics, scholars have tried to answer the question, What should I do? Part 2 of this book explored that quest. Theories that consider what proper human conduct is are often referred to as *ethics of conduct*.

There is a more ancient approach to ethics, and in the past few decades this older approach has experienced a revival. This form of ethics asks the fundamental question, How should I be? It focuses on the development of certain personal qualities, of a certain behavior pattern—in other words, on the development of what we call *character*. Because its foundation is in ancient Greek theories involving the question of how to be a virtuous person, this approach usually is referred to as *virtue ethics*. However, virtue ethics as a phenomenon is far older than the Greek tradition and is encountered in many other cultures. On pages 386–389, you'll see some examples of non-Western virtue ethics.

What Is Virtue? What Is Character?

The concept of virtue (Greek: *aretē*) is complex. For one thing, it carries certain associations, which it has acquired over the centuries; thus, in English, we may think of virtue as a basically positive concept—a virtuous person is someone you can trust. We also may experience, however, a certain negative reaction to it; sometimes, a virtuous person is thought of as being rather dull and perhaps even sanctimonious. (Being called a "Goody Two-Shoes" is not a compliment.) In everyday language, "virtue" often refers to sexual abstinence, and that can, of course, be a positive concept as well as a negative one, depending on one's viewpoint. A book titled *Raising Maidens of Virtue* was published in 2004, advocating raising teenage girls according to biblical principles of purity, modesty, cleanliness, and other traditional virtues.

However, the ancient Greek concept of *aretē* differs considerably from what we today associate with "virtue." For one thing, it has its origin in the name of the Greek god Ares, the god of war, and must originally have meant having warrior-like qualities. (Here we can add that the term *virtue* itself comes from Latin, and its origin is *vir,* or "male"!) But regardless of origins in deep antiquity, the word *aretē* would have had no negative connotations for a Greek-speaking person at the time of Socrates and Plato, because it signifies a different kind of person altogether: not a person of untainted thoughts and behavior, but a person who does what he or she does best

385

and does it excellently, on a regular basis. We still have a trace of the ancient meaning of *aretē* in the word *virtuosity*. Originally, a virtuous person was a *virtuoso* at everything he or she did, because of proper choices and good habits but, above all, because such a person had succeeded in developing a good character.

Is Character Innate?

Today we often take a deterministic view of the concept of character. It is something we are born with, something we can't help. If we try to go against our character, it will surface in the end. That viewpoint may or may not be correct, but in any event it is shaped by modern schools of thought in philosophy and psychology. Not everyone shares that view; it often is pointed out that we may be born with a certain character but our character can be molded to a certain extent when we are young, and it certainly can be *tested* throughout our lives. This point of view comes closer to the prevailing attitude toward virtue among Greek philosophers: Character is indeed something we are born with, but it is also something that can and must be shaped. We are not the victims of our character, and if we let ourselves be victimized by our own unruly temperaments, then we are to blame.

Non-Western Virtue Ethics: Africa and Indigenous America

As I mentioned in Chapter 1, Socrates gets credit for introducing the topic of ethics as a philosophical discipline in the Western intellectual tradition, meaning that he engaged in, and encouraged his students to engage in, theoretical discussions about values, good character, and good behavior. But, of course, that doesn't mean that Socrates invented morals, values, or even ethics. It is inconceivable that a culture can exist, and persist, without having some system of values, some moral rules identifying good and bad social behavior, so as far back as we can trace *Homo sapiens* cultures—according to current scientific views some 200,000 years or more—there must have been moral codes. (Even earlier forms of hominids may well have had basic rules of coexistence, such as "Be generous and don't hoard food," "Show respect toward the Old Leaders," and "Be loyal to your tribe.") And it is also almost certain that these ancient groups (as you read in Chapter 2) had stories—myths and legends—that would explain how everything came into being and why humans ought to behave in this way and not in that way. So if we identify ethics as explaining or questioning the moral rules (see Chapter 1), then ethics, too, has been part of the human social fabric for a very long time indeed. Some of those stories are part of the human memory banks to this day in the form of folklore, as well as ancient surviving religions or the surviving written works of dead religions. What is interesting in this context is that in some cultures (such as China; see Chapter 11), the moral value systems have emphasized *conduct*—doing the right thing—but the overwhelming number of ancient stories that we have, as well as examples of tribal cultures around the world, seem to have favored the *virtue ethics* approach: focusing on developing a good character.

Even if the main topic of this chapter is the philosophy of Plato and his teacher Socrates, we'll take a brief look at the phenomenon of *tribal virtue ethics* from two non-Western traditions: African and indigenous American tribal cultures.

African Virtue Theory

For the Akan people in West Africa (in the Ghana region), morality consists of having a good character. Although one probably cannot classify the Akan people of today as "tribal" in the classic sense, their cultural origin is that of a tribal community where religion, moral values, and folklore all help determine the common outlook on life. In his book *An Essay on African Philosophical Thought: The Akan Conceptual Scheme,* the scholar Kwame Gyekye, himself an Akan, emphasizes that Akan ethics is not perceived as something commanded by *Onyame* (God); the Akan people regard their ethics as having a humanistic origin. Gyekye says that insofar as religion is involved at all, the Akan people have a natural law approach to morality: If something makes sense morally, then that is its reason for being a moral law, not its connection to a supernatural being.

Gyekye describes the Akan ethics as focused on virtue and character; whenever a person commits an act of wrongdoing it is said not that "he/she did something wrong" but that "he/she is a bad person." How does one become a good person? As in every theory of virtue, that is a difficult question, because "character" tends to be something we are born with. However, the Akan ethics assumes, like the Aristotelian theory of the Golden Mean (see Chapter 9), that we can work toward acquiring a good character through good habits. And the best way to teach those good habits is through *storytelling*. Contrary to most traditional Western ethicists, the Akan thinkers have not forgotten that it is through stories that children get their first and perhaps their best exposure to the concepts of right and wrong. Those stories and proverbs habituate the children to moral virtues. Gyekye points out that people still have a choice of behavior and can be held accountable for that behavior because if they act in a morally wrong way, it means that they have not built up their own character the way they should have.

This forms a link between an ethics of conduct and an ethics of virtue, says Gyekye: It is because of what you do that you become a good person; you don't start out doing good things because of who you are. Originally, a human being is born morally neutral, according to Akan moral philosophies.

What kinds of virtues are favored by the Akans? Kindness, faithfulness, compassion, and hospitality are among the key virtues. Akan values are utilitarian in the sense that anything that promotes social well-being is a good thing. Even if God approves of virtue, the bottom line is that it is good for the people. The most important thing in Akan moral thought is the well-being of the community. The community thrives when the people cultivate social virtues. In *An Essay on African Philosophical Thought,* Gyekye says:

> Akan thought . . . sees humans as originally born into a human society (*onipa kurom*), and therefore as social beings from the outset. In this conception it would be impossible for people to live in isolation. For not only is the person not born to live a solitary life, but the individual's capacities are not sufficient to meet basic human requirements. For the person . . . is not a palm tree that he or she should be complete or self-sufficient.

The Akan view of storytelling as a path to moral understanding comes close to the premise of this book: that we, as socialized humans, can explore our ethical systems by listening to and making up stories. In every culture the first moral lessons seem to be taught through stories (see Chapter 2), and in the moral universe of the Akan people myths and legends guide the young toward becoming responsible members of the community. Similarly, you'll remember how the character of Tata Ndu (*The Poisonwood Bible,* Chapter 3) emphasized the importance of the community. This *communitarian* philosophy, with close ties to storytelling, can be found in the virtue ethics of ancient Greece as well.

Native American Values

The value system of North American Indian tribes has itself acquired a mythological status in America and indeed around the world. The values of the Native American have come to stand for *ecological virtue,* because it commonly is believed that these tribal people lived in harmony with nature, without abusing their own resources. One reason for this perceived harmony is the American Indian idea of what constitutes a *moral community;* for the traditional Native American, this community consists of the tribe, but also of their immediate nonhuman neighbors: the animals, and the spirits of the rocks, the trees, the winds, and the waters. In their compilation of Indian myths and legends, Richard Erdoes and Alfonso Ortiz include the White River Sioux account of the old days before Columbus when "we were even closer to the animals than we are now; many people could understand the animal languages; they could talk to a bird, gossip with a butterfly. Animals could change themselves into people, and people into animals."

The ecologist J. Baird Callicott says in his paper "Traditional American Indian and Western European Attitudes Toward Nature: An Overview" that although there is no such things as *the* American Indian belief system, there is still a predominant view shared by tribal Indians toward nature. According to Callicott:

> The Ojibwa, the Sioux, and if we may safely generalize, most American Indians, lived in a world which was peopled not only by human persons, but by persons and personalities associated with all natural phenomena. In one's practical dealings in such a world it is necessary to one's well-being and that of one's family to maintain good social relations not only with proximate human persons, one's immediate tribal neighbors, but also with the nonhuman persons abounding in the immediate environment. For example . . . among the Ojibwa "when bears were sought out in their dens in the spring they were addressed, asked to come out so that they could be killed, and an apology was offered to them."

It does appear that most Native American tribes had a quite different relationship with their environment than did the settlers from Europe or even from Asia. The hunter would evoke the spirit of the animal before the hunt, asking its permission to kill it and promising it some kind of sacrifice in return; the hunter would not kill in excess; the hunter would not let anything of his prey go to waste; the women of the tribe would utilize every bit of material from the kill; the women would supply a large percentage of food for the tribe by gathering tubers, berries, and so on; and because theirs was a nomadic existence, the people would not stay in one place long enough to deplete its resources. There is evidence of a close spiritual relationship between the tribal people and their environment, of an understanding of the seasons, of animal movements, and of interrelationships between animal and human spirits—

an understanding that humans have only a small part to play in the general order of things and are by no means all-important. There is evidence of a reverence for the mother of all (the earth) in the rejection of plowing by nineteenth-century Indians on the grounds that you don't plow furrows in your mother's breast. A Navajo chant praises the beauty of this world, "beauty before me, beauty behind me," not just empty land ripe for development.

Those values may seem very attractive to a modern, Western, nature-loving person in a world where there is little appreciation of the environment as an autonomous whole and where the word *development* seems to indicate that before the housing area there was "nothing," or at least "nothing of value." However, it may be another matter for a modern person to adopt Native American values. Callicott himself stresses that the American Indian attitude toward nature is not *conservationist* in the true sense, because it is not scientific but an integrated part of a moral and social order. We can't go to the American Indians and copy their way of life, because it involves social concerns that aren't ours anymore (such as taboos and hunting practices), but we can see it as an ideal, available as an option. So what is this option? In Callicott's words:

> The American Indian, on the whole, viewed the natural world as enspirited. Natural beings therefore felt, perceived, deliberated, and responded voluntarily as persons. Persons are members of a social order (i.e., part of the operational concept of a person is the capacity for social interaction). Social interaction is limited by (culturally variable) behavioral restraints, rules of conduct, which we call, in sum, good manners, morals, and ethics.

Does that mean that all American Indians have had a sense of a social order in their natural neighborhood? We can't assume that. It now seems clear that the reason the Anasazi tribe of Arizona and New Mexico abandoned their cliff cities after several hundred years was partly because of a drought but also because they had exhausted the environment: There was no more wood, no more topsoil, and so they had to move. It also is a fact that although the Plains Indians did not hunt more animals than they could process (and the animal population did not suffer as a consequence), part of their success was due to the fact that the hunters were not very numerous. Had they been *able* to process large numbers of prey, we might have seen a decline in the animal population back then. It is now speculated that the woolly mammoth disappeared from the face of the earth in part because of very well-organized human hunting in North America as well as in Eurasia. Humans, regardless of their tribe, have the potential for great care and great greed; we should be careful not to label whole populations "saints" and others "sinners." But if we look to the Native American tribes today, in the southwestern United States and elsewhere, we do find an attitude toward life and the role of humans in nature that indeed is based on a system of values that looks to the *balance* of things: Humans can be physically and mentally fit only if they are in harmony with their surroundings, and nature has to be in similar harmony for humans to stay healthy. The idea of internal and external harmony, which at one time seemed to be disappearing with the decline of Native American culture, is on the rise again, along with an interest and pride in cultural traditions. In Chapter 13 we return to the idea of respect for nature as a virtue and take a look at the ethics involved in the debate about global warming.

Virtue Ethics in the West

What happened to virtue ethics in ancient times in the West, and why has it been revived by scholars of ethics recently? By and large, what happened was Christianity—with its emphasis on following God's rules and conducting oneself according to the will of God. The ancient world had taught for many centuries that virtue is a matter of shaping one's character, the implication being that once one has succeeded, one can justifiably be proud of what one has become—one can take a legitimate pride in being a self-made virtuous person. (We shall see how that is an important part of Aristotle's virtue theory in the next chapter.) But in Christian thinking, one can accomplish nothing without the help and grace of God—meaning that one just can't take credit for having become a good person, for the credit or glory goes exclusively to God, *Soli Deo Gloria*. A chasm appeared between the teachings of the classical tradition and the moral and philosophical viewpoints of the rising religion. Disagreements exceeded verbal argumentation and turned violent for the first time in Christian history (but unfortunately not for the last time). See Box 8.1 for some examples of that violence. One result, nonviolent but with important symbolic consequences, was the closure of both Plato's and Aristotle's schools in Athens by the Roman emperor Justinian in 529 C.E., after those schools had been in existence for over eight hundred years. (In comparison, the oldest European university was founded in Bologna, Italy, in 1088. The University of Paris opened in 1160, and Oxford University in 1190. Harvard University was founded in 1636, and Columbia University in 1754.) Later in this chapter and in the next chapter, we return to the significance of the closing of Plato's and Aristotle's old schools.

To *do the right thing* became the main imperative of Christian ethics; however, the concepts of virtue and vice became main elements. Within the Christian tradition and within every aspect of our Western outlook on life that has been shaped by this tradition, the idea of virtue is central, but scholars of ethics point out that it is not so much the question of *shaping your own character* that is important in this tradition as it is recognizing the *frailty of human character in general* and believing that with the help of God one may be able to choose the right thing to do.

From the time of the Renaissance to well into the twentieth century, questions of ethics were less a matter of doing the right thing to please God and more a matter of doing the right thing because it led to general happiness—because it was prudent or because it was logical. However, present-day scholars interested in virtue ethics have put forth the following argument: You may choose to do the "right thing" to please God or to escape unpleasant consequences or to make some majority happy or to satisfy your inner need for logic—but you may still be a less than admirable person. You may give to charity, pay your taxes on time, remember your nieces' and nephews' birthdays, hold the door for physically challenged people, and still be a morose and mean person. As we saw in the chapter on psychological egoism, you may be doing all the "correct" things just to get a passport to heaven or to be praised by others or to make sure they owe you a favor. So "doing the right thing" doesn't guarantee that you are a good person with a good *character*. However, if you strive to develop a good character—to be courageous or protective or tolerant or compassionate—then, on the basis of this character trait, you will *automatically* make the right decisions about

Box 8.1   VICTIMS OF RELIGIOUS FANATICISM

Since 2001 we have heard much about fundamentalist Muslim terrorism and fanaticism, and devastating results of that fanaticism have been felt around the world, from 9/11 in the United States, to the bombings in Bali and elsewhere, to the beheadings of foreign civilians in Iraq and Pakistan. As most people are aware, that does not mean that all Muslims are violent fanatics. What most people don't know is that in the early days of Christianity, small groups of Christian fanatics set out to strike terror in the hearts of non-Christians, because those groups refused to accept the values of the traditional pagan Greco-Roman world. Two such examples of what could be called fundamentalist Christian terrorism took place in the Egyptian city of Alexandria. In the year 415 C.E. a mob of fanatical Christian monks, possibly inspired by the Bishop of Alexandria, attacked and murdered one of the first women philosophers on record, Hypatia, leader of the Neoplatonic Institute in Alexandria. As far as we know, Hypatia lectured on Plato, Aristotle, and Pythagoras, and thus the Christians associated her with paganism. As she was riding through town in her chariot during one of the many religious riots, the mob dragged her out of her cart, tore off her clothes, and flayed her alive with clamshells. Hypatia had done her research in the great library at Alexandria (or what was left of it), which was founded by one of Alexander the Great's generals, Ptolemy I, who became the founder of an Egyptian dynasty (fourth century B.C.E.). The library was expanded over the centuries and probably contained most of the works of Greek philosophy, literature, and science, either in the original or copied by hand. During the reign of Queen Cleopatra, one of Ptolemy's descendants (around 30 B.C.E.), a part of the library was burned down by the Roman army, possibly by mistake. When another section of the library went up in flames in 391 C.E. (along with a pagan temple), there was no doubt that the destruction was caused by Christian extremist fundamentalists. It is, of course, important to note that those small groups of fanatics were an exception. Most Christians in the Roman Empire were not extremist, nor did they advocate terror, any more than they do today. In 380 Emperor Theodosius had made Christianity the official religion of Rome; Emperor Constantine had converted already in 312 C.E., and at the Church Council in Nicea in 325 the Christian bishops had established what were to count as official Christian sacred writings of the Old and the New Testaments.

One last word about the library in Alexandria: Its ultimate destruction came at the hands of Islamic fundamentalist invaders in 646 C.E. Scholars estimate that science suffered a setback of perhaps a millennium from the loss of the library; humanity's loss in works of art— philosophy, literature, drama, and artifacts— cannot be measured. And there is a further lesson, that religious fanaticism is not the monopoly or invention of one religion, past or present.

what to do, what course of action to take. In other words, virtue ethics is considered to be more fundamental than ethics of conduct, yielding better results.

In today's discussions on ethics, opinions are divided as to the merits of virtue versus conduct; however, no virtue theory is complete without recognition of the importance of conduct. We can have a marvelous "character," but if it never translates into action or conduct, it is not of much use—and how do we develop a good character in the first place if not through *doing* something right? Also, one of the most conduct-oriented ethical theories, Kant's deontology, has the question of character embedded in it. For Kant, a good character in the form of a *good will,* a fundamental

Hypatia (370–415 C.E.), the leader of the Neoplatonic Institute in Alexandria and one of the first female philosophers that we know of, was driving through the streets of town in her chariot when she was intercepted, tortured, and killed by Christian extremists.

respect for other people, and respect for the nature of the moral law itself is essential to the moral decision process. Indeed, one-half of the book he wrote late in life, *The Metaphysics of Morals,* focuses on a doctrine of virtue (in Chapter 6 you read the section concerning *lying*), and what he used to call the good will is here renamed a *virtuous disposition.* The question of whether we should choose ethics of conduct or virtue ethics is a bifurcation fallacy or a false dilemma (see Chapter 1); we can certainly decide that there is room for both approaches.

In the rest of this chapter and in the next chapter, we look at the classical virtue theories of Plato and Aristotle. We then move on to some examples of modern virtue theory.

The Good Teacher: Socrates' Legacy, Plato's Works

The saying goes that a good teacher is one who makes herself or himself superfluous. In other words, a good teacher lets you become your own authority; she or he does not keep you at the psychological level of a student forever. As a matter of fact, great personalities who have had considerable influence on their followers often have failed in this respect. For a teacher it is hard to let go and consider the job done (whether one is a professor or a parent), and for a student it is often tempting to absorb the authority of the teacher, because life is hard enough as it is without having to make your own decisions about everything all the time. This is what the good teacher or parent prepares the student for, however—autonomy, not dependence.

The teacher-student relationship between Socrates and Plato would probably not have become so famous if Plato had remained merely a student, a shadow of the master. Indeed, we have Socrates' own words (at least through the pen of Plato) that the good teacher does not impose his ideas on the student but, rather, serves as a midwife for the student's own dormant intellect. In many ways Socrates has become a philosophical ideal. As we shall see, he stood by his own ideals in the face of adversity and danger; he believed in the intellectual capacities of everyone; he strove to awaken people's sense of critical thinking rather than give them a set of rules to live by, and, above all, he believed that "the unexamined life is not worth living."

Socrates, Man of Athens

What do we know of Socrates? There is no doubt that he lived—he is not a figment of Plato's imagination, as much as Plato may have made use of poetic license in his writings. Aristophanes, the author of comedies in Athens, refers to Socrates in his play *The Clouds* (albeit in a rather unflattering way). The fact is that we don't have any writings by Socrates himself, for his form of communication was the discussion, the live conversation—what has become known as the *dialogue*. From this word is derived the term for Socrates' special way of teaching, the *dialectic method* (sometimes also called the *Socratic method*). A method of teaching that uses conversation only, no written texts, is not exactly designed to affect posterity, but posterity has nevertheless been immensely affected by our indirect access to Socrates through the writings—the *Dialogues*—of Plato.

What we know of Socrates is that he lived in Athens from approximately 470 to 399 B.C.E. The son of a sculptor and a midwife, he was married to Xantippe and had children. He was one of several teachers of philosophy, science, and rhetoric in Athens at a time when internal politics were volatile (aristocrats versus democrats) and when Greece, which had experienced a golden age of cultural achievements in the wake of the Persian wars, was actually on the verge of decline. The most important political element of the time was the city-state, the *polis* (the origin of the word *politics*). With the peculiar features of the Greek countryside—the inland features of tall mountains and the seaside features of islands—the stage had been set for centuries for a specific power structure: small, independent, powerful realms warring and/or trading with one another. Two of the main areas were Athens and Sparta. Each area, a state in itself, considered itself to be geographically Greek but politically specific to its particular *polis*. Thus it meant more to an Athenian to be a citizen of Athens than it meant to be Greek. Being a free citizen of a particular *polis* carried with it an inordinate pride. Today some might condemn such a pride as being overly nationalistic or even chauvinistic (in the original sense of the word); for a Greek of the time it was a reasonable feeling. When Socrates was younger, he had been a soldier in the Athenian infantry and had distinguished himself as a courageous man. The loyalty to Athens that was expected of him then was something he lived up to his entire life; indeed, when he returned from the war, he stayed put in his hometown.

In one of Plato's dialogues, *Phaedrus,* Socrates and a friend, Phaedrus, have ventured outside the city walls, and Socrates carries on about the beauty of nature, the trees and the flowers, to such a degree that Phaedrus remarks that Socrates acts like a tourist. Socrates agrees, because he never ventures outside Athens, not even to go to the Olympic Games. The city of Athens is everything to him. It is the life among people, the communication, the discussions, the company of friends that are important to him, not nature, beautiful as it may be: "My appetite is for learning. Trees and countryside have no desire to teach me anything; it's only the men in the city that do."

It is not unusual to hear a big-city person say the same thing today—that New York or Paris or Rio has everything they could ever want. Most of us think such people are missing out on a few things, but Socrates' attitude becomes crucial to our understanding of his conduct toward the end of his life.

The Death of Socrates and the Works of Plato

Many cultures take the position that someone's life cannot be judged until it is over, that the ending helps define—sometimes even determine—how we think of the life spent. That may seem terribly unfair, for few of us are in full control of our lives, and we would prefer not to have our accomplishments judged primarily by circumstances beyond our control. In the case of Socrates, though, it seems fitting that his life is judged in the light of his death, for in the face of adversity, in the ultimate "situation beyond his control," he seems to have remained in full control of *himself.* This is another reason that Socrates has become not just the philosopher's ideal but also a human role model—because he did not lose his head but instead faced injustice with courage and rationality.

After what in antiquity passed for a long life (he was nearing age seventy), Socrates found himself in a difficult political situation, brought about by several factors. First, Socrates had great influence among the young men of Athens—those young men who might be of political influence in the future—and many were the sons of noblemen. Second, Socrates conducted his classes in public (this was customary at the time in Athens, before the formalization of classes, schools, and academy life), and his method was well known to his students, as well as to any city council member who might cross the *agora* (the public square) while Socrates was teaching. Socrates used a certain method of *irony* to get his point across, and it often involved engaging politicians in a discussion under the pretext of ignorance to trick the speaker into revealing his own ignorance or prejudice. His students adored him for it, because it was the ultimate "questioning of authority." The fact that Socrates himself may have been serious in a roundabout way about claiming his ignorance was something his listeners may not have realized. Socrates did not adhere to any one conception of reality unless it could be tested by reason; in other words, he would not profess to "know" anything for certain before investigating it and discussing it. That attitude, which was essentially one of humility rather than arrogance, seems to have been lost on his enemies, and over the years he acquired a considerable number of such enemies. Third, the most elusive factor but perhaps also the most important one: Athens was changing; what had been a place of comparatively free exchange of ideas, the undisputed center of the intellectual Western world, was

Jump Start by Robb Armstrong

JUMP START reprinted by permission of United Feature Syndicate, Inc.

The words of Socrates sometimes turn up in popular culture, such as in this comic strip about a young police officer and his family. Here his mother, an erudite woman, quotes Plato. Another introduction to Socrates from the realm of popular culture is the film *Bill and Ted's Excellent Adventure,* although Bill and Ted persist in pronouncing his name wrong.

becoming a place in which people expressed themselves more cautiously. Old laws against impiety were now more thoroughly enforced, and people were being banished for offenses against the state. The reason was complete exhaustion after thirty-seven years of war with Sparta, political upheavals, and an ensuing suspicion of dissidents. Most important, in Socrates' case, he had expressed reservations concerning the democratic government (not "democratic" in any modern political or partisan sense of the word, but a form of government in which male citizens of the city-state had a political voice, as opposed to the oligarchic form of government by the few). For most of Socrates' life Athens had had a democratic constitution, but during a brief, troubled time after Athens lost the long Peloponnesian War to Sparta, a group of aristocrats seized power and overthrew the constitution. The leader of this group of "Thirty Tyrants," Critias, had been a member of Socrates' circle, and although Socrates himself fell into disfavor with the tyrants, scholars speculate that some of his enemies had old scores to settle, even though the new Athenian democratic government had given amnesty to all involved in the affair after the fall of the tyrants. Another of Socrates' earlier associates, Alcibiades, had been responsible for a major naval expedition that went terribly wrong: He deserted, and the expedition was destroyed. Those connections may also have contributed to the downfall of Socrates.

Eventually his enemies took action. There was no way of getting rid of Socrates by political means, so they resorted to what appears to be a standard charge: that Socrates was "offending the gods and corrupting the youth." Socrates was tried and convicted by a jury of five hundred male citizens of Athens. The Athenian court would vote once for conviction or acquittal, and once again if the verdict was guilty, in what we today would call the "penalty phase," determining the punishment. Socrates himself gave two speeches, one in his defense and one concerning his punishment. His speech during the penalty phase featured an in-your-face suggestion that the proper punishment would be not death but a *reward* for services to the state, much like a sports hero: to be feted by the city of Athens.

The verdict was determined by a simple majority, not by a unanimous vote. The jury was almost split down the middle as to Socrates' guilt: Some speculate that if Socrates had had 30 more votes in his favor, he would have been acquitted. It seems that 280 voted for conviction, and 220 voted for acquittal. A tie vote—half the difference between 280 and 220—would have been resolved in favor of the accused. But the votes in favor of the death penalty after Socrates' "reward" speech were considerably higher than for his conviction—which means that some people who had thought him innocent were now so outraged at his behavior that they voted for capital punishment.

It seems possible that his enemies did not intend to get rid of Socrates by actually executing him. The standard reaction to such charges by accused citizens was to leave the city and go elsewhere within the Greek realm, and there were many places to choose from, because that realm extended from Italy well into the Middle East. But because Socrates chose to stand trial, arguing that by leaving he would be admitting guilt, his fate appeared sealed. Even so, to the last minute there were powers working to free him; his friends, many of whom were of considerable influence, conspired to spring him from jail and bring him to exile in safety. In Plato's dialogue *Crito* we hear how Socrates' good friend Crito pleads with him to listen to his friends and take their offer of escape and life, because "otherwise people will say we didn't do enough to help you." Socrates answers:

> In questions of just and unjust, fair and foul, good and evil, which are the subjects of our present consultation, ought we to follow the opinion of the many and to fear them; or the opinion of the one man who has understanding? . . . Then, my friend, we must not regard what the many say of us: but what he, the one man who has understanding of just and unjust, will say, and what the truth will say.

When Crito suggests that Socrates ought to escape because he has been convicted by unjust laws, Socrates replies that two wrongs don't make a right, and the laws of Athens have supported him throughout his life; even though unjust, they are still the laws of Athens. If he, Socrates, had been a less faithful citizen of Athens, he might choose to leave, but because he never left the city, he believes he has to live by his own rule of respecting the laws and the rules of reason and virtue and not turn his back on them.

So Socrates, the citizen of Athens, could not envision a life away from the city, even when the alternative was death.

Could Socrates have done a better job defending himself? Given that only a narrow majority of the five hundred jury members found him guilty, it seems clear it wouldn't have taken much for that small majority to change their minds. In Plato's dialogue the *Apology* (an excerpt of which appears as a Primary Reading at the end of this chapter), Socrates isn't exactly expressing himself cautiously or diplomatically in his address to his judges. He is assuming they will use rational judgment and see his point of view; he doesn't seem to understand the considerable animosity many feel toward him. The end result is, of course, a conviction. Since we can see in retrospect that another style of argumentation, or even just being slightly apologetic, might have saved his life, many have speculated that perhaps he didn't try too hard because

The Death of Socrates (1787) by Jacques-Louis David shows Socrates still exploring issues of life and death with his friends, even though he will soon drink the cup of poison prepared for his execution by the distraught jailer.

he *wanted* to die and make a point. This theory goes all the way back to Plato's contemporary Xenophon, who thought Socrates deliberately antagonized the jury to get a conviction. Others are convinced that he didn't and claim that he was arguing in a style completely true to his personality and outlook on life, that he fought in court, in his own way, until the very end. Box 8.2 speculates that the world we live in might have looked quite different had Socrates not been executed.

In the Narratives section you will find another historical figure, Sir Thomas More (*A Man for All Seasons*), who apparently made the same choice: that standing up for the truth is more important than staying alive. But that doesn't mean he, or Socrates, *wanted* to die. You might say they chose integrity over personal concerns, and that is probably what makes the Socratic example so compelling.

Was Socrates guilty? His accusers may have believed so, although we may find it hard to imagine why. Did he offend any gods? He seems to have been a religious man; he often made the traditional sacrifices to the gods, and Plato has him referring to gods or "the god" often in his dialogues. But Socrates also referred to what he called his *daimon* (spirit), a little voice inside him telling him what to do. It is hard to know whether he was just talking about his conscience or whether he believed in some guardian spirit, but it may have seemed to his accusers that he was trying to introduce new gods. Did he corrupt the youth of Athens? Well, yes, if you believe that

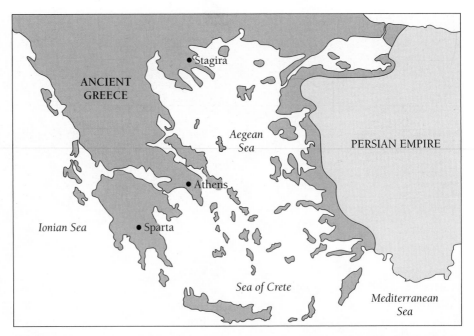

During the time of Socrates (fifth century B.C.E.) the Greek cultural realm stretched from Italy in the west to Asia Minor in the east; although people would consider themselves citizens of the Greek culture, their most important affiliation was with the city-state (*polis*) in which they were born.

teaching young people to think for themselves, to use their reason in search of the truth, is corrupting them. In his speech in his own defense (see *The Apology* in the Primary Reading section), Socrates asked those young people to come forth if they felt they had been corrupted; of course, none of the young people of his own circle did.

Plato tells us about the last, dignified minutes of Socrates' life, thereby giving history and philosophy the legacy of someone who chose to die for a rational principle. The scene is vividly described in the dialogue *Phaedo*. Plato writes that he himself wasn't present because of illness, and the story of Socrates' death is told by another student, Phaedo, but others have speculated that Plato may have already left Athens as a precaution, fearing reprisals against Socrates' supporters. In the end, Socrates' friends and students are gathered to say good-bye. They are on the verge of breaking down, while Socrates does his best to keep their spirits up. Even the jailer who brings in the poison apologizes to the old philosopher for having to cause him harm and hopes Socrates will not hold it against him. Socrates assures him that he will not and swallows the poison, an extract of hemlock. He continues talking, but the end approaches quickly. He lies down and pulls a blanket over himself, covering himself completely. But then—it must have been a dramatic moment for his friends—he removes the cover from his face for a final statement. And what are the last words coming from the Master's mouth? None of the wisdom they were used to hearing him speak, such as "The unexamined life is not worth living." No, he says to his old friend Crito, "I owe a rooster to Asclepius—will you remember to pay the debt?" Crito

Box 8.2   WHAT IF SOCRATES HADN'T BEEN EXECUTED?

What might have happened if the jury had been convinced of Socrates' innocence—or if Socrates had been convinced by Crito and had allowed himself to escape? If Socrates hadn't been executed, chances are Plato wouldn't have become a writer or a philosopher, for he wouldn't have felt compelled to preserve Socrates' name for posterity and give him philosophical immortality. And without Plato's writings we would have no Platonism, no school influencing antiquity for nine hundred years and beyond, into Christianity. And without Plato's school the young man from Stagira who came to the big city of Athens to get an education—Aristotle—might never have become a philosopher. And without Aristotle's philosophy? Universities would probably be structured differently, sciences would have other categories, ethics would be different, and elements of Christianity would be absent. Our world might look substantially different today if Socrates had died a natural death.

promises that he will, and within minutes Socrates is dead. The meaning of that request has been discussed by philosophers ever since. Was Socrates driven by the memory of an unpaid debt, or was he talking in symbolic terms? Asclepius was a common Greek name but also the name of the god of healing. Did he want his friends to sacrifice the rooster to the god because Asclepius had "cured" him—that is, released his soul from the prison of the body? We can only guess.

The effect of Socrates' death on Plato was profound. Born in about 427 B.C.E., Plato had been Socrates' student, in an informal sense, for thirteen years, and the death of his teacher caused him to take leave of Athens for a lengthy period, during which he traveled to Egypt and Sicily, among other places. Eventually he returned to Athens, and some time before 367 B.C.E. he founded his own school of philosophy, the Academy (Plato's own home—which he opened up to his students—named after the Greek hero Academus). This school appears to have been the beginning of a more formalized teaching institution, with regular lectures and several professors associated with the school. It remained open until 529 C.E., when it was closed by Christians. As Plato took on the mantle of his teacher, he began to reconstruct Socrates' intellectual legacy by writing the *Dialogues*. These books remain some of the most influential writings in philosophy, but they also are works of literature, as brilliant as any drama written in antiquity. That Plato from the very first dialogues reveals himself to be a great storyteller is all the more interesting, for, as you may remember from Chapter 2, he himself was not in favor of the arts, because he believed they spoke to people's emotions and made them forget the cool balance of reason. And, yet, Plato's own writings are works of art in themselves. Socrates and his friends and students come alive. We understand their way of talking, and we gain insight into their thinking, which, on occasion, is rather alien to our own day and age. The early dialogues of Plato give a picture of Socrates that is very fresh and probably quite accurate. However, scholars believe that in later dialogues Socrates changes into something that is more Plato's image of an ideal philosopher than Socrates himself. Indeed, in the last dialogues, Socrates appears as Plato's mouthpiece for his own

Plato (427?–347 B.C.E.) was the son of Ariston and Perictione. They named their son Aristocles, but he became known as Plato, literally "broad." Some people speculate that it meant "broad forehead," referring to his wide knowledge, but others trace the term back to—wrestling! Plato was a wrestler in his youth, and his nickname traveled with him into his career as a philosopher. It seems to have indicated that he had broad shoulders. His father died when Plato was a young boy. His mother, Perictione, was apparently a philosopher in her own right, although women in ancient Greece had virtually no independence.

advanced theories on metaphysics—theories that Socrates probably never held himself. That may mean that Socrates was indeed a good teacher who did not hinder Plato from "graduating" intellectually. It also means that through this life-long tribute to Socrates, Plato showed that you can kill a thinker but not his thoughts; so in a sense Plato made certain that Socrates, long dead at the hands of the Athenian judges, lived on to affect the history of thought well after his accusers had turned to dust.

The Good Life

Socrates' statement to Crito that some things are more important than life itself, such as being true to your principles no matter how others may feel about it, holds the key to what Socrates seems to have considered the "good life" or a life worth living. This would be a life in which one is not ruled by the opinion of others or even by one's own opinions, those ideas of ours that may or may not have some basis in the truth but that we haven't bothered to examine closely. If we stop for a minute and examine such opinions, we will probably discover that they constitute the basis for the majority of our viewpoints: We think we live in a great country, or perhaps we think we live in a deceitful, oppressive country. We think that chicken soup is good for colds. We may think that what scientists say must be true as long as they are wearing white lab coats. Perhaps we think that people who believe in UFOs are nuts, or we think that UFOs abduct humans from time to time. We hear actors weighing in on politics, and if they are our favorite actors, perhaps we value their opinion—but how exactly do actors get to be experts on politics? Some are indeed very well informed (and some actors also happen to be politicians); others just have *opinions*. And it is the opinion issue that interested and irritated Socrates. We think many things, and if we allow ourselves to examine those opinions, we will usually find that they are based on very flimsy evidence. Of course, on occasion we feel strongly about something precisely because we *have* examined it, but, in that case, Socrates would say, we are not talking about opinion (*doxa*) anymore—we are talking about knowledge (*epistēmē*). This, for Socrates, was the test of truth: Can it stand up to unprejudiced scrutiny? If so, it must override any sort of opinion we may have, even though it may hurt the feelings of others; if they see the truth, they, too, will understand, for *only ignorance leads to wrongdoing*. For Socrates as well as for Plato, this is a truth in itself: No one is willfully evil, provided that he or she understands the truth about the situation. And if a person still chooses the wrong course of action, it must be because his or her understanding is faulty.

For a modern person the response to that seems inevitable: What if there is more than one way of looking at the situation? In other words, what if there is more than one truth? We are so used to assuming there is more than one way of looking at something that we sometimes assume there is no truth at all. That, however, is very far from the intellectual attitude of Socrates. For Socrates, as well as for Plato, each situation has its Truth, and each thing can be described in one way that best captures its true nature, its essence. That does not mean that this was a common attitude among Greek thinkers. In Socrates' own time, contact with other cultures had brought about a certain amount of cultural relativism, and Greece was sufficiently heterogeneous to foster a tolerance of different customs. Accordingly, for many of Socrates' contemporaries, such as the Sophists, relativism became the accepted answer to the search for absolute truth. For Socrates, the theory that virtue might be a question of personal preference or relative to one's own time and culture was the epitome of misunderstanding, and much of the Socratic quest for the true nature, the essence, of a thing or a concept is a countermeasure to the prevailing relativism of the Greek intelligentsia. This also implies a fundamental Socratic principle: that truth should not be confused with appearance. The external appearance of something—a person, or a situation—is not necessarily the same as its true nature. Just as *doxa* must be discarded for *epistēmē*, appearance must yield to knowledge of the inner truth. In the Narratives section you'll find a film that, even if it is a comedy about cartoon characters, illustrates this principle that a later time has called "not judging a book by its cover": *Shrek*. Later in the chapter we return to the idea that the truth is somehow not to be judged by our senses but by our rational mind: Plato's theory of Forms.

Virtue for Socrates means to question the meaning of life and to keep one's integrity while searching, to not be swayed by one's physical longings or fear of unpleasant situations or concern for comfort. This ideal is attainable because the Truth can be found—in fact, it can be found by *anyone* who has as a guide a teacher with integrity. In other words, Socrates says we can't hope to attain virtue without the use of our *reason*. Later on (in particular during the Middle Ages), the link between virtue and reason was weakened, but for Plato and Socrates, as well as for Greek antiquity as such, the connection was obvious. Using our reason will make us realize what virtue is and will actually make us virtuous.

The good life, therefore, is not a pleasant life in which we seek gratification for the sake of having a good time. The good life is strenuous but gratifying in its own way, because one knows that one seeks and sees the Truth, and one is in control of oneself.

The Virtuous Person: The Tripartite Soul

Let us now focus on what makes a person good. You may remember from Chapter 4 that Plato's brother Glaucon told a story about the Ring of Gyges, stating that if you had the chance to get away with something and you didn't, you had to be stupid. For Socrates this matter was of grave importance, and this was his answer: A person who does something unjust to others is either ignorant or sick. If we inform that person that he is being unjust, he may realize his ignorance and improve himself. But there is the chance that he will laugh in our face. In that case, Socrates said, he is simply not well—he is out of balance. Glaucon's argument that an unjust person is happier than a just person carries no weight with Socrates, because an unjust person can't be happy at all; only a well-balanced person can be happy. But what is a well-balanced person?

Everybody has desires, and sometimes those desires can be very strong. We may want something to drink when we are thirsty, something to eat when we are hungry; we have desires for sex, for power, and for many other things. We also have desires to get away from things, as when we move away from a fire we're too close to. Those needs and wants Plato calls *appetites,* and they are what we must control if we are to achieve the good life. Appetites may rule a person's life, but that is not good, because the things we desire aren't necessarily the things that are good for us. So sometimes we pull away from what we want because we realize that it will be bad for us. The power that pulls us back is our *rational element,* our *reason.*

There is a third element at play; Plato calls it *spirit.* Sometimes he calls it *willpower.* We feel it when we sometimes let our appetites win out over our reason; afterward we feel disgusted with ourselves, and the anger directed at ourselves is our spirit. When we fall off our diet, our reason may have lost the battle, but our spirit will be angry at our weakness and will keep bothering us. What, then, should a person do? Establish a good working relationship between reason and spirit; let reason be clear about what it wants to do, and then train the spirit to help control the appetites. Reason and spirit will, side by side, keep the body healthy and the soul balanced. In his dialogue *Phaedrus* Plato describes the three-sided relationship by the following metaphor: A charioteer has two horses to pull his chariot; suppose one is well-behaved, whereas the other is wild and unruly. He is stuck with both and can't choose another horse, so he must make the well-behaved horse help him control the unruly horse and subdue it. So which roles do these figures play? The charioteer is Reason, the well-behaved horse is Willpower, and the wild horse is Appetites. Notice that a "balanced" individual to Plato does not have one-third of each element—he or she has total control by reason and willpower over appetites. When reason rules, the person is *wise;* when spirit controls the appetites, that person is also *brave* (because it takes courage to say no to temptation and yes to a painful experience); and when the appetites are completely controlled, the person is *temperate.* Such a person is well balanced and would not dream of being unjust to anybody; on the contrary, he or she would be the very picture of *justice,* and justice is the virtue that describes the well-balanced human being who is wise, brave, and temperate. Only that kind of person can be happy in the true sense of the word; Glaucon's idea that an unjust person is

Box 8.3   THE TRIPARTITE SOUL: PLATO AND FREUD

Plato

Elements of the Soul		*Virtues*
Reason	—corresponds to—	Wisdom
Willpower	—corresponds to—	Courage
Appetites	—corresponds to—	Temperance

Freud

Theory of the Psyche
Superego
Ego
Id

If an individual has succeeded in mastering his or her appetites by using reason to guide willpower, then a fourth virtue comes into play: *justice.* In that case Plato would say we have encountered a truly virtuous individual: a just person, a person of internal balance and integrity.

In the early twentieth century Sigmund Freud suggested a theory about the human psyche that has some parallels to Plato's theory: Freud's psyche comprises the Id (the Unconscious), the Ego (the conscious self), and the Superego (the codes and rules we have been taught). Can the Id be compared to appetites? Yes, as long as we remember that, for Freud, the Id can't be accessed, whereas Plato believed a person could understand his or her own appetites. As for the Ego and the Superego, they don't match Plato's schema too well: The Ego is part reason but also part willpower; the Superego has elements in common with both too. The similarity between Plato's theory of the soul and Freud's theory of the psyche is not a coincidence: Freud was a great admirer of Plato's dialogues.

---

happier than a just person can be discarded, because such a person is off balance. (For another thinker's view of the tripartite soul, see Box 8.3.)

Plato was not interested in just the virtuous individual; further on in his famous dialogue *The Republic,* he speculates that a well-balanced person can be compared to a society in harmony with itself; as appetites must be controlled by reason and willpower, so, too, must parts of the population be controlled by other parts. Who corresponds to *reason?* Wise rulers, says Plato, "philosopher-kings" who would rather not rule; they will get the job done without fuss and with reason as their principle of guidance. Who corresponds to *willpower* in a state? The "auxiliaries," soldiers and law enforcement. And what about all the rest of the population—merchants, businesspeople, educators, entertainers, private citizens? They correspond to the *appetites* and must be thoroughly controlled. If they are not—such as in a democracy—then that society is off balance and sick. This restrictive social plan did not correspond to

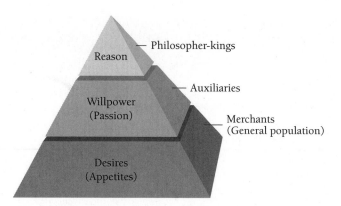

Plato himself never suggested that one might illustrate his theory of the balanced soul and the good state with a pyramid, but the image works, for several reasons. Plato imagines his ideal society to be a hierarchy of power, with the philosopher-kings on top, the auxiliaries in the middle, and the general population at the bottom. But Plato also insists that the ideal society has the same structure as the ideal soul. So when the pyramid illustrates the mind of a just person, the configuration looks like this: At the top of the pyramid we have Reason—the smallest part of our mind, but the most important one. Reason has to dominate and seek the aid of Willpower (sometimes called Passion) to control the Desires (Appetites). The result is a very balanced person who will not be swayed by his or her emotions—just as a pyramid is a very stable structure. Imagine placing the pyramid on its tip—then you'll have the image of a person who is out of balance, because his or her reason is ruled by desires. You may want to revisit Chapters 2 and 4, and apply the pyramid image to Plato's reluctance to go to the theater for fear of losing control and reread Socrates' argument against Glaucon that a person who lets desires control him is sick, and a sick person can't be a happy person.

democratic Athenian society at all, and Plato has been vilified by democratically minded thinkers ever since. See Box 8.4 for Plato's idea of a well-balanced society.

Among modern Plato scholars there is some disagreement about Plato's intentions in his social theory of the ideal state. Its radical principles include not only a strict hierarchy but also rules about marriage and children among the philosopher-kings. For one thing, Plato advocates that anyone would be eligible as a guardian (a ruler or a soldier), depending on his or her talent and regardless of *gender;* to his contemporaries (and even to some of our contemporaries) the idea of a woman ruler (or president) is outlandish or even outrageous, but Plato apparently found it a completely reasonable thought. Most people today, however, find his rules about childbearing among the guardians too extreme and certainly both outlandish and outrageous: For the sake of eugenics (creating a superior breed of people by mating selected men and women), guardians would be paired off and mated during their childbearing years, but the children would be removed from the mothers and raised in common so that no parent would know his or her own child. Plato envisioned such a plan to allow personal preferences and affiliations to be held to a minimum so that the guardians could focus on what was good for the state.

Those radical thoughts have caused some Plato scholars to say that Plato may not have meant one word of his political theory—it was all tongue-in-cheek, a big joke on his students told at a dinner party. Women in government! He couldn't possibly have

Box 8.4   A WELL-BALANCED PERSON IN A
WELL-BALANCED SOCIETY

On page 404, you'll find a graphic illustrating Plato's notion of a well-balanced soul—not Plato's own illustration, mind you, but a short-cut that to me gathers some of Plato's key ideas: The well-balanced person's reason rules; it is aided by his or her spirit or willpower; and the person's desires are controlled at all times. Here we expand it to cover Plato's theory of the ideal society, Plato's Republic (and it is because of Plato's social theory that I thought of using the pyramid as an illustration in the first place, since Plato says that society is simply the structure of the soul, in a large format). So, following the pyramid structure of the ideal balanced soul, we have the ideal balanced society ruled by philosopher-kings (reason) at the top, a small but powerful group. Next we have the auxiliaries, meaning the soldiers and law enforcement, helping the philosopher-kings keep law and order, and protecting everybody from unrest and enemy onslaughts (compare willpower or spirit). And at the bottom? "The people," what Plato calls merchants and tradesmen, meaning everybody who doesn't get to be in law enforcement or the military, or in government (appetites or desires). *That would mean most of us.* And following the parallel of the individual pyramid, the people never have a say about anything at all that goes beyond their own personal and professional lives—but they are not oppressed (supposedly), since the government is looking out for their interests and the interests of society as a whole (just as reason looks out for the interests of the entire body). This social model is what has caused critics—fairly or unfairly—to call Plato a supporter of totalitarianism, and the *Republic* the first blueprint for a totalitarian society.

been serious. However, at least two things speak for taking Plato seriously: For one thing, late in life he left his teaching position in Athens to return to Syracuse, presumably to tutor the young tyrant Dionysius II. Apparently Plato used his own principles as outlined in the *Republic* to try to groom Dionysius into a guardian, without much success. Even though Plato's family had intended for him to go into politics, it is obvious that Plato was much more a scholar and a writer than a successful politician. For another thing, Plato's student Aristotle had no doubt that Plato was serious, and who could be a better judge than a contemporary source who had heard Plato discuss his theories?

There is little evidence that Socrates himself ever had such political visions; his main interests seem to have been getting individuals to improve their thinking and become better persons. Examining the concept of virtue, he would begin with a concept, a word of common usage, such as *justice* or *piety,* and ask his partners in the dialogue to define it, under the assumption there would be one, and only one, description that would be the true one. At some point in the Platonic dialogues, we begin to lose the sense that it is Socrates talking, for a theory develops that is Plato's own: the theory of Forms.

Plato's Theory of Forms

When we ask about a person's view of reality, we generally want to know whether that person is religious or an atheist, pessimistic or optimistic about other people and events, interested in a historical perspective or mainly looking to the present and the

Box 8.5   THREE THEORIES OF METAPHYSICS

In philosophy we encounter three major theories of the nature of reality, or of metaphysics: *materialism, idealism*, and *dualism*. Through the ages people have leaned toward one or the other, and today the prevailing theory in the Western world is overwhelmingly *materialistic*. That does not mean people are overwhelmingly interested in accumulating riches, although that may be the case. Metaphysical materialism has nothing to do with greed; it merely means you think reality consists of things that are *material*—they or their effects can be *measured* in some sense. This category includes everything from food to briefcases to brainwaves. It follows that a materialist doesn't believe in the reality of things supposedly immaterial, such as souls or spirits. Typical philosophical materialists are Thomas Hobbes, Karl Marx, and Paul and Patricia Churchland.

Idealism is the theory that only spiritual things have true existence and that the material world is somehow just an illusion. Again, that has very little to do with the colloquial use of the word, which we associate with a person with high ideals. Few people in philosophy define themselves as idealists today, but this theory had a certain influence in earlier times. Bishop George Berkeley was an idealist, and so was the German philosopher G. W. F. Hegel. The Hindu belief that the world we see is a mere illusion, *maya*, is also an example of idealism.

The theory of *dualism* combines materialism and idealism in that a dualist believes reality consists of a matter-side and a spirit-side—in other words, that although the body is material, the soul/spirit/mind is immaterial and perhaps immortal. Although this theory seems to appeal to our common sense, it poses several logical problems, which philosophy has not been able to solve, for how exactly does the mind affect the body if the mind is immaterial and the body is material? René Descartes is the most famous of the dualists, but Plato also is often counted among them, although some might prefer to call him an idealist because of his theory of Forms.

future, and so on. Philosophically speaking, however, a person's view of reality is what we call *metaphysics*. What exactly is the nature of reality as such? In philosophy the answer will be one of three major types: Reality is made up of things that can be measured (*materialism*); or Reality is totally spiritual, all in the mind (*idealism*); or Reality consists of part matter, part mind (*dualism*). (These three theories of metaphysics are described in Box 8.5.) What, exactly, was Socrates' philosophical view of reality? The early dialogues indicate that he seems to have believed in an immortal soul that leaves the body at death, which would make him a dualist. In later dialogues, though, Plato chooses to let Socrates speak for a theory—which was obviously Plato's own—that says reality is very much different from what our common sense tells us. What we see and hear and feel around us is really a shadowy projection of "true reality." Our senses can't experience it, but our mind can, because this true reality is related to our mind: It is one of the Ideas, or *Forms*.

What exactly is a Form? Today it is hard to grasp Plato's concept, but for the Greek mind of Plato's own day it was not so alien. In early times the Greeks saw each good thing as represented by some divinity; there was a goddess for justice, another for victory. There were the Muses, lesser goddesses representing each form of art. The Olympic gods each had their own areas of protection. At the time of Plato many intellectuals, including Plato himself, had left traditional Greek religion behind. Some of the ancient tendency to personify abstract ideas, though, may have survived in his Forms. A Form is at once the ideal abstraction and sole source of each thing that resembles it. Let us look at an example. There are all kinds of *beds* today—double beds, twin beds, bunk beds, futons, waterbeds, hammocks. Plato would ask, What makes these things beds? We, today, would approach the question in a functionalistic manner and say something about them all being things to sleep on. Plato would say they are all beds because they all participate in the Form of Bed, a kind of ideal "bedness" not only that they have in common as a *concept* but also that actually *exists* above and beyond each singular bed. It is this quality that gives the bed its share of reality, as a sort of dim copy of the true Bed Form. This realm of Forms is true reality, and the entire world in which we move around is only a dim copy of the ideal Form. Where exactly *is* this world of Forms? It is nowhere that you can see and touch, because then it would just be another example of a copy. It has to be "out of this world," in a realm that our body does not have access to but that our mind does. So it is through our intellect that we can touch true reality, and only through our intellect. That is why Plato has Socrates tell Phaedrus that trees and countryside can't teach him anything—because there is nothing to be learned from the senses except confusion. The only true lesson in reality is achieved by letting the mind, the intellect, contemplate the Forms, because the world we see changes constantly, but the world of Forms never changes. The Forms are eternal, and for Plato (and for many other philosophers), the more enduring something is, the more real it is.

But how did Plato conceive of such a theory? And how does he propose to persuade us that he is right? One example answers both questions: Think of a circle; now think of a perfect circle. Have you ever drawn one? No. Have you ever seen one? No. Can you imagine one? Yes. Can you describe one mathematically (if you have the training)? Yes. If you have never experienced it, then how can you imagine it and describe it? Because your mind understands that the perfect circle really exists—not just as a mathematical formula, but in a higher, mental realm of reality. From this higher realm the perfect Form of a circle (and all the other Forms) lend their reality to imperfect circles and other things in our tangible world; if the Form of a circle didn't exist, then you wouldn't have a notion that a circle could be perfect! Today we would say we understand the perfect circle because we can describe it mathematically, but that doesn't mean it exists somewhere else. (See Box 8.6 for a discussion of how we can know Forms.)

Because the world of Forms is purely spiritual and immaterial, some philosophers choose to call Plato an idealist; however, more prefer to call him a dualist, because the world of matter is not "nonexistent" but merely of a lesser existence than the world of Forms.

Does everything have a Form? Concepts such as justice, love, and beauty have their natural place in the realm of Forms; they may be on this earth incompletely, but their Forms are flawless. Cats and dogs obviously have Forms; things of nature have a perfect Form in the spiritual realm, which gives them reality. Manufactured objects

Box 8.6   THE THEORY OF ANAMNESIS

How do we know about the Forms if we can't learn about them by observing the world around us? Plato believed that we remember the Forms from the time before we were born, because during that time the soul's home was the realm of the Forms themselves. At birth the soul forgets its previous life, but, with the aid of a philosopher "in the know," we can be reminded of the nature of true reality. This is one of the functions of Socrates in the literature of Plato: to cause his students to remember their lost knowledge. The process is known as *anamnesis,* a rerembering, or, literally, a non-forgetting. In Plato's dialogue *Meno,* Socrates shows that this knowledge is accessible to everyone, as he helps a young slave-boy "remember" truths of math and logic that he has never learned in this life.

Plato, furthermore, believed in *reincarnation* (transmigration of souls). Reincarnation was not a common belief among the ancient Greeks, who seem to have believed in a dreary, dark Hades to which all souls were destined to go, regardless of whether they had been good or bad in life. But Plato apparently saw it differently: Toward the end of the *Republic,* Socrates tells an evocative story of the soul's long journey after death, called "The Myth of Er." He claims that the soul must undergo several cycles of life before it is purified sufficiently to go back to the Forms to stay forever. We know that Plato was influenced by Pythagoras, who believed in reincarnation; but some scholars also speculate that Plato may have been under the direct or indirect influence of Hindu theories of karma and reincarnation, which had existed in India for at least five hundred years before Plato's own time. However, other scholars point out that Hinduism hadn't yet spread beyond isolated groups in India.

have Forms too, so in the realm of Forms there is a Form of a chair, a knife, a cradle, and a winding staircase. What about a Form of something that has not "always" been—such as a computer, an iPod, or a microwave oven? Here we are moving into an uncomfortable area of Plato's theory, because even if microwave ovens are a new invention, presumably their Form has always existed. But what about Forms for dirt, mud, and diseases? Plato gives us the impression that the Forms are perfect and somehow closer to goodness than things on this earth; however, it is hard to envision perfect dirt, mud, and diseases, even though the theory of Forms certainly implies they exist. (A generation later, Plato's student Aristotle was to criticize the theory of Forms for assuming that every phenomenon has a Form. Aristotle asserted that some phenomena are merely a "lack" or deficiency of something. A doughnut hole doesn't have a Form—it is just the empty middle of a doughnut.)

The Form of the Good

For Plato the world of Forms represents an orderly reality, nothing like the jumble of sensory experience. Forms are ordered according to their importance and according to their dependence on other Forms. Certainly worms and dirt have Forms, but they are very low in the hierarchy; at the highest level are abstract concepts such as justice, virtue, and beauty. At the very top of the hierarchy Plato sees the Form of the Good as the most important Form and also as the Form from which everything else derives.

Is the Form of the Good a god, in the final analysis? Followers of Plato around the fourth and fifth centuries C.E., the *Neoplatonists,* leaned toward that theory, but it is hard to say whether Plato himself had specifically religious veneration for his Forms; it is certain that he had intellectual respect and veneration for them and for the Form of the Good in particular.

The Form of the Good allows us to understand a little better what Plato means by saying that evil acts stem from ignorance, because, according to the theory of Forms, if a person realizes the existence of the Forms and in particular the highest Form of them all, the Good, it will be impossible for that person to deliberately choose to do wrong; the choice of wrongdoing can come only from ignorance of the Good. The choice to follow the Good is not an easy one, though, even when we have knowledge of it, because we have desires that pull us in other directions. Besides, Plato says the first time we hear about the Forms, the theory sounds so peculiar that we refuse to accept our own recollection of it. Plato tells a story to illustrate this, "The Myth of the Cave." (See the excerpt from Plato's *Republic* with the story of the cave at the end of this chapter.) In a large cave a group of prisoners are kept chained to their seats so they can look only in one direction, toward a huge wall. Behind them there is a fire that casts shadows on the wall. The prisoners, having never seen anything else, believe these shadows are all the reality there is. One prisoner gains his freedom and now sees the cave, the fire, and the world outside the cave for what they really are—but will the others believe him when he returns?

Because the cave is our everyday world of the senses, and because we are the prisoners who see only two-dimensional shadows instead of a multidimensional reality, we have the same problems the prisoners have when one prisoner stands up

Dilbert by Scott Adams

DILBERT reprinted by permission of United Feature Syndicate, Inc.

The influence of Plato's "Myth of the Cave" can be detected in this *Dilbert* strip that asks, What is reality? In the *Dilbert* universe we can be sure it is our worst nightmare.

and claims that he or she has "seen the light" and knows that reality is totally different from what we think. How do we respond to such "prophets"? We ignore them or ridicule them or silence them and continue to live on in our illusion. And what is the duty of the philosopher who has seen "the light" of true reality, the Good and the other Forms, according to Plato? To return to the cave, even if it would be wonderful to remain in the light of the Truth and forget about the world of shadows. The philosopher's duty is to go back and tell the others, and that, Plato believed, was what he himself was doing with his dialogues. For Plato, Truth was not something relative that differed for each person; it was an absolute reality beyond the deceptive world of the senses, a reality that never changes and that we, when we shed the chains of our physical existence—either intellectually or through death—will be able to see and be in the presence of. (For a contemporary Cave allegory with a twist, go to the Narratives section and read the summary of the film *The Truman Show*. Truman Burbank lives in a Cave of his own, unbeknownst to himself, but on live television to the rest of the world.)

Plato's Influence on Christianity

Plato's momentous influence on Western thinking is not measured by how many people took his theory of Forms to heart. As a matter of fact, not many scholars followed Plato's metaphysics to the letter; however, his idea of a never-changing realm of goodness, light, and justice to which our soul can have access made its way into Christianity, along with the Platonic disdain for the physical world as an obstruction to that access. Many early Christian thinkers had been trained in the Platonic and Neoplatonic schools of thought (which were probably taught by Hypatia in Alexandria, for one, before she was murdered), and the view of true reality as something that is not of this world came naturally to them; controlling the desires of the body and focusing on the afterlife are elements that Platonic philosophy and early Christian thinking have in common. Saint Augustine (354–430 C.E.), for example, had had a thorough pagan spiritual education before his conversion to Christianity at age thirty-two. He had studied Manichaeism, the then-popular Persian philosophical religion that taught that the powers of light and the powers of darkness are locked in battle until the final day and the powers of light will not win unless we humans help them in their fight for goodness. He had studied Neoplatonism, a philosophy developed by the thinker Plotinus on the basis of Plato's philosophy, which taught that this tangible, material world is unimportant compared with the world of the spirit and even that the material world is godless and should be shunned. This intellectual and religious legacy that Augustine brought with him subtly changed the direction of Christianity forever, according to historians. It is, of course, the ultimate irony that Plato's Academy in Athens was closed in 529 by the Christian emperor Justinian, as you read earlier in this chapter, presumably to stop the pagan influence of the ancient school or simply as a symbolic gesture that antiquity had come to an end—but the most influential of all Christian thinkers in the early centuries of Christianity, Augustine, was already well acquainted with the philosophical principles of Plato's metaphysics by the time he converted to Christianity. In the writings

In Plato's "Myth of the Cave," a group of prisoners are placed so they can see on the wall of the cave only reflections of objects carried back and forth in front of a fire behind them. Since this is all they see, they assume it to be reality. Had Plato been acquainted with movie theaters, he might have chosen the movie screen as a metaphor for the shadow world of the senses.

of Augustine, Christianity became a religion that, even more than previously, looked to the afterlife as the true reason for human existence and shunned earthly concerns and earthly pleasures. That disregard for the physical world and our physical existence has been heavily criticized since the end of the nineteenth century by scholars such as Nietzsche (see Chapter 10), who believe that it shows an abysmal contempt for what Nietzsche saw as the only true reality there is: the ever-changing reality of our physical existence on this earth.

Study Questions

1. What are the elements that constitute a person, according to Plato? What is the proper relationship between those elements? (In other words, what is a virtuous person?)

2. You read that Socrates' last words referred to paying a debt to Asclepius. What do you think he meant?

3. Explain Plato's theory of Forms, using his story of the cave as an illustration. Is Plato's theory of reality (metaphysics) materialistic, idealistic, or dualistic? Explain.

4. Imagine that you were assigned to be Socrates' legal counsel. What would you advise him to do or say to escape a death sentence? Do you think it might make a difference? Why or why not?

5. Compare African and American Indian tribal virtue ethics with the virtue ethics of Socrates. What are the similarities? What are the differences?

Primary Readings and Narratives

The two Primary Readings are excerpts from Plato's dialogues: one from his *Republic,* the wrap-up discussion about the virtuous person in the good state; and one from his *Apology,* his version of Socrates' speech in his own defense. The first two Narratives have Socratic themes: a summary of the film *A Man for All Seasons,* whose title character finds himself falsely accused by advisers to King Henry VIII and defends himself in a manner reminiscent of Socrates, and an excerpt from Plato's *Republic,* "The Myth of the Cave," in which people have been imprisoned all their lives so that the only reality they know is the shadows on the wall. The third Narrative is a summary of the film *The Truman Show,* a story that questions the nature of reality. The fourth narrative is a summary of the film *Shrek*—perhaps not an obvious choice as an illustration of Socratic thinking, but an eloquent defense of Socrates' argument that it is the inner truth that counts, not the world of appearances.

 Primary Reading

The Republic

PLATO

Excerpt from Book IV, **The Republic,**
fourth century B.C.E. Translated by Francis MacDonald Cornford.

In this excerpt from *The Republic,* you get the conclusion of Socrates' conversation with Glaucon about what constitutes a good, virtuous, or, in Socrates' terminology, *just* man. Like the ideal state, the ideal person must be controlled by reason and use the spirited element (willpower, passion) as its helper to control the appetites. And when the soul works according to this principle, he or she will be wise, courageous, and temperate. With these qualities of virtue, the just person will be highly unlikely to engage in behavior that will be harmful to others or harmful to the state: It is not a matter of mere external behavior but a matter of an inner character.

AND SO, after a stormy passage, we have reached the land. We are fairly agreed that the same three elements exist alike in the state and in the individual soul.

That is so.

Does it not follow at once that state and individual will be wise or brave by virtue of the same element in each and in the same way? Both will possess in the same manner any quality that makes for excellence.

That must be true.

Then it applies to justice: we shall conclude that a man is just in the same way that a state was just. And we have surely not forgotten that justice in the state meant that each of the three orders in it was doing its own proper work. So we may henceforth bear in mind that each one of us likewise will be a just person, fulfilling his proper function, only if the several parts of our nature fulfil theirs.

Certainly.

And it will be the business of reason to rule with wisdom and forethought on behalf of the entire soul; while the spirited element ought to act as its subordinate and ally. The two will be brought into accord, as we said earlier, by that combination of mental and bodily training which will tune up one string of the instrument and relax the other, nourishing the reasoning part on the study of noble literature and allaying the other's wildness by harmony and rhythm. When both have been thus nurtured and trained to know their own true functions, they must be set in command over the appetites, which form the greater part of each man's soul and are by nature insatiably covetous. They must keep watch lest this part, by battening on the pleasures that are called bodily, should grow so great and powerful that it will no longer keep to its own work, but will try to enslave the others and usurp a dominion to which it has no right, thus turning the whole of life upside down. At the same time, those two together will be the best of guardians for the entire soul and for the body against all enemies from without: the one will take counsel, while the other will do battle, following its ruler's commands and by its own bravery giving effect to the ruler's designs.

Yes, that is all true.

And so we call an individual brave in virtue of this spirited part of his nature, when, in spite of pain or pleasure, it holds fast to the injunctions of reason about what he ought or ought not to be afraid of.

True.

And wise in virtue of that small part which rules and issues these injunctions, possessing as it does the knowledge of what is good for each of the three elements and for all of them in common.

Certainly.

And, again, temperate by reason of the unanimity and concord of all three, when there is no internal conflict between the ruling element and its two subjects, but all are agreed that reason should be ruler.

Yes, that is an exact account of temperance, whether in the state or in the individual.

Finally, a man will be just by observing the principle we have so often stated.

Necessarily.

Now is there any indistinctness in our vision of justice, that might make it seem somehow different from what we found it to be in the state?

I don't think so.

Because, if we have any lingering doubt, we might make sure by comparing it with some commonplace notions. Suppose, for instance, that a sum of money were entrusted to our state or to an individual of corresponding character and training, would anyone imagine that such a person would be specially likely to embezzle it?

No.

And would he not be incapable of sacrilege and theft, or of treachery to friend or country; never false to an oath or any other compact; the last to be guilty of adultery or of neglecting parents or the due service of the gods?

Yes.

And the reason for all this is that each part of his nature is exercising its proper function, of ruling or of being ruled.

Yes, exactly.

Are you satisfied, then, that justice is the power which produces states or individuals of whom that is true, or must we look further?

There is no need; I am quite satisfied.

And so our dream has come true—I mean the inkling we had that, by some happy chance, we had lighted upon a rudimentary form of justice from the very moment when we set about founding our commonwealth. Our principle that the born shoemaker or carpenter had better stick to his trade turns out to have been an adumbration of justice; and that is why it has helped us. But in reality justice, though evidently analogous to this principle, is not a matter of external behaviour, but of the inward self and of attending to all that is, in the fullest sense, a man's proper concern. The just man does not allow the several elements in his soul to usurp one another's functions; he is indeed one who sets his house in order, by self-mastery and discipline coming to be at peace with himself, and bringing into tune those three parts, like the terms in the proportion of a musical scale, the highest and lowest notes and the mean between them, with all the intermediate intervals. Only when he has linked these parts together in well-tempered harmony and has made himself one man instead of many, will he be ready to go about whatever he may have to do, whether it be making money and satisfying bodily wants, or business transactions, or the affairs of state. In all these fields when he speaks of just and honourable conduct, he will mean the behaviour that helps to produce and to preserve this habit of mind; and by wisdom he will mean the knowledge which presides over such conduct. Any action which tends to break down this habit will be for him unjust; and the notions governing it he will call ignorance and folly.

That is perfectly true, Socrates.

Good, said I. I believe we should not be thought altogether mistaken, if we claimed to have discovered the just man and the just state, and wherein their justice consists.

Indeed we should not.

Shall we make that claim, then?

Yes, we will.

Study Questions

1. Compare this section of *The Republic* with what you have read in Chapter 2 and Chapter 4. What are the characteristics of a just person, according to Socrates and Plato? What are the characteristics of a just state? Do you agree? Why or why not?

2. Why do we need to control our appetites or desires at all times, according to Plato? Do you agree? What are the political ramifications of comparing the rule of reason over appetites to the rule of the guardians over the general population?

Primary Reading

Apology

PLATO

Dialogue excerpt, fourth century B.C.E. Translated by R. G. Bury.

In the *Apology,* the very first of Plato's dialogues, Socrates argues in his own defense while on trial. This is not a typical "dialogue," since Socrates does most of the talking, but we know he has listeners because he begs for their attention and asks them not to heckle him. Is this a true retelling of what Socrates actually said, or is Plato here (as often elsewhere) making things up? Scholars have speculated that Plato, being present at the trial, must surely have remembered every word of this traumatic, horrible event; however, the account was probably not written until some years later, perhaps as much as ten years, so we must assume that Plato tells it not only the way he remembers it but also the way he believes it *ought* to sound. Since Plato's account of the trial is not the only one in existence, we can assume that the general gist of Socrates' defense was the way Plato presented it.

I have said enough in my defense against the first class of my accusers; I turn to the second class. They are headed by Meletus, that good man and true lover of his country, as he calls himself. Against these, too, I must try to make a defense. Let their indictment be read; it runs like this: "Socrates is a doer of evil who corrupts the youth, and who does not believe in the gods of the state, but has other new divinities of his own." Such is the charge; now let us examine the particular counts. He says that I am a doer of evil and corrupt the youth; but I say, men of Athens, that Meletus is a doer of evil, since he pretends to be in earnest when he is only joking, and is so eager to bring men to trial from a pretended zeal and interest about matters in which he really never had the smallest interest. And the truth of this I will try to prove to you.

Come here, Meletus, and let me ask you a question. You think a great deal about the improvement of youth?

Yes, I do.

Tell the judges, then, who is their improver; for you must know, since you care so much.* You say you have discovered their corrupter, and are citing and accusing me before them. Speak then, and tell the judges who their improver is. Observe, Meletus, that you are silent and have nothing to say. But is not this disgraceful, and a clear proof of what I say, that you have never cared about this? Speak up, friend, and tell us who their improver is.

The laws.

But that, my good sir, is not my meaning. I want to know who the person is who, in the first place, knows the laws.

The judges, Socrates, who are present in court.

---

*A play on Meletus's name, which means "one who cares" in Greek. [Ed.]

What, do you mean to say, Meletus, that they are able to instruct and improve youth?

Certainly they are.

What, all of them, or some only and not others?

All of them.

By the goddess Hera, that is good news! There are plenty of improvers, then. And what do you say of the audience—do they improve them?

Yes, they do.

And the members of the Council?

Yes, they improve them.

But perhaps the members of the Assembly corrupt them? Or do they too improve them?

They improve them.

Then every Athenian improves and elevates them except me; and I alone am their corrupter? Is that what you affirm?

That is what I stoutly affirm.

I am very unfortunate if you are right. But suppose I ask you a question. How about horses? Does one man do them harm and all the world good? Is not the exact opposite the truth? One man is able to do them good, or at least not many; the trainer of horses does them good, and others who have anything to do with them rather injure them. Is that not true, Meletus, of horses or of any other animals? Surely it is; whether you and Anytus say yes or no. Happy indeed would be the condition of youth if they had one corrupter only, and all the rest of the world were their improvers. But you, Meletus, have sufficiently shown that you never had a thought about the young; your carelessness is seen in your not caring about the very things you bring against me. Now, Meletus, I will ask you another question—by Zeus I will. Which is better, to live among bad citizens or among good ones? Answer, friend, I say; the question can be easily answered. Do not the good do their neighbors good, and the bad do them evil?

Certainly.

And is there anyone who would rather be injured than benefited by those who live with him? Answer, my good friend, the law requires you to answer—does anyone like to be injured?

Certainly not.

And when you accuse me of corrupting the youth, do you allege that I corrupt them intentionally or unintentionally?

Intentionally, I say.

But you have just admitted that the good do their neighbors good, and evil do them evil. Now, is that a truth which your superior wisdom has recognized so early in life, and am I at my age in such darkness and ignorance that I do not know that if one of my associates is corrupted by me, I am very likely to be harmed by him? Yet I corrupt him, and intentionally too? So you say, although neither I nor any other human being is ever likely to be convinced by you. Either I do not corrupt them, or I corrupt them unintentionally; and in either case you lie. If my offense is unintentional, the law has no cognizance of unintentional offenses; you should have taken me aside privately and warned and admonished me. For if I had been better advised, I would have stopped doing what I only did unintentionally—no doubt I would; but you had nothing to say to me and refused to teach me. Instead you bring me up in court, which is a place not of instruction, but of punishment. It will be very clear to you, Athenians, as I said, that Meletus has no care at all, great or small, about the matter. But still I would like to know, Meletus, how you think I corrupt the young. I suppose you mean, according to your indictment, that I teach them not to acknowledge the gods the state acknowledges, but some other new divinities instead. These are the lessons by which I corrupt the youth, you say.

Yes, that I say emphatically. . . .

I have said enough in answer to the charge of Meletus; any elaborate defense is unnecessary. But I know only too well how many are the enmities I have incurred, and this is what will be my destruction if I am destroyed—not Meletus or Anytus, but the envy and detraction of the world, which has been the death of many good men, and will probably be the death of many more; there is no danger of my being the last of them.

Someone will say, "Are you not ashamed, Socrates, of a course of life which is likely to cause your death?" To him I may fairly answer: There you are mistaken; a man who is good for anything should not calculate the chances of living or dying; he should only consider whether in doing anything he is doing right or wrong—acting the part of a good or a bad man. . . . Wherever a man's place is, whether he has chosen it or has been placed in it by his commander, there he should remain in the hour of danger; he should not think of death or of anything but disgrace. For so it is, men of Athens, in truth.

Strange indeed would be my conduct, men of Athens, if I who, when I was ordered by the generals you chose to command me at Potidaea and Amphipolis and Delium, remained where they placed me, like any other man, facing death, and if now, when I believe the god orders me to fulfill the philosopher's mission of searching into myself and other men, I were to desert my post through fear of death or any other fear. That would indeed be strange, and I might justly be arraigned in court for denying the existence of the gods, if I disobeyed the oracle because I feared death, fancying that I was wise when I was not. For the fear of death is indeed the pretense of wisdom and not real wisdom, being a pretense of knowing the unknown; for no one knows whether death, which men in their fear think is the greatest evil, may not be the greatest good. Is not this ignorance disgraceful, the ignorance which is the conceit that man knows what he does not know? In this respect only I believe I differ from men in general, and may perhaps claim to be wiser than they are—that whereas I know but little of the world below, I do not suppose that I know; but I do know that injustice and disobedience to a better, whether god or man, is evil and dishonorable, and I will never fear or avoid a possible good rather than a certain evil. Therefore if you let me go now, and are not convinced by Anytus, who said that since I had been prosecuted I must be put to death (for otherwise I should never have been prosecuted at all), and that if I escape now, your sons will all be utterly ruined by listening to my words—if you say to me, "Socrates, this time we will not listen to Anytus and we will let you go, but upon one condition, that you do not inquire and speculate in this way any more, and that if you are caught doing so again you will die"—if this was the condition on which you let me go, I would reply: Men of Athens, I honor and love you; but I will obey the god rather than you. And while I have life and strength I will never cease from the practice and teaching of philosophy, exhorting anyone I meet and saying to him in my manner, "You, my friend, a citizen of the great and mighty and wise city of Athens, are you not ashamed of heaping up the greatest amount of money and honor and reputation, and caring so little about wisdom and truth and the greatest improvement of the soul, which you never regard or heed at all?" And if the person with whom I am arguing says, "Yes, but I do care," then I will not leave him or let him go at once, but will interrogate and examine him, and if I think he has no virtue in him, but only says he has, I will reproach him for undervaluing the greater and overvaluing the less. And I will repeat the same words to everyone I meet, young and old, citizen and alien, but especially the citizens, since they are my brothers. For this is the command of the god; and I believe no greater good has ever happened in the state than my service to the god. For I do nothing but go about persuading you all, old and young alike, not to think of your persons or properties, but first and chiefly to care about the greatest improvement of the soul. I tell you that virtue is not given by money, but that from virtue comes money and every other good of man, public as well as private. This is my teaching, and if this is the doctrine which corrupts the youth, I am a mischievous person. But if anyone says this is not my teaching, he is speaking an untruth. Therefore, men of Athens, I say to you, do as Anytus bids or not as Anytus bids, and either acquit me or not; but whichever you do, understand that I will never alter my ways, not even if I have to die many times.

Men of Athens, do not interrupt, but hear me; there was an understanding between us that you would hear me to the end. I have something more to say, at which you may be inclined to cry out; but I believe that to hear me will be good for you, and therefore I beg you not to cry out. I would have you know that if you kill such a one as I am, you will injure yourselves more than me. Nothing will injure me, not Meletus or Anytus—they cannot, for a bad man is not permitted to injure one better than himself. I do not deny that Anytus may perhaps kill me, or drive me into exile, or deprive me of civil rights; and he may imagine, and others may imagine, that he is inflicting a great injury on me; but there I do not agree. For he does himself a much greater injury by doing what he is doing now—unjustly taking away the life of another.

Study Questions

1. What does Socrates mean by saying, "The fear of death is indeed the pretense of wisdom and not real wisdom"?

2. What does he mean by saying that if the Athenians put him to death, they will hurt themselves more than him?

3. It has been speculated by philosophers that Socrates in his heart really wanted to die, and for that reason he said things in his argument for his defense that would irritate the jury of five hundred citizens (who voted guilty with only a small majority); however, newer research points toward Socrates being serious about defending himself. In your opinion, based on this excerpt, should Socrates have argued for his defense in some other way?

4. Socrates has been called a martyr to the principle of seeking the Truth. Could you imagine any principle so important to you that you would be willing to give up your life for it? Alternatively, can you think of any circumstances that to you would override even the most important principle?

Narrative

A Man for All Seasons

ROBERT BOLT (SCREENWRITER)
FRED ZINNEMAN (DIRECTOR)

Film, 1966. Based on a 1960 play by Robert Bolt. Summary.

This film, which won multiple Academy Awards, including best picture, best director, and best actor, portrays a real event in England's history. It is the sixteenth century; Henry VIII is king, and he has a problem: His wife, Catherine, whom the pope gave him dispensation to marry because she was his brother's widow (and as such, a relative), has not borne him any sons, and since he is concerned about the line of succession, he is looking around for another queen. The problem is that since England is Catholic, the king has no legal access to divorce, unless clever lawyers can find a loophole in his marriage. Churchmen, government officials, and legal experts, concerned with their own future, put together a strategy: to declare the marriage annulled on the grounds that the pope had no authority to grant the permission to marry in the first place. However, there is one legal expert who refuses to go along with the scheme: Sir Thomas More, a man whom the king considers a friend. Hoping to win him over, King Henry appoints him chancellor and shows up in person at More's estate on the River Thames to persuade him, but he leaves in anger when it becomes clear that More considers the word of the pope to have a higher authority. Why is it so important for the king to get More on his side, when he has the support of everyone else? Because, as the king himself remarks, More is an honest man who would not choose convenience over his conscience, and receiving More's blessing would make the plan legitimate to the king. But More refuses to budge, even though he knows that incurring the king's wrath can be a dangerous thing; indeed, this is the beginning of the end for More, as his erudite daughter Margaret soon realizes.

When Henry VIII institutes the English Reformation and outlaws Catholicism so he can divorce Catherine and marry his new love, Anne (who herself will be executed to make way for another queen a few years later), More withdraws from his position as chancellor in silence, never uttering a word in public or in private about the king's activities. A brilliant lawyer, More is trying to protect himself and his family by following both his conscience and the law to the letter, believing that his silence will be a shield, but he discovers that his silence does not protect him, as it should according to the law. As the king's man Thomas Cromwell remarks, More is an innocent and does not envision the schemes being prepared by his adversaries. A young man, Richard, who used to be part of the circle around More but believed he could find glory and fortune by attaching himself to Cromwell instead, now serves as an informant on More. But there is truly nothing to report: More is a man of integrity, the only lawyer in London who has not accepted bribes on a regular basis, says More's friend, the Duke of Norfolk. Since More refuses to sign a new oath of allegiance to the king and to accept the new rules of succession

In the 1966 film *A Man for All Seasons* we meet Sir Thomas More (Paul Scofield), a lawyer associated with the court of King Henry VIII. In this true story, More becomes a victim of his own high moral standards: The king wants More's support in annulling his marriage, but More's professional integrity won't allow him to give it. In this scene paralleling Socrates' speech in his own defense (see the *Apology*), More argues for his viewpoint and his life, well knowing that he is already condemned.

according to the Protestant Church of England, he is called in for a hearing, during which his sharp legal mind outwits Cromwell; but from now on he is considered an enemy of the court, and being his friend becomes dangerous. Norfolk tries to persuade him to do as everyone else, do the convenient thing to save himself and his career, but following one's principles is more important to More than life and safety. To save his friend Norfolk from the danger and embarrassment of their friendship, he provokes a quarrel that leaves Norfolk hurt and angry, so that he turns his back on More.

Soon More finds himself a prisoner in the Tower of London, the last stage in the lives of many political prisoners; through several seasons he languishes in the damp cell without being allowed to see his family, under constant pressure from Cromwell to either sign the oath or speak up against it. We see how his posture has deteriorated; his hair is gray, and his face shows the hardship of imprisonment. One day he is surprised and overjoyed to see his family—his wife, Alice, his daughter, and her husband—but when he realizes that they have been ordered to come just to put pressure on him, he understands that he will not be seeing them again and that staying in England will endanger their lives; he makes them promise that they will flee the country, by different routes, on the same day, and very soon.

His daughter asks him why he can't just sign the oath to save himself—speak it with his mouth and speak against it in his heart—and More answers,

> What is an oath, then, but words we say to God? Listen, Meg, when a man takes an oath, he is holding his own self in his own hands, like water—and if he opens his fingers then, he needn't hope to find himself again.

But Margaret is not satisfied; to her, it is not her father's fault if the state is three-quarters bad, and if he elects to suffer for it, then he elects himself a hero. More replies:

> That's very neat. If we lived in a state where virtue was profitable, common sense would make us saints, but since we see that avarice, anger, pride and stupidity commonly profit far beyond charity, modesty, justice and thought, perhaps we must stand fast a little, even at the risk of being heroes.

More knows that his daughter will understand, but his wife, Alice, is tormented by the suffering he is putting her through—she says she is afraid that when he is gone, she is going to hate him for what he has done to them; and, for once, at this moment, Thomas More begins to lose his composure. It means so much to him that his wife understand why he may be going to his death. He begs her to say she does, for without her understanding he might not be able to endure what is going to happen to him. And now she looks at him, embraces him, and tells him she understands that he is a good man and that he must do what his conscience tells him to do. Sad but relieved, he hugs his daughter and his wife one last time.

At last More stands trial; he has often told his family as well as his adversaries that there can be no trial because they have nothing on him; silence can be used only to signify tacit consent and not dissent. But now there is a witness: A man in fancy clothes, a rich and powerful man, approaches the bench. It is Richard, the young man who sold out to Cromwell, More's former friend who now holds a high public office, a position received in return for the perjury he is about to commit. He swears that he has heard More speak his mind, against the king and the new Church of England. Cromwell asks the questions, and his instructions to the jury consist of saying that the jury hardly need deliberate. Thus we know that they, too, must have been "instructed" before the trial. And indeed the verdict is "guilty." Almost deprived of his right to speak, More now rises, a condemned man, and breaks his silence, arguing that he is being executed for not agreeing to the king's divorce, which he certainly was against, because it nullified the authority of the pope. Cromwell decries this as treason; and soon after, on a sunny day in summer, More is executed by beheading.

Study Questions

1. Find similarities between Socrates and Thomas More; are there any significant differences?

2. What does More mean by saying, "When a man takes an oath, he is holding his own self in his own hands, like water—and if he opens his fingers then, he needn't hope to find himself again"?

3. If you were in More's position, what might you have chosen to do? If you had been in the position of More's daughter or wife, would you have understood and accepted his actions? Why or why not?

4. Virtue ethics, as you know, focuses not on what to do but on how to be; the film shows More as a man of honesty and integrity, two very important virtues. But would it be possible to criticize More for having failed the test of the virtues of family loyalty and flexibility? Why or why not? (This question actually reveals one of the problems with virtue ethics: What do we do about conflicting virtues?)

Narrative

The Myth of the Cave

PLATO

Excerpt from The Republic, *fourth century* B.C.E. *Translated by Francis MacDonald Cornford.*

There is no better fictional narrative that illustrates Plato's theory of Forms than the Myth, Fable, or Allegory of the Cave itself. Here you have it in its entirety; the two persons talking are Socrates, telling the story, and Plato's brother Glaucon, listening.

Next, said I, here is a parable to illustrate the degrees in which our nature may be enlightened or unenlightened. Imagine the condition of men living in a sort of cavernous chamber underground, with an entrance open to the light and a long passage all down the cave. Here they have been from childhood, chained by the leg and also by the neck, so that they cannot move and can see only what is in front of them, because the chains will not let them turn their heads. At some distance higher up is the light of a fire burning behind them; and between the prisoners and the fire is a track with a parapet built along it, like the screen at a puppet-show, which hides the performers while they show their puppets over the top.

I see, said he.

Now behind this parapet imagine persons carrying along various artificial objects, including figures of men and animals in wood or stone or other materials, which project above the parapet. Naturally, some of these persons will be talking, others silent.

It is a strange picture, he said, and a strange sort of prisoners.

Like ourselves, I replied; for in the first place prisoners so confined would have seen nothing of themselves or of one another, except the shadows thrown by the fire-light on the wall of the Cave facing them, would they?

Not if all their lives they had been prevented from moving their heads.

And they would have seen as little of the objects carried past.

Of course.

Now, if they could talk to one another, would they not suppose that their words referred only to those passing shadows which they saw?

Necessarily.

And suppose their prison had an echo from the wall facing them? When one of the people crossing behind them spoke, they could only suppose that the sound came from the shadow passing before their eyes.

No doubt.

In every way, then, such prisoners would recognize as reality nothing but the shadows of those artificial objects.

Inevitably.

Now consider what would happen if their release from the chains and the healing of their unwisdom should come about in this way. Suppose one of them was set free and forced suddenly to stand up, turn his head, and walk with eyes lifted to the light; all these movements would be painful, and he would be too dazzled to make out the objects whose shadows he had been used to see. What do you think he would say, if someone told him that what he had formerly seen was meaningless illusion, but now, being somewhat nearer to reality and turned towards more real objects, he was getting a truer view? Suppose further that he were shown the various objects being carried by and were made to say, in reply to questions, what each of them was. Would he not be perplexed and believe the objects now shown him to be not so real as what he formerly saw?

Yes, not nearly so real.

And if he were forced to look at the fire-light itself, would not his eyes ache, so that he would try to escape and turn back to the things which he could see distinctly, convinced that they really were clearer than these other objects now being shown to him?

Yes.

And suppose someone were to drag him away forcibly up the steep and rugged ascent and not let him go until he had hauled him out into the sunlight, would he not suffer pain and vexation at such treatment, and, when he had come out into the light, find his eyes so full of its radiance that he could not see a single one of the things that he was now told were real?

Certainly he would not see them all at once.

He would need, then, to grow accustomed before he could see things in that upper world. At first it would be easiest to make out shadows, and then the images of men and things reflected in water, and later on the things themselves. After that, it would be easier to watch the heavenly bodies and the sky itself by night, looking at the light of the moon and stars rather than the Sun and the Sun's light in the day-time.

Yes, surely.

Last of all, he would be able to look at the Sun and contemplate its nature, not as it appears when reflected in water or any alien medium, but as it is in itself in its own domain.

No doubt.

And now he would begin to draw the conclusion that it is the Sun that produces the seasons and the course of the year and controls everything in the visible world, and moreover is in a way the cause of all that he and his companions used to see.

Clearly he would come at last to that conclusion.

Then if he called to mind his fellow prisoners and what passed for wisdom in his former dwelling-place, he would surely think himself happy in the change and be sorry for them. They may have had a practice of honouring and commending one another, with prizes for the man who had the keenest eye for the passing shadows and the best memory for the order in which they followed or accompanied one another, so that he could make a good guess as to which was going to come next. Would our released prisoner be likely to covet those prizes or to envy the men exalted to honour and power in the Cave? Would he not feel like Homer's Achilles, that he would far sooner "be on earth as a hired servant in the house of a landless man" or endure anything rather than go back to his old beliefs and live in the old way?

Yes, he would prefer any fate to such a life.

Now imagine what would happen if he went down again to take his former seat in the Cave. Coming suddenly out of the sunlight, his eyes would be filled with darkness. He might be required once more to deliver his opinion on those shadows, in competition with the prisoners who had never been released, while his eyesight was still dim and unsteady; and it might take some time to become used to the darkness. They would laugh at him and say that he had gone up only to come back with his sight ruined; it was worth no one's while even to attempt the ascent. If they could lay hands on the man who was trying to set them free and lead them up, they would kill him.

Yes, they would.

Study Questions

1. To recapitulate: This is an allegory of what Plato sees as reality. What does it mean? Who are the prisoners? Where is the cave? What does it mean to see the sun?

2. What did Plato have in mind when he let Socrates speak the final sentences?

3. In what way might this worldview correspond to elements in the worldview of the Christian tradition? Are there significant differences?

4. Can you think of a modern story (film or novel) that speculates about the nature of reality? (Does it ask questions such as, Is reality the way we see it? What are we on this earth for? and Is there life after death?) Does it agree or disagree with Plato's version?

Narrative

The Truman Show

ANDREW NICCOL (SCREENWRITER)
PETER WEIR (DIRECTOR)

Film, 1998. Summary.

This film is one of those stories we can interpret in a number of ways. That it is a satire on the entertainment industry and its mixing of reality and fiction is the easy interpretation, but some also see it as an allegory about the freedom of the human spirit in a world that is overly regulated. It could also be one man's fantasy of being the center of the universe. But in essence *The Truman Show* is about seeking and finding true reality beyond the illusion that presents itself as everyday life, and as such it becomes a story with a Socratic twist, a parallel to Plato's "Myth of the Cave."

Truman (Jim Carey) is on television 24/7, but he doesn't know it. The world is real to him, but everyone else knows it is a soundstage, a world of fakery. The only thing that isn't faked in the show is Truman himself (a *true man,* as opposed to all the other characters in the show) and his emotional reactions. Once he realizes his world is not real, will he try to seek true reality, or be content with illusions and safety? Compare the question asked by Socrates in the Myth of the Cave: What is the philosopher supposed to do once he realizes he has been stuck in a cave of illusions all his life?

Truman Burbank is a young insurance salesman who lives with his wife, a nurse, in the small, pleasant island community of Seahaven, the kind of place where everybody knows everyone else—at least they all know Truman. It's a friendly town, and Truman has never been anywhere else. When he was a boy his father drowned during an outing in their sailboat: Surprised by a storm, Truman's dad fell overboard and disappeared in the waves. This traumatic experience gave Truman a fear of deep water, so the mere thought of going on the ferry to the mainland, or driving across the bridge, makes him anxious. Nevertheless, he has travel dreams: He wants to go to Fiji. As a boy he wanted to be an explorer, but his teacher was quick to tell him that all the places have already been discovered, so why would he want to go anywhere? His best friend since childhood does his best to discourage Truman's longing for exotic places, and Truman's wife points out that they can't afford to just take off, they have obligations and must meet house payments and so on. In fact, everyone seems to be trying to make Truman stay in Seahaven.

When he was in high school, he fell in love with Sylvia, a beautiful, elusive girl who seemed to have something important on her mind, but somehow they were always prevented from seeing each other—until a fateful evening at the library when they were able to sneak out and make a run for it to the beach. But within minutes a vehicle showed up, presumably driven by her father, who snatched Sylvia away from him. She wasn't normal, he said, and shouted that they were moving to Fiji. So we understand that the reason Truman wants to go to Fiji isn't just to see a faraway place—it is to look for Sylvia. Before her father took her away, she tried to convey to Truman that something was wrong—but he didn't understand what she meant.

Now, years later, he is beginning to feel that something *is* wrong. His wife is constantly telling him about new household products with unnatural enthusiasm, as if she is acting in a commercial. In his car on the way to work the radio malfunctions, and he hears a voice describing the route he is taking. He walks into a building on the spur of the moment and tries to enter the elevator, only to find that there is no back wall to the elevator—he can see clear through to a backstage area where people are having lunch. But first and foremost, he has a chance encounter in the street with a homeless person who looks awfully familiar to him. He turns, takes a second look—and realizes that it is Dad, returned from the dead! But at that moment, strangers turn up and whisk the older man away on a bus.

This is the turning point for Truman: Is somebody trying to prevent him from talking to his father? Increasingly, he has the feeling that his entire reality is somehow staged and that people are not what they seem. And as viewers we know that he is right: Everything *is* staged except for Truman and his reactions, because Truman is the hero of *The Truman Show,* a live, twenty-four-hours-a-day television series broadcast to the entire world. That was the secret that Sylvia was trying to tell him but never quite managed to convey.

It is a hugely popular show. Truman has been on TV from the day he was born, without having the slightest idea that his reality isn't normal. And in a way it is "normal"—an idealized normality that doesn't exist for anyone else. His mother is an actor, his wife is an actor, even his best friend whom he has known since childhood—everyone is in on it except Truman. *The Truman Show* is the brainchild of the brilliant director Christoph, who watches over everything on the set high above Seahaven, in a control booth disguised as a perennially visible full moon. The control booth makes the sun rise and set electronically, changes the weather, and cues everyone on the set through earphones. The words of friendship spoken by his best friend are lines fed to the friend by Christoph. In a rare interview the great director is asked why Truman has never questioned his reality, and he answers that we all believe the reality that is presented to us.

But Truman's gullibility is coming to an end: When he realizes that the travel agent has no intention of selling him a ticket to Fiji, he packs his suitcase and heads for the bus depot, and buys a ticket to Chicago. But the bus isn't going anywhere—the bus driver is an actor who can't get the bus started—and Christoph isn't about to let Truman leave. There is nowhere to go; the set is enclosed. But Truman doesn't give up. One night, as the TV crew relaxes because they think he is asleep, what they're really watching is a dummy under a blanket, with a tape recorder producing snoring sounds. Truman has sneaked out. For the first time in his life he is not on camera.

Christoph mobilizes the entire island: All the actors are now engaged in looking for Truman, but he is nowhere to be found—until they think to look for him in the unthinkable place: on the water, in a sailboat, headed for—Fiji? All over the world, viewers watch with bated breath. Will Truman succeed in his quest? Will he escape his confining, designed world? Even Sylvia is watching, praying that Truman will make it. Christoph does what he can to thwart Truman, even ordering his reluctant engineers to whip up a nearly fatal storm. In spite of his deep-seated fear of water, Truman hangs in there and outlasts Christoph's rage. He continues on his way toward the horizon—which comes up sooner than expected: All of a sudden the bow of his boat goes right through the sky, a beautifully painted backdrop. He has been sailing around in a huge tank on the soundstage.

Immediately ahead is a flight of stairs, leading up to a door. Truman steps off the boat, walks to the stairs along the edge of the world, and ascends to the door. And now Christoph, desperate, addresses him over the speaker system, a disembodied loving voice coming from above. He tells Truman about how long he has been observing him as a boy and a young man, all the kinds of experiences a parent would remember— and how well he knows him and his fears. Nothing bad can ever happen to him in Seahaven—the real world is a dangerous place. The door is open to the dark, mysterious real world. Is Truman going to go through it and disappear? Or will he act true to his conditioning and go back?

Study Questions

1. What are the similarities between Plato's "Myth of the Cave" and *The Truman Show,* and what are the differences? In Plato's myth the perfect world is outside the cave. Where is it in the film? You may also want to explore the concept of one person being deluded versus humanity as such being deluded. Is this exclusively Truman's story, or are we all "Trumans," stuck on the soundstage as in Plato's cave?

2. What is the significance of Truman's first name? What does it mean in the context of the story?

3. If you could choose, would you rather have a pleasant life based on a lie, or a difficult, unpredictable life founded on a true perception of the world?

Narrative

Shrek

TED ELLIOTT (SCREENWRITER)
ANDREW ADAMSON AND VICKY JENSON (DIRECTORS)

Film, 2001. Based on the book by William Steig. Summary.

To put a green ogre in the company of Socrates and Plato may seem sacrilegious to some, but as it happens, the film *Shrek* nicely illustrates one of the key lessons of Socrates: that you can't judge something by its appearance. Socrates himself was by no means a handsome man, according to the Greek ideal of beauty in his own day, but we have all learned to see the beauty of Socrates as something internal rather than external. And here comes Shrek, who teaches the same lesson to children and adults, many of whom will never get

Throughout Plato's *Dialogues* Socrates emphasizes that we shouldn't judge anything by its appearance—that we must look for the inner essence of things. This is, of course, a timeless lesson that can be taught in different ways to each new generation. In the *Shrek* films we learn that we shouldn't judge an Ogre by his frightening looks or bad reputation—or a beautiful princess by her daytime appearance—because beauty can be an inner quality. Here Fiona and Shrek are feeling a mutual attraction, even if Shrek at this point doesn't know Fiona's secret: that she, too, is part Ogre.

anywhere near a textbook featuring Socrates, let alone Plato's *Dialogues*. Contrary to most of the story summaries in this book, I have to reveal certain aspects of the ending, because otherwise the Socratic lesson isn't clear, and I apologize if I've revealed more than you'd like to know!

Down in the swamp lives an ogre, a great green monster; the countryside is terrified of him because he is mean and, above all, antisocial. As we get to know Shrek (whose name in German, *Schrek,* means *terror*), we come to understand that his seclusion isn't just because he wants it that way—he is convinced that because of his meanness and ugliness nobody will want to hang out with him. He needs no one, and nobody needs him. But fate has a job for Shrek: rescuing the Princess Fiona from her captivity in the tower guarded by the dragon so that she can marry her Prince Charming. The fairy tale demands that the prince himself rescue her, but he is a bit too comfortable and fastidious, so through blackmail, threatening to destroy Shrek's home in the swamp, he hires Shrek to be the knight in shining armor, by proxy. But no knight is complete without a squire, and an unlikely one presents himself: the talking donkey, Donkey. Now Donkey wants desperately to spend time with his new friend Shrek (he fantasizes about spending the night and making waffles in the morning), because he is even more lonely than the ogre, but Shrek is not interested.

Outsmarting the dragon, Shrek rescues the princess, who is as beautiful as her legend has foretold. But she is an impatient, haughty woman and can't quite believe that her Prince Charming has sent someone in his place—that just isn't done. She's supposed to love her rescuer, and he is not supposed to be working for someone else.

Together, the three make their way back to Prince Charming's kingdom, and on the journey we get to know the princess better. She and Shrek are developing a mutual liking for each other, and in a private moment, as the sun sets, we learn her secret: During the daytime she is a human beauty, but at night she is transformed into the shape of— an ogre, a chubby green woman. The transformation from one to the other is a punishment her parents tried to hide by placing her in the tower, and now she has to hide from her rescuers until she meets the prince because, as legend has it, love's first kiss will transform her into her true shape. Shrek has no inkling of her dual nature—but Donkey sneaks a peek and learns her dark secret. Now you'd think that if Fiona is a part-time ogre, she and Shrek could find common ground. Not so, because Shrek overhears her bemoan her ugliness and thinks she's talking about him. So for the rest of the journey they are alienated.

When Fiona is introduced to the prince, she is terribly disappointed—Prince Charming is a conceited little man with grandiose notions of himself. But she's convinced that he is her Prince Charming, and she will find rescue and redemption through him, so she follows him to the castle and engages in wedding preparations. Shrek goes home and sulks—and has to face an additional problem, because his swamp has been taken over by squatters, other fairy-tale beings who have been evicted from their traditional homes by the prince.

But it wouldn't be a fairy tale if it didn't have a happy ending: Shrek realizes that he can't just stand by and watch her get married, and she realizes that she has already met her true love, and it's not Prince Charming—it's Shrek. So Shrek invades the wedding and kisses her at the altar. Love's first kiss—which will transform her into her true form! And the transformation happens, miraculously. Before us stand—two ogres. Her true shape is the shape of the ogre, the dimply, chubby, sweet green woman, perfectly suited for Shrek, if you believe that couples have to be of the same physical type . . . and they have a wedding party, and everybody lives happily until the sequel. And even Donkey finds love— because the dragon, who is female, has fallen in love with him.

Now why is this a Socratic story? Shrek's true nature can't be gleaned from his threatening appearance—he is the Beast to Fiona's Beauty. But Fiona herself has a true nature that is hidden under her beauty, and it may be an ogrish nature, but she is neither threatening nor beastly. Her true nature lends understanding and grace to Shrek himself, and we learn that both of them have a sweetness that is on the inside, rather than the outside. It is the inner truth that counts, not the world of appearances.

Study Questions

1. Find other stories with a similar message: It is the inner beauty and truth that count, not the external appearance. Evaluate the message: Is it always true? Why or why not?

2. Fiona is transformed from a slim, haughty beauty to a chubby, lovable ogress. Does this transformation contain an underlying discrimination against overweight people, or does it work in the opposite direction—an acceptance of people for their inner worth, regardless of their shape?

3. If you have seen *Shrek 2* (2004) and *Shrek the Third* (2007), you may want to weigh in on the further story: Is it still a Socratic journey to find the inner truth, or has the theme changed? *Shrek 2*'s theme is, above all, the choices we make for love. What might love's choices have to do with seeing the inner truth?

Chapter Nine

Aristotle's Virtue Theory: Everything in Moderation

*A*fter Plato's death in 347 B.C.E., leadership of the Academy fell to his nephew Speusippus. History believes that another man had expected to take over, and with good reason, for he was by far the best student ever to be associated with the Academy. That man was Aristotle, who had studied for twenty years with Plato. Scholars now think that because of the amount of traveling Plato did, Aristotle may never have been especially close to his teacher; it seems certain that the closeness between Socrates and Plato was never repeated between Plato and Aristotle.

Because Aristotle was not a native-born Athenian but was born in Stagira in northern Greece (in 384 B.C.E.), he did not have the rights of Athenians and had no recourse when he was not chosen as the new leader of the school. He left Athens, presumably in anger. He traveled to Asia Minor, got married, and began his studies in biology. In 343 he went to Macedonia, where he became a tutor for the young prince, the son of King Philip. (In three short years, that boy would become the regent of Macedonia and later of an immense realm covering most of the classical world. He would come to be known as Alexander the Great.) Exactly what Aristotle's status was at court is a matter of speculation—some scholars think that his tutoring of Alexander was actually a minor job compared with the real purpose of his stay, which may have been completely political: King Philip hoped to get Aristotle elected as head of Plato's Academy even if he'd already been passed over for Plato's nephew Speusippus, because Speusippus was anti-Macedonian, and Philip apparently had expansionist ambitions and needed a pro-Macedonian leader of the most powerful school in the Greek culture. But when Speusippus died, Aristotle was passed over a second time, and King Philip focused on going to war with Athens instead. So Aristotle packed up and left for his home in Stagira, but his connection with the Macedonian court was by no means over: When Philip died suddenly, and Alexander became king, Alexander found use for his old teacher and sent him to Athens in 335 to open up a school of his own, in competition with Plato's school. There is some speculation that even at that point, Aristotle had hoped to become leader of the Academy, for he traveled to Athens with a huge amount of teaching material and an entire staff to run the school, but it never happened. Instead, Aristotle started teaching at the site of the public horse track, known as the Lyceum after Apollo Lykeion, and for twelve years—not a particularly long span, as academic careers go—he taught students and wrote books about issues that were of interest to him in philosophy, science, and what we today would call social and political science.

Empirical Knowledge and the Realm of the Senses

Making claims about someone's influence on history can be a risky business because such claims tend to be exaggerated. In Aristotle's case, however, it is quite safe to say that he is one of the persons in antiquity who has had the most influence on Western thinking and that even in modern times few people have rivaled his overall histori- cal importance. As Plato left his legacy in Western philosophy and theology, Aristotle opened up the possibility of scientific, logical, empirical thinking—in philosophy as well as in the natural sciences.

It is no wonder that Plato made no contribution in that area. He wouldn't have been interested in natural science, because its object is the world of the senses, far removed from the Forms. Although Aristotle was a student of Plato and did believe in the general reality of Plato's Forms, he believed that Forms are *not* separate from material things; as a matter of fact, Aristotle believed the Forms have no existence outside their objects. If we're enjoying the view of a waterfall cascading off a cliff face, we are at the same time, Aristotle believed, directly experiencing the Forms of cliff, of waterfall, and of falling. If we're in love with someone and think the person is beautiful, we are experiencing the Form of beauty right there in the person's face. And if we are studying a tree or a fossil, the Form that gives us knowledge about the history of that tree or fossil is right there. In other words, knowledge can be sought and found directly from the world of the senses. From the previous chapter, you may remember Socrates' remark in *Phaedrus* that he never ventured outside the city because trees and countryside could not teach him anything—in contrast, Aristotle would most definitely look to those trees for knowledge.

This turn in Aristotle's thinking—from Forms being separate to being insepara- ble from the thing or the experience—is what made it possible for him to think in terms of empirical research (gathering evidence, making hypotheses, and testing the- ories on the basis of experience). Legend holds that Alexander the Great, on his exploits deep into Persia and Afghanistan, had samples of flora and fauna collected and sent to his old teacher. Aristotle would have been delighted to receive such sam- ples and would have studied them carefully, because he believed in the possibility of empirical knowledge.

Aristotle the Scientist

Aristotle was instrumental in founding the sciences—not the exact disciplines as we know them today, but sciences in the sense that the concepts of *logic* and *observation* were combined. The extent of his influence, however, goes beyond that. It is hard for us to imagine that there was an era when a human being actually could "know every- thing," in the sense of having access to all available knowledge at the time, and yet it seems that Aristotle was such a person. He was the author of what we know as clas- sical logic; he laid the foundations of the classifications in biology; he developed theories of astronomy; he was interested in politics, rhetoric (the art of verbal persua- sion), and drama; he wrote books on the proper structure of tragedy and of comedy; he developed theories of the nature of the soul, of God, and of other metaphysical

Aristotle (384–322 B.C.E.), Greek philosopher and naturalist, here shown teaching the young Alexander. If one were to pick one scholar as the most influential in Western cultural history, it would have to be Aristotle. Not only did he leave influential writings in a multitude of fields such as biology, metaphysics, logic, ethics, drama, and politics, he also introduced the concept of empirical science to the ancient world. It is said about Aristotle that he knew everything there was to know at the time, and that may well be an accurate description.

questions. Indeed, the term *metaphysics* derives from Aristotle: He supposedly wrote a book on physics and then another book without a title about the nature of reality. Because it came after the book on physics, his followers called it the "book after physics," *ta meta ta physica.*

His book about ethics may prove to have the most enduring influence of them all. But he also wrote about the justification of slavery and the nature of woman as a lower being. Aristotle thus presents ideas in his writings that are deeply offensive to

During the Renaissance, Raphael painted this vision of Plato's Academy, titled *The School of Athens*—not a true representation of daily life in the school but, rather, a highly symbolic image of two schools of thought. Two figures are approaching the steps in the center: Plato and Aristotle. Plato, the older man, is on the left. On the left side of the painting are some of Plato's students; but most are historical figures, including some from Raphael's own day, who have subscribed to the Platonic way of thought. Plato is pointing upward to the world of Forms, his image of true reality, whereas the younger man next to him, Aristotle, is stretching out his hand toward us, palm downward. He seems to say that it is in this world we can find true knowledge, not in any intellectual realm removed from the senses. On the right we find the Aristotelians of history, the scientists. And on the far right, Raphael has chosen to place himself, peeking straight out at us.

most modern Western readers, but philosophers usually choose to read his more controversial writings as historical documents rather than as blueprints for how to live our lives. In many ways Aristotle was not what we call a critical thinker; indeed, Socrates would not necessarily have approved of him, for he often refrains from analyzing a viewpoint (such as the status and nature of women) but, rather, limits himself to mentioning it. He seems to assume that some things are obvious; most people who lived during his time probably agreed with him.

A great many of Aristotle's writings are lost to us. Aristotle, like Plato, wrote dialogues, and the Roman orator Cicero held them in high regard, but only some fragments

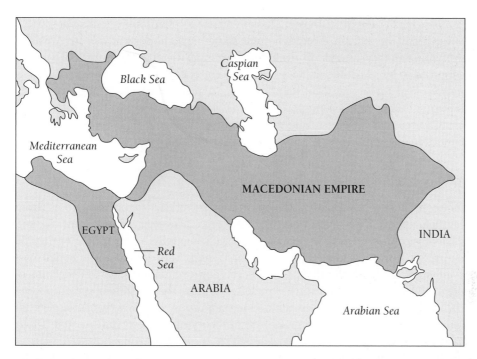

The realm conquered by Alexander the Great (356–323 B.C.E.) was immense by the standards of the time period and even of today; however, it was short-lived. On Alexander's death his generals divided the spoils and had to deal with local insurrections. Nevertheless, the memory of Alexander was kept alive in cultures as far apart as Egypt and northern India; in the mountainous reaches of Afghanistan, Pakistan, and northern India the name "Sikander" (Alexander) became a legend: For example, the Afghan city of Kandahar, which figured in the U.S. war on terrorism, is named after Alexander. In Egypt a dynasty was founded by his general Ptolemy, and a city was named after him that centuries later would become the new center of civilization, the city of Alexandria.

remain. For the most part, they're lecture notes and course summaries that he used in his classes; some were written for general audiences and some for more advanced students. Some of the works are supplemented by notes taken by his students.

Aristotle's Virtue Theory: Teleology and the Golden Mean

Virtue and Excellence

In the first part of Chapter 8, we saw that the Greek conception of virtue was slightly different from our colloquial use of the word. Although calling someone virtuous may for some imply a certain amount of contempt, no such meaning was implied by the ancient Greeks. If you were virtuous, you would not be considered dull or withdrawn from life, because being virtuous meant, above all, that you managed your skills and your opportunities well. To be virtuous meant to act with *excellence*—we might even say with *virtuosity,* because this term retains some of what the Greeks associated with virtue.

Nowhere is that more apparent than in Aristotle's philosophy: You might say that virtue lies in the difference between doing something and doing it well. To Aristotle, everything on this earth has its own virtue, meaning that if it "performs" the way it is supposed to by its nature, then it is virtuous. For one thing, this means that virtue is not reserved for humans; for another thing, it means that everything that exists, including humans, has a purpose. There is virtue to a sharp knife, a comfortable chair, a tree that grows straight, and a healthy, swift animal. For young, growing entities such as saplings and babies, one might talk about *potential virtue*.

Teleology: The Concept of Purpose

One concept that is essential for understanding Aristotle's ideas on virtue comes from his metaphysics: the concept of *teleology*. In Greek, *telos* means goal or purpose, and a teleological theory or viewpoint assumes that something has a purpose or that the end result of some action is all-important. Examples of teleological theories exist even today; we encounter them often in everyday discussions about "the meaning of life." Modern science, however, has preferred to leave the question of the purpose of the universe behind. Plato also believed in the purpose of things, but Aristotle built his teleology into a complete metaphysical theory of "causes." (For Aristotle's four causes, see Box 9.1.)

For Aristotle, everything that exists has a purpose, built into the fabric of reality from the very beginning. The idea of a purpose seems reasonable when we look at manufactured objects, because those objects must surely have started with an idea, a purpose, in the mind of their maker. To him, the universe was initially created by a great mind—but this "designer" had no further influence on its creation. If a cutler makes a knife, its purpose is to cut well, not just to make a dent. When you bake muffins you intend them to be edible, whether they turn out that way or not. But can't we have human actions without a purpose? Aristotle would say no, especially if we are creating an object; its purpose is a given thing.

What about nature-made objects? Does a tree have a purpose? Does a wolf? an ant? a river? Today we would hesitate before saying yes, because after all, who are we to make such assumptions? If we say the purpose of a tree is to give us shade, or apples, we are assuming that it is here for us humans and not just for its own sake in the order of things. Even if we say the wolf's purpose is to cull the herd of caribou, we hesitate to say that someone "designed" it that way, with purpose. Today, if we tend to use the term *purpose* or *function* to describe how things work in nature, we should probably remind ourselves once in a while that, scientifically, we are referring to how things work within the ecosystem, without implying that there is an underlying designed purpose to nature. (Aristotle himself was not particularly interested in the relations between things in nature, such as an ecosystem, but was more concerned with the separate characteristics of natural phenomena.) There may well be such a purpose, as well as a designer, but scientists today generally believe that such assumptions, sometimes referred to as Intelligent Designs, fall outside the scope of science. Few scientists, regardless of how they feel privately, would willingly mix up religious opinions and professional theories. Aristotle, however, had no such

Box 9.1   THE FOUR CAUSES

For Aristotle every event has four causes, or four factors that work on it and bring it into being. These are the *material cause,* or the "stuff" the thing is made of; the *efficient cause,* the force that has brought it into being; the *formal cause,* the shape or idea (the Form) of the thing; and the *final cause,* the purpose of the thing. Consider this illustration (for which I give credit to one of my students):

- Material cause: flour, water, and so on
- Efficient cause: me, the baker
- Formal cause: the idea of muffins
- Final cause: to be eaten!

The material cause and the efficient cause are fairly straightforward from a modern point of view: We have a general idea what Aristotle means when he says the material cause of a thing is the actual physical material that makes it what it is. But what about the efficient creative force? For a muffin, the creative force is the baker; for a wolf, it would be the wolf's parents; for a river, it would be mountain springs and precipitation. (Later religious traditions inspired by Aristotle have chosen to read God as the creative, efficient force.) But the formal and final causes are less intuitive. In the formal cause we see the last surviving element of Plato's theory of Forms in Aristotle's philosophy, but the Form is not outside the object in some intellectual realm; it is right there in the object itself. (Consider the painting by Raphael on p. 434: Aristotle is pointing downward, almost as if saying, "*This world* is where you find true reality.") A successful muffin displays the perfect Form of muffin, whereas a misshapen muffin is only a weak representation of the muffin Form.

For Aristotle, the final cause was by far the most important cause from a philosophical point of view, because it allows us to understand the purpose of a thing—in other words, its essential qualities and nature. We do not understand the nature of a thing—natural or manufactured—until we understand its purpose. It follows that Aristotle believed everything has a purpose given to it by nature; if the object realizes its potential, it has fulfilled its purpose and is a success. A sharp knife, a fast rabbit, and a smart human being would be examples of potential purpose actualized because each has become what it was supposed to be.

compunction about making statements that reflected anthropocentrism (the view that everything happens for the sake of humans) or speculations about the general structure of the universe (for he believed he understood it). For Aristotle, everything in nature does have a purpose, although it may not be easy to determine just what that purpose is. How *do* we go about determining what the purpose is? We investigate what the thing in question *does best.* Whatever that is will be the special characteristic of that thing. If the thing performs its purpose or function well, then it is *virtuous.*

The Human Purpose

For Aristotle, there is no question that a specifically human purpose in life exists. Each limb and organ of the body has a purpose, he says—the eye for seeing, the hands for grasping—so we must conclude that the person, as a whole, has a purpose above and beyond the sum of the body parts. (For Aristotle, that was an obvious conclusion; today we are not so quick to conclude anything about purposes. See Box 9.2.)

Box 9.2   TELEOLOGICAL EXPLANATIONS

We use teleological explanations quite often even today, although generally they are not acceptable as a scientific form of explanation. If we were to explain why giraffes have long necks, we might say something like "So they can reach tall branches." Saying "so they can" implies that somehow giraffes are designed for that purpose or else that they have stretched and stretched over the ages until they can finally reach those branches. (Such a theory of evolution was proposed in the nineteenth century, before Charles Darwin. Its proponent was Jean Lamarck, and the theory is referred to as "inheritance of acquired characteristics.") Even though we all know that giraffes do eat leaves off tall branches, it would not suit modern science to assume that that is their *purpose*. Darwin, with his theory of *natural selection*, proposed a new point of view: that giraffes don't come equipped with a purpose, nor does any other creature, but we all adapt to circumstances, and those who adapt the best survive and have offspring. We therefore must imagine the ancestors of giraffes as being rather short-necked, with some born with longer necks as a result of mutation. Because the ones with long necks could reach the leaves that the others couldn't reach, they were successful during times of hardship when many of the others perished. They gave birth to long-necked offspring, who gave birth to offspring with even longer necks, and so on. This is a *causal explanation;* it looks to reasons in the past to explain why something is the way it is today, instead of looking toward some future goal.

The idea that humans are born for a reason and with a purpose is irresistible even to many modern minds. We ask ourselves, "What is the reason for my being here on this earth?" "Why was I born?" We hope to find some answer in the future—some great deed we will do, a work of art we will create, the children we plan to raise, the influence we will exert on our profession, or the money and fame we plan to acquire. Some believe their greatest moment has come and gone, like an astronaut who has been on the moon—how do you top that? Such people may spend the rest of their lives searching for a new purpose.

Our belief in destiny, in one form or another, influences our perception of the purpose of our lives. But that is only half of Aristotle's concept of *telos*, because it applies only on a *personal* level. Aristotle is talking not only about the person becoming what he or she is supposed to become but also about the human being *as such* becoming what human beings are supposed to become. In other words, Aristotle believed not only that a telos exists for an individual but also that it exists for a species. How do we know what the purpose of an individual as a member of a species is? We investigate what that creature or thing does best—perhaps better than any other creature or thing. The purpose of a bird must involve flying, although there are flightless birds. The purpose of a knife must involve cutting, although there are movie prop knives that don't cut a thing. The purpose of a rock? To do whatever it does best: lie there. (That is true Aristotle, not a joke.) And the purpose of a human? To *reason*. We can't evaluate a person without taking into consideration the greater purpose of being human, which is to *reason well:*

Now if the function of man is an activity of soul which follows or implies a rational principle . . . [and we state the function of man to be a certain kind of life, and this to be an
activity or actions of the soul implying a rational principle . . . and if any action is well
performed when it is performed in accordance with the appropriate excellence: if this is
the case,] human good turns out to be activity of soul in accordance with virtue, and if
there are more than one virtue, in accordance with the best and most complete.

But we must add "in a complete life." For one swallow does not make a summer, nor
does one day; and so too one day, or a short time, does not make a man blessed or happy.

Scholars are usually generous here in labeling reasoning the purpose of *humans*—
for in Aristotle's terminology it is the "purpose of *man*." As we go deeper into Aristotle's
works, it becomes apparent that he is not using the word inclusively, to cover males
and females, as was to become the intellectual habit in the eighteenth, nineteenth, and
most of the twentieth centuries: He means *males*. For Aristotle, men are the creatures
who have the true capacity for reasoning; women have their own purpose (such as
childbearing) and their own virtues. That may seem controversial enough to a modern reader who believes that men and women should have access to the same social
opportunities, but the controversy doesn't end there: Aristotle has become nothing
short of notorious for proclaiming not only that men and women are fundamentally
different but also that, in his own words from his text *The Generation of Animals,* "the
female is, as it were, a deformed male." Man is the default gender for Aristotle, because
he sees the male as the perfect human being, and since women aren't male, they are less
perfect. In a nutshell: Men produce semen, and women don't. Aristotle believed that
semen was blood transformed, with the added element of *soul* or essence. It was thus
the father who gave the soul to the baby; the mother "only" provided the physical part,
the body. (Here it is interesting to recall that Aristotle believed himself to have a considerable amount of knowledge about the human body, probably because he came
from a family of physicians. In all fairness, it would have been impossible for him to
know that, biologically, the situation is, in fact, reversed: The early human fetus is, by
default, *female,* and if it has a Y chromosome, the male characteristics will develop
later in the pregnancy.) In believing woman to be a creature fundamentally different
from man, Aristotle seems to have joined forces with the public opinion of the times,
although not with the opinion of his own teacher, Plato, who believed that the role of
women depended on what they were well suited for, individually. (See Box 9.3 for
what others have said about the human purpose.)

The purpose for man, Aristotle would say, is to think rationally, on a regular
basis, throughout his life, as a matter of habit—in other words, to develop a rational
character. And that, according to Aristotle, is the same as *moral goodness.*

For modern thinkers this is a surprising twist: that moral goodness can be linked
with being good *at something* rather than just being good, period. Moral goodness
seems for us to have more to do with not causing harm, with keeping promises, with
upholding the values of our culture, and so on. For Aristotle, though, there is no difference between fulfilling one's purpose, being virtuous, doing something with
excellence, and being morally good. It all has to do with his theory of *how* one goes
about being virtuous.

Box 9.3   IS THERE A HUMAN PURPOSE?

Aristotle inspired an entire school of thought long after he was dead. The Catholic Church came upon his writings some fifteen hundred years after his death, and Saint Thomas Aquinas incorporated several of Aristotle's ideas into his Christian philosophy in the thirteenth century, including the idea that humans have a purpose. For Aquinas, that purpose included life, procreation, and the pursuit of knowledge of God. Other thinkers are not so certain that humans have a purpose; Jean-Paul Sartre (1905–1980) believed there is no such thing as human nature and that anyone who says there is is only looking for an identity to hide behind so that he or she won't have to make difficult choices (see Chapter 10).

Aristotle recognizes two forms of virtue, *intellectual* and *moral*. When our soul is trying to control our desires, we engage our moral virtues. But when our soul concentrates on intellectual and spiritual matters, we engage our intellectual virtues: When we think about objects of this world that are subject to change and try to make appropriate decisions, we engage our practical wisdom, our *phronesis*. But when we think about higher matters—the eternal questions of philosophy—we use our theoretical wisdom, our *sophia* (*philosophy* is a combination of *philo* = "love of" and *sophia* = "wisdom"). One may excel in other virtues, but the highest virtue of them all is *sophia,* actualizing the uniquely human potential for abstract thought. So the intellectual virtues involve being able to learn well, think straight, and act accordingly. The moral virtues also involve the use of the intellect, because the only way humans can strive for perfection is to engage their intellect in developing a keen sense of the needs of the moment.

The Golden Mean

Ancient Greece gave us the concept of moderation, or the "Golden Mean." Over the entrance to the temple of Apollo at Delphi were inscribed "Know Thyself" (*gnothi seauton*) and "Nothing in Excess" (*meden agan*). Socrates incorporated the idea of moderation in his teachings, as did several other thinkers, but above all it is at the heart of Aristotle's idea of virtue: an action or a feeling responding to a particular situation at the right time, in the right way, in the right amount, for the right reason—not too much and not too little. By using the Golden Mean, Aristotle believes he describes the "good for man"—where a human can excel, what a human is meant to do, and where a human will find happiness. We will return to the subject of happiness shortly.

In his *Nicomachean Ethics,* named for his son Nichomachus, Aristotle compares the Golden Mean to an artistic masterpiece; people recognize that you can't add anything to it or take anything from it, because either excess (too much) or deficiency (too little) would destroy the masterpiece. The mean, however, preserves it. That may remind some readers of a joke among artists: "How many artists does it take to make a great painting? Two—one to paint it, and the other to hit the painter over the head when the painting is done." Why the bash on the head? Because there comes a time, if the work is good enough, when more paint would be too much, and sometimes the artist doesn't recognize that moment. Aristotle would reply that the *virtuous* artist will know that moment—indeed, that is precisely what constitutes a great artist. If that is the case for art, then it must apply to moral goodness: We are morally good if we are capable of choosing the proper response to every situation in life, not too much and not too little:

> Virtue, then, is a state of character concerned with choice, lying in a mean, i.e., the mean relative to us, this being determined by a rational principle by which the man of practical wisdom would determine it. Now it is a mean between two vices, that which depends on excess and that which depends on defect; and again it is a mean because the vices respectively fall short of or exceed what is right in both passions and actions, while virtue finds and chooses that which is intermediate.

Aristotle tells us that every action or feeling must be done in the right amount. In many ways this is quite modern and a very down-to-earth approach to our daily problems. We all have to make big and little decisions every day: How much gratitude should I show when someone does a favor for me or gives me a present I didn't expect? How much is the right amount of curiosity to express about my friend's personal life? (I don't want to appear to be snooping, and I don't want to appear cold either.) How much should I study for my final? (I know when I've studied too little, but what exactly is studying too much?) How long should I leave the roast in the oven for it to be done to perfection when the kids like it gray and my spouse likes it bloody? How much love should I feel, and show, in a new relationship? We face those types of problems every day, and we rarely find good answers to them. In that sense Aristotle shows a feeling for what we might call the "human condition," common human concerns that remain the same throughout the ages. Very few philosophers have done as much as he to try to give people some actual advice about such mundane matters. Thus, even though Aristotle's ideas derive from an ancient, alien world of slavery and other policies that are unacceptable to us today, there are features of his works that make his writings relevant for modern times and modern people. At the end of the chapter you'll find two excerpts from Aristotle's *Nicomachean Ethics,* in which he explores the Golden Mean as well as the virtue of courage.

Does Aristotle actually tell us what to do? Not really. He warns us that we each are prone to go toward one extreme or the other and that we must beware of such tendencies, but the only help we can find on the road to virtue is the idea that we must try and try again.

There are three questions one might want to ask. The first is, If this is supposed to be a theory of *character,* why does it seem to talk about actions and conduct and what to *do?* The answer is that for Aristotle, this *is* a question of character because he is not so much interested in our response to singular situations as he is in our response in general. If we perform a considerate or courageous act only once, he would not call us considerate or courageous; the act must be done on a regular basis, as an expression of the kind of person we strive to be. In other words, we have to acquire some good habits. That means we can't hope to be virtuous overnight—it takes time to mold ourselves into morally good people, just as it takes time to learn to play a musical instrument well. The second question one might ask is, What does this have to do with the specific human virtue of rational thinking? The answer lies

An application of Aristotle's theory of virtue: Three women on a bridge see a drowning child being swept along by the waters. One woman is rash and jumps in without looking; the other is too cautious and frets so much that the time for action is past. But the third one reacts "just right": She has developed a courageous character; she chooses an appropriate action and acts at the right time to save the child. (See Box 9.4.)

in the fact that the way we find out what the mean is in every situation is through reasoning, and the more times we have done it and acted correctly as a result, the better we can build up the habit of responding correctly. Now let's ask the third question: Does this mean we are supposed to do *everything* in the right amount, not too much and not too little? It is easy to imagine eating in the right amount and exercising in the right amount, but what about acts like stealing? lying? or committing murder? Must we conclude that we can steal and lie and murder too much but also too little? that we will be virtuous if we steal, lie, and murder in the right amount? Hardly, and Aristotle was aware of this loophole; he tells us that some acts are just wrong by themselves and cannot be done in the right amount. Similarly, some acts are right in themselves and cannot be done too often. One such thing is justice: You can't be "too just," because being just already means being as fair as you can be.

How exactly do we find the mean? After all, it is not an absolute mean; we cannot identify the exact midpoint between the extremes the way we would measure the exact number of calories allowed in a diet. It is far more complex than that, and Aristotle warns us that there are many ways to go wrong but only one way to "hit the bull's-eye" in each situation. It takes a full commitment, involving the entire personality, over a lifetime of training. In his lectures Aristotle appears to have covered a wide variety of virtues. Let us look at a few of them.

Box 9.4 THE RIGHT DECISION AT THE RIGHT TIME

Imagine three women on a bridge: Heidi, Jill, and Jessica. Below them a dark river is rushing along, sweeping a little boy toward them, carrying him to certain doom. Heidi looks down at the swirling water and imagines all the things that could go wrong if she were to attempt a rescue: the submerged rocks, how heavy her shoes and jeans will get if she jumps in, the fact that she just got over a bad cold, and the fact that she doesn't swim well. Besides, she remembers, she has to make it to the library before closing time. While she has been doing all this thinking, Jill has already jumped in the river to save the boy. She jumped without thinking, however, and hit her head on one of the submerged rocks and knocked herself out. Jessica sees the boy, and as fast as lightning she calculates the swiftness of the river, the position of the rocks, her own swimming prowess—and she runs down the little staircase to the riverbed, throws in the life preserver that is hanging on the wall, saves the boy, and pulls ashore the unconscious Jill for good measure. Or maybe she sheds her shoes and jumps in and saves the boy. Or shouts to some men who are out fishing and asks them to give her a hand. The main thing is that she *thinks,* and then *acts,* at the right time, in the proper amount. That is courage to Aristotle. Jill acted rashly. Heidi may have had the right intentions, but she did not act on them. You must act on your intentions and succeed in order to be called virtuous.

But what if some time in the future, by some odd coincidence, Heidi finds herself in the same situation again? A bridge, a drowning child—or some other situation where she might be in a position to help by making the right split-second decision. Her previous failure might help her do better this time around. Aristotle believes we become virtuous through doing virtuous acts; and, if Heidi has learned anything from watching Jessica, then she, too, might do the right thing this time. (But she has to remember that no two situations are exactly alike. In another situation acting exactly as Jessica did could be to act either rashly or too timidly.) Similarly, Jill might have learned from the situation; next time around she might be too timid, but eventually she, too, might get it right. Now Jessica: Can we rely on her to always make the right choice from now on? Most of us would not have such lofty expectations and would forgive her for a future mistake, but for Aristotle it was clear: When you have ascended to the level of a virtuous person, then your future actions will generally also be virtuous, because you have developed virtuous habits. One brave deed does not make a person brave (as one swallow does not make a summer). If Jessica slips and makes a wrong judgment call, then she is not so virtuous after all.

If someone is in danger, that person can react in three ways: with too little courage (in which case he is a coward), with the right amount of courage, or with too much courage (in which case he is being foolhardy). Courage was for Aristotle a very important virtue, and you'll find his analysis of courage in the Primary Readings. Box 9.4 applies the virtue of courage as well as the vices of cowardice and foolhardiness to a specific situation, and two stories in the Narratives section focus on courage as a virtue: the ancient Icelandic *Njal's Saga* and the film based on Joseph Conrad's novel *Lord Jim*. In addition, the theme of courage is explored as a contemporary virtue in Chapter 11.

Box 9.5   THE CLASH BETWEEN CLASSICAL
AND CHRISTIAN VIRTUES

For a modern Western person, the idea that it is legitimate to take pride in an accomplishment is not strange; we understand why Aristotle says we should not humiliate ourselves by making ourselves less than we are. But his idea that we have a right to feel proud about things that aren't our own doing, such as being born of a certain class and race, is more problematic. To the traditional Christian mind, in fact, the entire idea of legitimate pride is a grave misconception. As much as Aristotle became an inspiration to medieval Christianity, there is a marked discrepancy between most of Aristotle's virtues and the Catholic lists of the cardinal virtues and the cardinal sins. For the Christian it is a cardinal sin to feel pride, because our accomplishments come through the grace of God and are not our own doing. This is expressed in the Latin words *Soli Deo Gloria,* the honor (glory) is God's alone. The cardinal virtues are justice, prudence, temperance, fortitude, faith, hope, and charity. The cardinal (deadly) sins are pride, lust, envy, anger, covetousness, gluttony, and sloth.

Let's consider the act of pleasure seeking. If you overdo it, you are intemperate—but suppose you are not capable of enjoying pleasures at all? That is not a virtue, and Aristotle doesn't know what to call such a person except "unimpressionable." The virtue is to know in what amount to enjoy one's pleasures; that Aristotle calls *temperance.* Thus for Aristotle, there is no virtue in staying away from pleasures, for "temperance" does not mean "abstinence." The key is to enjoy them *in moderation.*

Suppose we look at the art of spending money. For Aristotle, there is a virtuous way to spend money too. If you spend too much you are prodigal, and if you spend too little you are a miser. Spending just the right amount at the right time on the right people for the right reason makes you *liberal.*

For the Greek mind, for the man of the polis, *pride* is a natural virtue, and so it is for Aristotle. You can, however, overestimate your honor and become vain, or you can underestimate it and become humble. The virtuous way to estimate yourself and your accomplishments is through *proper pride.* (See Box 9.5 for a discussion of the differences between Aristotle's virtues, such as pride, and the traditional Christian list of cardinal virtues and vices.)

Is there a virtuous way to feel *angry*? Absolutely—by having a good temper or, as we might say today, being even-tempered. Being hot-tempered is a vice, but so is being meek. If you have been wronged, Aristotle believes, you ought to be angry in proportion to the offense against you.

Let us now consider the virtue of *truthfulness.* We probably would agree with Aristotle that this is a good thing, but what is his idea of a deficiency of truthfulness? Not *lying,* as we might expect, but *irony,* or as it is often translated, "mock-modesty" (in other words, downplaying the situation). Aristotle obviously would not have enjoyed Socrates' use of irony. The excess of truthfulness? Bragging. To the modern reader, the excess of truthfulness might be something different, such as being *rude* by telling someone, "You sure gained weight over the holidays!" But for Aristotle, it is not a matter of not harming others by lying or by being rude but a matter of assessing the situation properly, neither underplaying nor overplaying the truth. Here we touch on a hidden element of Aristotle's virtue theory: *Whom is the theory intended for?* Not necessarily young people who need to get their lives straightened out. It is, instead, directed at future politicians. The young noblemen and sons of wealthy landowners who had the leisure time to go to school were expected to become the pillars of Athenian society. What Aristotle is teaching them is, in many ways, to be good public figures. That is why it is necessary to know how much money to spend, in large sums. That is why it is important to know the extent of your pride and your anger. Of course, Aristotle's virtues are also applicable to other people, but some virtues—such as the virtues of wit or humor—carry a direct message to those young men who plan to enter public life. Most of us probably would like our partners to have a sense of humor. But imagine how important it is for a public figure not to be a boor, not to be a buffoon, and to have a ready wit. Aristotle recognized that fact. (See Box 9.6 for additional discussion of virtues.)

There are, then, three dispositions: two vices, one on either side, and virtue in the middle. How do we find the virtue? It may be difficult, depending on our own personal failings. If we have a hard time controlling our temper, we might try for a while to be so cool that nothing makes us angry, just to get out of the habit of being irascible; in other words, we might shoot *past* the target of good temper until we feel we can control ourselves and find the mean. If we tend to overindulge in desserts, we might try to lay off sweet things completely for a while. That is not the ideal situation, but Aristotle advises us to experiment until we get it right. Besides, if we find ourselves at one extreme, it is hard for us to see the difference between the other extreme and the virtue: A chocolate lover finds the chocolate hater and the person who has just a few bites of chocolate each week equally dull and unsympathetic. The political extremist may view the political moderate as just another extremist on the opposite front. Indeed, some extremes are closer to the mean, the virtue, than others. Being a coward is probably more opposed to being courageous than to being foolhardy. So if you don't know what path to choose, at least stay away from the extreme that is more opposed to the mean than the other extreme. We all have to watch out for our own personal failings, and we also have to watch out for temptations, because if we let ourselves indulge in too many pleasures we lose our sense of moderation and proportion. These matters are not easy, and Aristotle knew that we must judge each situation separately. At the end of the chapter you'll find the ancient Greek story of the "Flight of Icarus," which illustrates that virtue lies in following a middle course between too much and too little—not because it ensures a bland, average existence, but because it ensures survival.

Does Aristotle then propose a set of guidelines for what virtue is that can be applied in all situations? Nothing beyond the general range of the Golden Mean and an appeal to intuition, reasoning, and good habits. In other words, the virtuous person will know how to be virtuous! That has caused some ethicists to call Aristotle an ethical relativist, because virtue is, in a sense, relative to the situation. But labeling Aristotle an ethical relativist is wrong. He never states that morals are completely

Box 9.6   VARIATIONS ON ARISTOTLE'S THEME OF THE GOLDEN MEAN

Virtues on Aristotle's list include magnificence (spending large sums of money correctly), friendliness, modesty, and righteous indignation (a sense of justice). And Aristotle's approach can be applied to many situations we find ourselves in on an everyday basis; you might want to discuss this additional list of virtues and vices and add your own suggestions.

ADDITIONAL VIRTUES AND VICES

EXCESS (VICE)	MEAN (VIRTUE)	DEFICIT (VICE)
Loyalty without critical eye	Loyalty	Disloyalty
Passivity	Patience	Impatience
Judgment lacking; intrusion	Compassion	Absence of feelings
Sense of being perpetually indebted	Gratitude	Absence of any gratitude
Being too serious	Responsibility	Irresponsibility
Stubbornness	Perseverance	Unreliability
Rudeness	Honesty	Deceit; deception
Rigid adherence to rules	Rules set with exceptions	Leniency
Anxiety over everything	Awareness of real concerns	Obliviousness
Speeding	Maintaining speed limit	Driving too slowly
Excessive studying; workaholism	Sufficient studying to pass test	Insufficient studying; laziness

And so on and so forth! Can you think of a vice (one not mentioned by Aristotle) that has no mean? Can you think of a virtue that has no excess?

In Chapter 7 you read about a theory that it is right and appropriate for a victim of a crime to feel *resentment* toward the perpetrator, as well as for the community to feel *moral indignation* on behalf of the victim. Since Aristotle believes there is a Golden Mean for the feeling of anger—somewhere between being prone to rage and being cold or meek—and he also believes that *righteous indignation* is a virtue, his thinking is in harmony with this theory. Where, within the virtuous middle range, might the proper resentment/indignation response be for a person hit by a computer virus? for a rape victim? for a community targeted by bioterrorism?

culture-dependent or that each social group determines what counts as its moral code. On the contrary, Aristotle is quite adamant about virtues having a rock-bottom value for each situation; it is just that situations may differ, and one may be called upon to do more in one context than in another. If we want to apply a modern term to Aristotle, we might dare to call him a soft universalist (albeit with values typical for his day and age): Our responses to situations must remain flexible, and we each have our own ideals and failings, but the right, virtuous response reveals itself in being appropriate to the situation and falls within a range that is recognized by other people of virtue.

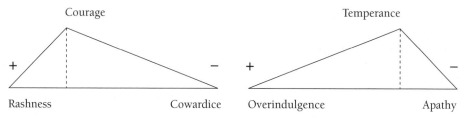

For Aristotle, the mean between the extremes is not an absolute middle; in other words, depending on the situation, the persons involved, and the virtue itself, the mean may be closer to one extreme than the other, and Aristotle advises us to stay away from the vice that is the further from the mean. If you imagine yourself at one of the extremes, you also can imagine that it might be hard to tell exactly where the mean is; that is why Aristotle says we must find it through trial and error. A mean that might be viewed as closer to the vice of excess than to deficiency would be *courage,* which can be said to be closer to rashness than to cowardice; a virtue that is closer to the vice of deficiency than the vice of excess might be *temperance.*

Is there such a thing as a perfectly virtuous person for Aristotle? Yes, it appears that he thought it was possible. Furthermore, he seems to have believed that if you are virtuous in one respect but fail miserably in another, then you have lost out completely. If you deviate only slightly, though, you are still a virtuous person—a person who is good at being human and at realizing the human potential.

In the Narratives section, I have included two stories that each illustrate Aristotle's idea that we become virtuous by doing virtuous things and thus developing good habits: The way to become courageous is to do courageous things, the way to become compassionate is to do compassionate things, and pretty soon it will become part of your character. One Narrative is Isaac Bashevis Singer's story "A Piece of Advice," about a cantankerous old man who becomes a decent human being by doing decent things, and the other is a remarkably similar story about another cantankerous old man who becomes a decent human being by doing decent things: the film *As Good As It Gets.*

Happiness

Being virtuous makes you happy—that is Aristotle's sole reason for designing the development of a virtuous character. But if the goal is happiness, why does he warn us about indulging in too many pleasures? Because pleasure and happiness are not identical, as most ancient thinkers would agree. We have to ask what exactly Aristotle means by happiness.

Happiness is what's "good for man," according to Aristotle. For most of us a good life means a happy life, but a good person means a moral person. For Aristotle, there was no conflict. We can be happy only if we're good, but in what way? The highest realizable goods are to live well, to be happy, to do well; what is good for man can't be something that harms him, and indulgence in too many pleasures can certainly be harmful. A further requirement of true happiness is that it must be steadfast; if we rely too much on pleasures, we'll find that they cease to give us a thrill after a while, so pleasure can't be the same as happiness. Nor can fame or fortune, because those things are certainly ephemeral—we can lose both overnight. So what is the thing that can be ours forever, that nobody can take away, and that is not harmful but beneficial to us as human beings? Good reasoning, or, as the ancient Greeks would put it, *contemplation*. This can be ours forever, and, as anyone who has struggled with an intellectual problem and solved it knows, it can even be exhilarating. For Aristotle, then, the ultimately happy life is the life of the thinker. But Aristotle is a realist too—he adds that, although the truly happy life may be a life of contemplation, it doesn't hurt to have friends, money, and good looks!

What about happiness as a reward for good behavior, in the afterlife? For Plato, the goal of a human life seemed to be a comprehension of the world of Forms and ultimately a reunification with that world in an afterlife. Aristotle seems to have had a different view of spirituality: As far as we can tell, he had no belief in an afterlife any more than he believes in a god who watches over humanity. He states that the soul is the *form* of a human and the body is one's *matter*, but form cannot exist separate from matter, so when the body dies, the soul ceases to exist in any personal way, even if (as he also says) the form of a human being may be immortal. In any event, whatever we are while we are alive will cease to exist when we die; therefore, happiness for Aristotle is exclusively a phenomenon for the living and must be achieved in this world for a person's life to have fulfilled its purpose. Whereas Plato's metaphysics (as we have seen in Chapter 8) could easily be incorporated into a religion that focused on life after death, Aristotle's metaphysics offers no "pie in the sky." Thus it is all the more extraordinary that Aristotle's philosophy became one of the great pillars of support for Christianity as it evolved in the high Middle Ages.

Was Aristotle himself happy in his lifetime? It appears that during his twelve years in Athens running his own school, he enjoyed contemplation, he had money, and he had friends. (Whether he was good-looking we just don't know, since no images of Aristotle have been preserved, but he reputedly liked to dress in the latest styles.) But with the death of his former student Alexander the Great in 323 B.C.E. at the age of thirty-two, it all came to an abrupt end. The anti-Macedonian feelings that were mounting in the realm controlled by Alexander's troops (including the city-state of Athens) no longer could be kept in check, and because Aristotle was considered pro-Macedonian, the Athenian city council decided to get rid of him. Ironically, their method was to charge him with the same offense that had been leveled against Socrates, of offending the gods. But whereas Socrates chose to stay and die for his principles, Aristotle packed up and left Athens for good so that "Athens wouldn't sin twice against philosophy." He took off for his country estate in Chalcis—a place he had inherited from his mother—but he died the year after of a stomach ailment.

Here we might want to ask ourselves, According to his own system of seeking the mean between extremes, did Aristotle in the end display courageous behavior, or was his behavior "deficient"? It is tempting to compare his choice with Socrates', and many would probably say that the comparison does not come out in Aristotle's favor. But here we should remember that the relationship Socrates had with the city of Athens was vastly different from that of Aristotle with the city-state; it had been Socrates' hometown, he had been concerned for its welfare all his life, and he had fought for it as a soldier. Aristotle was, for all intents and purposes, a foreigner, a "migrant worker" in the philosophy trade. He may have felt a certain loyalty to Athens from having spent over thirty years of his life in the city, but there was general discrimination against noncitizens, and Aristotle can't have been immune to that. He himself might have said that leaving was the perfectly rational, virtuous thing to do: the right action at the right time, for the right reason, not too much and not too little.

Aristotle's Influence on Aquinas

Today, Aristotle looms as one of the most influential persons in human history, but several times after his death it seemed as if his writings were destined to be totally forgotten. After his death, his books were collected by the new leader of the Lyceum, Theophrastus, who had been a student of Aristotle's; and subsequent generations of leaders hid the books to preserve them from theft and other threats—especially since the Lyceum was temporarily closed when foreign philosophers were kicked out of Athens around 300 B.C.E. The Lyceum did reopen and stayed open until its official closure by Emperor Justinian in 529 C.E., but it was never the great success story that Plato's Academy had become. Aristotle's own books were damaged in storage and would have been lost had it not been for an avid book collector, Apellicon, who simply appropriated them along with other classic writings and brought them to Rome in 100 B.C.E. Here they were copied, starting a new Aristotle fad among Roman philosophers, but even that was to fade away: When the Lyceum was finally closed by the Roman emperor along with Plato's Academy, the scholars working at Aristotle's school feared for their safety and fled to Persia with copies of Aristotle's books. Back in the Roman cultures around the Mediterranean, Aristotle's works were largely forgotten, and even the location of the Lyceum was lost, until its rediscovery in 1997 by archaeologists. Primarily in Alexandria, it was the Platonic spirit that survived to put its mark on the new world religion. In the Middle East, though, Aristotle's works were studied continually. As the scientific spirit declined in the West, Arabic scholars kept Aristotelian research alive until the advent of another new world religion, Islam, in which Aristotle's philosophy has remained influential. It was not until well into the next millennium that an interest in Aristotle was rekindled in the Christian world. Eventually his theories found their way back into Western philosophy through the works of Saint Thomas Aquinas (1225–1274). In the late Middle Ages and through the Renaissance, Aristotle eclipsed Plato as a philosopher and was known in European intellectual circles (as he had been for centuries in the Arabic world) as "The Philosopher." So for a man who for all intents and purposes didn't have an established career by the time he was thirty-eight, whose life's unfulfilled ambition apparently had been to become leader of Plato's school, and who eventually lost his job because of political persecution, Aristotle's posthumous career is nothing short of remarkable: His influence on philosophy itself is immeasurable; his theories of science laid the groundwork for the basic scientific concepts in the Western tradition after the so-called Dark Ages of the early Medieval period; his entire system of classification of sciences and humanities became, to a great extent, the inspiration for the structuring of the first universities in Europe in the high Middle Ages and the Renaissance; he provided inspiration for Islamic interpretations of the Koran; and some of his ideas became the cornerstone of the theology of Catholicism, through the works of Aquinas.

It was Aristotle's concept of teleology that became particularly fascinating for Aquinas: If everything has a purpose, then surely it was designed by God. And if we humans, with our free will, decide to follow God's purpose for us, then it must mean we are following God's will, and we are doing right; on the other hand, if we decide to go against God's purpose, we are doing wrong. So what is God's purpose for us? Aquinas identified four specific goals that together made up what has become known as Aquinas's *natural law:* (1) We are obliged to preserve our own lives. (2) We are obliged to procreate within marriage. (3) We are obliged to live as good citizens among other people. (4) We are obliged to seek knowledge, primarily about God and his creation. Those four rules are natural to us because we have been designed that way, says Aquinas. It doesn't mean those rules can't be broken—people commit suicide, people have babies outside of wedlock or take measures to avoid getting pregnant, some people care little about living in harmony with others, and some show no interest in seeking knowledge about God. However, they are going against God's will—a will that, for Aquinas, is knowable and understandable to humans, because that will is rational, and humans have been endowed with reason so we can understand God's rules. So if we decide not to follow our built-in purpose, it is because of a sinful willpower. (Aquinas's natural law is not to be confused with the *laws of nature* we are familiar with from science. Such scientific laws are descriptive, whereas Aquinas's natural law is normative: You can't break the law of gravity, but you can break the law of procreation.)

What happens to people who break the rules of the natural law? Aquinas is convinced that they will not get away with it—they might in this life, but certainly not in the next. That is why there is also *divine law,* for those offenses that God knows about but other humans haven't discovered. On this earthly plane there is also, of course, *human law,* so that criminal offenses that are discovered can be punished. And the entire universe is run by God according to eternal rules, the *eternal law.*

You may recognize some of Aquinas's views on natural law as contemporary Catholic doctrine. For example, it is Aquinas's rule of self-preservation that forbids suicide, and his rule of procreation that forbids abortion, contraception, and homosexual relationships (because all procreation must take place naturally between married couples, without hindrance, and in no other way). This was not always so: Aquinas's teachings were for centuries considered controversial by the Church, and not until a Church council in 1914 was it decided that they would from then on be considered official Catholic doctrine. So we can say that Aristotle long after his death not only made an everlasting mark on Western science and philosophy, as well as Middle Eastern philosophy, but also to this day has been influential within Christianity.

Some Objections to Greek Virtue Theory

As mentioned earlier, the particular brand of ethical theory known as virtue ethics that we find in the Greek tradition by and large disappeared from view with the rise of modern philosophy. That was not merely because the texts were forgotten; it was a concerted effort by scholars to find a better approach to ethics, because as the centuries passed it was becoming clear, for a number of reasons, that the Greek theories of virtue had several shortcomings. For one thing, Thomas Aquinas found it difficult to reconcile Aristotle's virtues not just with Christian virtues but also with the Christian respect for *God's laws*. In the Christian approach to morals, following commandments is far more important than striving toward virtues, and belief in the human ability to shape one's own character autonomously is considered to be a sin of pride. You become what you ought to be by God's grace, not merely by your own effort.

Philosophy, after parting ways with theology in the sixteenth and seventeenth centuries, began to look critically at virtue ethics from a secular point of view, for, as we have seen, Aristotle was talking about the virtues of a ruling class, virtues that could not be disputed by someone with a different point of view. The modern, political vision of equality does not enter into the Aristotelian moral theory, and from both a Christian and a social viewpoint, an egalitarian approach had become indispensable for an acceptable moral theory by the eighteenth century. For those scholars believing in "natural rights" for all people, it was necessary to set up a moral theory that everyone could follow regardless of status, birth, or intelligence, and such a theory could be based only on laws that were clear and reasonable. Virtues were criticized as being too vague and logically problematic, because what happens if two virtuous people disagree about what to do? How can one persuade the other? There is no recourse to reason in that case except to declare one person less virtuous than the other, so virtue ethics is not a tool in itself for solving conflicts. Such a problem does not arise if you have a clear set of moral and civil laws to refer to. That is what is needed if we regard each other as equals—not a theory with a static view of what makes a person virtuous. The rejection of virtue theory in favor of a rule- or duty-oriented moral theory was, therefore, considered a step forward in moral egalitarianism.

There is a more fundamental problem embedded in classical virtue theory: its basis in *teleology*. It was natural for Plato and Aristotle to assume that as human actions had a purpose, so did humans themselves have a purpose, and that purpose was to let their rationality shine because that was what human nature was all about. And because this is the human purpose, what is good for humans must begin and end with rationality. But that gives rise to a series of questions: (1) Must what is good for someone always be linked with what he or she does best? Suppose a man is excellent at forging paintings. Does that mean his life should include this as a purpose, to make him happy? Aristotle and Plato would reject this on the basis that forging paintings is bad in itself, but that is surely a lame answer because it assumes that we know beforehand which purposes are acceptable and which aren't. However, even if we stick to the idea of rationality, it is not very obvious that this is the human purpose. (2) Why must we talk about a human "purpose" at all? Science and philosophy today do not, as a rule, talk about purposes of nature, including human nature. A purpose requires that *someone* has that purpose; individuals may have purposes, but we hesitate to claim that nature has a purpose or even that there is a higher power with a purpose. This is outside the realm of science and also that of contemporary moral philosophy. (3) Even if humans are very good at being rational, they are not excellent at it, at least not everybody, and even the select few geniuses can't be rational all the time. We are instead good at *being able* to act rationally some of the time, and with those qualifications it is hard to claim that rationality is our overriding purpose. And (4) Why should there be just one purpose for humans? A knife can be used to cut, to throw, to clean your nails (don't try this at home), to hang on the wall, and any number of other things. A tree surely has more functions than to supply humans with shade and fruit—it provides oxygen, its leaves fertilize the ground, it provides a home for birds and squirrels and maggots, it supplies a subject for an art class to paint—and makes more trees. Why should we assume that each thing or species has one function that defines it? Humans surely have a multitude of functions. It is doubtful, then, whether a theory of virtue should, indeed, involve the question of function or purpose at all. Contemporary theories of virtue tend to steer clear of this ancient, problematic issue, as we will see shortly.

Study Questions

1. Explain Aristotle's theory of the four causes.

2. What is Aristotle's Golden Mean? Does it imply that the virtuous person is an average person of average talents and intelligence?

3. Explain Aristotle's theory of virtue in detail, using at least three examples. At least two of the examples must be Aristotle's own.

4. In the end, Aristotle was accused of the same crimes as Socrates, but, unlike Socrates, Aristotle chose exile. Evaluate Aristotle's choice: Was he himself displaying courage? Was he a coward? Was he rash? How do you think Aristotle would have defended his course of action?

Primary Readings and Narratives

The two Primary Readings are excerpts from Aristotle's *Nicomachean Ethics*. The first is from Book II, in which Aristotle explains the doctrine of the Golden Mean. The second is from Book III, in which he elaborates on the virtue of courage. The first Narrative is the ancient Greek myth of the flight of Icarus, illustrating Aristotle's theory that the virtuous person always seeks the middle way, avoiding the extremes of excess and deficiency: Flying on wings made of feathers and wax, Icarus disregarded his father's advice to take a middle course. The next Narrative explores the theme of courage; it is an excerpt from *Njal's Saga,* the Icelandic epic that takes place in the late Viking Age. In the excerpt, Njal, his wife, Bergthora, and their little grandson face death with stoic courage, choosing to perish together. This is followed by Joseph Conrad's novel and film *Lord Jim*, a story of cowardice, courage, and honor. The fourth Narrative is an excerpt from a twentieth-century short story by Isaac Bashevis Singer, "A Piece of Advice," in which a nasty, temperamental man learns virtue by developing the habit of pleasant behavior. In a parallel story, another nasty man experiences a character transformation by doing nice things for others: the Academy Award–winning film *As Good As It Gets*. In both cases, the man becomes less selfish by pursuing better habits *for their own sake*.

Primary Reading

Nicomachean Ethics

ARISTOTLE

Excerpt from Book II, fourth century B.C.E. Translated by W. D. Ross.

This excerpt contains some of Aristotle's most famous writings on virtue: He explains the relationship between virtue and conduct in Chapter 4, and in Chapter 6 he outlines the general theory of the Golden Mean. The excerpt from Chapter 7 gives us most of Aristotle's own list of virtues as examples of the relationship between the mean flanked by two extremes, too much and too little.

4   The question might be asked, what we mean by saying that we must become just by doing just acts, and temperate by doing temperate acts; for if men do just and temperate acts, they are already just and temperate, exactly as, if they do what is in accordance with the laws of grammar and of music, they are grammarians and musicians.

Or is this not true even of the arts? It is possible to do something that is in accordance with the laws of grammar, either by chance or at the suggestion of another. A man will be a grammarian, then, only when he has both done something grammatical and done it grammatically; and this means doing it in accordance with the grammatical knowledge in himself.

Again, the case of the arts and that of the virtues are not similar; for the products of the arts have their goodness in themselves, so that it is enough that they should have a certain character, but if the acts that are in accordance with the virtues have themselves a certain character it does not follow that they are done justly or temperately. The agent also must be in a certain condition when he does them; in the first place he must have knowledge, secondly he must choose the acts, and choose them for their own sakes, and thirdly his action must proceed from a firm and unchangeable character. These are not reckoned in as conditions of the possession of the arts, except the bare knowledge; but as a condition of the possession of the virtues knowledge has little or no weight, while the other conditions count not for a little but for everything, i.e. the very conditions which result from often doing just and temperate acts.

Actions, then, are called just and temperate when they are such as the just or the temperate man would do; but it is not the man who does these that is just and temperate, but the man who also does them as just and temperate men do them. It is well said, then, that it is by doing just acts that the just man is produced, and by doing temperate acts the temperate man; without doing these no one would have even a prospect of becoming good.

But most people do not do these, but take refuge in theory and think they are being philosophers and will become good in this way, behaving somewhat like patients who listen attentively to their doctors, but do none of the things they are ordered to do. As the latter will not be made well in body by such a course of treatment, the former will not be made well in soul by such a course of philosophy.

6   Virtue, then, is a state of character concerned with choice, lying in a mean, i.e. the mean relative to us, this being determined by a rational principle, and by that principle by which the man of practical wisdom would determine it. Now it is a mean between two vices, that which depends on excess and that which depends on defect; and again it is a mean because the vices respectively fall short of or exceed what is right in both passions and actions, while virtue both finds and chooses that which is intermediate. Hence in respect of its substance and the definition which states its essence virtue is a mean, with regard to what is best and right an extreme.

But not every action nor every passion admits of a mean; for some have names that already imply badness, e.g. spite, shamelessness, envy, and in the case of actions adultery, theft, murder; for all of these and suchlike things imply by their names that they are themselves bad, and not the excesses or deficiencies of them. It is not possible, then, ever to be right with regard to them; one must always be wrong. Nor does goodness or badness with regard to such things depend on committing adultery with the right woman, at the right time, and in the right way, but simply to do any of them is to go wrong. It would be equally absurd, then, to expect that in unjust, cowardly, and voluptuous action there should be a mean, an excess, and a deficiency; for at that rate there would be a mean of excess and of deficiency, an excess of excess, and a deficiency of deficiency. But as there is no excess and deficiency of temperance and courage because what is intermediate is in a sense an extreme, so too of the actions we have mentioned there is no mean nor any excess and deficiency, but however they are done they are wrong; for in general there is neither a mean of excess and deficiency, nor excess and deficiency of a mean.

7   We must, however, not only make this general statement, but also apply it to the individual facts. For among statements about conduct those which are general apply more widely, but those which are particular are more genuine, since conduct has to do with individual cases, and our statements must harmonize with the facts in these cases. We may take these cases from our table. With regard to feelings of fear and confidence courage is the mean; of the people who exceed, he who exceeds in fearlessness has no name (many of the states have no name), while the man who exceeds in confidence is rash, and he who exceeds in fear and falls short in confidence is a coward. With regard to pleasures and pains—not all of them, and not so much with regard to the pains—the mean is temperance, the excess self-indulgence. Persons deficient with regard to the pleasures are not often found; hence such persons also have received no name. But let us call them 'insensible'.

With regard to giving and taking of money the mean is liberality, the excess and the defect prodigality and meanness. In these actions people exceed and fall short in contrary ways; the prodigal exceeds in spending and falls short in taking, while the mean man exceeds in taking and falls short in spending. (At present we are giving a mere outline or summary, and are satisfied with this; later these states will be more exactly determined.) With regard to money there are also other dispositions—a mean, magnificence (for the magnificent man differs from the liberal man; the former deals with large sums, the latter with small ones), an excess, tastelessness and vulgarity, and a deficiency, niggardliness; these differ from the states opposed to liberality, and the mode of their difference will be stated later.

With regard to honour and dishonour the mean is proper pride, the excess is known as a sort of 'empty vanity', and the deficiency is undue humility; and as we said liberality was related to magnificence, differing from it by dealing with small sums, so there is a state similarly related to proper pride, being concerned with small honours while that is concerned with great. For it is possible to desire honour as one ought, and more than one ought, and less, and the man who exceeds in his desires is called ambitious, the man who falls short unambitious, while the intermediate person has no name. The dispositions also are nameless, except that that of the ambitious man is called ambition. Hence the people who are at the extremes lay claim to the middle place; and we ourselves sometimes call the intermediate person ambitious and sometimes unambitious, and sometimes praise the ambitious man and sometimes the unambitious. The reason of our doing this will be stated in what follows; but now let us speak of the remaining states according to the method which has been indicated.

With regard to anger also there is an excess, a deficiency, and a mean. Although they can scarcely be said to have names, yet since we call the intermediate person good-tempered let us call the mean good temper; of the persons at the extremes let the one who exceeds be called irascible, and his vice irascibility, and the man who falls short an inirascible sort of person, and the deficiency inirascibility.

There are also three other means, which have a certain likeness to one another, but differ from one another: for they are all concerned with intercourse in words and actions, but differ in that one is concerned with truth in this sphere, the other two with pleasantness; and of this one kind is exhibited in giving amusement, the other in all the circumstances of life. We must therefore speak of these too, that we may the better see that in all things the mean is praiseworthy, and the extremes neither praiseworthy nor right, but worthy of blame. Now most of these states also have no names, but we must try, as in the other cases, to invent names ourselves so that we may be clear and easy to follow. With regard to truth, then, the intermediate is a truthful sort of person and the mean may be called truthfulness, while the pretence which exaggerates is boastfulness and the person characterized by it a boaster, and that which understates is mock modesty and the person characterized by it mock-modest. With regard to pleasantness in the giving of amusement the intermediate person is ready-witted and the disposition ready wit, the excess is buffoonery and the person characterized by it a buffoon, while the man who falls short is a sort of boor and his state is boorishness. With regard to the remaining kind of pleasantness, that which is exhibited in life in general, the man who is pleasant in the right way is friendly and the mean is friendliness, while the man who exceeds is an obsequious person if he has no end in view, a flatterer if he is aiming at his own advantage, and the man who falls short and is unpleasant in all circumstances is a quarrelsome and surly sort of person.

Study Questions

1. According to Aristotle, can we become virtuous just by doing the right thing? Can a person be virtuous without doing the right thing?

2. Examine the virtue of proper pride. The modern equivalent of humility might be called low self-esteem. Do you think there is such a vice as too much self-esteem? Why is pride considered a sin by the Catholic tradition?

3. Set Aristotle's list of virtues and vices up in a schema with "too little" to one side, virtue (the mean) in the middle, and "too much" to the other side. Are there virtues missing that you think ought to be essential to a virtue ethics? If yes, which ones?

Primary Reading

Nicomachean Ethics

ARISTOTLE

Excerpt from Book III. Translated by W. D. Ross.

You may remember that the first virtue on Aristotle's list was *courage,* and we shall look at the theme of courage for the next few pages. Here Aristotle goes into detail examining what he considers true courage.

That it is a mean with regard to feelings of fear and confidence has already been made evident; and plainly the things we fear are terrible things, and these are, to speak without qualification, evils; for which reason people even define fear as expectation of evil. Now we fear all evils, e.g. disgrace, poverty, disease, friendlessness, death, but the brave man is not thought to be concerned with all; for to fear some things is even right and noble, and it is base not to fear them—e.g. disgrace; he who fears this is good and modest, and he who does not is shameless. He is, however, by some people called brave, by a trans-ference of the word to a new meaning; for he has in him something which is like the brave man, since the brave man also is a fearless person. Poverty and disease we perhaps ought not to fear, nor in general the things that do not proceed from vice and are not due to a man himself. But not even the man who is fearless of these is brave. Yet we apply the word to him also in virtue of a similarity; for some who in the dangers of war are cow-ards are liberal and are confident in face of the loss of money. Nor is a man a coward if he fears insult to his wife and children or envy or anything of the kind; nor brave if he is confident when he is about to be flogged. With what sort of terrible things, then, is the brave man concerned? Surely with the greatest; for no one is more likely than he to stand his ground against what is awe-inspiring. Now death is the most terrible of all things; for it is the end, and nothing is thought to be any longer either good or bad for the dead. But the brave man would not seem to be concerned even with death in all circumstances, e.g. at sea or in disease. In what circumstances, then? Surely in the noblest. Now such deaths are those in battle; for these take place in the greatest and noblest danger. And these are correspondingly honoured in city-states and at the courts of monarchs. Properly, then, he will be called brave who is fearless in face of a noble death, and of all emergencies that involve death; and the emergencies of war are in the highest degree of this kind. Yet at sea also, and in disease; the brave man is fearless, but not in the same way as the seamen; for he has given up hope of safety, and is disliking the thought of death in this shape, while they are hopeful because of their experience. At the same time, we show courage in situ-ations where there is the opportunity of showing prowess or where death is noble; but in these forms of death neither of these conditions is fulfilled.

What is terrible is not the same for all men; but we say there are things terrible even beyond human strength. These, then, are terrible to every one—at least to every sensible man; but the terrible things that are not beyond human strength differ in magnitude and degree, and so too do the things that inspire confidence. Now the brave man is as daunt-less as man may be. Therefore, while he will fear even the things that are not beyond human strength, he will face them as he ought and as the rule directs, for honour's sake;

for this is the end of virtue. But it is possible to fear these more, or less, and again to fear things that are not terrible as if they were. Of the faults that are committed one consists in fearing what one should not, another in fearing as we should not, another in fearing when we should not, and so on; and so too with respect to the things that inspire confidence. The man, then, who faces and who fears the right things and from the right motive, in the right way and at the right time, and who feels confidence under the corresponding conditions, is brave; for the brave man feels and acts according to the merits of the case and in whatever way the rule directs. Now the end of every activity is conformity to the corresponding state of character. This is true, therefore, of the brave man as well as of others. But courage is noble. Therefore the end also is noble; for each thing is defined by its end. Therefore it is for a noble end that the brave man endures and acts as courage directs.

Of those who go to excess he who exceeds in fearlessness has no name (we have said previously that many states of character have no names), but he would be a sort of madman or insensible person if he feared nothing, neither earthquakes nor the waves, as they say the Celts do not; while the man who exceeds in confidence about what really is terrible is rash. The rash man, however, is also thought to be boastful and only a pretender to courage; at all events, as the brave man is with regard to what is terrible, so the rash man wishes to *appear*; and so he imitates him in situations where he can. Hence also most of them are a mixture of rashness and cowardice; for, while in these situations they display confidence, they do not hold their ground against what is really terrible. The man who exceeds in fear is a coward; for he fears both what he ought not and as he ought not, and all the similar characterizations attach to him. He is lacking also in confidence; but he is more conspicuous for his excess of fear in painful situations. The coward, then, is a despairing sort of person; for he fears everything. The brave man, on the other hand, has the opposite disposition; for confidence is the mark of a hopeful disposition. The coward, the rash man, and the brave man, then, are concerned with the same objects but are differently disposed towards them; for the first two exceed and fall short, while the third holds the middle, which is the right, position; and rash men are precipitate, and wish for dangers beforehand but draw back when they are in them, while brave men are keen in the moment of action, but quiet beforehand.

As we have said, then, courage is a mean with respect to things that inspire confidence or fear, in the circumstances that have been stated; and it chooses or endures things because it is noble to do so, or because it is base not to do so. But to die to escape from poverty or love or anything painful is not the mark of a brave man, but rather of a coward; for it is softness to fly from what is troublesome, and such a man endures death not because it is noble but to fly from evil.

Study Questions

1. Aristotle is often assumed to have said that "a brave man is never afraid." Is this a fair statement?

2. What, according to Aristotle, is the most courageous behavior? Do you agree with him?

3. Would Aristotle consider Socrates' choice to stand trial a brave decision? Why or why not?

4. After September 11 a debate arose in the media about whether hijacking a plane and deliberately flying it into a building, causing death and anguish to civilians, was a

"cowardly act." In many people's opinion the terrorist actions were the very picture of cowardice, using innocent poeple as weapons against other innocent people. A dissenting view came from television talk-show host Bill Maher, who suggested that deliberately flying an airplane into a building was not cowardly (and for that remark his show was eventually cancelled). Media magnate Ted Turner chimed in, calling the hijackers "brave" but "a little nuts." In your view, were the terrorists brave or cowardly? Is there a third possibility? For a solution you might want to turn to Chapter 10 and the section on Philippa Foot, who suggests that a virtue without good intentions is no virtue at all.

5. In Chapter 11 you'll find an expanded discussion of courage, distinguishing between physical and moral courage. Apply Aristotle's Theory of the Golden Mean to both kinds.

 ## Narrative

The Flight of Icarus

Ancient Greek Myth.

This myth illustrates an element in Aristotle's virtue theory that most Greeks were familiar with because it corresponds to the classic Greek ideal of moderation, or what the Greeks called *sophrosyne;* in the *Nicomachean Ethics* we know it as the mean between extremes, not too much and not too little. The story of Icarus, part of Greek mythology, has been used often as a symbol in Western literature over the past several hundred years.

Wanted for the murder of his nephew, the great artisan Daedalus hid out on Crete, where he built King Minos a labyrinth to house the monster Minotaur (a creature with a bull's head and a man's body). Here Daedalus lived for years, fell in love with one of Minos's slaves, and had a son by her, Icarus. When Icarus was a young man, Daedalus decided to leave Crete. But Minos did not want to lose his master craftsman and so locked Daedalus and his son up in the labyrinth; they escaped with the help of Minos's wife. It was difficult to get off the island, because Minos kept all his ships under military guard, but Daedalus had an idea: He fashioned a pair of feather wings for himself and another pair for Icarus. The quill feathers were threaded together, but the smaller feathers were held together with wax. Daedalus was quite emotional when he told Icarus how to use the wings on the perilous journey, admonishing his son not to fly too high to avoid having the wax be melted by the sun and not to fly too low so that ocean water wouldn't soak his feathers. Then he told his son, "Follow me!" and they set out across the ocean toward the northeast. They had already traveled a considerable distance when Icarus, for whatever reason, disobeyed his father. He began rising toward the sun, enjoying the air currents and the sweep of his great wings.

When Daedalus looked back to see if his son was still following close behind him, there was nobody—but far below, on the waves, floated the feathers of Icarus' wings. He had risen too close to the sun, and the wax on his wings had melted, plummeting him

Pieter Bruegel the Elder, *The Fall of Icarus* (c. 1558). The inventor Daedalus made wings of feathers and wax for himself and his son, Icarus, so they could escape from Crete, but Icarus flew too close to the sun, and the wax melted. If you look closely, you can see the legs of poor Icarus in the water (right-hand corner). Bruegel was so fascinated by this story that he painted it twice, both times with the farmer in the foreground. This is the original painting; the second is nearly identical except that Daedalus is shown flying above the cliffs. The Roman poet Ovid, who retold the story, specifically mentioned in his *Metamorphoses* that the fall was witnessed by a plowman, a shepherd, and a fisherman, and that is why Bruegel put them in his painting. What do you think the significance might be of the artist's having placed the tragedy of Icarus off to the side?

toward the water below; Icarus had drowned. His father circled around and around until the body of his son rose from the waters; then he picked it up and carried it to a nearby island where he buried it.

Study Questions

1. Is this story meant to be taken literally? Why or why not?

2. Bruegel's painting shows the fall of Icarus, but you have to look hard to find him. Why do you think the artist didn't make Icarus the focal point of the painting?

3. In Western literature the story of Icarus has often been used as a metaphor for overextending yourself, or being overconfident. It has been taken as a warning not to reach above your station in life, to "know your place." Is this lesson exactly the same as the original story teaches? (What would Aristotle say? What lesson might a parent be trying to teach his or her child when telling this story?)

4. Is this a didactic story? Why or why not?

Narrative

Njal's Saga

Prose epic, ca. 1280. Author unknown. Summary and Excerpt.

This story is set in the latter part of the Viking Age (700–1000 C.E.). It isn't a story of Vikings, however, but of their relatives, who stayed in Iceland to farm the land. The area was settled by the Norsemen (mostly Danes and Norwegians) about 800, and by the time *Njal's Saga* was written it was a land of great unrest; blood feuds and various intrigues led to the Danish takeover of the country, which for four hundred years had been independent. *Njal's Saga* is one of many *sagas*, which are historical epics about past life in Iceland.

Nordic mythology teaches that the world as well as the gods eventually will perish in a natural disaster. Thus the Norsemen (the farmers as well as the Vikings) held to the belief in a gloomy fate looming ahead. Even though Christianity was by that time the official religion, the old view of life being ruled by fate still had a hold on people's minds.

This very brief outline cannot explain the complex plot of the saga and can only hint at the inevitable tragic ending. Njal, his wife, Bergthora, and their four sons are carrying on a blood feud with neighbors, not because either party is evil, but because over the years events have led in that direction. Through misunderstandings and gossip, the enmity between Njal's family and their neighbors grows, even though Njal does his best to avert it by talking sense to everybody. His negotiations backfire, though, and things get worse. At the *Alting* (the place of arbitration), it becomes clear that all hope of peace is lost, and Njal goes home and prepares for a siege. His adversary, Flosi, arrives with a hundred men, and Njal asks his sons to help him defend the house from inside. The enemy are quick to take advantage of the situation and set fire to the farmhouse.

> There was an old woman at Bergthorsknoll called Sæunn. She knew a lot about many things and had second sight. She was very old by this time, and the Njalssons called her senile because she talked so much; but what she predicted often came true. One day she snatched up a cudgel and made her way round the house to a pile of chickweed that lay there, and started beating it and cursing it for the wretched thing that it was. Skarp-Hedin [one of Njal's sons] laughed at this, and asked her why she was so angry with the chickweed.
>
> The old woman replied, "This chickweed will be used as the kindling when they burn Njal and my foster child Bergthora inside the house. Quickly, take it away and throw it into some water or burn it."
>
> "No," said Skarp-Hedin "for if that is what is ordained, something else will be found to kindle the fire even if the chickweed is not here."
>
> The old woman kept nagging them all summer to take the chickweed indoors, but they never got round to doing it. . . .

Months later, Flosi has now shown up with his force of one hundred men, and Njal has fortified himself and his household inside the farmhouse. Now the chickweed that figured in Sæunn's predictions becomes a weapon:

. . . They [Flosi and his men] brought the chickweed up and set fire to it, and before those inside knew what was happening, the ceiling of the room was ablaze from end to end. . . .

Njal said to them, "Be of good heart and speak no words of fear, for this is just a passing storm and it will be long before another like it comes. Put your faith in the mercy of God, for He will not let us burn both in this world and the next."

. . . Now the whole house began to blaze. Njal went to the door and said, "Is Flosi near enough to hear my words?"

Flosi said that he could hear him.

Njal said, "Would you consider making an agreement with my sons, or letting anyone leave the house?"

"I will make no terms with your sons," replied Flosi. "We shall settle matters now, once and for all, and we are not leaving until every one of them is dead. But I shall allow the women and children and servants to come out. . . ."

. . . Flosi said to Bergthora, "You come out, Bergthora, for under no circumstances do I want you to burn."

Bergthora replied, "I was given to Njal in marriage when young, and I have promised him that we would share the same fate."

Then they both went back inside.

"What shall we do now?" asked Bergthora.

"Let us go to our bed," said Njal, "and lie down."

Then Bergthora said to little Thord [their grandson], Kari's son, "You are to be taken out. You are not to burn."

The boy replied, "But that's not what you promised, grandmother. You said that we would never be parted; and so it shall be, for I would much prefer to die beside you both."

She carried the boy to the bed. Njal said to his steward, "Take note where we lay ourselves down and how we dispose ourselves, for I shall not move from here however much the smoke or flames distress me. Then you can know where to look for our remains."

The steward said he would.

An ox had recently been slaughtered, and the hide was lying nearby. Njal told the steward to spread the hide over them, and he promised to do so.

Njal and Bergthora lay down on the bed and put the boy between them. Then they crossed themselves and the boy, and commended their souls to God. These were the last words they were heard to speak. The steward took the hide and spread it over them, and then left the house. . . .

Study Questions

1. Do you think Njal, Bergthora, and the little boy display courage, or are they just giving up?

2. Would removing the chickweed have prevented the arson?

3. For the old Norsemen and -women, the name and reputation you left behind when you died was all-important. How do you think Njal and Bergthora were regarded after they died?

4. Would Aristotle recognize their final act as courageous? Why or why not?

Narrative

Lord Jim

JOSEPH CONRAD

Film by Richard Brooks (director and screenwriter), 1965. Based on the novel by Joseph Conrad, 1900. Summary.

Lord Jim is one of the finest fictional explorations of a human soul trying to do the right thing, at the right time, for the right reason. The film based on Joseph Conrad's classic novel tells the story of a young man named Jim who dreams of doing great deeds. As a newly appointed officer in the British Mercantile Marine, he spends quiet moments on board his ship fantasizing about saving damsels in distress and suppressing mutinies. After having been stranded in a Southeast Asian harbor because of a broken leg, Jim takes a job as chief mate to a crew of drunken, raucous white sailors with an equally unpleasant captain on the rusty old *Patna,* which is transporting a group of Muslim pilgrims to Mecca. Once they are at sea, a storm approaches, and Jim inspects the ship's hull. It is so rusty it is on the verge of breaking up. Back on deck Jim sees that the crew is lowering a lifeboat into the water—just one, for themselves. No measures are being taken to save the hundreds of pilgrims on the ship. Jim insists to the others that he is staying on board, but, at the last minute, as the storm hits, he comes face to face with his fear of death, which causes him to push aside all dreams of heroic deeds, and he jumps into the lifeboat after all.

Believing that the *Patna* is lost already, the men in the lifeboat set course for shore. When they arrive, they see that someone got there ahead of them; in the harbor lies the *Patna* herself, safe and sound. She was salvaged and towed to shore by another crew, and all the pilgrims are safe. Jim is relieved that no one was lost, but his dreams of valor have been shattered—he is tormented by guilt. There is an inquest, and Jim decides to tell all, to the dismay of his superiors, who believe that dirty linen should not be aired in public. His testimony so affects the prosecutor that the prosecutor later kills himself, leaving a note saying that if fear can break even one of us, how can anyone believe himself to be safe and honorable? Jim's officer's papers are canceled. Everywhere he goes from now on, the memory of the *Patna* will haunt him; somebody will recognize him or mention the scandal, and he will have to go somewhere else, to another port and another odd job.

Is Jim a coward? Were all the dreams of noble deeds just fantasies? He doesn't know. Months later, in some harbor in Southeast Asia, Jim is now a common dockside worker. One day, while transferring goods from shore to ship, he finds himself in a new, dangerous situation: A worker with a grudge against the shipping company lights a fuse that threatens to blow up the ammo being freighted to the ship, and he calls out to all hands to jump, before it blows. But Jim, on hearing the yell "Jump!," stands fast. The only man remaining on board, he puts out the fire and becomes a hero. The administrator of the shipping line, Stein, offers him a job, which Jim later accepts because he wants to get out of town. The job entails taking the guns and ammunition up river to the village of Patusan

To stay or to jump? Jim (Peter O'Toole) is about to make the decision that will ruin his life: During a storm, he abandons ship and the many passengers who had put their trust in him, in *Lord Jim* (Columbia Pictures, 1965).

to help the local people fight against a tyrant. He becomes the hero of the people, respected and trusted. They call him *Tuan Jim,* Lord Jim. He now believes that he finally has proved himself, but in fact the real test is yet to come. A band of pirates land in Patusan, and with the help of a traitor from the village, they trick Jim into believing that they have good intentions. They are white, they promise they will sail away without harming any of the villagers, and Jim chooses to believe them; he lets them go without disarming them, trusting their word. He vows to the chief of the village that if anyone is harmed because of his decision, he will forfeit his own life. As it turns out, the chief's own son is killed in a fight between the pirates and the villagers. The villagers expect Jim to flee to save his life, and Stein tries to make Jim leave the village with the native woman he loves, but this time Jim stands fast; he explains to Stein, "I have been a so-called coward and a so-called hero, and there is not the thickness of a sheet of paper between them. Maybe cowards and heroes are just ordinary men who, for a split second do something out of the ordinary." In the morning Jim goes to the chief, who is mad with grief over his son, and offers him his life. Does the chief kill Jim? Read the book or watch the film.

Study Questions

1. Is Jim a coward, or is he courageous? Is it possible to be both?

2. Do you think we all are like Jim in the sense that we all have a moral breaking point which, when we reach it, reveals the frailty of our character?

3. How would Aristotle rate Jim? Is he in the end a virtuous person?

4. Although the virtue of *honor* is not on Aristotle's list, it was an important concept in his day. Today it may not seem terribly important to many in the Western world, but in the time period of Lord Jim, the concept of personal honor was at least as important as when Aristotle was alive. Do you agree with the author (Joseph Conrad) that it is more honorable for Jim to confess his failings during the inquest than to keep quiet and follow the lead of his superiors? Is Jim an honorable man? Why or why not?

5. Compare the plot of *Lord Jim* with Aristotle's prescription for the perfect tragic plot (see Chapter 2): Something horrible happens to an ordinary man, not because of some vice or depravity of his character, but because of a great error in judgment. Does this fit Jim? If so, is Aristotle right that we feel pity and fear because we understand what he is going through—that we might react the same way?

Narrative

A Piece of Advice

ISAAC BASHEVIS SINGER

Short story, 1958. Translated by Martha Glicklich and Joel Blocker. Summary and Excerpt.

This story takes place in a pre–World War II Polish-Jewish village; Singer (1904–1991), who won the Nobel Prize in literature in 1978 for his "impassioned narrative art," drew on his Polish-Jewish background for most of his stories.

Baruch lives with his wife's family in the village of Rachev; it is a much grander household than his own childhood home was because his father-in-law is a wealthy man and likes to live in style. The father-in-law is a good man in many ways, and a learned man, but he has one major fault: He has a terrible temper. Unwilling to forgive and forget, he harbors resentments over any little offense. One time Baruch borrowed a pen from him and forgot to return it, and that sent his father-in-law into such a fit of rage that he struck Baruch in the face. This upset the family terribly because a father-in-law does not have that kind of authority over his son-in-law, but Baruch, being an easygoing young man, was quite willing to forgive the older man. The differences between the two men are noticeable: The older man is fastidious, and Baruch is lazy; his father-in-law is always sharp and on top of things, whereas Baruch is terribly forgetful and sometimes can't even find his way home because he doesn't pay attention to where he is. But after the incident with the pen, Baruch's father-in-law approaches him—a rare event—and asks his advice on how to control his anger, for he has alienated all his business partners. Baruch suggests that they go to see the Rabbi of Kuzmir, a neighboring town. At first the older man scoffs at the thought, but later he agrees to go.

They arrive in Kuzmir on a Friday afternoon (at the beginning of the Sabbath) after a long journey through the winter snows, and Baruch's father-in-law goes to talk with Rabbi Chazkele; for three-quarters of an hour he is alone with the rabbi, and then he emerges, irate, calling the rabbi a fool, an ignoramus, to the embarrassment of his son-in-law. What was the rabbi's advice that so infuriated Baruch's father-in-law? That he must become a flatterer. For a week he must flatter everyone he meets, going through the motions of saying nice but insincere things to all of them regardless of who they might be. And that, to the father-in-law, is worse than murder. But Baruch suspects there must be a deeper meaning to the odd piece of advice. The older man wants to go home immediately, but since it is the evening of the Sabbath they can't leave for home (because one does not travel on the Sabbath, between sunset on Friday and sunset on Saturday). So they stay in Kuzmir to celebrate the Sabbath and listen to the prayers of Rabbi Chazkele. Both Baruch and his father-in-law are deeply moved by the rabbi's chanting, and by his words.

> The rabbi commented on the law. And what he said was connected with what he had told my father-in-law at their meeting. "What should a Jew do if he is not a pious man?" the rabbi asked. And answered: "Let him play the pious man. The Almighty does not require good intentions. The deed is what counts. It is what you do that matters. Are you angry perhaps? Go ahead and be angry, but speak gentle words and be friendly at the same time. Are you afraid of being a dissembler? So what if you pretend to be something you aren't? For whose sake are you lying? For your Father in Heaven. His Holy Name, blessed be He, knows the intention and the intention behind the intention, and it is this that is the main thing."
>
> How can one convey the rabbi's lesson? Pearls fell from his mouth and each word burned like fire and penetrated the heart. It wasn't so much the words themselves, but his gestures and his tone. The evil spirit, the rabbi said, cannot be conquered by sheer will. It is known that the evil one has no body, and works mainly through the power of speech. Do not lend him a mouth—that is the way to conquer him. Take, for example, Balaam, the son of Beor. He wanted to curse the children of Israel but forced himself to bless them instead, and because of this, his name is mentioned in the Bible. When one doesn't lend the evil one a tongue, he must remain mute.

> Why should I ramble on? My father-in-law attended all three Sabbath meals. And when, on the Sabbath night, he went to the rabbi to take leave of him, he stayed in his study for a whole hour.
>
> On the way home, I said, "Well, father-in-law?" And he answered: "Your rabbi is a great man."
>
> The road back to Rachev was full of dangers. Though it was still midwinter, the ice on the Vistula had cracked—iceblocks were floating downstream the way they do at Passover time. In the midst of all the cold, thunder and lightning struck. No doubt about

it, only Satan could be responsible for this! We were forced to put up at an inn until Tuesday—and there were many Misoagids staying there. No one could travel further. A real blizzard was raging outside. The howling in the chimney made you shiver.

Misoagids are always the same. These were no exception. They began to heap ridicule upon Hasids—but my father-in-law maintained silence. They tried to provoke him but he refused to join in. They took him to task: "What about this one? What about that one?" He put them off good-naturedly with many tricks. "What change has come over you?" they asked. If they had known that he was coming from Rabbi Chazkele, they would have devoured him.

What more can I tell you? My father-in-law did what the rabbi had prescribed. He stopped snapping at people. His eyes glowed with anger but his speech was soft. And if at times he lifted his pipe about to strike someone, he always stopped himself and spoke with humility. It wasn't long before the people of Rachev realized that my father-in-law was a changed man. He made peace with his enemies. He would stop any little brat in the street and give him a pinch on the cheek. And if the water carrier splashed water entering our house, though I knew this just about drove my father-in-law crazy, he never showed it. "How are you, Reb Yontle?" he would say. "Are you cold, eh?" One could feel that he did this only with great effort. That's what made it noble.

In time, his anger disappeared completely. He began to visit Rabbi Chazkele three times a year. He became a kindly man, so good-natured it was unbelievable. But that is what a habit is like—if you break it, it becomes the opposite. One can turn the worst sin into a good deed. The main thing is to act, not to ponder. He even began to visit the ritual bath. And when he grew old, he acquired disciples of his own. This was after the death of Rabbi Chazkele. My father-in-law always used to say, "If you can't be a good Jew, act the good Jew, because if you act something, you *are* it. Otherwise why does any man try to act at all? Take, for example, the drunk in the tavern. Why doesn't he try to act differently?"

The rabbi once said: "Why is 'Thou Shalt Not Covet' the very last of the Ten Commandments? Because one must first avoid doing the wrong things. Then, later on, one will not desire to do them. If one stopped and waited until all the passions ceased, one could never attain holiness."

And so it is with all things. If you are not happy, act the happy man. Happiness will come later. So also with faith. If you are in despair, act as though you believed. Faith will come afterwards.

Study Questions

1. Is this an example of virtue ethics or ethics of conduct? Explain your answer.

2. Do you think someone can become a better person by constantly doing the right thing, even if his or her inclination is to do something else entirely? What might Aristotle say?

3. Comment on this quote: "One could feel that he did this only with great effort. That's what made it noble." What might Kant say to that? After you've read Chapter 10, return to this question and discuss what Philippa Foot might answer.

Narrative

As Good As It Gets

MARK ANDRUS AND JAMES L. BROOKS (SCREENWRITERS)
JAMES L. BROOKS (DIRECTOR)

Film, 1998. Summary.

Melvin Udall is a famous writer of romance novels. He is also a terrible person; he is an "equal opportunity offender," having epithets and other insults ready for anyone who crosses his path—blacks, Jews, foreigners, women, homosexuals, anyone at all. His gay neighbor's little dog irritates him, so he stuffs the dog down the disposal chute. Melvin is utterly obnoxious and self-centered. When eating at his favorite restaurant, he will sit at only one specific table and be served by only one specific waitress, Carol; he even insults other customers so that they will leave and he can claim "his" table. In addition, he won't use the restaurant's silverware but carries a sealed plastic set. We begin to realize that Melvin is not just obnoxious but also sick; he suffers from obsessive-compulsive disorder. But the disorder in itself doesn't excuse or explain away Melvin's selfishness and rudeness.

Melvin wants to continue his life with as few variations as possible: being careful not to step on cracks while walking from his Manhattan apartment to the restaurant and back; having no physical contact with anyone; eating at the restaurant, being served by and exchanging casual remarks with Carol; and spending his time alone and uninterrupted, writing his best-selling novels about people who experience the grand passion of their lives. But around him, things begin to change dramatically: His gay neighbor, Simon, an artist, is attacked and left for dead by one of his models and his pals. While Simon is in the hospital with terrible injuries, his good friend, an art dealer named Frank who is black, calls on Melvin to lend a helping hand. He figures Melvin owes Simon. They have exchanged words previously, when Simon had tried to confront Melvin about his dog (who came back safe from the chute experience) and Melvin closed the door in Simon's face. Frank then confronts Melvin and threatens him into behaving decently to Simon. Melvin is terrified of him, and when Frank insists that Melvin take the dog for a while, Melvin has no choice but to comply. And with this little change, a crack has opened in Melvin's armor.

As the weeks go by, Melvin doesn't just get used to the dog but dotes on him, feeding him bacon from the restaurant. When Simon gets back from the hospital, bruised and broke, he is devastated to find that his terrible neighbor is now his dog's favorite.

Other things change: One day Carol is no longer at work, and Melvin, being obsessive about who serves him, finds out why: Her little son Spence, who has asthma, has been getting worse. So Melvin makes a point of visiting her to try to persuade her to go back to work. Realizing the gravity of her son's condition, he arranges for a physician to make house calls to do for Spence what Carol's HMO hadn't done—make him better—thus freeing Carol to return to the restaurant and serve his meals. Carol tries to thank Melvin by writing him a long letter, but Melvin doesn't know how to accept gratitude and refuses to read it.

How do Aristotle, Isaac Bashevis Singer, and the movie *As Good As It Gets* (TriStar, 1998) propose transforming a cantankerous, mean-hearted, and selfish person into a kind and caring human being? By making him do things that a kind and caring person would, thus developing kind and caring habits. In this scene Melvin (Jack Nicholson) and Carol (Helen Hunt) share a tender, tentative moment in the midst of helping a mutual friend, although Melvin's transformation is not yet complete.

Frank talks Melvin into driving Simon to Baltimore to see his estranged parents; Simon is about to lose his apartment and needs financial help. Melvin doesn't want to travel alone with Simon and asks Carol to come along. The threesome embark on a strange journey that results in Simon's becoming able to paint again and to get his confidence back, Melvin's admitting to himself that he is in love with Carol, and Carol's disliking Melvin more than ever, because she had been close to falling in love with him until he began acting in his old selfish, insensitive way. Upon their return to New York, Simon and Carol have become the best of friends—and Melvin reveals that he has arranged for Simon to share his big apartment. Now what remains is for Melvin to convince Carol that she loves him and that life with him will be good.

This story almost has the character of a fable—the mean boy who became a good boy, the lost young woman who found love, the friendless man who found a friend in his enemy—but all of it is saturated with humor and sarcasm, so very little sentimentality is allowed to linger. But what is the connection to virtue ethics? Here is a man of despicable character, rude and selfish, who is changed—by what? *By changing his habits.* By doing things differently, he becomes a different person. Compare this with the story by Isaac

Bashevis Singer, and remember Aristotle's advice that "it is by doing just acts that the just man is produced."

Study Questions

1. Is Melvin a believable character? Is it likely that an insensitive, selfish person could become a better person by doing good deeds, even though they are done reluctantly and without good intentions?

2. Is Carol being too suspicious? How would you describe her character, referring to Aristotle's concept of the Golden Mean?

3. Compare Melvin and Baruch's father-in-law in Singer's story. What are the similarities? What are the differences?

4. Is it good enough to become a different and better person by having a change of habits forced on you, or is it better if you choose to change your habits yourself? Reread the first Primary Reading, Aristotle's *Nicomachean Ethics,* and explain what Aristotle would say. What do you yourself think? Has your character ever improved by being forced into a situation?

Chapter Ten

Contemporary Perspectives

*I*n the introduction to Chapter 8, I mentioned that the idea of a good character as one of the key elements in a moral theory was eclipsed by the general notion that all that matters is *doing the right thing.* With the advent of Christianity, virtue ethics was rejected in favor of an *ethics of conduct*—asking the kinds of questions introduced in Part 2 of this book. As we saw earlier, that was in part a result of a greater social awareness: There is more fairness in asking everybody to follow rules of conduct than there is in trying to make people adapt to vague principles of how to be, and there is a greater chance of developing rational arguments for your position regarding rules of conduct than there is of getting others to agree with your viewpoint concerning what is virtuous. In recent years, though, philosophers have turned their attention to the ancient thoughts about character building, and virtue theory is now experiencing a revival. (See Box 10.1 for a brief overview of virtue ethics and character.) This trend has been hotly contested by scholars such as J. B. Schneewind, who believe the original reasons for adopting ethics of conduct are still valid.

The revival of virtue theory has been primarily a British and American phenomenon, and we will look at some of the proponents of this new way of approaching ethics. In continental philosophy (European philosophy excluding the British tradition), there was a separate renewal of interest in Aristotle and his virtue theory in the twentieth century, but in a sense a version of virtue theory has been in effect in continental philosophy ever since the nineteenth century, and we will take a look at that tradition too. Because virtue theory is now associated with the new British/American theory, we will call its continental counterpart the "Quest for Authenticity."

Ethics and the Morality of Virtue as Political Concepts

As we have seen, there is a subtle difference between morality and ethics, and in the debate about virtue that difference becomes very clear. In an *ethics of virtue* the issue is to ask yourself what kind of person you want to be, to find good reasons to back up your view and to listen to possible counterarguments, and then to set forth to shape your own character, all the while being ready to justify your choice of virtue rationally or to change your mind. An ethics of virtue doesn't specify what *kind* of virtue you should strive for, although it is usually assumed that it will be something benevolent or at least nothing harmful. The important thing is that you realize you *can* mold your character into what you believe is right. The question of whether your chosen virtue really is a morally good choice is not necessarily part of the issue.

470

Box 10.1   CAN WE CHANGE OUR SPOTS?

Opponents of virtue ethics often claim that for people to be praised for what they do, or blamed for it, it must be assumed that they are *responsible* for their actions. But are we responsible for our character and disposition? Virtue theory asks us to look primarily at people's character. Suppose we ask someone to give to charity, and she doesn't have a generous disposition. Can we then blame her for her lack of virtue? If we can't, then virtue ethics is useless as a moral theory. It may praise people for dispositions that they already have, but it doesn't tell us how to improve ourselves. Virtue theory's response to that is that certain people have certain dispositions, and in that respect some are more fortunate than others, morally speaking; some people are just naturally thoughtful and generous, or courageous, or truthful. The rest of us have to work on these things. Just because we lack a good disposition doesn't mean we can't work on improving it, and just because we have a tendency toward a certain disposition doesn't mean we can't work on controlling it.

However, a *morality of virtue* focuses precisely on this issue: Which virtue is desirable to strive for, and which is no virtue at all? Parents of young children generally know that telling stories can be an excellent way to teach moral virtues, but lately politicians as well as educators have also taken notice. The politician and writer William H. Bennett has published several collections of stories with morals—didactic stories—meant to be read to young children; the best known of those collections is simply titled *The Book of Virtues* and contains stories from the Western cultural heritage, as well as from other cultures, all with a short added moral explanation. (Box 10.2 discusses stories that warn against following nonvirtuous role models.)

In the latter half of the twentieth century, virtue ethics made another entrance on the stage of British and American philosophy. For some thinkers it was an absolute necessity to make the switch from an ethics of conduct to virtue ethics because, as virtue ethicists say, you can do the right thing and still be an unpleasant person; however, if you work on your character, you will become a good person *and* do the right thing without even having to think about it. For others, virtue ethics has become a much-needed supplement to an ethics of conduct. Some see virtue ethics as a way for people to explore the issue of a good character; others view it as a way to teach what a good character should be all about.

The Political Aspect of Conduct Versus Character

In the last decade of the twentieth century, the political debate in the United States became polarized in a new way—which actually turned out to be a polished and updated version of the older polarization between *conduct* and *character.* Republican politicians brought up the issue of character: Is the candidate trustworthy? Does he or she have integrity? Does he or she keep promises? In short, is the candidate a virtuous person—in his or her private life as well? Democratic politicians responded by pointing to the public policies of the candidate: What has he or she accomplished

Box 10.2   NEGATIVE ROLE MODELS

Virtue theory usually focuses on heroes and saints who are to be emulated, but little attention is given to those characters who perhaps teach a deeper moral lesson: the negative role models. Whether we look to real-life figures or fictional characters, moral lessons can be learned by observing the destiny of "bad guys," provided that they don't get away with their misdeeds. (Twisted souls can, of course, learn a lesson from the evildoer who does get away with it, but that is another matter.) From childhood we hear of people who did something they were not supposed to do and suffered the consequences. Most of these stories are issued as a warning: Don't "cry wolf," because in the end nobody will believe you. Look what happened to Adam and Eve, who ate the fruit of the one tree they were not supposed to touch. Look what happened to the girl who stepped on a loaf of bread so she wouldn't get her feet wet. She was pulled down into the depths of hell (in a Hans Christian Andersen story). When we grow up we learn the lesson of politicians who turned out to be crooked, of televangelists who didn't practice what they preached, of rich and famous people who have serious drug problems. Movies and novels also bombard us with negative models: Darth Vader (*Star Wars*) sells out to the Dark Side, so we learn to beware of people who have lost their integrity. Charles

Foster Kane (*Citizen Kane*) forgets his humanity and dies lonely, his heart longing for the time when he was a small boy. The Count of Monte Cristo loses his own humanity through an obsession with revenge. Madame Bovary loses control of her life because she fantasizes too much. And Smeagol loses not only his self but even his identity as a hobbit when he becomes Gollum through allowing the Ring to take over his spirit (*The Lord of the Rings*). Through exposure to such characters we get a warning; we live their lives vicariously and find that bitterness lies at the end. Films such as *Money for Nothing, A Simple Plan, Goodfellas,* and *Fargo* show us that the life of selfish pursuits carries its own punishment. There are, however, works that fail to bring home the moral lesson because they are either too pompous or simply misinformed. Such a film is *Reefer Madness*, which is now a cult classic depicting the life of crime and madness that results from smoking marijuana. Another antidrug film but with a far superior story and impact is *Requiem for a Dream*. It realistically describes the downward spiral of drug addictions, in this case from diet pills as well as heroin. (If you remember your fallacies from Chapter 1, you'll be able to identify *Reefer Madness* as an example of the slippery slope fallacy, whereas *Requiem* depicts an actual, chilling slippery slope.)

politically so far? What social policies does the candidate support, and with what success rate has he or she had them implemented? This is not just an interesting revival of the philosophical question of conduct versus character; it goes to the heart of how we view the importance of values. Do we think the question of personal character and integrity is the most important form of ethics—perhaps even the only form of ethics? Or do we believe that the personal standards of someone who serves the public are less important than his or her social conscience and efforts to change things presumably for the better? For some politicians, the question of character has in itself become a matter of a person's outlook on social policies rather than a question of personal values: A person of good character is a person who supports

Zits by Jerry Scott and Jim Borgman

ZITS Partnership, King Features Syndicate.

Virtue ethics recommends that we emulate role models; however, in this culture we also encourage individuality and the characteristics that make people unique and natural. Immanuel Kant warns about holding siblings up as role models, because that may create resentment rather than inspiration to be good. In *Zits*, the teen Jeremy is inundated with conflicting advice to be like someone else but also to be himself—is it any wonder he is confused?

certain social policies. Regardless of how one feels about national politics, it is philosophically interesting that the revived debate between ethics of conduct and virtue ethics is not always a partisan story—the virtue concept is not in itself a Republican issue, and the policy issue is not by nature Democratic—it all depends on the political needs of the moment.

As with so many of the moral issues we have looked at, an extreme either/or turns out to be a *false dichotomy*—a false either/or with other possible alternatives. If we assume that character is important, why should we assume that a person's stand on social issues is less important? And if we assume that social views count, then why shouldn't character count as well? A person can have a perfectly squeaky-clean character and yet be completely ineffective as a decision maker or a negotiator or even have little grasp of or interest in social policies and the needs of society. And a highly effective politician, well liked and radiating understanding of social and economic problems in the population, can turn out to have a personal life that is in shambles because of a lack of character. At times, though, it does seem all-important that a political leader have character and integrity—even if there is disagreement about his or her policies.

The emerging pattern shows that each group focuses on what it considers most important: On the whole, conservatives focus on character and liberals focus on a variety of social policies, such as the right to abortion, affirmative action, gun control, welfare, and other causes related to the general question of what to do.

Have Virtue, and Then Go Ahead: Mayo, Foot, and Sommers

Bernard Mayo

In 1958 the American philosopher Bernard Mayo suggested that Western ethics had reached a dead end, for it had lost contact with ordinary life. People don't live by great principles of what to do ("Do your duty" or "Make humanity happy"); instead, they measure themselves according to their moral qualities or deficiencies on an everyday basis. Novelists have not forgotten this, says Mayo, because the books we read tell of people who try hard to be a certain way—who sometimes succeed and sometimes fail—and we, the readers, feel that we have learned something.

An ethics of conduct is not excluded from virtue ethics, says Mayo—it just takes second place, because whatever we *do* is included in our general standard of virtue: We pay our taxes or help animals that are injured in traffic because we believe in the virtues of being a good citizen and fellow traveler on Planet Earth. In other words, if we have a set of virtues we believe we should live by, we will usually do the right thing as a consequence. However, an ethics of conduct without virtue may not be benevolent at all; it is entirely possible to "do your duty" and still be a bad person— you do it for gain or to spite someone. (A good example of such a person is Dickens's Ebenezer Scrooge in *A Christmas Carol,* who may appear to be a pillar of society but only because it is profitable to him.) You can do something courageous without actually being courageous, says Mayo (although Aristotle would insist that if you do it often enough you actually *become* courageous, and utilitarians would insist that it doesn't matter why you do something, as long as it has good results).

So how should we choose our actions in an everyday situation? Mayo says we shouldn't look for specific advice in a moral theory (Do such and such); we should, instead, adopt general advice (Be brave/lenient/patient). That will ensure that we have the "unity of character" a moral system of principles can't give us. Mayo advises us to select a role model, either an ideal person or an actual one. Be just, be a good American—or be like Socrates or Buddha or choose a contemporary role model such as Jane Goodall or Maya Angelou. There are heroes and saints throughout history we can choose from, not necessarily because of what they have done, but because of the kind of people they were.

So when Mayo suggests that we learn from factual *exemplars* such as Martin Luther King, Jr., Mother Teresa, or perhaps our parents, he is not saying we should emulate their actual doings but, rather, that we should live in their "spirit" and respond to everyday situations with the strength that a good character can give. This is a much more realistic approach to morality than is reflected in the high ideals of principles and duty that an ethics of conduct has held up for people. People have felt inadequate because nobody can live up to such ideals, says Mayo, but everyone can try to be like someone he or she admires. Critics of this enthusiasm for role models have pointed out that just emulating someone you admire doesn't in itself solve your moral dilemmas: (1) What if your idea of a role model doesn't correspond to what other people consider models of decent behavior? This is one of the traditional problems with virtue ethics: Who gets the final word about what is to count as virtue? It provides no

Box 10.3   KANT'S REJECTION OF ROLE MODELS

Bernard Mayo points out that Kant rejected the idea of imitating others as a moral rule and called it "fatal to morality." Kant deplored holding up an example of an ideal, rather than striving for the ideal itself. Mayo thinks striving for the ideal itself is too much to ask of ordinary people. If we read Kant's *Lectures on Ethics,* we find an interesting argument for why it is not a good idea to point to *people* as worth emulating: If I try to compare myself with someone else who is better than I am, I can either try to be as good or try to diminish that other person; this second choice is actually much easier than trying to be as good as the other person, and it invariably leads to *jealousy.* So when parents hold up one sibling for the other to emulate, they are paving the way for sibling rivalry; the

one who is being set up as a paragon will be resented by the other one. Kant suggests that we should recommend goodness as such and not proffer individuals to be emulated, because we all have a tendency to be jealous of people we think we can't measure up to. So the Kantian rejection of role models is not merely an abstract preference for an ideal but also a realistic appreciation of family relationships and petty grudges. It may even serve as a valid psychological explanation for why some people have a profound dislike for so-called heroes and make consistent efforts to diminish the deeds of all persons regarded as role models by society. Such an attitude may just be another reaction against being told that someone else is a better person than you are.

easy method for solving moral disputes. (2) What if your role model turns out not to be so perfect after all? If he or she is still alive, you have to assume that anyone can make a wrong turn, even someone you have chosen to emulate. Are you supposed to keep a critical distance or just follow your model every step of the way? And even if your role model is a historical figure (who can't make any new mistakes), there is always the risk that new material will surface, showing another and less virtuous side to that person. Are you then supposed to drop your hero or find ways to defend him or her? (3) The most serious complaint may be the one that comes from several philosophers (from different time periods) who find fault with the very idea that one can be virtuous by just imitating someone else. (Mayo, of course, didn't invent that idea; he just made it part of a modern philosophy of virtue.) One is Kant, and you can find his thought-provoking criticism in Box 10.3. Another is the French philosopher Jean-Paul Sartre, who insisted that we ought to take responsibility for every single thing we do in order to be true to ourselves and become authentic human beings. Taking such responsibility precludes settling for just copying what others do, because that approach would give us a false sense of who we are and a false sense of security—by making us believe we can go through life and be good persons just by imitating others. In Sartre's terminology, we would then be living a life of inauthenticity.

Philippa Foot

Opponents of virtue theory ask how we can call beneficial human traits "virtues" when some humans are *born* with such traits and others don't have them at all. In

Philippa Foot (b. 1920), a British ethicist, is credited with being one of a handful of 20th century philosophers who have revived and modernized the concept of virtue ethics. For years she held the position of Griffin Professor of Philosophy at the University of California, Los Angeles. Her works include *Virtues and Vices and Other Essays in Moral Philosophy* (1978), *Natural Goodness* (2001), and *Moral Dilemmas: And Other Topics in Moral Philosophy* (2002).

other words, human responsibility for those dispositions doesn't enter into the picture at all. Good health and an excellent memory are great to have, but can we blame those who are sick and forgetful for not being virtuous?

The British philosopher Philippa Foot counters that argument in her book *Virtues and Vices* (1978) by stressing that virtues aren't merely dispositions we either have or don't have. A virtue is not just a beneficial disposition but also a matter of our *intentions*. If we couple our willpower with our disposition to achieve some goal that is beneficial, then we are virtuous. So having a virtue is not the same as having a skill; it is having the proper intention to do something good—and being able to follow it up with an appropriate action.

For Foot, virtues are not just something we are equipped with. Rather, we are equipped with some tendency to go astray, and virtue is our capacity to *correct* that tendency. Human nature makes us want to run and hide when there is danger; that is why there is the virtue of courage. And we may want to indulge in more pleasure than is good for us; that is why there is the virtue of temperance. Foot points out that virtue theories seem to assume human nature is by and large sensual and fearful, but there actually may be other character deficiencies that are more prevalent and more interesting to try to correct through virtue—such as the desire to be put upon and dissatisfied or the unwillingness to accept good things as they come along.

But what about people who are *naturally* virtuous? The philosophical tradition has had a tendency to judge them rather oddly. Suppose we have two people who make the decision to lend a hand to someone in need. Person A likes to do things for others and jumps at the chance to be helpful. Person B really couldn't care less about other people but knows that benevolence is a virtue, so he makes an effort to help in spite of his natural inclination. For Kant the person who makes an effort to overcome his or her inclination is a *morally better person* than the one to whom virtue comes easily. But surely there is something strange about that judgment, because in real life we appreciate the naturally benevolent person so much more than the surly one who grudgingly tries to be good for the sake of a principle. As a matter of fact, those are the people we *love,* because they *like* to do things for the sake of other people. Many schools of thought agree that it takes a greater effort to overcome than to follow your inclination, so it must be more morally worthy. Aristotle, however, believed that the person who takes pleasure in doing a virtuous action is the one who is truly virtuous.

Foot sides here with Aristotle: The person who likes to do good, or to whom it comes easily, is a morally better person than the one who succeeds through struggle. Why? Because the fact that there is a struggle is a sign that the person is *lacking in virtue* in the first place. Not that the successful struggler isn't good, or virtuous, but the one who did it with no effort is just a little bit better, because the virtue was already there to begin with. Foot's own example, in *Virtues and Vices,* is honesty:

> For one man it is hard to refrain from stealing and for another man it is not: which shows the greater virtue in acting as he should? . . . The fact that a man is *tempted* to steal is something about him that shows a certain lack of honesty: of the thoroughly honest man we say that it "never entered his head," meaning that it was never a real possibility for him.

In addition, Foot offers a solution to another problem plaguing virtue ethics: Can we say that someone who is committing an evil act is somehow doing it with virtue? Say that a criminal has to remain cool, calm, and collected to open a safe or has to muster courage to fulfill a contract and kill someone. Is that person virtuous in the sense of having self-control or courage? Foot borrows an argument from the one ethicist who is most often identified with an ethics of conduct, even though his work also includes the topic of virtue—Kant: *An act or a disposition can't be called good if it isn't backed by a good will.* Foot interprets it this way: If the act is morally wrong, or, rather, if the *intentions* behind the act are bad, then cool-headedness and courage *cease to be virtues.* Virtue is not something static; it is a dynamic power that appears when the intention is to do something good. The "virtue" value is simply switched off when the good intention is absent. And here we have an answer to the study question raised at the end of Chapter 9, after Aristotle's text on courage: *Can a terrorist be courageous?* Should we acknowledge that the September 11 hijackers were somehow brave, in spite of their evil intentions? Foot would probably say no: A virtue is nullified if it is done with an evil intention. The hijackers may have experienced some kind of spiritual fortitude, but it doesn't deserve the name *courage* if we view courage as a virtue. And saying that their intention may have been to do something good for somebody other than the victims doesn't count, in any moral theory: not in the religion of Islam, which forbids the killing of innocents; nor in Christianity and Judaism, which forbid the same thing; nor in utilitarianism, which sees the immensity of the massacre and psychological turmoil that followed throughout the world as unjustified by any local cause the hijackers may have had; nor in Kant's theory, which says we should never use any other person merely as a means to an end; nor in virtue theory, which, as we can now see, holds that it is *motivation* that determines whether or not a character trait can be called virtuous.

We find parallels in other situations in which there may not be any evil or criminal element. Hope, for example, is generally supposed to be a virtue, but if someone is being unrealistic and daydreams about wish fulfillment, hope is no longer a virtue. And temperance may be a virtue, but not if a person is simply afraid to throw herself into the stream of life. In that case it is a shield and not a virtue.

Critics of Foot's positive attitude toward the person who is naturally good with few selfish inclinations often point to Kant's argument against the storekeeper who decides not to cheat customers (similar to the version of the argument you know from Chapter 6): To say you like your customers so much that you would never cheat them is not enough, because what if you stopped liking your customers? Similarly, the person who has never been tempted because susceptibility to temptation is not in her or his nature may seem a higher moral person to Foot; but perhaps it is just because that person has never come across temptation before, and in that case it is easy enough to be virtuous. True virtue, say Kant's followers, shows itself precisely in the face of temptation—and not in its absence. However, when we have the choice between a store where they have a strict policy against cheating but the personnel are cold and grumpy and the store where they've known us for years and ask us how we're doing, don't we prefer to shop at the friendly place rather than at the unfriendly, but morally correct, place? Kant may think we should choose the unfriendly place, but Foot disagrees: We prefer friendliness, not principles. But what makes being friendly morally superior to being principled, in Foot's view? Remember, Kant rejected the storekeeper's third option because someone who wouldn't cheat his or her customers because of a sunny disposition toward them is really just doing what he or she wants, out of self-gratification, not out of principles. Of course, it is possible to be of a sunny disposition *and* be principled, but that is not the issue here. The issue is whether a sunny disposition is enough to make someone a moral person or whether having a character that isn't tempted is morally superior to being a person who encounters temptation and fights it. Foot says yes: The storekeeper who wouldn't dream of cheating her customers is a better person than the one who has had a moment's temptation and rejected it, because temptation simply wasn't a factor. Foot's assumption is that it takes a weak character to be tempted. But, realistically, perhaps all that was missing was exposure and opportunity. So perhaps Kant has a point after all.

Christina Hoff Sommers

Which, then, are the virtues to which we should pay attention? Foot leaves the question open to an extent, because people tend to differ about what exactly is good for others and desirable as a human trait. Another ethicist, however, prefers to be more direct; her aim is not so much to defend virtue ethics as such as to focus on specific virtues and moral failings in our Western world. Christina Hoff Sommers tells of the woes an ethics professor of her acquaintance would experience at the end of a term. In spite of the multisubject textbooks they had read and the spirited discussions they had engaged in, the professor's students somehow got the impression that there are no moral truths. Everything they had studied about ethics had been presented in terms of rules that can be argued against and social dilemmas that have no clear solutions. More than half of the students cheated on their ethics finals. The irony of cheating on an ethics test probably did not even occur to those students.

What is lacking in our ethics classes? asks Sommers. It can't be good intentions on the part of instructors, because since the 1960s teachers have been very careful to

Box 10.4   THEIR CHEATING HEARTS; OR, DO PRINCIPLES MATTER?

Christina Hoff Sommers brings up the question of cheating students and sees it as a problem of students being able to connect personally with the moral theories they have studied. A blatant case of cheating was revealed in the spring of 2007 at Duke University, where thirty-four out of thirty-eight students in the graduate business school were disciplined for plagiarism. Your author had occasion to blog about this matter, and the comments were profound. One student, "Charlette," wrote, "When a student makes the decision to cheat, their desire to gain whatever they may gain from cheating is greater than their desire to be 'morally right.' It seems to me that all you can do is influence how much people value being the latter. In this society, I'm sure most people know that cheating is considered 'wrong.' Simply 'teaching values' doesn't appear to greatly affect how a person would make decisions if they have already developed most of their values."

Another student, "Evan," responded, "Clearly these students value a letter grade over the acquisition of knowledge. This is perhaps a symptom of a dysfunctional academic system rather than a dysfunctional morality." "Thea" chimed in: "I think that this is what happens in a society when prestige and money become synonymous. In generations past, prestige could be acquired in myriad ways including benevolence, ethics, special skills and abilities, knowledge. Today, those things do not provide people with prestige automatically. Instead, they are relevant only so far as they can be translated to money." And "Eric" related cheating to theories learned in class: "Students may make a decision to cheat because they don't agree that doing so would be 'morally wrong.' . . . The college environment with its set rules of what cheating is applies Kant's ideas of ethics. These rules don't look at the consequences but instead say 'this is always wrong' even if there could be a net benefit to the students and world. If you are a college student who instead prefers Bentham's hedonistic calculus you might conclude that cheating in some situations is actually the 'right' thing to do."

In your view, is it wrong to cheat on a test? Is this a black-and-white issue, or are there shades of gray? After having studied a number of moral theories in this book, do you find that one or more theories can clarify such a question for you, or do you regard it as a matter for one's moral instinct to decide? Your answer may go to the heart of the current debate in value theory: Do our moral principles actually matter at all when we make decisions, or are we guided more by other factors, such as personal needs or feelings?

present the material from all sides and to avoid moral indoctrination. (Even this text, as you have noticed, contains sporadic mention of the difference between doing ethics and *moralizing*.) Somehow, though, students come away with the notion that because everything can be argued against, moral values are a matter of taste. The teacher may prefer her students not to cheat, but that is simply her preference; if the student's preference is for cheating as a moral value ("Cheat but don't get caught"), then so be it. The moral lesson is learned by the student, and the chance for our society to hand down lessons of moral decency and respect for others has been lost because of a general fear of imposing one's personal values on others. See Box 10.4 for a student "blog" discussion on the issue of cheating.

Christina Hoff Sommers (b. 1950), American philosopher, coeditor of *Vice and Virtue in Everyday Life* (1985), and author of *Who Stole Feminism?* (1994) and *The War Against Boys* (2000), argues for a return to virtue ethics in order for people in modern society to regain a sense of responsibility rather than leave it to social institutions to make decisions on moral issues.

Sommers suggests that instead of teaching courses on the big issues such as abortion, euthanasia, and capital punishment, we should talk about the little, everyday, enormously important things, such as honesty, friendship, consideration, respect. Those are virtues that, if not learned at a young age, may never be achieved in our society. Sommers mentions that in ethics courses of the nineteenth century, students were taught how to be good rather than how to discuss moral issues. When asked to name some moral values that can't be disputed, Sommers answered,

> It is wrong to mistreat a child, to humiliate someone, to torment an animal. To think only of yourself, to steal, to lie, to break promises. And on the positive side: it is right to be considerate and respectful of others, to be charitable and generous.

For Sommers, it is not enough to investigate virtue ethics—one must practice it and teach it to others. In that way virtue *theory* becomes virtue *practice*. If we study virtue theory in school, chances are we will find it natural to seek to develop our own virtues. Sommers believes a good way to learn about virtues is to use the same method that both Bernard Mayo and philosopher Alasdair MacIntyre (see Box 10.5) advise: to read stories in which someone does something decent for others, either humans or animals. Through stories we "get the picture" better than we get it from philosophical dilemmas or case studies. Literary classics can tell us more about friendship and obligation than a textbook in moral problems can. For Sommers, there are basic human virtues that aren't a matter of historical relativism, fads, or discussion, and the better we all learn them, the better we'll like living in our world with one another. Those virtues are part of most people's moral heritage, and there is nothing oppressive about teaching the common virtues of decency, civility, honesty, and fairness.

Too often we tend to think that certain issues are someone else's problem; the state will take care of it, whether it is pollution, homelessness, or the loneliness of elderly people. For Sommers this is part of a virtue ethics for grown-ups: *Don't assume that it is someone else's responsibility.* Don't hide from contemporary problems—take

Box 10.5   MacIntyre and the Virtues

The American philosopher Alasdair MacIntyre believes that our moral values would be enriched if we followed the examples of older cultures and let *tradition* be part of those values. We don't exist in a cultural vacuum, he says, and we would understand ourselves better if we'd allow a historical perspective to be part of our system of values. That doesn't mean that everything our ancestors did and thought should become a virtue for us, but a look back to the values of those who came before us adds a depth to our modern life that makes it easier to understand ourselves. And how do we understand ourselves best? As the tellers of stories of history, of fiction, and of our own lives. We understand ourselves in terms of the story we would tell of our own life, and by doing that we are defining our *character.* So virtue and character development are essential to being a moral person and doing what is morally good.

But virtues are not static abilities for MacIntyre any more than they are for Philippa Foot. Virtues are linked with our aspirations; they make us better at *becoming* what we want to be. It is not so much that we have a vision of the good life; rather, we have an idea of what we want to accomplish (what MacIntyre calls "internal goods"), and virtues help us accomplish those goals. Whatever our goal, we usually will be more successful at reaching it if we are conscientious and trustworthy in striving for it. Whatever profession we try to excel in, we will succeed more easily if we try to be courageous and honest and maintain our integrity. With all the demands we face and all the different roles we have to play—in our jobs, sexual relationships, relations to family and friends—staying loyal and trustworthy helps us to function as one whole person rather than as a compilation of disjointed roles.

them on and contribute to their solution. Do your part to limit pollution. Think of how you can help homeless people. Go visit someone you know who is elderly and lonely. Virtues like those will benefit us all and are the kind we must learn to focus on if we are to make a success out of being humans living together.

This vision of personal virtues is probably the most direct call to a resurgence of moral values that has been produced so far within the field of philosophy. Sommers, however, is arguing not for a revival of religious values but for a strengthening of basic concepts of personal responsibility and respect for other beings. Her claim is that few ethicists dare to stand by values and pronounce them good in themselves these days for fear of being accused of indoctrinating their students. For Sommers the list of values cited above is absolute: They can't be disputed. Herein lies one answer to why Sommers today remains one of the most controversial of American contemporary philosophers (another answer can be found in Chapter 12: her approach to feminism): In the intellectual climate of the 1990s, it was considered not only customary but even proper to view values as something more or less relative to one's culture and to one's personal life experience; we've explored the issue in Chapter 3. As you have heard, the entire intellectual juggernaut of academic instruction had, since the 1970s, been moving away from the very notion of "indoctrination," of instructors telling their students what to think about values. For Sommers, however, the end result has not been what was presumably intended—an enhanced individual

CALVIN AND HOBBES. Reprinted with permission of Universal Press Syndicate. All rights reserved.

Here is another stab at doing philosophy from Calvin, who is voicing rare scruples about cheating on an ethics test (scruples that apparently were not shared by the students of Christina Hoff Sommers's colleague or the graduate students caught cheating at Duke University). Is Hobbes right that "simply acknowledging the issue is a moral victory"?

moral responsibility—but, rather, the opposite: no sense of responsibility at all, since morals are perceived to be relative. So Sommers digs deeper into who we are as humans and finds a common ground of values.

But is she right? Can we just pronounce the virtues of decency, civility, honesty, and so forth the ultimate values without any further discussion? For many of her colleagues and readers, this is an unacceptable return to what we in this book have called *hard universalism.* Perhaps Sommers is right that most people would agree her values are good, and perhaps not. For many, what Sommers is doing is just old-fashioned moralizing (and some applaud that effort, but others don't). In effect, this isn't just Sommers's problem—it is a problem inherent in all genuine virtue ethics, as you'll remember from the previous chapter: When there is a dispute about virtues, among virtuous people, who gets to be right? How do we determine exactly what virtue is, if virtue is its own answer? How can college students be convinced that cheating is a bad thing? How can teens be convinced that sharing copyrighted material via the Internet is wrong? It can't be done by simply teaching them that honesty is a virtue; that might work for young children, but adolescents and adults need *reasons.* Reasons and reasoning are the key here. A moral story such as Charles Dickens's *A Tale of Two Cities* may tell us that self-sacrifice is a "far, far better thing" to practice than anything else, and it may make sense to me, but in your ears it may just sound like propaganda. What we need is to add rational argumentation to virtue ethics: give good reasons why something is a virtue, and a value. The stand-off between Sommers and many of her colleagues might, in this respect, be deflected by seeking an answer in what we've called *soft universalism* and in an approach you're familiar with from elsewhere in this book: looking for the common ground, plus finding good reasons why something is, or should be, a virtue. We return to soft universalism in Chapter 11.

The Quest for Authenticity: Kierkegaard, Heidegger, Sartre, and Levinas

Within what is called "contemporary continental philosophy"—by and large European philosophy after World War I—one school of thought holds there is only one way to live properly and only one virtue to strive for: that of *authenticity.* That school of thought is *existentialism.* Although existentialism developed primarily at the hands of Jean-Paul Sartre as a response to the experience of meaninglessness in World War II, it has its roots in the writings of the Danish philosopher Søren Aabye Kierkegaard and the German philosopher Friederich Nietzsche. In this section we take a look at Kierkegaard, Martin Heidegger, and Sartre, with a brief visit to the ethics of Nietzsche. In addition we will look at a philosopher, who in more recent years has emerged as a forceful voice for ethics as fundamental to human existence: Emmanuel Levinas. Whereas Kierkegaard's form of authenticity is ultimately conceived as a relationship between *oneself and God,* Heidegger's authenticity deals with one's relationship to *one's own form of existence,* and Sartre's authenticity deals with *one's relationship to oneself as a person making moral choices,* Levinas focuses on the relationship between *oneself and the Other*—our fellow human beings.

Kierkegaard's Religious Authenticity

During his lifetime (1813–1855), Kierkegaard was known locally, in Copenhagen, as a man of leisure who had a theology degree and spent his time writing convoluted and irritating attacks on the Danish establishment, including officials of the Lutheran church. Few people understood his points because he was rarely straightforward in his writings and hid his true opinions under layers of pseudonyms and irony. The idea that there might be a great mind at work, developing what was to become one of the most important lines of thought in the twentieth century, was obvious to no one at the time, in Denmark or elsewhere. As a matter of fact, Kierkegaard was working against the general spirit of the times, which was focused politically on the development of socialism and scientifically on the ramifications of Darwinism. People weren't ready to listen to ideas such as the value of personal commitment, the psychological dread that accompanies the prospect of total human freedom of the will,

Søren Kierkegaard (1813–1855), Danish philosopher, writer, and theologian, believed that there are three major stages in human spiritual development: the aesthetic stage, the ethical stage, and the religious stage. Not everyone goes through all stages, but true selfhood and personal authenticity can't happen until one has put one's complete faith in God.

the relativity of truth, and the value of the individual. As it happened, though, such ideas were to become key issues for French and German existential philosophers a couple of generations after Kierkegaard's death.

There are two major, very different ways of approaching the strange writings of Søren Kierkegaard. You can dismiss him as a man who had a difficult childhood and as a consequence developed an overinflated ego with no sense of proportion as to the importance of events. In other words, you can view his writings as simply the product of an overheated brain that pondered the "great mystery" of Søren Kierkegaard's life and times. Or you can view his writings as words that speak to all humanity from a uniquely insightful point of view, which just happens to have its roots in events in Kierkegaard's own life. Among current scholars this second approach has become the prevailing one.

What was so eventful about Kierkegaard's life? Nothing much, compared with the lives of other famous people; but, contrary to most people, Kierkegaard analyzed everything that happened to him for all it was worth and with an eerie insight. He was born into a family of devout Lutherans (Lutheranism is the state religion in Denmark and has been since the Protestant Reformation) and was the youngest boy born to comparatively old parents. Several of his older siblings died young, and for some reason both Søren and his father believed that Søren would not live long either. His father's opinion had an extreme influence on the boy—an influence that Kierkegaard later analyzed to perfection, years before Freud described conflict and bonding between fathers and sons.

When his father was young and a shepherd in rural Denmark, he was overcome by hunger and cold one bleak day on the moors, and he stood up on a rock and cursed God for letting a child suffer like that. Shortly after that incident his parents sent him to Copenhagen as an apprentice, and his hard life was over. That was a psychological shock to him, because he had expected punishment from God for cursing him, and he waited for the punishment most of his life. He grew rich while others lost their money, and for that reason he expected God to punish him even more severely. The first tragic thing that happened to him was that he lost his young wife; however, two months later he married their maid, who was already pregnant at the time.

When Søren's older siblings died, his father thought that God's punishment had struck again, but otherwise his luck held while his guilt grew. It is possible that he then got the idea of letting his youngest son somehow make amends for him—take on the burden and strive for a reconciliation with God. In the Lutheran tradition there is no such thing as making a confession to your minister to "get things off your chest"—you alone must face your responsibility and handle your relationship with God. That means that you have direct access to God at any time, in your heart; you have a direct relationship with God. Your faith is a personal matter, and for Kierkegaard in particular the concept of faith was to become extremely personal.

Søren turned out to be an extraordinarily bright child, and his father devoted much time to his education, in particular to the development of his imagination. The two made a habit of taking walks—in their living room. Søren would choose where they were going—to the beach, to the castle in the woods, down Main Street—and his father would then describe in minute detail what they "saw." It was intellectually and emotionally exhausting for the boy, and scholars have ridiculed the father for his fancy, but today it is recognized by many that the combination of imagination and intellectual discipline is just about the best trait a parent can develop in a child, although one might say that this was a rather extreme way of going about it. At the end of this chapter you can read an excerpt from Kierkegaard's *Johannes Climacus* in which he describes his father's vivid imagination.

Kierkegaard was a young adult when his father died, and he understood full well the immense influence his father had had on him. He wrote the following in *Stages on Life's Way* (1845), though he didn't let on that he was writing about himself:

> There was once a father and a son. A son is like a mirror in which the father beholds himself, and for the son the father too is like a mirror in which he beholds himself in the time to come. . . . the father believed he was to blame for the son's melancholy, and the son believed that he was the occasion of the father's sorrow—but they never exchanged a word on this subject.
>
> Then the father died, and the son saw much, experienced much, and was tried in manifold temptations; but infinitely inventive as love is, longing and the sense of loss taught him, not indeed to wrest from the silence of eternity a communication, but to imitate the father's voice so perfectly that he was content with the likeness . . . for the father was the only one who had understood him, and yet he did not know in fact whether he had understood him; and the father was the only confidant he had had, but the confidence was of such a sort that it remained the same whether the father lived or died.

So Kierkegaard *internalized* the voice of his father; as Freud would say, he made his father's voice his own *Superego*. This had the practical effect of prompting Kierkegaard finally to get his degree in theology (which his father had wanted him to do but which he hadn't really wanted himself). Kierkegaard also internalized his father's guilt and rather gloomy outlook on life. (See Box 10.6 for another event that may have been influenced by his father.) Kierkegaard believed that everyone, even a

Box 10.6   A KIND OF LOVE AND A MARRIAGE THAT WASN'T: REGINE OLSEN

An event of great importance in Søren Kierkegaard's life occurred when he fell deeply in love for the first and only time. The woman's name was Regine Olsen, and she was the daughter of a minister. Regine and Søren became engaged, and he engaged himself in a new intellectual scrutiny: What was this feeling? Was it constant or a fluke? What might go wrong? Was it right for him to try to do something "universal" that everybody did, like get married and have children, or would it somehow interfere with his father's plans for him to be a sacrifice to God? Regine, a kind and loving woman, was utterly puzzled at Søren's reluctance to accept that they were just young people in love. When they were together he was in a good mood and was confident about their future together, but when he was alone, the doubts started closing in on him. It appears that he felt he was not quite worthy of her, for some reason—perhaps because in years past he had visited a brothel, or perhaps because he couldn't quite explain his father's influence on him to her. Mostly, though, it was the shock of the physical attraction he felt toward her that distracted him, he thought, from becoming truly spiritual. During this period he began to understand one aspect of the Don Juan character: He realized that he loved Regine the most *when he was not with her* but was fantasizing about her. Once they were together his ardor cooled considerably. Eventually he decided that it was better for both of them if they broke up, but because nineteenth-century mores demanded that the woman, not the man, break off the engagement if her character were to remain stainless, he had to try to force Regine to break the engagement. This he did by being as nasty to her as he could, even though he still loved her. He embarked on a program he himself had devised, alternating between playing the fool and the cynic; once when she asked him

Regine Olsen, Søren Kierkegaard's fiancée, a gentle Copenhagen woman who did her best to understand the intellectual scruples of her boyfriend, who could not reconcile his devotion to God with the idea of physical attraction to a woman and a subsequent bourgeois marriage. This photo was taken a few years after Kierkegaard finally broke up with her. (Photo of Regine Schlegel [*née* Olsen] courtesy of The Royal Library, Copenhagen.)

if he never intended to marry, he answered as nastily as he could, "Yes, in ten years when I've sown all my wild oats; then I'll need a young girl to rejuvenate me." For a long time he persisted in being rude to her, and she continued to forgive him, because she was very much in love with him. In the end he himself broke up with her, however, and she appears to have talked about killing herself. Kierkegaard wanted her to despise him, and a short time later she actually became engaged to a friend of theirs and married him. After that, Kierkegaard never tired of talking about woman's fickle, stupid, and untrustworthy nature. But here we must remember that Kierkegaard had multiple author-personalities, and beneath the scorn lurked his love, which apparently never died: He approached Regine with the suggestion that they resume their friendship, but her husband wouldn't allow it. After Kierkegaard died, it was revealed in his will that he had left everything he owned to Regine, but she refused to accept the inheritance.

child, has an intimate knowledge of what anguish feels like; he believed that you feel dread or anguish when you look to the future—you dread it because you realize you must make choices. This feeling, which has become known by the Danish/German word, *angst,* is comparable, Kierkegaard says, to realizing that you're far out on the ocean and you have to swim or sink, act or die, and there is no way out. The choice is yours, but it is a hard choice, because living is a hard job. Suppose you refuse to make your own decisions and say, "Society will help me," or "The church will help me," or "My uncle will help me"? Then you have given up your chance to become a real person, to become *authentic,* because you don't accomplish anything spiritual unless you accomplish it yourself, by making the experience your own. Each person is an individual, but only through a process of individuation—choosing to make one's own decisions and take responsibility for them in the eyes of God—can a person achieve selfhood and become a true human individual. The truth you experience when you have reached that point is *your truth alone,* because only you took that particular path in life. Other people can't take a shortcut by borrowing "your truth"—they must find the way themselves. We can't, then, gain any deep insights about life from books or from teachers. They can point us in the right direction, but they can't spoon-feed us any truths. In the Primary Readings you'll find a short excerpt from *Either/Or* in which Kierkegaard describes the nature of making hard choices.

This attitude is reflected in Kierkegaard's cryptic and disturbing assertion that *truth is subjective,* an idea that has been vehemently disputed by scientists and philosophers alike. Some philosophers believe Kierkegaard meant there is no objective knowledge at all; we can never verify statements such as "2 + 2 = 4," "The moon circles the earth," and "It rained in Boston on April 6, 2002," because all such statements are, presumably, just a matter of subjective opinion, or what we call *cognitive relativism.* That would mean that we could never set any objective standard for knowledge. Although other philosophers, such as Friedrich Nietzsche, have actually worked toward such a radical viewpoint, Kierkegaard is not among them. He never says that *knowledge* is subjective, and to understand what he means we have to look more closely at what he says. His actual words are *"Subjectivity is Truth,"* and Kierkegaard scholars believe that to mean the following: There is no such thing as "Truth" with a capital *T* that we can just scoop up and call our own. The "meaning of life" is not something we can look up in a book or learn from anybody else, because *it just isn't there unless we find it ourselves.* There is no *objective* truth about life, only a *personal* truth, which will be a little bit different for each individual. It will not be

Edvard Munch, *The Scream* (1893). This image, which exists in more than fifty original versions, is the epitome of the feeling of angst. Munch described in his diary the moment that inspired him to do this work: "I was walking along the road with two friends—the sun was setting—all of a sudden the sky turned crimson—my friends walked on, and I froze, shaking with anguish—and I felt that through nature was passing a vast, endless scream." (Ulrich Bischoff, *Edvard Munch 1863–1944,* Köln: Benedikt Taschen GmbH & Co, 1989. Translated by Nina Rosenstand.)

vastly different, though, because when we reach the level at which we are truly personal, we will find that it corresponds to other people's experiences of individuation too. In other words, the personal experience becomes a *universal* one—but only if you have gone through it yourself. This is the ultimate meaning of life and the ultimate virtue: to become an authentic human being by finding your own meaning. If you settle for accepting other people's view of life, you are no better than the evil magician Noureddin (or Jaffar, in the Disney movie version) in the story of Aladdin; he has no personal magic or talent himself, so he tries to steal it from the one who has, Aladdin.

For Kierkegaard himself, truth is a religious truth: One must take on the concept of sin and responsibility and seek God's forgiveness directly, as an individual. But that is hard for most people to do because we are born with quite another character. Typically humans are born into the *aesthetic stage:* the stage of sensuous enjoyment. Children obviously have a very strong interest in the joys of their senses, but if that persists into adulthood it can result in unhealthy character development, symbolized by the Don Juan type who loves to pursue the girl but loses interest once he has seduced her. She wants to get married, and he wants *out.* He leaves, only to fall in love with and pursue some other girl, and on it goes. Today we would say this is a person who *can't commit.* Kierkegaard makes the same basic observation but explains that this happens because the Don Juan type is steeped in sensuous enjoyment, which sours on itself: Too much of the same is not a good thing, but a person who is stuck in the aesthetic stage doesn't have any sense of what is morally right or wrong. Such knowledge usually comes as people mature and enter the *ethical stage* (although some people are stuck in the aesthetic stage forever).

In the ethical stage people realize that there are laws and conventions, and they believe that the way to become a good person is to follow those conventions. A fictional character from nineteenth-century middle-class Copenhagen becomes Kierkegaard's prototype for the ethical stage: Judge William, the righteous man who tries to be a good judge and a good husband and father. Scholars don't quite agree on how to evaluate this good and kind man, because the fact is that we are rarely certain when Kierkegaard is being serious and when he is being sarcastic. Kierkegaard also cites Socrates (whom he greatly admired) as an example of an ethical person. Although Socrates is commonly recognized as a truly courageous and virtuous man who strove to live (and die) the right way, Judge William doesn't come across as a heroic person; we even get the impression that he is actually a pompous, self-righteous, bourgeois bore who has his attention fixed on "doing the right thing" merely because society expects it of him. So it seems Kierkegaard wants to tell us that it isn't enough to follow the rules and become what everyone else thinks you ought to be; that way you exist only in the judgment of others. You have to take on responsibility for judging yourself, and the way you do that is by making a *leap of faith* into the *religious stage.* It isn't enough to judge your own life in terms of what makes sense according to society's rules and rational concepts of morality; what you must do to become an authentic person is leave the standards of society behind, including your love for reason and for things to make sense, and choose to trust in God, like Abraham, who made that same choice when he brought his son Isaac to be

Martin Heidegger (1889–1976), German philosopher and poet and a member of the National Socialist Party, believed authentic life is a life open to the possibility of different meanings. The feeling of *angst* can help jolt us out of our complacency and help us see the world from an intellectually flexible point of view.

sacrificed, even though it didn't make sense to him. Reason and the rules of society can't tell you if the insight you reach as a religious person is the truth.

So why is Socrates not a perfect person? Why did he stay within the ethical stage and make no leap of faith to the religious stage, according to Kierkegaard? Because the leap was not available to him, since he didn't belong to the Judeo-Christian tradition. Socrates is an example of how far you can reach if you stay within the boundaries of reason. However, in the religious stage there is no objective measure of meaning. At this stage you take responsibility for yourself, but at the same time you give up your fate and place it in the hands of God. Finally you can become a true human being, a complete individual and person, because only in the religious stage can you realize what it means to say that "Subjectivity is Truth."

Heidegger's Intellectual Authenticity

Martin Heidegger is an enigmatic and controversial philosopher. He is enigmatic because he aims to make people break through the old boundaries of thinking by inventing new words and categories for them to think with. That means there is no easy way to read Heidegger; you must acquaint yourself with an entirely new vocabulary of key concepts and get used to a new way of looking at reality. In spite of his rather inaccessible style, though, Heidegger has become something of a cult figure in modern European philosophy. He is controversial because he was a member of the Nazi Party during World War II (see Box 10.7).

Heidegger sees human beings as not essentially distinct from the world they inhabit, in the same sense that traditional epistemology does: There is no "subject" on the inside of a person and no "object" of experience on the outside. Rather, humans are thrown into the world at birth, and they interact with it and in a sense "live" it. There is no such thing as a person who is distinct from his or her world of experience—we *are* our world of experience. This idea of interaction with the world from the beginning of life is one that Heidegger took over from his teacher and mentor Edmund Husserl, but he adds his own twist to it: What makes humans special

Box 10.7   HEIDEGGER AND THE NAZI CONNECTION

At the time of Hitler's takeover of Germany in 1933, Martin Heidegger's philosophy professor, Edmund Husserl, was head of the philosophy department at the University of Freiburg. Husserl was already a famous philosopher, having developed the theory of *phenomenology*, a philosophical theory of human experience. Its main thesis is that there is no such thing as a consciousness that is empty at first and then proceeds to order and analyze the objects of sense experience; instead, our mind is already engaged in the process of experiencing the world from day one. We can't separate the concepts of the experiencing mind and the experience of the mind, and, because it is impossible for philosophy to say anything about a nonexperiencing mind and the unexperienced object-world, phenomenology sees its primary task as describing, as clearly as possible, the phenomenon of experience itself. Husserl had been the essential inspiration for many of Heidegger's writings; in fact, he had taken Heidegger under his wing when Heidegger was a young scholar. Husserl was Jewish, though, which meant that

he was targeted for persecution by the new Nazi leaders. He was fired from his university position and eventually died as a result of Nazi harassment. Heidegger, his former student and protégé, profited from those events by taking over Husserl's position as department chair; indeed, it seems that he never raised any protest against the treatment of his old professor. At that time Heidegger joined the Nazi Party for, as he explained later, purely professional reasons: He couldn't have kept his university position without becoming a party member. That appears to be stretching the truth, for Heidegger never did anything at all to distance himself from the Nazi ideology during the war years. Today people are divided in their views on Heidegger; some feel that because of his Nazi association, his philosophy is tainted and must somehow contain elements of Nazi thinking. Others believe that Heidegger was essentially apolitical, although he was not very graceful about it; they think his philosophy should be viewed independent of his personal life.

is not that they are on the inside and the world is on the outside, but that they experience their *existence* differently than all other beings do. Humans *are there* for themselves; they are aware of their existence and of certain essential facts about that existence, such as their own mortality. So Heidegger calls humans "Being-there" (*Dasein*) rather than "humans." Things, on the other hand, don't know they exist, and to Heidegger neither do animals; an animal may know it is hungry, or in pain, or in heat, but it doesn't know its days are numbered, and that makes the difference. Our humanity consists primarily of our continuous awareness of death, our "Being-toward-death" (*Sein-zum-Tode*). On occasion we let ourselves get distracted, because that awareness is quite a burden on our minds, and we let ourselves forget. We become absorbed in our jobs, our feelings, the gossip we hear, the nonsense around us. According to Heidegger, we often refer to what "They" say, as if the opinion of those anonymous others has some obvious authority. We bow to what "They" say and believe we are safe from harm and responsibility if we can get absorbed by this ubiquitous "They" (*Das Man*) and don't have to think on our own. In other words, we try to take on the safe and nonthinking existence-form of things—we objectify ourselves.

That does not make an authentic life, however, and in any event it is doomed to failure because we can't forget so completely. Humans just can't become things, because we are the ones who understand the relationship between ourselves and things. When we do the dishes we understand what plates are for, what glasses are for, and why they must be cleaned. We understand the entire "doing dishes" situation. When we prepare a presentation on our computer, we understand what a report is, what a computer is, and why the two have anything to do with ourselves, even if we may not understand what the report is for or how the computer works. In the end, humans are different because we can ask, What is it for? and understand the interconnections of the world we live in. We are asking, thinking creatures, and to regain our awareness of that fact, we must face our true nature. We may pretend to be nothing but victims of circumstances (I have to do the dishes; there is no other choice), but we also can choose to realize that we interact with our world and affect it. In *Being and Time* (1927), Heidegger calls this phenomenon (in his exasperating style) "An-already-thrown-into-the-world-kind-of-Being who is existing-in-relationship-to-existing-entities-within-that-world" (*Sich-vorweg-schon-sein-in [der-Welt] als Sein-bei [innerwelt-lich begegendem Seindenen]*). But he also describes it, in a slightly more down-to-earth fashion, as the structure of *care*. "Being-theres" always "care" about something, Heidegger says. That doesn't mean humans care *for* others, or *for* things—it merely means we are always *engaged* in something (the state of being engaged in something Heidegger called care—*Sorge*). Sometimes this involves caring for others, but mostly it involves engaging in our own existence: We fret, we worry, we look forward to something, we're concerned, we're content, we're disappointed about something—our health, our promotion, our family's well-being, our new kittens, or the exciting experiences we anticipate on our next vacation. We are always engaged in some part of our reality, unless we get caught up in another and deeper element of human nature: a *mood,* such as dread or anguish—*angst.*

Heidegger's concept of *angst* is related to Kierkegaard's: It does not involve fear of something in particular; it is, rather, the unpleasant and sometimes terrifying insecurity of not knowing where you stand in life and eventually having to make a choice—perhaps with little or no information about your options. For Kierkegaard this experience is related to a religious awakening, but for Heidegger the awakening is metaphysical: You realize that all your concerns and all the rules you live by are *relative,* in the deepest sense; you realize that you have viewed the world a certain way, within a certain frame, and now for some reason the frame is breaking up. A woman may feel angst if she loses her tenured job at a university, not just because she is worried about how she will provide for her family, but also because her worldview—her professional identity and sense of security—has been undermined. A young man may feel angst if he learns he has an incurable disease—not just because he is afraid to die, but also because "this isn't supposed to happen" to a young person. Children may feel angst if they are drawn into a divorce battle between their parents. A hitherto religious person may feel angst if he or she begins to doubt the existence of God, because that is the breakup of the ultimate framework. And humans may feel angst when they realize that their worldview is somehow not a God-given truth.

People whose attitude toward the world is *inauthentic* may experience the most fundamental form of angst. Heidegger himself states that if a Being-there is open to the possibility of different meanings in his or her reality, then he or she is living an authentic life. If, however, a Being-there does not want to accept the possibility that something may have a different meaning than he or she has believed up until now, then he or she is inauthentic. A typical trait of those who are inauthentic is that they become absorbed in just reacting to the things in their world—in driving the car, loading the laundry into the dryer, working on the computer, shopping, watching TV. Such persons think the predigested opinions of others or of the media are sufficient for getting by; they let themselves become absorbed in "The They," *das Man.*

But what does authenticity mean? Is it a call to "get in touch with yourself" by pulling away from the world? Or is it just a banal reminder to "stay open-minded"? Even worse, is it a built-in feature of being human, something we can't escape? Some Heidegger scholars see it not just as a call to reexamine yourself or to avoid hardening of the brain cells; to them authenticity is a fundamentally different attitude from one by which we allow the readily available worldviews of others to rule our lives. Being authentic means, for Heidegger, that you stop being absorbed by your doings and retain an attitude that "things may mean something else than what I expect." Only through this kind of intellectual flexibility can we even begin to think about making judgments about anything else, be they facts or people. So authenticity is, in a sense, remaining "open-minded," but it also involves performing a greater task by constantly forcing yourself to realize that reality is in flux, that things change, including yourself, and that you are part of a world of changing relationships. And *this* causes angst, because it means you have to give up your anchors and security zones as a matter of principle. In the end, angst becomes a liberating element that can give us a new and perhaps better understanding of ourselves and the world, but it is hard to deal with while we are in the midst of it.

Sartre's Ethical Authenticity

For some people angst is simply an existential fact, something we have to live with all our days. Jean-Paul Sartre is one of those people. Sartre is the best known of the French existentialists of the mid–twentieth century; others include Albert Camus, Gabriel Marcel, and Simone de Beauvoir.

Sartre studied phenomenology (the discipline of the phenomenon of human consciousness and experience) in Berlin during the years between the two world wars, and he was well acquainted with the theories of Edmund Husserl and Martin Heidegger. During World War II Sartre was held by the Nazis as a prisoner of war, but he escaped and joined forces with the French Resistance movement. Those experiences in many ways influenced his outlook on politics and on life in general: His political views were socialist and at times even Marxist, to a certain degree. Always politically active, Sartre may well be considered the most influential philosopher in twentieth-century Europe and possibly elsewhere—perhaps not as much because of his philosophical or literary writings (for Sartre was also a dramatist and a novelist) as because of his intellectual inspiration. The existential movement may not

French philosopher and writer Jean-Paul Sartre (1905–1980) was recognized as the most influential thinker in the existentialist movement. His best-known works of philosophy are the lecture "Existentialism as Humanism" (1945) and the much larger, much more intellectually challenging *Being and Nothingness* (1943).

have reflected a completely faithful version of the Sartrean philosophy, but it is certain that in his own century Sartre inspired the most extensive philosophical movement ever to reach people outside the academic world—the movement of existentialism.

Although existentialism as a fad in the 1950s became stereotyped as the interest of morose young people who dressed in black, chain-smoked late at night in small cafés, and read poems to one another about the absurdity of life, Sartre's existentialism had a whole other and more substantial content. Partly inspired by his experiences during the war, Sartre came to believe that there is no God and that because there is no God, there are no absolute moral rules either. The concept that God's nonexistence makes everything permissible was not new at the time; it was well known to Western readers of Dostoyevsky and his novel *The Brothers Karamazov* as well as to readers of Friedrich Nietzsche. (See Box 10.8 for a discussion of Nietzsche's contributions to existentialism.) But it was given a new twist by Sartre. Instead of saying, as many other atheists did, that we can find our values in our own human context and rationality, Sartre held that without the existence of a God, there are no values, in the sense that there are no *objective* values. There is no master plan and, accordingly, nothing in the world *makes sense*; all events happen at random, and *life is absurd*. So what do we do? Give a shrug, and set about to make merry while we can? No, we must realize that because no values exist outside ourselves, we, as individuals in a community, become the *source* of values. And the process by which we create values is the process of *choice*.

When a person realizes that he or she has to make a choice and that the choice will have far-reaching consequences, that person may be gripped by *anguish*—Sartre uses the image of a general having to choose whether to send his soldiers to their death. It is not a decision that can be made lightly by a person of conscience, and such a person may worry about it a great deal, precisely because he doesn't know beforehand whether he will make the right decision. If he realizes the enormity of the situation and still makes his choice as best he can, shouldering whatever consequences may develop, he is living with *authenticity*. However, suppose the general says to

Box 10.8   NIETZSCHE AND EXISTENTIALISM

The German philosopher Friedrich Nietzsche (1844–1900), one of the truly controversial figures in Western philosophy, is often credited with being one of the contributors to the French existentialism of the twentieth century. Sartre's view that life is absurd because there is no God has an early counterpart in Nietzsche's statement that "God is dead"; by that Nietzsche did not mean that Christ had died, or that there is no God, but that faith in God was waning if not gone altogether, and as a result the guarantees of stable, universal values provided by a faith in God had disappeared. For Nietzsche, there are no absolute values in the absence of God; there are no values at all except those we as humans decide on. Whereas, for Sartre, the values we must decide on are the values that make us into beings who take responsibility for our lives as well as for the lives of others who look to us for guidance, Nietzsche suggested that the old Christian value system of loving one's neighbor and turning the other cheek must be scrapped, because it is the morality of a weak person, a "slave" who fears his "master," the strong-willed, self-made individual.

For Nietzsche, the "slave-morality" began in ancient times when slaves hated and feared their masters and resented anyone who wielded power over them. Whereas the values of the master would include pride, courage, and loyalty to one's clan, the values of the slave population included a fellowship with other slaves against the master. Because pride and courage are "master"-values, the slave prizes equality and meekness. Nietzsche speculates that when slavery was finally abolished in the ancient world, the former slaves took their value system with them and made it into social and religious ideals: social equality, resentment against anyone who stands above the crowd, and turning the other cheek in meekness. Nietzsche sees the

slave-morality as a form of spiritual slavery to majority opinion. In its place, he advocates a new "master-morality" in which values reflect respect for one's equal but disdain for weaker individuals; the person who is strong enough to create his own values in the face of absurdity has the right to forge ahead and make whatever life he wants for himself. (The use of the gender-specific *he* and *himself* here is deliberate: Nietzsche saw the powerful individual as male and displayed a generally misogynist approach to women in his writings.) For Nietzsche, that meant a liberation from the hypocrisy of the late nineteenth century, in which, as he saw it, Europe was suffering from the fear of excelling, of anybody being stronger or more clever than a neighbor; he saw it as an opportunity for a gifted individual (an "Overman") to seize the day and create a life worth living. (Sometimes Nietzsche's term *Übermensch* is translated as "Superman," but many Nietzsche scholars tend to avoid that translation, since it so easily, and wrongly, associates to the familiar flying figure in a red cape. Instead the more direct translation, *Overman,* is used.) Nietzsche abhorred political despotism and would never have wanted his idea of the Overman to be transformed into an ideology of a "master race" because he saw the Overman as an individual, not a member of a group. But that is what happened when certain German politicians of the early twentieth century did a deliberately selective reading of his works. Early Nazi thinkers saw Nietzsche's ideas of the Overman as legitimizing the idea that some people (meaning some *races*) are nobler and more valuable than others, and many of Nietzsche's thoughts were worked into Nazi ideology. That association with the Nazis tainted Nietzsche's writings for many readers in the second half of the twentieth century, although he himself would probably have greatly

(continued)

Box 10.8   NIETZSCHE AND EXISTENTIALISM *(continued)*

disapproved of what Nazi thinkers got out of his philosophy.

Nietzsche's thoughts on the Overman are generally referred to as a *transvaluation of values:* Through rejecting the herd mentality of the majority, the individual can reach an authentic set of values for himself. French existentialism has a clear line to Nietzsche's idea that life is absurd because God is dead, and there are no absolute values, but they part ways on the question of how to decide on a value system; there is no connection between French existentialism and Nietzsche's ideas of the right of the gifted individual to create his own values without taking other people into consideration.

himself, "I *have* to send the soldiers out, for the sake of my country/my reputation/the book I want to write." Then he is acting inauthentically: He is assuming that he *has no choice*. But for Sartre, we always have a choice. Even the soldier who is ordered to kill civilians still has a choice, although he may claim he will be executed if he doesn't follow orders and thus has no choice. For Sartre, there are some things that are worse than death, such as killing innocent civilians. So claiming that one's actions are somehow *determined* by the situation is inauthenticity or, as Sartre calls it, *bad faith*. Bad faith can be displayed in another way too: Suppose the general is so distraught at having to make a choice that he says, "I just won't choose—I'll lock myself in the bathroom and wait until it is over." In that case, Sartre would say, the general is deluding himself, because he is already making a choice—*the choice not to choose*—and thus he is in even less control of the consequences of his choice than if he actually had chosen a course of action. In our hearts we know this, and Sartre maintains we can never deceive ourselves 100 percent. There will always be a part of us that knows we are not like animals or inert things that can't make choices, simply because we are human beings, and human beings make choices, at least from time to time. (See Box 10.9 for Henri Bergson's view of choice—and the ethical choices he made.) Animals and things can exist without making choices, but humans can't, because humans are aware of their own existence and their own mortality; they have a relationship to themselves (they exist "for themselves," *pour soi*), whereas animals and things merely float through existence (they exist "in themselves," *en soi*). In *Being and Nothingness* (1943), Sartre says:

> Thus there are no *accidents* in a life; a community event which suddenly bursts forth and involves me in it does not come from the outside. If I am mobilized in a war, this war is *my* war; it is in my image and I deserve it. I deserve it first because I could always get out of it by suicide or by desertion; these ultimate possibilities are those which must always be present for us when there is a question of envisaging a situation. For lack of getting out of it, I have *chosen* it. This can be due to inertia, to cowardice in the face of public opinion, or because I prefer certain other values to the value of the refusal to join in the war (the good opinion of my relatives, the honor of my family, etc.). Any way you look at it, it is a matter of choice. . . . If therefore I have preferred war to death or dishonor, everything takes place as if I bore the entire responsibility for this war.

Box 10.9   HENRI BERGSON: LET YOUR TRUE SELF EMERGE

The French philosopher Henri Bergson (1859–1941) is not considered an ethicist per se, but his theories of consciousness and time perception involve an unusual concept of authenticity. For Bergson, humans live most of their lives subject to the demands of circumstances and customs and to the internalized opinions of others. Once in a while, however, their true selves break through. We can't live our lives without a certain amount of custom and regard for immediate circumstances, but if we are to remain true to what we really are, we need to listen to the murmurs of our own self that are hiding behind the facade of our civilized lives. And how do we know there is such a true self? We all have agonized over some decision, weighing the pros and the cons, coming up with the most logical answer or the one that will please us or seems to be the morally right thing to do. Then, sometimes, to our own surprise, we end up doing something else entirely. Afterward, when we are asked why, we answer that we just "had to do it"—we "couldn't help ourselves." That, says Bergson, is our true self emerging. It may happen to a person who has decided to marry someone, received all the gifts, ordered all the catering, and is standing at the altar—the person says NO! when she meant to say yes. If you experience, in the midst of your everyday life, a sense that all of a sudden there is *something you must do before it is too late,* such as running away with the circus, learning the art of fencing, going to Paris, or having a baby, that, says Bergson, is your true self trying to get your attention, and that is true authenticity—all the rest is a veneer. There are two major problems with Bergson's

view. The first is that we have no assurance that this "deeper self" is actually a *good* self; the urge that comes over us may be to kill or betray someone. So it is doubtful that Bergsonian authenticity can actually be called a "virtue." The second problem is that Bergson thought this deeper self was proof that we have freedom of the will, but the whole point is that we have *no control* over what that self wants, and that is hardly what we normally mean by having a free will. Bergson's philosophy became immensely influential for just about all the French thinkers of the twentieth century, either as an inspiration or in creating a critical reaction. Sartre himself was greatly influenced by Bergson, and so was Emmanuel Levinas.

As a private person Bergson seems to have been a man of much integrity; in 1917 he went to the United States to fulfill a moral duty, as he saw it—to put an end to World War I. He also was utterly devoted to his daughter, who was hearing-impaired. In 1941 he lined up in the rain to be registered as a Jew by the Nazis during the Paris occupation; he contracted pneumonia, and it caused his death. He had wished to convert to Catholicism, but in view of Hitler's persecution of the Jews he decided to remain a member of the Jewish faith as a gesture of solidarity. Those are the deeds of what we would call a person of moral virtue, so let us suppose we asked Bergson whether he did those things as a conscious, free decision. We might have received the answer that other people of moral virtue have given in similar situations: I did what I did because I could not do otherwise.

How does bad faith manifest itself? Sartre's famous example involves a young woman on a date. The woman's date makes a subtle move on her—he grasps her hand—and she doesn't quite know what to do. She doesn't want to offend him or to appear to be prudish, but she really doesn't know whether she wants to have a relationship with him either. So she does nothing. She somehow manages to "detach" herself from the situation, as if her body really doesn't concern her, and, while he moves in on her, her hand seems not to belong to her at all. She looks at his face and pretends that she has no hand, no body, no sexuality at all. This, says Sartre, is bad faith: The woman thinks she can turn herself into a thing by acting thinglike, but it is an illusion, because through it all she knows that sooner or later she has to say yes or no. What should she do to be authentic? She should realize that she has to make up her mind, even if she can't foresee whether she will want to have a relationship or not. Making up her mind will then create a new situation for her to react to, even though it is essentially unforeseeable. This openness to the unforeseen is part of being authentic. When we make a choice, Sartre says, we are taking on the greatest of responsibilities, for we are choosing not only for ourselves and our lives but for everyone else too. Whatever choice we make sends out the message to everyone else that "this is okay to do." Therefore, through our choices we become role models for others. If we choose to pay our taxes, others will notice and believe that it is the right thing to do. If we choose to sell drugs to little children, somebody out there will see it and think it is a good idea. (Interestingly, doing something just because someone else is doing it is not enough for Sartre; as we saw in the section on Mayo's theory of role models, true authenticity must come from personal choices and not from just following role models.) Whatever we choose, even if we think it will concern only ourselves, actually will concern all of humanity, because we are endorsing our action as a general virtue. That is why choices can be so fraught with anxiety—and for Sartre that anxiety never goes away. We must live with it, and with the burden of the choice, forever. We are free to choose, but we are not free to refrain from choosing. In other words, *we are condemned to be free.*

This emphasis on human freedom is one of the strongest in the history of philosophy and one of the most radical, demanding theories of freedom of the will. You'll remember from Chapter 4 (and also from the film *Minority Report* in Chapter 7) that historically, there has been a dispute between supporters of the idea of *free will* and supporters of what we call *hard determinism,* the theory that everything in human life as well as in nature is determined by causal factors: heredity and environment, or nature and nurture. Sartre is one of the strongest critics of the theory of hard determinism, claiming that every kind of explanation of human actions that refers to outside forces or some kind of inner compulsion—in other words, any view that that we have no choice—is bunk, a bad excuse, or—in the terminology of existentialism—bad faith. Free will is our only "nature" as human beings; it is in a sense our fate to have no fate, to always be faced with multiple possibilities and the need to make choices, without having control over their consequences—and live with the resulting anguish. That, to Sartre, is living as an authentic human being.

So can we at least find comfort in the company of other people, close friends, lovers, or relatives who also have to face hard choices? For Sartre, that presents no real solution; the presence of the Other—another person, different from myself—only reminds me of my absolute responsibility to make choices. And besides, the very presence of the Other is problematic in itself: When another person looks at me, and our eyes meet, he or she is always trying to dominate me, as I am trying to dominate him or her. For Sartre every human relationship is a game of dominance using the gaze as a tool of power, and this is especially the case for relationships between lovers. Essentially, we are alone with our choices and responsibilities. In the Narratives section you'll find two stories, each of which in its own way is a wonderful illustration of exactly what Sartre is talking about. The first is an excerpt from Sartre's own stage play *No Exit*—for Sartre was also a writer of plays and novels—in which three people face one another in their own self-made hell; and next you have a summary of the film *Good Will Hunting*, about a young man who lives in bad faith because he lacks the courage to make choices with consequences.

But how can we make a choice if the world is absurd and all our actions are meaningless? When we first experience the absurdity of existence, we may feel nauseated, dizzy from the idea that reality has no core or meaning. But then we realize we must create a meaning; we must choose for something to matter to us. For Sartre, the social conditions of France became a theme that mattered to him, but you might choose something else—your family, your job, or your Barbie doll collection. Any kind of life project will create values, as long as you realize that the world is still absurd in spite of your project! If you think you are "safe" with your family or your job or your doll collection—if you think you've created a rock-solid meaning for your life—then you've fallen back into bad faith. This is the case with the waiter (another of Sartre's examples) who wants so badly to become the perfect waiter that he takes on a "waiter identity" that provides answers to everything: how to speak, what to say, how to walk, where to go. The waiter has not chosen a project; he has turned himself into a thing, an "in itself" that doesn't have to choose anymore. Living authentically means living in anguish, always on the edge—confronting the absurdity of life and courageously making choices in the face of meaninglessness. When something you care about appears, then you will know what to do. The French philosopher and novelist Simone de Beauvoir, Sartre's significant other and his collaborator on the subject of existentialism, puts it like this: "Any man who has known real loves, real revolts, real desires, and real will knows quite well that he has no need of any outside guarantee to be sure of his goals."

Suppose you decide you'll do something about your life *tomorrow*. That *next year* you'll write that novel. Or go back to college. Suppose you decide you *should have* married someone else, had children, gone to see the Pyramids, or become a movie actor. Then there is not much hope for your authenticity, says Sartre, because your virtue lies only in what you accomplish, not in choices you make about things you are *planning* to do. If you never start that book, you have no right to claim you are a promising writer. If you never tried to become an actor, then you can't complain that you're a great undiscovered talent. We are not authentically anything but what we *do,* and we are hiding from reality if we think we are more than that. Like Aristotle, Sartre links the value of our virtue with the success of our conduct: Intentions may be good, but they aren't enough. (For an exploration of the issue of personal identity as it relates to authenticity, see Box 10.10).

Box 10.10   PERSONAL IDENTITY AS AN ETHICAL ISSUE

The question of *Who am I?* is something you may encounter in a philosophy class focusing on metaphysics, or theory of knowledge (epistemology), but you don't find it often within a discussion about ethics. The assumption is, presumably, that once we start worrying about how to behave with *others,* we're already fairly sure who *we* are. But that is, of course, not necessarily the case, and even if we are familiar with ourselves, there is more to the sense of self than just a descriptive level: We shouldn't forget the normative level. William Shakespeare says, in *Hamlet,*

> This above all: to thine own self be true,
> And it must follow, as night the day,
> Thou can't not then be false to any man.

Here Shakespeare assumes that we're fairly familiar with who we are but that this awareness also carries a moral virtue, and a duty: to have integrity and be true to ourselves—the best in ourselves, that is. (Presumably it doesn't imply that once you know your weaknesses, you should cultivate them!) Understanding who we are *so that* we can become better persons is an idea that dates back to Socrates—he interpreted the inscription "Know Thyself" at the Apollo temple in Delphi as meaning just that: introspection with self-improvement as a result. Let us take a look at three examples:

For the existentialists such as Sartre the concept of *authenticity* captures the moral value of knowing oneself; it isn't merely a question of being comfortable with who you are, or even of constantly questioning yourself and your role in life; more important, you must be able to act out of a sense of integrity, and with absence of bad faith, in everything you do.

For American psychologists, the idea of knowing oneself has been labeled as having *ego integrity* ever since the influential German-born analyst Erik Erikson (1902–1994) coined the term. Erikson, who also identified and named the phenomenon *identity crisis,* saw ego integrity as having inner harmony and balance of the mind; you don't dwell on what might have been, or how others have done you wrong, but accept things you have no control over.

For the thinker who is interested in storytelling, such as the French philosopher Paul Ricoeur (1913–2005), the quest for personal identity becomes a quest *for self-comprehension through telling one's own story.* Finding one's narrative self doesn't mean that we remember everything and then put it into words, or that we tell everything exactly like it was, but that we find our *character arc* (see Chapter 13) in the process of connecting the dots in our life—seeing a pattern in the events leading up to the present time.

In all these cases we are talking about a normative approach to personal identity: First we must understand who we are, and then that understanding must make a difference in the rest of our lives. In that way the quest for personal identity becomes a moral journey.

Levinas and the Face of the Other

Emmanuel Levinas (1905–1995) was born the same year as Sartre, but whereas Sartre became a philosopher of the mid–twentieth century, Levinas was a late bloomer and became one of the leading voices of French philosophy only in the last decades of the twentieth century. His most important works are *Totality and Infinity* (1961; translated into English, 1969) and *Otherwise Than Being or Beyond Essence* (1974; translated into English, 1981). In many ways his experience parallels that of

The Lithuanian-French philosopher Emmanuel Levinas (1905–1995) believed that ethics is the deepest and most primary human experience: We see the other person looking at us and we hear him or her talking to us, and we understand that this is someone whose life is precious and irreplaceable. The Other commands us not to kill, and we feel obliged to place his or her needs above our own.

Sartre. He, too, became interested in the philosophies of Husserl and Heidegger in Germany; indeed, his interest preceded Sartre's by more than a decade, and it was Levinas, not Sartre, who introduced those ideas to the French public with books on Husserl and Heidegger. (According to Simone de Beauvoir, Sartre, when reading Levinas's book on Husserl, exclaimed, "This is the philosophy I wanted to write!"— although Sartre afterward claimed he could do it better.) Like Sartre, Levinas was a prisoner of war during World War II, doing forced labor for the Nazis; also like Sartre, he developed a highly personal philosophy based on his early interest in German phenomenology. Both became recognized as distinguished scholars within the field of philosophy. But there the similarities end. Sartre was French by birth, whereas Levinas—born a Lithuanian—became French by choice. Whereas Sartre's Catholic belief in God came to an end, Levinas never lost his Jewish faith. Whereas Sartre developed his existential philosophy based on the fundamental anguish of the choice—an essentially lonely enterprise—Levinas sees the bottom line of all human existence as the encounter with the Other, not in a competition for dominance, as Sartre sometimes would express it, but in coming face-to-face with another human being and realizing that the Other is alive, looking at *you,* speaking to *you,* needing *you* to recognize him or her as someone who is fundamentally different from you and fundamentally vulnerable. Levinas maintains that "ethics precedes ontology": Understanding the needs of the Other and *my* own responsibility for the needs of the Other comes before any philosophy about existence. That is why Levinas has described ethics as "First Philosophy": This is the foundation and the beginning point, which we are normally not even aware of but where we encounter what is really important in life: the face of the Other.

As we have seen, many modern theories of ethics state that everyone ought to be treated as *equal.* Bentham talks about how each person has one vote in terms of his or her pain and pleasure; Kant claims that all persons should be viewed as ends in themselves; Rawls points out that justice consists of treating all persons with fairness regardless of who they are. The Golden Rule is in effect even in philosophical systems that are otherwise opposed to one another. For Levinas, there is nothing wrong with the political quest for equality, but that quest is not fundamental to ethics; what is fundamental is another experience altogether. When I meet another human being, another face, the ethical reaching out to that person consists in realizing precisely that we are *not* equal. Levinas is not saying I am "better" than the Other. On the contrary, the Other counts more than I: The Other, no matter who he or she is, is a person in need, always "poor" and asking for my help and understanding; first and foremost the Other is telling me, "You must not kill." As Levinas says in a dialogue with Richard Kearney:

> The approach to the face is the most basic mode of responsibility. As such, the face of the other is verticality and uprightness; it spells a relation of rectitude. The face is not in front of me (*en face de moi*) but above me; it is the other before death, looking through and exposing death. Secondly, the face is the other who asks me not to let him die alone, as if to do so were to become an accomplice in his death. Thus the face says to me: you shall not kill. . . . In ethics, the other's right to exist has primacy over my own, a primacy epitomized in the ethical edict: you shall not kill, you shall not jeopardize the life of the other. The ethical rapport is asymmetrical in that it subordinates my existence to the other.

Of course, that is not really a description of most actual encounters between people; fortunately, we rarely find ourselves in situations in which we are begging for our lives. But for Levinas, that encounter is the underlying foundation beneath all human encounters: The face is naked, the eyes are pleading, the voice speaks. For Levinas, the true ethical moment happens when we are being addressed by the Other. In response, it is not enough to say, "Well, he or she is just the same as I am, we are all humans." That, to Levinas, is not going far enough, or it is going too far: That would be making us all into some collective form of being, some anonymous humanity. Instead, we are supposed to say, "He/she is completely different from what I am, so his/her life is my responsibility." That is the unequal, asymmetrical situation, the *alterity* (otherness) of the Other, which makes the other human individual our responsibility. In particular, it is the Other's voice that calls to us, more so than looking into his or her eyes. Sartre's existential philosophy has often alluded to the power of the *gaze,* the eyes trying to dominate the other person's, but Levinas sees the typical encounter between humans as not only a visual but also an aural experience: You hear the voice speak to *you,* and you respond by being there for the other person. And when you respond with your whole being in acceptance that the Other is there, demanding attention, then you become special to the Other, you become *irreplaceable.* For Levinas, humans in an ethical relationship with each other recognize the Other as irreplaceable, "non-substitutable." The loss of the Other can't be made up for by finding another. (Box 10.11 explains how Levinas would look at the story of Abraham and Isaac in terms of the face of the Other.)

So is that the way things actually are between people, or is it the way Levinas thinks they ought to be? In other words, is he being descriptive or normative? Elegantly, Levinas answers that the encounter is something that happens before we even think in such categories: The encounter with the Other is not merely an actual situation but also the framework within which human encounters take place, so it is the way we actually meet, deep down before we start speculating about existence and responsibility and all the rest, but it is also in a sense the way one ought to meet each

Box 10.11   KIERKEGAARD, LEVINAS, AND ABRAHAM

You may remember a section in Chapter 2 dealing with the biblical story of Abraham about to sacrifice his son Isaac to God. To briefly recapitulate: Abraham believes that God has told him to sacrifice his and Sarah's only son, so he takes young Isaac up on the mountain, letting Isaac carry the firewood; Isaac is wondering where the sacrificial lamb is, but Abraham explains that God will provide. On the top of the hill, they build the sacrificial altar, and Abraham straps his son down and is ready to slaughter him when the voice of God intervenes and rewards Abraham for his faith in God's command. Kierkegaard (whom you now know better than you did in Chapter 2) said that Abraham's attempt to sacrifice his son violated the ethics of the community, but believing that he served God's purpose took Abraham to a higher stage—to the religious stage, which he had to ascend to by a leap of faith—bringing him into direct contact with God. Levinas, on the other hand, believes that Kierkegaard misunderstood the entire situation: The important moment is not that Abraham disregards his beloved son for God's sake but that Abraham through the voice of Isaac himself is called back from the brink, back to the ethical demands of life and fatherhood; in a sense, Isaac's face intervenes on his own behalf. Levinas says that for Kierkegaard ethics is the rigid rules of the community that have to be overcome to be religious. For Levinas, however, ethics is the Other's voice speaking to one. Essentially, Levinas sees Abraham as someone who almost made a monumental mistake, but he sees Kierkegaard as having made the mistake of believing that the leap of faith was a matter between the individual and God alone and that to get there one had to leave behind the world of the others with their rules and morals. For Levinas, ethics, and in a sense also faith itself, takes place between one person and the Other.

individual person—because (sadly) not everyone sees other people as unique individuals who are supposed to be held higher than one holds oneself; some people even see others as "merely a means to an end."

The ultimate disregard for the Other is to Levinas represented by the Nazi Holocaust (in which he lost his entire Lithuanian family). The Holocaust represents the utter evil of putting people through torture and to death not for their convictions but for their ancestry. The fact that Heidegger had been involved with the Nazi Party made Levinas say, in later years, that "one can forgive many Germans, but there are some Germans it is difficult to forgive. It is difficult to forgive Heidegger." And, yet, the dreadful event of the Nazi death camps, where, in Levinas's words, God was not present but the devil was, in some roundabout way did not destroy his belief in God; he says,

> Before the twentieth century, all religion begins with the promise. It begins with the "Happy End." It is the promise of heaven. Well then, doesn't a phenomenon like Auschwitz invite you, on the contrary, to think the moral law independent of the Happy End? That is the question. . . . It is easier to tell myself to believe without promise than it is to ask it of the other. That is the idea of asymmetry. I can demand of myself that which I cannot demand of the other.

Interview with Wright, Hughes, and Ainley, in Bernasconi and Wood (1988)

So ethics becomes the highest form of religious faith: Without the relief of a promise of heaven, we must be there for the Other, serve the Other for no reward at all. According to Levinas, "Faith is not a question of the existence or non-existence of God. It is believing that love without reward is valuable."

With his philosophy that we look to the Other as someone we must give our love to but who doesn't have to return it (an ethic that is sometimes used to describe the relationship between parent and child), Levinas's ethics stands as a complete renewal within the European tradition of autonomy, finding personal integrity in a relationship of the individual not to oneself but to someone else. In this he comes closest of all the modern European philosophers to an ethics of virtue, seeing the ultimate virtue as the willingness to serve the Other; as a thinker within the modern tradition of authenticity, he regards the asymmetrical relationship to the Other as the truly authentic relationship. Remember from Chapter 4 that Levinas's philosophy was presented as an example of *ideal altruism*. This ethic, which today perhaps more than any other philosophy stands for kindness and sacrifice of one's self for the sake of others, is nevertheless not without controversy.

Some critics see his thinking as a kind of throwback to a time when ethics were expressed in personal, even religious, terms, and further, in terms of male and female. And for some critics this throwback is a serious weakness. In a disarmingly innocent way, in his early writings Levinas insisted that the Other is, essentially, feminine (something that Sartre, by the way, has also been criticized for asserting): "The feminine is other for the masculine being not only because of a different nature but also inasmuch as alterity is in some way its nature."

In later years he modified his position, but it still generates discussion. Levinas's critics see this as just another statement in the long line of sexist philosophies in which a male point of view pronounces women to be "deviant" or "different" or "really kind of strange," and which assumes that women accept this as an objective truth. Seen in the light of this old tradition, it is small wonder that many women philosophers, most notably Simone de Beauvoir (see Chapter 12), have accused Levinas of being reactionary, deliberately taking a man's point of view, seeing himself as the Absolute and the woman as the Other.

But even if Levinas could be said to hold the opinion that woman is completely different from man, it does not mean he thinks woman is inferior to man; on the contrary, according to his theory of the Other, if anything is absolute, it is precisely the Other. In his later years, Levinas would talk about the feminine virtues of the home, of the welcoming feminine touch, the quality of "discretion" of the feminine face as opposed to the male face with its authority and self-assertion, but always in positive terms. (However, whether you regard "feminine" as inferior or superior, it is still sexism to a *classical* feminist, see Chapter 12) A feminist philosopher, Tina Chanter, suggests that Levinas is in fact praising the feminine qualities as true *human* qualities; "feminine" does not mean biologically female to Levinas, says Chanter, and "masculine" doesn't mean "male"; rather, each term stands for features in all of us. That interpretation (in some ways similar to the gender philosophy of the psychoanalyst Carl Jung) may give another dimension to Levinas's controversial words about the Other as feminine. In the Primary Readings you will find an excerpt from an interview with Levinas in which he talks about the "face of the Other." In the Narratives you will find a summary of one of the most famous Westerns of all time, *The Searchers,* in which the encounter with the face of the Other is beautifully illustrated.

Study Questions

1. Evaluate the question of character versus conduct in politics. Which do you think is of higher importance for a person running for (or elected to) office to have: personal integrity or a view on government that you agree with? Is there an alternative? Explain.

2. Discuss the question of character versus conduct in personal matters. Philippa Foot claims, with Aristotle, that a person who has a good character is better than a person who has to control himself or herself. Kant would say the opposite. Explain those viewpoints. Which do you agree with more and why?

3. Bernard Mayo wants us to emulate role models. Can you think of a person—a historical figure, a living person, or a fictional character—whom you would like to emulate? Explain who and why. What are some of the problems involved with the idea of emulating role models?

4. Kierkegaard believes that being ethical is not the ultimate ideal mode of existence—one must also have religious faith. Explore his viewpoint: What does he think faith can give that ethics cannot? Do you agree? Can we be ethical without faith? Can we have religious faith without ethics? Explain.

5. For Sartre, any explanation that deflects one's complete responsibility is an example of bad faith. Do you agree? Are there cases where people should not be held accountable for what they have done? or cases where it is legitimate to say, "I had no choice"? Explain.

6. Levinas is reluctant to include animals as beings with "faces." Do you agree that ethics can be extended to animals only as a secondary move patterned after ethics toward humans? Or should ethics toward animals be a primary form of ethics? Can Levinas's own theory be redesigned to include animals?

Primary Readings and Narratives

The first two Primary Readings are short excerpts from the writings of Søren Kierkegaard, one from *Johannes Climacus* and one from *Either/Or,* Volume II. The third Primary Reading is an excerpt from Jean-Paul Sartre's lecture "Existentialism Is a Humanism." The fourth Primary Reading is an excerpt from an interview with Emmanuel Levinas, conducted by three graduate students, Tamra Wright, Peter Hughes, and Alison Ainley, and published as "The Paradox of Morality: An Interview with Emmanuel Levinas." All four Narratives explore, in one way or another, the existential themes of choice, angst, authenticity, and responsibility. The first is a summary of Jean-Paul Sartre's classic play *No Exit* about three souls condemned to live in one another's company forever, in hell. The second is a summary of the existential aspects of the film *Good Will Hunting.* The third Narrative is a film summary that takes us to the Old West and issues of racism and the Other: *The Searchers.*

Primary Reading

Johannes Climacus

SØREN KIERKEGAARD

Written 1842–1843, first published 1912. Excerpt translated by Nina Rosenstand.

Kierkegaard used to speak through many aliases, and some we are not supposed to take seriously; Johannes Climacus became one of his most serious and personal aliases, and here we read about Johannes's childhood, which exactly resembles Kierkegaard's own.

> His father was a very strict man, apparently dry and prosaic, but under this coat of coarse weave he hid a glowing imagination which not even his advanced years managed to conceal. When Johannes on occasion would ask permission to go out, he was most often refused; however, on one occasion his father offered, as a form of compensation, to take a walking tour up and down the floor. This was at first glance a poor substitute, and yet this turned out to be like the coarse coat: It hid something else entirely. The suggestion was accepted, and the decision where to go was left entirely to Johannes. So they left by the gate, walked to a nearby castle in the woods, to the beach, or up and down the streets, anywhere Johannes wanted, because for his father nothing was impossible. While they were walking up and down the floor, his father would describe everything they saw; they said hello to people passing by, coaches rolled noisily past, drowning out his father's voice; the fruits of the vendor woman looked more inviting than ever. He related everything so accurately, so vividly; he described so immediately in the most minute detail things that were familiar to Johannes, and whatever Johannes didn't know he described in such elaborate and educational manner that he, after having walked with his father for half an hour, was just as tired as if he had been outside an entire day. . . . For Johannes it was as if his father was the Good Lord, and he himself was his favorite who was allowed to come up with silly ideas to his heart's content; for he was never turned down, his father was never perturbed, everything was included and happened to Johannes's satisfaction.

Primary Reading

Either/Or

SØREN KIERKEGAARD

Excerpt from Volume II, 1843. Translated by Nina Rosenstand.

In this text, written shortly after Kierkegaard broke up with Regine Olsen, he speaks with the voice of Judge Williams, admonishing a friend who refuses to make choices (about getting married, in particular). In his friend's words, "Get married, and you'll regret it. Don't get married and you'll regret it." Williams responds,

The choice itself is decisive for the content of one's personality. . . . If you imagine a first mate on his ship at the moment when it has to make a turn, then he might say, I can do either this or that. However, if he is not a poor navigator, he will also be aware that the ship is all the while moving ahead at its regular speed, and that he thus only has an instant where it is immaterial whether he does one thing or the other. So it is with a human being: Should he forget to take account of the speed, there comes at last a moment when it is no longer a question of an either-or, not because he has chosen, but because he has refrained from choosing—which is the same as saying, because others have chosen for him, because he has lost his own self.

Study Questions

1. Do you approve of Kierkegaard's father's teaching technique? Explain. Are there similarities between his technique and virtual reality? Are there differences?

2. Whom do you think Kierkegaard identifies most with: the friend who doesn't want to choose or Williams? or perhaps both?

3. Compare the second excerpt with Sartre's theory of the existential choice.

Primary Reading

Existentialism Is a Humanism

JEAN-PAUL SARTRE

Lecture, 1946, published in **Existentialism from Dostoyevsky to Sartre,** *1989. Translated by Philip Mairet. Excerpt.*

In his famous lecture on existentialism from 1946, Sartre expresses the key concepts of his philosophy: Traditionally, philosophers have expressed the thought that humans have an essence, given to us by our creator, or evolved as part of our human nature. But for Sartre, humans don't have a "nature," contrary to all other beings and things in the universe; we exist in the world, with freedom to choose our path, and thus our *existence precedes our essence*. But that puts us in a state of *anguish*, from which we would like to escape (in bad faith), but we cannot, because we are *condemned to be free*.

If one considers an article of manufacture as, for example, a book or a paper-knife—one sees that it has been made by an artisan who had a conception of it; and he has paid attention, equally, to the conception of a paper-knife and to the pre-existent technique of production which is a part of that conception and is, at bottom, a formula. Thus the paper-knife is at the same time an article producible in a certain manner and one which, on the other hand, serves a definite purpose, for one cannot suppose that a man would produce a paper-knife without knowing what it was for. Let us say, then, of the paper-knife that its essence—that is to say the sum of the formulae and the qualities which made its production and its definition possible—precedes its existence. The presence of such-and-such a paper-knife or book is thus determined before my eyes. Here, then, we are viewing the world from a technical standpoint, and we can say that production precedes existence. . . .

Atheistic existentialism, of which I am a representative, declares with greater consistency that if God does not exist there is at least one being whose existence comes before its essence, a being which exists before it can be defined by any conception of it. That being is man or, as Heidegger has it, the human reality. What do we mean by saying that existence precedes essence? We mean that man first of all exists, encounters himself, surges up in the world—and defines himself afterwards. If man as the existentialist sees him as not definable, it is because to begin with he is nothing. He will not be anything until later, and then he will be what he makes of himself. Thus, there is no human nature, because there is no God to have a conception of it. Man simply is. Not that he is simply what he conceives himself to be, but he is what he wills, and as he conceives himself after already existing—as he wills to be after that leap towards existence. Man is nothing else but that which he makes of himself. That is the first principle of existentialism. And this is what people call its "subjectivity," using the word as a reproach against us. But what do we mean to say by this, but that man is of a greater dignity than a stone or a table? For we mean to say that man primarily exists—that man is, before all else, something which propels itself towards a future and is aware that it is doing so. Man is, indeed, a project which possesses a subjective life, instead of being a kind of moss, or a fungus or a cauliflower. Before that projection of the self nothing exists; not even in the heaven of intelligence: man will only attain existence when he is what he purposes to be. Not, however, what he may wish to be. For what we usually understand by wishing or willing is a conscious decision taken—much more often than not—after we have made ourselves what we are. I may wish to join a party, to write a book or to marry—but in such a case what is usually called my will is probably a manifestation of a prior and more spontaneous decision. If, however, it is true that existence is prior to essence, man is responsible for what he is. Thus, the first effect of existentialism is that it puts every man in possession of himself as he is, and places the entire responsibility for his existence squarely upon his own shoulders. And, when we say that man is responsible for himself, we do not mean that he is responsible only for his own individuality, but that he is responsible for all men. The word "subjectivism" is to be understood in two senses, and our adversaries play upon only one of them. Subjectivism means, on the one hand, the freedom of the individual subject and, on the other, that man cannot pass beyond human subjectivity. It is the latter which is the deeper meaning of existentialism. When we say that man chooses himself, we do mean that every one of us must choose himself; but by that we also mean that in choosing for himself he chooses for all men. For in effect, of all the actions a man may take in order to create himself as he wills to be, there is not one which is not creative, at the same time, of an image of man such as he believes he ought to be. To choose between this or that is at the same time to affirm the value of that which is chosen; for we are unable ever to choose the worse. What we choose is always the better; and nothing can be better for us unless it is better for all. If, moreover, existence precedes essence and we will to exist at the same time as we fashion our image, that image is valid for all and for the entire epoch in which we find ourselves. Our responsibility is thus much greater than we had supposed, for it concerns mankind as a whole. . . .

This may enable us to understand what is meant by such terms—perhaps a little grandiloquent—as anguish, abandonment and despair. As you will soon see, it is very simple. First, what do we mean by anguish?—The existentialist frankly states that man is in anguish. His meaning is as follows: When a man commits himself to anything, fully realising that he is not only choosing what he will be, but is thereby at the same time a legislator deciding for the whole of mankind—in such a moment a man cannot escape from the sense of complete and profound responsibility. There are many, indeed, who show no such anxiety. But we affirm that they are merely disguising their anguish or are in flight from it. Certainly, many people think that in what they are doing they commit no one but themselves to anything: and if you ask them, "What would happen if everyone did so?" they shrug their shoulders and reply, "Everyone does not do so." But in truth, one ought always to ask oneself what would happen if everyone did as one is doing; nor can one escape from that disturbing thought except by a kind of self-deception. The man who lies in self-excuse, by saying "Everyone will not do it" must be ill at ease in his conscience, for the act of lying implies the universal value which it denies. By its very disguise his anguish reveals itself. . . . When, for instance, a military leader takes upon himself the responsibility for an attack and sends a number of men to their death, he chooses to do it and at bottom he alone chooses. No doubt under a higher command, but its orders, which are more general, require interpretation by him and upon that interpretation depends the life of ten, fourteen or twenty men. In making the decision, he cannot but feel a certain anguish. All leaders know that anguish. It does not prevent their acting, on the contrary it is the very condition of their action, for the action presupposes that there is a plurality of possibilities, and in choosing one of these, they realize that it has value only because it is chosen. Now it is anguish of that kind which existentialism describes, and moreover, as we shall see, makes explicit through direct responsibility towards other men who are concerned. Far from being a screen which could separate us from action, it is a condition of action itself.

And when we speak of "abandonment"—a favorite word of Heidegger—we only mean to say that God does not exist, and that it is necessary to draw the consequences of his absence right to the end. . . . In other words—and this is, I believe, the purport of all that we in France call radicalism—nothing will be changed if God does not exist; we shall rediscover the same norms of honesty, progress and humanity, and we shall have disposed of God as an out-of-date hypothesis which will die away quietly of itself. The existentialist, on the contrary, finds it extremely embarrassing that God does not exist, for there disappears with Him all possibility of finding values in an intelligible heaven. There can no longer be any good *a priori,* since there is no infinite and perfect consciousness to think it. It is nowhere written that "the good" exists, that one must be honest or must not lie, since we are now upon the plane where there are only men. Dostoevsky once wrote: "If God did not exist, everything would be permitted"; and that, for existentialism, is the starting point. Everything is indeed permitted if God does not exist, and man is in consequence forlorn, for he cannot find anything to depend upon either within or outside himself. He discovers forthwith, that he is without excuse. For if indeed existence precedes essence, one will never be able to explain one's action by reference to a given and specific human nature; in other words, there is no determinism—man is free, man *is* freedom. Nor, on the other hand, if God does not exist, are we provided with any values or commands that could legitimise our behaviour. Thus we have neither behind us, nor before us in a luminous realm of values, any means of justification or excuse.—We are left alone, without excuse. That is what I mean when I say that man is condemned to be free. Condemned, because he did not create himself, yet is nevertheless at liberty, and from the moment that he is thrown into this world he is responsible for everything he does.

Study Questions

1. What does Sartre mean by saying that we are "condemned to be free"?

2. Explain Sartre's concept of *anguish*—what is it, and when are we likely to experience it? Is there a difference between being afraid, and feeling anguish?

3. The concept of *making a choice* is at the core of existentialism. Compare Sartre's and Kierkegaard's emphasis on making choices—are they talking about the same process, or are there differences?

4. Explain in what way Sartre's existentialism is a theory about moral values.

 Primary Reading

The Paradox of Morality: An Interview with Emmanuel Levinas

Interview conducted in 1986 by Tamra Wright, Peter Hughes, and Alison Ainley. Excerpt.

Three graduate students from the University of Warwick interviewed Levinas after taking a seminar on one of his books, *Totality and Infinity*. In the section on Levinas, you read about one of the controversial points in his philosophy, his remarks about the feminine. Here you have a hint of another controversy: Levinas's statements about the face of another human being as the fundamental ethical experience; does this imply that we can't have an ethical relationship with a nonhuman—an animal, for instance?

> *Is the face a simple or a complex phenomenon? Would it be correct to define it as that aspect of a human being which escapes all efforts at comprehension and totalization, or are there other characteristics of this phenomenon which must be included in any definition or description of the face?*
>
> The face is a fundamental event. Among the many modes of approach and diverse ways of relating to being, the action of the face is special and, for this reason, it is very difficult to give it an exact phenomenological description. The phenomenology of the face is very often negative.
>
> What seems essential to me is, for example, the manner in which Heidegger understood the *Zeug*—that which comes to hand, the instrument, the thing. He understood it as irreducible prototype. The face is similar in that it is not at all a representation, it is not a given of knowledge, nor is it a thing which comes to hand. It is an irreducible means of access, and it is in ethical terms that it can be spoken of. I have said that in my analysis of the face it is a demand; a demand, not a question. The face is a hand in search of recompense, an open hand. That is, it needs something. It is going to ask you for something. I don't know whether one can say that it is complex or simple. It is, in any case, a new way of speaking of the face.
>
> When I said that the face is authority, that there is authority in the face, this may undoubtedly seem contradictory: it is a request and it is an authority. You have a question later on in which you ask me how it could be that if there is a commandment in the face, one can do the opposite of what the face demands. The face is not a force. It is an

authority. Authority is often without force. Your question seems to be based on the idea that God commands and demands. He is extremely powerful. If you try not doing what he tells you, he will punish you. That is a very recent notion. On the contrary, the first form, the unforgettable form, in my opinion, is that, in the last analysis, he can not do anything at all. He is not a force but an authority. . . .

Is it necessary to have the potential for language in order to be a "face" in the ethical sense?

I think that the beginning of language is in the face. In a certain way, in its silence, it calls you. Your reaction to the face is a response. Not just a response, but a responsibility. These two words [*réponse, responsabilité*] are closely related. Language does not begin with the signs that one gives, with words. Language is above all the fact of being addressed . . . which means the saying much more than the said.

In the word "comprehension" we understand the fact of taking [*prendre*] and of comprehending [*comprendre*], that is, the fact of englobing, of appropriating. There are these elements in all knowledge [*savoir*], all familiarity [*connaissance*], all comprehension; there is always the fact of making something one's own. But there is something which remains outside, and that is alterity. Alterity is not at all the fact that there is a difference, that facing me there is someone who has a different nose than mine, different colour eyes, another character. It is not difference, but alterity. It is alterity, the unencompassable, the transcendent. It is the beginning of transcendence. You are not transcendent by virtue of a certain different trait.

In totalization there is certainly the fact of inclusion, of adding up. Men can be synthesized. Men can easily be treated as objects. We speak to the other who is not encompassed, who, on the contrary, is the one who offers his face to you.

The analysis can go further. I'm not saying that it is completed. The idea that is very important to me is frailty, the idea of being in a certain sense much less than a thing. One can kill, annihilate. It is easier to annihilate than to possess the other.

For me, these two starting points are essential: the idea of extreme frailty, of demand, that the other is poor. It is worse than weakness, the superlative of weakness. He is so weak that he demands. This, of course, is the beginning of the analysis, because the way in which we behave concretely is different. It is more complex. In particular because, what seems to me very important, is that there are not only two of us in the world. But I think that everything begins as if we were only two. It is important to recognize that the idea of justice always supposes that there is a third. But, initially, in principle, I am concerned about justice because the other has a face. . . .

If animals do not have faces in an ethical sense, do we have obligations towards them? And if so, where do they come from?

It is clear that, without considering animals as human beings, the ethical extends to all living beings. We do not want to make an animal suffer needlessly and so on. But the prototype of this is human ethics. Vegetarianism, for example, arises from the transference to animals of the idea of suffering. The animal suffers. It is because we, as human, know what suffering is that we can have this obligation.

The widespread thesis that the ethical is biological amounts to saying that, ultimately, the human is only the last stage of the evolution of the animal. I would say, on the contrary, that in relation to the animal, the human is a new phenomenon. And that leads me to your question. You ask at what moment one becomes a face. I do not know at what moment the human appears, but what I want to emphasize is that the human breaks with pure being, which is always a persistence in being. This is my principal thesis. A being is something that is attached to being, to its own being. That is Darwin's idea. The being of animals is a struggle for life. A struggle for life without ethics. It is a question of might. Heidegger says at the beginning of *Being and Time* that *Dasein* is a being who in his being is concerned for this being itself. That's Darwin's idea: the living being struggles for life. The aim of being is being itself. However, with the appearance of the human—and this is my entire philosophy—there is something more important than my life, and that is the life of the other. That is unreasonable. Man is an unreasonable animal. Most of the time my life is dearer to me, most of the time one looks after oneself. But we cannot admire saintliness. Not the sacred, but saintliness: that is, the person who in his being is more attached to the being of the other than to his own. I believe that it is in saintliness that the human begins; not in the accomplishment of saintliness, but in the value. It is the first value, an undeniable value. Even when someone says something bad about saintliness, it is in the name of saintliness that he says it.

Study Questions

1. What does Levinas mean by saying, "The face is a hand in search of recompense, an open hand. That is, it needs something. It is going to ask you for something"?

2. Do you agree with Levinas that "there is something more important than my life, and that is the life of the other"? Why or why not?

3. Do you agree with Levinas that the prototype for all ethics, including ethical treatment of animals, is human ethics, based on the experience of the human face? Why or why not?

Narrative

No Exit

JEAN-PAUL SARTRE

Play, 1944. Translation by S. Gilbert (1989). Summary and Excerpt. The first presentation of the play was in Paris in May 1944.

For Sartre, there is no life after death, for there is no God to send the soul to one realm or the other. But as a dramatist and a novelist, Sartre played with the idea of hell nevertheless. In the drama *No Exit*, three characters find themselves in a locked room with no windows: a middle-aged man, Garcin; a young woman, Estelle; and a lesbian woman, Inez. They all know that they are dead and in hell, and they are highly surprised that there is no torture chamber—merely a room decorated in bad taste. They don't know one another, but they are forced to spend an unforeseeable amount of time together in this room, interrupted only occasionally by a prison guard, the "valet." For a while they can "glimpse" the life of the living, but that soon fades, and all they have is one another. Each pretends to wonder what the others have done to be sent to hell, but, as Inez says, they are all "murderers." Estelle killed her baby, Inez killed her lover's husband (or at least drove him to his death), and Garcin killed the spirit in his wife by his cruelty to her.

. . . INEZ: Yes, I see. [*A pause.*] Look here! What's the point of play-acting, trying to throw dust in each other's eyes? We're all tarred with the same brush.

ESTELLE [*indignantly*]: How dare you!

INEZ: Yes, we are criminals—murderers—all three of us. We're in hell, my pets; they never make mistakes, and people aren't damned for nothing.

ESTELLE: Stop! For heaven's sake—

INEZ: In hell! Damned souls—that's us, all three!

ESTELLE: Keep quiet! I forbid you to use such disgusting words.

INEZ: A damned soul—that's you, my little plaster saint. And ditto our friend there, the noble pacifist. We've had our hour of pleasure, haven't we? There have been people who burned their lives out for our sakes—and we chuckled over it. So now we have to pay the reckoning.

GARCIN [*raising his fist*]: Will you keep your mouth shut, damn it!

INEZ [*confronting him fearlessly, but with a look of vast surprise*]: Well, well! [*A pause.*] Ah, I understand now. I know why they've put us three together.

GARCIN: I advise you to—to think twice before you say any more.

INEZ: Wait! You'll see how simple it is. Childishly simple. Obviously there aren't any physical torments—you agree, don't you? And yet we're in hell. And no one else will come here. We'll stay in this room together, the three of us, for ever and ever. . . . In short, there's someone absent here, the official torturer.

GARCIN [*sotto voce*]: I'd noticed that.

INEZ: It's obvious what they're after—an economy of man-power—or devil-power, if you prefer. The same idea as in the cafeteria, where customers serve themselves.

ESTELLE: Whatever do you mean?

INEZ: I mean that each of us will act as torturer of the two others.

What tortures Garcin most, though, is that he is a deserter. He, who always thought he would live and die bravely, never had a chance to prove himself, he says—he died too soon.

GARCIN [*putting his hands on her shoulders*]: Listen! Each man has an aim in life, a leading motive; that's so, isn't it? Well, I didn't give a damn for wealth, or for love. I aimed at being a real man. A tough, as they say. I staked everything on the same horse. . . . Can one possibly be a coward when one's deliberately courted danger at every turn? And can one judge a life by a single action?

INEZ: Why not? For thirty years you dreamt you were a hero, and condoned a thousand petty lapses—because a hero, of course, can do no wrong. An easy method, obviously. Then a day came when you were up against it, the red light of real danger—and you took the train to Mexico.

GARCIN: I "dreamt," you say. It was no dream. When I chose the hardest path, I made my choice deliberately. A man is what he wills himself to be.

INEZ: Prove it. Prove it was no dream. It's what one does, and nothing else, that shows the stuff one's made of.

GARCIN: I died too soon. I wasn't allowed time to—to do my deeds.

INEZ: One always dies too soon—or too late. And yet one's whole life is complete at that moment, with a line drawn neatly under it, ready for the summing up. You are—your life, and nothing else.

GARCIN: What a poisonous woman you are! With an answer for everything.

Estelle is beginning to find Garcin attractive (she is used to men fawning over her). Inez is falling in love with Estelle, and Garcin is himself attracted to Estelle but prefers that each of them stay in their own corner rather than hurt each other. But the stage is set, and they can't help interacting. All three try to manipulate one another; they team up, two against the third one. They constantly scrutinize one another (for in hell you have no eyelids you can close). They need each other for comfort and support, but they have no trust in one another. They realize that there is no need for torture instruments and devils—they are each other's torturers. The room and the other two people in it *are* hell for them: Their punishment is spending an eternity with one another in a hostile triangle. In the end Garcin succeeds in opening the locked door to their room, but now all three are reluctant to leave, because for each that would mean the other two had won the dominance game. All three stay to torment each other, forever.

On the symbolic level Sartre is—probably—not talking about any real life after death but about the human condition. He is saying we make life a hell for one another, because we are so very good at manipulating one another, and every human relationship, even that between lovers, has at its core a battle for power and dominance. Sartre concludes with one of his most famous lines: "Hell is—other people."

Study Questions

1. Would you agree with Sartre that "hell is other people"?

2. Do you think Garcin, Estelle, and Inez might apply Sartre's own principles of existentialism to cope with their life in hell? How?

Narrative

Good Will Hunting

GUS VAN SANT (DIRECTOR)

MATT DAMON AND BEN AFFLECK (SCREENWRITERS)

Film, 1997. Summary.

Harvard math professor Gerald Lambeau challenges his students to prove an advanced theorem written on the board in the hallway; the following day someone has proved it. In high anticipation, students crowd the auditorium, expecting the math genius to step up, but both they and Lambeau as well as the students are disappointed: Nobody takes credit for the feat. However, we, the audience, know who the genius is—the young

The film *Good Will Hunting* (Be Gentlemen Limited Partnership, 1997) shows us that you can be extremely intelligent, and yet have much to learn about life. Will Hunting (Matt Damon) is a mathematical genius, but everything he knows is from books, and he is unwilling to use his math skills to improve his prospects. When the chance presents itself for him to create a future with a woman he is attracted to, Skylar (Minnie Driver), his courage fails him—because who knows if she will reject him? His close friend Chuckie (Ben Affleck) tries to teach him that he should not shy away from reaching out to an uncertain future.

janitor Will. We've seen him stop, look at the board, ponder the problem, and work it out. And then we've seen him after work hours interacting with his friends, playing baseball, going to bars, getting drunk, getting into fights, and eventually being arrested for hitting a police officer—a hands-on, violent physical existence that seems light-years away from the cerebral life at Harvard.

But when Professor Lambeau adds a more advanced problem to the board, the young janitor is almost caught red-handed. At first, Lambeau thinks he is defacing the board, but as the young man slinks away, the professor realizes that he has solved the problem. Thinking Will is a student who has taken on part-time work at the school, Lambeau sets out to find him.

Meanwhile, Will's life is taking a new direction: In a bar, his friend Chuckie tries to pick up two female college students by pretending to be erudite, and a male college student steps in and does his best to expose Chuckie as a fake. But the college student must now deal with Will, who exposes the student's knowledge as nothing more than sophomoric parroting of textbook material. Will doesn't understand only math—he shows himself to have a profound knowledge of American social history as well. And as we get to know him better, we realize that his knowledge extends to just about any field of research, and all of it learned through visits to the library, not from any college classes.

One of the girls Chuckie tried to impress has noticed Will. Later that evening she comes up to Will, introduces herself, and tells him she has been waiting for him to make a move. Since he hasn't approached her table and she has to go home, she gives him her phone number. The young woman, Skylar, is in her final year of college and shows no reluctance to go for what she wants. Will, however, has not shown any initiative toward her, even though he likes her, and this becomes one of the pivotal themes in the story.

Next morning Lambeau tracks Will down and finds him in court, at his arraignment for assault. Will defends himself eloquently, but we hear that he has a rap sheet that includes grand theft auto, mayhem, theft, and physical abuse. And we learn that he has been in and out of foster homes for years. This time there will be no mercy, because the person he assaulted was a cop. But Lambeau steps in and makes a deal with the court: Will is released into his custody with the provision that Will agrees to work with him on math theories and agrees to see a therapist.

Working with Lambeau amuses Will, because he truly is a self-taught math genius—far brighter than Lambeau himself, who is a Fields Medal winner. But Will chews up five therapists by running circles around them intellectually and emotionally until they give up. Lambeau, worried that the terms of Will's release will be violated, finds him a final therapist: Lambeau's old friend from school, the psychologist Sean Maguire. Will, doing what he is good at, sizes Maguire up and finds his weak spot: He is still grieving over the loss of his beloved wife, who died of cancer a few years earlier. Even so, Sean Maguire takes Will on, seeing the real person behind the mask of intellectual mastery—a person who is afraid of life, afraid of friendship, love, and commitment, because of the abuse and abandonment he experienced in childhood.

Skylar and Will go out on a date, fool around in a novelty store, and eat fast food on what it seems more like a two buddies' night on the town than a romantic date, and when they kiss, it is on her initiative. Our impression of Will as a smart but somewhat inexperienced human being is enforced during his next session with the psychologist. Sean tells him that he has much learning but no experience and that he is a genius but also a terrified orphan—terrified that someone might get power over him if he opens up too much, and abandon him. Even when Will tells a joke, it is about people and places he has only read about. Does he even date? Has he had sex? Sean whistles the tune "People" ("People who need people are the luckiest people in the world")—a little comment to Will that his choice of not needing people is the wrong choice. And Will's dating is certainly in question—he has called Skylar, only to hang up on her before saying anything. Sean calls him on the carpet: Will doesn't want to ruin their budding relationship by finding out that she is not perfect—or by letting her find out that *he* is not perfect. And Sean tells Will that his deceased wife was not perfect—she would fart—but when you love each other, he says, the imperfections become precious, and the question is not, Is he or she perfect? but, Are we perfect for each other? You'll never find out unless you take the chance, he says. On the other hand, as Will is quick to point out, Sean has not remarried. Is he afraid of engaging in life himself? Will presses Sean: How did he know his wife was the right woman for him? Sean tells the story of the great Red Sox game he chose to miss because he wanted to go on a date with her instead. In other words, the value of what you are willing to give up to be with the one you love will tell you how much you love him or her.

Meanwhile, Will takes Skylar out on dates, and they do have sex but never at his place, always at hers, because he doesn't want her to see his squalid living quarters. He tells her elaborate stories about being one of thirteen brothers and having no privacy. But he does share his three friends with her, including Chuckie, and to his delight she gets along with them. But Chuckie realizes that Will is not being up front with his girl.

Old tensions are coming to the surface between Sean and Lambeau: Lambeau wants to recruit Will for a think tank, which would make him both rich and famous, and Sean believes it is more important for Will to find himself and become an authentic human being. We realize that Lambeau is developing an inferiority complex over Will's genius but that he has always believed that Sean felt intellectually, or at least financially, inferior to *him*. But Will has no intention of being manipulated by Lambeau. He sends Chuckie in his place to do a tongue-in-cheek job interview while he himself goes on a date with Skylar, who gives him what amounts to an ultimatum: She is leaving for Stanford University to go to medical school, and she wants him to come to California with her—she loves him and wants to have a life with him. But what if she changes her mind, he asks? What if he changes his? She: "You're afraid I won't love you back!" He: "You don't want to hear I was abused, I was an orphan, I don't need help!" And Will leaves her, saying he doesn't love her.

It appears that Will is reaching a breaking point: He insults and alienates Lambeau, making it clear that he doesn't want his job offer or his help. He refuses a job offer from NSA, saying he doesn't want to be responsible for his research killing strangers. And when Sean asks him if he has a soul mate, and he refers to dead philosophers such as Plato, Nietzsche, and Kant, Sean confronts him with his analysis: Will sees only the negative possibilities, so he doesn't dare take chances.

Skylar leaves for California, and Will violates his parole, ending his sessions with Lambeau. He goes back to his day job with Chuckie as a construction worker and tells him that it's all over—with the girl and with the fancy job offers—and thinks Chuckie will approve. But to his surprise, his friend now takes him to task: He has the opportunity to do something better than manual labor, his math genius gives him a winning ticket, and he doesn't dare cash it in?

Will now goes back to Sean and arrives in the middle of a ferocious quarrel between Sean and Lambeau, who accuses Sean of having chosen to be a failure. When Lambeau leaves, Sean shows Will that he has Will's old file documenting the horrible abuse he had suffered at the hands of his father. Sean understands, because he was a victim of an abusive father himself. Finally, Will breaks down in tears, his defenses crumbling.

The following day he goes to a prearranged job interview in Cambridge. There is a sense of change in the air—Sean decides to take some time off and go traveling, and while he is packing, Lambeau shows up, and the two old friends patch up their differences. It happens to be Will's birthday; he is now twenty-one, and his friends spring a big surprise on him: They've scraped enough money together to give him his own wheels—a beat-up old car, but it has a good engine.

So now Will is looking at a future in which his math genius will come to fruition, as a researcher in Cambridge. He has a car, and he has friends—but he also loves a woman on the other side of the continent. What will he do? Will he choose the secure future, or will he follow Sean's example and choose love, even if he can't be sure it is going to work out? The lesson Sean tried to teach him was that the value of what you are willing to give up to be with the one you love will tell you how much you love him or her. So what does Will decide? See the movie for yourself and decide if he made the right choice.

Study Questions

1. Explore the similarities between Will and Sean: How do those parallels help Will find himself? Is Will also helping Sean?

2. Compare the relationships between Will and Skylar and between Kierkegaard and his girlfriend Regine. What are the similarities? What are the differences?

3. How do Will and his friends illustrate Kierkegaard's "three stages of life" theory?

4. How do scenes between Will and Sean display aspects of Sartre's ideas about choice, authenticity, and bad faith?

5. Explain the title of the film. How might it have an existential meaning? Might it also refer to an element in Kant's ethics (see Chapter 6)?

Narrative

The Searchers

JOHN FORD (DIRECTOR)

Film, 1956. Summary.

The Searchers was considered a run-of-the-mill Western when it first came out in 1956, but since then it has acquired a reputation for being perhaps the best Western ever made. It is without a doubt one of director John Ford's finest works, and one reason for its current high standing in American film history is that the actor playing the lead, John Wayne, gives a performance that puts an end to the story that he really wasn't much of an actor. Another is that its theme is unusually frank for its time period, displaying one of the less romantic, less palatable sides of the Old West: the prevailing racism directed against American Indians. *The Searchers* appears in a chapter that is otherwise predominantly European in its philosophical themes because of the pivotal scene in the film, which could have been concocted as an illustration of Emmanuel Levinas's theory of the "face of the Other." A word of warning: I will be giving away the surprise ending of this film, because it is in one of the final scenes that the "Levinas" moment happens.

A lone rider approaches a small ranch somewhere in the Southwest; it is Ethan Edwards, returning home from the Civil War. He is still in what remains of his Confederate uniform, even though the war ended years before. The ranch belongs to his brother and his family—Martha, his wife; their teenage daughter, Lucy; a son of about thirteen; the

In the film *The Searchers* (Warner Brothers, 1956) Ethan Edwards (John Wayne) ruthlessly pursues a Comanche Indian band that has murdered his brother, sister-in-law, niece, and nephew, and kidnapped his other niece Debbie. Ethan initially intends to kill the Indians and rescue his niece, but the pursuit lasts years, and Ethan later searches for the band with a different purpose: not to save Debbie but to kill her because he believes she has been "contaminated" living with the Indians. When he finds Debbie as a young adult woman, his racism is overwhelmed by sheer human empathy—what Levinas calls "the face of the Other." In this scene, Ethan finds evidence that his niece has been kidnapped and plots revenge.

youngest daughter, Debbie; and a grown foster son, Marty, who is one-eighth American Indian. We realize that Ethan has had a hard time adjusting to the fact that the South lost the war, and that he has taken his own time returning home because he has strong feelings for Martha—feelings that are reciprocated, in a shy, discreet way. That first evening, Ethan gets reacquainted with his brother's family, but we also hear him belittle Marty for his Indian heritage and looks: "Fella could have mistook ya for a half-breed!"

The following day, a raid on a neighbor's cattle by Comanche Indians lures Ethan and Marty away from the ranch; a troop of Texas Rangers ask them to come along in pursuit, but Ethan's brother stays behind to look after his family. This is the last time Ethan sees his blood relatives alive, except for one. Too late Ethan and Marty realize that they have been tricked into leaving the ranch. In the meantime, the Comanches attack the little ranch and murder Ethan's brother, Martha, and their son, and take the two girls captive. When Ethan and Marty return, all that's left is the burning ranch and the three bodies. Realizing that Lucy and Debbie have been abducted, Ethan and Marty join forces with Lucy's fiancé, Brad, and take off in pursuit. They soon come upon the Indian camp, where they think they see Lucy in her blue dress, but Ethan finds Lucy's body hidden in a canyon—she has been raped and murdered—and buries her with his bare hands. An Indian warrior took her dress and is now wearing it. Brad goes crazy from grief and rage, and rushes into the Indian camp, where he is promptly killed. Ethan and Marty back off and lose sight of the tribe. Weeks turn into months, and the Comanche band continues to be elusive. Their search takes them all over the Southwest, where they find sporadic clues as to the whereabouts of the Indians and hints that Debbie is still alive. Months turn into years, but Ethan has no intention of giving up. "That'll be the day," he says. The two men have one of their most grueling experiences when they come upon a cavalry post after the cavalry has conducted a raid on an Indian village. The soldiers have rescued white captive women and have left a number of Indians dead. Ethan looks on in dread—not at the slaughter of the Indians, but at the blank stares from the white captive women who have lost their minds from years of deprivation, and we sense that he is coming to a resolve about Debbie's situation. If she is still alive, she is now reaching puberty, and since Indian women marry early, she may have married one of the warriors. The search has changed Ethan; he wants to find the Indian tribe who killed his brother—and Martha—to take revenge, but to Marty's horror Ethan now also intends to kill Debbie, who he believes has been "contaminated" by living with the tribe. (This attitude reflects the general opinion of the white settler communities in the nineteenth century.) After years of obsessive searching, they finally catch up with the band of Comanches led by a chief called Scar, who is quite aware of the two searchers and their quest. Ethan and Marty pretend to be traders and are invited into Chief Scar's teepee, where his three wives huddle in a corner. One of them gets up, and Ethan and Marty recognize her instantly: It is Debbie, all grown up. They have to control themselves so as not to give themselves away, and they find a pretext to leave camp so they can make plans—but Debbie has also recognized them and follows them. She wants to warn them of an ambush planned by Scar, but she has no intention of coming with them—she needs to get back to "her people," as she says to Marty. Ethan, true to his word, draws his gun and tries to kill her. Marty steps in to protect her, but at that moment they are attacked by the Indians, and Debbie gets away.

Ethan and Marty barely escape with their lives. Severely wounded, Ethan dictates his will, leaving the ranch and his cattle to Marty, "having no blood kin." "But," says Marty, "Debbie is your blood kin!" Ethan's reply—"She's been living with a buck . . ." ("buck" was a derogatory term for an Indian warrior)—shows us how he has completely written Debbie off as a relative, perhaps even as a human being.

Ethan and Marty return to the little homestead community in Texas to regroup but receive information that the Comanche band is camped not too far away, and with the company of Texas Rangers they set out for one last attempt. Marty sneaks into the camp and smuggles Debbie out unseen, to prevent Ethan from killing her, while the rangers are preparing an attack on the village. Scar discovers him, and he kills Scar. During the attack, Ethan locates Scar's tent and, robbed of his revenge for the murders of his brother and Martha, he scalps the dead chief. Now he looks around for Debbie. Debbie is running toward the hills as fast as she can, but Ethan is on horseback; Marty, on foot, tries to intercept Ethan but is summarily brushed aside, and Ethan starts up the hill after Debbie. There is now no way Marty can save her from Ethan. Ethan jumps off his horse, confronting the terrified, cowering young woman. He looks at her face, sees her humanity and vulnerability, and instead of killing her he scoops her up into his arms, and tells her, "Let's go home, Debbie."

So Ethan puts her on his horse, and together with Marty they ride back to the homesteads, where Debbie is welcomed and Marty is met by his long-time girlfriend. Nobody seems to notice Ethan. We see him framed by the doorway, with the desert behind him; he is alone, and he turns around, away from civilization, and returns to the wilderness. He has been estranged from civilization too long to belong with other human beings. He has no home anymore.

The moment when Ethan sees Debbie for what she is, and his own humanity takes over, has been called "one of the most moving moments in film history" by the French film director Jean-Luc Godard. Here we might also call it a "Levinas moment."

Study Questions

1. Is Ethan Edwards a racist? Explain.

2. Evaluate the character of Marty, being of one-eighth American Indian heritage. What does he bring to the story?

3. Why is Ethan trying to kill Debbie? What happens to him at the moment he decides against it?

4. Why might that moment be called a "Levinas moment"? Explain, referring to Levinas's theory of the "face of the Other."

5. Does Ethan's acceptance of Debbie mean that he is now no longer the racist that he was (if he ever was a racist)? In other words, do you think he now views *all* other humans as an "Other" in need?

6. A few years later, John Ford made another Western, *Two Rode Together,* about a white captive woman rescued and returned to the white settlements, a woman who is *not* welcomed by the bigoted settlers because she is too "contaminated," and who wishes to return to the Indians. The story is similar to what happened to Cynthia Parker, the white captive woman who was the mother of the great Indian chief Quana Parker. What do you think Ford wanted to say in choosing to tell both stories?

Chapter Eleven

Case Studies in Virtue

*T*his chapter presents three classical virtues—*courage, compassion,* and *gratitude*—for closer examination. We look at how they have been perceived by some philosophers of the past and present and how they may affect our lives. Why these virtues? Why not also loyalty, honesty, honor, and other virtues held dear by various traditions? Just for the simple reason that the topics of courage, compassion, and gratitude have provoked some fascinating contributions to the study of ethics and I would like to share these with you. And there is another simple reason: We have to limit our discussion to just a few samples. However, if you should feel inspired to continue the debate with other virtues as topics, I would wholeheartedly encourage it!

Courage of the Physical and Moral Kind

In 1933, during the Great Depression, President Franklin D. Roosevelt reassured the nation when he said, "The only thing we have to fear is fear itself." Those words helped millions of Americans, not only through the Depression but also through the trying times of World War II, to find courage to carry on, but is it true that fear and courage exclude each other? You'll remember that the first virtue Aristotle had on his list was courage—the proper "Golden Mean" response to danger. But in the Primary Readings for Chapter 9, you also saw that even Aristotle believed that courage is not synonymous with the absence of fear—that would be foolhardiness. Rather, it is an appropriate response to fear, at the right time, and in the right place, and for the right reason. Just to recap: Aristotle says (see pp. 456–457), "Properly, then, he will be called brave who is fearless in face of a noble death, and of all emergencies that involve death; and the emergencies of war are in the highest degree of this kind. Yet at sea also, and in disease; the brave man is fearless. . . . The man, then, who faces and who fears the right things and from the right motive, in the right way and at the right time, and who feels confidence under the corresponding conditions, is brave." As you can tell from the excerpt, Aristotle himself does not say that the brave man has no fear but that properly managed fear distinguishes a courageous person.

Of course, fear can be paralyzing when we are faced with a difficult choice and a dangerous task, but many a brave man or woman has decided to do the courageous thing precisely because of being afraid, not just in spite of being afraid. In many ways, courage has been the exemplary virtue for many philosophers, often in a rather abstract sense, because they were most often speculating about other people's response to dangerous situations. Interestingly, we know that Socrates indeed had the reputation for being a courageous man in battle when he was a young soldier in the war against Sparta, but courage in battle just isn't one of Socrates' primary themes. Perhaps that is in itself significant: Those who are courageous generally don't talk about it. In this section we explore some of the many faces of courage. Courage in battle may seem like the most obvious example, and perhaps that is where the most extreme forms of courage manifest themselves; but not all defiant acts under fire qualify for the term *courageous*—some are pure instinct, some are done because one fears a worse consequence (such as being tried for desertion), and some are done for the sake of some future advantage (medals, a political career, and so forth). But even outside the battle situation, we of course encounter courageous people—"ordinary people in extraordinary situations," as they are often described.

What is courage, and why is it a virtue? You already know that Kant says a quality such as bravery is not virtuous unless it is backed by a good will (Chapter 6). That means we can't just declare somebody who is brave a virtuous person—it takes more than simple fearlessness. In Chapter 10 you saw Philippa Foot add her opinion to what makes an admirable character trait a virtue—not the character trait alone, but also the intent behind it.

Stories of Courage

In 2003–4 the confluence of several things led to a renewed debate about courage, especially courage in war. For one thing, the war in Iraq had elevated a number of people to the forefront of the news: Some of them lived through their ordeal, others did not. Private Jessica Lynch, the female prisoner of war who was rescued from her Iraqi captors and lived to set the record straight, was at first hailed as a truly courageous woman warrior who fought until her gun was empty. She was not a combat soldier but had received very basic combat training before being sent on a maintenance mission with her crew: They took a wrong turn and were captured by Iraqi soldiers. In the ensuing firefight, most of her group died, and the survivors were taken to a hospital. Exactly what happened next is unclear; the other female POW, Lori Piestewa, died from her injuries, but Jessica survived. When the Marines came through the hospital looking for her and announcing that they were American soldiers, she said the words that have become famous: "I'm an American soldier too!" Was she abused and tortured while in captivity? It appears not. But from her own mouth we have learned that she never fired a shot, and her survival was more or less a matter of luck; she even feels that it is inappropriate that she was given the Bronze Star for "meritorious service in combat." Many people who are in favor of the idea of women in combat pointed out that her courage was as great as any male soldier's and clear proof that women can function well in battle. Others said that she was an excellent example of why women should *not* be in combat—not necessarily because they can't handle it, but because their presence will make their fellow male soldiers focus on their safety rather than on the object of their mission. Returning home, Jessica steered clear of the entire debate about women in combat, went on TV, and declared that what she did was nothing special—that all the glory should go to the Marines who rescued her. Now, was she courageous in

During the early days of the war in Iraq, in March 2003, a U.S. army maintenance crew took a wrong turn and was ambushed by Iraqi forces. Eleven crew members died, and seven were captured. Private Jessica Lynch, one of the captured, was rescued on April 1 by U.S. special operations forces from the hospital where she had been kept prisoner. The story told by the Pentagon and the media was that she had fought valiantly and had been mistreated during her captivity. Afterward, a different picture emerged: Jessica's gun had jammed, and she hadn't fired any shots—and she had no recollection of what happened at the hospital. In subsequent interviews she graciously refused to be called a hero and pointed out that the real heroes were the soldiers who rescued her.

battle? We don't know—there are stories of soldiers doing far more heroic things. But was she courageous in standing up and revising her media image, playing down her role? Here we have a good example of two different kinds of courage, which often are related—*physical* and *moral courage*—and we'll talk about them in the coming text. Jessica's war experience probably can't be taken as either proof or disproof of the appropriateness of women in combat, but she does serve as a good example of an individual who shows courage in claiming that she did nothing extraordinary—which is extraordinary in itself. In Chapter 12 we return to the issue of women in combat.

Other stories coming out of Iraq, through the embedded journalists and the soldiers interviewed by them, have been giving us a picture of what courage is. In Iraq in 2003, Army Sgt. 1st Class Paul R. Smith held off an attack with his machine gun until he was mortally wounded. He posthumously earned the Medal of Honor for organizing a defense that held off a company-sized attack on more than one hundred vulnerable coalition soldiers. Marine Cpl. Jason L. Dunham received the Medal of Honor posthumously; he died in 2004 in Iraq shielding soldiers in his care from a grenade thrown by an insurgent. Since the Medal of Honor was established by George Washington in 1782, more than 3,400 men and women have received the honor, but the medal is not given lightly: At the time of this writing, only two Medals of Honor, reserved for "the Bravest of the Brave," have been given to soldiers in the Iraq war.

But often courage involves more than heroic actions in battle. Pat Tillman, a safety for the NFL's Arizona Cardinals, enrolled in the army after 9/11, giving up fame and fortune because he wanted to make a difference and fight for his country. That act itself is for many a shining example of courage: giving up a rewarding, exciting life to do what one considers the right thing. When Tillman was killed in Afghanistan in 2004, the nation heard that he died bravely in battle. That he did, to be sure—any volunteer soldier who dies in battle deserves to have that said about him or her—but what the nation wasn't told immediately was that he died as a result of "friendly fire," accidental fire by another Army Ranger, and that Tillman was awarded the Silver Star on the basis of a concocted battle scenario. In 2007 Jessica Lynch, who herself knew something about being misrepresented, testified to a congressional hearing on the charges of a cover-up of Tillman's death that "the bottom line is the American people are capable of determining their own ideals of heroes and they don't need to be told elaborate lies."

As chance would have it, 2004 was also the sixtieth anniversary of D-Day, the American and British invasion of Normandy that turned the tide in World War II and signified the beginning of the end of Hitler's regime. What became sadly apparent during the commemorative events in France, as well as the celebration at the new World War II memorial in Washington, D.C., was that the ranks of the surviving World War II veterans were thinning. Mostly in their eighties and nineties, these vets, called "the Greatest Generation," and their extraordinary experiences will soon be, literally, history; and many felt that it was high time their stories were recorded if they hadn't already been, and their courage and sacrifice celebrated. A swell of books and magazines were published, focusing on the D-Day stories in particular, the excruciating fight just to get off the landing beaches alive under heavy enemy fire. (In the Narratives section you will find the story of such a real-life individual, slightly fictionalized, in one of the episodes from the acclaimed HBO series *Band of Brothers*.) One of the books that came out in 2004 did not focus on either the war in Iraq or D-Day but on the concept of courage in general: John McCain's *Why Courage Matters*. For Senator McCain, himself a Vietnam War veteran and a POW, the notion of courage has been "defined down": We tend to confuse courage with fortitude, discipline, righteousness, or virtue; we call athletes courageous when they play a good game, we call people courageous if they just do their job—but real courage takes more. What is virtue without courage? he asks. We need courage to keep being virtuous even when our virtue is being tested. In McCain's words, "We can admire virtue and abhor corruption sincerely, but without courage we are corruptible."

Such courageous people are not just the heroes of famous battles or political struggles but also ordinary people who do their best, following their convictions even to the point of losing everything, including their lives, says McCain. One such person is Angela Dawson, a mother who decided to stay with her children in their neighborhood and fight the drug dealers—a decision that cost both her and her children their lives; the dealers burned her house down, trapping her and the kids inside. Some of the other examples McCain turns to include the Navajo chief Manuelito; John Lewis, a disciple of Dr. Martin Luther King, Jr.; Hannah Senesh, the young Jewish woman who worked to establish a Jewish homeland; and Aung San Suu Kui, the oft-imprisoned political activist in Burma (Myanmar). McCain tells their stories, and lets us see wherein their courage lies. Echoing Aristotle, he emphasizes that courage comes from doing courageous things—but in one important respect McCain and Aristotle differ: Consider the case of Angela Dawson. She certainly had the courage to stand by her convictions and stand up to the drug dealers, but the result was that her home was torched, and she and her kids were burned alive. Did she have courage? It would certainly seem so. But what would Aristotle say? She had too much of it—she was being foolhardy, stubbornly risking her own life and the lives of her children. Aristotle might have said that Dawson misjudged the situation, and because of that (although it is a harsh thing to say)

In thirteen episodes the acclaimed HBO television series *Band of Brothers* follows E Company from D-Day (June 6, 1944) to the end of World War II in Europe (May 1945). One of the frequent themes explored is courage, of both the physical and the moral variety. In the episode summarized in the Narratives section, "Carentan," you'll meet this man, Private Albert Blithe (Marc Warren), who must face his paralyzing fear of combat.

she was not virtuous. So McCain's theory that courage is the foundation of virtue perhaps needs to take into account Aristotle's theory of the Golden Mean—we can often discern when someone has too little courage, but can we also discern when someone has too much? Aristotle's criterion was, Did they succeed? Then they were virtuous. And how did they succeed? By using their *reason* in determining when something is too much and when it is too little. These are two different views of what courage means, and it is up to us to decide if they speak to us, if we prefer one over the other, or if we think it would make sense to modify one with aspects of the other.

Box 11.1 WHAT IS A HERO?

In the chapter text, you have read a discussion about what makes a person courageous. Another aspect of that discussion is the concept of *hero* itself. We approached it briefly, in the section about Private Jessica Lynch: Is anyone who displays courage a hero? Does it matter what the end result of a courageous deed is, or is it the display of courage that counts? Some critics have pointed out that we are much too quick to pronounce somebody a hero these days—the word has been inflated. If someone such as Private Lynch has displayed courage but hasn't done much more than simply survive an ordeal, the media will often slap a "hero" label on the person. But that label is offensive to people who set their standards for heroism higher: Saving the lives of others, with courageous disregard for one's own safety, is a suitable criterion for some. In that case, Officer Walwyn Stuart (Chapter 4)

would be a hero. For others, a true hero is someone who rises above what he or she has been hired or trained to do and performs an extraordinary deed that helps others—"ordinary people doing extraordinary things." In that case, some of the locals and tourists staying behind to help find survivors and victims of the 2004 tsunami would qualify as heroes, as would those civilians who chose to stay behind and help strangers rebuild their lives. The same criteria would apply to the events surrounding Hurricane Katrina in 2005. Mostly we tend to assume that courage is part of the picture—unless we choose to think that celebrities are heroes just because they are celebrities, or good at their job, like the so-called sports heroes or movie heroes. In your view, is it true that we have inflated the concept of hero? Can you be heroic without courage? What would be your definition of a hero?

Physical and Moral Courage

Your adrenaline is pumping, your heart rate is accelerated, you may even experience tunnel vision and a sense that time has slowed down. But it isn't a movie—it's you, in a dangerous situation, making split-second decisions. You do what you are trained to do, perhaps what seems the logical thing to do, or perhaps you just act out of instinct. Then, if you're lucky, you'll live to talk about it. So now people are calling you a hero—but you didn't feel that you were doing anything heroic; you just responded to the needs of the moment. Do you recognize the situation? If you do, I salute you. Most of us don't, but we have all heard of people who, after having done something that looks extraordinarily heroic, deny having done anything special. As a matter of fact, when is the last time you heard such a person stand up afterward and say, "Yeah, I'm a hero!"? So the title of hero, and the admiration of bravery, is usually something that is bestowed upon an individual by *others*. As we have seen in Chapter 4, we really can't look into the hearts of people and see their true motivation for the deeds they do. As long as it looks like an unselfish act, and involves physical danger, we're generous with our praise and call it courage. Box 11.1 explores the concept of "hero."

Indeed it may be courage. It could also be luck, or a misinterpretation of motive—in the film *Hero* (1992) a small-time con artist enters a crashed airplane, and in his quest for loot he manages to save every passenger on board. But disregarding physical danger for the sake of others' lives, liberty, property, or simply happiness is generally identified as courage. What we shouldn't forget is that this is only one of many types of courage: the *physical* kind. Although most of us will perhaps never be in a situation where we can prove to ourselves and the world that we can be physically brave, the other type of courage works in the shadows, is rarely recognized, and is perhaps so common that most of us don't even realize when we've had a courageous moment of the *moral* kind: the kind where you stand by your friend when it would be more convenient to distance yourself from him or her; the kind where you don't allow the powerful clique at school to exclude a newcomer, or someone who is a little different from them; the kind where you stand up to your boss because you know you're right, even if you may lose that job. A whistleblower such as Erin Brokovich certainly must have had physical courage, but the very thought of blowing the whistle takes moral courage to begin with, the kind of courage Rosa Parks displayed when she, in 1955, refused to give up her seat to a white bus passenger. Moral courage may not result in the spectacular saving of lives, yet we recognize it in particular when it is *absent.* We may understand, and forgive, friends who failed us when we really needed them, but we rarely forget. And if we have failed a friend in her or his moment of need—if we are decent human beings, that will come back to haunt us even long after our friend has assured us that it was okay, that he or she understands. McCain believes there isn't much difference between physical and moral courage when push comes to shove, and it may certainly be true that the person who has one kind also is likely to have the other; but even so, there is one big difference that we should take into account: Physical courage is *visible,* whereas moral courage often is not—it is often lived through without a sense of accomplishment, or reward, or even acknowledgment. In the Primary Readings section, we take a look at McCain's suggestion for how to teach our kids moral courage, by teaching them to do their "nearest duty."

An example of the moral courage that simply consists in standing up and being counted comes out of Spokane, Washington. In May 2005 it was disclosed that Spokane's conservative Republican mayor, Jim West, had an unusual hobby. Undercover work by the only daily newspaper in town revealed that West would troll gay chat websites and get in touch with young men, eighteen or about to turn eighteen. That might be regarded as part of the private life that we all want respected, but it turned out that he had offered a number of those young men positions as interns in City Hall and that he had used his office computers for this pastime—all of which the mayor admitted to, while claiming that he'd never done anything illegal. (And the FBI agreed that it wasn't *illegal,* but the FBI isn't hired to weigh in on whether actions are *ethical.*) As could be expected, many people in Spokane were outraged—but not because he was revealed to be gay; there was a general consensus among the voters that his sexual life was nobody's business. Some were outraged because the mayor had been a staunch anti-gay legislator in Olympia (Washington's capital), and one sensed a bit of *hypocrisy* there. But mainly people were angry because it just didn't seem right, or at least it seemed unprofessional, that the mayor would be (1) trolling for very young men and (2) using his position to offer them jobs that would keep them close to his office. Young men came forward to corroborate the story and told of job offers and harassment.

There was talk of circulating a recall petition, and an outraged citizen, Shannon Sullivan, a single mother working in a floral shop, showed up at City Hall to sign the petition. But there was no petition, and she was the only one there. So Ms. Sullivan took out the papers to file a petition herself, so that her young son would know that his mother had done the right thing and so that the citizens of Spokane would have the chance to decide either to keep the mayor or to recall him. Without any kind of legal background, and having been fired from the floral shop for being a "trouble-maker," Shannon Sullivan succeeded in taking the recall petition all the way through several legal challenges to the Washington Supreme Court. With her little son sitting in the audience, she held her own against the mayor's lawyers, who were fighting her every step of the way. The Supreme Court sided with her, the recall signature drive was completed, and in December 2005 the mayor was recalled by the voters of Spokane. Now this is the stuff Hollywood movies are made of: Everywoman against the establishment and the best minds money can buy, and winning because of her moral fortitude. Does that mean that if the Supreme Court hadn't sided with her, Sullivan would have been less courageous? Or does it mean that somebody who is fighting a moral battle that you, or I, might *not* agree with is *not* courageous? Or that simply being courageous guarantees that one is morally right? Of course not. The point I want to make is that there is *physical* backbone and then there is *moral* backbone, and Shannon Sullivan's standing in front of the Supreme Court, arguing from the point of view of a citizen because nobody else rose to the occasion and she thought somebody had to do it, *exemplifies moral courage.*

But on a smaller scale, there's plenty of moral spine to go around: Calling the doctor's office to get the result from a medical test can be a test of courage all by itself, and so can deciding to tell something to your best friend that she ought to know but won't appreciate your telling her. Mentioning some everyday occurrences that require us to step up to the plate and do things we generally don't enjoy doing can bring home the immediacy of the moral challenge and remove the notion that courage happens only on faraway battlefields or in rare, life-threatening situations. As Ayn Rand enjoyed pointing out (see Chapter 4), if we reserve our moral challenges only for extremely unlikely situations, we get into the habit of thinking that we may not be called upon to act morally on an everyday basis.

A controversial topic within the discussion of courage is the topic of suicide. Is a person who decides to commit suicide courageous or a coward? Or perhaps those categories don't apply at all. In Box 11.2 you'll find a discussion of the subject.

Let us suppose that we now have a better understanding of courage. It involves taking action, or just standing up for something or someone you believe in, when doing so may involve a risk to yourself, your job, your well-being, even your life—instead of remaining silent because it is easier or less risky, or because speaking up might be considered politically incorrect by some. It involves doing the right thing when it is difficult, not when it is easy. (In the Narratives section, the story of Tom Horn illustrates a certain kind of courage: choosing to protect your friends even to the point where it may cost your life.) But here we run into a new problem: When do we know whether our "cause" is actually morally righteous? Can we just trust our moral intuition? As you'll see later in this chapter, Hitler's right-hand man, Heinrich

Box 11.2   IS SUICIDE COURAGEOUS OR COWARDLY?

The issue of suicide has come up on occasion in this book; in Chapter 2 you read about young Werther, who killed himself out of unrequited love, and in Chapter 5 we used suicide as an example in the debate about John Stuart Mill's harm principle. Shocking to most of us, statistics show that suicide is the second greatest killer of American college students, more than all illnesses and birth defects *combined,* and takes a back seat only to accidents. So within a college environment, the debate does tend to gravitate toward the subject from time to time, and the issue sometimes comes up: Is committing suicide a courageous act, or is it cowardly? The question assumes there is one clear answer. If we grant that suicide can sometimes be attempted by sane people, then we can apply the issue of virtue and vice, of morally right and wrong (because we wouldn't use moral condemnation on mentally ill people who don't have a choice in their actions), and then the question of courage versus cowardice will have to do with the how and the why. Much of our attitude toward suicide is rooted in religion; Catholicism sees suicide as a deadly sin, condemning a soul to eternal damnation. Buddhism views suicide as a personal failure to deal with one's karma—a failure that will have negative results in the next life. But some moral systems, whether religious or secular, such as those in Imperial Japan and Imperial Rome, have had great respect for the suicide solution. It is hard to rise above the ethics of one's culture and upbringing in this regard, but if we can for a moment forget the issue of whether or not suicide is plain wrong, we can focus on the courage/cowardice issue.

What if a person allows himself or herself to die, or downright commits suicide so that others may live? Self-sacrifice is usually not even labeled suicide in our language, so that gives us a clue: There is supposedly something *selfish* in suicide. The question is, How much? And of what nature? If a person commits "suicide by cop," by forcing a situation where a police officer has no choice but to shoot, the selfishness extends beyond that person's own wants and usually is met by heavy condemnation because it also inflicts misery on others (the police officer will face a hearing, might lose his or her badge, and will have to live with killing another person to the end of his or her life). If people kill themselves because they can't face the shame of some personal situation being disclosed, the world usually pities them for their mental agony but would have admired them more if they had stayed alive to face the music—so there is some sense that suicide is an "easy way out." Generally, the only type of suicide that is met with a kind of silent acceptance or even admiration in this culture (where euthanasia is illegal in all but one state) is the decision by a terminally ill person to cheat the reaper and take matters into his or her own hands, shortening the time of torment. However, all these cases surely require a definite amount of personal guts, just to stand up and go through with it. So is there courage in the suicidal act? Undoubtedly, in the decision and in the act itself—but might there be more bravery in staying alive? That may be a very individual judgment call, but our willingness to call the act of suicide both brave and cowardly shows not only that we have mixed feelings about it but also that we may be referring to different aspects of the act: We judge the immediate decision to die, but we also judge the decision to avoid the future.

Himmler, thought he was doing the right thing by setting in motion the "Final Solution"—the mass extermination of the German Jews—and he found it a very hard thing to do. Did that make it right? Of course not. In the next section you'll see what virtue can be added to "courage" to make it less likely that courage is misspent: compassion. In addition, we'll look at the role of reason and reexamine why emotions may be morally relevant, but why we also need reason to moderate and give direction to the moral feelings.

Compassion: From Hume to Huck Finn

A story that is familiar to most people raised in the Christian tradition is the parable of the Good Samaritan: A victim of a robbery and an assault is passed over by several so-called upstanding citizens and is finally helped by someone who is moved by his plight: the Good Samaritan. You'll find the story in the Narratives section. It is generally recognized that people *are capable of* showing compassion—the debate usually centers on *why:* You'll remember Thomas Hobbes's view that humans are by nature self-centered and that compassion is something humans show toward others in distress because they are afraid the same calamity might happen to them. In other words, when people show sympathy and pity toward one another, either it is to make sure that others will help them if the same thing should happen to them, or else it is a kind of superstition, a warding off of the fate of others. There are scholars who think Hobbes's viewpoint was fostered by the political unrest of the seventeenth century, which might well have caused a thinker to focus on his own survival and to believe that self-love is the primary driving force.

In the eighteenth century, the Age of Reason, two philosophical giants shared a different idea. Both the Scottish philosopher David Hume and the Swiss philosopher Jean-Jacques Rousseau believed that humans are naturally compassionate toward one another. As you read in Chapter 4, Hume held that even a selfish person will feel benevolence toward strangers whenever his self-interest is not involved. Rousseau claimed that the more we are corrupted by civilization, the more we tend to forget our natural inclination to help others and sympathize with them, because it is not an aberration of nature that makes people selfish—it is *civilization* itself. Rousseau certainly agreed that there are people who show compassion only because they are afraid something might happen to them and because they have only their own interests at heart, but that is not a natural thing, he said; it is caused by human culture. If we would seek only the natural capacities in ourselves, we would find the natural virtue of compassion still intact. The best way to reestablish contact with our original nature is to educate children as freely as possible so that they don't become infected with the evils of civilization.

Philosophers in the Western tradition were not the only ones to speculate about human nature and compassion; in the third century B.C.E. the Chinese philosopher Mencius claimed, as Rousseau would some two thousand years later, that humans are compassionate and benevolent by nature but have been corrupted by the circumstances of everyday life. In an upcoming section we take a look at the philosophy of Mencius as well as those of Confucius and Lin Yutang.

Scientists Agree: Compassion Is Hardwired

As you have read in Chapter 1 as well as in Chapter 4, new research in neuroscience has revealed that, contrary to what most philosophers have emphasized for over two thousand years, it is not natural for the human brain to approach moral problems with logic only and without feelings. For those of you who remember the original *Star Trek* television and film series, that idea—which most people outside the field of philosophy would consider mere common sense—is illustrated beautifully in the character of Mr. Spock, the half-human, half-Vulcan character. With his brilliant mind, Spock attempts to control his emotional human side and cultivate his Vulcan all-rational heritage, but it doesn't work that way: Spock finds himself to be quite emotional from time to time. One might say that aside from Hume and Rousseau, most philosophers have, for a very long time, attempted to do the same thing: downplay the emotional element under the assumption that it will lead to corruption and favoritism, and perhaps even a slide backward to a less refined, more animal-like existence based on instincts (which is amusing, considering that some of those same thinkers have claimed that animals have no emotional life). But in several distinct studies released in 2006 and 2007, neuroscientists and other scholars presented their findings:

1. An Empathy Center in the Brain University of California neuroscientist Antonio Damasio pointed out that we have a center for empathy in the brain that serves as a buffer for decisions that are likely to harm other humans; persons with damage to this brain area feel less reluctance to make decisions that may benefit the many but will harm a few people. (And, I suppose, such impaired brains might also be less reluctant to make decisions that will benefit the few but harm the many.)

2. Mirror Neurons Italian researchers as well as University of California neuroscientist V. F. Ramachandran have found that we have a natural capacity for understanding what others feel through certain neurons labeled *mirror neurons.*

3. Thoughts of Harm Cause Negative Emotions Harvard psychologist Joshua Greene has, with brain imaging, shown that thoughts of hurting another human being generate negative emotions in the normal brain.

4. A Grammar of Morals Has Evolved Harvard evolutionary biologist Marc Hauser has suggested that we have a broad set of moral codes built into our brain by evolution, as surely as our language comes with a built-in grammar; but, just as languages can have a basic grammar in common but otherwise be different, so, too, can our moral responses.

5. Altruism Feels Good Neuroscientists Jorge Moll and Jordan Grafman have, through brain imaging, found that doing good things for others makes the pleasure area in the brain light up, in the same manner that we respond positively to food and sex. Rather than being a sophisticated override of selfish interests, it is an ancient, basic neurological response that may even predate *Homo sapiens.*

The common conclusion is that, contrary to what most philosophers, psychologists, and biologists thought, the bottom line for our moral universe is *empathy,* or, as David Hume called it, "fellow-feeling." We have instant emotional responses that seem to be universal, such as Greene's 2004 brain-imaging experiment in which volunteers were asked to imagine hiding in a cellar in a village with enemy soldiers hunting down all survivors. If a baby cries, should the child be smothered to protect everyone in the cellar? (This scenario was in fact the plot for the final show in the long-running and very successful television series *M*A*S*H*.) Everyone agrees that the baby should not be killed—but also that it is wrong to risk the lives of everyone else. Greene's conclusion is that, in essence, the "emotion" part and the "reason" part of the brain are in conflict, and that the emotional response (don't hurt the baby) is far older than the cooler evaluation of saving everyone else. That, says Greene, explains why we're more willing to help our neighbor than someone starving halfway around the world—our brains evolved in a tribal society where we needed to respond to those around us, and we had no information about distant places.

So the consensus is in among the scientists: *We have a moral intuition.* Interestingly, for Greene that doesn't mean that it is always more morally right to go with our emotions rather than with our reason, and the philosopher Peter Singer agrees: We have been tribal people for such a long time, and those responses were appropriate then, but we're in a different world now, and we can't just assume that we can trust our intuition. *Sometimes the right thing to do may be to override our moral intuition.* We get back to this question below, but for now we can consider it scientifically established: The normal human brain is hardwired for empathy. Now we have to see what philosophers make out of that—because even if scientists tell us we're naturally empathetic, it should come as no surprise that a great many people over the years have turned out either to be so brain-damaged that they have no empathy or to have a considerable talent for overriding their empathy and causing deliberate harm to others. That brings up the philosophical question of *when* we choose to, in very traditional terms, listen to our *heart,* and when to listen to our *head,* and *why*.

Philip Hallie: The Case of Le Chambon

We can now see that Rousseau was more right than he could have imagined when he speculated that we have a natural inclination to help others. But was he also right that it is *civilization* that causes evildoing, or does "civilized" mean "compassionate"? An indirect answer was given years ago by the American philosopher Philip Hallie (1922–1994), whom I once had the privilege of meeting. Hallie was an unusual philosopher, as today's philosophers go, because he was never afraid to talk about his own feelings and the feelings of others. You cannot understand evil unless you understand how it feels to those who are being victimized, he said, and you cannot understand goodness unless you ask those to whom goodness has been shown. Having been a U.S. soldier in World War II, Hallie had seen his share of bloodshed and cruelty, including the revelations of the Holocaust death camps. Deeply depressed about the apparent inability to fight evil without becoming as violent as one's enemy, Hallie was profoundly moved by learning about a concrete example of compassion that occurred in the midst of a civilization under the heel of barbarism. In the southern part of France, there is a small village called Le Chambon-sur-Lignon, where the population has had a long history of being persecuted for their Huguenot faith. During World War II the people of the village came to the aid of Jewish refugees from all over France in a rescue effort that was matched only by the prodigious efforts of Danish citizens to save the Danish Jews by smuggling them across the water to neutral Sweden, and the extraordinary courage and conviction of the Japanese consul-general in Lithuania, Chiune Sugihara, and his wife, Yukiko, who, against orders from their own government, hand-signed six thousand visas in twenty days for Lithuanian Jews, thus allowing them to travel to Japan and escape death at the hands of the Nazis. The people of Le Chambon also saved about six thousand lives (more than twice the number of their own population). The majority were Jewish children whose parents had already gone to the extermination camps. This took place all during the German occupation of France, even when southern France ceased to be a "free zone" governed by French collaborators.

As a contrast to the compassion of the French villagers, Hallie points to the sadism displayed during the Nazi reign. The Nazis regularly humiliated their prisoners; during marches prisoners were not allowed to go to the bathroom and had to perform their physical functions while on the march. Hallie describes this as an "excremental assault" and calls it an example of *institutionalized cruelty.* Hallie defines this type of cruelty as not only physical but also psychological. When a person's or a people's self-respect and dignity are attacked on a regular basis, the victims often begin to believe that somehow that cruelty is *justified* and that they really are no better than dirt. That is especially true when one population group commits this offense against another group. Thus cruelty becomes a social institution, endorsed by the victimizer and tolerated by the victim. Such instances of institutionalized cruelty can be seen not only in oppressive wartime situations but also in race relations throughout the course of history, in relations between the sexes, and in certain parent-child relationships. The general pattern is a demeaning and belittling of one group by another, so that soon such behavior becomes routine.

Why does institutionalized cruelty occur? Because one group is more powerful than the other, either in physical strength (it is bigger, is more numerous, or has more weapons) or in economic, educational, or political clout (as when one group can hold property, get an education, and vote, and the other group can't). Power can even be verbal, as when one group has the monopoly of using slurs against the other.

How can it be helped? By changing the power balance, says Hallie. That, of course, is hard—it is hard to acquire the right to vote, to own property, to get an equal education. It is hard to build up physical strength. And it is hard to reverse the trend of slurs and other insults. Even if all that is achieved, though, the insidious effect of institutionalized cruelty is not over when the cruelty ceases, because *it leaves scars.* The prisoners who were liberated from Nazi extermination camps were never truly "free" again; they carried their scars with them forever. And just being "kind" to a victim doesn't help—it only serves as a reminder of how far he or she has sunk. What truly helps is a gesture similar to what the people of Le Chambon did for the Jewish refugees in the face of the Nazi occupation.

Hallie heard of Le Chambon and went there to talk to the people; most of them didn't think they had done anything exceptional. What these people did for the refugees was to show them compassion in the form of *hospitality.* They showed the refugees that they were equal to the villagers themselves, that they deserved to live in the villagers' own homes while their escape across the mountains to Switzerland was being planned. This, says Hallie, is the only effective antidote to institutionalized cruelty: hospitality offered as an act of compassion, in a way that makes it clear to the victims that their dignity is intact.

The story of Le Chambon has a twist that makes it even more exceptional. How did the rescue effort succeed in an occupied country with Nazi soldiers everywhere? It wasn't that the villagers were tremendously discreet—no group can hide six thousand people who pass through over a five-year period. It was because of the courage of the town minister, André Trocmé, and his masterly organization of the smuggling operation that Nazi curiosity was deflected for the longest time. Trocmé's cousin Daniel Trocmé was arrested and executed by the Nazis, but that did not stop the rescue effort, because the villagers had an ally in a very unlikely person: the Nazi overseer of the village, Major Julius Schmäling. Schmäling's task was to keep the peace in the region—meaning, in Hallie's words, "to keep the French quiet while Germany raped the country and went about its business of trying to conquer the world." And Schmäling did keep the peace, but not through terror. Instead, he chose to ignore the steady stream of refugees and did not report the incidents to his superiors. One victim of the Nazis whom Schmäling could not save was one of the two doctors of Le Chambon, Le Forestier, who himself was not engaged in the underground movement. But one day he gave a ride to two hitchhikers from the underground, who hid their weapons in his Red Cross ambulance. When the ambulance was later searched by Nazi soldiers, the weapons were found and Le Forestier arrested. Intervention by Schmäling led the doctor's family to believe that he would only be sent to a work camp in Germany as a doctor, but in actual fact the Nazis intercepted the train taking the doctor to Germany. They took him off the train and executed him the following day with about 110 other people. The Trocmés found out the truth from Schmäling years after the war and realized that Schmäling, ever since that day, had agonized about the one life he hadn't been able to save.

In his posthumously published book *Tales of Good and Evil, Help and Harm* (1997), Hallie writes about the complex character of Schmäling: He and his wife tried for the longest time to avoid membership in the Nazi Party, but when it was finally imminent, Schmäling joined the army so that he wouldn't have to be a party member. Originally a schoolteacher in Munich, he had told his students that decency has no price, no market value, but as an overseer he was very efficient; otherwise he couldn't have stayed on the job. So that makes him a morally ambiguous man, says Hallie. "He served a government that systematically persecuted defenseless people, but he would not persecute them himself." And that refusal to persecute the weak did not go unnoticed by the people of Le Chambon: After the liberation of Paris in 1944, when Nazi officers were held accountable for their atrocities in trials all over France, Schmäling's trial was most unusual. As he walked up the aisle toward the judge, everyone rose to pay tribute to this man who had saved so many at the risk of his own life. When asked why he had not reported the Jewish children hiding in the village, he responded, "I could not stand by and watch innocent blood be shed." Schmäling spent some time in prison in France but later returned to Germany, where he lived in modest circumstances until his death in 1973. (See Box 11.3 for Hallie's views on one of the major Nazi leaders.)

Box 11.3   IS IT BETTER TO CRY OVER YOUR VICTIM THAN NOT TO FEEL SORRY?

In a celebrated paper the philosopher Jonathan Bennett claims that it is better to be a person guilty of wrongdoing who has compassion than it is to be an innocent person who has no compassion. An example of the first kind of person is Heinrich Himmler, who, as head of the Nazi SS (an elite guard unit), developed stomach troubles because of what he felt he had to do. The seventeenth-century American Calvinist minister Jonathan Edwards was the other type of person; although he presumably served the needs of his flock, he believed everybody deserved to go to hell. Philip Hallie responds to Bennett's point of view by referring to an incident in Lewis Carroll's *Alice in Wonderland.* The Walrus and the Carpenter lure some little oysters to take a nice

walk with them along the beach. After a while they all sit down on a rock, and the Carpenter and the Walrus begin to eat the oysters. The Walrus feels sorry for them and weeps, but he eats them nevertheless. The Carpenter couldn't care less about the oysters and is just concerned with eating them. Hallie asks, Are we really supposed to believe that the Walrus is a better creature than the Carpenter because he has sympathy for his victims? The Walrus ate as many oysters as he could stuff into his mouth behind his handkerchief. Likewise, Himmler killed more than 13 million people even though he was "feeling sorry" for them. For Hallie sympathy is no redeeming quality at all if it isn't accompanied by compassionate action.

To Hallie, virtue is this: the compassion one shows in reaching out to save others at the risk of one's own life. It it not necessarily the result of logical thinking—it may be an act of the heart. For Hallie, there are degrees of moral behavior, though. If you just refrain from doing harm, you are following the *negative command* "Do not cause harm." That is commendable, but there is a stronger command, a *positive command:* "Help others in need." It is much harder to follow a positive moral rule than a negative one, which just requires you to do nothing. The people of Le Chambon followed the harder path of the positive rule. In your opinion, what did Major Schmäling do? Did he follow the negative rule of no harmdoing, or did he, under the circumstances, also follow a positive rule of actively helping? At the end of this chapter we look at a powerful story of compassion similar to that of Le Chambon, Steven Spielberg's film *Schindler's List,* and in the Primary Readings, you'll find an excerpt from Hallie's *Tales of Good and Evil, Help and Harm.*

Richard Taylor: Compassion Is All You Need

In Chapters 3 through 7 we looked at a number of rules and principles regarding the nature of moral goodness and the proper conduct of human beings. Even in this section on virtue, most of the theories we have discussed involve using *reason* to evaluate the proper moral action. But on several occasions you have encountered a suggestion that, in the last decades of the twentieth century, seemed extremely controversial but that has gained considerable interest and acceptance lately among philosophers and scientists alike: the notion that reason isn't everything when it comes to moral evaluations and decisions, that *moral feelings* are highly important too. You'll remember Martha Nussbaum's claim that emotions can have a reasonable side that makes them indispensable to moral decision making (see Chapter 1). In his own way, Philip Hallie considers the virtue of compassion as an *emotion* that is essential for the moral makeup of a decent human being. However, neither Hallie nor Nussbaum suggests that we can dispense with reason. Such a radical view isn't held by many, but some thinkers do believe that the way to do the right thing and have virtue is very simple: We do the right thing *when our heart is in the right place;* moral goodness is simply a gut feeling that we all have, a conscience that speaks without words, an empathy that leads us to reach out in compassion to others. If we don't have that, we have no morality at all. For Richard Taylor, an American philosopher, reason has *no* role to play in making the right moral choice. Taylor belongs to a school of thought that says *moral principles are, in effect, useless,* because we can always find exceptions. You will remember that this was one of the issues we discussed in Chapter 6. But Taylor doesn't believe the alternative is a moral nihilism. On the contrary—in his book *Good and Evil* (2000) Taylor says:

> Moral principles are nothing but conventions, but they have the real and enormous value to life that conventions in general possess. They help us to get where we want to go. Without them social life would be impossible, and hence any kind of life that is distinctively human. Their justification is, therefore, a practical one and has nothing to do with moral considerations in the abstract. The moment such a principle ceases to have that value, the moment its application produces more evil than good, then it ceases to have any significance at all and ought to be scorned.

So if rational principles aren't the basis of ethics, then what is? It is the virtue of compassion, a phenomenon of the heart, not the brain. The eternal focus in ethics on reason needs an antidote, and Taylor finds it in an analysis of *malice versus compassion.*

Imagine a series of atrocities. A child pins a bug to a tree just to watch it squirm. Boys set fire to an old cat and delight in its painful death. Soldiers make a baby girl giggle before they shoot her, and force an old man to dig his own grave before they beat him to death. What is so awful about these stories? It is not just that the victimizers did not live by the categorical imperative, says Taylor (referring to Kant). It is not that they didn't try to maximize general happiness for everyone involved (referring to utilitarianism). It is not that they were ignorant (Socrates) or didn't follow the Golden Mean (Aristotle). The horror we feel—and for Taylor it is the *same kind of horror* in all three cases—stems from the fact that these incidents are simply malicious. The acts are horrible not because the consequences are so terrible (the death of one bug, one cat, and two war victims may not have widespread effects) but because the intent was to cause suffering for the sake of someone else's pleasure or entertainment. These are not crimes against *reason* but crimes against *compassion.*

True moral value, then, lies in compassion, Taylor believes, and he illustrates this with three more tales. A boy comes up to an attic to steal something and rescues some pigeons that are trapped there, despite his father's strict command to leave the birds alone. When his father returns home he gives the boy a beating. A white sheriff beats up a black rioter during the race riots of the 1960s and then, breaking down in tears, cleans the man up and takes him home, after which he goes and gets drunk. An American soldier who is trapped on an island with a Japanese soldier during World War II finally finds the Japanese asleep but is not able to kill him. In each of these cases, Taylor says, the people had been taught moral principles that told them to do one thing ("Obey your father"; "Uphold the law through violence"; "Kill the enemy"), but their heart told them something else, and *their heart told them right.* According to Taylor,

> There are no heroes in these stories. . . . Goodness of heart, tenderness toward things that can suffer, and the loving kindness that contradicts all reason and sense of duty and some-times denies even the urge to life itself that governs us all are seldom heroic. But who can fail to see, in these mixtures of good and evil, the one thing that really does shine like a jewel, by its own light?

In the end we can't trust our reason, but we can trust our heart; compassion is all we need to be moral human beings, compassion toward all living things. Even people who do the right thing can't be called moral if they don't have compassion—in other words, if they don't have the right intention.

This is a much more radical view than Hallie's because it tells us to *disregard* our reason. Let us look at how that might work in practice. Taylor assumes that we all have this compassion in us—he appeals to our *moral intuition.* But what about the boys who set fire to the cat? Where was their natural compassion? And what about soldiers who kill defenseless civilians? Obviously, not everyone has this compassion, not even the people in Taylor's own examples. What can we do about people who have no compassion? Well, we can try to tell them stories about malice and compas-sion, but chances are that they will think it is a great idea to set fire to a cat and that the boy in the attic should have left the pigeons trapped. How can we appeal to peo-ple who are not responsive to compassion? If we were to ask Kant, Mill, Aristotle, or just about any moral thinker, he or she would say we must try to appeal to their *reason.* If we all had compassion there might not be any need for reason, but as we have seen, not everyone has it, and not everyone has it at the right time, at the right place, and for the right people. Therefore we must have something that might con-vince people who are lacking in compassion, and this is where reason has to come in. What arguments can we use? We might say, "How would you like it if someone did that to you?" In other words, we might appeal to their logical sense of universal-izability and invoke the Golden Rule. Or we might say, "If you do this you will get caught and punished." In that way we appeal to their sense of logic and causality; they can't possibly get away with any wrongdoing. If those two arguments don't convince them to do right, we might just lock them up—protect them from them-selves, and us from them—until they display enough rationality to understand our arguments. Reason, then, is not a substitute for moral feeling (compassion), but it becomes the necessary argument when the moral feeling is absent or deficient. A moral theory that leaves room for only compassion is powerless when it comes to enforcing moral values and virtues.

There is one more problem with Taylor's idea that compassion is all we need, and to illustrate it we will turn to Mark Twain's novel *Huckleberry Finn*. In the story Huck, a young boy, helps Jim, a slave, escape from his owner, Miss Watson. Jonathan Bennett analyzes this famous literary incident—and Bennett is a philosopher who believes in reason as an important part of ethics. He concludes that Huck certainly did the right thing in helping Jim, but it still wasn't good enough because he did it for the wrong reason. Let's review what happens in the story. Huck wants to help his friend Jim, but he realizes that by doing so he will be going against the morals of the town, which require him to return stolen property, which is what a runaway slave is. Because nobody has ever told Huck that owning people is wrong, he has no principle of equality to hold up against what Bennett calls the "bad morality" of the nineteenth-century town. So in the end Huck ends up lying to protect Jim without understanding exactly why, and he resolves not to adhere to any moral principles from then on because they are too hard to figure out. Bennett's conclusion is that Huck did the right thing but for the wrong reason; he should have set up a new principle of his own, such as "It is wrong to own people" or merely "Jim is my friend, and one should help one's friends." That way Huck's sympathy for Jim would have been supported by his *reason,* and he would not have had to give up on morality because it was too puzzling.

But let us think beyond Bennett. Mark Twain himself probably wouldn't have shared Bennett's conclusion, because for Twain Huck is a hero who does the right thing for the best of reasons—because he has compassion for a fellow human being (a human being whom many educated readers of Twain's own day and age might have chosen to turn in). Huck has virtue, even if he doesn't think very well. So Twain and Taylor would be in agreement there. But that doesn't make Huck's attitude any better, philosophically speaking, because it is just a stroke of luck that Jim is a good guy and worthy of Huck's compassion. Suppose the story had featured not the runaway slave Jim but a runaway chain-gang prisoner, Fred the axe murderer? Huck still might have felt compassion for this poor, frightened man and decided to help him go down the river and get rid of his irons. But later that night, Fred might have repaid Huck by killing him and an entire farm family farther down the river to get money and take possession of Huck's raft. In other words, natural empathy is not enough. What Huck lacked was not compassion but *reason* to shape it, reason to help him choose when to act and when not to act—because surely not all people are deserving of our compassion to the extent that we should help them escape what society has determined is their rightful punishment. We may sympathize with mass murderers and understand that they had a terrible childhood, but that doesn't mean we should excuse their actions and help them go free.

This example serves another purpose too. Not only does it show that we can't dispense with reason; it also shows that there is something else missing in virtue theory: If we focus solely on building a good character and developing the right virtues, such as loyalty, compassion, and courage, we still have to decide *what to do* once we've developed the virtues. We may have a wonderfully virtuous character but still be stuck with deciding between several mutually exclusive courses of action. Huck might ask himself (once he has decided to be loyal to Jim) what exactly is the best way to enact that loyalty: Is it to take Jim up north where nobody can own slaves, or

Box 11.4   LOVE AS A VIRTUE

When we talk about love as a virtue, we usually are not talking about passionate love. Passionate love does involve virtue; the passionate lover should not be self-effacing or too domineering, for example. However, that is not the issue here. The issue is love that we can *expect* of someone, and we usually can't expect to receive passionate love on demand. During the marriage ritual, when we promise to love and cherish each other, are we promising our partner that we will be passionately in love with him or her forever? Some undoubtedly see it that way, and they often are in for terrible disappointment if the passionate love of their relationship turns out not to last forever. Of course, there are fortunate couples who remain passionately in love over the years or whose passion develops into even deeper feelings, but that is not something every couple can count on. The promise to love each other is, rather, a promise to *show* love, to show that you care about the other person's welfare and happiness and are 100 percent loyal to that person. That we *can* promise to do, even if passion might not last. So love can be a virtue between people who love each other. The Christian virtue of love does not imply any marital promises but is, rather, an impersonal reverence for other people. Because it also does not involve romantic passion, it can be a requirement in an ethical system too.

is it to hide him until his owner stops looking for him? Might it be to help him escape with his family, hire him a lawyer, or what? Philosophers who object to virtue theory complain that even if we are virtuous, we still may not have a clue as to what to do in specific situations. A possible answer is that virtue ethics need not necessarily stand alone; even Aristotle talks about finding the right course for one's *actions,* not just for one's character. But if virtue ethics needs some rules of conduct to be a complete theory, then surely an ethics of conduct would do well to include elements from virtue ethics. We will take another look at the possibility of a combination of theories at the end of this chapter.

Gratitude: Asian Tradition and Western Modernity

The Russian writer Ivan Turgenev tells the following story in his *Prose Poems* (1883): Once upon a time there was a party in heaven, and the Most High had invited all the virtues. Big and small virtues arrived, and everybody was having a good time, but the Most High noticed that two beautiful virtues didn't seem to know each other, so He went over and introduced them: "Gratitude, meet Charity; Charity, meet Gratitude." The two virtues were very surprised, because this was their very first encounter since the creation of the world. . . . Gratitude as a virtue usually implies that it is something that is *owed* to someone. The question is, Are we obliged to feel or show gratitude just because someone expects it, or are there guidelines for when we should express gratitude?

For one thing, gratitude is a feeling, like love (see Box 11.4). Either you feel love or you don't, and nobody can make you feel it if you don't. (This is something that is known by anyone who has experienced unrequited love.) Similarly, we can't make people feel grateful to us for something we have done for them; indeed, the more we point out how grateful they should be, the more distant and uncooperative they may become. So perhaps we should not talk about making people *feel* gratitude; perhaps we should talk instead about encouraging them to *show* it. Even if you don't *feel* grateful for the socks you got for Christmas, it would be virtuous to *show* gratitude to the person who gave them to you. Not everyone agrees with that viewpoint—I knew a European pedagogue who taught his children that they never had to say thank you or show gratitude for presents given to them, because they had not asked for those presents and to show gratitude without feeling was, in his view, hypocrisy. He may have been right, but life must have been hard for those children when they realized that few others play by the same rules as their father. There are limits to how far you can place yourself and your family outside the mainstream of your culture without getting your nose bloodied from time to time.

We Owe Our Parents Everything: Confucius, Mencius, and Lin Yutang

Most of the topics we have discussed in this book are part of the Western philosophical legacy, but other cultures around the world have their own philosophical traditions and moral values. Here we take a look at the moral philosophies of Confucius and his student Mencius and carry the theme into the twentieth century with the Chinese philosopher Lin Yutang. The subject is gratitude, and the natural recipients of our gratitude are the elderly.

Chinese culture was already ancient in 551 B.C.E. when Confucius was born. When he died in 479 B.C.E., his thoughts on the *superior man* had already changed life and politics in his country, and they were to remain influential, even during periods of opposition, until the twentieth century in China. For centuries the common Chinese attitude toward virtue and right conduct had been to ask the advice of the spirits through divination. However, a certain practical vision had by and large replaced that view by the time of Confucius—a realization that human endeavor was more effective than spiritual guidance. The more important questions became What exactly is a good person? and What is the best kind of human endeavor? The questions were important because whoever was best—a "man of virtue"—was considered to be the person best equipped to rule the country. Before Confucius, such a man was presumed to be a nobleman, but Confucius redefined the man of virtue, the superior man, as someone who is wise, courageous, and humane; someone who thinks well and acts accordingly; someone who models his behavior after virtuous men of the past; and someone who understands that life is a long learning process. The man of virtue exhibits his humanity by being benevolent, and he seeks not profit or revenge but righteousness. Right conduct may show itself in rectifying what is wrong or in particular in rectifying *names,* or titles (in other words, using the proper words to address others, in particular one's superiors). Studying proper conduct and developing proper character are the same as studying *the Way* (*Dao,* or *Tao*). The Way means the way to proper conduct and proper character—wisdom—and only through studying the Way do people become superior. How do we practice the Way? By developing good habits and continual good thinking. The evils to watch out for are, in particular,

Box 11.5   CONFUCIUS AND ARISTOTLE

There are some extraordinary parallels between the virtue theory of Confucius and that of Aristotle; both men greatly influenced posterity, each in his own way. For both thinkers, good habits are the proper way to develop a good character. Both Confucius and Aristotle emphasized the link between good thinking and subsequent action, and both believed that the virtuous human being is one who recognizes the *mean,* the middle state of moderation. But there are also considerable differences. For Confucius, the superior man is one who shuns pride and strives for humility; Aristotle would have considered such a man to have insufficient self-appreciation. Confucius also seems to have reached out to a more inclusive moral universe than Aristotle did, and that has caused some

scholars to compare him to Christian thinkers. Confucius is known to have expressed a version of the Golden Rule: Don't do to others what you wouldn't want them to do to you, sometimes called the "Silver Rule." (See Box 4.10.) We don't find this attitude in Aristotle's writings, because the general idea of *moral equality,* which is essential for the Golden Rule, is absent in Aristotle's code of ethics. Confucius's superior man also must appreciate *cooperation*—both between people and between people and Nature—whereas Aristotle stressed the hierarchy of rule. Both men, however, envisioned a state that is run according to the model of a well-functioning family, with the ruler as paterfamilias at the head, deciding what is best for his family.

greed, aggressiveness, pride, and resentment. It truly is possible to become a superior man, according to Confucius, because people can be transformed by learning. Once we have learned enough about the Way to recognize it, we will know that there is virtue in *moderation.* (Like the Greeks, Confucius believed in the virtuous nature of the *mean* between the extremes of deficiency and excess; see Box 11.5.)

Confucianism is closer to virtue ethics than to an ethics of conduct, although proper conduct is also part of Confucius's philosophy. For the Confucian philosopher, ethics is not a matter of rigid definitions of what to do or how to be but a matter of virtues and behaviors that depend on circumstances. To know whether an action is appropriate, you must know how it affects others and whether it might be conducive or detrimental to the harmony of society. Virtue, *te,* consists of both personal character formation and good use of power by a government with good intentions. A person or a government that has achieved *te* is living according to *tao* (*dao*) and has also attained the basic virtues of *jen, li,* and *yi.* As with the term *tao,* there are no easy Western translations for these concepts: *Jen* means having a caring attitude toward others, including nonhuman beings; *li* means understanding and performing rituals correctly, but *li* is empty without *jen* (just knowing how to perform ceremonies correctly is meaningless if you don't have a caring approach); and *yi* is the understanding of what is proper and appropriate, not just in terms of etiquette but also in terms of whether something is reasonable and rational. So to have *li* (the understanding of rituals) you have to have *jen* (caring), but you must definitely also have *yi* (reasoned judgment) so you know what rituals are important and why. The

Box 11.6 TAOISM

The Chinese philosopher Lao-Tzu was a contemporary of Confucius. The two men knew each other and disagreed politely on several essential points, the most important one being the usefulness of social action. For Confucius, the superior man must try to effect change, to make life better for others. For Lao-Tzu, that is a useless endeavor, because humans can't effect changes. Nature is a complex duality of opposite forces working together, the forces of yin and yang, he believed. These forces work according to a pattern that can't be observed by most humans, and things happen in their own time. The best humans can do is to contemplate that fact. This is the only access to the Way, or Tao: By doing nothing, by letting nature take its course, we are not obstructing this course; we are emptying our minds of the constant question What should I do next? And by letting our minds become still and

perfectly empty, we are opening ourselves to the truth of the Way. The Tao of Lao-Tzu is far more mystical than that of Confucius, which is why his ideas have acquired their own label, Taoism (Daoism). Virtue and proper conduct meld together in the concept of "doing nothing," or rather "not overdoing it," *wu wei,* which entails unselfishness and mental tranquility. Interestingly enough, that doesn't mean that you deliberately should refrain from doing things like taking a box of matches out of the hands of a three-year-old; indeed, not to do so would be a selfish, willful act. You *should* take the matches away from the child but without congratulating yourself that you've saved her life; after all, she may head straight for your medicine cabinet next. Do what you have to do, but don't think you can make a difference; eventually that will give you peace of mind. That is the hard lesson of Taoism.

classical Chinese society was burdened with many elaborate rituals and ceremonies, and Confucius allowed for one's critical sense to cut through and determine what was essential and practical and what was not, depending on the circumstances.

Confucius's ideas of the virtuous man and the well-run state became so influential that they were adopted as state religion in China for a period of several hundred years (618–907 C.E.) even though Confucius didn't concern himself with religious questions. He believed that because we know very little about death and any life after death, we must focus our effort on this life and our relationships with other human beings. (Box 11.6 explains some differences between Confucianism and Taoism.)

Mencius (371–289 B.C.E.) followed in Confucius's footsteps but took Confucianism one step further. He believed not only that humans can learn to be good but also that they are good from the beginning; they just have been corrupted by life and circumstances. Mencius thought the proper method of finding our way back to our lost goodness is to look inside ourselves and recapture our nature—our conscience and our intuition. If we pay proper attention to our own good nature, it will grow and take over. Only through ourselves can we find the right way, and that process requires a certain amount of suffering. When we suffer, our character is developed. Mencius doubts that someone who has led an easy life can be truly virtuous. The virtues we are supposed to develop through suffering are independence, excellence, mental alertness, courage, and quietude of spirit. When we have reached such a mental equilibrium, we can help others achieve the same, because benevolence is the prime virtue.

The following admonishments are quoted from *The Book of Mencius,* a collection of sayings probably compiled by his followers. This excerpt shows that for Mencius the development of one's character is fundamentally the most important moral task. Although one has duties (which is why there are rules for *conduct,* which one ought to follow), one is not able to fulfill those duties without being *virtuous*—in other words, without having retained one's moral character:

> What is the most important duty? One's duty towards one's parents. What is the most important thing to watch over? One's own character. I have heard of a man who, not having allowed his character to be morally lost, is able to discharge his duties towards his parents; but I have not heard of one morally lost who is able to do so. There are many duties one should discharge, but the fulfillment of one's duty towards one's parents is the most basic. There are many things one should watch over, but watching over one's character is the most basic. . . . Benevolence is the heart of man, and rightness his road. Sad it is indeed when a man gives up the right road instead of following it and allows his heart to stray without enough sense to go after it. When his chickens and dogs stray, he has sense enough to go after them, but not when his heart strays. The sole concern of learning is to go after this strayed heart.

The tradition of Confucius and Mencius continued into twentieth-century China and is noticeable to this day. A modern voice of that tradition is Lin Yutang (1895–1976). Aside from Mao Zedong, Lin Yutang may be the most influential of all twentieth-century Chinese writers in the West. He traveled extensively in the United States but never lost touch with his Chinese heritage and values. Even more than by Confucius, Lin Yutang was inspired by Mencius. Lin Yutang himself believed that Western philosophers were too fixated on the idea of reason and had forgotten what the ancient Greek thinkers saw as the most important element of their philosophy: human happiness. In his 1937 book *The Importance of Living,* he mentions with much modesty that he is uneducated in philosophy. His knowledge of both Chinese and Western philosophy is considerable, however. What is the importance of living? Knowing when to take things seriously and when to laugh at the solemnity of life; being so fortunate and living so long that one can become a serious intellectual and then return to a higher level of simple thinking and simple ways.

In several books Lin Yutang attempted to bridge the gap between East and West, especially at a time during the first half of the twentieth century when there wasn't much understanding between the two worlds. Writing about family values in a transitional period during which Chinese values were changing (the later Communist takeover forced a transfer of authority to the people as the feudal system was dissolved), Lin Yutang saw the greatest difference between East and West not in the area of politics or gender issues but in the way we treat our elderly—our parents in particular.

Whereas a Western man might think most about helping women and children, a Chinese man would think primarily about helping his parents and other elderly people. That is not because the elderly are thought of as being helpless; it is because

Lin Yutang (1895–1976), the author of *The Importance of Living* (1937) and *The Wisdom of China and India* (1955), may be the modern Chinese thinker best known in the Western world. He worked hard to create a cross-cultural understanding between East and West, but he himself believed that some traditional Eastern values, such as respect for the elderly, are fundamentally different from modern Western values.

they are *respected*. In the Chinese tradition, the older you are, the more respect you deserve. Lin Yutang describes this in *The Importance of Living*:

> In China, the first question a person asks the other on an official call, after asking about his name and surname, is "What is your glorious age?" If the person replies apologetically that he is twenty-three or twenty-eight, the other party generally comforts him by saying that he still has a glorious future and that one day he may become old. But if the person replies that he is thirty-five or thirty-eight, the other party immediately exclaims with deep respect, "Good luck!"; enthusiasm grows in proportion as the gentleman is able to report a higher and higher age, and if the person is anywhere over fifty, the inquirer immediately drops his voice in humility and respect.

Just as people under twenty-one in our culture may lie about their age to get into clubs that serve liquor, Chinese young people may pretend to be older to gain respect. But in the West there is a point at which most people don't want to seem older than they are; in fact, they might like to appear *younger* than they are. The Chinese traditionally want to appear *older* throughout their lives, because it is to their advantage.

Box 11.7   SELF-WORTH AND RETIREMENT

Lin Yutang chastises the West for its "throw-away" attitude toward the older generation. He praises respect and love for one's parents and grandparents as virtues that have to be learned. The West, however, has not always discarded its citizens at the onset of old age. In earlier farming communities in particular, elders not only were respected but also were considered an important part of the community because of their *usefulness.* Perhaps they couldn't knead bread or plow the field anymore, but they still could look after the children and share their wisdom. In some parts of the Western world, we still can find that type of relationship within a community. But as most people would agree, it is not the case in the larger cities of the West, where it is not customary for grandparents to live with their children. The general attitude seems to be that showing signs of aging is somehow a flaw. A British writer once wrote of Americans that they think death is optional—that if you die you must have done something wrong, such as not having taken enough vitamins.

It would appear that part of our problem with accepting the aging process is that as Westerners we have developed the attitude that when we stop being *productive,* we stop being *valuable* as human beings. When a person retires, that feeling often is reinforced, because the person is all of a sudden excluded from part of his or her habitual environment—the workplace. Especially during the early and middle years of the twentieth century, when people would stay in their jobs for over forty years, retirement forced a reevaluation of the person's identity, and all too often the retiree felt that he or she had been *reduced* in value, had been deemed useless by society. That may be one reason it is not uncommon for people to fall ill and even die a short time after retirement, even if they had initially looked forward to it.

There are signs that this trend may change; there is a growing awareness that older people are still people, and because nowadays people usually don't stay at the same job as long as they did in previous generations they may depend less on their jobs for their sense of identity. Also, many retirees reenter the workforce part-time, either because they want to or, sadly, because they can't afford not to. The baby boomers are beginning to retire, and they have no intention of going away quietly: second careers await, not just out of financial necessity, but also from personal choice. With potential for longer life spans and a growing understanding that mental powers don't automatically decline after sixty, the eighties may truly be becoming the "new sixties"—provided that there is health insurance and that the seniors do their part to stay in shape. Besides, the world of retail is beginning to realize that though it may be sexy to appeal to teens, their buying power doesn't even come close to the buying power of their grandparents. So the "Gray Gold" may be courted more than we have been used to in the past.

Lin Yutang saw the quest for youth in American culture as alien and frightening—and he was writing in the 1930s, when American teens still attempted to dress and act as "adults." Today, in the exaggerated youth cult that is part of the baby boomer legacy, the phenomenon has become even more extreme. As respect grows with age in the Chinese traditional culture, it seems to *diminish* with age in the West: Somehow we perceive ourselves and others as less powerful, beautiful, and valuable as we reach the far side of fifty or even forty. Lin Yutang quotes an American grandmother who says that it was the birth of her first grandchild that "hurt," because it seemed to be a reminder of the loss of youth. (Box 11.7 discusses our attitude toward aging and how it affects retirement.)

Box 11.8 THE DUTY TO TAKE CARE OF ONE'S PARENTS

For Lin Yutang, the duty to take care of one's parents is a quintessential feature of Chinese culture; as a legacy of Confucian virtue theory, which stresses respect for older people and caring for one's parents, it is a powerful cultural tradition even in today's China. However, the duty to care for aging parents is a near-universal moral rule, except in the less family-oriented lives of many modern city-dwellers. In more traditional cultures it is usually the oldest son who is expected to take care of his parents, as in China, but other traditions exist: On the website www.mhhe.com/rosenstand6e you can find discussion of the film. The family tradition of the youngest daughter's staying unmarried to take care of her mother or her aging parents is, in fact, widespread in several parts of the world. Whether we might call it a new tradition or simply the demands of circumstances, in our society it is quite often the daughter living closest to her aging parents who takes on the task of caring for them; this frequently places a particular strain on such middle-aged female caregivers, since they, in today's world, also are likely to work full-time outside the home and, in addition, may be in the process of raising teenage children.

American parents are afraid to make demands on their children, says Lin Yutang. Parents are afraid of becoming a burden, of meddling in their children's affairs, of being nosy. But in whose affairs would we meddle if not in the affairs of those who are closest to us? he asks. Parents do have a right to make demands of their children, he says; they do have a right to be cared for by their children. That is because *their children owe it to them.* We owe a never-ending *debt of gratitude* to our parents for raising us, for being there when we were teething, for changing those diapers and taking care of us when we were sick, and just for feeding and clothing us. (See Box 11.8 for further views.) Among Chinese who immigrated to the United States, for example, the guilt over not being with their parents in China is enormous, even if they have brothers and sisters who can perform the duty in their homeland.

According to the Chinese conception of virtue, letting his parents grow old and die without his support is the gravest sin a man can commit. That is true for a woman too, but less so, because it is the duty of the firstborn boy to take care of his parents. Whom is the daughter supposed to take care of? Her *husband's* parents. Herein lies the secret as to why it is so important for Chinese families to have male offspring— even today, when restrictions call for only one child per family. The state may take care of you in your retirement, but even so, life is not complete without a son to lean on in your old age. The pressure to have male babies is so intense that occasionally female babies are killed at birth so that the parents can try again to have a male child, or the birth of a girl is simply kept a secret: a difficult choice, since pregnancies are monitored by the state and abortions forced on women who already have one child. One alternative is paying a hefty fine for the second child. Another, in a twenty-first-century twist, is to take fertility drugs that increase the chance of twins or triplets. If parents choose to keep a little girl, the response from friends and colleagues is quite different from what it would be if they had a boy. A boy is cause for celebration; a baby girl may prompt friends and colleagues to send cards of condolence to the parents. Despite attempts to revise the policy, it appears that the Chinese government is committed to the one-child-per-family rule for now, but the rule has now been in place for sufficient time that long-term consequences are emerging: There are simply not enough young girls in China now to "go around" and become sexual partners and wives in the next generation—and a shortage of women may have far-reaching consequences. Already now we hear of female babies being purchased from neighboring countries or downright stolen—and the specter of a culture with a large number of "surplus" young males raises more questions: How will these young men cope, and what will the Chinese state do for its bachelor citizens?

So far, the system has provided for its elderly citizens. Much to the shame of traditional Chinese, there are now some nursing homes for the elderly in the villages of China, but they are presumably more humane than the "human storage tanks" we have in our Western civilization because the elderly are still part of the community, and the problems of the village are presented to them in their capacity as advisers. In this manner the traditional respect for the older people is maintained, at least on a symbolic level, even though the family patterns have been disrupted.

We Owe Our Parents Nothing: Jane English

A young American philosopher, Jane English (1947–1978), proposes a solution to the constant and very common squabbles between parents and their grown children. It seems rather radical: She suggests that we owe our parents nothing. That idea is not as harsh as it appears, however. English thinks the main problem between grown children and parents is the common *parental* attitude that their children somehow are indebted to them. This "*debt-metaphor*" can be expressed in a number of ways, such as, "We are paying for your schooling, so you owe it to us to study what we would like you to study"; "We've clothed you and fed you, so the least you could do is come home for Thanksgiving"; or "I was in labor with you for thirty-six hours, so you could at least clean up your room once in a while." The basic formula is "You owe us gratitude and obedience because of what we have done for you." For English, that attitude undermines all filial love, because the obvious answer a kid can give is "I didn't ask to be born." And there is not much chance of fruitful communication after that. (As one of my students remarked, a parent can always fire back with "And you weren't wanted, either," but that would surely be the end of any parent-child friendship.)

So what should parents do? English said they should realize that there are appropriate ways of using the debt-metaphor and that applying it to a parent-child relationship is not one of them. An appropriate way to use the debt-metaphor is shown in the following example given by English in her essay "What Do Grown Children Owe Their Parents?":

> New to the neighborhood, Max barely knows his neighbor, Nina, but he asks her if she will take in his mail while he is gone for a month's vacation. She agrees. If, subsequently, Nina asks Max to do the same for her, it seems that Max has a moral obligation to agree (greater

Box 11.9   DATING, DEBT, AND FRIENDSHIP

Many of the problems of dating stem from a difference in attitude, says Jane English. One person thinks of the date in terms of a friendship, and the other one sees it as a debt-metaphor situation. Suppose Alfred takes Beatrice out for dinner and a movie, and at the end of the evening Alfred expects "something" in return for his investment. Alfred has chosen to view the situation as a favor-debt situation; he sees Beatrice as being indebted to him. Beatrice, however, is upset, because she viewed the situation as a friendship situation, with no favors and debts. In essence, Beatrice doesn't owe Alfred a thing, because Alfred's gesture was not presented as a "quid pro quo" situation to begin with but as an overture to friendship. The situation would have been more complex had Beatrice *agreed with Alfred* in the beginning that the dinner and movie were to be a "business arrangement" to be "paid off" later in the evening. A survey from some years back showed that, shockingly, a majority of California high school students, females as well as males, feel that dating is in fact a favor-debt situation. In that case, we must say

that if both participants agree, then so be it. There is, however, a good old word for when someone sells physical favors for material goods; that word is *prostitution.* In such a situation the one who is "bought" becomes merely a means to an end.

What can you do if you want to make sure to avoid a favor-debt situation on a date? For one thing, you can insist on going dutch. The two of you probably make the same kind of money these days, so why should one of you pay for the other? Remember, nobody should expect payment for doing someone an unsolicited favor (if the people involved aren't friends), and nobody should expect payment for doing any kind of favor if the people involved are friends. So either way you shouldn't expect anything of your date, and you shouldn't feel pressured by your date to repay anything. Be careful not to abuse this rule, though. One girl commented that "it's great to be able to be taken to a dinner and a movie and not have to do anything in return!" With that attitude, she reduces her date to becoming merely the means to an end, and that's not the idea.

than the one he would have had if Nina had not done the same for him), unless for some reason it would be a burden far out of proportion to the one Nina bore for him.

English labels what Nina does for Max a "favor"—and favors incur *debts.* But once you have paid your debt—once Max has taken Nina's mail in—then the debt is discharged, and the matter is over. This is *reciprocity,* and it means that you must do something of a similar nature for the person you are in debt to. But what if Nina never goes out of town, so Max never has an opportunity to take in her mail and pay off the debt? Then he might mow her lawn, give her rides to work, or walk her dog. If she has no lawn or dog and likes to drive to work, then he might figure out something else to do for her, and chances are that they might become friends in the process. In that case another type of relationship kicks in, one that no longer is based on a reciprocal system of favors and debts. Instead, the relationship is based on a system of duties relating to *friendship.* (See Box 11.9 for further discussion.)

In friendship, according to English, the debt-metaphor ceases to be appropriate, because friends shouldn't think they owe each other anything. Although debts are

PEANUTS

BY SCHULZ

© United Feature Syndicate, Inc.

The philosopher Jane English suggests that parents adopt a conversational tone toward their adult children that avoids laying guilt on the child as a method of persuasion—because the child can always answer back, "I didn't ask to be born." Here is a classic *Peanuts* strip illustrating the issue from an unusual angle: Lucy and Linus are engaged in a discussion about whether we actually ever ask to be born!

discharged when a favor is reciprocated, friendships don't work that way; just because you do something for your friend who has done something for you doesn't make the two of you "even." Friendships aren't supposed to be "tit for tat," and if they are, then the people involved aren't real friends. Friendship means that you are there for each other when needed and that you do things for each other because you *like* each other, not because you *owe* each other. The fact that there can be no debts doesn't mean that there are no obligations, however; on the contrary, friendship carries with it the never-ending obligation to be there for each other, at least while the friendship lasts. It implies a mutual sense of duty toward each other. With friendship, instead of reciprocity, there is *mutuality*.

Let us speculate a bit beyond what English herself writes: Suppose you borrow fifty dollars from a friend, and then you have a falling-out with her. Because there are no debts in a friendship and because obligations last only as long as the friendship does, you don't have to pay back the money, right? Wrong, because owing money is a true debt in our society and money must be paid back regardless of whether it is owed to friends or strangers. Similarly, you have to fulfill your part of a contract, regardless of whether it is with a friend, business partner, or a stranger. Such transactions come under the proper use of the debt-metaphor and persist beyond the extent of friendships. (In fact, they often are the cause of the breakup of friendships.)

English believes we often fall into the trap of regarding friendship duties as debts. Most couples find themselves saying things like, "We've been over to Frank and Claire's four times now, so we owe them a dinner." For English, that is a gross misunderstanding of what friendship is all about. You can go visit Claire and Frank a hundred times, and you still don't owe them a thing because they aren't doing you a "favor"; they ask you over because they like you. To most readers, that may seem a trifle idealistic; after the twentieth dinner, Claire and Frank surely will think something is wrong and won't ask you over again. But English's idea is that you will be there if they need you and that you should contribute to the friendship in *some way or other*—she doesn't say how much you should contribute or in what way; how you contribute is up to you.

English says the relationship between parents and grown children should be modeled after the friendship pattern and not after the debt-metaphor pattern. Parents don't do their children a favor by raising them, and, accordingly, children don't owe any debt to them. But that doesn't mean grown children don't have *obligations* to their parents—they have the same obligations as they have to their friends. Those obligations are limitless as long as the relationship lasts; they cease when the relationship ends. No reciprocity can be evoked, such as "You fed and clothed me for eighteen years, so I'll take care of you for the next eighteen but not a minute longer." *Mutuality*, however, is expected at all times. (What is expected in terms of other relatives is discussed in Box 11.10.)

What is the basis for a good parent-child relationship, then? Above all, love and friendship. If those are present, all that must be considered are (1) the need of the parents and (2) the ability and resources of the grown child. The parents may be sick and in need, and their son may love them, but he also may be out of work and unable to help with the medical bills. In that case, helping to pay the bills would *not* be part of his obligations, but other things would, such as providing cheerful company, taking the trash out, or making other contributions.

Suppose the parents need help but there is *no friendship* between the parents and the child. Then, essentially, the grown child is not obliged to help, especially if the end of the friendship (if in fact it ever existed) was the parents' choice. One might imagine that this would be the time for the parents to approach their estranged child and ask for a favor in the hope of reestablishing the friendship. English seems to assume that all the parents have to do is announce that they are sorry and would like to be friends again—but what if they follow that approach with immediate requests for support? Then their son or daughter might soon get the idea that there is a calculated reason behind this renewal of friendship. (That works both ways, of course; if the son or daughter has left home in anger and later decides that he or she needs help from home, an approach of remorse and offers of renewal of friendship followed by requests for support will look equally suspicious to the parents.)

For a solution, we might want to turn to the American philosopher Fred Berger (whose theory we discuss in more detail shortly). In assessing the extent of the

Box 11.10   WHAT ABOUT RELATIVES?

Jane English's main concern is for parents and grown children to realize that their relationship ought to be like that between good friends, and in such a relationship there are limitless obligations. But do we have any obligations to people who aren't yet our friends (we may hardly know them) but aren't strangers either, because they are more distant relatives? Should they rank as friends or as strangers? English has no category for them, and yet many people are concerned about how much we can and should rely on the support of relatives other than those in our immediate family. When they come to visit, should we give up our bedroom to them? Can I, as a student, ask my mother's cousin in Paris if I may stay with her for a year while I study at the Sorbonne? How can we tell our aunt and uncle from Sweden/Los Angeles/Idaho/Mexico that it really is not convenient for them to stay six weeks in our apartment? Am I obliged to find a lawyer for my half-brother who is in trouble?

And so on. Many times we might *choose* to help, just as we might help a stranger, but often the old line "Blood is thicker than water" makes us feel that we do have a specific *duty* to our extended family. One solution might be to think of that duty as a "duty to do small favors"—such as finding your relatives a good, cheap hotel or showing them around town and taking them out a few times—but not as a duty to provide very large favors, such as letting them have the run of your home for six weeks. Instead of finding a lawyer for your half-brother who is in trouble, you might provide him with the number of a good legal agency but let him choose a lawyer himself and let him be financially responsible. By your doing these small favors, a small debt to reciprocate now rests with the relative. If that debt is discharged to everyone's satisfaction—through reciprocal hospitality or perhaps through an annual Christmas card—you can all proceed to becoming friends.

gratitude you ought to show others for acts of kindness toward you, Berger says you should look for the *motivation*. Were those acts of kindness done for your sake? for the doer's? or both? If done for your sake alone, you should show gratitude; if done for the doer's own sake, you have no obligation; if done partly for your sake and partly for the doer's own sake, you should show some gratitude, but there is no need to go overboard. In a similar manner, we might ask why the parents are approaching their grown child (or the children their parents). Is it because of a genuine wish to reestablish contact, is it solely because they want assistance, or is the truth somewhere in between? If the approached party can determine the motivation with reasonable accuracy, then he or she can decide how to react.

What should parents say if they very much would like their grown child to take a certain course of action but realize that he or she does not owe it to them to do so? Not "You owe us" but something like "We love you, and we think you'd be happier if you did x." Or, suggests English, "If you love us, you'll do x." But is the second example a very good one? To most people, that alternative would set off a tremendous guilt trip, because it plays on the notion that if you don't comply, you don't love your parents. Few people are able to follow their parents' advice all the time, no matter how much love and friendship there may be between them. One alternative approach, which was suggested by one of my students, is for the parents to explain the whole situation: "Because of our past experience, we believe it is best for you, but it's your choice."

Jane English never lived to develop her theory further; she died at the age of thirty-one while on a mountaineering expedition in Switzerland. In her short life she published several other thought-provoking papers, and one might wonder how this bright person might have felt about the same issue had she lived to become a parent of grown children.

Friendship Duties and Gratitude

English supplies some guidelines for how we should consider *friendship* as a virtue that applies to the relationship between parents and grown children; Lin Yutang believes the virtue that should be applied to such relationships is *gratitude*. But what about both friendship and gratitude in other types of relationships, such as those between friends, or lovers, or neighbors? How far do our duties of friendship go? Are we obliged to help our friends in every way? to help them cheat on their tax returns? to lie to their spouse about where they were last night? to hide them from the police? to buy them drugs? The answer is, of course, no—even if they would do those things for us. Friendship may be a virtue, but it doesn't entail giving up one's other moral standards merely for the sake of friendship; besides, your friend is hardly displaying the virtue of friendship toward you, since by helping him or her you may be considered "aiding and abetting" someone in trouble with the law. A good friend doesn't ask that of another. But that doesn't mean you can't do *something* for your friends when they are in trouble, such as being there for them to talk to or finding them an appropriate counselor. (Box 11.11 discusses how the Golden Rule applies to such issues.)

A more mundane but equally tricky situation arises when someone does something nice for us that we didn't ask for and then expects something in return. Jane English states that such "unsolicited favors" do not create any debt, so we don't have to reciprocate. However, the situation may be more complex than that: The favor extended may be in an emergency in which a person is not capable of requesting help (such as someone picking up a wallet a person has dropped and returning it, or giving someone first aid after an accident). Jane English doesn't address such issues. And what if a person doing an unsolicited favor for a stranger is truly trying to be nice? In that case, doing nothing in return seems rude, even if we didn't ask for the favor. Here Fred Berger answers that certainly we have an obligation, and that obligation is to *show gratitude*. A simple thank-you, verbal or written, may be all it takes. In some situations the person who did us an unsolicited favor (offered to give us a ride or gave us a present) may *insist* that we show gratitude and reciprocate by doing business with them, going out with them, or even having sex with them. In that case, Berger says, we have to look at the giver's *intentions*: Did he give us something or do us a favor just so that we would be indebted to him? In that case, we don't owe the person anything, not even gratitude, because he did it for *himself,* not for us.

Box 11.11   DOES THE GOLDEN RULE ALWAYS WORK?

The Golden Rule has been mentioned several times in this text, and it is certainly one of the most widespread rules of ethics in existence, finding expression in religions and moral teachings throughout recorded history. But is it always the best solution to do unto others as you would have them do unto you? Suppose a friend wants you to put her up for a few weeks. She tells you she has been involved in a hit-and-run accident, and now she wants to hide from the police. You are reluctant to let her stay, but she assures you that she would do the same for you or even that you would want her to do the same for you if you were in trouble. But that may not be the case; you may see the situation in quite a different light. If you were in trouble you might need a friend, but you might not ask that friend to hide you; chances are you wouldn't have left the scene of the accident in the first place. (Staying at the scene is, of course, the only ethical course of action—besides, it's the law.) Your friend's perception of what she wants done for her is not the same as what you might want a friend to do for you. In everyday life we find many examples of this type of situation: Maria gives Cheryl a bread machine for Christmas because that's what Maria would like to get. But she didn't think to find out whether Cheryl might also like one, and in fact

Cheryl doesn't like kitchen gifts. Even an episode of the television series *The Simpsons* has dealt with the phenomenon: Homer Simpson shops for a present for his wife, Marge, and ends up giving her—a bowling ball, because that's what *he* wants! Often, such misplaced acts of kindness are caused by a self-centered attitude or a lack of perception, but they also may happen because of a fundamental difference in the approach to life. In her book *That's Not What I Meant,* the linguist Deborah Tannen describes a classic situation of misapplied Golden Rule approaches between partners who have different visions of correct behavior (or what Tannen calls different "styles"):

> Maxwell wants to be left alone, and Samantha wants attention. So she gives him attention, and he leaves her alone. The adage "Do unto others as you would have others do unto you" may be the source of a lot of anguish and misunderstanding if the doer and the done unto have different styles.

It appears that if we are to act on the Golden Rule, we have to make certain that the others really want to "be done unto." You may want to revisit Chapter 4 for a discussion of "The Platinum Rule."

So how do we know when we owe people gratitude? Certainly we owe it when we have *asked* them to do us a favor. As far as unsolicited favors go, though, we should express gratitude when we can be reasonably certain that (1) they did it for our own sake—because they like and respect us, as Kant would say, as *ends in ourselves,* not because they viewed us as the *means to an end.* We also should make certain that (2) they did help us *on purpose* and didn't just blunder into the situation. Moreover, we have to ascertain that (3) they did it *voluntarily,* that no one else forced them to do it. In Berger's words, gratitude should be a response to benevolence, not benefits, and that applies to all relationships, even those between parents and children. We should express gratitude in proportion to the things that are done for our sake. (To be sure, not everything parents do is done for the sake of the child.) If something is done for other reasons, our duty to show gratitude diminishes proportionately. And, says Berger, when we do show gratitude to people who have done something for us, we show that we appreciate *them* as intrinsically valuable persons—as ends in themselves and not just as instruments for our well-being.

Suppose the people who do things for us like us and respect us but still hope to get something out of being nice to us? You'll recall that we discussed the issue of selfishness versus altruism in Chapter 4, and we can apply that lesson here. We shouldn't disqualify others from deserving our gratitude just because they were hoping for some little advantage themselves; it is when we were considered solely a means to an end that our duty to show gratitude disappears.

Suppose you have good reason to feel grateful for something someone has done. Let's assume you are a poor student and your neighbors have seven kids. They cook up a huge dinner every night, and at the end of the month, when you are broke, they always invite you over for dinner. They say, "We have to cook anyway, so come on over." And you do, month after month. You keep waiting for the moment when the family may need your invaluable assistance with something, but the time never comes. So you keep eating their food and feeling like a moocher. What can you do? Well, you might do the dishes once in a while or help babysit. In other words, you can contribute to the mutuality of a friendship even if you aren't specifically asked to do so.

Let's return to the question How much gratitude should I feel? The answer, says Berger, lies in Aristotle's theory of virtue: just enough—not too much and not too little. Vague as it is, it is still the guideline most people instinctively use when they try to figure out how to respond to an act of kindness. We know that enslaving ourselves for the rest of our natural lives, giving up our firstborn, and other such measures would be too much. We also know that being rude and doing or saying nothing to show our appreciation is too little. But where exactly lies the right amount? That is, as with all the Aristotelian virtues, a case-by-case matter. Sometimes the right amount consists of a thank-you note, a bottle of wine, or a batch of chocolate-chip cookies. Sometimes it is house-sitting for six months, and sometimes it is going across country to give someone a helping hand. If we manage to hit the bull's-eye and find the right response, perhaps Aristotle is right, and we are on the way to becoming virtuous. In the Narratives section, the film *Pay It Forward* suggests that gratitude should be handed on, as a favor to someone else, who then in turn shows her or his gratitude by doing something for someone else—"paying it forward."

How to Receive Gratitude?

One aspect of the question of gratitude rarely touched on by philosophers is a matter that, in everyday life, is almost as important as the questions of when to be grateful and how much gratitude to show, and that is the virtue of gracefully *accepting gratitude*. Just as it takes skill to be a good giver, so it takes skill to be a good receiver, regardless of whether we talk about gifts, favors, or reciprocation. What if you are the person who did someone else a favor without expecting anything in return? In other words, you treated that someone as an end in himself or herself, and the mere fact that you were able to help is enough reward for you. But now the other person wants to thank you and do something for you in return. What do you do? Saying you don't want any thanks may be telling the other person how you feel, but it may not be enough, because the other person may feel he or she *needs* to reciprocate; so you must be able to sometimes allow the other to do so, with the implicit understanding that it is not going to lead to a game of one-upmanship with returned favors. Sometimes a simple "You're welcome" is enough, and sometimes the proper way to accept gratitude may be to gracefully accept a favor or a gift in return, even if you did not do the original favor to be rewarded. And here Aristotle comes in handy again: Your guideline as to how big a favor you can accept in return for a favor should be the extent of the original favor ("just right").

Virtue and Conduct: The Option of Soft Universalism

In Chapters 3–7 we explored the most influential theories of what has become known as ethics of conduct, and in Chapters 8–11 we have looked at classical and contemporary versions of virtue ethics. The majority of ethicists over the years have perceived their task as defining in the simplest terms possible, and with as few rules as possible, a moral theory that would have universal application, one that would be valid in all situations. As we have seen, no theory so far can be said to work equally well in all situations; all theories, when put to the test, show some flaws or problems. For all its positive elements, ethical relativism allows for a tolerance that objects to nothing, not even crimes against humanity; egoism, though recognizing the right of the individual to look after his or her own interests, fails to recognize that humans may actually be interested in serving the interests of others; utilitarianism, though seeking general happiness for all sentient beings, seems to allow for the few to be used, and even sacrificed, for the sake of the many; Kantian deontology wants to do the right thing but is so focused on duty that it may overlook bad consequences of doing one's duty—consequences that otherwise could have been avoided. And virtue ethics, which is intended as an alternative to those theories of conduct, hasn't quite solved the problem of when and how to use one's reason and rational argumentation in defining moral standards, and it hasn't succeeded in coming up with a theory of action in which the general ideas of virtue can be brought into play in particular situations or in solving disagreements between people who consider themselves virtuous. For those who look for a good answer to moral problems, that can be more than discouraging, and some might even decide, like Huck Finn, that moral speculations are too confusing and it's better just to follow their gut feelings. But that would be taking the easy way out, and actually it is not a very satisfying solution. On occasion we all may have to justify an action, and "It seemed like a good idea at the time" is not an adequate answer. Furthermore, we may decide that ethicists haven't come up with a complete solution to moral problems, but that doesn't mean we don't have to keep on trying to solve them on an individual basis. Just because the experts haven't given us all the solutions on a silver platter doesn't mean we're exempt from seeking solutions on our own. There *are* alternative answers.

Most of the theories we have looked at originated in time periods when it was assumed that humans would someday know all the answers to everything. It also was assumed, from a scientific viewpoint, that a simple explanation was better and more pleasing than a complex one. To a great extent that is still true: A theory gains in strength if unnecessary elements are cut away. (This phenomenon is often referred to as *Occam's razor,* from the British medieval philosopher William of Occam.) But the late twentieth century also taught us that simple solutions may not always be available, or even desirable, because there may be many possible ways of looking at each situation. (A case in point is Deborah Tannen's example of different "styles" of behavior described in Box 11.11.) So we are not focused on seeking simple answers to complex issues in ethics any longer.

I often hear students remark, Why do all these philosophers have to be so single-minded about everything? Why can't their theories allow for nuances? It is a good question—but it is a question that is possible only because we have become a culture that allows for nuances and different perspectives. Many theories do, in fact, allow for nuances, but it is unfortunately in the nature of introductory courses that some of those nuances tend to fall by the wayside in the effort to express a theory as clearly, and as briefly, as possible. Some moral theories are strong and straightforward precisely because they don't allow for nuances and exceptions, as we have seen in previous chapters. But with the complexity of today's world, what may serve us best could be a moral approach that assumes the possibility that we can have certain basic values in common and at the same time allows for a relativistic tolerance of other values. We may be looking for what was introduced in Part 2 as *soft universalism:* the theory that deep down, we can agree on certain core values that are based on our common humanity. However, that is not going to be easy, because we have to agree on *which* values are supposed to be the ones we have in common, and here our different cultural upbringing and ethnic diversity may come into play.

Some philosophers have been trying for a long time to redesign the traditional theories (such as utilitarianism, deontology, or virtue theory) to make them more logical, more responsive to present-day sensitivities, or more tolerant of exceptions. But we can choose another path: seeking the best advice from a multitude of theories. The approach of Fred Berger to the question of compassion is an example of that approach: He uses both Aristotle's theory of the mean between extremes and Kant's theory of ends in themselves to explore the subject of compassion. In other words, he allows for several different theories to be used at the same time, letting them work together to achieve a functional solution. This is a very pragmatic approach, and some might even call it a very American approach, because Americans are (presumably) typically interested in whether or not something *works.*

Berger's approach may work if we don't expect too much. Letting the vast spectrum of ethical viewpoints and traditions become available as options will certainly be no easy road, primarily because we can't just decide to take the best elements of all theories and lump them together in the hope that they may work. For one thing, they may well contradict one another; for another, if we choose a theory for its advantages, we're stuck with its disadvantages too. We can't just decide to add deontology to utilitarianism, for example, and assume that a smooth theory will emerge; we may have doubled our range of solutions, but we have also doubled our problems.

It is, however, probably the only solution for a future theory of ethics. We need theories of conduct, and we need theories of virtue, from more than just a few cultural groups; besides, most of us already use an approach that combines theories on a day-by-day basis. Sometimes we consider consequences as vitally important (especially in matters of life and death); sometimes we think keeping promises and other obligations is more important than worrying about consequences; sometimes we feel we're entitled to look after ourselves and our own interests; and sometimes we are focused on developing a good character—based on compassion, courage, or another virtue. Sometimes what we really need is to listen to that "little voice," our moral intuition, which neuroscientists tell us is an innate capacity. Often we do combine those views in specific situations. But we have to be able to decide when one viewpoint or aspect is more appropriate than another, and we have to try to avoid contradicting ourselves by putting together principles that are in obvious opposition to each other. You can't claim at the same time that consequences don't count and that consequences are all-important. What you *can* claim is that there are times when consequences are supremely important (such as calling and waiting for the ambulance to come for your neighbor who keeled over with a heart attack, even if you have to break your movie date to do that), and at other times a principle may be more important than certain consequences (such as a jury turning in a guilty verdict based on clear evidence, even if it may result in rioting). So despite the reluctance of many ethicists to mix and match moral theories, we do it on an everyday basis, and we can train ourselves to do it better by making sure we don't just make loopholes for ourselves, but genuinely try to address and evaluate the various aspects of real-life ethics as they arise in real situations: duty theory, consequentialism, virtue ethics, respect for other moral traditions—and, on occasion, some legitimate self-interest (provided that it doesn't seriously disregard the interests of others).

For many ethicists today the answer lies in what is called *ethical pluralism,* multiple ethical viewpoints coexisting on our planet and within the same culture. At least that was the viewpoint of many before September 11; some still see ethical pluralism as being the only civilized way for all of us to live together, whereas others have taken a second look at our Western ideals and traditions and found them to be worth supporting and offering to the world as a sensible moral code. Where does soft universalism stand, in a post-9/11 context? That depends greatly on what we call ethical pluralism. If it simply means that our culture consists of disparate and mutually exclusive viewpoints—individuals and groups not conversing, isolating themselves within their group identities, whether they be religious, political, or just based on different ethnic traditions—then soft universalism and ethical pluralism have little in common. But if an ethical pluralist can support the idea of a diverse society that wishes to create an environment with mutual respect and interest in sharing the responsibilities and joys of the community, then soft universalism can lend a hand, with its credo that we can show respect for a variety of moral viewpoints, as long as we agree that we can find some common values underlying the differences. Because, contrary to ethical relativism, moral subjectivism, and ethical pluralism (sometimes simply lumped together as "moral relativism" by its critics), soft universalism recognizes that there are, or ought to be, basic moral truths such as respect for others and a love of freedom—moral ideals that our nation and the Western civilization in general are based on, even though those ideals have not always been held in equally high regard by everybody. So a soft universalist will be able to profess pride in the traditions and values that promote such a respect for other human beings and an ideal of individual freedom while at the same time recognizing the value of diversity—as long as it is a diversity that accepts the notion of a common ground in shared democratic values. Is that less "tolerant" than ethical relativism? Yes, it is, and I suppose it is one of the philosophical legacies of 9/11 that the thinker who wants to be at peace with the world and accept diversity is more willing to draw the line at what he or she is willing to accept.

In the end, the view of soft universalism is that those common values are *founded in our common humanity,* in the fact that we live in groups and bond with other human beings but are also competitive individuals within our groups. So the challenge of soft universalism is to provide justification for why certain values are to be considered common ground. It must begin with the recognition that we share a common human moral intuition, a reluctance to cause direct harm. Next, it must set up a system of justification for which moral values should be considered valid at all times (such as the United Nations' list of human rights, for example), which values should be considered a matter of cultural preference and tradition, and which values should be considered globally unacceptable (such as "Some people are born to be free, and others are born to be slaves" or "People of a different religion/race/gender should be considered as having no rights"). Given that there are, in these times, schools around the world where young boys learn to hate everything Western and prepare for a life dedicated to destroying Western values and human beings, a system of ethics for the twenty-first century must look for the common ground we share as human beings, while balancing on the razor's edge of respecting others' traditions and at the same time cherishing and holding on to the best elements of our own. Ethical relativism doesn't have the capacity to do that, and neither does hard universalism. Whether soft universalism can provide genuine solutions to the problems of our highly complex world remains to be seen, but, as the philosopher Dwight Furrow would say, we have to try.

Diversity, Politics, and Common Ground?

It is time to gather a few threads that have been spun at various times in this edition: In Chapter 1 you read about the division experienced by much of the nation during and after the 2004 presidential election, with the country dividing itself into "red" and "blue" states and counties. In the heated media debate right after the election, former Democratic vice presidential candidate Geraldine Ferraro said on Fox News that if all the "blue" states got together and seceded, "nothing" would be left, because "all the talent is on the sides," meaning the two coasts. Such statements echoed the feelings of many "blue state" voters and was terribly offensive to many "red state" voters. It illustrates a certain attitude toward people who do not share one's moral and political views: that they must be *ignorant or stupid or willfully evil*. That attitude can be found among liberals and conservatives alike, and if we subscribe to that attitude, it entails that people whose views differ drastically (or even moderately) from "ours" essentially have no right to think what they think, because they are by definition wrong. *We* are the reasonable, sensible people, and those who disagree with us must be taught the error of their ways—retrained, perhaps even rehabilitated. They must be taught to see the light. If they resist, they are people of bad faith. But is that really the world of democracy, diversity, and tolerance that most people believe the United States is supposed to exemplify? The belief that one's own attitude is the enlightened one and that the others just refuse to face the facts can evolve into dogmatism, whether it is from the right or the left.

We have focused on *diversity* in this culture for a couple of decades now: People of different ethnic and racial backgrounds have found a place and changed what we now see as mainstream America. Women have found a place in public life and changed the face of the nation. People of different sexual orientations have, likewise, been included as part of the mainstream. But some of us tend to forget that diversity is not just a matter of race, ethnicity, and gender but also a matter of *convictions*. An environment that welcomes diversity must also include moral and political diversity. That means that a traditional, conservative environment must learn to accept that liberal members in its midst are liberal because they believe their own values are good and rational—not just because they are too stupid or narrow-minded or immoral to accept other values. And liberals, likewise, must rise above the notion that a conservative is someone who has not revised, or refuses to revise, his or her traditional opinions about values and politics. They must realize that "conservative" is not a derogatory term, and a conservative is not someone who is ignorant, stupid, or evil, but whose choice of values can develop with as much rationality and critical soul-searching as the development of liberal values. We must get to a point where we *respect the fact that other people may have different convictions*—but we don't necessarily have to *respect* those convictions! I am allowed to try to change your view, and you can try to change mine. But in recognizing your right to have a different opinion, and in your recognition of mine, we will live up to the quintessential American attitude, voiced by Patrick Henry in the eighteenth century: "*I may disagree with what you have to say, but I will fight to the death for your right to say it.*" And thus we will share the fundamental value of this democracy: That people have a right to think what they want and speak their mind about it, and when decisions have to be made, *we will take a vote.* Whoever wins gets to determine the policies—and those who didn't win still have the right to their conviction and to try to change the course of the future in a democratic way. We don't all have to agree that late-term abortions should be banned or that same-sex marriage should be allowed. But we should be able to acknowledge that those who don't agree with us on the issues we care about are, in general, not evil scoundrels but people who also have good will and who also are trying to create the best nation possible—as long as their agenda does not allow deliberate harm of others. So within the setting of a democracy, we all must agree to draw the line somewhere: We don't want to have a thought police, but we can't allow the enactment of political and moral views that entail some people being less than persons. The core value of respect for others' humanity and human dignity is the bottom line.

In Chapter 3, I speculated that the issue of finding common ground in our American culture might have a great deal to do with whether we perceive an outside threat, or whether we choose to focus on internal differences. Suppose we look at the issue in light of the previous discussion about soft universalism. How do we distinguish this proposed moral and political diversity from moral relativism? Precisely through the realization that we must choose and agree on some core values. We shouldn't ask for tolerance of all political and moral views. Some views seem offensive, or ludicrous, to me, and I will not hesitate to say so if someone asks me. But I am suggesting giving people the benefit of the assumption that they, too, make rational decisions based on their worldview, and that is what soft universalism entails: a respect for a diversity that respects our common humanity.

Study Questions

1. Was American POW Jessica Lynch a courageous soldier? Explain. Do you think John McCain would call her courageous? Define McCain's concept of courage. Do you agree with him?

2. Should we trust our moral intuition, or should we listen to our voice of reason? Explain your position with concrete scenarios.

3. What does Philip Hallie mean by negative and positive commands? Explain. Do you agree with him that positive commands are harder to live up to than negative commands?

4. Evaluate Richard Taylor's view that morality is a matter not of rational principles but of having your heart in the right place. Explore the pros and cons of such a view.

5. Evaluate the respect for the elderly as expressed in the philosophies of Confucius, Mencius, and Lin Yutang. Are such values completely alien to Western culture? Do you think modern Western culture would be improved by incorporating such ideas? Why or why not?

6. Contrast the conclusions of Jane English and Lin Yutang concerning the parent–grown child relationship.

7. Discuss the issue of dating: Is it a favor-debt or a friendship situation? Is there a way of resolving the problem of different expectations for dating partners in the twenty-first century?

Primary Readings and Narratives

The first Primary Reading is an excerpt from John McCain's *Why Courage Matters*; the second is an excerpt from Philip Hallie's *Tales of Good and Evil, Help and Harm*. The third Primary Reading, an excerpt from Lin Yutang's essay "On Growing Old Gracefully," discusses traditional ideas of gratitude within the family; the summaries of the films *Eat Drink Man Woman* and *Pay It Forward* illustrate how that virtue can be practiced in modern life. Before those two summaries, we have summaries of two other films illustrating the virtue of courage: an episode from the television series *Band of Brothers,* "Carentan," and the film *Tom Horn,* with an added excerpt from Tom Horn's autobiography.

To illustrate the virtue of compassion, praised as the true universal virtue by Western as well as non-Western thinkers, I have chosen the parable of the Good Samaritan and the film *Schindler's List.* These stories explore not only when one should show compassion but also whom one should show compassion toward—in other words, who counts as a member of one's moral universe.

Primary Reading

Why Courage Matters: The Way to a Braver Life

JOHN McCAIN

Excerpt, 2004.

In this excerpt Senator (and, at the time of this writing, Republican presidential candidate) John McCain suggests that we teach our children about moral courage by teaching them to "do their nearest duty." McCain didn't invent that notion, nor does he claim to. He cites the Unitarian social reformer James Freeman Clarke, who in his turn cited Johann Wolfgang von Goethe, whom you'll remember from Chapter 2. For Goethe, one's nearest duty means focusing on one's personal obligations: "Let each man wheel with steady sway, Round the task that rules the day, And do his best."

First we must answer the question "So what?" What do we need courage for anymore? Not to quiet our anxieties caused by September 11. A sense of proportion and a little righteous anger ought to suffice for that job. So what do we need it for?

We need it because without courage all virtue is fragile: admired, sought, professed, but held cheaply and surrendered without a fight. Courage is what Winston Churchill called "the first of human qualities . . . because it guarantees all the others." That's what we mean by the courage of convictions. Not that our convictions possess an innate courage, but that if we lack the courage to hold them, not just when they accord with the convictions of others but against threatening opposition, in the moment of their testing, they're superficial, vain things that add nothing to our self-respect or our society's respect for the virtues we profess. We can admire virtue and abhor corruption sincerely, but without courage we are corruptible.[. . .]

Most of us see the need for moral courage. Most of us accept social norms: that it's right to be honest, to respect the rights of others, to have compassion. But accepting the appropriateness of these qualities, wanting them, and teaching our children to want them aren't the same as actually possessing them. Accepting their validity isn't moral courage. How honest are we if we tell the truth most of the time and stay silent only when telling the truth might get us fired or earn us a broken nose? We need moral courage to be honest all the time. It's the enforcing virtue, the one that makes all the others possible. And it really isn't different from physical courage, except sometimes in degree and sometimes in the occasions when it encounters risk. If you don't have the courage to keep your virtue when facing unwanted consequences, you're not virtuous.[. . .]

We do not begin life fearing losses suffered by others. We are born selfish and struggle against it all our lives. We are concerned with our self-regard, although we might recognize it is dependent on the approval of our family. Later, the circle of those whose good opinion we require widens to encompass our friends. When does the moment occur when concern for our dignity enlarges to encompass the dignity of others? I think the transformation must begin when our desire to be loved becomes love for the object of our desire. And it progresses when our desire to emulate the behavior of our beloved, to ensure their love, becomes a love for the virtues that constitute their character. In that moment our conscience is born, our capacity to see that what's right for us is right for others. "If a man be brave," wrote the Unitarian social reformer James Freeman Clarke, "let him obey his conscience."

Clarke had borrowed from Goethe his life's motto: "Do your nearest duty." It's not always as easy as it sounds, to see your nearest duty or to want to see it. It's even harder to anticipate when our children will recognize their nearest duty. It's as hard for us to recognize sometimes as it is for them. We may not want to recognize it because we fear for them more than they fear for themselves, and their nearest duty might contain risks to their immediate happiness or worse. We can pay attention to them as they recount their day at school or on the playground, and identify in the routine occurrences of their experience an occasion where a duty would have appeared to a good person, with the choice to risk something or not to do it. But we don't always want to, even if we know that what they risk isn't something of lasting value.

We want our children to be popular almost as much as our children want to be popular. Popularity offers temporary security, enhances confidence, eases the petty disappointments of youth, and can be confused for love. But it's not love. It has no moral quality. It's a condition that might be hard to attain for some but doesn't represent an achievement of lasting significance. Its effects aren't as determinative of the quality of life as you might think when you're young and crave it. But still our children want to be popular, and we want them to be. If they are not, if they have suffered some embarrassment, some reduction in their circumstances in the constant ups and downs of childhood society, we'll try to comfort and encourage them by observing how transitory and ultimately insignificant a thing is popularity. But they'll feel the loss of it just the same, as will we. We hurt for them, and while we might know the hurt will pass, we would not want them to risk it again unnecessarily.

Teaching them virtue in the abstract, without recommending it in a specific situation, is not such a demanding thing. We don't experience empathetic apprehension and pain by urging them to be always honest, always fair, always respectful, the virtues that will alert them of their duty. We don't usually imagine their possession of those virtues provoking much more than the admiration of adults, their teachers, our neighbors and friends. If we're honest, we have in the backs of our minds as we impart these lessons to our children our own pride, our regard for our children as a reflection of our parenting. We want them to be honest and respectful because they and we will be admired for it. It's the allure of popularity that afflicts adults no less than children.

So it can be quite hard to help our children recognize their nearest duty if by so doing they risk social embarrassment or alienation from the peers whose friendship they most desire. But for kids, those are the most common risks of doing your nearest duty. In fact, they are the most common risks we adults face in our settled, mostly tranquil country.

What do you do when, in the course of your children's recitation of the day's events, they mention how bad they felt when their friend, the most popular girl or boy in the crowd, was cruel to a child with few friends, made the child cry from embarrassment and loneliness? We tell them that it's right to feel bad about it, as we should about any cruelty inflicted on the innocent. But don't we hesitate to tell them what they should do beyond empathizing with the victim? Maybe we recommend that they seek out the child and offer their companionship, even though we recognize such an act of decency might risk some opprobrium from the person who caused the injury. But do we recommend our children confront that popular boy or girl whose friendship they enjoy and tell them they think less of them for their unkindness? We might, but usually not without hesitation, dreading the impact it might have on our children's happiness. It's hard to tell children to recognize their nearest duty and to make the choice to accept it, when we know they may suffer for it.

When the pangs of our conscience confront our dread of the consequences for our loved ones who answer the call of theirs, it's our own courage we must summon as much as theirs. We have to believe in the truths we utter to our children when they are the ones who have been hurt, treated unkindly for no reason. We have to believe that there really is no great significance to being popular. We have to believe that if we love and are loved, by our family, by our true friends, and from that love we become good, the loss of popularity will hurt no longer than a bee sting. People who have only popularity to recommend themselves to our memory are soon forgotten. People with virtue, who do their nearest duty as their conscience instructs, are remembered. They are remembered as a source of happiness, not someone who resents another's.

We cannot explain virtue just in the abstract to them and hope that somehow they'll be okay. We have to help them recognize virtue's opposite and to feel an outrage that incites us to action and to accept the consequences. Keep the consequences in perspective, know that they are not the worst things in life, but accept them; accept them and resolve to provoke them again when virtue demands.

Study Questions

1. What does McCain mean by saying that "without courage all virtue is fragile"?

2. Explain the concept of moral courage using an example. Is it different from physical courage?

3. What does McCain mean by "doing one's nearest duty"? Does the fact that McCain is a high-profile politician add an element to that idea? Explain why or why not?

4. For five years, McCain was a POW in Vietnam. At one point he was offered his freedom but chose to stay behind with his fellow soldiers. That decision resulted in torture by his captors. Evaluate McCain's decision in terms of physical and moral courage, and the concept of one's "nearest duty."

Primary Reading

Tales of Good and Evil, Help and Harm

PHILIP HALLIE

Excerpt, 1997.

In this chapter, you read about Philip Hallie's encounter with people in Le Chambon who saved six thousand Jews from Nazi death camps. Here Hallie speculates that doing good is morally superior to refraining from doing evil.

Most of the old ethical theories and commandments present ethics as a friend of life and an enemy of death. And so those theories and commandments praise help and condemn harm. They celebrate the spreading of life with two sorts of ethical rules or ideals: negative and positive. The negative rules are scattered throughout the Bible and other ethical documents, but Moses brought the most memorable ones down to the West from Mount Sinai: Thou shalt not murder, thou shalt not betray. . . . These rules say no to the deliberate extinction of life and joy. On the other hand, positive rules are also spread across many ethical documents. For instance, the Bible enjoins us to be our brother's keeper. These rules say yes to the protection and spreading of life.

The naysaying ethic forbids our doing certain harmful things, and the yeasaying one urges us to help those whose lives are diminished or threatened. To follow the negative ideals you must have clean hands; but to follow the positive ones you can be less hygienic—you can dirty your hands doing something helpful. If you would be your brother's keeper you must go out of your way. The negative ethic is the ethic of decency, of restraint. It is terrible to violate it—to be a murderer or a liar—but obey it and you could be a dead person. A corpse does not kill and does not betray. Moreover, you could obey the no ethic by being silent, and it was the silent majority in Germany and in the world who fed the torturers and the murderers with their silence. The murderers and the torturers drank the silence like wine, and it made them drunk with power.

On the other hand, the yes ethic demands action. You must be alive if you would meet its demands; sometimes you must even put your life on the line. You must go out of your way, sometimes very *far* out of your way. In combat I had to become a killer in order to help stop Germany in its tracks. I had to violate the no ethic in order to help stop the many tortures and murders that Nazi Germany was perpetrating in Central Europe.

. . . My experience had led me to believe that human beings are doomed either to be clean-handed and helpless or murderous and helpful. I knew no one who was both clean and noble.

But in that story about the village of Le Chambon I found people who were both. Here were people in this slaughterhouse of a world who avoided hating and hurting life and at the same time prevented murder. . . .

. . . .

If evil has to do with the twisting and diminution of human life, then the government [Schmäling] ably served was evil. In a mountainous part of France where there were many French guerrilla fighters, he helped keep the French from stabbing his fellow Germans in the back and hindering the cruel march of Nazism. He helped an evil cause ably, and importantly.

But if goodness has to do with the spreading of human life, and the prevention of hatred and cruelty and murder, then he was surely good. Good and evil have much to do with perspectives, points of view. If you want to know whether cruelty is happening and just how painful it is, do not ask the torturer. Do not ask someone like Obergruppen-führer [Lieutenant General] Otto Ohlendorff, the head of the special troops assigned to kill unarmed civilians in Eastern Europe. The victimizer does not feel the blows, the victim feels them. Do not ask a sword about wounds; look to the person on whose flesh the sword falls. Victimizers can be blinded by simple insensitivity, by a great cause, by a great hatred, or by a hundred self-serving "reasons." Victims too can be desensitized, but usually they are the best witnesses to their pain. They feel it in their flesh and in their deepest humiliations and horrors.

And if you want to know about goodness, do not ask only the doers of good. They may be doing what they do out of habitual helpfulness or for some abstract cause. They may not realize exactly how they are helping the people they have helped: They may not be looking deeply into the eyes and minds of the beneficiaries of their good deeds.

But usually the beneficiaries of those deeds know. Usually they have this knowledge in their flesh and in their passions. And usually if they do not have this knowledge, goodness is not happening, the joy of living is not being enhanced and widened for them. Do-gooders can in fact do great harm. The points of view of victims and beneficiaries are vital to an understanding of evil and of good.

Study Questions

1. What is the difference between naysaying ethics and yeasaying ethics? Explain. What does this have to do with the story of the people of Le Chambon?

2. What does Hallie mean by saying, "To follow the negative ideals you must have clean hands; but to follow the positive ones you can be less hygienic—you can dirty your hands doing something helpful"? Explain, and evaluate Hallie's viewpoint: Is he right?

3. What is Hallie's final verdict on Schmäling? Was he good or evil? Explain.

Primary Reading

On Growing Old Gracefully

LIN YUTANG

The Importance of Living, 1937. Excerpt.

In this excerpt Lin Yutang talks about the duty of the adult male toward his parents and about the process of aging, which, to him, ought to be a stage characterized by both happiness and wisdom.

Every one realizes . . . that orphanages and old age pensions are poor substitutes for the home. The feeling is that the home alone can provide anything resembling a satisfactory arrangement for the old and the young. But for the young, it is to be taken for granted that not much need be said, since there is natural paternal affection. "Water flows downwards and not upwards," the Chinese always say, and therefore the affection for parents and grandparents is something that stands more in need of being taught by culture. A natural man loves his children, but a cultured man loves his parents. In the end, the teaching of love and respect for old people became a generally accepted principle, and if we are to believe some of the writers, the desire to have the privilege of serving their parents in their old age actually became a consuming passion. The greatest regret a Chinese gentleman could have was the eternally lost opportunity of serving his old parents with medicine and soup on their deathbed, or not to be present when they died. For a high official in his fifties or sixties not to be able to invite his parents to come from their native village and stay with his family at the capital, "seeing them to bed every night and greeting them every morning," was to commit a moral sin of which he should be ashamed and for which he had constantly to offer excuses and explanations to his friends and colleagues. This regret was expressed in two lines by a man who returned too late to his home, when his parents had already died:

> The tree desires repose, but the wind will not stop;
> The son desires to serve, but his parents are already gone.

. . . It seems a linguistic misfortune that hale and hearty old men in America tell people that they are "young," or are told that they are "young" when really what is meant is that they are healthy. To enjoy health in old age, or to be "old and healthy," is the greatest of human luck, but to call it "healthy and young" is but to detract from that glamour and impute imperfection to what is really perfect. After all, there is nothing more beautiful in this world than a healthy wise old man, with "ruddy cheeks and white hair," talking in a soothing voice about life as one who knows it. The Chinese realize this, and have always pictured an old man with "ruddy cheeks and white hair" as *the symbol of ultimate earthly happiness*. Many Americans must have seen Chinese pictures of the God of Longevity, with his high forehead, his ruddy face, his white beard—and how he smiles! The picture is so vivid. He runs his fingers through the thin flowing beard coming down to the breast and gently strokes it in peace and contentment, dignified because he is surrounded with respect, self-assured because no one ever questions his wisdom, and kind because he has seen so much of human sorrow. To persons of great vitality, we also pay the compliment of saying that "the older they grow, the more vigorous they are." . . .

I have no doubt that the fact that the old men of America still insist on being so busy and active can be directly traced to individualism carried to a foolish extent. It is their pride and their love of independence and their shame of being dependent upon their children. But among the many human rights the American people have provided for in their Constitution, they have strangely forgotten about the right to be fed by their children, for it is a right and an obligation growing out of service. How can any one deny that parents who have toiled for their children in their youth, have lost many a good night's sleep when they were ill, have washed their diapers long before they could talk and have spent about a quarter of a century bringing them up and fitting them for life, have the right to be fed by them and loved and respected when they are old? Can one not forget the individual and his pride of self in a general scheme of home life in which men are justly taken care of by their parents and, having in turn taken care of their children, are also justly taken care of by the latter? The Chinese have not got the sense of individual independence because the whole conception of life is based upon mutual help within the home; hence there is no shame attached to the circumstance of one's being served by his children in the sunset of one's life. Rather it is considered good luck to have children who can take care of one. One lives for nothing else in China.

Study Questions

1. Explain this quotation: "Water runs downwards and not upwards." What does this have to do with the relationship between parents and children?

2. Evaluate Lin Yutang's view of gratitude toward parents: Is it dependent on parental love? Why or why not? Is that an important issue?

3. When evaluating two opposing viewpoints in this chapter, Lin Yutang's and Jane English's, whose approach do you find more appealing? Explain why.

Narrative

Band of Brothers, Third Episode, "Carentan"

TOM HANKS AND STEVEN SPIELBERG (PRODUCERS)

Television series, 2001. Summary.

The highly acclaimed HBO television series *Band of Brothers* is, in effect, a sequel to the film *Saving Private Ryan* (see the website)—not in the sense that we encounter the same characters, but because we move within the same time frame and subject: American soldiers on D-Day, June 6, 1944, and further into the final year of World War II. *Saving Private Ryan* star Tom Hanks and director Steven Spielberg wanted to explore in more depth the war experiences of real American soldiers on D-Day and afterward. In the series, we follow "Easy" (E) Company's campaigns, with each episode's prologue delivered by real survivors from that unit. In this narrative I've chosen to focus on a story that is part of, but by no means all of, the third episode: the story of Private Albert Blithe. I intend for it to illustrate the concept of *physical courage,* but that is an issue you may want to discuss afterward.

It is the day after D-Day and the soldiers of Easy Company, having parachuted through a storm of anti-aircraft fire, are still scattered around the Normandy country-side. Some soldiers were shot before they hit the ground; others head toward their objectives despite the loss of most of their equipment. As these stragglers from many different units encounter one another, they form impromptu teams to engage the enemy while they try to locate their brethren. Except Private Albert Blithe. When some E Company wanderers come across Blithe, we sense that something is dreadfully wrong with him—not physically, but psychologically. He stares up at the sky, as if he's a young bird fallen from its nest looking back up at the peaceful, safe haven from which it tumbled. His gaze is fixed, he barely hears his buddies' questions, and yet there is nothing wrong with him physically.

After rejoining E Company, and surviving a firefight with German soldiers in the streets of the town of Carentan, and after seeing fellow soldiers drop dead from bullets or have limbs torn from their bodies, Blithe sinks to the ground—not wounded, but struck blind by fear and the horrors he has seen. His superior officer, Lieutenant Winters, assures him that he will be sent back to England and treats him with kindness and understanding, even though there doesn't seem to be anything physically wrong with his eyes. Winters's compassionate words are enough to bring Blithe around; his vision apparently returns, and he rejoins his platoon. It is during a quiet moment with another officer that Blithe confesses what is troubling him. We learn that after he hit the ground on D-Day, he hid in a ditch and fell asleep, rather than seek out his comrades and pursue the enemy. He feels his own fear is greater than his brain can handle. At this crucial time in his universe of terror, the brave Lieutenant Speirs (who later in the series performs acts of unfathomable courage) offers Blithe a piece of advice: You hid, he says, not because of fear, but because you still had hope—hope of survival. That hope will paralyze your actions. The only way to do your job and be a soldier is to tell yourself you're already dead.

Another battle ensues: German tanks roll over American soldiers, gunfire is cutting down the soldiers of Easy, bullets whiz and splat around the screaming Private Blithe. But now something happens to him: He raises his rifle, and as if to shoot back at the madness assaulting him, he finds the trigger and fires (and we sense that this is the first time he has fired his gun in battle) and blindly fires again, and again. At the end of the battle when he spies a German soldier on the skyline, he stands up, and without regard for his own safety, *carefully* aims this time, shoots, and sees his enemy fall. Standing over his vanquished foe, Blithe notices the man he killed is wearing an *Edelweiss*—an alpine flower that denotes its wearer as a great warrior. He takes the Edelweiss and affixes it to his own tunic. From somewhere deep within himself, Private Albert Blithe has found courage in battle. Later when a necessary and dangerous mission calls for volunteers, he is the first to step up. But this act of selfless courage is his undoing: He is shot in the neck; and though he is saved by a medic, we learn at the end of the episode that he never recovered from his wounds, and died in 1948, three years after the end of the war. The last we see of Albert Blithe, he is lying in his hospital bed, eyes staring upward, toward the peaceful sky from which he tumbled.

Study Questions

1. What happened to Blithe? Did he lose his fear? Is loss of fear necessary to find courage?

2. Does Lieutenant Speirs's advice seem wise to you? Why or why not? Does such a piece of advice apply only in battle, or is it relevant in other dangerous situations too? Is there a downside to such a piece of advice? Explain.

3. If you are a veteran, you may want to share your reaction to this story with the class or in an essay: Does it ring true? Why or why not? If you have seen the entire *Band of Brothers* series, you may want to put this episode into the greater context of the series.

4. Imagine what John McCain might say to the story of Blithe. Was Blithe courageous? Why or why not? What would Aristotle say?

Narrative

The Life of Tom Horn

TOM HORN

Autobiography, 1903. Summary and Excerpt.

Tom Horn

THOMAS McGUANE AND BUD SHRAKE (SCREENWRITERS)
WILLIAM WIARD (DIRECTOR)

Film, 1980. Summary.

This example of moral as well as physical courage will be considered controversial by some historians because it involves a man who was executed for murder: the American army scout, cattle detective, author, and frontier legend Tom Horn. It rests on the theory, suggested by several historians, that he was "framed," and that the state of Wyoming executed an innocent man. While in jail, awaiting the appeal of his death sentence, Horn writes the story of his life. It is presented the way he would want to be remembered, probably not 100 percent accurately, but written with a sense of professional duty as well as a great deal of humor. Horn's life seems to fall into two phases, and historians have had a hard time reconciling them, because in his early forties he was a convicted child killer; but in his twenties Horn distinguished himself as a very courageous and resourceful man. He was an on-again, off-again scout and interpreter for the U.S. Army in Arizona during the Apache wars of the 1880s. He had lived in Mexico and among the Apaches and spoke German, Spanish, and several Apache dialects aside from his native English; and in his autobiography he displays an understanding of both Mexican and Apache customs and outlook that is light-years ahead of his "monocultural" employers. Chief Geronimo saw him as a friend of the Apaches. Even so, his loyalties were with his employers, in particular his boss, the famed scout Al Sieber. On one occasion in particular, he stood his ground in battle with the Apaches, and through his steadfast example he saved both Sieber and the troops who would otherwise have been overwhelmed by the Indians. Horn was not known to be a modest man, yet he describes the following situation in his autobiography with modesty as often characteristic of physically courageous people:

> I received a long complimentary letter from the Department Commander, General Wilcox, along in the fall or early winter, telling me I was an excellent man, and that he had taken proper steps to have a medal presented to me for bringing old Sergeant Murray out of the fight after he was wounded . . . describing how I, under heavy fire, took one man and gained a high commanding point over the troops and kept them from getting demoralized and annihilated, by yelling to the soldiers to keep cool and to send up another man or two . . . That was the first time I learned I had done anything very great. . . .

. . . Of course I brought old Sergeant Murray out of the fight, but I had taken him in also, and I could not very well leave the old man alone. . . . I was afraid that Sieber would get killed, for I could have run away myself easily enough, but Sieber kept with the soldiers and he and some men were carrying Hentig, who was dead. I could not run away and leave Sieber. He would not leave the soldiers, and when I saw that, I knew I would have to fight the Indians away till they all got out . . . I never thought of saving the rest of the command.

. . . So the whole letter, while highly complimentary, was simply based on some account of these affairs as reported to him by some army officer, and in reality there was nothing extraordinary about it.

By the way, that was the last I ever heard of that medal.

Eventually, the army had no further use for Tom's services, and he took on other careers, such as serving as an agent for the Pinkerton detective agency. Eventually he drifted north into Wyoming. At this point I'll let the summary of the film *Tom Horn* tell the rest of the story. Although the film isn't completely historically accurate, it captures the spirit and the essence of the last years of Tom Horn's life:

A scruffy trail-worn cowboy rides into a frontier town in Wyoming, and immediately gets into a saloon fight because he'd rather drink to Geronimo—there's a man he respects—than to a bragging prizefighter. The cowboy, who introduces himself as Tom Horn, is outnumbered, and takes a terrible beating—but his presence is noted in town, and he is approached by a local rancher, John Coble. Would Tom be interested in a job? It would be completely free rein, no questions asked, as long as he gets results. The ranchers are plagued by rustlers, stealing cattle and changing their brands (which, in the Old West, was a hanging offense). So they would like Tom to stop the rustlers—cold. That means if they can't get scared off the land, Tom is to eliminate them. Coble emphasizes, though, that this conversation has to be confidential. "We've never had this talk," he says, because Tom's job will take him outside the boundaries of due process, something the "civilized" ranchers wouldn't want to have associated with their good name. Tom accepts the job, and agrees to keep silent about his employers; and to a man steeped in the Old West's code of honor, his word is his bond. In Tom's world of the frontier, where peace officers are few and far between, it is not unusual even for people with good intentions to take the law into their own hands to protect themselves and their property. Tom is introduced to the other ranchers at an outdoor picnic. Here he encounters the New West, the West of the future where wealthy ranchers have live lobsters brought in from Maine (Tom looks at the strange sea creatures and declares, "I never ate a bug that big before!"), and civilization and the new century are just around the corner. Many people are eager to put the old violent days of the West behind them. One person who professes her love for the Old West and its ways is the local schoolteacher, Glendolene Kimmell, and there is a sense of immediate sympathy and attraction between the two.

Tom goes about his business as a cattle detective, tracking rustlers, scaring them off if he can, and otherwise doing what he believes he is hired to do—killing them—on the direct orders of the Cattlemen's Association: It's better to avoid bringing the rustlers to trial. And he is a very efficient employee. Coble has already assured him that he and the Association are behind him 100 percent (to which Tom says, "I'll have to take your word for it" and Coble answers, "You've got it"). Ironically, as he succeeds in his job, and the ranchers see fewer cattle thieves, his presence is becoming an embarrassment to the men who hired him; his ways are not of the new century, regardless of the fact that he is now making their modern way of life possible. And Tom knows way too much about who hired him. In short, it would be better if Tom were gone. One of the men of the new century, Marshall Joe Belle, has political ambitions, and he and the Association see eye to eye. And a conspiracy is formed to get rid of Tom.

Tom has a personal problem: He drinks, periodically, and when he drinks, he brags. Shortly after Jimmy Nolt (in real life: Willie Nickell), the fourteen-year old son of a sheep farmer, is murdered by a sniper, Tom finds himself in a saloon, getting drunk. He doesn't find it suspicious that Belle wants to talk with him in private and asks him questions about the Nolt murder. At some point Tom declares that if he had shot the boy, it would have been "the best shot and the dirtiest trick I'd ever done." But when he is arrested and charged with the murder, he realizes that it was a setup: Hiding behind the door was a stenographer who took down his "confession." In the transcript it says, "It was the best shot and the dirtiest trick I've ever done."

And so the system of injustice rolls on. John Coble hires a lawyer for Tom, but for some reason, his defense is uninspired The prosecution's theory is allowed to stand unchallenged, paving the way for Tom's conviction as well as Marshall Belle's career in politics; and Tom offers nothing in his own defense. Coble has already pleaded with him not to speak up—and he doesn't. Never giving up the names of those who hired him, including Coble, he just sits in the makeshift outdoor courtroom tent and stares at the mountains that are lost to him forever, while the prosecution paints him as a murderer whose blood lust has driven him to kill poor squatters all over the territory. So Tom is found guilty of murder, and the sentence is death by hanging. On November 20, 1903, he is walked to the scaffold and hanged according to a new, modern mechanical method involving water running into a trough, lifting a lever and springing the trap door. And so, just as they avoided sullying their hands in eliminating the rustlers, by using Tom, the men of the New West have now eliminated an embarrassing reminder of their own violent past.

In this film, Tom may have met his unjust end without flinching, but that is not why I chose his character as an example of courage. It is because of what he knew and didn't say when it might have saved his life. What about the ranchers who hired him? They faded away, never acknowledging that he was on their payroll or following their instructions. John Coble himself was present at the trial but offered no support for Tom other than hiring a useless lawyer. So it appears that out of loyalty toward Coble, and a sense of professional honor, Tom never spoke up for himself or gave up the names of his employers. Perhaps we can even apply the words of John McCain in *Why Courage Matters*: "Enduring an inescapable fate stoically is admirable, but it is not the same thing as courage. Suffering stoically a terrible fate that you could have escaped, but that your convictions, your sense of honor, compelled you to accept, is."

Is this the true story of the real Tom Horn? Some think it is pure fiction and that Horn was simply a bloodthirsty killer, but an increasing number of researchers believe that Tom

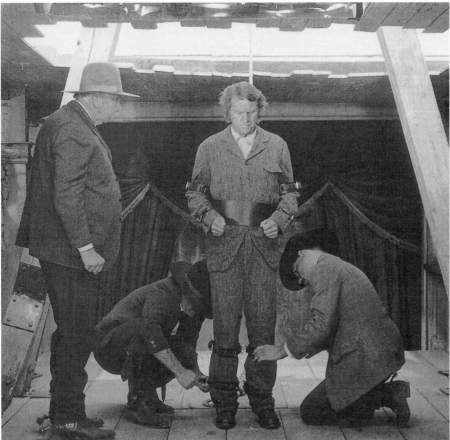

Was Tom Horn a cold-blooded child killer or a scapegoat who met his fate with moral courage? The film *Tom Horn* presents Tom as a victim of financial and political interests in the new twentieth century, staying true to nineteenth-century values of honor and friendship. Here Tom (Steve McQueen) is being prepared for his execution. According to witnesses, the real Tom Horn kept his composure throughout the process and even displayed a dry sense of humor.

was indeed a wronged man, sacrificed by the interests of the Cattlemen's Association. In real life Tom sat in his jail cell for one whole year, waiting for the Supreme Court to look at his appeal, which was eventually denied. He wrote numerous letters to John Coble and to lawyers, and judges, pointing out errors in the trial, to no avail—and he never did mention his employers. Glendolene wrote an eloquent tribute to Tom after his death, in which she describes him as being crushed between two civilizations, the old and the new. And Coble? After Tom's death he published Tom's book, with a moving preface. But by then it was too late to do something for Tom, and a few years later, Coble, now destitute and ill, and perhaps haunted by thoughts of things undone, shot himself to death in the back room of a local saloon.

Study Questions

1. Was Tom Horn brave in keeping silent about his employers? Or was he simply foolish? How far would you go to protect the identity of someone you considered a friend? or an employer?

2. What did Glendolene mean by saying that Tom was crushed between two civilizations, the old and the new?

3. The film presents Tom as an innocent man, framed and sacrificed by others' interests and ambitions. Would it make a difference in evaluating his courage if he really was guilty of killing the boy? What might Philippa Foot (Chapter 10) say? What might Aristotle say?

4. Would you say the quote by McCain fits Tom? Why or why not? Can you think of other examples of someone in history or in fiction who—because of his or her convictions—accepts a terrible fate he or she could have escaped?

Narrative

The Parable of the Good Samaritan

From the New Testament, Luke 10:30–37, King James Version.

For readers with a Christian background, the story of the Good Samaritan is the archetypal story of compassion. The Good Samaritan is one of the parables of Jesus of Nazareth, and it is intended to be taken as an allegory.

> A certain man went down from Jerusalem to Jericho, and fell among thieves, which stripped him of his raiment, and wounded him, and departed, leaving him half dead. And by chance there came down a certain priest that way: and when he saw him, he passed by on the other side. And likewise a Levite, when he was at the place, came and looked on him, and passed by on the other side. But a certain Samaritan, as he journeyed, came where he was: and when he saw him, he had compassion on him. And went to him, and bound up his wounds, pouring in oil and wine, and set him on his own beast, and brought him to an inn, and took care of him. And on the morrow when he departed, he took out two pence, and gave them to the host, and said unto him, Take care of him; and whatsoever thou spendest more, when I come again, I will repay thee. Which now of these three, thinkest thou, was neighbor unto him that fell among the thieves? And he said, He that shewed mercy on him. Then said Jesus unto him, Go and do thou likewise.

To the modern reader, the story illustrates that the Good Samaritan is the one who is truly good because he acts with compassion, whereas others, who are supposed to know the difference between right and wrong, do nothing. For contemporaries of Jesus, however, the story may have meant something slightly different. A Samaritan was, for the Jews of Israel, a social outcast; the Samaritans were a population politically

Arrival of the Good Samaritan at the Inn (1866) by Gustave Doré. The Good Samaritan has rescued a victim of a highway assault and here is taking him to be cared for. The Samaritan pays for the victim's keep and treatment out of his own pocket and lets the innkeeper know that if the costs add up to more, he will pay for that, too.

and ethnically distinct from the Hebrews, and people from Samaria were not held in high regard. The Jews, then, would have seen Jesus' purpose in telling the story as not so much instructing us to be compassionate as instructing us to recognize who our *neighbor* is (our neighbor is any person who acts with compassion toward us). The lesson is, "Even" a Samaritan can be our neighbor. But of course the overriding lesson is to "go and do likewise."

Study Questions

1. Explain what Jesus seems to mean by using the term *neighbor.* Is this story meaningful for Christians only, or might it also appeal to people of other faiths, agnostics, and atheists? Explain.

2. What might an ethical egoist say about this story? Why? Would you have a critical response, or would you agree? Why?

3. A university study conducted years ago tested people's willingness to stop and help someone in distress. A group of students were told to go to a lecture about the parable of the Good Samaritan, and on their way they encountered a man who appeared to be in severe pain. Apparently, the topic of the lecture didn't make any difference: Many of those students who thought they were early for the talk stopped to help, whereas few of the students who thought they were late stopped. Do you think it would make a difference to you, if you found yourself having to choose between helping or hurrying on, whether you remembered this story?

Narrative

Schindler's List

STEVEN ZAILLIAN (SCREENWRITER)
STEVEN SPIELBERG (DIRECTOR)

Film, 1993. Based on the 1982 book by Thomas Keneally. Summary.

All the story summaries in this book come with a strong suggestion: that you experience the stories in their original version because the summaries are intended only to highlight certain moral problems and can in no way do justice to the experience of reading the book or watching the film. That is especially true of the award-sweeping *Schindler's List,* based on a true story from Poland in World War II. The historical fact of the Holocaust is (or ought to be) familiar to everyone, but even if we think we know what happened, the experience of *hearing and seeing* people suffering (even in a Hollywood version) is more powerful than any words can convey. For the sake of the moral of the story, I have to tell you the entire story line, but I have, of course, omitted a great many details.

The year is 1939; the place is Kraków, Poland; the Nazi army has by now taken Poland, and Polish Jews are being moved to the 600-year-old Kraków ghetto. Deprived of the right to make a living, the Jews are trying to adjust. A German Gentile, Oskar Schindler, approaches the *Judenrat* (the Jewish Council) with a suggestion: Their investments and his business sense could make the start of a new factory. But Itzhak Stern, a member of the council, turns him down. We see Schindler getting cozy with top Nazi officials, showing himself to be a high roller and making friends, all for the sake of future business connections.

Two years later the overcrowded ghetto becomes a prison for Kraków's Jewish population; everybody of Jewish heritage is moved into the old city, and Schindler profits from the situation: He takes over the beautiful apartment belonging to a Jewish businessman. And now he again approaches the council with his suggestion; this time they are desperate for food and other goods unavailable to them, so investors agree to help Schindler set up his factory, making enamelware crockery. Stern becomes his production manager and immediately sees a way to help people in the ghetto by hiring them as skilled workers for the factory, people who have never done manual labor before—a rabbi, a musician, a history professor—because if they can't prove that they can contribute to the war effort, they will be deported.

Schindler sends for his wife from his hometown and proudly tells her that he is about to get rich—that all his previous failed business ventures lacked an essential ingredient that is now present: war. He is selling his crockery to his Nazi friends and making money hand over fist.

When Stern leaves his identification papers behind and is stopped without them, the Nazis are quick to put him on a train to Auschwitz. As the train pulls out, Schindler turns up and saves him by threatening the young Nazi officers with an end to their careers; Stern is grateful, but it is clear that Schindler didn't do it for Stern's sake. He says, "What if I'd got here five minutes later? Then where would I be?"

For the others being sent to Auschwitz there is no salvation; we see their suitcases opened by Nazi officials, the contents placed on shelves, their jewelry collected—and their gold teeth as well.

A new commander arrives at Plazov, the nearby labor camp: He is Amon Goeth, a ruthless and barely sane man who delights in shooting people at the slightest provocation or merely as target practice. On his order the Nazi storm troopers commence the liquidation of the Kraków ghetto: Everybody is rounded up and either shot on the spot or moved to Plazov. From a hilltop overlooking the ghetto, Schindler watches the horror of the mass murder. From afar he notices a little girl in a red coat (*Schindler's List* is a black-and-white film; the girl's coat is one of only a few items of color); we see his reaction when he understands that the girl will not survive.

Back in his factory, Schindler is all alone; the workers are gone. So he goes to Goeth to get his workers back, complaining that he is losing money. Goeth demands a cut of his profit and lets him have his workers back, all except Stern.

Up until now profit may have been the true drive behind Schindler's actions, but when he is approached by a young woman begging him to take in her parents as "workers" so they won't be killed, he agrees (after first refusing). We begin to see a change in him; he is beginning to see his Jewish workers, the "Schindler Jews," as people. Goeth is in no such frame of mind, though—he tells his maid, one of the young Jewish women, that he likes her, even if "she is not a person in the strictest sense of the word." When he is tempted to kiss the frightened young woman, he accuses her of almost seducing him and cuts her up with a piece of broken glass.

More prisoners are arriving at Plazov, and Goeth wants to make room for them; his method is to sort the healthy from the unhealthy, and so he forces the entire camp to take off their clothes and run around in a circle, naked, under the eyes of the camp doctors. Anyone looking less than completely fit is taken aside and shot. When the survivors are

Philip Hallie talks about the *institutionalized cruelty* of Nazi Germany and of the antidote of hospitality provided by the people of Le Chambon; another example of an antidote against the Nazi horrors is the true story of Oskar Schindler, told by Steven Spielberg in his 1993 film *Schindler's List* (Universal Pictures). By hiring Jews as workers in his factory, Schindler was able to cheat the Nazi extermination machinery of more than 1,100 men, women, and children. Here Schindler (Liam Neeson) argues desperately with an SS guard at the Auschwitz death camp that the children of his workers are also needed at his factory because their small hands can polish the inside of artillery shell casings.

allowed to dress, they are elated—but their joy is short-lived: In the meantime, the Nazis have rounded up the children and are now taking them away to be exterminated. A few children manage to hide, some of them inside the latrine.

After a period of more heartbreaks, Stern tells Schindler that he has been put in charge of the final "evacuation" to Auschwitz, with himself on the last train. Schindler is resigned to going home with his money and calling it quits, but as he is packing up all his money, he thinks of a use for it: He approaches Goeth and asks if he can *buy* his workers' lives, to have them transferred to another camp to set up a new factory. Goeth drives a hard bargain and agrees; now Schindler and Stern together must make a list of names of people to be saved: as many names as Schindler can afford. In the end, the list includes more than 1,100 Jews, and Stern tells him, "The list is life"—all around it is death. So the Schindler Jews are taken to the safe haven of Schindler's hometown in Czechoslovakia; but only the men and boys arrive. The train with the women and the girls has been sidetracked, through a clerical error—to Auschwitz.

By bribing the overseer at Auschwitz with diamonds, Schindler buys his women workers back but has to put up a fight to save their daughters. Finally the families are reunited, and for the remaining seven months of the war the factory produces useless artillery shells, for Schindler does not want to contribute to the killing. By the time the war ends, Schindler has no more money; he has spent his entire fortune saving 1,100 people. Saying good-bye to his Jewish friends (he is now considered a war criminal and must flee), he breaks down, thinking that he might have saved just a few more people if he had sold his car and his jewelry, but Stern and the others give him a letter, signed by everyone, and a gold ring with a quote from the Talmud: "Whoever saves one life saves an entire world." They collected the gold by extracting their own gold teeth and melting them down.

Study Questions

1. Explain the quote from the Talmud: "Whoever saves one life saves an entire world."

2. How does the compassion shown by Schindler compare with the virtue of hospitality shown by the people of Le Chambon? (See the discussion of Philip Hallie.)

3. Does the fact that Schindler originally hired the Kraków Jews for profit detract from his efforts to save them? Why or why not? (Here you might use Berger's criteria for gratitude.)

4. Compare the scene in which the prisoners are forced to run naked in front of the Nazi officers with Hallie's theory of institutionalized cruelty.

Narrative

Eat Drink Man Woman

HUI-LING WANG, JAMES SCHAMUS,
AND ANG LEE (SCREENWRITERS)
ANG LEE (DIRECTOR)

Film, 1994. Summary.

This film is an early film by Ang Lee, before his rise to U.S. fame with films such as *The Remains of the Day* and *Brokeback Mountain*. I chose it for its conflict between the old Confucian virtue of gratitude toward parents (in particular the virtue of children's sacrificing their happiness for the sake of their parents) and the virtue of seeking and creating happiness wherever you can find it.

The master chef Chu is preparing one of his fantastic meals—not at the restaurant where he has been working for many years, but at his home in Taipei, Taiwan. Everything is prepared with serious dedication, even though Chu has a problem: He has lost his sense of taste. His three grown daughters, whom he is cooking for, don't hesitate to point out if there is something amiss with the recipes; quarreling is not unusual in their home, and before she died, their mother used to quarrel with their father herself. It seems that the only way Chu knows how to express himself is through cooking, and it is through his efforts with his meals that we realize how much he cares for his daughters, especially the middle daughter, Jia-Chien.

Jia-Chien is a modern young woman: She is an airline executive, she has a once-in-a-while lover, and she is preparing to move out of her childhood home. We learn that she grew up in her father's restaurant kitchen and learned all the elaborate recipes, but her father wanted her to get a "real job," so she had to give up her dreams of becoming a great chef. The youngest daughter, Jia-Ning, is working as a waitress and trying very hard to steal her best friend's boyfriend away from her. The oldest daughter, Jia-Jen, a math teacher, has had a sad life: Nine years ago her boyfriend, a young student of chemistry, broke up with her and went to the United States, and she has never been able to get over it. Now she has converted to Christianity and believes she must resign herself to staying single to take care of their father.

Chu may love his daughters, but he does not understand them. After work at the restaurant (where he salvaged a botched dinner for important customers), he and his old friend, Old Wen, get drunk together and talk about life. Wen says, "Eat, drink, man, woman—food and sex—basic desires—can't avoid them!" Chu complains, "All my life, every day, all I do. . . . is that all there is? Is this the good life?" And Old Wen replies, "We're still alive, still cooking, thank God."

Dinners in the Chu household are the times when family announcements are made, and Jia-Chien announces that she is moving out, thus stealing her father's thunder, for he had an announcement to make too, but we don't get to hear it. And it looks as if things are going well for her: She is about to be promoted to a position in Amsterdam. A new colleague is introduced to her at work, a young man who has lived for years in the United States, and she finds herself attracted to him but is horrified when she realizes that he is her sister's former boyfriend, the man who broke her heart. She is even more horrified when she confronts him with the old story and learns that he has no idea who her sister is—the girl he used to date was her sister's best friend, Jin-Rong. So now Jia-Chien knows that her sister made the whole thing up.

Jin-Rong herself married someone else and is now getting divorced from him. They live close by Mr. Chu's house. She has a little daughter, Shan-Shan, and Mr. Chu finds himself becoming protective toward the little girl; he watches her get on the bus to school, a tiny child disappearing among pushy big adults, and we can tell that his heart goes out to her. Since her mother is not a good cook, he begins to prepare a lunchbox with elaborate little dishes for Shan-Shan; he takes Jin-Rong's food home and eats it (it is not very good). It soon turns out that Jin-Rong has found out, but she is not angry—she is grateful that Mr. Chu cares about her little girl. Changes are happening in Jin-Rong's household, too: Her mother is returning after having lived in the United States for many years. Mrs. Liang smokes, gossips, and loves to visit with Mr. Chu, and Chu's daughters soon believe they know what is happening: perhaps a permanent arrangement between their father and Mrs. Liang?

Old Wen collapses at work and is taken to the hospital, where Jia-Chien visits with him. Here he tells her that her father represses his emotions but that he loves her and is very proud of her. The next time she goes to visit Old Wen he has left for home, but further down the hallway she sees a familiar figure: her father, walking into the cardiovascular unit. At this moment her attitude toward her father changes: She believes he is keeping up a brave front but that his days are numbered, and when Old Wen dies on his first day back at work the reality of her father's age and the brevity of life overwhelms her.

The film *Eat Drink Man Woman* (Central Motion Pictures, 1994) explores updated versions of Confucian values in a modern Taiwanese family: When the oldest daughter believes that her father needs her, she gives up any idea of marriage (at least for a while); when, later, the middle daughter suspects that her father is ill, she gives up a career opportunity to stay with him. Here the middle daughter (Chien-Lien Wu) and her father (Sihung Lung) share a moment of understanding over an excellent dinner for two.

So when her promotion to the Amsterdam office comes through, she turns it down, to the surprise of her coworkers: She thinks her father needs her more.

Family developments continue, all announced during dinners: Jia-Ning has become pregnant and moves in with her new boyfriend; Jia-Jen falls in love with the new coach at her school and marries him in secret; and that leaves Chu and Jia-Chien alone in the big old house, except for visits from Mrs. Liang, her daughter, Jin-Rong, and little Shan-Shan.

But now Chu has an announcement to make, and he prepares a most elaborate dinner for everybody: the daughters and the two new husbands, Jin-Rong, her daughter and her mother. During the dinner he toasts his daughters, one toast after another, because he is trying to gather enough courage to say what must be said. The daughters, as well as Mrs. Liang, believe they know what he is going to say. Most believe that he will announce his engagement to Mrs. Liang; Jia-Chien believes the bad news about his health will finally come out. But Chu has something else on his mind. Proudly (and a bit drunkenly) he proclaims that he has sold the old house, shows Mrs. Liang his new health certificate to prove he is in great shape, and asks, formally, for her daughter's, Jin-Rong's, hand in marriage. Jin-Rong, the same age as his oldest daughter, Jia-Jen, sits modestly by his side, facing the incredulous family, and Mrs. Liang falls off her chair in a fainting spell. That was not the news she had expected. The evening ends in general emotional upheaval.

A few months later: Jin-Rong is pregnant and happy in their new house. Chu comes to visit the almost-empty old house for the last time and have a last meal there—but this time it is Jia-Chien who is cooking: Using her skills to prepare a meal the way her father has taught her, she proves that she really is a marvelous cook. And as they sit there, the two of them together, her father gently criticizing her food, he realizes that he can *taste* her soup—that his palate is functioning again and that for the first time in years he can taste food.

Study Questions

1. How does the filmmaker use food as a symbol in this film?

2. Describe the Confucian traditions in the film, and contrast them with the modern elements.

3. If you believed that your aging mother or father needed you, would you give up a promotion/transfer you had wanted in order to become a caregiver and stay at home for the remainder of your parent's life? Why or why not? How would Lin Yutang respond? How would Jane English respond?

Narrative

Pay It Forward

LESLIE DIXON (SCREENWRITER)
MIMI LEDER (DIRECTOR)

Film, 2000. Based on the book by Catherine Ryan Hyde. Summary.

This film can be viewed within several contexts in this book: One context is the virtue of gratitude, which is why it is placed in this chapter, but you could equally well view it in light of Chapter 4 and the discussions about selfishness and altruism.

On a rainy winter night, there is a hostage situation in Los Angeles. A young journalist's car is totaled by the fleeing hostage taker's SUV, and he is now stranded in the rain,

From the film *Pay It Forward:* For a short while, Trevor (Haley Joel Osment) is happy: He has brought his mother, Arlene (Helen Hunt), and his favorite teacher, Eugene Simonet (Kevin Spacey), together, and it looks as if things might be working out. But Trevor's violent, alcoholic father, Ricky, returns, and Arlene decides to give him another chance.

at night, in L.A. Out of the mist comes a man who hands the journalist the keys to his Jaguar. It's his to keep, says the stranger—"Call it generosity among strangers."

Cut to Las Vegas, four months earlier. It is the first day of school, and social studies teacher Eugene Simonet is giving his usual class introduction to the seventh grade. Simonet's face is disfigured after what looks like a burn accident, and he obviously has a chip on his shoulder. He asks the kids, Are they interested in the world? One of these days the world will be in their face, he says, and they may want to try to change it. So he gives them an assignment—the same he gives every year: "Think of an idea to change the world, and put it into action." An eleven-year old boy, Trevor, takes the idea to heart. On his way home he sees a homeless young man trying to eat garbage. The next thing we see is Trevor having dinner at home—cereal and milk—with the homeless man. Trevor's project is beginning to take shape, the *Pay it Forward* project. But his mother, Arlene, who is a waitress in a casino, comes across the homeless guy, Jerry, in her garage and is not enthusiastic; frightened and skeptical, she questions Trevor, who tells her it is an assignment. She goes to his school to confront Simonet. The meeting doesn't go well: Simonet is standoffish, and she resents him for being condescending. Arlene, divorced from Trevor's father, is an alcoholic. She comes home one day to find the homeless man, Jerry, in her garage—repairing her truck so she can sell it. He is already paying Trevor's good deed forward: Trevor gave him money so he could get cleaned up, and he found a job—and he'll try to kick his drug habit. Now Trevor explains his project in class: If we each help three strangers, and they in turn have to help three other strangers, then we will see a very rapid change for the better in the world. But each act of helping has to be a major, difficult thing, or it doesn't count. Simonet is impressed—it is the first new idea he has heard in his years of teaching.

Trevor experiences two setbacks—Jerry has a relapse into drugs, so now Trevor has to find someone else to help. He focuses on a small school friend who suffers from asthma and who is regularly tortured by two older boys; but when push comes to shove, Trevor can't make himself intervene. And the third person he has decided to help? Simonet. He wants him to date his mother, both for the teacher's sake and for Arlene's—because Arlene is an alcoholic and needs someone stable in her life, and if someone is there, then Trevor's father might not try to come back. We hear that Trevor's father, Ricky, has beaten up Arlene on several occasions, and we understand that Trevor is afraid the old pattern is going to repeat itself, in a never-ending circle of alcohol and violence. So now Trevor plays matchmaker for his mom and Eugene Simonet. Slowly the two warm up to each other and begin to understand that they are not trapped in roles where they are unloved and unwanted. For a short while they seem like a happy couple, and all three act like a content, normal nuclear family—until the return of Ricky puts an end to their happiness. Arlene decides to give Ricky another chance, and when Eugene blames her for exposing Trevor to danger, we finally hear the story behind Eugene's disfigurement: His own father was a violent alcoholic, and when Eugene was sixteen, he confronted his father—who beat him senseless, dragged him into the garage, doused him with gasoline, and set fire to him.

In the meantime, we hear more about the journalist who was given a Jaguar by a complete stranger. Intrigued, he has tracked down the owner and made him reveal why he gave away his car. He was "paying it forward"—after an immense gesture extended to him by a very unlikely character: He was in the emergency room with his daughter, who was suffering from an asthma attack, and the nurse wasn't paying attention to her. An injured man, a young black gangbanger, took charge and forced the nurse to help the gasping girl, firing his gun to make a point. The gunman went to prison, but the girl's life was saved. And the gunman told the father that he must pay the favor forward, to three people—so the journalist stuck in the rain was one.

The journalist seeks out the young black man in prison and gets him to tell his story by arranging an early parole date. The young man explains that he was running away from rival gang members in Vegas when an old white lady gave him a ride and saved his life—she was a bag lady, living out of her car, and she told him to pay it forward. So now the journalist must look for the old lady in Las Vegas, because he recognizes a good story when he sees one.

We meet Jerry one more time; he has left Las Vegas and gone up to the Pacific Northwest, without being able to kick his drug habit. Absorbed in his own misery, he crosses a bridge—and sees a woman about to jump to her death. He manages to talk her down and realizes that he is now paying it forward—Trevor's project is indeed spreading.

The journalist manages to find the bag lady, who tells her story. Her daughter had sought her out in one of the places where she'd normally drink herself into a stupor and spend the night, simply to tell her that she had forgiven her—for terrible things done to her when she was a child, by her mother's boyfriends while her mother was drunk. She will even let her mother visit with her son again, if the old lady can stay sober; and she has decided to forgive her mother because of an invention her son has made, which he calls "pay it forward." The daughter is, of course, Arlene, Trevor's mother. So now the journalist finally meets Trevor, the source of the project that is spreading like wildfire—to Los Angeles, San Francisco, Phoenix, and the Northwest. On his twelfth birthday he is interviewed by the journalist at the school. Trevor is not impressed with himself; he doesn't think he has succeeded, but he does tell the journalist that you have to try to make changes—that some people are so afraid of change, even for the better, that they just give up. Hearing these words, Eugene realizes that he is one of those people, and he and Arlene fall into each other's arms. And that night, Trevor's interview will be broadcast on national TV, and everyone will hear about the Pay It Forward project.

After the interview Trevor is about to leave the school and sees his friend, the asthmatic boy, again being attacked by the two older boys. Trevor wants so badly to make the world better, to make a difference—will he be able to help his friend this time? Will he be able to enjoy the changes he has indeed set in motion and have a real family life with his mother and Eugene? I will not reveal the ending of the film—you will have to watch it yourself.

Study Questions

1. What might Fred Berger say about showing one's gratitude by paying it forward? Would that be an appropriate reaction? Why or why not? What would Jane English say?

2. Could you undertake a project such as "Pay it Forward"? Whom would you choose to help? Remember the help must be big, and difficult for you, if it is to count. And what if someone chooses to do something special for you, as a "Pay it Forward" project—would you feel obliged to continue the project?

3. If you do a big favor for someone, would you be content with him or her paying it forward, or would you like a show of gratitude that is directed toward yourself?

4. From a realistic (some would say, cynical) point of view, is this a wise behavior model to follow? In 2003 a young girl was abducted and killed by a homeless man the family had invited home for dinner, and the same year Elizabeth Smart was abducted by a street person her father had hired as a handyman to help him out—but Elizabeth was rescued and returned safely nine months later. Is it advisable to do favors for strangers, as Trevor does? Are we being too cynical if we think of worst-case scenarios?

Chapter Twelve

Different Gender, Different Ethics?

*I*n this book we have examined prominent theories regarding ethics of conduct and virtue ethics, and their applications. As you have seen, both men and women have contributed to those theories, especially since the middle of the twentieth century. But in addition, there is a special branch of ethics dealing with the question of *gender*, and we generally label it *feminist ethics,* even if there is a great variety of opinions within this branch. Feminist ethics asks two separate, but related, questions: (1) Is there a morally correct way for society to approach the issue of gender equality? and (2) Is ethics gender-specific—meaning, is there an approach to ethics that is typical for women, and another for men? In this chapter we look at both issues.

If you ask a woman in the Western world today whether she is a feminist, chances are she will say no; if you ask her whether she believes that women and men should have equal opportunities, that women should not be discriminated against based on their gender, and that women and men should get equal pay for equal work, chances are she will say yes, and so will most men. That, according to classical feminism, qualifies anyone who agrees as a feminist, because those are the goals of classical feminism. But the word has today been weighed down by additional connotations to the extent that many people don't want to be associated with the idea of feminism; the term *feminazis,* coined by talk-show host Rush Limbaugh, hasn't helped any. Are feminists the same as feminazis? Not according to Limbaugh himself, who says he reserves the term "feminazis" for those he considers radicals. But the label "feminism" has caused some people to assume that all feminists somehow want to rule the world. If you believe that we should end sex discrimination and help create a friendly, cooperative working environment as well as private partnership for men and women based on equality, however, you are in fact a feminist, regardless of whether you are male or female according to many contemporary feminists.

Feminism and Virtue Theory

Originally, feminism was associated with acquiring political and social rights for women: the right to work, to own property, to vote, to get a divorce, and other rights considered irrelevant for women by most thinkers with political influence until well into the nineteenth century. Later in the chapter we take a brief look at that development. During its struggle for political equality, feminism rarely regarded itself as a separate moral theory; the male-dominated (often called *patriarchal* by feminists) world would often point to women's sensibilities as those of a higher moral view (think of the role of the schoolmarm in Western movies, exercising her civilizing influence), but because that was usually coupled with an assumption that women were unfit for life in the rough and heartless real world of men, early feminists usually placed little emphasis on that notion. However, a connection not just to ethics as such but to virtue theory as well has become apparent in the past decades.

For modern virtue theory the important question is, How should I be? In other words, What is the character I should strive for? The moral rules of "doing unto others," of "universalizing one's maxim," of "maximizing happiness for as many as possible," and of "treating everyone with impartial fairness" take second place to virtues such as loyalty to family and friends, generosity, compassion, and courage. A moral vice may, under such circumstances, very well turn out to be related to a famous rule of moral conduct: If you act only when you can imagine others being allowed to do the same thing (Kant's categorical imperative), then your child or friend may die while you wonder about allowing all others to defend their child or friend. If you insist on treating everyone with impartial fairness (John Rawls's "original position"), you have an equal obligation to a starving person on the other side of the world and to your niece down the street; you have no right to prefer helping your niece. Virtue ethics, however, discards that approach as a breach of loyalty and family responsibility and insists that you *should* help your niece before you spread yourself thin helping strangers. And you can be accused of the same vice if you are trying to make strangers happy (the principle of utility) at the expense of the needs of your family.

This is where the connection to modern feminism comes in. You have already read, in Chapter 7, that Rawls was criticized for assuming we can pretend to be just strangers to one another to achieve fairness. In this chapter we will take a look at the modern feminist theory that is the basis for that criticism, a theory that suggests that women and men tend to view the entire field of ethics from different viewpoints. Whereas men (who have written most of the theories about ethics, law, and justice

Baby Blues by Rick Kirkman and Jerry Scott

© Baby Blues Partnership. King Features Syndicate.

The dismayed homemaker mom in Kirkman and Scott's *Baby Blues* is observing her kids reenact a debate that has been known to happen but that was—arguably—not intended by most feminists: that gender equality should mean more advantages for the girls, and fewer for the boys! Do you think Mom is being serious in her answer to her young son?

Box 12.1   SEX OR GENDER?

By consensus, the term that is most commonly used today when people talk about sexual differences that go beyond mere biological functions is *gender.* Although this used to be a strictly grammatical term, it now is used as a sociopolitical term instead of the biological term *sexual.*

so far) tend to think of morality in terms of *rules of conduct,* justice, and fairness, says the theory, women tend to think of morality in terms of relationships, of staying friends, and of caring for those who are close to you or for whom you have accepted responsibility. In other words, women tend to think in terms of the *virtues* of caring, loyalty, and compassion. That theory is advanced by the psychologist Carol Gilligan, and we look at her ideas in further detail later. But first we must take a look at the idea of gender equality: What is it? Do we have it now? And what has been done to achieve it?

What Is Gender Equality?

The purpose of feminism throughout its history, with a few exceptions (such as the 1960s women's organization SCUM, Society for Cutting Up Men, which may or may not have been meant as a joke), has been to achieve equality for the sexes. Today many refer to that goal as *gender equality.* (See Box 12.1 for an explanation of "sex" versus "gender.") You know from Chapter 7 that the principle of equality does not imply that everyone is the same but that everyone should be treated as equals unless special circumstances apply. But what exactly does that entail when applied to the two sexes? Below we look at the concepts of cultural as well as biological equality.

Gender and Language

Since the Enlightenment and on into the twenty-first century, it has been customary to use words of the masculine gender to refer to both males and females. For many of us it is surprising to learn that the term *man* in some political statements, such as the American Declaration of Independence ("All men are created equal"), may not have been intended to cover women or people of color—an issue that is being discussed among constitutional scholars today.

It is not true, of course, that the term *men* can *always* be used to include women; it doesn't make any sense to say, for instance, that half of all men have ovaries and half don't. Today, the use of the terms *he* and *men* to include women is considered by many to be discriminatory. And even though very few men or women ever intended discrimination by using the word *he* for a man or a woman and *man* for all humankind, we now are moving away from what is known as "gender-specific" language toward "gender-neutral" language, because many believe that even when used with the best intentions, gender-specific terms subconsciously tell us that being male is somehow more important than being female and that certain social roles are best

Box 12.2   THE ISSUE IS MANHOLE COVERS

People often seem to feel that we are getting too radical in our elimination of gender-specific terms. It may make sense to do away with words such as *chairman* and *fireman* and use *chairperson* and *firefighter* instead, but what about all the words in the English language that just happen to include a gender-specific term but for which there is no graceful substitute? Will *freshman* now be *freshperson*? Do we have to say *personhole* cover instead of *manhole* cover? How about *manpower*? And *manned space missions*? (And, jokesters might ask, how about *man*-ipulate? and *his*-tory?) Other languages present similar challenges, but some languages have less of a problem finding a common word for humanity. German has a specific term for "human being"— *Der Mensch*—which is different from the terms for man and woman but which still includes a gender-specific term (*Mensch,* which is masculine in gender). In Danish the word for "human being" is a gender-neutral term, *Et Menneske.* And in Swedish, the term for "human being" is *En Människa,* a grammatically feminine word! To make matters even more interesting, there is a

word in ancient Icelandic, *man,* that means slave/maid/mistress! Apparently that word has no connection with the ancient Germanic word for man (*Madr*), which is the source for the term *man* in English.

So, getting back to the manhole covers, what should we do? Change some words and not others? Manhole covers have actually been referred to as "utility covers" in recent years. So should we change all such words? Leave them all the way they are? Two things are at stake here: the self-esteem of half the English-speaking population and the comfort of those used to an established language. We can choose from among four major courses of action: (1) Forcibly change language to some degree (and we have seen that this can be done within a generation). (2) Wait until a new gender-neutral terminology evolves by itself, in response to the changing times. (3) Make a distinction between sexist and nonsexist terms and change only the blatantly sexist ones. (4) Insist on keeping the traditional terms. What would you suggest?

performed by men. The real reason for being sensitive about gender and language is, of course, to achieve gender equality. (Box 12.2 provides a discussion of issues involved in gender-neutral language.)

Textbooks and cultural documents are continually being reworded to accommodate our new sensitivity toward gender and language. The Catholic Church has officially endorsed the use of non-gender-specific language in religious documents and biblical translations. Gender-specific words such as *mailman, chairman, housewife,* and *maid* have been changed to *mail carrier, chairperson, homemaker,* and *maintenance assistant* to signify that those terms cover both genders. Writers and speakers alike are instructed to avoid the use of *he* as a generic term and instead use *he or she, they, one,* or *you.* College students are urged to avoid gender-specific language in their term papers. Perhaps you think this is a subject of little importance—that it is merely a matter of semantic misunderstanding. But consider this: If you are male and you hear a statement such as "Now is the time for every man to stand up for what he believes in," there is a good chance you will feel somehow compelled to think hard about what you believe in. If you are female, you *may* feel the same way, but chances are you will feel, subconsciously, that somehow that statement does not apply to you; you may even think, "Yes, it is about time *they* pulled *themselves* together!" If even a few women feel excluded when they read or hear language that uses the masculine gender—excluded either in the sense of feeling left out or in the sense of not having to get involved—then that is enough reason to make some changes in the way we phrase things.

Is Biology Destiny?

When we ask whether sexual equality exists, we really are asking one of two questions: (1) Does cultural and social equality exist? or (2) Does biological equality? The first question is relative to the historical time period: Today we have reason to say that we have not reached total equality yet, but we hope to do so in the future. (In the past, in Western society, the answer would have been a flat no.) But if we ask the second question, we have to ask a follow-up question: What do we mean by "biological equality"? Do we mean that men and women are the same? or similar? That they will do similar things in similar situations? Or perhaps that they have a similar genetic makeup, even if there are cultural differences?

The bottom line is the difference between a descriptive and a normative approach. A descriptive theory of equality compares capabilities and pronounces people to be "similar" or "dissimilar." A normative theory of equality may or may not look at the "facts" presented by the descriptive theory but states that people *ought* to be treated a certain way—(1) the same, or (2) similarly under similar conditions, or (3) differently. And if a normative theory asserts that equality is a good thing, it will present a theory for how to achieve it.

Sexual equality, as an idea, is a complex issue. (The same is true of racial equality.) We must ask, Is sexual equality a biological fact? What does that mean? And is that important for an ethical policy? Let us look at what it means first. Are men and women biologically equal? We all know that, physically, most men are taller and stronger than most women, but that doesn't mean individual women can't be taller and stronger than individual men. In nature there is such a thing as *sexual dimorphism,* meaning that the two sexes of a species look very different, with one sex usually being much bigger than the other. (A consequence of dimorphism is usually that the bigger sex dominates the smaller sex and that one individual of the bigger sex can have many mates of the smaller sex, but not vice versa. Where the sexes are of the same size there are usually lifelong monogamous relationships and equal partnerships.) So do humans have sexual dimorphism? Not nearly to the extreme that gorillas do but slightly more than bonobo chimpanzees do; gorilla society is male-dominated, but bonobo chimpanzees, our closest relatives on this earth, have a gender-equal society with a tendency toward matriarchy. Biologically, there is no reason to assume that it is natural for one human gender to dominate the other, but neither can we conclude that we have an obvious natural tendency to be completely equal partners.

But are we then biologically equal when it comes to the *intellect*? The viewpoints on male and female intelligence are diverse, stretching from the old assumption that men are logical and women are not, to the assumption shared by many modern people that if we are intellectually different at all it is merely a subtle difference, to the view that women's intellectual style is superior to that of men. What exactly would intellectual equality mean? That we reach the same results when faced with the same problem? Or that we reach the same results *the same way* when faced with the same problem? Recent studies of the human brain have revealed that men and women actually use their brains differently when dealing with the same math problems, but they generally reach the same results in the same amount of time.

But whether we talk about physical or intellectual equality, some philosophers would call out a warning: Looking for actual equality is one thing, and perhaps a positive one, but if we intend our policy of gender equality to rest on a foundation of what we think is *actual, biological equality,* then we may be in trouble, because what if scientists someday prove that biologically we really are not the same at all? Then our reason for gender equality has disappeared, and we may slide back into some form of gender discrimination against women or against men. Better to forget about looking for actual similarities and concentrate on making a policy based on *what we would like to see happen:* Instead of using *descriptive* means to make us politically equal, let us use normative means, spelling out how we ought to treat each other. Remember from Chapter 5 that if we try to go from fact to policy, from an "is" to an "ought," then we are committing the *naturalistic fallacy,* basing a policy on fact without adding a moral premise. But that doesn't mean we can't take biology into account when we establish policies. The idea of sexual, or rather *gender,* equality is so important now that we have antidiscrimination laws against "sexism." In other words, we believe that regardless of whether equality between the genders is a natural fact, it should be a cultural institution. Box 12.3 explores one aspect of normative equality: The issue of women in combat.

Women's Historical Role in the Public Sphere

Gender equality is, of course, a novel idea in Western history. Until the mid–nineteenth century it was common practice in Western culture to assume that male and female natures were essentially different in their functions, aspirations, and potential, and that male nature was somehow more *normal* than female nature. It was not thought of as necessarily *better,* for, as I mentioned earlier, many men seemed to believe that women had higher moral standards; but it was considered more important in the sense that male nature was more representative of the human species than female nature was. What was that assumption based on? Today we might say *prejudice,* but it can't be dismissed as easily as that, because for a great many thinkers, objectivity was an important ideal. They tried to describe things as they saw them, not as they believed things ought to be, nor as they might appear to an undiscerning eye. And what they saw was that few women had any role to play in public life: There were few women politicians, few women artists, few women scientists. But why were there so few women in public life? The answer is tentative; not all the facts are in yet. It seems obvious, though, that a person's contribution to what we call public life is greatly dependent on that person feeling called or welcome as a contributor. If no one expects or wants you to become a good politician or mathematician or sculptor, you might not think of trying. Encouragement and expectation are major factors in such

Box 12.3   WOMEN IN COMBAT?

Should women be soldiers? Whether you agree or not, the fact is that women are in the armed forces, and have been, in some capacity, since before World War I, starting with the creation of the Army Nurse Corps in 1901 and the Navy Nurse Corps in 1908. It wasn't until 1948, however, that women got permanent status in the armed forces with President Truman's signing of the Women's Armed Services Integration Act. In 1967 president Johnson made it theoretically possible for women to advance to the top. Today women constitute nearly 15 percent of the U.S. Army, but only 6 percent of the Marine Corps. The issue today is not whether women should be soldiers but whether they should be allowed in combat.

The debate is, of course, more complex than a box can do justice to, but at least we can outline the main arguments:

Those in favor of allowing women in combat argue that

- It is a natural progression toward complete gender equality in a modern society.
- Qualified women can be as effective, and as brave, as their male counterparts.
- Many women want to serve their country in combat; and if they qualify, it would be unfair to exclude them.

- Since combat experience is necessary for officers' advancement within the military, it is discriminatory to exclude women officers—it maintains a glass ceiling.

Those against allowing women in combat argue that

- Women simply aren't "qualified," except for perhaps a very few. The training criteria for a combat soldier include carrying a heavy backpack plus weapon during a forced march, and the vast majority of even very motivated women just can't do that. And if standards are lowered so more women qualify, the effectiveness of the forces will be diminished, and soldiers put in unnecessarily dangerous situations.

- It is dangerous for the male soldiers to have female comrades-in-arms: Because of a natural chivalry and an instinct to protect, the male soldiers will be more focused on protecting their female colleagues and may become distracted from their battle training.

- Women POWs are in greater danger of being raped than male POWs, and threats or violence against the female POWs could become an element in the enemy's interrogation techniques, wearing down the resistance of the male POWs.

choices. On the other hand, if it appears that you are *destined* for a certain task, you might not question that either. For most women (until the arrival of dependable birth control), motherhood, several times over, was their destiny. And for those familiar with the demands of large families, it does not come as news that the person in charge of the *private sphere,* the home, has precious little time for anything else, unless she can afford domestic help. Indeed, throughout history—Western history as well as world history—most cultural contributions by individual women were made by those who did not play the role of homemaker.

"Woman's Work"

An interesting question is why women's contributions to the private sphere are rarely discussed. It's certainly true that when women could not own property, vote,

In March 2003 several women soldiers were among the prisoners of war in Iraq: You have already read about Jessica Lynch in Chapter 11; her close friend and comrade in arms, Private Lori Piestewa (right), a Hopi Indian, was killed in the ambush where Jessica was injured and taken prisoner. In the same ambush, Private Shoshana Johnson (left) became the first female black prisoner of war in U.S. war history. She, along with several male soldiers, was captured during the U.S. advance on Baghdad; but with the collapse of the Iraqi government, their captors vanished, and they were rescued by the advancing U.S. forces.

- It is simply uncivilized to have women in combat.

In your view, which arguments carry the most weight? Can you think of additional arguments for or against women in combat? In Chapter 11

you read about Private Jessica Lynch's ordeal and rescue as a POW during the war in Iraq. Two other women were captured in the same incident during the early weeks of the war: Private Lori Piestewa, Lynch's friend, and Private Shoshana Johnson, also an army maintenance soldier. Johnson made it back injured, but alive, while Piestewa died from her wounds. None of these three women had been trained for combat except for a few hours of basic weapons training: They were all members of a maintenance unit, but even so, they found themselves in a confrontation with the enemy. There is little doubt that they acted as soldiers with backbone and courage, and some advocates of women in combat have argued that their fortitude proves that women can be good combat soldiers. Others have pointed out that their ordeal proves what a thoroughly bad idea it is for military women to be present, not only in combat, but anywhere near the front lines. Has the story of these three women changed, or perhaps solidified, your view about allowing women to be trained for combat?

or hold a job without the permission of a guardian, many women still had considerable power within the four walls of their home. They managed the bookkeeping and purchases, planned and prepared meals for the household, educated the children, and kept things running on the farm—a full-time job in itself. Why were those management skills not considered important? In an odd way, they were; it is probably our modern-day prejudice to think that they weren't. A young woman chosen as a spouse was expected to have those skills, and "woman's work" was a vitally important social factor. But in the public sphere, women had no place and were not considered potential contributors until almost the end of the nineteenth century. (That assertion, of course, refers to women from middle- and upper-middle-class backgrounds; many working-class women have, for as long as there has been a working class, generally participated in the public sphere, simply because they have had no choice. If a widow with small children didn't enter the workforce, her children might starve to death—and she too.) Even today, many people accept the idea that the public sphere is the vital one—perhaps because work in the public sphere is *paid for* and work in the private sphere generally is not. However, asking whether women's work has been valued may in itself be choosing the viewpoint of the public sphere in which men have traditionally determined values; women have traditionally always valued one another's work, learned from it, criticized it, improved it, and shared it. From a traditional woman's point of view, the question of public (male) recognition for her work may not be the most important question: What may matter more is receiving recognition and appreciation for her work from her peers in the community, other women.

Another factor must be mentioned here. In early times, having women remain outside the public sphere was thought by most men (and women too) to be a way of *protecting* women; they were spared the unpleasantness and insecurity of the world of affairs. That is the viewpoint of the Arab fundamentalist culture, where much the same pattern prevails today. Some critics believe it can be interpreted as a way of treating women as *property* (namely the property of their fathers and husbands)—as an investment in the next generation and as a working resource.

The Goddess Theory: Women Before Patriarchy

This pattern of women being excluded from the public sphere may seem so ancient that we believe it has always existed. However, a theory advanced by many feminist scholars today is that the subjection of women to men (which we know as a historical fact going back at least three thousand years) may not have been the ancient order of things. You may remember that John Stuart Mill was a nineteenth-century advocate of women's rights (see Chapter 5). In his book *The Subjection of Women* (1869) he says that we don't know what it would be like for women not to be subjected to men because they always have been. But he may well have been wrong, because archaeological evidence (artifacts and written documents) now points to the possibility of women having had far more influence in early Middle Eastern and African cultures than we used to think. In what is now Turkey, there appear to have been civilizations more than ten thousand years ago who revered a mother goddess of fertility; in Greek and Middle Eastern legends, we find ancient myths of a creator goddess and powerful priestesses and queens. Similarly, African legends suggest a strong memory of a mother goddess and of women who had much social power in their communities. Whether we should call those ancient cultures *matriarchal* is open to question because we have no evidence that they were *ruled* by women, but there is tentative evidence that until some gradual cultural change toward patriarchy happened around thirty-five hundred years ago, women in the Old World had higher social standing than they did later. Part of that social standing may have derived from the local religions' belief in a creator goddess rather than a creator god.

Further challenges to the universality of patriarchy have come from other parts of the world: In the American Indian tradition, women were considered respected, full members of the community with rights to have their own opinions and to choose a husband and divorce him. Furthermore, in Eastern tribes it was not uncommon for the chief to be a woman. However, according to American Indian historian Paula Gunn Allen, the European settlers rarely reported that fact, and history books have most often referred to those chiefs as being male. At various times and places in human history, women seem to have had considerably more social influence than they have had in the Western world of the past several thousand years except for the past five decades.

A place where goddess worship may have lasted longer than most other places, and where women may have had comparatively more influence, was Ireland before the advent of Christianity with Saint Patrick in 435. And for centuries after Christianity took hold, the high public standing of women that was a legacy of the goddess religion remained a factor in Ireland. Saint Brigit of Kildare (453–525) was raised by the pagan Druid priesthood but was attracted to Christianity. She was ordained as a bishop by mistake, instead of as a nun, as a result of the wrong oath being administered. It initiated a new tradition, and from then on until the Vikings arrived several hundred years later, women in Ireland could become bishops. Irish bishops generally had a more gender-egalitarian view of women than the rest of Europe did, and when in 900 a European bishops' council convened to decide whether women had souls, the yes votes won—by one vote. That vote came from an Irish bishop.

Losing Ground: The Middle Ages

In the European convents of the early Middle Ages, women received an education that allowed them to become medical practitioners, illustrators, composers, and writers, aside from having clerical powers equal to the male clergy of the monasteries. One such woman was Hildegard of Bingen (1098–1179), a German abbess. She was given to the Church at the age of eight and began having visions at an early age. She wrote a number of books on God's plan for humanity, two about her visions, and another two on science and nature. She composed liturgical songs, and wrote what is recognized as the first morality play about the battle between good and evil, *Ordo Virtuem*. She founded her own convent, Rupertsberg, where her music was performed. Toward the end of her life she offered her writings to the new University of Paris, only to suffer the indignity of having them rejected on the grounds that she was a woman.

In the twelfth to fourteenth centuries, women lost ground within the Catholic Church. New policies deprived abbesses of their right to hear confessions, and convents that had functioned as hospitals and social safety nets for the community were closed down or transformed into isolated cloisters. No secular schools had been founded yet, and young women were now barred from a religious education. The reason may seem strangely arbitrary to a modern person: To be accepted as a student, receive an education, and communicate with God, the young acolyte's head had to be shaved into a tonsure. But according to Scripture (in particular

Box 12.4   SOR JUANA INEZ DE LA CRUZ

In seventeenth-century Mexico, still a colony of Spain, the concept of women's rights was advocated and, in a sense, embodied by a nun, Sor Juana Inez de la Cruz (1651–1695). Born Juana Inés de Asbaje y Ramírez de Santillana, she was the illegitimate child of a Spanish father and a Creole mother. A child prodigy, she educated herself by voraciously reading books in her grandfather's library. At the age of fifteen, she was introduced in court to the viceroy and his wife, who took her on as a lady-in-waiting and created an intellectual environment for her as entertainment for the court. At twenty she entered a convent but continued her intellectual pursuits, and over the years she amassed a library consisting of over four thousand volumes. Sor Juana wrote secular love poetry, songs, and plays, including comedies, received commissions, and lived to see her works published both in Mexico and in Spain. But with the departure of the viceroy and his family for Spain, she lost her protection against the pressures of the Catholic Church to conform to traditional convent life. Her professional struggle for her rights as an intellectual within the Church began in 1691: When attacked by a bishop whose sermon she had criticized, she wrote a statement that has earned her the title of the first feminist in the Americas, *Respuesta a Sor Filotea* ("Response to Sor Filotea," the bishop's pseudonym), in which she referred to the culture of Mexican women and to a woman's right to disagree with authorities. But shortly afterward she gave away all her books and artifacts, and in a statement signed in her own blood she resolved to dedicate the rest of her life to helping the poor. In 1695, when she was forty-four, she was helping infected nuns during an epidemic, caught the illness herself, and died.

Paul's first letter to the Corinthians), women not only weren't allowed to shave their heads but also were supposed to hide their hair under a veil when in the presence of God. And since you can't have a tonsure, and thus be eligible for a religious education, while having a full head of hair and wearing a veil, the tonsure policy kept women out of schools. Even so, some nuns, such as Sor Juana Inez de la Cruz, rose to intellectual prominence (see Box 12.4).

First-, Second-, and Third-Wave Feminism

We often hear feminism referred to as "first wave," "second wave," and "third wave." Those chronological terms form a time line for awareness of women's social situation. Box 12.6 gives a brief overview of this timeline. The first wave generally refers to the feminist movement in the West from its early beginnings in the seventeenth century to the accomplishment of its most urgent goal, the right for women to vote. In 1869 women in Wyoming gained the right to vote, but general suffrage for women wasn't obtained in the United States until 1920. In the meantime, New Zealand women had been included as voters in 1893; in 1902 Australia followed suit. Norway joined the list in 1913, and Denmark in 1915. So, too, did Canada, England, Germany, and Austria after World War I, in 1918. Sweden gave women the

English philosopher Mary Wollstonecraft (1759–1797), wrote *A Vindication of the Rights of Women*, which was much ridiculed at the time by male scholars but would have a lasting influence. Wollstonecraft died in childbirth, giving life to a second Mary Wollstonecraft, who, under her married name, Shelley, was to give life to another kind of creature with the story of Frankenstein and his monster.

right to vote in 1921, but it wasn't until 1944 that French women could go to the polls, and Mexico followed in 1947. Switzerland waited until 1971, and in 1994 black women gained full suffrage in South Africa. In 2004 Afghani women became voters, but women in Saudi Arabia still cannot vote. What began as furtive discussions four hundred years ago has still not reached full global implementation.

Early Feminism in France and England

A very early speaker for the rights of women was the French thinker Poulain de la Barre, who in 1673 argued that men and women are fundamentally similar because they have the same powers of reasoning. Poulain believed women should have access to all occupations in society, even as generals in the army and leaders of Parliament. Few people paid much attention to Poulain, however; he remained both unique and unknown as a seventeenth-century feminist. During the French Revolution (begun in 1789), things changed considerably in France. Women began to let their voices be heard in the pre-Revolution debate: Olympe de Gouges wrote the *Declaration of the Rights of Woman and the Female Citizen* in 1791, in which she argued for complete equality between men and women, including rights to vote, to own property, to serve in the military, and to hold office. During the Revolution she wrote over thirty pamphlets and considered herself a revolutionary, but since she was against the killing of the royal family, she was targeted as an anti-revolutionary and was beheaded during the Reign of Terror in 1793 at the age of forty-eight. Another high-profile woman was Madame Zepherine d'Epinay, who believed that women and men have the same nature and the same constitution and will display different virtues and vices only if they are brought up that way; any differentiation is due to social pressure, nothing else. Her ideas inspired the philosopher the marquis de Condorcet, who in 1792 suggested that education should be available to women because both men and women were, primarily, members of the human race. Condorcet's opponent, Talleyrand, who was inspired by the social critic Jean-Jacques Rousseau, managed to put a stop to those ideas, which, it seems, were too radical even for the revolutionaries. Thus the view of Rousseau, which had become popular in the late eighteenth century—that men should live in a democracy of equals but that their women belonged at home as intelligent but subordinate partners to their spouses—became the official view of the gender issue in France of the early nineteenth century.

In eighteenth-century England there were voices—male as well as female—that argued for the possibility of a different order. The British philosopher Mary Wollstonecraft (1759–1797) was one of the few women of the eighteenth century who directly addressed women's situation. (See Box 12.5 for a short list of other women ethicists before the twentieth century.) In *A Vindication of the Rights of Women* (1792), she suggested not only that it is unfair to women to socialize them to be uneducated, unthinking creatures who are only eager to please but also that it is unfair to men, because although a man may fall in love with that kind of woman, he certainly won't want to live with her. After all, what will the two have in common once the seduction is over and they are married? No, Wollstonecraft wrote, women should have the same opportunities as men. If they don't measure up, men will have reason to claim superiority; but to apply two different value systems—one that says what is proper for men and one that says what is proper for women—is to make a mockery of the concept of virtue itself:

> I wish to persuade women to endeavour to acquire strength, both of mind and body, and to convince them that the soft phrases, susceptibility of heart, delicacy of sentiment, and refinement of taste, are almost synonymous with epithets of weakness, and that those beings who are only the objects of pity and that kind of love, which has been termed its sister, will soon become objects of contempt. . . . Besides, the woman who strengthens her body and exercises her mind will, by managing her family and practicing various virtues, become the friend, and not the humble dependent of her husband.

In the nineteenth century John Stuart Mill, inspired by his longtime intellectual friend (and later wife) Harriet Taylor, wrote about how women's as well as men's characters are molded by society:

> All women are brought up from the earliest years in the belief that their ideal of character is the very opposite to that of men; not self-will, and government by self-control, but submission, and yielding to the control of others. All the moralities tell them that it is the duty of women, and all the current sentimentalities that it is their nature, to live for others.

Under different social circumstances, Mill says, we would see women acting no longer as the full-time slaves of their husbands but as independent individuals with original intellectual ideas to contribute to society. If women are capable of fulfilling social functions, they should be free to do so. If it is impossible for a woman to do certain things because of her nature, then what need is there to prohibit her from doing them? The old saying "'ought' implies 'can'" applies: You can't tell someone she ought (or ought not) to do something unless she is actually able to do it. Mill does believe that male and female qualities in general are not the same—that men and

Box 12.5   WOMEN MORAL PHILOSOPHERS

Carol Gilligan is right in saying that the famous and influential moral theories within the Western philosophical tradition have until recently all been expressed by male thinkers. That does not mean, however, that there have been no women moral thinkers in Western history aside from Mary Wollstonecraft and Harriet Taylor Mill; here is a small selection from a list of more than thirty names in the *Encyclopedia of Ethics* of women ethicists (Western as well as Eastern) from the earliest years of philosophy to the nineteenth century. I don't wish to imply that women's contributions to ethics until the twentieth century can be contained in a box. However, most of these names are not generally well known, and before the twentieth century women thinkers had very little influence in philosophy. This list demonstrates that there were women who could and did think and write during times when women were discouraged or even banned from taking part in intellectual life. In all probability there were many more thinking and writing women than history has recorded.

Phintys of Sparta (c. 420 B.C.E.) held that it was not unfitting for women to philosophize and that courage, justice, and wisdom were common to women as well as men; in the tradition of Greek moral thinking (which you will recognize from Aristotle, who was not born yet when Phintys wrote her book, *On the Moderation of Women*), she recommends moderation in all things as a virtue for women.

Makrina of Neocaesaria (c. 300 C.E.) so impressed her brother, the Bishop of Nyssa, that he cited her moral philosophy in his own writings. Makrina was familiar with Plato's philosophy and taught that women were created in God's image and had rational souls; with a rational soul, one is capable of becoming morally virtuous and thus eligible for entry into heaven after death, she believed.

Murasaki Shikibu (978–c. 1031) was a Japanese courtier who, in her novel *Genji Monogatari*

(*The Tale of Genji*), which is considered the first real novel, led her main character, the woman Ukifune, to a realization of freedom and moral responsibility in the face of existential dread. Today this story is seen as an early exploration of the key themes of existentialism as they were later defined in the Western world of the twentieth century.

Christine de Pizan (1365–1431) wrote a book, *Cité des Dames* (*The City of Women*), in which she envisioned women living in a community to protect themselves from physical and moral harm. She argued that oppression of women was counterproductive to the improvement of society and that women should strive to avoid activities that dull their intellect, since they were limited by certain social roles.

Marie le Jars de Gournay (1565–1645) was the editor of Montaigne's *Essays* and wrote in a work of her own, *Egalité des Hommes et des Femmes* (*Equality Between Men and Women*), that women are equal to men in their capacity for moral reasoning and action. She believed that sexual differences are related exclusively to reproduction and have otherwise no bearing on male or female nature.

Mary Astell (1666–1731) worked on a synthesis of the traditions of Locke and Descartes and believed that reason ought to govern our passions. The only way to accomplish that, she said, was to have universal education for women as well as for men.

Antoinette Brown Blackwell (1825–1921) was the first ordained American woman. She was a prolific writer of philosophy and theology and maintained that women and men make moral judgments differently; in a forerunner of Gilligan's argument about an ethic of justice and an ethic of care, Blackwell claimed that women bring compassion to justice and caring to the concept of rights.

Box 12.6   FIRST-, SECOND-, AND THIRD-WAVE FEMINISM: A BRIEF OVERVIEW

We generally talk about the development of feminism in America as a phenomenon in three waves: "first," "second," and "third" wave. The first wave is considered as having its official starting point in 1848 with the Women's Rights Convention in Seneca Falls, led by Lucretia Mott and Elizabeth Cady Stanton, and culminating with the Nineteenth Amendment in 1920, which granted women the right to vote. The philosophy and goals of the first wave of feminism were straightforward: rights for women to self-determination; rights to inherit and own property, even in marriage (as opposed to the ownership of one's inherited or earned property passing to one's husband); rights to raise one's children; and, above all, *suffrage* (the right to vote). The second wave was ushered in with the publication of Betty Friedan's book *The Feminine Mystique* in 1963. (In France, a similar reaction followed the publication of Simone de Beauvoir's *The Second Sex* in 1949; see chapter text). For most feminists of the second wave, the primary goal was the creation of an equal-opportunity society without discrimination because of one's sex—a society in which women, as well as men, would be able to freely choose their way of life and occupations; a common focus was on the upbringing of boys and girls, attempting to change the stereotypical gender roles to a more egalitarian pattern. (See the discussion of classical feminism in the next section.) For all second-wave feminists, a common goal was a complete and discrimination-free access for women to any education or profession they might be interested in and qualified for. Some feminists see that job as accomplished in the early twenty-first century, but others believe there is still much work to be done to achieve complete gender equality.

The beginning of the third wave is sometimes identified with the publication of Carol Gilligan's *In a Different Voice* (1982; see chapter text), and sometimes with the publication of Susan Faludi's *Backlash: The Undeclared War Against American Women* (1991). Other events that helped start the new wave were the 1991 Senate hearings into charges that Supreme Court nominee Clarence Thomas had sexually harassed law professor Anita Hill, his former aide. (Box 12.7 discusses the topic of sexual harassment.) Another was the 1992 election, which saw a large number of women elected to office, perhaps as a result of the much-publicized hearings. The philosophy of the third wave is less clearly defined than those of the first two waves: Radical feminism focuses on identifying and eliminating the roots of still-existing discrimination; other third-wave feminists focus on specific issues, such as feminist environmentalism, easier access to child care for working women, and combating racial and economic discrimination. For further discussion of the first-, second-, and third-wave phenomenon, visit the website (www.mhhe.com/rosenstand6e).

women are usually good at different things—but that from a moral point of view those qualities should be considered equally important. So what might Mill say about the current controversy as to whether women soldiers should be allowed in combat? Probably that most women would prefer not to and would not qualify but that those who want to and who do qualify should be allowed to do so. At the end of the chapter you can read Harriet Taylor Mill's own argument for why women should be allowed in the workforce.

Box 12.7 WHAT IS SEXUAL HARASSMENT?

Since the 1970s sexual discrimination has been unacceptable in most Western cultures, but it is only within the past few decades that *sexual harassment* has been identified as a related but separate problem. Unfortunately, there is little clarity about what exactly sexual harassment means. Does it mean that someone at your workplace or your school corners you and touches you? or cracks sexist or obscene jokes in your presence? Does it mean that someone compliments you on your looks? Or that someone from your workplace or your school asks you out? What seems like sexual harassment to one person may not look like it to another, and that is why there are now guidelines for the perplexed. According to the California Fair Employment and Housing Act, sexual harassment consists of

- Unwanted sexual advances
- Offering employment benefits in exchange for sexual favors
- Making or threatening reprisals after a negative response to sexual advances
- Visual conduct: leering, making sexual gestures, displaying of sexually suggestive objects or pictures, cartoons, or posters
- Verbal conduct: making or using derogatory comments, epithets, slurs, and jokes
- Verbal sexual advances or propositions
- Verbal abuse of a sexual nature; graphic verbal commentaries about an individual's body; sexually degrading words used to describe an individual; suggestive or obscene letters, notes, or invitations
- Physical conduct: touching, assault, impeding or blocking movements

From this list it is obvious that cornering and touching an employee is sexual harassment, regardless of whether the cornered person is male or female. But what about asking someone out? That should depend on whether the advance is considered sexual and whether or not it is wanted, and that would certainly be a case-by-case judgment. And could complimenting someone on her, or his, looks be construed as "verbal abuse"? Under certain circumstances it might, and that is what frustrates so many people, mostly men who are used to showing friendliness by complimenting female employees. To determine whether sexual harassment has taken place, review boards often ask the person making the complaint if he or she perceived the situation as being one of sexual harassment; it is thus the *perception* of the victimized person that will stand in many cases, not the *intention* of the perceived victimizer.

To avoid all such situations, some simple rules of the road are suggested: If you are in a superior position, at school or in the workplace, don't go out with someone in a position that you may be able to influence, because it can be seen as a "benefit/reprisal" situation of pressure, with the other person's job or grades on the line. In addition, others may view your date as now having an unfair advantage in terms of grades or the job. Some schools are moving toward banning all relationships between instructors and students, as some workplaces are banning relationships between coworkers, to avoid misunderstandings, ill will after relationships end, and (let's be realistic) lawsuits—because, as the guidelines based on the Fair Employment and Housing Act read, "If harassment occurs, an employer may be liable even if management was not aware of the harassment."

SALLY FORTH *by GREG HOWARD and CRAIG MacINTOSH*

Reprinted with special permission of King Features Syndicate.

Classical feminism taught that if gender differences are perpetuated, it is to the detriment of women's freedom. One of the traditions discarded by classical feminists was chivalry: men holding doors for women, pulling out chairs, and so on. The underlying assumption, said classical feminism, was that women are too weak or stupid to do things themselves, so chivalry was, in effect, demeaning to women. Now, in the age of third-wave feminism, opinion is divided as to traditional male chivalry. What do you think—can men be chivalrous to women without being sexists? Should women also hold doors for men? Would that be a veiled comment on a man's weakness?

Classical, Difference, and Radical Feminism

Today the idea of gender equality has several facets. Feminists generally agree that there should be gender equality, but they don't necessarily agree on what is female and male human nature, or on what exactly our policies should be to combat gender discrimination. The philosophies of feminism are in a process of development, responding to the pressures of the past and present and the challenges of the future. One facet is *classical feminism,* which calls for men and women to be considered as *persons* first and gendered beings second. Another is *difference feminism,* which holds that women and men possess fundamentally different qualities and that both genders should learn from each other. A facet of feminism that sometimes has received bad press is *radical feminism;* although some radical feminists indeed seem to be militant or extremist, the main point of radical feminism is not to mount the barricades but to seek out and expose the *root* of the problem of gender discrimination. ("Root" is *radix* in Latin; hence, radical feminism.) And then there is a breakout form of feminism severely criticized by many feminists that labels itself *equity feminism:* An equity feminist holds that the battle for equality has been won, that we should not think of women as victims of patriarchy any longer, and that we can now adopt any kind of gender roles we like because gender discrimination is by and large a thing of the past. (Box 12.8 discusses equity feminism.)

Classical Feminism: Beauvoir and Androgyny

For those taking the view that men and women should be considered as persons first, gender differences are primarily cultural. Biological differences are significant only in

Box 12.8   CHRISTINA HOFF SOMMERS'S EQUITY FEMINISM

In a highly controversial book, *Who Stole Feminism?* (1994), Christina Hoff Sommers (see Chapter 10) argues that feminism has been split into two movements: the "equity feminists," wanting equal opportunity for women and men, and the "gender feminists," "resenter feminists," or "feminist radicals," who, as Sommers sees it, have male-bashing as their main agenda. Sommers sees herself as an equity feminist. She also uses the terms "new feminists" and "gynocentric feminism" to describe the type of feminism she believes has done the movement a grave disservice by creating an atmosphere of general mistrust of men and of women who work with, support, or admire them. Here Sommers doesn't align herself exactly with any of the facets of feminism that we have discussed; although radical feminism comes closest to what she calls gender feminism, Sommers also finds that difference feminism has elements of misandry in that women's approaches are considered superior to those of men. And classical feminism, although being the form of feminism that probably comes closest to what Sommers calls equity feminism, also has elements of gender feminism for Sommers: Simone de Beauvoir, she says, had no intention of letting women choose gender roles freely but wanted to dictate the proper upbringing and life choices for women. Among contemporary gender feminists, Sommers counts Susan Faludi, Marilyn French, Carolyn Heilbrun, and Catharine MacKinnon. Sommers writes:

> Once I get into the habit of regarding women as a subjugated gender, I'm primed to be alarmed, angry, and resentful of men as oppressors of women. I am also prepared to believe the words about them and the harm they cause to women. I may even be ready to fabricate atrocities. . . . Resenter feminists like Faludi, French, Heilbrun and MacKinnon speak of backlash, siege, and an undeclared war against women. But

the condition they describe is mythic—with no foundation in the facts of contemporary American life.

Since women now have their political and personal freedom, says Sommers, they should be making use of it, instead of judging the authenticity of each other's attitudes:

> But women are no longer disenfranchised, and their preferences are being taken into account. Nor are they now taught that they are subordinate or that a subordinate role for them is fitting and proper. . . . Since women today can no longer be regarded as the victims of an undemocratic indoctrination, we must regard their preferences as "authentic." Any other attitude toward American women is unacceptably patronizing and profoundly illiberal.

The feminists Sommers criticizes generally respond that Sommers herself has misunderstood the goals and nature of feminism; although the overt oppression of previous times is over, it has now become covert and internalized, and it lives in the hearts of the critics of feminism, women as well as men. Although opportunities have opened to women, many women still grow up believing that the masculine cultural world is their only option; it takes a long time for such wounds to heal, and they don't heal without active interference. For that reason, and for their own sake, women must be shown that equality is still far away. So when Sommers says women have the right to choose a life in which they work at home, raising children, or work in a male-dominated environment or when she says they have the right to enjoy romance literature in which men are strong and women are seduced, then Sommers must herself have internalized the traditional male view of what a woman's proper place is, according to some critics.

Sommers responds by claiming that gender feminism simply does not represent the

(continued)

Box 12.8 CHRISTINA HOFF SOMMERS'S
EQUITY FEMINISM (*continued*)

viewpoint of most women today—women who are politically aware and concerned with gender equality—in other words, feminists. Most women today, says Sommers, have access to the professions of their choice and want to lead lives in which they have friendly relations with male coworkers and loving relations with male partners. Many want families, and some even want to live the traditional life of a homemaker, and they are not interested in being represented by women who tell them they have a false consciousness. As a fellow equity feminist, Sommers cites the author and fellow philosopher Iris Murdoch, who believed in a "culture of humanity," not in a "new female ghetto" of misandric feminism.

terms of procreation, they say; apart from birthing and breastfeeding infants, which can be done only by women, the sexual differences are irrelevant. Culture has shaped men and women, and a cultural change could therefore allow for another type of gender: the *androgynous* type.

In her groundbreaking work *The Second Sex,* Simone de Beauvoir, one of the most powerful voices for equal education and equal opportunities in the twentieth century, accuses the philosophical tradition of seeing man as the "typical" human being, so woman thus becomes "atypical." For man, woman becomes "the Other," an alien being who helps man define himself through her alienness, and with whom he communicates on an everyday basis but who never becomes "one of the boys." Woman, who has been placed in this situation for millennia, has also come to believe she is atypical. The female anatomy is seen as a psychological determining factor, whereas the male anatomy is not. In other words, women do what they do because they are women; men do what they do because they are normal. But this is a *cultural* fact, not a natural one, says Beauvoir. And the only way a woman can become *authentic* is to shed her role as "deviant" and become a true human being by rejecting the traditional female role. Society can assist in this process by treating little boys and girls the same—by giving them the same education and the same subsequent opportunities. Here we must remember that Beauvoir was engaged in issues other than feminism; she was, with her partner Jean-Paul Sartre, one of the strongest voices in the philosophical existentialist movement of the mid–twentieth century (see Chapter 10). Existentialism posits that there is no human nature; any attempt at claiming we *have to* do or be something is nothing but a poor excuse for not wanting to make a choice: *bad faith.* If we carry this over into Beauvoir's theory of feminism, we understand what she means when she says that a woman must shed her culturally given role as the second sex: There is no female human nature any more than there is any human nature in general; we must fight the cultural traps of gender roles and their assumption that this is how we have to be, because that is nothing but a poor excuse for not making our own choices. (However, if we should *want to* make the choice of traditional gender roles, Beauvoir would have little patience with us, since she believed the choice of gender freedom is best made if the traditional option of stay-at-home-mom is not available to women. Many contemporary feminists find that this hardly constitutes true freedom of choice.)

It is against the background of the traditional male philosophical approach to the gender question that Beauvoir criticizes Emmanuel Levinas and his view of the Other as essentially feminine (see Chapter 10). To Beauvoir, this is nothing but old-fashioned reactionary male-oriented thinking, because for a classical feminist like her, the attitude of seeing the sexes as fundamentally different also means that one is generally dominating the other; when Levinas praises feminine qualities as the nurturing and welcoming element in both men and women, the classical feminist still sees that as discrimination (against men as well as against women) because it persists in stereotyping the typically feminine as nurturing.

Until women begin to think of themselves as a group, Beauvoir says, they will believe that they are abnormal human beings. And as long as men and women receive different educations and different treatment from society, woman will not feel responsible for the state of the world but will regard herself as men regard her—as an overgrown child. Of course women are weak, Beauvoir says. Of course they don't use male logic (here we must remember that she is talking about uneducated women before World War II). Of course they are religious to the point of superstition. Of course they have no sense of history, and of course they accept authority. Of course they cry a lot over little things. They may even be lazy, sensual, servile, frivolous, utilitarian, materialistic, and hysterical. They may, in short, be all that some male thinkers thought they were. *But why are women all these things?* Because they have no power except by subterfuge. They have no education, so they have never been taught about the cause and effect of history and the relative powers of authority. They are caught up in a never-ending stream of housework, which causes them to be practically oriented. They nag because they realize they have no power to change their situation. They are sensual because they are bored. In *The Second Sex* Beauvoir says, "The truth is that when a woman is engaged in an enterprise worthy of a human being, she is quite able to show herself as active, effective, taciturn—and as ascetic—as a man." (See Box 12.9 for Beauvoir's influence on modern philosophy.) At the end of the chapter you can read an excerpt from this book as well as a summary of one of Beauvoir's short stories, "The Woman Destroyed."

So if we change our culture, we will change what has for so long been considered female nature—and with it, probably also male nature. We will create people who are responsible human beings above all and who will respect each other for that reason. This philosophy was adopted by many late-twentieth-century feminists, including Germaine Greer, Gloria Steinem, and Joyce Trebilcot.

The question is, Can we choose our gender at all? Obviously we can't choose our *sex* (not without going through major surgery, anyway). But the term *gender* also encompasses our *social roles* as male and female. Can we, then, decide which social role we wish to adapt—which gender we wish to be—or do biological factors exist that prevent people from exercising gender choice? In other words, is our gender determined by our biology to a greater extent than people who advocate androgyny realize?

Box 12.9   THE OTHER: SIMONE DE BEAUVOIR

Simone de Beauvoir (1908–1986), a feminist and an existentialist, was long considered a minor thinker by the philosophical community. One reason was that she was Jean-Paul Sartre's "significant other," and her books, such as *The Second Sex,* show considerable influence from Sartre's ideas. However, most philosophers now recognize that many of the fundamental ideas of existentialism came about through discussions between Sartre and Beauvoir, and many ideas first published by Sartre may well have originated during those discussions. There is even some suspicion that Sartre occasionally published ideas by Beauvoir under his own name. True or not, this new attitude reveals a changing perspective on women in philosophy. In the twenty-first century, Beauvoir's influence in the area of gender inequality has turned out to be just as viable as Sartre's philosophy. Beauvoir is primarily interested in the existence of woman as a cultural phenomenon; she analyzes woman's subjugation in a man's world—a situation that was far more common in the mid–twentieth century than now. She hopes that instead of a world where woman is considered deviant and man normal, we will have a society of *human beings,* not just males and females, and people will interact with each other equally as productive, authentic beings. Beauvoir has come

under heavy criticism from some feminists for not realizing that she herself regards man as the norm and wants women to be treated and to act like men, rather than rejoice in their inherent female nature. It appears that Beauvoir herself decided to live a child-free life to escape the female stereotype.

Psychologists of the 1960s and 1970s generally assumed that sex roles were purely a matter of upbringing, or *nurture.* The theory of *psychosexual neutrality,* inspired by the theory of behaviorism, which arose earlier in the century, held that a child can be molded into being male or female but is born neither except by virtue of the genitals; if a person seems stereotypically male, it is because of his upbringing, and not a biological fact. This theory also suggests that if we'd like our children to be less stereotypically male or female than tradition expects, we just have to give them a more unisex upbringing. But the theory of psychosexual neutrality has come under severe criticism within the past few years: Cases that had been reported as successful molding of children born with ambiguous genitalia (formerly called hermaphrodites, they're now referred to as *intersexual* children) are now under scrutiny for simply having assigned a sex to the child and assuming that upbringing and hormone treatment would take care of the rest.

A disturbing story is that of David Reimer, who lost his penis to a botched circumcision as an infant in the late 1960s and was raised as a girl, Brenda. In spite of the parents' well-meaning efforts to convince Brenda that she was a girl, she never felt comfortable, and upon discovering the truth at the age of fourteen, promptly discarded the female persona for that of David. He had reconstructive surgery and married a woman whose children he adopted. But the stresses of his abnormal childhood proved to be too much for David, and after being divorced he took his own life in 2004. The case of Brenda/David as well as cases of intersexual children do seem to point toward *nature* as being more important in forming a person's sexual identity than *nurture* is. (See Box 12.10 for a discussion of homosexuality and gender choice.) But we shouldn't discount the influence of nurture completely: The manner in which we express our sexuality and whether or not we become "typically" male or female may well be a matter of our upbringing, at least to some extent.

Difference Feminism: Gilligan and the Ethic of Care

The idea that nature will prevail over nurture has given a boost to the theory of *difference feminism,* which emerged in the 1980s to claim that women and men should be viewed as equal but fundamentally different. By the beginning of the 1980s women had been in the workforce long enough for people to begin to evaluate the situation, and although some women felt good about working in what used to be a "man's world" and conforming to its standards (to a greater or lesser degree), others felt that somehow those standards were damaging to their female identity. Few provisions for child care existed, there was little understanding of family demands, and the overriding atmosphere was one of competition and isolation rather than cooperation and teamwork. For those women, survival in the male-dominated public sphere was possible only if they were willing to give up some of their female values. Difference feminism proposed that the feminist agenda could include not just equal opportunity and equal pay for men and women but also an acknowledgment that many women want something different from what men want and some of women's capabilities lie in areas other than those of most men.

Interestingly enough, that was not the first time such ideas have been advanced—Western history, and certainly the history of philosophy, is rich with statements about the nature of women being different from that of men. Some famous examples include Aristotle, who believed that women were deformed men; Kant, who found it thoroughly improper for a woman to display any interest in intellectual or technological pursuits, even if she might be good at them; Rousseau, who saw a woman as a man's helpmate and little else; and Nietzsche, who admired women for being more "natural" than men but vilified them for being inconsistent. Theories such as those all state that women and men have different abilities and thus different places in society. However, those theories were not advanced with any notion of gender equality. John Stuart Mill was the first influential philosopher to suggest that although men and women have different capacities, they should nevertheless be given equal

The psychologist John Gray theorizes in his best-selling self-help book *Men Are from Mars, Women Are from Venus* that men and women have very different approaches and expectations. Difference feminism agrees. Classical feminism, on the other hand, assumes that if we minimize gender differences in a child's upbringing, a new generation of people who are persons first and gendered beings second will appear. Here is a classical feminist, Cathy, with a classical feminist dilemma: how to buy for children without perpetuating gender stereotypes. Does cartoonist Cathy Guisewite touch on a real problem? If so, what can be done about it?

Box 12.10   CAN GAYS CHOOSE NOT TO BE GAY?

In talking about the possibility of choosing gender roles, it is reasonable to discuss the issue of homosexuality and the gay lifestyle. There is still considerable political and moral opposition to homosexuals in Western societies, in some more than in others. In some societies homosexuals can now marry; in others homosexuality is still illegal. Why is there a traditional opposition to homosexuality in Christian countries? It is because of several traditional Christian assumptions, such as (1) homosexuality is a *moral choice,* and one that goes against nature (nature calls for procreation), so homosexuality is morally wrong; and (2) homosexuals are primarily seducers of adolescents, who will then become homosexual. In the early 1990s scientists reached the *tentative* conclusion (based on brain autopsies) that male homosexuality is not a matter of choice but of biology. In that case both of the above objections would be invalid, because (1) gay men don't choose their lifestyle or sexual orientation but are born with it (so it is *natural* for them); and (2) boys can't be seduced to become homosexuals; they either are born that way or not. (Besides, being gay does not imply that one is primarily interested in young boys.) But there is as yet no extensive research about lesbianism or about bisexualism. The advantage for homosexuals of a conclusive result pointing to biological factors is obvious: There could be no more reason for discrimination based on the belief that homosexuality is an "immoral choice." But such a finding might open the door for new areas of discrimination: Might we see parents take their young children to the doctor to have them "screened" for homosexuality, and if they test positive, ask to have them "cured"? In this way homosexuality would be labeled a *defect,* a disease. Some homosexuals might say they would prefer to be heterosexual if that were possible, but certainly not all would.

In 2004 the issue of same-sex marriage became headline news in several states around the country, as well as in Europe. In several European countries gay civil marriages had already been legal for years, but in some European communities the issue became one of allowing gays to have church weddings. In the United States the focus was on civil marriages versus civil unions; although many states allow what are called civil unions, same-sex partnerships that are recognized by employers, insurance companies, and health care officials, some mayors and judges around the country thought it only fair to extend the possibility of a civil marriage to gay couples. In San Francisco it became a media event, with gay celebrities getting hitched in front of the cameras. Later that year, the California Supreme Court nullified the marriages as being against state law, but in 2005 a judge found the ruling unconstitutional. The issue continues to be politically volatile: In 2007 the California State Assembly voted to allow same-sex marriage, facing a veto by Governor Arnold Schwarzenegger—a repeat of the situation in 2005, when the California Senate approved a similar bill, which was then vetoed by the governor. In 2008 the California Supreme Court struck down the ban on same-sex marriages, making California the second state (Massachusetts was the first) to legalize such unions, but Connecticut, Vermont, New Jersey, Maine, and Washington allow civil unions or domestic partnership. Although there seems to be a growing acceptance of the concept of civil unions by the American public, the majority of voters find the idea of same-sex marriage unacceptable: In the 2004 election eleven states decided on constitutional amendments that defined marriage as an institution between a man and a woman, and in most cases the amendment won by a large margin.

opportunities and equal respect for their abilities. It is that concept toward which the new feminism looks. That the question of gender equality is still a very sensitive one was demonstrated by the resignation of Harvard president and economist Larry Summers in 2006 after a 2005 conference speech in which he speculated that the fact that more men than women have successful careers in science and engineering was due not just to social factors but also to innate abilities—in other words, that men and women are fundamentally different by nature in terms of their typical talents. The speech caught the attention of the media, and an outcry ensued, labeling Summers a sexist, even though difference feminists as well as neurobiologists have speculated along the same lines for decades. However, what critics in the media and at Harvard heard was a throwback, a biased attempt to exclude women based on a traditional mistrust of women's rational capabilities.

In general, the values we've celebrated for so long as good human behavior have been predominantly male values, say the new feminists, because the male person has been considered the "real" person, whereas women have been thought of as slightly deviant. The man is the typical human being. In older textbooks on human development, the earlier forms of hominids, such as *Homo habilis* and *Neandertal,* have usually been depicted as males ("Neandertal man"). Only recently in textbooks and articles have humans been symbolized by both male and female figures. Even recent theories of psychology seem to use boys and men as their research material rather than girls and women, and the medical community must now face the problems resulting from years of conducting research with primarily male subjects. The statistics regarding women and certain diseases (heart disease, for example) are unreliable, and the administration of medicine to women is often decided on the basis of research on male subjects. This is not just a matter of a slanted ideology; it is a very practical problem. Women have for a long time been judged by the standards of men, as though women were what Aristotle claimed so long ago—deficient males. Difference feminism wants to replace the image of one of the genders being more "normal" than the other with an image of both genders, with all their unique characteristics, being equally representative of the human race. This shift involves upgrading the female tasks of motherhood, housekeeping, caring for family members, and so on, tasks that for some people seemed to fall by the wayside in the first rush to get women into the workforce. Typical female virtues that arise from concentrating on those tasks are generosity, caring, harmony, reconciliation, and maintenance of close relationships. The virtues that typically have been considered male are justice, rights, fairness, competition, independence, and adherence to the rules.

Psychologist Carol Gilligan has been a major inspiration in the gender debate. Her book *In a Different Voice* (1982) analyzes reactions of boys and girls, men and women, and concludes that there is a basic difference in the *moral attitudes* of males and females. In one of her analyses she uses an experiment by a well-known contemporary psychologist, Lawrence Kohlberg; it is called the *Heinz dilemma.* An interviewer using Kohlberg's method asked two eleven-year-old children, Jake and Amy, to evaluate the following situation: Heinz's wife is desperately ill, and Heinz can't afford medication for her. Should Heinz steal the medication? Jake has no doubts; he says yes, Heinz should steal the medication, because his wife's life is more important than the rule of not stealing. Amy, though, is not so sure. She says no, he shouldn't steal the medication, because what if he got caught? Then he would have to go to jail, and who would look after his sick wife? Perhaps he could ask the pharmacist to let him have the medication and pay later. Since the interviewer didn't get the expected response, Amy changed her answer. The interviewer concluded that Jake had a clear understanding of the situation: It would be just that the wife should receive the medication, because her rights would override the law of not stealing. The interviewer thought that Amy's comprehension of the situation was fuzzy at best. Jake understood what it was all about: rights and justice.

Gilligan rereads Amy's answer and comes up with another conclusion entirely: Although Jake answered the question *Should Heinz steal the drug or not?* (in other words, a classical dilemma requiring a choice between two answers), Amy heard it differently: *Should Heinz steal the drug, or should he do something else?* In effect, the children were answering different questions, and Amy's response makes as much sense as Jake's. But Amy is not concerned with the issues of rights and justice as much as she is with what will happen to Heinz and his wife; she even takes the humaneness of the pharmacist into consideration. In other words, she thinks in terms of *caring.* She acknowledges that there are laws, but she also believes people can be reasoned with. The interviewer, Gilligan says, didn't hear that in Amy's answer because he was looking for the "justice" answer. Gilligan concludes that boys and men tend to focus on an *ethic of justice,* whereas girls and women look toward an *ethic of care.*

Gilligan's influence on modern thinking about gender issues has been enormous, although other philosophers, psychologists, and linguists have also approached them in similar ways, and some of them long before Gilligan's book came out. Perhaps the first person to suggest that women tend to think in terms of caring whereas men think in terms of justice was not a philosopher, or a psychologist, but a playwright: the Norwegian Henrik Ibsen, in his monumentally influential play *A Doll's House* from 1879. You can read an excerpt from this play in the Narratives section. Also, you may remember the debate in Chapter 7 about justice, in which John Rawls suggested that we adopt "the original position," pretending that we don't know who we are when our policy takes effect; you may also remember the responses from Wolgast and Friedman that we can't just assume we are strangers who don't know one another, because part of being a social person is precisely that we have caring relationships with others and don't just exist in some abstract legal universe. That is, in essence, similar to Gilligan's criticism of a traditional ethic of justice as being the traditional male approach to moral questions and emphasizes that we can't just pretend we don't have our own gender. In the Primary Readings you'll find an excerpt from Gilligan's *In a Different Voice.* On the website (www.mhhe.com/rosenstand6e) you can read the summary of a film that explores the notion that women are, or should be, caring and nurturing: *Like Water for Chocolate.*

Does that mean Gilligan is claiming that all women are always caring? That is a matter of interpretation. Some readers see her theory as a description of what we might call the "female condition": Because of either nature or upbringing or both, most women *are* caring human beings. Others see that as a preposterous statement. Not all women are caring, and few women, even if they are generally caring persons,

Carol Gilligan (b. 1936), American psychologist and author of *In a Different Voice* (1982) as well as coauthor of several books on women's and girls' psychology. She became Harvard University's first professor of gender studies. Like Simone de Beauvoir, Gilligan believes that throughout Western history men have been considered the "normal" gender and women have been viewed as not-quite-normal. However, unlike Beauvoir, Gilligan does not argue for a monoandrogynous society, believing instead that men and women are fundamentally different in their approach to life—different but equal.

are caring all the time. Gilligan's theory of the ethics of care does not have to be read as a description of how women really act, though; with its emphasis on values it is a theory about how most women believe they *ought to act.* It is a theory of women's normative values—we might call it a theory about the *caring imperative*—not a theory about some inevitable female nature.

What does the Gilligan theory add up to? For many women, it means that their experiences of attachment and their focus on relationships are normal and good and not "overly dependent," "clinging," or "immature"; it means an upgrading of what we consider traditional female values. The point of Gilligan's book is to prompt the mature woman to understand rights and the mature man to understand caring so we all can work and live together in harmony. Her hopes may not be realized for decades to come, however, for although some may argue that they know some very caring men and some very justice-oriented women, it seems Gilligan is right in claiming that most women in the United States grow up believing that caring is what is most important, and most men grow up believing that individual rights and justice are the ultimate ethical values.

There are risks involved in Gilligan's theory. Some think we may end up elevating female values far above male values. In that case we will have reversed one unfair system but created another unfair system by declaring women "normal" and men "slightly deviant." A more pressing problem is the following: If we say it is in a woman's nature to be understanding and caring, we may be forcing her right back into the private sphere from which she just emerged. Men (and also women) may say, Well, if most women aren't able to understand "justice," then we can't use them in the real world, and they'd better go home and do what nature intended them to do: have babies and care for their man. Similarly, if a job calls for "caring" qualities, employers may be reluctant to hire a man, because men are not "naturals" at caring. So instead of giving people more opportunities, Gilligan may actually be setting up new categories that could result in policies that exclude women from "men's work" and men from "women's work." It is not enough to say that the qualities of one gender are not supposed to outweigh the qualities of the other, because we all know that even with the best intentions, we tend to rank one set of differences higher than the other. We may all be equal, but remember George Orwell's *Animal Farm?* In that novel, which is a metaphor for political despotism, Orwell warns against some being considered "more equal than others." Critics have claimed that what Gilligan is doing is throwing a monkey wrench into the philosophy of gender equality, and her "ethic of care" theory may result in statements such as this: "We need a new executive with a good head for legal rules—but we can't hire a woman, of course, even though she seems otherwise qualified, because science says that women have a lousy sense of justice." In short, there is a danger that a psychological theory of gender may shift from describing what seems to be the case to prescribing a set of rules about who ought to do what.

Although her theory of the ethic of care may raise problems for the concept of equality, there is no doubt that Gilligan has touched on something a vast number of women have been able to relate to. I'll let this anecdote illustrate her talent for seizing the situation: Some years ago she gave the keynote address at an ethics conference at the University of San Diego. Gilligan, who is a petite woman, arrived at the podium in the great lecture hall—and completely disappeared behind the imposing lectern, designed in a more traditional age for taller male scholars. No provisions had been made for shorter speakers. Causing a storm of applause, she reappeared on the other side of the lectern and grabbed the microphone, calmly commenting, "There is obviously still work to be done!"

Some years ago, Gilligan and other feminists engaged in a written debate in the *Atlantic Monthly* with Christina Hoff Sommers (see Box 12.8 and Chapter 10), who by then had acquired a solid reputation among some feminists as being no feminist at all. Sommers had just published a book, *The War Against Boys* (2000), in which she claimed that because of what she calls gender feminism, young boys are now facing a hard time in school. Contrary to the standard wisdom that girls are overlooked in the classroom in favor of the more assertive boys, Sommers says it is in fact the girls who nowadays are getting all the attention from the teachers and are being held up as role models as smarter and better behaved than the boys. That makes boys lose self-esteem. Sommers's claims caused consternation and disbelief among readers of the *Atlantic Monthly,* where her views were first published. But she has also found an audience who agree that conditions in schools have changed dramatically over the past decades to the benefit of girls, and we need to look at the possibility that in some cases it may have come at a price: the shortchanging of boys. Since her book came out in 2000, her claims have, to a great extent, been supported by further studies as well as a growing appreciation in the court of public opinion. An article in *Newsweek,* January 30, 2006, "The Trouble with Boys," echoed Sommers's analysis with statistics and case studies, claiming that the attention given to girls has made boyhood itself somehow questionable and that what is needed is a positive reevaluation of *masculinity* itself. Critics were quick to point out, however, that this is nothing but a backlash, attempting to undo the great strides women made in the twentieth century and to undermine the intellectual and professional gains of women in the twenty-first century. However, it is clear that the observation that boys are being shortchanged in today's educational climate has hit a nerve with parents, and students, based on personal experience. The debate rolls on, and by the end of this chapter you'll have met two thinkers—one a linguist and the other a neuropsychologist—who have, each in her and his own way, weighed in on the issue: Deborah Tannen and Michael Gurian.

Radical Feminism: Uprooting Sexism

The term *radical* alone is often enough to make some people tune out. We are used to the term meaning "extremism." For some, a radical feminist is a stereotypical male-basher. But we must be cautious here, because much depends on how we interpret the term *radical*. If we read it as "extremist feminism," then it will generally be used by antifeminists to describe anything they disagree with as being too extreme. The feminists themselves who are tagged with the label may think of themselves as mainstream. It is thus a relative concept and often used in a disparaging sense, meaning any feminism that goes further than you're willing to accept. ("Equal pay for equal work" could sound like radical feminism to some traditionalists.) To be sure, there are feminists who think in more sweeping terms than others. Some see sexual intercourse with men as inherently humiliating for women. And there are misandric feminists who assume that all men are incapable of wanting or working for gender equality, just as there are misogynist men who think ill of all women. But most of those who today call themselves radical feminists have a different agenda: They take the term *radical* in its original Latin meaning, going to the *root* (*radix*) of the matter. Such radical feminists ask, How did gender discrimination arise? What were the structures that kept it in place? And do we still have elements of those structures today? The answers are generally: *It arose in patriarchy;* those structures have kept gender discrimination alive to this day. A child is still considered to be of the father's family more than of the mother's; yet a mother is still considered to be the primary caregiver of a child taken ill at school, even though the father's profession might be less demanding than hers and his workplace closer to the child's school. A woman is still expected to take her career less seriously than a man is, and to adopt her husband's last name, and some continue to consider a woman's career contributions as less important than a man's. Sexual liberty is still considered more acceptable for boys and men than for girls and women. Little girls' toys are still in the pink section in the toy stores, and little boys' toys are still action figures from a world with practically no equal women participants. The radical feminist doesn't necessarily want boys to play with dolls or girls to play Mortal Kombat, but she or he wants us to understand *where those choices are coming from* and to decide to discard any tradition that sees women as lesser beings than men. The "Princess" phenomenon, explored in Box 12.11, would indicate for the radical feminists that the roots of gender stereotypes are deep.

A famous radical feminist, Andrea Dworkin (1946–2005), wrote in her book *Right-Wing Women: The Politics of Domesticated Females* (1983):

> To achieve a single standard of human freedom and one absolute standard of human dignity, the sex-class system has to be dismembered. The reason is pragmatic, not philosophical: Nothing less will work. However much everyone wants to do less, less will not free women. Liberal men and women ask, Why can't we just be ourselves, all human beings, begin now and not dwell in past injustices, wouldn't that subvert the sex-class system, change it from the inside out? The answer is no. The sex-class system has a structure; it has deep roots in religion and culture; it is fundamental to the economy; sexuality is its creature; to be 'just human beings' in it, women have to hide what happens to them as women because they are women—happenings like forced sex and forced reproduction, happenings that continue as

long as the sex-class system operates. The liberation of women requires facing the real condition of women in order to change it. 'We're all just people' is a stance that prohibits recognition of the systematic cruelties visited upon women because of sex oppression.

Dworkin says that one of the toughest challenges to women is to realize that all women have a common condition, even women you don't like, women you don't want to be compared to. The common condition is that women are, in Dworkin's words, "subordinate to men, sexually colonized in a sexual system of dominance and submission, denied rights on the basis of sex, historically chattel, generally considered biologically inferior, confined to sex and reproduction: this is the general description of the social environment in which all women live."

The goal of radical feminism is thus to raise the individual awareness of what the patriarchal tradition has done to us, men as well as women. We must try to undo the social and psychological damage done by centuries of male-dominated culture—by making women aware of how much in their personal and professional lives has been dominated and designed by men. Radical feminism sees women's minds as by and large shaped by men's accomplishments and thinking, and unless women learn to focus on women's talents and accomplishments, they/we will always have a "false consciousness": We think we understand, but all we have to work with are mind tools and concepts invented by men. Another radical feminist, Gerda Lerner, says that women have until recently been excluded from the "power of naming and defining." Men have defined the problems deemed worthy of attention, as well as the vocabulary with which they should be described. Being able to put a name to a problem is part of solving it, and if women are deprived of naming their own problems, the problems remain unrecognized. For that reason, sex discrimination isn't uprooted simply by listening to the private wishes and professional ideas of women, because those wishes and ideas may be favored by the male tradition we all grew up within. Radical feminism insists that both women and men must be educated to see that tradition as one of oppression and be encouraged to create a new one based on a female perspective.

The Bridge Builders: Tannen and Gurian

For many people, regardless of whether or not they call themselves feminist, the gender debate in the late-twentieth/early-twenty-first century has become too divisive: The classical feminist view seems to fly in the face of the fact that gender appears to be a true natural characteristic, not something that we can change through upbringing and education. The difference feminist view, on the other hand, seems to solidify some old stereotypes that many are happy to have escaped, and radical feminists haven't been making many friends among women and men who enjoy and believe in traditional gender relations. But a few researchers have weighed in with an alternative approach—one that sounds promising if you happen to lean toward soft universalism, like your author. Two names in particular deserve to be mentioned: the linguist Deborah Tannen and the neuropsychologist Michael Gurian. I have chosen to call them bridge builders, because for both researchers the primary goal is to make it possible for women and men to *understand* each other, not to become like each other or to compete against each other. Deborah Tannen gained national attention with her second popular book, *You Just Don't Understand,* based on her research into differences in conversation styles between women and men, and girls and boys, and through a subsequent series of works, both scholarly and popular, exploring why we tend to misunderstand each other and what we can do to bridge the gap between us.

Tannen's theory is that although many differences in our conversational styles may be due to hardwiring (nature), some of them have to do with our environment (nurture), and she thus places herself in between classical and difference feminism, although she does point out that cross-culturally, all over the planet, some male-female behavioral differences seem to be universal. For Tannen, we are sufficiently similar that we can learn to understand where our significant other—or colleague or boss—of the other gender is coming from, so we can learn to see life through the eyes of our partner and make mutual adjustments to take his or her expectations into consideration. You'll perhaps remember reading about Tannen and the Golden Rule in Chapter 11—this is one of her suggestions: If a man prefers to relax and not have to say anything when he comes home, and his wife or girlfriend is yearning to talk about her day and hear about his when she comes home, it is no good if we torture each other by one being noncommunicative and the other being overly communicative. What we must do is try to see it from the other's perspective: If you're a woman who wants to talk, give him a little quiet time! If you're a man who just wants peace and quiet, put yourself in her place and be interested in what she has to say about her day, and don't try to solve her problems! She just wants to share her day with you, not get a twelve-step program.

Michael Gurian is a psychotherapist who has staked out a slightly different territory: In a series of very popular works that can be described as self-help books, he has outlined not only the psychological characteristics and needs of boys and girls but also the neurobiological science behind their behavior. In his book *What Could He Be Thinking? How a Man's Mind Really Works* (2003), he explores what he considers typical male brain patterns, presented for female readers in particular to help in making relationships less rocky and providing a basis for a mutual understanding. Although many books written by difference feminists explore the natural differences between women and men, Gurian's book is an exception because he, like Tannen, seeks to emphasize *understanding* the differences. In addition, Gurian contributes to the gender debate with a concept that is uniquely his own: *Bridge brains.* Neurologically, says Gurian, there are "typical" masculine men and "typical" feminine women. But in addition, there are women who are comfortable thinking and acting in ways that some would describe as more masculine than feminine, and men who act and think in more feminine than masculine ways. Sometimes such bridge brains are gay or lesbian, but often the bridge brains are heterosexual—they're just really good at understanding the other gender, because neurologically, their brains are less typically male or female. Although some have criticized Gurian for being a traditionalist, his books, like Tannen's, have provided much practical relief and insight to readers who have been turned off by the divisiveness of twentieth-century feminism as well as the oppressiveness of the traditional gender roles. The final word has by no means been said about male and female human nature, and about what roles we ought to play in the dance of human relationships, but there is something to be said for people who try to make the dance smoother for the rest of us, rather than more complicated.

Box 12.11   THE PRINCESS PHENOMENON

While second-wave feminists were focused on the classical feminist concept of strict gender equality, some feminists took the radical view that any display of traditional femininity was playing into the hands of patriarchy and male dominance: Skirts gave way to pants, jewelry and makeup disappeared, high heels became flat heels, and life became, perhaps, less glamorous, but also more comfortable. Little girls were dressed in unisex coveralls, and the frilly look was retired. So it was quite disturbing for older second-wave feminists to see the princess look emerge in the new millennium with a new push by the Disney Corporation to recapture the minds of romantic little girls and their romantically starved mothers. The pink Princess line of merchandise was a hugely successful result, with clothes, bedding, alarm clocks, everything that a little girl might beg to have in her room. Little girls love it—but some parents are worried that the gender brainwashing has started up again, trying to make the girls into conventional women who focus more on being cute than on creating a meaningful future for themselves. So does that mean that the new generation of girls will grow up to be vain robots—or is it simply opening up more possibilities for self-expression, as third-wave feminism advocates? Lately it appears that little girls aren't stuck with the princess identity in the Disney universe; they can also opt to be fairies (like Tinkerbelle)—and pirates!

In the chapter text, you'll find theories of classical and difference feminism; how might a classical and a difference feminist each view the princess phenomenon?

Study Questions

1. Give a brief account of the similarities and differences between classical, difference, radical, and equity feminism. Can those facets overlap? Explain.

2. Which brand of feminism do you think is the most relevant today? Are you a feminist? If yes, why? If no, why not?

3. Outline the advantages and the problems associated with difference feminism.

4. Evaluate Gurian's concept of "bridge brains." Is it useful? Why or why not?

Primary Readings and Narratives

The first Primary Reading is an excerpt from Harriet Taylor Mill's "Enfranchisement of Women," and the second is from Simone de Beauvoir's *The Second Sex.* The third is an excerpt from Carol Gilligan's *In a Different Voice.* The first Narrative is a summary of and an excerpt from the classic play by Henrik Ibsen, *A Doll's House,* in which a nineteenth-century housewife, treated as a beloved but mischievous child by her husband, proves to be very much an adult person. The second Narrative is a summary of and excerpts from Beauvoir's short story "The Woman Destroyed," in which the title character's husband leaves her for another woman. The final Narrative is a summary of the film *Mona Lisa Smile,* about a young art professor at Wellesley in the 1950s.

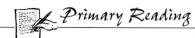

Primary Reading

Enfranchisement of Women

HARRIET TAYLOR MILL

Excerpt, 1851.

You have read about Harriet Taylor Mill in Chapter 5, as being John Stuart Mill's soul mate and intellectual partner, and in this chapter you have read about their collaboration on the philosophy of women's rights in mid-nineteenth-century Great Britain. Here you have an excerpt from Harriet Taylor Mill's text, written in 1851—sixteen years before John Stuart Mill's own book about women's rights, *The Subjection of Women,* was published. In 1851 Harriet and John were also finally married, two years after the death of Harriet's husband and after a relationship of twenty-one years. Until Harriet's untimely death from tuberculosis in 1858, she and John went on collaborating about other projects such as an analysis of domestic violence, property rights, and the work that was to become John Stuart Mill's first book after her death: *On Liberty.*

In this excerpt H. T. Mill dismisses three standard nineteenth-century arguments against women in the workforce: that allowing women in the workforce would (1) go against the duties of motherhood, (2) be unfair competition to men, and (3) mean an unsuitable hardening of the female character.

Concerning the fitness, then, of women for politics, there can be no question: but the dispute is more likely to turn upon the fitness of politics for women. When the reasons alleged for excluding women from active life in all its higher departments, are stripped of their garb of declamatory phrases, and reduced to the simple expression of a meaning, they seem to be mainly three: the incompatibility of active life with maternity, and with the care of a household; secondly, its alleged hardening effect on the character; and thirdly, the inexpediency of making an addition to the already excessive pressure of competition in every kind of professional or lucrative employment.

The first, the maternity argument, is usually laid most stress upon: although (it needs hardly be said) this reason, if it be one, can apply only to mothers. It is neither necessary nor just to make imperative on women that they shall be either mothers or nothing; or that if they have been mothers once, they shall be nothing else during the whole remainder of their lives. Neither women nor men need any law to exclude them from an occupation, if they have undertaken another which is incompatible with it. No one proposes to exclude the male sex from Parliament because a man may be a soldier or sailor in active service, or a merchant whose business requires all his time and energies. Nine-tenths of the occupations of men exclude them *de facto* from public life, as effectually as if they were excluded by law; but that is no reason for making laws to exclude even the nine-tenths, much less the remaining tenth. The reason of the case is the same for women as for men. There is no need to make provision by law that a woman shall not carry on the active details of a household, or of the education of children, and at the same time practise a profession or be elected to parliament. Where incompatibility is real, it will take care of itself: but there is gross injustice in making the incompatibility a pretence for the exclusion of those in whose case it does not exist. And these, if they were free to choose, would be a very large proportion The maternity argument deserts its supporters in the case of single women, a large and increasing class of the population; a fact which, it is not irrelevant to remark, by tending to diminish the excessive competition of numbers, is calculated to assist greatly the prosperity of all. There is no inherent reason or necessity that all women should voluntarily choose to devote their lives to one animal function and it consequences. Numbers of women are wives and mothers only because there is no other career open to them, no other occupation for their feelings or their activities. Every improvement in their education, and enlargement of their faculties—everything which renders them more qualified for any other mode of life, increases the number of those to whom it is an injury and an oppression to be denied the choice. To say that women must be excluded from active life because maternity disqualifies them for it, is in fact to say, that every other career should be forbidden them in order that maternity may be their only resource.

But secondly, it is urged, that to give the same freedom of occupation to women as to men, would be an injurious addition to the crowd of competitors, by whom the avenues to almost all kinds of employment are choked up, and its remuneration depressed. This argument, it is to be observed, does not reach the political question. It gives no excuse for withholding from women the rights of citizenship. The suffrage, the jury-box, admission to the legislature and to office, it does not touch. It bears only on the industrial branch of the subject. Allowing it, then, in an economical point of view, its full force; assuming that to lay open to women the employments now monopolized by men, would tend, like the breaking down of other monopolies, to lower the rate of remuneration in those employments; let us consider what is the amount of this evil consequence, and what the compensation for it. The worst ever asserted, much worse than is at all likely to be realized, is that if women competed with men, a man and a woman could not together earn more than is now earned by the man alone. Let us make this supposition, the most unfavourable supposition possible, the joint income of the two would be the same as before, while the woman would be raised from the position of a servant to that of a partner. Even if every woman, as matters now stand, had a claim on some man for support, how infinitely preferable is it that part of the income should be of the woman's earning, even if the aggregate sum were but little increased by it, rather than that she should be compelled to stand aside in order that men may be the sole earners, and the sole dispensers of what is earned. Even under the present laws respecting the property of women,[1] a woman who contributes materially to the support of the family, cannot be treated in the same contemptuously tyrannical manner as one who, however she may toil as a domestic drudge, is a dependent on the man for subsistence. . . .But so long as competition is the general law of human life, it is tyranny to shut out one-half of the competitors. All who have attained the age of self-government, have an equal claim to be permitted to sell whatever kind of useful labour they are capable of, for the price which it will bring.

The third objection to the admission of women to political or professional life, its alleged hardening tendency, belongs to an age now past, and is scarcely to be comprehended

---

[1]The truly horrible effects of the present state of the law among the lowest of the working population, is exhibited in those cases of hideous maltreatment of their wives by working men, with which every newspaper, every police report, teems. Wretches unfit to have the smallest authority over any living thing, have a helpless woman for their household slave. These excesses could not exist if women both earned, and had the right to possess, a part of the income of the family.

by people of the present time. There are still, however, persons who say that the world and its avocations render men selfish and unfeeling; that the struggles, rivalries, and collisions of business and of politics make them harsh and unamiable; that if half the species must unavoidably be given up to these things, it is the more necessary that the other half should be kept free from them; that to preserve women from the bad influences of the world, is the only chance of preventing men from being wholly given up to them.

There would have been plausibility in this argument when the world was still in the age of violence; when life was full of physical conflict, and every man had to redress his injuries or those of others, by the sword or by the strength of his arm. Women, like priests, by being exempted from such responsibilities, and from some part of the accompanying dangers, may have been enabled to exercise a beneficial influence. But in the present condition of human life, we do not know where those hardening influences are to be found, to which men are subject and from which women are at present exempt. Individuals now-a-days are seldom called upon to fight hand to hand, even with peaceful weapons; personal enmities and rivalities count for little in worldly transactions; the general pressure of circumstances, not the adverse will of individuals, is the obstacle men now have to make head against. That pressure, when excessive, breaks the spirit, and cramps and sours the feelings, but not less of women than of men, since they suffer certainly not less from its evils. There are still quarrels and dislikes, but the sources of them are changed. The feudal chief once found his bitterest enemy in his powerful neighbour, the minister or courtier in his rival for place: but opposition of interest in active life, as a cause of personal animosity, is out of date; the enmities of the present day arise not from great things but small, from what people say of one another, more than from what they do; and if there are hated, malice, and all uncharitableness, they are to be found among women fully as much as among men. In the present state of civilization, the notion of guarding women from the hardening influences of the world, could only be realized by secluding them from society altogether. The common duties of common life, as at present constituted, are incompatible with any other softness in women than weakness. Surely weak minds in weak bodies must ere long cease to be even supposed to be either attractive or amiable.

But, in truth, none of these arguments and considerations touch the foundations of the subject. The real question is, whether it is right and expedient that one-half of the human race should pass through life in a state of forced subordination to the other half. If the best state of human society is that of being divided into two parts, one consisting of persons with a will and a substantive existence, the other of humble companions to these persons, attached, each of them to one, for the purpose of bringing up *his* children, and making *his* home pleasant to him; if this is the place assigned to women, it is but kindness to educate them for this; to make them believe that the greatest good fortune which can befall them, is to be chosen by some man for his purpose; and that every other career which the world deems happy or honourable, is closed to them by the law, not of social institutions, but of nature and destiny.

When, however, we ask why the existence of one-half the species should be merely ancillary to that of the other—why each woman should be a mere appendage to a man, allowed to have no interests of her own, that there may be nothing to compete in her mind with his interests and his pleasure; the only reason which can be given is, that men like it. It is agreeable to them that men should live for their own sake, women for the sake of men; and the qualities and conduct in subjects which are agreeable to rulers, they succeed for a long time in making the subjects themselves consider as their appropriate virtues. . . . Under a nominal recognition of a moral code common to both, in practice in self-will and self-assertion form the type of what are designated as manly virtues, while abnegation of self, patience, resignation, and submission to power, unless when resistance is commanded by other interests than their own, have been stamped by general consent as pre-eminently the duties and graces required of women. The meaning being merely, that power makes itself the centre of moral obligation, and that a man likes to have his own will, but does not like that his domestic companion should have a will different from his.

Study Questions

1. What are Harriet Taylor Mill's counterarguments to the three standard arguments against women in the workforce? Are they convincing to you? Why or why not?

2. Might the three arguments (motherhood, unfair competition, and hardening of the character) be valid in any conceivable modern context? Explain why or why not.

3. Apply H. T. Mill's arguments to the idea of women in combat. Do you see the same arguments supporting the idea? Or is there a difference? Explain.

4. Comment on H. T. Mill's statement that the only reason women have been ancillary (subordinate) to men is that men like it; is that a fair statement within the context of the nineteenth century, as far as you can tell? Would it be a fair statement in the twenty-first century?

Primary Reading

The Second Sex

SIMONE DE BEAUVOIR

Excerpt, 1949.

In this excerpt, Beauvoir demonstrates her commitment to what we have called classical feminism: If boys and girls were raised as human beings rather than two different species, sexism would no longer exist. The "castration complex" and the "Oedipus complex" are references to Sigmund Freud's psychoanalytic theories that little girls feel inferior to boys because they have no penis (and believe they have been deprived of one). Here you should remember that the style of child rearing Beauvoir criticizes is, for most educated people in the Western world, a thing of the past. Her critical assessment of the traditional upbringing of boys and girls has been a powerful factor in changing that tradition.

A world where men and women would be equal is easy to visualize, for that precisely is what the Soviet Revolution *promised:* women raised and trained exactly like men were to work under the same conditions and for the same wages. Erotic liberty was to be recognized by custom, but the sexual act was not to be considered a "service" to be paid for; woman was to be *obliged* to provide herself with other ways of earning a living; marriage was to be based on a free agreement that the spouses could break at will; maternity was to be voluntary, which meant that contraception and abortion were to be authorized and that, on the other hand, all mothers and their children were to have exactly the same rights, in or out of marriage; pregnancy leaves were to be paid for by the State, which would assume charge of the children, signifying not that they would be *taken away* from their parents, but that they would not be *abandoned* to them.

But is it enough to change laws, institutions, customs, public opinion, and the whole social context, for men and women to become truly equal? "Women will always be women," say the skeptics. Other seers prophesy that in casting off their femininity they will not succeed in changing themselves into men and they will become monsters. This would be to admit that the woman of today is a creation of nature; it must be repeated once more that in human society nothing is natural and that woman, like much else, is a product elaborated by civilization. The intervention of others in her destiny is fundamental: if this action took a different direction, it would produce a quite different result. Woman is determined not by her hormones or by mysterious instincts, but by the manner in which her body and her relation to the world are modified through the action of others than herself. The abyss that separates the adolescent boy and girl has been deliberately opened out between them since earliest childhood; later on, woman could not be other than what she *was made,* and that past was bound to shadow her for life. If we appreciate its influence, we see clearly that her destiny is not predetermined for all eternity.

We must not believe, certainly, that a change in woman's economic condition alone is enough to transform her, though this factor has been and remains the basic factor in her evolution; but until it has brought about the moral, social, cultural, and other consequences that it promises and requires, the new woman cannot appear. At this moment they have been realized nowhere, in Russia no more than in France or the United States; and this explains why the woman of today is torn between the past and the future. She appears most often as a "true woman" disguised as a man, and she feels herself as ill at ease in her flesh as in her masculine garb. She must shed her old skin and cut her own new clothes. This she could do only through a social evolution. No single educator could fashion a *female human being* today who would be the exact homologue of the *male human being;* if she is raised like a boy, the young girl feels she is an oddity and thereby she is given a new kind of sex specification. Stendhal [a nineteenth-century French novelist] understood this when he said: "The forest must be planted all at once." But if we imagine, on the contrary, a society in which the equality of the sexes would be concretely realized, this equality would find new expression in each individual.

If the little girl were brought up from the first with the same demands and rewards, the same severity and the same freedom, as her brothers, taking part in the same studies, the same games, promised the same future, surrounded with women and men who seemed to her undoubted equals, the meanings of the castration complex and of the Oedipus complex would be profoundly modified. Assuming on the same basis as the father the material and moral responsibility of the couple, the mother would enjoy the same lasting prestige; the child would perceive around her an androgynous world and not a masculine world. Were she emotionally more attracted to her father—which is not even sure—her love for him would be tinged with a will to emulation and not a feeling of powerlessness; she would not be oriented toward passivity. Authorized to test her powers in work and sports, competing actively with the boys, she would not find the absence of the penis—compensated by the promise of a child—enough to give rise to an inferiority complex; correlatively, the boy would not have a superiority complex if it were not instilled into him and if he looked up to women with as much respect as to men. The little girl would not seek sterile compensation in narcissism and dreaming, she would not take her fate for granted; she would be interested in what she was *doing,* she would throw herself without reserve into undertakings. . . .

I shall be told that all this is utopian fancy, because woman cannot be "made over" unless society has first made her really the equal of man. Conservatives have never failed in such circumstances to refer to that vicious circle; history, however, does not revolve. If a caste is kept in a state of inferiority, no doubt it remains inferior; but liberty can break the circle. Let the Negroes vote and they become worthy of having the vote; let woman be given responsibilities and she is able to assume them. The fact is that oppressors cannot be expected to make a move of gratuitous generosity; but at one time the revolt of the oppressed, at another time even the very evolution of the privileged caste itself, creates new situations; thus men have been led, in their own interest, to give partial emancipation to women: it remains only for women to continue their ascent, and the successes they are obtaining are an encouragement for them to do so. It seems almost certain that sooner or later they will arrive at complete economic and social equality, which will bring about an inner metamorphosis.

However this may be, there will be some to object that if such a world is possible it is not desirable. When woman is "the same" as her male, life will lose its salt and spice. This argument, also, has lost its novelty: those interested in perpetuating present conditions are always in tears about the marvelous past that is about to disappear, without having so much as a smile for the young future. It is quite true that doing away with the slave trade meant death to the great plantations, magnificent with azaleas and camellias, it meant ruin to the whole refined Southern civilization. The attics of time have received its rare odd laces along with the clear pure voices of the Sistine *castrati,* and there is a certain "feminine charm" that is also on the way to the same dusty repository. I agree that he would be a barbarian indeed who failed to appreciate exquisite flowers, rare lace, the crystal clear voice of the eunuch, and feminine charm.

When the "charming woman" shows herself in all her splendor, she is a much more exalting object than the "idiotic paintings, overdoors, scenery, showman's garish signs, popular chromos," that excited [French poet Arthur] Rimbaud; adorned with the most modern artifices, beautified according to the newest techniques, she comes down from the remoteness of the ages, from Thebes, from Crete, from Chichén-Itzá; and she is also the totem set up deep in the African jungle; she is a helicopter and she is a bird; and there is this, the greatest wonder of all: under her tinted hair the forest murmur becomes a thought, and words issue from her breasts. Men stretch forth avid hands toward the marvel, but when they grasp it is gone; the wife, the mistress, speak like everybody else through their mouths: their words are worth just what they are worth; their breasts also. Does such a fugitive miracle—and one so rare—justify us in perpetuating a situation that is baneful for both sexes? One can appreciate them at their true value; if these treasures cost blood or misery, they must be sacrificed.

Study Questions

1. Identify the characteristic elements of classical feminism in this excerpt.

2. Comment on Beauvoir's remark that one can appreciate the beauty of flowers, the charm of women, and "appreciate them at their true value; if these treasures cost blood and misery, they must be sacrificed."

3. What does Beauvoir mean by saying, "Let the Negroes vote and they become worthy of having the vote; let woman be given responsibilities and she is able to assume them"?

4. Evaluate the criticism that the gender-free model of upbringing Beauvoir envisions for boys and girls is really just patterned after the traditional upbringing of boys; does Beauvoir want women to become men in order to achieve social and political freedom?

 Primary Reading

In a Different Voice

CAROL GILLIGAN

Excerpt, 1982.

In this excerpt, Gilligan refers to the psychoanalyst Erik Erikson, whom you encountered briefly in Chapter 10. Erikson's theory of development focuses on the importance of the adolescent boy's separating himself from his parents to achieve a personal identity before he can experience any intimacy. For the adolescent girl it is different, says Erikson; she doesn't experience the same kind of separation. However, it is the boy's development that becomes the typical individual development for Erikson, according to Gilligan. In this excerpt she also refers to how fairy tales may give similar portrayals of male and female psychology. Gilligan here introduces the experience of the ethic of care from the woman's point of view.

> Erikson's description of male identity as forged in relation to the world and of female identity as awakened in a relationship of intimacy with another person is hardly new. In the fairy tales that [psychoanalyst] Bruno Bettelheim describes [in *The Uses of Enchantment*] an identical portrayal appears. The dynamics of male adolescence are illustrated archetypically by the conflict between father and son in "The Three Languages." Here a son, considered hopelessly stupid by his father, is given one last chance at education and sent for a year to study with a master. But when he returns, all he has learned is "what the dogs bark." After two further attempts of this sort, the father gives up in disgust and orders his servants to take the child into the forest and kill him. But the servants, those perpetual rescuers of disowned and abandoned children, take pity on the child and decide simply to leave him in the forest. From there, his wanderings take him to a land beset by furious dogs whose barking permits nobody to rest and who periodically devour one of

the inhabitants. Now it turns out that our hero has learned just the right thing: he can talk with the dogs and is able to quiet them, thus restoring peace to the land. Since the other knowledge he acquires serves him equally well, he emerges triumphant from his adolescent confrontation with his father, a giant of the life-cycle conception.

In contrast, the dynamics of female adolescence are depicted through the telling of a very different story. In the world of the fairy tale, the girl's first bleeding is followed by a period of intense passivity in which nothing seems to be happening. Yet in the deep sleeps of Snow White and Sleeping Beauty, Bettelheim sees that inner concentration which he considers to be the necessary counterpart to the activity of adventure. Since the adolescent heroines awake from their sleep, not to conquer the world, but to marry the prince, their identity is inwardly and interpersonally defined. For women, in Bettelheim's as in Erikson's account, identity and intimacy are intricately conjoined. The sex differences depicted in the world of fairy tales, like the fantasy of the woman warrior in Maxine Hong Kingston's recent autobiographical novel [*The Woman Warrior,* 1977] which echoes the old stories of Troilus and Cressida and Tancred and Corinda, indicate repeatedly that active adventure is a male activity, and that if a woman is to embark on such endeavors, she must at least dress like a man. . . .

"It is obvious," Virginia Woolf says, "that the values of women differ very often from the values which have been made by the other sex." Yet, she adds, "it is the masculine values that prevail." As a result, women come to question the normality of their feelings and to alter their judgments in deference to the opinion of others. In the nineteenth-century novels written by women, Woolf sees at work "a mind which was slightly pulled from the straight and made to alter its clear vision in deference to external authority." The same deference to the values and opinions of others can be seen in the judgments of twentieth-century women. The difficulty women experience in finding or speaking publicly in their own voices emerges repeatedly in the form of qualification and self-doubt, but also in intimations of a divided judgment, a public assessment and private assessment which are fundamentally at odds.

Yet the deference and confusion that Woolf criticizes in women derive from the values she sees as their strength. Women's deference is rooted not only in their social subordination but also in the substance of their moral concern. Sensitivity to the needs of others and the assumption of responsibility for taking care lead women to attend to voices other than their own and to include in their judgment other points of view. Women's moral weakness, manifest in an apparent diffusion and confusion of judgment, is thus inseparable from women's moral strength, an overriding concern with relationships and responsibilities. The reluctance to judge may itself be indicative of the care and concern for others that infuse the psychology of women's development and are responsible for what is generally seen as problematic in its nature.

Thus women not only define themselves in a context of human relationship but also judge themselves in terms of their ability to care. Women's place in man's life cycle has been that of nurturer, caretaker, and helpmate, the weaver of those networks of relationships on which she in turn relies. But while women have thus taken care of men, men have, in their theories of psychological development, as in their economic arrangements, tended to assume or devalue that care. When the focus on individuation and individual achievement extends into adulthood and maturity is equated with personal autonomy, concern with relationships appears as a weakness of women rather than as a human strength. . . .

The discovery now being celebrated by men in mid-life of the importance of intimacy, relationships, and care is something that women have known from the beginning. However, because that knowledge in women has been considered "intuitive" or "instinctive," a function of anatomy coupled with destiny, psychologists have neglected to describe its development. In my research, I have found that women's moral development centers on the elaboration of that knowledge and thus delineates a critical line of psychological development in the lives of both of the sexes.

Study Questions

1. Examine "The Three Languages," the first fairy tale cited in the excerpt, and compare it with "Snow White" and "Sleeping Beauty" (which I assume you are familiar with). Explain how each can be said to contain a view of the male and female psyche. You may want to read the section on fairy tales in Chapter 2 again.

2. How does this excerpt on women's moral values relate to virtue theory?

3. Evaluate Gilligan's statement that "women's deference is rooted not only in their social subordination but also in the substance of their moral concern. Sensitivity to the needs of others and the assumption of the responsibility for taking care lead women to attend to voices other than their own and to include in their judgment other points of view." How do you think Levinas (Chapter 10) would comment on that statement? What do you think Christina Hoff Sommers might say? And what is your own opinion?

 Narrative

A Doll's House

HENRIK IBSEN

Play, 1879. Translated by William Archer. Summary and Excerpt. Two British film versions exist, both from 1973; one stars Claire Bloom and Anthony Hopkins; the other stars Jane Fonda and David Warner.

By the time the Norwegian playwright Henrik Ibsen wrote *A Doll's House,* isolated voices had been speaking out for the liberation of women for over a hundred years, but there was not a single country in the Western world where women had yet achieved the right to vote. When Ibsen's play was performed on the stages of Europe, the final act turned out to be a bombshell; Ibsen allows us to see Nora's situation from her own point of view and shows us that this viewpoint is heroic in its own way. In her quest to be regarded as a mature human being, Nora sent signals to men and women all over the Western world and made a considerable impact on the gender debate in Scandinavia at the end of the nineteenth and the beginning of the twentieth century. The story has been considered so compelling that the play is still performed today.

Some contemporary readers may prefer to look for literature about the condition of women written by *women,* not by *men.* But, for one thing, Ibsen's play has had historical importance in helping men as well as women see the traditional woman's role as a political question; for another thing, good writers gifted with clear powers of observation and an imaginative genius, such as Ibsen, are often quite capable of seeing a situation from the other gender's point of view.

The conflict between the feminine virtue of caring and the masculine focus on justice may seem new to many readers of Carol Gilligan, but in these excerpts you can see the outlines of that very same debate, anticipated by Ibsen more than a century ago.

Nora and Torvald Helmer are a happily married middle-class couple with three young children. Helmer regards his lively wife as another child, always happy and singing; his pet names for her are his songbird, his lark, his little squirrel. He accuses her of being a spendthrift, of always asking for more pocket money, but he forgives her because she is so sweet and amusing. And even to her friends she seems like a carefree, coddled woman with no worries other than choosing what clothes to wear for parties. But things are not what they seem on the surface. An old friend of Nora's comes to visit, and Nora tells her a deep secret of which she is very proud: Some years ago Helmer was very ill, and the doctor recommended an expensive trip to Italy as a cure. Helmer believes that Nora's father lent them the money, and he is now dead, so he can't tell. But Nora paid for the trip all by herself, with no income or fortune of her own: She took out a private loan, with high interest, and that is why she has been asking Helmer for so much pocket money, buying only the cheapest things for herself, and paying the loan off, always on time, with interest. And it won't be long now before the loan will be paid off: Helmer is being promoted to bank manager, and their finances will improve.

But disaster waits in the wings: An employee at the bank, Krogstad, turns up and begs her to ask her husband to let him keep his job. Why might he lose it? Because he has a criminal record; he has forged papers. And why would he come to Nora? Because Nora knows him well—he is the man who lent her the money for the trip to Italy. He threatens to tell Helmer, but what is worse, he has done some research. Nora's father cosigned the loan, as security—but the signature is dated days after her father died. The conclusion is obvious: Nora forged her father's signature, and now Krogstad threatens her with the law and tells her that his crime was no worse than her own.

> *Krogstad:* May I ask you one more question? Why did you not send the paper to your father?
>
> *Nora:* It was impossible. Father was ill. If I had asked him for his signature, I should have had to tell him why I wanted the money; but he was so ill I really could not tell him that my husband's life was in danger. It was impossible.
>
> *Krogstad:* Then it would have been better to have given up your tour.
>
> *Nora:* No, I couldn't do that; my husband's life depended on that journey. I couldn't give it up.
>
> *Krogstad:* And did it never occur to you that you were playing me false?
>
> *Nora:* That was nothing to me. I didn't care in the least about you. I couldn't endure you for all the cruel difficulties you made, although you knew how ill my husband was.

Krogstad: Mrs. Helmer, you evidently do not realise what you have been guilty of. But I can assure you it was nothing more and nothing worse that made me an outcast from society.

Nora: You! You want me to believe that you did a brave thing to save your wife's life?

Krogstad: The law takes no account of motives.

Nora: Then it must be a very bad law.

Krogstad: Bad or not, if I produce this document in court, you will be condemned according to law.

Nora: I don't believe that. Do you mean to tell me that a daughter has no right to spare her dying father trouble and anxiety?—that a wife has no right to save her husband's life? I don't know much about the law, but I'm sure you'll find, somewhere or another, that that is allowed. And you don't know that—you, a lawyer! You must be a bad one, Mr. Krogstad.

Krogstad: Possibly. But business—such business as ours—I do understand. You believe that? Very well; now do as you please. But this I may tell you, that if I am flung into the gutter a second time, you shall keep me company.

[*Bows and goes out through hall.*]

Nora: [*Stands a while thinking, then tosses her head.*] Oh nonsense! He wants to frighten me. I'm not so foolish as that. [*Begins folding the children's clothes. Pauses.*] But—? No, it's impossible! Why, I did it for love!

Later, Helmer talks to her about what a despicable man Krogstad is, and how vile his crime. Shortly after, Helmer fires Krogstad, in spite of Nora's pleas, and Krogstad shows up again. Now he wants more: Unless Nora makes Helmer reinstate him and give him a promotion, he will reveal all. And if Nora should think of drastic solutions, such as killing herself, her husband will still be told everything. Now Krogstad wants Helmer to know, so he can blackmail the two of them, instead of only her, and he leaves a letter for Helmer, telling him everything. Nora is desperate and tries to distract Helmer when he comes home by dancing for him, and she makes him promise that he will not open the letter until the next day. Meanwhile, she pleads with her friend and confidante to go to Krogstad and persuade him to stop his threats.

The following night Nora and Helmer are at a dance, and Nora dances as if it is her last night on this earth. Coming home, there is still the letter waiting for them, and Nora, deep in despair, is waiting, too: for a miracle, for without it she is going to kill herself.

But Helmer reads the letter, and is horrified: the woman he loved, a liar and a criminal! He blames her weakness of character and her father's bad influence and sees himself as a ruined man. He insists that Nora can no longer see her children—they must be protected from her evil influence. Nora threatens suicide, but Helmer scoffs at it: How is that going to help *him* and *his* ruin? And now it dawns on Nora that her motivation for forging her father's signature is utterly lost on Helmer; the miracle she was hoping for, and dreading, is far from happening.

But now comes the salvation: Nora's friend has succeeded in persuading Krogstad to drop the matter (through a personal sacrifice which Nora knows nothing about). Krogstad returns Nora's I.O.U. with an apologetic letter, and Helmer is ecstatic, exclaiming that now he is saved. And, magnanimously, he now sees Nora as a poor, misguided soul who has not understood what she has done, and he forgives her. All she needs now is his guidance, he says—from now on he'll be her will and her conscience, and everything will be as before.

Meanwhile Nora, stone-faced, has changed out of her masquerade dress and into her ordinary clothes. For her, the masquerade is over, and although he doesn't know it yet, it is, too, for him. She asks him to sit down, for she has much to talk over with him.

Helmer: You alarm me, Nora. I don't understand you.

Nora: No, that is just it. You don't understand me; and I have never understood you—till tonight. No, don't interrupt. Only listen to what I say.—We must come to a final settlement, Torvald.

Helmer: How do you mean?

Nora: [*After a short silence.*] Does not one thing strike you as we sit here?

Helmer: What should strike me?

Nora: We have been married eight years. Does it not strike you that this is the first time we two, you and I, man and wife, have talked together seriously?

Helmer: Seriously! What do you call seriously?

Nora: During eight whole years, and more—ever since the day we first met—we have never exchanged one serious word about serious things.

Helmer: Was I always to trouble you with the cares you could not help me to bear?

Nora: I am not talking of cares. I say that we have never yet set ourselves seriously to get to the bottom of anything.

Helmer: Why, my dearest Nora, what have you to do with serious things?

Nora: There we have it! You have never understood me.—I have had great injustice done me, Torvald; first by father, and then by you.

Helmer: What! By your father and me?—By us, who have loved you more than all the world?

Nora: [*Shaking her head.*] You have never loved me. You only thought it amusing to be in love with me.

Helmer: Why, Nora, what a thing to say!

Nora: Yes, it is so, Torvald. While I was at home with father, he used to tell me all his opinions, and I held the same opinions. If I had others I said nothing about them, because he wouldn't have liked it. He used to call me his doll-child, and played with me as I played with my dolls. Then I came to live in your house—

Helmer: What an expression to use about our marriage!

Nora: [*Undisturbed.*] I mean I passed from father's hands into yours. You arranged everything according to your taste; and I got the same tastes as you; or I pretended to—I don't know which—both ways, perhaps; sometimes one and sometimes the other. When I look back on it now, I seem to have been living here like a beggar, from hand to mouth. I lived by performing tricks for you, Torvald. But you would have it so. You and father have done me a great wrong. It is your fault that my life has come to nothing.

Helmer: Why, Nora, how unreasonable and ungrateful you are! Have you not been happy here?

Nora: No, never. I thought I was; but I never was.

Helmer: Not—not happy!

Nora: No; only merry. And you have always been so kind to me. But our house has been nothing but a play-room. Here I have been your doll-wife, just as at home I used to be papa's doll-child. And the children, in their turn, have been my dolls. I thought it fun when you played with me, just as the children did when I played with them. That has been our marriage, Torvald.

. . . .

Helmer: To forsake your home, your husband, and your children! And you don't consider what the world will say.

Nora: I can pay no heed to that. I only know that I must do it.

Helmer: This is monstrous! Can you forsake your holiest duties in this way?

Nora: What do you consider my holiest duties?

Helmer: Do I need to tell you that? Your duties to your husband and your children.

Nora: I have other duties equally sacred.

Helmer: Impossible! What duties do you mean?

Nora: My duties towards myself.

Helmer: Before all else you are a wife and a mother.

Nora: That I no longer believe. I believe that before all else I am a human being, just as much as you are—or at least that I should try to become one. I know that most people agree with you, Torvald, and that they say so in books. But henceforth I can't be satisfied with what most people say, and what is in books. I must think things out for myself, and try to get clear about them.

. . . .

Nora: I have waited so patiently all these eight years; for of course I saw clearly enough that miracles don't happen every day. When this crushing blow threatened me, I said to myself so confidently, "Now comes the miracle!" When Krogstad's letter lay in the box, it never for a moment occurred to me that you would think of submitting to that man's conditions. I was convinced that you would say to him, "Make it known to all the world"; and that then—

Helmer: Well? When I had given my own wife's name up to disgrace and shame—?

Nora: Then I firmly believed that you would come forward, take everything upon yourself, and say, "I am the guilty one."

Helmer: Nora—!

Nora: You mean I would never have accepted such a sacrifice? No, certainly not. But what would my assertions have been worth in opposition to yours?—That was the miracle that I hoped for and dreaded. And it was to hinder that that I wanted to die.

Helmer: I would gladly work for you day and night, Nora—bear sorrow and want for your sake. But no man sacrifices his honour, even for one he loves.

Nora: Millions of women have done so.

So, in the end, Torvald is the one who understands nothing; he promises to love her, to do anything if she will only stay with him. But she sees him now as a stranger and prepares to leave. In her final words to him she says that to get together again, they would both have to change so much that "communion between them shall be a marriage." And Nora leaves, closing the door behind her.

Study Questions

1. What does Nora mean by the final line in this excerpt?

2. If you were in Nora's position, would your reaction be similar or different? Why? If you were in Helmer's position, would your reaction be similar or different? Why?

3. Examine the excerpts and find evidence of virtue ethics as opposed to an ethics of justice.

4. Ibsen refers to his characters as "Nora" and "Helmer" rather than "Nora" and "Torvald." What kind of effect might that have on the reader of the play? Do you think it is intentional?

Narrative

The Woman Destroyed

SIMONE DE BEAUVOIR

Short story, 1967. Translated by Patrick O'Brian. Summary and Excerpts.

As you know from Chapter 10, Jean-Paul Sartre was not only a philosopher but also a novelist and a playwright. The fact that his longtime partner, Simone de Beauvoir, also wrote fiction is not quite as well known. Here we look at passages from her short story "The Woman Destroyed," about Monique, who has been married to Maurice for more than twenty years. Their two daughters are grown and no longer live at home, and Monique is under the impression that now she and Maurice will continue with the pleasant life they've established and which has become a habit. So it is a dreadful shock to her to discover that he has been having an affair with an acquaintance of theirs, Noëllie, for quite some time.

In these excerpts you will see Monique swing between extremes of blaming Noëllie, her husband, and herself for the situation that has developed. Maurice doesn't deny the relationship, and initially he doesn't want to lose either woman. He wants to have his cake and eat it too.

Maurice will see anything I say against Noëllie as the effect of my jealousy. It would be better to say nothing. But I really do find her profoundly disagreeable. She reminds me of my sister—the same confidence, the same glibness, the same phonily offhand elegance. It seems that men like this mixture of coquetry and hardness. When I was sixteen and she was eighteen Maryse swiped all my boyfriends. So much so that I was in a dreadful state of nerves when I introduced Maurice to her. I had a ghastly nightmare in which he fell in love with her. He was indignant. "She is so superficial! So bogus! Paste diamonds, rhinestones! You—you're the real jewel." Authentic: that was the word everyone was using in those days. He said I was authentic. At all events I was the one he loved, and I was not envious of my sister anymore; I was happy to be the person I was. But then how can he think a great deal of Noëllie, who is of the same kind as Maryse? He is altogether gone from me if he likes being with someone I dislike so very much—and whom he ought to dislike if he were faithful to our code. Certainly he has altered. He lets himself be taken in by false values that we used to despise. Or he is simply completely mistaken about Noëllie. I wish the scales would drop from his eyes soon. My patience is beginning to run out. . . .

"I don't want any sharing: you must make your choice."

He had the overwhelmed look of a man who is saying to himself, *Here we are! It had to happen. How can I get myself out of this one?* He adopted his most coaxing voice. "Please, darling. Don't ask me to break with Noëllie. Not now."

"Yes, now. This business is dragging on too much. I have borne it too long by far." I looked at him challengingly. "Come now, which do you like best? Her or me?"

"You, of course," he said in a toneless voice. And he added, "But I like Noëllie too."

I saw red. "Admit the truth, then! She's the one you like best! All right! Go to her! Get out of here. Get out at once. Take your things and go."

I pulled his suitcase out of the wardrobe, I flung clothes into it higgledy-piggledy, I unhooked coat hangers. He took my arm: "Stop!" I went on. I wanted him to go; I really wanted it—it was sincere. Sincere because I did not believe in it. It was like a dreadful psychodrama in which they play at truth. It is the truth, but it is being acted. I shouted, "Go and join that bitch, that schemer, that dirty little shady lawyer."

He took me by the wrists. "Take back what you have said."

"No. She's a filthy thing. She got you by flattery. You prefer her to me out of vanity. You're sacrificing our love to your vanity."

Again he said, "Shut up." But I went on. I poured out everything I thought about Noëllie and him. Yes: I have a confused recollection of it. I said that he was letting himself be taken in like a pitiful fool, that he was turning into a pretentious, on-the-make vulgarian, that he was no longer the man I had loved, that once upon a time he had possessed a heart and given himself up to others—now he was hard and selfish and concerned only with his career.

"Who's selfish?" he cried. And he shouted me down. I was the one who was selfish—I who had not hesitated to make him give up a resident post, who would have liked to confine him to a small-time career all his life long so as to keep him at home, I who was jealous of his work—a castrating woman. . . .

Evening

I had an inspiration this morning: the whole thing is my fault. My worst mistake has been not grasping that *time goes by.* It was going by and there I was, set in the attitude of the ideal wife of an ideal husband. Instead of bringing our sexual relationship to life again I brooded happily over memories of our former nights together. I imagined I had kept my thirty-year-old face and body instead of taking care of myself, doing gymnastics and going to a beauty parlor. I let my intelligence wither away: I no longer cultivated my mind—*later,* I said, *when the children have gone.* (Perhaps my father's death was not with-out bearing on this way of letting things slide. Something snapped. I stopped time from that moment on.) Yes: the young student Maurice married felt passionately about what was happening in the world, about books and ideas; she was very unlike the woman of today, whose world lies between the four walls of this apartment. It is true enough that I tended to shut Maurice in. I thought his home was enough for him: I thought I owned him entirely. Generally speaking I took everything for granted; and that must have irritated him intensely—Maurice who changes and who calls things in question. Being irritating—no one can ever get away with that. I should never have been obstinate about our promise of faithfulness, either. If I had given Maurice back his freedom—and made use of mine, too, perhaps—Noëllie would not have profited by the glamour of clandestinity. I should have coped with the situation at once. Is there still time? . . .

It is only now that I realize how much value I had for myself, fundamentally. But Maurice has murdered all the words by which I might try to justify it: he has repudiated the standards by which I measured others and myself; I had never dreamed of challeng-ing them—that is to say of challenging myself. And now what I wonder is this: what right had I to say that the inner life was preferable to a merely social life, contemplation to trifling amusements, and self-sacrifice to ambition? My only life had been to create happiness around me. I have not made Maurice happy. And my daughters are not happy either. So what then? I no longer know anything. Not only do I not know what kind of a person I am, but also I do not know what kind of a person I ought to be. Black and white merge into one another, the world is an amorphous mass, and I no longer have any clear outlines. How is it possible to live without believing in anything or in myself?

Study Questions

1. In your opinion, does Beauvoir want us to identify with Monique, or criticize her atti-tude, or perhaps a little bit of both? Identify the passages that support your view.

2. Compare these excerpts with the text excerpt from *The Second Sex* (pp. 621–624). How might Beauvoir analyze Monique's situation and attitude from the viewpoint of her own classical feminism?

3. Monique seems to think she has no moral right to hold on to her husband. Do you agree? Why or why not?

Narrative

Mona Lisa Smile

LAWRENCE KONNER AND MARK ROSENTHAL (SCREENWRITERS)MIKE NEWELL (DIRECTOR)

Film, 2003. Summary.

It is 1953, the beginning of the fall semester at Wellesley College, a women's college in Massachusetts with many proud traditions. The semester starts with a ritual: A young student (who later, with an ironic twist, turns out to be one of the main characters,

Joanie) knocks on the massive wooden doors of the college. The school president asks, "Who knocks at the door of learning?" The student answers that she is everywoman, and the president replies that anyone who seeks knowledge and wants to dedicate her life to knowledge is welcome. The professors at Wellesley are competent men and women, and the standards for teaching are high, but as the film progresses, we realize that the main reason most of the girls are receiving a very expensive, highly respected education is not to dedicate their life to knowledge but mainly to learn what a well-mannered high-society wife needs to know. Few students actually end up using their degree.

Into this school of traditions comes a young progressive art professor and graduate student from California on a one-year probation hire: Katherine Watson. She has idealistic notions about opening the eyes of other young women eager to learn, but her first "History of Art 100" class is a disaster: She is lecturing from the textbook, but all the students have already read the book and end up ignoring her and leaving for independent studies. It seems that Katherine's stay at Wellesley is going to be difficult: The alumni and the professors find her proposed thesis on Picasso much too avant-garde, and a professor scolds her for losing control of her first class. She rooms with another teacher, who teaches classes in etiquette and promptly tells Katherine that she would have been married except for her fiancé's dying in World War II. We get the impression that getting married is the ultimate ideal for everyone, professors and students alike—except for Katherine's other roommate, the school nurse Amanda Armstrong, a woman with a strong personality and a good sense of humor but with a tragedy in her life: Her "companion" has just died—and so we know that Amanda is a lesbian. She warns Katherine that too much independence will frighten the establishment at Wellesley.

Next class Katherine is better prepared: Instead of following the official syllabus, she introduces her own and starts showing the students modern art, to shock them into a realization that art appreciation doesn't come out of a book but is a lived experience: The question What is Art? is more important than the answer. But immediately she is up against the traditionalists among her students, above all Betty, daughter of a socialite, who is about to have all her dreams fulfilled and get married. Betty is "popular" because she wields power, but she is not well-liked; she is always putting the less popular, less attractive girls down and does her best to undermine not only Katherine but also the nurse Amanda, who has been distributing illegal contraception to the students. Writing a tell-all column in the school paper about the birth-control issue, Betty effectively gets Amanda fired. But in her own life Betty is under the strict influence of her mother, who arranges all wedding preparations, including telling Betty how to manipulate her future husband.

Other students begin to awaken to Katherine's persuasively fresh outlook: Joanie, Betty's friend, begins to see things Katherine's way; and above all, the free-spirited Giselle takes her art lessons to heart and begins to see Katherine as a role model. Giselle is looking for love, dates her handsome Italian language professor Bill Dunbar for a while, and isn't ready to accept that the relationship is over. Dunbar himself tells fascinating stories of when he was a soldier in Italy in World War II, in his classes as well as on dates, and Katherine herself begins to take a liking to him.

Joanie has a heart-to-heart talk with Katherine and reveals that she would like to go to Yale Law School but doesn't consider it an option, since she's getting married to Tommy. Katherine insists that she can do both and helps her submit an application to Yale,

From the film *Mona Lisa Smile*: Katherine Watson (Julia Roberts) does her best to teach her students at Wellesley College to appreciate modern art. At the same time, she tries to persuade them not to let their education, and their intellect, go to waste.

in secret. To Joanie's enormous surprise, she is accepted. In the meantime, Betty marries Spencer in a lavish wedding to which the "movers and shakers" of the community are invited, and Betty stops taking classes so she can go on her honeymoon and set up her new home.

Right before the Christmas break, President Carr lets Katherine know that her job indeed is in peril—if she doesn't change her ways and lecture less on modern art, her contract will not be renewed.

During the break, Joanie and her boyfriend are visiting Betty and Spencer in their new home, and Betty shows off her washer and dryer, her home, and "everything she ever dreamed of." When she hears Joanie has been accepted to Yale, she can't believe Joanie would even consider it—she is so close to having her dreams fulfilled, and now she's about to throw it all away! But perhaps Betty's life isn't so perfect after all: Spencer gets a call from New York and has to leave on business right after dinner, and Betty is stuck with her dinner guests and a bunch of unanswered questions.

Katherine gets a Christmas surprise: Paul, her boyfriend from California, shows up and proposes to her. He's so miserable without her that he's willing to move back East to be with her. So now it looks as if she really can have both too—but that same evening she realizes that she really doesn't want a marriage with Paul at all—especially since she inadvertently calls him *Bill,* and we know it's professor Dunbar who is on her mind.

Betty returns to classes in the new semester and expects to pick up where she left off so she can graduate. This procedure seems to be acceptable to everyone at Wellesley, but Katherine comes down hard on her: If she doesn't catch up, she will be failed—and Betty responds that Katherine's position is by no means certain. The power struggle between the two is in full bloom. After the girls hear Katherine's view that marriage is not a necessity, Betty writes a scathing column in which she denounces Katherine as subversive. Katherine responds by running a series of commercial ads in art class, showing women as housewives, in girdles, with their intellect being wasted, and goes to President Carr, telling her she resigns—Wellesley is not a real college, she says; it's just a glorified finishing school. They're not educating future leaders—but their wives! Carr responds angrily that a hundred years ago women couldn't even get an education, so they've come a long way.

Bill Dunbar persuades Katherine to give Wellesley another chance because they need someone like her, and she and Bill start dating—but before long she finds out, through encountering an old war buddy of Bill's, that he was never in Italy but merely at the Language Institute in Long Island. All his stories were lies, and she breaks up with him in disappointment. He tells her that she is disappointed in everybody—but perhaps she should not expect people to change according to her way but according to their own.

Joanie herself voices the same opinion when Katherine finds out that she and Tommy eloped and got married, and now she'll follow him to Washington instead of going to Yale. To Katherine's desperate plea for her to continue with her education, Joanie says, "You're the one who said I could do anything I wanted—this is what I want." She says she would regret not having a husband and a family more than she'll regret not going to law school.

Meanwhile, of all the students who have come under Katherine's influence, it is Betty who has the greatest change of heart: In an important scene she looks at a photo of Leonardo's Mona Lisa, and says, "Mona Lisa is smiling, but is she happy?" When her husband turns out to be a philanderer, and her mother tells her to put up with it and keep quiet about it, she stands up to her mother and demands a divorce. At the graduation ceremony, Betty announces that she is going to move to Greenwich Village with Giselle and become a law student.

Will Katherine be invited back to teach at Wellesley? Will she accept such an invitation? Will she patch it up with Bill? I'll leave that for you to experience for yourself, but I will tell you that the story of Katherine Watson is told, in retrospect, by her best student, Betty, in her final column for the school paper before she graduates and embarks on a career of her own.

Study Questions

1. Would you say this film is told from the perspective of a predominantly classical feminist, a difference feminist, a radical feminist, or an equity feminist? Explain.

2. What would Simone de Beauvoir say to Joanie's decision to be a homemaker rather than go to law school? What would Christina Hoff Sommers say? What do you think of her decision?

3. What do the screenwriters want us to conclude about traditional values, marriage, and same-sex relationships, judging from this film? Do you agree?

4. Try to retell the story from Wellesley President Carr's point of view, pointing out the problems of having a "subversive" teacher undermine the good conservative values of the school. Is Katherine more right than President Carr? Why or why not?

5. The mission statement of Wellesley College is, according to its website, "to provide an excellent liberal arts education for women who will make a difference in the world." It was founded in 1870 and remains a highly prestigious school to this day. You may want to do some research of your own and determine whether the film accurately portrays the school in 1953 and whether the school today differs from that depicted in *Mona Lisa Smile*.

Chapter Thirteen

Applied Ethics: A Sampler

*T*his final chapter is a result of increasing reader requests for more detailed discussions of issues involving applied ethics, drawing on the previous chapters on ethics of conduct and virtue ethics. In general, this book is conceived of not as an applied ethics approach but, rather, as a discussion of fundamental theories of ethics, using stories as examples. However, if theories are not applied to issues in the real world, then ethicists can indeed be accused of living in ivory towers. So in this chapter I present to you a sampling of discussions from the field of applied ethics; each topic is intended to be a starting point for further discussions, because space does not allow me to go into great detail about the pros and the cons. The topics featured are *abortion, euthanasia, media ethics, business ethics, just war theory, animal rights, environmental ethics,* and *the death penalty.* The last section will bring the book full circle: the ethics involved with *storytelling,* in particular as a tool for self-improvement.

The Question of Abortion and Personhood

The landmark decision by the Supreme Court in 1972 known as *Roe v. Wade* made abortion on demand a possibility for American women, because it made the decision to seek abortion within the first trimester a matter of privacy for the pregnant woman. For decades the abortion debate, which had been very polarized and very public in the late 1960s and early 1970s, lived on in two marginal arenas: pro-choice and pro-life movements. The groups known as "pro-choice" looked back to the years of struggle as though the right to seek abortion had become a constitutional certainty, like the right to vote. The groups known as "pro-life," generally coming from conservative religious backgrounds, were more vocal in insisting that abortion should be considered murder; they demonstrated in front of Planned Parenthood offices, and extremists occasionally resorted to violence, targeting and on a few occasions murdering abortion doctors. Even so, *Roe v. Wade* looked as though it couldn't be challenged. And yet, within the first decade of the new millennium, new judges were appointed to the Supreme Court who may, if the matter comes up, decide that the abortion issue should be a matter for the individual states, not a federal matter—which would mean a reversal of *Roe v. Wade.* Political candidates no longer regard the right to abortion as written in stone, whether or not they approve of the right to choose abortion.

In the following section we first look at the abortion issue from a historical viewpoint. Next we examine the question of what constitutes personhood (referring to Chapter 7). Last, we apply two contrasting philosophies to the issue: utilitarianism and Kant's deontology (Chapters 5 and 6).

The Catholic Church on Fetal Personhood

The debate over whether abortion should be generally available often focuses on the question of whether the fetus is a person. In some cultures the fetus is not a person at all; even the newborn infant is not considered a person until after a waiting period that usually is imposed to see if the baby will live. The view adopted by the Catholic Church (but not by all churches or religious communities) is that the fetus is a person from conception. This has not always been Catholic dogma, however. The idea underlying this viewpoint is that the soul is present when the fetus *looks* human; thus, in earlier times, a fetus was not considered a person until well into the pregnancy. Saint Augustine specifically states that terminating a pregnancy before the fetus is able to *feel* anything should not be considered homicide, because until that time the soul is not present. However, in the late seventeenth century, a primitive microscope seemed to show that a tiny, fully formed person (a *homunculus*) could be seen in the spermatozoon, and so church policy considering the fetus a person from conception was established. The policy remained unchanged even with the advent of better microscopes, which conclusively refuted the previous theory, and when the existence of the ovum was established in 1847. One can of course choose to view the beginning of life as the beginning of personhood regardless of church policies and misunderstandings about microscopes. In that case the argument against abortion is generally that if it is wrong to kill a human being, a person, then it must also be wrong to kill a fetus, who is either a person from conception or a potential person and should therefore have the same rights as a born person. Within the Catholic tradition one can circumvent the ban on killing a fetus through the principle of the *double effect,* which states that one mustn't take a life under normal circumstances but that it is permissible under very special circumstances: (1) Death must be an *unintended* side effect of accomplishing something else (a primary effect), such as saving a life; (2) the primary effect must be *proportionately* very serious so as to outweigh the death; and (3) causing the death is *unavoidable* and the only way to accomplish

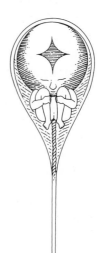

In the seventeenth century a young scientist reported that he saw a small person, a homunculus, inside a sperm cell while looking through a primitive microscope. Presumably, he saw something like this image. He was never able to duplicate the experiment; nevertheless, since then, the official Catholic policy is that a fetus is a person from conception.

the primary effect. Thus a pregnant woman who has cancer of the uterus will get permission from the church to have an abortion because it will be part of the necessary medical process to remove the uterus. The removal of the uterus will kill the fetus, but it is an unavoidable and unintended side effect of saving the woman's life. However, a pregnant woman whose pregnancy itself is in danger of killing her receives no such permission because killing the fetus would in that case be intentional—regardless of the woman's life being in danger. We will meet the double effect again in the section on euthanasia, as well as in the discussion of the just war concept.

Warren and Thomson: Rights and Personhood

What does it take for us to identify a fetus as a person? There are thinkers today who believe that we can surely call the fetus a human being but we can't call it a person because it takes more to be a person than just having human genetic material. The philosopher Mary Ann Warren argues that a being has to have (1) consciousness and ability to feel pain, (2) a developed capacity for reasoning, (3) self-motivated activity, (4) capacity to communicate messages of an indefinite variety of types, and (5) self-awareness in order to be considered a person; thus even the most developed fetus does not qualify. But neither do newborn babies, according to this viewpoint; so to avoid the specter of infanticide, Warren argues that as long as anyone in our culture objects to infanticide, then it should be outlawed—not for the sake of the infant (who is not a person yet), but for the sake of people's feelings in general.

A slightly less radical view is presented by another philosopher, Judith Jarvis Thomson, who argues for a woman's right to an abortion by saying that it does not matter whether the fetus is a person: What matters is that a woman has a *right to defend her body against intrusions*—even if the fetus should qualify for personhood. Thomson (who wrote her famous contribution to the abortion debate in 1971, just before *Roe v. Wade*) compares the pregnant woman to a person—any one of us—who wakes up in a hospital bed and finds herself (or himself) attached with intravenous tubes to someone in the next bed, a famous violinist. Suppose, Thomson says, you are told that the violinist can't be moved, or else he will die, so he must be sustained by you for the next nine months (or eighteen years). Do you have a right to unplug yourself? Yes, even if it would mean an innocent violinist's death. For Thomson there is a small catch, however: You must have tried to take precautions not to be in that situation. Furthermore, if it is only a small sacrifice to you, then you have a moral duty to go through with it—but the violinist still doesn't have any right to demand your life and freedom.

Other positions put forth by abortion rights advocates, based on the view that the fetus may be a person, at least late in the pregnancy, argue that even so, the rights of the fetus as a person do not outweigh the rights of the woman as long as the fetus is not viable (can't survive outside the woman's body).

Utilitarianism Versus Deontology

It is possible to approach the abortion issue from both a utilitarian and a deontological point of view, regardless of whether one is pro-choice or anti-abortion (pro-life). The utilitarian approach focuses on the *consequences* of abortion: The anti-abortion utilitarian will point to the many deaths of unborn children, and the utilitarian who is an abortion rights advocate will point to the back-alley deaths that occur when women seek illegal and unsanitary abortions. The deontological approach focuses on the issue of *rights:* The anti-abortion deontologist will argue that the fetus, as a person, is being used merely as a means to an end, its life and rights disregarded; the deontologist who is an abortion rights advocate will argue that the rights granted by the personhood and life of the woman outweigh the rights of the fetus, at least until viability (in the third trimester). Box 13.1 explores the broader issue of bioethics from utilitarian and deontological viewpoints.

Euthanasia as a Right to Choose?

You'll remember from Chapter 7 that the discussion in social and political ethics often has centered on the concept of rights—in particular, *positive* and *negative rights.* Positive rights are identified as *entitlements* and belong to the political spectrum to the "left" of the middle. To the "right" of the middle we find the concept of negative rights, rights of noninterference by the state: the rights to *life, liberty,* and *property.* For many political moderates (such as John Rawls), a mixture of positive and negative rights is essential for the creation and maintaining of a good society.

Below we look at the topic of euthanasia from a "rights" point of view.

The Definitions of Euthanasia

First of all, what is euthanasia? Literally, it is Greek for "good death." There are four major distinctions: *voluntary* and *involuntary* euthanasia and *active* and *passive* euthanasia. "Voluntary" implies that the patient requests euthanasia. "Involuntary" has two meanings: (1) The patient clearly doesn't want to die but is killed anyway (this is the kind of "euthanasia" performed by doctors in the death camps of Hitler's Holocaust); (2) the patient is incapable of communicating his or her wish, leaving the decision to the family (this is also sometimes called *nonvoluntary* euthanasia to distinguish it from outright killing). "Active" euthanasia refers to the patient's life being taken directly, by means such as drugs or the use of a weapon; "passive" euthanasia usually refers to the withholding of treatment from the patient that would otherwise have kept the patient alive longer. At the time of this writing, Oregon is the only state that allows active voluntary euthanasia, under specifically defined circumstances (and this law is in conflict with federal law, according to former U.S. Attorney General John Ashcroft). Passive voluntary euthanasia is common: The patient wishes life-prolonging treatment to end. Active involuntary euthanasia is not a legal option, whether it means killing someone who doesn't want to die or assisting someone whose family requests assisted suicide for him or her. Passive involuntary euthanasia is common, if we take "involuntary" to mean "nonvoluntary": The family requests a stop to life-prolonging measures.

Kevorkian and the Double Effect

When Dr. Jack Kevorkian began his work of either helping suffering people end their lives or killing misguided patients (depending on which view you hold), the idea of doctor-assisted suicide was still considered a radical one by most Americans. In 1999

Kevorkian stood trial for the third time. Acquitted of assisting suicide on two previous occasions, this time he was convicted of second-degree murder. The main reason Kevorkian had been acquitted twice was, in fact, the principle of the double effect, which you know from the section on abortion: His lawyer argued that his primary intent had been to alleviate the patients' suffering (allowing them to inject themselves with a large dose of painkiller), with death as an unintentional and unavoidable side effect. Some of us may think that such an argument was a bit of a stretch, since by Kevorkian's own admission the fatal outcome was intentional, but legally it made a difference between a direct and an indirect action. Also, when Kevorkian was eventually convicted, it was partly because the double effect argument couldn't be used. He had himself administered the lethal dose to a patient who subsequently died. Kevorkian served eight years in prison and was released in 2007. He insisted that he had not changed his mind about the right to die but that he would not engage in helping anyone die in the future.

The Key Arguments for and Against Euthanasia

The key arguments in favor of active voluntary euthanasia (which is what the debate usually focuses on) are that (1) it should be the right of individuals to decide the manner and time of their own death; (2) it should be a person's right to avoid otherwise inevitable suffering (in other words, the right to death with dignity); (3) we help others we love when their lives are at an end and they are facing severe pain—our pets—so we should be able to do the same for our human loved ones; (4) we might want to have that option ourselves someday.

The most common counterarguments are that (1) it is not up to patients or doctors to play God—there is a time to die for everyone, and we shouldn't interfere; (2) it goes against the Hippocratic oath, by which doctors are sworn to heal, not to take lives; (3) having opened up the possibility of doctors assisting in people's death, the step from voluntary to involuntary euthanasia (the kind where the patient has not given his or her consent) is only as short as the doctor's and family's conscience; (4) financial pressures might be brought to bear on a terminally ill family member whose insurance is about to run out.

Could the right to die be considered a *negative* right? Yes, if one's body is considered property, then we may argue that we have a right to do with our bodies what we please, provided it doesn't infringe on other people's rights. But it doesn't entail that we have a right to *assisted suicide,* which is the issue. Could the right to die be considered a *positive* right? This is more probable. We may argue that the right to death with dignity is an entitlement all people have, similar to the right to food, shelter, clothing, work, education, and so forth. However, it would be hard to compel others, such as doctors, to help in *taking* lives as a professional duty; nor does a woman's right to seek abortion mean that a doctor is obliged to perform the abortion.

The Legacy of Terri Schiavo

In 2005 the nation's attention turned to a case in Florida that became the ultimate case study for the topic of euthanasia, both from a pro-euthanasia and from an anti-euthanasia point of view: the life and death of Terri Schiavo. In 1990, at the age of twenty-seven, Terri suffered a collapse that left her brain-damaged and, as far as the doctors could determine, nonresponsive; she was dependent on a feeding tube, since she couldn't swallow. (The ultimate cause of the collapse was never completely determined, even after an autopsy.) Her husband, Michael, was for the first year after her accident engaged in getting her help and therapy, with the assistance of her parents, but after a while he became an advocate of letting Terri die. The doctors diagnosed her condition as a "persistent vegetative state," a state not quite like a coma but without signs of brain activity.

Schiavo claimed that Terri had said before her collapse that she would never live the life of a "vegetable"; he maintained that he wanted her to die with dignity, so eventually he got a court order to have her feeding tube removed. That would lead to death within one to two weeks, a process that people outside the medical community know as "passive euthanasia" but that the medical community refers to as "end of treatment." Terri's parents, Robert and Mary Schindler, however, saw the situation in quite a different light. First, to them, she was not nonresponsive; they believed they were in contact with her, through her smiles and eye movements—Terri was not in a coma, and she was not in any way terminal. With the feeding tube she was actually quite healthy. And second, they had no recollection of her ever having said she didn't want to live like a "vegetable"—she was a young, healthy woman when she collapsed, and she hadn't given much thought to end-of-life issues. Furthermore, they were willing to step up to the plate and take care of her, if Michael would divorce her and give her up to them. (As Terri's husband, he was her next-of-kin, with all rights to make decisions on her behalf.) From 2001 to 2005 the issue of Terri's right to die was bounced from court to court, involving removals and reinstatements of the feeding tube, until in 2003 it reached the Florida Senate, which passed "Terri's Law" to protect her life. Over the next two years, the case gained international attention. The U.S. Supreme Court refused to review the case, thus revoking "Terri's Law," and the matter went straight to the U.S. Senate, which delayed its Easter recess to pass a bill to keep Terri alive. The House of Representatives passed the bill, but it was overturned by the Supreme Court of Florida, and the U.S. Supreme Court refused to hear the appeal. All appeals exhausted, the Schindlers could only watch while Terri's feeding tube was removed for the last time. The media attention was intense as Terri's life trickled away from dehydration, and on March 31, 2005, she died. Schiavo later went public, saying that he was gratified that he was finally able to give Terri the peace she wanted.

Who was right—her husband or her parents? Did Terri want to live, or to die? The autopsy showed that her brain was so deteriorated that she could not have had conscious brain activity in her final years. Was Schiavo's decision appropriate or inappropriate? Was her parents' fight to keep her alive a valiant battle for their daughter's life, or ultimately selfish? And what of the involvement of Congress, making a law for one particular person? Those were the topics for discussions in the media as well as among private citizens. But from the point of view of the euthanasia debate, the Terri Schiavo case illuminated the battleground. Terri's husband became the voice for the right to die with dignity when life offers no more positive aspects (whether

Box 13.1   BIOETHICS: HUMANS ARE NOT COMMODITIES

One area in which utilitarian and deontological approaches clash is in the moral debate about access to health care. We all want policies to live up to the ideals of equality as well as of justice, but we also know that some people's needs are greater than others'. Since resources seem to be dwindling, it is a question of how to distribute such social goods in a manner that is "fair." In the health care debate the question is becoming urgent, because whatever ethical viewpoint we adopt as the basis for our policies will determine the way in which people with health problems are going to be treated in the future. The utilitarian viewpoint of creating as much happiness for as many as possible was a genuine improvement over the lack of concern for ordinary people that was common in the public policies of Bentham's day, but in Chapter 5 we saw some problems that have arisen from the principle of utility: The majority may be happy, but what if the price of their happiness is the misery of a minority?

Kant's rule that we should never treat a rational being as merely a means to an end has become an antidote to the utilitarian disregard for the minority. In the health care debate the discussion is forming along those same lines: The utilitarian view points to the limited resources of society and the overall capacity for pain and pleasure of the individual and suggests that resources should be directed toward people whose quality of life will be improved in the long run, rather than toward people whose quality of life might not improve dramatically. Bentham's idea of quantifying a qualitative experience (putting numbers on feelings) is in the forefront again, because that may help doctors decide which patient to help: a thirty-five-year-old person or a ninety-three-year-old person (under the assumption that society can't afford to help both). Since the thirty-five-year-old may enjoy life and contribute to society for many years, resources should probably go there instead of to a person close to the end of life whose quality of life might not be improved much; whereas the concept "quality of life" used to refer to extreme situations in which a person was suffering so much that life was no longer enjoyable, it has

that was a correct interpretation or not); Terri was used by pro-euthanasia groups as a symbol of a person's right to decide not to linger in a situation that holds no promise of recovery—in fact, an argument for *active euthanasia*. Terri's parents, on the other hand, became the voices for life having a right of its own, of hope against hope—and as such, their anguish and their plight were used by anti-euthanasia groups, against the idea of "doctors playing God." And the whole long battle could have been avoided had Terri made a living will specifying her wishes. That is perhaps the most significant legacy of all: After Terri's death—which took fourteen grueling days after her feeding tube was removed—people across the nation made living wills to prevent their situation from becoming like Terri's.

Media Ethics and Media Bias

When ethicists say "media ethics," they usually mean the rules of ethical conduct associated with the *news media*, but, to be sure, the issue is broader than that: In the greater area of the media (television and film entertainment, sports, game shows, even magazines of all varieties), we could address issues such as product placement now come to mean an overall "global" evaluation of a person's life, a concept that has become known as Quality Adjusted Life Years (QALY). Some utilitarian doctors argue that it is the overall QALY calculation that will tell where funding is going to go, and that means that the care of elderly or terminal patients (which has a low QALY yield) will receive less priority than will the care of younger patients whose lives may be saved.

Some doctors and philosophers are disturbed by this development, because they see it as a complete disregard for the respect for *all* individuals (regardless of their age) that Kant argued for and that Rawls was working for in his theory of the original position (in which everyone must have at least minimal care and security, no matter who he or she is). As a modern equivalent of Kant's idea, these philosophers suggest the concept *irreplaceability*. In his essay "Social Justice," the Danish philosopher Peter Kemp writes,

> The irretrievable loss of another is one of the most universal human experiences. If I smash a plate I can buy another one. If my house burns down I can build another one in the same style as the old one. Everything we appreciate solely in material terms can be replaced. But another human being can never be replaced. . . . The death of another (which also occurs when e.g. a marriage or friendship breaks down irreversibly) is the fundamental reality from which the irreplaceable ethic springs.

According to the ethics of irreplaceability, each person, no matter how old or how isolated and lonely, is unique and should be respected as a person, never to be sold out to the happiness of the majority. That also means that individuals can't be reduced to a resource for society—their bodies as incubators or their organs for transplants—without their consent. The discipline of bioethics is continually struggling to create policy suggestions for all the areas in which human needs may collide, such as the abortion issue, genetic profiling, euthanasia, and organ transplants; but the underlying philosophy is that human beings and their bodies are not commodities to be used for someone else's purpose, even if that purpose may be the greater good.

(the "accidental" appearance of products such as soft drinks and alcohol), rigged contests, prizes, and roles and other jobs going to friends and relatives of the producers. Such ethical concerns would come under the general umbrella of *ethics within a profession*. Here we'll focus on the more specific area of news media ethics—because, for one thing, the news media have been part of the heightened focus on controversial issues in applied ethics in the last couple of decades: Stories about people transgressing the moral rules can be "good copy" (news that sells papers or commercial air time), because many people find such stories interesting or just salacious. News stories about the rich and famous being engaged in moral controversies have "legs," such as the in-the-spotlight life and drug-related death of heiress Anna Nicole Smith, the child-molestation court trial of Michael Jackson ending in acquittal, and the drunk-driving convictions of heiress and model Paris Hilton, not to mention the first wall-to-wall media-coverage murder trial of O. J. Simpson. But for many people, the truly interesting media focus is on the fundamentally different views on matters such as abortion, euthanasia, the death penalty, gun ownership, and same-sex marriage; and whenever political candidates run for office, their opinions on such matters are closely examined.

But we can also turn the spotlight on the news media itself: What constitutes ethical reporting, and what is ethical broadcasting? Is it unethical, for example, for a reporter to make public a matter of national security? And does the public always have a "right to know"? Journalists who gain access to sensitive material and publish it may be said not only to report the news but also to create conditions for more "news" to report. In other words, they may play an active role in situations that they supposedly are merely reporting. The film classic *Network* (1976) speculated that a TV network might actually generate news of terrorism for the sake of ratings. In the seventies, that sounded shocking and outlandish, but with the creation of twenty-four-hour cable news, the Internet, YouTube, and the Blogosphere, such scenarios are not only possible but probable. In the Netherlands in 2007, the network BBN ran a game show in which three kidney-failure patients competed for the organs of a young, dying woman. The show was heavily criticized for being in poor taste—but then the producers admitted that it was, in fact, a hoax. The "patient" was a healthy actress, and the contestants (who were real patients) were in on the hoax from the start. The point of the hoax was to raise public awareness about the dearth of transplant organs. The producers felt that their cause was noble, but many viewers saw it differently: They felt that they had been had—that their good faith had been exploited. This was a game show, not a news show or a documentary, but since the show itself created a news storm, intentionally, it does come under the "media ethics" umbrella, in a broad as well as a narrower, news-related sense. In your view, is such a hoax acceptable if the cause is noble, or is this kind of fake story unacceptable in itself because it disrespects the viewers? Philosophers disagree.

The Right to Know

The public's "right to know" has become questionable in the aftermath of hugely publicized court cases and human tragedies of the 1990s. After examining the effects of televised high-profile trials, some now question the wisdom of allowing cameras in the courtroom, because their presence may actually affect the trial, at least turning it into a circus, as it did in O. J. Simpson's criminal trial in 1995. And does the public really have a "right" to see TV close-ups of relatives grieving over grisly photos of murder scenes? Sensationalism in the mainstream media seems to have become the order of the day. Decades ago, the tabloid ("yellow") press was where you'd find subjects with salacious content, and not much evidence of journalistic concern for verifying facts. But according to some media commentators, the line between mainstream and tabloid media has blurred, to the extent that people have been demonized in the "court of public opinion" with the help of the mainstream media, relying primarily on leaks and rumors. And once the story has hit the press, the genie can't be put back in the bottle. Hasty accusations of wrongdoing published by the media, although later proven to be untrue, may hang over a person's head for years, perhaps for life. When the media decided to go with the story that Richard Jewell, the suspect in the 1996 bombing of Olympic Park in Atlanta, had a history of aberrant behavior, the story was disseminated nationwide. When he was later exonerated (and took the media to court for libel), it wasn't front-page news. And most of us just happen to remember sensational headlines on front pages rather than the follow-ups on page 13. At the end of the chapter, you'll find an excerpt from "Ethics as a Vehicle for Media Quality" in which Andrew Belsey and Ruth Chadwick explore the concept of virtue in journalism.

Media Ethics and Free Speech

An aspect of media ethics that has come under scrutiny lately is not the traditional question of what reporters can investigate, or reveal, but what television and radio hosts can *say* without being unacceptably offensive. That raises a new set of issues, especially in cases where media hosts are hired for their abrasive, confrontational style. Don Imus is a case in point. Imus, a veteran radio and television host known (and hired) for his aggressive style and offensive language, got into hot water in the spring of 2007 for using disparaging racial language about the Rutgers University women's basketball team, calling them "nappy-headed hos." The media response was multifaceted: Rutgers team players went on TV, eloquently pointing out that they were thrust into the spotlight through no fault of their own and that the sweetness of their sports victory was stolen from them by the Imus fallout. Although nobody condoned the term used by Imus, some people called for him to be fired for being racially insensitive, and others pointed out that the issue was sexism as much as racism. Some felt the discussion was sidetracked from the start, since the context of the remark was apparently a discussion of how *tough* the Rutgers team was, not what race they were (and they weren't all African American); others pointed out that it was essentially unfair for Imus, a white man, to be vilified for such a remark while some media personalities of color have uttered discriminatory statements about other population groups without being heavily criticized. Interestingly, conservative author Ann Coulter and rap singer/actor Snoop Dogg made the same point: The Rutgers women didn't deserve that kind of epithet or attention, being good students with a fine sports record (implying that there are some women who *do* deserve the epithet!). The end result was that Imus was fired from his radio show, even though he apologized to the Rutgers women and they accepted his apology.

For the Rutgers team there was hardly any upside to this unpleasant episode, but for the media culture and its viewers/listeners perhaps there is a silver lining. Not only did it become clear that there are certain words and attitudes that are no longer acceptable in the media, but also the greater question of *fairness* has been introduced: Should there be a separate set of rules for what media personalities of one race can utter, and another set of rules for another race? a certain set of rules for conservative media personalities and another for liberal media people? The philosopher Lawrence Blum stated in his landmark paper from 1991, "Philosophy and the Value of a Multicultural Community," that racial discrimination is unacceptable, no matter who expresses it, but "white" discrimination against people of color is worse than discrimination against white people by people of color because of the historical ramifications of oppression. But the British philosopher Mary Wollstonecraft (see Chapter 12) argued that it is fundamentally unfair to set up separate systems of virtue for separate groups of people (she was talking about men versus women), because, ethically, what is wrong for one group ought to be wrong for the other. Perhaps the Imus case has brought us to the point where we have to decide whether we should have separate standards of virtue in the media or whether we ought to recognize the same sensitivities, live by the same rules, be ready to cut one another the same slack that we would like to be cut if we make mistakes, and be ready to forgive those who later regret using certain expressions, and who apologize for using them. In the end, it ties in with the discussion about *freedom of speech* that you read in Chapter 7: Should this freedom be curtailed for the sake of sensitivities, and if so, should it be curtailed across the board, including art forms such as Snoop Dogg's music, which uses the same kind of slurs against women as Imus used? Or should the airwaves be available for offensive statements, artistic expressions, and opinions—provided that we can shut off the TV and radio if we don't want to hear them?

The News Media and Credibility Problems

The news media have had to face issues of sensationalism and insensitivity, but it is a far graver problem for a news distributor to face accusations of stretching the truth, or downright *lying*. Over the past decade the credibility of mainstream news media has been damaged by instances of journalists inventing characters (Patricia Smith at the *Boston Globe*), plagiarizing material (Mike Barnicle at the *Globe*, Jayson Blair at the *New York Times*, Jack Kelly at *USAToday*), and "inventing" entire autobiographies (James Frey, *A Million Little Pieces*, Misha Defonseca, *A Mémoire of the Holocaust Years*, and Margaret Jones, *Love and Consequences*, in reality written by Margaret Seltzer). In addition, both *CNN* and *Time* magazine brought uncorroborated stories about the United States using nerve gas to kill defectors during the Vietnam War and had to issue retractions; Great Britain's *Daily Mirror* likewise had to issue a retraction after publishing fake photos of abuse of Iraqi prisoners of war. And the career of famous CBS news anchor Dan Rather came to an end after he aired documents two months before the 2004 presidential election, allegedly from 1973, stating problems with President Bush's National Guard service. Internet bloggers pointed out that the documents had to have been forged, since they contained superscript, proportional spacing, and other modern computer features that few typewriters had the capacity for in 1973; Rather later admitted that he had not been careful enough in checking the authenticity of his sources, although he stated that he believed the information to be essentially correct.

A sobering statistic: Numerous studies in the late 1990s and early 2000s, including a Gallup Poll, show that we are losing our faith in the media: According to Gallup, we rate journalists below politicians and just above used-car salesmen in trustworthiness and ethical standards. (On a personal note, I have a bumper sticker on my office wall that reads "I think, therefore I don't trust the media." Not exactly in Descartes' spirit, but reflecting a certain cynicism of our times.)

Media Ethics in Wartime

The idea that the public has a "right to know" certain things is at the core of the notion of freedom of the press, a constitutional right embedded in the First Amendment. In peacetime we generally consider the right of reporters to investigate and publish

In the film *15 Minutes,* a television station acquires a videotape depicting the murder of a popular police detective. A tabloid-TV journalist (Kelsey Grammer) makes the decision to air the video as an exclusive, because, as he says, "If it bleeds, it leads." In the scene depicted here, the journalist has acquired yet another tape, this one showing the killer's confession. Do you think a TV station would deliberately air a murder? In an accelerated, sensationalist news environment, might the scenario of *15 Minutes* become possible—here or abroad?

their findings as something fundamental—so much so that reporters generally go out of their way to protect their sources and not reveal them, even under the threat of incarceration. But how about during wartime? All of a sudden, the notion that the public has a right to know takes a back seat to national security. We have been engaged in the "war against terror" since 2001. Since 2002, this nation has been at war with the Taliban and al Qaeda in Afghanistan, and in 2003, we went into Iraq. (Box 13.2 discusses the subject of terror and violence shown on television.) And since it became clear that CNN and Fox News were watched not only by American audiences but also by the enemy, the issue of national security loomed large even in the everyday details of reporting. Here we are, of course, talking about a fine line: How much information should the journalist have access to, and reveal to the public, without compromising national security?

A dramatic shift in the role of the media happened with the war in Iraq in 2003. In previous wars the press have usually stayed behind the lines, except for a few individuals who have chosen to go it alone and report from the front lines; the war in Iraq introduced the concept of "embedded journalists," reporters from TV stations, newspapers, and magazines traveling with the military as they moved toward Baghdad and other key cities. The skeptics were many, warning that reporting would not be fair to the soldiers or to the readers, or would impede the progress of the

Box 13.2   HOW FAR WOULD—AND SHOULD—TELEVISION GO?

How far are the news media willing to go to secure an exclusive story—or to provide unique footage? And how far is too far? There is an unwritten rule that TV stations should not show people dying. Over time, live TV has inadvertently shown unexpected deaths, such as the shooting of Lee Harvey Oswald in 1963, the police shooting of a tank hijacker in San Diego in the 1990s, and in the early stages of September 11, TV stations showed footage of people jumping from burning World Trade towers; but such deaths rarely are rebroadcast on the evening news. Does that mean we are not likely to see violent deaths broadcast, live or canned, on network or cable TV in the future? CBS, on *60 Minutes,* chose to air a videotape of the assisted-suicide death of one of Dr. Jack Kevorkian's patients. When *Wall Street Journal* reporter Danny Pearl was executed by terrorists in Pakistan in 2002 and the process videotaped by those same terrorists, CBS aired part of his interrogation, but not his death itself—it was,

however, posted to the Internet on several websites. And this now seems to have become a standard procedure: In Iraq, after the major battles of 2003, al Qaeda (and possibly also Iraqi insurgents) has kidnapped and executed numerous civilians who were in Iraq as part of the reconstruction effort: The first one to be executed was Nick Berg, an American citizen who had gone to Iraq of his own accord, presumably to help out as well as make some money for himself. Berg's headless body was found after his disappearance, and a videotape was posted to an al Qaeda website with Berg in an orange jumpsuit being interrogated by masked men and then being beheaded by those same men. Whereas the news media stopped at showing the execution itself, or chose to run the gruesome soundtrack but not the video, numerous websites posted the whole video. Since then, many other civilians, including citizens of Italy and Nepal, have been executed in Iraq, usually by being beheaded. And this is where opinions are

armies, or would present a problem if journalists were taken prisoner, and so forth. And all the fears were probably realized; some reporting was not fair, some journalists were probably somewhat of a hindrance, and many journalists were indeed killed, including veteran CBS reporter Paul Douglas. Some journalists shot footage that created great controversies, such as NBC reporter Kevin Sites's filming of a marine shooting a wounded Iraqi insurgent, and Fox News's Geraldo Rivera inadvertently revealing U.S. troop positions in his live report. But overall, the public probably received a more nuanced picture of the war than ever before, and in some cases, the presence of the media in the thick of battle, as well as during more tedious phases of the war, turned out to be a morale boost for troops who could send instant greetings home to their loved ones via TV, and in some cases challenge perceptions of the war proliferating on the home front.

But how about the home front? In the years right after 9/11 the world of the media was rocked by rumors and scares: In 2001 and 2002, letters containing anthrax were sent to prominent politicians and other individuals; at the time of this writing, the culprit or culprits have still not been identified. Rumors of other types of terror threats have come and gone, and to this day it is impossible for a layperson to beginning to differ: Before, and immediately after 9/11, proper media ethics included not showing violent deaths or other shocking scenes, for the sake of the individuals involved and their loved ones. When Saddam Hussein was executed in late 2006, his execution was videotaped on a cellphone, but only the beginning was shown on U.S. television. In the Narratives section you'll find the film *15 Minutes,* where the following scenario is suggested: What if the videotaped murder of a famous, popular person is being offered to the networks? Will they take the high road and refuse to air it, or will they air it because if they don't, someone else will? The moral of *15 Minutes* is that airing it would be the wrong, and greedy, thing to do—but what if we are talking about footage of terrorists killing American citizens? For some, that makes no difference—showing the footage plays into the hands of the terrorists and furthers their agenda. But for others this represents a different situation: If we don't actually see how vicious and evil these terrorists are, we may think they can be reasoned with and negotiated with—so the media, by protecting us from shocking footage, may actually be preventing us from judging the situation correctly.

But technology sometimes has a way of circumventing our moral debates: With the introduction of YouTube, where private citizens inside or outside interest groups from around the world post videos, the question of what we should be able to watch on TV has become moot for anyone who has a computer: Saddam Hussein's execution could be seen in its entirety on numerous websites, including YouTube, within hours after it had taken place, and although YouTube has been sued by Viacom over copyright issues, and sets certain restrictions on what can be posted, other Internet venues can easily pop up out of reach of censorship. Teen gangs post their videos of attacking innocent civilians—*cyberbashing*—and young girls post home videos of other young girls being beaten. Now we have reached beyond the control of regulated news media and are, in a sense, back to the question of personal ethics and character, which was explored in previous chapters.

say which were actual terror dangers that were averted by Homeland Security, and which were just rumors. The official terror level has been raised from a permanent "orange" to a higher "yellow" and back to "orange," under the policy that it is better that we be informed about the rumors rather than surprised by an actual attack. But exactly how much is too much? When is the media providing vital information, and when is it "crying wolf"?

How much a journalist should report and an editor release, and when, of course depends on the situation. Aristotle's theory of the Golden Mean provides a good starting point for solving the media ethics problem. For each situation there is one correct answer, somewhere within the middle range. Sometimes the media need to freely share information, unpleasant though it may be, in the interest of the public's right to make decisions based on informed consent. At other times the proper amount of coverage called for is the bare minimum, either because no more information is available at the time (and excessive speculation may hurt more than help the public) or because the dissemination of the information might threaten the security of the country. Crying wolf is poor journalistic ethics, but so are apathy and indifference. It is a brilliant journalist or editor who knows the difference in each instance.

Bias in the News Media?

Above we have explored the kinds of issues that media professionals have to deal with regardless of their own political affiliations or those of their news organizations: National security awareness, overall sensitivity, and credibility are demands on the profession that exist for all reputable news outlets. But in addition there is a concern, shared by many viewers and critics, that a *bias* exists in the very selecting and reporting of the news. When asked about the choices reporters make when bringing stories to the forefront, reporters often answer that they just report the facts, they don't invent them or doctor them—but that can surely be dismissed as a media myth: Before journalists *report* the facts, they *select* which facts to report (or their network does it for them, with so-called talking points), having already decided what is going to count as newsworthy. Why are some world events reported, and others not? Why do we hear of some disasters (such as the 2005 tsunami), but others (such as the Darfur genocide tragedy) come to the media surface only slowly, if at all? Why were we inundated with stories of celebrities while former chief of staff to Vice President Dick Cheney, Lewis "Scooter" Libby, was sentenced to two and a half years in prison for obstruction of justice and "outing" a federal agent's name? Conspiracy theorists among us will suggest that it is all nefarious reporting: Some news stories are suppressed, and others are enhanced, for personal or political gain. The truth, however, is often simpler than that. Some news events (such as natural disasters or rebellions) occur while network reporters are already in the vicinity; others simply happen below the radar. And some stories are not picked up because they aren't "sexy" enough for news media that sell ads and airtime.

NON SEQUITUR   by WILEY

Much of the criticism of the press in the past few years, and especially in the wake of September 11, is that it has become a fearmonger because a good dose of anxiety ("Anthrax found in a post office! More news at 11!") keeps people glued to their television sets or makes them buy more papers and magazines. Is that a fair criticism? Do the media just report the news, or do they also select what news to report and when and how to report it? Where do we draw the line between the media giving out information, including warnings and alerts, and whipping up panic?

But we should not be oblivious to the fact that bias does exist in the news media. Some papers and networks find themselves politically to the left of the middle, and some to the right. That, in itself, is not against the rules of media ethics, as long as the political bias is kept within editorials or is expressed by hosts or columnists who are clear about their personal convictions. Often, such hosts have guests who express different viewpoints, and it is all part of the give-and-take of live, and lively, television. The problem arises if it is the presentation of the *news itself* that is preselected on the grounds of somebody's political conviction. The suspicion among liberal viewers and critics is that networks with predominantly conservative hosts (FoxNews) are selecting and twisting the news to fit a conservative agenda; the suspicion among conservative viewers and critics is that the majority of the networks (CBS, NBC, ABC, CNN, and MSNBC) are selecting and twisting the news to fit a liberal agenda. And perhaps that is not just political paranoia: What many people see as persuasive evidence, enough to substantiate some of those perceptions, has been presented by media analyst Bernie Goldberg, writing about the time when he was a reporter for CBS. To the viewer who would just like to get some objective reporting, that is intensely disturbing. However, although some of the bias may be part of an underlying scheme, there is a more straightforward explanation: We all have some fundamental worldview, and news that corresponds to that worldview looks to us like "sensible" news. Often, what some viewers call a bias is for the reporter the "default" position of a reasonable person—in other words, the reporter may not even be aware that his or her reporting is grounded in a political viewpoint. So what can we do? A website, NewsHounds, has as its tagline "We Watch FOX so You Don't Have To," but that is not an option if you want to be cognizant of the entire spectrum of opinions! You can't delegate the watching to someone else, because you might be misinformed, miss something important, or be the victim of someone else's agenda. Watch and read the news from several sources, every day! Watch CNN *and* FoxNews, listen to conservative talk radio *and* NPR, go on the Internet and read the blogs, subscribe to your favorite newspaper and then go online and read the competition's viewpoint. That's probably a little too "fair and balanced" for most of us, but at least it allows for insight into a variety of views in an increasingly complicated media world.

Business Ethics: The Rules of the Game

In some ways, media ethics and business ethics are overlapping phenomena: Whenever decisions in the media are made with an eye toward profit, we might as well be talking business ethics. And even in other ways there are similarities: Whenever media ethics involve ethics of the workplace, we are also talking business ethics, and whenever the news media ponder moral issues caused by the dissemination of news, we might also be talking about business ethics. All these aspects are part and parcel of responsible decision making within any kind of profession, and the world of business is, of course, an environment of professional standards. The question is, are these standards different from the moral values we find in personal relationships and elsewhere in our society? In this section we look at the question of whether "business

Dilbert by Scott Adams

© Scott Adams/Dist. by United Feature Syndicate, Inc.

This is one of many *Dilbert* strips in this book on big business. It can hardly get more graphic: For marketing dishonesty is a practical value. Is this a fair representation of "business ethics"?

as usual" implies a disregard for moral values; we take a tour of the most common themes in business ethics; and we look at two issues in some detail, one abstract, and the other a concrete case: business ethics as grounded in the concept of *property,* and the 2007 scandal of Chinese products containing poisonous substances.

Are Businesspeople Amoral?

For many people, "business" and "ethics" is an oxymoron, as though the concepts are mutually exclusive. Some might say that the business world has not been particularly encumbered by ethical sensitivities for most of its existence—it is almost expected to be a dog-eat-dog type of environment, as if the rules of ethics don't apply. However, Richard T. de George, University of Kansas Distinguished Professor of Philosophy and author of *Business Ethics,* calls this the "Myth of Amoral Business." De George asks, If businesspeople were really expected to do business without an eye to value judgments and ethical standards, then why are we so shocked when a business or a corporation acts immorally or without any regard for moral standards? In other words, we expect an adherence to the general code of ethics that we find in our greater society; that doesn't mean the Myth isn't correct sometimes. Sometimes businesspeople are greedy, and sometimes there are bribes and kickbacks, but it is our outrage at the revelation of such goings-on that shows that this is not the normal or expected state of affairs. Increasingly, businesses recognize that the greater community will react negatively to such revelations, and this is why *business ethics* has become established as a discipline for businesspeople.

As often happens in ethics, we don't notice when things are going right, only when they're going sideways. We pay much attention when managers, executives, and other business leaders break the rules for selfish gain (such as when prominent businesswoman Martha Stewart went to prison for five months for conspiracy and lying to federal investigators about her sale of stocks the day before the stock value fell dramatically); but in the vast majority of cases, businesspeople abide by the rules and provide the normal, smooth business climate that simply works.

There is a value system *within* the workplaces in the world of business; sometimes this is written down in a code of ethics, and sometimes it is an unwritten set of rules. This can range from rules that one should not take home pens and Post-it pads from the supply room, to rules for dating practices in the workplace, to more serious rules against insider trading. But in addition, there is a value system *for the business as such,* governing the entire business world where capitalism is the norm, and that is the system acknowledging *free enterprise,* with *profit* as the desired result. If you'll recall Karl Marx's critique of the concept of profit in Chapter 7, you already know that Marx and his followers did not consider profit morally justifiable. The discipline of business ethics does ask fundamental philosophical questions, such as the justifiability of profit, but in general, the business world operates under the assumption that there is nothing odious in generating profit. The question more frequently addressed by business ethics is, *how* is the profit obtained? Through fair and honest marketing, or through incomplete or even false advertising? Below we return to a case of dishonest marketing with devastating results.

Often colleges offer courses in business ethics, and often corporations themselves do the same thing for their employees. Is that because there is a general interest among businesspeople in learning about issues in ethics—or it is because companies believe that their employees are in severe need of some guidance when it comes to professional standards? Maybe a bit of both, and sometimes the teachers have to admit that the lessons weren't learned, after all. You'll remember from Chapter 10 that thirty-four out of thirty-eight graduate business students at Duke University cheated on their take-home exams. What you didn't hear was that all students had agreed to abide by an honor code, posted in the classroom, and that they were, on the average, twenty-nine years old, from many different countries, with six years of work experience on the average, which means they weren't "kids." And even so, they chose to cheat. A study released by the Center for Academic Integrity at Duke University in September 2007 showed that 56 percent of MBA students cheat, compared with 54 percent in engineering, 48 percent in education, and 45 percent in law school, despite having taken ethics courses. Representatives for the Center for Academic Integrity were disappointed, and expressed suspicion that the students were just thinking of themselves, despite the ethics classes. Christina Hoff Sommers (Chapter 10) might reply that perhaps what was taught in those classes was not presented in a way that the students could relate to: Were they taught abstract principles, along the lines of *ethics of conduct?* Or were they given role models, and taken through concrete examples dealing with real people where the student response becomes a matter of having a good character—in other words, according to *virtue ethics?* There is a high probability that the human connection that is at the heart of virtue ethics can bring the lesson home more efficiently than learning about principles. After all, bank and train robbers in the Old West often prided themselves at never having stolen anything from a person; that stealing was wrong in principle didn't impress them as much as the face-to-face realization of the other person's humanity, and a reluctance to violate that humanity. Would the graduate students at Duke have cheated as readily if cheating had been presented to them as a character failing, a breach of trust vis-à-vis their professor? In the Primary Readings you'll find a summary of a report from the Ethics Resource Center, "Critical Elements of an Organizational Ethical Culture," in which the authors, Amber Levanon Seligson and Laurie Choi, argue that being immersed in an "ethical culture" has more of an impact on employees than an actual ethics program.

General Business Ethics Topics

So if you take a course in business ethics, what themes are you likely to encounter? First and foremost the rights and duties of the *corporate world,* examining whether businesses should be responsible for public welfare. When is a corporation liable for damages to the environment? How important is product safety? Is the corporate world responsible to the community for creating jobs and revitalizing low-income sections of town, or do they just have moral obligations to the shareholders? Is there such a thing as ethical investing, or is that an area where ethics doesn't apply? Other questions that involve corporate ethics include marketing and truth in advertising; the entire discussion that has become so prominent in the past decades concerning trade secrets and insider trading; and the ethics of accounting and corporate takeovers. A new area that has received much attention is computer ethics, a morally gray area for many when as long as something is online, it must be fair game; this has led to a series of regulations, concerning both computer privacy and copyright issues, not to mention security issues. An area that promises to become even more prominent in future debates about business ethics is international trade and multinational companies.

Business ethics courses may also focus on *workers' rights.* Above all, the right to fair wages, the right to join unions, and the right to strike qualify as workers' rights issues; but, in addition, the focus may be on protecting against health hazards on the job, discussing conflicts between drug testing and privacy, and determining the proper relationship boundaries between employer and employee, or even among workers. Such discussions might focus on determining what constitutes sexual harassment, or simply outline what the company considers acceptable dating practices. Another set of issues are discrimination and affirmative action.

Whistle-blowing is a sensitive issue in business ethics, contrasting loyalty to the company with the right, and even the duty, to speak up when observing wrongdoing. In the Narratives section you'll find one of the most famous cases of whistle-blowing, as depicted in the film *The Insider,* about one man's moral decision to reveal to the world how the tobacco companies deliberately misrepresented their products.

As you can see, many of these topics in business ethics courses display the same tendency that you saw in Chapter 1 about the relationship between ethics and the law: In many cases the ethics of business is just that, ethics—a sense of right and wrong when dealing with coworkers, employers, employees, customers, shareholders, and the general population. But sometimes the question of wrongdoing becomes a matter for the law; as business venues change and technology progresses, new forms of crime also evolve, such as cybercrime, and it is an ongoing task for business ethics theory to identify these new crimes and make them known to the world of business as well as to anyone else who may be affected by them.

The Property Question

As you'll remember from Chapter 7, John Locke pointed out that we have three negative or natural rights: to *life, liberty,* and *property*. This theory of negative rights has become part and parcel of the *laissez-faire* ("hands-off") policy advocated by fiscal conservatives (see Chapter 5), but it has also become a cornerstone of business philosophy. So how does Locke identify property? In his *Second Treatise on Government,* Chapter 5, he says,

> Though the earth, and all inferior creatures, be common to all men, yet every man has a property in his own person: this no body has any right to but himself. The labour of his body, and the work of his hands, we may say, are properly his. Whatsoever then he removes out of the state that nature hath provided, and left it in, he hath mixed his labour with, and joined to it something that is his own, and thereby makes it his property. It being by him removed from the common state nature hath placed it in, it hath by this labour something annexed to it, that excludes the common right of other men: for this labour being the unquestionable property of the labourer, no man but he can have a right to what that is once joined to, at least where there is enough, and as good, left in common for others.

This quotation, and in particular the last line, is known as *the Lockean Proviso.* A famous interpretation from C. B. Macpherson reads into this that we have three restrictions: (1) We can only take and keep as much from nature as we can use before it spoils; (2) we have to leave enough for others, and not take it all for ourselves; and (3) we can acquire property only through our own labor. A debate has gone back and forth over whether Locke implies that you can be a voter only if you own property, and whether you can only acquire your own property or pay others to work it for you; also, the acquisition of property may depend on one's own labor when there is plenty of land in common for all, but once land becomes scarce, and society is well-established, then some will have land and others won't, setting the stage for political inequality. And if you acquire land from the amount of land available to all, do you need everyone else's consent to acquire it? The American libertarian philosopher Robert Nozick (1938–2002) has supplied this interpretation in his influential book *Anarchy, State and Utopia* (1974)—his so-called Entitlement Theory:

> If the world were wholly just, the following inductive definition would exhaustively cover the subject of justice in holdings:
>
> a. A person who acquires a holding in accordance with the principle of justice in acquisition is entitled to that holding.
>
> b. A person who acquires a holding in accordance with the principle of justice in transfer, from someone else entitled to the holding, is entitled to the holding.
>
> c. No one is entitled to a holding except by (repeated) applications of (a) and (b).
>
> The complete principle of distributive justice would say simply that a distribution is just if everyone is entitled to the holdings they possess under the distribution.

For Nozick, acquiring property is just or fair if others (who used to be co-owners of the land in common) aren't worse off by your acquiring the property. And that leads to the entire realm of business transactions, because if you have acquired property without violating others' right to property, then you also have a right to transfer it. This is the very foundation of commerce. Critics have pointed out that this is hardly a guarantee of fair distribution of property, or of rectification if injustices have occurred. But it is also sometimes pointed out that critics may have been particularly eager to find flaws in Nozick's embracement of the concepts of property and profit, because his critics in academia have usually been further to the left on the political spectrum, preferring thinkers who themselves are critical of the capitalistic ideology, such as the liberal John Rawls and his theory of the Original Position (Chapter 7). Rawls's philosophy strives for social fairness, not only as an abstract idea where property is, theoretically, there for the taking by anyone with the will and skills to acquire it, but also as a continued redistribution of social goods so no one is left worse off than anyone else. And here we should also remember that further to the political left than John Rawls, among socialist and Marxist thinkers, property is itself not a *right* but a *problem,* leading to social inequality. In his *Discourse on the Origin of Inequality among Mankind* (1754), Rousseau said that "the first man who, having fenced in a piece of land, said, 'This is mine,' and found people naive enough to believe him, that man was the true founder of civil society." There are significant differences between Rousseau and Karl Marx, but Marx took Rousseau's cue and in his *Communist Manifesto* (1848) declared property, along with the concept of profit, the cause of social evils. So for some thinkers on the far left to this day, libertarian and other defenders of the entire enterprise of business are simply in the wrong no matter how they define and redefine business ethics, because the concept of property for far left thinkers is fundamentally illegitimate.

Profit Versus Respect for Life?

Last, we look at a specific story of business ethics, or rather the lack of it. The power of this extreme example will, to some extent, depend on whether you have ever had, and lost, a pet. In the fall of 2006, veterinarians across the country encountered an unusual phenomenon: Otherwise healthy dogs and cats were being brought to their offices dying of what appeared to be a kidney ailment. No common denominator seemed to be present—they were from different environments, had not been exposed to any environmental poisons, were of different breeds and species, and had been fed a variety of pet food brands. So what was happening? In the winter and spring of 2007, the scandal unfolded: The animals were dying because of contaminated pet food; unknown to most consumers, much of the pet food sold under various brand names is actually manufactured by just a few producers; and even if the pet food came from other producers, there was indeed a common denominator: a wheat gluten additive from China. To make a long story short: The imported wheat gluten was not completely organic; to stretch the raw materials and increase profit, the Chinese suppliers had added *melamine,* an industrial chemical, to the gluten. Why would the Chinese manufacturers do that? Allegedly because the melamine nitrogen reads as a protein nitrogen in a chemical analysis and thus makes the gluten look as if it has more protein in it than it actually does. Melamine is a material used in making furniture, particularly shelving; it is a nonfood and extremely hazardous to one's health. In layman's terms, the melamine, when ingested, combines with a chemical, cyanuric acid, that attacks the kidneys and causes renal failure; the smaller the animal, the faster its health is going to deteriorate. This resulted in a huge pet food recall, reaching global proportions. In the United States and Canada, the culprit was contaminated wheat and rice gluten; in South Africa, it turned out to be corn gluten; but all the original sources came from a few Chinese companies. Skeptics pointed out that only sixteen confirmed cases of animal deaths could be attributed to the poison, but veterinarians across the country joined the debate, in the daily media as well as in animal health magazines, pointing out that there is no centralized database where we can find data about animal deaths. According to the vets' assessment, at least 100 pets died from the poison, and perhaps as many as 3,600, according to an online database. The Veterinary Network sets the pet losses as high as possibly 7,000 animal companions. (I present as anecdotal evidence the following: Out of approximately twenty-five families frequenting the dog park where we take our own dog, two families reported that their dogs had died because of the pet food additives, and one fell ill but recovered. If we imagine those numbers repeated across the country, with an eye toward exaggerations and misdiagnoses, the numbers will still be staggering.) And the story is ongoing: In the April 2008 issue of *BARK, The Modern Dog Culture Magazine,* scientists reported that the melamine additive risk had actually been known in veterinary literature since the 1940s, and that in the 1980s, Italian researchers warned against melamine used for fraudulent purposes. In low doses, cattle and sheep can convert the nonprotein nitrogen to amino acids; but with higher doses, even cattle and sheep die. Dogs and cats can't convert the melamine and die much faster. The problem is that few people read international veterinary literature from past decades.

Is this a story that makes you angry? If you love pets, I assume you feel outrage; veterinarians did: Here they were, trying to save the lives of what most pet owners these days consider four-legged family members, and often out of ignorance recommending the dog food that was in fact killing their patients. If you don't love pets, perhaps you reserve your outrage for when human lives are at stake. But consider this: As Scott Gottlieb's article "How Safe Is Our Food?" in the Primary Readings section states, the FDA (Food and Drug Administration) is not up to speed when it comes to imported food substances in this global economy. Poison scandals have already hit Panama, with fifty-one people dead after using cough syrup tainted with antifreeze; the additive came from China. Gottlieb argues that the FDA simply can't keep up—they are understaffed, and even if they go out and inspect the offending factories abroad, they don't speak the language or know the local culture and its standards. We import more and more food *and* drugs with raw materials from India and China, where local quality controls aren't what we are used to.

Let us assess the situation: If contaminated gluten can turn up in animal food, how about imported gluten for human consumption? So far, none has turned up, but some analysts believe that a healthy amount of caution will be advisable. Tainted toothpaste from China is another of the latest scandals. If we go beyond foods to items that may end up someone's mouth, such as toddler toys, 2007 also saw a recall of toys painted with lead paint—also from China. Their oversight methods may be lax, but furthermore, their entire sense of right and wrong in business may differ from ours—the lessons of ethical relativism shouldn't be forgotten. And this assumes that we're merely talking about what we would call shoddy business practices, not a *deliberate* tainting of our food and drug supplies, as we might see it in a *bioterrorist* attack.

So whose fault was the melamine scandal? Pet owners can't be blamed, because most of us try to feed our pets things that are good for them. U.S. and Canadian vets can't be blamed, because they didn't know. Can the importers be blamed? The FDA? Some blame should be shared, yes, because there was insufficient oversight. But the primary blame falls on Chinese companies who rate profit higher than respect for business partners as well as consumers (interesting, considering that China to this day is known as a Communist country, with inherited disdain for profit and property). But this is not necessarily a matter of Chinese manufacturers trying to poison the "decadent capitalist consumers" in the West, as some have speculated: Reports out of China tell of poisoning scandals with nonfood additives sold to the Chinese consumers themselves. A business ethics analysis of this case would have to address that issue, as well as the overall issue of international trade imbalances (as for example, do we really want almost everything in our stores these days to have originated in China? And so forth), lack of oversight, and other ethical issues arising from the globalization process. In any event, this grim example bears out what de George says: If we expected the business world to be amoral, we would not be shocked and outraged whenever that turns out to be the case. So under normal circumstances, we do expect a certain code of ethics to be upheld by the business world. Whether it is for selfish purposes, such as keeping the profit margin and ensuring repeat customers, or for less selfish purposes, such as recognizing the needs of the community, is a debate that belongs in Chapter 4; regardless of the underlying motivations, the fact remains that we do expect the business community to live by the same general set of values that are in effect elsewhere in our society.

Just War Theory

World War II has been referred to as "the last good war," meaning the last one that had clearly identifiable good and evil sides. But even World War II was, in the beginning, not considered clear-cut at all by many Americans; even after the Japanese attack on Pearl Harbor (December 7, 1941), some argued that more violence was not a proper response to violence. In addition, victories over the Nazis and imperial Japan during the war didn't come without heavy cost in civilian lives.

For many Americans—young as well as older people—during the Vietnam War, the very idea that a war could be "just" was an oxymoron. During the late sixties and early seventies, the war in Vietnam was widely perceived as an *unjust war,* since the principles being fought for were unclear or downright objectionable to many, involving mainly politics. Conscription was in effect, and many of the young men drafted against their will saw the war they were being asked to fight as not being a matter of national self-defense. Some veterans returning from the war, such as John Kerry, raised critical voices against the war. Conscientious objectors found the entire idea of a just war self-contradictory.

When the United States and its allies engaged in the Gulf War against Iraq, liberating occupied Kuwait, some people who, two decades before, had stood against the idea of the Vietnam War had mixed emotions: Liberating another country from an occupational force seemed a noble enough cause, but then there was the question of oil and the availability of it for an oil-dependent nation. The suspicion remained for many that the underlying motivation for U.S. involvement was tainted with self-interest. Of course, it is a good question exactly why it is supposed to be suspect for a country to pursue its own interests; it becomes questionable only when that self-interest prevents other countries from pursuing *their* own interests. (You'll remember the harm principle from Chapter 5; you'll also remember from Chapter 4 and Chapter 11 that an action that is motivated not just by self-interest but also by concern for others cannot be labeled as straight egoism.)

As I am writing this, the United States has been engaged in two wars for almost the entire time we have been moving further into the twenty-first century: the war in Afghanistan and the war in Iraq. To date, the lives of more than four thousand American soldiers have been lost. The war in Iraq, in particular, has become an issue of controversy, but both military conflicts have inspired a renewed discussion of what constitutes a just war. Whether directly or indirectly (an issue that is itself controversial) a result of the terrorist attacks of September 11, 2001, our military engagements in the Middle East have changed how we perceive the phenomenon of war—almost as the rise of the Cold War in the post–World War II years redefined what was then considered typical warfare.

Traditionally, the concept of war has been applied to a conflict between nations. In the eighteenth century, Jean-Jacques Rousseau identified within his social contract theory the end of war hostilities as the moment when soldiers lay down their arms; at that point they are no longer to be considered "enemies." However, in many ways that was when the lengthier phase of the war in Iraq began—with defeated Iraqi soldiers melting into the landscape, and reappearing as guerrilla fighters. Now the concept of war has been expanded to include warfare against terrorists without a nation backing them up, and against "insurgents," local or imported guerrilla forces engaging a conventional military force in conventional battle or through terrorist suicide attacks, roadside bombings, or other forms of ambush. This expansion of the definition of war is appropriate according to some, but illegitimate according to others, because in their viewpoint terrorism should be dealt with as a criminal act, not an act of war. One of the difficulties in discussing war and terrorism is that the definition of a terrorist is itself in dispute, and Box 13.3 explores that issue further.

For several months after the terrorist attacks on September 11, an extraordinary feeling of bipartisanship permeated the American political scene, but with the war in Afghanistan in 2002, there were already signs that the unity between right and left, between Republicans and Democrats, couldn't hold. There was a sense of united purpose in sending troops to Afghanistan, because that was where the al Qaeda training camps were, where Osama bin Laden had been operating for years, and where the Taliban, the absolute governing power, had allowed al Qaeda to operate. However, as the war continued with Taliban guerillas and warlords engaging our troops continually

Box 13.3   TERRORIST OR FREEDOM FIGHTER?

A terrorist is someone who terrorizes others in order to obtain a goal, usually of a political nature, and usually by means of violence or threat of violence. That's the easy definition. Terrorism has been used as a political weapon by political subgroups in the West particularly since the 1970s, when left-wing terrorist groups emerged in Germany and the United States, with stated goals of overthrowing the government. In the last decades we have also seen right-wing terrorists, such as abortion clinic bombers and snipers; left-wing terrorism has branched off into *eco-terrorism*, terrorist attacks on behalf of the environment. Generally, most people in democratic cultures frown on the use of fear and violence as a means of making a political point, and that attitude was only strengthened by the 9/11 attacks. But after 9/11 a saying was quite often heard in political discussions: "One person's terrorist is another person's freedom fighter." Does that expression merit consideration? Given the fact that Osama bin Laden, the supposed mastermind behind 9/11, received support from the United States back in the days when he was fighting in Afghanistan with underground Afghani troops against the Soviet occupational forces, the question is legitimate. Perhaps all that matters is from whose perspective one sees it: When we approve of their fight, they become freedom fighters, and when we disapprove, they're terrorists? But we don't have to accept that relativistic definition if we can decide on a distinction. Some, including myself, suggest that you can be a freedom fighter with a political goal, and even use violence and fear to obtain your goal, as long as your target is an occupational or other oppressive force within a country you call your own, and violence is not directed deliberately against civilians. An additional important element is the ultimate goal: If your goal is increased freedom for your people to achieve self-determination, then you can indeed be called a freedom fighter. But if your goal is to achieve power without any intention of establishing a democracy, the term "freedom" fighter would be a travesty. (And of course you can be a freedom fighter without resorting to violence at all. Gandhi was such a freedom fighter, and so was Martin Luther King, Jr. I doubt that anyone today would call them terrorists, although their nonviolent, passive-resistance policy did strike fear in the hearts of opponents.) A terrorist directs his or her acts of violence not only against military and/or occupational forces but also against civilians. The only way a terrorist can claim to be a freedom fighter is to claim that there are no innocents among his or her targets, which was indeed a claim made by bin Laden on video in the fall of 2001, but it was a claim that most Americans found hard to accept, since we distinguish between military and civilian targets and victims, and there were no military victims anywhere except at the Pentagon on 9/11. An argument sometimes used by people targeting what most of us would call civilians is that if you don't actively rebel against your government, then you are an accomplice in its transgressions, so you are not a civilian. But the 9/11 attacks didn't follow that definition either, since there were children (who don't make political decisions) among the victims—and apparently there was no attempt to weed them out or ascertain whether any adults on board the planes or at the World Trade Center harbored ill feelings toward the U.S. government (and should thus have been excluded as targets).

Of course, there is still some leeway in the interpretation of what qualifies as an occupational or oppressive force—some would say that the American and British forces in Iraq themselves took on the role of occupiers, while others regard us as liberators—but not nearly as much when it comes to a definition of civilians. In the Primary Readings the philosopher Jan Narveson explains what he thinks characterizes a terrorist.

even after a new democratic Afghan government was in place, the fragile political homefront unity was further fragmented, until, with the war in Iraq, we were left with what you read about in Chapter 1: a "50-50 nation," a nation divided. Many citizens believed it was morally right and patriotic to *support* the war, but a perception was also frequently voiced that it was patriotic in itself to *oppose* the war. In Box 13.4 we take a look at the phenomenon of patriotism. The topic of *just war* has been revived and debated around the country, in academic institutions and in the media, but just war theory has in fact been a topic for military leaders and students of military history for centuries. A revival of the topic actually predates September 11, 2001, by more than two decades, with the publication of professor of political philosophy Michael Walzer's book *Just and Unjust Wars* (1977). Has the war in Iraq been conducted according to the criteria of a just war? Below we take a closer look at what constitutes a "just war," and you may want to use whatever knowledge you have of the war in Iraq to come up with your own evaluation.

So is there such a thing as a just war? For a *pacifist,* the answer is no: Nothing on this earth—no attack on our loved ones, no danger to our life or our country—warrants raising our hand or using weapons of any kind against another human being. If you're a pacifist, say critics, you can't make an exception such as "I don't believe in war, but I'd of course want to defend my family," for two reasons: (1) If you have proclaimed that you reject the idea that force can solve a problem, then it doesn't matter if we talk about it on a grand or a small scale: Force is impermissible, period. (2) If you believe that it is okay for you to resort to force to save your family from harm, what about those who don't have family members to save *them* from harm? That is traditionally the state's role: to protect its citizens from enemies, both domestic and foreign. When it is engaged in protection against harm caused by a foreign force, we call it war. And if you find it acceptable for an individual to protect his or her family from harm, then, logically, you should accept that the state takes on a similar action to protect its citizens.

So, according to the critics, the only consistent viewpoint for a pacifist is to reject the notion of using force to defend one's family against harm. Other forms of defense are acceptable, such as calling 911 (but if you don't approve of violence, you can't allow the police to use violence to save your family, either). Or you can put yourself in harm's way and use passive resistance, hoping that harm to your family will be deflected onto you, or that the harm-doer will think twice. In the 1930s and 1940s, Mohandas K. Gandhi (1869–1948), known by the reverent title of Mahatma, headed a movement to make the British pull out of their colony of India and give it its independence. His method, passive resistance, provided an alternative for countless people—in India as well as elsewhere—who would like to express their disapproval of an idea or a policy without resorting to violence. Gandhi's approach helped bring about Indian independence in 1946, but in 1948 he himself became a victim of violence, being gunned down by an assassin. Martin Luther King, Jr., met the same fate in 1968 after being a life-long admirer of Gandhi's philosophy of passive resistance and advocating the same method in his civil rights movement. King's commitment continues to inspire people who seek to create political change without resorting to any form of violence.

Box 13.4   PATRIOTISM: TOO MUCH, TOO LITTLE, OR JUST THE RIGHT AMOUNT?

In the weeks following September 11, 2001, we saw flags go up by the thousands in just about every neighborhood in the country, from billboards to bumpers. To some, that was a positive sign of love for one's country; to others, it was an oppressive display of excessive nationalism. A debate about what exactly patriotism is arose, and as the war against terror morphed into the war in Afghanistan, and then the war in Iraq, pro-war and anti-war viewpoints began to differ drastically in their definition of proper patriotism.

But what exactly is patriotism, and when is it too much, too little, or just the right amount? In the 1970s the opinion was voiced among philosophers that patriotism is like racism and sexism: It is an unfounded preference for one's own country just because it is one's own country, just as sexism is a preference for one's own sex and a disregard for the other sex, and racism is a preference for one's own race and a disregard for other races. One of the visions of Marxism, for example, is people shedding their national affiliations and boundaries and becoming international, because the plight of workers is presumably the same everywhere. The final words of the original French song and rallying cry for Communism from 1871, *The Internationale,* are "The Internationale unites the human race." Less radical views of patriotism have been suggested, based on the criticism that it makes no sense to say we aren't allowed to love our country more than other countries—just as it would make no sense to say we shouldn't love our own family more than we love strangers. In a paper from 1989, "In Defense of 'Moderate Patriotism,'" Steven Nathanson, an American ethicist, argues against critics of patriotism that "patriotism is a virtue as long as the actions it encourages are not themselves immoral. . . . That a morally acceptable form of patriotism is possible can be seen by comparing patriotism to love or family

loyalty. People may (and, one hopes, typically do) have a special interest and concern for their parents, spouses, and children. They really do care more about those 'near and dear' than about strangers. Yet, so long as this concern is not an exclusive concern, there is nothing the matter with it." In other words, it is acceptable to be a patriot as long as one is mainly expressing a love for one's country and homeland and isn't implying that one's country is always automatically right—in other words, this view rejects the notion of "my country, right or wrong" but allows for a personal sense of affiliation and love for one's roots. Part of the American tradition is the right to question authority—to ask good questions and expect them to be answered. One might say that it is a matter of pride in one's tradition, of patriotism, to keep asking good questions. Something that is deeply American and an ingrained feature in both the political left and the political right is to want the United States to be the best that it can be, because we love this country and wish it well. What has been disturbing to many in the years after 9/11 is that the debate over who is a better patriot has become shrill at times: There is an assumption among the Left that they are not *allowed* to voice a critical opinion of the war in Iraq or the Bush administration—that the Right has monopolized patriotism itself. Conversely, there is a sense among the Right that the Left is speaking with a voice of treason, criticizing the administration at a time when displaying disagreement in the nation makes us more vulnerable to enemy attacks and plays into the hands of the terrorists. For some, love of country means loving what it *could be,* whereas for others, it means loving what it *has been,* and is. Wherever we find ourselves in this troubled spectrum, it is good to remind ourselves that conservatives don't have a monopoly on patriotism, and neither do liberals.

But critics of pacifism point out: (1) If you put yourself in harm's way to save your family without personal use of force and lose your life, and your act of sacrifice doesn't save your family, nothing has been gained. (2) You may have the right to refuse to use any form of force or violence yourself, but if you have responsibility for others, such as small children, your right does not extend to them, because they are under your protection, morally and legally.

If you are not a pacifist and believe in the concept of a just war, the alternative isn't simply to be a "hawk," a "warmonger," or a belligerent, violent person. On the contrary: The doctrine of just war is based on the assumption that the ideal condition is peace; war is seen as the last resort to restore peace. Once that is a given, several other conditions must be in place to call a war just (*jus ad bellum*). These rules were worked out in the late Middle Ages by the so-called Schoolmen or scholastics, building on Roman law and early Christian thinkers such as Augustine and Ambrose, and they have become the foundation for military ethics in the West ever since. Here we look at an overview of these rules, as they are taught in military ethics courses:

- **Last resort** As stated above, a war can be just only if all other ways of restoring peace have been exhausted, such as negotiations and economic sanctions.

- **Just cause** If going to war is the only way a country can defend its values and lives of innocent citizens against aggression and restoring peace, then the cause is considered just. In modern-day terms, identified by Michael Waltzer in his influential book *Just and Unjust Wars* (1977), this boils down to a response to an aggression and a defense of rights.

- **Legitimate, competent authority** War can be declared only by a competent governmental authority. A clarification may be necessary here: A "competent authority" doesn't refer to the leader's intelligence or lack thereof, but exclusively to whether or not the leader is the legitimate representative of the people and whether he or she has the constitutional authority to declare war. Some over-enthusiastic general can't start a war on his or her own.

- **Comparative justice** The values and rights that are being defended must be so important that their defense outweighs the horrors of war.

- **Right intention** The intention must be to defend the rights in question, and not have some ulterior motive, such as gaining territory or enhancing business.

- **Probability of success** There has to be a reasonable assumption that the war will accomplish its goal.

- **Proportionality of ends** The costs of the war must not exceed the presumed benefits. Some victories are too costly, as any utilitarian will tell you. The term for such a victory is *Pyrrhic,* from Pyrrhus, the king of Epirus who won a battle against the Romans in 279 B.C.E. but sustained such huge losses that it put the value of the victory in doubt.

Those are the rules that have to be in place when war is declared; in addition, there are rules that must be followed while conducting the war, "justice in war" (*jus in bello*).

Over the past few centuries there has been a tendency to emphasize justice in war rather than just war, because the "just cause" concept is hard to define: After all, any nation (or terrorist group) can claim that its values are at risk and then march off to war. Instead, scholars have focused on limiting the damage done by war through these two rules:

- **Proportionality of means** Although some harm will of course be caused, one should avoid causing unnecessary damage.

- **Discrimination** The term *discrimination* here means discerning, or "discriminating" between combatants and noncombatants. This rule was added to Just War theory in the Middle Ages; before then, Western thinking did not discriminate between soldiers and civilians (as some would argue that certain non-Western cultures are still not doing). Since everyone knows that wars usually involve civilian casualties, especially modern wars, the last rule doesn't exclude the loss of innocent noncombatants altogether, but they can't be *deliberately* targeted. Having some civilian casualties—on the enemy side, but also on one's own side—is considered acceptable as long as the overall result furthers the goal of peace. This falls under the principle of the *double effect,* which you read about in the discussion of abortion, a principle based on Catholic theology: An action that is prohibited under normal circumstances can be permitted if part of the outcome is (1) unintended, (2) doesn't exceed the goal in magnitude, and (3) unavoidable in order to accomplish its goal.

Even if two warring nations do follow those rules (which, of course, is not a given), there are still plenty of gray areas where one group can interpret the rules differently than another. And just wars can involve unjust acts. Some would cite the internment of Japanese Americans during World War II as an example of an unjust action during a just war.

A "third pillar" has been suggested in recent years: *jus post bellum,* or justice after war. In recognition that war crimes are often part of the fabric of war, some legal measures are thought to be necessary in the wake of a war. In *Parameters, US Army War College Quarterly,* Autumn 2002, professor of military science Davida E. Kellogg points out that although there may be difficulties setting up an international war-crimes tribunal, it is still a necessity so that injustices committed against citizens can be addressed and so that the citizens don't embark on revenge on their own. A problem facing the new kind of warfare of today is what to do with terrorists who are not innocent civilians but who are not soldiers of a nation either. Kellogg suggests that in the aftermath of a war, such criminals or "unlawful combatants" be treated as prisoners of war with rights, but still regarded as criminals, contrary to the tradition reaching back to the Middle Ages, when such irregular combatants were simply regarded as "pirates" without any rights whatsoever. (Thus, the handful of surviving defenders of the Alamo in Texas in 1836 were executed by Mexican General Santa Anna after the battle precisely because they were considered pirates without the rights of a soldier to honorable treatment.) In "Justice After War" in *Ethics & International Affairs*

(2002), Brian Orend argues that the goals for a *jus post bellum* theory would include the following principles:

- There ought to be proportionality and publicity in the postwar settlement, and unjust gains from aggression must be eliminated.
- The settlement should address the basic rights that were violated.
- The settlement must distinguish between leaders, soldiers, and civilians.
- There ought to be punishment of leaders, as well as of soldiers.
- The compensations must be proportional to the losses.
- The aggressor should be rehabilitated under acceptable terms.

The addition of *jus post bellum,* in accordance with the rules of the Geneva Convention, can obviously apply to the aftermath of a war that one nation or coalition of nations has won and the other has lost; but it is harder to apply these principles to the aftermath of a war that has been fought between nations and bands of terrorists.

So has the war in Iraq been a just war? Some will answer flat out no, others will say yes, and some will say that we simply haven't been presented with all the facts yet. Let us look at the seven criteria for a just war: The critics point out that (1) the war can't be described as a *last-resort effort,* since the UN inspectors hadn't completed their search for the so-called WMDs, the weapons of mass destruction. The war supporters have countered that the accumulated results of twelve years of trying to make Saddam Hussein comply with the restrictions following the Gulf War of 1991, and finally reaching a point where everything had been tried, meant there was no further reason to try again. The critics have said that (2) it was not a *just cause,* because the WMDs simply were not there, and Iraq was not a threat to us after all. The war supporters have answered that various intelligence sources claiming that WMDs existed had either misled the government or had been misinterpreted. Furthermore, WMDs had indeed been used on previous occasions, such as the extermination attempt on the Kurds, so it was a given that Saddam Hussein had possessed them earlier, and they might still be found—and, further still, there were other reasons for going to war, such as liberating 20 million people from tyranny. (3) The critics have claimed that President Bush was not a *legitimate authority,* since his 2000 election was determined by the Supreme Court, not by the voters; the supporters of the Bush administration have answered that, aside from the election result's being constitutionally valid, eventually, after recounting all the Florida votes that were in dispute in the 2000 election, in 2001 it was reported by the *Miami Herald* and *USAToday* that Bush indeed had won by a small majority. (4) For the critics, the war did not represent *comparative justice,* since, in their eyes, our values and way of life were not genuinely threatened by Iraq but, rather, by al Qaeda, and no connection between al Qaeda and Saddam Hussein had been established—and besides, for all intents and purposes, it looked as if the hunt for bin Laden had been given up, or at least put on the back burner, for the sake of the war in Iraq. The supporters have said that had Hussein had the power to attack us in the future, he would have done so, and it was right not to sit back and wait for that to happen—and, furthermore, the very fact that al Qaeda showed up in Iraq during the war was proof enough that a connection indeed was there—and that the search for bin Laden never stopped during the war in Iraq but, rather, continued quietly. (5) According to the critics, the *right intentions* have not been shown, given that Iraq is rich in oil and provides the United States with business opportunities; supporters point out that defense of our country, prevention of future wars, liberation of a country from abuse and tyranny, and establishing a democracy in the Middle East for the sake of stability and freedom are all very powerful, right intentions. (6) And how about the *probability of success*? Critics have been very vocal, pointing out that the United States and its allies have had no exit strategy, meaning that once the war was won, there was no blueprint for "winning the peace," and chaos ensued, placing a burden on Iraqi families as well as on the families of fallen U.S. soldiers. Supporters, on the other hand, have pointed out that success has already been achieved: 20 million people are free to pursue their chosen destiny, Iraq is no longer a threat to the United States, there are no more political murders, and Iraq had its first truly democratic election in 2005. (7) And *proportionality of ends*? That is something posterity will have to judge—as it will have to judge the entire war against terrorism in general. Will the war in Iraq have proved to be too costly? The critics say yes, the loss of American lives—by the spring of 2008 numbering over four thousand men and women—was too high a price to pay. The monetary sums being poured into the reconstruction of Iraq at a time when the homeland economy hadn't been doing well were just over the top. And with little assurance that a free Iraq would not be overwhelmed by the totalitarian influence of the Islamic Republic of Iran, the end result may not necessarily be a democratic Iraq, Western-style. Even supporters of the war effort, including military experts, conceded that mistakes had been made; the phenomenon of Iraqi "insurgents" attracting al Qaeda sympathizers from around the region had not been anticipated sufficiently, and the lack of cooperation between the various factions of Iraqi ethnic, religious, and political groups had been underestimated. However, supporters expressed the viewpoint that they would rather fight the war against terror in Iraq than at home, and that losses of American lives have still been light compared with losses in previous conflicts, such as World War II and the Vietnam War. And with the apparent success of the "2007 surge," an expanded military effort that effectively reduced the number of roadside and marketplace attacks by insurgents by some 70 percent, combined with reports that daily life was returning to some semblance of normality in Baghdad neighborhoods and elsewhere, supporters see both a probability of success and a proportionality of ends, in the long run. Whether we find that the critics or the supporters of the war in Iraq have the better arguments, the debate illustrates that even if we have rules of just war, they are by no means unambiguous, and they can serve only as guidelines, not as a clear and easy checklist.

When we look to discussions of a just war and terrorism by contemporary philosophers, most papers and books written before 9/11 have one thing in common: They imagine a future enemy to be a nation with an identifiable government, rarely a shadowy association of international terrorists. At the end of the chapter you will find a selection of text excerpts on the subject predating 9/11, including a famous text by Immanuel Kant. In war-torn eighteenth-century Prussia, Kant wrote one of his last works, "Perpetual Peace." With a clarity that wasn't apparent to readers until after World War II, Kant envisioned the slippery slope of escalating wars of the future leading to a war of mutual extermination and admonished that the only way civilization will survive is for all governments to become republican (that is, a democracy instead of various forms of dictatorship that regard their citizens as merely a means to an end). You will remember the concept of the *kingdom of ends* from Chapter 6, and this is what Kant was dreaming of: a world where people respect one another and their laws, where no nation abuses its own citizens, where nations will join together in a federation of free states, and where strangers are considered people too. In his essay, Kant suggests the formation of a "League of Nations" to prevent future wars—a feat that was not accomplished until 1919 on President Woodrow Wilson's initiative. It became a precursor of the United Nations. Although some might say Kant's vision is both a trifle naïve and incomplete, one might hope there is a profound truth to his observation that truly democratic countries, where each citizen knows he or she has constitutionally protected rights, are less likely to generate wars of aggression—or have individuals embark on terrorist ploys against their own government or other nations—than countries where the individual has few or no rights and feels like a pawn in the political games of others. An active global effort toward democracy might thus go a long way toward preventing future terrorist actions as well as future wars. The American philosopher John Rawls, whom you know from Chapter 7, focused in his final book, *The Law of Peoples,* on some of the same issues, and you'll find an excerpt in the Primary Readings.

Animal Welfare and Animal Rights

There was a time when animals were considered morally responsible, to a degree. It was assumed, almost as in the fairy tales we knew as kids, that animals have a form of reason, and when they hurt one another or humans, they do it on purpose. Until the mid–nineteenth century, animals could be held legally responsible for their actions (although they had very few recognized rights); all through the European Middle Ages rats, roaches, and other pests were put on trial (usually in absentia) for the damage they caused to human lives and property. Even in the United States, animals were put on trial for hurting their masters or their own offspring, and they were "executed" if found guilty. Today, when an aggressive dog attacks a small child and is put to death, do we consider ourselves to be "executing" the dog? Some might argue that that is exactly what we are doing—we are punishing the dog for transgressing a human law. But legally we are simply disposing of the dog's owner's property not as a punishment against the dog but as a precaution in the public interest. Who *does* get punished? Not the dog, but the *owner,* who receives a fine or even a jail sentence. In San Francisco in 2002, a dog owner even received a second-degree murder sentence after her dogs attacked and killed a neighbor, but a judge later reduced the sentence to four years for manslaughter. Today we don't consider animals to be legally responsible for their actions, because we don't consider them to be moral agents. A dog who wakes up his owners when the house is on fire may be praised for it afterward, but if she fails to react, nobody will call her "callous" or "evil." (In previous times, when animals were put on trial, the issue of whether they were moral agents still was not solved because it was commonly considered that they had no souls and thus had no free will. Were the people who put them on trial contradicting themselves? Yes. But so do we sometimes, and one of the objectives of discussing these issues is to get into the habit of thinking more consistently.)

Ironically, even if animals in the past were considered as having some form of moral responsibility, they were not considered eligible for rights, or even humane treatment.

In Chapters 5 and 6 we touched on the issue of animals as candidates for moral respect. Chapter 5 introduced you to Descartes's idea that animals cannot feel pain because they have no minds and Bentham's and Mill's view that since animals obviously can feel pain and experience pleasure, consideration for animals should be included in whatever moral decisions we make that might affect them. Today, research by animal behaviorists has established that nonhuman animals are capable of feeling physical pain. In addition, animal studies in the wild as well as under more controlled conditions in animal behavior labs support the old anecdotal assumption that animals can also feel emotions; and the criticism, raised repeatedly throughout the twentieth century, that animal researchers are just "anthropomorphizing" their subjects is rarely heard now. Animal researchers and writers are increasingly affirming the observations of David Hume and Charles Darwin that if animals act as if they feel emotions similar to fear, joy, and sadness, then it is the simplest and most likely explanation that they do in fact feel such similar emotions—although we will have a hard time showing exactly how similar, until the day when we can hook up animals (and people) to monitors and read their minds electronically and chemically, or in fact talk to the animals themselves and ask them, as some ape researchers are already doing. (The question of animal *intelligence* is considered in Box 13.5.)

The Utilitarian Approach

Within the utilitarian philosophy the recognition that animals can feel pain— physically, and even emotionally—obviously doesn't mean we as humans are not allowed to cause animals pain or distress, any more than it means we are not allowed to cause other humans pain: When great results can be obtained for a majority (of humans and/or animals), then causing pain to sentient creatures is morally acceptable and even commendable. For that reason, classical utilitarians such as Bentham and Mill and most utilitarians today rarely use the term "animal rights." Rather, modern utilitarians talk about "animal welfare." As you'll remember from Chapter 7, Bentham thought the notion of human rights was "nonsense upon stilts," and obviously a utilitarian would view animal rights in the same light, inasmuch as a utilitarian doesn't believe it serves any good purpose to talk about rights that are absolute and can never be infringed on, if the protection of such rights would be detrimental to the majority in a society.

A utilitarian believes we should take animal pain and pleasure into consideration whenever there are no overriding concerns that would justify causing pain for the sake of achieving good consequences for the many. As we saw in Chapter 5, a typical

Box 13.5   RATIONAL ANIMALS?

The question of animal intelligence has been a challenge ever since Aristotle claimed that animals can think in a practical sense, but only humans can think rationally and abstractly. What does it take to think rationally? You'll remember that our working definition of rationality in Chapter 6 was the ability to identify a goal and take the shortest route to it (and that definition itself was questionable). For Kant the true test of a rational being is whether he or she can understand the categorical imperative: Could you allow yourself to do something you wouldn't accept as a universal law? Most of us, however, have a less strict view of what it is to think rationally. If someone solves a problem through trial and error, we usually view it as a rational method, but it is even better if someone can envision a solution to a problem without having encountered the problem before, and solve it on the first try simply by having thought about it abstractly.

Most of us are probably willing to accept that nonhuman animals have some sort of mental activity whereby they associate time and place, link past fears and joys with present persons and places, and anticipate events in the near future, such as dinner. But can nonhuman animals solve abstract problems and even conceive of a kind of categorical imperative? Throughout the twentieth century, that question was so controversial that most scholars steered clear of it for fear of ridicule; in 1900 a horse in Germany, Clever Hans, believed by his owner and numerous scientists to be able to do math because he could thump out the correct answers to math questions when asked, was revealed to be "simply" a good reader of human body language, and research into animal intelligence carried the stigma of Clever Hans with it well into the last half of the twentieth century. But since new research into animal intelligence was made public during the 1980s and 1990s, many researchers have been less reluctant to consider nonhuman animals as having a rudimentary capacity for rational thinking and even for language comprehension. Close observation and interaction with dolphins, orca whales, monkeys, pigs, dogs, and even birds have led to a new appreciation of the possibility of nonhuman animal reasoning. In particular, research into the behavior and language capacity of nonhuman great apes (bonobo chimpanzees, chimpanzees, gorillas, and to a lesser extent orangutans) has made it conceivable that the great apes have a grasp of abstract rational thinking as well as trial-and-error thinking.

Of the great apes, the bonobo chimpanzee Kanzi may be the most famous example of nonhuman animal intelligence today, although his sister Panbanisha now seems to surpass him in linguistic talent. They both live at the Great Ape Trust in Iowa under the tutelage of psychologist Sue Savage-Rumbaugh. Having taught himself how to use a lexigram (an electronic "talking" board with symbols for English words) by watching the humans try, unsuccessfully, to teach his mother its use, Kanzi answers questions or tells his human friends what he wants, including watching videos that feature humans in ape costumes. Panbanisha has been raised in the human-language environment and has learned to use the lexigram as well. Kanzi's feats include understanding new sentences and reacting accordingly (such as "Put the key in the refrigerator"), as well as displaying logical thinking, going through a series of actions to achieve a goal (such as cutting a string to get into a box with a key that opens another box with a treat). Panbanisha has shown an interest in copying the words she sees on the computer screen and has reportedly taken up writing words in English on the floor with chalk. In addition, Panbanisha serves as an interpreter for her and Kanzi's mother, who never learned the use of the lexigram.

(continued)

Box 13.5   RATIONAL ANIMALS? (*continued*)

The bonobo chimpanzee Kanzi is today perhaps the most outstanding, and controversial, example of a nonhuman being using and understanding language and demonstrating rational thought—at the approximate level of a human child of three (and occasionally even older). Never having been trained to understand human language or use a lexigram (a talking board with symbols signifying nouns, verbs, and names), Kanzi picked up both skills as an infant from watching his mother in training. Here, at sixteen years of age, Kanzi is working with his lexigram, answering questions for Sue Savage-Rumbaugh at Georgia State University's Language Research Center.

Would Kant recognize these behaviors as evidence of rational thinking and welcome Kanzi and Panbanisha as persons instead of things? That would depend on whether it is possible for the apes to grasp the concept of universalization: Might they understand the idea of "Don't do that—how would you like it if we did that to you?" Kanzi's and Panbanisha's language comprehension is now presumably at the level of a three-year-old human child's. If we are ready to recognize a small child as having some grasp of rational thought and as understanding the preceding sentence, and are willing to call a three-year-old child a person, why not be as open-minded about the personhood of an ape if he or she is on the approximate same intellectual level? For some thinkers, the entire ape language experiment hinges on whether it's merely some smart animals "aping" human behavior for rewards, or whether apes can really communicate freely (within limits) in a human language. Since one of the first apes who learned American Sign Language, Washoe, taught her son the ASL signs and communicated with him using signs even when they thought themselves to be unobserved by humans, and Panbanisha is now teaching her young son, Nyota, how to use the lexigram, the answer seems to be yes.

utilitarian response to animal experiments would be to frown on the use of animals in research on household products or cosmetics, because the contentment or protection each individual human would gain from the pain of animal experiments—a safer hairspray, a milder detergent—does not outweigh that pain, especially since humans can choose to avoid products that make your eyes sting and dry out your hands. However, when the focus shifts to medical experiments possibly resulting in the cure for terminal or debilitating illnesses, many utilitarians change their minds: The beneficial outcome of such research, which uses a limited number of animals, could be so overwhelming that there is no excuse not to perform such experiments. (You will recognize the problem from the film *Extreme Measures*, summarized in Chapter 5, even though the film addresses the problem of *human* test subjects.)

The Kantian Approach

As you will remember from Chapter 6, Kant excludes animals from moral consideration as ends in themselves because, to him, they are not rational creatures. Rational creatures are capable of understanding moral rules and, above all, moral duties and responsibilities. Kantians believe that only those who are capable of entering into a mutual relationship involving moral responsibilities are eligible for rights, and since animals are not perceived as having such capabilities, the deontological tradition reserves rights for humans. So what happens to human beings who, for some reason, are not capable of taking on duties and responsibilities? Some modern Kantians, such as the philosopher Carl Cohen, choose to solve that problem by saying that as long as most people are capable of rational thinking and understanding duties, then respect should also be extended to the few who aren't. However, even if it may appear as though an animal is capable of understanding its "duties," what that understanding really amounts to is training based on rewards or punishment—not a true understanding of moral duties—so from a Kantian point of view, animals are by their very nature excluded from having rights. This is what Cohen and others refer to as *contractarianism:* If your mind is capable of comprehending the obligations involved in a contract—written or oral—then you are a rational being and should be treated with respect. A creature that doesn't understand the implications of a contract can't have duties and consequently can't have any rights either. That doesn't mean we can't or shouldn't choose to be kind to animals, because there is no excuse for causing needless suffering, but although we may take on the responsibility of caring for an animal, our pet has no moral claim on us.

Rights and Interests

From the viewpoint that having rights entails having an understanding of duties, the path to animal rights ought to remain blocked. However, there is an alternative viewpoint linking rights not with *duties* but with *interests.* You were introduced to the ideas of Australian philosopher Peter Singer in Chapters 4 and 5, and you may remember the title of one of his books, *The Expanding Circle.* The circle Singer would like to see expanded is our moral universe: Who counts as a morally important being? Singer sees our view of who counts as having expanded from the family or the tribe to nations and to all humans. Singer and others would now like to see that circle expanded further to include the great apes and possibly other intelligent, social species, such as whales, dolphins, and wolves, in what is called "the community of equals," as stated in the Declaration on Great Apes. The argument used by many thinkers advocating rights for animals is that if a living being is capable of having interests, then those beings should have at least some moral standing (they should be taken into our moral universe). But what does it mean to have an interest? It may seem as if our cars have an interest in regular maintenance, because otherwise they break down. But presumably our cars don't suffer when they break down (only we, the owners, do). So the capacity for suffering and the interest in not suffering must be included in the basic description of a being with moral standing. But is an interest something that some individual really wants, or is it something that is good for that individual? And if interests imply rights, does it mean that individuals with interests have a right to have the interest fulfilled? For Singer, it is the capacity for interests that makes an individual eligible for rights, but that capacity doesn't mean those individuals have a right to have their wishes (or even their needs) fulfilled; however, they have a right to have their needs taken into consideration as morally relevant. In concrete terms, Singer's suggestions for "rights for the great apes" would include the right not to be tortured, not to be deprived of their freedom, and not to be killed, but it would not include any right to a steady supply of jellybeans (if that's what some individual ape might prefer). Some critics have remarked that it is unusual for a utilitarian philosopher such as Singer to use a concept such as *rights* instead of *welfare,* since traditionally any right for a utilitarian must be superseded by overriding social concerns. But Singer's philosophy of the ethical treatment of animals comes as close to the concept of rights as is possible for a utilitarian, since he believes the possibility that those rights would ever be overridden by other concerns is remote. For Singer, harming an animal would be permissible only in extreme cases, such as saving all of humanity.

Other thinkers sharing Singer's view that beings with interests should have rights include Joel Feinberg and Steve Sapontzis. For Feinberg it is obvious that individual animals have interests, perhaps more interests than some humans who are severely mentally impaired, so individual animals should have rights. However, an entire species can't have "interests," so Feinberg doesn't favor the rights of endangered *species,* only those of *individuals,* nonhuman or human. But, says Feinberg, if the criterion for being a member of the moral universe is that you can make moral claims against someone else, then animals already have such rights, because they can be represented in court by humans protecting their interests.

Sapontzis looks at the issue from both a utilitarian and a Kantian point of view: If we agree that animals probably have an overall narrower range of interests than humans, that is still not a sufficient reason to disregard such interests. In "The Moral Significance of Interests," he writes: "It certainly does not follow on utilitarian grounds that because an individual has a narrower range of interests he may be treated as a tool for the gratification of the interests of a being with a wider range of interests. If that did follow, renaissance men could eat specialists and peasants for dinner." Utilitarians aren't obliged to treat humans and animals in *the same* way, just to take their interests into equal consideration (so there won't be a question of giving animals the right to vote or to a good, well-rounded education, as some critics are fond of speculating).

What if we apply Kantianism to the issue of animal interests? Sapontzis points to the wealth of new research in animal intelligence, as well as to our common experiences with animals: It is about time, he says, that we put the debate over whether animals are rational behind us; of course they are—not to the degree of human rationality, but rational nevertheless. They may not be able to use the categorical imperative, but they are courageous, loyal, and devoted, and if we want to extend moral worth to humans with the same qualities, then we must let many animals into the moral fold too. As Sapontzis says, "Anyone still inclined to believe that only humans are rational should adopt a dog and get to know him personally."

What if you still think that granting rights to animals is too big a step, since humans, after all, have such a wide range of moral interactions that animals may never comprehend or participate in? You may consider a solution suggested by the philosopher Mary Ann Warren, whom you met earlier in this chapter: *partial rights*. Because many animals do have the same rudimentary intellectual capabilities as small children and the same (or an even greater) capacity for suffering, they should have some moral standing; but since human capacities for both reasoning and suffering are more extensive, they may override the rights of animals. Animals can probably never be morally autonomous the way humans can, but moral autonomy need not be the only criterion for having rights. It is, however, an important factor. So Warren suggests that humans should be the only beings granted full, equal rights (at least until we find other morally autonomous creatures), but nonhuman animals can be the bearers of partial rights, to be superseded by human rights only in extreme cases. In Box 13.6 you'll find a discussion about whether great apes should be considered *persons*.

Ethics of the Environment: Think Globally, Act Locally

In the 1970s a new concept arose: *environmentalism*. The Western world had suffered an energy crisis, and oil dependency was all of a sudden becoming an issue. Energy consumption in the West had skyrocketed after Word War II, outpacing everywhere else on the planet. In addition, it was becoming noticeable that there were fewer bees than before, and fewer birds, and the culprit was tracked down: pesticides sprayed on the fields of grain and on flowering trees and bushes. Birds' eggs had a hard time developing because the shells were thinner and more porous, also because of pesticides. Frogs were disappearing from the wetlands, and indeed the wetlands themselves were disappearing, being drained and turned into farmland or subdivisions. This was a wake-up call for an entire generation, and for a decade or so people scaled back their energy consumption, alternative energy forms were being developed, and people used the stairs instead of the elevator, turned off the lights when they left the room, recycled cans and newspapers, lowered the thermostat in winter, carpooled to work and school, and so forth—all the things that, we hear today, will help us save the environment. The slogan of environmentalism became "Think globally, act locally." And the concerted efforts did indeed make a difference, at least to some extent, in

Box 13.6   APES AND PERSONHOOD

You'll remember the debate in Chapter 7 concerning the distinction between a human being and a person, and how the term "person" is more useful when discussing rights than "human," because it signifies that the "entity" in question is capable of interacting in a morally and socially significant way with others, whereas the term "human" merely refers to someone having human DNA. A legal case in Austria in 2007 illustrates the need for the term "personhood" in addition to the term "human": Matthew Hiasi Pan was in danger of being sold unless the Vienna Supreme Court granted him personhood, because Pan was a chimpanzee, and the animal shelter where he had lived for twenty-five years was in bankruptcy. However, the Austrian legislators recognize only the status of a *human* and the status of a *thing*, and Matthew Hiasi Pan had been ruled a thing. (You'll recognize Kant's dichotomy, which we discussed in Chapter 6: Either you are a rational being, or you are a thing.) In England, New Zealand, and Australia, great apes are considered hominids with limited rights, but not so in Austria. The matter was brought before the Austrian Supreme Court, which decided against Hiasi: He was again found to be a thing, with no rights. The problem with the court ruling seems to be that the court has decided against making a distinction between "humanity" and "personhood." It goes without saying that Hiasi is not a human being, genetically, but being a "person" requires (among other characteristics) the capacity for meaningful communication, a sense of purpose, and self-awareness, characteristics that apes share with us at least to some extent. The Great Ape Project, spearheaded by Peter Singer, has undertaken a census of all living great apes, publishing the biographies of individual apes in captivity. The census is intended to be a reminder that apes are not "things" or pets—they are intelligent beings with a long history of abuse by another species of great ape—the humans.

In your view, should the United States follow Great Britain, New Zealand, and Australia in declaring apes fellow hominids, and go along with New Zealand in granting apes personhood? The Spanish Socialist Party introduced a bill in 2006 granting apes personhood, and in 2007 the Spanish legislators were debating the bill. This would make Spain the first European country to recognize apes as persons. Would it be the morally right thing to attempt to establish legal personhood globally for apes? Would it be more reasonable to choose *partial rights* for apes (see chapter text)? Or do you agree with the Austrian Supreme Court? In the Primary Readings section you'll find two texts related to this issue.

some parts of the Western world: The bees bounced back, and the birds did too. But then oil became cheap again, and we forgot to be energy conscious. For the next decades climatologists debated whether we might be moving toward a "greenhouse effect" because of the steadily climbing levels of CO_2 (carbon dioxide) that are part and parcel of modern energy use. It seemed like a fairly remote theory to most people until reports came in about glaciers melting and the polar ice pack shrinking.

Global Warming: An Inconvenient Truth?

In the late twentieth century, environmental concerns spawned a variety of approaches. One was a recycling movement, which has had broad success—just look at those blue recycle bins in your workplace, at school, and at the curbside on recycle days. Another was the "save water" approach in restaurants where ice water is no longer served automatically—you have to ask for it. Some hotels ask you to keep your wet towels for one more use to save laundry water. And some communities experiment with "gray water," cleansed recycled water. But more radical environmentalist viewpoints were already in existence, culminating in the concept of *deep ecology*, coined by the Norwegian philosopher Arne Næss and supported by scientists such as Rachel Carlson and Aldo Leopold: According to the philosophy of deep ecology, humans are only one of many equally worthy species on the planet, without any species having more right to live than any other. The entire land with all its inhabitants is a moral entity. (Box 13.7 explores the concept of respect for nature from the American Indian point of view.) Aldo Leopold had already in 1948 introduced the concept of *land ethic* in his book *A Sand County Almanac*:

> All ethics so far evolved rest upon a single premise: that the individual is a member of a community of interdependent parts. His instincts prompt him to compete for his place in that community, but his ethics prompt him also to cooperate (perhaps in order that there may be a place to compete for).
>
> The land ethic simply enlarges the boundaries of the community to include soils, waters, plants, and animals, or collectively: the land.
>
> This sounds simple: do we not already sing our love for and obligation to the land of the free and the home of the brave? Yes, but just what and whom do we love? Certainly not the soil, which we are sending helter-skelter downriver. Certainly not the waters, which we assume have no function except to turn turbines, float barges, and carry off sewage. Certainly not the plants, of which we exterminate whole communities without batting an eye. Certainly not the animals, of which we have already extirpated many of the largest and most beautiful species. A land ethic of course cannot prevent the alteration, management, and use of these 'resources,' but it does affirm their right to continued existence, and, at least in spots, their continued existence in a natural state.
>
> In short, a land ethic changes the role of *Homo sapiens* from conqueror of the land-community to plain member and citizen of it. It implies respect for his fellow-members, and also respect for the community as such.

This ethic of respect for the land inspired and invigorated many people, but for others, the problem with environmentalism was that it became an "ism." Like any other ideology, it has turned many people off because of its radicalism: Ranchers and farmers saw their rights to use their streams, fields, and woods diminish because of the presence of endangered species on the premises, such as rare mice and birds, and the almost notorious spotted owl. And when activist movements such as Earth Liberation Front (ELF) and Animal Liberation Front (ALF) arose, commonly referred to as eco-terrorist groups, environmentalism itself acquired a tainted reputation among many people.

Enter global warming: By the early 2000s the idea that the planet's temperatures are heating up because of industrial and vehicle emissions of CO_2 gases, creating a "greenhouse effect" that, in turn, will force temperatures even higher, was a theory advanced by groups to the left of the political spectrum. From 1997 to 1999 the Kyoto Protocol was established, with more than 160 countries as members, and coming into force in February 2005. The purpose of the Kyoto Treaty was to reduce the emissions of carbon dioxide and other greenhouse gases to a level where "anthropogenic" activity (caused by humans) will not present a danger to the world climate. The United States and Australia did not ratify the treaty. The United States was in 2005 the top emitter of carbon dioxides, but we were bypassed in late 2007 by China, which is allowed certain exemptions from the Kyoto Protocol. Those exemptions were one reason the United States did not want to ratify the treaty. Other reasons cited were an unfair strain on the U.S. economy and scientific ambiguity as to the effect of greenhouse gases.

By 2006 it appeared that the global warming issue was a "liberal" cause: Liberal politicians advocated energy restraints, public transport, hybrid cars, no gas-guzzling SUVs or Hummers, and so forth. Conservative politicians pointed out that in a free country, people should be free to choose their lifestyle; that public transport may work in big cities and an Eastern environment, but doesn't work for Western demographics; that the connection between global warming and greenhouse gases had not been established; and that global warming itself had not been established. But by 2007 the picture had changed for many: Former Vice President Al Gore produced an Academy Award–winning documentary, *An Inconvenient Truth,* in which he argued that global warming is a reality: The polar ice caps are melting, raising global water levels; glaciers around the world are disappearing, rain belts are shifting; deserts are spreading. Life will change for most people on the planet; some areas will become uninhabitable, some nations will see a reduction in crops, and some will have to change their entire agricultural systems. And with visuals to prove it, many felt vindicated or changed their minds. As of the time I am writing this, there is general agreement that we are experiencing a climate change, but the extent of it is still under debate; most politicians and media voices in the West are treating it as a fact, although critics such as meteorologist John Coleman, founder of The Weather Channel, calls it "the greatest scam in history." In addition, the question of *why* it is happening is still in dispute: Are Al Gore and the liberal media pundits right in claiming that the global warming is due to human, *anthropogenic* activity? Or are conservative politicians and media pundits right that we may be witnessing one of many climate cycles that, according to climate research, the world has seen a number of over the past 20,000 years, and further back in time—cycles that have little or nothing to do with human activities? In the Primary Readings section you can read two reviews of Al Gore's movie, one positive and the other negative.

Be that as it may, we are probably facing a time of great change, and as you'll remember from Chapter 1, many from "blue" and "red" political zones find themselves meeting in the middle—and the middle, they say, is *green*: We can't afford not to pay heed to the climate changes, so we have to shift gears and commit to curbing the greenhouse gases and look for alternative energy sources. For some conservative analysts, this is a question of a misreading of scientific data for the purpose of political control.

Box 13.7 AMERICAN INDIANS AND LAND ETHIC

As you saw in Chapter 8, traditional American Indian values include a respect for the environment—or, rather, for the spirits of the environment. Since all features of nature are thought to be inspirited (what historians of religion call *animism*), then every living and every natural thing deserves to be treated with respect. That doesn't mean you can't hunt animals, or pick berries, or cut trees, but it does mean that you must do it responsibly, without waste of resources, and that you must engage the environment in a dialogue, asking for permission to hunt or to cut firewood, and giving thanks once your mission has been accomplished. This attitude toward nature was thought by the American philosopher J. Baird Callicott in the late twentieth century to be the ideal *land ethic* (a concept coined by Aldo Leopold; see chapter text): a respect for the entire environment as a whole. But critics (including your author, in a paper titled "Everyone Needs a Stone,") have pointed out that (1) this is just a modern version of Jean-Jacques Rousseau's eighteenth-century concept of the *noble savage;* tribal peoples such as eighteenth- and nineteenth-century American Indians were no more "noble" than they were "savage"— they were people dealing with their environment the best they could, in their own way; and (2) the assumption that the Indians were some early form of environmentalists is a *romantic misrepresentation:* Indians had, in tribal days, respect for the land and its inhabitants, not because they appreciated the interconnectedness of everything, but because nature was dangerous, life was precarious, and if you didn't stay on the good side of nature/the spirits, it/they could destroy you. And it actually shows more respect for the American Indian cultures to view their cultural history from a more realistic and less romantic viewpoint. But that doesn't mean we can't learn from their understanding of nature as a functioning whole that must be respected. Indeed, perhaps the real lesson is here *that if you mistreat nature, it will come back to bite you—* which is exactly what the American Indian land ethic seems to have been all about.

Ethics of the Environment: For Us, or for Itself?

For the header of this section I chose "Ethics of the Environment" rather than "Environmentalism" because of the controversial undertone of the latter. Ethics of the environment implies, in a very broad sense, that we consider the environment as something that should be included in our moral deliberations—for the sake of either *the human beings* whose existence depends on the environment, or *the humans and nonhuman animals* who make this planet their home, or *the humans, the animals, and the organic or even inorganic elements of nature.* The concern about global warming can imply all three. We can choose to be concerned because of immense changes in store for human beings—and most of the changes will probably not be pleasant (except perhaps in Scandinavia, where the tourism industry is gearing up for a Mediterranean-style beach climate to go with the long summer days, and a blossoming quality-wine industry within the next fifty years). But we can also choose to be concerned for the plight of animals around the world whose habitats will change, and shrink—at a time when extinction is threatening most of the large mammals in the wild. And we can certainly also choose the *Gaia* philosophy (Gaia was Mother Earth in Greek mythology) and be concerned for the entire planet, whose ancient forests and rivers and deep waters face climate changes of the human or nonhuman kind.

Environmentalism, in its holistic, deep-ecology version, implies that all elements of nature have a right to exist, but that, in itself, raises new questions, drawing on what you have read about rights in Chapters 6 and 7 and in the preceding section on animal rights in this chapter: Can a being or a thing have rights without having responsibilities? Should trees have rights?

In 1974 Christopher D. Stone wrote a paper, "Should Trees Have Standing? Towards Legal Rights for Natural Objects" (in *People, Penguins, and Plastic Trees*). Many dismissed the paper as complete nonsense at the time. However, it has gained in influence since then. In the paper Stone states that every time we have opted to include another group in our welfare concern, such as slaves, women, minorities, children, or animals, the decision has been met with ridicule before it has achieved common acceptance. He proposes that we now expand our moral universe to cover not only individual animals but also entire species and natural objects such as lakes and streams, mountain meadows, marshes, and so on (who really can't be said to have interest since they are not "alive"):

> Whenever it carves out "property" rights, the legal system is engaged in the process of *creating* monetary worth. . . . I am proposing we do the same with eagles and wilderness areas as we do with copyrighted works, patented inventions, and privacy: *make* the violation of rights in them to be a cost by declaring the "pirating" of them to be the invasion of property interest. If we do so, the net social costs the polluter would be confronted with would include not only the extended homocentric cost of his pollution [. . .] but also cost to the environment *per se*.

What Stone suggests here is a grand solution not only to the problem of whose rights should be protected but also to the problem of *how* they should be protected. He proposes fining polluters because pollution is *bad for nature*, regardless of whether it might affect a local human population or visitors to a polluted wilderness area. It would take us too long to discuss in detail the concept of giving rights to plants and natural objects such as rocks and streams (and of course we'd want to include cultural objects such as historical buildings, old baseball fields, statues, and favorite movie locations). The question is how far we want to go, not in assigning protection for the environment—because we can take that as far as we want to go—but in assigning rights per se, regardless of human interest in the subject. If nobody cares about a certain meadow or about the building in downtown Los Angeles where they filmed *Blade Runner* (the Bradbury building, incidentally), then should we give it rights on the basis that someone may someday care, or because it has acquired those rights just by hanging around?

If we do assign rights to plants, where do we stop? It is all well and good to preserve a good-looking row of trees, but what about preserving a scraggly row of carrots on the grounds that they have a right to life? What we have here is a *slippery slope argument*, the logical fallacy, you'll remember from Chapter 1, claiming that some idea will lead to a series of increasingly unacceptable consequences (such as: "If you refuse to wear fur because of concern for living creatures, then you shouldn't eat meat, either; as a matter of fact, you shouldn't fight the roaches and ants in your kitchen because they, too, are living creatures, nor should you use antibiotics or antibacterial mouthwash out of concern for the living bacteria"). A slippery slope is usually advanced as a satirical criticism of some idea (here, refusing to wear fur) by pointing to ridiculous consequences. (Another term for this type of slippery slope is a *reductio ad absurdum,* a reduction to absurdity.) To respond to a slippery slope, we can take one of three paths: (1) abandon our original idea, because the consequences now seem silly; (2) agree that we should take the consequences seriously; or (3) *draw the line* between one part of the slope and another by arguing that there is a moral difference between, for example, eating meat and killing roaches that spread disease. Concerning the question of giving rights to trees, one could argue that there is a moral difference between granting rights to trees (if that is one's conviction) and granting rights to carrots. However, if we choose to draw the line, it is up to us to have good arguments as to why there is a moral difference between one step of the slope and the next.

The Death Penalty

When the moral question of punishing criminals comes up today, it is usually related to the issue of sentencing children as adults or that of the death penalty. The issue of trying children in adult court was examined briefly in Chapter 7, and here we explore the issue of capital punishment. To get the most out of the debate, it is recommended that you have the punishment discussion from Chapter 7 fresh in your mind, particularly the five categories of punishment: deterrence, rehabilitation, incapacitation, retribution, and vengeance.

Two Philosophers on Capital Punishment

Until the twentieth century, most philosophers had no compunction about arguing in favor of the death penalty. Two voices coming from two different traditions have been particularly influential, and you are familiar with both of them: John Locke, in seventeenth-century England, stated that humans have rights even before the social contract, in the state of nature. These are the three negative rights, to *life, liberty,* and *property.* But since there is no government in the state of nature to enforce those rights, one must take on that task oneself. Therefore, if a person has infringed on your rights, you are free to punish the perpetrator (if you can catch him or her, that is). And, says Locke, if someone in the state of nature has taken a life, then he has given up his own right to life and can be hunted down and killed like a wild animal. Locke believes such action will have two effects: (1) *deterrence*—those who see how a killer is treated will think twice about doing the same thing—and (2) *retribution,* restoring the balance that was disrupted by the murder. So Locke uses both a forward-looking and a backward-looking argument in favor of killing a killer.

THE WIZARD OF ID   Brant parker and Johnny hart

© 1993 by permission of Johnny Hart Studios and Creators Syndicate, Inc.

With a particularly dark sense of humor, this *Wizard of Id* strip deals with capital punishment—a topic that isn't usually a source of laughter. The strip creates a perverted application of a utilitarian principle of punishment: As long as punishment has good consequences (such as deterrence or rehabilitation), then the issue of guilt or innocence is of minor importance.

The other familiar voice in favor of the death penalty is Immanuel Kant, speaking to us from eighteenth-century Prussia. Kant argues that capital punishment is a rational response to a capital crime—and he argues exclusively in favor of *retribution:* If we execute a criminal to obtain some good social consequences, such as safe streets, then we are in effect using the killer as merely a means to an end—we are using him or her as a stepping-stone to safe streets. Indeed, executing an *innocent* person would probably have the same kind of deterrent effect. Instead, Kant insists that there should be one reason, and one reason only, for punishing a person: because of his or her *guilt.* And for us to proceed according to the principle of *lex talionis,* we should punish the guilty in proportion to the crime, not with an eye toward any further social consequences. That means the only proper punishment for murder is death—even if good social consequences might actually come out of imprisoning the killer for life or letting him or her go free after a period of rehabilitation.

We see how seriously Kant takes this principle by his example: If a society decides to disband but still has people waiting on death row, then the last action of that society should be to execute its convicted murderers, even if there will be no society afterward to enjoy the safer streets. Furthermore, it is only right and proper to execute a murderer for his crime—and in a sense it is showing the convicted killer the utmost *respect* as a human being: Instead of using him for some social purpose (such as deterrence), or trying to rehabilitate him under the assumption that he didn't know what he was doing, we give him credit for actually having made up his own mind to commit a crime—and then we hold him accountable for it.

It wasn't until the nineteenth century that strong voices began to speak up against capital punishment as such, and not merely in opposition to executions for lesser crimes such as burglary. In the twentieth century opposition to the death penalty became known as *abolitionism* (whereas "abolition" in the nineteenth century referred to abolishing slavery in America).

Today's Capital Punishment Criteria

From 1968 to 1976, there was a moratorium on the death penalty in the United States, but since 1976 individual states have been able to decide whether they want to make certain crimes punishable by death, as long as their laws meet guidelines established by the U.S. Supreme Court. In 2008 thirty-six states allowed capital punishment, and fourteen states didn't. Local governments all over the United States, as well as a number of professional organizations such as the American Bar Association have called for a new moratorium on capital punishment. A moratorium on executions by lethal injection was lifted in 2008, and executions were resumed.

What crimes are today punishable by death in the thirty-eight states that allow capital punishment? Theoretically, treason is, but the death penalty is evoked only under rare circumstances, as with the execution of Julius and Ethel Rosenberg for espionage in 1953—still a controversial judicial decision, especially since 2001, when a witness for the prosecution admitted that he lied on the stand. In previous decades, murder, even if committed in a state of rage or panic, might lead to the gas chamber or the electric chair, but today one or more "special circumstances" have to apply, depending on the state legislation. In California, for example, some of the special circumstances are killing more than one person; raping and killing a person; stalking a victim before killing him or her; killing a police officer, a judge, or a jury member; killing with poison; and killing while carjacking. Richard Allen Davis, who abducted, sexually assaulted, and killed twelve-year-old Polly Klaas in Petaluma, California, in 1993, is on death row: He pleaded not guilty but was convicted. Brandon Wilson, who killed nine-year-old Matthew Checci in 1998 in Oceanside, California, after following him into a restroom (stalking), is now on death row. Those are cases in which the California law of special circumstances applies. In other death penalty states, other rules may apply. In the state of Washington, for example, a killer of multiple victims must be shown to have had a "common scheme" in killing them, such as robbery. The simple fact of there being more than one victim isn't enough in itself to warrant the death penalty; Washington legislators have been debating changing the law in the wake of the capture of several serial killers.

Abolitionist Arguments

Abolitionists make the following general arguments:

1. Cruel and Unusual Punishment   The death penalty is an uncivilized, cruel, and unusual form of punishment, depriving the criminal of the ultimate right: the right to life. Abolitionists often cite the fact that among Western nations, the United States is the only country that still executes its citizens, and abolitionist nations around the world usually refuse to extradite a murderer to the United States if he or she may be executed. Proponents of the death penalty, called *retentionists* because they want to *retain* the penalty, reply that of all Western nations, the United States is the only country in which serial killers operate on a regular basis and that the homicide rate is generally higher than in other Western nations, so special measures have to be taken.

2. State-Sanctioned Murder   Executing a murderer is no better than stooping to the level of the murderer, making murder state-sanctioned. Retentionists reply that this is a false analogy: The murderer kills innocent people, whereas the state executes someone who has been found guilty.

3. Discrimination   As it is administered today, at least in certain states, the death penalty shows patterns of discrimination: The poor, the uneducated, and African American men are more likely to receive the death penalty than are people from other population groups, regardless of the crime rate. Retentionists reply that this is not an argument against the death penalty as such, only against the way it has been administered—which admittedly has been discriminatory. But such slanted approaches can be avoided in the future, and according to a recent report from the Justice Department such approaches are virtually a thing of the past, at least in federal cases. Be that as it may, the general perception among abolitionists as well as many retentionists is that the discrimination issue is still far from having been resolved.

4. Innocents Executed   Mistakes have been made and innocent people executed—twenty-three known innocents in this country in the twentieth century. A person wrongly incarcerated cannot have the years he or she spent behind bars restored, but he or she can be compensated financially. An innocent person who has been executed can't be compensated in any way, because everything has been taken from him or her. To many, this argument is the strongest abolitionist point, leading to the adage that it is better that many guilty go free than that one innocent person be punished. In the Primary Readings you'll find an excerpt from Mark Fuhrman's *Death and Justice* (2003), in which he argues that since mistakes *can't* be avoided, it is better to abolish the death penalty.

5. Political Ambition   An aspect that is rarely brought forth, but that may be very important, is the influence of politics. As Mark Fuhrman mentions in his book *Death and Justice,* as long as the death penalty is a factor in local and state politics, there is a danger of its being abused, to secure votes and look "tough on crime." Because judges, sheriffs, and district attorneys are *elected* in many states and have to run election campaigns, their stance on the death penalty and their history of convictions will be part of those campaigns. Deliberately or inadvertently, isn't there a risk that this external factor may slant the view of what is "the worst of the worst" among criminals—those cases deserving the death penalty? Fuhrman cites examples in Oklahoma to that effect: While Bob Macy was District Attorney, executions were at an all-time high, with twenty-one executions in 2001 alone. When there is even the slightest suspicion that such a factor may play into seeking the death penalty, there is reason for caution.

6. Primitive Emotions   Some abolitionists argue that you can choose to be a retentionist only if you are ignorant, sadistic, or emotional, and that if you bothered to examine exactly what goes on at an execution, and to distance yourself from your emotional response to the victims, then you would become an abolitionist. (These arguments are set forth in the abolitionist book *Who Owns Death? Capital Punishment, the American Conscience, and the End of Executions* [2000] by Robert Jay Lifton and Greg Mitchell.) Retentionists answer that even botched executions are no argument against the death penalty as such, only against incompetence; that most retentionists don't *like* the thought of putting people to death and regard capital punishment as a necessary evil; and relating to the suffering of the victims is extremely relevant to the entire issue of punishment. You'll remember the argument from Berns, Strawson, and Whiteley in Chapter 7 that if we are incapable of feeling some form of morally righteous indignation and anger on behalf of the victim—and all the more so on behalf of a murder victim—then we have in effect lost respect and empathy for other human beings.

7. Cost Across the board, abolitionists and retentionists agree with the stark numbers: It costs more to put a criminal to death than it does to keep him or her alive in prison without the possibility of parole. These are some statistics from the Death Penalty Information Center: In California, having the death penalty costs $114 million per year more than keeping convicts in prison for life. Each of the state's executions has cost the taxpayers more than $250 million. A Duke University study showed that North Carolina taxpayers pay $2.16 million for the death penalty over what life sentences would cost. In Florida, having the death penalty costs $51 million more, and the bill for each execution amounts to $24 million. Now, why would it be more expensive to execute someone than to keep him or her alive for perhaps forty years? Not because of the cost of a rope or bullets, obviously. That was way back when, in the Old West. It is the cost of the *appeals,* which can go on for fifteen years or more. Abolitionists hope to appeal to people's wallets and purses through this argument; retentionists reply that (1) justice should have no price tag and (2) the disparity in costs can be fixed easily enough by limiting the access to appeals. Abolitionists reply that without the appeals system, more innocents are sure to become the victims of a flawed legal system.

Another angle is the *emotional cost* of the death penalty: Abolitionists point out that with the many appeals, the families of victims will be expected to be present in court, reliving their tragedy again and again, whereas if a killer is sentenced to "life without," he or she disappears into the prison system, and the family will never have to face the killer again.

8. Lack of Closure Perhaps one of the emotionally most powerful arguments from the abolitionists is that the assumption that the victim's family will find closure after the execution of their loved one's murderer simply isn't true. Closure is a myth, they say. The majority of murder victims' relatives who witness the execution of the murderer say that nothing "feels better" after the execution, and it doesn't bring back the murder victim. Retentionists argue that to some bereaved family members, the only thing that can bring about some measure of justice and peace of mind is the knowledge that the murderer is no longer breathing the air that he or she deprived the victim of.

Retentionist Arguments

Just because the list of retentionist arguments is shorter than the list of abolitionist arguments, you shouldn't jump to the conclusion that retentionists don't have powerful arguments on their side. It is not a numbers contest. Remember that for each abolitionist argument you have just read, the retentionist has a counterargument. But the strongest retentionist arguments can be concentrated within three major areas:

1. A Matter of Justice   Only capital punishment can fit the severity of the crime of murder, and a person who murders has forfeited his or her own right to life. In other words, the issue for many retentionists is *justice,* and the only adequate justice they see for a capital crime is one of retribution. The murderer deserves to die; the victim's family deserves closure; and society deserves to have the books balanced: Commit a crime, and you will pay for it in proportion to the crime. Abolitionists reply that the whole issue of proportionality ("an eye for an eye") has been distorted by retentionists. Only in murder cases do they invoke the principle—does anyone ever talk about "an eye for an eye" when the issue is burglary? Does the court go in and take something from the home of the thief as punishment? Or how about carjacking, embezzlement, or prostitution? How do you punish someone proportionately to that? In the Primary Readings you'll find an excerpt from Tom Sorell's paper "Two Ideals and the Death Penalty," in which he argues that the death penalty is a just and proper form of punishment, and an excerpt from Mark Fuhrman's book *Death and Justice* in which he argues against the death penalty.

2. Elimination of the Murderer   The only way to protect the public effectively from future killings is to eliminate the murderer (the argument of *incapacitation*). An abolitionist may argue that keeping a murderer in prison for life without the possibility of parole is just as effective, but the retentionist will answer that the prison has not yet been built that is 100 percent escape-proof. Even science fiction contains escape scenarios from asteroid penal colonies! And even if prisons were escape-proof, we may still have gubernatorial decisions pardoning murderers. A serial killer of children may appear to be completely rehabilitated in prison and given a pardon, but recidivism in these cases is very high. Here an abolitionist may point to the slippery slope, implying that perhaps any criminal who can't be rehabilitated should be executed regardless of his or her crime. Or perhaps we should even try to anticipate what criminal tendencies a first-time offender has and execute him or her on the basis of what he or she will probably do later on! But though some retentionists would welcome a broadening of capital punishment to cover rapes and child molestation, no serious philosophers of law argue that a person should be punishable for something he or she has not done yet, and most retentionists reserve capital punishment for murders with special circumstances.

3. General and Specific Deterrence   Some retentionists argue that a conviction followed by execution is a deterrent (whereas almost everyone agrees that the longer the time lag between conviction and execution, the less deterrent effect the execution has). It will certainly be a specific deterrent for that criminal, because he or she is not going to commit murder again! In the general sense of the word, others will be deterred by the threat of sure and swift punishment. Some retentionists cite swift justice as a formidable deterrent in countries where civil liberties are not on the main political agenda: If you know you will have your hand amputated if you steal, are you really going to take the chance? But other retentionists claim that the loss of civil liberties and rights is too high a price to pay for safe streets. The effectiveness of general deterrence is undecided statistically: Some statistics show some deterrence factor after an execution; other statistics actually portray the crime rate as going up after executions. (Deterrence seems to be a fact in noncapital crimes. However, it is hotly debated whether the "three strikes and you're out" law in California and similar laws in other states have had any deterrent effect.) Abolitionists sometimes point out that if a person has killed once and knows that he or she is likely to get caught, convicted, and executed, then what is to deter the murderer from killing again, perhaps witnesses? They can suffer the penalty only once. And retentionists answer back by saying that a murderer in prison for life might well (and often does) go on murdering in prison, knowing that there can be no stricter penalty than the one he or she is already suffering, so the only way to prevent further killings is to retain and use the death penalty.

The five reasons for punishment discussed in Chapter 7 all have a role in the death penalty debate. As we just saw, *deterrence* can be used as a retentionist argument. The effect is usually assumed to be that others are deterred from committing the same crime; the intention is less to deter the criminal from doing it again (specific deterrence). (See *The Wizard of Id* on page 682, a spoof of a retentionist utilitarian argument: The wrong man may be executed, but the real killer learns a valuable lesson.) *Incapacitation* can likewise be a retentionist argument, but what about *rehabilitation*? Rehabilitation is not relevant here, for obviously an executed person doesn't learn not to commit the same crime again. *Retribution,* on the other hand, is highly relevant, for a retributivist will usually argue that the death penalty is the ultimate form of justice: It fits the crime, provided that society can be certain it has caught and convicted the guilty person. *Vengeance,* the supposedly nonlegitimate reason for punishment, is generally the most prevailing retentionist view among laypeople, who often argue that a murderer ought to die because he or she ought to suffer the way the victim suffered and that the suffering of the murderer will make society feel better. An abolitionist will generally argue that a life term can be as effective a deterrent as death, that a life term also incapacitates a murderer, and that there is always a chance that a murderer can be rehabilitated. Few retributivists are abolitionists, but it is possible to argue that a life term is the proportionate punishment for a murder, so we can have proportionality and still have respect for life, even the life of a murderer; vengeance is never an option for an abolitionist, who generally sees the death penalty as an expression of primitive social revenge.

It has been customary among scholars to view this insistence on how we *feel* as a primitive trait, but before we reject all references to emotions in the death penalty debate outright, we should remember that several philosophers have recently argued that emotions are not altogether irrelevant in our moral decision process. Martha Nussbaum (Chapter 1) argues that emotions can have their own logic; Richard Taylor

(Chapter 11) says that the fundamental morality of compassion comes from the heart, not the brain; Walter Berns (Chapter 7) says a society that punishes without feeling anger toward the criminal doesn't care for its victims; Diane Whiteley (Chapter 7) argues that a proper understanding of justice includes a sense of moral indignation over harm done to a victim. And neuroscientists point out that it is *natural* for us to consult our emotions where making moral decisions. No thinkers today argue that punishment should take place along exclusively emotional lines, because in that case we'd probably quickly see the punishment exceed the severity of the crime, but maybe justice should not be completely separated from emotions either. Should we be seeking a Golden Mean between impartial justice that punishes according to a set scale with neither rage nor compassion and a system of justice that allows a measure of emotion to enter into the picture, as an outlet for society's righteous anger against an identified and justly convicted perpetrator, as well as an opening for mercy when an unusual set of circumstances warrants it? Or is that a dangerous step toward legitimatizing revenge? In the Narratives Section you'll find two stories dealing with the death penalty; one is Larry Niven's" science fiction short story "The Jigsaw Man," and the other is the 2003 film *The Life of David Gale*.

The DNA Issue

Recently, a number of people serving life sentences or waiting on death row have been exonerated and released as the result of DNA testing. According to the Death Penalty Information Center, an abolitionist website, over 120 death row inmates had been freed between 1973 and June 2007. It should be pointed out, however, that of those 120, fewer than 20 have been exonerated because of DNA testing—the rest have been freed because of other factors. These reversals have prompted both retentionists and abolitionists to question the procedures that convicted these people in the first place. In Idaho, Charles Fain was on death row eighteen years for raping and killing a nine-year-old girl. When DNA analyses cleared him in 2001, he magnanimously said that he had no hard feelings but was just looking forward to resuming his life after years of incarceration. It appears that the small town where he had been convicted had conveniently pounced on him as a newcomer to the area, even though he had an alibi. And in Oklahoma City it was revealed in 2001 that a forensic chemist whose testimony had contributed to 23 people being sent to death row and 11 already executed had lied on the stand on at least six occasions. Given such cases, one doesn't have to be an abolitionist to wonder how many other executions may have involved a less-than-fair trial. But a retentionist will state that such cases still don't provide a compelling argument against the death penalty as such, only against the way it has been administered, and retentionists as well as abolitionists are generally in favor of introducing mandatory DNA testing of suspects in a wide array of criminal cases so the risk of convicting an innocent person can be minimized.

However, not all crime scenes contain DNA from the perpetrator; only if the criminal leaves blood, saliva, hair with follicles, body tissue, or semen at the crime scene can DNA be used to rule out other suspects and point to one suspect in particular. And it is equally important to realize that DNA is not the only important evidence that can convict a criminal. Eyewitnesses *can* be reliable and, contrary to the popular conception, circumstantial evidence can sometimes be extremely strong.

When Gary Ridgway was apprehended in December 2001 in Seattle and charged with the Green River serial killings of the early 1980s, most people who had followed the case were astonished that an arrest had actually been made. The case had dragged on so long, with several suspects but not enough evidence, that only a few dedicated police detectives were still on the case. But those clear-thinking officers had collected a saliva sample from one of the suspects years earlier on the off chance that science at some time in the future could do something with it, and in the late 1990s the DNA technology was available. When the Washington State lab got around to testing the sample in 2001, the perseverance of the detectives paid off: There was a DNA match between semen found on three Green River victims and the saliva sample. Confronted with an overwhelming amount of evidence and a possible death sentence, Ridgway confessed to forty-eight murders after a long series of chilling interviews with the police, in which he talked, in extremely callous terms, about the individual victims and their deaths. The confession was part of a plea bargain, and thus Ridgway exchanged a trial and a near-certain death sentence for life imprisonment without the possibility of parole. It seems that with the new, faster DNA tests, there is no legal or moral downside: Innocent people are being set free, and killers are being matched up with their victims even decades after their murders. In addition, it isn't just the criminal's DNA left at the crime scene that can help convict him or her—the victim's DNA speaks loudly too. If the victim's blood, for example, has been found in the suspect's home or on his or her clothes, it provides important evidence, such as in the case of seven-year-old Danielle van Dam, abducted from her San Diego home in the middle of the night and murdered in the spring of 2002. Her blood found in David Westerfield's motor home and on his clothes gave the judge reasonable cause to order him to stand trial. He was found guilty in August 2002 and sentenced to death.

You may have wondered why it is that police and lawyers talk about DNA matches as being one in 5, 6, or even 10 billion, since there are "only" 6 billion humans on the planet these days. How can there be a match between a suspect and a nonexistent person? The fact of the matter is that talking about matches of one to several billion is just another way of saying that the DNA points *exclusively* to the accused. The roundabout way of saying it is, in effect, a consequence of a scientific problem you are well acquainted with from Chapter 3, the problem of induction. Since DNA research is an empirical science, a good scientist can't make statements about anything being 100 percent certain, but referring to the actual statistical possibility of another person being born with the exact same DNA (which would be, presumably, 10 billion to one), you can make a statement in court that translates into common English as a complete and indisputable identification of a criminal, even better than with a fingerprint.

If the American criminal justice system in the future *can* eliminate most of the doubt as to someone's guilt or innocence through DNA analysis, would that also eliminate the abolitionist argument that the death penalty sometimes kills innocents? In cases where no DNA evidence exists, there would still be a danger of an innocent person being executed. And it is the principle of the state taking a life that the abolitionist is protesting more than anything. But for reluctant retentionists the increased certainty of guilt might pave the way for a *greater* confidence in the justification of capital punishment. Proposals of mandatory DNA tests for all criminals and even a DNA profile for all children born in the United States might go a long way toward helping to solve crimes and avoid wrongful convictions.

Even with these new scientific safeguards against convicting the wrong person, there appears to be a growing unease in the United States about the very nature of the death penalty, at least at the legislative level. Case in point: In 2000 the state of Illinois declared a moratorium on the death penalty, and in 2002 a fourteen-member panel recommended a major reform of capital punishment in the state, including a statewide DNA database, an independent forensic lab, videotaping of interrogations, and a ban on executing mentally retarded murderers. The bipartisan commission stopped short of recommending an end to capital punishment, but a narrow majority on the panel concluded that since no system can guarantee that no innocent person is ever sentenced to death, the death penalty should be abolished in the state of Illinois. The concept of having all criminals tested for DNA has won bipartisan support in Washington, and in October 2004 the Advancing Justice through DNA Technology Act was signed into law by President Bush after having passed the House and the Senate, making funding available for states to help pay for postconviction DNA testing. In addition, the Supreme Court banned executions of teens under the age of eighteen in 2005. Could this be the beginning of the end of the death penalty in America? Many people think so, despite the end of the moratorium on lethal injections in 2008.

The Ethics of Self-Improvement: Narrative Identity

The final sampling of applied ethics brings us full circle to Part 1 of this book: "The Story as a Tool of Ethics." As you read in those chapters, philosophers and scholars from other academic fields have lately been turning to stories and storytelling to add meat to the bones of their professional theories. But storytelling has perhaps had its most dramatic impact, psychologically as well as philosophically, in the area of personal ethics, and that is the concept of becoming the raconteur of one's own life. It has become clear to philosophers as well as psychologists that we humans are storytelling animals (an expression coined by the American philosopher Alasdair MacIntyre). Therapists observe that patients with mental disorders, or simply in need of some structure to their chaotic lives, get a better grasp of their past, their present, and their future if they try to tell about their life in story-form, sometimes even in the third person. Neuroscientists realize that people strive to *make sense* of events, and thus look for *cause and effect* so they can predict future events of the same kind. And philosophers focus on two areas: *ontology* (theory of being) and *ethics*. Ontologically, we understand ourselves as strung out between our beginning and our end, our birth and our death. As the French philosopher Paul Ricoeur (1913–2005) says, we don't remember our beginning, and we won't live to tell about our ending, but while we're living in the middle we look back and look ahead, and try to find a direction, so we insert the missing pieces from family stories, and our hopes and dreams. For Ricoeur, we have a *narrative identity,* a self that is the central figure in our own story. But even more important, we *ought to* work on our narrative identity, so storytelling becomes a normative, moral imperative for Ricoeur: We must learn to see our life as a story, to make ourselves better people, and to connect with others, who then become part of our story, as we become part of theirs. Thus, we become *accountable* to one another. In 2004, at the age of ninety-one, Ricoeur received the Kluge Prize for his life's work in philosophy, and in his acceptance speech he said,

> . . . Change, which is an aspect of identity—that of ideas and things—reveals a dramatic aspect on the human level, which is that of a personal history entangled in the innumerable histories of our companions in existence. Personal identity is marked by a temporality that can be called constitutive. The person is his or her history. . . . In this vast panorama of capacities affirmed and exercised by the human agent, the main accent shifts from what seems at first a morally neutral pole to an explicitly moral pole, where the capable subject attests to himself as a responsible subject. . . . The "power to recount" occupies a preeminent place among the capacities inasmuch as events of every kind become discernable and intelligible only when recounted in stories; the age-old art of recounting stories, when applied to oneself, produces life narratives articulated in the works of historians. . . . We can then speak of a narrative identity: it is that of the plot of a narrative that remains unfinished and open to the possibility of being recounted differently, and also of being recounted by others.

A few examples: Have you ever been in a situation where someone you have just met asks you to talk about yourself? You may have found yourself answering, "Oh, there isn't much to tell," and then immediately felt that this was a poor answer—especially if you were trying to make a good impression. And perhaps later, when alone, you thought of all kinds of things to say about yourself. This is a common experience, and the good thing about it is that it serves as a wake-up call: That time around you were caught by surprise, but next time you will have a story to tell, because we all do. It is sometimes said that we could all write one good novel, the novel of our life—although the saying assumes a great deal about our ability as storytellers. Most of us aren't very good at telling our own story and must develop a talent for shaping it and adjusting it to our audiences. Talking about ourselves makes us realize that, as much as we may try to be completely accurate, it's not possible. We simply can't remember everything that has happened to us; we also realize that even if we could remember, it would not all be equally interesting. So *selectivity* is part of the secret of effective storytelling. And we select different things to tell depending on the audience. If you are telling your story to a new boyfriend or girlfriend, you will emphasize certain things in your life, but if you are describing yourself in front of a panel of strangers during a job interview, you will most definitely emphasize other things. And if you are updating your parents about recent events in your life, you will probably choose quite a different story to tell.

Another feature of telling one's own story is a result of being alive: The story is *incomplete*. We are always in the middle of it; we may be closer to the beginning than to the end or closer to the end than the beginning, but we never view our own story from the same point of view as that of an author telling a story—because our story is not finished yet. We don't know how it will end.

FOR BETTER OR FOR WORSE by Lynn Johnston

In this *For Better or Worse* comic strip, life is viewed as a story, written perhaps by fate, perhaps by God, but definitely with an individual's input. What do you think is meant by "writing our own story"? Is it the same as *telling* our own story, or is there a difference?

A third feature is that, contrary to what we might think, the telling of our own story is to a great extent *fictional,* put together with *poetic creativity.* We may try to remember to be objective, but telling a story generally involves not only a beginning, a middle, and an ending but also a movement from one situation to the next. We don't just say, "And then this happened, and then that happened"; we say, "And *because* this happened, *then* that happened." We assume causality—and since we rarely know all factors involved, we make use of interpretations and make assumptions. (And then, of course, we may be outright lying, but that is a different story!)

So if telling one's own story is such an unreliable enterprise, why bother? Because it is good for us; it helps us find out where we have been and where we are going. As you read in Chapter 2, storytelling is now part of many therapy sessions, and it involves not only listening to stories but also telling them, mostly about oneself. If we see our past as a story, we might be able to identify things to be proud of and things to improve upon. In other words, we may get a better grip on our identity. And when we realize that we are also part of other people's stories, and they are part of ours, then we begin to see ourselves as part of a much bigger story, that of our community and culture.

Searching for Meaning

The psychoanalyst Erik Erikson believed that if we are lucky enough to have become psychologically mature, we will have developed *ego integrity,* and we will stop asking useless questions such as "Why did I do that? Why didn't I do such and such?" We will learn to accept the events in our lives, those we are responsible for and those that just happened to us, as facts with which we must contend. Knowing individuals who have attained this peace of mind may help us along the way.

One challenge to our ego integrity occurs when something happens in our life that we didn't expect and that we find grossly unfair. A man works hard and saves his money so he can enjoy his later years, and then he dies six months after retiring. Parents give up everything they have so that their daughter can go to college, and she ends up on skid row because of drug abuse. A promising young football player is gunned down in gang-warfare cross fire, although he isn't a gang member.

Is there a good way to deal with such calamities? One approach that has provided comfort to many people over the ages has been to view such an event as an act of God or of Fate: It had to happen, we don't know why, but to God it makes sense. Now, we see "through a glass darkly" (1 Corinthians 13:12) but later, in heaven, we will see why it happened. Another source of comfort for some is to view it as *karma*: It is the consequence of something you did earlier or in a previous life. In other words, it is your own fault, and it will do you no good to rage about it or blame someone else. The best you can do is to realize it and try to create good karma for next time around.

A popular modern Western way of approaching the problem is to assign guilt, or blame. We say the retiree brought on his death himself; he never exercised, and his cholesterol level was too high. The parents of the girl who became a drug addict must have done a terrible job of raising her. And the football player's parents should have moved to another neighborhood. Our accusations are sometimes justified, but they can also be unnecessarily cruel. Sometimes, common sense will tell us, people really can't be blamed for what happens to them or to those they love. But it is reassuring to bystanders to blame the victim—it's a way of believing that if they're careful to avoid the victim's mistakes, they'll escape disaster. Although it may be true in some cases that a person's conduct contributed to what happened to him or her, that is far from being a universal pattern. In any case, we have no right to infer *guilt* from *causality;* in other words, just because someone's conscious or unconscious conduct led to some problem, we can't automatically conclude that he or she is guilty of some *moral wrongdoing.* Such an attitude often reflects a double standard: If it happens to strangers, they must have done something "wrong"; if it happens to me or to one of my heroes, we are just unfortunate victims.

An enormously popular self-help book and CD with the enticing title *The Secret,* by Rhonda Byrne, claims that anything is within reach if you make an effort to visualize it. This idea is the latest version of the old concept that positive thinking can make good things happen, and there is surely something to that. It is better to take charge of your life than to leave the control to others. However, some caution is appropriate. What if people try to visualize good things, and nothing happens? or bad things happen? Is that just a sign that they aren't following the program—that they're somehow not putting enough effort into it? That is what we call the *fallacy of begging the question:* a circular definition. And does that mean that if bad things happen to people, they are somehow to blame for it because they didn't focus hard enough on good things happening? Then what happens to our compassion for people down on their luck—or our hope of receiving compassion from others when it is our turn at the bottom of the barrel? Those are disturbing questions about a popular phenomenon, showing that if we choose to view life's good things as being within our control, then (1) we're buying into magical thinking and (2) we display a certain heartlessness toward people who are truly the victims of circumstance.

An alternative way of dealing with life's crises is to see them in the light of *stories*. Humans—at least modern humans in the Western world—seem to have a need for history and their own lives to make sense; we need to understand *why* something happened. Even people in traditional cultures with little written history have the same concern about a life well spent. In such cultures the models are usually the myths and legends of that culture: Do as the cultural hero did, and you will have lived well. In our pluralistic culture the emphasis is much more on doing something *new*— blazing a trail, inventing something, writing a paper about an idea nobody has thought of before. We like our children to be different from their friends, to be individuals. Martha Nussbaum says that stories teach us to deal emotionally with the unexpected. Of course, the unexpected situation in our own life is not likely to be the same as the one in our favorite story—then it wouldn't be unexpected. But we can react to the unexpected in the same way our favorite characters do, and in that way we may be able to rise to the occasion. Persons from a traditional culture might find such efforts at being ready for the unexpected, as well as efforts at being different, incomprehensible, for what makes persons good in their culture is precisely that they do the *same* as their ancestors. The urge to act well, however, is the same for members of both modern and traditional cultures. To live an accomplished life, you must follow a pattern ("Do like the ancestors" or "Do something new"), and others will deem it a good thing if you succeed. *Havamal,* "The Word of the High One," the ancient Norse poem of rules for living, says, "Cattle die, kindred die, every man is mortal. But the good name never dies, of one who has done well." That doesn't just mean that good people will be remembered—but also means that *we pass judgment* on people according to how they handled themselves in life.

When things go our way, we don't ask about the meaning of life. We find that the whole development makes sense. The mythologist Joseph Campbell compares it to being at a fun party: You don't stop and ask yourself what you are doing there. But at a boring party you might ask yourself that question. Similarly, when things go wrong in someone's life, he or she may question the meaning of life—because somehow, life doesn't make sense anymore. An unexpected element interrupts our life's story, and we lose the thread—we experience an *identity crisis* (an expression introduced by Erikson). So how can stories help?

When we change direction in life, we change our future; we don't know what it may be, but we can assume that if we decide to have a child or switch majors or move to another city, our future will at least contain elements different from what it would have otherwise. But when we change direction in our life, we also change our past, because we now see it in a different light, *redescribing* and *reinterpreting* it. When our viewpoint shifts and we interpret our past in the light of the present, we rewrite our own story and sometimes even the story of our community and our culture. When I decide to major in pre-med instead of business because of my sister's illness, I rewrite my story from then on. If my uncle dies just after retiring, I rewrite his story, and it *does* become a moral lesson; I tell myself I will try not to do what he did or try to avoid what life did to him, or at least to make every day count. (In that way I rewrite my own story as well.) If I lose my money because of bad investments, I may rewrite the story in a number of ways: I was victimized, but now I'm smarter; or I was too concerned with money, but now I'm smarter. (Of course, we are not always smarter, but it makes us feel better to think so.) At any rate, we rewrite our past so it will make sense to us in the present and give a new, meaningful direction to our future. It is when we feel incapable of finding a new story line in our life—when the change has been so dramatic that there seems to be no new purpose lurking among the rubble— that the identity crisis may be hard to shake. In that case, it takes courage to choose to view the world and human life the way the British philosopher Bertrand Russell described it—as a collection of atoms brought together at random, with no rhyme or reason other than the rules of science and biology. But even that is a story: It is a story of natural forces and how each human fits into the greater whole of biology— rather a romantic notion. In the face of meaninglessness, we also might choose, with certain existential philosophers, to say that life is its own meaning. In that case the force and will of life in any shape or form become a story we can relate to when no other stories present themselves. We may, of course, choose to say that we just don't know. We would like to think that there is some story, some purpose, but we don't know what it is or whether there is one at all. In the Primary Readings you'll find an excerpt from a self-help book by Tristine Rainer, teaching readers how to tell their own story.

When we tell our own story and the story of our culture, it is most often an attempt to see the overall pattern, or impose one, to find some sense behind chaotic events. But we tell personal and cultural stories to try to improve ourselves and perhaps to make up for cultural errors or wrongdoing of the past. This level of storytelling doesn't just *describe* the situation but also *prescribes* what we ought to be doing next. That is Paul Ricoeur's point in suggesting we work on a narrative identity. This *normative* element contains what may be the deepest moral dimension of the so-called true stories of oneself and one's culture: looking forward to the future, trying to shape it into an ideal image, and reshaping the past so that it appears to lead toward the ideal. (Fictional stories that warn against an unwanted future are part of this moral effort.) Do we have any guarantees that such stories, told to make the future better, actually match reality at all? An actress says she has had a drug prob- lem, but now she is clean and wants to teach others about the dangers of drugs. A schoolteacher tells her class that their culture has elements of discrimination and persecution in its past but that this will never happen again if they will all work together. A politician tells of the hardships we have endured and of the great things we can accomplish if we stand together and vote for him. Or a couple get together again after having broken up and tell each other how they were both wrong and how this time it is going to be different. In some cases those projections are, of course, just wishful thinking, or they are expedient "spin." But well-told stories have a power all their own: *They can make the future happen.* So while we listen to, and create, great stories that can change our lives and our culture, we should remember to retain our critical sense and our sense of moral responsibility: Do our stories prescribe a future that we would actually want to happen?

A trend has developed lately that literally addresses the future, attempting to change it through stories: the phenomenon of ethical wills. An increasing number of people choose to leave to their heirs not only their material but also their spiritual

Box 13.8   ETHICAL WILLS

In an iterview with the *Christian Science Monitor,* workshop leader Susan Turnbull characterizes what she calls "personal legacy letters," or ethical wills, as a way of capturing "the spark of your soul." In her workshops she suggests starting out with questions such as these:

- What do you want your loved ones to know about your family history?

- What is your vision for your heirs' use of their inheritance?

- Have you made mistakes for which you want to ask forgiveness? Or is there forgiveness you want to offer?

- Why have you made certain decisions about your estate, such as donating a portion of it to charity?

- How does your use of money reflect your most important values?

- What are some values and life lessons you'd like to share regarding education, the workplace, marriage, and parenting?

- What have your friendships meant to you over the years?

Workshop leaders suggest updating one's ethical will every five years, reflecting new life experiences. Although most people might think that the writing of an ethical will is an exercise that should be postponed until the end of one's life, it may also be a useful way to do an overview of what one's life story is all about—and there is no age restriction on such an exercise; there can be moral wisdom in the life experience of a twenty-five-year-old as well as in that of an older person.

goods. People write long or short essays, or create videos or audiotapes, all for the purpose of leaving some kind of statement to their children and grandchildren—and perhaps to the world in general—about their values. And the way those values are expressed is generally by telling one's story, specifying the moral of one's own story. To be sure, it isn't the first time in history such ethical wills have been written—in 1050 a Jewish father wrote such a letter in which he gave his son advice about how to live a good life. Box 13.8 explores some questions raised by ethical will workshops.

Living in the Narrative Zone

We humans are temporal beings. We live in the present, but we are always reaching back to the past and forward to the future, in a constant state of tension between memory and anticipation. We live our own story, which has its own beginning and its own end, although we can't describe them. Furthermore, we live the stories of our culture; we identify with them or criticize them or rewrite them. We seek moral lessons in our own stories and in the stories of our culture. We also just like to hear stories, watch stories, and tell stories; and when we do, the time period we experience multiplies. We are still living our own life, but there is a new element: *narrative time,* a concept also introduced by Paul Ricoeur. Narrative time is the compressed time of a novel or a movie, the time it takes for the story to unfold. So although it may take us three days to read a book, its narrative time may span generations. Two hours at the movies, and we may have lived through years of narrative time, following the lives of the characters from youth to old age. In this way we share multiple experiences with fictional characters and expand our moral horizons, as Nussbaum suggested in Chapter 1.

There is a story, "Mantage," by the science fiction writer Richard Matheson, about a man who wanted his life to be the way things are in the movies, because he thought his life was extremely dull. His wish was granted, and this is what happened: He found that time had sped up, and before he knew it he had fallen in love, was married and had kids; now he found himself making money, living in style, and having love affairs, but when he looked at his watch, only an hour had passed. He found that he was living out his life in abbreviated chunks of time, the same as in a movie. After two hours he was old and dying, and the last thing he saw before his eyes was the letters DNE EHT—"The End" to the audience watching him. As the saying goes, when the gods want to punish us, they give us what we wish for.

Obviously that is not what the man truly wished for—he wanted a life with an exciting story line, not a life lived in the time it takes for a film audience to watch a movie. We readers and viewers are luckier, because we can have the best of both worlds. We can retain our own real-life time while we share in the accelerated, telescoped time of books and movies. When we open a book or sit down in a movie theater, we enter what we might call the *Narrative Zone,* where we can live other lives vicariously, acquire skills and experiences that we might never know of otherwise.

We may be emotionally cleansed by experiencing the strong feelings in a story, as Aristotle suggested. We may get an idea of what it feels like to be a member of the other gender or another race, of another time and place, or of another species entirely—and those experiences may help us decide how to live once we leave the Narrative Zone. Nothing else provokes our empathy as effectively as a good story: We weep and rejoice with our friends in the novel or in the movie, even if we know that it is only make-believe. They are not wasted tears or smiles, for they are, ultimately, the building blocks of our character.

If we happen to read the story of the Good Samaritan, there is a chance that we will stop to help the victim should we happen to see a mugging in progress. There is also a chance that the "victim" will end up mugging us, but that doesn't mean we should not have read the story or that we should have come to the victim's aid; it means that life doesn't always conform to the stories we read, and we shouldn't think it does.

So sometimes we get hurt when we are inspired by stories, and sometimes we are inspired by the wrong stories. The essayist and science fiction writer Ursula K. Le Guin compares our existence as readers and listeners to the hoop snake that bites its own tail: It hurts, but *now you can roll!* What is the moral? If the hoop snake doesn't make a hoop, it won't move, and it will be as though it never lived. So we must take chances—we mustn't shy away from taking part in the listening process, in becoming engaged in the story—and we mustn't shy away from becoming engaged in our own story. For Le Guin, telling stories and listening to stories is a kind of life affirmation and an incentive to live life to the fullest.

As a final word, I'd like to make a full circle myself, figuratively speaking, and remind you of Nussbaum's words from *Love's Knowledge* in Chapter 1. Why do we need *stories* on this journey toward becoming more morally responsible persons? Because "we have never lived enough." Even if our life span stretches into the three digits, there will always be experiences we haven't had, places we haven't traveled to, and lives we haven't lived. Great authors, and filmmakers, help us broaden our horizon so we understand a little more about what it means to be a traveler on Planet Earth, and even beyond—and see other lives in a broader perspective. With the help of great storytellers, you may be able to understand what life must be like for someone born in another time period, on another continent, into the body of someone of another gender, race, or perhaps even species. And perhaps you will be able to tell your own story along the way.

A Final Word

I hope that you will make use of the theories we have explored throughout this book to embark on discussions of some of these other issues as well, since you now have the theoretical background to weigh in with more than how you *feel* about an issue. As we have seen numerous times in this book, feelings about moral issues need not be irrelevant, but feelings can't take the place of rational arguments—primarily because an appeal to feelings rarely solves conflicts, but an appeal to logic might. In addition, I hope you will approach the world of stories with an enhanced appreciation for issues raised in television shows, in movies, and in literature, be they stories about cloning and genetic engineering, media ethics and responsibilities, human relations involving compassion and gratitude, or perhaps courage in wartime and peacetime. In this book we've used summaries and excerpts of such stories to illustrate and explore some intricate moral issues, and I hope you've felt inspired to seek out and experience the original stories in their entirety by yourself, because a summary or even an excerpt doesn't do a good story justice. My hope is that as the access to a moral theory has perhaps been made easier or more relevant by a movie or a novel, so, too, might a good background knowledge of moral theories enhance your enjoyment of a fictional story. I know it has for me. There are many issues out there, nationally and globally, and many stories about them. Enjoy the exploration!

Study Questions

1. If you were a journalist, how might you describe the proper balance between the public's right to know and the need for national security? Would it make a difference if you were not a journalist but a member of law enforcement? or a schoolteacher? or a military person?

2. In your view, is the "Myth of Amoral Business" true? Why or why not?

3. In your view, can a war be just? Explain in detail, referring to the text.

4. What is patriotism? Can we apply Aristotle's concept of the Golden Mean and talk about too much, the right amount, and too little patriotism? Explain.

5. Should animals have rights? If no, explain why not. If yes, explain whether your view is based on their ability to suffer, their ability to think, both, or neither.

6. In your view, should the great apes be granted personhood so that they are guaranteed right to life, liberty, and protection from torture? Why or why not?

7. Do we have a moral responsibility to try to slow down or even stop global warming? Explain why or why not. If your answer is yes, how would you propose we do that?

8. Which, in your view, is the strongest argument in favor of the death penalty? Which is the strongest argument against it? In your view, should we retain or abolish capital punishment? Explain.

Primary Readings and Narratives

The Primary Readings are many in this chapter, reflecting the many topics; they are not intended to reflect the complete debate but merely to be a collection of ideas that may whet your appetite for more. The first Reading is an excerpt from "Ethics as a Vehicle for Media Quality" by Andrew Belsey and Ruth Chadwick, exploring the concept of a "virtuous journalist." Next there are two short Readings from the field of business ethics: "Critical Elements of an Organizational Ethical Culture" by Amber Levanon Seligson and Laurie Choi, a 2006 Ethics Resource Center report summary, and a *USAToday* blog by Scott Gottlieb, "How Safe Is Our Food? FDA Could Do Better." Next we have two texts covering the topics of just war and terrorism: an excerpt from John Rawls's book *The Law of Peoples* and an excerpt from Jan Narveson's essay "Morality and Violence: War, Revolution, Terrorism." On the animal rights issue, the Great Ape Project is represented by two texts: *The Declaration on Great Apes* and an excerpt from a brief by Lee Hall and Anthony Waters, "From Property to Person: The Case of Evelyn Hart." Environmental ethics is represented by two reviews, one positive and the other negative, of former Vice President Al Gore's documentary *An Inconvenient Truth*. You'll find two Readings on the death penalty: an excerpt from Tom Sorrell's pro–death penalty paper "Two Ideals and the Death Penalty" and an excerpt from Mark Fuhrman's anti–death penalty book, *Death and Justice: An Exposé of Oklahoma's Death Row Machine*. The last Primary Reading is an excerpt from Tristine Rainer's guide to writing an autobiography, *Your Life as Story*. The Narratives are the film *15 Minutes*, about media ethics; the film *The Insider*, a true story about a man accusing the tobacco companies of misrepresenting their products, which serves as an illustration of business ethics; the short story "The Jigsaw Man," about a utilitarian rationale for capital punishment; and the film *The Life of David Gale*, about an abolitionist activist on death row for murder.

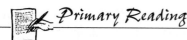 *Primary Reading*

Ethics as a Vehicle for Media Quality

ANDREW BELSEY AND RUTH CHADWICK

Excerpt, 1995.

In this paper Belsey and Chadwick argue that if the media have too many legal restrictions, journalists are going to be distracted by trying to get around them, rather than behaving with professional ethics. The fewer legal constraints a journalist has, the higher his or her ethical standards will have to be, according to the authors, because a legal right to publish is not equivalent to a moral right to publish. The authors use the concept of a "virtuous journalist," linking the notion of journalism to virtue ethics. Virtues mentioned are fairness, integrity, objectivity, trustworthiness, and accuracy, among others. In addition, the authors suggest that an ethical code of practice would be useful. Such a code of practice would involve both "dos" and "don'ts" of the profession.

The Ethical Route to Media Quality

No legal framework guarantees ethical behavior in any area of life, though the law does provide an arena in which some forms of behavior are encouraged and some discouraged. There will be (dis)incentives in the form of sanctions and penalties, but ultimately a society depends on the sense of morality and responsibility of its members. This is how it ought to be in a democracy. Similarly, neither the negative nor the positive aspects of the legal route will guarantee media quality. Unless media professionals have a sense of morality and responsibility too, the quality will be lacking. But in relation to the media there is an important interplay between law and ethics. To put the point simply: too many legal prohibitions and restrictions force journalists to concentrate on what they can get away with in legal terms, and thus distract their attention away from matters of ethics. This has a distorting and a trivializing effect on the output of the media, to the detriment of quality. Conversely, giving legal rights and freedoms to journalist places them under an obligation to pay attention to the ethical issues of their profession. As Klaidman and Beauchamp put it in their influential discussion of media ethics, "freedom from legal constraints is a special privilege that demands increased awareness of moral obligation."

This is because a legal right to publish does not mean that it is morally right to publish. Even when the law is satisfied there are still ethical questions in areas such as obscenity, character assassination, privacy, confidentiality, deception, sexism, and homophobia. Journalists need to select from the mass of possible information what should be included and what should not, and judgments about what is important, significant, trivial, or tasteless are, basically, ethical judgments. Similarly, judgments about presentation are also ethical, inasmuch as they raise issues of sensitivity and taste on the one hand, and sensationalism and vulgarity on the other. All these ethical issues can be summed up in the concept of professional competence, as this requires not just a command of technical skills but also the ability to deploy moral qualities (Klaidman and Beauchamp, 1987, 12). Thus, for example, a commitment to truth-telling, often put forward as constitutive of journalism (and therefore basic to journalistic competence), requires honesty, integrity, tenaciousness, and no doubt other ethical qualities, too, on the part of the journalist.

One interesting and important way of spelling out further what is involved in this ethical notion of competence in the media is by referring to Klaidman and Beauchamp's prescription for journalism in terms of virtue and the virtues: every journalist the "virtuous journalist" (Klaidman and Beauchamp, 1987). The virtuous journalist will display a commitment to many virtues, including fairness, accuracy, honesty, integrity, objectivity, benevolence, sensitivity trustworthiness, accountability, and humor. More important, though, than a list of specific virtues is virtue: the virtuous journalist is one who has a virtuous character, one who therefore has a disposition to act virtuously not only in familiar but also in novel situations. It is in this sense that the competent journalist is the virtuous journalist and is also the journalist with a commitment to quality.

In such a way, then, can ethics be a vehicle for media quality. As before, it is a vehicle which can travel the ethical route in two ways, a positive aspect emphasizing the ethical requirements for maintaining quality in the media (the virtues, like truth-telling), and a negative aspect emphasizing the prohibitions (the corresponding vices, such as lying).

The Ethical Route via a Code of Practice?

The ethical route to media quality requires a commitment by individual journalists and other media practitioners to certain ethical principles and standards—a commitment which can be conveniently expressed by the notion of the "virtuous journalist." But should this commitment be further demonstrated by adherence to an ethical "code of practice," incorporating the various principals and standards?

While not essential, such an approach has advantages. It joins journalism with other occupations that have promulgated codes of practice, and is one of the moves which demonstrate an aspiration to move beyond mere occupation to professional status. Adherence to a code brings journalists together as professionals recognizing common aims and interests and accepting responsibilities to the public. Adherence to a code thus shows a collective public commitment to acknowledged ethical principles and standards, rather than a purely solitary conscientiousness about ethical matters. Putting ethical principles and standards into a published code is a convenience, announcing to both professionals and the public that there is a commitment to quality and to the standards of behavior and practice necessary to achieve quality.

An ethical code of practice will have both positive and negative aspects, detailing what is required and what is prohibited. Both aspects clearly have a contribution to make to media quality. A code of practice for the media, for example, could require journalists to be honest and accurate in all matters, to be impartial and objective in reporting news, to publish corrections, to offer a right of reply, to protect the identity of confidential sources. It could also, presumably, prohibit deception, harassment, invasions of privacy, doorstepping the victims of traumatic events, exploiting children, buying the stories of criminals. It is noticeable that these prohibitions tend to be much more specific than the positive requirements.

However, a code of practice could be seen as having functions other than just listing the requirements and prohibitions. First, a code could have a disciplinary function, linking breaches of requirements and prohibitions with sanctions. A code could also have an educative function, in that it would teach what was expected of a journalist and would both state and encourage the standards of competence and the underlying thinking that constitute journalism as professional practice. Related to this a code could also have a "utopian" function, which would be a statement of the ideals and aspirations of the profession, going beyond a list of requirements and prohibitions. In the case of a code of the media, such ideals could go back to First Amendment aspirations, linking press freedom with the requirements of democracy.

Study Questions

1. What is a *virtuous journalist,* according to the authors? And what do they mean by an "ethical code of practice"?

2. According to this excerpt, is it legitimate for a journalist to have a political agenda in his or her writings? Explain why or why not.

3. Evaluate the case of Jayson Blair (*New York Times*) according to this text. Why were his actions a breach of journalistic ethics?

4. Evaluate the case of Dan Rather (CBS, *60 Minutes*) according to this text. Did Rather go against the rules of ethical journalism? Explain why or why not.

Critical Elements of an Organizational Ethical Culture

AMBER LEVANON SELIGSON AND LAURIE CHOI

Ethics Resource Center Report, 2006.

Executive Summary

In the 2005 National Business Ethics Survey® (NBES), the Ethics Resource Center (ERC) finds that a formal ethics and compliance program alone does not substantially impact outcomes. Additional analysis reveals that ethical culture often has more of an impact on achieving an effective ethics and compliance program than do program inputs and activities.

NBES measures eighteen dimensions of ethical culture by asking employees if their top and middle management, supervisors, and coworkers demonstrate various "Ethics Related Actions" (ERAs) in the workplace. ERC found that employees who perceive their managers, supervisors, and coworkers displaying ERAs are more likely to observe outcomes expected of an effective ethics and compliance program than those whose colleagues and managers exhibit fewer ERAs. This paper builds upon the NBES findings on ethical culture and explores which ERAs have a greater impact on program outcomes. In addition, this paper presents new analysis on whether ethics training is more useful for junior employees than for senior employees.

Key Findings

1. Three ERAs have an especially large impact on outcomes expected of an ethics and compliance program: Setting a good example; Keeping promises and commitments; and Supporting others in adhering to ethics standards.

2. Formal ethics training does not have the same impact on all levels of employees.

Key Conclusions

• Actions speak louder than words. Results regarding the three ERAs with the greatest impact on outcomes imply that having a general organization-wide ethics communication strategy is not enough to create desired outcomes. Employees need to see their superiors and peers demonstrate ethical behavior in the work they do and decisions they make every day.

• Training needs to be different for management versus non-management employees. Ethics training is more useful in helping junior employees feel prepared to handle situations that invite misconduct than it is for senior employees. This does not suggest eliminating all ethics training for top and mid-management employees. What it does suggest is developing training curricula that takes these differences into account.

Study Questions

1. Why do you think setting a good example works better as a training tool in business ethics than learning about principles? How does virtue ethics play into this phenomenon?

2. Why do you think training needs to be different for management and non-management employees?

Primary Reading

How Safe Is Our Food? FDA Could Do Better

SCOTT GOTTLIEB

blogs.usatoday.com/oped/2007/05/, May 21, 2007.

Scott Gottlieb is a resident fellow at the American Enterprise Institute and was deputy commissioner of the FDA from 2005 to 2007.

> Our system for inspecting food and drug imports into the USA is woefully outdated, designed to regulate a mostly domestic industry, not to deal with a globalized world.

Attention has turned to these shortcomings after popular brands of pet food were contaminated with a chemical that killed or sickened thousands of cats and dogs. The pet food episode is only the latest in a string of problems stemming from raw materials to food and drug products imported from developing countries. In Panama, for example, at least 51 people have died since October after using cough syrup tainted with a chemical cousin of antifreeze. The deadly ingredient originated in China.

The Food and Drug Administration (FDA) has primary responsibility for inspecting shipments of drugs and most foods. Though no regulatory system can eliminate every risk, our present approach isn't adapted to deal with the fact that companies are sourcing more of their raw materials from less developed countries that don't have the same regulatory protections in place as the United States does.

To address these gaps, many in Congress have proposed to merely increase the FDA's current activity, testing more shipments of raw goods, for example, or adding inspectors to peer inside more cartons at the border. Buffing up our inspection model doesn't help us better address the changing nature of risks we face.

Staffing Shortage

It's true that FDA never permanently received the number of inspectors it was promised shortly after 9/11 to improve oversight of food from deliberate tampering. I recently left the FDA, where I worked as a deputy commissioner, and staffing shortfalls were a daily burden. But adding manpower won't go very far. Neither will merely testing more batches of goods, which can be prohibitively expensive.

Our inspection model at FDA worked better when the volume and complexity of imported products were small, grew slowly and were limited to a smaller set of goods. But the FDA can no longer be globally dispersed, sending its dwindling cadre of increasingly reluctant inspectors into every foreign factory. They don't speak the language, understand the culture or know the local criminals. FDA needs to target its inspection resources more effectively to areas of highest risk and monitor reputable firms empowered by the agency to police their own supply chains.

The United States still has the safest food and drug supply in the world, but the need for a new approach is necessitated by the dramatic changes in the nature of the food and drugs arriving in the USA from other countries. FDA processed 15 million shipments of goods in 2006, up 60% since 2003. Products arrived from more than 230 countries and more than 300,000 manufacturers. More and more drugs, especially generics, get their raw material from China and India, where local controls are weak. Against this, FDA has about 625 inspectors for foods and 260 for pill-type drugs.

Innovations in distribution and supply chains also mean imported products can be widely distributed shortly after crossing our border, amplifying risks. Many imports come from countries that don't have the same market pressures as the USA's. American brands can be decimated when things go wrong. That serves as a more potent deterrent to bad behavior than any sanction that a regulator can levy.

The FDA also needs to be able to better identify and prioritize risks from imported products all along their life cycle, and not just at the border. Rather than remaining a primary line of defense, the border needs to be a checkpoint to make sure foreign firms have complied with health and safety requirements along the supply chain. This requires better information about goods coming in and more cooperation with foreign agents so FDA can identify highest-risk products.

Some Progress

Recent FDA changes in the inspection of some imported food in response to concerns about terrorism are working and provide a foundation for building a more modern, risk-based approach to inspecting all of our imports. The bioterrorism-focused system uses information that FDA collects from importers, and greater cooperation with overseas law enforcement and regulatory agencies, to make targeted decisions about which imports to sample based on the possibility for tampering. Top-secret software used to analyze risks means that products such as loose spices imported from the Middle East probably will get far more scrutiny than whole produce from Canada.

Firms also need to take more responsibility for the quality and safety of ingredients they buy overseas. In China, U.S. drug companies are turning to private outfits to independently audit raw material suppliers, and a private U.S. drug standards outfit recently set up shop there for this purpose. Ultimately, FDA needs to enable companies to be inspected by private third parties certified by the agency.

Our current system was never given appropriate resources or direction to address the complex problems posed by globalization. Dealing with modern risks will require not just jerry-rigging our existing model, but a fundamentally new blueprint.

Study Questions

1. What is the main point in Gottlieb's article?

2. Whose fault is it if poisons and other health risks get into the food we eat from international sources? Can rules within business ethics help us?

Primary Reading

The Law of Peoples

JOHN RAWLS

Excerpt, 1999.

John Rawls, whom you met in Chapter 7 as well as in this chapter, hopes in his *Law of Peoples* to outline a *realistic utopia* according to the principles of justice, recognizing that peoples should view one another as free and independent. He sees five kinds of domestic societies: *Reasonable, liberal peoples* and *decent peoples* ("nonliberal societies whose basic institutions meet certain specified conditions of political right and justice") together form the category of *well-ordered peoples;* then there are *outlaw states; societies burdened by unfavorable conditions;* and *societies of benevolent absolutisms* (societies that recognize human rights but don't allow their citizens a political voice). Here Rawls explores the right of well-ordered peoples to go to war.

Role of Nonideal Theory

To this point we have been concerned with ideal theory. In extending a liberal conception of justice, we have developed an ideal conception of a Law of Peoples for the Society of well-ordered Peoples, that is, liberal and decent peoples. That conception is to guide these well-ordered peoples in their conduct toward one another and in their designing common institutions for their mutual benefit. It is also to guide them in how to deal with non-well-ordered peoples. Before our discussion of the Law of Peoples is complete, we must therefore consider, though we cannot do so wholly adequately, the questions arising from the highly nonideal conditions of our world with its great injustices and widespread social evils. On the assumption that there exist in the world some relatively well-ordered peoples, we ask in nonideal theory how these peoples should act toward non-well-ordered peoples. We take as a basic characteristic of well-ordered peoples that they wish to live in a world in which all peoples accept and follow the (ideal of the) Law of Peoples.

Nonideal theory asks how this long-term goal might be achieved, or worked toward, usually in gradual steps. It looks for policies and courses of action that are morally permissible and politically possible as well as likely to be effective. So conceived, nonideal theory presupposes that ideal theory is already on hand. For until the ideal is identified, at least in outline—and that is all we should expect—nonideal theory lacks an objective, an aim, by reference to which its queries can be answered. Though the specific conditions of our world at any time—the status quo—do not determine the ideal conception of the Society of Peoples, those conditions do affect the specific answers to questions of nonideal theory. For these are questions of transition, of how to work from a world containing outlaw states and societies suffering from unfavorable conditions to a world in which all societies come to accept and follow the Law of Peoples.

There are . . . two kinds of nonideal theory. One kind deals with conditions of noncompliance, that is, with conditions in which certain regimes refuse to comply with a reasonable Law of Peoples; these regimes think a sufficient reason to engage in war is that war advances, or might advance, the regime's rational (not reasonable) interests. These regimes I call *outlaw states*. The other kind of nonideal theory deals with unfavorable conditions, that is, with the conditions of societies whose historical, social, and economic circumstances make their achieving a well-ordered regime, whether liberal or decent, difficult if not impossible. These societies I call *burdened societies*.[1]

I begin with noncompliance theory, and recall that the fifth initial principle of equality of the Law of Peoples gives well-ordered peoples a right to war in self-defense but not, as in the traditional account of sovereignty, a right to war in the rational pursuit of a state's rational interests; these alone are not a sufficient reason. Well-ordered peoples, both

---

[1]There are also other possibilities. Some states are not well-ordered and violate human rights, but are not aggressive and do not harbor plans to attack their neighbors. They do not suffer from unfavorable conditions, but simply have a state policy that violates the human rights of certain minorities among them. They are therefore outlaw states because they violate what are recognized as rights by the Society of reasonably just and decent Peoples, and they may be subject to some kind of intervention in severe cases.

liberal and decent, do not initiate war against one another; they go to war only when they sincerely and reasonably believe that their safety and security are seriously endangered by the expansionist policies of outlaw states. In what follows, I work out the content of the principles of the Law of Peoples for the conduct of war.

Well-Ordered Peoples' Right to War

No state has a right to war in the pursuit of its *rational,* as opposed to its *reasonable,* interests. The Law of Peoples does, however, assign to all well-ordered peoples (both liberal and decent), and indeed to any society that follows and honors a reasonably just Law of Peoples, the right to war in self-defense.[2] Although all well-ordered societies have this right, they may interpret their actions in a different way depending on how they think of their ends and purposes. I will note some of these differences.

When a liberal society engages in war in self-defense, it does so to protect and preserve the basic freedoms of its citizens and its constitutionally democratic political institutions. Indeed, a liberal society cannot justly require its citizens to fight in order to gain economic wealth or to acquire natural resources, much less to win power and empire.[3] (When a society pursues these interests, it no longer honors the Law of Peoples, and it becomes an outlaw state.) To trespass on citizens' liberty by conscription, or other such practices in raising armed forces, may only be done on a liberal political conception for the sake of liberty itself, that is, as necessary to defend liberal democratic institutions and civil society's many religious and nonreligious traditions and forms of life.[4]

The special significance of liberal constitutional government is that through its democratic politics, and by following the idea of public reason, citizens can express their conception of their society and take actions appropriate to its defense. That is, ideally, citizens work out a *truly* political opinion, and not simply an opinion about what would best advance their own particular interests, of whatever kind, as members of civil society. Such (truly political) citizens develop an opinion of the rights and wrongs of political right and justice, and of what the well-being of different parts of society requires. As in *Political Liberalism,* each citizen is regarded as having what I have called "the two moral powers"—a capacity for a sense of justice and a capacity for a conception of the good. It is also assumed that each citizen has, at any time, a conception of the good compatible with a comprehensive religious, philosophical, or moral doctrine. These capacities enable citizens to fulfill their role as citizens and underwrite their political and civic autonomy. The principles of justice protect citizens' higher-order interests; these are guaranteed within the framework of the liberal constitution and the basic structure of society. These institutions establish a reasonably just setting within which the background culture[5] of civil society may flourish.

Decent peoples also have a right to war in self-defense. They would describe what they are defending differently from the way a liberal people would; but decent peoples

---

[2]The right to war normally includes the right to help to defend one's allies.

[3]Of course, so-called liberal societies sometimes do this, but that only shows they may act wrongly.

[4]See *A Theory of Justice,* sec. 58, pp. 380ff.

[5]See *Political Liberalism,* p. 14.

also have something worth defending. For example, the rulers of the imagined decent people, Kazanistan, could rightly defend their decent hierarchical Muslim society. They allow and respect members of different faiths within their society, and they respect the political institutions of other societies, including non-Muslim and liberal societies. They also respect and honor human rights; their basic structure contains a decent consultation hierarchy; and they accept and abide by a (reasonable) Law of Peoples.

The fifth kind of society listed earlier—a *benevolent absolutism*—would also appear to have the right to war in self-defense. While a benevolent absolutism does respect and honor human rights, it is not a well-ordered society, since it does not give its members a meaningful role in making political decisions. But *any* society that is nonaggressive and that honors human rights has the right of self-defense. Its level of spiritual life and culture may not be high in our eyes, but it always has the right to defend itself against invasion of its territory.

Study Questions

1. What are the two kinds of nonideal theories, and what is Rawls's purpose in introducing the concept?

2. When do well-ordered peoples have a right to go to war, according to Rawls? Would you agree? Why or why not?

3. What are "the two moral powers"? What roles do they play in society, and how do they complement each other?

Primary Reading

Morality and Violence: War, Revolution, Terrorism

JAN NARVESON

Essay published in the anthology Matters of Life and Death, *1993. Excerpt.*

Jan Narveson, a libertarian philosopher, explores the nature and function of terrorism in this essay written years before September 11, 2001, but well within the modern era of terrorist acts. He asks the question whether terrorism is ever justified, and whether terrorists deserve to air their grievances and be heard.

In recent times, the use of political terrorism has been much too prominent for comfort. As the term suggests, terrorism has a major psychological dimension. Hooded figures appear out of nowhere, spraying an airport with bullets from automatic weapons; car bombs go off; civilian hostages are taken. These things do physical damage, indeed; but their main purpose is to frighten us, thus (so the terrorist reasons) to compel us or our leaders to accept a political program or act that we would not otherwise accept. "Terror" arises because the terrorist is intentionally indiscriminate: anyone can be targeted, and even those not targeted can easily be in the way of an assassin, especially one whose modus operandi is the time bomb or other means lacking immediate control. The fact that damage to the innocent might well ensue doesn't worry the terrorist at all—but it *does* worry *us.*

Terrorism is, then, a sort of war, waged on behalf of political causes; but unlike ordinary wars, which are "up front," this war is in the shadows. And it is so because those fomenting it are too weak to wage open warfare, where it is clear who the combatants are. So terrorism is (quite reasonably) seen as underhanded, "sneaky," disreputable.

This characterization calls for an important distinction between two very different contexts of employment of terror. On the one hand we have "insurgent" terrorism, that used by groups on the *outside* of official political power, as exemplified by the Red Army in Germany and Italy, the Irish Republican Army, several Palestinian organizations, and so on. On the other hand we have "state" terrorism, employed by those very officials themselves: the Stalinist regime with its "Gulag Archipelago," the dread SS troops of the Nazis, the Czarist secret police, assassination squads in some Latin American countries. What these two kinds of terrorism have in common is their shadowy, extralegal (or in the case of state terrorism, often spuriously legal) character, so that victims can't predict what will happen to them nor appeal to regular sources of redress. But they differ drastically in the extent of their effects.

Of the two, state terrorism is the overwhelmingly greater in the extent of evils done. Millions of victims fell to Eastern European Communism, Nazism, and other evil regimes, as against thousands at the hands of "insurgents." Condemnation of state terrorism is easy. There is no question about whether to disapprove of regimes that resort to such methods to secure themselves in power and defend their policies: they are simply evil, ghastly monstrosities masquerading as real governments devoted, however fuzzily, to the good of their people. For that reason we will talk only of insurgent terrorism from here on, hoping that we will have sufficiently averted the risk of leaving the reader with the impression that this is the only sort there is.

Insurgent terrorists are characteristically weak. If they could command real armies with a serious chance of winning, they would engage the forces of the state in open battle. As it is, they can do little real damage—the number of victims of this kind of terrorism is comparatively small. (Even in Ireland, the total number of deaths from terrorism doesn't nearly equal the rate from auto accidents, say.) This type of terrorist is, then, in a kind of strategic dilemma. Can he create enough fear to win the concessions he aims for? But there is a problem. He cannot do anything else, being too weak. And a rare outburst will not do the trick. On the other hand, a really substantial campaign of terror, if he can manage that, will have at least two drawbacks from his point of view: first, it will put the established order's counterterrorism facilities in high gear, which could easily be fatal to the Movement. Second, if terrorism becomes the order of the day, people become calloused and blasé, as in Lebanon: the terrorist no longer inspires the sort of terror by which alone he can hope to be effective. Terrorists become a terrible nuisance, but that is all.

The trouble in this regard is that the terrorist trades on what is in fact an irrational tendency in human nature—the tendency to magnify unexpected and "mysterious" evils out of their true proportion. And the cure is a dose of rationality, plus a modicum of courage. The life expectancy of the average citizen is very little reduced by terrorism, whereas the expected evil if we accede to the terrorists' demands is great. The statesman, therefore, won't be cowed, but will soldier on.

There are other problems inherent in the use of terrorist methods as well. To forward their cause, terrorists must publicize the fact that it was they who threw the bomb, or whatever. But such publicity sets people on the road to tracking them down and destroying them, for terrorist groups are never strong enough to resist real armies or well-organized and well-armed police. Besides, those who resort to terrorist tactics inspire hatred, which is hardly a propitious environment for an aspirant to political power. If we know what these evil people can do when they are weak, what could we expect if they were strong? Our motivation to make sure they do not become so is redoubled with every victim.

Is terrorism ever justified? Are there any circumstances and any causes which would allow moral resort to such tactics? One is tempted to answer in the negative. Unfortunately, terrorism has been disconcertingly effective in the past: in Ireland, earlier in this century; in Israel in the late 1940s; and on many other occasions. And while we may take the view that no possible end could justify such evil means, this may be just lack of perspective. The German officers' plot to assassinate Hitler in 1944 was of the same general kind of terrorism, but few of us think it was morally unjustified.

Insofar as terrorism has worked, why has it? For two rather different reasons, I believe. On the one hand, those in charge have concluded that they're better off knuckling under to the threats than attempting further to resist them. On the other, and I believe more importantly, those in charge have concluded that their own position is untenable. Sometimes what they conclude is that it is *morally* untenable. The terrorists are seen, after all, to be supporting the just cause.

Clearly that should not happen. Terrorism is prima facie unjust, as is all violence. If people resort to using terrorist methods, why do they do so? It must be because they see no chance of their proposals being adopted by the powers that be if they confine themselves to more civilized methods. But if their proposals are just, they should be acceptable to people, and hence popular. Either those proposals are not so good after all, or the state against whom the terrorist methods are being used is unjustly subjugating its populace. In the latter case, if terrorist methods are used in a selective manner, against the officials of the regime rather than the general populace, there may be some expectation of success, since the populace may be presumed to sympathize with the aims of the terrorists. The efforts of officials to track down the terrorists and root them out will be thwarted by a populace not inclined to cooperate with them. A government that rules only by force can perhaps be brought down by determined persons using such tactics. The cost of doing so is high, of course. But there may be literally no other way, in which case the question is whether the result is worth the cost. Many of those killed will surely be innocent even if they are officials of the regime, not to mention others who are not connected with nor sympathetic to it. One who throws bombs and the like has a lot to answer for, and the answers had better be good ones. But it is difficult to argue that the use of terrorist tactics cannot possibly be morally justified, for the same reason that military means cannot be ruled out when all else (or at least, enough else) fails. Thus, we have noted the existence of terror inspired in a populace by its own government: people snatched from their beds and dragged off to the gulag, or tortured and shot in miserable dungeons, opposition members disappearing without a trace. Governments that rule by these methods are, one may plausibly argue, the most purely and absolutely evil of all human agencies on earth. Such regimes do not deserve the support of their people or of anyone else, and almost any sort of rebellion that has any chance of success against them is likely to be justified. Indeed, the fact that a regime is seen as a *terrorist regime* in that sense, ruling exclusively by force, is itself a principal cause of counterterrorism by insurgents. The least we can do is be aware of, and publicize as much as possible, the facts about such regimes, hoping to inspire some kind of redress by whatever means—and be thankful that democratic governments, whatever their other vices, are at least largely free of such tactics. (We should also not complacently think that they are entirely free of them, nor that the relatively civilized impositions of democratic governments on their citizens are of no account.)

In conclusion, we cannot condemn terrorists absolutely, without giving their cause a hearing. Indeed, the impossibility of *getting* a sufficient hearing by standard means is probably one of the main causes of the resort to terrorism. And if our hearing finds that they have a point, then we must do something about it; else we leave the terrorists in the situation of saying, "Well, that's our point: we *must* act like this, for otherwise we just continue to suffer." But beyond that? Clearly we must not knuckle under to the terrorists' threats simply because they are threats. To do that is to give way to greater evils to come.

Study Questions

1. Define the two types of terrorism according to Narveson's guidelines. Do the terrorist attacks of September 11 fall within either category? Explain.

2. What, to Narveson, is it in particular that terrorists trade on? And what is the antidote? In light of September 11, do you agree? Why or why not?

3. What should a civilized nation do to combat terrorism, according to Narveson? How does that compare with the war on terrorism? Do you agree with Narveson? Why or why not?

4. Narveson argues that we should not altogether refuse to listen to the grievances of terrorists. In light of September 11, do you agree? Why or why not? In your view, are there any grievances that would legitimate the deliberate targeting of civilians? Explain.

Primary Reading

The Declaration on Great Apes

GREAT APE PROJECT

1993.

The Declaration on Great Apes came out of the Great Ape Project commenced in 1993 by philosophers Peter Singer and Paola Cavalieri, as expressed in their book, *The Great Ape Project: Equality Beyond Humanity* (1994). Your author was herself an advance reader on the GAP FAQ website and had occasion to review and evaluate many of the moral problems arising from the declaration.

> We demand the extension of the community of equals to include all great apes: human beings, chimpanzees, bonobos, gorillas and orangutans.

The community of equals is the moral community within which we accept certain basic moral principles or rights as governing our relations with each other and enforceable at law. Among these principles or rights are the following:

1. The Right to Life

The lives of members of the community of equals are to be protected. Members of the community of equals may not be killed except in very strictly defined circumstances, for example, self-defense.

2. The Protection of Individual Liberty

Members of the community of equals are not to be arbitrarily deprived of their liberty; if they should be imprisoned without due legal process, they have the right to immediate release. The detention of those who have not been convicted of any crime, or of those who are not criminally liable, should be allowed only where it can be shown to be for their own good, or necessary to protect the public from a member of the community who would clearly be a danger to others if at liberty. In such cases, members of the community of equals must have the right to appeal, either directly or, if they lack the relevant capacity, through an advocate, to a judicial tribunal.

3. The Prohibition of Torture

The deliberate infliction of severe pain on a member of the community of equals, either wantonly or for an alleged benefit to others, is regarded as torture, and is wrong. . . .

Study Questions

1. What are the implications of this declaration for apes as well as for humans? What will happen to apes in zoos? apes in medical research labs? apes in behavior research labs? apes used in movie productions?

2. Do you agree that apes should be granted legal personhood, at a time when not even all humans on the planet are treated like persons? Why or why not?

3. Some people see this as a positive first step toward protecting all animal life; others view it as a dangerous slippery slope. Where do you stand on this issue?

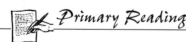

From Property to Person: The Case of Evelyn Hart

LEE HALL AND ANTHONY JON WATERS

Seton Hall Constitutional Law Journal, 2000. Excerpt.

In a legal brief, Hall and Waters argue that the seven-year-old chimpanzee Evelyn Hart should not be classified as property but as a person. Evelyn was due to be shipped to Emory University to take part in a viral study as a test subject, as the property of the National Institutes of Health. Hall and Waters argue that Evelyn is a person because of the following factors: (1) rationality and self-awareness; (2) self-control; (3) a sense of the future; (4) a sense of the past; (5) capacity to relate to others; (6) concern for others; (7) curiosity; (8) communication.

Included here is the conclusion to their brief.

Conclusion

From time to time, but not too often, society as a whole must admit that it was wrong. Collectively, we grow out of certain habits of mind, certain modes of behavior. Examples abound, but human slavery and its abolition is a familiar example as is, more recently, the end of apartheid in South Africa. When the collective prejudices, or unexamined assumptions, which have shaped a particular set of laws are later shown to be wrong— morally wrong, perhaps, as a result of changed morality; factually wrong, perhaps, in light of advances in our knowledge—the right response is for the law to take account of the changed morality, or the new knowledge, or, as in this case, both. We now know that it was wrong to classify Evelyn Hart, and others like her, as property. The law as it now stands cannot be defended, save as a product of the ignorance of its time.

But even recognizing and accepting our moral obligation to the Evelyn Harts in this country does not conclude our inquiry. The next question we must ask is whether the practical consequences of affording Evelyn Hart the minimal protections she seeks would be so far reaching, so disruptive of the status quo, as to render the idea infeasible.

Let us look, then, at the consequences. We may assume that if there were a well organized, well funded group opposed to protecting non-human great apes, we would be treated to a parade of horrors. "Next President Could Be A Chimpanzee," the New York Post might proclaim. "Orang-utans To Get Drivers' Licences?" asks the New York Times, reporting that "people on the street worry that it will be difficult to determine which rights non-human great apes do have, and which they do not. 'I don't want come in one day and find that I've been replaced by an orang-utan,' observed Anil Khan, a driver with the Yellow Cab Company."

There are at least two good answers to this anticipated parade of horrors. The first is that a moral imperative is just that: imperative. Worldwide condemnation of apartheid and resultant pressure for its abolition were not, in the main, tempered or restrained by questions of practicality. The fact of the moral imperative was enough. And so it is here.

The second answer to the parade of horrors is that they bear no relation to what Petitioner is asking of this Court. She is asking, quite simply, for the same fundamental protections as are afforded other persons. This Court can, of course, grant Petitioner rudimentary protections against physical and psychological harm without also being understood to have granted her the right to vote, to drive, or to hold public office. To be free from abuse, and to be free to accept the sanctuary being offered her: that is all she is asking.

Evelyn Hart has answered the philosophic objection that there can be no rights without duties. The answer is two-fold. First, as a matter of law, there is nothing novel about protecting those in need without imposing a countervailing obligation on them. *Youngberg v. Romeo* demonstrates that United States law can recognize rights commensurate with a Plaintiff's needs and capacities, despite the fact that there may be no correlative responsibilities imposed. Second, although one consequence of this reclassification— from Property to Person—is that arrangements must be made for her care, we would do well to remember how she came to be "property" in the first place. We have invaded, disrupted, and largely destroyed her world, for our purposes. Therefore, if non-human great apes who were long ago captured in the wild, enslaved, and shipped here, are no longer able to fend for themselves in what was their natural habitat, the very least we can do is to provide safe and peaceful sanctuary.

A primary purpose of justice is to correct "the arbitrariness of the world." The plight of Evelyn Hart demonstrates that such arbitrariness is not limited to human relations. But here, the arbitrariness is of human making. For all of these reasons, the Petitioner respectfully requests this Court to reverse the judgment of the District of Columbia Circuit of the Court of Appeals, and to enjoin the National Institutes of Health from assuming ownership of her.

Study Questions

1. Why, according to Hall and Waters, is the "parade of horrors" not implied by granting Evelyn Hart personhood? Explain.

2. Compare the case of Matthew Hiasi Pan to Evelyn Hart, and focus on the similarities. In your view, is the request for personhood status reasonable? Why or why not?

3. Amnesty International has come out against personhood rights for the Great Apes, claiming that it is inappropriate to focus on apes as long as humans are still suffering from oppression. What do you think about their argument?

 Primary Readings

Ethics and the Environment

Below you'll find two reviews of former Vice President Al Gore's film *An Inconvenient Truth*. The first one, by A. O. Scott, is from the *New York Times* and praises the film for its style as well as its content. The second one is by Michael Barone of *U.S. News and World Report* and lambastes the film for being inaccurate and based on faith in a credo rather than facts.

Warning of Calamities and Hoping for a Change in "An Inconvenient Truth"

A.O. SCOTT

Review in the **New York Times Movie Review**, *May 24, 2006.*

CANNES, France, May 23—"An Inconvenient Truth," Davis Guggenheim's new documentary about the dangers of climate change, is a film that should never have been made. It is, after all, the job of political leaders and policymakers to protect against possible future calamities, to respond to the findings of science and to persuade the public that action must be taken to protect the common interest.

But when this does not happen—and it is hardly a partisan statement to observe that, in the case of *global warming*, it hasn't—others must take up the responsibility: film-makers, activists, scientists, even retired politicians. That "An Inconvenient Truth" should not have to exist is a reason to be grateful that it does.

Appearances to the contrary, Mr. Guggenheim's movie is not really about Al Gore. It consists mainly of a multimedia presentation on climate change that Mr. Gore has given many times over the last few years, interspersed with interviews and Mr. Gore's voice-over reflections on his life in and out of politics. His presence is, in some ways, a distraction, since it guarantees that "An Inconvenient Truth" will become fodder for the cynical, ideologically facile sniping that often passes for political discourse these days. But really, the idea that worrying about the effect of carbon-dioxide emis-sions on the world's climate makes you some kind of liberal kook is as tired as the image of Mr. Gore as a stiff, humorless speaker, someone to make fun of rather than take seriously.

In any case, Mr. Gore has long since proven to be a deft self-satirist. (He recently told a moderator at a Cannes Film Festival news conference to address him as "your Ade-quacy.") He makes a few jokes to leaven the grim gist of "An Inconvenient Truth," and some of them are funny, in the style of a college lecturer's attempts to keep the attention of his captive audience. Indeed, his onstage manner—pacing back and forth, fiddling with gadgets, gesturing for emphasis—is more a professor's than a politician's. If he were not the man who, in his own formulation "used to be the next president of the United States of America," he might have settled down to tenure and a Volvo (or maybe a Prius) in some leafy academic grove.

But as I said, the movie is not about him. He is, rather, the surprisingly engaging ve-hicle for some very disturbing information. His explanations of complex environmental phenomena—the jet stream has always been a particularly tough one for me to grasp—are clear, and while some of the visual aids are a little corny, most of the images are stark, illuminating and powerful.

I can't think of another movie in which the display of a graph elicited gasps of hor-ror, but when the red lines showing the increasing rates of carbon-dioxide emissions and the corresponding rise in temperatures come on screen, the effect is jolting and chilling. Photographs of receding ice fields and glaciers—consequences of climate change that have already taken place—are as disturbing as speculative maps of submerged coastlines. The news of increased hurricane activity and warming oceans is all the more alarming for being delivered in Mr. Gore's matter-of-fact, scholarly tone.

He speaks of the need to reduce carbon-dioxide emissions as a "moral imperative," and most people who see this movie will do so out of a sense of duty, which seems to me entirely appropriate. Luckily, it happens to be a well-made documentary, edited crisply enough to keep it from feeling like 90 minutes of C-Span and shaped to give Mr. Gore's argument a real sense of drama. As unsettling as it can be, it is also intellectually exhila-rating, and, like any good piece of pedagogy, whets the appetite for further study. This is not everything you need to know about global warming: that's the point. But it is a good place to start, and to continue, a process of education that could hardly be more urgent. "An Inconvenient Truth" is a necessary film.

Gore Twists Science, History

MICHAEL BARONE

Review in *Creators Syndicate*, March 27, 2007.

Al Gore likes to present himself as a tribune of science, warning the world of imminent danger. But he is more like an Old Testament prophet, calling on us to bewail our wrongful conduct and to go and sin no more.

He starts off with the science. The world's climate, he reports, is getting warmer. This accurate report is, however, not set in historic context. World climate has grown warmer and cooler at various times in history. Climate change is not some unique historic event. It is the way the world works.

Not this time, Gore says. What's different is that climate change is being driven by human activity—to wit, increasing carbon dioxide emissions. Which means, he says, that we have to sharply reduce those emissions. But what the scientists tell us is that some proportion of climate change is caused by human activity and some proportion by natural causes—and that they can only estimate what those proportions are. The estimates they have produced have varied sharply. The climate change models that have been developed don't account for events of the recent past, much less predict with precision events in the future.

To which the prophet replies, with religious intensity, that all debate should be over. Those scientists with inconvenient views should be defunded and silenced. We should replace scientific inquiry with faith. We should have faith that climate change—"global warming"—is caused primarily by human activity. And we should have faith that the effects will be catastrophic, with rising oceans flooding great cities and pleasant plains and forests broiled by a searing sun.

Even the New York Times bridles at this. After Gore's film on climate change won an Academy Award for best documentary, the Times printed an article in which respected scientists—not Republicans, not on oil company payrolls—charged that Gore has vastly exaggerated the likelihood of catastrophic effects.

When you read the fine print of even the scientific reports that Gore likes to cite, you find the same thing. Gore foresees a 20-foot rise in sea level—240 inches. The Intergovernmental Panel on Climate Change report foresees a maximum of 23 inches. Gore says that "our civilization has never experienced any environmental shift remotely similar to this." Geologist Don Easterbrook says there have been shifts up to "20 times greater than the warming in the past century."

Science says that we should learn more about possible bad effects of climate change and calculate rationally how we can mitigate them. As the economic journalist Robert Samuelson points out, there is little that we can feasibly do in the short term to reduce carbon emissions, though over the long term we may be able to develop substitutes for carbon fuels.

As the environmentalist Bjorn Lomberg points out, the Kyoto Treaty that Gore helped to write (but which the Clinton administration never asked the Senate to ratify) would produce very little reduction in climate change at very high cost.

But religious prophets are not concerned about costs. Gore calls for an immediate cessation of new carbon-burning facilities. In other words, stop economic growth. But stopping economic growth in the developing world means consigning millions to miserable poverty. And we know what stopping economic growth in the developed world can mean.

Read the history of the 1930s: fascism, communism, world war. There are worse things than a rise of 1 or 2 degrees Centigrade.

The natural human yearning for spirituality has produced in many people educated in secular-minded universities and enveloped in an atmosphere of contempt for traditional religion a faith that we vulgar human beings have a sacred obligation not to inflict damage on Mother Earth. But science tells us that the Earth and its climate have been constantly changing.

Gore and his followers seem to assume that the ideal climate was the one they got used to when they were growing up. When temperatures dropped in the 1970s, there were warnings of an impending ice age. When they rose in the 1990s, there were predictions of disastrous global warming. This is just another example of the solipsism of the baby boom generation, the pampered and much-praised age cohort that believes the world revolves around it and that all past history has become irrelevant.

We're told in effect that the climate of the late 1950s and early 1960s was, of all those that have ever existed, the best of all possible climates. Not by science. But as a matter of faith.

Study Questions

1. What are the key arguments for and against Gore's film, as presented by Scott and Barone? Which of these two do you find to have the better arguments on his side?

2. If you have seen Al Gore's film, give an account of your impression of it. Were you convinced that we are facing global warming and that it is caused primarily by human factors? Why or why not?

3. Whether or not global warming is caused by humans, there seems to be evidence that temperatures are rising. If humans can in any way help to slow down the process, what are you prepared to do, or what are you already doing, about it?

4. If global warming is indeed a scam for political gain, as claimed by some critics, would that absolve us from all responsibility toward our planet? Explain why or why not.

Primary Reading

Two Ideals and the Death Penalty

TOM SORELL

Excerpt, 2002.

In 2002 the John Jay College of Criminal Justice's biannual journal *Criminal Justice Ethics* had a special symposium on the death penalty. In his paper British philosopher Tom

Sorell argues in favor of the death penalty, stating that in principle capital punishment is justified for aggravated murder. Within a just society, and with safeguards in place, it would be wrong not to have access to capital punishment, because of the concept of *responsible agency*. For Sorell, the death penalty is a kind of punishment that is appropriate not only in an ideal society but also within the real world, what Sorell calls the "worldly ideal." An explanatory note: The ICCPR that Sorell refers to is the International Covenant on Civil and Political Rights.

I now return to the question of whether there is a tension between the ideal of a just state, when it is taken to be the sort of state that protects and promotes the rights mentioned in the ICCPR, and the ideal of taking responsibility. The rights outlined in the Universal Declaration of Human Rights, the ICCPR and the International Covenant on Economic, Social and Cultural Rights were first declared against the background of the then recent experience of state-directed atrocities by the Nazis and the systematic denials of individual freedoms by countries in the Soviet bloc. No one believed that these injustices would immediately be eradicated or that they would even be significantly reduced throughout the world in a short time. The human rights instruments at best indicated a trajectory of improvement from what, in some parts of the world, were very low levels of access to fair trials, elections or legislative bodies at the time those instruments were formulated. The idea of taking responsibility has different degrees of force depending on where on that trajectory a state's courts, punishments, and penal institutions can be located. A state that imposes the death penalty for a greater range of crimes than the ICCPR allows, say for theft or corruption, does not encourage the criminal to take responsibility. In such a state, the wrongdoer has more of an excuse for not confessing to his crime than someone who faces a year or two of imprisonment in a humane and modern prison system. The same goes for someone who is liable to be stoned to death for adultery or who can have his hand amputated for theft. The more disproportionate the punishment, the more unequal the treatment is in the courts, or the less attention that is paid to evidence, the more the evasion of responsibility by wrongdoers is counterbalanced and excused by the injustice present in the social response to wrongdoing. On the other hand, in a state whose institutions and protections are high on the development trajectory indicated by the ICCPR, and thus close to the ideal, the scope for justifiable evasion of responsibility would seem to be correspondingly small.

What about evasion of responsibility for a crime that attracts the death penalty? Is this, too, unjustifiable in a state with good legal protections for the accused? A prior question is whether a state whose institutions and protections are close to ideal can impose the death penalty at all. If the answer is "Yes," then the evasion of responsibility, even for capital crimes, is hard to justify. A natural interpretation of the ICCPR is the following: as long as the death penalty is reserved for the most severe crimes, is not imposed on minors, and can be commuted, its existence is not by itself a violation of rights or sufficient to constitute a legal regime as unjust. Given general legal protections, the ICCPR seems to be saying, a state can apply the death penalty sparingly without failing to satisfy the ideal of a just state. On the other hand, in view of the 1989 protocol to the ICCPR calling for the abolition of the death penalty, which identifies the abolition of the death penalty as a means of protecting the right to life, things are not so clear.

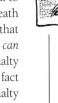

I believe that the argument justifying the abolition of the death penalty by appeal to the right to life, as is found in the 1889 protocol, is unstable in cases in which the death penalty is reserved for aggravated murder, and the only other grounds for supposing that the death penalty and the just state to be incompatible are weak. The death penalty *can* be applied by a just state. The fact that a state can be just and apply the death penalty does not, of course, mean that the death penalty cannot be applied in error, but the fact that it can be applied in error does not by itself justify the abolition of the death penalty in cases in which the burden of proof is high. Possible miscarriages of justice do not justify the abolition of the death penalty across the board, for they do not justify those who are guilty of capital crimes evading responsibility for their crimes in legal systems that protect human rights. On the contrary, the ideal of taking responsibility justifies nothing less than cooperation with the prosecuting authorities in such states. It justifies confessions, and it justifies willing submission to proportionate punishment, including, for the worst crimes, capital punishment.

I begin my argument for this with the reasoning implicit in the 1989 protocol that calls for the abolition for the death penalty. The preamble to the protocol asserts twice that the abolition of the death penalty takes further the enhancement of the right to life guaranteed by Article 6 of the ICCPR. But what exactly is this right to life? It is not an absolute right to life, one that rules out, for example, killing in self-defense or killing in war. Again, the protocol itself permits death as a penalty for a serious crime of a military nature committed in wartime. At most, the right to life recognized by the ICCPR is a right to life for those who are blamelessly going about their business in accordance with other rights that are supposed to be extended to members of civil society. According to the ICCPR, the right to life can lapse when the life is that of someone who takes away life. It seems consistent with the ICCPR for threats to the existence of civil society or the right to life of individuals to be countered with threats of proportionate punishment on the part of states. If death is a proportionate response to certain kinds of murder, large scale terrorism, or serious military crimes in wartime, then it may be threatened; and if it may justly be threatened, then it may justly be carried out on those who are genuinely guilty. Safeguards against error in the identification of the guilty are of course also required by justice, but not safeguards against self-identification *by* the guilty where punishments are proportionate to crimes.

Unless the death penalty is always disproportionately severe, no matter *what* the crime to which it is applied, or unless Hobbes is right and one has the right to do *anything* one can to save one's life (something I have already disputed), there is something wrong with evading responsibility, even in cases in which taking responsibility means death. Part of what is wrong with the evasion of responsibility for capital crime is the same as what is wrong with the evasion of responsibility for *any* crime. But the more serious crime, the greater the wrong of evading responsibility for it. Serious crimes taint a whole life and sometimes a whole era, and for the guilty person to proceed as if nothing has happened, or as if nothing much has happened, or as if it is all right for *him* to have committed a crime because he got away with it against great odds, is a denial of the difference between big and small wrong-doing. Since the more things *look* like small wrongdoing the less things look wrong at all, denying the difference between big and small wrongdoing is a way of eroding the category or wrongdoing itself. Therefore it is important to maintain scales of wrongdoing. This does not mean refusing to revise them, but it does place the burden of proof on those who revalue downwards the seriousness of serious crime.

Proportionality, which is rightly insisted upon as a condition of just punishment, cannot operate in the absence of such scales. And proportionality cannot be a norm that only the authorities are expected to respect; it has to constrain the thinking and action of ordinary agents as well. One does not have to be an angel to meet this condition. A thief who avoids guns because he draws the line at armed robbery and does not want to get involved in murder reflects in his behavior the relative seriousness of armed robbery and murder. A computer hacker who penetrates the security codes of a major corporation but would not dream of infecting a hospital's computer system with a virus represents a similar type of case. The argument that someone should not be allowed to get away with, or get away lightly with, serious wrongdoing, is as much an argument from proportionality as the argument that death should not be the penalty for tax evasion or perjury. And the proportionality reflected in certain kinds of criminal behavior show that proportionality is a value accessible to the immoral as well as to the moral. Just as you do not need to be an angel to do your best to avoid killing and kidnapping in your criminal activities, you do not need to be an angel to recognize that people who kill and kidnap and act as if nothing has happened are sometimes far lower in the hierarchy of non-angels than you are.

This line of thought has a bearing on miscarriages of justice. I said at the beginning that in the case of the most severe penalties, the greatest precautions need to be taken against their wrongful imposition. But the duty to avoid miscarriages of justice is not only a duty on states. It is a duty on everyone. It is a duty on those who have evidence that clears the innocent person to make that evidence public. But it is also a duty on the guilty to take responsibility. In saying this, I am not, of course, making an *appeal* to the guilty to take the rap. I am trying to point to an ideal that shows that guilt and the evasion of responsibility have weight in our thinking about the abolition of the death penalty, and that those things are left out in arguments against the death penalty from the ideal of the just state. I am not claiming that things will be morally better on balance if all the guilty are caught and punished and a few of those executed along the way are innocent. It *may* be better for the guilty to go free than for the innocent to be punished. It may, accordingly, be better for those guilty of horrible crimes to go free than for an innocent person to be executed for one of them. But there is still something wrong with the guilty going unpunished, and there is something wrong, too, with those who are guilty of horrible crimes being punished as if their crimes were minor. Part of the source for these thoughts is the ideal of responsible agency, and a theory or a rhetoric that ignores this ideal is defective as a theory of or rhetoric about the death penalty.

Study Questions

1. Sorell argues that the death penalty is the only true way to achieve a just punishment for extreme crimes. Would you agree with him? Why or why not?

2. In Sorell's opinion it is possible to create a sufficiently safe judicial system so that no innocent person is sentenced to death. Do you agree? Return to this question after reading Fuhrman's text (next) and reevaluate Sorell's argument.

3. If you are in favor of the death penalty, which crimes would you make eligible for execution, and why? What would Sorell say?

Primary Reading

Death and Justice: An Exposé of Oklahoma's Death Row Machine

MARK FUHRMAN

Excerpt, 2003.

Law enforcement officers are traditionally retentionists; they see horrific crimes committed, and they witness the suffering of the victims and, in murder cases, the victims' loved ones, who in turn become victims too. They are closer to the experience of pain and loss because of crime than most people in academia, who view such issues perhaps with much interest and sympathy, but generally from a remove and abstractly. It is a natural, and widespread, reaction among police officers that the only appropriate punishment for murder is death—not because they are particularly bloodthirsty, but because they see, with their own eyes, what murder does to human beings, and they view the death penalty as the only real form of justice. For that reason *Death and Justice* is a highly unusual and thought-provoking book. Mark Fuhrman, a former LAPD homicide detective and now an author of true-crime books as well as a talk-show host and a television commentator, undertook an investigation of the death penalty expecting to see his retentionist views confirmed, but the opposite happened: During the course of his investigation he found himself changing his mind about the justification of the death penalty. His focus was on death penalty cases in Oklahoma City, where the district attorney, Bob Macy, was such a firm believer in capital punishment that he chose to overlook (and perhaps even encouraged) shoddy work and mishandling of evidence by the forensic scientist Joyce Gilchrist. Macy's zealousness and Gilchrist's less-than-professional work raised doubt about the guilt of people on Oklahoma's death row as well as people who have already been executed; and Fuhrman cites example after example of Oklahoma prisoners whose cases have been reexamined. Some have been exonerated and released, some are awaiting new trials, and some have had their death sentences changed to life without parole.

Because of his research, Fuhrman changed his mind—going from being a retentionist to being an abolitionist—not because he is against the death penalty in principle, but because, as he says, in the real world you simply can't have a judicial system in which district attorneys and judges are political players running for election and reelection and still have a guarantee of a fair trial at the state level, because some of those officials will take a "tough-on-crime" stance for the sake of their own political future. Interestingly, Fuhrman believes a *federal* death penalty should still be an option for the worst crimes, such as terrorism and serial murders. In addition to his misgivings about the practical feasibility of a fair legal system that includes capital punishment, his book concludes with a reexamination of the notions of justice and revenge.

> I used to believe in the death penalty. It was an article of faith for a cop. During my twenty years on the force, I saw so much death, pain, and misery that I never questioned whether or not capital punishment was just. There were some people who deserved to die. That's what I thought, and so did my fellow cops.

We often expressed our support for the death penalty with crude terms and lofty rationalizations. We never used the word *revenge*. Instead, we called it justice, but it was cloaked in hate and anger. When we talked about the death penalty it was always with contempt for the suspect. "Fry the fucker," we'd say, "drop the pill on that asshole." That was the way we talked and the way we felt. I was empowered by my peers and that led to a feeling of self-righteousness. I had a closed mind about the issue and refused to accept any facts that might shake my worldview. There was no good reason, that I saw, to be against the death penalty, unless you wanted criminals to get away with murder. It seemed absolutely right and justified. . . .

When I started working on this book, I thought that since death penalty cases carry the highest punishment, they would be investigated more thoroughly and professionally. I quickly realized that the opposite is true. Catastrophic errors occur in many death penalty cases, because of the pressure to make a strong case and get a capital conviction.

Death penalty cases are all high-profile. Maybe you don't see them on the evening news, but within that jurisdiction, even in Oklahoma County, where they were so commonplace, a death penalty case creates the same pressure and scrutiny, the same temptations to cheat or cover up that I saw in the Simpson trial.

Once a prosecutor announces the death penalty will be sought, anything less than a capital conviction is seen as a failure. If Bob Macy hadn't asked for the death penalty in these cases, Joyce Gilchrist and the rest of the OCPD wouldn't have felt so much pressure to not only solve the case but also ensure a capital conviction. That pressure was self-reinforcing among those involved in a death penalty case. It gathered a momentum that swept everybody along with it. No one could afford to go against the flow.

The first place where a death penalty case goes wrong is with the detective. His investigation is the foundation on which the prosecution is built. It is up to him whether the crime is investigated thoroughly, professionally, and responsibly. It would be easier if the detectives were simply incompetent, yet certain efforts to hide the mistakes and holes in their cases indicate that they were competent enough to know when they were wrong.

Cops are supposed to follow the rules. That's what makes us different from criminals. What I saw in Oklahoma was that the more law enforcement felt superior to criminals, the more they started to act like them.

The problem isn't just Okalahoma County or Bob Macy or Joyce Gilchrist. It's the death penalty itself. Capital punishment is driven by two emotions—revenge and ambition. The public says it wants revenge for horrible crimes. But they want that revenge secondhand, carried out discreetly by clinical professionals in a small room very far away. The mob cries for blood—they just don't want to actually see it. And so they are never satisfied with, or sickened by, the revenge that is carried out for them. They never learn that revenge has no end; it just completes the circle of violence. The loss that the family of a murder victim feels is not made any less painful by the execution of their loved one's killer. If there ever is any closure for the family of murder victims, it should be based on forgiveness, not revenge. . . .

If we didn't feel guilty about the death penalty, we wouldn't have to erect such a complex mechanism in order to achieve it. Lately, that guilt has expressed itself in concern that innocent people are being convicted and possibly executed. From the reinstatement of the death penalty in 1977 to the time I am writing this, of the one hundred people released from death row, only eight of those cases involved DNA evidence.

Statewide, Oklahoma has one wrongful conviction for approximately every forty death sentences passed since 1973. These are cases of demonstrated innocence, not cases overturned because of reversible error. Of the seven innocents released from McAlester's death row, two of them, Clifford Henry Bowen and Robert Lee Miller, had been prosecuted by Bob Macy. . . .

"What if an innocent person is executed?" I asked Bob Macy. "Is that sacrifice worth keeping the death penalty?"

"I'd have to say yes," Macy replied.

I don't agree with Macy. I think that one innocent man's life is worth losing the death penalty. I'll go one step further. I think the nearly eleven years that Robert Lee Miller spent in prison are reason enough to lose the death penalty.

When you work in law enforcement, it's us versus them. Good guys and bad guys. You erect a wall between yourself and the criminals. Sometimes during my police career I let down that wall and developed a rapport, even an understanding, with a suspect. This often happened during interrogations. For a moment, I would see the suspect as a man. I would have empathy for him. That made it difficult to do my job, so the wall went back up again.

In order to execute people, we have to demonize them, deny their humanity, and mark them with the stigma of evil so great that there is no choice but to kill them. The system is built to minimize any feelings of empathy or responsibility. There is a sense of inevitability in death penalty cases that gradually achieves momentum until nothing, not even the United States Supreme Court, can stop an execution.

Justice is supposed to be blind, but we all know it's not and never will be. We want it to be perfect and flawless, unlike any other human endeavor.

"As long as the criminal justice system is administered by human beings," Jim Fowler said, "we should not have a punishment that is one hundred percent irrevocable."

Throughout my research and writing of this book, I wanted to have it both ways. I wanted to support the death penalty. When I found problems with it, I wanted them to be identified and fixed. I soon came to realize that the problem was the death penalty itself. We have tried tinkering with the system, when the Supreme Court overturned the death penalty nationwide in *Furman v. Georgia* and then established guidelines for state legislatures in *Gregg v. Georgia.* It took only a few years before prosecutors like Bob Macy were arguing that almost every murder was "heinous, atrocious and cruel" and therefore satisfied the aggravators that the Oklahoma legislature had established in accordance with the Supreme Court's decisions. Bob Macy used the vagueness of the Oklahoma statutes and court precedent concerning the death penalty to create a system in which almost any murder, from domestic violence to armed robbery to a drive-by shooting, was deserving of the death penalty.

Every murder is "heinous, atrocious and cruel." By executing the innocent we have committed an act just as "heinous, atrocious and cruel" ourselves.

In my career as a detective, both as a police officer and an author, I have always followed the evidence, wherever it led. My investigation of the death penalty in Oklahoma County has brought me to this conclusion: death penalty cases are not investigated or prosecuted at a level that can guarantee justice, or even that the accused is actually guilty.

I no longer believe in the death penalty. I no longer have faith that it is administered fairly or justly. I fear that innocent people have been executed.

That's why I am calling for the abolition of the death penalty. Not only in Oklahoma but in every state. The federal government should reserve the right to execute only those guilty of treason, terrorism, and political assassination. In these circumstances, we as a nation would be executing the criminal, and it would no longer be up to individuals like Bob Macy and Joyce Gilchrist. These federal executions should be televised and broadcast on the Internet. If we don't have the stomach to watch executions, we shouldn't be performing them.

I could make all sorts of arguments about deterrence, cost-effectiveness, wrongful convictions, politics, philosophy, and so on. But it boils down to this—the death penalty brings out the worst in all of us: hatred, anger, vengeance, ambition, cruelty, and deceit.

This book has been a journey. I had to reach deep down within myself to come to this conclusion and the words to express it. I was wrong about the death penalty. I chose revenge instead of justice. And I was not alone. Instead of being an individual, I was just another ugly face in the crowd, chanting for death. Now I recognize the need to change not just our laws but ourselves.

Murder creates a pain that can't be forgotten or ignored. Our efforts to bring justice to those responsible should not make that pain any worse. In seeking the death penalty, horrible mistakes were made that cannot be undone. However, once we admit these mistakes, we have taken the first step toward reconciling and working together to ensure those mistakes don't happen again. Then we can begin to right the terrible wrongs that have been committed, not just against death row inmates but against our system of justice and therefore all of us.

Study Questions

1. Do you think Fuhrman is right in his assessment that death penalty proponents may think they want justice, but what they really want is revenge?

2. Would you agree with Bob Macy that executing an innocent person is a price worth paying for retaining the death penalty? Why or why not?

3. Would you agree with Fuhrman that it is not possible to have a judicial system that allows for the death penalty and at the same time elects judges, sheriffs, and district attorneys through a process that makes them vulnerable to political pressures?

4. Compare Fuhrman's and Sorell's stance on the death penalty: Taking both texts into consideration, do you think the death penalty can be applied justly?

5. As an interesting aside, executions in Oklahoma City went down from twenty-one in 2001 to fourteen in 2003, and six in 2004. In comparison, Texas executed twenty-three people, and Ohio came in second with seven executions in 2004. Fuhrman's book came out in 2003. Do you think a book such as *Death and Justice* might be able to influence the attitude toward the death penalty within a state's judicial system?

Primary Reading

Your Life as Story

TRISTINE RAINER

Book, 1997. Excerpt.

Rainer's book is a practical guide to writing one's autobiography and includes chapters such as "The Nine Essential Elements of Story Structure," "Genres of the Self," "Truth in Autobiographic Writing," and "Finishing the Unfinished Story." She suggests looking for patterns in your life and the lives of others as a stargazer looks for constellations. Her book is more than a guide to writing a best-selling story about yourself—it is intended as a guide to make you understand yourself better. In this selection she gives the first lesson in finding the story of your life.

What is a story anyway? We all know intuitively. As children we gobble them up and never feel too full for more. Myths are stories, fairy tales and folktales are stories; so are novels, movies, and sitcoms. But you can't touch, taste, smell, hear, or see a story—only the images and words it assumes. To say what a story is, is like trying to get your hands around a ghost shape.

Though they are intangible, stories are powerful and their power seems to come from another realm. They appear to be a way in which the sacred enters our lives. Myths, stories to explain how and why we are here, begot religion. The morality tales of Moses, Jesus, Mohammed, and Buddha—stories that tell us what to value and how to live—have determined the course of world history for more than nineteen centuries. Stories remembered within a community or family transport the beliefs and values of past generations into the future. The individual stories of our own lives tell us who we are and infuse our personal existence with excitement, meaning, and mystery.

Myths, parables, family stories, and the innumerable media stories of our popular culture are offered to us already embodied in the words or images of others. However, the stories of our own lives require active searching—learning to look through our memories in a new way. To find story in your life, you must engage imagination with memory; you must invent a line of continuity—not from nothing, but from the raw materials of your life. It's like reading a pattern in DNA or figuring out the possible anagrams in a word. To find story in your life, you have to know what you are looking for. Fortunately, though you can't see a story, if you learn what its features are, when you look you will recognize one—and then many.

So what are the features of a story? A story isn't just a plot, a series of interconnected events. A story is a meaningful narrative with a beginning, a middle, and a conclusion. You started out at point A, the beginning, and because of what you did and what happened to you in the middle, point B, you ended up at point C, the conclusion. At point C you were a different person than you were at A, not just because you were older, but because you saw things differently.

In its simplest form a story is: what you wanted, how you struggled, and what you realized out of that struggle. A story is a series of interrelated events that you made happen and that happened to you, and the consequence. The consequence is a change in you. In an autobiographic story, change may occur in other characters, but it must also occur in you, because you are the protagonist. The change may come from an event (you married, you got old), but it is also a moral change. You had a realization, a shift in values or perception.

In other words, within the story you made a "character arc," you had a change in character. Gradually, because of what happened to you in life and the minirealizations you had along the way, you went from "there" to "here" as a person. What you believed, what you valued, and how you acted toward others changed, even if only slightly. You track this character arc in an autobiographic story by including your feelings, reactions to the events you experienced, and your realizations. You give the events of your life significance because of what they meant to you and how you changed from your engagement with them. An autobiographic story is not just an account of events; it is the charting of your emotional, moral, and psychological course, which gives meaning to those events.

It is worth taking some time to think about the inner course you wish to trace before you start putting down everything you can remember about your past. It is worth considering what story you want your life to tell. Why? Why not just write down everything you can remember, like so many people do? Because it won't be alive, it won't tap into the power of myth, it won't participate in the kind of truth that we read narratives for.

Study Questions

1. What does Rainer mean by a "moral change" in a story?

2. What is a "character arc"?

3. Write three pages of autobiography (the story of your life so far) using Rainer's method. Have a friend who knows you well critique it: Did you mention points in your life he or she would recognize? Are there important events you chose to omit? Does he or she recognize your self-image? Write a new version using your friend's critique, and compare the two.

4. In the first season of the television series *The Sopranos,* young Chris, a mobster as well as an aspiring screenwriter, is experiencing an existential crisis. Feeling that nobody takes him seriously enough, he shoots a deli manager in the foot because he doesn't get preferential treatment. Afterward he agonizes that his life seems disjointed and meaningless, because he has no "character arc." He proceeds to try to establish a reputation as a tough mobster. Is that what Rainer means by a character arc? If you are a *Sopranos* fan, what do you think the screenwriter had in mind by having Chris talk about character arcs?

Narrative

15 Minutes

JOHN HERZFELD (SCREENWRITER AND DIRECTOR)

Film, 2001. Summary.

The American avant-garde artist Andy Warhol once said that in the future, everyone will be famous for fifteen minutes. He was referring to the mass-media hunger for news, feeding on brief stories about individual lives. You will see this quote again, in the summary of *The Insider.*

Movie reviewers weren't very kind to the film bearing the promising title *15 Minutes,* and it wasn't much of a box office success either, but I find that it is far better than its reputation, especially in raising the question of media responsibility. As you read in Box 13.2, opinions differ on how far a TV network might go to secure an exclusive story. Would network executives choose to air a videotaped murder? *15 Minutes* speculates that some tabloid show might do just that, for the sake of ratings.

In addition, the theme of what might happen when a fascination for Hollywood and the movies goes bad links this film up with our discussion about Hollywood influence in Chapter 2.

Two men go through immigration in New York; one, Oleg, is a Russian with a Hollywood fixation. He explains to the immigration officer that he has come to America because he saw *It's a Wonderful Life.* The other is Emil, a Czech, who has acquaintances in New York who owe him money. On the way to visit Emil's acquaintances Oleg steals a video camera. When they reach their destination and it turns out that his friend can't pay Emil what he owes him, Emil kills him and his wife with a kitchen knife. Meanwhile, Oleg is filming the event in detail, the first step toward fulfilling his dream of becoming an American film director.

Emil, having no intention of letting a couple of murders stop him, seeks to cover up the crime by setting fire to the apartment—but someone is watching from an adjacent bathroom: a woman. She flees down the stairs but has left her purse behind. So Emil and Oleg set out to find her.

Meanwhile, we encounter the host of a New York tabloid show, Robert Hawkins. His producer is trying to tone down the violent style of his show, but Hawkins is adamant: If they don't run a violent story, someone else will—and besides, what is a better lead story? "If it bleeds, it leads," he says.

A frequent guest on his show is popular New York police detective Eddie Fleming. His face is on the cover of magazines, and he is quite aware of his own celebrity status—but not merely because he enjoys the attention. He explains that if his fame can buy him just a little extra goodwill from the public so more crimes can be solved, then that's what he'll use it for. He may be narcissistic, but he is also a pro.

The apartment where Emil committed the murders and set the fire is now burned out, and the New York Fire Department takes control of the scene. A young arson inspector, Jordy Warsaw, finds to his dismay that NYPD and star detective Fleming are already there. At first Fleming thinks it is an accident, but he bows to the younger man's expertise when he shows him evidence of its being arson, and thus a murder scene.

In the meantime, Oleg and Emil are watching TV in a cheap hotel room and see Hawkins interview a serial killer who has been deemed temporarily insane. Emil's reaction: "I love America—nobody is responsible for what they do!" In an attempt to find the female witness, they call an escort service, dialing a number they found on a card in her purse. The woman who shows up from the escort service isn't the witness—but they murder her when she won't give out the escort service's address. (And Oleg films the entire incident.) Later, when the police and Fleming investigate this new crime scene, they find that she has been murdered with the same knife that was used in the arson murders.

Fleming, at home, hears a noise outside, investigates, and sees nothing—but in the meantime Emil and Oleg make their way into his apartment, attack him, and tie him to a chair with duct tape while Oleg films it all. Emil, with the logic of a madman, explains his plan to Fleming: They will kill someone famous and film it—which will prove they're crazy, because who else but crazy men would film their crimes? Then a judge will sentence them to a mental hospital instead of prison, but in the hospital they will reveal that they are sane, and because of the American double-jeopardy law (you cannot be tried for the same crime twice), they will be set free, sell their film to Hollywood, and become rich.

Fleming, knowing himself to be in a desperate predicament, fights back every way he can, using the chair he is strapped into as a weapon, but in the end it does him no good: While Oleg films everything, Fleming is knifed by Emil and dies.

Now Hawkins is approached by Emil and Oleg. They have a story worth a lot of money: a tape of Fleming's death. Will he buy it? And will he air it? Indeed, Hawkins shows up at the arranged place and buys the tape. Oleg films the exchange of the tape and the briefcase full of cash. When Hawkins arrives back at the TV station, Fleming's police colleagues try to talk sense to him and beg him for the tape, but it is too late: Minutes later, it is being broadcast all over New York and beyond, with Hawkins's introduction stating that he, as a journalist, feels obliged to show it.

As Oleg and Emil are watching the broadcast in a restaurant, their fellow patrons are horrified by what they see on the giant TV in the middle of their dinner, and when they hear the two men quarreling over the movie rights, they recognize them from the televised tape. In short order Emil is caught; Oleg disappears into the crowd.

Several twists and turns of the plot lead us to a final resurfacing of Oleg. Enraged that Emil, having found a lawyer who will argue that he was legally insane and that Oleg planned the whole thing, is found incompetent and indeed will escape punishment, Oleg has a trump card: the tape on which Emil tells Fleming of his plan, effectively proving that he was legally sane and responsible for his crimes. What does Oleg do with this tape? Will he succeed in becoming a famous American film director? Will Hawkins have a change of heart about what constitutes media ethics? I will leave that for you to experience on your own.

Study Questions

1. In your opinion, was Hawkins acting responsibly as a journalist when he chose to air Fleming's death scene? Why or why not? Remember that Hawkins says, "If it bleeds, it leads," but that he also says it is his duty as a journalist to show the tape. If you answered no, then what, in your view, might be the responsible action of a journalist faced with Hawkins's moral choice?

2. Oleg is obsessed with American movies, to the point that he wants to make his own. However, he also seems to think that Hollywood has given an accurate portrayal of American society. Hollywood films shown around the world may indeed give people a skewed view of life in America—but do you think there are many such as Oleg who believe that view is true? If so, what can be done about it?

3. Do you think it possible that a "reality show" such as *Survivor* might air scenes in which its participants are injured or perhaps killed? Why or why not? Should they? Why or why not?

4. Emil is misinformed about the rules of double jeopardy: If a legally insane convict recovers his sanity, he can be tried as a sane person. But for someone to be judged insane, he or she has to be unaware of the difference between right and wrong. Might Emil, in a real-life situation, be found legally insane? Explain why or why not.

5. What does the title refer to in the context of the film?

Narrative

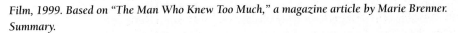

The Insider

ERIC ROTH AND MICHAEL MANN (SCREENWRITERS)
MICHAEL MANN (DIRECTOR)

Film, 1999. Based on "The Man Who Knew Too Much," a magazine article by Marie Brenner.
Summary.

This film is based on the true story of one man making the decision to go public against the tobacco companies with his expert knowledge of the addictive nature of nicotine. In the context of Chapter 6, the plot illustrates the story of two men's sense of duty, regardless of the consequences, acting for the sake of a moral principle. In light of Chapter 7, you may want to apply theories of respect for persons, and negative and positive rights (the negative right of free speech, and the positive right of receiving truthful information). But, in the context of Chapter 8, you might also view it as the story of a person of integrity choosing to fight for what is right, even if the outcome may cost him everything—a story paralleling that of Socrates. In the context of this chapter, you can choose to view it as a story of business ethics as well as media responsibility: What is the bottom line for a television show doing investigative reporting—doing business or serving the public? Do tobacco companies have moral responsibilities to their customers?

One day in the mid-1990s, Jeffrey Wigand comes home from work early. His wife is horrified when she learns that he has been fired. They live in an expensive home and have lots of medical expenses: Their oldest daughter has asthma, and his wife can't work because someone has to look after the little girl in case she has an attack. Wigand was a corporate VP in charge of research and development at Brown & Williamson, the tobacco giant. He has a severance package, but the future looks grim. It is only as the story unfolds that we realize just how grim it is going to get. By coincidence, at the CBS studios in New York, the producer of *60 Minutes,* Lowell Bergman, is putting together a story about a tobacco study and calls Wigand. To his surprise Wigand won't talk to him—but he faxes him cryptic messages, indicating that he'd like to be able to talk but has a confidentiality agreement with his former company. Later, Brown & Williamson executives let

Wigand know that since they suspect he has broken the agreement, they want him to sign a new, expanded one—and if he doesn't, he'll lose all benefits. Now Wigand is furious—at B&W for threatening his family and at Bergman, who he believes has leaked the story. Bergman flies down from New York to Wigand's home to persuade him that he, Bergman, can be trusted, and Wigand then tells him the story: At a congressional hearing on the tobacco industry and nicotine some years back, seven CEOs—the Seven Dwarfs, as Wigand calls them—from the tobacco industry testified that nicotine was not an addictive drug. But Wigand knows that to be false. So why was he working for the tobacco company? The pay was good, and there was good medical coverage, even if he perceived that integrity within the industry was a problem.

Mike Wallace, the investigative journalist for *60 Minutes* who early in the film has been introduced as a man of integrity himself, suggests a way for Wigand to be able to speak on his show: What if he were subpoenaed as a witness in a smoker's lawsuit in Mississippi? Then his statement would be on record, and in this way he could get around the confidentiality agreement. So Bergman links Wigand up with the lawyer for the plaintiffs in the Mississippi lawsuit. Meanwhile, the Wigands have had to move out of their beautiful home and into a more modest house. He begins a new career as a high school science teacher and forces himself to adjust to the situation, but his wife finds the transition hard. When they start to receive death threats, Wigand decides that it is time to go public.

He agrees to an interview with Wallace on *60 Minutes*. During the taping he reveals that the tobacco CEOs perjured themselves when they claimed nicotine isn't addictive: Cigarettes, he says, are "delivery devices for nicotine." In addition, he reveals that Brown & Williamson is enhancing nicotine chemically so it is absorbed more rapidly by the brain and that he was fired because he wouldn't keep quiet. Mike Wallace asks him if he wishes he hadn't blown the whistle. At times, Wigand says, but he'd do it again, because he thinks it was worth it. Now things start to happen quickly for Wigand, but in a way he hadn't imagined: Security guards are moving into his home because of the threats, and his wife is leaving him, taking their children with her. They keep the house, so he has to move into a hotel room. He testifies in the Mississippi lawsuit, specifically stating that nicotine is a drug, but his deposition is sealed, unavailable to the public. And the *60 Minutes* crew is in for a surprise: CBS executives lean on them to cut Wigand's interview, claiming the broadcasting company may be sued by the tobacco company for "tortious interference," a third party interfering in a contract situation, creating damages for the first party (the tobacco company).

Bergman is livid: Why should lawyers be able to determine the content of *60 Minutes*, a program of investigative journalism that has proved its integrity over and over again? Is the priority business or news? To Bergman's enormous disappointment, Wallace caves: In the twilight of his career, he has to consider his legacy, and sides with the corporate lawyers. And now the tobacco company embarks on a smear campaign against Wigand, digging up any old secret they can find, such as a dismissed shoplifting charge, so his word will be discredited. Jeffrey watches the cut, gutted interview air and becomes despondent. Both Bergman and Wigand have so much to lose: one his self-esteem and reputation for professional integrity, the other his family and perhaps his life. After a heated, then conciliatory, talk with Wigand, Bergman decides it is time for

In this scene from *The Insider* (Touchstone, 1999), Jeffrey Wigand (Russell Crowe) is being interviewed by Mike Wallace for *60 Minutes*. When the actual interview between Wigand and Wallace aired in 1998, the impact was tremendous. Wigand told the inside story about nicotine that the tobacco companies didn't want us to know: that it is an addictive drug, and cigarettes are the delivery device for the drug. The film uses blurry images (such as the foreground in this picture) and mirror reflections with much effectiveness, perhaps symbolizing the contrast between truth and falsehood.

desperate measures: He leaks the story to the *New York Times*. When the story appears on the front page of the paper, Wallace changes his mind: He will air the original interview. The CBS executive tries to argue that this story will last only fifteen minutes and then people will forget it, but Wallace reminds him that it is fame that lasts only fifteen minutes—infamy lasts longer than that. So Jeffrey Wigand gets to tell his side of the story on national TV. After the airing, Lowell Bergman quits. What was broken doesn't get put back together again.

Study Questions

1. Apply George's analysis of the Myth of Amoral Business of this case: Does it apply to the tobacco companies? To CBS? Why or why not?

2. Apply the criteria of courage from Chapter 11 to the case of Wiegand: Does he have physical courage? Moral courage? Explain.

3. Use Kant's second rule, that people should never be used merely as a means to an end, to evaluate Wigand and Bergman's actions.

4. If you were in Jeffrey Wigand's position, what do you think you would have done? Is Wigand doing his "nearest duty"? Is that important?

Narrative

The Jigsaw Man

LARRY NIVEN

Short story, 1967. Summary.

This science fiction story explores a topic that seemed far-fetched in 1967 to most readers, illegal trade in organs. But reality seems to be catching up: For years Chinese dissidents who had escaped to the West told stories about the Chinese organ trade, but it wasn't until 2000 that the rumors were corroborated: Chinese prisons tailor executions of death row inmates according to the organs needed. Kidneys are especially popular; Chinese recipients pay less for them than foreign customers do, and such customers have been traced worldwide, including transplant recipients in the United States. Stories in the West about people turning up with kidneys missing may be an "urban legend," but a five-year-old Russian boy was close to being sold for parts by his grandmother in 2000, for $90,000. Niven not only speculates about the future but also seems to express a viewpoint on capital punishment: Young Lew is in jail, awaiting his trial. He knows that the outcome will be a sentence of death. They have evidence enough to convict him, and many people are being convicted and executed these days. We are in the late part of the twenty-first century (in Larry Niven's "Known Space," a future history of Earth and the universe).

In jail, Lew is confronted with a grisly story: Two fellow inmates tell about their crime of organlegging. Organs for transplant are in high demand among wealthy people, and high prices are paid for illegally acquired organs. How does one acquire organs illegally? One kidnaps healthy people, murders them, and sells their organs. One of Lew's cellmates is the bodysnatcher; the other is the doctor performing the organ extractions. They are both scheduled for execution.

Are there no legal organ transplants in this future society? Of course there are. By this time a method has been developed to keep organs fresh indefinitely, and worthy recipients are always waiting for life-saving organs, but there are more people needing organs than there are organs made available through accidents. As a result, an alternative method has been in use for almost a century (since the 1990s): On death row are people whose death, some say, doesn't do society any good, so they are made to "atone" for what evil they did in life by having their organs serve others when they die. Organ harvesting of condemned murderers is part of the system of punishment now, so Lew's two cellmates know what awaits them: an injection, instant freezing, death, and organ extraction. However, society needs more organs than the murderers on death row can supply. So, although kidnapping was already punishable by death in some states, now other crimes have joined the list.

Suddenly there is activity in the cell: The two cellmates are pressing themselves up against the bars and invite Lew to join them: They are about to commit suicide in a way that will make the organ banks reject them. The doctor has a hollowed-out space in his leg with a bomb implanted, and in a gruesome display of blood and gore the two inmates are blown to pieces—but so is the outside wall! Lew manages to squeeze out the hole in the wall, but he is very far off the ground, up close to the roof of the building. Driven by fear, he manages to swing himself upward toward the roof, and he lands on a pedwalk moving from the jail to the adjoining building. From there he jumps to a ledge and breaks through a window, into an office. While looking for something he can use to make himself less conspicuous—a change of clothes, shaving gear, anything—he notices what building he is in. A hospital. The hospital where criminals are executed and their organs removed. He has landed in the organ bank. Moving from room to room, he tries to find a way out, but he is being tracked, and beams of tranquilizer sounds are hitting him. Desperately he looks around and realizes that he is in the room of organ tanks. Refusing to die for what he considers nothing, he grabs a chair and starts smashing tanks, and he keeps smashing tanks until he blacks out.

Final scene: Lew is in court, hearing prosecutor and defense argue about his case; to his amazement, nobody mentions the organ tanks. They have plenty on him as it is; extra charges are considered only as a backup. Lew knows that he will lose his life, but at least he also knows that he has put up a fight. And now we learn what Lew is accused of, with plenty of ironclad evidence: "The state will prove that the said Warren Lewis Knowles did, in the space of two years, willfully drive through a total of six red traffic lights. During that same period the same Warren Lewis Knowles exceeded local speed limits no less than ten times, once by as much as fifteen miles per hour."

Study Questions

1. How does this story illustrate the type of argument called a "slippery slope"?

2. In your view, can the harvesting of organs from executed criminals be justified? If so, how? If not, why not?

3. Is this story a criticism of a forward-looking reason for punishment or a backward-looking one? Explain.

4. How would a utilitarian respond to this story? How would a deontologist respond? Explain in detail.

Narrative

The Life of David Gale

CHARLES RANDOLPH (SCREENWRITER),
ALAN PARKER (DIRECTOR)

Film. 2003. Summary.

This film is viewed as a powerful argument against the death penalty—and yet, because of the surprise ending, it is not a one-dimensional abolitionist argument but, rather, an exploration of people's commitment to a cause. For that reason I am summarizing the entire story, including the ending—because the moral of this story lies in seeing the beginning in light of the end.

In the film *The Life of David Gale,* David Gale (Kevin Spacey) is a philosophy professor who likes to challenge his students. He is a firm believer in the abolition of the death penalty and constructs a way to influence the debate significantly. Here, in the beginning of the film, he is lecturing on the philosophy of controversial French psychoanalyst Jacques Lacan. Study question 5 explores the Lacan angle of the film.

An investigative reporter at a magazine gets a dream assignment: an exclusive interview with a death row inmate, just days before his execution for murder. The prisoner, David Gale, has selected the young reporter because of her reputation: She has spent a week in jail because she would not give up her source for one of her stories. So Gale knows that the reporter, Bitsey Bloom, has tenacity and integrity. Gale himself has spent six years on death row in Huntsville, Texas, for the rape and murder of Constance Harraway. He has now exhausted his appeals and has only three days left before he will be put to death. He used to be a professor of philosophy at the University of Austin and—what's more significant—he used to be a high-profile death penalty abolitionist, a member of "Death Watch," who debated capital punishment on TV with the governor of Texas. And now, having kept silent for six years, he wants to tell his story. When Bitsey first sits down in front of David Gale, with guards monitoring the interview, he says to her that someone on death row is no longer a person, just a crime—and he wants to be remembered for his life, not just for his death. He has claimed innocence from the beginning, but we also sense that he has no hope that his life will be spared—he is resigned to die. And in three days of interviews we get his story in flashbacks, as he tells it (and as viewers, we should remember that since he tells the story, it is the version he wants us to believe is true).

First we see Gale as a philosophy professor, lecturing on the French twentieth-century psychoanalyst Lacan, summarizing one of Lacan's theories: that we can't have our fantasy and still want it—that our desires must remain unfulfilled for us to still want them—and so to be fully human is to live by ideals and ideas, not through wishes. And, "In the end, the only way we can measure the value of our lives is to value the lives of others." Only later do we, the viewers, realize that this is the blueprint for Gale's entire purpose in life.

A pretty female student, Berlin, approaches him after class—she is failing the class and will do "anything" to pass. Gale whispers to her, suggestively, that he'll give her a very good grade if she will . . . study hard. That same evening, things take an ugly turn: David is at a party for students and professors. His young son is at home with a sitter, and his wife is in Spain, apparently with a lover. At the party, Berlin shows up, and Gale learns that she has been dropped because of failing grades—she puts up a brave front and makes it clear to Gale that since she is no longer a student, they are now free to have an affair. Gale is drunk, and they end up having rough sex in the bathroom. Next day he relates this folly to his good friend Constance Harraway, a fellow professor and Death Watch member—and the later murder victim. Constance is appalled that David would be so stupid, but she has more important things to focus on: The TV debate with the governor is coming up, David hasn't done his homework, and what they need is an example of an innocent man or woman who has in effect been executed—and they can't come up with evidence to that effect. She says that finding an innocent man on death row will only show that the system works—they need an *executed* innocent man to force a moratorium on capital punishment in Texas. During the debate Gale loses his cool and is caught by the governor because he can't come up with evidence that an innocent person has been executed in Texas. But the day is about to get much worse: Outside the studio David Gale is arrested for rape—Berlin has accused him of sexual assault. As David relates the story to Bitsey, we hear that the charges are eventually dropped, and Berlin sends him a postcard in which she writes how sorry she is for the whole thing. But even so, the consequences are devastating: He loses his job; his wife leaves him and takes his son along to Spain; he loses his house and starts drinking heavily. At some point, in a flashback, we see him reduced to being a drunk on a downtown street, ranting about the Greek philosophers he used to teach in his classes—Socrates was ugly, Plato was fat, and Aristotle was a prissy dresser! And yet, because of a chance he might get custody of his son, he cleans up his act, goes to AA meetings, and gets a blue-collar job—and he keeps on being an abolitionist. But eventually he is even kicked out of Death Watch—he is a liability. The final blow is when he learns that Constance is dying from leukemia.

Bitsey has become engaged in David's story in spite of herself—she prides herself on being objective. Two days earlier she believed that David was guilty and deserved death, but strange things start happening after she and an intern go to Constance's house, which has been turned into a ghoulish museum. A gothic girl shows them around, and Bitsey sees the layout of the kitchen and the chalk marks on the floor where the body was found. Later that night she finds a tape placed in her hotel room, with the actual death scene: Constance, naked on the floor, quietly dying, handcuffed, with duct tape over her mouth and a plastic bag tied around her neck—and according to court reports, with the key to the cuffs in her stomach, swallowed before her death. Bitsey is now convinced that Gale has been framed, to make abolitionists look crazy—but we also hear from the intern that Gale apparently could have received a life sentence had his lawyer not messed up. Even so, Gale stood by him and didn't request another lawyer.

The interview series with Gale continues. On the last day of Constance's life, she and David talk philosophically about death: She is not resigned to go, but she is so tired and frightened—and she regrets not having had more sex than she's had. In his own way David loves her, and they make love—which is why Constance had his semen in her when she was found. A close friend of Constance's and a fellow Death Watch abolitionist, Dusty (who wears a cowboy hat), has shown up from time to time, and he is also there now. And then there is a gap in Gale's story—he meanders around town, sleeps in his car, and is arrested, for the rape and murder of Constance.

What happened that night? Can Bitsey find out before Gale's execution the next day? She is determined to help, but he tells her that she is not there to save him but to save his son's memory of his father. And sometimes, maybe death is a gift . . .

Now Bitsey is on a mission. She goes back to Constance's house with the intern and puts heself in the spot of the victim, to perform an experiment—she cuffs herself and places a bag over her head. Sure enough, after a minute she begins to struggle; it is not a quiet agony. When she is freed, she has found the clue: Constance did it herself, David didn't kill her. But why make it look like a murder? Because Death Watch needs an *executed innocent* person to further their cause! And to Bitsey, Dusty is the only possible suspect. She and the intern lure Dusty away from his home and ransack his place—and find a videotape, addressed to Bitsey herself. This videotape has the whole death scene on it, with Dusty stepping into the frame after Constance's death—but Bitsey wasn't meant to see it until *after* David's execution.

Desperate, Bitsey tries to reach the prison before David's execution; does she make it in time? Outside the prison the crowd is howling, "ugly faces screaming for revenge," to quote a previous Reading. But David is executed right on schedule—Bitsey doesn't manage to save him. Devastated, she believes this to be the end, as we, the audience, do. But there is an epilogue: As the nation watches, Constance's death tape implications hit the news; it becomes clear that an innocent man has been executed—and the debate about a Texas moratorium on the death penalty has begun. As a commentator says, in death David Gale achieved what he worked for in life. But was this the death of a martyr? In the mail Betsey receives yet another tape—the original, with the final scene. We see who steps up to the camcorder to shut it off, and that man is David Gale himself.

Study Questions

1. What does it mean for our understanding of the whole story that David himself removed the tape? Look for clues in the summary to the ending of the film.

2. Is David a hero, or is he a deceitful conspirator? Can one be both? Is there another possibility? Does the final scene of the tape undercut David's own intentions of sacrificing himself? And what do you think about Constance's decision to participate in her own death, to make a moral point?

3. Is this a film about the death penalty, about believing in a cause, about making one's life count, or perhaps a bit of all of those elements? In the end, is it an abolitionist film? Who, in effect, are we supposed to root for?

4. From Chapter 5 you'll remember the theory of utilitarianism. Would it be fair to say that David Gale believes in the idea that the end (ending capital punishment) justifies the means (faking a murder)? Does that make him a utilitarian?

5. The reference to the French psychoanalyst Jacques Lacan may have intrigued you. It is indeed not just a passing reference but adds a deeper meaning to the film, according to Rose Pacatte, the director of the Pauline Center for Media Studies. In an essay, "Sex, Lies, and Videotape: What Is the Value of a Human Life," she writes,

> If you are familiar with linguistic theory (not as boring as it sounds—honest!), then the script for *The Life of David Gale* takes on deeper levels of meaning and shows an intelligence that goes beyond ordinary entertainment. Why so? Because the reference to Lacan makes the film become an invitation to viewers to examine the structures of language, meanings and values that the powers in our nation, such as government, the news media and the Church, use to communicate. Whether we think that capital punishment "makes sense" or not, it behooves us to examine how we reached that conclusion. Thought and language are inextricably entwined with how we live within our culture. As Alan Parker [the director] hoped, his film offers us a "space" to examine and "deconstruct" the place of the human person in society, especially in relation to capital punishment, and just how "free" we really are.

Is Pacatte right? Is the film an invitation for us to reexamine our thoughts and language about who we are as persons? If you are familiar with Lacan, you may want to engage in a discussion about that.

Credits

Glossary

ableism: Discrimination against the disabled.

abolitionism: Today: the viewpoint that the death penalty ought to be abolished. *See* retentionism.

absolution: Forgiveness; usually God's forgiveness.

absolutism: The ethical theory that there is a universal set of moral rules that can and should be followed by everybody. Also referred to as *hard universalism.*

absurdity: The existentialist concept that life is meaningless because there is no God to determine right and wrong (or because we can't know what God's values are, if God happens to exist).

acculturation: Cultural development.

act utilitarianism: The classical version of utilitarianism that focuses on the consequences of a single act.

ad hominem argument: A logical fallacy (a formally faulty argument) that assumes that because a person is who he or she is, his or her viewpoint must be wrong.

ad misericordiam fallacy: Appeal to pity.

ageism: Discrimination against elderly people (or anyone from a different generation) because of their age.

agnosticism: The view that God is unknown or that it cannot be known whether or not there is a God.

altruism: Concern for the interests of others. Extreme (ideal) altruism: concern for the interests of others while disregarding one's own interests. Moderate altruism (also known as Golden Rule altruism or reciprocal altruism): taking others' interests into account while being concerned for one's own interests as well.

ambiguity: Quality exhibited in an expression or statement that can be interpreted in different ways.

anamnesis: Greek: re-remembering. Plato's theory of remembering the truth about the Forms, forgotten at birth.

androgynism: Male and female nature in the same individual, in terms of either sex (biological) or gender (cultural).

android: An artificial intelligence; a robot made to resemble a human being. Literally: manlike. There is no accepted word for a female android, but the equivalent would be *gyneoid.*

angst: Existentialist term for anxiety or anguish, a feeling of dread without any identifiable cause. Most frequently felt when one has to make important decisions. Different from *fear,* where the object of the emotion is known.

anime: A Japanese genre of animated films.

animism: The form of religion that sees all elements of nature as enspirited.

anthropocentrism: Viewing everything from an exclusively human perspective.

anthropology: The study of humans. Physical anthropology: the study of human biology and biological prehistory. Cultural anthropology: the study of human cultures.

anthropomorphism: Literally: making into a human shape. Projecting human characteristics into the behavior of other animals.

antiquity: Usually refers to the historical time period in ancient cultures around the Mediterranean after the invention of writing (about 6,000 years ago) and before the early Middle Ages (approx. 500 C.E.).

anxiety: *See* angst.

approximation: To approach something with as much accuracy as the conditions allow.

arbitrary: Coincidental, without meaning or consistency.

artificial womb: Medical environment allowing a fetus to grow to maturity outside a mother's womb.

asceticism: Denying oneself physical pleasures and indulgence.

ataraxia: Epicurus's highest form of pleasure, having peace of mind as a result of freedom from pain.

atheism: The conviction that there is no God.

authenticity: Being true to yourself, having personal integrity. Existentialism: not succumbing to the idea that you have no free choice. *See* bad faith.

auto-icon: An image of oneself that consists of oneself. Bentham's term for his own planned future position as a stuffed corpse on display.

autonomy: Independence; a state achieved by those who are self-governing. Autonomous lawmaker: Kant's term for a person using the categorical imperative without regard for personal interest, arriving at something he or she would want to become a universal law. Moral autonomy: being capable of and allowed to make moral decisions on your own.

backward-looking justice: Correcting past wrongs.

bad faith: Existentialist term for the belief that you have no choice; the belief that you can transform yourself into a thing with no will or emotions.

begging the question: A logical fallacy whereby a person who is supposed to prove something assumes from the start that it is a fact.

Being-there: Heidegger's term for human beings, or at least for beings who are self-aware.

benevolence: Interest in the well-being or comfort of others.

bibliotherapy: Using books, usually stories of fiction, in therapy sessions to facilitate patients' understanding of themselves and their situation and options.

bipartisan: "Of two parties," politically neutral or objective.

blog, blogger: From *weblog,* personal websites devoted to opinion and observations, often political.

care: (1) Heidegger's concept of human existence, involving a *Care-structure,* being engaged in living; (2) Gilligan's concept of ethics as it is typically viewed by women—*an ethics of care* rather than an *ethics of justice.*

catalyst: A person or agent that causes something to happen.

categorical imperative: Kant's term for an absolute moral rule that is justified because of its logic: If you can wish for your maxim to become a universal law, your maxim qualifies as a categorical imperative.

catharsis, cathartic: Cleansing. *See* Aristotle's theory of drama, Chapter 2.

causality, causal explanation: The chain of cause and effect. Aristotle's theory of causation: material cause (the material aspect of a thing), efficient cause (the maker of a thing), formal cause (the idea of a thing), and final cause (the purpose of a thing).

character arc: A concept used in screenwriting and narrative theory. A character in the story undergoes a certain development leading to a conclusion.

chauvinism: Originally: excessive feeling of nationalism, from the Frenchman Chauvin. Today it usually means male chauvinism (sexism from a male point of view).

classical feminism: The feminist view that women and men ought to be considered persons first and gendered beings second. Gender differences are due to "nature" rather than "nurture."

cloning: Creating a genetic copy of another individual, either through a process whereby multiple twins are created or through a process whereby a cell nucleus is taken from the original individual, implanted in an emptied ovum, and allowed to develop into an embryo. If the embryo is terminated within ten to fourteen days, *stem cells* may be harvested. If an embryo can survive and be carried to term, a cloned individual is the result. Cloning will not result in a perfect copy of another individual, physically or mentally, because of the variety of circumstances surrounding the growth process that can't be duplicated. *See also* reproductive cloning *and* therapeutic cloning.

cognitive, cognition: The faculty of knowing, examining something rationally.

collateral damage: Unintentional and unavoidable civilian casualties during a war.

communitarianism: A moral and political theory that the individual receives his or her identity from his or her community and can flourish only within the community. The theory is found in the ancient Greek tradition but is also evident in traditional African tribal cultures. Modern communitarians mentioned in this book include Alasdair MacIntyre and Elizabeth Wolgast. In addition, Hillary Rodham Clinton has declared herself a communitarian with the publication of her book, *It Takes a Village.*

conceptualize: Make a vague notion into a concept with a clear definition that can be used in a description or an argument.

condition of possibility: What makes something possible, or what makes it come into being.

consequentialism: A theory that focuses exclusively on the consequences of an action. Utilitarianism is the best-known consequentialist theory, but ethical egoism also qualifies as an example of consequentialism.

Continental philosophy: Philosophical traditions from the European continent (excluding British traditions).

contractarianism: The theory that only humans can have rights, because only humans can enter into agreements (contracts) and recognize duties springing from those agreements.

correlative: A term or a concept that is understood in its relation to other concepts. The fallacy of the suppressed correlative: If terms are correlative, like *hot/cold,* and *tall/short,* they help define each other. If one is suppressed, the other ceases to have any meaning.

counterfable/countermyth: A story/fable/myth told deliberately to prove another story, type of story, or idea wrong.

criminal justice: Punishment of people found guilty of crimes.

criterion: A test, rule, or measure for distinguishing between true and false, relevant and irrelevant. A standard for a correct judgment. Plural: *criteria.*

Crusades, the: Military expeditions undertaken by European Christians from the eleventh through the thirteenth centuries to recover the Holy Land from the Muslims.

cultural diversity: The recognition of a variety of ethnic and racial groups within a given region (all the way from a neighborhood to planet Earth).

cultural imperialism: A critical term for the attitude of imposing one's cultural accomplishments and moral convictions on other cultures.

cultural relativism: The theory that different societies or cultures have different moral codes. A descriptive theory.

culture war: Ideological disagreement between liberal and conservative values.

cynicism: Distrust in evidence of virtue or disinterested motives. Pessimism. Originally a Greek school of thought believing that virtue, not pleasure or intellect, was the ultimate goal of life. Deteriorated into the idea of self-righteousness.

debt-metaphor: English's term for using the terms *owing* and *debt* in situations where they may or may not be appropriate. Appropriate use: a situation in which favors are owed. Inappropriate use: a situation of friendship or family relationship.

deduction: The scientific and philosophical method of identifying an item of absolute truth (an axiom) and using

this as a premise to deduce specific cases that are also absolutely true.

deep ecology: Coined by philosopher Arne Næss, it is a radical environmentalist concept that humans are only one of many species on the planet, and that all species have an equal right to live.

deontology: Duty-theory. An ethical theory that disregards the importance of consequences and focuses only on the rightness or wrongness of the act itself.

descriptive: Describing a phenomenon without making an evaluative or judgmental statement. Opposite of normative.

deterrence: A concept of criminal justice: punishing criminals with the intent to deter them (*specific* deterrence) or others (*general* deterrence) from committing the same crime.

dialectic method: Socrates' method of guiding his students to their own realization of the truth through a conversation, a dialogue. Also called the Socratic method.

dichotomy: An "either-or" statement. A false dichotomy: an either-or statement that ignores other possibilities.

didactic: Done or told for the purpose of teaching a lesson.

difference feminism: The feminist view that women and men are fundamentally different, morally and psychologically due to human nature.

dilemma: The situation of having to choose between two courses of action that either exclude each other or are equally unpleasant.

distributive justice: Fair distribution of social goods.

divine command theory: A theological theory that God has created the laws of morality; in other words, something is right because God commands it. Opposed to *natural law theory,* which claims that God commands something because it is right. *See also* natural law.

double effect: A principle primarily found within Catholic ethics: An action that is otherwise prohibited can be permitted, provided that it is an *unintended* side effect to some other, necessary action; that the effect of the primary action is *proportionately very serious,* and the effect of the secondary action is *unavoidable.* The principle is used to justify rare cases of euthanasia and abortion, among others.

dualism: The metaphysical theory that reality consists of matter and mind. Also used as a term for any theory of opposite forces.

egalitarian: A theory that advocates social equality.

Ego: Freud's term for the human experience of the self. *See also* Superego *and* Id.

ego integrity: Erikson's term for mental equilibrium, accepting one's past, and not playing the "what if" game with oneself.

elitism: The belief that a certain advantage (for instance, knowledge, education, or wealth) should be reserved for a small part of the population, an elite.

embedded journalist: A journalist who travels with a military force.

emotionalism: The moral philosophy that moral values derive from emotions, not from reason. David Hume is considered the primary emotionalist.

empiricism: The philosophical school of thought that claims humans are born without knowledge, that the mind is an empty slate (*tabula rasa*) at birth, and that all knowledge comes through the senses.

end in oneself: Kant's term for a person. Persons (rational beings) should be regarded as dignified beings who have their own goals in life; they should not be used as a means to an end only. *See* means to an end, merely.

end justifies the means, the: The statement of a consequentialist: Only the consequences count, not how they are brought about.

enfranchisement: Having rights, and thus political power. (*Disenfranchisement* means having those powers taken away.)

Enlightenment, the: In the European and American cultural tradition, the eighteenth century saw a new focusing on the rights of the individual, the importance of education, and the objectivity of science. Also called the *Age of Reason* or the Western Enlightenment; rationality was considered the ultimate cultural goal by scientists, philosophers, and many politicians.

epistemology: Theory of knowledge. One of the main branches of traditional philosophy.

equilibrium: In this book: A well-balanced mind, capable of fair judgment.

equity feminism: The feminist view that the battle for equality has been won and that further insistence on women's inequality only serves to make women into victims.

essence: A thing's inner nature. "Essence precedes existence": the traditional philosophical conception of reality, including human nature; the theory that there is a design or purpose that nature must follow.

ethical egoism: The theory that everybody ought to be egoistic/selfish/self-interested.

ethical pluralism: Several moral systems working simultaneously within one culture.

ethical relativism: The theory that there is no universal moral code and that whatever the majority of any given society or culture considers morally right is morally right for that culture. A normative theory. *See also* cultural relativism.

ethical will: Personal legacy letter summarizing one's values and life lessons.

ethicist: A person professionally or vocationally involved with the theory and application of ethics.

ethics: The study, questioning, and justification of moral rules.

ethics of conduct: The study of moral rules pertaining to decisions about what course of action to take or "what to do."

ethics of virtue: The study of moral rules pertaining to the building of character or "how to be."

ethos: The moral rules and attitudes of a culture.

eudaimonia: Greek: well-spirited, contentment, happiness. Aristotle's term for the ultimate human goal.

Eurocentric: A critical term meaning that American culture is overly focused on its European roots. Possibly a misnomer, since Americans rarely focus on European traditions, politics, and history but, rather, on the European *legacy* for mainstream American culture.

euthanasia: Mercy killing; doctor-assisted suicide. Literally: "good death," from Greek. Voluntary euthanasia: requested by the patient. Involuntary euthanasia: (a) The patient is killed against his or her will; (b) The patient cannot communicate his or her wish, so the decision is made by the family (also called nonvoluntary euthanasia). Active euthanasia: helping someone to die at his or her request. Passive euthanasia: withholding treatment that will not help a terminally ill patient.

evidence: A ground or reason for certainty in knowledge. Usually empirical evidence; facts gathered in support of a theory.

exemplar: A model, an example for others to follow.

existence precedes essence: Existentialist belief that humans aren't determined by any essence (human nature) but exist prior to any decision about what and how they ought to be.

existentialism: A Continental school of thought that believes all humans have freedom of the will to determine their own life.

extrinsic value: *See* instrumental value.

fable: A short narrative with a moral, introducing persons, animals, or inanimate things as speakers and actors.

fallacy: A flaw in one's reasoning; an argument that does not follow the rules of logic.

falsification, principle of: The concept that a valid theory must test itself and allow for the possibility of situations in which the theory doesn't apply. In a sense, part of the verification process of a theory is being able to hypothetically falsify it.

fatalism: The theory that life is determined by a higher power and that our will can't change our destiny.

faux pas: French: a misstep, a social blunder.

fecundity: Being fruitful, having good consequences.

first-wave feminism: Feminism from the eighteenth century until approximately 1920. *See* second- and third-wave feminism.

forensic: Related to the use of scientific or medical procedures to investigate a death.

Forms, theory of: Plato's metaphysical theory of a higher reality that gives meaning and existence to the world we experience through our senses. This higher reality is accessible through the mind. Example: a perfect circle; it doesn't exist in the world of the senses, but it does exist in the intelligible world of Forms.

fortitude: Strength of mind and courage in the face of adversity.

forward-looking justice: Creating good future social consequences. *See also* consequentialism.

free will: The notion that we can make choices that are not completely determined by our heredity and our environment.

fundamentalism: A religious approach to reality that interprets the dogmas and sacred scriptures of the tradition literally.

gender-neutral: Not gender-specific. Usually used when referring to language. Examples: Scientists must do their research well. Nurses should take good care of their patients.

gender-specific: Applying to one sex only. Examples of gender-specific language: A scientist must do *his* research well. A nurse should take good care of *her* patients.

genetic engineering: Scientific manipulation of the DNA code of an individual (human, animal, or plant), usually to enhance certain desired characteristics or eliminate congenital diseases.

genetic fallacy, the: Assuming that something can be fully explained by pointing to its original/first condition.

genocide: The murder of all or most of a population.

genre: A literary type of story (or film), such as horror, Western, or science fiction.

Golden Mean, the: The Greek idea of moderation. Aristotle's concept of virtue as a relative mean between the extremes of excess and deficiency.

golem: A Jewish legend of an artificial person that must be controlled lest he overpower his human maker.

good will: For Kant, having good will means having good intentions in terms of respecting a moral law that is rational and deserves to be a universal law.

greatest-happiness principle, the: *See* utility.

hard determinism: The theory that everything can, in principle, be predicted and understood with 100 percent accuracy, because everything is an effect of a previous cause.

hard universalism: *See* absolutism.

harm principle, the: John Stuart Mill's idea that one should not interfere with other people's lives unless those people are doing harm to others.

hedonism: Pleasure-seeking. The paradox of hedonism: The more you look for pleasure, the more it seems to elude you. Hedonistic calculus: Bentham's pros-and-cons system, in which pleasures are added and pains subtracted to find the most utilitarian course of action.

heterogeneous: Consisting of dissimilar or diverse elements.

hierarchy: A structure of higher and lower elements, ordered according to their relative importance.

homogeneous: Consisting of similar elements.

human condition, the: What it means to be a human being, usually in terms of inevitable facts: having physical and spiritual needs, being a social creature, and being subject to illness and aging.

hyphenated: A political term for the distinction between one's national or ethnic ancestry and one's American identity, such as *Swedish-American*. To be "hyphenated" indicates for some people that one's loyalties are divided. Today it is common to omit the hyphen, as in *Swedish American*.

hypothetical imperative: A command that is binding only if one is interested in a certain result. An "if-then" situation.

Id: Freud's term for the Unconscious, the part of the mind that the conscious self (the Ego) has no access to but that influences the Ego.

idealism: The metaphysical theory that reality consists of mind only, not matter.

immutability: The quality of remaining stable and unchanged.

inalienable: Incapable of being taken or given away.

incapacitation: A concept of criminal justice: punishing a criminal with the intent of making the public safe from his or her criminal activity. May refer to incarceration as well as other forms of punishment, including capital punishment.

incredulity: Skepticism; refusal to believe something.

induction: The scientific and philosophical method of collecting empirical evidence and formulating a general theory based on those specific facts. The problem of induction: Because one never knows if one has collected enough evidence, one can never achieve 100 percent certainty through induction.

institutionalized cruelty: Hallie's term for cruelty (psychological or physical) that has become so established, it seems natural to both victimizer and victim.

instrumental value: To have value for the sake of what further value it might bring. Also known as extrinsic value; good as a means to an end. *See* means to an end.

intersexual: A person with both male and female genitalia.

intrinsic value: To have value in itself without regard to what it might bring of further value. Good in itself, good as an "end in itself." *See* end in oneself.

intuition: Usually, an experience of understanding that is independent of one's reasoning. Can also mean the moment of understanding, an "Aha" experience. Moral intuition: a gut-level feeling of right and wrong.

ipso facto: By the fact itself.

irony: Ridicule through exaggeration, praise, or understatement.

jus ad bellum: Just war: a war conducted in self-defense according to set rules.

jus in bello: Justice in war. Rules for proper conduct of war.

jus post bellum: Justice after war, in terms of punishment of war crimes and compensations for victims.

karma: Originally a belief associated with Hinduism that actions have consequences, either in this life or in the next. Now a modern expression of the concept that "what goes around, comes around."

kingdom of ends: Kant's term for a society of autonomous lawmakers who all use the categorical imperative and show respect to one another.

land ethic: Introduced by Aldo Leopold: Environmentally, humans are members of the entire community of animals, plants, soil and water, and should act responsibly.

leap of faith: Kierkegaard's concept of the necessary step from the ethical to the religious stage. It involves throwing yourself at the mercy of God and discarding all messages from your rational mind or your self-interested emotions.

lex talionis: The law of retaliation; an eye for an eye. A retributivist argument for punishment.

liberalism: A political theory that supports gradual reforms through parliamentary procedures and civil liberties.

libertarianism: (1) A theory of government that holds the individual has a right to life, liberty, and property; that nobody should interfere with those rights (negative rights); and that the government's role should be restricted to protecting those rights. (2) A theory that humans have free will independent of mechanistic causality.

master morality: Nietzsche's view of the morality of strong individuals in ancient times; includes respect for the enemy, loyalty to friends and kin, and scorn for weaker individuals. Leads to the concept of the Overman (Superman), the strong individual who has gone beyond the moral rules and sets his own standards of good and evil.

materialism: The metaphysical theory that reality consists of matter only, not mind.

matriarchy, matriarchal: A society in which women have great social influence and the words of older women within the family carry much weight. Sometimes taken to mean a society ruled by women.

maxim: Kant's term for the rule or principle of an action.

means to an end: Something used to achieve another goal, an end. *See* instrumental value.

means to an end, merely: Kant's term for reducing others to a stepping-stone for one's own purpose.

mental state: Any mind activity or mental image.

metaethics: The approach to ethics that refrains from making normative statements but focuses on the meaning of terms and statements and investigates the sources of normative statements.

metaphor: An image or an illustration that describes something in terms of something different. A figurative image such as "My boyfriend is a tiger."

metaphysics: The philosophical study of the nature of reality or of being.

misandry: Misgivings about, hatred of, or lack of trust in men.

misanthropy: Misgivings about, hatred of, or lack of trust in the goodness of human nature.

misogyny: Misgivings about, hatred of, or lack of trust in female human nature. There is no traditional equivalent term for mistrusting male human nature, but such a term might be *misandry*.

monism: A type of metaphysics that holds that there is one element of reality only, such as materialism or idealism.

monoculturalism: As opposed to multiculturalism. The concept of a dominant culture, viewing its history and cultural practices as the only significant contributions to the culture in question.

moral agent: A person capable of reflecting on a moral problem and acting on his or her decision.

moral cannibalism: Ayn Rand's description of any moral theory that advocates altruism.

morality, morals: The moral rules and attitudes that we live by, or are expected to live by.

mores: The moral customs and rules of a given culture.

multiculturalism: The policy of recognizing cultural diversity to the extent that all cultures within a given region are fairly represented in public life and education. Sometimes includes gender as cultural diversity. *See also* cultural diversity, pluralism, *and* particularism.

myth: A story or a collection of stories that give identity, guidance, and meaning to a culture. Usually these are stories of gods and heroes, but they may involve ordinary people too. In common language myth has come to mean "falsehood" or "illusion," but that is not the original meaning.

narrative: A story with a plot. Narrative structure: perceiving events as having a logical progression from a beginning through a middle to an ending.

narrative time: The time frame within which a story takes place. The experience of sharing this time frame as one reads or watches the story unfold.

naturalistic fallacy: The assumption that one can conclude from what is natural/a fact ("what is") what should be a rule or a policy ("what ought to be"). Not all philosophers think this is a fallacy.

natural law: A view introduced to the Catholic Church by Thomas Aquinas that what is natural for humans (in other words, what God has intended) is good for humans. What is natural for humans includes: preservation of life, procreation, socialization, and pursuit of knowledge of God.

natural rights: The assumption that humans (and perhaps also nonhumans) are born with certain inalienable rights.

negative command: Hallie's term for a moral command involving a prohibition, such as "Don't lie" or "Don't cause harm." *See* positive command.

negative rights: Rights not to be interfered with; usually includes the right to life, liberty, and property. Originally an element in John Locke's political philosophy; has become a defining element of modern Libertarian philosophy.

neo-classicism: A style of art and architecture in the seventeenth and eighteenth centuries that revived classical Greek and Roman forms. Also, any spiritual and philosophical movement that tries to recover the classical ideals of moderation and order.

nihilism: From the Latin *nihil,* nothing. The attitude of believing in nothing. Moral nihilism: the conviction that there are no moral truths.

normative: Evaluating and/or setting norms or standards. Opposite of descriptive.

objectification: Making an object, a thing, out of someone: disregarding his or her human dignity. Also reification, making a thing out of someone.

objective: The kind of knowledge that is supported by evidence and that has independent existence apart from experience or thought.

ontology: A philosophical discipline investigating the nature of existence.

original sin: The Christian belief that the disobedience of Adam and Eve is inherited by all humans from birth, so all humans are born sinful.

Other, the: A philosophical concept meaning either something that is completely different from yourself and all your experiences or someone who is different from you and is thus hard to understand.

Overman, or Superman: Nietzsche's term for the individual who has recognized his will to power and created his own system of values based on an affirmation of life.

pacifism: The belief that war and violence are morally wrong, regardless of the circumstances.

parable: A short narrative told to make a moral or religious point.

particularism: The branch of multiculturalism that believes people not belonging to the dominant culture should retrieve their self-esteem by learning about the traditions and accomplishments of their own cultural group rather than those of the dominant group or any other group. Also called exclusive multiculturalism.

paterfamilias: The male head of the household.

patriarchy: A society ruled by men, or a society in which men have great social influence.

philanthropy: Greek: loving humans. Doing good deeds, being charitable.

philology: The study of language, its structure and history.

phronesis: Aristotle's term for practical wisdom, our everyday decision-making process.

pleasure principle: Freud's term for the oldest layer of the human mind, which caters selfishly to our own pleasure. For most people it is superseded by the reality principle, at least most of the time.

pluralism: The branch of multiculturalism that believes racial and ethnic discrimination in a population of cultural diversity can be abolished by a shared orientation in one another's cultural traditions and history. Also called inclusive multiculturalism. Also: any theory or culture that includes several different viewpoints.

positive command: Hallie's term for a moral command to actively do something rather than merely refraining from doing something wrong (a negative command). Example: "Help another being in distress."

positive rights: Rights of entitlement. The theory that each individual has a right to the basic means of subsistence against the state, such as food, shelter, clothing, education, welfare, health services.

preconceived notion: An idea that is formed before actual knowledge or experience and that you don't think of questioning.

prerational: Before the use of reason; instinctive; belonging to human nature before the development of reason.

prescriptive: *See* normative.

presocial: Before the existence of society.

principle of utility: *See* utility.

procreation: Having offspring, giving birth.

protagonist: The hero of the story.

psychological altruism: The theory that everyone is always unselfish.

psychological egoism: The theory that everyone is selfish, self-interested.

psychosexual neutrality: The behaviorist theory that human sexuality is a matter of upbringing (nurture) rather than a hardwiring of the brain (nature).

radical feminism: The feminist view that the root cause of male dominance of women and discrimination against women must be examined.

rational being: Anyone who has intelligence and the capacity to use it. Usually stands for human beings, but may exclude some humans and include some nonhuman beings.

rationalism: The philosophical school of thought that claims humans are born with some knowledge, or some capacity for knowledge, such as logic and mathematics. Opposite of empiricism.

reality principle: Freud's term for the knowledge that we can't always have things our own way.

reductio ad absurdum: A form of argument in which you reduce your opponent's viewpoint to its absurd consequences.

rehabilitation: A concept of criminal justice: punishing a criminal with the intent of making him or her a better socialized person at the end of the term of punishment.

reification: *See* objectification.

relevance: Direct application to a situation; pertinence.

Renaissance: Literally: rebirth. The European cultural revival of the arts and sciences in the fourteenth through sixteenth centuries. This period marked the end of the Middle Ages.

reproductive cloning: Creating an identical individual from an existing person's cells. *See* therapeutic cloning.

restorative justice: Rehabilitation of criminals, and restitution to the victims.

retentionism: The viewpoint that the death penalty ought to be retained (kept as an option).

retribution: A concept of criminal justice: the logical dispensing or receiving of punishment in proportion to the crime. Sometimes known as "an eye for an eye," *lex talionis.* To be distinguished from vengeance, which is an emotional response that may exceed the severity of the crime.

retributive justice: Punishment of criminals in proportion to their crime.

revisionism: Advocacy of revision of former values and viewpoints. Today: refers mostly to a cynical revision of heroic values of the past.

rhetoric: The art of verbal persuasion.

Romanticism, the Romantic movement: A movement among artists, philosophers, and social critics in the late eighteenth and nineteenth centuries, partly based on the idea that emotion is a legitimate form of expression and can give access to higher truths without necessarily involving the intellect.

rule utilitarianism: The branch of utilitarianism that focuses on the consequences of a type of action done repeatedly, and not just a single act. *See* act utilitarianism.

satire: The use of sarcasm in a narrative criticism of conditions one doesn't approve of.

second-wave feminism: Feminism in the United States and Europe from the mid-1950s on. Some consider second-wave feminism to have ended by the mid-1980s; others see it as continuing.

selfish gene: Dawkins's theory that humans as well as animals have a disposition that favors themselves, but also the survival of their genes. Occasionally, animals (or humans) will sacrifice themselves so that their closely related relatives or offspring may survive.

Silver Rule, the: Do not do to others what you would not like them to do to you. A negative version of the Golden Rule, Do unto others as you would have them do unto you.

skepticism: The philosophical approach that we cannot obtain absolutely certain knowledge. In practice it is an approach of not believing anything until there is sufficient evidence to prove it.

slave morality: Nietzsche's concept of the morality of the "herd," people who in his view resent strong individuals and claim that meekness is a virtue.

slippery slope argument: A version of the *reductio ad absurdum* argument; you reduce your opponent's view to unacceptable or ridiculous consequences, which your opponent will presumably have to accept or else abandon his or her theory. Your opponent's argument must "slide down the slope" of logic. A way to defeat the slippery slope argument is to "draw the line" and defend your viewpoint on the basis that there is a difference between the "top of the slope" and the "bottom of the slope."

social contract: A type of social theory, popular in the seventeenth and eighteenth centuries, that assumes humans in the early stages of society got together and agreed on terms for creating a society.

soft universalism: The ethical theory that although humans may not agree on all moral rules or all customs, there are a few bottom-line rules we can agree on, despite our different ways of expressing them.

sophia: Greek: wisdom. Aristotle's term for theoretical wisdom, the highest intellectual virtue.

spatial: Associated with space.

straw man (straw dummy) argument: A logical fallacy that consists of attacking and disproving a theory invented for the occasion.

subjective opinion: One that is not supported by evidence, or is dependent on the mind and experience of the person.

subjectivism: Ethical theory that claims that your moral belief is right simply because you believe it; there are no intersubjective (shared) moral standards.

Superego: Freud's concept of the human conscience, the internalized rules of our parents and our society.

teleology: A theory of purpose. A teleological theory such as Aristotle's may assume that everything has a purpose. Also used to designate theories interested in the outcome of an action, that is, consequentialist theories.

temperance: In virtue theory this means moderation. In a modern context it may mean abstinence from alcohol.

temporal: Associated with time. Temporal being: a being living in time and understanding himself or herself in terms of a past, a present, and a future.

theology: The study of God and God's nature and attributes.

therapeutic cloning: Generally, duplicating and growing stem cells (cloning) as a form of medical treatment of illnesses. *See* reproductive cloning.

third-wave feminism: Feminism from the mid-1980s to the present day.

totalitarianism: A form of government that views the state as all-important and the lives of its citizens as disposable.

transgenic: Genetic engineering of an animal or a plant (or, theoretically, a human) with some genes from another species.

universal law: Kant's term for a moral rule that can be imagined as applying to everybody in the same situation and accepted by other rational beings.

universalizability: A maxim that is acceptable as a universal law.

universalization: The process by which one asks oneself whether one's maxim could become a universal law: "What if everybody did this?"

unrequited: Unreturned, nonreciprocal.

utilitarianism: The theory that one ought to maximize the happiness and minimize the unhappiness of as many people (or sentient beings) as possible.

utility: Fitness for some purpose, especially for creating happiness and/or minimizing pain and suffering. Principle of utility: To create as much happiness and minimize suffering as much as possible for as many as possible. Also: the greatest-happiness principle.

Utopia: Literally, no place. Sir Thomas More's term for a nonexistent world, usually used as a term for a world too good to be true. Utopia can also mean "good place." A bad place is known as "Dystopia."

Veneer Theory: The theory that values are merely a thin social veneer covering our basically selfish nature.

vengeance: Revenge. When used as a concept of criminal justice: an emotional response to punishment.

viability: The time in a pregnancy where a fetus could survive outside the mother's body.

vicariously: To experience something through the experiences of others.

Voir dire: The questioning of potential jurors during jury selection.

Way, the: Chinese: Tao (Dao). The morally and philosophically correct path to follow.

yin and yang: The two cosmic principles of Taoism, opposing forces that keep the universe in balance.

Selected Bibliography

Works of Nonfiction

Ammitzbøll, Marianne. *Den skjulte skat*. Copenhagen: Olivia, 1995.

Aristotle. *Nichomachean Ethics*. In *Introduction to Aristotle*, edited by Richard McKeon, translated by W. D. Ross. New York: Random House, 1947.

———. *Poetics*. In *Introduction to Aristotle*, edited by Richard McKeon, translated by Ingram Bywater. New York: Random House, 1947.

Arrison, Sonia. "New Anti-Terrorism Law Goes Too Far." Op-ed, *San Diego Union-Tribune*, October 31, 2001.

Austin, Jonathan D. "U.N. Report: Women's Unequal Treatment Hurts Economies." CNN.com, September 20, 2000.

Badinter, Elisabeth. *The Unopposite Sex*. Translated by Barbara Wright. New York: Harper & Row, 1989.

Beauvoir, Simone de. *The Ethics of Ambiguity*. Translated by Bernard Frechtman. New York: Philosophical Library, 1948.

———.*The Second Sex*. Translated by H. M. Parshley. New York: Knopf, 1952.

Bedau, Hugo A., ed. *Justice and Equality*. Englewood Cliffs, N.J.: Prentice-Hall, 1971.

Belenky, Mary Field, et al. *Women's Ways of Knowing*. New York: Basic Books, 1986.

Belsey, Andrew, and Chadwick, Ruth. "Ethics as a Vehicle for Media Quality." In *The Media and Morality*, edited by Robert M. Baird, William E. Loges, and Stuart E. Rosenbaum. New York: Prometheus Books, 1999.

Benedict, Ruth. "Anthropology and the Abnormal." *Journal of General Psychology* 10 (1934).

Bentham, Jeremy. *Principles of Morals and Legislation*. In *The Utilitarians*. New York: Anchor Books, 1973.

———. *The Works of Jeremy Bentham*, vol. 2. Edited by John Bowring. Edinburgh, 1838–43.

Berger, Fred. "Gratitude." In *Vice and Virtue in Everyday Life*, edited by Christina Hoff Sommers and Fred Sommers. Fort Worth: Harcourt Brace Jovanovich, 1985.

Bergson, Henri. *Time and Free Will*. Translated by F. L. Pogson. New York: Harper, 1960.

Bernasconi, Robert, and Wood, David, eds. *The Provocation of Levinas*. New York: Routledge, 1988.

Berteaux, John. "Defining Racism in the 21st Century." *Monterey Herald*, January 17, 2005.

———. "Unheard, Unseen, Unchosen." *Monterey Herald*, March 6, 2006.

Bok, Sisela. *Strategy for Peace*. New York: Random House, 1989.

Bonevac, Daniel, ed. *Today's Moral Issues*. Mountain View, Calif.: Mayfield, 1992.

Bonevac, Daniel, et al., eds. *Beyond the Western Tradition*. Mountain View, Calif.: Mayfield, 1992.

Booth, Wayne C. *The Company We Keep*. Berkeley: University of California Press, 1988.

———. "Why Ethical Criticism Fell on Hard Times." In *Ethics: Symposium on Morality and Literature* 98, no. 2 (January 1988). Chicago: University of Chicago Press.

Boss, Judith A. *Ethics for Life*. Mountain View, Calif.: Mayfield, 1998.

"Boy Sentenced to Watch *Saving Private Ryan*." Associated Press, August 20, 1998.

Brickhouse, Thomas B., and Smith, Nicholas D. *Socrates on Trial*. Princeton, N.J.: Princeton University Press, 1989.

The Cambridge Companion to John Stuart Mill. Edited by John Skorupski. New York: Cambridge University Press, 1998.

Carmody, Denise Lardner, and Carmody, John Tully. *How to Live Well: Ethics in the World Religions*. Belmont, Calif.: Wadsworth, 1988.

Chan, W., ed. *A Source Book in Chinese Philosophy*. Princeton, N.J.: Princeton University Press, 1963.

Chandler, Raymond. "The Simple Art of Murder." *Atlantic Monthly*, January 1945.

Cohen, Carl. "The Case for the Use of Animals in Biomedical Research." *New England Journal of Medicine* 315 (October 2, 1986).

Confucius. *The Analects*. New York: Dover, 1995.

Coren, Stanley. *The Intelligence of Dogs*. New York: Macmillan, 1994.

Dawkins, Richard. *The God Delusion*. New York: Houghton Mifflin, 2006.

———. *The Selfish Gene*. Oxford: Oxford University Press, 1976, 1989, 2006.

De George, Richard T. *Business Ethics*. New York: Macmillan, 1990.

"The *Discover* Interview: Marc Hauser." *Discover Magazine*, May 2007.

Donn, Jeff. "Company Says It Cloned Human Embryo." Associated Press, November 25, 2001.

Douglas, John, and Olshaker, Mark. *Obsession*. New York: Scribner, 1998.

Dworkin, Andrea. *Right-Wing Women*. New York: Perigree, 1993.

Dworkin, Ronald. *Taking Rights Seriously*. Cambridge, Mass.: Harvard University Press, 1977.

"Editor Sacked over Fake Photos." *The Globe and Mail*. May 15, 2004.

Ehrenburg, Ilya. "Bøger." In *Evige Tanker*, edited by Anker Kierkeby. Copenhagen: Westmans Forlag, 1951.

The Elder Edda. A selection translated from the Icelandic by Paul B. Taylor and W. H. Auden. London: Faber and Faber, 1973.

Encyclopedia of Ethics. Edited by Lawrence C. Becker and Charlotte B. Becker. New York: Garland, 1992.

English, Jane. "What Do Grown Children Owe Their Parents?" In *Having Children: Philosophical and Legal Reflections on Parenthood,* edited by Onora O'Neill and William Ruddick. New York: Oxford University Press, 1979.

Erikson, Erik. *Childhood and Society.* New York: Norton, 1964.

Ethics, Literature, Theory. Edited by Stephen George. Lanham, Md.: Rowman & Littlefield, 2005.

Ethics as First Philosophy: The Significance of Emmanuel Levinas. Edited by Adriaan T. Peperzak. New York: Routledge, 1995.

Ethics for Military Leaders I—II. Edited by Aine Donovan, Donald E. Johnson, George R. Lucas, Jr., Paul E. Rousch, and Nancy Sherman. American Heritage Christian Publishing, 1997.

Existentialism from Dostoyevsky to Sartre. Edited by Walter Kaufman. New York: Meridian Publishing Company, 1989.

Feinberg, Joel. "Psychological Egoism." In *Ethical Theory,* edited by Louis P. Pojman. Belmont, Calif.: Wadsworth, 1989.

———. "The Rights of Animals and Unborn Generations." In *Philosophy and Environmental Crisis,* edited by William T. Blackstone. Athens: University of Georgia Press, 1974.

Foot, Philippa. *Virtues and Vices.* Berkeley: University of California Press, 1978.

Freeman, Derek. *The Fateful Hoaxing of Margaret Mead.* Boulder, Colo.: Westview Press, 1999.

Friedman, Marilyn. "Feminism and Modern Friendship: Dislocating the Community." *Ethics* 99 (1989), University of Chicago Press.

Fuhrman, Mark. *Death and Justice: An Exposé of Oklahoma's Death Row Machine.* New York: HarperCollins 2003.

———. *Murder in Spokane.* New York: HarperCollins, 2001.

———. *Silent Witness: The Untold Story of the Death of Terri Schiavo.* New York: HarperCollins, 2005.

Furrow, Dwight. "Of Cave Dwellers and Spirits: The Trouble with Moral Absolutes." In *Moral Soundings: Readings on the Crisis of Values in Contemporary Life,* edited by Dwight Furrow. New York: Rowman & Littlefield, 2004.

Genovese, E. N. *Mythology: Texts and Contexts.* Redding, Calif.: C.A.T. Publishing, 1991.

George, Stephen. "The Ethical Dimensions of Richard Wright's *Native Son.*" In *Ethics, Literature, Theory,* edited by Stephen George. Lanham, Md.: Rowman & Littlefield, 2005.

Gilligan, Carol. *In a Different Voice.* Cambridge, Mass.: Harvard University Press, 1982.

Glenn, Linda MacDonald. "Ethical Issues in Genetic Engineering and Transgenics." June 2004. Retrieved January 13, 2005, from http://actionbioscience.org/biotech/glenn.html.

Gonzales, John Moreno. "Shacks, Tidy Yards and Tight-Lipped Neighbors Surround the Long-Time Home of a Suspect in the Killings of 3 Civil Rights Workers 40 Years Ago." Newsday.com, Jan. 10, 2005.

Graves, Robert. *The Greek Myths.* 2 vols. Penguin, 1960.

Gross, Hyman. *A Theory of Criminal Justice.* New York: Oxford University Press, 1979.

Guillo, Karen. "Study Finds No Death Penalty Bias." Associated Press, June 7, 2001.

Gyekye, Kwame. *An Essay on African Philosophical Thought: The Akan Conceptual Scheme.* New York: Cambridge University Press, 1987.

Hallie, Philip. "From Cruelty to Goodness." In *Vice and Virtue in Everyday Life,* edited by Christina Hoff Sommers and Fred Sommers. Fort Worth: Harcourt Brace Jovanovich, 1985, 1989.

———. *Tales of Good and Evil, Help and Harm.* New York: HarperCollins, 1997.

Harris, C. E., Jr. *Applying Moral Theories.* Belmont, Calif.: Wadsworth, 1986.

Hart, Richard E. "Steinbeck, Johnson, and the Master-Slave Relationship." In *Ethics, Literature, Theory,* edited by Stephen George. Lanham, Md.: Rowman & Littlefield, 2005.

Hauser, Marc D. *Moral Minds: How Nature Designed Our Universal Sense of Right and Wrong.* New York: HarperCollins, 2006.

Heidegger, Martin. *Being and Time.* Translated by John Macquarrie and Edward Robinson. New York: Harper & Row, 1962.

Herodotus. *The Histories.* Translated by Aubrey de Sélencourt. New York: Penguin Books, 1996.

Hertel, Hans. *Verdens litteraturs historie,* vols. 1–7. Copenhagen: Gyldendal, 1985–93.

Hinman, Lawrence. *Ethics, A Pluralistic Approach.* Austin: Harcourt Brace, 1993.

Hobbes, Thomas. *English Works.* Vol. 3. Edited by Sir W. Molesworth. London: J. Bohn, 1840.

Hohlenberg, Johannes. *Søren Kierkegaard.* Copenhagen: Aschehoug Dansk Forlag, 1963.

Horn, Tom. *The Life of Tom Horn, Government Scout and Interpreter.* 1904. Reprinted by Triton Press, 1988.

David Hume. *An Enquiry Concerning the Principles of Morals.* Oxford: Oxford Clarendon, 1957.

———. *An Enquiry Concerning the Principles of Morals.* In *Enquiries Concerning Human Understanding and Concerning the Principles of Morals,* 3rd ed., edited by L. A. Selby-Bigge, revised by P. H. Nidditch. Oxford: Clarendon, 1975.

Jalbert, Shana. "U.S. Must Address Real Problems, Forget Military Might, Turner Says." *Brown* (University) *Daily Herald,* February 12, 2002.

Johnson, Charles. "The Education of Mingo," 1977. *The Sorcerer's Apprentice.* New York: Macmillan, 1986.

Kalin, Jesse. "In Defense of Egoism." In *Ethical Theory,* edited by Louis P. Pojman. Belmont, Calif.: Wadsworth, 1989.

Kant, Immanuel. *Grounding for the Metaphysics of Morals.* Translated by James W. Ellington. Indianapolis: Hackett, 1981.

———. *The Metaphysics of Morals.* Introduction, translation, and notes by Mary Gregor. Cambridge: Cambridge University Press, 1991.

———. "On the Distinction of the Beautiful and Sublime in the Interrelation of the Two Sexes." In *Philosophy of Woman,* edited by Mary Briody Mahowald. Indianapolis: Hackett, 1983.

Kaplan, Alice. "The Trouble with Memoir." *Chronicle of Higher Education,* December 5, 1997.

Katz, Eric. "The Rings of Tolkien and Plato: Lessons in Power, Choice, and Morality." In *The Lord of the Rings and Philosophy: One Book to Rule them All,* edited by Gregory Bassman and Eric Bronson. Chicago: Open Court, 2003.

Kearney, Richard. *Dialogues with Contemporary Continental Thinkers: The Phenomenological Heritage.* Manchester: Manchester University Press, 1984.

Kellogg, Davida E. "Jus Post Bellum: The Importance of War Crimes Trials." *Parameters,* Autumn 2002.

Kemp, Peter. *Das Unersetzliche: Eine Technologie-Ethik.* Berlin: Wichen-Verlag, 1992.

———. "Etik og narrativitetens tre niveau'er." *Psyke & Logos,* Copenhagen, no. 1, vol. 17.

———. "Social Justice." In *The Good Society: Essays on the Welfare System at a Time of Change,* edited by Egon Clausen. Copenhagen: Ministry of Social Affairs, 1995.

Kemp, Peter, Lebech, Mette, and Rendtorff, Jacob. *Den bioetiske vending.* Copenhagen: Spektrum/Forum Publishers, 1997.

Kierkeby, Anker, ed. *Evige Tanker.* Copenhagen: Westmans Forlag, 1951.

Kierkegaard, Søren. *Enten-Eller. Anden Deel.* Copenhagen: H. Hagerup's Forlag, 1950.

———. *Johannes Climacus* (written 1842–43, first published 1912). Copenhagen: Gyldendal, 1967.

Kimmel, Michael. "A War Against Boys?" *Dissent Magazine,* Fall 2006.

Kittay, Eva Feder, and Meyers, Diana T., eds. *Women and Moral Theory.* Savage, Md.: Rowman & Littlefield, 1987.

Körner, Stephan. *Kant.* Harmondsworth, England: Penguin, 1955.

Kurtz, Stanley. "Free Speech and an Orthodoxy of Dissent." *Chronicle of Higher Education,* October 26, 2001.

Leake, Jonathan. "Scientists Teach Chimpanzee to Speak English." *The Sunday Times,* UK, July 25, 1999.

Le Guin, Ursula K. "It Was a Dark and Stormy Night." In *On Narrative,* edited by J. I. Mitchell. Chicago: University of Chicago Press, 1981.

Lehrer, Johan. "Hearts and Minds." *The Boston Globe,* April 29, 2007.

Leopold, Aldo. *A Sand County Almanac.* New York: Oxford University Press, 1987.

Lerner, Gerda. *The Creation of Feminist Consciousness.* New York: Oxford University Press, 1993.

———. *The Creation of Patriarchy.* New York: Oxford University Press, 1986.

Levin, Richard. *The Question of Socrates.* New York: Harcourt, Brace & World, 1961.

Levinas, Emmanuel. *Ethics and Infinity: Conversations with Philippe Nemo.* Pittsburgh: Duquesne University Press, 1985.

Lifton, Robert Jay, and Mitchell, Greg. *Who Owns Death? Capital Punishment, the American Conscience, and the End of Executions.* New York: Morrow, 2000.

Lin Yutang. *The Importance of Living.* London: Heinemann, 1937.

Lloyd, *Genevieve. The Man of Reason.* Minneapolis: University of Minnesota Press, 1984.

Locke, John. *Second Treatise on Government.* 1823. Works, 10 vols. London. Reprint, Germany: Scientia, Verlag Aalen, 1963.

Louv, Richard. "Line Between Reality and Science Fiction Has Been Eroding." *San Diego Union-Tribune,* October 28, 2001.

———. "War on Terrorism Calls for Re-evaluation of Military Ethics." *San Diego Union-Tribune,* October 21, 2001.

MacIntyre, Alasdair. *After Virtue.* Notre Dame, Ind.: University of Notre Dame Press, 1981, 1984.

Mackie, J. L. *Ethics: Inventing Right and Wrong.* New York: Penguin, 1977.

Mahowald, Mary Briody, ed. *Philosophy of Woman.* Indianapolis: Hackett, 1983.

Malinowski, Bronislaw. "Myth in Primitive Psychology." In *Magic, Science, and Religion.* Garden City, N.Y.: Doubleday Anchor, 1954.

Maltin, Leonard. *Leonard Maltin's TV Movies and Video Guide.* New York: Signet, 1996.

Mappes, Thomas A., and Zembaty, Jane S., eds. *Social Ethics.* 4th ed. New York: McGraw-Hill, 1992.

Mayo, Bernard. "Virtue or Duty?" In *Vice and Virtue in Everyday Life,* edited by Christina Hoff Sommers and Fred Sommers. Fort Worth: Harcourt Brace Jovanovich, 1985, 1989.

McCormick, Patrick T. "Adult Punishment Doesn't Fit the Underage Criminal." *Spokesman-Review,* September 4, 2001.

McLemee, Scott. "What Makes Martha Nussbaum Run?" *Chronicle of Higher Education,* October 5, 2001.

Medlin, Brian. "Ultimate Principles and Ethical Thought." In *Ethical Theory,* edited by Louis P. Pojman. Belmont, Calif.: Wadsworth, 1989.

Mencius. Translated by D. C. Lau. Harmondsworth, England: Penguin, 1970.

Mill, Harriet Taylor. "Enfranchisement of Women." In *Philosophy of Woman,* 3rd ed., edited by Mary Mahowald. Indianapolis: Hackett, 1994.

Mill, John Stuart. *Autobiography.* New York: Columbia University Press, 1924.

———. *On Liberty.* In *The Utilitarians.* New York: Anchor Books, 1973.

———. *The Subjection of Women.* Cambridge, Mass.: MIT Press, 1970.

———. *Utilitarianism.* In *The Utilitarians.* New York: Anchor Books, 1973.

Mitchell, J. I., ed. *On Narrative.* Chicago: University of Chicago Press, 1981.

Mitrovich, George, and Winters, Timothy. "Separated by a Hyphen." Op-ed, *San Diego Union-Tribune,* October 11, 2001.

"Moderates, Liberals Hear Call to Morality Debate." *Los Angeles Times,* November 10, 2004.

Morality in Criminal Justice. Edited by Daryl Close and Nicholas Meier. Belmont, Calif.: Wadsworth, 1995.

The Moral Philosophy of John Steinbeck. Edited by Stephen George. Lanham, Md.: Scarecrow Press, 2005.

Morlin, Bill, and White, Jeanette. *Bad Trick: The Hunt for Spokane's Serial Killer.* Spokane, Wash.: New Media Ventures, 2001.

Mulhauser, Dana. "National Group Rallies Students Who Question Campus Feminism." *Chronicle of Higher Education,* October 5, 2001.

Narveson, Jan. "Morality and Violence: War, Revolution, Terrorism." In *Matters of Life and Death,* 3rd ed., edited by Tom Regan. New York: McGraw-Hill, 1993.

Nathanson, Stephen. *An Eye for an Eye? The Morality of Punishing by Death.* Savage, Md.: Rowman & Littlefield, 1987.

———. "In Defense of 'Moderate Patriotism,'" *Ethics,* vol. 99 (April 1989).

Nestle, Marion, and Nesheim, Malden. "Who Knew? Melamine, the Not-So-Secret Ingredient." *BARK: The Modern Dog Culture Magazine,* April 2008.

"News Media's Credibility Crumbling." *Insight Magazine/ World Net Daily,* May 8, 2004.

Nietzsche, Friedrich. *Beyond Good and Evil.* Translated by Helen Zimmern. Riverside, N.J.: Macmillan, 1911.

———. *On the Genealogy of Morals.* Translated by Walter Kaufmann and R. J. Hollingdale. New York: Random House, 1969.

Nozick, Robert. *Anarchy, State and Utopia.* Basic Books, 1974.

Nussbaum, Martha. *Hiding from Humanity: Disgust, Shame, and the Law.* Princeton: Princeton University Press, 2004.

———. *Love's Knowledge.* New York: Oxford University Press, 1990.

"N.Y. Times Uncovers Dozens of Faked Stories by Reporter." *Washington Post,* May 11, 2003.

O'Brian, William. *The Conduct of Just and Unjust War.* Westport, Conn.: Praeger Publishers, 1981.

Oden, Thomas C., ed. *Parables of Kierkegaard.* Princeton, N.J.: Princeton University Press, 1978.

Orend, Brian. "Justice After War." *Ethics & International Affairs,* vol. 16.1 (Spring 2002).

Orenstein, Peggy. "What's Wrong with Cinderella?" *New York Times Magazine,* December 24, 2006.

Packe, Michael St. John. *The Life of John Stuart Mill.* New York: Capricorn, 1954.

Plato. *Apology.* In *Dialogues of Plato.* Translated by Benjamin Jowett. New York: Washington Square Press, 1968.

———. *Plato's Phaedrus.* Translated by W. C. Helmbold and W. G. Rabinowitz. New York: The Liberal Arts Press, 1956.

———. *The Republic.* Translated by G. R. U. Grube. Indianapolis: Hackett, 1974.

———. *The Republic of Plato.* Translated by Francis MacDonald Cornford. London: Oxford University Press, 1945.

Pojman, Louis P., ed. *Ethical Theory.* Belmont, Calif.: Wadsworth, 1989.

Punishment and the Death Penalty: The Current Debate. Edited by Robert M. Baird and Stuart E. Rosenbaum. New York: Prometheus, 1995.

Race and the Enlightenment: A Reader. Edited by Emmanuel Chukwudi Eze. Oxford: Blackwell, 1997.

Rachels, James. *The Elements of Moral Philosophy.* New York: Random House, 1986, 1999.

Rand, Ayn. "The Ethics of Emergencies," "Man's Rights." In *The Virtue of Selfishness.* New York: Penguin, 1964.

Rawls, John. "Justice As Fairness." *Philosophical Review* 67 (April 1958).

———. *The Law of Peoples.* Cambridge, Mass.: Harvard University Press, 2001.

———. "Two Concepts of Rules." *Philosophical Review* 1–13, 1955.

Rendtorff, Jacob Dahl, and Kemp, Peter. *Basic Ethical Principles in European Bioethics and Biolaw.* Vol. 1, *Autonomy, Dignity, Integrity and Vulnerability.* Copenhagen: Centre for Ethics and Law, and Barcelona: Institut Borja de Bioètica, 2000.

Rescher, Nicholas. *Distributive Justice.* Indianapolis: Bobbs-Merrill, 1966.

Ricoeur, Paul. *Interpretation Theory.* Fort Worth: Texas Christian University Press, 1976.

———. "Narrative Time." In *On Narrative,* edited by J. I. Mitchell. Chicago: University of Chicago Press, 1981.

———. *Time and Narrative.* 3 vols. Chicago: University of Chicago Press, 1985–1989.

Rosenstand, Nina. "Arven fra Bergson: En Virknings-historie." In *Den Skapende Varighet,* edited by Hans Kolstad. Oslo, Norway: H. Aschehoug & Co., 1993.

———. "Everyone Needs a Stone: Alternative Views of Nature." In *The Environmental Ethics and Policy Book,* 2nd ed., edited by Donald VanDeVeer and Christine Pierce. Belmont, Calif.: Wadsworth, 1998.

———. *The Human Condition: An Introduction to Philosophy of Human Nature.* New York: McGraw-Hill, 2002.

———. "Med en anden stemme: Carol Gilligans etik." In *Kvindespind—Kønsfilosofiske Essays,* edited by Mette Boch et al. Aarhus, Denmark: Forlaget Philosophia, 1987.

———. *Mytebegrebet.* Copenhagen: Gads Forlag, 1981.

———. "Myths and Morals: Images of Conduct, Character, and Personhood in the Native American Tradition." In *Tribal Mythologies,* edited by Helmut Wautischer. Aldershot: Ashgate, 1998.

———. "Stories and Morals." In *Ethics, Literature, Theory,* edited by Stephen George. Lanham, Md.: Rowman & Littlefield, 2005.

Rousch, Paul E. "Justification for Resort to Force." In *Ethics for Military Leaders,* edited by Aine Donovan, David E. Johnson, George R. Lucas, Jr., Paul E. Rousch, and Nancy Sherman. American Heritage Christian Publishing, 1997.

Rousseau, Jean-Jacques. *Confessions.* Baltimore: Penguin Books, 1954.

———. *On the Social Contract.* Translated by Donald A. Cress. Indianapolis: Hackett, 1983.

Ruth, Sheila, ed. *Issues in Feminism.* Mountain View, Calif.: Mayfield, 1998.

Sapontzis, Steve F. "The Moral Significance of Interests." *Environmental Ethics,* Winter 1982.

Sartre, Jean-Paul. Excerpt from *Being and Nothingness.* In *Reality, Man and Existence: Essential Works of*

Existentialism, edited by H. J. Blackham. New York: Bantam, 1965.

———. "Existentialism Is a Humanism." In *Existentialism from Dostoyevsky to Sartre,* edited by Walter Kaufmann. Translated by Philip Mairet. New York, Meridian Publishing Company, 1989.

Savage-Rumbaugh, Sue, and Lewin, Roger. *Kanzi: The Ape at the Brink of the Human Mind.* New York: Wiley, 1994.

Schmidt, Kaare. *Film-historie, kunst, industri.* Copenhagen: Gyldendal, 1995.

Schneewind, J. B. "The Misfortunes of Virtue." *Ethics* 101, October 1990. Chicago: University of Chicago Press, 1990.

Seligson, Amber Levanon, and Choi, Lauri. "Critical Elements of an Organizational Ethical Culture." *Ethics Resource Center Research Report,* 2006.

"Sexual Harassment Is Forbidden by Law." San Diego State University pamphlet, November 1994.

Shaw, William H. *Morality and Moral Controversies.* Englewood Cliffs, N.J.: Prentice-Hall, 1981.

Singer, Peter. *The Expanding Circle.* Farrar, Straus and Giroux, 1981.

Sommers, Christina Hoff. "Teaching the Virtues." *Imprimis.* Hillsdale College, Michigan, November 1991.

———. *The War Against Boys.* New York: Touchstone, Simon & Schuster, 2000.

———. *Who Stole Feminism?* New York: Simon & Schuster, 1994.

Sommers, Christina Hoff, and Sommers, Fred, eds. *Vice and Virtue in Everyday Life.* Fort Worth: Harcourt Brace Jovanovich, 1985, 1989.

Steifels, Peter. "Emmanuel Levinas, 90, French Ethical Philosopher." Obituary, *New York Times,* December 27, 1995.

Steinbeck, John. "Paradox and Dreams." *America and Americans.* New York: Viking Press, 1966.

Steindorf, Sara. "A Novel Approach to Work." *Christian Science Monitor,* January 29, 2002.

Stone, I. F. *The Trial of Socrates.* New York: Doubleday, 1988.

Stone, Oliver, and Sklar, Zachary. *JFK: The Book of the Film.* New York: Applause Books, 1992.

"Study of Monkeys Hints at a Thinking Ability Without Language." New York Times News Service, October 24, 1998.

"Sudanese Criticize Governor's Decree on Women." CNN.com, September 6, 2000.

Tannen, Deborah. *The Argument Culture.* New York: Random House, 1998.

———. *That's Not What I Meant!* New York: Ballantine, 1986.

———. *You Just Don't Understand.* New York: Morrow, 1990.

Taylor, Mark C. *Journeys to Selfhood: Hegel & Kierkegaard.* Berkeley: University of California Press, 1980.

Taylor, Paul W. *Principles of Ethics: An Introduction.* Belmont, Calif.: Wadsworth, 1975.

Taylor, Richard. *Good and Evil.* New York: Prometheus, 2000.

Trebilcot, Joyce. "Two Forms of Androgynism." *Journal of Social Philosophy,* January 1977.

2004 Child Fatality Report. State of Washington Office of the Family and Children's Ombudsman, May 30, 2006.

Tyre, Peg. "The Trouble with Boys." *Newsweek,* January 30, 2006.

"USA TODAY Editor Resigns After Reporter's Misdeeds." *USAToday,* April 20, 2004.

Waal, Frans B. M. de. "Do Humans Alone 'Feel Your Pain'?" *Chronicle of Higher Education,* October 26, 2001.

———. *Good Natured: The Origins of Right and Wrong in Humans and Other Animals.* Cambridge, Mass.: Harvard University Press, 1996.

———. *Primates and Philosophers: How Morality Evolved.* Princeton, N.J.: Princeton University Press, 2006.

Waltzer, Michael. *Spheres of Justice.* New York: Basic Books, 1984.

Warren, Mary Ann. "Human and Animal Rights Compared." In *Environmental Philosophy: A Collection of Readings,* edited by Robert Elliot and Arran Gare. State College: Pennsylvania State University Press, 1983.

———. "On the Moral and Legal Status of Abortion." *The Monist,* vol.57, no.1 (January 1973).

Weiss, Rick. "Test-Tube Baby Born to Save Ill Sister." *Washington Post,* October 3, 2000.

Wesley, John. "Reel Therapy." *Psychology Today,* February 2000.

Wilgoren, Jodi. "Death Knell for the Death Penalty?" New York Times News Service, April 15, 2002.

Williams, Bernard. *Morality: An Introduction.* New York: Harper & Row, 1972.

Williams, Ian. "China Sells Organs of Slain Convicts." *Observer* (UK), December 10, 2000.

Wolgast, Elizabeth. *The Grammar of Justice.* Ithaca, N.Y.: Cornell University Press, 1987.

Wollstonecraft, Mary. *A Vindication of the Rights of Women.* Excerpt in *Philosophy of Woman,* edited by Mary Briody Mahowald. Indianapolis: Hackett, 1983.

Wright, Tamra, Hughes, Peter, and Ainley, Alison. "The Paradox of Morality: An Interview with Emmanuel Levinas." In *The Provocation of Levinas,* edited by Robert Bernasconi and David Wood. New York: Routledge, 1988.

Zack, Naomi. *Thinking About Race.* Belmont, Calif.: Wadsworth, 1998.

Zimbardo, Philip. *The Lucifer Effect: Understanding How Good People Turn Evil.* New York: Random House, 2007.

Works of Literature

Andersen, Hans Christian. *Eventyr og Historier.* 16 vols. Odense, Denmark: Skandinavisk Bogforlag, Flensteds Forlag.

Beauvoir, Simone de. *The Woman Destroyed.* Translated by Patrick O'Brian. New York: Putnam, 1969.

Bennett, William J. *The Book of Virtues.* New York: Simon & Schuster, 1993.

Conrad, Joseph. *Lord Jim: A Tale.* New York: Bantam, 1981.

Dostoyevsky, Fyodor. *The Brothers Karamazov.* New York: Signet Classic, New American Library, 1957.

Euripides, *Medea.* In *Classical Mythology: Images and Insights,* by Stephen L. Harris and Gloria Plazner. Translated by Moses Hadas. Mountain View, Calif.: Mayfield, 1995.

Goethe, Johan Wolfgang von. *The Sorrows of Young Werther.* Translated by Elizabeth Mayer and Louise Bogan. New York: Vintage Books, 1973.

Graves, Robert. *The Greek Myths.* 2 vols. Harmondsworth, England: Penguin, 1960.

Grimm's Complete Fairy Tales. Garden City, N.Y.: Doubleday.

Huxley, Aldous. *Brave New World.* New York: Bantam, 1958.

Ibsen, Henrik. *A Doll's House.* In *The Collected Works of Henrik Ibsen,* vol. 7: *A Doll's House, Ghosts.* Introductions and translations by William Archer. New York: Scribner, 1906.

Jewkes, W. T., ed. *Man the Myth-Maker.* New York: Harcourt Brace Jovanovich, 1973.

Kafka, Franz. *The Basic Kafka.* New York: Simon & Schuster, 1979.

Kingsolver, Barbara. *The Poisonwood Bible.* New York: HarperTorch, 1998.

Lee, Spike, with Lisa Jones. *Do the Right Thing.* New York: Simon & Schuster, 1989.

Le Guin, Ursula K. "The Ones Who Walk Away from Omelas." In *The Wind's Twelve Quarters.* New York: Harper & Row, 1981.

Matheson, Richard. "Mantage." In *Shock I.* New York: Berkeley, 1961.

Niven, Larry. "The Jigsaw Man." In *Tales of Known Space: The Universe of Larry Niven.* New York: Ballantine, 1975.

Njal's Saga. Translated by Magnus Magnusson and Hermann Palsson. Baltimore: Penguin, 1960.

Poe, Edgar Allan. *Complete Tales and Poems.* New York: Barnes & Noble Books, 1992.

Rand, Ayn. *Atlas Shrugged.* New York: Signet, 1957.

Sartre, Jean-Paul. *No Exit.* New York: Random House, 1989.

Shelley, Mary. *Frankenstein.* New York: Bantam, 1981.

Singer, Isaac Bashevis. "A Piece of Advice." From *The Spinoza of Market Street.* Translated from Yiddish into English by Martha Glicklich and Joel Blocker. New York: Fawcett Crest, 1958.

Tarantino, Quentin. *Pulp Fiction, A Quentin Tarantino Screenplay.* New York: Hyperion, 1994.

Walker, Alice. *Possessing the Secret of Joy.* New York: Simon & Schuster, 1993.

Wessel, Johann Herman. "Smeden og Bageren." In *De gamle huskevers.* Edited by Fritz Haack. Copenhagen: Forlaget Sesam, 1980.

Selected Website Sources

Aldo Leopold, "The Land Ethic"
http://home.btconnect.com/tipiglen/landethic.html

Altruism is innate
http://www.washingtonpost.com/wpdyn/content/article/2007/05/27/AR2007052701056.html

Anti-terrorism vs. counterterrorism
http://www.tamilcanadian.com/page.php?cat=74&id=4946

AP falsification incident
http://www.worldnetdaily.com/news/article.asp?ARTICLE_ID=40331

Ape language research
http://www.gsu.edu/~wwwlrc/

Aristotle's biography
http://www.gradesaver.com/ClassicNotes/Authors/about_aristotle.html

http://www-history.mcs.st-andrews.ac.uk/Mathematicians/Aristotle.html

Aristotle's Lyceum
http://www.newadvent.org/cathen/01713a.htm

Army Sgt. 1st Class Paul Smith, Medal of Honor recipient
http://www.medalofhonor.com/PaulSmith.htm

Atlantic Monthly websites, Christina Hoff Sommers debate
http://www.theatlantic.com

Barbara Kingsolver
http://www.english.eku.edu/SERVICES/KYLIT/KINGSLVR.HTM

California's same-sex marriage bill
http://www.mercurynews.com/news/ci_6069432?nclick_check=1

California's Three Strikes Law
http://www.rand.org/publications/RB/RB4009/RB4009.word.html

CBS document scandal
http://www.southerndigest.com/vnews/displays.v/ART/2004/09/14/41472eba1033d

http://www.azcentral.com/news/articles/0910bush-memos10.html

Challenged in House of Lords
http://news.bbc.co.uk/2/hi/uk_news/politics/7190530.stm

Charles Dickens
http://www.worldwideschool.org/library/books/lit/charlesdickens/ATaleofTwoCities/Chap1.html

Charles Garner, Abu Ghraib trial
http://www.msnbc.msn.com/id/6795956/

Chiune and Yukiko Sugihara
http://www.jewishvirtuallibrary.org/jsource/Holocaust/sugihara.html

Christianity's development in the Roman Empire
http://www.roman-empire.net/religion/religion.html

Christine Korsgaard interview 2003
http://www.people.fas.harvard.edu/~korsgaar/CPR.CMK.Interview.pdf

Cloned wolves
http://www.telegraph.co.uk/news/main.jhtml?xml=/news/2007/03/27/wclone27.xml

http://www.timesonline.co.uk/tol/news/uk/science/article1571502.ece

CNN poll on support for the war in Iraq
http://www.cnn.com/2007/POLITICS/03/19/iraq.support/index.html

Congress passes anti-genetic discrimination bill
http://ap.google.com/article/ALeqM5g9PKo1Dr67gVSZWb-B4tOfMvmgDwD90D626G0

CSI: Crime Scene Investigation series
http://www.cbs.com/primetime/csi/main.shtml

Criminal justice ethics
http://www.lib.jjay.cuny.edu/cje/html/cje.html

David Hume online, A Treatise of Human Nature
http://www.class.uidaho.edu/mickelsen/texts/Hume%20Treatise/hume%20treatise3.htm

Death penalty facts
http://www.deathpenaltyinfo.org/

Death Penalty Information Center June 5, 2007
http://www.deathpenaltyinfo.org/FactSheet.pdf

Debating torture
http://www.pbs.org/newshour/bb/military/july-dec05/torture_12-02.html

Deliberate poisoning in Libby, MT
    http://www.spokesmanreview.com/breaking/
    story.asp?ID=11625

The Don Imus controversy
    http://www.spokesmanreview.com/opinion/
    story.asp?ID=184054&page=all

"Duke Probe Shows Failure of Post-Enron Ethics Classes"
    (Update2)
    http://www.bloomberg.com/apps/news?pid=20601103
    &sid=aEL5ZnKhQuXY&refer=u

Duke University business students cheating on tests
    http://www.bloomberg.com/apps/news?pid=20601103
    &sid=aEL5ZnKhQuXY&refer=u

Dystopia film discussion
    http://blogs.takepart.com/2008/02/13/top-10-dystopian-
    future-films-telling-us-to-act-now/

Ed Koch on Michael Moore's Farenheit 9/11
    http://www.newsmax.com/archives/articles/2004/6/28/
    190852.shtml

Ethical wills
    http://www.csmonitor.com/2004/0707/p11s02-lifp.html

Ethics in space
    http://www.cnn.com/2007/TECH/space/05/01/death.in
    .space.ap/index.html

Ethics Resource Center Research Report 2006
    http://www.ethics.org/erc-publications/organizational-
    ethical-culture.asp

Ethics Updates, edited by Lawrence Hinman
    http://ethics.acusd.edu/index.html

"Existentialism Is a Humanism"
    http://evans-experientialism.freewebspace.com/sartre02
    .htm

Fired because of use of word
    http://www.adversity.net/special/niggardly.htm

Gandhi
    http://www.mkgandhi.org/

The Golden Rule in 21 religions
    http://www.religioustolerance.org/reciproc.htm

The Great Ape Project
    http://www.greatapeproject.org

"Hearts and Minds," on the cognitive revolution
    http://www.boston.com/news/education/higher/articles/
    2007/04/29/hearts__minds/

Herrad of Hohenbourg
    http://home.infionline.net/~ddisse/herrad.html

"How Safe Is Our Food? FDA Could Do Better."
    http://blogs.usatoday.com/oped/2007/05/how_safe_is_
    our.html

Human-animal hybrid ban lifted in UK
    http://news.bbc.co.uk/2/hi/health/7193820.stm

Ibn Fadlan
    http://www.luth.se/luth/present/sweden/history/viking_
    age/Viking_age4.html

Illinois death penalty report
    http://www.cnn.com/2002/LAW/04/15/death.penalty.
    report/index.html

Immanuel Kant's "Perpetual Peace"
    http://www.mtholyoke.edu/acad/intrel/kant/kant1.htm

An Inconvenient Truth reviews
    http://www.nytimes.com/2006/05/24/movies/24trut.html?
    ex=1181188800&en=bdf41cd59071a377&ei=5070

    http://www.realclimate.org/index.php/archives/2006/05/
    al-gores-movie/

    http://www.reason.com/news/show/116471.html

Iraq had no link to al-Qaida
    http://www.chron.com/disp/story.mpl/world/5608384
    .html

Italian prisoners for life want to be executed
    http://politiken.dk/udland/article315769.ece

Jeremy Bentham's Auto-Icon
    http://www.ucl.ac.uk/Bentham-Project/info/jb.htm

Jessica Lynch on Pentagon cover-ups
    http://blog.oregonlive.com/breakingnews/2007/04/
    _getty_imagesjessica_lynch_tes_1.htm

    http://www.capitolhillblue.com/cont/node/2334

*John Jay College of Criminal Justice study of child abuse by
    priests*
    http://www.jjay.cuny.edu/churchstudy/main.asp

Jus post bellum
    http://www.carlisle.army.mil/usawc/Parameters/
    02autumn/kellogg.htm

    http://www.cceia.org/resources/journal/16_1/articles/
    277.html/_res/id=sa_File1/277_orend.pdf

Kierkegaard and Regine Olsen
    http://sorenkierkegaard.org/kw25.htm

Life of David Gale, *Analysis*
    http://www.daughtersofstpaul.com/mediastudies/reviews/
    filmdavidgale.html

Linda MacDonald Glenn
    http://www.actionbioscience.org/biotech/glenn.html

Locke's theory of property
    http://plato.stanford.edu/entries/locke-political/

Lord of the Rings, *list of characters*
    http://www.lord-of-the-rings.org/books.html

Lynndie England, Abu Ghraib trial
    http://www.usatoday.com/news/nation/2005-09-26-
    england_x.htm

Marine Cpl. James L. Dunham, Medal of Honor recipient
    http://www.mcnews.info/mcnewsinfo/moh/

Martin Luther King's "A Letter from (a) Birmingham Jail"
    http://almaz.com/nobel/peace/MLK-jail.html

Match Point
    http://en.wikipedia.org/wiki/Match_Point

Michael Gurian
    http://www.michaelgurian.com/

Michael Walzer, *Spheres of Justice*
    http://books.google.com/books?id=dtFbhw7-wZEC&
    dq=%22spheres+of+justice%22+walzer&pg=PP1&
    ots=hqL0_3RiyP&sig=_fGe849vRPlL2bPP4Yy2q_
    qp8cM&hl=en&prev=http://www.google.com/search?
    hl=en&q=%22spheres+of+justice%22+walzer&sa=
    X&oi=print&ct=title&cad=one-book-with-thumbnail#
    PPR11,M1

Military Commissions Act of 2006
    http://en.wikipedia.org/wiki/Military_Commissions_
    Act_of_2006

    http://www.nytimes.com/2006/09/28/opinion/28thu1.
    html?ex=1317096000&en=3eb3ba3410944ff9&ei=
    5090&partner=rssuserland&emc=rss

Mississippi Burning *reviews*
    http://www.cinepad.com/reviews/mississippi.htm

http://www.law.umkc.edu/faculty/projects/ftrials/price&
bowers/movie.html

The Molly and Adam Nash story
http://www.amednews.com/2001/prse0115

"Movies with a Message"
http://www.jsonline.com/onwisconsin/movies/oct04/
266611.asp

Nathaniel Abraham
http://www.wsws.org/articles/2000/jan2000/abra-j14.
shtml

Oldest European universities
http://www.unbf.ca/psychology/likely/scholastics/
universities.htm

Olympe de Gouges
http://www.pinn.net/~sunshine/march99/gouges2.html

Paul Ricoeur's acceptance speech at receiving the Kluge Prize
http://www.loc.gov/loc/kluge/prize/ricoeur-transcript
.html

Peter Singer, "A Convenient Truth;" NY Times article, 01/26/07
http://www.utilitarian.net/singer/by/20070126.htm

*Peter Singer, "Should We Trust Our Moral Intuitions?" Project
Syndicate, March 2007*
http://www.utilitarian.net/singer/by/200703.htm

Philosophers on the Mesa
http://philosophyonthemesa.wordpress.com/

The Primates Home Page
http://www.dwebsoft.com/PrimatesWeb/

Ray Killen's sentencing
http://www.cnn.com/2005/LAW/06/23/mississippi.
killings/index.html

Raymond Chandler, "The Simple Art of Murder"
http://www.en.utexas.edu/amlit/amlitprivate/scans/
chandlerart.html

Recount in Florida
http://www.pbs.org/newshour/media/media_watch/
jan-june01/recount_4-3.html

Retributive and restorative justice
http://www.georgetown.edu/centers/woodstock/report/
r-fea61a.htm

Review of Walzer's *Spheres of Justice*
http://query.nytimes.com/gst/fullpage.html?res=9A0CE
5DC1738F937A15757C0A965948260

"Robert Nozick, Libertarianism, and Utopia," by Jonathan
Wolf
http://world.std.com/~mhuben/wolff_2.html

Robert Nozick and Locke's Proviso
http://www.cooperativeindividualism.org/fremery_nozick
_review_of.html

Robert Yates investigation files
http://www.krem.com

Ronald Dworkin, "The Threat to Patriotism"
http://www.nybooks.com/articles/15145

Ronald Dworkin's Freedom's Law
http://www.hup.harvard.edu/catalog/DWOFRE.html

The Silent Scream of the Asparagus
http://www.weeklystandard.com/Content/Public/
Articles/000/000/015/065njdoe.asp

The Society for the Study of Ethics and Animals
http://mail.Rochester.edu/~nobs/ssea.html

Sor Juana Inez de la Cruz
http://www.mexconnect.com/mex_/history/jtuck/
jtjuanainescruz.html

http://www.edwardsly.com/ines.htm

Stanford Encyclopedia of Philosophy: Distributive Justice
http://www.seop.leeds.ac.uk/archives/win1998/entries/
justice-distributive/

Stem cell research
http://www.latimes.com/news/local/politics/cal/la-
me-stemcell17may17,1,4139407.story?coll=la-news-
politics-california

http://www.medicalnewstoday.com/healthnews.
php?newsid=73381

Stories of fake memoirs
http://sycamorereview.com/blog/2008/3/4/fake-memoirs
.html

Sue Savage Rumbaugh, William M. Fields
http://www2.gsu.edu/~wwwlrc/savage-rumb-srcd-
mono.pdf

Torture in Nazi Germany
http://andrewsullivan.theatlantic.com/the_daily_dish/
2007/05/verschfte_verne.html

"Truth Falls Victim to Politics"
http://www.spokesmanreview.com/opinion/
topstory.asp?ID=32295

Tuskegee syphilis study
http://www.med.virginia.edu/hs-library/historical/
apology/

The 2007 pet food scandal
http://en.wikipedia.org/wiki/2007_pet_food_recalls
http://www.petconnection.com/recall/index.php

U.S. Constitution
http://www.nwbuildnet.com/nwbn/usconstitutionsearch
.html

The Virginia Tech massacre
http://www.latimes.com/technology/la-na-heroes18apr
18,1,2123657.story

*Weather Channel Founder: Global Warming 'Greatest Scam
in History'*
http://icecap.us/images/uploads/JC_comments.doc

White House press releases on the Patriot Act
http://www.whitehouse.gov/news/releases/2005/06/
20050609.html

"Who's a terrorist and who isn't?" AP article, 10/03/01
http://www.msnbc.com/news/636814.asp

Women in the armed forces
http://www.womensmemorial.org/historyandcollections/
history/learnmoreques.htm

Women's suffrage
http://www.rochester.edu/SBA/history.html

Women's suffrage, global
http://www.womenshistory.about.com/library/weekly/
aa091600a.htm

Index

Page numbers in **boldface** refer to primary readings and narratives. Page numbers in *italics* refer to illustrations.

Ableism, 316
Abolitionism, 682, 683–685, 721–724, 733–737. *See also* Death penalty
Abortion
artificial wombs and viability, 321–322
Catholic Church on, 639–640, *639*
definition of personhood and, 640
embryonic stem cell research and, 324
Libertarian Party on, 337
pro-life *vs.* pro-choice groups, 251, 638
Roe v. Wade decision, 638
utilitarianism *vs.* deontology and, 640–641
"About Magnanimous-Incident Literature" (Twain), 60–61
Abraham and Isaac story, 57–60, *58*, 503
Abraham on Trial: The Social Legacy of Biblical Myth (Delaney), 59–60
Absolutism (hard universalism), 117–118, 128, 278, 482
Abstract individualism, 343–344
Abu Ghraib prisoner abuse scandal, 6, 30–33
Academy of Athens, 399, 410, 431, *434*
Accepting gratitude, 555–556
Acculturation, 123, 124
Act utilitarianism, 253–255
Adam and Eve, 54
Adams, Evan, *35*
Adamson, Andrew, **427–430**
Ad baculum fallacy, 21
Ad hominem fallacy, 21, 141
Ad misericordiam fallacy, 21
Adolf Eichmann in Jerusalem (Arendt), 6–7
Aeschylus, 86
Aesop's fables, 47, 60
Aesthetic stage, 489
Affirmative action, 331, 345
Affleck, Ben, **514–518**, *515*
Afghanistan, 127, 661, 663
Africa
communitarianism in, 186
female genital mutilation in, 127, **157–159**, *157*
folktales in, 66
sense of morality in, 17
tribal virtue ethics, 387–388
African Americans
backward-looking justice for, 344–346
civil rights movement, 345–346, 360–361, 374–377
in *Do the Right Thing*, **160–162**, *161*
searching for their roots, 142
slavery of, 288, 319, 345–346
in Tuskegee syphilis study, 174, 236
in Westerns, 74
Afterlife, reincarnation in, 408
Agamemnon (Aeschylus), 86
Aged, respect for, 544–547, 566–568, 579–582
Agent Orange, 174

Age of Reason (Enlightenment), 225, 285, 289–290
Agnosticism, 18
Agora, 394
Aiello, Danny, *161*
Akan people, virtue ethics among, 387–388
Alchemists, 63
Alcibiades, 395
Alcohol intake, 250
Alexander the Great, 431, *435*, 448
Alexandria, library at, 391, *392*
Alexie, Sherman, **33–36**, *35*
ALF (Animal Liberation Front), 677
Alice in Wonderland (Carroll), 536
Allegorical stories, 57
Allen, Paula Gunn, 595
Allen, Woody, **307–311**
All Quiet on the Western Front (film), 70, *71*
Al Qaeda, 114–115, 649, 668
Alter ego, 64–65
Alterity, 502, 504
Altruism
by animals, 191–192, 196–198
in films, 582–585
neurological response to, 532
prisoner's dilemma and, 190, 215–216
psychological *vs.* ethical, 188–190
reciprocal, 190, 224
selfish-gene theory and, 191–192
Amendments, constitutional
First, 332–334, 647–648
Second, 333
Fourth, 335
America and Americans (Steinbeck), **149–151**
American Indians
Golden Rule in religion of, 184
land ethic and, 679
myths and legends of, 54, 66
philosophy of harmony, 17
in *Smoke Signals*, **33–36**, *35*
status of women among, 594–595
value system of, 388–389
in Westerns, 74
Americans. *See* United States
American Sign Language (ASL), 672
Amoral value judgments, 9, 654–656
Amygdala, 234
Anamnesis, 408
Anarchy, State and Utopia (Nozick), 657–658
Andersen, Hans Christian, 60, 65, 75
Androgyny, 604
Androids (artificial persons), 77–79, 292
Andrus, Mark, **467–469**
Angel Heart (film), 64
Anger, 351–353, 444, 446
Angst
Heidegger on, *490*, 492–493
Kierkegaard on, 487
Munch on, *488*

Anguish, in existentialism, 494
Animal Farm (Orwell), 613
Animal food, melamine contamination of, 658–660
Animal Liberation: A Practical Guide (Singer), 235
Animal Liberation Front (ALF), 677
Animals
altruism by, 191–192, 196–198
cloned, 326–327
Descartes on, 234, *236*
emotions in, 670
empathy towards, 171
great apes, 674, 676, 711–712, 712–714
Hume on, 670
Kant on, 292, 294, 673
in lab testing, 235, 673
morals of, 191–192, 196–198, 292, 669–670
personhood of, 671–672, 676, 712–714
pet food contamination, 658–660
protection of humans by dolphins, 191–192
rescued from Katrina damage, 171
rights of, 319, 673–675, 711–712, 712–714
thinking ability of, 293, 671–672
torture of, 294
utilitarianism on, 233–235, 670–673, 674–675
Animal testing, 235, 673
Anime, 82
Animism, 679
Anthrax letters, 650
Anthropocentrism, 437
Anthropology, ethical relativism and, 118–124, *123*, 136–137, **145–147**
"Anthropology and the Abnormal" (Benedict), 122, 134, **145–147**
Anti-authoritarianism, 341, 394
Antiterrorism Act, torture and, 121, 240
Apellicon, 449
Apes, rights for, 674, 676, 711–712, 712–714
Apollo, 85
Apology (Plato), 396, 398, **415–418**
Appeal to authority fallacy, 21
Appetites, Plato on, 402–405, *404*
Apted, Michael, **268–271**
Aquinas, Saint Thomas, 440, 449–450, 451
Archetypes, 62
Arendt, Hannah, 6–7
aretē, 385–386. *See also* Virtue ethics
Argument, in philosophy, 20
Aristophanes, 393
Aristotle, 435–449
Alexander the Great and, 431, 448
on animals, 671
on communitarianism, 342
Confucius and, 542
on courage, *447*, 456–458, 522, 525–526
on drama, 24, 85–86, 88, 96–98

Aristotle (*continued*)
  on empirical knowledge, 432
  on excellence and virtue, 435–436
  on four causes of every event, 437
  The Generation of Animals, 439
  Golden Mean of, 88, 387, 440–447,
    442, 447, 453–455, 542, 651
  on happiness, 230, 447–449
  on human purpose, 437–440
  influence on Thomas Aquinas, 440,
    449–450, 451
  life of, 431, *433,* 448–449
  on logic, 15
  Nicomachean Ethics, 339, 440–441,
    453–455, 456–458
  objections to, 450–452
  on pity, 171
  Poetics, 85, 86, **96–98,** 98–100
  Politics, 330
  on relationship of history and poetry, 54
  as scientist, 432–435
  teaching by, 89, *434*
  teleology of, 436–437, 438, 450,
    451–452
  on virtue, 477
  on women, 433, 439, 607
Arrival of the Good Samaritan at the Inn
  (Doré), *575*
Artificial Intelligence (AI), 77–78
Artificial persons, 77–79, 292
Asclepius, 399
As Good As It Gets (film), **467–469,** *468*
Ashcroft, John, 641
Asian philosophy, 15, 17, 184, 541–543
ASL (American Sign Language), 672
Astell, Mary, 599
Ataraxia, 228
Atheism, 18
Athens, as *polis,* 393–394, *398*
Atlas Shrugged (Rand), **219–221,** 337,
  338–339
Atomistic model, 341–343
August, John, **36–39**
Augustine, Saint, 410–411, 639
Aung San Suu Kui, 525
Austen, Jane, 61–62
Authenticity
  Bergson on, 497
  equity feminism and, 603–604
  Heidegger on, *490,* 492–493
  Kierkegaard on, 487–490
  as only virtue to strive for, 483
  personal identity and, 500
  Sartre on, 494–499, 500
Authority, just war and, 665, 667
Autobiography (Mill), 241–242
Auto-Icon, 226
Autonomy, Gender, Politics (Friedman), *343*
Ayres, Lew, 71

Baby Blues (comic strip), *587*
The Bacchae (Euripides), 86
Backlash: The Undeclared War Against
  American Women (Faludi), 600
Backward-looking justice, 344–346, 350
"Bad faith," 496–499, 604
Baigent, Michael, 67
Balkanization, 142
The Ballad of Little Jo (film), 74
Banality of evil, 6–7

Banality of heroism, 7
Band of Brothers (TV series), *526,* **568–569**
The bargain, 62–64
BARK, The Modern Dog Culture
  Magazine, 659
Barnicle, Mike, 648
Barone, Michael, **716–717**
The Basketball Diaries (film), 87
Bay, Michael, **367–371**
B.C. (comic strip), *140*
Beach, Adam, 35
Beauvoir, Simone de
  classical feminism of, 603–605
  on Husserl, 501
  influence on Sartre, *606*
  on Levinas, 504
  on life choices, 499, 501, 504
  The Second Sex, 600, 604–606,
    621–624
  "The Woman Destroyed," **631–633**
Beavis and Butt-head (TV series), 87
Begging the question fallacy, 21,
  177–178, 693
"Beginning" stories, 51
Behaviorism, 606
Beheadings, shown on television, 650–651
Being and Nothingness (Sartre), 496
Being and Time (Heidegger), 492
Being-there (*dasein*), 491–493
Belsey, Andrew, **700–702**
Benedict, Ruth, 120–123, *123,* 128, 134,
  145–147
Benét, Stephen Vincent, 63–64
Bennett, Jonathan, 50, 536, 539
Bennett, William H., 471
Bentham, Jeremy
  on animal suffering, 234
  body of, 226, *226*
  on equality, 501
  on hedonistic calculus, 229–232, *231*
  An Introduction to the Principles of Morals
    and Legislation, 227, **256–258**
  Mill on, 241
  on rights, 329
  on utilitarianism, 225–229
Berg, Nick, 650
Berger, Fred, 551–552, 553
Bergson, Henri, 497
Berkeley, George, 406
Berns, Walter, 351, 688
Berteaux, John, 362–363, 363–364
Beyond Essence (Levinas), 500
Bias in the media. *See* News media ethics
Bible
  Abraham and Isaac, 57–60, *58,* 503
  Adam and Eve, 54
  Golden Rule in, 184
  Good Samaritan parable, 57, **574–576,**
    575, 697
  Jephtha's daughter, 63
  prodigal son parable, 57
Bibliotherapy, 48
Bidinotto, Robert James, 347
Bifurcation fallacy, 21, 293
Big Fish (film), **36–39,** *37*
Bigotry, freedom of thought and, 316
Bill and Ted's Excellent Adventure (film), 395
Billy Budd (Melville), 318
Bin Laden, Osama, 662, 667
Bioethics, 644–645

Biological equality of sexes, 590–591, 604
The Birth of a Nation (film), 50
Bisexualism, 609. *See also* Homosexuality
Bizarro (comic strip), *49, 324*
Black Americans. *See* African Americans
"The Blacksmith and the Baker" (Wessel),
  263–265, *264*
Blackwell, Antoinette Brown, 599
Blade Runner (film), 78, 326, 680
Blair, Jayson, 648
Blair Witch Project (film), 87
Blame, 693
Blue states *vs.* red states, 2–4, 559–560.
  See also Conservatives, political;
  Liberals, political
Blum, Lawrence, 647
Boas, Franz, 120
Bobo's Progress (comic strip), *117*
Bolt, Robert, **419–422**
Bonobo chimpanzees, 590, 671. *See also*
  Great apes, rights for
The Book of Mencius, 544
The Book of Virtues (Bennett), 471
Bowling for Columbine (film), 89–90
"The Boy Who Cried Wolf" (Aesop), 47
Bradbury, Ray, 79–80
Brain
  accountability after brain damage, 11
  altruism and, 532
  bridge, 616
  computer model of, 352
  decisions causing deaths of others and,
    22–23, 352
  moral compass in, 10–11, 22–23,
    532–533
  thoughts of hurting others and, 532
Brandt, Michael, **304–307**
Brave New World (Huxley), 68–69, 321,
  322–323, 326
Bridge brains, 616
Brigit of Kildare, Saint, 595
Brokeback Mountain (film), 74
Brokovich, Erin, 528
Brooks, James L., **467–469**
The Brothers Karamazov (book by
  Dostoyevsky and film),
  265–266, 494
Brown, Dan, 54, 67–68
Bruegel the Elder, Pieter, *459*
Buddhism, 184, 530
Buffalo Girls (film), 74
Bumfights (film), 288
Burke and Hare case, 226
The Burning Bed (film), 87
Burton, Tim, **36–39**
Business ethics, 653–660
  amorality of business people, 654–656
  cheating by business students, 655–656
  justifiability of profit, 655
  organizational culture and, 702–703
  in pet food contamination case,
    558–560
  profit *vs.* respect for life, 658–660,
    729–731
  property rights and, 657–658
  sexual harassment, 600, 601, 656
  whistle-blowing, 656
  workers' rights, 656
Business Ethics (de George), 654
Byrne, Rhonda, 693

California, death penalty criteria in, 683
Callatians, funeral customs of, 119, *120, 135*
Callicott, J. Baird, 388–389, 679
Calvin and Hobbes (comic strip), *125, 173, 182, 482*
Campbell, Joseph, 694
Capital punishment. *See* Death penalty
Carbon dioxide, global warming and, 677–678
Cardinal sins and virtues, 444
Care, Heidegger on, 492
"Carenant," *Band of Brothers*, **568–569**
Caring imperative, 612–613
Carroll, Lewis, 536
Carson, Rachel, 677
Cash, David, 188
Castration complex, 621
Categorical imperative, 278–288. *See also* Kant, Immanuel
    beings who are things and, 292–295
    conflicts between duties and, 282–283
    effect of consequences on, 282
    health care access and, 644–645
    hypothetical imperatives *vs.*, 279
    the kingdom of ends and, 295–296, 669
    lack of exceptions to, 286–288
    loophole in, 283
    overview of, 278–282
    rationality and, 281, 284–286
    statement focused on respect for persons, 291
Catholic Church
    child molestation scandal in, 175, 317
    on fetal personhood, 639–640, *639*
    influence of Aristotle on, 440
    Irish women in, 595
    non-gender-specific language in, 589
    on suicide, 530
    Thomas Aquinas' natural law and, 450, 451
    women during the Middle Ages, 595–596
Cathy (comic strip), *285, 608*
Causal explanations, 438
Cavalieri, Paola, 262
Cavendish, Margaret, 234
Censorship, 88, 90
Center for Academic Integrity, 655
Cervantes, Miguel de, 59, 67
Ceteris paribus, 346
Chadwick, Ruth, **700–702**
Le Chambon-sur-Lignon, France, 533–536
Chandler, Raymond, **100–102**
Chanter, Tina, 504
Character
    ability to change, 471
    actions and conduct and, 441
    definition of, 385–386
    innateness of, 386, 471
    Mayo on, 474–475
    political aspect of conduct *vs.*, 471–473
    as purpose of man, 439
    telling the story of our life and, 49, 481, 570–574
Character arc, 500
Cheating by students, 478–479, 482, 655
Cherokee myths, 54
Child molestation, 175, 317, 335

Children. *See also* Schools
    in aesthetic stage, 489
    Andersen's stories for, 60, 65, 75
    cloned, 326–328
    crimes by, 318–319
    didactic stories for, 471
    duties toward parents, 544–547, 566–568, 579–582
    ethical egoism in, 183
    infanticide, 127, 135–136
    intersexual, 606–607
    Kant on, 293–294
    minimizing gender stereotypes in, *608*
    molestation of, 175, 317, 335–336
    moral development in, 12–13
    one-child policy in China, 547–548
    personhood of, 315, 317–318
    Plato on, 404–405
    potential virtue in, 436
    utilitarianism and, 251–252
    as victims in September 11 attacks, 662
Chimpanzees, 590, 671–672, 712–714
China, export of contaminated dog food by, 658–660
Chivalry, *602*
Cho, Seung-Hui, 4, 163–164, 287
Choi, Laurie, **702–703**
Choice, Sartre on, 496–499
Christianity. *See also* Catholic Church
    Aristotle's influence on, 440, 449–450
    on cardinal sins and virtues, 444
    closure of Plato's Academy, 399, 410
    fanaticism in, 391
    on Golden Rule, 184
    on homosexuality, 609
    Irish women in, 595
    Nietzsche on, 495
    Plato's influence on, 410–411
    on suicide, 530
    on virtue ethics, 390–392, 450–452
    on women during the Middle Ages, 595–596
Christine de Pizan, 599
A Christmas Carol (Dickens), 474
Churchland, Paul and Patricia, 406
Cicero, 434
Cinderella (film), 55
Cinderella tale, 55–57
Cité des Dames (Christine de Pizan), 599
Civil codes of ethics, 20
Civil disobedience, 360–361
Civil rights movement, 345–346, 360–361, 374–377
Civil unions, 609
Classical feminism, 602, 603–605, *608,* **621–624**
Classical liberalism, 250
Cleopatra (queen of Egypt), 391
Clever Hans, 671
Clinton, Hillary, 186, 342
Cloning
    eugenics and, 371–374
    personhood and, 320
    reproductive, 325–328
    therapeutic, 325
Cloonan, Jack, 239–240
Closure, death penalty and, 685
The Clouds (Aristophanes), 393
Code of Hammurabi, 19
Cognitive relativism, 487

Cohen, Carl, 673
Coleman, John, 678
College students. *See* Students
Columbine High School shootings, 87
Combat, women in, 523–524, 592–593
Coming of Age in Samoa (Mead), 136–137
Common decency, 130
Communication, gender differences in, 616
Communism, 338–339
Communist Manifesto (Marx), 658
Communitarianism, 186, 342–344
Community of equals, 674
Comparative justice, 665, 667
Compassion, 531–540. *See also* Empathy
    in animals, 196
    Bennett on, 536
    as emotion, 537
    in films, 576–579
    in Good Samaritan parable, 57, **574–576,** *575,* 697
    Hallie on, 533–536
    hardwired in brain, 10–11, 532
    Le Chambon story, 533–536
    malice *vs.*, 537–538
    neuroscience and, 532–533
    role of reason and emotion in, 536–540
    Taylor on, 5, 536–540
Competition, cultural relativism and, 119
Computer ethics, 656
Conditional decisions, 279
Condorcet, marquis de, 597
Conduct. *See* Ethics of conduct
Conflict resolution
    categorical imperative and, 282–283
    ethical egoism and, 187
    ethical relativism and, 116–118
    moral subjectivism and, 130
Confucius, 17, 184, 541–543
Connery, Sean, 69
Conrad, Joseph, 62, **462–464,** *463*
Consequentialism
    ethical egoism as, 182
    example of, 224
    Kant's criticism of, 275–278, 282
    uncertainty of the future and, 232–233
    utilitarianism and, 224–225
Conservatives, political, 473, 559–561, 664, 678
Contemplation, happiness and, 448
Contractarianism, 673
"A Convenient Truth" (Singer), **261–263**
Convictions, diversity of, 560
Cooper, Gary, *302*
Cooperation, Confucius on, 542
Corporate ethics, 656
Costner, Kevin, 73
Coulter, Ann, 647
Council of Nicea, 391
Counterfables, 60–61, 76
Courage, 522–531
    Aristotle on, *447,* 456–458, 522, 525–526
    heroism and, 527
    McCain on, 239, 525, 528, **562–564**
    physical *vs.* moral, 524, 527–531, 568–569
    stories of, 460–461, 523–526, 534, 570–574
    suicide and, 529–530
    wartime stories, 69–70, *71,* 523–525, *524,* 568–569

Craig, Larry, 175
Crime and Punishment (Dostoyevsky), 62
Crime stories, 80–83, *81, 83, 84,* **100–102,** 133
Criminal justice, 346–353. *See also* Justice
in ancient Greece, 395–396, 403
anger and, 351–353
for animals, 669–670
approaches to punishment in, 348–351
crimes by children, 318–319
crimes by women, 319
DNA evidence and, 688–690
precognition and, 381–384
racism and, 374–377
retributive *vs.* restorative, 347
television cameras in the courtroom, 646
use of stories in, 49
victims and, 353, 364–367
Crises, dealing with, 693–694
Critias, 395
Critical Elements of an Organizational Ethical Culture (Seligson and Choi), **702–703**
Critique of Judgment (Kant), 276
Critique of Practical Reason (Kant), 276
Critique of Pure Reason (Kant), 276
"Critiques," 276
Crito (Plato), 396
Crockett, David "Davy," 137
Cromwell, James, *84*
Crowe, Russell, *84, 731*
Cruel and unusual punishment, death penalty as, 683
Cruelty, institutionalized, 534–535
Cruz, Sor Juana Inez de la, 596
CSI: Crime Scene Investigation (TV series), *81*
La Cucaracha (comic strip), 2
Cultural difference argument, 124
Cultural diversity. *See* Multiculturalism
Cultural identity, 142–143
Cultural imperialism, 124
Cultural relativism
anthropology and, 119–120, 122
definition of culture and, 129–131
in diverse society, 129–131
in Greek culture, 401
rulers who break the standards, 137
Cultural tolerance, 122–123, 124, 127
Culture. *See also* Cultural relativism; Multiculturalism
African (Akan), 387–388
American, 139, 143
of business organizations, 702–703
defining, 129–131
dominant, 139
female nature defined by, 605
of online communities, 129
value of stories in, 51–52
Curtis, Michael, **213–215**
Cusack, John, 237
Cyberbashing, 651
Cyberpunk, 75–76
Cynicism, 173–175
Cynics, 174

Daily Mirror, 648
Daimon, 397
Damasio, Antonio, 10–11, 22, 195, 352, 532

Damon, Matt, **514–518,** *515*
Dances with Wolves (film), 74
Dao, 541–543
Darius (king of Persia), 119, *120,* 135
Darwin, Charles, 670
Dasein (Being-there), 491–493
Dating, as debt-favor arrangement, 549
David, Jacques-Louis, *397*
The DaVinci Code (Brown), 54, 67–68
Davis, Richard Allen, 683
Dawkins, Richard, 191–192
Dawson, Angela, 525–526
The Day After Tomorrow (film), 77
D-Day invasion, 525
Deadwood (TV series), 75
Dean, James, *41*
Death. *See also* Euthanasia
Heidegger on awareness of, 491
morality of taking a life, 639–640
persistent vegetative state and, 643
shown on television, 650–651
Death and Justice: An Exposé of Oklahoma's Death Row Machine (Fuhrman), 684, **721–724**
"The Death of Iván Ilyich" (Tolstoy), 48
The Death of Socrates (David), *397*
Death penalty, 681–690
arguments against, 683–685, 721–724, 733–737
arguments for, 686–687, 717–720
costs and, 685
current criteria for, 683
DNA evidence and, 688–690
emotions and, 351, 353
Kant on, 682
Locke on, 681
Debt-metaphor for dating, 548–549
Decisions. *See* Moral decisions
Declaration of Independence, American, 330
Declaration of the Rights of Man, French, 330
Declaration of the Rights of Woman and the Female Citizen (Gouges), 597
Declaration on Great Apes, 674, **711–712**
Deductive arguments, 15
Deep ecology, 677, 680
"Defining Racism in the 21st Century" (Berteaux), **362–363**
Defonseca, Misha, 648
De George, Richard T., 654
Delaney, Carol, 59–60
Democracy, 395, 669
Deontology, 275–311. *See also* Categorical imperative
abortion and, 640–641
beings who are things, 292–295
categorical imperative criticisms, 282–288
categorical imperative overview, 278–282
ends in themselves in, 288–291
intentions in, 275–278, 280, 477–478
the kingdom of ends and, 295–296, 669
D'Epinay, Zepherine, 597
Descartes, Renè
on animals, 234, *236*
as dualist, 406
on epistemology, 15
individualism and, 341

Descriptive ethics, 120, 121, 166
Descriptive soft universalism, 138
Detective stories, 80–83, *81, 83,* 100–102
Determinism, 176, 498
Deterrence, punishment as, 348, 349, 681, 686–687
"The Devil and Daniel Webster" (Benét), 63–64
De Waal, Frans, 196, 197, **211–213**
Dialectic (Socratic) method, 17, 393
Dialogue, in Socratic method, 17, 393
Dialogues (Plato), 16, 89, 167, 393, 399
Dickens, Charles, 1, 483
Didactic stories, 47, 170, 471
Difference feminism
definition of, 602, *608*
Gilligan on, 607–613, *612*
Sommers on, 603
Dilbert (comic strip), *11, 14, 247, 409, 654*
Dilemmas, 190, 215–216, 610–611
Diogenes, 174
Dionysius II, 405
Dionysus, 85–86
Disabilities, people with, 316
Discourse on the Origin of Inequality among Mankind (Rousseau), 658
Discrimination
in death penalty administration, 684
of noncombatants in a just war, 666
against people with disabilities, 316
personhood and, 316
Disgust, moral values and, 26
Dislocated communities, 344
Distributive justice, 339–344
affirmative action as, 331, 345
forward- and backward-looking justice, 344–346, 350
Friedman on, 343–344, *343*
Nozick on, 657
Rawls on, 339–341
Wolgast on, 341–342, *342*
Diversity. *See* Multiculturalism
Divine law, 450, 451
DNA evidence, 688–690
Doctor-assisted suicide. *See also* Euthanasia
double effect and, 641–642
ethical relativism and, 128–129
harm principle and, 249
The Doctrine of Right (Kant), 299
The Doctrine of Virtue (Kant), 299
Dog food, contaminated, 658–660
Doing the right thing, 160–162, 390, 467–469. *See also* Ethics of conduct
A Doll's House (play by Ibsen and film), 611, **626–631**
Dolphins, protection of humans by, 191–192
Domestic violence, 352
Dominant culture, 139
Dominant population, 141
Don Quixote (Cervantes), 59, 67
Doré, Gustave, 58, *575*
Dostoyevsky, Fyodor, 62, 254, **265–266**
Do the Right Thing (film), **160–162,** *161*
Double character, 64–65
Double effect, principle of, 639–640, 642, 666
Douglas, Paul, 650
Doxa, 401

Doyle, Sir Arthur Conan, 80
Dr. Faustus (Mann), 64
Dr. Jekyll and Mr. Hyde (Stevenson), 64
Dr. Quinn, Medicine Woman (TV series), 74
Drama
  Aristotle on, 24, 85–86, 88, 96–98
  existentialist, 512–514, 514–518
  Plato on, 84–86, 88, 92–96
Drug legalization, harm principle and,
  249–250
Drugs, as quick fixes, 321
Drugstore Cowboy (film), 50
Dualism, 406
Dual-nature stories, 64–65
Dunham, Jason L., 524
Duty theory. *See* Deontology
Dworkin, Andrea, 614–615
Dworkin, Ronald, 331–334
Dystopia stories, 75–76

Earth Liberation Front (ELF), 677
East of Eden (Steinbeck), 9–10, **40–46**,
  41, 65
Eat Drink Man Woman (film),
  579–582, *581*
Eco, Umberto, 88, **98–100**
Ecological virtue, 388–389
Ecology. *See* Environmentalism
Ecosystems, teleology and, 436
Eco-terrorism, 602, 677
Educating Rita (film), 79
Education. *See also* Schools; Students
  of Mill, John Stuart, 240–242, *241*
  teaching values in, 13–14
  use of stories in, 49–50
  of women, 600, 604, 605
"The Education of Mingo" (Johnson), 79,
  107–110
Edwards, Jonathan, 536
Efficient cause, Aristotle on, 437
Egalitarianism, 229, 341
Egalitarian liberalism, 250
De l'égalité des deux sexes (Poulain), 244
Egalité des Hommes et des Femmes
  (Gournay), 599
Ego, in Freud's tripartite psyche, 403
Ego integrity, 500, 692–693
Egoism. *See also* Psychological egoism
  egotism *vs.*, 164
  ethical, 181–188
  group, 188–189
  morality of animals, 196–198
  rational ethical, 190
  selfish reasons for good deeds,
    172–173, 178–179, 213–215
  selfish *vs.* self-interested, 166
  selflessness and, 188–190
Egotism, 164. *See also* Egoism
Either/Or (Kierkegaard), **506–507**
Elderly, respect for, 544–547, 566–568,
  579–582
Elements of Moral Philosophy (Rachels),
  135, *137*
ELF (Earth Liberation Front), 677
Elliott, Ted, **427–430**
Embedded journalists, 649–650
Emotionalism, 194–195, *194*
Emotions
  in the Age of Romanticism, 83–84
  in animals, 670

compassion as, 537
death penalty and, 684–685, 687–688
Hume on, 194–195, *194*
moral issues and, 21–23
Nussbaum on, 24–27, 28–29
origin of values and, 191
Plato on, 84–85
punishment and, 350–353
storytelling as teacher of, 25
Empathy. *See also* Compassion
  hardwired in brain, 10–11, 532
  Hobbes on, 171
  towards animals, 171
Empirical knowledge, 432
End-of-civilization science fiction, 75–76
Ends in themselves, 288–291
Enfranchisement of Women (Mill, Harriet
  Taylor), **618–621**
England, early feminism in, 598–600
English, Jane, 548–553
Enlightenment, 225, 285, 289–290
Entitlements (positive rights), 338–339,
  641, 657–658
Entitlement Theory, 657–658
Environmentalism, 675–681
  deep ecology, 677, 680
  ecological virtue, 388–389
  ecosystems and teleology, 436
  ethics of, 679–681
  global warming, 3, 77, 676–678,
    679–680
  land ethic, 677, 679
  pesticides, 675–676
  recycling movement, 676–677
  rights of natural objects, 680–681
Epicurus, 228
Episkin, 235
Epistēmē, 401
Epistemology, 15
Equality
  Aristotelian moral theory and, 451
  biological, of sexes, 590–591, 604
  definitions and types of, 329–331
  gender, 523–524, 588–596
  rights not traded for benefits,
    331–334
  sameness and, 331
  social, 330, 331–334
Equality Between Men and Women
  (Gournay), 599
Equal treatment for equals, 330
Equity feminism, 602, 603–604
Erdoes, Richard, 388
Erikson, Erik, 500, 624, 692
An Essay on African Philosophical Thought
  (Gyekey), 387–388
Eternal law, 450
Ethical altruism, 189
Ethical egoism, 181–188
  emotional criticisms of, 187–188
  ethical altruism *vs.*, 189
  Golden Rule and, 22, 182–184
  imprudence of, 187
  inability to solve moral conflicts
    using, 187
  as normative theory, 181
  obligation to look after oneself and,
    181–185
  Rand on, 184–185
  rational, 190

  as self-contradictory, 186–187
  shortcomings of theory of, 185–188
  theory of, 181–185
  universalizability and, 183
Ethical pluralism, 558–559
Ethical relativism, 116–162
  anthropological findings and, 118–124,
    123, 136–137, **145–147**
  Aristotle and, 445–446
  on colonialism, 252
  conflict solving and, 116–117
  cultural difference argument, 124
  cultural relativism, 119–120, 122,
    129–131, 401
  cultural tolerance and, 122–123,
    124, 127
  definition of, 116
  definition of culture and, 129–131
  definition of majority and, 128–129
  descriptive *vs.* normative ethics in,
    120, 121
  difficulty of defense of, 138
  ethical pluralism and, 558–559
  "flat earth" argument against, 132
  hard universalism and, 117–118, 128
  inability to criticize or praise other
    cultures, 125–127
  induction as argument against,
    132–134
  majority rule under, 128–129, 130,
    141–142
  metaethics and, 121
  moral differences and, 114–118
  moral subjectivism and, 130
  multiculturalism and, 139–143
  as normative theory, 120, 122
  problems with, 124–132
  professed *vs.* actual morality, 128
  soft universalism and, 116–117,
    134, 142
  tolerance as universal virtue and,
    131–132
Ethical stage, 489
Ethical wills, 696
Ethic of care, 611–613
Ethics. *See also* Virtue ethics
  bioethics, 644–645
  as branch of philosophy, 15
  business, 653–660
  cheating on tests in, 478–479,
    482, 655
  computer, 656
  of conduct, 470–478, 489
  descriptive, 120, 121, 166
  environmental, 675–681
  ethic of care, 611–613
  as "First Philosophy," 501
  of irreplaceability, 645
  limitations of, 58–59
  medical, 48, 322
  morality *vs.*, 14
  news media, 644–653
  normative, 120, 121, 122, 128, 181
  personal identity and, 500
  within a profession, 645
  of self-improvement, 690–698
  Socratic beginnings of, 16–17
"Ethics as a Vehicle for Media Quality"
  (Belsey and Chadwick), **700–702**
Ethics of an Artificial Person (Wolgast), *342*

Ethics of conduct
  Foot on, 477–478
  Kierkegaard on, 489
  Mayo on, 474–475
  political aspect of, 471–473
  replacement of virtue ethics by, 470
"The Ethics of Emergencies" (Rand), **207–211**
Ethnicity and culture, 129, 131, 139–143. *See also* African Americans; Multiculturalism
Eugenics, 322, 371–374
Euripides, 86, **102–106**
Euro-Americans, multiculturalism and, 140
Eurocentrism, 124, 139, 140
Euthanasia
  active *vs.* passive, 641, 643, 644
  definitions of, 641
  doctor-assisted suicide, 128–129, 249, 641–642
  ethical relativism and, 128–129
  harm principle and, 249
  Kevorkian and, 641–642
  key arguments for and against, 642
  legality of, 530
  Schiavo case and, 642–644
  voluntary *vs.* involuntary, 641
Ever After (film), 56
"Everyone Needs a Stone" (Rosenstand), 679
Evil, 5–7, 80–83
Evolution, moral codes in, 532
Excellence, Aristotle on, 435–436
Exclusive multiculturalism, 140
Executions, shown on television, 650–651
Exemplars, 474
Existentialism
  authenticity in, 483
  Beauvoir on, 499, 604, *606*
  in films and plays, 512–514, *514*–518
  Murasaki on, 599
  Nietzsche on, 495–496
  Sartre on, 493–494, *494*
"Existentialism Is a Humanism" (Sartre), **507–510**
The Expanding Circle (Singer), 190, 557, 673–674
Expansionism, moral, 132
Experience, in phenomenology, 491
The Experiment (film), 6
Extreme Measures (film), **268–271**, *269*
Eyre, Chris, **33–36**

Fables, 47, 60–61, 76
Fahrenheit 9/11 (film), 89–90, 175
Fahrenheit 451 (film), 79–80
Fain, Charles, 688
Fairness, justice as, 358–360
Fairy tales, 54–56, 60, 66
Fallacies
  ad baculum, 21
  ad hominem, 21, 141
  ad misericordiam, 21
  appeal to authority, 21
  begging the question, 21, 177–178, 693
  bifurcation, 21, 293
  false dichotomy, 21, 293, 473
  genetic, 197
  hasty generalization, 21
  naturalistic, 246, 591
  red herring, 21

  slippery slope argument, 21, 472, 680–681
  straw man, 21, 324
  suppressed correlative, 180–181, 193
The Fall of Icarus (Bruegel the Elder), *459*
False dichotomy fallacy, 21, 293, 473
Falsification requirement for good theory, 177–178
Faludi, Susan, 600
Faust (Goethe), 63
Faust legend, 63–64
Favor-debt situation, dating as, 549
FDA (Food and Drug Administration), 659–660, 703–705
Fear, courage and, 522
Feinberg, Joel, 674
Female genital mutilation, 127, **157–159**, 157n
Feminazis, 586
Feminine, the Other as, 504, 604–605
The Feminine Mystique (Friedan), 600
"Feminism and Modern Friendship: Dislocating the Community" (Friedman), 343, 344
Feminism/feminists, 586–637. *See also* Gender equality
  bridge-builders among, 615–616
  classical, 602–607, *606, 608,* **621–623**
  difference, 602, 603, 607–613, *608, 612*
  early, in France and England, 597–600
  equity, 602, 603–604
  first-, second-, and third-wave, 596–600
  language and, 588–590
  princess phenomenon, 617
  radical, 600, 602, 614–615
  virtue theory and, 586–588
Feminist ethics, 586. *See also* Feminism/feminists
Ferraro, Geraldine, 559
Fetal personhood, 639–640, *639*
15 Minutes (film), *649,* **726–729**
Films. *See also names of specific films*
  anime, 82
  censorship of, 88, 90
  as moral events, 72
  storytelling of moral issues in, 24
  as therapy, 48–49
  violence in, 87
Final cause, Aristotle on, 437
First Amendment rights, 332–334, 647–648
First-wave feminism, 596–600
The Fisher King (film), 68
"Flat earth" argument against ethical relativism, 132
Flaubert, Gustave, 62
Fleder, Gary, **271–274**
"The Flight of Icarus" (Greek myth), **458–459**
Food and Drug Administration (FDA), 659–660, 703–705
Foot, Philippa, 475–478, *476*
For Better or For Worse (comic strip), *289, 692*
For Capital Punishment: Crime and the Morality of the Death Penalty (Berns), 351
Force Majeure (film), 216
Ford, Harrison, 69

Ford, John, 67, **518–521**
Foreman, Carl, **301–303**
Form, Plato's theory of, 405–410, *411*
Formal cause, Aristotle on, 437
Forward-looking justice, 344–346, 349
Fourth Amendment rights, 335
Fox News, 653
France, early feminism in, 597–598
Frank, Scott, **381–384**
Frankenstein's monster, 77, 326, *597*
Franklin, Benjamin, 335
"Freedom and Resentment" (Strawson), 351
Freedom fighters *vs.* terrorists, 662
Freedom's Law (Dworkin), 331
Free speech, right of, 332–334, 647–648
Free will, 176, 326–327, 498
French Revolution, gender equality and, 597–598
Freud, Sigmund, 197, 285, 403
Frey, James, 648
Friedan, Betty, 600
Friedman, Marilyn, 343–344, *343*
Friends (TV series), **213–215**, *214*
Friendship
  feminism and, 343, 344
  between parents and grown children, 551–552
  reciprocity in, 549–551
  unsolicited favors in, 553–555
"From Property to Person: The Case of Evelyn Hart" (Hall and Waters), **712–714**
Frontal lobes. *See* Brain
Fuhrman, Mark, 684, **721–724**
Fundamental Equality Principle, 330–331
Funeral customs
  cadavers for medical research, 226
  Callatian, 119, *120,* 135
  Greek, 135
Furrow, Dwight, **147–149**

Gaia philosophy, 680
Galaxy Quest (film), 80
Gandhi, Mohandas K., 662, 663
Gandolfini, James, *83*
Gattaca (film), 320, **371–374**, *372*
Gay men, 74, 609
Gaze, Sartre on, 502
Gender, use of term, 588, 605
Gender differences
  biological, 590–591, 604
  in communication, 616
  difference feminism, 602, 603, 607–613, *608, 612*
  in ethic of care, 611–613
  in language, 588–590
  in moral judgments, 599
Gender equality. *See also* Feminism/feminists
  biology and, 590–591, 604
  in combat, 523–524, 592–593
  ethic of care and, 613
  goddess theory, 594–595
  in language, 588–590
  psychosexual neutrality, 606
  in rationality, 285–286, *285*
  in second-wave feminism, 600
  women's historical role in public sphere and, 591–596
Gender feminism, 603

Gender identity, 609
Gender studies, *612*
General deterrence, 348, 686–687
The Generation of Animals (Aristotle), 439
Genetic engineering, personhood and, 320, 322–323, 325–328
Genetic fallacy, 197
Genetics
  cloning, 320, 325–328
  definition of human and, 312
  eugenics, 371–374
  human gender and, 439
  Human Genome Project, 321
  stem cell research, 323–325
Geneva Convention, 121, 240
Genital mutilation, female, 127, **157–159**, 157n
Genji Monogatari (Murasaki), 599
Genocide, 6–7, 126
George, Terry, **377–381**
Gerolmo, Chris, **374–377**
Geronimo (film), 74
The Getaway (film), 87
Ghost Rider (film), 64
Gilgamesh, 65–66
Gilligan, Carol
  on difference feminism, 610–613, *612*
  In a Different Voice, 600, **624–626**
  on emotions in decision-making, 50
Gilroy, Tony, **268–271**
Glaucon, 167–170, 182, 185, *185,* 198–202, 402
Glenn, Scott, 73
Global warming, 3, 77, 676–678, 679–680, 714–717
Glover, Danny, *73*
God, 495–496, 594–595
The God Delusion (Dawkins), 192
Goddess theory, 594–595
Goethe, Johann Wolfgang von, 63, 83–85, 88–89, **106–107**
Goldberg, Bernie, 653
Golden Mean
  in African virtue theory, 387
  Aristotle on, 88, 440–447, *447,* **453–455**
  bridge metaphor for, *442,* 443
  in courage, 443
  death penalty and, 688
  news media ethics and, 651
  variations on, 446
Golden Rule
  altruism from, 190
  Confucius on, 542
  effectiveness of, 554
  ethical egoism and, 182–184
  Kant on, 278, 281, 288
  moral decisions based on, 22
  utilitarianism and, 253, 254
Golden Rule altruism, 190
Golem character, *8,* 77, 78–79, 107–110
Gollum (in *Lord of the Rings*), *8,* 77, 203–204, 472
Good, Plato's Form of, 408–410
"Good" and "evil," 4–10, 80–83, *81, 83*
Good and Evil (Taylor), 537
"Good life," Socrates on, 400–401
Good Natured: The Origins of Right and Wrong in Humans and Other Animals (de Waal), 197

Goodness, 7–10
Good Samaritan parable, 57, **574–576,** *575,* 697
Good twin/bad twin story, 64–65
Good will, Kant on, 280, 281, 391–392
Good Will Hunting (film), *499,* **514–518,** *515*
Gore, Al, 3, 678, 714–717
"Gore Twists Science, History" (Barone), **716–717**
Gorillas, altruism by, 196. *See also* Great apes, rights for
Gottlieb, Scott, **703–705**
Gouges, Olympe de, 597
Gournay, Marie le Jars de, 599
Grafman, Jordan, 532
The Grammar of Justice (Wolgast), 342, *342*
Grammer, Kelsey, *649*
Grandmother Spider myths, 54, 66
Grant, Hugh, *269*
Gratitude, 540–556
  Berger on, 551–552
  of children toward parents, 544–547, 566–568, 579–582
  Confucius on, 541–543
  English on, 548–553
  feeling and showing, 540–541
  how to receive, 555–556
  Lao-Tzu on, 543
  Lin Yutang on, 544–547
  Mencius on, 543–544
  motivation of kindness and, 552
  for unsolicited favors, 553–555
Gray, John, *608*
The Great Ape Project, *262,* 676, 711
Great apes, rights for, 674, 676, 711–712, 712–174
Greatest-happiness principle, 224–225, 254–255. *See also* Utilitarianism
Greeks. *See also* Aristotle; Plato; Socrates
  criminal justice, 395–396
  funeral customs, 135
  historians, 119
  myths and legends, 66, **458–459**
  religion, 406–407
  storytelling by, 84–86, 88
  theater, 85–86
"Green" attitude, 3
Greene, Joshua, 532
Greenhouse effect, 676. *See also* Global warming
Green River Killer, 315
Griffith, Melanie, 74
Grimm brothers' fairy tales, 54–56, 66
Grounding for the Metaphysics of Morals (Kant), 277–278, 280, 288, 290, 292–293, 295, **297–298**
Group egoism, 188–189
Guilt, 693
Gulf War, 661
Gulf War Syndrome, 174
Gun control, 333
Gurian, Michael, 616
Gyekye, Kwame, 387–388

Habermas, Jürgen, 320–321
Haley, Alex, 142
Hall, Lee, **712–714**
Hallie, Philip, 5, 7, 50, 533–536, **565–566**
Hamlet (Shakespeare), 500

Hammurabi, legal code of, 19
Hanks, Tom, **568–569**
"Hansel and Gretel," 55
Happiness
  Aristotle on, 230, 447–449
  defining, 230
  greatest-happiness principle, 224–225, 254–255
  hedonistic calculus, 229–232, *231*
  higher and lower, 243–247
  Mill on, 230
  pleasure *vs.,* 230
Happy Future, stories of, 76
Hard determinism, 176, 498
Hard universalism, 117–118, 128, 278, 482
Harm principle, 247–253, 329, 536
"Harrison Bergeron" (Vonnegut), 331
Hasty generalization fallacy, 21
Hauser, Marc, 11, 532
Havamal ("The Word of the High One"), 694
Hawke, Ethan, *372*
Hays Office, 90
Health care access, 268–271, 644–645
Heat (film), 87
Heche, Anne, 217
Hedonism, 227
Hedonistic (hedonic) calculus, 229–232, *231,* 239
Hedonistic paradox, 228, 242
Hedonistic utilitarianism, 227
Hegel, G. W. F., 406
Heidegger, Martin
  connection with Nazis, 490–491, *490,* 503
  on experiencing existence, 490–491
  influence on Levinas, 501
  on intellectual authenticity, 492–493
Heinz dilemma, 610–611
Helgenberger, Marg, *81*
Henry, Patrick, 560
Heraclitus, 15
Hermaphroditic children, 606–607
Hero (film), 527–528
Herodotus, 119
Heroes, definition of, 527
Heroism
  by animals, 196
  in drug wars, 525
  by Japanese consul-general in Lithuania, 534
  at Le Chambon-sur-Lignon, France, 533–536
  on September 11, 2001, 165, 238–239
  by terrorists, 188
  in the Virginia Tech school shootings, 163–164
  in wartime, 69–70, *71,* 523–525, *524,* 568–569
  in Westerns, 72, 301–307, *301*
Herzfeld, John, **726–729**
Hesse, Herman, 65
Hiasi Pan, Matthew, 676
Hidden premise, 246
Hiding from Humanity (Nussbaum), 24
High Noon (film), 74, **301–303,** *301*
Hildegard of Bingen, 595
Hill, Anita, 600
Himmler, Heinrich, 530, 536

Hinduism, 406, 408
Histories (Herodotus), 119
Hobbes, Thomas
    on individualism, 341
    Leviathan, **206–207**
    as materialist, 406
    on natural rights, 328–329
    on self-interest, 170–171, *170,* 182, 191
    on war of everyone against everyone,
        76, *170*
Hollow Man (film), 168
Holocaust, 6–7, 533–536, 576–579.   .
    See also Nazis
Holy Blood, Holy Grail (Baigent et al.), 67
Holy Grail legend, 67–68, *69*
Homosexuality, 74, 609
Homunculus, 639, *639*
Honor-killing, 114
Horn, Tom, autobiography of, **570–574**
Hospers, John, 337
Hotel Rwanda (film), **377–381,** *378*
"How Safe Is Our Food? FDA Could Do
    Better" (Gottlieb), **703–705**
Huckleberry Finn (Twain), 539
Hugo, Victor, 62
Human–animal hybrid stem cells, 325
Human beings. *See also* Meaning of life;
    Personhood
    Aristotle on purpose of, 437–440
    definition of, 312–313
    gender-specific words for, 589
    human nature, 476, 604
    what it means to be, 76
Human Genome Project, 321
Human law, divine law *vs.,* 450
Human nature, 476, 604
Humanoids (artificial persons), 77–79, 292
Human purpose, Aristotle on, 437–440
Human rights, **354–357,** 559
Hume, David
    on animals, 670
    on emotionalism, 194–195, *194*
    on "fellow-feeling," 134–135, *194,* 532
    on naturalistic fallacy, 246
    on utilitarianism, 227
Hunt, Helen, 583
Husserl, Edmund, 490–491, 501
Huston, Anjelica, 74
Huxley, Aldous, 68–69, 321, 322–323, 326
Hypatia, 391, *392,* 410
Hyphenated Americans, 142
Hypocrisy, 528
Hypothetical imperatives, 279

I, Robot (film), 77–78
Ibn Fadlan, 118
Ibsen, Henrik, 611, **626–631**
Icarus, **458–459,** *459*
Id, 403
Idealism, 406
Identity
    American, after September 11
        attacks, 143
    crisis, 500, 694
    cultural, 142–143
    gender, 606–607, 609
    narrative, 690–698, 725–726
    personal, 500, 690–698
Identity crisis, 500, 694
Immoral value judgments, 9

Immortality, myths of loss of, 54
The Importance of Living (Lin Yutang), 544
Impossibilium nulla est obligatio, 168
Imprisonment, 346
Imus, Don, 647–648
In a Different Voice (Gilligan), 600,
    610–613, *612,* **624–626**
Incapacitation argument for death
    penalty, 686
Incest, 137
Inclusive multiculturalism, 139–141
An Inconvenient Truth (Gore), 3, 678,
    714–717
In Defense of Animals (Singer), 235
"In Defense of 'Moderate Patriotism'"
    (Nathanson), 664
Indiana Jones and the Last Crusade (film),
    68, *69*
Indians. *See* American Indians
Individualism
    abstract, 343–344
    atomistic model, 341–342
    Friedman on, 343–344, *343*
    Wolgast on, 341–342, *342*
Indoctrination, teaching ethics as, 481
Induction, 132–135
Inductive arguments, 15, 132–134
Infanticide, 127, 135–136
Inheritance of acquired characteristics, 438
Innocence Project, 133–134
The Insider (film), 656, **729–731,** *731*
Institutionalized cruelty, 534–535
Instrumental value, 227, 229, 288
Intellect, gender equality in, 590–591
Intellectual virtue, 440
Intelligence, of animals, 293, 671–672
Intentions
    in deontology, 275–278, 280, 477–478
    gratitude for unsolicited favors and,
        553–555
    in just wars, 665, 668
"Internal goods," 481
The Internationale, 664
International war-crimes tribunals, 666
Intersexual children, 606–607
Intrinsic value, 227, 229, 288
*An Introduction to the Principles of Morals
    and Legislation* (Bentham), 227,
    256–258
Inuit culture, infanticide in, 135–136
The Invisible Man (Wells), 168
Iraq War
    Abu Ghraib prisoner abuse scandal,
        6, 30–33
    American soldiers killed in, 661
    civilian deaths in, 650
    ethical relativism and, 126, 253
    just war theory and, 661, 663, 667–668
    news media ethics and, 648–651
    noncombatants, 666
    public opinion of, 3
    2007 surge, 668
    unlawful combatants, 240, 666
Ireland, goddess worship in, 595
Irony, 179, 394, 444
Irreplaceability, ethics of, 645
Islam, 19, 184, 391, 449–450
The Island (film), 320, **367–371,** *368*
"I think, therefore I am," 234, *236*
It Takes a Village (Clinton), 342

Jacobsen, J. P., 62
Jaggar, Alison, 286
Japanese-Americans, internment of, 666
Jason and the Golden Fleece, 66
Jaws (film), 67
Jefferson, Thomas, 330, 334
Jen, 542
Jensen, Shelley, **213–215**
Jenson, Vicky, **427–430**
Jephtha's daughter, 63
Jessica's Law, 335–336
Jesus of Nazareth, parables of, 57
Jewell, Richard, 646–647
JFK (film), 141
"The Jigsaw Man" (Niven), **732–733**
Johannes Climacus (Kierkegaard), **506**
Johnny Guitar (film), 74
Johnson, Charles, 79, **107–110**
Johnson, Lyndon B., 345
Johnson, Shoshana, 593, *593*
Jolivet, Pierre, 216
Jones, Margaret, 648
Journalism. *See* News media ethics
Juana Inez de la Cruz, Sor, 596
Jump Start (comic strip), 395
Jurassic Park (film), 321
Jus ad bellum, 665
Jus in bello, 665–666
Jus post bellum, 666–667
Just and Unjust Wars (Walzer), 663, 665
Just cause, in just war, 665, 667
Justice. *See also* Criminal justice
    in ancient Greece, 395–396, 403
    anger and, 351–353
    comparative, 665, 667
    death penalty as, 686 (*See also*
        Death penalty)
    distributive, 331, 339–346, 350, 657
    equal treatment for equals, 330
    forward- and backward-looking,
        344–346, 349, 350
    Rawls on, 358–360
    retributive *vs.* restorative, 347
    Socrates on, 186
"Justice After War" (Orend), 666–667
"Justice as Fairness" (Rawls), **358–360**
Just war theory, 660–669
    discrimination of noncombatants, 666
    Iraq and Afghanistan wars and,
        661, 663
    pacifism and, 663, 665
    patriotism and, 664
    postwar settlements, 666–667
    rules for, 665–666
    terrorists *vs.* freedom fighters, 662
    unlawful combatants and, 666

Kaczynski, Theodore, 284
Kafka, Franz, 59
Kanka, Megan, 335
Kant, Immanuel. *See also* Categorical
    imperative; Deontology
    on animals, 292, 294, 673, 675
    on beings who are things, 292–295
    on capital punishment, 682
    Critique of Judgment, 276
    Critique of Practical Reason, 276
    Critique of Pure Reason, 276
    on ends in themselves, 288–291
    on evil, 6

Grounding for the Metaphysics of Morals (Kant), 277–278, 280, 288, 290, 292–293, 295, **297–298**
on intentions, 275–278, 477–478
on the kingdom of ends, 295–296, 669
Lectures on Ethics, 475
life and work of, 276, 277
The Metaphysics of Morals, 276, 286, 293–295, **299–301**, 392
on natural predisposition, 295
"Perpetual Peace," 668–669
racism and, 289, 290
on retributive justice, 347, 349
on role models, *473*, 475
on virtue vs. conduct, 391–392
on women, 289, 607
Kanzi, 671–672, *672*
Karma, 56, 408, 693
Katrina, Hurricane, 171
Katz, Erik, 170, **202–206**
Kearney, Richard, 502
Kellog, Davida E., 666
Kelly, Jack, 648
Kemp, Peter, 645
Kevorkian, Dr. Jack, 641–642
Kierkegaard, Søren
on Abraham and Isaac story, 58–60, 503
Either/Or, **506–507**
Johannes Climacus, 506
life of, 484–487, *484*
religious authenticity of, 487–490
on stages of life, 489
Killen, Ray, 346
Killer bees, 323
King, Martin Luther, Jr., **360–361**, 662, 663
Kingdom of ends, 295–296, 669
Kingsolver, Barbara, 124, **151–156**, *152*
Kinsley, Michael, 9
Kline, Kevin, 73
Knowledge and Interest (Habermas), 320–321
Kohlberg, Lawrence, 610–611
Konner, Lawrence, **633–637**
Koppelman, Brian, **271–274**
Korsgaard, Christine, 287
Kurtzman, Alex, **367–371**
Kwakiutl Indians, 122–123
Kyoto Protocol, 678

L.A. Confidential (film), 82, *84*
La Fontaine's fables, 60
Laissez-faire, 187, 250, 657
Lamarck, Jean, 438
Land ethic, 677, 679
Language
American Sign Language, 672
animals and, 671–672, *672*
gender and, 588–590
psychological egoism and, 179–181
Lao-Tzu, 543
The Last of the Mohicans (film), 74
Last resort, just war as, 665, 667
Law. *See also* Criminal justice; Punishment
Bentham on, 227, 242
of Hammurabi, 19
human vs. divine, 450
lex talionis, 346, 682
moral issues and, 19–20
natural, 450, 451
naturalism vs. legal positivism, 19
use of stories in legal community, 49

The Law of Peoples (Rawls), **705–708**
League of Nations, 669
Leap of faith, 59, 489–490, 503
Le Chambon-sur-Lignon, France, 533–536
Lectures on Ethics (Kant), 475
Lee, Ang, **579–582**
Lee, Spike, **160–162**, *161*
Legal positivism, 19
Legends, fact vs. fiction in, 52, 55
Le Guin, Ursula K., **267–268**, 697–698
Leopold, Aldo, 677
Lerner, Gerda, 615
Lesbians, 609. *See also* Homosexuality
"A Letter from Birmingham Jail" (King), **360–361**
Leviathan (Hobbes), **206–207**
Levinas, Emmanuel
on Abraham and Isaac story, 503
life of, 500–501, *501*
on the Nazi death camps, 503
on the Other, 189, 501–505, 605
"The Paradox of Morality," **510–512**
Lewis, John, 525
Lexigrams, 671, *672*
Lex talionis, 346, 682
Li, 542
Libby, Lewis "Scooter," 652
Liberalism, egalitarian, 339
Liberals, political, *473*, 559–561, 664, 678
The Libertarian Alternative (Hospers), 337
Libertarian Party, 249, 250, 337
Library at Alexandria, 391, 392
Librescu, Liviu, 163–164
Life
choices in, 499, 501, 504
the "good life," 400–401
meaning of, 437–440, 487–489, 494, 500
profit vs. respect for life, 658–660, 729–731
quality of, 232, 268–271, 644–645
respect for, 658–660
right to, 337–338
telling one's story, 49, 570–574, 690–692, 725–726
The Life of David Gale (film), **733–737**
The Life of Tom Horn (film), 72, **570–574**
Lifton, Robert Jay, 685
Limbaugh, Rush, 586
Limitations of ethics, 58–59
Lincoln, Abraham, 178–179
Lin Yutang, 544–547, *545*, **566–568**
Literature, Arts, and Medicine Database, 48
Little Big Man (film), 74
"Little Red Riding Hood," 52, 55
Livingstone, Neil, 239
Living wills, 644
Locke, John
on capital punishment, 681
harm principle and, 250
on individualism, 341
influence on founders of United States, 336
on natural rights, 329, 334, 657
Second Treatise on Government, 334, 336, 657
Lockean Proviso, 657
Logic, 15, 20–21, 136, 532

Logical fallacies. *See* Fallacies
Lonesome Cowboys (film), 74
Lonesome Dove (film), 74
Looking after oneself, obligation of, 181–185
Lord Jim (Conrad), 62, **462–464**, *463*
The Lord of the Rings (books by Tolkien and film)
effects of evil in, 8
Gollum character in, *8*, 77, 472
as Holy Grail legend variant, 8
invisibility ring in, 168–170, *169*, 202–206
overview of key characters, **221–223**
Love, as a virtue, 540
Love and Consequences (Jones), 648
Love's Knowledge (Nussbaum), 24, 26, **28–29**, 698
The Lucifer Effect (Zimbardo), 6, **30–33**
Lung, Sihung, *581*
Lyceum, in Athens, 431, 449
Lying, 136–137, 299–301, 307–311, 648
Lynch, Jessica, 523–525, *524*

Machiavelli, Niccolò, 225
MacIntyre, Alasdair, 51–52, 480, 481
Macpherson, C. B., 657
Macy, Bob, 684
Madame Bovary (Flaubert), 62
MADD (Mothers Against Drunk Driving), 250
Majority rule
in ethical relativism, 128–129, 130, 141–142
in utilitarianism, 248, 253–254
Makrina of Neocaesaria, 599
Malice, compassion vs., 537–538
A Man for All Seasons (film), **419–422**, *420*
Mangold, James, **304–307**
Manhole covers, 589
Manichaeism, 410
Mann, Michael, **729–731**
Mann, Thomas, 64
"Mantage" (Matheson), 697
Manuelito, 525
Marie Grubbe (Jacobsen), 62
Marlowe, Christopher, 63
Marriage, 486–487, *486*, 609
Marx, Karl, 338, 406, 658
Marxism, 338–339
M*A*S*H (TV series), 533
Matchpoint (film), **307–311**
Material cause, Aristotle on, 437
Materialism, 406
Matheson, Richard, 697
Matriarchal societies, 594
Mayo, Bernard, 474–475, 480
McCain, John, 239, 525, 528, **562–564**
McGregor, Ewan, *37*
McGuane, Thomas, **570–574**
McQueen, Steve, *573*
McVeigh, Timothy, 284
Mead, Margaret, 136–137
Meaning of life
absence of, in existentialism, 494
Aristotle on human purpose, 437–440
personal identity, 500
as subjective, 487–489
writing one's story, 692–696
Medea (Euripides), 86, **102–106**

Media ethics. *See* News media ethics
Medical ethics, 48, 174, 236, 322
Medical research, gender equality in, 610
Megan's Law, 335–336
"Me-ism," 255
Melamine in dog food, 658–660
Melting pot image, 139
Melville, Herman, 66–67, 318
A Mémoire of the Holocaust Years
    (Defonseca), 648
Men Are from Mars, Women Are from Venus
    (Gray), *608*
Mencius, 543–544
Meno (Plato), 408
Metaethics, 121, 239
Metaphysics
    as branch of philosophy, 15, 433
    dualism, 406
    idealism, 406
    major theories of, 406
    materialism, 406
The Metaphysics of Morals (Kant), 276,
    286, 293–295, **299–301**, 392
Micro-inequities, 139
Middle Ages, women's status in, 595–596
Midgley, Mary, 5, 179–180, *180,* 192–194
Milgram, Stanley, 6
Milgram obedience experiments, 6
Military, women in, 523–524, 592–593
Military Commissions Act of 2006,
    121, 240
Mill, Harriet Hardy Taylor, 243, 244, *245,*
    598, **618–621**
Mill, James, 240, 252
Mill, John Stuart, 240–253
    on abuse of minorities, 237
    Autobiography, 241–242
    on Bentham, 241
    on colonialism, 252–253
    education and breakdown
        of, 240–242, *241*
    on happiness, 230
    harm principle of, 247–253, 329
    on hedonistic calculus, 233
    on hedonistic paradox, 242
    on higher and lower pleasures, 243–247
    on Kant's categorical imperative, 282, 291
    On Liberty, 245, 248, 319
    naturalistic fallacy and, 246
    on self-determination, 319
    The Subjection of Women, 244, 594, 618
    on tyranny of the majority, 248,
        253–254
    Utilitarianism, 243, 248, **258–261**
    utilitarianism revision by, 242–247,
        258–261
    on women's rights, 244, 598, 600,
        607, 609
Millican, James, *302*
A Million Little Pieces (Frey), 648
Minority Report (film), **381–384**
Mirror neurons, 11, 532
Les Misérables (Hugo), 62
Missing (film), 74
Mississippi Burning (film), 345–346,
    374–377
Mitchell, Greg, 685
Moby Dick (Melville), 66–67
Moderation. *See also* Golden Mean
    Aristotle on, 444
    Confucius on, 542

    in Flight of Icarus myth, 458–459
    Phintys on, 599
Modoc legends, 66
Moll, Jorge, 532
Mona Lisa Smile (film), **633–637,** *635*
Monoculturalism, 139
Monoculturalism, 139
Monster's Ball (film), 50
Moore, Michael, 89, 175
Moral absolutism (hard universalism),
    117–118, 128, 278, 482
Moral agents, persons as, 313
Moral autonomy, 295
Moral awareness, in science fiction, 75
"Moral cannibalism," 337
Moral community, 388
Moral conflicts. *See* Conflict resolution
Moral courage, 524, 527–531
Moral decisions
    causing deaths of others, 22–23, 352
    conditional, 279
    emotion and, 21–23, 50, 194–195
    golden mean example, 442, *442,*
        443, *447*
    Heinz dilemma, 610–611
    law and, 19–20
    logic and, 20–21
    moral intuition and, 533, 558
    by Nazis, 530–531
    religion and, 17–19
    Socrates on, 16–17
    storytelling and, 23–24, 25, 51–52
Moral differences, 114–118
Moral expectations, 20
Moral goodness, Aristotle on, 439
Moral intuition, 533, 558
Morality. *See also* Moral decisions
    compassion required by, 536–540
    development of, before age of seven,
        12–13
    ethics *vs.,* 14
    evolution and, 532
    good and evil concepts in, 4–10
    hardwired in the brain, 10–12, 532
    homosexuality and, 609
    legality *vs.,* 19
    nihilism, 115, 130, 142
    "slave-morality," 495
    of taking a life, 630–640
    teaching, 479–481
    virtue ethics and, 470–471
"Morality and Violence: War, Revolution,
    Terrorism" (Narveson), **708–711**
Moralizing
    in didactic stories, 60, 471
    negative associations of, 14
    in politics, 5
    teaching ethics and, 482
Moral judgments, in normative *vs.*
    descriptive ethics, 121, 122
Moral nihilism, 115, 130, 142
Moral relativism
    ethical pluralism and, 558–559
    Furrow on, **147–149**
    moral subjectivism, 115–116, 130
    prefrontal cortex and, 10–12
"The Moral Significance of Interests"
    (Sapontzis), 674
Moral skepticism, 115–116
Moral subjectivism, 115–116, 130
Moral values, 12–13
Moral virtue, 440

More, Sir Thomas, 397, **419–422,** *420*
Mothers Against Drunk Driving
    (MADD), 250
Mott, Lucretia, 600
The Mountains of the Moon (film), 68
"The Mouse and the Lion," 60
Movies. *See* Films
Multiculturalism
    acknowledging, 560–561
    dominant viewpoint in, 141
    ethical pluralism, 558–559
    ethical relativism and, 139–143
    Eurocentrism and, 124, 140
    moral and political, in United States,
        4, 560
    salad bowl metaphor of, 139–140
    soft universalism and, 142–143
    use of storytelling in understanding, 49
Munch, Edvard, *488*
Muntz, Peter, 54
Murasaki Shikibu, 599
Murder, 136, 314–315, 684
"The Murders in the Rue Morgue"
    (Poe), 80
Murdoch, Iris, 604
Mutuality, in friendship, 550–551
My Fair Lady (musical), 79
Mystery stories, 80–83, *83,* 100–102
Mystic River (film), 50
Myth of Amoral Business, 654
"The Myth of Er" (Socrates), 408
"The Myth of the Cave" (Plato), 409–410,
    409, 411, **422–424**
Myths, 54, 66

Naess, Arne, 677
The Name of the Rose (Eco), 88, **98–100**
Narrative identity, 690–698
    ethical wills, 696
    living in the narrative zone, 696–698
    rewriting one's story, 694–695
    searching for meaning, 692–696
    telling one's story, 49, 690–692, 725–726
Narrative time, 696–697
Narveson, Jan, **708–711**
Nathanson, Steven, 664
"50-50" nation, United States as, 2–4
National security, civil liberties *vs.,*
    335–336
Native Americans. *See* American Indians
Natural Born Killers (film), 87
Naturalism, 19, 450, 451
Naturalistic fallacy, 246, 591
Natural law, 19, 450, 451
Natural predisposition, Kant on, 295
Natural selection, 438
Navajo legends, 66
Nazis
    Bergson and, 497
    ethical relativism and judgment of,
        125–126
    firm moral principles of, 50
    harassment of Husserl, 491
    Heidegger's connection with, 490–491,
        490, 503
    Holocaust, 6–7, 533–536, 576–579
    Le Chambon village resistance to,
        533–536
    Levinas on, 503
    medical experiments by, 322
    moral decisions of, 530–531

rescue of people from, 533–536, 576–579
Sartre's opposition to, 493
in *Schindler's List*, 165, **576–579**, *578*
use of Nietzsche's philosophy by, 495–496
who felt sorry for their victims, 536
Neeson, Liam, 578
Negative command, 536
Negative rights, 334–338, 641, 642
Negative role models, 62, 472
Nelson, Hailey Anne, *37*
Neoplatonic Institute, Alexandria, 391, *392*
Neoplatonism, 391, *392,* 409–410
Network (film), 646
Neuroscience and moral values, 10–12, 13, 195
Newell, Mike, **633–637**
News media ethics, 644–653
    active generation of news for ratings, 646
    business ethics and, 653–654
    credibility problems, 648
    embedded journalists, 649–650
    free speech and, 647–648
    legal restraints and, 700–702
    political bias, 652–653
    public's right to know and, 646–647, 649
    violent deaths shown on television, 650–651, 726–729
    in wartime, 648–651
New Testament. *See* Bible
Niccol, Andrew, **371–374, 424–427**
Nicomachean Ethics (Aristotle), 339, 440–441, **453–455, 456–458**
Nietzsche, Friedrich, 411, 494, 495–496, 607
Nihilism, 115, 130, 142
Niven, Larry, **732–733**
Njal's Saga, **460–461**
Noble savage concept, 679
No Exit (Sartre), 499, **512–514**
Nolan, Pat, 347
Noncombatants, 666
Nonhumans (artificial persons), 77–79, 292
Nonmoral value judgments, 9
Non Sequitur (comic strip), *652*
Nonviolent protest, 360–361, 663
Nonvoluntary euthanasia, 641
Normative ethics, 120, 121, 122, 128, 181
Normative soft universalism, 138
Northwest Coast Indians, 122–123
Novels, 25, 26, *286*. *See also* Storytelling; *names of specific novels*
Nozick, Robert, 341, 657
The Nuremberg Files, 251
Nussbaum, Martha
    Hiding from Humanity, 24
    importance of emotions in work of, 24–27, *24,* 50, 352, 537, 687
    Love's Knowledge, 24, 26, **28–29,** 698
    on novels, *286*
    on stories, 694
    Upheavals of Thought: The Intelligence of Emotions, 24

Objectivism, 207–211
Occam's razor, 192, 557
Oedipus complex, 621
Oedipus Rex (Sophocles), 86
"Of Cave Dwellers and Spirits" (Furrow), **147–149**

"Of the Principle of Utility" (Bentham), **256–258**
Oklahoma City federal building bombing, 284
Okonedo, Sophie, *378*
Old people, respect for, 544–547, 566–568, 579–582
Olsen, Regine, 486–487, *486*
"The Ones Who Walk Away from Omelas" (Le Guin), **267–268**
"The One Where Phoebe Hates PBS," *Friends,* **213–215**
"On Growing Old Gracefully" (Lin Yutang), **566–568**
On Liberty (Mill), *245,* 248, 319
Online communities, cultural ethics in, 129
"On the Different Races of Man" (Kant), 290
On the Moderation of Women (Phintys), 599
Ontology, 690
Open Range (film), 74
Ordo Virtuem (Hildegard of Bingen), 595
Orend, Brian, 667
Organs, availability for transplant, 646, 732–733
"Original position," Rawls on, 340, 344–345, 587, 611, 658
Original position theory, 340, 344–345
Ortiz, Alfonso, 388
Orwell, George, 613
Osment, Haley Joel, *583*
The Other, 78, 501–505, 604–605
Otherwise Than Being (Levinas), 500
O'Toole, Peter, *463*
"Ought implies can," 168, 189
Ovid, 78, 459

Pacifism, 663, 665
Palma, Michael, **268–271**
Pan, Matthew Hiasi, 676
Panbanisha, 671–672
"The Parable of the Good Samaritan," 57, **574–576,** *575*
Parables, 56–57, **574–576**
"Paradox and Dream" (Steinbeck), **149–151**
"The Paradox of Morality: An Interview with Emmanuel Levinas," **510–512**
Parameters, US Army War College Quarterly, 666
Parents
    advice from, 552–553
    duties of children towards, 544–547, 566–568, 579–582
    friendship with grown children, 551–552
    lack of duty towards, 548–553
Parker, Alan, **374–377, 733–737**
Parks, Rosa, 528
Parmenides, 15
Parsimony, principle of, 192
Partial rights, 675
Particularism, 140
Passionate love, 540
Passive resistance, 360–361, 663
Paterfamilias, 542
Patria potestas, 317
Patriotism, 664
Patterns of Culture (Benedict), *123*
Pay It Forward (film), 555, **582–585,** *583*
Peanuts (comic strip), *550*
Pearce, Guy, *84*
Pearl, Danny, 650
Pearson, Keir, **377–381**

Perictione, *400*
"Perpetual Peace" (Kant), 669
The Persians (Aeschylus), 86
Persistent vegetative state, 643
Personal identity, 500, 690–698
Personal legacy letters, 696
Personhood, 312–328. *See also* Right(s)
    of children, 315, 317–318
    cloning and, 325–328
    crimes and, 314–316
    of criminals, 316–317
    definition of human being, 312–313
    of fetuses, 639–640, *639*
    genetic engineering and, 320, 322–323
    of great apes, 671–672, 676, 712–714
    medical advances and, 321–322
    of prostitutes, 314–315
    responsibility and, 318–319
    stem cell research and, 323–325
    of women, 313, 319
Persons as ends in themselves, 288–291
Petersen, William, *81*
Peterson, Scott and Laci, 353
Pet food, melamine contamination of, 658–660
Pets. *See* Animals
PGD (preimplantation genetic diagnosis), 323
Phaedo (Plato), 398
Phaedrus (Plato), 394, 402
Phenomenology, 491, 493, 501
Philadelphia (film), 48
Philip (king of Macedonia), 431
Philosophy
    argument in, 20
    four classic branches of, 15
    questioning values, 13
    role of reason in, 18–19
    storytelling in teaching of, 49–50
"Philosophy and the Value of a Multicultural Community" (Blum)
Phintys of Sparta, 599
Phronesis, 440
Physical courage, 524, 527–531, 568–569
Picturing Justice website, 49
"A Piece of Advice" (Singer), **464–466**
Piestewa, Lori, 523, 593, *593*
Pity, Hobbes on, 171
Plagiarism, 479, 648
"Platinum Rule," 184
Plato. *See also* Socrates
    Academy of Athens, 399, 410, 431, *434*
    on anamnesis, 408
    Apology, 396, 398, **415–418**
    bust of, *92, 400*
    Crito, 396
    Dialogues, 16, 89, 167, 393, 399
    on drama, 84–86, 88, 92–96
    as dualist, 407
    on the Form of the Good, 408–410
    on ideal society, 403–405, *404*
    influence on Christianity, 410–411
    life of, 399–400, *400*
    Meno, 408
    "The Myth of the Cave," 409–410, *409, 411,* **422–424**
    Phaedo, 398
    Phaedrus, 394, 402
    on psychological egoism, 167–170, 185–186, *185,* 202–206
    on reincarnation, 408

Plato (continued)
  The Republic, 85, 92–96, 167–170,
    198–202, 412–414, 422–424
  theory of forms, 405–410, 411
  theory of metaphysics, 15
  on the tripartite soul, 402–405, 404
  on utility, 227
  on women, 404, 439
Pleasure, hedonistic paradox and, 228
Pleasure principle, 197
Plotinus, 410
Pluralism, 139, 558–559
Poe, Edgar Allan, 80
Poetic creativity, 52, 692
Poetics (Aristotle), 85, 86, 96–98, 98–100
The Poisonwood Bible (Kingsolver), 124,
    151–156
Polis, 393–394, 398
Politics
  Aristotle on, 330
  conduct vs. character in, 471–473
  conservatives, 473, 559–561, 664, 678
  ethics of conduct and, 471–473
  liberals, 473, 559–561, 664, 678
  red states vs. blue states, 2–4, 559–560
  September 11, 2001 terrorist attacks
    and, 143, 335–336, 664
Politics (Aristotle), 330
Popper, Karl, 177
Positive command, 536
Positive rights, 338–339, 641
Positive thinking, 693
Possessing the Secret of Joy (Walker), 127,
    157–159
Postwar settlements, justice in, 667
Potential virtue, 436
Poulain de la Barre, François, 244, 597
The Poverty of Historicism (Popper), 177
Prefrontal cortex. See Brain
Preimplantation genetic diagnosis
    (PGD), 323
Pride, 444
Pride and Prejudice (Austen), 61–62
Priests, child abuse by, 175, 317
Primates and Philosophers: How Morality
    Evolved (de Waal), 197–198,
    211–213
"Primitive" societies, 120, 122
Primoratz, Igor, 347
Princess (film), 82
Princess phenomenon, 617
Prisoner's dilemma, 190, 215–216
Privacy, right to, 250–251
Probability of success, in just wars, 665, 668
Problem of induction, 132–134
Prodigal son parable, 57
Professed vs. actual morality, 128
Professional ethics, 645
The Program (film), 87
Propaganda films, 50
Proper pride, 444
Property rights, 336–337, 657–658
Proportionality of ends, 665, 668
Proportionality of means, 666
Proportionality principle,
    in punishment, 686
Prose Poems (Turgenev), 540
Prostitutes, personhood of, 314–315
Proulx, Annie, 74
Prudence, 184
Psychological altruism, 189

Psychological egoism
  animal altruism and, 196–197
  cynicism and, 174–175
  as descriptive theory, 166
  excuses and, 175
  free will and, 176
  Hobbes on, 170–171
  language problems in theory of, 179–181
  Midgley on, 179–180, 180
  "ought implies can," 168, 189
  pity and, 171
  psychological altruism vs., 189
  selfish reasons for good deeds,
    172–173, 178–179, 213–215
  Socrates and Plato on, 167–170,
    185–186, 185
  theory of, 163–166
  unfalsifiability of theory of, 177–178
Psychology, moral values and, 13
Psychosexual neutrality, 606
Psychotherapy, storytelling in, 49
Ptolemy I, 391
Public's right to know, 646–647, 649
Pulp Fiction (film), 64, 111–113
Punishment
  anger and, 351–353
  capital, 351, 353, 681–690
  cruel and unusual, 683
  cultural differences in, 124
  as deterrence, 348, 349, 681, 686–687
  imprisonment, 346
  proportionality principle in, 686
  as rehabilitation, 347, 348–349
  as retaliation, 346
  as retribution, 349–350, 351,
    681–682, 687
  as vengeance, 350–351, 687
Pygmalion (Shaw), 78–79
Pyrrhic victories, 665

Quality Adjusted Life years (QALY), 645
Quality of life, 232, 268–271, 644–645
The quest, 65–66
Quest for Fire (film), 68

Race, culture and, 131
Rachels, James, 134–138, 137, 179, 255
Racism
  civil rights movement, 345–346,
    360–361, 374–377
  criminal justice and, 374–377
  in death penalty administration, 684
  in the Enlightenment, 290
  freedom of speech and, 333–334,
    647–648
  freedom of thought and, 316
  phenomenon of "privileged race,"
    362–363
  in Westerns, 518–521
Radical feminism, 600, 602, 614–615
Raiders of the Lost Ark (film), 68
Rainer, Tristine, 725–726
Raising Maidens of Virtue (McDonald), 385
Ramachandran, V. F., 11, 532
Rand, Ayn
  on American culture, 143
  Atlas Shrugged, 219–221, 337, 338–339
  on moral courage, 529
  on objectivism, 207–211
  The Virtue of Selfishness, 184–185,
    207–211, 208, 336–337

Randolph, Charles, 733–737
Raphael, 434
Rather, Dan, 648
Rational element. See Reason
Rational ethical egoism, 190
Rationality. See also Reason
  in animals, 293, 671–672
  categorical imperative and, 281, 284–286
  in the Enlightenment, 225
  gender differences in, 285–286, 285
  values originating from, 191
Rawls, John
  "Justice as Fairness," 339–341,
    358–360
  The Law of Peoples, 705–708
  on the original position, 340, 344–345,
    587, 611, 658
  on property rights, 658
  A Theory of Justice, 340, 358
  "Two Concepts of Rules," 350–351
Reality TV shows, 53, 237–238
Reason. See also Rationality
  in the Enlightenment, 225, 285
  in moral choice, 537–539
  Plato and Socrates on role of, 185–186,
    185, 401, 402–405, 404
  as purpose of being human, 438–439
  as tool of ethics, 18–19
Reciprocal altruism, 190, 224. See also
    Utilitarianism
Reciprocity, 190, 224, 549–551, 553
Recycling movement, 676–677
Red herring fallacy, 21
Red states vs. blue states, 2–4, 559–560.
    See also Conservatives, political;
    Liberals, political
Reductio ad absurdum (slippery slope
    argument), 21, 472, 680–681
Reefer Madness (film), 50, 472
"Reel Therapy," 48–49
Rehabilitation, punishment as, 347, 348–349
Reimer, David, 607
Reincarnation, Plato on, 408
Relatives, obligations to, 552
Relativism. See also Ethical relativism
  cognitive, 487
  cultural, 119–120, 122, 129–131,
    137, 401
  moral, 10–12, 115–116, 130, 147–149,
    558–559
Religion. See also Christianity
  ancient Greek, 406–407
  animism, 679
  Aristotle and, 437
  Confucianism, 17, 184, 541–543
  goddess, 594–595
  Golden Rule in, 184
  "good" and "evil" in, 5
  Hinduism, 406, 408
  Islam, 19, 184, 391, 449–450
  Manichaeism, 410
  moral issues and, 17–19
  parables in, 57
  reproductive cloning and, 326–327
  stories and legends in, 51, 53–54
  Taoism, 543
  victims of religious fanaticism, 390, 391
  virtue ethics and, 390–392
Religious stage, 489–490
Remarque, Erich Maria, 71
Reproductive cloning, 325–328

The Republic (Plato)
    on art and drama, 85, **92–96**
    on ideal society, 403–405, *404*
    on the just person, **412–414**
    "The Myth of the Cave" (Plato),
        409–410, *409, 411,* **422–424**
    on psychological egoism, 167–170,
        198–202
    on reincarnation, 408
    on utility, 227
Requiem for a Dream (film), 50, 472
Responsibility, 318–319, 480–482
Responsible agency, 718
Restorative justice, 347
Retentionism, 683, 686–687, 717–720.
        See also Death penalty
Retirement, self-worth and, 546
Retribution, punishment as, 349–350,
        351, 681–682, 687
Retributive justice, 347
Retro-Westerns, *73*
Return to Paradise (film), 190, **215–218,** *217*
Ricoeur, Paul, 500, 690–691, 695, 696
Ridgway, Gary, 315, 689
Right(s). *See also* Personhood
    abortion and, 641
    of animals, 320, 673–675, 676, 711–712
    Bentham on, 329
    civil liberties *vs.* security, 335–336
    civil rights movement, 345–346,
        360–361, 374–377
    to death, 642
    Dworkin on, 331–334
    of free speech, 332–334, 647–648
    Hobbes on, 328–329
    human, **354–357,** 559
    to know, 646–647, 649
    to life, 337–338
    Locke on, 329
    natural, 328–329, 451
    of natural objects, 680–681
    negative, 334–338, 641, 642
    not traded for benefits, 331–334
    partial, 675
    positive, 338–339, 641
    to privacy, 250–251
    property, 336–337, 657–658
    public's right to know, 646–647, 649
    racism and, 345–346, 360–361, 362–363
    in slavery, 320
    United Nations Universal Declaration of
        Human Rights, **354–357,** 559
    of women, 244, *245,* 319–320, 598,
        600, 607, 609
    workers', 316, 338–339, 656
Righteous indignation, 446
*Right-Wing Women: The Politics of
    Domesticated Females* (Dworkin),
    614–615
Ring of Gyges (Plato), 167–170,
    198–202, 402
"The Rings of Tolkien and Plato" (Katz),
    170, **202–206**
Rio Bravo (film), 74
Rivera, Geraldo, 650
Robinson, Bruce, **215–218**
Robots (artificial persons), 77–79, 292
Roe v. Wade, 638
Role models
    Kant on, *473, 475*
    Mayo on, 474–475

negative, 472
Sartre on, 498
siblings as, *473, 475*
stories with, 61–62, 472
Romeo and Juliet (Shakespeare), 68–69
Roosevelt, Franklin D., 522
Roots (Haley), 142
Rosenberg, Julius and Ethel, 683
Rosenstand, Nina, 679, 711
Rosenthal, Mark, **633–637**
Roth, Eric, **729–731**
Rousseau, Jean-Jacques
    on the noble savage, 679
    on property and inequality, 658
    on war, 661
    on women, 597–598, 607
Ruben, Joseph, **215–218**
Rule utilitarianism, 254–255
Runaway Jury (film), *237,* **271–274**
Rusesabagina, Paul, **377–381,** *378*
Russell, Bertrand, 695
Rutgers women's basketball team, 647

Sacrifice
    Abraham and Isaac story, 57–60, *58, 503*
    of the few for the many, 236–238
    self-sacrifice, 530
Saddam Hussein, 651, 667–668
Sadism, by Nazi soldiers, 534
Salad bowl metaphor of multiculturalism,
    139–140
Sally Forth (comic strip), *602*
Sameness, equality and, 331
Same-sex marriage, 609
A Sand County Almanac (Leopold), 677
Santa Anna, Antonio Lòpez de, 666
Sapontzis, Steve, 674–675
Sartre, Jean-Paul
    on choice and authenticity, 496–499
    "Existentialism Is a Humanism,"
        507–510
    on imitating good persons, 475
    influence of Beauvoir on, *606*
    influence of Bergson on, 497
    on lack of human purpose, 440
    No Exit, **512–514**
Satire, 174
Savage-Rumbaugh, Sue, 671, 672
Scapegoats, 349
Schamus, James, **579–582**
Scheck, Barry, 133–134
Schiavo, Terri, 642–644
Schindler, Robert and Mary, 643
Schindler's List (film), 165, **576–579,** *578*
Schmäling, Julius, 535–536
Schneewind, J. B., 470
Scholastics (Schoolmen), 665
The School of Athens (Raphael), *434*
Schools. *See also* Education; Students
    gender feminism and, 613
    multiculturalism in, 139–141
    school shootings, 4, 87, 163–164, 287
Schwarzenegger, Arnold, 77
Science, 320–321, 432–435
Science fiction, 75–80, 367–371,
    371–374, 732–733
Scofield, Paul, *420*
Scott, A. O., **714–715**
Scream (films), 87
The Scream (Munch), *488*
SCUM (Society for Cutting Up Men), 588

Search and seizure, 335
The Searchers (film), 67, 72, **518–521,** *519*
Second Amendment rights, 333
The Second Sex (Beauvoir), 600, 604–606,
    621–624
Second Treatise on Government (Locke),
    334, 336, 657
Second-wave feminism, 600
The Secret (Byrne), 693
Selectivity, in storytelling, 691
Self-determination, Mill on, 319
Self-esteem, multiculturalism and, 140
Self-interest, 166, 181–182, 186, 661
The Selfish Gene (Dawkins), 191
Selfish-gene theory, 191–194
Selfishness, 166, 179–181
Selflessness, 188–190
Self-sacrifice, 530
Self-worth, retirement and, 546
Seligson, Amber Levanon, **702–703**
Seltzer, Margaret, 648
Senesh, Hannah, 525
Seniors, respect for, 544–547, 566–568,
    579–582
Senses, empirical knowledge from, 432
Sepoy Mutiny, 252, 253
September 11, 2001 terrorist attacks
    American identity following, 143
    civil liberties *vs.* security after, 335–336
    downing of the fourth plane, 238–239
    ethical relativism and, 114–115
    examination of Western ideals after, 558
    heroic acts, 164–165, *172*
    patriotism and, 664
    possibility of virtue in terrorists, 477
    psychological egoism and, 165
    Sepoy Mutiny experience compared
        with, 253
    terrorists *vs.* freedom fighters after, 662
Serial killers, animal torture by, 294
Serkis, Andy, *8*
Set It Off (film), 87
Sexism. *See also* Gender equality
    freedom of thought and, 316
    invisibility of women in the classroom,
        363–364
    Levinas and, 504
    radical feminism and, 614–615
Sex offenders, registration of, 335
Sexual abuse of children, 175, 317, 335–336
Sexual behavior, 90, 251
Sexual dimorphism, 590
Sexual harassment, 600, 601, 656
Sexual identity, 606–607, 609
Shakespeare, William, 68–69, 500
Shame, moral values and, 26
Sharia, 19
Shaw, George Bernard, 78–79
Shelley, Mary Wollstonecraft, 77, 597
"Should Trees Have Standing? Towards
    Legal Rights for Natural Objects"
    (Stone), 680
Shrake, Bud, **570–574**
Shrek (films), 65, 90, **427–430,** *428*
Sibling rivalry, *473, 475*
Sideshow (Tepper), 131
Silverado (film), 73–74, *73*
Simenon, Georges, 80
Simone (film), 79
"The Simple Art of Murder" (Chandler),
    100–102

Simpson, O. J., 21, 646
The Simpsons (TV series), 554
Singer, Isaac Bashevis, **464–466**
Singer, Peter
    on animal rights, 233, 235
    "A Convenient Truth," **261–263**, *262*
    The Expanding Circle, 190, 557,
        673–674
    The Great Ape Project, *262*, 676
    on moral intuition, 533
    prisoner's dilemma variation by, 190
    as a utilitarian, 224
Sites, Kevin, 650
Situation awareness, of cloned beings,
    326–327
Skepticism, 115–116
Slave-morality, Nietzsche on, 495
Slavery
    Aristotle on, 433
    backward-looking justice for, 345–346
    denial of rights in, 319
    in the Enlightenment, 288
    of genetically altered population,
        326–327
Slippery slope argument, 21, 472, 680–681
Smith, Patricia, 648
Smith, Paul R., 524
Smoke Signals (book by Alexie and film),
    33–36, *35*
Snoop Dogg, 647
Snow White and the Seven Dwarfs (film),
    55–56
Social classes, 227–229, 289
Social contract theory, 167, 334, 340, 661
Social equality, 330, 331–334
Social goods, 344
Socialism, 338–339
Socialization, values from, 191, 197
"Social Justice" (Kemp), 645
Social utility, 339
Society for Cutting Up Men (SCUM), 588
Socrates. *See also* Plato
    death of, 394–400, *397*
    as dualist, 406
    on ethics, 15, 16–17
    on the good life, 400–401
    on justice, 186
    Kierkegaard on, 489, 490
    life of, 393–394
    on personal knowledge, 500
    Plato on, 89
    on psychological egoism, 167–170,
        185–186, *185*
    on utility, 227
Socratic method, 17, 393
Soft universalism
    Benedict on, 134
    common humanity and, 559
    dealing with moral differences with,
        116–117, 117n
    descriptive *vs.* normative, 138
    ethical pluralism, 558–559
    Hume's emotionalism as, 195
    moral intuition in, 533, 558
    multiculturalism and, 142
    Rachels on, 134–138, *137*
Soldier Blue (film), 74
Soli Deo Gloria, 444
Sommers, Christina Hoff
    on cheating by students, 655
    on equity feminism, 603–604

hard universalism and, 482–483
    on personal responsibility, 480–482, *480*
    on teaching ethics, 478–480
    The War Against Boys, 613
    Who Stole Feminism?, 603–604
Sophia, 440
Sophists, 401
Sophocles, 86
Sophrosyne, 458
The Sopranos (TV series), 82–83, *83*, 87
Sorell, Tom, **717–720**
Sor Juana Inez de la Cruz, 596
The Sorrows of Young Werther (Goethe), 63,
    83–85, 88–89, **106–107**
Soul, tripartite, 402–405, *404*
Sound deductive arguments, 15
"The Sour Grapes," 60
Spacey, Kevin, *84, 583, 734*
Spain, status of great apes in, 676
Spanish Inquisition, 63, 240
Sparta, as *polis,* 393, 398
Specific deterrence, 348, 686–687
Speusippus, 431
Spielberg, Steven, **381–384, 568–569,
    576–579**
Spirit (willpower), Plato on, 402–405, *404*
Spitzer, Elliot, 175
Spock (character), 532
Stages on Life's Way (Kierkegaard), 485
Stand By Me (film), 87
Stanford Prison Experiment, 6, 30–33
Stanton, Elizabeth Cady, 600
Star Trek (TV series), 76
Star Trek: The Next Generation (TV series),
    76, 78
Star Wars (films), 76
Steinbeck, John
    East of Eden, 9–10, **40–46**, *41*, 65
    "Paradox and Dream," **149–151**
    photograph of, 150
Stem cell research, 323–325
Steppenwolf (Hesse), 65
Stevenson, Robert Louis, 64
Stewart, Martha, 654
Stone, Christopher D., 680
Stone, Oliver, 141
Storytelling
    about life's crises, 693–694
    about the beginning, 51
    about the value of stories, 79–80
    the bargain, 62–64
    courage stories, 460–461, 523–526,
        570–574
    crime, 80–83, *81, 83, 84,* 100–102
    didactic stories, 47, 170, 471
    fables and counterfables, 47, 60–61, 76
    fact *vs.* fiction in, 52
    fairy tales, 54–56, 60, 66
    good twin and bad twin, 64–65
    Greek philosophers on, 84–86, 88
    Holy Grail legend, 67–68, *69*
    impact of stories, 83–91
    moral issues and, 23–24
    mysteries, 80–83, *83,* 100–102
    myths, 54, 66
    narrative identity and, 49, 690–698,
        725–726
    parables, 56–57
    personal legacy letters, 696
    the quest, 65–66

in religion, 51, 53–54
    role models in, 61–62, 472
    science fiction, 75–80, 367–371,
        371–374, 732–733
    selectivity in, 691
    self-comprehension through, 500
    tall tales, 137
    teaching morality through,
        387–388, 480
    telling one's story, 49, 570–574,
        690–692, 725–726
    use of, in professions, 48–51
    in video games, 87
    wartime stories, 69–70, *71*
    Westerns, 70–75, *73,* 301–307,
        518–521
    in world cultures, 51–52, 387–388
Straw man fallacy, 21, 324
Strawson, P. F., 351
Strick, Wesley, **215–218**
Strohmeyer, Jeremy, 188
Stuart, Walwyn, 165, *165,* 527
Students. *See also* Education; Schools
    cheating by, 478–479, 482, 655
    gender feminism effects on, 613
    gender-neutral language in term
        papers, 589
    invisibility of women in the classroom,
        363–364
    suicide by, 530
    teaching ethics to, 479–480
Styles of behavior, 554
The Subjection of Women (Mill), 244, 594, 618
Subjectivism, moral, 115–116, 130
Subjectivity, as truth, 487, 490
Suffering
    by animals, 234–235, 294
    in utilitarianism, 234, 236–238
Sugihara, Chiune and Yukiko, 534
Suicide
    courage and, 529–530
    doctor-assisted, 128–129, 249, 641–642
    lovesickness and, 106–107
    The Sorrows of Young Werther and, 63,
        83–85, 88–89, **106–107**
    "suicide by cop," 530
    utilitarianism and, 251–252
Sullivan, Shannon, 529
Summers, Larry, 610
Superego, 403, 485
Superheroes, 170
Suppressed correlative fallacy, 180–181, 193
Suu Kui, Aung San, 525
"The Swamp King's Daughter"
    (Andersen), 65
Sweatshops, 316

Taking Rights Seriously (Dworkin),
    331, 332
The Tale of Genji (Murasaki), 599
A Tale of Two Cities (Dickens), 1, 483
Tales of Good and Evil, Help and Harm
    (Hallie), 535, **565–566**
Taliban, 127
Talking points, 652
Talleyrand, Charles Maurice de, 597
Tall tales, lies in, 137
Talmud, Golden Rule and, 184
Tannen, Deborah, 554, 615–616
Tao, 541–543
Taoism, 543

Tarantino, Quentin, **111–113**
Taxi Driver (film), 87
Taylor, Richard, 5, 536–540, 687
Te, 542
Teaching ethics, 479–480
Teleological explanations, 438
Teleology, Aristotle and, 436–437, 438, 450, 451–452
Television. *See also* News media ethics; *names of specific shows*
  generating news for ratings, 646
  reality shows, 53, 237–238
  shows as moral events, 72
  sitcoms, 213–215
  violence in, 87
  violent deaths shown on news, 650–651, 726–729
Telling one's story, 49, 570–574, 690–692, 725–726. *See also* Narrative identity; Storytelling
Temperance, Aristotle on, 444, *447*
Tepper, Sheri S., 131
Terminator (films), 77–78
Terri's Law, 643
Terrorism. *See also* September 11, 2001 terrorist attacks
  anthrax letters, 650–651
  benefits to news media, *652*
  death of journalists, 650
  eco-terrorism, 602
  Narveson on, **708–711**
  official terror level, 651
  Oklahoma City federal building bombing, 284
  terrorists *vs.* freedom fighters, 662
Terrorists, heroic acts by, 188
Testing theories, 126
Thales, 15
That's Not What I Meant (Tannen), 554
Theatre. *See* Drama
Theophrastus, 449
Theories, viability of, 126, 177–178
A Theory of Justice (Rawls), 340, 358
Therapeutic cloning, 325
"Think globally, act locally," 675–676
Third-wave feminism, 600
The 13th Warrior (film), 118
"Thirty Tyrants," 394, 395
Thomas, Clarence, 600
Thomas Aquinas, Saint, 440, 449–450, 451
Thomson, Judith Jarvis, 640
Thought experiments, 75
Three-strikes law, 348
3:10 to Yuma (film), **304–307**
Thurman, Uma, *372*
Tillman, Pat, 524
Titanic (film), 174
Tolerance
  cultural, 122–123, 124, 126–127
  as universal virtue, 131–132
Tolkien, J. R. R., 169–170, 202–206, **221–223**
Tolstoy, Leo, 48
Tombstone (film), 74
Tom Horn (film), **570–574**, *573*
Tonsure policy, 595–596
Torturing and killing
  Abu Ghraib prison, 6, 30–33
  of animals, 294
  Congress on definition of torture, 121
  evil and, 5

Geneva Convention on, 121, 240
  Kantians on, 291
  in utilitarianism, 239–240, 254
Totalitarianism, Plato and, 405
Totality and Infinity (Levinas), 500
Toys, lead contamination in, 659
"Traditional American Indian and Western European Attitudes Toward Nature" (Callicott), 388–389
Traditional myths, 54
Tragical History of Dr. Faustus (Marlow), 63
Transgenic animals, 323
Transplant organs, availability of, 646, 732–733
Transvaluation of values, 496
A Treatise of Human Nature (Hume), 195
Trebilcot, Joyce, 609
Tredwill-Owen, Caspian, **367–371**
Tribal virtue ethics, 387–389
Tripartite soul, 402–405, *404*
Trocmé, André, 535
True self, Bergson on, 497
The Truman Show (film), 410, **424–427**, *425*
Truth, 487, 489, 490
Truthfulness, Aristotle on, 444–445. *See also* Lying
Turgenev, Ivan, 540
Turnbull, Susan, 696
Turner, Jahi, 193
Tuskegee syphilis study, 174, 236
Twain, Mark, 60–61, 539
Twins, stories of, 65
"Two Concepts of Rules" (Rawls), 350–351
"Two Ideals and the Death Penalty" (Sorell), **717–720**
2001: A Space Odyssey (film), 68, 77
Tyranny of the majority, 248, 253

Übermensch (Overman), 495–496
Unconscious, reason and, 285
Unforgiven (film), 74
United Nations Universal Declaration of Human Rights, **354–357**, 559
United States. *See also* Iraq War; September 11, 2001 terrorist attacks
  Abu Ghraib prisoner abuse scandal, 6, 30–33
  American identity following September 11 attacks, 143
  Congress on definition of torture, 121
  conservatives in, 473, 559–561
  culture of, 139, 143
  death penalty in, 683, 685
  Declaration of Independence, 330
  First Amendment rights, 332–334, 647–648
  Fourth Amendment rights, 335
  liberals in, 473, 559–561, 664, 678
  moral and political diversity in, 4
  multiculturalism in, 4, 139–140, 560
  as a "50-50" nation, 2–4
  politics in, 473, 559–561, 664, 678
  Rand on, 143
  red states *vs.* blue states, 2–4, 559–560
  Second Amendment rights, 333
  sexual harassment in, 600, 601, 656
  U.S.A. Patriot Act of 2001, 335
  Westerns, 70–75, *73*, 301–307, 518–521
Universal Declaration of Human Rights, **354–357**, 559

Universal good, tolerance as, 131–132
Universalism. *See* Hard universalism; Soft universalism
Universalizability, 183, 287
Universal moral law, 279
Unlawful combatants, 240, 666
"Unseen, Unheard, Unchosen" (Berteaux), **363–364**
Unselfishness, 179–181
Unsolicited favors, 553–555
Upheavals of Thought: The Intelligence of Emotions (Nussbaum), 24
U.S.A. Patriot Act of 2001, 335
Usefulness, self-worth and, 546
Utilitarianism, 224–274
  on abortion, 640–641
  act and rule, 253–255
  on animals, 233–235, 670–673, 674–675
  Bentham on, 225–229, *226*, **256–258**
  defining happiness in, 230
  on disabilities, 261–263
  on drug legalization, 249–250
  on ethical egoism, 190
  on forward-looking justice, 344, 349
  greatest-happiness principle in, 224–225, 254–255
  harm principle in, 247–253, 329
  on health care access, 268–271, 644–645
  hedonistic, 227–229
  hedonistic calculus, 229–232, *231, 239*
  higher and lower pleasures and, 243–247
  Mill's revision of, 242–247, **258–261**
  in political thought, 250–251
  problem of sheer numbers in, 235
  sacrificing a few for the many, 234, 236–238
  on torture, 239–240
  tyranny of the majority and, 248, 253–254
  uncertainty of consequences and, 232–233
Utilitarianism (Mill), 243, 248, **258–261**
Utility, principle of, 254

Valid deductive arguments, 15
Values
  in art theory, 9
  for businesses, 655
  definition of, 9, 12
  development of, before age of seven, 12–13
  humans as value-givers, 289–291
  intrinsic *vs.* instrumental, 227, 229, 288
  moral, 12–13
  multiculturalism and, 141
  origin of, 191
  in science, 320–321
  teaching, 13–14
  transvaluation of, 496
Van Dam, Danielle, 193
Van Sant, Gus, **514–518**
Van Zandt, Steven, 83
Vaughn, Vince, 217
Veil of ignorance, 340, 341
Veneer Theory, 191, 211
Vengeance, 350–351, 687
Verne, Jules, 75
A Very Long Engagement (film), 70

Viability, abortion and, 322
"The Victim and the Justification of
    Punishment" (Whiteley), 351–352,
    364–367
Victim impact statements, 353
Video games, 87
Vietnam Westerns, 74
A Vindication of the Rights of Women
    (Wollstonecraft), 244, 597, 598
Violence. See also Terrorism
    advocating, 251
    domestic, 352
    as evil, 5
    in the media, 86–87, 88, 650–651,
        726–729
    from rising religion, 390, 391
    school shootings, 4, 87, 163–164, 287
    torture, 5, 30–33, 121, 239–240,
        291, 294
    in video games, 87
Virginia Tech school shootings, 4,
    163–164, 287
Virtue(s). See also Virtue ethics
    Aristotle's Golden Mean and, 444, 446,
        447, 453–455
    cardinal, 444
    in Christianity, 444
    definition of, 385–386
    excellence and, 435–436
    intellectual vs. moral, 440
    love as, 540
    Mencius on, 544
    teaching, 480–481
    virtuous disposition, 392
Virtue ethics, 385–430
    African tribal, 387–388
    Aristotle on, 435–449
    character and, 385–386, 471
    in cheating by students, 655
    Christianity and, 390–392
    contemporary revival of, 470
    definition of virtue, 385–386
    feminism and, 586–588
    Foot on, 475–478
    indoctrination and, 481
    Kant and, 391–392
    Levinas and, 504
    Mayo on, 474–475
    morality and, 470–471
    Native American, 388–389
    objections to, 450–452
    prehistoric cultures, 386
    of reason in, 401, 402–405, 404
    ...es on, 394–401, 397, 398
    ...rs on, 478–483
    ... and, 451–452
    ...oul and, 402–405, 404
    ...lfishness (Rand), 184–185,
        336–337
    ...Foot), 476–477
    ...n, 392

    596–597, 600

    158

Walzer, Michael, 341, 663, 665
Wang, Hui-Ling, 579–582
Wanjiru story, 66
War. See also Nazis; Terrorism
    in Afghanistan, 127, 661, 663
    French Revolution, 597–598
    Gulf War, 174, 661
    heroism in, 69–70, 71, 523–525, 524,
        568–569
    in Iraq (See Iraq War)
    as just, 70, 660–669
    Narveson on, 708–711
    news media ethics during, 648–651
    postwar settlements, justice in, 667
    torture during, 6, 30–33, 121, 240
    war-crimes tribunals, 666
    wartime stories, 69–70, 71
The War Against Boys (Sommers), 613
War-crimes tribunals, 666
Warhol, Andy, 726
"Warning of Calamities and Hoping for a
    Change in 'An Inconvenient Truth'"
    (Scott), 714–715
Warren, Mary Ann, 640, 675
Washington, death penalty criteria in, 683
Washoe, 672
Waterboarding, 121, 240
Waters, Anthony Jon, 712–714
Watterson, Bill, 125
the Way, 541–543
Weapons of mass destruction (WMDs), 667
Weir, Peter, 424–427
Weisz, Rachel, 237
Welles, Halsted, 304–307
Wells, H. G., 75, 168
Wessel, Johann Herman, 263–265
West, Jim, 528–529
Westerfield, David, 689
Westerns, 70–75, 73, 301–307, 518–521
What Are Friends For? (Friedman), 343
What Could He Be Thinking? How a Man's
    Mind Really Works (Gurian), 616
"What Do Grown Children Owe Their
    Parents?" (English), 548–549
Whistle-blowing, 656
White lies, categorical imperative and, 286
Whitely, Diane, 351–352, 364–367, 688
"The white man's burden," 252
Who Owns Death? Capital Punishment, the
    American Conscience, and the End of
    Executions (Lifton and Mitchell), 685
Who Stole Feminism? (Sommers),
    603–604
Why Courage Matters (McCain), 90, 525,
    562–564
Wiard, William, 570–574
William of Occam, 192, 557
Wills, ethical, 696
Wilson, Brandon, 683
Wilson, Edward O., 191
Wilson, Woodrow, 669
Wiretapping, 335
Wiwel, Nils, 264
The Wizard of Id (comic strip), 682
WMDs (weapons of mass destruction), 667
Wolgast, Elizabeth, 341–342, 342
Wolheim, Louis, 71
Wollstonecraft, Mary, 77, 244, 597, 598,
    647–648

"The Woman Destroyed" (Beauvoir),
    631–633
"Woman's work," 592–594, 610
Women. See also Feminism/feminists;
    Gender equality; Women's rights
    Aristotle on, 433, 439, 607
    in combat, 523–524, 592–593
    communitarianism and, 343–344
    education for, 600, 604, 605
    ethical relativism and treatment
        of, 127
    ethic of care and, 611–613
    female genital mutilation, 127,
        157–159, 157n
    goddess theory, 594–595
    historical role in the public sphere,
        591–596
    as human, 313
    invisibility in the classroom, 363–364
    Kant on, 289, 607
    Kierkegaard and, 486–487, 486
    Levinas and, 504
    in the Middle Ages, 595–596
    Mill, Harriet Hardy Taylor, on, 245
    Mill, John Stuart, on, 244, 598, 600,
        607, 609
    moral philosophers, 599
    Nietzsche on, 495, 607
    as the Other, 504, 604–605
    Plato on, 404, 439
    princess phenomenon, 617
    rationality and, 285–286, 285, 289
    sexual harassment of, 600, 601
    suffrage for, 596–597, 600
    "woman's work," 592–594, 610
Women's rights
    in first-, second-, and third-wave
        feminism, 600
    legal responsibility and, 319
    Mill, Harriet Hardy Taylor, on, 244,
        245, 598
    Mill, John Stuart, on, 244, 598
    Wollstonecraft on, 598
Workers' rights, 316, 338–339, 656
World War II. See Nazis
Wu, Chien-Lien, 581
Wu wei, 543
Wyatt Earp (film), 74

Xenophon, 397
The X-Files (TV series), 81

Yates, Robert L., Jr., 314–315, 317
Y chromosomes, 439
Yi, 542
You Just Don't Understand (Tannen),
    615–616
Young Guns I and II (films), 74
Your Life as Story (Rainer), 725–726
"The Youth Who Could Not Shiver and
    Shake," 66
YouTube, 651

Zaillian, Steven, 576–579
Zehr, Howard, 347
Zimbardo, Philip, 6, 30–33
Zinneman, Fred, 301–303, 419–422
Zits (comic strip), 473
Zorro legend, 52